Reformed Dogmatics

Lexham Press, 1313 Commercial St., Bellingham, WA 98225
LexhamPress.com

ISBN 9781683594192
Library of Congress Control Number 2020940436

Transcribed from lectures delivered in Grand Rapids, Michigan
First publication hand-written in 1896
Originally printed in 1910

REFORMED DOGMATICS

GEERHARDUS VOS, PH.D., D.D.

Translated and edited by

Richard B. Gaffin, Jr.

LEXHAM PRESS

Contents

Contents

PREFACE

The welcome decision of Lexham Press, the publisher, to make this single-volume edition available will facilitate easier access to the *Reformed Dogmatics* and further its study and usefulness as a whole. The contents of this edition, including prefaces, are unchanged.

Several points made in prefaces to the volumes previously published separately bear repeating here. The goal has been to provide a careful translation, aiming as much as possible for formal rather than functional equivalence. Nothing has been deleted, no sections elided or their content summarized in a reduced form. Vos's occasionally elliptical style in presenting material, meant primarily for the classroom rather than for published circulation to a wider audience, has been maintained. The relatively few instances of grammatical ellipsis unclear in English have been expanded, either without notation or placed within brackets.

This is not a critical translation. Only in a very few instances has an effort been made to verify the accuracy of the secondary sources cited or quoted by Vos, who usually refers to no more than the author and title and sometimes only to the author. No exact bibliographic details have been provided, and explanatory footnotes have been kept to a minimum.[1]

---

1   Further details related to producing the translation, with some observations about its contents, are in the prefaces to the individual volumes. A fuller overview is available in Richard B. Gaffin, Jr., "The *Reformed Dogmatics* of Geerhardus Vos," *Unio Cum Christo: International Journal of Reformed Theology and Life*, 4/1 (April 2018): 239–45.

As previously noted, English readers are now able to explore the relationship between the early Vos of the *Reformed Dogmatics* and his subsequent groundbreaking work in biblical theology.[2] I continue to be confident that whatever differences such comparisons may bring to light, the end result will confirm a deep, pervasive, and cordial continuity between his work in systematic theology and in biblical theology.

The *Reformed Dogmatics* makes a valuable contribution for anyone looking for a uniformly sound and often penetrating presentation of biblical doctrine, particularly for students and others interested in an initial in-depth treatment of systematic theology.

May God grant that the *Reformed Dogmatics* be used for the well-being of His church and its mission in and to the world in our day and beyond.

R. Gaffin, Jr.
June 2020

---

2   There are some observations concerning this relationship in the items mentioned in the previous footnote, including books and articles cited in them. See also the recent important, thoroughly researched biography of Danny E. Olinger, *Geerhardus Vos: Reformed Biblical Theologian, Confessional Presbyterian* (Philadelphia: Reformed Forum, 2018).

REFORMED DOGMATICS

VOLUME ONE

THEOLOGY PROPER

Translated and edited by

Richard B. Gaffin, Jr.

with

Kim Batteau, Associate Editor
Annemie Godbehere
Roelof van Ijken

✦

Contents

CONTENTS

PREFACE

The *Reformed Dogmatics* of Geerhardus Vos (1862–1949), here appearing for the first time in English, is a welcome publication for anyone wishing to benefit from a uniformly sound and often penetrating articulation of biblical doctrine. It will be of particular interest to those who are already familiar with the work of Vos—the father of a Reformed biblical theology.[1] Few, if any, among them have not experienced a growing appreciation of his profound and singular insights into Scripture. F. F. Bruce's characterization of *The Pauline Eschatology* is an apt description for his work as a whole: "indeed outstandingly great … a rare exegetical feast."[2]

The *Reformed Dogmatics* stems from the period 1888–1893, when among other subjects the young Vos taught systematic theology (dogmatics) at the Theological School of the Christian Reformed Church, later renamed Calvin Theological Seminary. This *Dogmatiek* was first published in Dutch as a hand-written manuscript in five volumes, in 1896. It was subsequently transcribed and printed in 1910. While the 1896 version is apparently in Vos' own hand, the transcription is almost

---

1   For some reflections on his work in biblical theology (or "History of Special Revelation," the designation he much preferred), and its significance, see my "Vos, Geerhardus," in *Dictionary of Major Biblical Interpreters* (ed. Donald K. McKim; Downers Grove, IL: IVP Academic, 2007), 1016-19, and the literature cited there, 1019, and my "Introduction" in Geerhardus Vos, *Redemptive History and Biblical Interpretation: The Shorter Writings of Geerhardus Vos* (ed. Richard B. Gaffin, Jr.; Phillipsburg, NJ: P&R, 1980/2001), ix-xxiii; see also J. T. Dennison, Jr., *The Letters of Geerhardus Vos* (Phillipsburg, NJ: P&R, 2005), 36-41, 49-59, and the editor's "Introduction: The Writings of Geerhardus Vos," in Danny E. Olinger, ed., *A Geerhardus Vos Anthology: Biblical and Theological Insights Alphabetically Arranged* (Phillipsburg, NJ: P&R, 2005), 1-27.

2   On the front cover of the 1953 Eerdmans reprint.

certainly by some other person or persons. But there is no good reason to question that it was done with Vos' full knowledge and approval. That transcription is the basis for this translation project.

While this is not a critical translation, the goal has been to provide a careful translation, aiming as much as possible for formal rather than dynamic equivalence. The accuracy of the secondary sources Vos cites or quotes—usually by referring to no more than the author and title and sometimes only to the author—has not been verified nor the exact bibliographic details provided. Explanatory footnotes have been kept to a minimum. Nothing has been deleted, no sections elided or their content summarized in a reduced form. Vos' occasionally elliptical style in presenting material, meant primarily for the classroom rather than for published circulation to a wider audience, has been maintained. The relatively few instances of grammatical ellipsis unclear in English have been expanded, either without notation or, where the expansion is more extensive, placed within brackets.

Concerning the use of Scripture a couple of things are to be noted. Effort has been made to verify Scripture references, and occasional instances of typographical error, where the intended reference is clear, have been corrected without that being indicated. In Vos' original, Old Testament verse references are to the Hebrew text, which varies occasionally from the numbering used in English Bibles. These references have been changed in this translation to be consistent with English versification. Also, quotations occasionally follow the Statenvertaling[3] but are usually Vos' own translation, whether exact or a paraphrase. Accordingly, rather than utilizing a standard English translation, they are translated as Vos quotes them.

English readers will now be able to explore the relationship between the early Vos of the *Reformed Dogmatics* and his subsequent work in biblical theology, begun in the fall of 1893 when he moved from Grand Rapids to Princeton Seminary as the first occupant of its newly created chair of biblical theology.[4] Whatever differences that comparison may bring to light, it is safe to anticipate that the end result will substantiate

---

3   The state-commissioned Dutch translation first published in 1637.

4   The most extensive bibliography of Vos' writings is in Dennison, *Letters of Geerhardus Vos*, 89–110; on the *Dogmatiek*, 92. For a thorough survey of Vos' life, see 13–85; on his time teaching in Grand Rapids, 25–26.

deep, pervasive and cordial continuity between his work in systematic theology and biblical theology. An important reference point in this regard is provided by Vos himself in his comments on the thoroughly positive, complementary relationship he as a Reformed theologian saw between the two disciplines. This point was present in his Princeton inaugural address in the spring of 1894[5] and echoed decades later, well after his retirement.[6]

Another interesting question concerns the antecedents of the *Reformed Dogmatics*, particularly those Vos may have considered its more immediate predecessors. Calvin is quoted most often, and there is occasional reference to various figures in late 16th and 17th century Reformed theology. However, there is no indication of current or more recent Reformed theologians who substantially influenced him and upon whose work he sees himself as building. There are only two passing references to Charles Hodge in Volume One (both dissenting!). There is no mention of Abraham Kuyper or B. B. Warfield, although Vos was personally acquainted with both and corresponded with them during his time in Grand Rapids, sometimes touching on matters theological. This silence may be explained by the fact that their major works were yet to appear.

The appearance of the *Reformed Dogmatics* will disclose substantial affinity with the *Reformed Dogmatics* of Herman Bavinck. This is to be expected, since the slightly younger Vos (by seven years) considered Bavinck a good friend as well as a close theological ally. The first volume of Bavinck's work (in Dutch), however, did not appear until 1895, after Vos' Grand Rapids period.[7] Perhaps the later volumes of the *Reformed Dogmatics* will shed more light on the question of influences on Vos' work.[8]

---

5   "The Idea of Biblical Theology as a Science and as Theological Discipline," *Redemptive History and Biblical Interpretation*, 23–24.

6   Geerhardus Vos, *Biblical Theology: Old and New Testaments* (Grand Rapids: Eerdmans, 1948), Preface, 23.

7   Vos provided lengthy and appreciative reviews of volume 1 (1895) and volume 2 (1897) of the *Gereformeerde Dogmatiek* soon after each appeared; see *Redemptive History and Biblical Interpretation*, 475–93.

8   For Vos' side of ongoing correspondence with Kuyper, Bavinck and Warfield, see Dennison, *Letters of Geerhardus Vos*, 116–203, for the time prior to and during his Grand Rapids period, 116–78. None of this correspondence sheds any light on the existence of the *Dogmatiek*.

Volume One, appearing here, deals with theology proper. Subsequent volumes, scheduled to appear as the translation of each is readied, treat in order anthropology, Christology, soteriology, and in the final volume, ecclesiology and eschatology.[9]

This project represents a collaborative effort without which it would not have otherwise been possible. Particular thanks are due to the translators for their efforts in providing base translations of the various parts of Volume One and also to Kim Batteau for some translation review. I have reviewed and revised their work and given the translation its final form.

Thanks are due to Lexham Press for its commitment in initiating and supporting this project, and to its editorial staff for their work. Special thanks to the project manager, Justin Marr, for all his time and efforts, not least his ready availability to make suggestions and answer questions about procedures. Finally, it would be remiss not to acknowledge indebtedness to the unknown person or persons responsible for the careful transcription work done over a century ago. Those labors have made this translation project immeasurably more feasible.

R. Gaffin, Jr.

January 2013
Reissued August 2014

---

9   Interestingly, and no doubt of some disappointment to some readers today, there is no introduction (prolegomena) to systematic theology. It is unclear if—and if so, where—this area was covered in the curriculum of the Theological School at this time and whether Vos or someone else taught it. My thanks to Dr. Mark A. Garcia for verifying this state of affairs from the resources available in the Heritage Hall Archive at the Calvin College and Seminary Library, Grand Rapids, Michigan.

CHAPTER ONE

The Knowability of God

1. *Is God knowable?*

Yes, Scripture teaches this: "that we may know the One who is true" (1 John 5:20), although it also reminds us of the limited character of our knowledge (Matt 11:25).

2. *In what sense do Reformed theologians maintain that God cannot be known?*

   a) Insofar as we can have only an incomplete understanding of an infinite being.

   b) Insofar as we cannot give a definition of God but only a *description*.

3. *On what ground do others deny God's knowability?*

On the ground that God is All-Being. They have a pantheistic view of God. Now, *knowing* presumes that the object known is not all there is, since it always remains distinct from the subject doing the knowing. Making God the object of knowledge, one reasons, is equivalent to saying that He is not all there is, that He is limited.

4. *What response is to be made against this view?*

   a) The objection that this view presents stems entirely from a philosophical view of God, as if He were All-Being. This view is wrong.

God is certainly infinite, but God is not the All. There are things that exist, whose existence is not identical with God.

b) It is certainly true that we cannot make a visible representation of God because He is a purely spiritual being. But we also cannot do that of our own soul. Yet we believe that we know it.

c) It is also true that we do not have an in-depth and comprehensive knowledge of God. All our knowledge, even with regard to created things, is in part. This is even truer of God. We only know Him insofar as He reveals Himself, that is, has turned His being outwardly for us. God alone possesses ideal knowledge of Himself and of the whole world, since He pervades everything with His omniscience.

d) That we are able to know God truly rests on the fact that God has made us in His own image, thus an impression of Himself, albeit from the greatest distance. Because we ourselves are spirit, possess a mind, will, etc., we know what it means when in His Word God ascribes these things to Himself.

✦

Chapter Two
Names, Being, and Attributes of God

1. In what does the importance of the names of God lie?

In this, that God through them draws our attention to the most important attributes of His being. This being is so rich and comprehensive that we need to have some benchmarks in order to understand the rest. God's names are not empty sounds (like the names of people), but they have meaning and contribute to our knowledge of God.

2. What is the meaning of the name Elohim?[1]

"He who is to be feared," "the One who is full of majesty." The ending im[2] is a plural ending. The singular is *Eloah* and appears first in the later books of the Bible as a poetical form. The plural ending does not point to an earlier polytheistic conception, but signifies the plenitude of power and majesty there is in God.

3. What are the meanings of the names El and Adonai?

El means "the Strong One," "the Mighty One." *Adonai* means "Ruler," "Lord"; originally, "my Ruler," "my Lord."

---

1 Throughout Vos' transliterations of Hebrew and Greek words are preserved—they have not been updated to conform to current transliteration systems.

2 In this version, italics represent emphasis, per underlining in the original manuscript—not transliteration, although italics often occur on transliterated words. This style is included for each time a word is underlined in the original manuscript.

4. *Give the meaning of the name Eljon.*

It means "the Exalted One," namely "above all other so-called gods"; cf. Genesis 14:18.

5. *What is the meaning of the name El Shaddai?*

"The Mighty One," "the Sovereign One."

6. *What is the derivation and what is the meaning of the name Jehovah?*

Very early the Jews thought that Leviticus 24:11, 16 forbade them to pronounce the holy name of God. They always replaced it with Adonai. Later, when vowels were added to the Hebrew text, the vowels of Adonai were used. Thus, the pronunciation "Jehovah" came into existence. We cannot ascertain with certainty what the original pronunciation was, but most probably the pronunciation was *Jahweh*. However, we are already so used to the sound of Jehovah that it would almost be irreverent to change it at this stage. According to Exodus 3:14, Jehovah is a covenant name and signifies: (a) self-existence; and (b) God's immutability and faithfulness.

Elohej[3]

7. *What does the name Jehovah Zebahoth affirm?*

It means "the God [or the Lord] of Hosts." This name was first used in the time of Samuel. In that connection, one has thought that it indicates Jehovah as *Captain of Israel's battle array* (Psa 44:9). However, in Scripture, two other things are also called "hosts," namely the stars and the angels (Deut 4:19; Job 38:7). Thus along with the meaning mentioned above, included also in the name is this: God all-powerfully rules over angels and stars, and Israel should not fear them as the heathen do.

8. *Has God made Himself known to us only through His names?*

No, also through His attributes. God's attributes are the revealed being of God Himself insofar as it is made known to us under certain circumstances.

---

3   Elohej occurs in the original manuscript, but it's not certain why.

9. *What two questions arise for us in connection with God's attributes?*

   a) In what relation do they stand to His being?

   b) In what relation do they stand to each other?

10. *What do the ancients teach concerning God's being?*

   a) As has been noted above, we cannot give a definition of God's being. After all, every definition presupposes a higher concept of genus and a distinction between a concept of genus and a concept of species, as well as a composition of the two. Now there is nothing higher than God, and God is simple, without composition.

   b) There is no distinction in God between essence and existing, between essence and being, between essence and substance, between substance and its attributes. God is *most pure* and *most simple* act.

11. *May we make a distinction in God between His being and His attributes?*

No, because even with us, being and attributes are most closely connected. Even more so in God. If His attributes were something other than His revealed being, it would follow that also essential deity must be ascribed to His being, and thus a distinction would be established in God between what is essentially divine and what is derivatively divine. That cannot be.

12. *May we also say that God's attributes are not distinguished from one another?*

This is extremely risky. We may be content to say that all God's attributes are related most closely to each other and penetrate each other in the most intimate unity. However, this is in no way to say that they are to be identified with each other. Also in God, for example, love and righteousness are not the same, although they function together perfectly in complete harmony. We may not let everything intermingle in a pantheistic way because that would be the end of our objective knowledge of God.

13. *From what other matters in God must we clearly distinguish His attributes?*

a) From God's names, derived from the relation in which He stands to what is created. Thus, He is called Creator, Sustainer, Ruler (we call these predicates or descriptions).

b) From the personal qualities that are unique to each person of the Holy Trinity and whereby they are distinguished from one another, e.g., begetting, being begotten, and being breathed (these are called properties, "particularities").

14. *In how many ways have theologians attempted to make a classification of God's attributes?*

a) They have been classified in three ways according to which, it is thought, one must arrive at knowledge of the attributes:

1. The way of causality
2. The way of negation
3. The way of eminence

However, this is not so much a classification of attributes as of ways in which *natural theology* has attempted to establish God's attributes.

b) Another classification is *affirming* and *negating* attributes. Pure negations only tell us what God is *not* and are therefore not attributes in the fullest sense of the word. When we consider this more closely, these so-called negative attributes mostly include something affirming, so the distinction disappears. For example, God's eternity says more than that He has no beginning and no end. It also says that for Him everything is an indivisible present, etc.

c) A third classification divides into *absolute* and *relative* attributes, or what comes down to the same thing, *inherent* and *transitive* attributes. However, strictly speaking, all God's attributes are absolute. In other words, the ground for them resides in His being, apart from the existence of the world, although we must admit that we could not conceive of some of them in action (e.g., grace and mercy) if the world did not exist. On the other hand, there is no attribute in God that is not in a certain sense transitive, that is, which He has not revealed. We cannot claim that we know everything in God, but what we know, we only know because God has revealed it to us, because He has communicated and disclosed it to us.

d) In the fourth place, there are some who want to differentiate between *natural* and *moral* attributes. Moral attributes are, e.g., goodness, righteousness. The remaining attributes that lack this quality are called natural. Against this distinction, there are two objections.

   1. The word natural is ambiguous. It could give occasion here for thinking that God's moral attributes do not belong to His nature, His being.

   2. In addition, the error could arise as if in God the moral is separated from the natural and the latter is a principle of lower order in God.

e) Fifth, we have Schleiermacher's classification along the same lines as his system. He divides according to the different ways in which our feeling of dependence expresses itself in response to God's attributes. This feeling does not arouse resistance within us against God's eternity, omnipotence, etc. Such attributes form one class. But against God's holiness, righteousness, etc., this feeling arouses resistance. These form a second group. This resistance has been removed by Christ, and the attributes with which we come into contact through Christ are summed up in a third group.

f) The most common classification, which we also follow, distinguishes between *incommunicable* and *communicable* attributes.

   1. To the incommunicable attributes belong:

      a. Self-existence

      b. Simplicity

      c. Infinity

      d. Immutability

2. To the communicable attributes belong:

    a. Spirituality and personality

    b. Understanding

    c. Will

    d. Power

    e. God's Blessedness

15. *What must be noted regarding an objection raised against this ancient division into communicable and incommunicable attributes?*

It has been said that the differentiation is relative, that is, that the incommunicable attributes when viewed from another perspective are communicable and vice versa. For example, God's eternity is infinite in relation to time; in man there is a finite relation to time. Thus, there is an analogy between God and man. Conversely, there is only limited goodness and righteousness in us; in God both are perfect. Thus, there is an infinite distance. Each attribute, one says, is at the same time incommunicable and communicable according to one's perspective.

This view is entirely wrong. God's eternity says much more than that He stands in an infinite relation to time. It says that He is wholly exalted above it. Clearly, there is not a shadow or trace of this in man. God's eternity is indeed incommunicable, not only in degree but also in principle.

16. *What else do we observe about incommunicable and communicable attributes in relation to each another?*

That the former determine the latter. For example, God is infinite and possesses understanding. Now, we are able to connect infinity with understanding and say God possesses infinite understanding. We could do this as well with all the other attributes. The two sets are at no point separated from each other; they penetrate each other.

17. *What is God's self-existence?*

That attribute of God by which He is the self-sufficient ground of His own existence and being. Negatively expressed, *independence* says only what God is *not*. Self-existence is precisely the adequate affirmation here. Proof texts: Acts 17:25; John 5:26.

18. What is God's simplicity?

That attribute of God whereby He is free of all composition and distinction. God is free:

a) Of logical composition; in Him there is no distinction between genus and species.

b) Of natural composition; in Him there is no distinction between substance and form.

c) Of supernatural composition; in Him there is no distinction between slumbering capacity and action. Proof texts: 1 John 1:5; 4:8; Amos 4:2; 6:8.

The Socinians and Vossius[4] deny this attribute in order better to escape the Trinity, that is, the oneness in being of the three Persons.

19. What is God's infinity?

That attribute whereby God possesses within Himself all perfection without any limitation or restriction.

It is further distinguished into:

a) Infinite perfection

b) Eternity

c) Immensity

20. Is the concept of infinity negating or affirming?

It has been claimed that it is purely negating and therefore has no content. This is not correct. Certainly it is true:

a) That we cannot form a graphic image of the infinite or of an infinite thing. Beholding is always limited, and what is limited does not comprehend the infinite.

b) That we cannot make a concept of the infinite with our thinking. Thinking also is always limited; thus it is inadequate for comprehending the infinite.

---

4   Vorstius is possibly meant here (see the answer to question 32 below).

Nevertheless, it remains true that we must hold with conviction that:

a) Behind the finite we comprehend, the infinite exists. It is with the infinite God as it is with space. However far we proceed in our imagination, we know that we have not yet arrived at the end, that we could still take one more step.

b) This infinity for God Himself is not something indeterminate as it is for us, but He Himself perfectly encompasses and governs it. However inconceivable this may be for us, in God it is a reality.

21. *Is God's infinity limited by the existence of other things that are not God?*

No, for to be infinite does not mean to be everything, although the pantheists claim the latter.

22. *Where does Scripture teach us God's infinite perfection?*

In Job 11:7–9 and Psalm 145:3.

23. *What is God's eternity?*

That attribute of God whereby He is exalted above all limitations of time and all succession of time, and in a single indivisible present possesses the content of His life perfectly (and as such is the cause of time).

24. *How many concepts of eternity are there?*

Two:

a) A more popular concept: Eternity as time without beginning and without end.

b) The more abstract and more precisely defined concept: Eternity is something that lies above time and differs entirely from time.

c) Both belong together and serve to supplement each other. According to the first, time in itself would be the original, and eternity only an extension of time. The latter taken to an extreme brings us to the pantheistic error that time is only an alteration of eternity. But both exist, eternity in God, time in the world. Scripture has both descriptions of eternity: Psalm 102:12; 90:2, 4; 2 Peter 3:8.

25. *What question presents itself to us here?*

How God can have knowledge of temporal things, without, with this knowledge, time, as it were, penetrating God's thinking and thereby His entire being? In other words: How does God relate to time?

26. *What must the answer to this be?*

a) That we may not follow those who deny a real existence to time and space and think that they are merely subjective forms in which man represents things. So Kant and many others. Time and space are objective and real.

b) That it is difficult to decide whether time and space are independent entities or modes of existence, or are relations of things to each other, or an entirely different kind of reality, or something about which we can say nothing further. These questions belong to the realm of metaphysics. God's Word does not give a further explanation.

c) That time and space as realities are also realities for God, the existence of which He knows.

d) That, however, a great difference remains between the relationship in which we stand to these realities and in which God stands to the same realities. We have time and space not only as real outside us, but they are also created in our mind as forms for representation, so that our inner life is governed by them and we cannot be rid of them. We can only see in space and think in time. For God it is entirely different. His divine life does not unfold or exist in those forms. He is exalted above them and just that fact makes His eternity His omnipresence. He knows the finite as existing in time and space, but He does not know and see it in a temporal or spatial manner.

27. *Is it right to say that all "occurring" takes place in time and that thus there must also be passage of time in God?*

No, for we know that there is causing and being caused, thus a real occurring, outside of time, namely, in the generation of the Son and the spirating of the Holy Spirit.

28. *What do you understand about God's immensity?*

That perfection of God whereby He is exalted above all distinction of space, yet at every point in space is present with all His being and as such is the cause of space.

29. *Wherein lies the distinction between immensity and omnipresence?*

Both express the same thing but from two different perspectives. The first teaches how God is exalted above space and the second how He nevertheless fills space at every point with His whole being.

30. *How should we not think of this omnipresence of God?*

Not as extension over space; "God is entirely within all and entirely outside all," as one theologian has stated.

31. *In how many ways can existing beings be considered in relation to space?*
In a three-fold way:

    a) Material bodies exist in space in a delimited way. They are completely delimited and encompassed by space.

    b) Pure spirits, which are created, exist in space in a determinate way, that is, although they themselves have no extension unlike material bodies, they are still determined by space and its laws. Our soul cannot function everywhere.

    c) God, lastly, is in space in an effecting way, that is, space is sustained by the upholding power of His providence, as He has created it in the beginning and He wholly fills it.

32. *Is God omnipresent with only His power and knowledge or also with His being?*

The older Socinians, Vorstius, and some Anabaptists claimed the first. The latter is the case, as demanded by the infinity of God's being.

33. *Is God present everywhere in the same way?*

No, He reveals His presence in a different way in heaven than in the place of the lost, and differently on earth than above.

34. *How do you prove God's immensity from Scripture?*

From the following: Ephesians 1:23; Jeremiah 23:23–24; Psalm 139:7–12; Acts 17:24–28.

35. *What is the answer to the objection that the infinity of space limits God's infinity?*

a) That we have no ground for claiming space is infinite. It is true that we cannot imagine an end to space, but that is due to our own limitation.

b) Admitting that space were infinite, even then it need not limit God's infinity. That God is infinite does not mean that He *is all*. Since they fall into different spheres, the two infinites need not limit each other.

c) If space were infinite, it would not be independent of God. God alone is self-existent; also note His immensity.

36. *What is God's immutability?*

That perfection in God whereby He is exalted above all becoming and development, as well as above all diminution, and remains the same eternally.

37. *Why is it necessary to emphasize this attribute?*

Because pantheism teaches that within God there is development, indeed, that the development of the world is nothing other than the process whereby God comes to self-consciousness. Martensen, a Christian theologian tainted by pantheism, says, for example, "God's immutability is not the immutability of the lifeless, for he is only as in eternal fruitfulness *he becomes of himself*. His eternity is therefore not a stagnant eternity like the eternal mountains, or a kind of crystalline eternity like the eternal stars, but a living eternity, continuously blossoming in unfading youthfulness." Beautiful language, but a God-dishonoring thought!

38. *How are the creation of the world and God's actions in time to be brought into agreement with His immutability?*

We must believe that all these deeds do not effect any change in God, since they do not require time in Him, although naturally their realization falls within time.

39. *How can we further distinguish God's immutability?*

One can speak of:

a) An immutability of being.

b) An immutability of essential attributes.

c) An immutability of decrees and promises.

40. *Prove this from Scripture.*

See James 1:17; 1 Timothy 1:17; Malachi 3:6.

41. *What is the first of the communicable attributes?*

God's spirituality.

42. *What does Scripture mean when it calls God Spirit?*

The Hebrew and Greek words that mean "spirit" are both *wind*. From this starting point we discover the following:

a) Wind is that power among material powers that seems to be the most immaterial and invisible. We feel it but we do not see it (John 3:8). When God is called Spirit, it therefore means His immateriality (John 4:24).

b) Wind or breath is the mark of life and thus stands for life or in place of enlivening power. Thus it is the case that God's spirituality also means His *living activity*. As Spirit God is distinguished from man, indeed all that is created, that is flesh, that is powerless and inert in itself. Spirit is thus what lives and moves *of itself*. Jeremiah 17:5; Isaiah 31:3.

c) Wind as the spirit of life or the breath of life belongs with something else enlivened or activated by it. God can also in this sense be called Spirit insofar as He is the enlivener and source of life for the creature. That is so both in a natural sense as well as in a spiritual sense. That agrees with the fact that man can be called flesh in a twofold sense, both insofar as he naturally has no power of life in himself and insofar as he is spiritually dead and cut off from God. In the latter sense, the word takes on its bad meaning, which it has throughout the entire Scripture. Psalm 104:30; 2 Corinthians 5:16.

d) The spirituality of God implies that He is a rational being, with understanding, will, and power.

43. *Whereby does the doctrine of God's spirituality acquire a practical significance?*

Through the use of images in Roman Catholic and Lutheran churches (cf. Rom 1:23).

44. *What else does God's spirituality involve?*

That God's being also exists as personal. However, we should consider that God's being may not be called personal in the abstract but only in His threefold existence as Father, Son, and Holy Spirit. In God personality is not one but three. There are not four but only three persons in the Godhead.

45. *Do not infinity and personal existence exclude each other?*

Almost the whole of modern philosophy claims that they do and therefore will not acknowledge any communicable attributes or personality in God. This claim is based on the idea that an "I" cannot exist without a "not-I" and that the nature of infinity excludes such an opposite.

The answer to this:

a) That God is not all that exists and that therefore in His thinking He can most certainly place other things vis-à-vis Himself without canceling out His infinity.

b) That personal consciousness is not caused by the consciousness of another outside us, but completely the reverse; the former makes the latter possible. Only where there is personal consciousness can one distinguish something else from one's self.

c) That in us, human beings, consciousness of personality is certainly awakened and developed by contact with the world outside us, but that we may not make this a rule for God. He is wholly independent from all that is outside Him.

d) That within God's being itself there is a distinction that should explain completely how there can be consciousness of personal existence in God apart from other things. The Father is indeed conscious not to be the Son, and the Son not to be the Father, and the Holy Spirit not to be the Father and not to be the Son. And these three do not limit each other but together are the one, infinite God.

46. What do we consider concerning God's understanding?

His knowledge and His wisdom.

47. What is God's knowledge?

That perfection by which, in an entirely unique manner, through His being and with a most simple act, He comprehends Himself and in Himself all that is or could be outside Him.

48. What distinguishes divine knowledge from that of human beings?

a) It occurs by a most simple act. Human knowledge is partial and obtained by contradistinction. God arrives immediately at the essence of things and knows them in their core by an immediate comprehension.

b) It occurs from God's being outwardly. With us the concept of things must first enter our cognitive capacity from outside us. God knows things from within Himself outwardly, since things, both possible and real, are determined by His nature and have their origin in His eternal decree.

c) In God's knowledge, there is no cognition that slumbers outside His consciousness and only occasionally surfaces, as is the case for the most part with our knowledge. Everything is eternally present before His divine view, and in the full light of His consciousness everything lies exposed.

d) God's knowledge is not determined through the usual logical forms, by which we, as by so many aids, seek to master the objects of our knowledge. He sees everything *immediately*, both in itself and in its relation to all other things.

49. *Is God's knowledge the same as His power?*

Some have claimed this. Augustine said, "We see the things that you have made because they exist; they exist, on the other hand, because you see them." In the same sense, Thomas Aquinas speaks of God's knowledge as the "cause of things." Likewise, many Reformed and Lutheran theologians. Against this idea we note:

a) That it is certainly true that every act of will in God and every expression of His omnipotence is accompanied by knowledge, and thus one may speak of an effectual knowledge.

b) That this, however, will always be a figurative way of speaking that may not lead us to identify the knowledge and power of God.

c) That God's knowledge and power must be distinguished is clearest from the fact that they have different objects. God *knows* all that is *possible*. His power is active only with respect to all that is real, and in a very different sense.

50. *How does one distinguish God's knowledge with reference to its objects?*

a) Into *necessary* knowledge and a *free* knowledge.

b) Into a knowledge of *simple comprehension* and a knowledge of *vision*.

51. *What is meant by the distinction between necessary and free knowledge?*

The objects of necessary knowledge are God Himself and all that is possible. It is called necessary, because it is not dependent on an expression of will in God. God is as He is, an eternal necessity reposing in Himself; also what is or is not possible is determined with equal necessity by God's perfect nature. One should note, however, that this necessity does not lie in a compulsion above God but in God's being itself.

The objects of *free* knowledge are all actual things outside God, that is, that actually have been, still are, or will be. It is called free because the knowledge of these things as existing depends on God's omnipotent decree and was by no means an eternal necessity.

One should note that the objects of free knowledge are simultaneously objects of necessary knowledge, but then not as actual but as purely possible.

52. What is meant by the distinction between a knowledge of simple comprehension and a knowledge of vision?

It is the same as the previous distinction. The knowledge of simple comprehension extends to all that is possible; the knowledge of vision, to all that is actual in the sense described above.

53. In which two respects, however, is the knowledge of simple comprehension distinguished from necessary knowledge?

a) God is clearly the object of necessary knowledge but not of the knowledge of simple comprehension. Yet, the latter, as the name indicates, comprises only that which is *purely possible*.

b) Actual things are also objects of necessary knowledge insofar as they are likewise possible. It seems that they must be excluded from the knowledge of simple comprehension because we are dealing here with a simple comprehension, that is, a comprehension that excludes all that is actual.

54. Why are these classifications of the objects of God's knowledge important?

Because they include a protest against the pantheistic identification of God and the world. By these distinctions, we confess that for God more is possible than exists in reality, that His power and thoughts extend beyond the world, that the latter is the product of His free will.

55. What is so-called middle knowledge?

It is something that Jesuits, Lutherans, and Remonstrants introduce between necessary and free knowledge.

By this is meant the knowledge that God possesses of certain things that would occur independently of God by the free determination of human will, provided that certain conditions would be fulfilled beforehand. For example, God gives to some His Word and the Holy Spirit, but not to others. We conclude from this His omnipotence in granting the means of grace. No, the proponent of middle knowledge responds, God knew which persons would convert themselves by a free determination of will when these means are presented to them, and therefore He brings these means only to them.

56. *What must be said against this conception?*

a) That knowledge, indifferent to whatever kind or origin, pre-supposes absolute certainty. Only what is certain and sure can be known.

b) That, therefore, whatever is free and uncertain in itself cannot be the object of knowledge, nor can it be a particular kind of knowledge.

c) That the opponents have only invented this knowledge in order to unite God's foreknowledge with their free will. And that they seek to unite two things here that logically exclude each other. Freedom of action in a Remonstrant sense and advance knowl-edge of that action are not compatible.

d) Some have appealed to God's eternity in order to defend the knowledge of absolutely free actions. They say that God stands wholly above time, that the future is always present for Him, and therefore that He can know it despite its absolute freedom.

This is certainly true, but God's eternity, to which they appeal here for help, is simply overthrown by this doctrine of absolutely free will, withdrawn from God's decree. If in this way God must expect an increase in His knowledge of things outside Himself, if He must, as it were, wait if He thus must take up within Himself the influence of the temporal, then this destroys His eternity. The doctrine of middle knowl-edge denies precisely what could make it comprehensible.

57. *Is not such middle knowledge taught in 1 Samuel 23:9–12 and in Matthew 11:22–23?*

No, in the first case David is simply told what the consequence would be given the present attitude of the people among whom he found himself if he remained in the town. In Matthew 11:22–23, we have a hy-perbolic mode of speech used by Jesus to indicate the hardening of His contemporaries.

58. How far does the knowledge of God extend?

It comprises all things great and small, free and necessary, past, present, and future. Therefore, it is called *omniscience*.

59. What is the relation between God's decree, His free knowledge, and the free actions of men?

God's decree grounds the certainty of His free knowledge and likewise the occurring of free actions. Not foreknowledge as such but the decree on which it rests makes free actions certain.

60. How do you describe the wisdom of God?

That perfection of God by which He uses His knowledge for the attainment of His ends in the way that glorifies Him most.

61. How can one demonstrate God's knowledge and wisdom from Scripture?

From Hebrews 4:13; Psalm 139:16; Proverbs 15:11; 1 Timothy 1:17.

62. In how many different senses can the word "will" be understood?

It can have three meanings:

    a) All morally determined attributes, insofar as these are active powers that can operate in a twofold direction. In this sense, holiness, righteousness, etc. belong to the will.

    b) The *capacity* to make a decree or a plan, and such a decree or plan *itself*. In this sense, the will (never the understanding) is the capacity by which God decrees or is the decree of God itself.

    c) The capacity by which God executes a decree of His will by a manifestation of power outwardly. In this sense, God's will is most closely connected with His active might.

63. Is there a particular reason for classifying the following attributes of God under His will?

Yes, for while in us rational attributes lie for the most part below our consciousness and thus hardly resemble a conscious volition, in God they are entirely different. All His rational perfections, such as His holiness, righteousness, etc., lie in the full light of His consciousness, that is, they are a conscious inclination of His nature. Clearly, conscious inclination is *will* in the wider sense of the word. Thus, the older theologians were entirely correct when they dealt with holiness and righteousness, etc., under the attributes of God's will.

64. *How can one describe God's will?*

That perfection of God by which in a most simple act and in a rational manner He goes out toward Himself as the highest good and toward creatures outside Him for His own sake.

65. *Is then God's will (speaking reverently) a selfish will?*

We could say this in a good sense. In man, selfishness is evil because the highest good lies outside himself. In contrast, God is the all-sufficient one, who delights in the highest good within Himself.

66. *Can we say that God's will and understanding are the same?*

No, against this identification others have rightly observed that God is clearly *omniscient* and *omnipotent*, but not *omni-volitional*.

67. *Must one also distinguish between God's will and His active power?*

a) God's omnipotence as the capacity to do, including what He does not actually do, is naturally distinguished from God's will. God does not will all that lies within the scope of His omnipotence.

b) But also between God's will and His active power one must make the greatest distinction. Certainly, God's decree, in which His will is active, is not the same as the powerful execution of His decree.

c) Still, we need to keep in view that God's active power has much more the character of a bare willing than our active power. With us, too, all exercising of power begins with willpower. That, however, is accompanied by various things that have no place in God as a pure spiritual being. God's simple will is powerful enough to call a thing into being. One needs to consider, however, that in saying this, one takes the word *will* as meant in question 62 under c and not as it is under a and b. Scripture itself says that by God's will things are and are created.

68. *How do we further distinguish God's will?*

a) Into *necessary* and *free* will. The first has reference to God Himself, the second to things existing outside of Him.

b) Into *absolute* and *conditional* will. This distinction, established by some older theologians, was rightly rejected by later ones. God's will is not conditional, but only the object willed by Him can be conditional in its nature, that is, dependent on something else. God does not will the one thing because He wills the other, but He certainly wills that there will the one for the sake of the other.

c) Into *antecedent* and *consequent* will. When the Reformed used this distinction, they did not mean anything other than that there is a logical order in God's decrees and that He makes one thing subject to another as a means to an end. They were certainly very conscious that things do not have their capacity to serve as means apart from God but that that capacity is derived from God's will. God wills A with an antecedent will and is not then forced to choose B with a consequent will, but omnipotently makes B an effective means for reaching A.

With this distinction the Lutherans and Remonstrants intend something entirely different. For them the *antecedent* will is a general rule established by God in indeterminacy, the *consequent* will a determinate application of it after God has first taken note of free human choice. By an antecedent will, God decrees to save all who believe. Then He sees who the believers are and then decrees with His consequent will to give them salvation. This, of course, is rejected by all the Reformed.

69. *Which distinction is of much greater importance?*

The distinction between the *secret* will of decree and the *revealed* will of precept.

70. *Are there also other names in use for this distinction, and why are they less suitable?*

Also spoken of is a will of good pleasure and a will of sign. God's *preceptive* will, however, also expresses His good pleasure, and sometimes His *decretive* will is brought to our attention by a sign. So, these terms express less accurately what is meant (Matt 11:26, εὐδοκία; Rom 12:2, θέλημα ... εὐάρεστον).

71. What do we understand, respectively, by the will of decree and the will of precept?

The *will of decree* is God's free determination of all that will come to pass and how it will occur. The *will of precept* is the rule laid down by God for rational beings to direct their conduct accordingly.

72. What difficulty does this distinction cause?

Many things that God forbids occur, and many things that He commands do not occur. Therefore, the will of decree and the will of precept seem to directly oppose each other.

73. Can all attempts to remove this difficulty be considered successful?

a) Some have denied that the existing will has the character of a will, and they wish to degrade it to merely a prescription. One must observe, however, that in God's prescriptions His holy nature speaks and that in fact they are founded upon a strong desire in God. More precisely, the problem here is this: How can there be two desires in God, one that wills the good and abhors the evil, and one that leaves the good unrealized and permits the evil to appear?

b) Some have distinguished between the *existence* of an action and the *manner* of its existence (the action equals the material and the formal). God's preceptive will, it is said, has reference only to the latter. That is true. But His decretive will also has reference to the latter, and in that respect both wills thus again stand side by side unreconciled.

c) Still others thought that everything was settled when they pointed out how God's decretive will also includes making known His preceptive will. When A sins, then God's decretive will has determined it, and His preceptive will has forbidden it. But now one needs to consider that God's decretive will also comprises that God would forbid it. So, they think, the will of precept is joined with that of the decree, and all is resolved in a higher unity. However, this resolution is pure illusion. Both wills now fall under the decree but such that they have become only out-wardly parallel but are not internally in harmony. The question is clearly how God can decree to permit something that He must at the same time by virtue of His holiness decree to forbid.

74. Does Scripture also distinguish between a twofold concept of will in this matter?

Yes, "to will" sometimes means the natural inclination or intent of the soul and sometimes the determination of the decree. (Compare above, question 62, a) and b); Matthew 27:43, θέλω; and Psalm 22:9, חָפֵץ.)

75. Can we sufficiently solve the difficulty here for our thinking?

No, because it comes down fundamentally to the problem of permitting sin and is identical to that problem. With our limited insight into God's ways, this question is not capable of a solution. All we can do is to guard against looking for the difficulty at a point other than where it lies.

76. Where then does the difficulty really lie?

In this, how in His decree God can permit things that violate and offend His rational attributes.

77. What needs to be said regarding this difficulty?

We must not forget that included within God's rational attributes there is one that can remove this temporal violation and offence, namely His punitive righteousness, so that, as it were, in the end the balance is once again restored. By this, however, we have not explained how it agrees with God's absolute holiness that He first decrees this removal in order then to maintain it.

78. Wherein may we not seek the difficulty?

We may not imagine that God would do us an injustice if He conducts Himself toward us in this double manner by decree and command. We do not find a rational problem here concerning the relation between God and the creature. If someone thinks of having discovered something like this, then it is the result of humanizing God. If we order someone to do something, then we are at the same time obliged to do everything in our power to advance the fulfillment of this order. If we neglect to do this, then we sin against a brother. The same thing cannot be said of God. He has no obligation at all with His decree to act for the realization of His command beyond what pleases Him. Just as little does His truthfulness demand that He decree and command the same thing. In the above-mentioned case, we would not only transgress against our brother through lovelessness, but also through deceitfulness. This, too, we cannot transfer to God.

79. *How are we to evaluate the case when the Lord prophesied to Hezekiah, "You will die of this disease," and nevertheless healed him?*

The prophecy was not a revelation of God's decretive will that would later be changed, but was simply an announcement of the fact that the illness was deadly in its nature. Hezekiah was healed by a miracle. God's decretive will was clearly that He should be healed. God speaks in human idiom. When we say, "He will die of this illness," we mean the same thing.

80. *How are we to evaluate Abraham's case where he was first commanded to sacrifice Isaac, and this command was later withdrawn?*

Here God commands something that He does not will. The great problem, however, was just how God can decree something that He does not approve. In Abraham's case, one could at most find a difficulty concerning God's truthfulness. How can God say to Abraham, "It is my will that you sacrifice your son," while in reality it was not His will? One must so understand this that God did not really say to Abraham, "It is my positive will that it come to pass (will of decree), but it is my will of precept prescribed for you," that is, "I demand of you that you should feel commanded to do it."

81. *Do all the earlier theologians give the same scope to the concept of God's holiness?*

No, there are those who include all the rational attributes under holiness, e.g., love, grace, mercy, etc. Others identify righteousness and holiness, e.g., Cocceius.

82. *Is it necessary to take the concept of holiness in such a broad sense?*

No, for although holiness stands in the closest relation to the remaining rational attributes, it is not to be identified with them. Also, the close connection in which these attributes stand to each other is already sufficient to point out that they are called attributes of the will, and that God's will is presented as having God Himself as the first object and having all the other objects for the sake of His will.

83. What is the original concept of holiness?

The root קדשׁ originally means, "to be set apart," "to be separated." God is therefore called, "the Holy One," because He exists in Himself and nothing can be compared to Him. The metaphysical gap that exists between Him and the creature is therefore expressed by the concept of holiness. A very clear Scripture is 1 Samuel 2:2, "There is none holy like the Lord: for there is none besides You; there is no rock like our God" (see Exod 15:11; 1 Sam 6:20).

84. Is the concept of holiness exhausted by this?

No, this is already clear from the fact that God can also communicate a likeness of His holiness to the creature. Of course, God can never give up His eternity. From this it is therefore apparent that the concept as described above needs supplementing. This supplement must be sought in the following: God is holy not only insofar as He is the eternal One, but also insofar as in His dealings with His creatures He claims everything for Himself and makes it subservient to His purposes, sets it apart, hallows it.

85. How is this second element in the concept of holiness distinguished from the first?

By accenting the rational significance of God's holiness. God is not only distinguished from all that exists outside Him, but He also knows Himself, seeks Himself, and loves Himself as the supreme embodiment of rational perfection. And from this determination of God toward Himself, it follows that He also makes the creature subservient to Himself and separates it for Himself. For the creature being holy means "consecrated to God."

86. What results from this consecration of the creature to God?

That sometimes the appearance can arise as if God's holiness is synonymous with His grace. When God sets a person or a nation apart for Himself, He at the same time takes them into His special favor. Grace follows consecration, for in being dedicated to God lies the beatitude of the creature; compare Psalm 103; Hosea 11:8; Psalms 22:3; 33:21; and the name "the holy One of Israel" in Isaiah 43:14 and other such places.

87. *How then can we describe the holiness of God?*

As that attribute of God by which He seeks and loves Himself as the highest good and demands as reasonable goodness from the creature to be consecrated to Him.

88. *Can one rightly call God's love the central attribute of His being according to which all the others must be classified?*

No, because all attributes are God's being. What is more, theologians who venture to make God's love the central attribute do this at the expense of other attributes, e.g., holiness, as if God were nothing other than pure self-sacrificing love. Scripture teaches us that there is such self-sacrificing love in God, but at the same time it teaches that there is more than this love and that it also is subordinate to the highest law of the rational life of God, namely, that in the first place He wills Himself and glorifies Himself.

89. *Does the attribute of love need to be understood rationalistically as an insight into and approval of the excellent attributes of the object that is loved?*

No, love has its rational sense within itself and does not lose that sense even when it extends to the most unworthy object. Scripture ascribes to God such a love for lost sinners who did not have anything in themselves that would arouse God's approval and His good pleasure.

90. *What distinguishes God's love from His holiness?*

Holiness has reference to God's love of Himself as the highest good. Thus, it is God's self-determination. Love, on the other hand, has reference to the disposition of God's good pleasure toward what lies outside of Him, or to the affection of the three Divine Persons for each other as well.

91. *How has one attempted to make an argument for the Trinity from the attribute of love?*

It has been pointed out that love demands a personal object that is distinct from the person who loves. This is true, but one should observe that in this way we do not yet come to the conclusion that there are precisely three persons in the Godhead.

92. *Is self-love permitted in the creature in the same way that it is in God's holiness?*

a) God can and must love Himself as the highest good. The creature may not aim at making itself the highest good and final purpose of its aspirations. In us absolute self-love is forbidden; indeed, strictly taken, so is absolute love for another creature where the honor of God would be left aside.

b) Still, one may speak of self-love in a good sense. The obligations, through whose fulfillment we must glorify God, must vary in nature. There are some that call us to self-sacrifice, others that we must have a regard for self-preservation. Ill-considered self-sacrifice can become sin. Nobody may hate his own flesh. Matthew 22:39; Romans 13:9; Galatians 5:14; James 2:8.

93. *In what ways does God reveal His love toward His creatures?*

By (a) His goodness; (b) His grace; (c) His lovingkindness; (d) His mercy or compassion; (e) His longsuffering.

94. *What is God's goodness and what is it sometimes called?*

It is His love toward personal and sentient creatures in general and can also be called *Amor Dei generalis*, "God's general love."

95. *What is the grace of God?*

The undeserved love of God toward sinful beings who lie under the judgment of His righteousness.

96. *Which two elements does the concept of grace contain?*

a) That it is unmerited. In a certain sense, one may say of all God's demonstration of favor that it is undeserved. By the presence of sin, however, it becomes especially apparent that the creature has no claims. Thus, grace in a narrower sense is favor toward sinners, that is, favor so great that it even overcomes the obstacles of sin and of righteousness.

b) Naturally connected with this element is the second, namely, that when God's love works in sinners, it is a monergistic principle. If in its origin God's love toward sinners is without obligation and freely acting, it must therefore be sovereignly divine in its outworking, that is, an undivided work of God. For the first aspect, compare Romans 4:4, 16; for the second, 2 Corinthians 12:9; Ephesians 4:7.

97. What is grace called in Hebrew and Greek?

The Hebrew word is חֵן; the Greek is χάρις.

98. What is God's lovingkindness?

The love of God insofar as it, as a special tenderness, seeks to lead the sinner to conversion. It is called חֶסֶד, Numbers 14:19 and Psalm 31:17; χρηστότης, χρηστός, Romans 2:4; πραΰτης, ἐπιείκεια, 2 Corinthians 10:1.

99. What is God's compassion or mercy?

God's love and pity toward sinners, who are considered as wretched. It is called רחום, οἰκτιρμός, ἔλεος, σπλάγχνα. The mercy of God flows from free antecedent love; cf. Ephesians 2:4–5: "rich in mercy *because of* the great love with which he has loved us."

100. What is God's long-suffering?

God's love to those who deserve punishment, demonstrated in postponing punishment and in calling to conversion. It is called אֶרֶךְ אַפַּיִם, Psalm 103:8; μακροθυμία, 2 Peter 3:15.

101. How may we describe God's righteousness?

As the natural disposition of His being not only to maintain Himself against every violation of His holiness but also to show in every respect that He is holy (Psa 7:12; Acts 17:31).

102. *What is the difference between the holiness of God and His righteousness?*

These two attributes are most closely connected to one another, yet they are not to be identified with each other. The difference is mainly twofold:

a) We call holiness the rational goodness of God as He possesses that in Himself, without our understanding that goodness as moving outside of Himself. On the other hand, righteousness is specifically that attribute of God's being that compels Him to make His holiness a power outside of Himself.

b) Holiness is, as we have seen, God's determination toward Himself. It is, as it were, a centripetal property, by which God moves toward Himself, toward the center of His being. On the other hand, righteousness is more a centrifugal property, by which God works from Himself outwardly, although this also occurs to reveal and maintain His holiness.

103. *What results from this righteousness of God?*

That every rational creature must serve as a means to reveal God's righteousness and therefore represents a certain worth for God. Thus, the righteousness of God toward man and the righteousness of man toward God can be named with the one and same word; both run parallel (cf. Rom 1:17; 3:21–22; 5:17, 21; 8:10, etc.). In all these places, the righteousness of God is used as a predicate that can be imputed to man. The righteousness of God for man consists in this, that he meets the demands that God establishes and must establish for him.

104. *Why is righteousness of such great importance for a devout life?*

Because it is just that attribute of God that highlights most sharply the dependence of the creature on God insofar as it makes that dependence a means to carry out the right of God. Hence, the aversion that every one-sided ethical conception of religion has for this concept of righteousness. If one places God and man next to each other as having equal rights, then it is out of the question to speak of God's righteousness. As soon as a deeply devout life awakens, then a hungering and thirsting after the righteousness of God is also present again.

105. *Does it depend on God's discretion whether or not He will exercise His righteousness?*

No, this is a claim of the Scholastics of the Middle Ages, the Socinians and the Remonstrants, but it is contradicted by Scripture.

106. *Is it necessary for God's righteousness to reward goodness?*

No, Scripture teaches that all reward is not *ex condigno*, according to worthiness, or *ex congruo*, in proportion to, but only *ex pacto*, from a free agreement that God has established with the creature. Naturally, when once God's grace has chosen this mode—that He wills to reveal His approval of good by reward—then righteousness demands that He also keep this promise. Besides, if we have done all that we were indebted to do, we are still unworthy servants.

107. *Which diverging concepts of righteousness are there besides the one being developed here?*

   a) The concept founded on the theory of improvement. Righteousness would then be the form that God's love assumes toward the transgressor when it would improve him. This is the theory found in the case of the Pelagians, Socinians, and universalists.

   b) The concept founded on the theory of deterrence. Righteousness is then the form that God's love assumes when it seeks to deter other people from misdeeds by the suffering of the transgressor. This is the theory of most jurists, such as Clement of Alexandria, Tertullian, Origen, Leibniz, Grotius. These all make Scripture subservient for promoting moral good as an end in itself. However, there are also those who take moral good itself in a utilitarian sense and therefore use terror as a means of promoting bliss.

108. *What objection is there against the theory of improvement?*

   a) There are two different kinds of suffering—punishments and corrections. Only the latter can count as a means for improvement, and Scripture clearly differentiates it from the first. Proponents of this theory must therefore show that *all suffering* possesses the character of correction. This they cannot do, for Scripture teaches that we first become children of God when we are justified by the punitive suffering of our surety (Gal 4:4–5).

b) In many cases punishment removes all possibility of improvement for the offender. This theory has no place for the death penalty, the *jus talionis* warranted by Scripture.

c) Even where this is not the case, one cannot claim that physical evil of itself has the tendency to improve someone. Just as often it results in hardening. Punishment only improves when one feels how it is deserved. But this presupposes that righteousness is exercise according to what is deserved and not only for improvement. This means that the theory of improvement can only be maintained with the help of our theory.

d) The theory has a superficial view of physical evil, of pain. That pain has a beneficial side is true. But God could just as well have reached the same goal, which He now reaches by pain, in other ways if there had been no pain. Indeed, as we think away the punishment of sin, all pain as a means of prevention would have been superfluous. Thus God uses a means to repentance that entails misery without needing to do so. This is cruelty in God.

e) The general consciousness of man says that evil must be punished apart from all its consequences. The sentiment for righteousness is much more in danger of degenerating into bloodthirstiness rather than into real philanthropy. This shows us its original significance.

109. *What objection is there to the deterrence theory?*

a) It makes one person entirely a means for another, at least if it wants to maintain the good right of the death penalty or lifelong imprisonment. This, however, cannot be, for considered apart from God, every human being is important in himself, which does not allow him to be reduced to a bare means.

b) It deprives those who are punished of exactly what it wants to cultivate in others, namely obedience to the law. The theory leads to forming a quantitative concept of virtue. It is concerned with the greatest virtue for the greatest possible number, and to this end some are sacrificed.

c) In reality this theory, too, is based on the forensic. Only when the punishments of sinners are merited and legitimate will they truly exercise a reforming influence. If they only lead to ceasing from evil for fear of punishment, they do not promote true morality. In order for this theory to be maintained, it must incorporate the concept that virtue has worth only insofar as it promotes human happiness. That is, it is eudemonistic in nature. So, it is to be judged with eudemonism.

110. *Must the exercise of punishment be understood as a purely commercial transaction?*

No, it may not. There is a manifold difference between paying a financial debt and punishment for guilt, as the doctrine of the atonement will show. Punishment is the restoration of a relationship, of the status of sinners in relation to God, not taking back something that first was taken from God.

111. *What is the pantheistic and philosophical concept of the righteousness of God?*

In this point of view, righteousness is merely a term used to express that, in the impersonal ground of the universe, there must be a cause that sin and misery appear to be linked to each other.

112. *Are there also those who take a mediating point of view between the pantheistic opinion and ours?*

Yes, some concede that God is personal, but limit the punishment of sin to its natural consequences. From this, however, the preposterous view could result that a rational and tenderhearted person is punished the most severely, a hardened sinner the lightest.

113. *How can you prove that our understanding of righteousness is correct?*

a) Such consciousness of right and wrong is inborn in every human being.

b) The spiritual experience of the regenerate bears witness to this. They all side with God in what is right as one designates it.

c) This consciousness of righteousness is not a product of evolution but something natural. It already has a name in the oldest languages. The rites and ceremonies of all religions testify to this.

d) God's holiness demands the existence of such righteousness. Everywhere in Scripture it is presented under the symbol of fire. That is, it must glow and be active outwardly.

e) It is impossible to maintain the concepts of "must" and obligation in their full force if they do not have the concept of punishment to support them.

f) The doctrines of the atonement and of justification, as Scripture develops these, rest entirely on this attribute of divine righteousness.

114. *How do theologians further distinguish the righteousness of God?*

a) *Justitia dominica* or "the righteousness of rule." This indicates that in governing the world God gives a reliable expression of the rectitude of His being. It describes God's relationship to sin as first *originating* as a relationship that *is* just.

b) *Justicia judicialis* or "judicial righteousness." This indicates that God in His judgment over rational beings speaks justly and therefore demonstrates His relationship to sin as a *given fact* as a relationship that *does* justly.

115. *What is included in God's "ruling righteousness"?*

a) That He is exonerated of collaboration in the origin of evil as such. God's activity with respect to evil is only a permitting activity.

b) If God nevertheless permits evil and it does not originate outside His decree, then it seems as if the presence of sin and the majesty of the law would never have made such a deep impression on people as is now the case.

c) The same is true of God's love. It only appears to the fullest in its greatness now that it is tested and has triumphed in the most terrible of all crises, the crisis of sin.

d) We may not go as far as maintaining that the contrast between good and evil is a necessary factor in the divine economy.

116. *How do you further divide the "judicial righteousness" of God?*

Into

a) *legislative righteousness* that expresses itself toward sin and the good as merely future or possible.

b) *executive righteousness* that expresses itself toward sin and the good as actually present, and then

    1. as punitive or avenging righteousness;

    2. as remunerative or rewarding righteousness.

One may not say, however, that either reward or punishment is a *necessary* form of revelation of divine righteousness.

117. *Which proof texts can you supply for righteousness?*

Exodus 22:5–6; Romans 2:6ff.

118. *What is the understanding of the attribute of divine truthfulness?*

a) *Metaphysical* truthfulness. God agrees with His own understanding, and therefore in opposition to idols is the only true God (Jer 10:11).

b) *Ethical* truthfulness. God reveals Himself as He actually is.

c) *Logical* truthfulness. God causes the concepts that we must necessarily form of things, in keeping with the structure of our cognitive capacities, to agree with reality (see Num 23:19; Titus 1:12–13).

119. *Is there emotion or feeling in God?*

Not in the sense of an intense transitory movement of emotion, something passive, whereby the will retreats into the background (compare *affectus* from *afficere*, "to be affected"). Certainly, however, in the sense of an inner divine satisfaction that accompanies the energetic expression of His will and His power and His understanding.

120. *What is meant, for example, by God's wrath?*

Not a sudden surge of passion but an evenly strong yet lasting and rational impulse of God's holy will. Only with us human beings is a sudden surge of emotion possible. In the New Testament God's wrath regularly means the decree of God to punish in the Day of Judgment those who remain unrepentant. Θυμός is the disposition of wrath in God; ὀργή its active result outside of God.

121. *What is the zeal of God?*

The jealousy of the love of God with respect to His covenant people who are betrothed to Him (Exod 20:5).

122. *What is the repentance of God?*

By it is indicated anthropomorphically that He is mindful of man's deviation, in all its antithetical sharpness, from his destiny (Num 23:19; Gen 6:6).

123. *What is God's power?*

The capacity to put His will into effect outwardly. As *omnipotence* it is the capacity to accomplish what is not in conflict with God's own being.

124. *Is God's power limited by the reality of what exists?*

No, this would be a pantheistic thought. God is able to do more than He actually does.

125. *Is God's power the same as His will?*

No, at least not if will means God's good pleasure or His decree. Certainly, however, if we take will as the expression of will (not *voluntas*, but *volitio*).

126. *What are the objects of God's power?*

a) God Himself, insofar as He governs His own being.

b) All that is possible, insofar as God would be able to realize it.

c) All that is actual, insofar as it is in fact realized.

127. *What is the distinction between power and strength?*

We have taken the word "power" here in the sense that "strength" generally has, that is, the capacity to act. In the contrast just mentioned, however, power generally means "authority," "competence," "the right to act," "sovereignty." This, however, is more a matter of a relationship of God to the creature than an attribute of God Himself.

128. *For distinguishing the power of God, what does one call power that concerns what is possible and power that concerns what is actual?*

a) Necessary power (*potentia necessaria*).

b) Free power (*potentia libra*).

129. *What other distinction do theologians make concerning the power of God?*

That between:

a) *Absolute* power, that is, that capacity by which God intervenes in the course of the world directly, without making use of second causes.

b) *Ordaining* power, that is, that capacity of God that works in the once established manner of natural causes. Pantheistic philosophy naturally also rejects this distinction. It will know of nothing other than *potestia ordinata*.

130. *Is it a correct expression to say that God cannot do the impossible?*

No, for the impossible cannot exist, not even partially in concept, and therefore insofar as it is logically impossible, it is not an object. Eternal rational truths are rightly eternal because they are true in the thinking of God. What conflicts with these, conflicts with the being of God Himself. God cannot deny Himself. The ideal of power is not absolute indifference, which is also exalted above itself, but a self-determined reasonable and rational freedom.

131. *Which proof texts can you supply for God's power?*

Genesis 17:1; Jeremiah 32:17; Matthew 19:26.

132. *What is God's blessedness?*

It is the inner sense of His perfection and His glory. It is called μακάριος as the one blessed.

133. *What, in distinction, is God's glory?*

The revelation of the perfections of God outwardly like brilliant light. In Hebrew, כָּבוֹד, הוֹד (Psa 24:8); in Greek, δόξα (1 Tim 1:11; 6:15–16).

CHAPTER THREE

The Trinity

1. *Why must we not seek a decisive proof for the Trinity in the Old Testament?*

    a) Because Old Testament revelation was not finished but only preparatory. The perfect comes only at the end.

    b) Under the Old Testament's dispensation the concept of the oneness of God had to be deeply impressed upon Israel's consciousness in the face of all polytheistic inclinations.

    c) We must not imagine that the Old Testament saints were able to read in the Old Testament everything that we can read there in the light of the New. Yet, what we read in it is clearly the purpose of the Holy Spirit, for He had the Scripture of the Old Testament written not only for then but also for now.

2. *Which traces of the doctrine of the Trinity can we nevertheless discover in the Old Testament?*

    a) The distinction between the names Elohim and Yahweh. Elohim is God as He works among both Israel and the heathen by creation and providence. Yahweh is God as He has made Himself known by theocratic guidance and revelation. Compare Genesis 1:1 with 2:4. Where God reveals Himself, He therefore bears another name, that is, one knows Him in that respect not only more than elsewhere but also as another.

b) The plural form of this name Elohim (see Eloah).

Since Peter Lombard many have found a proof for the Trinity in this form. For example, Luther, but not Calvin. Elohim, however, is used of Father and Son (see Psa 45:8); the name also appears for people and idols (Exod 22:8, 1 Sam 28:13). The plural is to be understood intensively, as "heavens," "waters" are extensive. It points to the inexhaustible fullness of God, and is therefore a *pluralis majestatis* in the deeper sense of the word.

c) The concept of the angel of the Lord, יְהוָה מַלְאַךְ.

Concerning this are the following hypotheses:

1. The Angel of the Lord is a finite spirit, a created angel. Thus Augustine, Jerome, and later Kurz and Delitzsch. This Angel, they say, can speak as if He were God, as the messenger speaks *ex persona* for the one who has sent Him and is identified with Him. However, how could such a messenger receive religious honor for the one who sent Him? Judges 6:11, 18, 22–23.

2. The Angel of the Lord is the *Logos*, the Second Person of the Trinity. Thus Irenaeus, Tertullian, and later, Lutheran and Reformed dogmaticians (Calvin hesitates at some places, yet seems to choose 1 above), Hengstenberg. Some assume that the *Logos* has *personally* united Himself for a time with a created being.

3. The Angel of the Lord is not a person but only an impersonal appearance of God, a momentary entering of God into the sphere of the visible. מַלְאָךְ is to be understood as an abstract noun.

We accept the interpretation under 2 since only it does justice to all the givens. Additionally, however, we also note:

1. Those who shared in this appearance did not have a clear and distinct concept of the doctrine of the Trinity.

2. The Angel, the Messenger, was uncreated, the eternal *Logos*, but the visible form in which He revealed Himself was created, and the *Logos* was not personally united with it, as He was with the human nature assumed later.

The grounds for this interpretation are as follows:

1. The Angel speaks with God's authority (Gen 16:13).

2. He is addressed as God (Gen 16:13).

3. He does divine works (Exod 23:20).

4. He has divine attributes (Gen 16:8).

5. He accepts divine honor (Josh 5:14).

6. He is distinguished from a created angel, Exodus 33, where the Angel of the Presence is distinguished from an ordinary angel (Isa 63:9; Deut 4:37).

7. His name alternates with the name Elohim (Zech 12:8).

d) The concept of *Chokma*, חָכְמָה, "wisdom," as it appears in Proverbs 8:22 and following and Job 28:12–27. Here wisdom is personified, so that it becomes objective for God Himself and yet it stands in the closest relation to Him. It is the image of His thought, the perfect imprint of His inner existence—within Him and outside of Him at the same time. In the prologue of the Gospel of John such things are said of the *Logos*.

e) To the word of God in the Old Testament are also ascribed divine attributes (e.g., Psa 33:4; Isa 40:8; Psa 119:105).

f) The doctrine of the Spirit of God in the Old Testament. The Spirit is the principle of the natural, rational, reasonable life of the world and thus represents the self-conscious immanence of God. He is also the Spirit of revelation. Finally, He is also the Spirit who lives with each believer (see Pss 51:13; 143:10). The Spirit acts as a person standing objectively vis-à-vis God (Isa 63:10; 48:16).

g) Old Testament passages in which God speaks of Himself in the plural. The church has always had a Trinitarian conception of these passages. The following are diverging sentiments:

1. It is a *pluralis majestatis* as the Oriental rulers used of themselves. There are no antecedents for this in Scripture. Only relatively late does something like this appear (Gen 20:15; cf. Ezra 6:8).

2. It is a *pluralis communicationis* by which God includes Himself together with the angels (cf. Isa 6:8); thus Philo, also the younger Delitzsch. However, in Genesis 1:26 one cannot attribute an active part in creation to the angels.

3. It is a *pluralis* of self-generation, in which the subject considers and addresses Himself as object, so that the appearance of a plurality arises. See Hitzig. This is unproved, see Genesis 2:18; Psalm 12:5.

h) Old Testament passages where more than one person is expressly named; Psalms 45:6–7; 110:1. Hebrews 1:8–9 shows that these passages must be understood in this way.

i) Passages that speak of *three* persons; Numbers 6:24–26; compare 2 Corinthians 13:14; Psalm 33:6; Isaiah 61:1; 63:9–10.

3. *In what way must proof for the Trinity be provided from the New Testament?*

One will have to prove:

a) That there is one God.

b) That there are nevertheless three distinct persons named, respectively, Father, Son, and Holy Spirit, called God and considered as God.

c) That there is, therefore, unity in trinity and trinity in unity.

4. *Which New Testament texts speak of the three persons alongside each other?*

Luke 1:35; 3:21–22; Matthew 28:19; 2 Corinthians 13:14; 1 Corinthians 12:3–4; 1 Peter 1:2. Also, above all, in chapters 14–16 of the Gospel of John the teaching of the Lord bears a Trinitarian character.

5. *Which two matters are primarily of concern in argumentation for the Trinity?*

The deity of the Son and the personality of the Holy Spirit. The personality of the Son and the deity of the Holy Spirit, in contrast, are so certain that argumentation is virtually superfluous.

6. *Is there anywhere in the New Testament that provides us with a complete doctrine of the Trinity?*

No, as in the case with other dogmas, here also it was left to the church, under the guidance of the Holy Spirit, to gather the givens spread abroad throughout Scriptures and then to formulate the dogma gradually and in contrast to all kinds of error.

7. *Who used the name Trinity first?*

In its Latin form the first to use the term was Tertullian, who speaks of a *Trinitas Unius Divinitatis*. Before him, however, related terms were already used in Greek. Theophilus, bishop of Antioch in Syria, spoke of ἡ τρίας τοῦ θεοῦ. This was in the last half of the second century after Christ.

8. *Who in the Greek church has contributed the most to the dogmatic development of the doctrine of the Trinity?*

Apollinaris of Laodicea, who, however, was heretical in his Christology, and the great Cappadocians.

9. *Who in the West has contributed most?*

Tertullian. With him, however, much was still unclear. He had the Son and Spirit as proceeding from the Father only for the sake of the creation. They do not have the entire substance of the Godhead but are "parts" or "portions" subordinate to the Father, etc.

10. *What lies between Tertullian and the Cappodocians?*

The official presentation of the church's doctrine at Nicaea and Constantinople. The creed accepted there is also received by our Belgic Confession, article 9, and is therefore binding for us for formulating the doctrine of the Trinity.

11. *How does this creed read?*

As originally accepted at Nicaea (apart from later changes) it reads:

We believe in one God, the Father Almighty, the Maker of all things visible and invisible.

And in one Lord Jesus Christ, the Son of God, begotten as Firstborn of the Father, who is of the substance of the Father, God of God, Light

of Light, very God of very God, begotten, not made, being of one substance (*homoousios*) with the Father. By whom all things are made,
both in heaven and on earth. Who for us men and for our salvation
has come down and become flesh, and became man and has suffered,
and on the third day He rose and ascended into heaven, and who
shall come to judge the living and the dead.

And in the Holy Ghost....

Those who, to the contrary, say, "There was a time when He was
not"; "He was not before He was begotten"; and that He was made out of
nothing or is of another substance or essence (or is created), or that the
Son of God is variable or changeable—these the catholic (and apostolic)
church anathematizes.[1]

12. *In which theses can you state the doctrine of the Trinity?*

a) There is only one divine being. Scripture expresses itself decisively against all polytheism (Deut 6:4; Isa 44:6; Jas 2:19).

b) In this one God are three modes of existence, which we refer
to by the word "person" and which are, each one, this only true
God. In Scripture these three persons are called, Father, Son, and
Holy Spirit.

c) These three persons, although together the one true God, are nevertheless distinguished from each other insofar as they assume
objective relations toward each other, address each other, love
each other, and can interact with each other.

d) Although these three persons possess one and the same divine
substance, Scripture nevertheless teaches us that, concerning
their personal existence, the Father is the first, the Son the
second, and the Holy Spirit the third, that the Son is of the Father,
the Spirit of the Father and the Son. Further, their workings outwardly reflect this order of personal existence, since the Father
works through the Son, and the Father and Son work through the
Spirit. There is, therefore, subordination as to personal manner
of existence and manner of working, but no subordination regarding possession of the one divine substance.

---

1   It is not clear what source for the creed Vos is incorporating here.

e) The divine substance is not divided among the three persons as if each possesses one-third. Neither is it a new substance beside the three persons. Finally, neither is it an abstraction of our thinking in a nominalistic sense. But in a manner for which all further analogy is lacking, each of these persons possesses the entire divine substance.

13. *On which two points has the agreement of the Nicene Confession of Faith with the preceding description been called into question?*

a) Doubt has been raised whether with the use of the word *homoousios* the Nicene Fathers truly meant that the Son is of *one being*, that is of one and the same substance with the Father. Repeatedly, also in recent times, the assertion has been made that *homoousios* says no more than "similar." That these doubts are unfounded appears from the following points:

   1. If the Nicene Fathers had meant no more than that the Son is *similar* in being with the Father, then they would not have needed to reject the Arian *homoiousios*, whose precise meaning is "similar." However, they rejected it.

   2. The confession of Nicaea says explicitly: The Son is begotten of the substance of the Father.

   3. If there is nothing more than similarity, and the Son is still God, one then falls into tritheism, that is, into "tri-godhood."

b) It has been proposed that the Nicene Confession has the Son receiving not only His personal existence but also His deity from the Father. In fact, there are expressions that allow being explained in this sense: "begotten of the substance of the Father, God of God, Light of Light." One must admit that on this point the framers of the Confession had not yet come to complete clarity. Already the Cappadocians used the more careful and more exact description, begotten and spirated "*within* the divine substance." To Augustine belongs the honor that, on the basis of Scripture, he completely eliminated this element of subordination concerning substance from the doctrine of the Trinity. It was a dangerous element.

14. *Give a description of the most important terms that have been used and are still being used by theologians in their doctrine of the Trinity.*

a) First, we have the words *ousia* and *hypostasis* (οὐσία and ὑπόστασις). *Ousia* is the being of God in the abstract that is common to the three persons. *Hypostasis*, on the other hand, means the personal existence mode of this being, what we call person.

   Both these terms originate from Greek philosophy. *Ousia* is Platonic, *hypostasis* is Stoic. The latter originally means "self-existence" and could therefore be used by theologians for a long time to express the same as *ousia*. Later it took on more the sense of "person." But not at once. Consequently, great confusion arose because one could now hear at the same time the assertion that there was one *hypostasis* and that there were three *hypostases* in the Godhead.

b) Another Greek word is *physis*, "nature." This also indicated the substance of God in distinction from the persons. However, *physis* and *ousia* are not the same. *Ousia* is the being of God in the abstract. *Physis* is inclusive of the attributes in Father, Son, and Holy Spirit, that is, those unique to the divine being. The attributes, however, are inseparably joined to the being (Greek φύσις).

c) Still another Greek word was *prosōpon* (πρόσωπον). The original meaning is "face" or "mask." The Latin *persona*, from which we get "person," had the same meaning. Naturally, the heretical Sabellians, who wished to know only of a revealed trinity, eagerly made use of these words in order to gain acceptance for their sentiments. The consequence of this, however, was that the orthodox avoided these words. The Greeks therefore used the above-mentioned *hypostasis* for "person," even where they had earlier used *prosōpon*.

d) The western Latin church also found it difficult at first to find unambiguous terms. There were two Latin words, namely, *substantia* and *subsistentia*. Sometimes both were used for substance, and sometimes both for person, sometimes the one for substance and the other for person. The solution was as follows:

   1. The term *substantia* was abolished in relation to God. *Substantia* is associated by contrast with *accidentia*, "accident," "chance,"

and by calling God "substance" one did not want to give the
impression that in God, too, there is chance.

2. This rejected word was replaced by the more precise term *es-
sentia*, "being," "essence," which corresponds to the Greek *ousia*.

3. The nature of God, as inclusive of the attributes of His being,
is called *natura* in Latin, which agrees with the Greek *physis*.

4. The word *subsistentia* remained in use in order to indicate
the personal mode of existence. Thus, it means what we call
person. In the same sense is *suppositum*, a translation of the
Greek words *hypostasis* and *hypokeimenon* (ὑποκείμενον).

e) The ancients also spoke of a *perichoresis* or *enyparxis* (περιχώρησις,
ἐνυπάρξις); Latin: *circumcessio* or *inexistentia mutua*, "mutual
in-being." One wished to say that the persons of the Godhead are
in each other reciprocally (John 14:2;[2] 17:21; 1 Cor 2:10–11). There is
a kind of internal circulation of the Godhead, an eternal movement within the being of God.

f) The persons of the Trinity are distinguished from each other by
their character (*character hypostatius sive personalis*; Greek: τρόπος
ὑπάρξεως). This personal factor is expressed in the names Father,
Son, and Holy Spirit, which make known the uniqueness of the
three persons. This factor is incommunicable, that is, it belongs
only to one person. Thus, it serves to distinguish the persons.
With the Father, it is His begetting the Son (but not in His causing by breathing the procession of the Spirit, for He has that in
common with the Son). With the Son, it is His being begotten
by the Father. With the Holy Spirit, it is His being breathed out
(spirated) by Father and Son.

g) Regarding the relation between persons and substance, and, in
particular, regarding the question how the persons are distinguished from the substance, complete unanimity does not
reign among the orthodox. Two extremes must be avoided here:
Sabellianism that admits only one person, who is said to have
revealed himself in three forms, and tritheism that does not comprise the three persons within the unity of substance. In order

---

2　Perhaps John 14:20 is meant.

to find the proper middle way, some say that the persons are distinguished from the substance *modaliter*, "according to the mode," that is, as the substance in the abstract and as the substance in a certain mode with certain ways of existence (but not *realiter*, *formaliter*, or merely *ratione*). Others say that the persons are distinguished from each other *realiter*, "actually" (but not *essentialiter* or merely *ratione*). Mastricht says, "If someone cannot follow this scholastic style of discourse, then let him simply believe with Scripture that the persons are distinguished as *three* and declare that beyond that he does not know what kind of distinction, since Scripture has not revealed these things, or that they are distinguished supernaturally, not in a natural manner."

h) Concerning the idea to be connected with the words *hypostasis*, *subsistentia*, *suppositum*, *persona*, unanimity also does not reign. Calvin admits that the word "person" is only an aid but still does not disapprove of its use. Socinians, Remonstrants, Anabaptists, Cartesians, and also Cocceius have disputed its use. The oldest definition was: "Person is the divine being itself distinguished by a certain independent character and by its own manner of existence." Later further descriptions were added. The accepted definition of the older dogmaticians goes back beyond Melanchthon to Boethuis. It reads, "Person is an independent entity, indivisible, rational, incommunicable, not sustained by another nature and not a part of something else."

In order to arrive at clarity regarding this matter one first needs to make clear demands that a theological definition of person must satisfy. These are:

1. It may not detract from the unity of the being of God. If one says, for example, "Person is what does not exist in another nature," that appears to exclude the persons of the Trinity. These persons surely do not exist in themselves but in the divine nature.

2. It must have an element in itself that is common to divine and human personality. In Christology, specifically the divine person of Christ serves to represent the human person of the

elect in the justice of God. If a point of likeness does not exist, then this could not happen.

3. It must be Reformed in that it allows the human nature of the Mediator to be impersonal. If I say, "Person is a being with self-consciousness and self-determination (free-will)," then the human nature of the Savior is included.

In order to satisfy these three conditions at the same time, one can now formulate approximately in the following manner, "Person is an independent entity, indivisible, rational, incommunicable, not sustained by another nature but possessing in itself the principle of its operation."

Or, one can be content with the more modest description, "Person, with reference to the Trinity, means the divine essence in a specific mode of existence and distinguished by this specific mode of existence from that essence and the other persons." On this point further, see Christology.

i) The activities by which each of the persons of the Trinity exists distinct from each other, one calls "internal works" (opera ad intra). They are personal activities not common to all the persons and are incommunicable. As such they are the begetting and spirating of the Father, for the Son, being begotten and spirating, for the Spirit being spirated. These works, for the reasons mentioned, are called divided works (opera divisa).

j) In contrast to the "internal works" are the "external works" (opera ad extra). These may not be divided but belong to the whole being (Gen 1:26; John 5:17, 19).

1. The external works are performed by God's power, and power as an attribute belongs to the being.

2. In the economy or management of God each person has His unique task. For example, creation is ascribed to the Father, salvation to the Son, etc. Yet here, too, the three persons in a certain sense work together, namely, the Father through the Son and the Spirit, the Son through the Father and Spirit.

3. Moreover, in the economy in a narrower sense, that is, in the economy of salvation, the persons of the Trinity exist in

a judicial fellowship. Nothing can take place in which each one is not involved judicially. The Father, as Judge, represents violated holiness and is wrathful. But at the same time the thought of salvation wells up in the depth of His Fatherly heart and He ordains the Son as Mediator and the Holy Spirit as the one who applies salvation. The Son accomplishes the Mediator's work, but He does so officially for the Father's sake, and through the Holy Spirit He applies His merits. The Holy Spirit works in the hearts of the elect, but He does so for the sake of the Father and the Son.

4. This order of working points us back to the order of existence. Just because the Father is the First Person, He occupies that place in the plan of salvation and in the external works in general. Just because the Son is the Second Person, He also assumes in both respects the position He assumes. And the same is true for the Holy Spirit.

15. *Why is this doctrine of the economy of God important?*

Because it contains a powerful protest, both against pantheism that identifies God and the world as well as against deism that keeps God and the world separate. God is not the unconscious background of the world, but in Him there is an abundance of conscious distinctions. Neither does God stand at a distance from His world but is present as Creator and Sustainer, as Savior and Sanctifier, as the source of all being, of all thought, of all life in the world.

16. *Have analogies for the doctrine of the Trinity been drawn from nature?*

Yes, this was already done very early.

a) Many church fathers adduced physical images.

b) Augustine, in particular, worked out the analogy that exists between the Trinity and the unity of intellect, will, and emotions in the human soul. On careful reflection, this analogy could lead to Sabellianism or Modalism. In man these three principles are certainly summed up in the unity of person. Augustine had a strong impression of the unity of God and therefore sometimes actually verges on Sabellianism. "Three persons, it is said, not so much because they wanted to say this, as that they did not want to keep silent about it." This analogy reoccurs in Anselm, Melanchthon, among the Reformed, Keckermann, and in many later theologians.

c) For the medieval Scholastics the point of departure is that all positive relationships must be ascribed perfectly to the most perfect being of all. It must therefore have been created in itself and creating, creating and not being created; thus, for example, Duns Scotus.

d) Still others take their departure in the goodness or love of God; thus recently, Müller and Dorner. Goodness and love presuppose fellowship between more than one person. In this way, however, one does not arrive at the Trinity, at most at a bi-unity.

e) Finally, we have the pantheistic distortion of the doctrine of the Trinity. The ecclesiastical scriptural names are used to attach an entirely new sense. An example is the construction of Hegel: The Father is God in His eternal idea of Himself and for Himself; the Son is the eternal idea of God in its otherness, the world as objectified out of God; the Spirit is the idea returned again to itself in the element of community.

17. *Must we ascribe personality to God's being in itself?*

No, for then we obtain four persons. The essence, however, is not impersonal for it exists in three persons. Only if one abstracts the essence from the latter can one say that it is not personal.

18. *What are the two extremes between which the orthodox doctrine of the Trinity lies?*

a) Modalism or Sabellianism. It will recognize only the divine Person, who assumes three forms of revelation.

b) Tritheism or tri-godhood. It emphasizes the threeness of persons to such an extent that it thereby loses sight of the unity of the being.

19. *How do you refute Sabellianism?*

By showing:

a) That Scripture everywhere places the divine Persons in distinction from each other. The Father speaks to and of the Son and the Son to and of the Father.

b) In God's economy, as it reveals itself in the plan of salvation, the persons appear in judicial relationships with each other. Thus, they must have the capacity and competence to undertake such relationships. For example, what is said about the Counsel of Peace would all be a mere show if the persons were not distinguished from each other.

c) That this heresy denies the immutability of God as soon as it takes the distinction between the persons more seriously. Some Sabellians do teach that the Godhead from eternity was one and unipersonal but for the sake of revelation has divided itself into a trinity of persons. This is the pantheistic doctrine of a self-developing of God in the world.

d) That Sabellianism does not allow justice to be done to the humanity of the Mediator. According to this point of view, it is merely a revelatory from of God, like the appearance of the Angel of the Lord.

20. *Is the name Father always used of God in the same sense?*

No.

a) Sometimes God is called Father as the origin of all that is created. In this sense one can say that the name refers to the Trinity as a whole and to the Father insofar as within the divine economy the work of creation falls to Him (compare Eph 3:16).

b) In by far the most instances, God is called Father of men insofar as He is the one who begets His children. Therefore, the name indicates God's sovereignty in the work of grace. Thus, it is not in agreement with Scripture if we call God the Father of all. Neither is this true when it can be said to be the truth that all are His children in the deeper sense of the word.

c) Entirely distinct from these two meanings is the meaning of the name of Father applied to the First Person of the Trinity in His relationship with the Second Person. The Father is Father of the Son and this is a supernatural relationship, of which all human sonship can only be called an image.

21. *Is the Second Person always called the Son of God in the same sense?*

No, when some claim that the name Son is only an official name for Christ, we reject this, not because this name never occurs in this sense, but because this is not its primary and basic meaning. The Socinians maintained that Christ is called Son as the Messiah. But we hold:

a) That He is called Son as, in a supernatural manner within the Trinity, He is eternally generated by the Father.

b) That even as Messiah He can only be called Son because He is Son supernaturally, for Christ can only be Messiah because He is the eternal Son of God. The clearest confirmation for this is the many places that bring His Sonship into the closest connection with his worth as Mediator and His resurrection. (Acts 13:13; Rom 1:4)

22. *Show that the first and foremost reason why the Second Person is called Son lies in His eternal and supernatural relationship with the Father and is independent from His position as Mediator.*

This appears:

a) From those places where the Word is called Son *before* His incarnation (Gal 4:4; John 1:14, 18).

b) From the places in which the name Son of God is used such that it includes the deity of the Lord (John 5:18–25; Heb 7).

c) From the places in which He is called the *only begotten* Son of God (John 1:14, 18; 3:16, 18; 1 John 4:9).

d) From the fact that Christ nowhere prays to God as "*Our* Father" or speaks of Him as "*Our* Father." It is always "Father." In these places the Lord does not place Himself on the same line with His disciples. For Him, God is a Father in an entirely other, infinitely higher sense than for them.

e) From the fact that in Mark 13:32 the Lord presents Himself as "the Son" in distinction from angels and men.

f) From the fact that in Matthew 11:27 a wholly unique knowledge of God, which no one else can possess, is derived from His Sonship.

g) From the fact that by accepting the title Son of God, Christ could be charged with blasphemy.

23. *Is it correct to speak of the Father as the "Fountain of Deity," as many have done?*

This expression is not biblical. It can also lead to misunderstandings. Scripture uses the name Father relative to showing the personal existence of the Son. Of this the Father is the source and not of His deity. The deity of the three persons is one and undivided, belonging to each of the three persons. On the other hand, the Son and the Holy Spirit have their personal existence from the Father, the Holy Spirit from the Father and the Son.

24. *If this is true, how is it nevertheless that the Father in some places is placed as God toward the Son and the Holy Spirit?*

In such places, Christ is not in view as the eternal Word, except for His incarnation, but specifically as Mediator and Guarantor of the covenant of grace. This happens in 1 Corinthians 8:6; John 17:3; Ephesians 4:5, 6; 2 Corinthians 11:31; and Ephesians 1:3.

25. *What comment did Augustine make regarding the personal existence of the Father?*

He said that the Father has His personal existence precisely in generating the Son and spirating the Holy Spirit, and that thus in a certain sense the personal existence of the Father is determined by the Son and the Spirit.

26. *What is the personal character of the Father?*

Negatively considered, it is His not being generated. Positively considered, it is His both generating and spirating. In itself spirating also belongs to the Son, but in this connection with generating it is only present with the Father.

27. *Which external works are more specifically attributed to the Father?*

  a) The first planning of the counsel of redemption, including election.

  b) The work of creation and providence, especially their first results.

  c) Representation of the Trinity in its rightly maintained deity in the work of redemption.

28. *Which attributes, as a result, are preeminently ascribed to the Father?*

  a) Power, Matthew 11:26.

  b) Righteousness, Genesis 18:25; John 17:25; 2 Thessalonians 1:6.

29. *With reference to the Second Person of the Trinity, what, in turn, must be treated?*

  a) The personal existence of the Son, its ground and nature.

  b) His deity.

  c) His economic function.

30. *What information does Scripture provide for us to determine more exactly the relationship that exists between the First and Second Persons within the Trinity?*

  a) The names Father and Son, which presuppose each other.

  b) The words "only begotten" and "firstborn" (John 1:14, 18; 3:16–18, 1 John 4:9; Col 1:15; Heb 1:6).

  c) The doctrine of the Word of God, the *Logos*-doctrine, and the designations of Christ that appear to be connected with it, namely "the radiance of the glory and the express image of His substance" (Heb 1:3), "the image of the invisible God" (Col 1:15; 2 Cor 4:4); further, "Wisdom" in the Old Testament.

31. *What must be observed about the names Father and Son?*

That from them one derives at times too much and at other times too little. Too much if one thinks to have found proof here for a communication of being from the Father to the Son; too little if one maintains that these terms are only to be taken figuratively and do not express a real relationship between the two persons.

32. Show that in the names of Father and Son there does not need in itself to be a communication of being.

If this were the case, it would have to rest on the supposed fact that among men a son obtains his being by communication from his father. This, however, is not the case. Only Traducianists maintain that it is and then only when at the same time they are Realists. According to the Reformed view, God is continuously creating the being of men. Naturally this cannot be applied even remotely to the Son. He was not created, but generated. One will therefore have to admit that in the common use of the names father and son for divine and human relationships the point of comparison cannot lie in the communication of being.

33. Does not John 5:26 speak of a communication of being?

No, it does not speak about a communication of life from the Father to the Word before His incarnation, but only about a communication of life to the Mediator. Already Calvin correctly explained this passage in the last mentioned sense. One should peruse the context.

34. When does one derive too little from the names Father and Son?

When one wishes to find only an expression of the unity of being or of the equality of the persons with each other.

35. In what does the true meaning of these names reside?

In the concept of *causality*. The Father is called Father and the Son, Son because the former is the *cause* of the personal existence of the latter.

36. What needs to observed concerning the designation "only begotten Son"?

Regarding its meaning differences of opinion are prevalent. All must certainly admit that this designation belongs to Christ as the eternal Word, thus before and apart from His incarnation. But some maintain that nothing more is involved than that from eternity Father and Son are bonded by love as an earthly father and his only son would be. It is figurative language to express the greatness of this love.

Against this view we observe the following: If one already acknowledges that the name *Son* expresses an eternal, supernatural relationship, it is in all respects necessary to discover in "only begotten Son" a more exact description. It would be very unnatural in this latter designation to take one half literally, the other half figuratively. We take both literally. For us, therefore, the name "only begotten Son" includes that the relationship of causality is a relationship of generating on the one side and of being begotten on the other. Moreover, that the one relationship is of the most intimate unity, completely different from God's unity with the children spoken of in John 1:12. This difference lies in *only* begotten. The others are not born in this fashion. Finally, John 1:14 teaches us that the possession of divine glory by the Son coheres in a certain manner with this generation. It reads, "a glory as of the *only begotten* of the Father."

37. Where does the name "firstborn" occur?

In Colossians 1:15, "firstborn of all creatures." Primarily at issue in the explanation of these words is the genitive πάσης κτίσεως. Is this a partitive genitive or a comparative genitive? In the first instance the sense becomes "the firstborn of all creatures." Christ would then be included under the concept of creature. Some who dispute the deity of Christ maintain that this is the meaning of the apostle.

In the second instance the sense is "who is *born* before, then all creatures were *created*," so that Christ lies outside the circle of creatures. The genitive then depends on the comparative concept included in "first."

The latter view is the correct one. The text does not say, of "all *the* creation," as one would expect on the first view, but only of "each creature," "every creature," which only fits the latter view. One should note the clear distinction the apostle makes here between being *born* and being *created*. The latter is true of all other things; only the first can be said of Christ. He is born but not created.

38. Where else do we find the name "firstborn"?

In Hebrews 1:6, where it is added that He can bear that name because He has inherited the divine nature, "having become so much more superior than the angels as He has inherited a more excellent name than they." The name alluded to is "firstborn" (cf. v. 4, 6, 9).

39. *Did the name Logos appear elsewhere before its use in the Gospel of John?*

Yes, the Old Testament already spoke of a "word of God" by which the heavens are made, as was seen above.

In the non-sacred writings of Philo and the earlier and later Jewish theology this name is also used, although with a basically different meaning, to which one needs to pay attention. With Philo and others the word is means of revelation and creation. The idea is that God is so high and far above the finite that He cannot come into immediate contact with His creation. One therefore tries to lessen this infinite distance by an intermediate being, a kind of cosmic mediator, who then reveals God to man and thus is called *"logos,"* word.

In the Gospel of John and in Scripture in general it is quite different. There in the first place Christ is not called *Logos*, "Word," for what He does with respect to the world, but for what He is with respect to the Father. Here is where one must pay attention most carefully in order to grasp the deep meaning of this *Logos*-doctrine. The other thought is present, too. God spoke and can speak to man though Christ, because the Son is His eternal Word. But this thought is subsidiary and derives from the first.

40. *Specify which elements are included in this being the Word of the Second Person of the Trinity.*

a) The word is something caused by the speaker.

b) Nevertheless this word is not created out of nothing. Its rationale is already inherent in the speaker.

c) The word reproduces an image of the speaker; it is an imprint of his personal existence. There is equivalence between the speaker and his word.

d) Speaker and word remain tied to each other in the most intimate way. Even after it has been spoken, the word lives on in the consciousness.

41. *Has one sometimes wanted to find more in the Logos-doctrine?*

Yes, some have found in it a confirmation of their philosophical conception of the Trinity. Even some Reformed theologians have taught that generation was an act of the divine thinking of the Father. *Logos*, however, can have a twofold meaning: (1) word in its external sense, that is, *speech*; (2) word in its internal sense, that is, *reason*. If it is taken in the latter sense, the thought would be that the Son is called the Word as the one brought forth from eternity by the Father's thinking. Scripture, however, provides no occasion for understanding the *Logos* designation in this sense.

42. What more is taught in John 1:1 and 18 regarding the Logos?

That He was "with God" (πρὸς τὸν θεόν) and "in the bosom of the Father" (εἰς τὸν κόλπον τοῦ πατρός). Here both times a preposition is used that suggests direction. The Son is "toward the Father" and "toward the bosom of the Father." The thought appears to be that Christ, continually through generation, turns, as it were, through the impulse of His personal life toward the Father.

43. Which expressions connected with the Logos-doctrine are present in Hebrews 1:3?

Here the Son is called ἀπαύγασμα τῆς δόξης καὶ χαρατὴρ τῆς ὑποστάσεως of God; that is, "reflection of His glory and image of His substance."

44. What in the Letter to the Hebrews is distinctive about its argumentation for the deity of Christ?

This argumentation is distinctive in reasoning from the greatness of His inheritance as Mediator and His honor as Mediator to His eternal Sonship. Someone who is Mediator in this way can only be God's supernatural Son or, more exactly, "God's natural Son." Such is also the reasoning in the third verse being discussed here. One must consider the connection between this verse and what follows in this way: "*Since* He is the reflection of the Father's glory, etc., He has been able to obtain this place of power and honor and to take His place at the right hand of the majesty in the highest heaven."

45. To what purpose do the expressions "reflection of the Father's glory," etc. appear to be used by the writer of Hebrews?

They are used in order to connect the deity of the Son with the unity of God. The Son is, as it were, a reflection, an imprint of the Father, and is yet distinguished from Him. By "reflection of His glory" unity in being is expressed, by "imprint of His substance," equality of persons. One image was not able to express these two truths at the same time. Therefore two images were chosen. Of one being with the Father and yet begotten of the Father—that is what the two images teach us. Here "imprint" means "stamp" in the sense of "what is stamped," for example, the impression on a coin.

46. *Which names are attributed to Christ in Colossians 1:15 and 2 Corinthians 4:4?*

Here He is called "the image of God." In 2 Corinthians 4 that is brought into connection with that fact that God's glory is revealed in Him. As the image of the Father, Christ shares in this divine glory that belongs to God alone (Rom 1:23). When it is now said, "He is the image of the invisible God," that implies, "the *visible* image of the invisible God." In other words, the incarnate Word is spoken of here. But the incarnate Word would not be able to be the image of God unless He was that image as the eternal Word.

47. *What follows from all the givens from Scripture discussed so far?*

   a) The relationship between Father and Son is one of causality.

   b) It is also a relationship of unity of being.

   c) It is a relationship of equality of persons.

   d) It is a relationship connected with the possession of the divine nature by the Son, for from that possession it is repeatedly inferred that the Son shares in the glory of God.

48. *What judgment is to be made about speaking of the communication of being from the Father to the Son?*

If by that one thinks of the being as it were first existing in the Father and then taken by Him and communicated to the Son, then that language appears very dubious.

49. *What objections are there against such an idea?*

   a) It appears to us not to do justice to the absolute deity of the Son. A communicated deity is not an absolute deity but a contradiction. Deity cannot be communicated. It is always of itself, self existing.

b) It can easily lead to viewing the Son as a created being. Where something is communicated, one must think of a person to whom it is communicated. If now the Son is there before being is communicated to Him, then He is also generated from this communication of being. But how? Out of nothing? That cannot be. And yet the communication of being appears to lead to such a consequence.

c) The old theologians have not really intended a communication of being. What they meant was a *communicatio* that makes being to be in common. The Father does not first generate the Son in order then to communicate being to Him. But *within* the one divine being He generates the Son from that being and thereby makes this one being common between Himself and the Son.

50. *Is the generation of the Son a temporary, transitory or an eternal, abiding act?*

It is eternal and abiding. There can be no thought of continuation or progression in time. In his *Institutes of the Christian Religion* 1.13.29, Calvin appears to deny this eternity. It follows directly from the eternity of God.

51. *Is generation an act of will of the Father or an eternal, necessary act?*

The latter. Otherwise the Son would be a creature, for all that proceeds from the will of God and so could not have been, is created. Of course generation is not contrary to the will of the Father. All that is meant is that it is not in the same sense as, for example, the creation is the free result of this will.

52. *Does generation imply a division or split in the divine being?*

No; its result is that the Son completely possesses the divine being, like the Father. There is but one God and the Son is that God.

53. *How do you describe the generation of the Son?*

It is the eternal, necessary act of the First Person of the Trinity, by which, within the same divine being, He is the ground for the existence of a second person, equal to His own person, and by which He makes this second person to share in the possession of the divine being without, thereby, any split taking place.

54. What is the difference between deity and divinity?

Many who argue against the Trinity are willing to attribute divinity to the Son. Arians, semi-Arians, Socinians and other Unitarians deny unity of being. To all these people one must pose this question: Is the Son God in the sense that one can speak of only one God? That decides everything and faced with that question everyone must take sides. No one can be saved from it with vague answers.

55. What kinds of proofs are there for the deity of the Son?

These are two kinds:

a) Indirect proof, that is, proofs drawn from facts and data that presuppose deity.

b) Direct proof, consisting of biblical passages that intentionally teach the deity of the Son.

56. In what does the first category of proofs consist?

In places that:

a) Ascribe divine names to the Son (Psa 45:7-8 compared with Heb 1:8-9; Isa 9:6; 7:14 compared with Matt 1:23; Mal 3:1 compared with Mark 1:2 and Luke 1:16; 1 Tim 3:16 and Heb 1:10-11 compared with Psa 102:26; and Eph 4:8-9 with Psa 68:18).

b) Attribute divine properties to the Son, specifically:

1. *Eternity* (Mic 5:2 compared with Matt 2:6; Isa 9:6; Heb 7:3; Rev 1:8; John 8:58).

2. *Immensity* and *omnipresence* (Matt 18:20; 28:20; John 3:13).

3. *Omnipotence* (Rev 1:8; John 5:19; Heb 1:3).

4. *Omniscience* (John 21:17; 16:30; 2:24-25; 1:49; Rev 2:23 compared with 1 Kgs 8:29). Mark 13:32 is no objection. Augustine speaks of an official not-knowing of His human nature.

5. *Immutability* (Heb 1:11-12 compared with Psa 102:26; Heb 13:8).

6. *Fullness of deity* (Col 2:9).

c) Attribute divine works to the Son, specifically:

1. The work of creation (Prov 8:27; John 1:3; Col 1:16–17; and Heb 1:2, 10).

2. The work of providence (Heb 1:3; Col 1:17; John 5:17).

3. The working of miracles (John 5:21; 6:40; [5:36]).

4. The works of redemption (Acts 20:28; John 13:18; 10:16; Eph 5:26, John 16: 7, 14).

d) Attribute divine honor to the Son, specifically:

1. *Faith* directed to Him (John 14:1). He teaches differently than the Pharisees and the Scribes, even than Moses and the Prophets, having authority and whose word does not allow for any higher appeal.

2. *Hope* (1 Cor 15:19; 1 Thess 1:3; 1 Tim 1:1).

3. Formal *worship* (Heb 1:6; Psa 2:12; John 5:23; Phil 2:9–10).

4. The invoking of grace from Him (2 Cor 13:13; 1 Cor 1:2; Acts 7:59; 9:14; Rev 5:13; 1 Pet 4:2; 2 Tim 4:18; Rev 1:6; 2 Pet 3:18).

57. Which texts speak directly and intentionally of the deity of the Son?

John 1:1; Romans 9:5; Philippians 2:6; Titus 2:13; John 5:20; 20:28.

58. What is in John 1:1?

"The Word was God." By this, absolute deity is attributed to the Son, for He bears the same name with the Father, with whom He was in the beginning.

59. How many translations are there of Romans 9:5?

a) The customary translation, "…from whom is Christ according to the flesh, who is God above all, to be praised forever, Amen." So understood, these words provide the strongest evidence for the deity of the Son.

b) Others, however, would have it translated, "From whom Christ is to be praised forever." The final words would then refer to the Father.

c) Still others would translate, "From whom is Christ according to the flesh, who is above all. God is to be praised forever." The final words must then refer to the Father.

60. *Why is the first translation the correct one and the latter two to be rejected?*

a) Because Christ is the antecedent, and it is not arbitrary here to think of Him when the apostle continues, "who is ..."

b) Because the words "according to the flesh," by virtue of the contrast implied, demand a description of the deity of the Lord (cf. Rom 1:3).

c) The words applied to Christ stand in the closest connection with what precedes, since they add a new link in the chain of Israel's privileges.

d) If a doxology to God the Father occurred here, the word order in the original would not agree with what is always the word order in such doxologies.

e) After Paul has lamented the sad apostasy of Israel, one does not expect a doxology to God in this context.

61. *What is the answer when one says that nowhere else does Paul call the Lord, God?*

That he certainly does so, namely in Titus 2:13 and Acts 20:28.

62. *How then can the apostle sometimes distinguish so sharply between God and Christ (e.g., 1 Corinthians 8:6; Ephesians 4:5)?*

This distinction is meant economically. Here Christ is placed as Mediator in contrast to God, not as Son to the Father.

63. *What is the answer if someone says that there are no praises (doxologies) to Christ in later letters by apostles?*

This claim is based on the denial of the authenticity of 2 Peter and of the apostolicity of the Epistle to the Hebrews, as well as on a faulty explanation of 1 Peter 4:11. In any case, 2 Timothy 4:18 and Revelation 1:6 and 5:13 may not be dismissed.

64. Give a short explanation of Philippians 2:6.

We can render this much-discussed and variously interpreted passage as follows: "The one possessing the same being with God the Father (being in the form of God) did not consider equality in the economy of God's working as something to be robbed (did not view equality with God as a matter for robbery), but humbled Himself, etc."

That is, as far as His divine being was involved, Christ, like the Father, was in the form of God. In the order of persons, however, He was the Second Person, so that in the counsel of peace it fell to Him to be the Surety, with all that is bound up with that. The apostle, then, intends to say: In this division of the work of redemption Christ did not consider being equal with the Father as something to be robbed, as something that He must take for Himself by force. As the second person He submitted to this second work, with which suffering and death are associated, and thereby has become the great example of self-denial. The text therefore teaches:

a) That with the Father the Son possesses the same divine being.

b) That, nevertheless, in the order of persons, in mode of existence, He is not the first but the second person.

65. What is the Son called in Titus 2:13?

"Our great God and Savior." Despite the desire of some, the initial words do not refer to God the Father, so that one would have to translate, "of our great God and of our Savior." They refer to Christ:

a) Because the expression "appearing" is never used of the Father but always means the return of the Son for judgment.

b) Because what follows only concerns the Son.

c) Because if the reference were to God the Father, the expression "*great* God" would be superfluous. On the Day of Judgment, the apostle intends to say, Christ will be revealed as great God and Savior. So, the addition of "great" makes good sense.

66. What is in 1 John 5:20?

That the Son is the true God and eternal life. Here, too, these words must refer to the Him and not to the Father, for:

a) Otherwise the same thing would be said twice.

b) In this sense, it is not said of God the Father that He is eternal life.

c) Here the words must show that Christ is able to do what is attributed to Him in the beginning of the verse, namely, come and give us understanding so that we may know the One who is true. He is able to do this, says the apostle, because He is the true God and eternal life.

67. What judgment is to be made about John 20:28?

What we have to consider here is not an outcry of amazement, but of amazement addressed to Christ, for:

a) The text states, "Thomas *answered* and *said*."

b) "My God" could perhaps be an outcry of astonishment, but "my Lord" can only refer to Christ.

c) The context demands this explanation, that Christ is being addressed. The words contain Thomas's acknowledgment of the Lord's resurrection. One should note that the Lord accepts this acknowledgment of His deity.

68. What comprises the work of the Son in the economy of God's working?

He occupies the second place in the external works [*opera ad extra*] of God. *Through* Him all things are created. On behalf of the Father He takes on the role of Surety in the counsel of peace and accomplishes in time His mediatorial work on earth in order to continue His intercession in heaven before the Father.

69. Is there a connection between the eternal Sonship of Christ and His work as Mediator?

Yes; Scripture joins these two with each other. Because He is the Second Person in the Trinity and so has His personal existence from the Father, it is appropriate that of the three persons He shall be the one sent, who comes to fulfill the servant-work of the covenant. The Son is therefore presented in Scripture as a servant.

70. *Does the Son also have a close relationship to what is created, considered apart from His position as Mediator?*

Yes; for as all things are created *through Him,* so they are also created *for Him.* That comes out especially in Paul's letters from his first imprisonment (Eph 3:9, 11; 1:3–4; Col 1:16; Eph 1:10; 5:5; cf. 1 Cor 15:2).

One should note, however, that in this relationship the Son is not called Mediator. The name "Mediator" always has in view the relationship in which the incarnation brings the Word to stand in relation to creation. This latter relationship results entirely from the demands of the work of redemption.

71. *Which attributes are primarily attributed to the Son as a result of His work in the economy of God's working?*

   a) Wisdom (1 Cor 1:24; Prov 8).

   b) Faithfulness, as that is particularly characteristic of a steward (cf. 1 Cor 4:2 with Heb 3:1–2; John 5:30; 8:29, 49–50).

   c) Power, both in the sense of authority and force (1 Cor 1:24; Heb 1:3).

   d) Mercy and grace (2 Cor 13:14; Eph 5:2, 25).

God the Holy Spirit[3]

72. *What three points must be discussed here?*

   a) The personal existence of the Holy Spirit, its nature and degree.

   b) His deity.

   c) His economic involvement.

73. *Which is most disputed, the personality or the deity of the Holy Spirit?*

His personality. Once this has been established it will be impossible any longer to cast doubt on His deity. With the Son the situation is just the reverse. He is the one who appeared and became personally revealed in the flesh. On the other hand, the Holy Spirit only seldom does his work in visible forms. He is the person who dwells and prays within believers

---

3　This heading is in the original manuscript, although no previous headings were given to indicate sections dealing with the Father and the Son.

and thus in a certain sense is identified with them. He therefore stands less in a personal relationship *toward* believers.

74. *What error results from a false understanding of these characteristics?*

The old Sabellian error that the Holy Spirit is only an expression of God's power. This is also the view of all Unitarians, earlier and more recent. It is the view as well of the modern Sabellianism of the school of Schleiermacher, according to which the Holy Spirit is God in the church as a whole. The Holy Spirit first began to exist, it is said, when the Christian church made its appearance. This error is facilitated because Lutherans ascribe more to the sacrament itself and to the word itself than do the Reformed. Thus they do not feel the need to the same degree as we do of the personal activity of the Holy Spirit.

75. *With what data do we have to reckon in order to determine the personal existence of the Holy Spirit?*

  a) With the name "Spirit" (Hebrew, *ruach*; Greek, *pneuma*).

  b) With the expression "proceeding from," by which Scripture describes the relationship between Father and Son and Holy Spirit.

  c) With texts that speak of a unity between the Spirit and the Father or the Spirit and Christ (1 Cor 2:10–11; 2 Cor 3:17; Eph 1:17; and the Gospel of John).

  d) With texts that attribute all the qualities of personality to the Holy Spirit.

76. *Is something in particular expressed by the name "Spirit" that belongs to the Third Person of the Trinity as person?*

Yes, everything favors that it does. The name Son for the Second Person has such a significance. Therefore, that will also be the case with the name Spirit. The name cannot have in view being in the abstract, for in that Father and Son likewise share. If the Third Person is called the Holy Spirit specifically, there must also be a specific reason. Finally, in the Apostolic Benediction the name "Spirit" stands side by side the personal names "Father" and "Son."

77. *What then does the name Spirit teach about the personal existence of the Holy Spirit?*

a) The Hebrew and Greek words for Spirit both originally mean "breath" and subsequently "wind" and any invisible power. Now, however, breath is the distinguishing mark of life. In Genesis 2:7 the inbreathing of life means the communication of life. Therefore the Third Person of the Trinity is called Spirit because, as far as His personal existence is concerned, He is brought forth from eternity by the Father and by the Son, because the personal breath of life passes over as it were from them to Him. In this connection it must be kept in view, just as with the generation of the Son, that we have to do here not with a mere human figure used by God in Scripture to indicate relationships within His being. The reverse is true. Breath as a sign of life in living beings is an image in what is created of the particular way in which the Holy Spirit, who is the supervisor of life, receives His personal existence from the Father and Son.

b) Breath or wind is something active, something that acts with force. Just so the Holy Spirit is the person of the Trinity that brings life and movement into what is created.

c) If the breath of one person is breathed into another, then that involves at the same time that there is some likeness between the life that thus originates and the life from which the breath issues. So, between the Holy Spirit, the Son, and the Father, besides unity of being, there is also a resemblance of the persons, with the result that they are each other's image.

78. *Can we further distinguish "out-breathing" [spiration] from generation?*

No, not as far as the action itself is concerned. On the formal difference we will speak later.

79. *What does John 15:26 teach us about the personal existence of the Holy Spirit?*

That He "proceeds from the Father." The great question is how this procession is to be understood. Should it be understood as a description of eternal spiration or of temporal sending? On the former understanding the Holy Spirit receives His personal existence from all eternity; on the latter, the Third Person of the Trinity is sent to the church after the accomplished work of redemption.

80. *How can you prove that the former and not the latter understanding is meant?*

   a) In the immediately preceding verses where the temporal sending of the Holy Spirit is mentioned, Scripture uses another word, not "whom I will cause to proceed from the Father," but "whom I will send from the Father."

   b) It is not said, "who will proceed from the Father" but "who proceeds from the Father," in the present tense. Thus, an eternal, ever-present act must be meant.

   c) If temporal procession were meant, the Lord would say, "I will send the Spirit, whom the Father (otherwise or usually) sends."

   d) The preposition used here is the same that is used elsewhere regarding the Son.

81. *If this understanding of the verse is correct, how is it that here the Holy Spirit is said to proceed "from the Father" and not from the Father and the Son?*

Because the Son speaks here as Mediator, He does not include Himself. Although the Spirit certainly proceeds from Him as Son, considered in terms of His deity, it is less appropriate that He would speak of that as Mediator.

82. *Does it follow from 1 Corinthians 2:10 and 11 that the Spirit with respect to God is the same as what the spirit of man is to man—in other words, not personally distinguished from Him but only one of His faculties?*

No; that in no way follows from this text. The apostle wishes only to say that the Spirit stands in an equally close relationship to the depth of God as the spirit of man to man. The Spirit is in God as the spirit of man is in man. The point of comparison therefore lies in the close union between the Spirit and God. It is just as close as in man, as close as the unity there is between human nature and the spirit of man. As the one is a being-in, so is the other a being-in. But the similarity goes no further and one has to force the image in order to find in it something more. With man the unity is such that man and his spirit are only one person. With deity, unity is such that there nevertheless can be three persons in the one divine being. In spite of the comparison there is a great difference.

83. What does 2 Corinthians 3:17 teach?

That "the Lord," that is the divine person of the Mediator, is the Spirit. This is so in the sense that in turning to the Lord, Israel will at the same time turn to the Spirit and be delivered from all veiling and bondage because the Spirit works freedom (see the context). In view here first of all is the economic unity between the Spirit and the Mediator in the work of redemption. But this unity points back to the unity in the divine being.

84. What does Ephesians 1:17 teach?

Here the Spirit is called "Spirit of wisdom and of revelation in the knowledge of" God and Christ. This means that the Holy Spirit possesses this knowledge of God by nature and can therefore communicate it.

85. What does the Lord teach us about the Holy Spirit in His last discourses transmitted in the Gospel of John?

That, like the Son, He teaches, proclaims, and witnesses, and that for Him these acts, just as is true for the words of Christ, result from a hearing and receiving (John 16:13–14). With Christ, however, all this resulted from His eternal abiding at the side of the Father, from the close, entirely unique relationship in which He stood and stands to the Father. Therefore, such a relationship must also exist with respect to the Holy Spirit (cf. John 14:26; 16:13; 1 John 2:20–21).

86. How does more recent Sabellian theology dispose of those texts that prove the personality of the Holy Spirit?

By finding nothing more in them than an emphatic personification. One must at all costs avoid seeing personality, for the deity of the Holy Spirit is so firmly established that as His personality is proven, there is no more evading the doctrine of the Trinity.

87. *Why can one not admit that in these texts there is a personification?*

a) A personification may never be accepted where it would nullify the sense of a statement and would defeat the purpose for which the statement is made. This would be the case in Romans 8:26. If the Holy Spirit is not really a person, then there is no comfort in His praying for us. One does not comfort someone with personifications.

b) One cannot expect such a large number of figurative sayings in the New Testament and in its prose style. Especially in dogmatic argumentation there is no place for such sayings.

c) Personifications are always easy to distinguish from all other things. In John 3:8; Hebrews 12:24; and 1 Corinthians 13:1–8, everyone senses immediately that he is dealing with personifications. But this is not the case in texts that speak of the Holy Spirit.

88. *What proofs are there for the personality of the Holy Spirit?*

a) The personality of the Spirit is seen from His procession because the latter is the ground of the former, as generation is the ground of the personality of the Son.

b) The Spirit speaks of Himself in the first person (Acts 10:19–20;[4] 13:2). In the three significant proof texts in the Gospel of John, Christ refers to Him with the masculine personal pronoun ἐκεῖνος (John 14:26; 15:26; 16:13–14).

c) All the distinguishing marks of personality are attributed to Him, such as:

1. *Intellect* (1 Cor 6:11; John 14:26; 15:26; Rom 8:16; 1 Tim 4:1; Isa 61:1; Acts 13:2; 5:3; 20:28).

2. *Will* (1 Cor 12:11; Acts 16:7).

3. *Emotions* (Eph 4:30; Isa 63:10; Matt 12:32).

d) Our relationship to the Holy Spirit is such as is possible only toward a person (Matt 28:19; 2 Cor 13:13).

---

4 The original manuscript only lists v. 19.

e) The Holy Spirit has appeared in separate personal forms, like a dove (Matt 3:16), like fiery tongues (Acts 2:3–4).

f) The Holy Spirit is distinguished as a person from His own power (Luke 1:35; 4:14).

89. *Distinguish between the generation of the Son and the spiration of the Holy Spirit.*

a) Generation takes place by the Father alone; spiration takes place by Father and Son.

b) Some say that generation not only causes a new mode of existence in the divine being but also a mode of existence that is like that of the One who generates. The latter then is not true of spiration. The reason offered for this point is that a mode of existence can only be an image of one and not of two. But how if the two are already like each other, as is the case with Father and Son? This point is doubtful to say the least.

c) The result of generation is the communication of the capacity, in turn, to grant participation in the divine being. Through generation the Son receives the necessary attribute of actual breathing. In spiration such a necessary attribute is not communicated to the Holy Spirit. In Him the inner movement of the Trinity comes to conclusion and rest.

d) Concerning logical order, generation comes first and then spiration. But this is not a distinction in time. Both are equally eternal.

90. *Does the Holy Spirit proceed only from the Father or from the Son as well?*

Also from the Son, although the Greek church denies this. Different motives underlie this denial. It agreed above all with the mystical direction of the Greek church. In this way the saving work of the Holy Spirit within the soul could be more easily detached from the objective work of the Mediator. Proofs for procession from the Son also are the following:

a) If the Spirit does not proceed from the Son, then there is a point in the Godhead where Son and Spirit do not affect each other but are separated. They would then find their unity only indirectly, that is to say, in the Father.

b) The Son sends the Spirit in time. He would not be able to do this if the Spirit did not also proceed from Him eternally, for the order of working in the Trinity follows the order of existence among the three Persons (John 16:7).

c) The Spirit is called the Spirit of the Son and the Spirit of Christ no less than the Spirit of the Father (Gal 4:6; Rom 8:9; Phil 1:19).

d) All that the Spirit has, He has from the Son no less than from the Father (John 16:13–15).

91. *If the Holy Spirit has His personal existence from the Son, who in His turn has His from the Father, is there thereby no derogation of the Holy Spirit's deity?*

No, for by spiration the Holy Spirit does not receive His deity but only His personal existence. As He receives the latter, at the same time He is made to share in the one indivisible divine being.

92. *How many kinds of processions of the Holy Spirit are there?*

Only one. The Holy Spirit proceeds as a unique Spirit within the divine being (not out of nothing). But there is a twofold breathing, one from the Father and one from the Son.

93. *How do you prove the deity of the Holy Spirit?*

By proving that:

a) He bears divine names. Not valid as proofs are those places that present words from the Old Testament as spoken by the Holy Spirit. Such places do not directly concern His deity but simply follow from His work in the economy of God's working as the author of Holy Scripture. Words of men from the Old Testament are therefore sometimes presented in the New Testament as spoken by the Holy Spirit (cf. Isa 6:9 with Acts 28:25). Certainly valid as proof, however, are Acts 5:3, 9; 1 Cor 3:16; 6:19; and 1 John 4:13.

b) Divine attributes are ascribed to Him:

1. Eternity (Gen 1:2).

2. Omnipresence (Psa 139:7–8; 1 Cor 3:16).

3. Omniscience (1 Cor 2:10; John 16:13; 2 Pet 1:21).

4. Omnipotence (Luke 1:35).

c) Divine works are attributed to Him:

1. Creation (Gen 1:2; Psa 33:6).

2. Preserving and governing (Psa 104:30).

3. Miracles (Matt 12:28; 1 Cor 12:4; Luke 1:35).

4. Forgiveness of sins and regeneration (1 Cor 6:11; John 3:5).

5. Governing the church (Acts 13:2; 15:28; 20:28).

6. Foretelling future events (John 16:13).

7. Illumination and sanctification (Eph 1:17–18; 2 Thess 2:13; 1 Pet 1:2).

8. Resurrection from the dead (Rom 8:11).

d) Divine honor is given to Him (Matt 28:19; 2 Cor 13:13; Rev 1:4; 1 Cor 6:19–20).

e) One can sin against the Holy Spirit and then, in fact, commit the most severe, unforgivable sin.

94. *In what does the distinguishing work of the Holy Spirit consist, in distinction from the work of the Father and of the Son, within the economy of God's working?*

In perfecting things by bringing them to their goal. As the Holy Spirit is the person that completes the Trinity, so His work completes the work of God in every area. Some have found here a ground for the designation *Holy* Spirit. (Holiness, however, is the "separateness" of God.) The Holy Spirit would then be called "Holy" because in Him the three-and-one being of God is complete in itself and Father and Son again come together in one point. Scripture, however, does not speak of this.

95. *How is the Holy Spirit designated as a consequence of this, His distinguishing work?*

As the One *to whom* are all things, as can be seen from a comparison between Romans 11:36 and 1 Corinthians 8:6. As the preposition "from" belongs to the Father, the preposition "through" to the Son, so the preposition "to," to the Holy Spirit.

96. *How does the work of the Holy Spirit relate to that of the Son?*

It follows in order, as the work of the Son follows in order that of the Father. This must always be kept in view, for one arrives at a false mysticism if one detaches the work of the Spirit from the objective mediatorial activity of the Son.

97. *In what different respects does the Holy Spirit carry out His distinguishing work?*

a) In *creation*, where He is the superintendent of life, as the Father is the source of being and the Son, the architect of thought (cf. Gen 1:2; Job 26:13; 33:4; Psa 33:6; 104:30; Isa 40:13). The Holy Spirit lays the final hand on what is created, as is sufficiently shown by the expressions "brother," "made ... the heir," and "to adorn."

b) The Holy Spirit is continuously the one who prompts and enables in science, art, and official service (Exod 28:3; 31:6; 35:35; Psa 51:12; Isa 45:1; and elsewhere).

c) The Holy Spirit has prepared the body of the Messiah, according to the promise of God the Father made to the Surety in the counsel of peace (cf. Psa 40:7-8 with Heb 10:5). To the preparation of this body also belongs the inspiring of this Scripture passage, since it is intended to form a picture of Christ.

d) The Holy Spirit has also worked continuously in the human nature of the Mediator and provided it with gifts of grace, which it needed for discharging the offices of mediator. This happened especially at His baptism in the Jordan River and in His exaltation. Of course, this equipping only has reference to His human nature.

e) The Holy Spirit also works in the body of Christ, the church. He has formed the church already under the old order by regenerating individual believers, converting them, bringing them to make confession, and joining them together. After the exaltation of the Mediator, the Holy Spirit has begun to form the mystical body of the Lord, in which He dwells and unites the head, Christ, with the individual members. This began with the outpouring of the Holy Spirit on the day of Pentecost, which finds its explanation in this outpouring (Eph 2:22).

f) Also, the Holy Spirit works in individual believers by:

1. Preparatory grace.

2. The grace of regeneration and calling.

3. Conversion, to which faith belongs.

4. The application of justification.

5. Sanctification. This includes the recreating work that occurs at the death of believers in their souls and at the resurrection of the dead in their bodies.

98. *Which attributes are particularly ascribed to God the Holy Spirit as a result of this distinguishing work?*

a) Holiness.

b) Goodness (Psa 143:10).

c) Grace (Heb 10:29; Zech 12:10).

d) Might and power, especially perfecting power (Luke 1:35).

e) Glory, in an active sense, as in, making glorious (1 Pet 4:14).

Chapter Four

Of God's Decrees in General

1. Where have we now arrived in our treatment?

To a consideration of the external (*ad extra*) works of God.

2. Into how many kinds can one divide these external works?

Into two kinds:

a) In the most general sense, an external work has reference to something that is not God, thus to a creature, although it is not therefore true that the external work devolves directly upon the creature. If we so understand an external work, we must reckon the decrees to the external works. They differ, however, from generation and spiration because they have reference to what is not God, to creatures.

b) In a narrower sense, an external work of God devolves directly upon something that is not God. So understood, the external works begin with the creation. But the decree does not therefore begin with the latter, for the decree and execution of the decree are to be sharply distinguished. One can certainly say of the decree that it revolves about created things, but not that it directly affects them.

3. *What t u s do we emphasize when we attribute decrees to God?*

a) Go   overeignty. Someone who makes a decree concerning a
ma   stands above that matter; it falls under his authority. He
can   with it as he wills. Thus God stands sovereignly above all
poss   e things. Whether they will receive existence or how they
will   ist depends entirely on His eternal purpose.

b) God' *freedom*. When we decide on something, that includes that
we make a free choice. While our freedom, however, is always
relative and as creatures we are bound by many things, the freedom of God in His decree is utterly unlimited and stands under
no other rule than that of His own glorious virtues that form His
being itself. By this freedom the decree of God is distinguished
from the internal [*ad intra*] works, the generation of the Son and
the spiration of the Holy Spirit. It is not an act of free will of the
Father that He generates the Son, nor an act of free will of the
Father and the Son that they cause the Spirit to proceed from
themselves and their being. With that said, however, in no sense
do we maintain that these internal works are compelled or are
again st the will of the divine persons. All that is meant is that
they do not depend on an act of free will. Expressed differently,
the decree is completely tied to everything that pertains to created things. They could also not exist and God would still remain
God, perfect and fully glorious in Himself. That may not be said of
the internal works, for these belong to the necessary acts of God
without which He would not be the Triune God.

c) God's *wisdom*. A decree is always guided by motivations. A
Pelagian freedom of the will, which would be without grounds,
does not exist, not even for God. Moreover, such freedom would
not connote a perfection, but an imperfection. Absolute arbitrariness is an imperfection. Thus, at the same time God's decree
is completely free and governed by wise motives. There are no
grounds from outside Him that determine Him in making His
decree but grounds derived from Himself, which therefore do
not compel Him but give direction to His own perfect will. Both
must be maintained by us, the freedom and the wisdom of God's
decree, especially the first against pantheism, which makes everything to be a necessary effluence of God's nature. If God could

not have omitted the decree or made it otherwise, the thought intrudes that the existence of the universe is necessary, given the existence of God. But that thought is impermissible. The transition between God's eternal-necessary existence and the temporal existence of the created universe is a completely free transition. Conversely, we must also maintain that God has had wise and sufficient reasons for His decree. In by far the most cases we may not be able to specify them. All we affirm, and that based on Scripture, is that:

1. There are such reasons.

2. They all may be reduced to a final ground, namely the glorification of God Himself. But the different links by which they are tied to this final and highest goal can by no means always be specified by us.

   From this knowledge that God's decree is wise, it follows, in connection with the universality of God's decree, that everything in the universe is governed by thought that has an ideal meaning. There is no blind, purposeless existence in which no thought would be present. A transparent plan of the entire world of real things is present in the counsel of God.

4. *Which words in the original languages does Scripture use where it speaks of God's decree?*

   a) In the Old Testament:

   1. The word עֵצָה, "counsel" (Psa 33:11; Prov 19:21; Isa 28:29; 46:10–11). This word comes from the root יעץ, whose basic meaning in a material sense is "to penetrate into something"; "to press into something"; "to press one's self for something." It is used especially for giving counsel to others. The rational element of God's decree thus comes to the fore here (2 Sam 16:20; Prov 27:9).

   2. Further is the word סוֹד, "council," from the root יָסַד in the *hip'il*, "to be crowded closely together for confidential deliberation" (Pss 2:2; 31:14). Of God's decree, Jeremiah 23:18, 22. Thus here, too, the emphasis is on deliberation, resolution.

3. Yet another term is זָמַם, "to begin," alluding to the concentration of thoughts (Jer 4:28; 51:12; Prov 30:32).

4. Again, another word is חֵפֶץ, "inclination," "liking," "volition," "good pleasure" (Isa 53:10). Here, in distinction from the words mentioned above, the emphasis falls more on the willing, the free element in God's decrees.

5. A fifth term has a similar meaning, namely רָצוֹן, from רצה, "to hang on something," "to cling to something," then "sovereign will," "good pleasure," sometimes even "arbitrariness" (e.g., Neh 9:24, 37; of God, Psa 51:20; 145:16; Isa 49:8).

b) In the New Testament:

1. Here εερε ε, "good pleasure" (Matt 11:26; Eph 1:5, 9), corresponds to the two last mentioned Hebrew words. Here the element of free good pleasure comes emphatically to the fore (Luke 2:14; 3:22).

2. Not much different is the adjective δεκτός, "accepted with pleasure"; Luke 4:19, "the acceptable year of the Lord"; 2 Corinthians 6:2, "at an acceptable time."

3. Next are the words that mean "willing," βούλεσθαι and βουλή, as well as θέλειν and θέλημα. The difference between these two sets of terms appears to come down to the following: βούλεσθαι looks at the will as consulting, deliberating, and thus has the emphasis fall on the rational element in God's decree. Θέλειν, on the other hand, focuses more on the free inclination expressed in the decree and thus places the willing element in the foreground. But both words belong together and complement each other. Compare Matthew 1:19, where θέλειν is used ("Joseph had an aversion against putting her to shame"). In Romans 7:15 θέλειν is the opposite of μισσειν, "to hate." With that agrees the fact that θέλειν is also used of the revealed counsel of God, in which He demands and commands, thus in which the tenor of His Holy nature is expressed, while βούλεσθαι is only used of God's ordaining. In Ephesians 1:11 both terms occur together: "the counsel of His will" = "the plan that meets with His approval." Compare further for βουλή, Luke

7:30; Acts 2:23; 4:28; 13:36; Hebrews 6:17; for θέλημα, Matthew 26:42; Luke 22:42; Acts 21:14; Matthew 18:14; 1 Peter 3:17; 4:19; Ephesians 1:5; of God's revealed will, Romans 12:2.

4. Another New Testament word is πρόθεσις, "purpose," literally "presentation," "what someone proposes." The prefix "pre-" (or "pro-") is not meant in a temporal sense, but figuratively in a spatial sense. God places the decree, as it were, before Himself by His reason and then holds His will fixed on it (Rom 8:28; 9:11). Both elements of the decreeing of God are thus present here: wisdom and sovereignty, thinking and willing.

5. *What is the relationship of God's decree to His reason and His will?*

a) In decreeing, an activity of reason and an activity of will accompany each other.

b) To be more specific, God's necessary knowledge provides the material for His decree.

c) From this material thus given, God's free will, led by sufficient reasons, chooses what will become real.

d) On this act of free will rests the free knowledge of God that proposes the objects of the decree not as purely possible but as they will become real in time.

6. *What are the further properties of God's decree?*

a) It is *eternal* and is that in a specific sense, not simply as all God's acts are eternal. Viewed from God's side, every act of God is eternal simply because there is no passage of time in the being of God. But some of His acts terminate in time, such as creation, providence, the justification of sinners, etc. We do not call these latter acts eternal but temporal acts. With God's decree it is otherwise. It has reference to matters outside of God but as an act nevertheless remains within God, and we therefore call it eternal in the strictest sense of the word. In this eternity there is no temporal sequence in the different parts or portions of the decree.

In the execution of the decree the fall follows creation without it being able to be said that [in the decree] the one precedes the other. And although there is certainly an order in the decree of God and its different parts are not in isolation alongside each other, this can never be a temporal order. Also, one may not so conceive of the situation as if God, in willing a certain end, is forced to will as well the means for attaining that end. In this sense as well the choosing of the one does not precede the necessity of the other. God causes the means completely freely, so that they can be means for attaining His purposes. What we call laws of nature are not absolute necessities for God. He could have made them otherwise. Only insofar as God's attributes come into contact with things is one decree tied to another or involved in the other. For example, if God determines to permit sin, necessarily tied to that is that there shall be punishment for sin, for His righteousness demands that. So there is:

1. An order of free dependence, where means and end are freely conjoined.

2. An order of necessary connection, where the unchangeable attributes of God affect things decreed and cause new decrees, as it were, to originate.

The eternity of God's decree is expressed in Ephesians 3:11, "the eternal purpose that He has accomplished"; Acts 15:18, "to God all His works are known from eternity"; 2 Timothy 1:9, "before times eternal"; 1 Corinthians 2:7, "before the world was" (Eph 1:4; 2 Thess 2:13; 1 Pet 1:20).

b) God's decree is *one* and is oriented to one highest goal: the glorification of His name, of Himself. Especially for His creatures, angels and men, this is the goal to which God's decree is directed. The proof for this lies in the simplicity and self-existence of God.

c) God's decree is *universal*; it encompasses all things. What concerns the decree itself (not what concerns its execution) there is no distinction in the firmness with which things are determined, between the physical and the moral, the good and the evil. All are equally established by God with equally essential certainty. Because in the universe everything is related, the firmness of the decree in its entirety would also vanish with the universality of God's decree. For that to which the decree does not extend remains uncertain and would intrude in an unsettling fashion into what is certainly determined. On this all-encompassing character of God's decree and the certainty attendant on it rests the possibility of all knowledge, for without reality as certain, knowledge is not possible.

This universality of God's decree is the foundation for His free knowledge, as previously noted. This knowledge cannot have another foundation. In order to be the object of knowledge something must be certain. In order to be the object of eternal knowledge it must be eternally certain. But to posit that something would be eternally certain outside of God's decree would of course come down to positing a second deity beside Him. But what is an independent eternal certainty other than God? Foreknowledge must therefore rest on the decree.

Socinians deny that God's foreknowledge pertains to future free acts. Arminians help themselves with the defense that future free acts are always already present for God by virtue of His eternity, humanly speaking even before they happen. He knows them accordingly, without having made a decree about them. That view has been refuted earlier, in considering the doctrine of God's attributes. Here the Socinian is more consistent.

1. The all-encompassing character of God's decree is taught us by Holy Scripture in so many words. He works all things to the counsel of His will (Eph 1:10-11); all His works are known to Him from eternity (see Prov 16:33; Dan 4:34-35; Matt 10:29-30; Acts 17:26; Job 14:3; Isa 46:10).

2. The good acts of men are included. Believers are created for good works, which God ordained beforehand for them to walk in them (Eph 2:10).

3. The evil acts of men are also included. Acts 2:23, "this man then being delivered up according to the definite counsel and foreknowledge of God"; Acts 4:28, "to do whatever Your hand and Your counsel had predestined to take place"; Psalm 76:10, "The wrath of man shall praise you"; Proverbs 16:4, "The LORD has wrought everything for the sake of His own will, even the ungodly for the day of evil." Of course, this does not mean that

there is no distinction between God's decree concerning moral evil and His decree concerning other things. We will come back to this matter later. But here it must be noted that the difference cannot be as if evil were decreed by God with less firmness. Everything is equally firm. Something is decreed or is not decreed, and a third supposedly lying in between may not be entertained.

4. God's decree also includes so-called chance; Proverbs 16:33, "The lot is cast into the lap ..." (Gen 45:8; 50:20; John 19:36; Psa 34:20; Exod 12:46; Num 9:12). This really needs no demonstration because chance is not a scientific but purely a popular concept. Only that is called chance for which we do not know how to indicate the cause or causes. In each particular case, however, there are certainly causes. Where the lot is cast into the lap, there the way it falls and the result are just as determined and certain as where we decide something by premeditation. A die has no free will in a Pelagian sense so that it can fall on whatever side it chooses. But even apart from this natural determination there is in all natural things, there is still a direct determination of God from which they cannot escape.

5. God's decree concerns the means as well as the end that is to be reached. It is therefore foolish to exclude the means, with the thought that God's counsel will still be realized.

The latter is certainly true, but man deceives himself if he thinks his aversion and his unwillingness to use means is unconnected with the outcome. In many instances that aversion and unwillingness are precisely the means that God uses to prevent one or another outcome.

Under this rubric belongs as well the question whether God has decreed a fixed lifetime and specific time of death for every man. The Remonstrants and Socinians answer this question negatively; the Reformed, naturally, affirmatively. Voetius has devoted an extensive writing to this question. He laid emphasis on this point, especially to guard against the popular misconception that if someone's death were a miraculous occurrence that would suddenly interrupt the chain of natural causes and effects. Here, too, causes and effects go together, and if medications do not prevent death, that can be due to the nature of the disease and one must not immediately think of a miracle that prevented their working. But naturally that disease in its nature and the power of the medicine are together included in God's eternal decree (Job 14:5; Psa 39:5; John 7:30).

One says, however, that fifteen years were added to Hezekiah's life after it was first announced to him that he would die. But this announcement of the prophet was not a revelation of a divine decree that would later be changed but only a declaration of the deadly nature of the disease that would certainly have brought an end to Hezekiah's life, had God not miraculously intervened.

6. The decree of God also embraces the free acts of man. This is by far the most difficult point of all. On the one hand, it is completely absurd and impossible that what is most important in what takes place in world history would be beyond the control of God's decree. If arbitrariness rules in this area, then the entire course of the world is abandoned to what is arbitrary, and God would have to wait for what the final outcome will be. On the other hand, one wishes to hold that just here an exception must be made, since our consciousness of rationality appears to demand some kind of chance factor in our acts of will. Man says involuntarily, "If I will be responsible for my deeds, then I must have also been able to do otherwise. And if God's eternal decree has already determined my doing, then I could not do otherwise." In other words, eternal certainty and moral freedom exclude each other; they are incompatible concepts.

One must keep a sharp eye open for this objection. It is not that the execution of God's decree and my rational freedom conflict with each other. Freedom is uncertainty, so one thinks. In that is its essence, and certainty and uncertainty naturally cannot go together. Now in any case this much is clear, that the certainty of God's decree may not be changed. If these two are incompatible and one of these must give way, then it is settled in advance that the second will have to give way. In other words, we will have to change our concept of freedom; we will have to form a conception of human freedom such that it no longer finds its essence in uncertainty and absolute chance. The great question appears here then: What is moral freedom? That is, what is that freedom in which everyone's moral consciousness tells him that it is inseparable from responsibility? To shift the question to the execution of God's decree makes no sense, for, as we said, the objection lies in the certainty of the decree of God and decidedly not in its execution. The execution, for example, is different for good or evil acts of free will, and yet for both the objection that appears here is in principle the same.

7. *How many concepts of freedom are there?*

a) The Pelagian concept of free will that amounts to uncaused self-determination. If a man is to be free in this sense, there must be no grounds on which he acts that determine his actions. He must determine his actions at every point. At every point in his willing he must be able to do precisely the opposite, and if this cannot be said, he is not free. The character of man therefore does not determine his will, but will stands above character and forms character. Man, as he comes from God's hand, is neutral, neither good nor evil. His nature is a rational scale in a state of equilibrium, and only if the scale tilts to the right or to the left does man become good or evil, holy or unholy. As it happened with Adam, so it still happens in principle with every man, only the circumstances for Adam were more favorable than for us.

b) The concept of freedom that we must attribute to Adam must also freely grant that in the state of rectitude the outlook for Adam had two sides. He could fall or remain standing, he was not forced to sin, he did not possess a principle that must lead to sin, and yet the possibility that he sinned existed, as the outcome shows. Now it is of the highest importance to distinguish this concept of freedom from the Pelagian concept. The difference lies in the fact that we do not think of Adam's nature like a scale in equilibrium. Adam was completely holy and good. The scale was thus tilted to the good side from the beginning. According to Pelagians, a morally neutral Adam can become, as he chooses, either good or evil. According to us, a good Adam can become evil. From that flows another distinction to which equally close attention must be given. The Pelagian concept extends to include both sides. It applies to the transition both from evil to good and from good to evil. The concept we apply to Adam holds only for his position before the fall; later it never and nowhere occurs again. Adam could produce evil from good, but no one after the fall, including Adam, can produce good from evil. Further, those regenerated are unable again to produce evil from good. Even the perfected saints in heaven are unable to do that.

Our result, then, is that this freedom for Adam is something entirely unique. It is related to the covenant of works, and instead of being excluded by Adam's holiness is properly connected with it insofar as this holiness was a mutable and not an immutable holiness.

c) The third concept of freedom is inseparable from the concept of man or the concept of a "rational being," so that besides man it applies to pure spirits and, in the most perfect sense, to God.

It all comes down to the fact that man does what he does from an inner impulse because there is something in his very being that impels him to his actions. Thus he is not moved from the outside, like a machine, but from the inside out, like a living organism. One can often hear the defense that man in a state of sin no longer possesses free will. That is true if one understands freedom in the sense described under b) above. He can do nothing else but sin. But it is untrue if one thereby thinks that man sins against his own inclinations. He sins just because his sinful soul, his sinful character, impels him to sin. This is again true if one juxtaposes conscience and character in man. His conscience tells him that he must do what is good, his sinful habits impel him to do what is evil. One may therefore certainly say he is driven to do what is evil against his own conscience, but not against his own will, his own character. Conscience and character, with its will, are not the same. There is something in sinful man that is not compatible with sin, that protests against sin. But that is not something good in him. It is the voice of God in him who bears witness to what is right. Still, it preserves a good sense if one says:

Man in his fallen state does not have free will because he must do what is evil against his better knowledge and the testimony of his conscience. He is a slave of sin and his conscience tells him that it is sin.

8. *What then is the status of the connection between God's decree and these three kinds of freedom?*

   a) It immediately catches the eye that the first, the so-called Pelagian freedom of the will, is incompatible with God's decree. In essence it is uncertainty and therefore incompatible with any sort of certainty, therefore also incompatible with the certainty of God's decree. Thus, indifferent to whether we are dealing with Adam or with fallen man, if he has a free will as the Pelagian teaches, then he stands outside God's decree. It is important, therefore, to hold for Adam, too, that he was not free in a Pelagian sense.

   b) It is somewhat different for the second freedom as, based on Scripture, we attribute to Adam before the fall the possibility to turn from good to evil.

      1. First of all, we must note that here there is no causeless freedom. Adam's initially holy nature turns to sin—not, his neutral nature decides for evil.

      2. Next, we are unable to explain how a cause can exist in the holy nature of Adam that turned him to sin. We must pronounce the origin of the first sin in Adam an unsolvable problem.

      3. Thirdly, we must say that the relationship of God's decree to this first free sin is also inexplicable. One thing is certain: Sin, as far as its reality is concerned, did not come from God, although it receives its certainty from God's decree. The cause of sin lies in man, but sin, too, has not obtained its determination and certainty apart from the permissive decree of God.

   c) The third kind of freedom does not conflict with God's decree. God can so act on man that he still acts freely of himself. If by grace God makes someone holy so that his unconscious life as a whole is holy, then also of himself his thoughts, words and deeds will be holy, necessarily holy. But thereby they will be no less free.

Here freedom and certainty are fully compatible. To understand this well one must be clear about what belongs to this freedom and what is incompatible with it.

Freedom in the third sense we define in general as: motion of character, in accord with itself, in a rational being.

This includes:

1. That all expressions in the conscious life are revelations of the character that lies beneath and in back of them. Man's individual acts and expressions of the will are not free and detached from his character but are determined by it. Their freedom consists just in the fact that their acts flow from inner character and are in accord with it. If that were not the case, man would not be responsible. Only an act that is exponential of character is covered by the moral law. Acts that are not occur among those who are insane but whom one then rightly views as not responsible. Instead of nullifying freedom, this causality is the only true foundation of freedom.

2. That all such expressions are accompanied by thinking; they must be rational acts. Motions that we make mechanically and without rational awareness, although they flow from an inward disposition, we do not call free. Someone who acts freely and wills freely accompanies his acting and willing by conceptualizing them. He is aware that therein his being is expressed, that it is he himself who acts and acts in such a way, since his character brings it about.

3. Man's character, however, must also have a certain freedom. As the will is certainly determined from the inside out by character but nonetheless is freely and rationally determined, so must character be naturally free and rational. Thus one can certainly affect the character of a person without the loss of freedom. But it is not an indifferent matter how one affects the character of a person. There are influences conceivable that could eliminate freedom of character. And similarly character may be determined and stable, but with a rational stability that is governed and controlled by a rational tendency in a deeper sense.

4. From what has just been said it follows that character may not be controlled by blind material forces. Whoever makes the human spirit and thus the human will a product of matter, that is, the materialist, abolishes the freedom of character. One calls this materialistic determinism. Determinism is incompatible with the freedom that a rational being must possess in order to be responsible.

5. There is, however, another determinism that we will call pantheistic. This teaches that the being of man, his character, is only a phenomenon, a random, passing phenomenon issuing with necessity from the activity of All-Being that is not conscious of itself and causes all things in a blind fashion. This, too, cannot exist along with freedom, because here not only is an external influence exercised on character but it also loses its independence. It no longer exists in itself; it has become a manifestation of something else. It no longer acts of itself; something else acts on and through it. Pantheism is thus incompatible with the freedom of rational beings.

6. Finally, there is still a third form of determinism that one could call rationalistic. It comes down to this, that our thoughts, the verdict of our reason, control the will with necessity. Thinking, then, dictates the law for willing, and nothing else is left for the will than to follow the verdict of reason. One easily perceives that such a rationalistic conception abolishes freedom. Now it is certainly true that the verdict of our reason will influence the decision of our will. But in that decision reason has only a serving task, insofar as it teaches me, namely, what in the various possibilities that present themselves most agrees with my disposition, with my will. The verdicts of reason are thus subservient to the will and not independent of the will. One can act on someone's will by motives of reason only if one has a point of contact in that person's will to which one can appeal. By presenting someone with the shamefulness of an act, one will perhaps be able to prevent the act, provided that the person possesses feelings of shame.

7. It should now be clear that God can realize His decrees with reference to His creatures without needing to limit their

freedom in a deterministic manner. Their free acts are not uncertain and the certainty to which these acts are connected is not brought about by God in a materialistic, pantheistic, or rationalistic manner. As the omnipresent and omnipotent One, the personal One, He can so govern man that man can do nothing without His will and permission and still do everything of himself in full freedom. When God sanctifies someone, He is at work in the depths of his being where the issues of life are, and then the sanctified will acts of itself and unconstrained outwardly no less freely than if it never had been under the working of God. The work of God does not destroy the freedom of the creature but is precisely its foundation.

9. Is God's decree also efficacious?

Yes, in this sense, that it reaches fulfillment with certainty. Nothing ever happens with greater certainty than what God has decreed. However, one must not so conceive of this as if the decree is the cause of the reality of all things. The decree is the ground of the certainty of all things. To decree something is not yet to carry out or to do something. Everything is equally subject to God's decree. In the execution of God's decree there is a great difference between the particular parts. So, by the efficacy of God's decree, we only mean that an unbreakable connection exists between the certain determination of the decree in God and its execution in time. In God's decree there is an efficacious will to realize it. The decree is not present in God as a mere idea but is an abiding thought or will. There is a unity between having decreed, being decreed, and efficacious willing what is decreed (βούλεσθαι and βεβουλῆσθαι, not βουληθῆναι alone.)

10. Is God's decree also immutable?

Yes, this is already included in the preceding attribute. It is also involved in His eternity, in which there is no thought of change. It arises further from God's independence and wisdom. For the last-mentioned attributes one may compare Isaiah 46:10; Job 23:13; Psalm 33:12; and Hebrews 6:17.

11. How then do you define God's decree?

As "the free determination of His rational will concerning everything outside Him that will be and how it will function."

12. What is the relationship of God's decree to His providence?

Creation aside, decree and providence are identical in scope and coincide completely. Providence is the execution of the decree. Their content is the same. Nothing with which God's providence is concerned may be excluded from the decree, and just as something becomes reality under God's providential governance, it is comprehended in God's decree. A comparison with the doctrine of providence is therefore the best means to cure a wrong view of God's decreeing. The decree is providence in outline, but then it is an approved outline that bears in itself the seal that it is to be realized. The one who thinks that God has decreed certain things, apart from the means, need only be pointed to providence, which shows us means and ends in their permanent connection.

13. What do the more or less Pelagian-minded introduce against God's decrees?

They continually speak of conditional decrees (*decretum conditionatum*). Like the Pelagians are the Remonstrants and Socinians. First, one says, there comes to pass in God the establishing of the general rule that faith will result in eternal life, and lack of faith in perdition. For Socinians God's decree must determine this provisionally and can only proceed further if man has decided the question, still open to that point, whether or not he will believe. When man has decided, then the second part of the decree follows that applies the general rule in specific instances. For Socinians this takes place in time, since they deny eternal foreknowledge of free acts; for the others it takes place already in eternity, since they do attribute such foreknowledge to God. But it comes down ultimately to the same thing, namely that God in His decree not only determines the creature but is also determined by the creature.

14. What objection do you have to such a conditional decree?

The subsequent decree is no longer a decree in the strict sense of the word. It is only a taking note of what man has decided before God. After the general rule has first been established and the creature has applied this rule to himself, nothing more remains for God to determine. A new element of certainty no longer enters.

15. What is the relationship between God's decrees and the being of God?

The Socinians say, in order to maintain the contingent character and the variability of the decrees, that they are essentially (*realiter*) separate from God. That is why the relationship between God's being and His decree was a much-discussed question in the old dogmatics. Some set the question aside as useless (so, e.g., Cocceius). One usually answered by making distinctions in this vein:

a) God's *thinking* and *willing*, as they are the active causes in His decreeing, are naturally not divorced from His being. If therefore decree means decreeing itself as a certain act or movement of God's mind and will, then decree is the same as God's being. God's decree is to such an extent God Himself, the decreeing God.

b) The *direction* and *relation* of this decreeing act outward, the inclining of the will toward the objects of the decree. This is entirely free, since God could have just as well not decreed or could have decreed differently. One must therefore say that taken in this sense, the decree is distinct from God's being and separable from it.

c) The *thing decreed* itself, that is, not yet so much the real thing outside God after the execution of the decree, but the idea of it as decreed in God's mind. This, too, does not coincide with God's being and can therefore be removed from it.

Although these matters are very abstract, it is good to emphasize them here. Complete identification of God's being and decree in every respect exposes to the danger of pantheism and leaves the impression that the universe must necessarily emanate from God's being.

16. How does one designate God's decree as it functions with respect to sin?

A *permissive* decree (*decretum permissivum*). This term has become accepted in Reformed dogmatics and is even found in most confessions. Our own [Belgic] Confession, on the doctrine of providence (Article 13), says, "[A]ll our enemies cannot harm us without His permission and will."

Here and there objection is made to this distinction. Beza states it is not difficult to show that it is completely misunderstood by some, in a way that removes the devils and evil men from God's control except that He keeps their actions and the consequences of their actions within certain limits. Nevertheless, Beza also wishes to see the terms *decernius* and *permissivum* (decreeing and permitting will) maintained, provided that they are explained correctly.

Danaeus speaks more dismissively: "From this it follows that that sophistical distinction that one is accustomed to make between God's permission and His decree ought to be abandoned, because what happens by God's permission happens with His will and consequently by virtue of His decree."

a) First, it should be observed that by permissive decree the Lutherans understand something entirely negative. By it they mean that God does not decree to prevent or hinder sin by a positive act. Thus, sin itself is fully present in God's decree as sure and certain. Concerning it God has nothing more to decide. His permissive decreeing, taken strictly, means to say that He does *not* decree rather than that He *certainly* decrees *not*, namely, to counter sin. This, of course, is a wrong and inadequate view. It teaches that sin has its reality and certainty from man. The former is true, as we have seen; the latter cannot be conceded. For, as for all things, so also for sin, certainty must lie in the decree of God. A permissive decree cannot be a bare budding in our spirit.

b) Others understand the permissive character of God's decree concerning sin more in another sense, namely as follows:

God decrees in a positive manner that certain things will happen. However, sin as an unavoidable consequence adheres to these things that God decrees. Thus, if He wills these things, He must also permit sin. So, it comes down to this: God has permitted sin not for itself but because of its necessary connection with other things that He willed.

Usually this is worked out further as follows: At issue above everything was the freedom of the human will, that man, therefore, should choose for himself what he wanted, good or evil. Thus, involved as well in this freedom, in this possibility of going in either direction, was the permitting of evil, of sin.

This view is entirely unacceptable. It still makes only the possibility of sin an object of God's decree, but not the certainty of sin. We must not only maintain that God tolerated that possibility but also that its certainty is the result of His permissive decree. It may not be thought as though God decreed to create man and then to wait on how the choice of man would turn out. That would be the Pelagian conditional decree applied to the situation of man before the fall. This view, then, is also completely at home within the orbit of Pelagian ideas.

c) There are different conceptions of God's permissive decree that do not really pertain to the decreeing act but more to its execution and so need not be discussed here—for example, the difference between the formal and the material in sin. This is a point that has its place in the doctrine of providence and not here. Although one would see this distinction as a solution, it is of no help here, for God's decree concerns both the formal and the material.

d) It is not possible to explain fully in a corroborating way how we are to think about God's permissive decree. We wish, in general, to maintain the following:

1. The permissive decree is no less a certain decree than any other. Any thought as though we can speak of hesitation or uncertainty in God must be excluded by far. God is certain in everything He decrees, and for all things their certainty is secure solely in the decree of God. Also sin, in order to be certain, must be through God's decree. The one who denies this deviates from Reformed doctrine. Just on this point lies the one great error of the church father Augustine, who wanted to make sin only an object of God's foreknowledge but not of God's decree. Calvin says as decisively as possible, "Man falls because God's providence has so ordained it, but he falls by his own fault" (*Institutes*, 1.18.4); "I acknowledge that it is a horrible decree. Still, no one can deny that God certainly has known how it would turn out with man and that therefore He has known because he has so foreordained it in His decree." "For the first man has fallen because the Lord judged that it ought to be so. Why He judged that remains hidden to us" (3.23.7, 8).

But Calvin also lets the reverse come out, as we immediately hope to see.

2. As its object the permissive decree had sin in view as something contrary to God's holy nature and on which His displeasure must rest. To permit something always means that it arouses my disapproval. Therefore, because on the one hand sin is against God's holy nature, on the other hand there must have been considerations in God that nonetheless caused Him to decree to permit it. It is not granted to man to know these considerations in detail. It must be enough for us to know that through sin God knew to glorify Himself by His righteousness and His redeeming love.

3. By permitting sin in His decree God remains completely free of any wrong. Calvin: "The destruction of the godless depends on God's decree such that the cause and nature of that destruction is to be sought in man himself." "Through his own malevolence, man has corrupted the nature that he had received from his God." "God could not have judged other than that man ought to fall, because He saw that thereby the honor of His name would properly come to light. And where one speaks of God's honor, there His justice must immediately be in view, for what deserves praise, must be just." Thus, according to Calvin, it is a just decree, both in its origin as in its content (cf. *Institutes*, 2.4.3–5, where Calvin goes much further than we would presume to and where in principle he rejects the permissive decree).

In the execution of this decree, too, there is nothing that can make God a cause of sin. On this point Scripture speaks as emphatically as possible. God tempts no one to evil (Jas 1:13). God is light and in Him there is no darkness (1 John 1:5). God made man upright, but they have sought out many schemes (Eccl 7:29). The Spirit of God teaches His children to praise all that is good as the work of God but also to ascribe blame for all that is evil only to themselves. This testimony of the Spirit in the believer, founded on God's word, teaches us how this matter appears in God's light, and we must believe it though that same light does not illumine our understanding.

CHAPTER FIVE

The Doctrine of Predestination

1. *What parts, in succession, come up for discussion concerning this doctrine?*

   a) The grounds why we assign it a separate place in the doctrine of the decrees.

   b) The scriptural terms that are important for predestination and election.

   c) The systematic development of the doctrine of election in connection with other areas of doctrine.

   d) The major deviating opinions and our criticism of them.

2. *Why in Reformed dogmatics is the doctrine of election treated separately after the doctrine of the decrees?*

In order to show the importance of this doctrine in the entire system. Also, as the doctrine of salvation follows consideration of creation and providence, so here the particular decree of predestination follows the general decree of God.

3. *Did Lutheran dogmatics also usually put predestination toward the beginning in its treatment?*

Yes; certainly initially. Melanchthon began his *Loci Communes* with its treatment. Later, it was different. The doctrine of election was now placed at the beginning of soteriology. This came about because Lutheran theology had undergone a total change.

4. *At what points is the doctrine of predestination or election related to the rest of Reformed doctrine as a whole?*

   a) It is a direct consequence of the Reformed concept of God's sovereignty, as that has been shaped based on Scripture. In the century of the Reformation one arrived at the doctrine of election along a twofold path. Luther came to predestination from man and his salvation. Zwingli and Calvin did so from God. Zwingli deduced predestination directly from providence (the decrees) and comes close to pantheism. Calvin expressed himself more soberly. But he, too, postulated that God is everything and the creature is nothing, that the creature, even in its highest importance, remains subordinate to God and must serve Him. Whoever gives up the doctrine of predestination must therefore also drop the doctrine of the sovereignty of God and subsequently falsify biblical teaching at numerous places.

   b) The doctrine of human inability after the fall is inseparably connected with predestination, so that one must maintain them both together or drop them both together. One of the two; it depends on God or it depends on man who will be saved. If one chooses the first, then one has accepted predestination. If one chooses the second, then this is possible only under two presuppositions. Either one must be Pelagian and say man has not become lacking in ability through his fall; then he is able to decide for himself. Or one must say man was at first lacking in ability, but God does something to man, in fact to all men without distinction, whereby they again become able to make a decision. But then A, who is saved, must have something good that B, who is not saved, does not have. And A must have this good of himself because he received precisely the same grace as B. In any case, here the inability of man is denied, whether one propounds that denial in a Pelagian or a semi-Pelagian fashion.

   Luther arrived at election by reasoning back to it from man's inability (*Concerning the Bondage of the Will*, against Erasmus). Later Lutheran theology had to give up absolute predestination.

8. *Is the concept "foreknowing" in this sense completely absent in the New Testament?*

It appears, but nowhere in relation to election as having for its object foreseen faith and good works. See 2 Peter 3:17: "You ... knowing this beforehand, take care lest you are led astray by the seduction of heinous men"; Acts 26:5: "As they have previously known me for a long time."

9. *From what at the outset does it appear that the concept cannot have such a meaning in the places it is used for election?*

From the fact that nowhere is added what God had known in advance in man. If we had to do with foreknowledge in this sense, such an addition would be essential. If I know something beforehand, then everything depends on what I know or sense beforehand.

Now, "foreknowing" and "foreknowledge" occur for election (in Rom 8:29; 11:2; 1 Pet 1:2, 20). "Knowing" in its special meaning is used (in Matt 7:23; 1 Cor 8:3; Gal 4:9; 2 Tim 2:19). Nowhere here is it mentioned that God has foreknown or known in persons. Compare that with the two texts mentioned in the answer to question 8, where something *is* mentioned.

10. *Prove that in Romans 8:28–29, God's "foreknowledge" cannot mean foreseeing.*

The context as a whole and the aim of the apostle's argument as a whole make that impossible here. The apostle intends to show that for those who love God, all things work together for good. He reasons as follows: Love for God is a consequence of the calling of God, that is, of that omnipotent act by which God has made alive those who are His.

This calling of God as an act in time does not stand alone. It had a reverse side in eternity. Believers are called according to the purpose of God. Again, however, this purpose did not stand alone as a cold determination of will, but something lay behind it that the apostle calls "foreknowledge."

Here the ascent backward from link to link ceases: calling—purpose—foreknowledge, and the descent begins from foreknowledge. The foreknowledge was such that a predestinating to the form of son resulted: "Those whom He has known beforehand, He has also ordained beforehand to be conformed to the image of His Son, in order that He might be the firstborn among many brothers." Hereby the sense of "foreknowledge" is already decided in principle. It is something like what a father feels toward his son, his future son. It is a knowing of love. Since behind God's purpose such a fatherly love functioned with respect to the elect, it ordained the form of son for all those who were the objects of its free choice. Given the fatherly and free character of this love, it is absolutely excluded for the apostle that this fatherly love can be blocked by anything in the realization of its being decreed. With divine certainty and with irresistible power this love aims at its highest goal, the complete glorification of the children in the image of likeness to Christ. It must carry through step by step in its working: "Those whom He knew, those He also called; those whom He called, those He also justified; those whom He justified, those He also glorified." That is the sense of the sequence. Everything follows with infallible certainty from the unique character of the foreknowledge of God.

Now one may wonder whether anything still remains of this beautiful argument and this natural tie, if one is forced to give "foreknowledge" the meaning of "foreseeing." Then everything becomes unintelligible and artificial. The divine act that stands at the beginning of the entire sequence then becomes something dependent and is no longer fit to be the basis, firm in itself, of the rest. We have a root that must draw its sap from the trunk and branches and at the same time must still also guarantee that trunk and branches will not wither—a contradiction.

Further, it may be noted that the likeness to the image of the Son to which believers are predestined refers to His glory as Mediator, not to the divine glory that He possessed from eternity. Only of the former will the elect obtain a likeness (though at a far distance).

11. *Prove that in Romans 11:2, as well, "foreknowledge" must have a similar meaning and cannot be "foreseeing."*

Here the apostle intends to show how impossible, indeed, how absurd it would be that God would reject Israel, His people. "Rejecting" and "knowing in advance" therefore exclude each other according to the thinking of the apostle. In the midst of Israel's apostasy and disobedience, he maintains its future salvation, for God, having once foreknown His people, cannot again reject them. One need only attempt to insert the concept of "obtaining knowledge beforehand" and the argument immediately becomes nonsense. In the face of Israel's actual apostasy how can it ever serve as an argument for its future restoration that God has still foreseen something good in Israel? It is completely the reverse: Precisely because in His free choice God took into account not what Israel would be in itself but exclusively His own good pleasure, precisely because the covenant relationship did not originate with Israel but with Him, precisely because of that, He cannot reject them.

12. *May something be deduced from 1 Peter 1:2 concerning the nature of God's foreknowledge?*

No, but certainly from 1 Peter 1:20. Here Christ is the object of foreknowledge. And then, of course, according to His human nature. Now by the nature of the case it makes no sense to say that the Father knew something beforehand in the human nature of the Mediator, for that human nature was entirely the result of God's election itself. Without election the Son would not have assumed a human nature. What is a result cannot at the same time be a ground or source. Therefore, it is certain that here this foreknowledge cannot be considered foresight of something that already existed for God outside His counsel.

13. *What is the meaning of the word "know" in Matthew 7:23?*

Here the word does not refer to "election" in the strict sense but is nonetheless used in a way that can shed light on its meaning elsewhere. Christ says that on the day of judgment He will say to many, "I never knew you." This cannot mean, "I did not know anything of or about you, ... you worker of iniquity." A knowing in the sense of "having knowledge of" is thus certainly present, but not a knowing in the other sense. Christ means to say, "I have not entered into a personal relationship with you." On the day of judgment the lost, as it were, will insist forcefully on the knowledge Christ has by saying: "Did we not prophesy in your name?" However, He says to them, "I never knew you!" On His side had been lacking just that knowing love, that friendship, to which from their side they now appeal.

14. *What about 1 Corinthians 8:3?*

Here Paul contrasts with the pride of those who think they know something love for God as that in which the inner worth of Christian character lies. That worth must not be sought in knowledge that puffs up. That it lies in love is shown by Paul from this, that all who love God are known by God, as Calvin says, are valued, highly esteemed. Here there is a fine play on words in the contrast between the knowledge of man in his confusion and being known by God that truly settles everything.

15. How about Galatians 4:9?

First, the fact that the Galatians know God is advanced by the apostle as the ground why they must not turn back again to the weak and impoverished elementary principles of the world. But according to the apostle, there is something else that weighs even more heavily. God has known them. That is, He has placed Himself to them in a relationship of love, as a father to His children. If now, knowing this, they turn back to the weak and impoverished elementary principles of the world, they make themselves guilty of ingratitude to the worst degree. All this shows that being known by God must be something still greater and more glorious than knowing God. That rules out the explanation that foreseeing is in view.

16. What is the case in 2 Timothy 2:19?

Here, too, the words, "The Lord knows those who are His," must not be taken as an intellectual knowledge. It means that God stands in the closest relationship to His children. The apostasy of those who had occupied a prominent place in the congregation is spoken of, and that from their apostasy one could despair of his own perseverance, especially since the pernicious doctrine of these erring spirits was spreading like gangrene. It is of no comfort in the face of that to consider that God indeed knows who are His and who will remain faithful to Him. But it is certainly a comfort in such circumstances to be able to remember that the Lord stands in the closest relationship of love to His own and therefore cannot allow them to fall away. Compare in John 10:27–28 the bond there is between the shepherd's knowing and the sheep's not perishing.

17. What is the main objection to the conception of God's foreknowledge maintained here?

That it does not indicate what it is that God could have foreknown in the objects of His choice.

a) Some answer, faith. That is the old Remonstrant answer, but it is simply inconsistent with the teaching of Scripture that calls faith a gift of God and in particular, with the Pauline contrast between faith and works that does not permit that one make of the former a kind of work of man, an evangelical obedience.

b) Others say, love. This conflicts even more with the antithesis just mentioned, which would then have to say that man is saved not by external works but by internal works of the law.

c) There is no place for something that God would have been able to foresee or to know beforehand in man. However subtly one may also sublimate the little He must have seen in man by speaking of a kind of *receptivity* that must be the opposite of all doing and working, it is still always a receptivity that man himself has rendered and to that extent an *activity* must correspond to it so that again it is "of those who work" and not of the God who shows mercy.

18. *What is the development of the idea of foreknowledge?*

The Hebrew יָדַע, "to know," is as good as the same in meaning as בָּחַר, "to choose," "to know." It takes on that meaning as follows: To take note of something closely, to be interested in it, to penetrate to its essence, to care about it—it is in all cases a sign of loving interest that wants to be most closely united with its object. We say, "To understand someone in some matter," or, "He has not understood me in this." Accordingly, divine knowing includes the following:

a) God was first in this act of predestination. The relationship between Him and the objects of His choice originated entirely from Him. Only because He willed to know them and in fact did know them did they become something for Him. That is the element of sovereignty. As an earthly sovereign, if he is pleased with his knowledge of someone or takes note of him, only through this knowledge makes him something of significance, so it is with the knowing of God.

b) This knowledge or foreknowledge of God is not an act of cold arbitrariness but an act of love in which the Lord, as it were, has been absorbed in knowing and contemplating His beloved from eternity.

  c) It does not stand on its own but carries in itself the impulse for a range of divine acts of salvation. The knowing of God is fruitful; it brings forth grace and glory.

19. *Can you show this by some citations from the Old Testament?*

Yes, in Hosea 13:4–5, just where Israel's sin and declensions are spoken of, "But I am the LORD your God from the land of Egypt … I knew you in the wilderness, in the land of great drought"; in Amos 3:2, where Israel's unfaithfulness is no less in the foreground, it is said, "You only of all the families of the earth have I known; therefore I will afflict you for your unrighteousness." In Psalm 144:3 the question is raised: "O LORD, what is man that you know him, or the son of man that you consider him?" (cf. also Psa 8:4). By means of the Septuagint the Hebrew meaning was then transferred to the Greek word.

20. *What does the preposition* προ *mean in the compound verb* προγιγνώσκειν?

  a) From Romans 8:29 it appears that προ is placed precisely with those acts of God that do not take place in time, namely, with foreknowledge, foreordination, purpose; not, on the other hand, with those acts that do take place in time, namely, calling, justification, and glorification. From this the conclusion may rightly be drawn that προ indicates the eternity of these acts.

  b) At the same time there is included here that the acts are done while their objects did not yet exist, whereby God is first in every respect. When God calls, justifies, and glorifies a person, then that person already exists. When, on the other hand, He foreknows, foreordains him, then that person does not yet exist. One must not therefore view the προ exclusively as a "before" in time but also as a "before" in order.

21. *What is the second word that Scripture uses in connection with this doctrine?*

Ἐκλέγεσθαι. In biblical Greek this verb occurs only in the middle voice. It corresponds with the Hebrew בָּחַר. The meaning of the Greek word contains the following elements:

a) Giving preference to a certain object in distinction from other objects that could also have come into consideration.

b) Choosing accompanied by good pleasure, that is, with an inclination of the will.

c) Setting apart for a certain relationship in which the chosen object must become mutually related to the one who chooses.

22. *How do you prove that the first element, distinction from others, is in fact in this word?*

It is in the preposition "out," "to choose out of." The Hebrew verb also sometimes expressly indicates this by having מִן follow it. In the Greek ἐκ is sometimes repeated. In Deuteronomy 18:5, Levi is chosen out of all the tribes of Israel; John 15:9, "I have chosen you out of the world"; Luke 6:13, "And chose from them twelve." Sometimes this concept of being chosen out of can recede into the background because the emphasis falls more on one of the other two elements mentioned above, but it is never entirely absent; Isaiah 58:5, "Is that a fast that I have chosen?" (= that, especially in distinction from other ways of fasting, meets my approval).

23. *How do you prove that the second element mentioned above is also in "election"?*

In itself it need not be in ἐκλέγεσθαι. One can choose without good pleasure, for example, the most evil out of evils. But generally all choosing is accompanied by an inclination to a preference. One may compare the connection between the Latin verbs *diligere* and *delectari*, which are both connected with "to pick," "to pick out" (λέγειν); Genesis 6:2, "And they took wives from all whom they chose"; Psalm 78:68, "He chose the tribe of Judah, Mount Zion, which He loved."

24. *Does this then mean that in the objects of His election God saw something good, something well-pleasing, in which He could delight Himself?*

No, that is not at all what is meant. In fact, in back of "election" lay "foreknowledge." One may compare with each other Deuteronomy 7:7-8, where it is emphatically stated that no good quality of Israel contributed to Israel's election, and Genesis 6:2, where the situation is quite different.

25. *Where in the word "election" is the third element mentioned above?*

In the use of the middle voice. We should actually have to translate it, "to choose for himself." In the Hebrew that is seen even more clearly (for example, in Num 16:7 and 2 Chr 7:16, where it is said of the person or thing chosen that it is holy, set apart for the Lord; Pss 105:26; 33:12; 135:4).

26. *Is the word "election" always used in the specific sense of election to salvation?*

No, it is evident from what has been noted above that it often occurs with another sense. This, however, does not eliminate that it also has this specific sense.

27. *Must one add "to salvation" to "election"?*

No, that is not its primary meaning. It is for another word that this meaning must be added. To "election" one must add "to a special relationship of belonging to God." This relationship is such that eternal salvation is connected to it, but one should not shift the biblical point of view. God chooses for Himself a possession. He predestines to eternal salvation. And both continually accompany each other.

28. *What is your proof for this?*

One may compare the meaning of the word in the middle voice in Deuteronomy 14:2 and texts like Ephesians 1:4, "that we should be holy and blameless before Him in love."

29. *What is the third word mentioned here?*

Προορίζειν, which we find used in Romans 8:29, where it immediately follows "foreknow." It means "to predestine." It is distinguished from both preceding terms because it requires an addition. To say that someone is foreknown or elect provides, at least in the language of Scripture, a complete thought. To say that someone is predestined immediately elicits the question, "To what?" Ὁρίζειν means "to establish boundaries," "to make a determination, a reckoning." Furthermore, it is a completely neutral word, that is, it can be used for good as well as for evil. Election and foreknowledge have only a good sense; predestination also has a bad sense. Compare Acts 2:23, where the ὡρισμένη βουλῇ ... τοῦ θεοῦ, "the determined counsel of God," occurs as that by which Christ was handed over (cf. also 4:28).

Besides in Romans 8:29, the more specific meaning of "predestined" appears in Ephesians 1:5, 11, "Who has predestined us for adoption as sons," and, "in Him we have obtained an inheritance, we who were predestined according to the purpose of Him who works all things according to the counsel of His will."

The purpose of election is a certain relationship; the purpose of predestination is a certain status, a condition, an image, a destiny. Compare "those whom He has also predestined to be conformed to the image of His Son." Thus, here it is a likeness, conformity to Christ, which is the object of predestination. In this connection one should think of His glory as Mediator, as was noted above.

30. *Are the two concepts of "election" and "predestination" always so sharply differentiated?*

No, sometimes the former can also be used for the latter; for example, in James 2:5, "Has not God chosen the poor of this world to be rich in faith and heirs of the kingdom?"

31. *Is there still another word in use for election?*

Yes, namely the word "purpose," for example in Romans 8:28, "who are called according to His purpose."

Purpose, πρόθεσις from προτιθέναι. The word differs from προορίζειν by the emphasis falling more on the willing side of God's decree of predestination. In all God's decree there is an act of the mind and an act of the will; so also in the decree of predestination. By the former the idea is formed, its destiny delineated, by the latter God with a resolute will establishes what He has thus determined for Himself in order to bring about its reality.

Sometimes "purpose" can also be understood in a more comprehensive sense, so that it includes "foreknowledge" and "election"; 2 Timothy 1:9, "Who has saved us and called us to a holy calling ... in His own purpose and grace, which He gave us in Christ Jesus before times eternal."

Romans 9:11 speaks of a "purpose according to election." By this the apostle means that God's purpose was an electing, approving purpose, a purpose that makes distinctions. It was a purpose of choice.

32. Does Scripture use as many words for reprobation as it does for election?

No, we hardly find a single word that can be juxtaposed with the words mentioned above as their opposite. That is certainly to be ascribed in part to the slight degree of practical interest that the congregation has for the darker side of this comforting doctrine.

33. What is the opposite of the word בָּחַר *(to choose)?*

The Hebrew מָאַס, "to reject." But nowhere in the Old Testament does this word have the meaning, "not to choose." It always speaks of rejecting again what was first chosen (Jer 33:24, "Has the LORD rejected the two clans that He chose?"; Psa 78:67–68, "But He rejected the tent of Joseph, He did not choose the tribe of Ephraim; but He chose the tribe of Judah, Mount Zion, which He loved"; cf. Exod 32:32ff.). Hence Isaiah 14:1 speaks of a repeated election of Israel, "The LORD will have compassion on Jacob and will again choose Israel." Only in Isaiah 41:9 does the contrast appear to be clearly antithetical; "I have you chosen and not rejected."

34. May we deduce from this that there is no reprobation alongside of election?

This would be very rash. The "out" in "to choose out" already shows that alongside of election there is something else.

35. What is the Greek word for מאס*?*

Ἀπωθεῖν, "to reject," "to cast off" (Rom 11:2).

36. May we deduce from the meaning of these words "reject" and "cast off" that God's predestination is not immutable?

No, this conclusion, too, is not permissible. Predestination has two senses. There is a foreordination that can end, but predestination in the proper sense, about which we are concerned here, will prove to be irrevocable.

37. Have the different meanings that the word election or foreordination can have sometimes been used to refute the doctrine of predestination?

Yes, it has been claimed that where Scripture speaks of election only a *national election* is meant. That God chooses means only that He establishes the administration of His covenant of grace amongst one or other nation to the exclusion of other nations. Also, it is maintained, now election only concerns the question in which century one or other pagan nation will be reached by Christian missions. Such predestination will still certainly be called absolute because it is independent of the condition of its objects and of the attitude they adopt. But otherwise one may not speak of an absolute predestination. Whether among such a nation or tribe there will be those who will be born again and converted and receive salvation depends, it is thought, not on God's sovereign decree, but lies in the use that men themselves make of their freedom of choice.

38. What must be observed against such a view?

a) That we in no way deny the existence of such a national election. God's decree is not exclusively concerned with individuals but also comprises nations and establishes the bond between generations. The destiny of a nation is weighed by Him, as is the destiny of a person. There is not the slightest interest, indeed it is completely impossible on Reformed grounds, to deny national election or whatever it may be called.

b) It must be pointed out that such national election leads directly to personal reprobation. It is firmly established that without the knowledge of God's word there is no salvation. When, therefore, God sovereignly decrees that certain nations will live on for a long time without the knowledge of the truth, this obviously includes that all the individuals who belong to such nations are lost. Election of a nation or predestination to the enjoyment of the presence of the means of grace is thus simply unthinkable without personal reprobation. And once personal reprobation is admitted then there is no reason for seeing why objections against a personal election can be maintained. If one will not recognize this, then one must posit three classes of men:

1. Those who have reprobated themselves.

2. Those who are reprobated by God.

3. Those who have elected themselves.

   This view, however, is highly unacceptable.

39. *In theological parlance what is the distinction between predestination and election?*

We will note here provisionally that these words differ in significance.

a) Predestination is a predetermination to a certain destiny. It therefore has the end of the state of affairs in view. Election is the appointment or determination of certain persons for one or other matter; it thus has persons in view.

b) Predestination is wider in scope than election. The former is usually seen as comprised of two parts: (1) election (*Electio*) and (2) reprobation (*Reprobatio*). So understood, election therefore becomes a part of predestination. Election then becomes "ordaining to eternal bliss."

c) Election only has reference to specific persons, in order to place them in a specific relationship. Predestination also comprises, with the goal toward which ordaining takes place, the means leading to that goal. When in Romans 8:29 the apostle says that the children of God are foreordained to be conformed to the image of His Son, he evidently means that this predestinating also ordains the means and the ways that lead to this reality. Hence there follows, "And those whom He predestined, those He has also called, and those whom He has called, those He has also justified, and those He has justified, those He has also glorified."

40. *Where does Paul speak explicitly about predestination?*

In Romans 9 and the following chapters.

41. *Does this passage speak of an external election that has reference to certain nationalities?*

No; that was already asserted long ago, and in modern times opponents of the Reformed doctrine of election repeatedly advance that assertion. That it is wrong appears from the following:

a) From the entire course of the apostle's reasoning. Here his discussion of predestination has a very specific immediate cause. The greater part of Israel in his time did not believe in Christ, and the Gentiles had obtained the privileges that were brought to maturity under Israel by its centuries-long development. That caused Paul deep sorrow. He sums up all the glorious things that Israel had possessed earlier (v. 4–5). Among those things, the "covenants" and the "promises of the covenant" also belong. But he was not ignorant that the promises of the covenant applied to the offspring as well as the fathers. How then could the fathers have had the promises of the covenant and yet their offspring be lost?

Has not then the word of God failed? (v. 6). "No" is the apostle's answer, for those promises did not hold good, strictly speaking, for all the offspring; they had in view the children of the promise. And if one takes it in this way, he means to say, there is no contradiction between the promises of the covenant made to Abraham and God's free foreordination. Now it certainly goes without saying that spoken of here is personal, not national predestination. Or, to express it with complete accuracy: personal election but national rejection. The promise of God continues, but not by incorporating Israel as a whole into the New Testament church but rather by joining together individuals out of Israel and the Gentiles to be the true seed of the promise to which the covenant promise made with Abraham pointed.

b) In so many words we are told to what this foreordination pointed. It is an ordaining to being God's children, to being the true spiritual children of Abraham (v. 7–8), to which, consequently, the full glorification of God's children is tied (v. 23). In contrast to this there is a foreordaining to dishonor (v. 21), to wrath (v. 22), to destruction (v. 22). God has called individuals *out of* Israel and *out of* the Gentiles (v. 24). And these who are called are the same of which it was just said that they were vessels of mercy prepared beforehand for glory.

Examples of persons are produced, both of election and hardening (Moses, v. 15; Pharaoh, v. 17). It is not out of a principle of usefulness that God temporarily prefers one and passes by the other, but He does it for the glory of His virtues (v. 17, 22). From v. 14 on everything is strictly individual.

42. Is it not true then that before v. 14 national matters are discussed?

In a certain sense that must be admitted. "In Isaac shall your offspring be named" certainly means in the first place that Isaac is the son from whom the covenant people will originate, while Israel will be placed outside the administration of the covenant. The thought is certainly not: Isaac is elected to eternal salvation (although we would naturally not deny that). Isaac's election is therefore still something other than an election to salvation. Likewise v. 9 speaks of the birth of Isaac from Sarah, not of his regeneration as a consequence of his election. Verse 12 is even clearer, where it is seen that the relationship prophesied to Rebekah does not have in view the salvation of Esau and Jacob but the national relationship of both peoples that would originate from them. The older will serve the younger. Likewise, v. 13 (a quote from Mal 1:2–3) is to be understood of a love that had as a result national, theocratic advantages for Esau and Jacob. All this is not subject to any doubt. But anyone who derives from it that here Paul in no way teaches a personal predestination to an eternal destiny is reasoning very superficially and completely bypasses the deep sense of his argument. It is a settled conclusion that he is dealing with the personal unbelief of his brothers according to the flesh, takes his point of departure from that (v. 1–2) and comes back to it (v. 24). The question therefore becomes how Paul can deduce from national matters a conclusion that he then maintains for personal matters. How can he conclude from the election of Isaac and Jacob the election of all who believe and of their being destined to eternal glory?

The answer is as follows: Paul has seen in what happened with Isaac and Ishmael, Jacob and Esau, a type for what takes place in a spiritual respect with all who live under the dispensation of the Gospel. Also, that the spiritual promises do not necessarily have in view every fleshly descendant but that God in His election and in making good on His covenant promises remains free—that is clear from the fact that God had already said to Abraham, "I will not produce a son and posterity for you in a natural way, but in a miraculous way" (v. 7). That is (i.e., "that is to be understood typologically"), the birth stemming from the promise accomplishes everything. That was already true in the case of Isaac regarding the origin of the covenant people, Israel. And it is still also true now regarding entrance into glory. Therefore, the conclusion is drawn in v. 8, "the children of the promise are counted as offspring." Thus, it is entirely a typological argument that the apostle makes use of here, but his theme remains, before as after, the election of individuals out of Jews and paganism.

43. *Does the apostle also teach that this election or foreordination of God is completely free, independent of something in man by which he would deserve preference?*

Yes, this is taught as emphatically as possible, so that all Remonstrant views are cut off at the root. One might still have been able to say for Isaac and Ishmael that the one, the elect, was born of the free woman, the other, the reprobate, of the slave woman. No wonder then that God made a distinction (Gal 4:22). But Paul has anticipated that objection. And therefore he is not satisfied with referring to the example of Isaac and Ishmael. At the same time he pointed to another example that by the nature of the case does not permit this objection. For Isaac and Ishmael the mothers differed, but for Jacob and Esau there was no trace of such a difference. Not only did they each have a mother equal in status, not only did they have the same mother, not only did they have one mother and one father, but they were children born as twins from the same conception. Rebekah, too, is a proof of this when she was impregnated by one man, namely Isaac our father, for when the children were not yet born neither had done anything either good or bad, so that the purpose of God according to election might stand, not by works but by Him who calls (v. 10–12). There was nothing outstanding whatsoever in Jacob that would have been a cause to move God to make him a ruler and Esau his servant. The word that determined their destiny already went out before they had done anything either good or bad. And this word was intentionally proclaimed well in advance so that later when the distinction came to light, one would not think it was for the better qualities of Jacob that he was given preference. Rather, it must be seen that the destiny of these two, and the nations that would descend from them, depended on the free will of the One who called. For that reason their destinies were different, and in this way it was seen in all its clarity that it was not by works. God of Himself had determined that He would have only the one for the work that He does in His covenant people. If that work had only been revealed later to Jacob and not to Esau, the possibility existed that one would have attributed the honor for this to Jacob himself, to his better qualities. That must not be. It must become clear: not of works, but of the One who calls. And in order to prevent this, God proclaimed well in advance, already before their birth, what will occur when the children grow up.

This happened in this way so that it would be clear how the God who calls is the fountain of all grace by which people are distinguished. But the same thing is also expressed still differently. It also had for its goal "so that the purpose of election (purpose of choice) might stand." Here we are presented with a work in an area where otherwise the works of Scripture are so sparse. A motive is spoken of by which God is guided in His sovereign and mysterious election. The purpose of choice and the "not of works, but of the One who calls" here stand beside each other as matters of identical content and of identical purport. The apostle thus evidently intends to teach that God makes a distinction between man and man in His predestination, because in that way it emerges into the clearest light that the elect have everything from His sovereignly working (= calling) grace. Where God from persons completely alike takes the one and leaves the other, there it is indisputable that He is the source of grace. This indication must be received by us thankfully. And what Paul teaches us is entirely in accord with Scripture. Sovereign election and free grace, then, are always in connection with each other. Whoever deprives us of election deprives us of free grace. That holds for election in general, but according to these words of the apostle it also holds for election in the specific sense, for the choosing, discriminating element in predestination. Whoever teaches a general salvation that includes everyone in its end results still certainly need not fail to do justice to the reality of free grace. But he necessarily fails to do justice to the revelation of free grace. And for this Paul has an eye here.

44. *How do some attempt to negate this teaching of Paul on predestination?*

By pointing to its other side, which is discussed in Romans 9:30–10:21.

Both of the following are settled for the apostle:

a) The free, sovereign ordination of God, which does not derive its grounds from the activity of man.

b) The full responsibility of man toward his Creator.

He then discusses both in succession. The apostle has not made an attempt to reconcile these two with each other logically. Nor may we make such an attempt. But it is even more impermissible to bend and distort the contents of Romans 9 up to v. 30, so that in one way or another it conforms to what follows. Both sides must remain next to each other, unreconciled for our thinking but each in its full right. To want to explain Romans 9 by Romans 9 is rationalistic exegesis.

45. What does Paul teach concerning the national election related to Israel?

In Romans 9 and following he discusses this in detail.

He asks: "Has God rejected His people?" And the answer is: "By no means! God has not rejected His people whom He has foreknown" (11:1-2).

a) A nation once foreknown cannot be rejected entirely so that nothing of it would remain; no seed would be saved out of it.

   Paul therefore points to himself as an example that God is fulfilling the promises made to the fathers. He himself is a Jew. Also in Elijah's days 7,000 men were left. Israel's election, as a national election too, is thus first of all irrevocable in the sense that there always remains a remnant according to election (v. 5).

b) There is another way in which this national election is carried out. Although it is true that there is a remnant, nevertheless the great mass is rejected. In 11:15 there is also talk of "their rejection," which parallels "their decrease" in v. 12. God has indeed rejected Israel as a whole, as a nation; the majority of the people is placed outside the administration of the covenant. But if one looks away from the present and does not consider the near future, then it remains the case that also this nation as an organism, this totality, is elect and once again will be placed into the dispensation of the covenant. The fullness of the Gentiles will enter and all Israel will be saved. So also can it be maintained that the gifts and the calling of God are without repentance (v. 29).

c) From this then is to be inferred how verses 17 and 19 must be understood when they speak of broken off and engrafted branches. This has frequently been viewed as proof of the relativity and changeability of election, and it is pointed out that at the end of v. 23 the Gentile Christians are threatened with being cut off in case they do not continue in the kindness of God. But wrongly. Already the image of engrafting should have restrained such an explanation. This image is nowhere and never used of the implanting of an individual Christian into the mystical body of Christ by regeneration. Rather, it signifies the reception of a racial line or national line into the dispensation of the covenant or their exclusion from it. This reception of course occurs by faith in the preached word, and to that extent, with this engrafting of a race or a nation, there is also connected the implanting of individuals into the body of Christ. The cutting off, of course, occurs by unbelief; not, however, by the unbelief of persons who first believed, but solely by the remaining in unbelief of those who, by virtue of their belonging to the racial line, should have believed and were reckoned as believers. So, a rejection (= multiple rejection) of an elect race is possible, without it being connected to a reprobation of elect believers. Certainly, however, the rejection of a race or nation involves at the same time the personal reprobation of a sequence of people. Nearly all the Israelites who are born and die between the rejection of Israel as a nation and the reception of Israel at the end times appear to belong to those reprobated. And the threat of v. 22 is not directed to the Gentile Christians as individual believers but to them considered racially.

46. *How does the reasoning of the apostle in Romans 9 oppose election by foreseen faith and good works?*

It rules out this Remonstrant understanding decisively. It is said of Esau and Jacob that their destiny was decided and that decision was announced before they had done anything, good or bad. But the whole argument is also overthrown if one must accept that even the slightest good is foreseen in man. The question of v. 14, "What shall we say then? Is there injustice with God?" becomes completely inexplicable if Paul considered the difference between belief and unbelief as the reason for the distinction between elect and reprobate. Then even the slightest appearance of injustice would be absent, and it would occur to no one to bring such a charge against God's doing.

That was not so for Jacob and Esau. But now there are a large number of people, even a majority, whose destiny is decided while they are still just like Jacob and Esau, not yet having reached the age of discretion. There is no speaking of faith as an act for children before their use of their minds. Therefore, the Remonstrant conception is not applicable to them. Now one can of course easily say that all children who die before they use their minds are elect. But the question is whether anyone would dare to apply this to the children who live outside the administration of the covenant of grace. If one does not venture to do so, and Scripture certainly does not give grounds for this, then it appears that for children election and reprobation takes place according to a different rule than foreseen faith and good works.

Furthermore, faith and good works always appear elsewhere in Scripture not as the occasion for God's election but as the fruit and result of election (John 6:44; Eph 1:4; 2:8–10; Acts 13:48; Phil 1:29; 1 Thess 1:2–4).

Already Augustine said, "A wheel does not run well in order to become round, but it runs well because it is round."

47. What is the meaning of the question in Romans 9:14?

It appears from the words with which it is introduced here that it is an objection that Paul anticipated. The objection is directed to the biased, discriminating element in election. Justice is one of God's virtues, and that would appear to have to include strict impartiality. Thus, one who is not elect would be able to object that God has not dealt with him justly. Paul gives the answer to this objection in a quote from the Old Testament. It is taken from Exodus 33:19 according to the Septuagint. There God speaks to Moses, "I will make all my goodness pass before you and will proclaim the name of the Lord before you. But I will be gracious to whom I will be gracious and will show mercy to whom I will show mercy." Here the Lord ascribes it to His free mercy that He grants Moses this vision and expresses this as a general proposition. He will (in fact) show *in the future* His grace and mercy to those whom He has *now* sovereignly decreed in his grace and mercy.

With this the objection is not refuted, but with an appeal to God's own declaration it is declared inadmissible. God Himself declares in Scripture that He reserves for Himself this so-called biased and unjust action and this way of acting against which men murmur. The apostle simply ascertains the fact without going further into its explanation and draws directly from his quotation the conclusion, "So then it is not of the one who wills or of the one who runs, but of the merciful God." These words are to be understood in a wholly general sense, without an allusion to certain facts having to be sought in them—for example, the willing of Abraham with respect to Ishmael or the running of Esau for the venison. Willing is simply human desiring, running is the strenuous attempting of man.

By appealing to this axiom Paul has naturally not wanted to suggest that there was no other explanation. It is certainly necessary to pay attention to how such an explanation is obvious. Partiality and impartiality, justness and injustice are opposites that presuppose particular relationships. If a dispute exists between two people over the right of ownership to a certain sum of money, and I am called in as arbiter and in distributing the sum give more to the one, less to the other than is due them, then I certainly show partiality and injustice. Here there was an original right violated by my choice. Where there is a right there can be injustice. But, conversely, where a right is lacking, that is not the case. If I decide to distribute a certain sum among the poor and I decide to be more generous to the one than to the other, then it is absurd to speak of injustice and partiality. None of those poor can claim any right to his gift. I act in a discriminating fashion, but am beyond all partiality, provided there are no parties involved. I remain beyond all injustice, provided there are none with rights. Now the apostle does not intend to say this directly, but it still comes through by implication in his answer. In what is said there is nothing of willing and running, whereby rights would originate, but exclusively of God's mercy. Mercy is not a judicial function or attribute, but a gift. Giving is a free action not bound by rights. Matthew 20:15, "Am I not permitted to do what I want with what is mine? Or is your eye evil because I am good?"

Of course the vindication of God, if one wants to seek such, is not to be sought in the equal sin of all. Here there is no speaking of a right; hence it can also not be a right forfeited by sin. Further, sin is equal in everyone. From an equal condition one can never justify a discriminating course of action. The only answer must be: Election is an action of God whereby no rights of persons comes into consideration, an act that God performs not as judge but out of the fullness of His sovereignty. He will have mercy on whom He has determined to have mercy.

48. *Give an explanation of Romans 9:16–18.*

These verses serve to provide the apostle with a conclusive proof for the sovereignty of election. He could have left matters with his argument that according to God's own express declaration there is no injustice with Him that He grants grace to whom He wills. But with marvelous resoluteness he goes a step further and shows that God is just as free in apportioning evil. That must thus shut the door [to all objections]. For God (= Scripture) says to Pharaoh, etc.

God's words to Pharaoh are, "Just for this have I raised you up so that in your person I might show my power and so that my name might be fully manifested in all the earth." This is a quotation from Exodus 9:16, partly according to the Septuagint but with a single apparently intentional change. The Septuagint has διετηρήθης, "You have been preserved alive." The Hebrew has הֶעֱמַדְתִּיךָ, "I have caused you to stand." The question here is not in the first place what the Hebrew in Exodus 9:16 means according to the letter. It occurs repeatedly that New Testament Scripture changes the letter of the Old Testament in order to give a better explanation of the purpose and the deeper intention that a word has. This has also happened here.

To begin with, in New Testament Greek ἐγείρειν, "to raise," consistently has the meaning "to raise up," "to cause to appear" (Matt 11:11, "Among those born of women there has arisen no one greater," etc.; Matt 24:11, "Many false prophets will arise"; John 7:52, "No prophet is arisen from Galilee").

Next, if Paul had wanted to say, "I have preserved your life" or "brought you to the throne" or "raised you up from an illness" or whatever of the like, then the changing of the words from the Septuagint becomes inexplicable.

Third, the Hebrew and what Paul says agree in principle entirely if we translate, "I have raised you up." The Hebrew simply says, "I have let you stand," that is, while many others must fall away, you remain. Paul explains that further. This happened, he says, because with the historical appearance of Pharaoh God had His purpose, and Pharaoh may not fall until this purpose was attained. Therefore, he remained standing.

Fourth, with every weakening explanation one blunts the point of Paul's reasoning if thereby the conclusion no longer follows logically that the apostle himself draws in v. 18, "So then He hardens whom He wills." That God has put Pharaoh on the throne, has kept him alive, or has raised him from his sick bed, that at the same time supplies a conclusion, that He has raised him up in his entire personality.

This is also the exegesis of Calvin, "…from which it follows that one now disputes with Him in vain, as if He were bound to give an account of Himself, since He of Himself proceeds to remove this objection, saying that the reprobate come out of the hidden treasure of His providence, in which He will have His name praised." So also Beza, Piscator, Bengel, Olshausen, Rüchert, Beck, Tholuck, Philippi, and many others.

If one wants to lessen something of the harshness of these words, then it must happen along a different path. One, one choosing this course, can say that this producing of Pharaoh's personality did not happen from abstract, still indeterminate humanity, but from sinful humanity. It has in view mediate creation. Of course, no one can object to that, although it cannot be proven that Paul had thought specifically of that. In any case, Pharaoh was raised to be an example of God's power. He was created for that. And that was the main purpose of "just for this end."

49. Give an explanation of v. 18.

The emphasis falls on the initial words, "*On whom He wills* He shows mercy, *whom He wills* He hardens." The apostle intends to say there is no other reason for the different assignments of destiny than the *absolute* will of God. And this is true both for the destiny of misery as well as for the destiny of blessedness.

Concerning the term "harden" (σκληρύνειν), here, too, there are many ready who think they are obliged to help the apostle by giving his words the blandest possible sense, so that he would not be ascribing anything preposterous to God. Calvin says, "Moreover, the word 'harden,' when it is attributed to God in Scripture, not only means permission, as some who insipidly mitigate wish, but also the activity of divine wrath," as Solomon also teaches that the perdition of the wicked has not merely been foreseen but that the wicked themselves are created with the purpose that they perish (Prov 16:4).

50. *What does v. 19 contain?*

An objection that Paul takes from the mouth of the opponents of predestination. This time it is not an objection against the partiality of God but against the fairness of God when He complains about the evil of sinners. It is within God's decree that sinners are like this; His sovereignty has predestined them to everything they are. Thus, they are in their entire appearance the result (not the product) of God's foreordination. But how then can God complain about them? Who has resisted His will—that is, who has ever successfully resisted His omnipotent will? The answer, no one! Thus we, too, have not been able to resist successfully. And we have to let ourselves become what God will have us to be. Therefore, God may not complain.

This is the objection. And now, the answer. In order to understand it well one will have to recall how Paul has answered the objection of v. 14. Not by removing the objection by reasoning and subtle distinctions, but simply by setting over against it God's emphatic declaration itself and then, with a bold turn, by placing alongside it a still more impressive example of God's sovereignty: You complain that God shows mercy to one and not to the other? I will answer you with what God Himself declares concerning this. He says to Moses, etc. But I will still tell you something else. He is not only free to withhold mercy. He also is free to harden and to bring about hardening. For he says to Pharaoh, etc. Do you complain that then nobody can resist His will and that the wicked must necessarily become as they are in their hardening? I will still tell you something else. Who are you, O man, to answer back to God? Does not the potter have power over the clay, etc.?

Such is the large-scale course of the apostle's reasoning. From it is evident how one misunderstands it totally if one advances all sorts of restrictions in order to tone it down. Undoubtedly, the apostle has also known about these restrictions and in fact he has himself used them on other occasions. He was just as much at home as we are with teaching on human responsibility and on the subjective development of human sin. He certainly knew that God is strictly just as well as sovereign. But he has intentionally left that to the side here and viewed the matter from the side of sovereignty. Why? Would he not have stopped the mouths of these blasphemers with more effect by pointing out to them that, although rejected by God, they are lost because of their own guilt? Did he now not expose himself to the danger that one goes on to say, Paul has no answer to our counter argument? The answer: It appeared to Paul in this connection to be beneath God's dignity to conduct a defense of His justice against these blasphemers. One does not convince such people; one stops their mouth. Furthermore, what Paul could and may have brought forward for the vindication of this sovereign way of proceeding by God would have been so difficult to understand that it probably would still have missed its mark. Here lie depths we can never fathom, difficulties that we will see solved by no one. The reasoning to which Paul has kept himself is in this case in fact the most effective.

Now comes the image of the potter and the clay. In order to explain it one needs to remember for what purpose an image or a parable is intended. It is not to be applied point for point. Whoever does that with the ordinary images and parables of Scripture will end up with the greatest absurdities. Every image has a *tertium comparationis*, the main point about which the comparison turns, about which it deals. All the rest is accessory. Applying this rule here, we ask: What is the main point of the comparison used here?

a) It is not the condition of the material from which the potter forms vessels. This can be coarse clay or fine clay meant for the most delicate porcelain. But that makes no difference in the relationship of the potter to the lump. So too here. The purpose of the image is absolutely not to show us whether the lump of humanity was pure or impure, refined or unrefined. In itself both can have been the case. Suppose the lump was sinful, impure. Is thereby God's sovereignty toward the lump less? If so, then one must consider the idea of the impurity of the lump as having been included.

b) It is also not the manner of working the clay followed by the potter that constitutes the point of comparison. One potter works with coarse, another with fine tools, one artistically and with nimble fingers, another tastelessly and without feeling for beauty. They all handle the lump of clay mechanically as lifeless material that they knead and form according to their heart's desire without the lump reacting to their working. All this cannot be carried over to God's treatment of man. He does not work on us as lifeless material but as living spirits. We are not dead and inanimate in His fingers. He does not deal with us mechanically. All such considerations lie outside the scope of the comparison. The image teaches us absolutely nothing concerning the mystery of how the formation of man takes place in God's decree. Whether that happens by mere permission or by withdrawing grace or by positive unfathomable acts, nothing about that is told us here. The one as well as the other is entirely within the terms of the image.

c) The *tertium comparationis* evidently consists of two things:

1. The allotment of a certain quality.

2. In connection with that, the assignment of a certain destiny.

These are surely the two things the potter does with respect to his vessels. He determines first of all *for what* they will serve, and then he determines *how* they must be made in order to serve this purpose. And in both cases He has authority over the clay. One should note that here "authority" is spoken of, not "power" (Greek ἐξουσία, not δύναμις). "Power" is a physical concept; "authority" is a moral concept. No one will deny that God has power over His creatures as the potter possesses power to work the clay. But that God possesses the authority for that, the authorization, the critics of divine predestination deny. But, Paul says to these critics, the relationship of God to you is like the relationship of potter to vessel. God can rightly, without in any sense detracting from His virtues, deal with you in the two respects mentioned above, as a potter deals with the clay. When He does that, He acts with the authorization that belongs to Him as God. And concerning that authorization, which conforms to God's perfect holiness, the creature is not free to pass judgment. That fact is contained in the question, "Who are you, O man, who answers back to God?" As man, as creature, the elect or the reprobate is not in a position to pass judgment about whether the actions of the Most High are just or not. The creature has no absolute standard of justice in himself that he could apply to God to evaluate His acts. This is not in the least denying that there is such a standard. God bears it in Himself, in His holy nature. In this point, too, we cannot extend the comparison between the potter and God. For concerning the potter in forming his vessels no ethical issues at all come into consideration. He does not need to respect any ethical laws toward his clay. The clay has no ethical qualities. It is a purely physical lump. But also when God orders the destiny of man in His eternal foreordination, He thereby acts according to ethical principles and from ethical motives. Only, the apostle intends to say, the creature has just as little right to pass judgment on these moral principles and motives as a clay vessel has a right to make a judgment about the intentions and thoughts of its maker. And a vessel has no right in this respect, indeed cannot have such a right.

So it comes down to the two elements in the image mentioned above. This cannot be difficult. The first, the allotment of a quality, is contained in the question of the thing formed: "Why have you made me like this?" From this it appears convincing that here in fact the determining of quality is spoken of. The thing formed knows, as it were, that its condition and its destiny cohere, that its destiny is given with its condition. Therefore it says: "Why like this?" Further, this first element is present in the name that God bears here, "The One who forms" (πλάσας). Forming is not merely the assigning of a destiny, but also the allotting, the granting of certain characteristics. We repeat here: Concerning the way that forming took place, the text tells us nothing. But that it took place is certainly evident in the text, and an unbiased exegesis will have to grant this.

The second element mentioned, the assignment of a destiny, is present in v. 21, where it is said of the potter that he makes one vessel "for honor," the other "for dishonor." That has in view the destiny that the vessels have. The one has a noble use, the other a shameful one. Likewise, people are destined for a noble or for an ignoble use. The apostle has transferred these traits to people insofar as they are the objects of God's predestination. He says that some people are "vessels of wrath, prepared for destruction." Others are "vessels of mercy, prepared for glory."

It is clear that in these expressions the two concepts, "destruction" and "glory," correspond to "honor" and "dishonor" in the image of the potter. As the potter predestines to dishonor, so God predestines to destruction; as the potter predestines to honor, so God predestines to glory. And from that it follows almost of itself that the two other concepts, "wrath" and "mercy," must agree with the qualitative element in the image. Calvin says, "They are vessels prepared for destruction, that is, given up and ordained to destruction. At the same time they are also vessels of wrath, that is, made to be demonstrations of God's punishment and anger." Wrath and destruction correspond to one another, the one demands the other. And likewise one must not take "vessels of mercy" to be vessels that were objects of mercy. Then all correspondence with the image is lost. They are vessels intended to serve for showing mercy. The genitive is a genitive that describes destiny. Calvin, "So then we believers are quite rightly called vessels of mercy, whom the Lord uses as instruments for manifesting his mercy; and the reprobate are rightly called vessels of wrath because they serve to demonstrate the judgments of God."

51. *How is v. 22 to be understood?*

Many who thus far agree with the exegesis just given think that a turn in the apostle's argument occurs here. They find this indicated by the particle δέ, "but if." They think that the sense is, "I insist that this is the absolute right of God and that He can and may act in this way. But what if He has not made use of this right?" But it has been quite rightly pointed out that such a contrast demands a much stronger word than the simple δέ. The sentence is to be paraphrased as follows: "If now, however, God when He had determined to reveal His wrath and to make known His power in certain persons (the reprobate), instead of immediately implementing this decision, bore these vessels prepared for destruction with much patience, with the intention that thereby it would be possible for Him to show the riches of His glory through vessels of mercy prepared for glory, must not then there be silence and must not one acknowledge that God in this particular implementation of His absolutely sovereign decree is no less right than if He had implemented it immediately?" The answer to this must naturally be in the affirmative.

We add the following for clarification. God could have immediately carried out His decree with regard to the reprobate. As soon as they became vessels of wrath by their willful sin, He could have given them up to destruction. But He did not do that. He bore them in much patience, that is, by postponing and delaying their punishment. He did this with a certain purpose, as is indicated by "so that." This purpose lay in the determination that He had made concerning the elect. He willed to show the richness of His glory concerning the vessels of mercy, and those vessels of mercy were included in the organism of the world. Therefore, had the Lord immediately abandoned the vessels of wrath to destruction, then the organism of the world would have been disrupted and the revelation of mercy could not have taken place in a gradual manner.

A point has been made of κατηρτισμένα εἰς ἀπώλειαν, "fitted for destruction," in antithesis to ἃ προητοίμασεν, "that He had prepared beforehand" (v. 23). Supposedly this would indicate a distinction between the vessels of mercy being prepared by God and the vessels of wrath preparing themselves. Nothing is against this view in itself. Everyone would agree that God in His governance of all things lets people go to destruction by their sin in a different way than He leads others to glory by His grace. The one is active, the other permissive, although not inactive. But it may be rightly doubted whether the apostle meant to express that by his words here. Actually, Paul is not at all speaking here about the effecting of God's counsel but about that counsel itself. One can certainly also posit a distinction in this counsel between the ordinary decree and the permissive decree. But even that is not expressed by the word κατηρτισμένα. Calvin writes, "So it is nonetheless without doubt that both these preparations are located in the secret counsel of God. Otherwise Paul would have said that the reprobate proceed or cast themselves into destruction. But now he means that before they are born, they are ordained to and left in their condition."

That in the one instance is "prepared" (passive), in the other, "that He had prepared beforehand" (active) will have no other ground than aiming at variation in expression. Besides, Calvin is certainly right when he thinks that here preparing and making ready do not refer to the actual leading and governing of men in the execution of God's decree, but to the forming and preparing of the destiny of men in God's decree itself. That is clearly reflected in "prepared *beforehand* for glory." In His long-suffering God spares the reprobate, not only for those elect who have already been prepared in reality but also for those who do not yet exist in reality but nevertheless are prepared in God's counsel. Concerning those whose life and fate He has already made a determination, such is thus the apostle's reasoning in this significant pericope.

We do not have to occupy ourselves at length here about whether this reasoning is infralapsarian or supralapsarian. However, if our explanation is correct, then an infralapsarian explanation will not do justice to the words of the apostle. The question of the vessel would then have never read, "Why have you made me thus?" but at the most, "Why when I already was as I was did you ordain me to this end?" But the question now is, "Why have you made me thus?" We believe therefore that also included in predestination here is God's foreordination of everything by which man becomes everything he becomes. And since the fall of our first parents is a prominent part of that, we also include this. By no means are we saying, on the other hand, that the apostle presents God here as the cause of sin. How God's decree, which comprehends all this, is executed does not at all come into consideration for the apostle. It was a permissive decree with respect to sin, and in its execution God remains entirely free of evil. God did not drive or incite man to sin. Man sinned entirely of himself. The image of the potter does not intend to teach us that by virtue of His predestination God makes man a sinner. But there is certainly involved, we think, that in His decree regarding the destiny of creatures, God includes the sin that men themselves commit, and that the concern of His decree with sin occupies a place in His predestination of what men will be and to what end they will serve.

52. Is election also discussed in the other letters of the apostle?

Yes, in the letters from the first imprisonment the wisdom of the decree of election comes to the fore, while in the Letter to the Romans the point is more the sovereignty of God. Ephesians 1:4 teaches that believers are chosen *in Christ*, that it happened *before* the foundation of the world, and that it had as its purpose that God's children be holy and blameless before Him in love.

The first of these points means:

a) Not that Christ was the basis or meriting cause of election, as if the reconciling love of the Father could only have been active because of the surety of Christ. Scripture teaches us above all that Christ with His incarnation, His mediatorship and everything connected with it must be regarded as a gift of God's electing love. Thus one must not say that God's love cannot rest on the elect except in Christ. For Christ Himself as Mediator was already a gift of that love.

b) It also does not mean that Christ was elected first and then believers, so that in the election of Him as head the election of the members as decreed would have been included. That also cannot be, for then one comes to the conclusion that believers exist just as well for the sake of Christ as Christ does for believers. Scripture teaches the opposite. He has been given to us by the Father.

c) The right meaning is that the children of God are chosen in order to be in Christ for the purpose that in Christ they would be included as members of His body. Compare Galatians 1:6: "Who has called you in the grace of Christ"; that is, "so that you would be in the grace of Christ." Thus contained in the election of God is the determination that believers would form a unity with Christ and that only in fellowship with Christ would they share in all the saving benefits intended for them. They are blessed with all spiritual blessings in heaven in Christ. Certainly, Christ thus duly enters into the decree of election but, one must note, as *object*. Of course we are speaking here of Christ in His quality as Mediator and not as eternal *Logos* in the abstract. Christ as Mediator was object and means in the decree of predestination.

By "before the foundation of the world" (πρὸ καταβολῆς κόσμου), election is delineated as an eternal act, an important point against many who maintain that for Paul election was a temporal act, like calling and justification. The purpose of election is holiness and blamelessness before God. That is, it is aimed in the first place at the glory of God. When God chooses something, He sets it apart for Himself that it be holy.

The plan of salvation is repeatedly portrayed in these letters as a creation of the wisdom of the Lord, who is worthy of the admiration of angels and men. The elect congregation is by preference called a body (Eph 4:4; Col 3:15).

It also coheres with this, then, when here the entire history of the world is placed under the viewpoint of being a single great outworking of this counsel of God. The purpose of God is called a πρόθεσις τῶν αἰώνων, "a purpose of the ages" (Eph 3:11). It is made "before the foundation of the world." That, therefore, is to say that the Lord who made it is the same God who created all things through Christ Jesus (Eph 3:9, 10).

Likewise, enough is made of a certain relationship of Christ in this counsel of God to the angels. It was the good pleasure of the Father in Christ to reconcile to Himself all things, whether on earth or in heaven. Among the things in heaven here the angels will certainly have to be understood (cf. Eph 1:10–11; Col 1:20).

53. *For the doctrinal exposition of the doctrine of predestination what subjects must be discussed in succession?*

a) The *subject* of predestination, the predestinating *God*.

b) The *point of departure* of predestination, divine foreknowledge.

c) The *distinguishing element* of predestination, divine election.

d) The *effective and formative element* of predestination, foreordination.

e) The *objects* of predestination, angels, men, the Mediator.

f) The *quality* in which the objects of predestination appear; expressed differently, the *scope* of predestination.

54. *To whom is predestination generally ascribed in Scripture?*

To God the Father. In 1 Peter 1:2 believers are therefore called "elect according to the foreknowledge of God the Father." In Ephesians 1 emphasis is placed on the fact that the love of election is a fatherly love. Election bears the marks of a fatherly act. Insofar as it governs the fate and destiny of creatures, it has in a certain sense a creative character. It is the Father who in order first forms the idea of election, although, of course, as an *ad extra* act the entire Trinity must be involved. However, nowhere in Scripture is election ascribed to the Son or the Holy Spirit. When in John 6:70; 13:18; 15:16, 19; Acts 1:2, 24 the word "chosen" is used of Christ, eternal election to salvation is not meant, but temporal choice and ordaining to an office.

55. *What is included when we ascribe election to the Father within the divine economy?*

That the so-called "counsel of peace" does not precede election but follows it in order. The former must be viewed as the first step in the implementation of the idea of election. The counsel of peace comprises the eternal suretyship of Christ, on which all God's gracious treatment of sinners in time depends. If now that surety is particular, that is, is not entered into for the human race in general but very specifically for the elect and for the elect only, then it follows that there must already have been a determining of the elect, an establishing of their persons, before the undertaking between the Father and the Son concerning sure-tyship began (this "before" and this "began" are not to be understood temporally). The opposite view, it occurs to us, must lead to a doctrine of universal atonement. In that case Christ was given for all and has accepted the suretyship, without limitation, for all, and only later in order has there entered into God's counsel the limitation by which the suretyship of Christ is put in force and made effective only for certain persons. That would come close to resembling the Amyraldian scheme, about which we will still speak later and which also begins with the universal in order to end with the particular. God's intention and love is initially all-embracing and later reduces to individual persons. This cannot be. We may think of a particular love of God provided it is there from the beginning.

56. *What was the starting point of predestination with respect to believers?*

Scripture teaches us that it is to be found in God's eternal love. To begin with, that is present in the word "foreknowledge" as we have developed its meaning above. This foreknowledge is a free sovereign love. And "foreknowledge" is put first by the apostle in the series of acts that form the foundation of the salvation of the sinner (Rom 8:29). Furthermore, this love of God is characterized for us by foreknowledge as a personal love. God did not merely love a part, a kernel, a remnant of humanity. God, we must say, loved particular people, a John, a Paul, etc. It was a knowing by name, a personal knowing, something moreover already included in the term "knowing" itself. A love other than personal is in itself not possible. Love is in its nature something personal. Finally, we must hold that for us nothing lies in back of this love. One may not even put mercy in back of it. And certainly not for the following reasons: Mere mercy is not something personal. Anyone who is in misery has as such a claim to our mercy. Mercy distinguishes itself just by this natural, general character from love. Thus, if in election one wishes to make mercy the starting point, one abandons a personal starting point. It would then have to be said: God saw us in our sin and by this, our miserable condition, was moved to compassion to save us in Christ. And that compassion then set God's love into motion. But then one could rightly ask whether all sinners did not stand equally miserable before God and whether equal misery should not have produced equal mercy for all. If one answers "no," then one concedes that besides mercy there was still something else that caused it to remain specifically with certain specific persons. And this something else can only lie in the love of God. It was there before mercy. And by it mercy was awakened and actuated. Only so is it also true that the ground of election does not in any respect lie in us, not even in our miserable lost condition. God loved us and saved us not *because* but *despite* our being miserable. Scripture considers this from the same point of view: "God who is rich in mercy *on account of* His great love with which He has loved us..." (Eph 2:4). Here mercy is clearly derived from love and not the reverse.

57. In what does the distinguishing element of election lie?

In the word "election" itself; That of itself makes us think of an antithesis and excludes every universalistic conception, every doctrine of a restoration of all things. God elected certain persons with the clear intention that He did not wish to elect others. One must bring these two sides into relationship with each other.

In us attention can so focus on a few things or persons that the remaining things or persons, although belonging to the same rubric, can remain in the background, and we, as it were, do not think of them. Thus one can only say in a relative sense that a decision concerning them has been made by us. It happens despite ourselves, because we neglect to make a decision concerning them. But with an omniscient God something like that is wholly impossible. There are no consequences in His determination that would not be completely clear to Him. His election has reprobation as its reverse side. This must be emphasized in our day because one readily presents the matter differently. Reprobation is described as the absence of any decision. God says otherwise in His Word.

He declares that He has made a distinction between Jacob and Esau, Isaac and Ishmael and has done that not because He ignored Ishmael and Esau but because He willed specifically to withhold from them what He gave the others.

58. Was there some reason for this discrimination present in the objects of election themselves?

No; that, too, is denied by Scripture. Election as a discriminating election is at the same time an entirely free election. But free is still something other than arbitrary. Election would not be free if God were led by motives that He had not derived from Himself. Election would have been arbitrary if God had been entirely without any motives, something that cannot be reconciled with His wisdom. For everything the Lord has a most sufficient and wise ground. It is enough for us to know that this ground came from Himself and not from those He elected. They were ordained to form one body with Christ the Mediator. Therefore it could not be a matter of indifference who they would become in the end. But that was not a ground for God, for they were that first by election and not the reverse. Suitability for the purposes of election is not the motivating cause in God but is much more its fruit.

59. May one say that there was only reprobation for the sake of election, that is, so that God's love and mercy with respect to the elect would appear so much the stronger?

No; this, too, is not presented by Scripture as the only purpose. It teaches us that there are two purposes of God with reprobation.

a) The one just mentioned—so that by the just rejection of some, the sovereign work of God's grace would appear so much the better as an exclusive work of God in the others. Therefore it is said, "So that the purpose of God according to election might stand, not of works but of Him who calls" (Rom 9:11). Esau was rejected so that it might appear how in Jacob everything was God's promise and God's work. In the same sense it is said, verses 22–23, that God with much patience has tolerated the vessels of wrath prepared for destruction in order to make known the riches of His glory in the vessels of mercy. Also in this some have found a proof for the proposition that reprobation is exclusively for the sake of election. But this is not the sense of these words. It is only said how enduring with patience the vessels of wrath (which apart from this were already vessels of wrath) stood in connection with the salvation of the elect.

b) There is still a higher ground in God as to why He also places the reprobate beside the elect. Scripture says He intends to establish vessels of dishonor to show His wrath, to make known His power (Rom 9:22). This is therefore an independent purpose, subordinate next to the purpose in election.

60. *What do you understand by the effective and formative element in predestination?*

We have already seen how Scripture gives us the acts of predestination in this sequence: foreknowledge, foreordination.

This foreordination emerges from foreknowledge. It determines the destiny and the condition of the elect of God, which they will finally reach when election has reached its goal. According to Romans 8:29, it is an image that is effected by foreordination. But now one must not limit foreordination by restricting it in a one-sided fashion to defining this image. It also comprises, beside this final state, all the means and ways by which this state will be reached. That is meant by the effectual and formative element in predestination. It is often presented in practice as if the means were disconnected from the end. One then posits election as something incomprehensible, above the operation of the grace of God. And it appears as if it is realized in a miraculous fashion apart from the means God had established. This is entirely contrary to Scripture. Paul teaches us that with election all the means and ways are also taken into account by which it must become reality. Therefore, "those He has first foreordained, those He has also called; those He has called, those He has also justified; those He justified, those He has also glorified." Thus, to extract the means is, humanly speaking, to provide a ground for thinking that one does not belong to the elect. Passively waiting to see whether election will take effect always rests on the mistaken understanding that election can operate outside the means.

This ordaining of means in the predestination of God must be taken in the widest sense. Everything belongs to it that contributes to bring the elect to where God will have them in the end. Included, then, is not only the ministering of grace, the external call, etc., but also preparatory grace in the sense to be defined later. Before God's children come to Him, the course of their life is not left to arbitrariness and chance. God appoints their destinies and their circumstances exactly in a manner as can be most serviceable for their subsequent place in the body of the elect. This was the case with Paul, who was set apart from his mother's womb, with Augustine, Luther, and Calvin, and this is also the case with the most insignificant believer. And after the external call this disposition also extends to the slightest detail. In connection with his discussion of election the apostle teaches precisely that all things, for those who are called according to God's purpose, must work together for good. That shows clearly how all things in God's counsel are placed under this viewpoint and so ordained that they must lead to this result, the good of God's children.

61. Who are the objects of predestination?

Scripture mentions angels, men, the Mediator. Thus far we have only spoken about men. We will now first answer the question whether the Mediator can be called predestined and elect. In 1 Peter 1:20 Scripture speaks of Christ, "who was foreknown before the foundation of the world but has been made manifest in these last times for your sake." In Luke 23:35 He is called "the elect of God"; in 1 Peter 2:4 "a living stone rejected by men but in the sight of God elect and precious." From the latter two verses it appears that "elect" must be understood as equivalent to "precious" and "beloved." This points us in the right direction. For Christ we ask how far one can speak:

a) Of foreknowledge. Foreknowledge means the personal love of God for the objects of His election. Now, the person of the Mediator was the person of God's Son. Can one speak then of a personal love of the Father for the Son, where the Father already perfectly loves the Son from eternity to eternity, apart from redemption? We think the answer is yes. There is a special love of God the Father that does not rest on Christ as Son but as Mediator, thus extends to His person insofar as He became the surety who willed to assume human nature. When at His baptism at the Jordan it is said so emphatically, "This is my beloved Son, hear Him," then that is certainly connected with carrying out the work of Mediator. And in this sense we must understand it when Scripture teaches a foreknowledge of Christ. Thus it is the particular pleasure of love that rested on the person of Christ in His capacity as Mediator.

b) Of election. We have seen above how in the doctrine or in the understanding of election two elements above all are present: (1) making a distinction, and (2) taking pleasure in the one elected.

Now it is self-evident that making a distinction is not applicable to Christ. He was the only one who could act as Mediator. Thus, here there can be no speaking of choosing and electing, but certainly of the second element. That, however, comes down to approximately the same thing as the foreknowledge of Christ as Mediator. And if one considers setting apart for a certain purpose, then the election of the Mediator coincides with His foreordination.

c) Of foreordination. It is true that it is not said directly that Christ has been foreordained. But on the one hand mention is made of how believers are ordained to be conformed to the image of Christ so that He might be the firstborn among many brothers (Rom 8:29). Indirectly included is that Christ, too, is ordained to this image. For the image, as we saw, we are not to think of moral quality but of mediatorial glory. At a great distance the members of Christ's body share in this His glory. The foreordination of Christ therefore means that for Him as Mediator a glory is intended by the Father, an image is ordained and delineated.

In agreement with this Christ speaks of the promise of this glory solemnly given to Him by the Father: "I ordain for you the Kingdom, as my Father has ordained it (established it by covenant) for me." If one can speak of an ordaining in this sense, then with reason an ordaining in the sense of determining must be antecedent. On the other hand, this ordination of Christ certainly encompasses all that is related to His mediatorial work—not only His glory but also His suffering with all its means and ways. God's plan and hand ordained beforehand what would take place, that toward which Herod and Pilate conspired (Acts 4:28).

62. Must one refer this predestination to Christ as Logos or as Mediator?

Christ can only be predestined as Mediator, and then only as Mediator in the specific soteriological sense. Of an incarnation of Christ apart from sin Scripture knows nothing. It is certainly true that the *Logos* as the Second Person in the Trinity stands in a certain relationship to all things. But one cannot derive this relationship from predestination, because it follows from the existence mode of the divine being itself and is not the fruit of a free ordaining that could also be otherwise. As all things are created through Christ, so also all things are created for Christ (Col 1:16). Still it is true that this economical relationship, in which Christ stands as Second Person of the Trinity to every creature created by Him, is also extended into His mediatorship. As creation was through Him and for Him, so that is now also true in re-creation.

63. Where does Scripture speak of an election of angels?

In 1 Timothy 5:21, where they are called "the elect angels." Apparently this is in contrast to non-elect angels. The question now is in what sense that can be understood of the angels.

    a) One could say, the election of angels exists in the fact that those who did not fall were ordained by God, from the moment of their remaining steadfast on, to be forever immutable. And conversely, the reprobation of the rest consisted in this, that those who fell were ordained to remain in their fallen state without redemption. There is, however, an objection to this view. In this way the election of angels is made dependent on something good that was foreseen in them, namely, their remaining steadfast. This conflicts with the entire analogy of Scripture. It would also lead us to think that the man who remained standing in the covenant of works and on that basis was made immutably blessed could for that reason be called elect.

    b) One will therefore have to consider this matter in more depth. Foresight of the steadfastness of angels was not the basis of their election, but on the contrary, election was the basis of their steadfastness. And, conversely, that the non-elect angels did not also manifest steadfastness did not have any other basis of certainty than that they were not elect. Calvin (*Institutes*, 3.23.4), "The angels who have persevered in their upright state are called "elect" by Paul (1 Tim 5:21); if their steadfastness was grounded in the good pleasure of God, then the apostasy of the other angels shows these were forsaken. For that no other cause can be adduced than reprobation, which is hidden in God's secret counsel."

c) This at the same time involves the conclusion that the election and reprobation of the angels are not to be understood in an infralapsarian but a supralapsarian way. Taking it in an infralapsarian way is equivalent to saying that the good angels' remaining steadfast fell outside the decree of election. And if that falls outside of the decree of election, then their election, which still depends on the decree, will rest on something in themselves and not on the free good pleasure of God. Now it is certainly true that one may not simply argue from the election of angels to the election of men. It can be that the two cases were not identical. But this much appears undeniable, that for the angels the determination of God concerning the angels falling or not falling must be reckoned as election. This electing is thus in itself not a term that should only be used where sin is already a settled given.

d) Are the angels elect in Christ? Some have answered, in Christ as Mediator; others, in Christ as head. Those who hold the former views add as a further explanation: in Christ as Mediator of preservation and of confirmation. But the name of Mediator definitely cannot be used here. In Scripture the term always means someone who, as surety, takes upon Himself the obligations of another who cannot fulfill these himself. Further, all proof is lacking:

1. That the angels could not fulfill their obligation.

2. That Christ took upon Himself their obligations vicariously.

Therefore, it is better to say that the angels are elect in Christ as their *head*. In the first place, then, this certainly has in view the *Logos*, through whom and for whom the angels were also created. In the second place, however, one can also think of the dominion that Christ exercises over the angels in the service of His congregation. The elect angels are certainly predestined to the end that they would serve in the work of redemption. They are called "ministering spirits" (Heb 1:14); they serve Christ their head and strengthened Him in His suffering. That Christ is already their head by creation entails of itself that He also remains their head and uses them as His servants in re-creation. Only note, however, that here head does not mean head of the body in an organic sense. Head has two meanings:

1. Ruler over others.

2. The thinking and governing part of a living body.

In the first sense Christ is the head of the angels; in the second sense Christ is the head only of elect men.

e) The language of Ephesians 1:10 and Colossians 1:20 has disposed some to find a reconciliation wrought by Christ for the angels there: "In order in the dispensation of the fullness of times to gather together all things as one in Christ, things in heaven and things on earth." "And that He having made peace through Him by the blood of His cross, through Him, I say, to reconcile to Himself all things, whether things on earth or things in heaven." But how can one speak of a reconciliation with regard to the angels? Neither can one speak of a mediator for them. Calvin understands Ephesians 1:10 as sustaining the elect angels in their state, both at the beginning when the non-elect angels fell as well as in its continuation when these angels had fallen. He calls Christ the Mediator insofar as this sustaining was effected in Him (cf. his commentary on this passage). On Colossians 1:20 Calvin says that "reconciliation" can be understood as prevention of apostasy. Peace with God was established and maintained and that is called reconciliation. And at the same time he calls to mind that the righteousness that the angels possessed could not be entirely adequate to satisfy God, with a reference to Job 4:18. Therefore, they needed a kind of grace, a kind of covering and reconciliation before God. Ephesians 1:10 cannot have in view election and the initiation of the ongoing sustaining of angels, for what is mentioned here happens "in the fullness of time," something that in any case cannot be understood of a time that would precede the coming of the Messiah (cf. Gal 4:4). It seems to us that this passage may be explained appropriately in the following way: Originally heaven and earth as they were created by God were united with each other and united with God. Then by sin a rupture took place.

The angels fell in part and men fell. Heaven and earth became divorced. Since God now redeems the elect in Christ and unites them again to Himself, He also restores the true unity between earth and heaven and brings back everything to Himself in a unity. The good angels had not been separated from God but they had been separated from men, and it is now the case that through Christ they, with God, become united in unity with all remaining creatures. Conversely, reprobate angels and reprobate men were banned from the earth and heaven and committed to hell, so that it is entirely true: "all things in heaven and on earth." One should now note what these words comprise:

1. All things in heaven and earth were initially one with each other and together were one before God. This is present in "again to gather all things into one" (ἀνακεφαλαιώσασθαι).

2. "All things" is neuter. Therefore, there is no reason to think exclusively of angels and men. The entire sphere of heaven and that of earth are meant. The split went through all creation, rational and irrational, living and lifeless. And all that creation is brought back into unity.

3. The gathering into one occurs in Christ as Mediator, who became man (in the fullness of times). By that it is already excluded to speak here of a reconciliation for the angels.

4. It is a gathering into unity before God whereby everything forms a unity because it is now harmonious in its being unanimously oriented toward God. This is contained in the middle voice of ἀνακεφαλαιώσασθαι, "to Himself." Colossians 1:20 is somewhat difficult. It occurs to us, however, that the meaning here is in the main the same as in Ephesians 1:10. "All things were reconciled to God," when by an effected reconciliation all things were led back to God. For example, "to set all things on fire" does not mean to say that fire has been put to each piece separately but simply that something is done with some pieces by which they all burn. So also here. To reconcile all things does not mean that reconciliation by the blood of Christ took place with respect to them all but only that reconciliation took place with regard to some, by which everything again came

into a right relationship to God. Here, too, one should note what is in the text, τὰ πάντα, τὰ ἐπὶ τῆς γῆς, τὰ ἐν τοῖς οὐρανοῖς. Everything is in the neuter.

64. In which quality did the objects of predestination appear in this matter before God?

With respect to the angels we have already seen that they appeared as they were still able to fall and would fall: the elect angels as still able to fall, the reprobate angels in the twofold circumstance of still being able to fall and as having fallen. Therefore, the predestination of the latter consisted in this: that God decreed to permit their fall and decreed to leave them in this fall and to be glorified by their just punishment. The predestination of the former consists in this: that God decreed to preserve them from the fall and thereafter to endow them with blessedness that could never be lost.

With regard to men at issue is the dispute between supra- and infralapsarians.

This dispute has three aspects: (a) an exegetical aspect; (b) a dogmatic aspect; (c) a historical aspect.

Since the principal *sedes* [place] for this dispute, Romans 9, has been discussed extensively above, the exegetical aspect of the matter can here be considered as sufficiently treated. We therefore go on immediately to the dogmatic aspect.

65. Indicate beforehand what is not at issue in the difference between the two parties.

a) The question in the first place is not whether there is a temporal sequence in God's decrees. With Scripture everyone Reformed confesses the absolute eternity of God's being. It is an eternity elevated above all temporal duration, in which a thousand years are as yesterday when it has passed and as a watch in the night (Psa 90:4). In this eternity everything is present that is hidden in the depths of the divine mind or has ever passed over from it into time as a work of His creative omnipotence. What will happen at the consummation of the ages is in that respect not sooner than that which took place at the dawn of creation. Every conception as if the differing parts of God's decree arise by stages of His observation must be rejected as incompatible with this eternity. That there would have first been a decree of creation, then of the fall, and then of predestination, or that these parts would have followed one another in reverse temporal order—both are in conflict with Scripture. It may be impossible for our thinking, bound by time, to grasp this eternity of divine life; nevertheless we must acknowledge it and may maintain nothing that is in conflict with it. To express it as briefly as possible: There are in God not many decrees, but it is one, single, completely present decree.

As a matter of fact, all this is already contained in the names of supra- and infralapsarianism. If it was a matter of a temporal order it should have been called ante- and postlapsarianism. The question would then have to be, "Do you believe in predestination before or after the decree of the fall?" Now, however, not a time but a space image has been chosen, apparently to avoid every trace of a temporal conception in conflict with God's eternity.

b) Nor is the question whether creation and the fall of man fall under the decree of God. With respect to creation, nobody doubts that. But whoever would deny that for the fall would become un-Reformed instead of infralapsarian since he would abandon one of most momentous turning points in world history, on which the work of redemption is entirely dependent and with that the course of well nigh all things, to chance. Almost all the Reformed confess unanimously with Calvin, "Man falls according to God's decree, but he falls by his own guilt." In His decree God has not only known of and reckoned with the fall, but since all things must have their certainty and fixity in His counsel, if we do not wish to posit a second ground of things beside God, then it also cannot be otherwise for the fearful fact of sin. That, too, must receive its certainty from God's decree. However great and however insurmountable the difficulties that follow closely on this position, still nothing may diminish it. Whoever begins to doubt here stands on the edge of a bottomless dualism. Only in the beginning, when theological perception was not entirely clear, could one remove the fall from the absolute decree of God. Augustine did this, who thought that for the events following the fall, God's foreknowledge rested on His decree while, converse-ly, for the fall the decree was dependent on a foreseeing. This and the other point (the apostasy of the saints) were the two weak points in Augustine's soteriology. Among truly Reformed theologians, only a few spoke of a foreseeing. Walaeus (*Leiden Synopsis*, xxiv, 23) says, "God, foreseeing with the infinite light of His knowledge how it would happen that man created after His image stood, together with his entire posterity, to misuse his free will, has deemed that it better accorded with His omnipotent goodness to show beneficence to the wicked, rather than not to allow there would be evil, as Augustine rightly reminds us."

c) In the third place it needs to be pointed out that according to the Reformed, supra- as well as infralapsarians, sin stands under a permissive decree. True, some have objected to this because it reminded them too much of the Formula of Concord, article 5, and had a Lutheran ring. Calvin protested against it (*Institutes*, 3.23.7). After him, Beza and Danaeus. But we cannot do without this expression. It is found in strict supra- as well infralapsari-ans. Germanus (*Opera Omnia*, II, p. 28), "Therefore, the creation of men, together with permitting and controlling the fall, are means ordained to the final end of man." And the same again and again. A permissive decree is naturally not an idle decree, a decree based on foreseeing, a decree simply not to prevent. It is a decree that brings certainty for sin as a fact and yet it is not the cause of the reality of sin. If one says that this sentence is meaningless words and distinctions, we grant that in a certain sense but at the same time point out that we are not able to get beyond them. They are beacons that we place at the edge of the unfathomable depths of mysteries.

d) The question is not whether sin comes into consideration as a factor in the decree of election and of rejection. On this point much misunderstanding reigns. One frequently hears the claim that those who place election above the fall teach that God has ordained men for eternal bliss and eternal misery only because He willed to do so and without considering their sin. But that is a conclusion that is not present in supralapsarianism and has never been intended by its advocates. With equally good right one could derive a variety of conclusions from infralapsarianism from which everyone must recoil, since they seem to attack the foundations of God's virtues. We will let Perkins speak here, who himself was disposed to supralapsarianism. He says, "Some accuse us of teaching that God has ordained men to hellish fire, and created them for destruction. ... To this I answer in the first place that reprobation, insofar as it pertains to the first act, that is, insofar as it refers to the purpose to abandon the creature and in this to demonstrate justice, is absolute. That we teach and believe. ... Sin itself occurs after the abandonment and the just permission of God. ... However, reprobation, insofar as it pertains to the second act, that is, the purpose to damn, is not absolute or indefinite but it takes account of sin. For no one perishes other than by his own guilt, and no one is ordained to hell or destruction without regard to anything, but because of his own sin. ... Secondly, I answer that God has not created man simply to destroy him, but so that by His just destruction of the sinner He would demonstrate His justice. For it is something quite different to will to punish man insofar as he is a sinner by a just destruction" (*Of Predestination and the Grace of God*, 1.770–772).

In the same way Calvin (*Institutes*, 3.23) reasons by pointing on the one hand to the absolute will of God in permitting sin and emphasizing on the other hand that none of God's creatures is ordained to destruction except insofar as he is sinful and in view of his sin.

It is therefore entirely false and heinous when one attributes to supralapsarianism the concept of a so-called tyrannical God. If permitting sin is included in predestination, then two things are certainly being affirmed:

1. That it was not to make God like a tyrant for the destruction of His rational creatures as such, but for the glorification of His own virtues.

2. That God in permitting evil and in including it in predestination has not acted arbitrarily, but according to perfect justice, although we are not able to judge that justice (cf. here Calvin, *Institutes*, 3.23.4 and what was observed above concerning Rom 9:21).

e) Positively we can say that the difference between the two views is:

1. A difference in the extent of predestination, since supralapsarians draw God's decree to permit the fall within predestination, the infralapsarians leave it outside. Here we let Trigland speak (*Advice Concerning the Concept of Moderation*, Second Part). "I say that the teachers of the Reformed Churches, both those who place predestination above the fall as well as those who place it below the fall, certainly agree on the substance of the matter but differ only in various ways of explanation that are made of the same matter. According to Junius ... 'We do not differ from those godly and learned men who state that in predestinating God has contemplated man before he was created. Nor from those who say that man is regarded as created and fallen. For what the latter and the former say in truth, that we devoutly confess, for we say both. ... When the latter say that in the predestinating of God man is considered as fallen, they do not actually have in view the cause of election and reprobation, but the order and pattern of causes from which damnation follows. ... But when the former say that in predestinating God has considered man as not yet created, they do not exclude God from considering mankind's fall.' " Trigland continues, "Indeed, if one pays careful attention to the matter itself in the writings of Reformed teachers, one will find that it is entirely in accord with Junius' explanation above. As, for example, can be seen from these words of Beza, 'Christ is presented to us as Mediator, therefore it is necessary that according to the order of causes, depravity take precedence in God's purpose, but before depravity, creation in holiness and righteousness, so that a way would be open for God, etc.'"

Trigland again, "...so that I cannot see in the latter [infralapsarians] any other difference than that the former [supralapsarians] who, going before the fall, take the word predestination or foreordination somewhat more broadly, namely, for the whole decree of God concerning the entire conduct and order of salvation and damnation of men, and of all the means that are conducive to that end, both of creation as also of the permission of the fall, as well as the raising up again of some and the forsaking of others. ... But the latter who remain below the fall take the word predestination somewhat more narrowly, so that they refer the creation of man and the permission and directing of the fall, not to predestination but to God's general providence. From this it is evident that the difference does not lie in the doctrine itself but in the explanation of the doctrine."

2. A difference in connecting the various parts of the divine decree. The older supralapsarianism at least maintained that in God's decree the permitting of the fall of man together with creation was subordinated to the highest end, the glorification of His justice and mercy. Thus, permitting the fall appears here as a means. Note carefully, not as a means for punishment itself but as a means for revealing God's justice and mercy. Infralapsarianism did not maintain a connection here between means and end in this sense. It certainly acknowledged that the fall was permitted for God's glorification, but did not dare to go further than this general proviso. It declared itself unable to explain how the fall was for God's glorification. It let the various parts of God's decree stand unconnected beside each other.

3. A difference in extending the personal-distinguishing character of predestination, especially of election, to include the decree of creation and the fall. The supralapsarian taught that in His decree to create God already had in view the elect as His personal beloved; likewise for the decree to permit the fall, there was not a moment in God's counsel in which the elect stood outside this personal relationship to God of being beloved. The infralapsarian, on the other hand, thinks that the personal relationship, the distinguishing, only begins after the decrees of creation and of fall, that therefore in these two decrees the elect were included in the general mass of men and did not appear as objects of God's special love.

One will perceive how the question whether in predestination God viewed man as still having to be created and still having to fall (*creabilis et labilis*), or as created and fallen (*creatus et lapsus*), is only a short formula for this difference.

It would perhaps be better to say *creandus* [to be created] *et lapsurus* [to be fallen] for characterizing supralapsarian sentiments. *Creabilis et labilis* leads to the idea that sin was not at all taken into account. "Will be created" and "will be falling" gives a sense of how sin was certainly taken into account.

66. In what respects do various supralapsarians still differ from one another?

The older supralapsarians taught that from its very outset predestination (election) was personal. God determined to create with these or those particular persons in view as His elect and beloved and likewise to permit the fall with them in view. On the other hand, later supralapsarians understood the decree at its outset less personally. So, for example, Mastricht. He distinguishes:

a) The purpose of God to reveal the glory of His mercy and His retributive justice. This is impersonal.

b) The purpose to create all men in one common root and permit them to fall in that one root. This also is impersonal.

c) The purpose to elect some specific persons and reject some specific persons out of this created and fallen humanity.

d) The purpose to prepare the means and ways fitting for carrying out the preceding decree. This is supralapsarianism for the two parts of humanity, not for specific persons.

67. In what does the distinctiveness reside of the supralapsarianism taught in "The Examination of the Concept of Tolerance" (Alexander Comrie)?

That sin accidentally becomes a transition point for a double predestination idea that lies above it and is maintained above it. Originally God predestined some to great beatitude, others to a natural state outside that beatitude (not, however, to permit sin). The former would reach that state of supernatural bliss because the Second Person of the Trinity would take on human nature and be most closely united with them in that human nature. The latter would remain outside that union. That was the pinnacle in God's decree of predestination. Now, however, the decree appears that God will permit sin to lay hold of both these predestined groups. Thereby the predestination of the elect is changed insofar as it becomes a predestination to save from sin and by that salvation to glorify them with Christ. A simple glorification is replaced by a glorification after antecedent redemption. At the same time the predestination of the nonelect is changed in the sense that it now becomes a decree not to leave them in their natural state but to leave them in sin and destruction.

68. *What are the objections against this opinion?*

a) It considers predestination as operating initially apart from redemption, while Scripture constantly brings it into connection with redemption. The entire dispensation that flows from election is a dispensation of redemption, "vessels of mercy."

b) It necessitates positing an incarnation of Christ even apart from sin. On this point it agrees with many more recent opinions that otherwise have an entirely different origin.

c) It teaches an addition of something supernatural to nature apart from sin, which in an objectionable way calls to mind the Romish system.

69. *What objection is to be made against the opinion of Mastricht?*

That it lets predestination originally be impersonal and thus removes its practical and comforting element. Scripture always provides a personal representation. It says that the first act of election is already a personal love (that is, "foreknowledge").

70. *Are the logical objections against supralapsarianism conclusive?*

No, because:

a) There always remain objections in such an abstract matter. We can never explain these things completely.

b) The objection that for the supralapsarian the object of predestination is a *non-ens* (a non-entity) rests on a misunderstanding. It is not a *non-ens* concerning the knowing part of God's decree but only concerning the willing act. Also, if this reasoning is extended, God could never have made a decree of creation.

71. Does not supralapsarianism suffer from great harshness?

We must acknowledge this. However, one should certainly keep in view that this harshness resides in the doctrine of God's decree as such, and supralapsarianism merely brings it out clearly. Supralapsarianism teaches, for example, that God has permitted that for the glorification of his justice certain persons, through their own fault, would fall into sin in order not to be redeemed from it. The infralapsarian also says that God permits man to fall into sin for His own glorification. Now, is it so much harsher when the supralapsarian says, for the glorification of His own justice? Does something harsh become harsher by strengthening the splendor of God's justice?

72. Can we question God's action in this?

No, we cannot and must not attempt that. This must remain certain as it was for the apostle: It is strictly just and not tyrannically arbitrary. But on the other hand, we have no right to apply the standard of our concept of disinterested love to God's action, as if He were not the center of all things, the highest good of everything, who can therefore also make all things subordinate to His own glory.

73. How does the Mediator figure in the decree of election?

Logically, only after sin. As Mediator He is surety. A surety presupposes a debt that must be paid. Debt presupposes sin. Christ as Mediator can only appear where sin is present. On this point one must judge as Beza does (see above in the quote of Trigland [65. e) 1.]). This must be so unless one wants to make Christ the Mediator of human nature for its glorification even in its sinless state and thus teach an incarnation apart from sin, as Comrie does. But this peculiar view does not flow from supralapsarianism as such, but from supralapsarianism connected with certain other ideas. A logical connection (nexus causalis) cannot exist between supralapsarianism and other doctrines, already simply because all the other parts of the doctrine of salvation presuppose sin.

74. Give a historical overview of the conflict between infra- and supralapsarianism.

Augustine, who first worked out the doctrine of predestination, was an infralapsarian, since he derived the fall from God's foreknowledge. Later the doctrine of Augustine was presented in supralapsarian terms. The presbyter Lucidus, who did this, was obliged to recant. In the Middle Ages the monk Gottschalk and Thomas Bradwardine appeared as supralapsarian defenders of predestination.

There has been dispute about Calvin. The truth is that sometimes he expressed himself in one way and at other times in another. But while his infralapsarian-sounding expressions can be explained as partial *a posteriori* representations, it is impossible to give a minimizing sense to his decidedly supralapsarian statements. One may compare the entire 23rd chapter of book three of his *Institutes*, where in connection with predestination he speaks very explicitly about the fall and the decree of the fall. Further, there is the following (*Opera*, IX.713), "Before man was created, in His eternal decree God established what He willed would happen with the entire human race. By this secret decree of God it has happened that Adam fell from the state of his natural rectitude and by his fall drew all his posterity with himself into the guilt of eternal death." We find more such expressions. Finally, Calvin's declaration, "God has created us in order to redeem us."

Among Reformed theologians after Calvin the following were supralapsarians: Beza, Peter Martyr Vermigli, Marlorat, Whitaker, Ferrius, Zanchius, Perkins, Gomarus, Maccovius (in part also, as appears from what was quoted above, Junius).

75. What has the Synod of Dordt declared regarding this issue?

It has maintained an infralapsarian position but without the intention of wanting to condemn supralapsarianism. In general one must keep in mind that an infralapsarian can never claim that what the supralapsarian says cannot be true. Were he to insist on this, he himself would have to give a positive explanation concerning the purpose of God in permitting sin. And he neither wants nor dares to enter precisely into that explanation. Therefore he says, "I keep to below the fall." But, he does not judge the supralapsarian. At the most he could demand that the supralapsarian also leave the matter as uncertain or pass over it in silence.

That the Synod of Dordt did not wish to condemn supralapsarianism is evident from the following:

a) Not a few of its members were supralapsarians: the president, Bogerman, Gomarus, Lydius, Voetius, Festus Hommius, in general the delegates from Gelderland and South Holland. These all signed the Canons of Dordt. So, they would have signed their own condemnation if supralapsarianism had been condemned.

b) Gomarus protested against the recommendation of Polyander, Thysius and Walaeus, but not against the canon [concerning predestination] itself. The first mentioned of these wanted to see infralapsarianism adopted in such a way that supralapsarianism was thereby excluded. On the other hand, Gomarus did not ask that his supralapsarianism be adopted, but that the question remain open. The canon was formulated differently than the recommendation of the professors named above against whom Gomarus protested.

c) Evidently, the supralapsarians who were at Dordt did not find their complete doctrine of predestination in the canon, but still a part of it was there and they could be resigned to the other part remaining unexpressed. Gomarus had clearly not meant that his position should replace what Walaeus and the others wrote, but only that it must be added if one wished to understand the matter in depth.

d) Among the charges that were brought against Maccovius was "that he taught that the object of predestination were not fallen man." The Synod, however, did not wish to condemn him.

e) Supralapsarianism is later taught by theologians of good repute who were considered in the Netherlands as being orthodox, namely Heidanus, Burmann, Braun, Voetius, Engelhardus, and others.

Speaking against supra- and for infralapsarianism were Polyander, Walaeus, Rivet, Cocceius, Henry Alting, Molinaeus, Fr. Spanheim, Fr. Turretin, Johann Heinrich Heidegger, Picket.

Initially the Westminster Assembly appeared to intend to adopt supralapsarianism. In the end, however, it adopted a formulation with which both views could identify. Its Prolocutor Twisse was a strong supralapsarian.

In the Netherlands Maresius firmly contended for infralapsarianism against Gomarus and Voetius.

76. *What is the difference between the infra- and supralapsarians on the doctrine of reprobation?*

According to infralapsarians, reprobation has two parts: (a) *praeteritio*, "passing by," God's decree not to grant the grace of salvation to certain persons lying in sin; and (b) *praedamnatio*, "predamnation," God's decree to commit these persons to eternal destruction because of their sin.

According to the supralapsarians, reprobation has three parts: (a) the decree to set apart certain persons for the revelation of God's retributive justice in the punishment for their sins; (b) permission in God's decree for the fall of man; (c) the decree not to grant grace to these persons, being once fallen, but to condemn them because of their sin.

Thus, in the latter sense reprobation is God's sovereign and just decree to ordain certain persons known to Him for the revelation of His punitive righteousness and therefore to permit them to fall into sin by their own fault and thereafter not to grant them grace in Christ.

77. *Where must the infralapsarian seek the cause of reprobation?*

This can be answered in three ways:

a) If one asks for the reason why just this or that particular person perishes, then the infralapsarian answers: that flows from God's sovereign good pleasure. It cannot result from sin, for in God's decree all Adam's posterity is also equally subject to sin, without all being reprobate.

b) If one now asks for the reason for the withholding of grace, then from an infralapsarian standpoint the answer must again be: God's sovereign good pleasure is the reason for this withholding. He was not obliged to grant His grace to anyone.

c) If one now asks for the reason why in general—without considering the antithesis with the elect, the reprobate perish—then for the infralapsarian the answer is that the reason did not lie in God's predestination, but in man's sin. If one asks further where the ground of certainty for sin lies, then the infralapsarian answers: in God's decree. If one asks still further what moved God to permit sin, he answers: I want to stay out of that question. Someone perishes because of his sin; the certainty of the sin comes from God's decree (although not the reality). But that God decreed to permit his sin for glorifying His justice, the infralapsarian dare not say. Therefore he does not include it in predestination.

The supralapsarian says: The legal ground why men perish lies in sin that they deliberately commit within time. Nobody perishes other than because of his own sin. But this sin itself cannot occur apart from the permission of God's decree. Therefore, this permission, that is, God's predestination, is the highest ground for the reality of perishing, although not the legal ground. Naturally sin cannot be the ground for God's decree that sin would occur. It had other grounds that we cannot fathom as far as their justness is concerned but that are nevertheless just.

78. *What do we understand concerning the hardening that God causes to come upon man?*

Regarding this Scripture teaches the following:

a) That generally hardening is the consequence of contact with the revelation or the truth of God against which sinful men rebels (so, for Pharaoh, Exod 7:3; Isaiah's contemporaries, Isa 6; Matt 13:11–16). "An odor of death to death."

b) That hardening is also caused by God simultaneously withdrawing the common grace of the Holy Spirit and permitting sin to break out and spread unhindered. Here, then, is a real act of God, but it is an act of withdrawing. God does not cause sin to arise in man but withdraws all influences that work for good. This is called, "given over to a depraved mind," "to dishonorable passions," "to the desires of their hearts" (Rom 1:28, 26, 24; Psa 81:13).

c) That sometimes hardening arises from resistance to extraordinary enlightenment that God has given man, but with no regenerating grace accompanying it. Something like this is indicated in Hebrews 6:4–8.

d) That becoming hardened by God can at the same time be called the hardening of oneself. That is said of Pharaoh.

79. *Is Christ the meriting cause of election?*

No, this would imply that the gift of Christ preceded election and so was generally intended for all mankind. One says, God cannot condescend to grant election to a sinful humanity if Christ is not already there as Mediator. We answer, He also cannot condescend to a sinful humanity with the gift of a mediator if the mediator is not already there. And so one never reaches a conclusion.

Turretin says, "The question is not whether Christ is the foundation and the meriting cause of a decreed salvation with respect to its matter but whether Christ is the meriting cause and the foundation of the decree of salvation with respect to God. The first question must be answered affirmatively, the second negatively. Everything that in reality comes to us flows from Christ, but Christ Himself, with all that flows from Him, has been given to us out of the free mercy of God. Scripture speaks this way everywhere (1 Cor 1:30)."

CHAPTER SIX

Creation

1. *What is creation?*

That external work of God by which He has produced heaven and earth, that is, the universe, out of nothing and has imparted to all things their nature.

2. *How do theologians divide the external works of God?*

    a) Some divide them into the works of creation and providence. The work of grace then falls under the latter. But there are objections to this division:

        1. Grace becomes a subdivision of providence which, although it can be that, is less accurate.

        2. It is as if one would separate the beginning of a thing from the rest of it. Creation must be understood more widely, as in the definition given above. It is not a bare beginning, but more. It is the once-for-all establishing of the natural order and is most closely connected with providence insofar as the latter is its continuation.

    b) For these reasons better is the division into *naturae opera* and *gratiae opera*, works of nature (creation and providence) and works of grace (re-creation and the order of salvation). Both are in the decree of God and there find their unity, a unity that we in any case cannot indicate in its details.

3. *Where does the doctrine of miracles belong?*

Usually this subject has been treated under God's providence because miracles form a contrast with God's ordinary governance. But two considerations should be noted:

a) This is not the only point of view from which miracles can be considered. They are more than unordinary acts of God. Lying outside of the order of nature, they belong in fact to the higher order of things, to the kingdom of grace, accompanying revelation, and thus should be closely connected with the *opera gratiae* [works of grace].

b) Seen in this way, miracles are correlated with each other; they form a plan in which nothing is accidental.

4. *Is the doctrine of creation an articulus purus [pure article] or an articulus mixtus [mixed article]?*

Articuli puri [pure articles] are those that cannot be derived both from reason and from revelation but depend entirely on revelation. *Articuli mixti* [mixed articles] flow from both reason and revelation. The question then is whether creation can be proven by reason. That has been attempted by starting from the concept of God. God, one says, could not remain shut up within Himself. He needed a world in order to love it, etc. Such reasoning is not legitimate. As far as we can judge, had the creation remained nonexistent, God would have been all-sufficient, as He is now. We can certainly reason from the world up to God, but we cannot by logic descend from God to the world. We believe that creation, as an incomprehensible, almighty act, cannot be proven or deduced by us. Nature may lead us to a point where we must cease our investigation and have an inkling of something mysterious and completely unique in its kind, but we cannot logically conclude that this has been a creation out of nothing. Creation is an *articulus purus*. We understand this to be true of creation out of nothing, not of the idea of a forming of the universe by God in general.

5. *In how many parts can we treat the doctrine of creation?*

In three:

   a) The significance of this doctrine in relation to the whole of Christian truth.

   b) The scriptural data for this doctrine and its exposition.

   c) A short discussion of deviating theories.

6. *At what points does the doctrine of creation cohere with Christian truth in general?*

   a) The doctrine of creation emphasizes the transcendence of God. That God has created the universe out of nothing is the most powerful expression of the fact that He is distinct from the universe, is exalted above the universe, and exists in Himself as the all-sufficient One. "He gives to all life, breath, and all things." Therefore what the doctrine of the Trinity proclaims with respect to God's inner existence, the doctrine of creation proclaims to us outwardly.

   b) The doctrine of creation teaches the infinity of God. The forms of finitude, in which all that is finite exists, namely time and space, have been created by God and may not be viewed as something in which He Himself exists by nature.

   c) The doctrine of creation reminds us of the complete freedom and sovereignty of God toward the universe. If, as pantheists believe, the universe had grown out of God, had developed out of Him, then He would Himself be involved in the degeneration and decline of the world. But since He has created it in His freedom, we can be assured that everything in this world, in spite of all the error and sin of human beings, will necessarily serve to glorify Him. This teaches us, in the midst of our misery, the higher, the only true theological optimism. Again, that the creatures have been brought forth out of nothing proves that they cannot claim as valid over against God any rights they imagine to possess. All their rights rest precisely on what God, in accordance with His perfect nature, has given to them. Pantheism leads to a philosophy of what is right that makes the creature to share in God's right, since the creature was eternally in God and present with God. Arminians say in principle that God has exactly as much right to us as He manifests benefits. We reverse that and say: Every right that God gives us is originally a benefit.

d) The doctrine of creation proves the omnipotence of God. Creating something out of nothing is an act of absolute, infinite power, something that completely transcends our concept of power (which is always tied to an object). The distance between being and nonbeing is an infinite distance. Therefore Scripture, in order to portray God's power, very often points to creation. He is the Creator of the ends of the earth, who does not tire or grow weary. Therefore creating is also an exclusively divine work. Creaturely creating is a *contradictio in adjecto* [a contradiction in the adjective].

e) The doctrine of creation secures for the creature a certain measure of glory. Divine interest is expressed when the Lord prepares, as creator, to create, which is a free act. That the universe comes into being is not its fate, even less God's; it is rather its creation. By the activity to which it owes its origin it is consecrated, the finger of God has touched and formed it, and in the midst of all its defection and sin the imprint of God's finger clings to it. God stands toward it not as a gardener who lets a plant or flower grow, but as the artist who forms an image according to his own vision, whose work was first in his heart and whose heart is therefore reflected in his work.

f) The doctrine of creation forms the basis of the doctrine of revelation. A God who by a self-conscious act of freedom brings the universe into existence cannot desire to do anything other than to reveal Himself directly in an unmistakable way to the world thus created. A God who as Creator of the world maintains interest in the world will not let that world exist without proper, sufficient knowledge of Himself. Conversely, a God who is not apart from the world nor elevated above the world but is developing within the world first comes to consciousness slowly and imperfectly in the world.

There must be something awkward in a revelation conceived of in this way. Many today are forming a concept of revelation that clearly betrays its affinity with pantheism and may absolutely not be combined with the theistic doctrine of creation.

7. *How many categories of scriptural data are there concerning the doctrine of creation?*

Two.

a) Texts spread throughout the whole of Scripture that speak of creation.

b) The detailed narrative in Genesis 1 and 2.

8. *What belongs to the first category?*

a) Texts that lay emphasis on what is new, previously not present, that appears as the product of creation (Exod 34:10; Num 16:30; Psa 51:12; Jer 31:22; Rev 4:11).

b) Texts that lay emphasis on the absolute, infinite power of God as revealed in the creation (Pss 33:9; 95:4–7; 121:2; Isa 40:26, 28; 41:20; 42:5; 45:12, 18; Jer 10:11; 32:17; Amos 4:13; Rev 10:6).

c) Texts that point to the exaltedness of God above the created world, attributing to Him an existence outside of and above it, thus to the transcendence of God (Pss 90:2; 102:26; 104:29; John 1:3; Acts 17:24; Rom 1:20, 25; Heb 1:10–12).

d) Texts that make mention of the creation as a work of wisdom (Job 28:24, 28; Isa 40:12–14; Jer 10:12–16; John 1:3; Heb 1:2).

e) Texts that present the creation as an organism infused with life (Pss 33:6; 104:30; Job 26:13; 33:4).

f) Texts that place the creation under the aspect of the sovereignty of God, demonstrating that He has created everything for His own sake (Isa 43:7; 45:18; Rom 1:25).

g) Texts that view the creation as something forward-looking, as a foundational act whereby the ordinances and laws of things are established once for all. The word for this is κτιζεῖν, "to found." The creation as such is therefore κτίσις, a "founding," "foundation."

From this a parallelism is developed between creation and re-creation (1 Cor 11:9; 2 Cor 5:17; Col 1:16; 3:10; Eph 2:10, 15; 4:24; Gal 6:15, κτίσις; Jas 1:18, κτίσμα). In this sense the Greek fathers spoke of a first, a second, and a third creation, as a threefold laying of the foundation, through which a world order arises (1 = creation, 2 = regeneration, 3 = consummation of things).

9. *Is it accidental that the Bible opens with a history of creation?*

No. The reason for this, however, is not to be sought in the effort to bring everything up out of the deepest depth. Such a thought is foreign to Scripture. Scripture does not intend to be an encyclopedia for us. The doctrine of creation is presented here in connection with God's saving revelation.

10. *How many kinds of interpretation are there of Genesis 1 and 2?*

Mainly three: the allegorical, the mythical and the historical. The first two views, however, are untenable because within the narrative of Scripture the creation narrative is interwoven like a link in the chain of God's saving acts. God does not make a chain of solid gold, in which the first link is a floral wreath. If the creation history is an allegory, then the narrative concerning the fall and everything further that follows can also be allegory. The writer of the Pentateuch presents his work entirely as history. Against those that believe in the results of higher criticism, it can perhaps be useful to note that according to the critics who carve the Pentateuch into pieces, Genesis 1 belongs to the Priestly Codex, that is, to the more sober, nonpoetic part of the Torah. The same writer who describes the layout of the tabernacle and the clothing of the priests gives us the narrative of creation, and he connects both. Further, elsewhere in Scripture Genesis 1 and 2 are treated as history (Exod 20:11; 31:17; Pss 8; 104; Matt 19:4; 2 Pet 3:5). See also the Sabbath idea in the Letter to the Hebrews.

11. *What is the mythical interpretation of the creation narrative?*

That a conscious, intentional invention is not to be understood here but an unintentional, naive poetry that developed gradually and for those among whom it first formed was taken as reality. Valid objections against this view are the same objections made against the allegorical view.

12. *How did Moses become acquainted with this creation narrative?*

Certainly revelation is at its basis. Another question is whether that revelation was given to Moses or originated long before him. Many, such as Kurz, Ebrand, Lange, and Hugh Miller maintain the first view and think that the entire revelation was shown to Moses in a vision. Thus, it is a prophecy in retrospect. Objections to this view are the following:

a) There is no analogy for such a retrospective vision in Scripture.

b) Visions in Scripture always have a symbolic element, whereas here we have pure history.

c) Visions in Scripture provide only bits and pieces of the history of the future, never a connected narrative.

d) How should one explain the marks of similarity between the biblical narrative and the creation sagas of pagan peoples? This similarity seems to demand that the creation story was known before Moses and that traces of it were preserved by pagans. Of course, if the narrative came to Moses completely or in part by tradition, this in no way detracts from the inspiration by which he was enabled to record it fully and infallibly.

13. *Can one who rejects the allegorical and mythical interpretations of Genesis 1 and 2 also fall into error on the other side?*

Yes, some want to give a hyperscientific exegesis that satisfies the latest perception and newest fashion. All sorts of theories from physics, geology, and astronomy have been projected onto the narrative. Some maintain that the theory of evolution in its entirety is contained in these chapters. This is perhaps apologetic zeal, but it is bad exegesis. Every interpretation of Genesis 1 and 2 must be justified exegetically. That science has discovered this or that, or thinks to have discovered it, is not enough to cause us to discover it in Genesis. The creation narrative provides pure truth, but in such a general form that it can serve equally for the instruction of God's people in centuries past and His children at the present time. (The hyperscientific interpretation loses sight of that.) That is precisely what makes the creation narrative such a great artistic achievement of the Spirit of God.

14. How is the first verse of Genesis 1 to be interpreted?

"In the beginning" means "before all things." Thus it does not refer back to subsequent deeds of creation, but speaks of the absolute beginning of time.

Concerning the creating mentioned here there are two explanations:

a) It is the initial bringing forth of material out of nothing, thus the so-called immediate creating, while in the following verses mediate creation is described.

b) It is a heading prefaced to the creation account. That is, first it is reported to us in general that God created heaven and earth and first in what follows is that further explained to us. We accept the first explanation, because:

1. Otherwise any reference to the first act of creation would be lacking.

2. The Hebrew word בָּרָא appears precisely to indicate the immediate creation in its divine uniqueness (see Num 16:30). In the *qal* form it is never used of human creating. That the basic idea is "to cut" is certainly true and to such extent refers to material out of which something has been cut. But that only shows that human language is unsuited for expressing with complete accuracy divine actions such as the act of creation. God must reveal Himself to man, must speak human language. Here He has at least chosen a word that comes closest to the reality in view.

3. "Heaven and earth" is equivalent to the universe, for which Hebrew does not have any word.

15. What more is contained in the twofold expression, "heaven and earth"?

Simultaneously this expression already contains a division. The creation at its first beginning, when everything was still intermixed, already lay under the goal to be split into two great spheres of heaven and earth. God draws lines from the beginning on. Even the chaos is called "heaven" and "earth."

16. *What does the so-called Restitution hypothesis want to maintain?*

Focusing on Genesis 1:2, this hypothesis teaches that there was an original earth before there was the creation or preparation that is described
from v. 3 on. It therefore translates v. 2, "the earth *became* formless
and empty," or "the earth *had become* formless and empty." (The first
translation is that of Kurz and Zöckler.) The goal of this hypothesis is to
harmonize Scripture with geology. The original earth became "formless
and empty" by numbers of upheavals, before God prepared our earth.
Against this view are the following considerations:

    a) An undefined period of such earthly catastrophes is in conflict
       with God's intention to make the earth a dwelling place for man
       (Isa 45:18). Such periods of emptiness are suitable only for a pan-
       theistic development of the universe.

    b) All the scientific objections are not solved by this hypothesis, in
       particular biological ones. Can there have been life on an earth
       without light?

    c) [The Hebrew] *tohu wabohu* is a negative then positive expression,
       indicating what has yet to receive its form.

17. *What has been done to remove the first objection?*

The formlessness and emptiness of the earth is connected to the fall
in the kingdom of the angels. But then men with their world become a
kind of second experiment, after the failure of the experiment with the
pure spirits. Scripture, however, nowhere presents matters in this way.
Angels are obliging, etc.

18. *How then do we interpret the second verse?*

As the introduction to v. 3. It describes the state of the earth when God
sent forth His first word of creation.

19. *What is to be concluded from the fact that in v. 2 there is no further
    mention of heaven?*

    a) That the aim of the creation account is not astronomical but sub-
       ordinate to the history of redemptive revelation.

    b) That v. 1 cannot be a heading. If this were the case, then we would
       have to say that only half of the heading is treated.

20. What is said further concerning the chaos?

That it was a "roaring flood" or abyss (see Psa 106:9; Isa 63:13). From Psalm 104:6 it is clear that this expression must not be understood to refer to a muddy material, in which land and water are still thoroughly mixed together, but to a solid core of earth, flooded by water (see also 2 Pet 2:5).

21. Explain the words, "the Spirit of God was hovering over the waters"?

The Spirit here is not a "wind from God," sent out to dry what was created, for that is first spoken of in what follows. According to Psalm 33:6 it is the personal spirit, the Third Person of the Trinity (see Psa 104:30). The word translated by "hovering," רְחַף, is used elsewhere of a bird that hovers protectively over its young (Deut 32:11). Already in the first instance where the Holy Spirit is mentioned in Scripture His activity is portrayed for us in an image borrowed from the kingdom of the birds, just as He elsewhere appears as a dove. Here "hovering," "brooding," has in view the stirring of life within lifeless material. The brooding of birds brings out very aptly that life originates from outside by fructification. In the world there is at first no life. The Spirit of God must hover above the roaring flood, for its roaring is a dead noise. But the Spirit of God hovers on and above the waters. He does not mingle with them. Even where God's immanence comes to the fore, God and the world still remain unmixed.

22. What is the meaning of "And God said" (v. 3)?

a) One must compare these words with Psalm 33:6 and with the teaching of the New Testament regarding the creative activity of the *Logos*, the uncreated Word (John 1:3; Eph 3:9; Col 1:16; Heb 1:2). That God speaks indicates that God's thought is going to form the chaos, that ideas are introduced concerning it. And that is precisely the particular work of the *Logos*, the Second Person of the Trinity. As being is from the Father and life from the Spirit, so thought is from the *Logos*. Naturally this must be so understood that nevertheless the undivided *ad extra* [external] working of the three persons is maintained.

b) It can also include that God can call His works into being by a word of power, without exertion of effort.

c) It shows that the world is something outside God, something distinct from God. It appears at the word of God. And the word is accompanied by thought; the external *logos* presupposes the internal *logos*.

23. What is the first thing called into being by this speaking of God?

Light. This is prerequisite, not only for the appearance of living beings where it shines, but for all distinguishing and grouping. Light is the image of clarity, of thinking. Consequently, the works of the *Logos* begin with the creation of light. The same connection, the same sequence, between life and light that we meet here we find in the work of re-creation, where regeneration and calling follow each other, just as in creation we see the hovering of the Spirit and the word of power, "Let there be light!"

24. What is said about this light?

"God saw that it was good." God thus recognizes it as a faithful image of His own light-nature, for He is a light and there is no darkness in Him. Its being good consists in its likeness to God. It was not said of the chaos that it was good, nor is that said of the darkness in v. 4 and 5.

25. How does light appear here?

As not yet concentrated in bodies of light ("lights"). It is thus something distinguished from its bearers. The sun has light, but is not light. Only of God is it said that He is light. According to Job 38:19 there is a place of light, and God asks Job if he knows the way to where light dwells (see also v. 12). The treasure of light of the Father of lights is thus much greater than we can conceive or can derive from sun and stars.

26. What is meant with the division between light and darkness (v. 4)?

The light must have its reverse if it is to become completely light. God's naming "day" and "night" is naturally not to be understood as if God gave the two periods of time the Hebrew names יוֹם and לַיְלָה. God's naming is something other. It is a naming that effects something from the outside; gives to things their specific, distinguishing character; makes them what they will continue to be. Augustine said: "All light is not day and all darkness is not night, but light and darkness following each other in regular order make day and night." The naming of day and night means that therefore light and darkness now receive from God this rhythmic character by which they follow each other. And this physical rhythm, this natural contrast, without doubt reflects the series of spiritual contrasts there are between truth and lies, between good and evil, between beauty and ugliness.

27. *How are we to understand, "And it was evening and it was morning, one day"?*

It is not as if the first creation day began with evening, for a sufficient distinction would not be made between the preceding darkness and the night. It is probable that here the later, ordinary way of reckoning is not being followed (from evening to evening), but that the days run from morning to morning. The closing words of v. 5 then indicate successively the two halves of the first day. The first half closed with the evening, the second half with the morning.

28. *Must the word "day" here be understood in the ordinary sense or in the sense of an indefinite period?*

There has been much dispute about this point. Here, too, the decision must not be made dependent on geological considerations but on purely exegetical ones.

29. *Is it right to say that the nonliteral interpretation is an innovation to which the development of modern science has driven theologians?*

No, those who say that are mistaken. Augustine already said: "What kind of days they were is extremely difficult, or even impossible, for us to imagine, much less to say."

30. *To what is appeal made to support the nonliteral interpretation?*

a) To the fact that sun and moon (or rather the rotation of the earth around its axis in relation to the sun) were not yet present. As we know, the length of an ordinary day is determined by this rotation.

b) To the indefinite use of the term "day" in other places in Scripture (Gen 2:4; 5:1; 2 Sam 21:12; Isa 11:16), also to the expression "day of the Lord" (= day of judgment) in the prophets, and to Psalm 90:4; 2 Peter 3:8.

c) To the analogy with other things of God. Here we have to do with *God's days*. Now the "things of God" are certainly archetypical (exemplars) for the things of men, but they are not completely identical. Thus we have no right, it is thought, to judge that God's days are like the days of men.

d) To the fact that the duration of God's Sabbath is eternal. That is one of the days here, the seventh day. If the seventh day is not limited to 24 hours, then the six previous days need not be limited to that time span.

On these grounds many, including those who are not intent on a reconciliation of the Scripture with science, accept an extraordinary length for the creation days. This includes many church fathers and theologians of the Middle Ages, and, among more recent theologians, even Charles Hodge inclines to this view.

3 1. *What supports the interpretation that takes "day" in its ordinary meaning?*

a) The entire creation aimed at man as its completion. It is difficult to accept that preparing for this goal took thousands of years.

b) All the creation days must have been of the same length. Who can accept, however, that a day on which nothing else occurred than the separation between light and darkness was a day of thousands of years?

c) The fact that the sun and moon, as measures of time, were not present does not mean that there was no time. Already from the beginning God ordained a rhythm and created the light so that it would alternate with the darkness. When later this light was concentrated in the sun and the other bodies, we are told nothing about it being only then that the 24-hour day began. There was no change at that point. Therefore we have a reason for assuming that before that time the rotation of the earth took place at the same speed and that light was so positioned as was necessary for an alternation of day and night within 24 hours.

d) From v. 14 on the days are unquestionably ordinary days of 24 hours. There God says emphatically of the lights in the expanse that they will be "for days and years." One might rescue the non-literal view by assuming for the fourth to the sixth days an extremely slow rotation of the earth about its axis, but what about plant life during those long nights? The night has to have been half of the full day.

e) It is not accurate to say that the days are God's days. God *ad intra* does not have days. Creation is an act proceeding outwardly from God. Appealing to the eternal Sabbath is also of no avail. Although God's Sabbath is certainly endless, that cannot be said of the first Sabbath (after the six-day creation) for mankind.

f) The use of the term "day" in Genesis 9:4 is figurative, but in Genesis 1 figurative language is not used. What one must show is another place in Scripture where a first, a second, a third day, etc., are just as sharply separated and nevertheless describe periods of time. The "day of the Lord" in the prophets refers to a specific day—that is, a day on which the Lord appears for judgment, even though His judgment may last longer than one day.

32. *Must someone who holds that the days are long time periods be regarded a heretic?*

No, in this sense the question is not an essential one. It would only become so if it provided the occasion for granting priority in principle over the Word of God to the so-called results of science.

33. *How is the work of the second day related to that of the third day?*

By the fact that both works serve the same goal, namely to prepare the earth for the origination of life.

34. *Does the separation on the second day have an additional significance?*

Yes. Here again one of the lines is drawn whereby clarity and differentiation takes place in what is created. Here spatial relationships with their contrast of below and above are made clear. And these relationships between above and below reflect the relationship between heaven and earth. The rain, which as God's blessing comes from above, is a symbol for heavenly blessings. Also, in relation to the Holy Spirit Himself an "outpouring" is spoken of. Thus Scripture also teaches us that almost all atmospheric processes come from God. It is His rain, His snow, His hail, His thunder, His lightning.

35. Does the expanse in view refer to a solid firmament?

No, it cannot be proven that Scripture is thinking of something like this with the word רָקִיעַ (Psa 104:2, "curtain"; Job 37:18, "mirror").[1] But one may not forget that the optical phenomenon of the expanse, although it is not held to be something solid, still represents a real idea. Limiting our view and our horizon, it reminds us, on the one hand, of our limitations and earthliness and, on the other hand, it places before our eyes, for our elevation and comfort, the heaven of God's glory.

36. How should we understand the waters "above the expanse"?

For this reference has been made to Revelation 4:6; 15:2; 22:1. But whatever these heavenly waters may be, it is not conceivable that they are made of the same material as the earthly waters under the expanse. The simplest and most natural understanding is that they are clouds.

37. How many parts are there in the work of the third creation day?

Two: (a) the separation of water and land on the earth; (b) the producing of plant growth on the resultant dried land.

The first will have occurred either by the elevation of land masses, or by the sinking of the sea floor, or by both at the same time (Psa 104:8).

A formal naming follows the separation of land and water, as above (Psa 104:9). The great chaos, the *tehom*, was not yet the sea, just as the darkness in itself was not yet night. The *tehom*, the "roaring flood," did not yet possess those characteristics by which the ocean affects us aesthetically. The grand poetry of the sea in its distinctiveness is willed by God. It shows us the eternal majesty and self-sufficiency of the Lord. That is why seeing the sea has a calming influence. In the presence of this picture of the sublimity and infiniteness of God one feels lifted above all petty cares and thoughts and loses himself in the sovereign will of God. At the same time, the way the ocean is prevented from overflowing the land is a proof of God's power that set this boundary for the sea (see Job 38:8–11; Psa 65:8).

---

1   While the verses cited above reflect the concept of God spreading out the heavens, they do not explicitly use the Hebrew word רָקִיעַ. For use of רָקִיעַ in the sense under discussion, see Genesis 1:6–8.

With respect to the second part of the work on this day, one may note that the earth can only bring forth plant growth because seeds were already planted earlier when the Spirit was hovering. Three kinds of plants are distinguished:

a) דֶשֶׁא, so-called cryptogams, that is, flowerless plants that do not fertilize each other in the usual way.

b) עֵשֶׂב מַזְרִיעַ זֶרַע, "seed-sowing herbs," that is, herbs and grains that grow in gardens and fields.

c) Fruit trees, that is, every fruit-bearing tree in the widest sense of the word. And all this is "according to its kind." מִין comes from a verb that means "split, divide." "Kind," then, is intended to substantiate a fixed idea, thought of in contrast to other "kinds." Pluriformity, not simplicity, is the starting point. This is opposed to the hypothesis of evolution that derives everything from simplicity and sees forms as the chance product of matter, forms that appear and disappear, while only matter is eternal. Rather, Scripture teaches that matter exists for the sake of forms. The merging of kinds is a "degeneration," a violating of the creation ordinance that made everything "according to its kind."

38. What belongs to the work of the fourth day?

a) The making of the "lights" or "light-bearers," מְאֹרֹת, φωστῆρες (Septuagint). These are the substantial objects, but the material for them will have been present earlier. Perhaps the "lights" were created out of superearthly materials. Does the narrative here speak of all the stars, including those that are invisible to the naked eye? That cannot be proven. Strictly speaking, mention is made here only of those heavenly bodies that give light and are signs for the earth. Reserve is fitting for us here. We have no right to maintain that the earth is the center of all heavenly bodies. On the other hand, the little earth is certainly *a center*. And that involves nothing incongruous. God does not reckon merely quantitatively. The world constantly plays up what it deems matters of great magnitude against the smallness of God's work. But God is a personal God, not a universal cosmic being, and it is the prerogative of His personality if He is divinely partial, choosing earth, as it were, over against the heavenly bodies.

b) Determining the assigned role of these bodies. This perhaps contains, in advance, a protest against all pagan superstition regarding these spheres. Their purpose is positive:

1. To separate between day and night. It is not as if day and night had not existed earlier. But now for the first time light is concentrated in the day and makes its full and specific appearance. The sun begins to rule over the day and the latter must comply with the sun. The earth now receives its light specifically from above. The night, which before this appears to have been completely dark, now receives a light as well.

2. To be signs, אֹתֹת. They are thus a kind of writing, written by God in the sky with His fingers. These signs indicate the climate, the weather and its changes, and sometimes by their constellations or by their sudden appearances proclaim important events in advance. There is, however, their misuse (Jer 10:2; see, however, Matt 2:2; Luke 21:25).

3. To be for set times, מוֹעֲדִים. This has in view the rhythm of the seasons and what is connected to the seasons in activities like farming, raising cattle, or commerce. The moon, too, has significance here, insofar as it regulates the months, and by it the festival times in Israel will be calculated (Psa 104:19; Jer 8:7).

4. To be for days and years, that is, for determining the lengths of the days and for measuring the length of a year.

c) Establishing the significance of a part of these bodies for organic life on earth. They are "to give light upon the earth." Therefore the sun and moon are called "the great lights," since they provide a large amount of light upon the earth, not so much because of their size. It is simply a question of how big they appear on earth, what they are for us.

39. *What follows on the fifth creation day?*

On the fifth day birds and fish appear, of which the first belong to the sky, the second to the water. Here there is a backward glance to the separation of the second and third day, respectively. Heaven and water were there before the dry land, therefore they are the first to be populated.

There is also a correspondence of organic structure between water animals and animals of the air. They are transient and mobile and share these characteristics with their distinctive element and with each other, in contrast to the stability of the earth. They also are similar in the way they reproduce. We read, "Let the waters swarm with swarms of living creatures," that is, "full of schools of fish." Nothing is said about what such birds and fish are made of. "In the expanse of heaven" means "air," for which Hebrew does not have a word. "Birds" and "fish" of course mean all water animals and flying animals. Scripture recognizes that here a higher level of organic life appears. Therefore these products are addressed and blessed. The animals are spoken *to*, while the plants were only spoken *of*. The animals have נֶפֶשׁ חַיָּה, "living soul," or, more properly, are "living soul"; sentient life is concentrated in them. Here, too, the creation is a creation in sorts, "according to its kind." It does not appear that for every kind only one pair was created. Rather the opposite is to be derived from the text. The animals could have been created at the same time in different places on earth. In the case of the creation of man it was different. There the creation of one pair at one point was necessary.

40. *What belongs to the sixth creation day?*

The creation of land animals and of men. Land animals are of three kinds:

a) בְּהֵמָה; large, tame animals. Thus man is not related to all animals in the same way; there are tame and wild animals. God shows this by creating tame animals as a separate class, and man has commensurate responsibilities toward these animals. It is not a matter of indifference how man treats them. In בְּהֵמָה, from בהם, "to be mute," there is an indication of the benign character of these tame animals.

b) "Creeping animals," that is, creeping animals on land, for there are also creeping animals in the oceans.

c) חַיְתוֹ־אֶרֶץ; "wild animals of the ground." This need not indicate "ferocious animals"—here again "according to their kind." The animal world is most closely connected with the earth on which it lives. Therefore, "Let the earth bring forth living creatures." Such language does not occur later concerning man.

41. *In what in particular does the importance of the creation of man appear?*

In the solemn words of deliberation that precede, "Let us make man after our image and after our likeness." For the meaning of "us," see the doctrine of the Trinity. Man is intended to reveal the image of God, also insofar as He is a triune God. The *Logos* and the Spirit specifically have, with the Father, placed their stamp on man.

42. *Is there a difference between the expressions "image" and "likeness"?*

No, both expressions say the same thing and reinforce each other. Should one wish to make a distinction, one may say, "in our image," בְּצַלְמֵנוּ, that is, "in the quality of the image of God, as God's image." For this meaning of the preposition בְּ, see Exodus 6:3, "as God almighty," בְּאֵל שַׁדָּי; Psalm 35:2, "rise up as my help," בְּעֶזְרָתִי; Isaiah 40:10, "as a mighty one," בְּחָזָק; Psalm 37:20, "as smoke," בְעָשָׁן. The second expression, "after our likeness," כִּדְמוּתֵנוּ, does not refer to the image in man, but to the knowledge of the image that is present in God's consciousness of God Himself and after which man is created as after a model.

43. *Does the image of God consist in dominion over the lower creation?*

No, this dominion is certainly brought into connection with the image of God and depends on the image, but it is not the image. Also, the reference here is not to all dominion but to that which all human beings possess equally by virtue of their being human. Compare, on the other hand, 1 Corinthians 11:7–8, where the reference is to an image and ruling in another sense, specifically with the male person in view. The dominion man has over the lower creation is not the same as the dominion God has, and therefore cannot constitute the image of God.

44. *What is made evident by the fact that creation after the image of God is mentioned first?*

That the image of God lies above the distinction between man and woman, in what is human in general and belongs to woman as well as man.

45. *What is the sense of the distinction here between "man" and "woman"?*

It appears here as a natural distinction of gender and does not yet come into view as an ethical relationship with marriage in view. That comes later. Therefore here, זָכָר and נְקֵבָה; later, אִישׁ and אִשָּׁה.

46. *What was the original mandate according to the creation ordinance for man?*

To subdue the earth, thus to lead an active, industrious life. Naturally such work is meant by which powers are not exhausted but multiplied.

47. *Of what did the food of man consist according to v. 29?*

From seed-bearing plants and from trees with seed-bearing fruit. Thus, vegetables for food. See the later command after the flood. Also, for the future, Isaiah 11:6ff. When food in heaven is mentioned, whether figuratively or where sacramental food is mentioned, Scripture always speaks only of plant food.

48. *May we conclude from this that originally animals were immortal?*

No, that would be to conclude too much. But certainly death with pain, the groaning of the creature (Rom 8:20), first entered the creation later with sin. In the plant world death certainly existed before the fall.

49. *Is it not true that the human body is designed for the use of animals as food?*

One may not reason back from the current condition of the body to its original design. Sin has brought about a radical change. As an organism man stands in the middle between plant-eating and flesh-eating animals. He can, if need be, still live only from plants.

50. *Why is it said at the end that everything was "very good" (v. 31), while earlier everything is said to be merely "good"?*

Because each product of creation, corresponding to God's higher idea, was nevertheless in its isolation not the complete expression of that idea. The idea of the world that God willed to realize was a harmonious whole. Only in the whole can the crowning goodness, which is spoken of here, be present.

51. *What elements are there in the "resting" of God?*

a) A negative element of ceasing from creating.

b) A positive element of taking pleasure in the finished work. This element is essential for the scriptural concept of "rest." When the work is finished and the supervisor looks upon it with inner satisfaction, then his capacities rest, and, still, he is all eyes, all ears, all attentiveness, all admiration. He focuses all his energies on what he made in order to comprehend it and to penetrate it. This for the first time is true rest, and so is the rest of God, the joy with which He recognizes and greets the created world as the image of His own glory. The rest of God is thus not a withdrawing of the Lord into the depths of His being, from which He had emerged in order to create. When God is refreshed at the sight of His work, then that look of enjoyment goes out as a blessing over the creation, and man, in whose consciousness the creation is reflected, receives in his heart that peace, as sharer in the Sabbath of God. That is the meaning of the "blessing" of the Sabbath.

52. *What do some claim about the creation narrative in Genesis 2?*

That it is not only independent of Genesis 1 but also at different points contradicts this chapter, since it comes from another source. Here, they say, man is created first (2:7). Here the earth is dry before the growth of the plants. Adam is first created separately.

53. *How is this claim to be answered?*

That there is no difference, if we only keep in view that Genesis 2 is not nor does it intend to be a creation narrative. The name תּוֹלְדוֹת (v. 4) never means the "birth" of something in the sense of its "beginning," but always the "births" [plural] of something, that is, its history after it has already originated. The expression stems from the time when history was still a description of generations, that is, in its most primitive form (Gen 10:1). Genesis 2:4 is thus a heading for what follows and not the conclusion of what precedes. And here only as much of what precedes is recapitulated as is necessary to understand what follows. Given that understanding, we can account for all the differences between Genesis 1 and 2.

54. *Is creation a work of the Father only?*

No, as an external [*ad extra*] work it is to be attributed to the triune God. Economically, however, it can be ascribed to the Father. The Father appears in the economy of God, especially in the economy of grace, as our Judge. And He is that as our Creator. As far as the act of creation is concerned, we observe that the three Persons of the divine being work together. From the Father, then, as we noted above, comes being, the bringing forth of substance out of nothing; from the Son comes individuated being, the idea; from the Spirit, living being. In this sense the creating of the substance of the spirits is permanently attributed to the Father, while the Son as *Logos* enlightens each of these spirits that comes into the world, and the Spirit of God causes the spirits to live. In re-creation this is likewise the case (see 1 Pet 1:3).

In the creation of the universe by the triune God lies the guarantee that nature also, as far as it extends, provides a trustworthy revelation of the being of God. It is not as if the natural revelation must lead to Unitarian results and then suddenly, in a totally unprepared fashion, the idea of the Trinity appears before us on the basis of God's supernatural revelation. The more and better we get to know nature, the more will we be brought face to face with the triune God.

55. *Is creation an eternal act?*

No, as a transitive act of God that has an object outside of God, it is an act in time, at least an act that coincides with the beginning of time. It is certainly true that in God's being itself no time distinction exists, and that thus creation, too, as an activity of God, may not be drawn within time. But that kind of eternity is proper to all of God's acts. One must only hold that the creation is not eternal in the same sense, for example, as the generation of the Son is eternal and the decrees are eternal. The latter not only proceed from eternity but also remain within eternity; they terminate with something eternal. That is not the case with the creation.

56. *Does not the creation of the universe detract from the immutability of God?*

No, when Scripture appears to speak as if there is a succession and change in God Himself, it is expressing itself in a human way. For example, in Psalm 90, where the absolute eternity of God is taught so clearly, it is however also said, "Before the mountains were born and You had brought forth the earth and the world, yes, from everlasting to everlasting You are God." (v. 2). The word "before" appears to introduce time into eternity, but that is because of the weakness of human language.

One must distinguish between active and passive creation (*creatio activa* and *passiva*). The former has in view the act of creating in God, the latter, the universe as created. Of the former Voetius says, "Creation, actively considered, is not a real change because by it God is not changed by that act; it only requires a new relationship of the Creator to what is created. And this new relation, which is not real in God, can therefore not effect a real change in Him." And Wollebius says: "The creation is not a change in the Creator, but a change in the creature, a change from potential being to actual being."

57. *If God's act of creating does not take place in time, how then can the passive creation, what has been created, manifest a distinction in time between its different parts?*

The reason lies in the distinction in order that was conceived and willed in God's act of creating. Included in God's idea of creation and in God's will to create is that one thing follow the other, and therefore in passive creation there is a sequence of time corresponding to this logical order in God. In other words, time and differences of time are products of creation, not the forms in which the creating God Himself moves.

58. *How must we answer the question: Could God have created the universe earlier or later?*

Here, too, one must distinguish between active and passive creation. As far as the universe's being created is concerned, this could have occurred earlier or later, if God had so willed. On the other hand, as far as the *creativa activa*, the creating act of God, is concerned, this could not have happened earlier or later by hastening or delaying the existence of the universe. We may not posit time before the existence of the universe, whereby something would have been taken away if the universe had been there earlier, or where something would have been added if the universe had come into existence later. There is no time before creation. There is only eternity, and time can make no intrusion into eternity, no creature can by its existence or nonexistence add something or take away something from eternity. Already Augustine said very accurately, "Without doubt the world did not come into existence in time, but with time" (*De Civitate Dei* [*The City of God*], 10.6).

59. Is it possible to defend the doctrine of an eternal creation (as product)?

As is well known, this was defended by Origen. Others have viewed it as an open question, that is to say, philosophically, apart from the witness of Scripture; so, Thomas Aquinas and Duns Scotus.

Against this doctrine are the following considerations:

a) The concept of an eternal creation cannot be reconciled with that of a creation out of nothing. Of itself the idea of creation out of nothing includes a transition from nonbeing to being.

b) The concept of an eternal creation leads to a confusion of creation and providence. If the universe is from eternity and nevertheless created, then it is also eternally created and is continually being created. Providence then becomes a continuous creation, or creation eternal providence, which amounts to the same thing.

c) An eternal existence of the world conflicts *a priori* with the theological character of world history. A history is something that must have a beginning and an end. We can conceive of an ocean of motionless water as having no shore, but for a swiftly moving stream we ask about its beginning and end.

Other arguments are less convincing. Some argue that if the universe were eternal, there would no longer be a difference between creation and the generation of the *Logos*. But the distinction would remain that the creation is out of nothing, while the generation of the *Logos* is out of the being of God. Also, it is hardly convincing to say that the eternity of the universe limits God in His eternity and infinity. God's infinity is in any case of a completely different sort than a universe without a beginning (see H. E. Gravemeijer [*Leesboek over de Gereformeerde Geloofsleer*] in the section where he discusses this issue).

60. How does Scripture speak about this question?

Genesis 1 speaks of an absolute "beginning." Similarly, John 1 speaks of a "beginning," in which the Word was through whom all things were made (v. 3). When Origen helped himself by assuming a series of worlds before this world, this idea is in conflict with what Psalm 90 says, "Before the mountains were born ... from everlasting to everlasting You are God." Behind this universe lies no other, but rather eternity.

61. Is the universe created out of nothing or out of already existing material?

Out of nothing, and that indeed out of *nihil negativum* [negative nothing]. Philosophers, it is true—Plato, for instance—have sometimes spoken of a nothingness that is only relative, compared with a higher reality. That was called *nihil privativum* [privative nothing]. By nothing was meant a certain kind of reality. The expression "out of nothing" does not come from the canonical Scriptures but from 2 Maccabees 7:28 in the Latin Vulgate, "*ex nihilo.*" See *Sapientia Solomonis* [*Wisdom of Solomon*] 11:18, where mention is made of creation out of formless matter, which however could refer to the second creation. For creation out of nothing Hebrews 11:3 is emphatic.

62. What is the difference between first and second creation?

The same as the difference between immediate and mediate creation (*creatio prima sive immediata; creatio secunda sive mediata*). The former refers to bringing matter out of nothing; the latter to the further preparation of created matter. For both the word "creation" is used. The ongoing creation of spirits belongs to the first, immediate creation.

63. What are the main divergent theories regarding the origin of the universe?

a) *The dualistic theory.* God formed the universe from something that existed along with Him from eternity. Sometimes this matter is seen as ethically evil. Objections to this theory are the following:

1. Matter is not worthy to be made absolute and eternal in this manner, much less evil matter or matter as evil. Only matter that is the product of the eternal Spirit is acceptable, not an eternal, blind matter, which then must be evil *per se*. The latter is the view of Plato and Aristotle.

2. The law of parsimony prohibits accepting two basic principles, where one can suffice.

3. Creation out of nothing does not violate the law of causality. For the law of causality does not teach us that all matter must come from other matter but only that all change must have a cause. Thus every origin must also have a cause. The cause of the origin of the material of the universe lies in the creating act of God.

4. For dualism, which teaches the eternity of a spiritually evil principle, every guarantee is lacking that the good will maintain the upper hand in the world. What is absolute and eternally necessary, we should say, cannot perish. Such an eternal antithesis does not allow itself to be removed by anything in world history, no matter how long it lasts.

b) *The emanation theory*, the doctrine that the universe flowed out of God. Here God and the universe are one in principle. The emanation is pantheistic. God is called the absolute insofar as the universe has not yet emerged from Him. This theory can be worked out in different ways, each according to whether it is based on identity pantheism or idealistic pantheism.

A particular, more recent form of this theory distinguishes in God between form and matter. Form is the divine spirit. Matter is the so-called "nature" in God. For the universe, form comes out of God's form, matter out of God's matter. Thereby God is thought of as self-conscious, which is usually denied by pantheism. The transition from form and matter in God to form and matter in the universe is pictured as an overflowing of God, although others speak of an act of His free will. Rothe is one of the proponents of this theory.

The emanation idea originates in the East, the theory of evolution in the West. The path of the former runs from above to below, the path of the latter is the reverse. The theory of evolution is atheistic, the emanation theory is pantheistic. We oppose these systems on the following grounds:

1. They do not do justice to God's transcendence and mix God and the universe.

2. The infinity of God's infinity is changed into God's being everything. And God does not remain infinite, since He can be

just as little outside the universe as the universe can be outside Him.

3. The more recent form of this theory, such as we find it in Rothe, consciously shifts dualism into God Himself, something to which all emanation theory must lead if it in some sense wants to maintain the distinction between God and the universe. "Matter," however refined it may be, is present in God. And this matter, a part of God, will have to descend outside God to become a lower form. Thus, a "fall" in God or out of God.

4. The emanation theory robs God of His sovereignty as well as His omnipotence. The concept of revelation is completely falsified by it. It makes God to be a partner of all the evil, both ethical and physical, that is in the universe.

5. The concept of moral evil is completely modified, since God is no longer thought of as a personal being.

6. The only true emanation, in the higher sense of the word, lies within the triune being of God Himself. But there are differences between emanation and generation. They differ:

   a. In the object: in emanation it is finite, in generation, infinite.

   b. In the object: in emanation it is impersonal, in generation, personal.

   c. In the subject: in emanation it is impersonal, in generation and spiration, personal.

   d. In the outcome: Son and Holy Spirit remain within the being of God, the emanated universe falls out of God.

c) *The theory of evolution.* This theory claims that everything has developed, and is still developing, from a single instance of matter by the working of certain natural laws. The theory of evolution, however, does not have an answer to the question where that matter and those laws come from. It can therefore not be a substitute for the doctrine of creation and is based, moreover, on deism or pantheism.

CHAPTER SEVEN

Providence

1. What is providence?

The eternal work of God by which He causes the created universe, as far as its substance is concerned, to continue to exist. Concerning its power, He causes it to operate, and concerning its operations, to reach the goal intended by Him.

2. What is the relation of this work of God to His other works?

a) Providence differs from creation *modaliter* [in its mode], insofar as creation effects the transition for the universe from nonexistence to existence. Providence, in contrast, is the cause of the continuation and continuing operation of the already established existence of the universe and of the powers already present in it.

b) Providence is the execution of the decree of God, insofar as the decree is related to the continuing existence and the natural development of the created universe and because the decree has a willing and efficacious side closely connected with the universe.

c) Providence belongs to the *ad extra* works of God and in particular to the works of nature, which are to be distinguished from the works of grace. Therefore we do not speak of the works of grace under God's providence. This distinction has not always been made by theologians, for even those who speak of the *opera naturae* [works of nature] and the *opera gratiae* [works of grace] classify miracles, which are in the closest connection with the works of grace, under providence.

3. *What is the basis for the doctrine of God's preservation of the universe?*

   a) On the continual representation of Scripture that the creature, although possessing a real existence, nevertheless at no moment and in no respect can be independent of God. If it existed of itself, then so far as its being is concerned it would be like God.

   b) On the doctrine of divine immanence, according to which God with His eternal power and divine nature can be excluded from nothing in creation. Therefore it will not do to exclude Him from the ongoing existence of the substance of creation.

   c) On the explicit declarations of Holy Scripture (see Neh 9:6; Col 1:17; Heb 1:3).

4. *Is providence, as far as preservation is concerned, a purely negative work, consisting in the fact that God does not destroy the created universe?*

No, it is a positive work, for only of God can it be true that He remains where He always is. God alone is absolute being. That the universe exists is not in itself sufficient grounds for its continuing to exist. For this, a new work of God is necessary, which we call preservation. Failure to appreciate that necessity is based on a deistic concept of God and on a deistic worldview. The biblical, Reformed doctrine navigates between the two extremes of pantheism and deism.

5. *How does it come about that we are so inclined to fall into this deistic error, as if given with the existence of a thing is its continuing existence, unless a positive act of destruction intervenes between the two?*

Because we have made for ourselves a god in our image and our likeness. Our relation to things outside of us is more or less deistic. When we have made something, then the sufficient grounds for its continuing to exist seem to us to lie in the fact that it exists. We do not then preserve it further, but it remains because it is. That way of thinking we then transfer to God. Of course this involves a huge *petitio principii*. For that something continues to exist when it is made by us does not depend on the fact that it exists, but exclusively on the preserving power of God.

6. *What is the opposite extreme with respect to the doctrine of preservation?*

That in a pantheistic fashion the continuity of the substance of the universe is abolished, and the universe is seen as being created every moment by God out of nothing. Preservation thus becomes a continuous creation. Supporters of this view are:

a) Many old dogmaticians, who desired to lay the emphasis on the creaturely and dependent existence of the universe. Therefore they call *conservatio* [conservation] a *creatio continua* [continuous creation]. For example, Ursinus, Heidegger, Alsted, Rijssen do this. This was not wrongly intended, but is, however, less happily formulated.

b) Many who under this formulation conceal a pantheistic worldview. One can already find the principles of this view in Descartes, which is then given a pantheistic coloring later in Malebranche and in Spinoza became a full-blown pantheism. Jonathan Edwards, who brought the sovereignty of God dangerously close to the borders of pantheism, defended this opinion in his book on original sin.

7. *What objections must be brought against this identification of creation and preservation?*

a) It abolishes all continuity in the existence of things. The element of what is abiding, of permanence, thereby disappears from the concept of substance. The universe comes into existence anew every moment; its existing at moment A is in no regard the basis for its existing at moment B, etc. So then, for B it is also completely indifferent whether an A instead of a P or a Q preceded. The real connection between moments of existing falls away.

b) The opposition between this opinion and the biblical view lies completely on the line of the opposition between pantheism and theism. According to this theory everything flows constantly out of God, everything must be created anew every moment. Since time is divisible into infinity, no one can determine a limit for how short the moments of creation are and so finally they will become so short that there no longer remains any room for existence, that is, the universe is constantly being created, but it never actually *is*. This comes dangerously close to the illusionism that asserts that finite things are an illusion.

c) This theory can also lead to Idealism. Fundamentally, here all *Vermittelung* [mediating] of things by each other is abolished, just at the point where it is most obvious, namely in the continuing existence of identical objects. If A in moment *A* is not the basis for the existence of A in moment *B*, how then will *A* ever be able to be the basis of *B*? In other words, how will we be able to maintain causality as real?

d) This theory becomes its most dangerous if its consequences are drawn for the life of man. It breaks up that life into a number of unconnected parts and thereby takes away the basis for moral life, for continuity of character, and for the responsibility of man.

8. *How then ought we to think about the preservation of God?*

As the act by which He, by a positive expression of His will, causes a thing, as it already exists or in connection with that existence, to remain itself. This does not mean that what exists in moment *A* does half the work necessary to perpetuate itself, and God does the other half. It is not a divided work. Rather God works so that He makes use of the existence of A in moment *A* in order to cause this identical A to continue to exist in moment *B*. Beyond this, the way in which this occurs must remain incomprehensible for us. We may not, however, abandon the continuity of things. As we shall see, this same co-working of God with what already exists returns in connection with other acts of providence.

9. *What then ought to be considered as belonging to preservation?*

a) First of all, maintaining the substance of things, both spiritual and material, and of both in their specific identity. The continuity of spirits is other than that of matter, and God preserves both of them according to their nature.

b) Besides matter and spiritual substance, there is, however, still more reality.

There is form, attribute, power, and still more. The question arises, therefore, as to whether maintaining these belongs to preservation. The answer, in brief, must be the following: Insofar

as these things are not active powers or actions, their maintenance must be subsumed under the category of preservation.
On the other hand, insofar as they are nothing other than active
powers, they belong to the act of concursus, if one will continue
to make a logical and clear distinction between preserving and
co-working. Gravity, for example, is, as far as we know, always at
work; it is identical with its action. There is as well, however, a
latent or dormant gravity, not active as such, that would thus fall
under preservation. It appears, then, that with regard to powers
God need cause their action to continue only by concursus. It is,
however, extremely difficult to indicate the boundary between
latent and constantly active powers. Scripture does not distinguish between such things, and we may therefore be satisfied
with pointing out this distinction in general.

c) Many also reckon the maintenance of type for organic genera and
kinds to preservation. One should bear in mind, however, that
here creation (creationism) in part and co-working and governing in part intersect, and that further the identity of kinds and
genera cannot be called an identity in the strict sense, but only a
similarity, unless one explains the propagation of individuals in
a realistic fashion.

10. *What is the second work of providence?*

Co-working, which has reference not to the substance of things but to
their action. If substance and activity differ, then with respect to the
latter a specific immanence of God must exist, an immanence that at
least *modaliter* [as to its mode] differs from that with respect to the
former. The same arguments that are valid for preservation can be
made for co-working. God may no more be excluded from the activity of
things than from their substance. When Charles Hodge maintains that
the theory of concursus seeks to make comprehensible what is incomprehensible, that is not the case, at least it does not have to be the case.
Nothing more is present in the postulate of concursus than in that of
preservation. We see that both must be accepted, but *how* that is so we
comprehend as little for the one as the other.

11. *What grounds, besides what has been mentioned, do we have for assuming a co-working of God?*

a) Scripture says that we are not only in God but also live and move in Him.

b) God works in all of nature down to the smallest and most insignificant matters, or what are such for us (Psa 104:21; Matt 5:45; 10:29; Acts 14:17). If we were to accept that God in a deistic fashion lets nature work of itself, then all these texts would have to be taken figuratively and the consolation of our religion and worship would be lost.

c) The entire teleology of nature and of history speaks of an immanent working of God (cf. Job 12:7–9; Dan 4:35).

d) Every individual has only to look at his life history to discern that there was a higher hand that governed it. At this point faith in God's co-working is most closely connected with our dependence upon Him. He directs even our free acts, and however far above our comprehension may be the manner in which he does that, in any case it must be a co-working, a concursus. Not matter, not fate, not chance can affect us, if our freedom is to be maintained, but only the co-working of God (Psa 104:4; Prov 16:1; 21:1).

12. *How are we to think about this concursus?*

Here, too, two extremes will have to be avoided, deism and pantheism. According to the first, the powers and the laws of nature certainly come from God and as such are not necessary for God but now work of themselves such that God remains excluded. That eliminates God's immanence. According to the other extreme, God alone does everything in nature, that is, there are not two causes that work together; the laws of nature and the powers of nature are just abstractions from God's modes of working. Thus, nature and God are identified. That can happen (like the theory of preservation as *creatio continua*) in a twofold manner:

a) In the consistent pantheistic sense, so that God is not only immediately all power and motion of the universe but is also the ground and the substance of the universe.

b) In the sense of inclining toward pantheism, so that the universe is certainly distinguished from God substantially but the power of the universe is still viewed exclusively as divine power; God = nature.

13. *What must be urged against this opinion that inclines toward pantheism?*

Although there are glimmers of this view in Zwingli and Calvin and other Reformed theologians, one can still not say that they were conscious of eliminating the action of second causes. In their views we have to do more with dangerous formulations than real error. Nevertheless, Reformed theology must guard against such formulations much more than against deism because our basic principle does not drive us in the direction of the latter, but toward pantheism. We note:

a) That this conception, as if God is the only acting cause in the universe, is based more on a philosophical concept of the absolute than on scriptural grounds.

b) That this conception is in conflict with the experience that we acquire from our own inner actions. We know ourselves as *causa secunda* [second causes] and will have to assume that, after discounting the difference between the activity of spirit and the activity of matter, something similar to what we call (spiritual) causality also takes place in material substances when we act.

c) That this conception brings us extremely close to Idealism and pantheism. It is inconsistent to posit a universe outside of God in which God nevertheless is the only acting cause. If He is thus made the doer of all doing, then one must also go a step further and make Him the being of all being.

d) That this conception is irreconcilable with the rational responsibility of man, insofar as that responsibility depends upon the causality of our will.

14. *What must be maintained regarding concursus?*

a) That it, like preservation, has to do with what is already created. In creating, God has placed powers in substances. These are realities, however uncertain we may be about the kind of reality that is to be attributed to them. There is something in the earth by which it exercises an attracting power. God has created it there and connected it in a certain way with the matter of earth. Just as He preserves the matter that makes up the earth, so He co-works together with that power that is joined to matter so that it endures. It is not God in the literal sense who attracts in the earth, but rather the earth itself that attracts by the concursus of God.

b) It is not a physical or metaphysical power but His omnipotent will by which God exercises His concursus, the same will by which He created the universe and preserves it. Making this distinction avoids the pantheistic formulations that hyper-Calvinistic theology has often fallen into. If God as *causa prima* [first cause] acts in the universe by physical or metaphysical power and if, as in fact is the case, this physical or metaphysical power is completely sufficient to explain what is effected, then no place remains for *causae secundae* [second causes], unless one divides power in two and attributes half to God and the other half to the creature. If, on the other hand, one holds that God is to be distinguished from the universe, not only with respect to substance but also with respect to its activity, then we arrive at recognition of the fact that what is at work *propro sensu* [in the proper sense] in the universe is the power not of God but of the universe, and that this power, however, at every point and in every moment, is dependent on the omnipotent will of God and without that will cannot express itself. In this way both the transcendence and the immanence of God are maintained, although here too we must confess our ignorance regarding the way in which God's omnipotent will is involved in the power of the creature.

c) What we call the laws and the powers of nature is a reality, a propensity placed in things by God to act and also to act in this way and not otherwise. These wills and powers are made suitable to the matter to which they belong. There is congruence between them and the substances to which they adhere. However, we may not go so far as to think of these laws and powers as already given with these substances or as inseparably bound to them. In that case the difference between preservation and concursus would vanish. And it would be impossible for God to change natural law, to abolish it, without changing or destroying substance. By His omnipotent will God can join to the same substance new and different powers than were previously proper to it. He follows the order of nature as He Himself has established it, but He by no means does that because He cannot do otherwise. It is important to keep this in view for describing the concept of miracle. It has been observed, correctly, that in an absolute sense no miracles exist for God. For Him it is no more miraculous for iron to float on water than for it to sink. He can exercise the influence of His will on the co-working factors involved so that iron floats and just as well exercise that influence so that it sinks. When, however, by His will He exercises other such influences, that is always accompanied by a real change in the powers of things themselves, for these really exist and are not simply the power of God.

d) How we ought not to think of God's concursus follows from what has already been said. Different wrong conceptions must be rejected:

1. Concursus is not general and indifferent (*concursus generalis et indifferens*), as the Jesuits, the Socinians, and the Remonstrants maintain. This general concursus is thought of as a neutral power imparted by God to all *causae secundae* [second causes], as the result of which they can act, while, further, the manner of their action is dependent on the kind of *causae secundae*. The sun imparts the same heat and power to grow to all plants on earth, yet these plants do not all grow in the same way because they differ from each other in kind.

   The motives for this conception lie on an ethical terrain. One wished to keep God free from co-working in sin and to leave room for the *liberum arbitrium* [free will]. One distinguished between *materia* [matter] and *forma* [form] in the act of sin. The former was attributed to God, who effected it by His *concursus generalis et indifferens*, the latter (the form) came from man. (Even Reformed theologians, like Gravemeijer, make use of this distinction). Although we ought to have all respect for the first motive mentioned above and to recognize every difficulty of the problem that emerges for us through the presence of sin in the world, nevertheless we can only see in this generalizing of concursus a failed attempt to maintain God's holiness at the expense of His absoluteness. God is kept free from evil (at least apparently), but at the same time He is kept apart from a part of the activity of the creature. God with His eternal power and capability also cannot be excluded from that doing by which His general influence becomes specific. There is in sin not only a metaphysical substrate as a real act; there is also reality in the form of sin, activity that is specifically culpable, and even of this culpable activity it is the case that it cannot be initiated or carried out against God's will and without His concursus. It is much better here to let what is inexplicable stand in its inexplicability than to make do with solutions that do not do justice to another, acknowledged truth.

2. Neither is concursus to be conceived of as partial, so that God and the creature would share the activity involved. The same act, it is to be emphasized much more, is at the same time entirely an act of God and entirely an act of the creature. It is an act of God in its entirety insofar as there is nothing in it that does not depend on His eternal will and insofar as at each moment of its occurring it is determined by this will. At the same time it is an act of the creature insofar as by the creature and from its center the will of God causes the act to occur and be manifested as a reality. As on so many other points where we deal with the relationship between the finite and the infinite, here we encounter two spheres into which one and the same object falls without the one limiting the other. Just as the infinity of space is not the infinity of God and still is borne by the infinity of God and does not limit the infinity of God, so also the activity of second causes is not the activity of God in a proper sense but is nonetheless borne by the activity of God without limiting the activity of God. God can do everything and the creature can do everything in the same instance, since the spheres of doing are different and need not exclude each other.

3. From what has been said it is now also excluded that the activity of God and that of the creature may be placed entirely

on the same line. God's activity has the primacy in order. Also, it is not to be thought that God pairs His concursus with the act of the creature as the same *causa occasionalis* [occasional cause]. We must rather affirm the following for concursus— with respect to the working of the creature God's activity is:

    a) *Concursus praevius sive praedeterminans* [prior or antecedent co-working]. In created things there is not a principle that works of itself and to which God then attaches. Rather, in every specific case the first impulse to activity and movement comes from God. God is first active before the creature can act. Every action and reaction of things that interact with each other depends in this way on God's omnipotent will. When a spark and gunpowder come in contact with each other, then all the conditions for an explosion are supplied by the preservation of God that maintained the particular powers of both, but those powers cannot cause this new phenomenon of an explosion by reacting with each other unless God co-works *per concursum praevium* [through prior concursus]. It is obvious that this *prae* [before] in *praevius* does not mean priority in time. It is entirely a question of order. It must be noted further that this *concursus praevius* does not terminate on the action of the creature, but on the creature itself.

    b) *Concursus simultaneus* [simultaneous concursus]. Once the action has begun, the efficacious will of God must also accompany it reciprocally at every moment if it is to continue. This *concursus simultaneus*, in distinction from the *concursus praevius*, does not concern the creature but its action. While the Jesuits among Roman Catholic theologians wanted to conceive of the concursus only as simultaneous and thus deny a *concursus praevius*, some Reformed theologians have accepted the latter as applying only to good and gracious actions and for the rest remained satisfied with the demands of a *concursus simultaneus*. However, one cannot make a distinction here between good acts and acts that are not good. With respect to their reality they are on the same line, and if a good action cannot take place without a *concursus praevius*, so the same must be maintained about an evil action.

c) *Concursus immediatus*, that is, an immediate concursus. We often make use of means to bring about some action, and although God uses means for His governing in order to realize His purpose, this cannot be said with regard to concursus. When God destroyed Sodom and Gomorrah by letting fire rain out of heaven, that is a mediate act of governing, but at the same time it is God's immediate concursus by which He enables fire to fall, to glow, to burn, to consume. In all the means that His governing utilizes, God's concursus is therefore immediately active. This immediateness is further described in detail by dogmaticians as an immediateness *quoad suppositium* and *quoad virtutem*. The first means an immediacy with respect to a being, the second an immediacy with respect to power. When God exercises His concursus, no other being, no other thing, interposes itself between this concursus and its object, as, for example, the sculptor places his chisel between himself and the block of marble. Even the *causa secunda* [second cause], although action is rightly attributed to it, does not in this way lie between God and the result. God's act adjoins and is involved directly in what is done. With respect to power God's concursus is likewise "immediate." It is not as if power issues and is separated from Him in order to be then further transferred apart from Him, to bring other power into action and thus cause a certain final action to exist. Rather, in every transposition and transmission of power, God is present at every moment with His *concursus praevius* and *simultaneus*. Here, too, the power that really belongs to *causae secundae* [second causes] does not form a link between God and the end result.

15. *After considering what belongs under preservation and co-working,*
    what belongs to the governing of God as a unique act of providence?

This question is not so easy to answer as it appears at a first glance. It may
not be denied that the three spheres of providence more or less touch
each other. With regard to God's preservation and co-working we have
already seen that. That is even clearer with respect to the distinction between co-working and governing. Thus one may reason as follows: Given
that God preserves things in their being, preserves the powers resident
in them, and by His *concursus praevius* [prior concursus] maintains them
in their action and generally works through second causes, that is, His
providence does not belong to the *opera gratiae* [works of grace] but to
the *opera naturae* [works of nature] and does not rest on immediate intervention but on the use of powers previously placed in the world, what
then remains for His governing? Consequently, some have proposed
to apply another scheme than the old conventional one to providence.
Many distinguish only between *conservatio* [preservation] and *rectio* or
gubernatio [ruling or governing]; see the Heidelberg Catechism; see also
Keckermann, Alting, Heidanus, Maresius. They then reckon concursus
as belonging to *gubernatio*, ruling. Conversely, however, one could just
as well classify the latter with the former, that is, be able to think of the
gubernatio as taking place by concursus. Nevertheless, it occurs to us
that room remains for a distinction. One may note the following:

   a) That God concurs still only means that He causes the natural
      powers to work when they work and to work as they ordinarily
      work. To say that does not yet specify the way in which these
      natural powers interact or group themselves, on which the
      end result will depend entirely. That fire glows and burns is
      already determined by concursus, and for that no special act of
      God's governing is needed. That fire must burn me precisely in
      the moment that I come in contact with fire by moving myself
      toward it, or that fire from heaven must strike me, does not in
      itself lie in the specificity of the power of nature. To regulate this
      happening would therefore fall to God's ruling. In other words,
      in the area of natural science, where one adheres strictly to the
      laws of nature and seeks to explain everything from its natural
      causes, there still remains a large area of possible connections
      and groupings of the powers of nature not already determined

by the laws of nature. In the language of the world one calls that the area of chance. We have already treated this concept earlier. It was defined there as the occurrence of things whose causes for us are unknown and indeterminable. Chance, then, has an exclusively subjective meaning. That the lot falls this or that way is for us chance. Still, we do not maintain that there are no natural causes for its falling as it does. From the vantage point of God's governing, however, we could speak of chance in a more objective sense, namely as the occurring of those things that are not already determined by natural causes—occurrences, thus, whose determination is not entirely given by *causae secundae* [second causes]. The Latin word for "chance," *accidens*, seems to be connected with this concept (from *ad* [toward] and *cadere* [to fall]). It would be called chance in this more than subjective sense, for example, if someone crosses the street and a roof tile falls on his head. His crossing the street had natural causes, the falling of the roof tile likewise had natural causes, but that he was crossing the street just when the roof tile fell at that exact spot is called chance, for it was an *accidentia* [accident], a coinciding of these two series of natural occurrences.

Now it is obvious that in this instance also we may not speak of chance from a Christian and theological standpoint. The use of this word is and remains a worldly way of speaking. God collocates and arranges the series of things so that they occur and coincide. At the basis of occurring there is everywhere an *apponere*, an arranging. The fact that on a strictly scientific basis room remains for chance shows sufficiently that there is also a place in the doctrine of providence for a divine governing along with preservation and co-working.

b) Apart from the above considerations, we do not have the least guarantee that God does not sometimes intervene immediately in the course of the universe by introducing a new power, no guarantee that He could not, for example—besides by *providentia ordinata* [ordained providence], by natural causes—also in a direct manner make a rain cloud move through the air so that it deposits its raindrops on our fields. Meteorology and physics, in general, certainly do not start from that idea, and everywhere

where miracles do not appear, one must allow them the right to insist on the demand that there must be natural causes and to investigate according to that demand. That is their prerogative and their method of investigation is based on it. Without it they certainly could not have made such advances as they have made in the modern era. Thus the full right remains for them, as much as they can, to trace back to natural laws the movements of rain clouds, the flashing of lightning and whatever more of such phenomena. We on our standpoint cannot believe otherwise on the basis of Scripture than that this quest will never succeed completely. We accept that there is a sphere of God's direct governing in which He is at work along with preservation and concursus, a third element that does not let itself be searched or classified. Considered from this viewpoint, too, the doctrine of providence thus gives us occasion to continue to speak of governing.

c) Here and there among dogmaticians an idea comes to the fore that the governing of God is specifically that action that leads the action of second causes to the end determined for them. Governing would then have in view the outworking of things more than their working. That they work and how they work would flow from concursus, that they with this specific working power would reach a specific end should be attributed to governing. It is, however, not clear that a new act of God is necessary for this. One cannot really distinguish between the quality of working and the result of working. That second causes work in just this or that way is the same as saying, in other words, that they reach this or that goal.

d) We ought to assign miracles, as well, to the governing of God, were it not rather that miracle belongs to the area of supernatural revelation, of the order of salvation. In any case, miracles do not belong to concursus, for they are not expressions of the natural power that is in things and appears under given circumstances. We will discuss the concept of miracle further later.

16. *Is the immanence of God dependent on the scope of this immediate governing of God?*

No. One has so presented it as if the concept of a governing of God would only be the correlate of our ignorance about second causes. According to this representation, we speak of a directing by God where we are not in a position to explain phenomena from the ordinary order of nature. However, the more natural science expands its boundaries, draws new spheres into its domain, and investigates the laws that govern there, to that same degree in proportion the domain that falls under God's free governing will contract. In its development, then, science would have to result in a systematic banning of God from His creation. The more science, the less faith in the providence of God.

This representation is totally false. It stems from a deistic conception of the relation between God and the universe. It has *causae secundae* [second causes] working outside of God's almighty will. In opposition, we must maintain that God's immanence would not be damaged in the least if natural science had already succeeded in drawing everything within its scope and in explaining every phenomenon, with the exception of miracle, on the basis of fixed laws. Even then it would not be these laws, and not these powers reduced to these laws, to which the course of the universe would be attributed, but exclusively to the will of God, who has established these laws, who preserves them, who has placed them in time and space and arranged them in a way that accords with His plan to realize their working in each other and with each other. God's governing in its proper sense would not vanish. It would simply be absorbed in concursus, and we would still stand just as far as always from the deistic caricature of the universe.

Logically it may most certainly be conceived that God has drawn His governing of the universe completely within fixed lines that He does not cross. A law is simply the manner of His working. That everything is to be explained from the laws of nature would thus simply mean that everything has been arranged by God as working in a series of His workings without it thereby ceasing to be God's working.

17. *Which two errors are opposed to this doctrine of the governing of God and at the same time to each other?*

The pagan idea of fate and the equally pagan idea of chance. The difference between the former and the Christian idea of God's governing lies in the teleological character of the latter. The difference is not as if in governing there were an element of uncertainty. Providence is just as inexorable (one may use this term) as fate. Nothing escapes it; it is never thwarted. But, as the word indicates, it involves foresight; it rests on the decree of a self-conscious, all-wise God, who forms His plans and carries out His plans. If everything happens according to His counsel, then this is so because the content of that counsel is arranged with wisdom for the goal He has planned. He foresees the needs of His plan. Pagan fate, on the contrary, is something that works with blind certainty, to which gods and men are equally subject. It is on a line with pantheism, insofar as pantheism teaches an unconscious absolute.

Chance has already been discussed. These extremes touch each other, for one can say that no more terrible fate for the universe can be conceived than that it would be abandoned to chance in the sense of the absence of causality. Carried out consistently, this so-called "casualism" then leads to atheism, just as teaching on fate leads to pantheism.

18. *How far does governing extend?*

This must be answered in different ways. If by governing one means that act of providence distinguished from preservation and concursus, then one can naturally not make it general. If we speak of *conservatio* [preservation], concursus, and *gubernatio* [governing] as three distinct acts, then we will then have to define governing as follows: "The governing of God is the action of His providence by which, everywhere it is necessary, He gives to *causae secundae* [second causes], maintained by Him in their existence and in their powers while they are working under His concursus, a specific direction or combines them in a certain way for reaching the end intended by Him."

If one otherwise understands under God's governing in the widest sense everything that He does in the created universe in order to bring to pass His plan for it, then naturally nothing can be excluded from this governing of God. Then, however, it includes much more than is only ascribed to governing by definition in the strict sense. Not only does it assimilate concursus entirely, but *conservatio* [preservation] as well may be viewed under this aspect, for by their continuing existence things also serve a goal. Governing, then, is identical with providence seen from its teleological side. It is a concept formed to express that God's hand is in everything, that in the unity of His consciousness and His will He comprehends all parts of the course of the universe, that under His approval and by His power everything occurs that occurs. Governing as such is that side of God's decree by which it is realized.

For the scope of God's governing, concretely considered, we need only refer back to what has been said about the doctrine of the decree. All the rubrics taken up there may be discussed in connection with the doctrine of providence. And Scripture teaches us that nothing is excluded from God's governing, be it small or large, free or necessary, good or evil. Only the Socinians and a part of the Arminians, and in a certain sense Roman Catholics and Lutherans, deny this all-inclusive governing of God. Amongst the ancients, Jerome agrees with them. For pagans the opinion was widespread that the gods concern themselves only with what is important and ignore what is less important. *Magna dii curant, parva negligunt.* ["The gods care about great matters, but ignore small ones"] (Cicero, Aristotle). Jerome thought that one diminishes the majesty of God if one holds that He knows every second how many mosquitoes are born and die, how many flies there are on earth, etc. Over against that way of thinking stands the decisive witness of Scripture (Pss 36:7; 145:15–16; Matt 10:29–31). Likewise to be taken into consideration here: One is thinking of God's heavenly majesty precisely in an earthly fashion if one wants to grant for it the quantitative distinction between great and small. If one applies that distinction to God, that is a "dangerous and evil distinction." A third objection against every exception to the principle of the universality of God's governing lies in the close connection that one thing has with another. One has expressed that paradoxically by saying that no particle of matter can move without all the matter in the universe sharing in that movement and feeling something of it. That is exaggeration, but in it is this element of truth, that nothing is indifferent to or superfluous for the whole. The universe is an organism and in an organism one cares for the small as well as the large parts. Moreover, it has frequently proven to be the case that small matters in the course of the world can occasionally be of incalculable importance, and the historical evidences for that are well known.

19. *May one not speak of a special governing of God toward His rational creatures?*

Yes, God governs them by addressing their consciousness by means of law-giving. This fact is perhaps important enough to provide occasion for it as a subdivision of the doctrine of governing. One should note, however, that this special governing does not exclude the concursus of God and His governing in other respects. When God writes His law in the heart of man, then He must:

a) Continually preserve that law there.

b) Again and again influence by co-working when that law bears witness.

c) When the law exercises influence on us, convincing us and bending our will, then in that case, too, the co-working of God cannot be lacking, provided it is a real working.

d) God must, by His direction in such circumstances, bring us to the place where we are confronted with His law. The governing of God by laws in the sphere of rational life is thus, again, not one that encroaches upon the all-encompassing reality of His providence.

20. *What is the relationship between God's providence and moral evil?*
Concerning that we note the following:

a) Lutherans deny *concursus praevius* [prior concursus] in general in order to avoid the difficulty this issue raises.

b) Some Reformed do not deny *concursus praevius* in general, but do deny it with respect to moral evil.

c) Lutherans have appealed to God's foreknowledge, where the question at issue is how God, without waiting for the first movement of the freely acting creature, can exercise His *concursus simultaneus* [simultaneous concursus].

d) For the further course of sin, Lutheran dogmaticians likewise seek to safeguard God from co-responsibility with the proviso that God only co-works *ad effectum* [with respect to realization or outcome], not *ad defectum* [with respect to fault or defect], *ad materiale* [materially], not *ad formale* [formally].

e) In all these respects Roman Catholic theology, which first worked out in detail teaching on concursus, agrees with the Lutheran conception.

f) The best and the most Reformed dogmaticians hold to *concursus praevius* as well for moral evil.

g) At the same time, concerning sins they have also wanted to distinguish between *causa efficiens* [effecting cause] and *causa deficiens* [faulting cause], between *formale* [formal] and *materiale* [material].

h) Against these restrictions we must remark that they are in part unsatisfactory, in part wrong. Regarding the distinction between *causa efficiens* and *deficiens*, it is wrong insofar as it seems to represent the activity of God with respect to sin as entirely negative and thereby carries the danger of reducing sin to something negative. In order to keep God pure, so it is said, we may not rob sin of its reality and of its positive character. As far as the distinction between *formale* and *materiale* is concerned, this is certainly right, but it does not explain how then God is active with respect to this *formale*.

i) With regard to the course of sin as indwelling *habitus* [disposition] and *actus* [act] in man, we must confess our ignorance when the question is raised about the relationship between that course and God's providence. Illustrations that have been produced in abundance only apparently solve this problem. In contrast, of the activity of sin in its consequences it may be said with the old theologians that these are determined and directed by God.

j) That unknown, about which we have just reminded, is expressed by the dogmaticians as *actuosa permissio peccati*, "active permission of sin."

VOLUME TWO

ANTHROPOLOGY

Translated and edited by

Richard B. Gaffin, Jr.

with

John R. de Witt, Associate Editor
Daan van der Kraan
Harry Boonstra

ANTHROPOLOGY

Richard B. Goffin, Jr.

Contents

CONTENTS

Preface

My thanks to the base translators of this volume, without whose work its appearance would not be possible, as well as to John Richard de Witt for some translation review. As with volume one, I have reviewed and revised their work and given the translation its final form. Again, thanks are due as well to the project manager, Justin Marr, and to the copy editors for their work.

Volume two sheds no light on a question raised in the preface to volume one concerning what Reformed theologians, contemporary or in the recent past, may have directly influenced Vos. What does come out clearly in a number of places, more so than in volume one, is Vos' impressive familiarity with the work of theologians, primarily Reformed, from the 17th century. With an eye to matters of continuing debate in Reformed theology, many readers will find particularly interesting his lengthy treatment of the covenant of grace in the final main section of this volume.

R. Gaffin, Jr.
November 2013

CHAPTER ONE

The Nature of Man

1. According to Holy Scripture, of what does the nature of man consist?

The Scripture teaches:

    a) That man consists of two parts, body and soul.

    b) That the soul is a substance.

    c) That it is a substance distinct from the body.

2. How does Scripture teach these truths?

Not so much explicitly as by assuming and presupposing them everywhere. More specifically:

    a) In places like Genesis 3:19; Ecclesiastes 12:7.

    b) In places that depict the body as clothing, a tabernacle (2 Cor 5:1).

    c) In all the places that teach that the soul exists and acts after death.

3. What does God's Word teach concerning the relationship between soul and body?

This is a mystery. The following, however, is certain beyond all doubt:

    a) The union between them is a life-unity. The organic life of the body and the life of the soul are not in parallel. Only on the presence of the soul in the body does the possibility rest that the organic bond of the latter is maintained.

b) Certain conditions of the body are dependent on the self-conscious acting of the spirit; others are independent of this.

c) Some functions of the soul are bound to the body; others can be done independently of the body.

d) In antithesis to Materialism, Idealism, occasionalism, etc., one may call this realistic dualism. It is most closely connected with some of the principal doctrines of the Bible.

4. *What does one mean by trichotomy?*

The doctrine that man does not consist of two but of three specifically different parts, namely:

a) πνεῦμα, *animus*, the principal and most noble part; "the spirit" to which the capacities of reason, will, and conscience belong.

b) ψυχή, *anima*, the soul; the principle of animal, bodily life that ceases to exist with death. Animals also have a ψυχή.

c) The body, σῶμα, considered solely as matter.

5. *What are the principal objections against this trichotomy?*

a) It is philosophical in origin (Pythagoreans, Plato) and rests on a disparaging of the body and a one-sided elevation of the nonmaterial existence of man. Because one fails to appreciate the organic bond between body and soul, the functions with which the soul works within the body must be detached from the soul and viewed as a third, independent principle. This motif is completely unbiblical and anti-Christian. Christianity wants a redemption of the body as well as of the soul.

b) Genesis 2:7 shows how God created man consisting of two parts: dust of the earth that was first inanimate, and spirit blown into it, through which man became a living soul.

c) Scripture nowhere uses the terms רוּחַ and נֶפֶשׁ, πνεῦμα and ψυχή arbitrarily, but where they are in contrast, that contrast is not the trichotomic one given above but an entirely different one. רוּחַ, πνεῦμα, "spirit" is the principle of life and movement in man, and is that insofar as it enlivens and moves the body. That, according to philosophical terminology, should be called ψυχή.

Hence, according to Scripture, the animals have that just as well as man. This, of course, in no way means that there is no specific difference between a human spirit and an animal soul but simply informs that by רוּחַ the principal feature is expressed that is the higher principle common to man and animals, namely the enlivening and moving of the body. To indicate the distinction between the animals and the human soul, the Scripture has used other words ("heart," etc.). So one sees how Scripture and philosophical terminology are diametrically opposed to each other.

Ψυχή, נֶפֶשׁ, on the other hand, is not the lower part of man but the principle of emotion, desiring, self-conscious life—the entity that comprises the multiplicity of impressions in the unity of consciousness. In this way the soul is the seat of emotion because all receptivity presupposes a receptive subject: In Scripture, I = my soul. The soul desires, hates, loves, wills (1 Sam 18:1, 3; Deut 13:7). Souls = persons in the Old Testament, as it still does according to our modern use of language (Gen 12:5). It is characteristic that a deceased person can still be called a soul—insofar as something personal and individual still always clings to the body—but, of course, never πνεῦμα, רוּחַ, spirit; that would be a *contradictio in adjecto*. Hence also the close connection there is between soul, blood, heart.

d) Scripture mentions the soul in poetic language as the most precious thing someone can possess. It is called the "glory of man," "his alone," etc. (Gen 49:6; Psa 6:6).

e) From a comparison of the places in which spirit and soul alternate, every appearance of a basis for a substantive distinction must vanish. The soul is spirit and the spirit is soul, depending on whether one considers it from one side or the other. Spirit refers to the life-power that sets the body in motion; however, it also has in view the capacity for motion of the soul itself. God is called "God of the spirits of all flesh" [Num 16:22; 27:16] on account of His immanence in the world of living beings.

f) One should note that spirit has become a religious concept—or, stated more accurately, is so innately. That man consists of two parts, spirit and flesh, of which the one is dependent on the other for its mobility and functioning, has the deeper meaning that it pictures the dependence of man on God. Just as our spirit breathes into our body in order to make it an organic instrument, so God's Spirit must breathe into the entire man in order to qualify him for spiritual good.

g) The trichotomy does contain an element of truth that may not be overlooked. It is to be absolutely rejected as an ontological theory of three specific and different constituent parts in man. It only contains truth as a formula for the empirical discord there is between the sensual impulses and the higher capacities of the spirit in man. Through sin, that part of the soul that is related to the *sōma* [body] has obtained independence in opposition to the higher inspirations of the soul. That is to say, there is discord in the spiritual life of man himself: The more spiritual sinful dispositions clash with the more sensual inclinations. But that higher part is also sinful, and the lower part also belongs to the soul.

h) The trichotomy conflicts with the testimony of our self-consciousness. No mortal man is aware of possessing a *psychē* in distinction from a *pneuma*. What the philosophers call *psychē* is simply the manifestation of the spiritual principle in relation to the material of the body.

i) The places in Scripture that seem to speak of a trichotomy may easily be explained differently. These are mainly 1 Thessalonians 5:23 and Hebrews 4:12. The truth is that through Platonic philosophy, trichotomic usage was brought into the vernacular and so became common usage. If one wanted to indicate the entire man, one spoke of body, soul, and spirit, without thereby intending to present himself as a supporter of Platonic philosophy. Scripture makes use of human language and so appropriates this common usage. When it does that through the mouth of Paul, that in no way indicates that Paul taught a trichotomy. The expression is nothing else than a rhetorical form of enumeration.

6. *What is Realism?*

The doctrine that every man is the manifestation of one human race in relation to a bodily organism. That is to say, all souls are not merely individual but one and the same substance that can only be personal in relation to a body.

This great generic human soul is a reasonable, rational, volitional entity. When a man dies, the personal existence of the soul ends (at least according to consistent realists), and it returns to the generic substance of which it was an individuation.

This doctrine is advocated by many because it best explains, so it is thought, the imputation of Adam's guilt. We were one with him when he sinned, actually in him.

7. *What are the principal objections against this Realism?*

a) It is a philosophic hypothesis, perhaps possible in itself but nothing more.

b) It finds no support in Scripture. One could call it one of the many ways by which one has tried to explain some scriptural facts—for example, original sin. Of these ways, however, it is by no means the best or what is presented to us by Scripture itself.

c) Our self-consciousness testifies against it, because it is a personal self-consciousness. The awareness that we possess a substantial soul is so interwoven with the consciousness of our personality, with our self-consciousness, that it is impossible for us to separate the two. From this it follows that we conclude that our soul can only exist as an individual and not generically.

d) It conflicts with the express teaching of Scripture, which tells us that our soul continues to exist personally after separation from the body. It is the consequence of a pantheistic Realism when Schleiermacher asserts that all philosophy testifies against the doctrine of immortality.

e) According to Realism, the entire human race was sinful as one substance. This substance Christ must have assumed when He became human, so that the man Christ became sinful. It is no wonder, then, when realists radically change the work of redemption. According to them, it occurs in Christ according to His human nature, not as a payment of debt by a surety but as an ethical purification process. Or, where one still wishes to retain the aspect of surety, one is forced to require justification as necessary for the human nature of Christ because it, of course, is under guilt, just as ours is. Shedd, who among recent American theologians advocates Realism, says: "Theologians have confined their attention mainly to the sanctification of Christ's human nature, saying little about its justification. But a complete Christology must include the latter as well as the former. Any nature that requires sanctification requires justification, because sin is guilt as well as pollution. The *Logos* could not unite with a human nature taken from the virgin Mary and transmitted from Adam unless it had been previously delivered from both the condemnation and corruption of sin. The idea of redemption also includes both justification and sanctification, and it is conceded that that portion of human nature, which the *Logos* assumed into union with Himself, was redeemed. His own humanity was the 'firstfruits' of his redemptive work. Christ the firstfruits, afterward they that are Christ's!"[1] This is an unequivocal explanation that shows where Realism in soteriology must lead. If Christ needed a justification for the human nature that He Himself possessed, then for us the consolation of His suretyship is gone. One should therefore be warned.

8. How many theories exist with reference to the origin of human souls?

Three: that of preexistence, traducianism, and creationism.

9. Where, respectively, have the latter two theories been advocated?

The Greek church has been creationist from the beginning. Tertullian, in the West, was traducianist. Jerome and Augustine were creationists. The latter, however, at the time of his conflict with Pelagius, held more to traducianism. The Latin church as a whole was creationist. That was so for the entire church of the Reformation up until the Formula of Concord. The Lutheran theologians of the 17th century first began to advocate traducianism. The Reformed maintained creationism. Most modern German theologians follow a middle course and teach that creationism is applicable to the soul and traducianism to bodily-animal life.

---

1 William G. T. Shedd, *Dogmatic Theology*, Part 4, Chapter 1.

10. *What does the traducianist theory teach and on what grounds?*

That the entire person is generated by the parents, body and soul. Some even go so far as to assume the divisibility of the soul. Others speak in vaguer terms about the origin or derivation of one soul from the other. The grounds on which one appeals from a traducianist side are:

a) That nothing is reported about a creation of Eve's soul. This is an *argumentum e silentio* [argument from silence] and lacks all force.

b) God rested on the Sabbath from creating. The creation was, as we have seen, *ktisis*, and as such closed, without the continuing creation of single souls thereby becoming impossible.

c) The transmission of Adam's sinful nature to his posterity. We will return to this later, only noting for now that traducianism does not offer the only nor the best solution for this fact.

d) One points to Christ's miraculous conception and birth and reasons as follows: If the soul were created immediately by God, then it is not to be seen why an extraordinary working of the Holy Spirit would be necessary to keep it pure at birth from Mary. We will also return to this later, and only say now in general that it is unscriptural and wrong and in part a consequence of realist-traducianist tendencies when one places all the emphasis of the incarnation on the moment of purification. The Holy Spirit also had entirely different activities to perform with regard to the incarnation.

e) Traducianists think their strongest ground is to be found in the transmission of ethical, national, familial, and other characteristics of spirit and character. In other words, traducianism is summoned to help explain the mystery of heredity. This, however, is an explanation that explains too much, for then the result would not only be partial but complete similarity between parent and child. Moreover, heredity is such a mysterious, and such a complicated, matter (one need only think of atavism = the reemergence of seemingly eliminated characteristics and dispositions in later generations) that one hardly can use an explanation as simple as traducianism.

There is another explanation that seems to us more likely. It leaves the empirical origin of heredity a mystery (what it will certainly always have to remain, as all reproduction is in its essence a mystery) but understands it to point to something better for the logical ground, namely the once-for-all established ordinance of God that like will originate from like. One has to concede to traducianists that all these phenomena cannot be accounted for by the influence of the body. Such an explanation sounds materialistic, and the traducianist explanation would be far more preferable.

11. What is to be said in favor of creationism?

a) It is more in agreement with the overall ideas of Holy Scripture. In that it gives us a doctrine concerning the origin of man, it gives us creationism. Compare Ecclesiastes 12:7; Zechariah 12:1; Hebrews 12:9.

b) It accords better with the nature of the soul. The difference between creationism and traducianism, as far as metaphysics and psychology are concerned, is as follows. It is either one or the other: Traducianism has to be explained in a realist sense or must seek help from creationism. That the soul is generated by the parents can mean only one of two things: that it separates from the soul of the parents (Realism), or that it is created by God in the actus generationis [act of generating]. If one chooses the former, one is saddled with all the objections to which Realism is subject, summarized above. If one chooses the latter, one is saddled with the impossible concept of a creatio mediato, a creation by means of the parents. This concept was already rejected earlier in considering the doctrine of creation. Moreover, it is no longer purely traducianist. And there is no escaping this dilemma. The substance of the individual soul is there in any case. If it was not there earlier, then it is created; if it was there earlier, then (according to the teaching of Realism) it had to separate from the soul of the parents. When many attempt to find a middle course between these two and speak about the origin of the soul of the child from the souls of the parents, as one flame is ignited by another, the entire explanation rests on a metaphor. In the case of the flame, nothing new results; the matter that burns, the flammable material through which it burns, the elements into which it changes through burning—all these were there earlier. Only a new chemical combination results. One need only attempt to apply this to the soul and one will see immediately to what untenable positions it leads. Taken strictly, it is materialistic to speak in this way about the soul in its generation. Even Shedd falls into such doubtful ways of speaking: "It is as difficult to think of an invisible existence of the human body in Adam as it is to think of an existence of the human soul in him." We reply: It is not only difficult but even impossible and entirely unnecessary to speak about an existence of our souls in Adam. Only in a very figurative sense can that be risked. If the material of our bodies already changes during our short span of life, our material parts were certainly not present in Adam.

c) Also, traducianism is certainly not compatible with the dogma concerning the person and the natures of Christ. Like Realism, it makes His human nature sinful in the way it explains original sin. And one should certainly pay attention to this, that traducianism gives an explanation of original sin only when it adheres to Realism. If it goes its own way, it gives the empirical ground of the transmission of sin but not the legal ground that satisfactorily explains this empirical fact. Concerning this legal ground, it does not in any respect extend further than creationism does. In other words, it has no speculative but only empirical value.

12. *What, finally, should be observed concerning this question?*

a) That we must not be wise beyond what is written.

b) It is dangerous to say, as do some traducianists, that if traducianism falls, then the entire dogma of original sin falls. We have no right to hang the millstone of our philosophy around the neck of God's truth in this manner.

c) The argument that God does no creative work after the creation Sabbath leads to a deistic worldview. What, then, is regeneration? Is it not presented in Scripture as a new creation? It is certainly true that it is a higher, spiritual creation, but by its occurring it shows sufficiently that God can also act creatively after the creation Sabbath. If He can do that in the higher sphere of grace, then surely also continuously in the sphere of nature.

d) Creationism does not presume to remove all objections and to re-solve all difficulties. It only intends to warn against the following false positions:

1. That the soul is divisible.

2. That numerically all men are of the same entity.

3. That numerically Christ assumed the same humanity that fell in Adam.

13. What does one understand by the preexistence view?

The doctrine that the human soul has existence as an individual soul al-ready before its joining with the organic body. In that lies the difference between Realism and the preexistence view, for the former denies an individual preexistence.

14. Who in theology has defended this doctrine of preexistence and from what motive?

Origen held the preexistence view. He assumed that in the beginning of the world in which we exist, souls were created by God and that they now, in succession, each in its time, unite with a natural product of generation. In modern times, this theory is defended, in connection with Kant's teaching on intelligible nature, by Julius Müller in his work *The Christian Teaching of Sin*. He thinks he is able thereby to explain the empirical depravity (original sin) of man during this life. Individual souls sinned in an existence outside or above time, and for that they are punished by a phenomenal existence in time, full of sin and misery.

15. What is to be said against this preexistence view?

a) If we attribute to the soul a prolonged existence outside the body (in time, according to Origen), then its joining with and appear-ance in the body becomes something accidental. The preexistence view stems from the same disparaging of the body on which tri-chotomy rests. The body belongs to man, and man cannot exist prior to his body. If, with Kant and Julius Müller, we assume an act of uncaused freedom outside time, then man, in conflict with his own limitedness and destiny, is elevated above a form that, as far as we can judge, is inseparable from his life.

b) The preexistence view is related to and gives rise to all kinds of doubtful mythological notions of the prior state of the soul; it is related to pagan teaching of the transmigration of the soul, etc. The early Christian church already sensed that this view was more pagan than Christian and therefore rejected it (as Origenism) at the Fifth Ecumenical Council in 553.

16. *In how many different ways has the expression "image and likeness of God" been understood?*

a) Some taught that "image" referred to the body and "likeness" to the soul.

b) Augustine said that "image" pointed to the intellectual and likeness to the "moral" capacities of the soul.

c) Bellarmine held that "image" designated the natural and "likeness" the supernaturally added.

d) Still others say that "image" expresses innate similarity to God, "likeness" similarity to God acquired by man.

e) The truth seems to be that both expressions form a ἐν διὰ δύσιν [a hendiadys], that is, they serve to describe one and the same concept from two sides. Or, if one wishes to make a distinction, one can do so in the way given above (in the section on creation). "Image" then becomes the impression in man, "likeness" the archetypical knowledge of the image of His nature that God bears in His own consciousness.

17. *What conceptions have been formed concerning the scope and meaning of the image and likeness of God in man?*

a) According to Reformed theologians, the image of God comprises both the intellectual and the moral nature of man.

b) The Greek church, the Socinians, and the Remonstrants err by thinking exclusively of the intellectual capacities.

c) Others (the Lutherans) err by entirely excluding these natural qualities and only take into consideration the moral qualities.

d) The Reformed conception maintains a middle course when it distinguishes between:

    1. The essential and amissible image of God, namely the possession of intellectual capacities and capacities for making ethical distinctions.

    2. The accidental and losable image of God, namely the good moral quality of the capacities in view in 1.

e) According to the general Protestant conception, "the image of God" and "original righteousness" (*justitia originalis*) are the same. The Roman Catholics, as we will see, dissociate them.

18. *Why is this doctrine of the image of God of such great importance for theology?*

It is self-evident that by "image of God" is expressed what is characteristic of man and his relation to God. That he is God's image distinguishes him from animals and all other creatures. In the idea that one forms of the image is reflected one's idea of the religious state of man and of the essence of religion itself.

a) According to the Roman Catholic conception, as we saw, *imago*, "image," has another meaning than *similitudo*, "likeness." Man was created with the "image." So by nature he is God's image-bearer. Now we have already seen that with "image" is meant the metaphysical correspondence of the human spirit with God. According to Rome, the natural relationship to God exists in the fact that in this way he is similar to Him. There is no thought of a close relationship between man and God, of a similarity of communal endeavor by the human will being subject to God. For all this belongs to the *similitudo* [likeness], and this, otherwise called *justitia originalis*, "original righteousness," is called an added gift, *donum superadditum*. Only by something that raises him above his created nature does man become a religious being, able to love, to enjoy his God, and to live in Him. Out of this follows entirely the externalist character of Roman Catholic religion. It becomes something added to man, that he has but is not identified with him, does not enter into his essence. That man is like God in this natural sense is a purely deistic relationship. There is room for something else if with the *imago* the *similitudo* would also be added as naturally belonging to the conception of man.

b) The Roman Catholic denial of the utter inability of man in his fallen state and its weakened conception of original sin is likewise connected to this teaching concerning the image of God. According to Rome, man can only lose what was not essential to him, namely the supernaturally added gifts, the *dona superaddita*. Because of his fall, these are lost. The essence of man, the *imago*, consisting in formal existence as spirit, in the *liberum arbitrium* [freedom of the will], remained. Because, however, there was no inner connection between the *similitudo* and the *imago*, the removal of the former cannot essentially change the latter. The *liberum arbitrium* might be weakened a little; in reality it is unharmed. In other words, by loosening the moral powers from the will, from the capacity of the will, and by denying that the former are natural in man, Rome has in principle appropriated the Pelagian conception of the will as *liberum arbitrium*. That capacity of free will has remained, and with that, the possibility that man, even after the fall, can do something good.

c) In both respects mentioned, the Protestant—and more specifically the Reformed—doctrine of the image of God is different than the Roman Catholic doctrine. That man bears God's image means much more than that he is spirit and possesses understanding, will, etc. It means above all that he is disposed for communion with God, that all the capacities of his soul can act in a way that corresponds to their destiny only if they rest in God. This is the *nature* of man. That is to say, there is no sphere of life that lies outside his relationship to God and in which religion would not be the ruling principle. According to the Roman Catholic conception, there is a natural man who functions in the world, and that natural man adopts a religion that takes place beyond his nature. According to our conception, our entire nature should not be free from God at any point; the nature of man must be worship from beginning to end. According to the deeper Protestant conception, the image does not exist only in correspondence with God but in being disposed toward God. God's nature is, as it were, the stamp; our nature is the impression made by this stamp. Both fit together.

d) If then the image of God and original righteousness are to be identified, if life in communion with God belongs to the nature of man and can nowhere be excluded, and if now, by sin, this original righteousness is lost, then the consequences will be twofold:

1. By falling away from something to which he was wholly disposed, which constitutes his proper and highest destiny, man will be changed in the deepest depths of his being; a radical reversal will take place within him. What clings to us outwardly can be removed without making us different inwardly. On the other hand, what coheres with every part of our spiritual organism can, if it is withdrawn, only bring about a powerful revolution by which the organism itself becomes disorganized. The loss of original righteousness follows spiritual death, because death in its essence is disorganization, a process of dissolution. From this, one can assess most clearly the Protestant and Roman Catholic conceptions concerning the capability of man to do spiritual good in his fallen state. According to us, man is dead and therefore does no good toward God. According to Roman Catholics, he is weakened or ill but nonetheless still always capable with his free will to move himself to do good.

2. The fact that original righteousness belongs to the nature of man has yet another consequence. Because the being of man was placed from the beginning in a necessary relation with God, because he is made in the image of God in the stricter sense and this image is his nature, sin therefore cannot be just a mere privation. This would mean that something that belongs to his nature can be removed and the rest left undamaged. This is impossible. Man has to be in relation with God in everything he is and does. So, if original righteousness falls away, unrighteousness replaces it as the natural state. That is, sin is a positive principle of enmity against God, as Paul taught us about the mind of the flesh. If the image of God, original righteousness, had not been the nature of man, perhaps he might have been able to remain in a neutral standpoint. Now,

the latter is cut off. He is either positively good or positively evil; there is no middle state. One can therefore say that the deeper conception of sin, especially of original sin, that rules in Protestant theology flows directly from the view one has of the original state before the fall.

e) If the question is posed how man can lose what belongs to his nature and whether he has lost his human nature by the fall, then that must be answered with a twofold observation:

1. The image in the broader sense has not been lost, and given also that his nature existed in that sense, it has remained at least to that extent.

2. The moral quality of the capacities of man is certainly fallen, but that it belongs to his nature is also seen in the fact that man could not remain neutral. He must either stand for God in original righteousness or against Him in natural unrighteousness. This characteristic of his nature does not take away that man in all his being and acting takes a position toward God. When he is sinful and in conflict with God, he is still morally *toto genere* [as to entire genus] something other than an animal that exists in *puris naturalibus* [in a purely natural state].

f) One will now, after all that has been said, understand why a diverging opinion concerning the image of God must be formed by the Socinians and Arminians. They could not choose the Roman Catholic supernaturalism. Neither was inborn virtue (= original righteousness) a concept that fit with their line of thinking. As a consequence of this, there was no other way out than to limit the image of God in a religiously neutral sense to dominion over the lower creatures. For, according to the Socinians and Arminians, the state of rectitude is a state of neutrality, of innocence, which had not yet been determined for virtue or for sin.

g) It requires no detailed demonstration that what has been said is of importance not only for determining the relationship of man to God in the abstract, but also is of the utmost moment for soteriology—what concerns God's work of grace that must renovate the image in man.

19. *What must be said concerning the question whether Adam was mortal or immortal?*

The word "mortality" can be used in different, very divergent meanings, which one does well first to distinguish before being able to answer this question unambiguously.

a) Immortal can mean, what cannot be destroyed but has to remain forever. In this sense there is nothing immortal except God, of whom it is said, "Who alone has immortality" (1 Tim 6:16).

b) Immortal can mean what in the course of things established by God cannot be destroyed but retains its being. In this sense Adam was immortal, fallen man is immortal, all spiritual beings (higher than the animals) are immortal, in every state, for none of these are abandoned by God to destruction.

c) Immortality can indicate that attribute of the soul as a consequence of which continuing personal existence is guaranteed to it. Not only so that it continues to exist as substance, but also that it abides as a substance conscious of its own identity. This immortality is like that mentioned above in b), belonging to all spiritual beings in every state. Only pantheists and materialists deny this.

d) By immortality one can understand not a condition but a state. That is, the suffix expresses the modality of the judgment, "man cannot die," as an apodictic one. In this sense, before the fall Adam was not immortal. For him the abstract possibility existed that by the entrance of spiritual death into his soul the principle of death would also extend to his body. Both for his soul and for his body he was mortal in the sense that he was susceptible to change. And all change in the moral sphere, all apostasy, was death for him, for soul and body. One can attribute immortality, in the sense meant here, only to the blessed after the resurrection from the dead, to the angels that were confirmed in their state. For neither does the abstract possibility of dying exist any longer. Yet it is very difficult to decide whether a condition of immortality also corresponds to this state of immutability and immortality and if so, to indicate precisely in what it consists. One might be able to say that this immortality means nothing other than that by God's grace both body and soul will be protected forever against the entrance of death. However, the intimations that Scripture gives us point further. If the body is resurrected in imperishability, then that certainly must be more than just that there is not a positive principle of corruption in it (a purely contradictory contrast). It will have to mean that it is changed and recreated in such a way that corruption no longer has power over it, that as a spiritual body it is not susceptible to chemical dissolution. And in accordance with this, the confirmation of the soul in its perfect state (= the *non posse peccare*) will also be a positive characteristic with which it will be endowed by God. Or better still, in accordance with all analogy, one will have to think of it as follows: that from the soul this condition of immutability and immortality will be communicated with the body. Still, it must be noted that this immortality, what concerns the soul, is already given to believers at bodily death, for in that crisis every principle of death is driven from the soul. Given, however, that the body belongs with the soul and because the latter is not complete without the former, in a strict sense one may have this immortality as a condition beginning only at the resurrection. As a state, one would be able to place it already before bodily death; for, understood as the state of the soul, it is nothing other than the direct consequence of the perseverance of the saints, as we have seen earlier.

e) One can understand immortality as the absence in soul and body of every positive principle of death, from which it [i.e., death] would necessarily result. That a man is mortal would then mean that he must die, that the process of dying is already begun in him, although it is at work for the moment in secret. In this sense, Adam was immortal before the fall, not after the fall, and this is the principal point in dispute between us and others. The Socinians and Arminians consider bodily death as a natural characteristic of man understood as an ethically neutral natural being. They do not have an eye for the immense difference that exists between a solely animal natural being and man. That is why, on this point, they place man on the same line with animals—with this difference, however: that liberation from this nature is held in prospect for him as the higher destiny of man. Just as his ethical neutrality has to develop into positive virtue, so his bodily mortality has to develop into immortality. Modern science in recent times points out that the human organism as it now exists is completely oriented to dying. Some theologians have wanted to grant to science the right to decide concerning the condition of the body before the fall. One may read what Charles Hodge writes on this point. He asserts that Scripture nowhere teaches explicitly that Adam's body was immortal in the sense in which the heavenly bodies [of believers] will be (see 1 Cor 15:42–52). One must of course concede this to him, and one could even go further and say that according to the representation of all the data of Scripture, Adam would have first received this immortality of 1 Corinthians 15 as the reward for perseverance in the covenant of works. The question, however, is not solved with this. Even after conceding this, two options remain: Adam was mutable with reference to his soul, and mortal insofar as he was also mutable with reference to his body, as described above, and at the same time immortal because there was no principle of death in his soul and in his body. This, however, is not what the Socinians and Remonstrants intend. This is also not what modern science means; and it seems that Hodge, too, does not mean this. The *Apology for the Confession ... of the Remonstrants* says, "It is untrue that Adam's body was immortal, that is, imperishable, for sound reason teaches that every animal body is perishable." And Hodge remarks that God knew beforehand how the testing of man would turn out and that therefore he could have created Adam with a mortal body. This strikes us as an anomaly for the following reasons:

1. As shown above, it does not follow from 1 Corinthians 15 and the covenant of works. No one can conclude from the denial that Adam had a body like believers will possess that his body was positively mortal, for there is a degree of difference between the two.

2. Bodily death is everywhere presented as a consequence of spiritual death. Yet according to this conception, we would have the consequence without the cause. One could, if necessary, defend this with supralapsarianism, but even supralapsarianism does not teach that the different purposes of

God's counsel that are subordinated to one another theologically are confused with each other temporally. When science
thinks it is able to determine that the human organism has
always been mortal, then it exceeds its rights. One may concede this: At this moment the body is *per se* mortal—that is,
has to die—that even apart from its relation to the soul it must
already be called a perishable body. But if we concede this,
there is still nothing gained for the theory intended. From this
would only follow that by its influence sin totally changed the
bodily organism, so that it received into itself a seed of death
that by extension is transmitted from parents to children. To
that there is no objection, and a conclusion from it about the
condition of Adam before the fall would not be justified. We
believe, however, that even this concession does not have to be
made. It is indeed true that the body exists of natural earthly matter, that in it a constant metabolism is taking place and
that all those materials that constitute it are in themselves
subject to decomposition. It always remains possible, however, that this natural tendency to decomposition, present in
the material of our bodies, can be so neutralized by a wholesome (= not sinful) soul that the body would remain fresh and
youthful forever. One can say one of two things: Either before
Adam fell the matter of which his body existed was essentially
different than it is now but it has also been cursed because of
sin, or although even then it already possessed a tendency to
dissolution, this was neutralized by a wholesome soul. In both
cases, this theory fails.

3. We know of only one instance of mortality of the body togeth-
    er with moral integrity of the soul. This is the instance of the
    human nature of the Savior before His resurrection from the
    dead. For in His case the carrying about of the seed of death
    in the likeness of sinful flesh, of which Paul speaks, indeed
    this animation in itself, showed that in Him the sinless soul
    had to dwell in the decaying tabernacle of the body in order in
    that way to come into the closest connection with death. This
    in itself made up an important part of His suffering. Because,
    however, the state of Christ's humiliation was of an entirely

unique sort, it does not permit drawing a conclusion about other cases. One cannot infer from it that Adam was mortal.

20. *How does one prove the unity of the human race?*

a) It is a generally accepted principle that the instances of the same species can have a common origin.

b) As a consequence of this, it is only necessary to show that the human races, notwithstanding all their diversities, form one species.

c) A species is determined by:

1. Organic structure. When differences in bodily organism appear for two animals that are not accidental divergences but apparently have a purpose, this difference proves difference of species. One does not find such differences among the human races. All points of difference between the races are accidental, not intentional.

2. Physiological characteristics, that is, everything related to the functions of the organism (blood circulation, digestion, etc., etc.). Even in this respect the human races do not show the slightest difference. They are physiologically alike.

3. Psychological predisposition. Neither here does a difference occur. All human races have the same mental capabilities.

4. The ability to procreate. Two species can frequently intermingle, but what is produced is infertile and does not reproduce. All human races can intermingle and still preserve their fertility in the offspring of this intermingling.

d) In addition, there is as well important linguistic evidence that counts not just for the possibility but also for the reality of common descent.

CHAPTER TWO

Sin

1. *What are the principal philosophical theories concerning sin, and what must be introduced against them?*

We have:

a) The dualistic theory, that sin is an inseparable characteristic of matter. Spirit = good, matter = evil.

> Against it counts:
>
> 1. This theory, if it does not wish to see God as author of sin, must posit something that exists as a substance independently of God.
>
> 2. It removes the moral element from the concept of sin to replace it with a physical element and thereby weakens the concept of sin.
>
> 3. It also removes the responsibility of man by making sin necessary.

b) The theory that sin is merely a limitation of existence. All existence is good; only the lack of existence, that is, finitude and limitedness, is evil. Finite man must always remain sinful. This view: (1) is pantheistic; (2) removes all responsibility. Only weakness, viewed in this way, is evil. Might is right.

c) The theory that sin is a necessary reaction against what is good. For its existence, everything in the world rests on opposition. There is no rest without weariness, no joy without sorrow, no desire without pain, no good without evil. This also makes sin necessary.

d) Schleiermacher's theory. Sin is the imperfection that arises because the higher principle of God-consciousness does not rule the lower principle of self-consciousness and world-consciousness. According to this conception:

   1. Sin is general and absolutely necessary. Even in the original state of man it was unavoidable.

   2. Here the concepts of sin and guilt become merely subjective.

e) The theory that the sensual nature of man is the seat and origin of sin. However:

   1. The worst and most sinful beings, namely the devil and the demons, are not sensual because they have no body.

   2. The most hateful of all sins have nothing to do with the body; for example, pride.

   3. This view would justify the monastic system and asceticism, which, however, are not approved by Scripture.

   4. According to this theory, the older a man gets and the more the sensual nature in him dies down, the more he should also grow in holiness. This is not the case.

   5. When Scripture speaks of sin as "flesh," this has another basis, for thereby is expressed not one's sensual character but ungodliness, God-forsakenness, the spiritual death of the state of sin.

f) The theory that all sin is selfishness. Of all theories, this one comes closest to the truth. Against it, however, we have to note the following:

   1. There is unselfish sin. When, for example, a mother, out of an excessive love for her deceased child, in despair takes her

own life, this suicide is sin. This, however, is plainly not to be called selfishness.

2. In some sense there is selfish virtue. Man has duties toward himself. He has to esteem the image of God that is in him, and he cannot hate his own flesh. God's Word requires love to our neighbor as ourselves.

3. All attempts to give a material definition of sin proceed from the presupposition that what they describe as sin also contains the property of sin *per se*, apart from any relationship to God. That is, one searches for a definition that will not only be material but also excludes God. And every definition that satisfies this demand is rationalistic and deistic in character, therefore useless for the Christian concept of sin. Sin, in the strict sense, is only conceivable as sin against God, and one can speak of sin against one's neighbor only in a derivative and figurative sense. The feature of a relationship to God is essential for the concept of sin and so has to be made part of the definition. If there were no God, one could not speak of sin. There would be selfishness and sensuality and love of the world, but all this, though one could call it evil, does not have a specifically sinful character because it is entirely lacking any relationship to God. It is absolutely necessary to grasp this clearly. It is not selfishness as such that constitutes the essence of sin, but selfishness as shutting oneself off toward God, as seeking after our own honor while *not* wanting God's honor. If one remains committed to the negative concept of selfishness, sin is still presented as separate from relationship to God. However, to the negative side turned inward corresponds a positive side turned outward: enmity against God. Conversely, if one seeks the essence of the good in love, then this love, too, if it is thought of apart from relationship to God, is not the genuine, holy, spiritual love to which the predicate "good" can be attributed in the fullest sense of the word. So, if the mother commits suicide out of love for her deceased child, then love toward God, which should be more to her, recedes into the background and her first love becomes sin to her. And if one spares oneself and out of self-love does not follow a

blind impulse to self-sacrifice because one knows that because of God's will one may not sacrifice or endanger oneself, then in such selfishness a kernel of genuine, spiritual good can be veiled. One sees, therefore, how relationship to God determines everything, making sin to be sin and good to be good.

2. *What characteristics, in consequence, belong to the scriptural concept of sin?*

a) Sin is a specific evil. It is not to be confused with physical evil, with what is unpleasant. Above the terrain of the physical lies that of the ethical, where the antithesis between good and evil reigns. All beings that belong to this reasoning sphere must be one or the other, good or evil. An in-between state, a neutral state between these two, is not possible. There are stages in good and stages in evil, but there are no stages between good and evil. The transition between evil and good is qualitative, not quantitative. A being that is good becomes evil not by a decrease in his goodness but by a radical change in it, by passing over to sin. And one is not to think of stages in evil and good, as if in being less advanced in evil an element of goodness still lurks and, vice versa, in a less developed holiness an element of sin still lurks. In the former, everything is sin, and in the latter, everything is good. But, as with the former, all the sin potentially present need not yet have come to development, so with the latter, goodness can be present as a seed while it has not yet increased. Thus, on both sides, progression is possible without thereby sin and virtue having to be set in opposition to each other as quantitative entities. It is certainly true that everything less good is an evil, but that only says that for man the quantitative lessening of the good is impossible without it being accompanied by the qualitative changing of good to evil. Only in the case of a reduction of the entire development of man would a reduction of good be conceivable in which evil does not immediately enter in. All that man is, should, as moral power, work goodness in him. But also in the good man there is expansion, the capacity for growth. It is likewise with sinful man. He is entirely evil, but his evil nature can develop, and to the same degree the level of sin also increase.

b) Sin always has reference to a law—and not just to a law in general, but specifically to a law of God. Precisely because they saw clearly that one cannot arrive at a correct understanding of sin if one does not establish it beginning with God, the old dogmaticians placed much emphasis on this element when they said that sin is nonconformity to God's law. That is the formal aspect of sin. If one can now describe the content of the law materially, then the problem would be solved as to what the material aspect of sin is. Now Scripture teaches that the law is fulfilled in love, and all its demands may be reduced to the one demand of love. That law, however, is the expression of God's being insofar as it is a *norm*. Therefore, we cannot go further than to affirm that love for God is the material aspect of moral goodness and that the opposite of this is the material aspect of moral evil.

c) God's law has to do not merely with already actually present persons, but also with representative and ideally present persons. Without yet being nonconformed to it *habitu* and *actu* [in disposition and act], one can be so by imputation, by reckoning. That is why sin extends to *status*, to being reckoned in the judgment of God. And here the rule holds that originally in Adam the *actus* [act] determined the *status*, but that subsequently for all his posterity *status* has determined *actus*. To give a complete definition of sin, we will have to say that it is nonconformity to God's law in *status* [status], *habitus* [disposition], and *actus* [act].

d) Sin includes *guilt* and *pollution*. Pollution is understood as spiritual, inherent depravity to which a sinful soul falls prey. Pollution is therefore not present before the soul itself is present. It is inconceivable without antecedent and subsequent guilt. Guilt, however, is conceivable without pollution. In Adam's first sinful motion, guilt and pollution coincided. Guilt does not necessarily presuppose the actual presence of the soul. One can be guilty covenantally. It is not something that was a reality in man but a reality with respect to man. Guilt exists in the judgment of God. It is called *reatus* [liability] by the theologians.

One distinguishes, then, between (a) *reatus culpae* [liability to guilt] and (b) *reatus poenae* [liability to punishment].

By *reatus culpae*, one means the turpitude and criminality that is inseparable from any sin in the judgment of God and men. As something individual, it cannot be transmitted to another. It is otherwise for *reatus poenae*, obligation to punishment. This is transferable.

e) As concerns its center, sin resides in the will of man. Its effects extend also to the intellect and the capacity for emotions, to the entire man, the body included. The entire man is, in his sinful state, the object of God's displeasure. In its origination, however, sin comes from the will, namely from the will understood as *voluntas*, as the deeper spiritual orientation of man. To conceive of a human being that at the same time would possess a perfect will and a deficient intellectual and emotional life is impermissible. But if we imagine such a being, it could not be called sinful. In Christ there was something like this during His state of humiliation, but in His will there was nothing sinful, and therefore He was pure in Himself and had no need of ethical sanctification, just as He did not need justification for Himself. One should keep in view, however, that the will of man is a reasoning will and not blind instinct, and furthermore that it is the will of a responsive being that necessarily has to react to the objects of its will. Man can only desire by means of his intellect and emotions, and so these three are closely connected such that they act together in every sinful deed. And the same is true for the *habitus* [disposition]. Our *voluntas* [will], too, is a moral tendency and inclination, going together with emotion. One may never forget that the three faculties of the soul in their distinctions are abstractions of what is given to us in our experience only as a living unity.

f) We can be in a sinful *status* without possessing pollution, but guilt and pollution are both connected to a sinful *habitus* [disposition]. According to the Pelagians, in contrast, one cannot speak of a sinful *habitus* in a proper sense. Every sin, according to their conception, exists *in actus* [as act]. Only with the free act, with the choice of the will, do guilt and pollution emerge for man.

3. Describe in its general features the Pelagian doctrine of sin.

The principal position of the Pelagians is that our ability is the measure of our obligation and our responsibility to do good. In contrast, Augustine's consciousness of his dependence is expressed in the prayer, *"Da quod jebes et quod vis"* ["Give what you command, and command what you will"].[1] The following positions were contained in the Pelagian postulate:

a) The freedom of the will is *liberum arbitrium* [free will] as abstract possibility at every moment to turn in either direction. The will is thus formed, concerning its quality, without a cause. The will arises from a willing subject, but in this subject no basis is to be found or indicated in advance exactly why the will becomes good or evil.

b) Accordingly, all sin exists in a clear, conscious, direct choice of evil.

c) There is no original sin. Men today are born without virtue and without sin, morally neutral. Heredity and sin are two concepts that clearly exclude each other.

d) This postulate also has a retroactive effect. That is to say, as little as innate virtue or innate sin is conceivable, just as little may innate holiness be thought of in Adam before the fall of our first parents. He was created by God in a state of innocence that stood below developed reasoning. Adam was neither good nor evil. He could only become either by his own free choice.

e) When Adam fell, only his own nature was thereby changed. Cain, Abel, and Seth only became worse as the bad example of their parents was constantly before their eyes. The power of this example, however, does not at all necessarily lead to sin in all situations. Thus, every man is put to the test individually. Death is not a punitive evil because children, who cannot have sinned, also die. There have also been adults, however, who have actually lived without sin.

f) Redemption from sin apart from the gospel is possible. The light of the gospel makes easy, however, the complete obedience that is

---

1 *Confessions*, 10.29.40.

required. When the Pelagians nevertheless speak of grace, then by that they do not understand, as we do, the supernatural grace of the Holy Spirit, but everything we receive from God's goodness in the broadest sense of this word.

g) Children do not have a moral character. Their baptism is only to be viewed as a sign of dedication to God. Augustine uses infant baptism as one of his most powerful arguments against the teaching of Pelagius. This is one of the strongest historical proofs for the antiquity of infant baptism, for if Pelagius had seen any chance to challenge the apostolic character of the baptism of infants, he surely would not have neglected to do it. He, to the contrary, had to make do with a symbolic interpretation of baptism and left the fact, as fact, stand untouched.

4. *On what basis does this Pelagian doctrine of sin have to be condemned?*

a) The main proposition that our ability is the measure of our responsibility to do good conflicts with all testimonies of our conscience. It is an indisputable truth that with the increase of sin our inability to do good increases. Now if the Pelagian teaching were true, sin would free its own victims by relieving them of their responsibility. The more sinful a man would become, the smaller would be his responsibility. One may flatter oneself here and there with such a conception, and the sinful heart may try to hide behind its own inability; the conscience continues to testify against it. It teaches that our obligation and our responsibility are independent of what we are able to do in our sinful condition. Not what we can but what we ought to be determines our responsibility.

b) To say that man by nature does not possess a moral character is to call him an animal. Everything that is not expressly a conscious choice of the will is thereby robbed of its moral quality. Now every man feels that his inclinations, his moods, his expressions of emotion are subject to the contrast between good and evil, that they possess a moral character. God's children delight in His law according to the inner man [Rom 7:22]. Sin and virtue that are not connected with the root of his life are made superficial appendages to man.

c) An uncaused choice of free will is not only metaphysically and psychologically inexplicable but also ethically worthless. If no other ground than coincidence can be given why a good deed did not turn out differently, then there is also no essential distinction in the deed itself by means of which both these products, respectively, would be produced. If the man as a character does not stand behind his act, the latter loses all value. Only as an exponent of character does an act possess the ethical quality that we are accustomed to ascribe to it.

d) The Pelagian theory leaves the universality of sin entirely unexplained. The bad example of parents and ancestors is no basis of explanation. The possibility that all have sinned, as an abstract possibility, does not explain why they all have actually sinned. It is much more plausible to assume a universal predisposition to sin as basis for the universality of sin.

e) The theory leaves no room for the activity of God's grace. It is irreligious insofar as the essence of religion is situated in our dependence (both in willing and working) on God. The prayer for the influence of God's Spirit to fit us for doing good is for the Pelagian an impossibility. Or if he can pray, he becomes in the same moment in which he prays rightly an Augustinian Christian.

5. *What are the causes of the ambiguity of Roman Catholic teaching concerning sin?*

   a) Before the Council of Trent little consensus ruled among theologians.

   b) The pronouncements of the council itself are not unambiguous.

   c) They are interpreted in different senses.

6. *In what difficulty did the Tridentine Council find itself?*

On the one hand, it had to reject the teaching of the Reformers, and on the other hand, it could not openly abandon the teaching of Augustine. And yet both agreed with each other. Augustine had taught what the Reformers taught.

7. *What appears to be the actual Roman Catholic teaching concerning sin as natural or inherent evil?*

    a) That sin in its essence must always exist in a conscious act of the will.

    b) That, consequently, indwelling concupiscence, which through the loss of original righteousness has the upper hand, can as such not yet be considered punishable sin.

    c) That the sinfulness of Adam's posterity is a status rather than a condition, or at least is only a negative condition. It exists in the lack of something that should be present; it is the absence of original righteousness.

    d) Just for that reason, it is removed in baptism *quoad materiam* [materially]. Concupiscence does remain but does not have the character of sin.

8. *What is meant by original sin, peccatum originale?*

By that we understand:

    a) The sinful, guilty state into which we have come by Adam's first sin.

    b) The inherent corruption with which, as the result of this state, we are born, is called (a) hereditary guilt, (b) hereditary pollution.

9. *Do all assume a connection between Adam's sin and ours?*

No.

    a) As was shown above, Pelagian teaching on sin denies any real connection.

    b) The older Arminian theory teaches a natural impotence inherited from Adam, which, however, does not include any guilt for which we are not responsible and for which, rather, God owes us a remedy.

    c) The later Wesleyan Arminianism no longer denied that guilt adheres to this inborn corruption but still gave no explanation regarding on what legal ground this guilt rested.

d) The New School theory teaches that the ground for their later becoming sinful is inborn in all men but that this ground in itself cannot be called sin because sin exists exclusively in the clearly conscious, intentional violation of law.

10. *What different theories have been formed to explain the data of Scripture concerning Adam's fall and our sinful condition?*

a) The federal theory, which, by positing a covenant of works, has Adam representing us in his probation, as a consequence of which his sin becomes legally our sin. This is called immediate imputation.

b) The theory of mediate imputation. This means that we are responsible for Adam's sin only insofar as we possess the same sinful nature with him.

c) The realistic theory, also called the Augustinian theory, according to which Adam's sin has become our sin not only representatively but also really because we existed in Adam and sinned with him (compare also the preexistence theory).

11. *Give the principal propositions that constitute the federal theory.*

a) Adam by nature was obliged to obey God, without thereby having any right to a reward.

b) God had created him mutable, and he also possessed no right to an immutable state.

c) His natural relationship to God already included that he, if sinning, must be punished by God.

d) All this was a natural *relationship* in which Adam stood. Now to this natural relationship a *covenant* was added by God, which contained various positive elements.

e) These positive elements were the following.

1. An element of representation. Adam stood not just for himself but, by virtue of a legal ordering of God, for all his posterity.

2. An element of probation with limited duration. While previously or otherwise Adam's period of testing could have lasted

forever with a constant possibility of a sinful choice, so now a fixed period of perseverance would have led to a condition of immutable virtue.

3. An element of reward, *ex pacto* [by covenant]. By the free ordination of God, Adam received a right to eternal life if he fulfilled the conditions of the covenant of works.

f) Now when it is said that these three elements are positive, that does not mean that within God's being there was not an inclination to reveal Himself in such unremitting kindness to man. He is the God of the covenant, and it is intrinsic to His being that He wants to be. But man had no right to expect and to demand it; insofar is the covenant of works positive.

g) By assuming the positive character of the covenant of works in this sense, we in no way intend to assert that Adam existed even for a single moment outside of the covenant of works. He was apparently created destined to be under it, and the garden in which he was placed was created to be a stage for his probation. The distinction between natural relationship and the covenant of works is logical and judicial, not temporal. That is, even when the covenant of works has served its purpose, the natural relationship remains in force in all circumstances, and also all the demands that stem from it still apply to man.

h) The organic unity that exists between Adam and his posterity is not the ground but the means for the transmission of Adam's sin to us. Now it can certainly be said that Adam must have one nature with us if he were to be our covenant head and his sin were to be imputed to us. An angel, for example, could not represent us federally. But, conversely, it does not follow that Adam, because he possesses our nature, now *must* represent us. The unity of the nature is only a *conditio sine qua non*. It is in no way the ground that excludes the possibility of the opposite. The actual relationship is such that God, with an eye to the covenant unity for which He intended humanity, also created it as a natural unity. As being reckoned in Christ by election entails that in God's time one is born again of Christ through the Spirit, so being reckoned in Adam by the covenant of works entails that in God's time one is born of Adam.

i) The ultimate legal ground for this representation in Adam cannot be specified by us. We only can say that it:

1. Was strictly juridical insofar as it reckoned with persons and not with the nature of man in the abstract.

2. Has an archetypical example in the economy of the divine persons, in which the one person appears representatively for the others.

3. Must be just simply because it is already factual. No other legal norm exists for us than the acts of God. Therefore, it is foolish to ask whether something that God does is right, as if we possessed an independent standard by which we could know that.

4. Runs completely parallel with the representation of the elect in Christ, against which no Protestant Christian can object. If one has an objection to the imputation of sin and no objection to the imputation of righteousness, one thereby betrays that the objections that one advances rest more on self-interest than on a sense of justice. The covenant of grace is nothing other than a covenant of works accomplished in Christ, the fulfillment of which is given to us by grace.

j) One can even go further and assert that in that covenant of works there were several stipulations that must be beneficial for man. As already seen,

(1) his probation was temporally limited; (2) it was concentrated in one man; (3) it was made as clear and objective as possible; (4) the reward promised was as glorious and as great as possible. For all these reasons, man cannot do otherwise than accept gratefully the covenant of works in which God placed him.

k) Through the covenant of works it is explained why the sin of our natural ancestors outside of Adam is not imputed to us. Imputation rests on the covenantal relation, and we stand in such a covenantal relation only to Adam and not to others.

l) The covenant of works explains why Christ, though He assumed a human nature, was not under the curse as we are and why He could therefore assume human nature undefiled. The covenant of works was established with human persons in Adam. Because the person of Christ is the person of the Son of God, He was not included in the covenant of works.

m) Adam's first sin as act is representatively our sin. It is just as if we had sinned in it. God reckons it so according to His justice, and this verdict of God is called the *imputation* of Adam's first sin. Imputation thus means "to put something on someone's account," whether it is required of him or is to his benefit. It is, however, only the *reatus poenae* [liability to punishment], not the *reatus culpae* [liability to guilt], of this first sin that is imputed to us. That *reatus culpae* is not transmittable. The *reatus poenae*, on the other hand, is imputed to us in the fullest sense of the word so that by this alone we are already condemned before God. It is a dangerous, and in its consequences far-reaching, error when one teaches that no one is condemned by God other than on the basis of his own inherent depravity and the guilt that is connected with it. Related to this error is the other error that all children (of whatever parents) who die before their use of reason are saved without exception. This goes a step still further than the preceding error, insofar as it denies that original corruption is condemnable but otherwise is completely on the same line. We must take a stand against this error: Something is sin or not sin, guilt or not guilt. If sin is guilt, then it is that fully. Every sin and guilt is in itself worthy of eternal death. (The parallel with Christ would require that we do not yet become fully righteous by Christ's imputed righteousness but only by our inherent righteousness that enters us based on the first.) Finally, it is illogical to say that I will not perish because of imputed original pollution but only on the basis of inherent original pollution if the latter is viewed as the necessary result of the former.

n) Original pollution, inherent corruption, was both for Adam and for us a *punishment* for the first sin. For Adam it appeared immediately; for us it can only appear when our persons come into being. It is not the only but still the principal punishment of sin, and potentially contains eternal death, since it is *separation from God* of the σάρξ, "flesh." While on the one hand it must thus be viewed as a penal consequence, on the other hand one can also view it as the basis of guilt. For there is no pollution without guilt. From all this it appears how sin perpetuates itself without end, how one sin flows from the other in order, in its turn, to give life to a third.

o) The federal theory does not deny that smaller groups of humanity, considered apart from the covenantal relation with Adam, are also in many ways in solidarity and are punished for common sins. We hold, however, that this solidarity in smaller groups is limited, does not extend down to all following generations, and does not stem from Adam through all preceding generations. Also, it is not a covenantal solidarity but it rests, so far as its legal ground is concerned, on the presence of the covenant of works. God can visit the sin of the parents upon the children, but He does not do that because, juridically, the children have sinned in their parents as they have in Adam. He can do that because the children have already forfeited all life in Adam, are under the wrath of God, and God is free in the choice of the form in which He wills to bring the punishment of sin upon them. This fact stands on a line identical to the order that God follows in the covenant of grace, where He grants His promises to children of believing parents and generally extends the grace of the covenant. This does not happen because the children are justified in the parents, but because they, too, were personally reckoned in Christ.

12. *On what grounds do we accept this theory of a covenant of works?*

a) On the general ground that, if all the data are present, it is allowable for us to connect them with each other and to give a suitable name to the connection so constructed. This is the case here. Here is a free covenant alongside the natural relationship. Although it is true that one cannot speak of a formal enacting of a covenant, God had only had to announce the covenant and that Adam was perfect before God guaranteed of itself that He accepted it.

b) All, whatever theory they may follow in this matter, admit that the right to reward, and certainly such a glorious reward, did not proceed from the natural relationship of Adam to God and, thus, had to have another foundation. However, as soon as one must agree that there was something positive, a special condescension of God, in these matters, he also accepts the covenant of works in principle, although one may still take exception to the designation.

c) The covenant of grace is the implementation of the covenant of works in the surety for us. That the former possesses the marks of a covenant is not subject to any doubt. From this, it follows that the latter must also have been a covenant. In fact, Scripture repeatedly sets the old and new covenants in opposition with each other (cf., e.g., Heb 8:8). To be sure, in such places the opposition is not directly between the covenant in Christ and that in Adam but between the new dispensation of the covenant of grace and the old. However, one must bear in mind that the old dispensation of the covenant of grace bore a legal character for Israel as a nation and, therefore, in its external form once more kept the covenant of works in view, although the core of what God established with Israel was of course the continuation of the Abrahamic revelation of the covenant of grace.

d) In Hosea 6:7, the translation "they have broken the covenant like Adam" seems to deserve preference, despite every objection.

e) The parallel that is drawn in Romans 5:12–21 between Adam and Christ, in relation to the doctrine of justification developed elsewhere by Paul, cannot be explained other than by the theory of the covenant of works. In justification, this is what was essential for Paul: that the righteousness of Christ is imputed to us without our personally contributing something to its acquisition. This applied to Adam immediately gives all the relationships of the covenant of works.

f) All other theories are subject to such objections that the federal theory is to be preferred over them.

13. *To whom does the theory of mediate imputation owe its origin, and what does it intend?*

It was constructed by the Saumurian theologians Amyraut, Cappel, and Laplace (Placaeus). For the doctrine of election, it has been pointed out how this Saumurian conception is most likely closely connected with the system of conditional satisfaction. If I posit that Christ (also in God's purpose) has made satisfaction for you conditionally, on the condition of your believing, then I posit a condition or act in man as the basis of the imputation of the righteousness of Christ, as the foundation of the state. Likewise, the doctrine of mediate imputation asserts that Adam's sin is only imputed to us because we possess with him the same depravity. The Formula of the Helvetic Consensus expressed itself against this conception decisively and unambiguously. The theory was adopted by the younger Vitringa, Venema, Stapfer, and, so it seems, by Edwards. The New School theory is associated with it.

14. *What must be observed against this theory?*

a) That it is completely untenable and explains nothing. One cannot "mediate" a thing by its own consequences. Original pollution already proceeds from Adam's sin, and yet [on this view] it will also provide the basis that we are guilty for the sin of Adam. Plainly stated, one must still end up with immediate imputation.

b) It leaves the transmission to us of Adam's corruption as an unexplained and inexplicable fact, since it does not want to view this corruption as punishment.

c) It can maintain the parallels with Christ in Romans 5 only by a non-Reformed and unbiblical conception of the covenant of grace.

d) According to it, a mediate imputation must take place of all the sins of the preceding generations to the following generations, where these are passed down to descendants.

e) If inherent corruption is already present in the descendants of Adam, and if one already thinks he is able to use that as a legal ground for explaining something else, then one no longer needs mediate imputation. In other words, the theory reasons in a circle.

15. *What has to be observed concerning the realistic or Augustinian theory?*

a) That it is a *very old* theory that goes back to Augustine and, concerning its basic principles, even further in history. Up until the elaboration of the doctrine of the covenant by Cloppenburg and

Cocceius, it was the orthodox theory with which the Reformers also agreed (with the exception of Zwingli). It does not follow from this, though, that with further knowledge of covenant theory they would have rejected it. This cannot be assumed, because these same Reformers remained creationists. The situation is simply that they had not arrived at a clear insight into the legal ground of the propagation of the sinfulness of the human race. Although God creates souls, the rational quality of these souls follows the propagation of *nature*. Here, the ethical still follows the physical; and although one continued to be convinced that this could not be unjust, one was still unable to provide a ground for this anomaly. When, later, the doctrine of covenant was applied to the original situation of man, this provided a natural explanation for this fact and was accepted gratefully by Reformed theology. It would therefore be ill-advised if we wished to go back to the Augustinian theory because of its antiquity. One might wish the same with regard to the covenant of grace, for this doctrine also is not so clearly developed by the old theologians as it was by those who were later.

b) That this theory, when it is explained, must amount to traducianism. If God creates souls, then it amounts to Materialism to maintain that these created souls in their moral quality now must be determined by a physical law of the propagation of the *body*. That our body was in Adam could still not be the legal ground why God counts us guilty with Adam. Matter or even organic life cannot rule the moral state in this way. Thus, if we wish to accept this theory, we must also become traducianists and accept that our souls are propagated from the souls of our ancestors, and so all souls go back to Adam, from his soul.

c) Even this, however, is not sufficient. If we posit that in a mysterious way all souls came from his, we do not yet have the legal ground of our condemnation. It is true that we have now made progress, in that we are no longer faced with a merely physical law of bodily reproduction. We are now faced with a higher—a metaphysical—relationship, by virtue of which soul is connected to soul and soul derives from soul, its nature with its existence. But this, too, is not a legal ground. In the legal sphere, the metaphysical cannot even so rule over the ethical. We cannot base the fact that we fall with Adam and are abandoned to perdition on God's establishment of the metaphysical law of traducianism rather than some other way. In God's way of acting, every law of reproduction is determined by strictly judicial considerations. We have to maintain this. And because this is so, we cannot remain content with a mysterious traducianism but have to move on to the terrain of Realism.

d) When we arrive there, we encounter new difficulties. The question arises how we are to think about this realistic existence of our souls in Adam's soul. Every conception one would give of that must appear, upon closer examination, to be based on a materialistic course of thought. In general, two conceptions are possible:

1. The soul of humanity was generic substance, only individualized in Adam. This point of individualization sinned for the entire substance. One must then assume, however, that this individual point controlled the entire generic substance, that it contained the whole in itself. This leads to the divisibility of souls whereby we end up with Materialism. Or one will have to accept that this point of individualization, though not controlling the entire generic substance, is nonetheless used by God to allow it to decide for the entire substance. With that, the idea of the covenant, which one wishes to exclude, enters again through the back door.

2. The second possible conception would speak of souls being included in the soul of Adam (compare what was quoted above from Shedd and the image of the different levels in a soul). This again is clearly materialistic; and, moreover, such a mode of being in Adam is not an identity on which ethical solidarity could be based. Thus Realism also does not help us over this difficulty.

e) The theory of the realistic mode of being in Adam leaves entirely unexplained how Adam's sin can be imputed to us and the sins of all our other ancestors cannot. One might say that the ground of the imputation is in the mode of being in another. If this is the case, then all being in another would have to include imputation.

If one then replies that the entire human race was only present in Adam, this is no solution to the difficulty. Complete or partial existing in another does not make the slightest difference, as long as one derives the legal ground from being in another. That there were in Adam 1,400 million people, and in Seth and Cain each only half of these 1,400 million people, makes no difference in the matter. Those who were in Seth and Cain were entirely in them. And also saying that only in Adam, with his decision, could the human race result in two lines and that later this possibility never existed again, does not provide the desired explanation. For, according to the Augustinian concept (= scriptural concept), the imputability of sin in no respect depends on the possibility that a sinner can choose either line. Our responsibility is not limited by our impotence. That I already have become impotent in Adam does not offer the least ground why the aggravation of original sin by actual sin in my grandfather would not be imputed to me, for I was also naturally existing in him. On this point, covenant theory does provide an explanation and is therefore to be preferred above the Augustinian as the best hypothesis for explaining all the facts.

f) The greatest difficulty for this theory is in the areas of Christology and soteriology. If the legal ground of our guilty standing before God is because of our really being in Adam, then this legal ground must extend to Christ. This can have a twofold consequence. One can either place the human nature of Christ that is born from Mary in the status of guilt, not only as he is surety but also for itself. Or, going still further, one can make that human nature share in the pollution that is passed over from Adam to his posterity. In both cases, the human nature of Christ must pay for itself; in the latter case, it cannot even pay for itself. A sacrifice that has to first be justified and purified is not the sacrifice pleasing to God that can bear sin and can obtain eternal life.

16. *How can one show that there was a specific promise in the covenant of works?*

a) From the analogy of Scripture. The angels who did not fall were confirmed in their state. Believers cannot fall away from the state of grace. Accordingly, we must assume that, if Adam had not fallen, the human race would have become immutably good and immortal in the strictest sense of the word.

b) Even after the covenant of works is broken, perfect keeping of the law is presented as a hypothetical means for obtaining life, a means that must work infallibly. "The man who does these things will live by them" (Lev 18:5). Now, if keeping of the law (if that were possible in the fallen state) would lead to the gift of life, then obedience in the situation before the fall must have had even more a promise of life.

c) The same follows from the parallel between what Adam should have done and what Christ has done. The latter has brought eternal life and immortality to light (2 Tim 1:10). Adam, too, would have done this if he had not succumbed in his probation.

d) Although man had no right to this promise of eternal life, still there is something in the nature of God that disposes Him to this justice-inflecting kindness[2] and takes man up into a fixed and unbreakable covenant where he cannot again fall away. This is also one of the characteristics of the concept of covenant, that there is the most intimate solidarity between the parties making the covenant. In the covenant of works, this perfect solidarity by which man would be taken up into the favor of God, incapable of being lost, is presented as the ideal. That would have been the covenant of works in its highest and most glorious unfolding if it would have become established as a covenant that could not be undone, on which Satan would no longer have an effect. The covenant of grace is distinguished from the covenant of works insofar as this absolute unity is not its end but its starting point. In Christ that unity is here, given from the beginning. But it is in view in both the covenant of works and the covenant of grace.

17. *With what punishment was breaking the covenant threatened?*

It consisted, according to Genesis 2:17, in "dying the death." Here death has to be taken in its broadest sense. One distinguishes temporal

---

2   *deze rechtsbuigende goedheid*

(bodily)/spiritual/eternal death. The general concept of death includes two elements:

a) Being cut off from the source of life.

b) Being abandoned to a process of dissolution.

The source of life for man as bearer of the image of God is God. "Life," however, can be understood in a twofold sense, in a natural and in a spiritual sense. In the natural sense, death only extends as far as the body and then only for a time, for the body of the spiritually dead must also be resurrected in natural immortality. Death in the spiritual sense extends to include both soul and body.

One may still ask whether a separate place may be assigned to eternal death. In principle, it is nothing other than the outworking of spiritual death, just as eternal life, in principle, already begins here for believers. Yet it has its distinctiveness in that it is a process in which body and soul will be inseparably united. An eternal death for the body in this dispensation is still a *contradictio in adjecto* [contradiction in the adjective]. The body must first be bound to the soul with the bonds of eternal destiny before death can reveal its full power therein.

Death, as spiritual and bodily death, made its entrance immediately after the first transgression of Adam. By his fall, Adam cut himself off, in a way incomprehensible to us, from the supply of life by the Holy Spirit, so that the Spirit departed from him. Death was the natural result of this.

18. *Under what twofold aspect must we consider Adam?*

He was at the same time a private person and *persona publica* [a public person]. In the latter respect, he represented all persons who would be born from him as human persons in the way of natural generation.

One should note the following considerations:

a) Guilt and imputation are conceptions that are not applicable to an impersonal nature, but only to persons. The law does not reckon with a nature but with persons. Conversely, the federal concept of representation is precisely a concept that is entirely personal. Accordingly, both fit together.

b) One could ask whether such a theory of imputation does not require as its reverse side that all who are counted in Adam should
be born immediately from Adam. If according to us, the organic
connection of humanity in all its branches is not the ground but
only the result and reflection of the legal relation in which it
stands before God, how is it then that the latter is so simple, the
former so complex? To this objection it must be answered that
the further development of humanity from Adam is not ruled
exclusively by the principles of the covenant of works, but that
it finds its place much more under the dispensation of the covenant of grace. Just because God had elected those persons, had
elected persons from such and such nations, and had ordained for
the earthly life of His elect such and such an environment—just
because of that, the stream of humanity had to flow through that
bed, as has occurred since Adam's fall. Thus the history of humanity does not reflect exclusively the simple relation of representation in Adam; it reflects much more complex relationships.

19. *Was it possible that Adam would have fallen before the temptation by
Satan and at a different point than the probation command?*

In the abstract, that possibility did not exist. God knew that with the
probation command Adam would be forced to a choice pointedly by the
temptation of Satan. It is another question, however, whether that possibility did not exist for Adam. There is no reason to assume that God
prevented him from sinning earlier by means of a special grace. And
as long as we cannot explain the mystery of the fall, as long as we must
confess that the temptation is the occasional cause but not the *causa
sufficiens* ("sufficient cause"), we cannot show or affirm that, considered
subjectively, an earlier fall for Adam would be impossible. It is, however,
useless to argue at length about these questions. Some theologians say
that Adam could only sin representatively at this one point.

20. *How must one view the manner in which the covenant of works was
revealed to Adam?*

As we have seen, in the covenant of works there were two elements,
one natural and one positive. Now since Adam was perfect in every respect, along with his natural relationship to God belonged a completely
clear awareness of this relationship. He knew from nature, by innate

knowledge, what God could demand of him—that he stood, as bearer of the image of God, under the moral opposition between good and evil, that upon breaking this natural relationship punishment would follow. All this and still more: He was assured of the favor of God and of life, provided that he persevered in the good. All of this Adam could know naturally. Fallen man still knows the same by nature.

It was otherwise with the actual stipulations of the covenant. These must have been communicated by God, at least in their general features, to the head of the covenant, although Scripture does not describe this explicitly. We know that the probation command was communicated (Gen 2:17). Likewise, it seems to follow from Genesis 3:22 that man had a grasp of the promise of life. Concerning the mystery of the propagation of his race, he will not have been wrongly ignorant. And concerning the deeper significance of this natural law, the Lord will surely have given him further instruction, so that he broke the covenant of works clearly aware of and certainly understanding his representative position.

21. *What should be observed concerning the abiding force of the covenant of works?*

a) Insofar as the covenant of works was a concrete application of the natural legal relation that obtains between God and man, man can never be released from it. Even where Christ fulfills the law for us, we do not become lawless creatures by this fulfillment of the law. Natural law remains in force as the rule of life for the redeemed elect. What Christ does frees us, not from the natural law under which all personal creatures as such must stand, but from the federal form of the law in which this law functioned as the means ordained by God for obtaining eternal life. By this distinction, all antinomianism is excluded.

b) Insofar as the covenant of works went beyond the natural relationship between God and man, it has passed away for those who are under the covenant of grace. Still here, too, one should distinguish carefully:

1. It has not passed away absolutely, as if they would attain to eternal life by another way than that of probation and representation. But they no longer come to that life by a probation and a representation in their natural head, Adam. Their

probation and representation has now taken place, according to God's dispensation of grace, in the supernatural head, Christ. Also, this probation is no longer an uncertain one that can have two different outcomes. Thus, if one considers believers in their head, they are saved under the same general system. If one considers them in their relation to Adam, they are saved by grace, for the juridical transfer from the one head to the other (from Adam to Christ) is not something that can in any way be derived from the covenant of works.

2. The consequences of the covenant of works for believers do not pass away at once. God's eternal judgment of damnation, under which they lie because of Adam's fall, is testified to in their conscience by the law of nature and Scripture until the hour of justification dawns and the judgment of acquittal, pronounced in Christ, is proclaimed in the same forum of the conscience. Neither can one say that what believers feel before their justification is only the general disfavor of God toward sin as breaking the law of nature, so that their sense of guilt would not be essentially different if anyone, entirely apart from the covenant of works, would have incurred the guilt for himself. This is not the case. All who are led to [recognize] their guilt know themselves to be guilty because of a federal sin. The covenant of works enters into the sense of guilt in an awakened soul, just as the awareness of satisfaction in the covenant head, Christ, becomes food for every soul that hungers and thirsts for personal righteousness. Even natural death and the necessity of the resurrection of the flesh may be viewed as consequences of, though not punishments for, Adam's breaking of the covenant. This is what the older [theologians] understood with their doctrine of the step-wise abrogation of the covenant of works.

c) The nonelect natural man is also still under the covenant of works, if one takes the covenant of works only in its broadest sense. He is not under it in the sense that his life here on earth would still be a probation, for he is put to the test and succumbed in Adam. He is one fallen, not one who is tested. He is under it insofar as his punishable culpability is at its root connected with

Adam's breaking of the covenant, whether he would acknowledge it or not. By the breaking of the covenant of works, he did not revert to his natural relationship.

Emphasis must be placed on this in yet another respect. By the covenant of works, the idea of covenant is introduced into humanity, and fellowship with God incapable of being lost and life flowing from that fellowship presented as the ideal. This ideal is not subsequently removed. God does not lower His demand and does not hypothetically waive His promise. He does not say, "Provided that, and as long as, you keep the law, you have life," but He still incites even the guilty man by keeping [before him] that lost ideal, *eternal life*. Thus the covenant idea continues at work in man's memory of a state that will be elevated above probation and change. Later, we will see that this thought is of importance for an appreciation of the Mosaic law. It stands in a certain relation to the covenant of works, and just for that reason can become a tutor [leading] to Christ, in whom the latter is realized with full glory.

22. *What have theologians taught concerning the sacraments of the covenant of works?*

Many speak of two sacraments, namely of paradise and of the tree of life (Braun, Cocceius). One arrives at this view in the following manner. Revelation 2:7 speaks of the tree of life, which is in the midst of the paradise of God. By that, Christ is meant. Apparently, therefore, the tree of life in the earthly paradise after the fall was a symbol of the power of life that is in Christ, and before the fall a sign that the power of life for man was not to be sought in himself but outside himself in God. Because, moreover, this tree is in the midst of the heavenly courtyard, it therefore has a central meaning and summarizes, as it were, all the glory and enjoyment of heaven. It will, accordingly, have formed the center point of paradise on earth, from which it follows directly that paradise itself was an image of heaven. To this attaches the widely shared conception that man, if he would have remained unfallen, would have enjoyed the state of bliss not on earth but in heaven. The sacrament thus becomes an image and seal of higher spiritual good.

Others speak of two sacraments, namely, both trees from the account of paradise (Mastricht). By the tree of knowledge of good and evil the threat was sealed; by the other tree, the promise.

Still others designate three or four sacraments, by adding to the three mentioned above the Sabbath as a seal of heavenly rest.

23. What must be observed with respect to this idea?

a) It is essential to the concept of a sacrament that the sealed sign is administered or enjoyed. Since there is no proof that man in the state of rectitude has eaten from the tree of life, and enjoying the other tree is excluded by the nature of the case, neither of the two can be called sacraments in the strict sense.

b) Further, it belongs to the concept of a sacrament that the thing signified and the sign shall not be identical, but sharply distinguished. For the Sabbath, such a distinction is difficult to maintain, for although it is in a certain sense the image of higher rest and heavenly bliss, it was at the same time a foretaste of that rest and insofar the signified thing itself.

c) That a sacrament would seal a threat is against all analogy. Even if one does not wish to maintain strictly that sacraments have to be means of grace, they will still have to be signs of God's covenantal favor in the widest sense. Therefore the tree of knowledge of good and evil, too, cannot pass for a sacrament.

d) One can certainly continue speaking of *signs* of the promised bliss. It is most obvious, then, to think of the tree of life and of paradise. The significance of the tree of life is sufficiently indicated in what has been said above.

24. From what does the tree of knowledge of good and evil derive its name?

The reason for that is not stated clearly. One could think of the following:

a) Because by this tree it would be made known and brought to light whether man would fall into the state of evil or would be confirmed in the state of immutable goodness.

b) Because by this tree man, who for the present knew evil only as an idea, could be led to the practical knowledge of evil. Or also because he, remaining unfallen, would still, by means of temptation overcome, gain clearer insight into the essence of evil as transgression of God's law and disregard of His sovereign power, and likewise would attain the highest knowledge of immutable moral goodness.

c) Because by this tree the essence of evil was, as it were, objectified for Adam. This essence of evil came most clearly to the fore when it was rid of all incidentals, harmful consequences, etc. In the usual transgression of law, the seed of evil is always more or less covered over with other things. If God had commanded Adam to treat the animals well and had made this the point of probation, then in the ill-treatment of the animals, which was in opposition to it, evil would have revealed itself as cruelty to the animals and not so directly as transgression against God. One therefore can say that the form of the probation command in itself already communicated a certain knowledge of evil, and, in contrast, of good.

25. What is the rationale for the probation command?

That God made a morally neutral thing the point of decision appears, as was just noted, to have had the purpose of ridding sin of all incidental features and to lay it bare at its core. If man sinned against this command, then it could be for no other reason than that he choose evil as evil and rejected good as good. Because God's will is for us the binding power, and love toward God should permeate all our moral relationships, a command that depended solely on God's will was extremely well suited to place man before the pointed choice: only because of God's will, or not.

Now, however, it has been proposed that *only* by such a probation command did the possibility exist for Adam to do something because of God's will. This is not the case. By the probation command, the possibility was given that it would come to light how Adam could also do good only because of God's will. Even considered apart from the probation command, Adam was obligated not do anything because of his own will, and he did nothing only because his inclination urged him to do it. In everything, the deepest motivation had to be love to God, and it was in fact so as long as Adam remained unfallen. Thus if one maintains that Adam could do something on account of God's will only through the probation command and the choice before which it placed him, then one has accepted in principle the Pelagian theory of a state of innocence in which man has inclinations that lead to doing good but in which the good as a moral power is still not yet awakened in him. Thus one must reject this view. One ought to also hold, despite all difficulties, that the abstract and in itself neutral command, "You shall not eat of it," resonated in Adam and that he, being perfectly holy, felt an inclination and natural tendency of the soul to obey the command. So for Adam, the choice was not between his inclination to eat the fruit and an abstract command that aroused no resonance in him but between two inclinations: the one toward the fruit, the other toward keeping God's command. The question, then, was which of those two he would follow. And when he followed the former, then this could only reside in the fact that the other inclination out of love for God to fulfill His command had receded or was weakened.

With this, we stand before the mystery of sin and of its first appearance. In Adam's disposition toward God Himself lies the mysterious ground of the origin of sin. In an inexplicable way, that inclination ceased, reversed. In it itself lay the beginning point of sin. The rationale for the probation command is thus to be sought in the fact that it only isolated Adam's holy disposition to fulfill God's will entirely from other considerations and influences in order, then, in a mysterious way to place before it the occasion for decision. It does not appear that the sensual inclination to eat the fruit came into conflict with the initial spiritual inclination. The way in which Satan approached Eve is not along the line of sensual inclination. He first arouses unbelief, distrust, desire for illicit knowledge, then achieves the latter with her consideration of the fruit in this respect with a view to the act of eating. From all this it is apparent what little logical warrant one has in saying that Adam and Eve could not fall other than in this way. We know absolutely nothing about how they are now fallen and could fall. How then should we presume to make a judgment about whether or not they could have fallen in another way?

26. *What significance in the account of the fall does the temptation of Satan have?*

   a) It cannot serve to explain the origin of sin rationally. To tempt is not to produce sin; usually it is the arousing of a sinful inclination already present in the heart so that it would express itself and result in action. That is not the case with Adam. A nonsinful inclination can be aroused—for example, the desire for more knowledge—but this arousal does not explain how it became sinful.

   b) It shows us that the first origin of sin is to be sought in a higher world than that of man. However, it is not true that due to this, as it is often said, the problem of the first origin of sin is shifted back out of the world of man into the world of angels. We will have to say that by this temptation a second problem is posed along with the first. We cannot understand: (1) how temptation can gain a hold on a holy man; (2) how a holy angel can fall without temptation.

   c) From the fact that the fallen angels do not again receive grace, while fallen man remains redeemable, the conclusion has naturally been drawn that sin originating from temptation can be remedied. On the contrary, sin that had no starting point outside the sinner cannot. This conclusion is obvious. It is not possible, however, to show in detail how this being and not being savable are related to the different origins of sin.

27. *From what does it appear that the serpent was not a mere animal but the instrument of a higher being?*

   a) From the entire course of the temptation. What the serpent says and does is beyond the scope of an irrational animal.

   b) The principle that the lower nature is only an image of the higher leads us to discover in the serpent an image of sin. Two traits especially make it such an image.

      1. The trait of temptation, for the serpent coils and creeps and attacks in secret.

2. The trait of poisoning, for the serpent's venom, when it is mixed with blood, can no longer be stopped in its action (Gen 3:1).

c) In the New Testament it is said, directly and indirectly, that it was Satan who tempted our first parents by means of a serpent (Rev 12:9; 20:2; Rom 16:20; John 8:44).

d) That Satan spoke by means of a serpent was therefore so that sin would reveal itself in a fitting form. Adam and Eve, who knew the character of the serpent, had to have considered that.

28. How did it happen that not only Adam but Eve also fell, and that Satan first tempted Eve?

For explaining the latter fact, one has thought of the character of the woman as more receptive. This could be true, provided that care is taken not to understand this receptivity in an ethical sense, as a greater susceptibility to evil. Eve was just as holy as Adam. That not only Adam but both our first parents sinned will also be connected to the fact that they sinned not as private persons but as representing the entire human race that would issue from them. Adam *alone* was not the origin of the human race. Nevertheless, the sin and covenant-breaking of Adam is always spoken of, and Adam is placed in contrast with Christ, because as man he represents the woman judicially.

29. In what is the material principle of Eve's or Adam's first sin to be sought?

a) This matter has been judged very differently. In general, we can anticipate from the outset that what generally constitutes the essence of sin will also have constituted the seed in this first sin. Our consideration of the probation command given above leads directly to this conclusion.

b) We find the essence of sin in general to be this: that man (1) divorces himself and his relationships from God; (2) places them as a separate center in opposition to God; (3) makes them act against God. We will have to discover all three of these traits in the first sin. We find, in fact, that Satan incites Eve to regard God's prohibition as a limitation of human rights and freedoms. In his question he presents it as worse than it is and asks whether God has also forbidden eating of *every* tree. Eve does deny that this prohibition was general, but she takes up the representation of the evil one insofar as she, in turn, presents the prohibition more strictly than it was given ("nor touch it"), speaks about it with a note of an aggrieved sense of justice, and ascribes to God the obligation above all to have to care for man's well-being ("in order that you do not die"). One sees here how all three elements mentioned above are already potentially present. The two spheres of divine justice and human justice are already separated. They are no longer concentric. This happened as soon as Eve began to reflect on the relationship there was between her own rights and freedoms and the prohibition of God. This is *temptation*: to shift the center of our lives from God to a point outside God; and this, therefore, is already the actual fall.

c) This fall *equally* underlies all the different forms in which sin immediately appears outwardly. It is, therefore, a hopeless task to say that this or that sin has been the first. At the most, one can say that this or that form of sin has manifested itself first. And so we find:

1. The manifestation of this fall is in the consciousness; there man recognizes himself as no longer living from God and for God. This is the sin of unbelief. Man no longer feels solidarity with God. He has the sense that God wishes to deceive him and therefore considers His words to be untruth.

2. The manifestation of the fall is in the alignment of the will of man. He no longer makes himself subject to God but seeks to be *like* God, above all not *less* than God.

3. The manifestation is in the emotional life of man. That he looks with lust and desire at the fruit that was forbidden by God shows how his emotion, too, functions in a wrong way, that it is no longer an enjoying of things in God but a godless losing of himself in things outside God.

d) Although all these were only manifestations of sin and not the real root itself, they still belong to the fullness of the first sin. Because it is of the essence of sin that it does not remain hidden but acts itself out, in this respect the first sin, too, had to be typical. The relation that exists between sinful disposition, sinful thoughts, the summoning up of the will, and sinful action is not external but organic. That it turns into action reveals just how deeply sin has taken hold. It is, therefore, useless speculation to ask what would have happened if Adam and Eve had not proceeded to the sinful act. Humanly speaking, the act could not have remained in abeyance.

e) The difficulty that remains in all this is here: We can certainly understand how inciting motives from the outside can be at work on man, provided that first from within, in an immediate way, the disposition is produced to which those motives are directed. God acts in this manner in the re-creation of man. He also works from the outside through His word. That can be because He has first awakened life from within in a direct manner. But Satan could not do that. He cannot reorder the inner being of man, and if he had been able to, then man could hardly be considered responsible for it. From this follows the mysteriousness of this conjoining process. Just as it is, it seems to be nothing but an enticing to outward expression of a sinful principle that was present already from within. Yet it is more. What we can understand is the working of sin from the inside out. To that precedes the penetration of sin from the outside to the inside. This precedence, this wonder, we do not understand. With us, the disposition determines the deed, both in the natural state and in regeneration; with Adam, the deed determined the disposition.

f) One may not say that Adam fell because the grace of God left him, but through his fall, one must say, Adam fell in an incomprehensible way from the grace of God.

30. *What were the consequences of Adam's first sin for himself?*

a) Coinciding immediately with the first sin, and therefore not to be called a consequence in the strict sense, was the total corruption of human nature—thus, that there was now nothing more in it that was in accord with the demand of God's law.

b) Related most closely to this was the loss of the gift of fellowship with God through the Holy Spirit. This is just the other side of what is noted in a). Both can be summarized in the proposition that man by his first sin lost the image of God—that is, insofar as it was losable.

c) This radical change in man took place not only in the reality of his condition, but it also was reflected immediately in his consciousness. Hence the accusing conscience, the fear of God, the sense of shame.

d) From His side, God also showed by actions how the condition of man and the relationship to Him was changed. Because paradise and the tree of life had been images and seals of the blessings promised in the covenant of works, man must be deprived of the sight of them. Hence banishment from paradise, the cherubim with the burning blade of a sword, and the declaration that "he may not reach out his hand and take of the tree of life."

e) The relationship of guilt is discussed above.

31. *With what designation do theologians indicate what we in Dutch call* erzonde *["hereditary sin"]?*

For that they use the term *peccatum originale* (English, "original sin").

32. *Why is this terminology more accurate than the one used in Dutch?*

Because it comports better with everything considered to be hereditary sin. If one distinguishes two things, (a) the guilt imputed to us for Adam's first sin, and (b) the corruption inherent in us as punishment for this imputed guilt, then one sees immediately that, strictly speaking, only the latter is inherited. The former is not inherited but is imputed to us. It is transmitted from Adam to us in the tribunal of God, but in an immediate way, not by heredity. *Peccatum originale* [original sin] expresses that better than hereditary sin [Dutch *erzonde*].

33. *How then is the expression* peccatum originale *[original sin] to be understood?*

a) Sin is called *peccatum originale* insofar as in its origin it stems from the root of the human race.

b) Insofar as it has originated in us, not, according to the Pelagian conception, by imitation, but is original in us. We bring it with us inherently.

c) Insofar as it is the origin of all other sin, namely actual sinning. Although the terminology was not consciously calculated by someone to express all these ideas, still it is, once in use, an excellent instrument to summarize all this in just a couple of words.

34. *In what does this original sin consist insofar as it is inherited* (= peccatum inhaerens = *hereditary pollution; in distinction from* peccatum imputatum = *hereditary guilt)?*

It consists of two parts:

a) The absence of the original righteousness. This is an inherited deficiency, a privation, the lack of something that should be there. Man is not only obliged to the bearing of punishment when he sins, because this sin is positively against God, but also because through this sin God is denied the obedience that is due Him. As was seen above, Roman Catholics make this the only element in inherited original sin.

b) The presence of positive evil that has entered in place of positive good.

35. *What must be observed concerning this second, positive element of inherent original sin?*

a) That it is sin essentially and in the proper sense of the word. In opposition to all who go along with us only halfway and here want to speak of sin in the figurative sense (the Greek fathers, the Remonstrants), one has only to pose the question whether personal guilt adheres to it. The answer to that decides everything. Whoever denies it does not hold to the biblical doctrine of inherent corruption.

b) That, nevertheless, it is not a substance that is infused into the human soul, nor a change of substance in the metaphysical sense of this word. This was the error of the Manichaeans and of Flacius Illyricus at the time of the Reformation. By making sin a substance, one outstrips one's self in zeal to maintain it as a reality. Sin as substance ceases to be sin. It is inseparable from the concept of sin in that it is within the sphere of quality and not of substance.

c) In his polemic against the Manichaeans, Augustine introduced a philosophical element into the concept of sin that subsequently has never disappeared from it. He taught not only that sin is not a substance, but further that it is deprivation of being, that is, a negation. He used here the terminology of the Neoplatonists and of Origen. This view in its turn, however, is related to the pantheistic theory that sin is limitation. Therefore, it is better to exclude this philosophical element from the concept of sin. Augustine wanted to point out that sin was not necessary and was not caused by God, and therefore he thought he had to make it negative. With him, we believe both, but deem it unnecessary to make this philosophical consideration the foundation of this belief.

1. It shows only that God need not be the cause of sin, but it does not prove that He is not the cause. There we also stand. We reject with indignation the proposition that God has in any way caused sin, but we cannot make it clear logically that He has nothing to do with the origin of sin. We recognize a mystery here.

2. It seems to us dangerous for the right view of sin to describe it as negative. It is a positive power in life.

3. Orthodox theology of later times has dropped this philosophical element in the teaching of Augustine, where it has insisted that sin should not be viewed as *mera privatio* ("mere deprivation"), but as *actuosa privatio* ("active privation").

d) Thus sin is not a substance, but it is also not mere privation. Rather, it should be called a *habitus*, a disposition, that is inherent in the substance and can be changed without essential change of the latter. Furthermore, it is a *habitus* [disposition] that forms an antithesis with what is opposed to it, from which the substance of the soul cannot escape. As it belongs to the nature of matter to possess extension, so it belongs to the nature of the substance of the human soul to possess a moral disposition, good or evil.

e) Because the sinful *habitus* is inherent in the soul as a whole, it extends to every capacity of the soul, to the entire life of the soul, and leaves nothing untouched. The corruption of sin resides not only in the lower capacities, as if the higher remain sound, but in both lower and higher. Everything is alienated from God and therefore the object of His displeasure. One calls this "total depravity." The meaning of this term is to be derived from the description we gave of the essence and the form of sin. If the distinguishing characteristic of sin is in relation to God, so total depravity will also have to be thought of in relation to God. By it is not meant:

1. That everyone is as bad as he can be or become. Although alienated from God and hostile toward God, in this hostility man can still have different grades of intensity.

2. Nor does it mean that the sinner carries about no knowledge of the will of God in his conscience. The conscience is an action of the moral consciousness of man. Even this moral consciousness is affected by sin, but since man has remained a rational being, the recognition of this fact can never disappear entirely from his consciousness. The conscience is the recognition of it. That it has remained, however, does not in the least prove that there is any good toward God in him. It is something cognitive. The conscience does operate on the will and on the emotions, but it does so through selfish motives.

3. Nor thereby is it meant that the one man cannot be more selfish than the other. All are sinful and selfish toward God, but within this circle of selfishness, in which the natural man moves, there are many concentric circles. A sinner, despite his selfishness toward God, can have a generous heart for his surroundings. Thus, while the one person includes much within himself in order to set it with himself against God, the other remains in almost complete isolation toward both God and world. There is thus a *justitia civilis* [civil righteousness], although at the same time for God everything that belongs to it is sin.

4. Sin has different forms in which it can manifest itself. No one ever has displayed all these forms in himself. The adjective "total" in the expression "total depravity" does not have in view that all possible depravity would be present in man.

Total depravity, on the other hand, does mean that by nature no love for God is present as the motivating principle of our life; that it does not dwell in us as a disposition and therefore never determines our deeds, thoughts, and words; and, conversely, that in our entire life there is an undertow of hostility toward God that only needs an external stimulus to develop into conscious opposition toward the Lord. There is no spiritual good in us.

f) Considered from another side, this inherent depravity is "inability for spiritual good." If man is sinful in everything and nothing but sinful, then from that it already follows that the sinner does no good. In this sense, inability is the impossibility of doing spiritual good. Inability, however, is also understood in another sense, namely as the impossibility of reversing the direction of one's own will, so that from being evil it would become good. In this second sense, too, man is incapable.

36. *What is meant by the distinction between natural and moral inability, and why should it be rejected?*

Many wish to deny the natural inability of man and maintain our moral inability. By that they mean that man, even in his fallen state, possesses the natural capacities that could be used in doing spiritual good. He has a rational understanding, a capacity of the will, etc. The basis for what is good is completely present in him. He is, however, morally incapable—that is, not able to put these natural capacities into operation in a right way. Against this distinction the following should be noted:

a) The opposition between moral and natural is wrong and misleading. Moral and natural do not exclude each other. Something can be both at the same time. When it is said of man that he is incapable of spiritual good, this inability is natural because it is innate to his corrupt nature and with this corrupt nature is passed down from parent to child. Whoever then denies that the inability is natural appears to deny that it is natural in any sense of the word, while he only means what is explained above.

b) One usually uses the opposition between natural and moral inability to emphasize man's responsibility. Because both adjectives, "natural" and "moral," belong with the word "inability," the appearance arises as if there are two degrees of inability, one less strong that is "moral" and one stronger called "natural." In common usage, in a more or less Pelagian manner, one associates with the term "moral" an idea of variability that is not associated with the term "natural." So the misconception arises that the inability of man for spiritual good is only a relative inability.

c) The distinction conceives of the will far too much as an abstraction. It is true that the sinful and good *habitus* [disposition] of the will have in common this abstract character of the will that they are both dispositions of the will. By that is not meant, however, that this abstraction exists in itself, apart from its inherent determination. Only if that were the case would it have any meaning to say that man is incapable because he has an *evil will* but still not incapable by nature because he has a *will*. One senses that the possession of a will takes away nothing from its inability unless one conceives of this will in a Roman Catholic-supernaturalistic sense, undetermined by nature. Then its natural presence can be viewed as a lessening of inability. The entire distinction, therefore, belongs in the Roman Catholic system and not on Reformed terrain.

d) The element of truth in it amounts to this: When it is said of man that he is spiritually incapable, then the idea appears to be present that he would want to change himself if only he could. This idea is completely wrong. In fallen man there is no spark present of this desire to change himself. Now the advocates of the distinction being discussed here say that man could do spiritual good, if only he wanted to. They stress that he is willingly evil. To place emphasis on that is far from unnecessary. Still, the idea is too much in vogue, as if spiritual inability is our fate and not our will, as if we groan under it but with the best will cannot escape it. This idea is prevalent especially in circles where one hides behind his inability and by appealing to it tries to avoid responsibility toward the gospel. Therefore, it must always be pointed out that inability and unwillingness are two sides of one and the same matter. We do not will what is good, and we cannot change our will. Still, it is not necessary, in order to put emphasis on this point, to adopt the distinction between natural and moral inability. One could just as well appeal to the continuing presence of the image of God in the broader sense. In it is already included that man has not lost his capacities of the will, intellect, and emotion.

e) The proposition that man is naturally not incapable also seems to deny that his capacities of intellect, will, etc., are weakened by sin to the greatest extent. The reason man is and remains evil is not *only* that those capacities operate in a perverse direction. Even if this moral direction were changed for a time, if with that change a change of these capacities themselves did not also take place by which they received their old power and perfection again, man could still not do a single deed that counts as perfect for God. The clarity of the intellect, the power of the will, the tone of the emotions—all are damaged in sinful man. In that, too, his inability exists, and this is one of the reasons why, for example, the good deeds of God's children here on earth are never perfect. So, even if one would accept the distinction between natural and moral, natural inability must still be maintained.

37. *Does the spiritual inability of man consist of the loss of his free will, his* liberum arbitrium?

This question should be answered in different ways. If by "free will" one means the spontaneity that the soul works from itself without compulsion, this characteristic is inseparably connected with the concept of will. An unfree, enslaved will, then, is a *contradictio in adjecto*, something that never has existed and never can exist.

If, however, by "free will" one means the abstract possibility that the will of man turns from good to evil or from evil to good, then this *liberum arbitrium* existed before the fall but no longer after the fall. This is also what theologians meant when they listed the loss of the *liberum arbitrium* as one of the consequences of sin. Man did possess the capacity to make evil from good, but not the capacity to make good again from evil. The latter, the bringing about of something good as well as the abolishing of something evil, is the exclusive prerogative of the omnipotence of God. And inasmuch as now, after his fall, man must always do evil contrary to the testimony of his conscience, and sin hinders the development and free movement of all his powers, one may speak in this sense, too, of a lack of freedom and bondage in which he exists as sinner.

38. *How can you prove this teaching of the inability of man for doing spiritual good?*

It is proven:

a) From the fact that Scripture nowhere ascribes to fallen man any capacity to do good of himself.

b) From the express declaration of Scripture that the opposite is the case. Compare John 15:4, 5; 6:44; Romans 8:7; 1 Corinthians 2:14.

c) From the form in which Scripture presents to us the doctrine of original sin. In this connection two features especially must be noted. The natural condition of sinful man is portrayed as a condition of death and as a fleshly condition. The point of comparison in both of these images includes the utter inability for spiritual good. As little as a dead person can stir or lifeless flesh can achieve an expression of life, just so little can the natural man do what is good toward God.

d) From the explanation of Scripture that man is not only negatively dead toward God and fleshly passive but also, moreover, that in this death lurks a principle of development and of hostility against God. Man, therefore, is not shackled in total inability by a single bond, but by two bonds.

e) From the necessity that the favor and fellowship of God are indispensable for man if he will produce spiritual good. As long as the wrath of God rests on him, nothing in his life can prosper. The consciousness of the judgment under which he lies, without having yet reckoned with other things, cuts off every good deed at the root.

f) From the necessity of the immediate working of grace by the Holy Spirit in regeneration. This is the other side of what was said under c). Everywhere the Holy Spirit is presented as the one who awakes life and the source of life. Nowhere in Scripture does the human soul appear as a self-changing subject, but always as an object that becomes changed from the outside by affecting grace. Hence there is spoken of a new birth, a new creation, a resurrection from the dead.

g) From the experience of the children of God. None will assert that he is capable of doing what the law demands of him. The awareness of guilt of an awakened sinner also includes, among other things, the conviction that he is bound by sin and cannot save himself. This sense of helplessness is precisely the characteristic of true repentance. Inasmuch, then, as the latter is nothing other than a coming to be aware of the real condition of man, we can infer from it that this in fact is a condition of inability.

39. *Which objections have been advanced against this doctrine of total inability?*

a) That it is incompatible with the moral responsibility of man. To this we respond with the following:

1. Inability to do good is only incompatible with responsibility if this inability has a nonmoral origin. For man this is not the case. He cannot, but that is because the direction of his will is wrong, going against God. It is not a natural capacity to will that is lacking in him, but the good moral quality of his capacity. This is what we found to be the kernel of truth in the distinction between natural and moral inability. Only we would also want to call this moral inability natural, inasmuch as it belongs to the nature of man to be moral and to be good.

2. In human judicial proceedings, which are carried out in the name of God, responsibility is not limited by inability. No judge will maintain that the guilty person was always capable of desisting from the act for which he was condemned. Nevertheless, he pronounces the verdict on it. Still more than this, the judge will rightly seek the ground for his verdict in the relationship between character and deed. That is why it always counts as valid evidence when one seeks to show that there is no correspondence between the character of the accused and the deed with which he is charged.

b) That it removes every impulse to act. However, it does so only with respect to doing acts of holiness. Hence it is presented more clearly in the New Testament than under the old covenant, when the economy was still a legal one. With respect to the activities of the soul directed toward receiving the benefits of the covenant of grace, there can be no thought of removing an impulse, simply because these activities do not come into consideration as spiritually good acts but as instrumental acts. When the demand of the covenant of grace for faith and repentance comes to someone, the meaning of it is not "perform a spiritually good deed, then you will be saved," but "acknowledge that your salvation is in Christ." Of course, it therefore remains the case for faith and repentance that in them a principle of spiritual good is present, for we teach that they are impossible without regeneration. But in the appropriation of the benefits of the covenant of grace, they do not figure under this aspect. Moreover, even the faith by which one is justified, viewed materially, is still an expression of a soul stained with sin and unrighteousness, which for its cleansing, which faith itself imparts, is in need of the righteousness of Christ. The faith, by which we are justified, is itself not righteous before God.

c) That it leads to postponing conversion. One says that it leads man to the thought, "I must wait on God's time." This, however, is by no means the case. If man lives with the consciousness of being able of his own power and on his own initiative to effect his conversion or even his regeneration, this could be for him a source of indifference and carelessness. It is capable of psychological proof that those actions that are in our own power result in no deeper movement in the life of our soul, while, on the contrary, the consciousness of inability and helpless passivity in important concerns can shake man in his deepest depths. So too here. Whoever preaches to man that he can change himself must expect that he will delay this easy change from one hour to the next. On the other hand, it can never have harmful consequences to tell man the full truth concerning his condition, provided that one but takes care that this inability itself is impressed on the conscience as guilt and responsibility.

40. From what can one determine extensively the scope of original sin?

a) Scripture everywhere teaches that all flesh is sinful and has corrupted its way before God (Job 14:4; John 3:6; Rom 3:9 ff.; 1 Kgs 8:46; Psa 143:2; Prov 20:9; Eccl 7:20; Gal 3:22; 1 John 1:8). If now every man, for whom this holds true, committed no actual sin (for example, newborn children), then that involves that they are guilty because of original sin.

b) Sin reveals itself in man so early that there can be no thought of becoming sinful by imitating the example of others. Scripture teaches that this sin clings to us from the first moment of our existence (Psa 51:5). (One should note that in this psalm David does not cite indwelling corruption as an excuse but as an aggravating circumstance for his sin of adultery.) "By nature children of wrath" (Eph 2:3; cf. Psa 58:3). That sin is nature means that it is given with our being human and follows the natural line of reproduction. Moreover, this text includes that this innate sin is under the wrath of God—thus not in the Zwinglian or Arminian sense of sickness or defect but fully doom-worthy sin.

c) The consequences of sin are common. Temporal death extends to all, even to children who did not sin in the likeness of Adam's sin. Where the consequence is present, the cause has to be present. Therefore, it was rightly seen by the Socinians and Remonstrants that, according to their system, corporal death could have no ethical meaning but must be a process of nature. Compare Romans 5:12–14. New School theology has seen itself compelled to return to this un-Christian and unscriptural position and to consider children before their use of reason to be on the same level with animals, although there are many who dare not take this position.

d) Scripture everywhere teaches that every single person has need of redemption through Christ. Now this redemption is in the first place redemption from the guilt of sin and the power of sin. If one wishes to limit the scope of original sin, then at the same time one thereby limits the necessity of redemption through Christ. Children are baptized as a sign and seal that they are washed in Christ's blood. Infant baptism, then, is a proof of the reality of original sin. To say that for children redemption is not deliverance from evil (but merely a means of preventing evil) is of no avail because it conflicts directly with the continuous significance of the means of grace. Compare John 3:3, 5, where the absolute necessity of regeneration for every person is taught (cf. Acts 17:30; Mark 16:16). If one does not believe in Christ, then one does not only then come under the wrath of God, but the wrath of God *remains* on such a person (John 3:36).

e) If some places in Scripture seem to teach that sin is not universal to man, then one must consider three things in that regard.

1. There is a *justitia civilis* [civil righteousness]. In civil matters, one can be free from intentional violation of the law without therefore being sinless before God.

2. There is a covenantal righteousness within Israel. The one who, as much as is within him, fulfills all the ceremonial commandments of the Mosaic law, possesses this covenantal righteousness, which at the most has only a typical significance but is not the righteousness of faith itself, much less the righteousness of works. Many places in the Psalms should be understood in this way.

3. There is an imputed righteousness that one possesses in Christ, which, instead of presupposing inherent righteousness, pointedly excludes it. One will be able to take all texts that speak of the righteousness and sinlessness of man back to one of these three groups.

f) Experience shows that no sinless creature has lived. Even those who deny original sin in principle cannot deny this fact and try to give it as good an explanation as possible. Every other explanation than that of an inborn depravity that extends to all is, however, unsatisfactory. That not everyone recognizes himself as such is no proof of the contrary. Sin has a blinding power by which it tries to conceal its own presence, and, on the contrary, it is a fact that progress in grace goes along with a deeper insight into sin and the inability of the natural heart.

41. *What answer should be given to the question how this inherent depravity of Adam is transmitted to us?*

a) Negatively, the answer to that question given by most Reformed theologians was that sin as something immaterial cannot lurk in the seed of the father—that therefore the propagation of sin must have another ground than the origin of the body from this seed.

b) That neither can the propagation of sin be ascribed to the sinful quality of the *actus* [act] of generation. This was the opinion of Augustine. It is tied to a one-sided view of sin as *concupiscentia carnis* [the lust of the flesh]. That the act by which a man is born is entirely sinful still need not be the cause that the product of this seed also becomes sinful, for sin is a quality and not a substance; it is resident only in the soul of those who perform the act, and in their body only insofar as it is the organic instrument of this soul. In the deed as such, taken metaphysically or physically, there is nothing sinful.

c) A third conception, likewise rejected by the leading dogmaticians, has the sinfulness of the soul taking its origin from its contact with the body. The soul would then be created without sin and first become sinful at the moment of union with the body. One then adds, however, to avoid materialistic (or, as well, traducianist) consequences, that it is not the corruption of the body or of the embryo in itself that causes sin—that it is much more the union of a soul, deprived of its original righteousness, with such a disharmonious body that does this. So, while sin in the strict sense cannot reside in the body in itself, it is possible, one thinks, that a certain condition of the body appropriated by the soul can become sin for it, because it lacks the positive holiness to suppress the passions of the flesh. And so sin would reside neither in the body in itself nor in the soul in itself but in nature, because it is just the nature of man that consists in the organic bond of body and soul. Peter Martyr Vermigli, Polanus, Benedictus Aretius, Hyperius, and Keckermann hold this view.

d) The opinion of most is that:

1. God imputes to the soul the guilt of Adam's first sin by virtue of the covenant.

2. After this has already occurred (in the judgment of God), before the actual existence of the soul, God appears, where it concerns the origination of souls, in the double capacity of creator and judge. As creator, He calls forth the substance of the soul out of nothing. As judge, He withholds from this substance, already at the point of this creation, the *habitus* of original righteousness. (Only a few, Zanchi for example, teach that for a short while the soul possesses *justitia originalis* [original righteousness], then loses it immediately thereafter.)

3. A human soul thus coming into being without original righteousness must immediately pass over into positive inherent depravity. This, therefore, is a necessary and immediate consequence of what God withholds from the soul. It is a reality, a real process, but it is not something God does to the soul, only something that the soul undergoes through the particular way in which God creates it.

This last explanation appears to us to be the most probable. We have to admit, however, that it does not remove all objections. The great difficulty present here is that one: (a) wills to keep God free from creating sin; (b) will not have the soul existing a single moment without sin. Now both conditions appear unable to be united in a consistent theory. If God does not cause sin, then it must originate in the already-existing soul. It is then a transition from not being sinful to being sinful, and if one posits this starting point and this end point, one is obliged to let the soul exist sinless for at least in a small moment of time; hence what Zanchi taught regarding the initial possession and immediately following loss of original righteousness. The difficulty here is the same as we found in the section on providence with respect to God's involvement in the evil deeds of man. There, too, we could not specify a point where the activity of God can be excluded. Everything that was in the deed had to be sustained and brought about by God, and yet at the same time this deed had to take a direction and a quality that could not be called God's work. One may transfer that to the origin of the soul, and one will feel the difficulty. One could produce images here in great number, but they would all give only a more or less accurate general view of the matter; they cannot resolve the true problem.

Further, it should be observed that the soul is not created by God outside the body but in close communion with it. Insofar as the embryo is no longer formed from the outside by the maternal organism but itself bears within itself a forming principle, this principle must be found in the soul. And insofar as the embryo developing in this way thus still constitutes a part of the maternal organism, the soul enters also into the closest connection with the latter. Herein is the truth of traducianism. Soul and body stand in the most intimate connection with each other and are organically one. So if the body still constitutes a part of the mother, then this cannot remain without influence on the soul. However, it does not seem permissible to draw this out to the point where it would also extend to the propagation of sin. Thinking, the will, and the emotions are entirely or in part tied to bodily mechanisms, from which it follows that, conversely, their development is determined by the formation of these organs. The same cannot be said of sin. It may manifest itself by means of the body, and that it manifests itself by means of the body might be a measure of its intensity. In the strict sense, sin is purely psychical in nature.

Sin belongs to the natural condition of man once it became so by the fall. Everything that belongs to nature has to reproduce. God's ordinance is such that natural traits and characteristics will be common to parents and children. Conversely, what is purely personal and individual need not reproduce. Nature is the term under which we summarize everything that is common to man. Personality is not something specific to all in the same sense, but differs for everyone. We must hold that sin is natural sin and therefore follows the line of natural reproduction. How this happens we cannot explain further. The ground on which it happens is not located only in a natural law. And the natural character of this sin does not exclude that it also takes on a personal shape for each person. All have a sinful will and a darkened intellect and a depraved emotional life, but because the personality that possesses these capacities is different in each particular instance, sin will nowhere occur equally and develop equally in two individuals.

42. *What is meant by the distinction between original sin and actual sin?*

In this contrast, "act" should be taken in a broader sense than the word usually has. Here it does not mean external action that is manifested by means of our body, but every conscious welling up of the depravity that is unconsciously present in us. Evil thoughts in this way fall under this concept of actual sins as well as evil words and deeds. One can make the following division:

I. *Peccatum Originale* [original sin]	II. *Peccatum Actualis* [actual sin]
a) Adam's first deed imputed to us = *peccatum imputatum*. b) Inherent depravity as punishment for that = *peccatum inhaerens*.	a) Sinful thoughts by which inherent depravity enters into our consciousness = *peccata interna sive cordis*. b) Sinful words and deeds by which sinful thoughts take shape externally = *peccata externa sive oris et operis*.
1. *absentia justitiae originalis* = absence of original righteousness. 2. *praesentia mali* = presence of positive evil as *habitus* [disposition].	

43. *Can one defend the distinction between "mortal sins" (peccata mortalia) and "venial sins" (peccata venialia)?*

Some of the older theologians, proceeding on the true proposition that there are degrees of intensity in the development of sin and that therefore all sins cannot be placed on the same line, wished to adopt this Roman Catholic distinction. Very quickly, however, one saw that it had a completely erroneous meaning for Rome. According to Rome, there are still sins that, considered in themselves, are not worthy of eternal death but only of temporal punishments or punishments in purgatory. Such sins are called *peccata venialia*. Contrary to this, Scripture teaches that every sin, without distinction, renders [one] guilty of death. All sins, viewed in this way, are mortal sins. There are no sins pardonable in themselves.

If, on the other hand, one wishes to call pardonable those sins for which, by God's mercy, forgiveness can be received, all sins are pardonable, the sin against the Holy Spirit excepted. Then the latter is the only mortal sin.

In Lutheran dogmatics, the distinction between *peccata mortalia* and *venialia* has yet another sense. Namely, it was taught that man can fall from the state of grace by certain transgressions because they are irreconcilable with faith. These are called *peccata mortalia*. Other sins of a less serious sort are compatible with the continuance of faith and for that reason are called *peccata venialia*. Since we reject the teaching of the falling away of the saints, we also naturally cannot accept this distinction.

44. *What should be observed concerning the distinction between sins of commission and omission (peccata commissionis et omissionis)?*

That in the strict sense true sins of omission do not exist. At the basis of all omission is a principle of commission in a wrong direction. If I love God less and forget God, then it is because something else has taken the place of God in my heart. Still, the sin of commission is greater if to this forgetting of God it adds conscious opposition to God.

45. *How is the distinction between sin committed against God and against neighbor to be judged?*

Here, too, sin against neighbor can be spoken of only in a figurative sense. If we wrong our neighbor, then this becomes sin for us only because God is involved with it. Thus the contrast between sin against God and against neighbor as a contrast between more and less grievous sin is false. Still, one can say: Provided that in our sinning against neighbor the thought of God recedes into the background, this contrast can be traced back to the preceding contrast between sins of commission and omission. Viewing the matter in this way, here, too, one could allow a distinction in degree.

46. *What should be observed concerning many additional distinctions?*

That their discussion belongs more in ethics than in the field of dogmatics. One further distinguishes:

a) Between spiritual and fleshly sins (*peccata spiritualia* and *peccata carnalia*). This distinction points to a substantive difference. Since, however, Scripture uses the terms "flesh" and "spirit" in another sense, it would be better to speak of psychological and sensual sins. According to scriptural usage, all sin is fleshly.

b) Between intentional and unintentional sins (*peccata deliberata* and *peccata fortuita*). What, however, is completely unintentional can be a consequence of sin but not a sin itself. One should only take care not to identify the contrast of intentional and unintentional with the contrast of conscious and unconscious.

c) Between blatant sin and sins that are tolerated (*peccata clemantia* and *peccata tolerantiae*). By the former one understands those sins that, because of their actual character, demand an immediate revelation of punitive justice—for example, the shedding of innocent blood, withholding from a laborer his just wages, etc., etc. The others are sins whose punishment, with the preservation of God's honor in the well-being of society, can be deferred.

d) Between reigning and nonreigning sins (*peccata regnantia* and *non regnantia*). A reigning sin is a sin that has become so strong in a person that it cannot be suppressed by any other sort of inclinations or considerations (whether they, in turn, are sinful or not). A nonreigning sin can be resisted.

47. *What opinions have been offered concerning the sin against the Holy Spirit?*

a) Some think that this sin, mentioned in Matthew 12:31, 32; Mark 3:28, 29, could only be committed during the time of Christ's presence on earth according to His human nature. This sin would then consist in a failure to appreciate the miracles of the Lord and in ascribing them to the action of Satan, although one was convinced in his heart that Christ had performed these miracles by the power of the Holy Spirit.

b) Augustine, the Melanchthonian dogmatics in the Lutheran church, and some Scottish theologians (Guthrie, Chalmers) understand by this sin against the Holy Spirit the *impoenitentia finalia*, that is, impenitence to the end. From this it would follow that anyone who dies in an unrepentant state commits this sin (cf. Calvin, *Institutes*, III, iii, 22).

c) The later Lutheran theologians held, in connection with their doctrine of the apostasy of the saints, that only the regenerate can commit the sin against the Holy Spirit, because according to their view, the state described in Hebrews 6:4–6 was that of the regenerate. The Canons of Dordt enumerate among the errors that are to be rejected the error that the regenerate could commit the sin against the Holy Spirit.

d) The Reformed conception, which since Calvin is accepted by all dogmaticians, may be presented and justified as follows:

1. The designation "sin against the Holy Spirit" is a little indefinite, for Scripture makes mention of a sin against the Holy Spirit that it nevertheless does not portray as unpardonable (Eph 4:30). In the Gospels, then, mention is also made specifically of "speaking against the Holy Spirit" (Matt 12:32) and of "blaspheming against the Holy Spirit" (Mark 3:29; Luke 12:10).

2. Apparently this blasphemy against the Holy Spirit is not persisting in sin in general but a specific form, distinguished from all other forms of unrighteousness. It takes place at a particular moment in time during this life and then makes conversion and forgiveness of sin here and on the day of judgment impossible.

3. The specific character of this sin is its intentional depreciation and blaspheming of the work of the Holy Spirit, insofar as He reveals the deity of the works of Christ and His glory. And this blaspheming of the Holy Spirit is distinguished from the blaspheming of the Lord Himself. A word spoken against the Son of Man can be forgiven; a word spoken against the Holy Spirit cannot. From this it is sufficiently evident that in order to be able to commit the sin against the Holy Spirit, one has to have recognized His personal activity and has to have entered

into a personal relationship with Him. It was rightly observed, however, that the terrible character of the sin against the Holy Spirit is not so much in the person against whom it is committed as it is in the official work of this person. Thus, he who has acknowledged his conviction concerning the truth of the gospel as the work of the Spirit and for whom, consequently, its reliability is beyond all doubt, and who nevertheless blasphemes against it, that person becomes guilty of this sin. If one rejects this specificity, then naturally every sin is a sin committed against the triune God and to this extent is also a sin against the Holy Spirit. The characteristic of intentionality and of violation of the conscience is peculiar to the sin against the Holy Spirit.

4. Still, Chrysostom and Jerome had no right to limit the possibility of committing this sin to the time of the Lord's stay on earth. The miracles He performed were a revelation of the Holy Spirit ("If I by the Spirit of God cast out devils," Matt 12:28), but the working of the Holy Spirit extended much further. He convinces of sin, righteousness, and judgment [John 16:8]. He worked by extraordinary gifts in the apostolic church. He also still works now through common and special grace. Everywhere He appears working officially under the dispensation of the gospel, the sin against Him can be committed.

5. It has been asked whether the apostasy described in Hebrews 6:4–6; 10:26–29, is to be identified with the sin against the Holy Spirit. To this a differentiating answer should be given. The Gospel teaches that there is only one unpardonable sin. If, now, the Letter to the Hebrews is speaking about an unpardonable sin, then this in general must be the same sin. Further, however, this sin, as it is described in Hebrews 6, is a particular form of the sin against the Holy Spirit that it could assume only in the apostolic age when the Spirit revealed Himself by extraordinary powers and gifts. Because one overlooked this, one so often found portrayed in this passage the state of the regenerate. What one reads here in fact exceeds the usual historical faith of our days, but therefore need not be regenerating grace.

6. Theologians have emphasized that not every blaspheming of the work of the Holy Spirit in a surge of passion or under severe temptation is to be deemed the sin against the Holy Spirit. They chose to think more of a persisting evil resistance, so that this sin becomes the end point of a willful self-hardening. It is therefore difficult to specify when and in whom unbelief has reached this stage. First John 5:16 speaks of a sin unto death, for which one shall not ask for forgiveness. So, the sin against the Holy Spirit was recognizable. It was that at least in the apostolic age, which possessed the gift of testing the spirits. It will be much more difficult to recognize it where no extraordinary gift of grace qualifies for this spiritual diagnosis. One therefore can never say decisively, "He or she has committed the sin against the Holy Spirit." It is easier to indicate the negative criterion: Truly fearing that one has made himself guilty of this sin, an expression coming from a tender conscience, is one of the signs of the latter. Because this sin is settled as a permanent disposition of malice, it is incompatible with such apprehension. Hence the rule: Only subsequently, when someone dies after persisting in that disposition, can one with reason decide that the person committed this sin.

7. To the question regarding the reason why this sin is unpardonable, a twofold answer has been given. Some seek this reason in the essence of sin itself. Because it is the activity of the Spirit that must regenerate and convert man, by blaspheming the Holy Spirit in this exercise of His office one rejects the sole means of salvation that God has ordained for man. This should not be understood as if the sinful opposition expressed in this transgression is invincible for the Holy Spirit. God's grace is stronger than every opposition. Indeed, since it works in and under the will itself, no opposition even comes into consideration so far as the metaphysical aspect of its working is concerned. Also, it should not be understood as if the sin against the Holy Spirit is so much more abhorrent that the possibility ceases for God to show mercy and let a surety intervene for it. We have no right to assert that any sin in itself is deeper than

the unfathomable mercies of God. On the other hand, one may indeed so understand it that God for wise reasons has decreed to reckon among His elect no one who would commit this deed, that He considered it to be an anomaly that such as who had come to this pernicious opposition to the Holy Spirit would nevertheless become temples of the Holy Spirit and would receive that same Spirit as pledge. So the ground of being unpardonable is in God's free ordination, which at the same time is a moral ordination. He has willed that the number of those in whom He would permit this sin would remain completely separated from the number of His children. So we have here an example of the rejection of a class. Whoever blasphemes against the Holy Spirit thereby shows that he has no part in the sacrifice of Christ, inasmuch as he does not belong to the elect. Christ has not died for him; and if he nevertheless would be saved, humanly speaking, a new sacrifice would be necessary. Hence it is said of such people that they again crucify the Son of God to themselves and put Him openly to shame (Heb 6:6).

8. By the sin against the Son of Man, contrasted with blaspheming the Holy Spirit, seems to be meant a rejection of Christ that has not developed into a clear awareness of His deity and His worthiness as the Messiah, as that is testified to the heart by the Holy Spirit. Thus Christ prayed for forgiveness for those who crucified Him because they did not know what they were doing. So, too, Paul persecuted the church of God, but he did so ignorantly, and grace was shown to him. In the Gospel, it is not said directly that the Pharisees, whom Christ warned about this sin, were actually guilty of it, but in any case it is to be presumed that they were bordering on it.

Chapter Three

The Covenant of Grace

1. *What words are used in Scripture to express the idea of the covenant, and what is their meaning?*

   a) In the Scriptures of the Old Testament, the word for covenant is בְּרִית. In the past, there was general agreement in deriving this word from the root ברה, with application of its meaning, "to cut," to the slaughter and dividing of sacrificial animals that took place in the establishment of a covenant. Compare כָּרַת בְּרִית (Gen 15:9 ff.), which literally means "to cut a covenant"; that is to say, to make a covenant by cutting up sacrificial animals.

   More recently, some have proposed a return to the indemonstrable older meaning of בְּרִית. It would then be designated a "determination" or "establishment," and thus be connected with its root that all determination is a demarcation, a cutting off, whereby the one thing is distinguished from the other. There are no places where בְּרִית occurs that compel this revision of the etymology of the word. That some deemed this necessary arose from the following: A covenant is always a reciprocal relationship between parties; this is essential to the concept. However, since one of the parties takes the initiative and, in view of His sovereign position, can regulate and promulgate this covenant relationship in advance, it appears as if "covenant" means "sovereign determination," "law," "establishment." This is not the case. Though בְּרִית may have this feature in common with חק and other similar words by which God proclaims the covenant, after the promulgation it always retains this characteristic: that the result is and remains a reciprocal relationship. With חָק, etc., that is not so. Compare the expression קוּם in Genesis 6:18; 9:9, 11; and נתן in Genesis 17:2, "to establish the covenant," "to grant the covenant." In both of these expressions, the priority lies with God in establishing the covenant. It is not He and men who mutually make the covenant. He alone makes it in His condescending goodness. But the condescending character of that goodness is seen precisely in its bringing to pass a genuine covenant. Although God gives man everything, by this giving He enables him to accept it freely and to enter the covenant relationship willingly. The covenant is unilateral in its origin, bilateral in its essence.

b) In the Septuagint, the Hebrew בְּרִית, with a few exceptions, is rendered by διαθήκη. It cannot have been the intent of the translators to replace the common concept of "covenant" with something else. In Isaiah 28:15, they translate, "We have made a covenant (διαθήκην) with hell and an agreement (συνθήκας) with death." Here διαθήκην and συνθήκας (= "treaty," "pact") are parallel, so that no doubt remains with regard to the usual meaning of the former. It means "pact," "covenant." However, διαθήκη is not the usual Greek word to express "treaty, covenant"; in fact, its occurrence with this meaning is extremely rare. The Greek generally employs συνθήκη for "pact," "covenant," and for the most part understands διαθήκη to mean "final disposition in a will." So here the Septuagint departed from the usual meaning, when it rendered בְּרִית with διαθήκη and not with συνθήκη. Other Greek translations of the Old Testament regularly use the latter; for example, Aquila and Symmachus. However, how did it come about that the Septuagint made this choice? The answer must be this: because the Greek world based the covenant idea, expressed by συνθήκη, so completely on the view of the equal standing of the parties involved that it could not simply be appropriated in order to bring it over into the sphere of thought of revelation. It first had to be altered and improved if it were to be able to do service as the translation of בְּרִית.

The distinguishing element that the priority belongs to God and that He sovereignly establishes His covenant among men is missing in the customary Greek word. The translators allowed themselves to be led by a more precise insight when they gave preference to διαθήκη over συνθήκη. By virtue of its usual sense of "testament" or "last will," the former was exceptionally well suited to focus attention on what was missing in the other word. This choice naturally elicited the objection that only for the sake of that one element one must now begin using διαθήκη with an entirely different meaning than the word had previously. This element had to be preserved. The result is therefore that the Septuagint did not change the Old Testament concept of the covenant, but, just in order to retain it intact, it modified the meaning of the Greek word διαθήκη, which originally meant "testament," and now for them became "covenant."

c) This designation became of great significance for the usage of the New Testament. In the New Testament, διαθήκη occurs in the following places: Luke 1:72; Acts 3:25; 7:8; Romans 9:4; 11:27; Galatians 3:15, 17; 4:24; Ephesians 2:12; Hebrews 7:22; 8:6, 8, 9, 10; 9:4; 13:16; Revelation 11:19. In all these passages, our theologians have translated the word with "covenant." They used "testament" as the translation of διαθήκη in Matthew 26:28; Mark 14:24; Luke 22:20; 1 Corinthians 11:25; 2 Corinthians 3:6, 14; Hebrews 9:15, 16, 17, 20; 10:29; 12:24; 13:20.

The question now is the meaning of the word in the New Testament. Two answers have been given: (a) Some maintain that everywhere in the New Testament it has retained its old classical Greek sense of "testament," "testamentary disposition," so that in the places where our theologians have translated with "covenant," it ought to be "testament." (b) Others maintain that in some places διαθήκη does indeed have the meaning of "testament," but that nonetheless in the vast majority of cases the concept of "covenant" remains in the foreground, so that there is no essential difference between the usage of the Septuagint and the New Testament. We agree with the latter view for the following reasons:

1. That in Hebrews 9:15–17, 20, διαθήκη is understood as "testament" is indisputable. There the reference is surely to the death of the maker of the testament that must come between the two, between granting the inheritance and possession of the inheritance, since a testament is only in force in case of death.

2. That διαθήκη would have this meaning in all places is *a priori* already very unlikely. If we consider how closely in its usage the New Testament links to the Septuagint, then we cannot expect anything other than that this rule will pertain here as well. As long as the contrary has not been proved, we will continue to ascribe to διαθήκη the meaning of "covenant," "treaty."

3. In many of the passages cited above, διαθήκη is used for what in the Old Testament is called בְּרִית, "covenant." Since Scripture remains the same, at least this much ought to be established: that the New Testament writers knew and used διαθήκη as the translation for בְּרִית in the sense of "covenant" (cf. Luke 1:72–73, "So that He was mindful of His holy covenant and of the oath that He swore to Abraham, our father, to give to us …"; Acts 3:25, "You are children of the prophets and of the covenant that God made with our fathers, saying to Abraham, 'And in your seed shall all families of the earth be blessed' "; cf. also Rom 9:4; Eph 2:12).

4. The concept in the third chapter of the Epistle to the Galatians speaks decisively for the translation "covenant." Consider the following: (a) There is a contrast between the διαθήκη of a man and the διαθήκη of God. Even the former no one dares to annul or change (v. 15); how much less the latter. Here the underlying thought is that where a man is bound to his obligations that he has taken upon himself, how much more is the immutable God bound to His freely made promise (cf. v. 18). (b) If one wishes to translate with "testament" here, then the contrast between a human covenant and God's covenant would include the thought that God could die. Such a thought is not applicable to God *qua talis* [as such]. That the Epistle to the Hebrews applies this to the mediator is irrelevant. Here it is not the mediator who makes the διαθήκη but God, for the

mediator appears here as the "seed to whom it was promised" (v. 19). (c) Here (v. 16) ἐπιδιατάσσεται has the meaning of "to add new conditions to those established earlier." This does not comport with the idea of a "testament," but certainly with the concept of a "covenant." (d) In Galatians 4:24, where the two covenants, the Abrahamic and the Sinaitic, are pictured under the allegory of Sarah and Hagar, the expressions employed require the meaning not of "testament" but of "covenant." One can hardly say of a testament that it gives birth to bondage or freedom, but certainly of a covenant dispensation, in consequence of which the children of the bondservants are born in a certain condition.

5. In the Epistle to the Hebrews itself, the διαθήκη is in no sense presented exclusively from the viewpoint of a testament. Only in the ninth chapter, cited above, is that the case. And even there the author moves imperceptibly from the concept of covenant to that of a testament. The motive for this was the idea of inheritance and also the idea that this inheritance was assured to us by the death of Christ. In 7:22, there is mention of a διαθήκης ἔγγυος, "a surety of the covenant"; in 8:6; 9:15; 12:24, of a διαθήκης μεσίτης, "a mediator of the covenant"—expressions that can only be interpreted in a forced manner if here, too, one wishes to retain the translation "testament." So, one sees that even in the Epistle to the Hebrews the idea of testament is in no way in the foreground.

6. That in the words of the institution of the Lord's Supper the reference is to a "covenant" and not in the first place to a "testament" will become clear from an attentive reading. Matthew 26:28 reads, τοῦτο γάρ ἐστιν τὸ αἷμά μου τῆς διαθήκης τὸ περὶ πολλῶν ἐκχυννόμενον εἰς ἄφεσιν ἁμαρτιῶν, "This is my blood of the covenant, which is shed poured out for many for the forgiveness of sins" (so also Mark 14:24). In Luke 22:20, we read, τοῦτο τὸ ποτήριον ἡ καινὴ διαθήκη ἐν τῷ αἵματί μου τὸ ὑπὲρ ὑμῶν ἐκχυννόμενον, "This cup is, by means of My blood shed for you (what the cup represents), (the essence and confirmation of) the new covenant." Here we have two sacramental expressions: The blood of the covenant stands for the covenant itself;

the cup stands for the blood. In Matthew, the expression "this is my blood of the covenant" refers back to what is recounted in Exodus 24:8, of the blood of the covenant as a type that Moses sprinkled on the altar and on the people. As the covenant between God and Israel was confirmed by the slaughter of sacrificial animals and the sprinkling of blood, so by the shedding of the blood of Christ the covenant between Him with His people and God was confirmed. Of that the Lord's Supper is a sign and a seal, and therefore the cup is said to contain the covenant blood of Christ. The Exodus passage reads: דַּם־הַבְּרִית.

7. We come now to those places where our theologians have translated the word with "testament," and where it appears to occur with approximately the same meaning we attach to the expressions "Old Testament" and "New Testament," whether we understand by this the old and new dispensations of the covenant of grace, or whether we conceive of this as a collection of writings given by God to His Church during the old and new dispensations, respectively. Second Corinthians 3:6, 14 belong to this category: "Who has also made us competent to be His ministers of the new covenant, not of the letter, but of the Spirit" ... "for to this day, in the reading of the Old Testament, the same veil remains, without it being lifted, which is done away with by Christ." Here, too, the reference can only be to a *covenant* and not to a testament. Ministers are appropriate to a covenant. Two covenants can be so contrasted that the one is presented as external, in the letter, the other as internal, in the bond of the Spirit. Accordingly, it is the Sinaitic covenant on its legal side that is distinguished here from the new, spiritual dispensation of the covenant of grace. And in verse 14, the reading of the Old Testament (better, of the old covenant) stands for the reading of the law of Moses, in which this covenant was inscribed in letters. For Israel, a veil falls over this reading. When Moses came down from the mountain and his face shone with the glory of God, he covered his face with a veil (Exod 34:29ff.). According to Paul, the purpose for this was that the Israelites should not see how that glory gradually disappeared from his face. This disappearing and passing, this

ending of the glory (v. 7), had the typical significance that the entire dispensation of the law is of a transitory nature. For the present, the Israelites could not yet know this, and therefore for them the viewing of that by which the type was pictured had to be retained. However, in the days of the New Testament, now that the veil had to fall away, a clear insight for them into the transitory character of the Old Testament dispensation was needed. But the minds of the Jews were hardened (v. 14). The veil remained; they saw Moses still covered with that veil and persisted in thinking that the old glory must shine under it, even though in reality it had already been replaced by a much more excellent glory. Here, then, "old covenant" is a metonymy for those Scriptures in which the old dispensation is expressed, and there is not the slightest reason to regress from the concept of covenant back to the idea of a testament.

8. The question still remains how, in spite of this scarcity of data, the concept "testament" could have come so much to the fore and in many expressions has been able to supplant the covenant idea. The answer: (a) The reason for this is the same as that which prompted the Greek translators to use διαθήκη everywhere for בְּרִית. They wanted to emphasize the priority and sovereignty from God's side. (b) One reasoned too much from Hebrews 9 and thought that the other passages had to conform to that one passage. (c) The influence of the Latin translation contributed to this. This translation used "*testamentum*" everywhere for διαθήκη, and this usage was followed without thinking. It would be chiefly due to this that the designation "Old Testament" and "New Testament" for both parts of Scripture became fixed. This was already the case toward the end of the second century, although Tertullian still regularly uses "Instrument" in place of "Testament."

2. *What can already be derived from this collection of scriptural data?*

a) That the relationship in which man, redeemed or to be redeemed, has to God his redeemer is a covenant relationship. Here it is not so much a matter of individual Scripture passages that deal in particular with this covenant idea as the fact that the whole of

God's revelation is governed by this idea. For the old covenant, that needs no demonstration. And if we consider that this covenant in its entirety was identical in essence with, and as to form marked by types for, the new dispensation, it will immediately become clear that it also applies to the latter.

b) In this covenant, God and man do not appear as equals, but God has the priority. His covenant with us is such that in its entirety it is at the same time a free gift to us. He gives His covenant as a testament, establishes the covenant relationship, by creating grace. From the outset, then, we need to distinguish these two elements: (1) the element of the efficacious priority of God; (2) the element of reciprocity, which is inseparable from every covenant and as a consequence of God's gracious working is also found here. All covenants, then, contain two parts. This all follows from the unique meaning of the term διαθήκη, whose introduction by the Septuagint is legitimized in the New Testament.

c) In one passage of the N.V. [Statenvertaling], the covenant dispensation of the new day is spoken of as a "testament" and thereby connected to the thought that Christ through His death and the shedding of His blood has bequeathed and sealed to us the benefits of the covenant of grace as a testament. The same thought comes to the fore in the words of institution of the Lord's Supper, although there is no mention of a testament. In both instances, it is clear that its permanence, its indissoluble character, is expressed by this idea.

3. *What different conceptions have been formed regarding the parties in this covenant of grace?*

a) Some regard God as one party and man as the other party, the latter with differing degrees of specificity.

b) A second conception makes the parties God the Father as representing the Trinity and God the Son as representing the elect. So, among others, the Westminster Larger Catechism (Q&A 31): "With whom was the covenant of grace made? The covenant of grace was made with Christ as the second Adam, and in Him with all the elect as His seed."

     c) The most common conception, especially since the time of
        Cocceius, was that there are two covenants—a covenant of re-
        demption among God the Father, the Son, and the Holy Spirit,
        and, based on that, a covenant of grace between the Triune God
        and the elect sinner, believers with their seed.

Though the second conception has much to commend it from a systematic and theological perspective, and there is also not a little found in
Scripture that favors it, the third is easier to understand and clearer,
and therefore more useful for the practical treatment of the matter.
Hodge says (*Systematic Theology*, 2:358), "This is a matter which concerns
only perspicuity of statement. There is no doctrinal difference between
those who prefer the one statement and those who prefer the other;
between those who comprise all the facts of Scripture relating to the
subject under one covenant between God and Christ as the representative of His people, and those who distribute them under two."

4. What then does one call this first covenant?

The covenant of redemption or the counsel of peace. The latter expression is drawn from Zechariah 6:13: "Even He shall build the temple of the
LORD; and He shall bear the glory, and shall sit and rule upon His throne;
and He shall be a priest upon His throne: and the *counsel of peace* shall
be between those two." This was so understood by the old divines that
the two parties are Jehovah and the man named Branch (v. 12); that the
covenant obligation of this Branch is the building of the temple of the
Lord (= the church of God); that the covenant reward would consist in
bearing the glory, as well as sitting and ruling upon a throne and being
a priest on this throne; that the stability stemming from the mutual
accord of the parties is found in the fact that all these things occur here
as they will surely come to pass. What took place here with Joshua the
son of Jehozadak was certainly a type of the Messiah. It appears, however, that the expression "the counsel of peace shall be between the two"
was wrongly applied by Cocceius and others to the agreement between
Jehovah and Christ, and should be understood of the union of the priestly and royal offices in the Messiah, by which the counsel or the covenant
of peace came into being. Even though the scriptural origin of the term
itself vanishes, in no sense does the thing need to be denied. That it is a
reality appears from the following considerations:

a) If from eternity the plan of redemption has been established in God's decree and in it the task of the Son to execute that plan, then it follows from the concept of the Trinity that an eternal communication of this idea of redemption between Father and Son and of their reciprocal good pleasure in it must be assumed. The Trinity is not after all a set of abstractions, but a living unity of living persons, and after removing all that is human that may adhere to such a conception of the counsel of peace, this still remains as the essence of the matter: There is such an eternal exchange of thought between the divine persons.

b) It is generally granted that the Triune God is the origin of the covenant of grace. If election is by preference attributed to the Father, then it seems fitting that the Son and the Holy Spirit were also involved in the eternal action from which grace flowed, in particular the former through His suretyship. This, however, is no different from what is meant by the counsel of peace.

c) There are passages in Scripture that have reference to such an eternal action in the Trinity. Paul speaks of the wondrously glorious plan of redemption and how it was hidden for ages in God, before the foundation of the world. Christ Himself speaks of the promises of the Father made to Him before His incarnation, and how He received a mission from the Father in consequence of which He came into the world. In Psalm 40, which is certified to us as messianic in the New Testament, the Christ appears saying: "Lo, I come: in the volume of the book it is written of me, I delight to do your will" [vv. 7–8]. And the Epistle to the Hebrews, citing this verse, says, "By which will we are sanctified" [10:10]. In John 17:4, the Savior declares in His prayer to the Father, "I have finished the work that you gave me to do." Cf. also Luke 2:49; 22:29 (διέθετο, appointed by way of *covenant*); Isaiah 42:1, 6, "my servant," "covenant of the people."

5. *What was the nature and scope of this counsel of peace?*

The requirement of the Father was:

a) That the Son assume our nature, enter into time with that nature, assume it in a humiliated state, and so become the surety for those specific persons whom the Father had in view in His election.

b) That the Son, who as a divine Person stood above the law, place Himself in His assumed nature under the law, that is to say, not only under the natural relationship under which man stands toward God, but under the relationship of the covenant of works, so that by active obedience He might merit eternal life. Considered in this light, the work of Christ was a fulfillment of what Adam had not fulfilled, a carrying out of the demand of the covenant of works.

c) That at the same time the Son in His human nature pay the penalty for the guilt that had come upon believers by their transgressing God's law, thus providing passive along with active obedience.

d) That the Son, after having obtained life for His own, effectually apply His merits to them by regenerating them, bringing them to repentance, working faith in them, all by the effectual influences of the Holy Spirit.

The pledge of the Father (equivalent to what was required of the Son) was:

a) That everything necessary for the assumption of human nature would be arranged; that a body would be prepared for Him.

b) That for the carrying out of His messianic offices He would be anointed with the Spirit without measure, as occurred especially at His baptism.

c) That in fulfilling His task He would be sustained and comforted, and Satan crushed under His feet.

d) That having entered into the depths of death, He would not remain there, but would arise exalted to the right hand of the Father and receive all power in heaven and on earth.

e) That through His exaltation and in His ascension, when He brought His perfect sacrifice into the heavenly sanctuary, He would be able on behalf of the Father to send the Holy Spirit in a special manner for the formation of the body of His people.

f) That by the working of that Spirit all those whom the Father had given Him would also actually come to Him and would be kept by His power, so that they cannot again fall away from His body.

g) That by this entire marvelous arrangement, in Him and through Him the highest revelation of the most glorious virtues of the Triune God would take place.

6. *What is Christ called as the result of this counsel of peace?*

"Surety." Christ also bears this name in relation to the covenant of grace, which flows from the counsel of peace. He became "surety" by taking upon Himself in eternity the obligations of His own. But He is also presented in time as the surety for believers, and appears as such where the covenant of grace between God and them is formally concluded. This suretyship thus binds the counsel of peace and the covenant of grace to each other.

"Surety" in the Greek is ἔγγυος, from γύαλον, "cupped hand," "palm of the hand." This has in view the giving of a pledge in the palm of the hand or the shaking of hands whereby one binds himself to another. (There are those, however, who doubt this derivation, cf. Cremer *in loco*; Prov 6:1). A surety, in any case, is one who makes himself personally responsible for fulfilling the obligations of another. In most places in the New Testament, the designation, "mediator," μεσίτης, also has the sense of "surety." But more on that point later in connection with the covenant of grace. For ἔγγυος, one may compare Hebrews 7:22, "Jesus has become the surety of a much better covenant." This is the only place where the word occurs for the Mediator.

7. *Is this counsel of peace the same as the decree of election?*

Some have identified these two, but wrongly so. Election has reference to the persons for whom grace and glory are intended. The counsel of peace, on the other hand, has in view the way along which, and the Mediator through whom, this grace and glory will be accomplished and effected. In election, Christ was certainly *in view* and *taken into account*, for which reason believers are said to have been chosen in Him. But in this counsel of peace, Christ is *treated* as surety. Election precedes the counsel of peace—that is, in order, naturally not in time, because in eternity there is no time. This must be the sequence, because Christ's suretyship, as His satisfaction, was particular. If election had not preceded, it would not have been particular but universal.

8. *In this counsel of peace, how has the Son become surety, conditionally or unconditionally?*

This is the question debated between Cocceius and the anti-Cocceians. Roman law recognized two kinds of surety, namely:

1. *Fidejussor.*
2. *Expromissor.*

By *fidejussio* was understood a suretyship, whereby the principal debtor remains under the debt until the actual payment. Thus, someone appears as surety in order to pay for another, provided that the person himself cannot, which still has to be determined. In consequence, the debt remains provisionally on the debtor.

By *expromissio*, on the other hand, is understood a complete and unconditional suretyship that relieves the first debtor of his obligation and transfers it immediately to the surety.

Cocceius and his school made use of this distinction to maintain their position that under the Old Testament believers did not have complete forgiveness of their sins. From Romans 3:25 it was concluded that for those believers, until the actual satisfaction of Christ, there was only a πάρεσις, a "passing over," and not an ἄφεσις, "a remission." And that came from the fact, they asserted, that Christ appeared not as *expromissor* but as *fidejussor*. Therefore, the guilt was not simply removed from the elect by His suretyship.

In contrast, the remaining Reformed theologians maintained that through His eternal suretyship the Son promised payment or satisfaction completely and unconditionally, without any withholding of benefits (Mastricht, V, I, 34).

The grounds for this latter opinion are:

a) Old Testament believers received full justification. As for all gifts of grace, the consciousness of this was less clear and robust than under the new dispensation, but there was not a difference in principle (Pss 103:4, 5; 51:2, 3, 9, 10, 11; 32:5).

b) It makes no sense to say that Christ became the surety conditionally, as if there were still any possibility that the sinner could pay for himself. In God's counsel, the sinner appeared as absolutely helpless, and therefore only an absolute suretyship could avail for anything.

One must not confuse this Cocceian view with another true opinion, namely, the view that until His justification God deals with or at least addresses the sinner as unjustified and therefore as personally guilty. Eternal suretyship is not the same as an eternal justification. The distinction between this treatment of the sinner as guilty and the Cocceian thesis is clearly apparent from this, that the former holds both under the old and under the new covenant, while the Cocceians only allowed their πάρεσις to hold for the Old Testament. We say one must consider God's treatment of the still-unjustified sinner under two points of view:

a) So far as his conscious legal relationship to God is concerned, he is a guilty person whom God condemns, who in his conscience carries about within himself the sentence of doom for his guilt, who lies under the wrath of God and is not released from his liabilities. So considered, he is not free before God through the suretyship of Christ, but must still be justified.

b) With regard to his unconscious state, in it God can already intend for him the benefits of the covenant of grace prior to his justification, on the ground of the suretyship of Christ. He does this in fact in regeneration. He treats him, therefore, as reckoned in Christ, and at the same time as someone personally guilty, who must still be justified. The explanation is to be sought in this: With the permission of a suretyship, the creditor is free to determine when and with which steps the initial debtor is to be acquitted. This is so when one has to do with a penal debt in distinction from a monetary debt. Now, in His freedom, God has determined that the sinner would not receive conscious forgiveness of guilt on the ground of the suretyship and the satisfaction of Christ until he believes and by faith is united with Christ. But that has nothing to do with the distinction between the Old and New Testament dispensations. That was true for Paul as well as for Abraham.

9. *After the Father had presented Him with the task of surety, could the Son withdraw from it or, after having accepted it, lay it down again?*

To posit this would be entirely unworthy of God. In the Trinity, complete freedom and perfect agreement go together. And the Surety was a divine and therefore immutable person. Thus Scripture also alludes to the immutability of God's counsel (Heb 6:18). The Remonstrants teach the opposite.

10. *How do you describe this counsel of peace in a few words?*

We can say that it is the agreement between the will of the Father in giving the Son as head and redeemer of the elect and the will of the Son in presenting Himself for them as surety.

11. *What does one usually associate with this counsel of peace?*

The use of sacraments by the Surety, to which some theologians devote a separate discussion. Christ made use of the sacraments of both the old and the new dispensations of the covenant of grace. Now, it goes without saying that these could not be for Him what they are for the believer. There can be no question of saving faith for Him, or of a use of the sacraments that would indicate the nourishing of faith. If we separate the counsel of peace and the covenant of grace, then for Christ the sacraments were not sacraments of the covenant of grace, but must be associated with the counsel of peace. And these are usually regarded from a twofold viewpoint.

a) That Christ subjected Himself to it accorded with His subjection to the law. It was the law, upon the fulfillment of which eternal life would follow, to which Christ subjected Himself. But that law had assumed a particular form, and for Israel it was overlaid with many positive regulations that did not otherwise belong to it essentially or necessarily. It was under that law in this specific form that Christ came. The sacraments constituted a part of that law. Hence, He was circumcised on the eighth day like every infant Jewish boy. So also is to be understood what He says to John the Baptist, "Thus it becomes us to fulfill all righteousness" (Matt 3:15).

b) At the same time, those sacraments could be construed as a means of sealing the promises made by the Father to the Son and, as some think, also of the promises, in turn, made by Christ to the Father. Hence the emphatic pronouncement at the baptism in the Jordan that the Father is well pleased with Christ.

It is not to be denied, however, that there are some objections to this conception. The difficulty is located in the following: The sacraments have a form such that they only appear to be able to seal what takes place with the believer, the members of the covenant of grace. Take, for example, baptism or circumcision. The primary thing consists in signifying and sealing a grace that cleanses from guilt and pollution. The symbolism points to regeneration, to mortifying the old man, to enlivening the new man. There is no question of this for Christ. Therefore, the symbolism of the sacraments was not appropriate to sealing or signifying anything to the Surety (cf. Witsius, *Verbonden* [*Economy of the Covenants*] II, 10). For these reasons, some theologians have endeavored to find a kind of general meaning in the sacraments that would also be applicable to Christ as surety. But in doing that, the significance of the sacrament dissipates too much; the core is lost.

The correct conception seems to us to be as follows. Removal of sin (to which the symbolism of circumcision and baptism points) can be sealed to Christ in the same sense in which, for example, it is said of Him that He was made sin. If the one can be said, then so can the other; and *insofar as* the one can be said, the other can also be said. Christ is made to be sin by the imputation of the sin of believers; that is to say, because their guilt was laid upon Him. Not the *pollution*, but the *guilt*. Considered according to His state and condition He was completely pure, but considered according to His status He was a sinner. In the language of Scripture, guilt is called "sin." And that imputed guilt lay upon Christ. Through His merit, His obedience, that guilt would be canceled. In consideration of His merits, God would take it from Him. In the state of His humiliation, Christ stood before the judgment of God as a guilt-bearing surety. Afterward, in His exalted state, He is a surety relieved of guilt who has fulfilled all righteousness. And between the states of humiliation and exaltation, therefore, lies the removal of the guilt through the judicial declaration of God, including that it satisfied. The sacraments sealed to Christ that this removal of the guilt would take place upon His merits. Circumcision and the water of baptism represented that for Him. Meanwhile, one goes too far if one says that the sacraments have sealed the forgiveness of sins to Christ. That cannot be, because in Scripture the forgiveness of sins always has a very specific meaning that is not applicable to the surety. To forgive is to remit A from punishment because B bears it. Thus it always involves remission for the person concerned. But for Christ, there was no question of remission. He must bear, endure, in order that His own people could be forgiven. To declare the debt removed because the person on whom it lay has paid it and to forgive the debt are two entirely different concepts that one may not confuse.

Therefore, one can also say that the sacraments have sealed to Christ what is depicted in them for the elect. The Father promised and assured Him that, on the basis of His merits, everything represented in the sacraments would occur in the members of His body.

Not saving faith, which there could not be in the Mediator, but faith in the broader sense as a holding to be true, and a trust in the promise of the Father, can, through the use of these signs, provide strength in Christ with respect to His human nature (cf. Matt 3:16, 17, with Matt 4:11; 17:1ff.; John 12:28; Luke 22:43).

12. *How do you define the covenant of grace?*

It is the gracious bond between the offended God and the offending sinner in which God promises salvation in the way of faith in Christ and the sinner receives this salvation by believing.

13. *What is the nature of the connection between the covenant of grace and the counsel of peace?*

a) The counsel of peace is the eternal pattern for the temporal covenant of grace. Hence many combine these two and make one covenant of them. According to our distinction, the first is eternal and the second temporal. The first is between God and the Surety; the second between the Triune God and the sinner in the Surety.

b) The counsel of peace is the secure foundation for the covenant of grace. If God had not from eternity entered into a counsel of peace with Christ the surety, then there could have been no question of a bond between God and sinful man. The counsel of peace makes the covenant of grace possible.

c) The counsel of peace secures the covenant of grace, provided that, in accordance with the indications given above, provision is made for all the means and ways that serve the establishment and implementation of the covenant of grace. Only in the way of faith can the sinner attain to the benefits of the covenant of grace. In that counsel of peace, this way of faith has now been opened for him. To Christ has been promised the Spirit, through whom the sinner will be brought to faith, and Christ has reciprocally guaranteed that the sinner will advance along this way in true faith. Thus, not only wherever the external administration of the covenant of grace is, but also its internal essence, flows from the counsel of peace.

14. *Where do the covenant of works and the covenant of grace coincide, and wherein are they to be differentiated?*

They agree:

a) In the author, who in both is God, to whom alone belongs the right to enter into such a covenant with the creature.

b) In the covenanting parties, namely God and man.

c) In the general purpose, namely the glorifying of God.

d) In the external form, namely requirement and counter-requirement, or requirement and promise.

e) In the content of the promise, namely heavenly, eternal blessedness.

They differ:

a) In the aspect under which God appears in both. In the covenant of works, God appears as creator and Lord; in the covenant of grace, as redeemer and father. In establishing the covenant of works, the motivation was God's love and benevolence toward unfallen man; in establishing the covenant of grace, God's mercy and particular grace toward the fallen creature.

b) In the aspect under which the parties appear in their relation to each other. In the covenant of works, there is no mediator; in the covenant of grace, there is.

c) In relation to the foundation on which both covenants rest, namely the covenant of grace upon the obedience of the mediator, which is firm and certain; the covenant of works on the obedience of mutable man, which is uncertain.

d) In relation to what man has to perform in this covenant. In the covenant of works, "Do this and you shall live." In the covenant of grace, on the other hand, there is only one way, the way of faith. If in the first covenant faith also functioned in the most general sense, it was as a part of merited righteousness. In the second, faith functions as the organ that takes possession.

e) In promulgation. The covenant of works was known in part from nature through the law written in the heart of man. The covenant of grace can only be known through positive revelation.

15. *What is to be understood concerning the mediator in the covenant of grace?*

"Mediator" is the translation of the Greek word *mesitēs*, μεσίτης. This is a term that does not occur in Classical Greek, but it does appear in Philo, Josephus, and later Greek writers. In the Old Testament, in the Septuagint translation, it is found once, in Job 9:33: "There is no arbiter between us who might lay His hand upon us both." The word has two somewhat different meanings.

a) That of surety, in the classical Greek, ἔγγυος (see above); that is to say, someone who, by assuming a debt, restores to a normal relationship with each other two parties divided at law. In Hebrews 8:6 it has its meaning as "He is also the mediator of a better covenant, which is confirmed with better promises." In 7:22, it is replaced: "Jesus has become surety (ἔγγυος) of a much better covenant." In 9:15 and 12:24, μεσίτης has the same meaning. Mediator, therefore, in this meaning, is "debt-assuming covenant surety." One should be sure to note this here, because the sound of the Dutch word *middelaar* has been appropriated to lead us in another direction. We think simply of mediation. But the biblical concept is much richer.

b) There is at least one place in Scripture where the term "mediator" has a meaning that corresponds more to the sound of our Dutch word: namely, the meaning of "one who makes peace between two separated, hostile parties." That passage is 1 Timothy 2:5-6, "There is one God, and there is one mediator between God and people, the man Christ Jesus, who gave Himself a ransom for all." In the counsel of peace, Christ took it upon Himself to bring to God the sinner estranged from God and hostile to God, subjectively too, through the operation of the Holy Spirit whom the Father would place at His disposal. It is therefore Christ's work to interpose Himself between the sinner and God through His servants, who preach His word, to make known what God has done and thus to lead the sinner predestined for the covenant to God. It is in this way that the ministry of Christ's word takes place. Therefore the apostle says, "Now then we are ambassadors for Christ, as though God appeals by us. We entreat you on behalf of Christ, be reconciled to God" (2 Cor 5:20).

One will then have to distinguish two stages in the mediatorship of Christ, which we can designate the mediatorship of suretyship and the mediatorship of granting access. The mediatorship of access consists in engendering faith. For the consciousness of the sinner, the mediatorship of the suretyship has its realization through the perfecting and strengthening of faith. As long as the sinner has not yet come to assured trust, he, as far as his consciousness is concerned, still stands more or less outside Christ and therefore makes use of Christ as mediator of access. On the other hand, as soon as assured trust reaches maturity, Christ will appear more as the surety, who has taken all his guilt upon Himself, in whom he is reckoned, who advocates for him in the covenant as his representative. From this point of view proceed those who regard the covenant of grace as a continuation of the counsel of peace and speak of an eternal covenant of grace established with Christ as covenant head. For this view, there are points of contact enough in Scripture, to some of which we will refer briefly in what follows. In Isaiah 42:6, Christ is called a "covenant of the people." The Messiah realizes in Himself the covenant of God's people, the spiritual, the true Israel. In Romans 5, Paul draws a parallel between Adam as the head of the first and Christ as the head of the second covenant. In 1 Corinthians 15, the same principle is also presupposed. All that is obtained for believers through Christ, insofar as it does not include moral imperfection, is first realized in Christ

Himself. There could of course be no repentance and sanctification in Christ the Mediator, for He was completely spotless, without sin. But if we exclude this, there are nonetheless many steps on the path to the glorification of God's children that were first trodden by Christ and then by those in the covenant. They have become one with Him in the likeness of His death and His resurrection; they have been buried with Him by baptism into death (Rom 6:3). The Spirit of Him who raised Jesus from the dead, will also make alive their mortal bodies, through His Spirit who lives in them [Rom 8:11]. In His resurrection, which justified Him, they are also justified with Him; they are seated and exalted with Him in heaven. They carry about in their bodies the dying of the Lord Jesus, so that the life of Jesus may also be revealed in their bodies [2 Cor 4:10]. He has become the firstfruits of them that slept [1 Cor 15:20]. In Galatians 3:16–17, the apostle says that the covenant was previously confirmed by God in Christ, that Christ is the "seed," and that in this word in the singular the oneness of believers with their Mediator in the covenant promise of God is intended by God Himself.

It is not necessary to make use of these scriptural data just for the doctrine of an eternal covenant of grace with Christ as the head. One can also deal with them properly in other ways. But it is necessary to place more emphasis on the mediatorship of Christ as surety than is usually done. That has been pushed back too much into the counsel of peace. In Scripture, it is a present reality that governs the Christian life. In that reality, the doctrine of a covenant of grace in Christ as covenant head has its enduring worth that may not be undervalued.

16. *How can Paul, in speaking of the covenant of grace, express himself in Galatians 3:20 as if no mediator came into consideration?*

It does in fact appear as if the reasoning of the apostle here excludes any mediatorship in the covenant of grace. He sets the law as was promulgated at Sinai over against the promise as was given to Abraham—thus over against the covenant of grace. He argues that this law cannot have been intended to force in a new covenant in place of the old. For, he says, with the law there is a mediator who brings two parties together, and in His arrangement of grace God is always the only party. God is one.

It should be remembered, however, that this argument only excludes a human mediator for the covenant of grace. In the covenant of grace, there is no mediator as there was with the law, namely, no mediator like Moses. There can, however, be a divine Mediator, for that there is such takes away nothing from the truth that in the covenant of grace God accounts for everything. The Mediator is Himself God. In the Mediator, it is but another person of the Trinity who Himself comes to accomplish the ministry of the covenant. The covenant of grace is Trinitarian in nature; it makes the Trinity to emerge in sharp relief.

17. How does Christ appear here as Mediator?

Not as the *Logos* considered apart from His incarnation, but as the *Logos* to become flesh or having become flesh. That is precisely the distinction between the counsel of peace and the covenant of grace. In the former, the Second Person of the Trinity appears as the *Logos* and decides concerning His incarnation. In the counsel of peace, the incarnation was an outcome, but in the covenant of grace it is a given, something of a presupposition. It makes no difference whether it has actually taken place or is still in the future; in both cases it is in the same manner made the basis for all of God's dealings with man. Therefore, the first announcement of this covenant already points forward to the seed of the woman, and not back to the eternal *Logos* who had assumed the suretyship. With Abraham, too, it points not backward but forward. It is entirely in accord with this principle that the Apostle Paul says in Galatians 3:16–17: The promises previously confirmed by God were in Christ. The covenant has its unity in Christ as Mediator, Surety, Covenant Head, but then in Christ as He becomes a figure in history—He has been promised beforehand and appeared in the fullness of time. Thus, when one calls Christ the surety of the covenant of grace, he must keep this historical Christ in view. On this point, the doctrine of an eternal covenant of grace is the weakest because it has the believer living too much in eternity.

18. With whom is the covenant of grace established in this Mediator?

The most and best Reformed theologians answer: with the elect sinner. To establish this historical fact, we append here a number of definitions from the heyday of Reformed covenant theology.

The title of Olevianus's primary writing, published after his death in Geneva (1585), is *On the Essence of the Covenant of Grace Between God and the Elect.*

Witsius: "The covenant of grace is an arrangement between God and the elect sinner, in which God declares His free and willing pleasure concerning eternal salvation, and to give all things pertaining thereto to those in covenant with Him, gratuitously, through and for the sake of Christ the mediator; and man by a true faith assents to that good pleasure."

Braun: "The gracious accord by which God promises eternal life to man, sinful and elect from eternity, on the condition of faith in Christ the surety and whereby the elect man in true faith assents to this, and with full confidence asks eternal life from God."

Lampe: "What is the covenant of grace? The accord between the Triune God and the elect sinner, in which God, for Christ's sake, promises the sinner everything he needs for his salvation, the sinner assents to these promises, and thus receives a right to claim them."

Mastricht: "That gracious accord between the Triune God and the elect sinner in and through which He to the elect, each in particular, ... promises redemption, calling, regeneration, and other means to salvation, absolutely and without limit, without any prerequisite conditions," etc. (V, I, 14).[1]

A Marck: "The gracious accord between God and the elect sinner, revealed to men through the gospel in different ways and stages since the fall, in which, for the sake of the suretyship of Christ, to those who believe in Him and repent all saving grace and glory is assigned, sealed by the use of the sacraments, and brought about through the activity of the church."

Franken: "Who are the involved parties? The blessed God and the elect sinner. ... The gracious agreement of God with the elect sinner, in which God on His side, for the sake of the merits of Christ, promises him complete salvation and a sinner on his side accepts this promise."

Brakel: "An ... accord ... between God on the one side ... and the one who is elect on the other ... in which God promises deliverance from all evil and the dispensing of all beatitude by grace," etc.

---

1   Editor's note: There is a substantial ellipsis in the transcription from here to the point indicated below in the answer to question 19. I have supplied this missing material from the handwritten 1890 edition.

19. *What motives led to thus presenting the covenant, while at the same time in this way one was threatened with difficulty in practice?*

   a) One wished to emphasize that only the elect are partakers of the entire essence of the covenant and all the benefits of the covenant. In them alone does the covenant reach its ideal. It must be realized in them according to its essence, so that it consists not only in an external relationship but also[2] in an internal affinity and bond. Because they had this in view and only this appeared to them to express the full concept of covenant, the theologians therefore said: between God and the elect. One will have to agree that this is a scriptural idea (cf. Jer 31:31-34; Heb 8:8-12).

   b) A second consideration was that, in a very special sense, the covenant of grace is presented in Scripture as an indissoluble covenant, in which God always keeps His promise. Mountains may depart and hills be removed; the covenant of His peace does not depart and is not removed [Isa 54:10]. Now, one could suppose this is intended conditionally, namely, that God keeps His promise if we meet our obligation. But that would not be a specific mark of the covenant of grace; that could apply just as well to the covenant of works. And the covenant of grace is distinguished from the covenant of works precisely by the fact that it no longer depends on human willing or running but on the faithfulness of God.

20. *Did the theologians mean with this definition that all the nonelect had no relationship to the covenant of grace?*

Although for some of them the concept is so tightly drawn that they in fact arrive at this assertion, one cannot say that for most of them. They had an eye for the other side and viewed the covenant as an entity that is ongoing historically. Then it goes without saying that the definition reads: with believers and their seed. The covenant of grace proceeds in families. It extends from the fathers to the children, to distant generations.

---

2 The transcription continues at this point (see the preceding footnote).

21. In what does the great difficulty of the doctrine of the covenant of grace lie?

In reconciling these two aspects with each other. Everyone senses that we may not place them side by side unrelated. There must be a certain relationship. Although the two aspects cannot be presented as completely overlapping, they must still be brought into connection with each other.

22. Which conceptions fail to do justice to this requirement?

a) All those views that proceed from the idea of an external covenant of grace or a national covenant, or however one may term it, in which one could have a right standing merely by fulfilling external religious obligations, somewhat in the Roman Catholic sense.

This idea can be developed in different forms and worked out with greater or lesser consistency. The result is always that one has to take for granted a dualism as a consequence. That is to say, there are then two circles distinct from each other, and the external one is not penetrated by the internal and accompanied by it at any point. If I tell people that God has established an external covenant with them, that of itself will rob the claim of the internal covenant of its force, so that for many the essence of the covenant of grace becomes a lifeless thing with which they no longer feel any personal connection. Moreover, with this external view, it does not matter where one draws the line between these two circles. One can do that with the Lord's Supper, so that the use of this covenant seal is tied to the spiritual, internal covenant, but baptism and profession of faith with the external. One can also do this with profession, so that it and the Lord's Supper continue to go together as both pertain to the internal covenant, while baptism is drawn into the external. Or one may not draw the line through any external means and attach the sacraments entirely to the external. This occurs when one teaches that historical faith is sufficient for the person himself to come to the Lord's Supper. In all these cases, one falls into an untenable ambiguity.

b) Nor is the other extreme to be commended. This occurs when in practice one reckons only with the essence of the covenant of grace, with election and the sharing of the elect in the promises.

Brakel is a representative of this line of thinking. Not only does he rightly deny that God can establish an external covenant with the sinner, but he also decisively denies that the nonelect unconverted are in any sense in the covenant. Later, he also says in connection with the doctrine of baptism that it seals only the elect.

23. *What distinctions have the Reformed generally made in order to do justice to both sides of this matter?*

A threefold distinction may be considered here:

a) Between an external and an internal side of the covenant of grace.

b) Between the essence and the administration of the covenant of grace.

c) Between an absolute and a conditional covenant of grace.

24. *Where does one find the first distinction?*

It is found, among others, in Mastricht (V, I, 28): "[B]ecause the required obligations of the covenant of grace are accepted by some (that is to say, in a spiritual sense and with sincere faith) or merely with an external profession of the mouth ... a twofold or double fellowship of the covenant of grace arises here: the one *total* or, as others say, *internal*, whereby those who sincerely, that is, with heart and mouth, pledge and promise the requirements of covenant making, or who are children of the promise, become partakers of all the promises, both spiritually and physically ... the other *partial* or only *external*, whereby the children of the kingdom who do not accept the conditions of the covenant sincerely but only with the mouth, without the heart, or just with an outward profession, become partakers of external ecclesiastical privileges and only temporal benefits." He points to 1 Corinthians 10:1-6; Psalm 95:9-11; Judas Iscariot, Simon the Magician, temporary believers, the branches that do not bear fruit in Christ, and the many who are called alongside the few who are chosen.

25. *Where is the second distinction found?*

In Olevianus, among others. In his work, the title of which is cited above, he distinguishes between the *essence* of the covenant of grace and the *attestations* of the covenant of grace, and deals first with the former and then with the latter. Turretin also expresses himself in this sense ([*Institutes*] XII, VI, 5): "They (the Reformed) propose further that this covenant can be regarded in two ways, according to its internal essence and its outward administration. The first matches the internal call and the invisible church of the elect that is formed by it. The second answers to the external call and the visible church of the called. In the latter respect, the covenant has in view only the proclamation and offer that takes place through the external call, and the external benefits that result from it in the preaching of the word, the administration of the sacraments, and the communion in holy things, in which as many participate among the people or in the church as hold to the same confession. And taken in this way, the covenant extends to many reprobates who remain in the visible church. In the former respect, on the other hand, it extends further to the acceptance, communication, and reception of all the covenant benefits and internal communion with Christ by faith, and in this sense pertains only to the elect."

26. With whom, among others, does one find the third distinction mentioned above?

The distinction between the conditional and the absolute covenant can be found, among others, in Koelman, who formulates it in the following words: "To avoid misconception, one must know these three things: *First*, that when reference is made to an external and internal covenant, or rather to making an external and internal covenant, by that two covenants are not understood, the one the covenant of grace, the other a covenant distinguished from it ... for the covenant is one and the same. But they all are not in the covenant in one and the same way. Some are in it only through external privileges, but some are also in it through whole-hearted acceptance, for the enjoyment of the saving benefits by means of those privileges. *Second*, if we say that some are in the covenant with God outwardly, through visible confession and conditionally, then we do not understand that, with respect to the covenant, as if they were not truly in the covenant, and as if that conditional covenant did not have the complete essence and nature of a covenant. But we have in view the thing promised in the covenant, which no one receives but those who fulfill the condition of the covenant. *Third*, if we say that those who are inwardly in the covenant, are actually (*realiter*) in the covenant, that word 'actually' has in view the actual fruit of the fulfilled covenant.

And so those who are in the covenant only outwardly are not actually in the covenant, for God never gave it to them, and did not intend to give to them the blessing that was promised in the covenant ... even so, they are still actually and truly in the covenant, that is, they are truly and actually bound by their assenting profession to fulfill the covenant. The commandments and threats of the covenant of grace impose on them an actual obligation to obey or suffer punishment, as the promise of the covenant imposes on them the obligation to believe the promise."

27. How is the first of these conceptions to be judged?

That it is unsatisfactory is immediately obvious. It makes it appear as though the members of the visible church who are not elect and not regenerate are regarded as covenant members only by coincidence and human shortsightedness. They are in the covenant with the mouth, outwardly, etc. Thus in our eyes they are covenant members, but not before God. They possess at most from the covenant that they share in the external privileges of the church. But that does not address the point in question. The question is precisely *whether* and *how* the nonelect, the unregenerate, the members of the visible church, are also members of the covenant *before God*.

28. What is to be brought out regarding the second distinction?

a) The distinction between the *essence* and the *administration* of the covenant certainly expresses a correct idea, but the terms are not entirely clear. They do not form a contrast. "Essence" and "form" would do that. But essence–administration can be understood in more than one way and does not provide a clear idea. It can be conceived of as the contrast between the invisible and the visible church, as Turretin seems to intend. Then essence and manifestation would be clearer. It can also be conceived of as the contrast between the purpose and its realization or proclamation. Olevianus takes it in this way. Why not [speak of] the purpose of the covenant of grace and the means for its realization? However, we keep in view the idea expressed in the distinction in order to return to it later.

b) Also left unresolved here is whether and in what sense before God they are covenant members who have nothing to do with this essence of the covenant rooted in election.

c) The identification of the administration of the covenant with the external call is skewed. All those who are outwardly called are not yet under the administration of the covenant; all are not yet externally in the covenant, or however one may designate it. A child born into the covenant is a covenant member, but is a pagan to whom the external call comes through missions likewise a covenant member? That cannot be. Outward calling and visible church do not coincide. One senses the lack of clarity in the distinction best in Turretin when one considers that on the one hand he identifies this administration of the covenant with the visible church and on the other hand with the external call. But then the visible church and those who are outwardly called must be identical. Which of course, according to Turretin himself, they are not.

29. How should the third distinction be assessed?

One must grant that of the three it is the most clear and useful. Naturally, it can also be misused. And in Koelman it in fact appears in an adulterated form that borders on the external covenant and then gives rise to all kinds of contradictions, so that one can hardly agree with Koelman when he asserts: "I do not intend two covenants but one."

That had two causes. First, at work here is the principle of a national covenant, a state church. As an argument to prove that the unregenerate and nonelect are in the covenant, Koelman employs the thesis that under the New Testament, God will accept whole nations and kingdoms as members in covenant with Him. This is certainly an Old Testament idea. Further, in play here was an overreaction against the Labadists, who fell into the opposite extreme. But apart from this erroneous school, there is a sound principle in the distinction.

30. What can you say further to clarify what is intended by these distinctions?

a) We shall first have to make clear that the concept of covenant can be taken in a twofold sense. It can be a relationship between two parties with reciprocal conditions, thus is an entity in the sphere of law. The covenant in this sense exists even when nothing has yet been done to realize its purpose; it exists as a relationship, as something that ought to be. And the persons or parties who live under such a relationship are in the covenant because they are under the reciprocal conditions. In the sphere of law, everything is considered and regulated in an objective manner. There one does not inquire about inclination or interest toward one or another relationship, but exclusively about the relationship itself.

b) Covenant can, however, also be taken in another sense, as meaning the same as *fellowship*. Then it does not have in view what should be and is expected and required but what is actually present in the sphere of being. Every covenant in the first sense looks forward and is intended to become a covenant in this second sense, a living fellowship or a fellowship of life. What the first is in law, the second is in actuality. The first remains barren and misses its purpose entirely if it does not move on to the second.

c) The application of this distinction to the concept of the covenant of grace can shed light on many points over which the diverging answers of the theologians have spread darkness. One asks, "Who is in the covenant of grace?" If one has in view the legal side of the matter, that is, if one poses the question, "Who is included and of whom can it be expected that they will live in the covenant?," the answer is, "All who by stipulation or by birth have become members of the covenant"; thus, believers and their seed. If one looks at the actual side, one poses the question, "In whom has this legal relationship become a living fellowship?" The answer is, "All who have been regenerated and have faith, at least in principle." Here, therefore, one has the two sides of the matter that emerged with greater or lesser clarity in the three distinctions discussed above. And one perceives how, according as the emphasis fell more on the one side or the other, the answer to the question, "Who are in the covenant?," had to turn out differently. So it was argued on the one side: All the members of the visible church are in; on the other side: Only they who have saving faith are in. Both of these are true, but in a different sense. This will appear further.

d) From this it now appears how one has to judge the concepts "being-outwardly-in," "being-under-the-administration," and "being-conditionally-in." "Being-outwardly-in" contrasts with "being-inwardly-in." The latter means covenant fellowship and describes this as something inward. "Being-outwardly-in," however, expresses precisely what is properly meant. The covenant, then, lays claim to the whole of the life of man, even where it has not yet come to real covenant fellowship. To be under the administration of the covenant has to mean that the covenant begins to be realized. Covenant fellowship first occurs for us and engages us as covenant promise and covenant requirement. In Olevianus, the covenant idea is borne entirely by this conception. It has to do with the inward relationship with God, with the essence of the covenant, covenant fellowship. In order that this be realized, the attestations of the covenant of grace come to us. The administration and the essence stand in the closest relationship with each other.

"Being-conditionally-in" the covenant of grace is an improper—better, an incorrect—way of speaking. One is in the covenant or one is not in it. A middle status lying between the two is impossible. But the intention is as follows. Being in covenant relationship is a being conditionally in covenant fellowship. When from man's side the covenant is appropriated by faith, the covenant emerges in its fullness, as it should do according to its design. So, man is first under and then in it. He is under the promise and the requirement, then he enters into the benefits of the covenant. But he is under the former completely, and he comes into the latter completely. The transition from the one to the other is in a certain sense tied to a condition.

e) One enters into a covenant in two ways: by freely acceding to and accepting its condition, or by being born into it. In the former case, the inclination to live in the covenant is of course to be assumed. Applied to the covenant of grace, this leads us to the conclusion that an adult hitherto standing outside the covenant relationship can only enter it by faith. By his entering into the covenant, he shows that he will live in and according to the covenant, and this he cannot rightly do without faith. It is thus to be assumed that here entrance into covenant relationship and entrance into covenant fellowship coincide. The first exercise of faith leads, of itself, to both. Supposing that acquiescing in the covenant was not sincere, that all faith was lacking, then the covenant relationship would continue to apply, but from the first moment on it would be a violated and broken covenant relationship; and fellowship, the essence of the covenant, would be lacking. In the second case, where one is born into the covenant, the covenant relationship precedes, in the expectation that covenant fellowship will follow later, so far as conscious life is concerned. That it can already be present earlier in the unconscious life of the covenant child is therefore not denied.

f) If one is under the covenant relationship and covenant fellowship, the essence of the covenant, is missing, one is nevertheless treated as a covenant member in the sense that nonobservance of the covenant incurs guilt and causes covenant-breaking. This explains how there is covenant-breaking and yet no apostasy of the saints. Note carefully, not merely temporary covenant-breaking is in view—for in believers that is compatible with perseverance—but final covenant-breaking. Everyone who is under the covenant is treated as though he lived in the covenant. It is so with the covenant of works, and is so with the covenant of grace. And therefore, one does not have the right to say that the nonelect are in no way in the covenant. For them there is no true covenant fellowship, but their accountability is determined according to the covenant relationship. This accountability is greater than that which an ordinary person outside the covenant has in relation to the gospel. Being-in-the-covenant may never be diminished to a life under the offer of the gospel. It is more than that.

g) The issue here comes down to finding the connection between this being-in-the-covenant and living in the fellowship of the covenant. It is obvious that there must be a close tie. There cannot be a dualism between these two. By freely entering the covenant, these two must immediately coincide if no discrepancy is to arise. But what if one is born into the covenant? Is then the one possible without the other? We here face the difficulty that the covenant relationship appears powerless to bring covenant fellowship in its wake. We get a covenant that remains unfruitful. A barren, juridical relationship, an "ought to be," appears to take the place of the glorious realities that mention of the covenant brings to our minds. This is in fact the point where, by means of the covenant idea, the Pelagian error could gain access to Reformed doctrine. If the covenant idea is in fact the all-encompassing expression of life under and in grace, how then can it be that in this form it comes to us first of all as something that "ought to be," a relationship that still lacks realization?

When in the realm of nature one enters into a commitment with someone else, one has the reasonable expectation that the person will keep to that commitment, that it will not remain an abstract concept, but something that is realized in life and becomes a relationship in life. Consequently, here, too, there is a difficulty. It makes no sense that God enters into a covenant with man unable to help himself, yet in terms of which faith and repentance are expected of him, if absolutely no provision is made to cause the covenant to become reality. But the Lord does not establish a covenant of grace with believers and their seed only in order to obligate them from the heart and increase their responsibility toward the gospel. The covenant relationship must be something more than a bond of obligation.

h) In order to remove these two difficulties, one will have to emphasize that in this covenant of grace, God in fact makes promises that enable the members of His covenant to really live in the covenant, to receive its essence, to make it a reality. God, when He establishes the covenant of grace with a believer, appears as a *giving*, a *gracious*, and *promising* God, for He witnesses in the gospel that it is He Himself who has generated faith in the soul, whereby the covenant is sealed and received. He further assures such believers that He is not only their God, but also the God of their seed. And that if they raise up their seed for Him, He will grant the grace of regeneration, whereby the covenant will be perpetuated, and that not only as a bond but also as a real, spiritual covenant fellowship. God has pledged to the members of His covenant His promises of regenerating grace for their seed as well. From their seed, He will call believers to Himself. And therefore, that seed is not merely under a conditional bond, but also under an absolute promise. For those who do not venture to accept this, the covenant concept must more and more lose its spiritual and gracious character. They make it an arid system of obligations, in which all comforting and enlivening power is lacking. Because God has thus established in the parents the covenant with the children, He has also given the promise that He will bestow the operations of His grace in the line of the covenant. He can also work outside that line and does so frequently. But then it is a free action, not to be explained further for us. It is an establishing of the covenant anew. In accordance with His sovereignty, He can also make exceptions within the sphere of the covenant. However, if experience later shows such exceptions, we may not seize on them to say, "God's covenant was powerless; His word has failed." In such a case, we must always follow the rule of Paul in Romans 9:6–8. The presumption is always that the children of the covenant, who are under the covenant bond, will also be led into covenant fellowship. Election is free, but it is not on that account arbitrary. Therefore, we say: Of those born under the covenant, not only is it required with double force that they believe and repent, but it is likewise expected and prayed for with a double confidence that they will be regenerated in order to be able to believe and repent.

i) Only in this way do we obtain an organic connection between being-under-the-covenant and being-in-the-covenant, between bond and fellowship. The former is, as it were, the shadow that the latter casts. The covenant relationship into which a child enters already at birth is the image of the covenant fellowship in which it is expected to live later. And on the basis of that expectation or, more accurately, on the basis of the promise of God that entitles us to that expectation, such a child receives baptism as a seal of the covenant. The child is regarded as being in the covenant. As it matures, it is again and again pointed out how it lives under the promises and how the reasonable expectation is that it will live in the covenant. The attestations of the covenant precede the substance of the covenant. These promises and this requirement as they apply to the child are precisely the means appointed by God as the way to be traveled, along which the communion of the covenant, the being "in" in a spiritual sense, is reached. Being-under-the-covenant not only precedes, but it is also instrumental. An impetus proceeds from this that is greater than from the preaching of the word that does not come to someone in this manner, in the way of the covenant.

j) Of the children born under the covenant, as long as they are children and if they die as children, it is to be assumed that they also share, or will have a share, in the spiritual fellowship of the covenant and the salvation coupled with it. On this basis, the Reformed church assumes the salvation of the children of the covenant who die in infancy. Here, too, there could be exceptions, but one may not for this reason allow himself to be robbed of comfort.

For the children of the covenant who are grown, matters are different. God's ordinance is such that only by exercising faith can each personally obtain assurance of his share in the benefits of the covenant. If for a long time he remains unconverted and unbelieving, the covenant relationship does not immediately end, and the requirement also does not cease, and the comfort likewise is not removed. But for the person himself, by his unbelief and impenitence, that comfort diminishes with every moment. He must give an account for the expectation cherished in relation to him not having been fulfilled, that he is therefore regarded as a covenant-breaker. This, at least, must be maintained so that the covenant relationship will not be seen as degenerating into a cloak of mistaken passivity.

k) One can ask: how does one come into the fellowship of the covenant? The answer can only be: through regeneration, or through faith and repentance. The former has in view the unconscious basis of fellowship, the latter the conscious enjoyment of fellowship, and here we have to do only provisionally with it. Now, however, an apparent objection arises. How can something be at the same time acquiescing in the covenant and a fulfillment of the conditions of the covenant? So Koelman reasons that the internal covenant is not properly a covenant because it involves no conditions or proposals for man, given that the exercise of the conditions of the covenant is itself his entry into the internal covenant. Whoever believes and repents keeps the covenant. Nothing more is expected by God or promised by man. In other words, a covenant always has in view something still to be done. Here the idea of commitment is simply employed in order to deny fellowship the name of covenant. But Scripture does not speak in this way (Jer 31:31–32). This whole objection is an apparent objection. It immediately collapses as soon as one makes a distinction between the initial assent of faith and the ongoing exercise of faith. Faith is not something that needs to be exercised only for a moment, as a condition for sharing in the benefits of the covenant forever. It is the ongoing activity that unlocks continual access to the good things of the covenant. So, if I say that by faith one enters into the inward fellowship of the covenant, this does not exclude that the continuing act of faith is also covenant-keeping. It all depends on how one views the matter. How else will such as those who were not born into the covenant gain a true agreement to the covenant than by an acquiescing faith? For such persons, therefore, faith is an entering into the covenant relationship and the fellowship of the covenant at the same time.

31. *In what sense can unregenerate and unbelieving persons be said to be in the covenant?*

a) They are in the covenant with regard to covenant obligation. As members of the covenant, they owe God faith and repentance. If they do not believe and repent, they are judged to be covenant-breakers.

b) They are in the covenant with regard to the covenant promise, made to believers when God establishes His covenant with them. God ordinarily takes the number of His elect from those who are in covenant relationship and from their seed.

c) They are in the covenant with regard to cultivating the covenant. They are continually roused and admonished to live in accordance with the covenant. The church treats them as members of the covenant and offers them the covenant seals, even stirs them up to use them. They are the guests who are first invited, the children of the kingdom, those to whom the word of God must first be spoken (Matt 8:12; Acts 13:46; Luke 14:16–24).

d) They are in the covenant with regard to the outward work of the covenant, the exercise of the power of the church. The words of God are entrusted to them, as Paul says of the greater part of the unbelieving Jewish church (Rom 3:2).

e) They are in the covenant with regard to common covenant blessing. Koelman: "The members of the covenant, the unregenerate, too, have splendid influences and operations of God's Spirit ... I confess that even the lost experience powerful operations of the Spirit for enlightenment and enabling; the Spirit of the Lord strives in their midst (Gen 6:3) and distributes common gifts (Heb 6:4–5; 1 Cor 12:8)."

32. *In what manner can one say that the covenant of grace is conditional?*

It has already been observed that the idea of conditionality is not applicable to being in the covenant, to the establishment of the covenant relationship. It can only have in view participating in the covenant fellowship, receiving the covenant benefits. The question therefore becomes, is there something placed upon man as a condition, that he on his side must do, in order to share in the covenant blessing promised from God's side?

Turretin has discussed this issue extensively and with clarity (*Institutes*, II, XII, 3). He says that one must give attention to four things:

a) A condition can be regarded as something that has meriting power and by its own nature confers a right to the benefits of the covenant, but also as prerequisite and means, as an accompanying disposition in the member of the covenant.

b) A condition can be regarded as to be fulfilled through natural capabilities, or to be fulfilled through supernatural grace.

c) A condition in the covenant can have in view the end of the covenant—salvation—or the way of the covenant—faith and repentance. One can ask, what is the condition in order to gain the end of the covenant? And also, what is the condition in order to attain to the way of the covenant?

d) The covenant can be viewed according to its institution by God, according to its first application in the believer, and according to its consummation.

The answer to the question above, according to these points of view, is governed by the opposition between Roman Catholics and Remonstrants on the one side and the Reformed on the other side. This question was contended over in both the 16th and 17th centuries. In the former it was Junius, for example, in the latter it was Witsius, among others, who maintained that the covenant of grace knows no conditions. By making it conditional, one feared falling back into the Roman Catholic or Remonstrant confusion of law and gospel, something that must be avoided at any cost. We say:

a) The covenant of grace is not conditional in the sense that in it there would be any condition with meriting power. Our faith and repentance never stand in a meriting relationship to the benefit of the covenant. We deny that against Roman Catholics as well as Remonstrants.

b) The covenant of grace is not conditional in the sense that what is required of man would have to be accomplished in his own strength. When the requirement is presented to man, he must always be reminded that he can get the strength for fulfilling it only from God. God Himself, by His grace, fulfills the condition in His elect. What is a condition for all is thus for them also a promise, a gift of the covenant.

c) The covenant of grace is not conditional in its whole scope concerning the covenant benefits. Let us say, for example, that justification is a covenant benefit. Now, this is bound to the covenant as a *conditio sine qua non*, or however one may wish to characterize it. But now, what about faith itself? Is that, in its turn, again tied to something else? Evidently not, for otherwise we would get an infinite series, and nowhere would there be an absolute beginning where the grace of God intervenes. Therefore, we say that the covenant of grace is conditional with respect to its completion and final benefits, not as concerns its actual beginning. Without sanctification, no one will see the Lord [Heb 12:14].

d) If we look at the foundation of the covenant of grace as it rests in Christ's suretyship, then it does have conditions for Him, the Mediator, not for the believer, for whom everything is secured in the passive and active obedience of the Mediator. If we consider the initial inclusion of members of the covenant into the fellowship of the covenant, then faith is the condition. If we consider the completion of the covenant, then the condition is not only faith, but also sanctification.

e) When we speak of faith as condition, by that is meant that the exercise of faith is the only way along which one can come to conscious enjoyment of the benefit of the covenant. For our understanding of the covenant, our consciousness of it, everything depends on faith. Whoever does not have faith, so far as his awareness is concerned, in practice stands outside the covenant, and to the degree one has more faith, one stands more firmly in the covenant. This faith as such comes into view here for reasons that will be set forth later in the treatment of faith. Law and gospel are not hereby confused, for one must note that faith, although Scripture itself calls it a work (John 6:29), is not considered a perfect work. The faith that justifies us perfectly and gives us complete access to the treasure of grace in its entirety is as *actus*, as a work, imperfect through and through. This alone already shows that it does not belong to the law, for the law recognizes only perfect work, in which nothing is lacking. Faith does not at all appear as the legal ground for our justification. That we believe does not make justification any less an act of pure grace. This must be emphatically underscored. Judicially, our faith does nothing for our justification. So far as the judicial aspect is concerned, God could just as well justify us without faith—something that does not eliminate the reasons there still are for the position faith occupies in the matter of justification. But those reasons do not lie within the sphere of law. They lie elsewhere. It is otherwise for work if one is in the covenant of works. Then his work is legally necessary for justification.

f) Now one asks whether faith only appears as a condition, or whether, along with faith, repentance must also be mentioned. On this, too, there was debate among Reformed theologians.

The correct answer is that in the widest sense repentance may also be posited. There is no true faith without repentance, and where repentance is lacking, one cannot be assured on good grounds of his sharing in the benefits of the covenant by faith. But there is, however, a difference between faith and repentance as so-called conditions. In this case, faith functions *causaliter*, that is, with causality. It is obviously in the nature of faith that it gives us access to the enjoyment of the covenant. It is a receptive organ, one that takes possession. One cannot say that of repentance. No one will be able to make his repentance an inherent means of bringing himself into covenant fellowship. It is simply, negatively, a condition-without-which-not. Justification is of course not coextensive with the benefits of the covenant. In the matter of justification, only faith functions. There it is *sola fide*. But the covenant is broader, so that one may well say: faith plus repentance (whereby, of course, both are not taken as momentary acts, but as ongoing activities).

g) Evidence that in this sense conditions are attached to the covenant of grace:

1. The Scriptures speak in this way (John 3:16, 36; Rom 10:9; Acts 8:37; Mark 16:16; and in many other places).

2. If there were no conditions, there would be no place for threats, for threatening only makes sense to those who reject the conditions; that is to say here, those who do not walk in the God-ordained way of the covenant.

3. If there were no conditions, God alone would be bound by this covenant, and no bond would be placed on man. Thereby the character of the covenant would be lost. All covenants contain two parts.

33. How is the testamentary nature of the covenant of grace to be assessed?

From this testamentary character it has been inferred that the covenant of grace admits of no conditions, properly called. A testament, it is said, has no conditions; it is an absolute declaration. It is necessary, therefore, that we look more carefully at the testament idea in relation to the covenant of grace. As has been shown above, the testament concept occurs in only one New Testament passage, namely Hebrews 9:16–17. Here, the testator is Christ. In His death, the covenant of grace is confirmed as a testament. This means that by His death, all the benefits of the covenant of grace have been secured for us, so that they come to us, as it were, as an inheritance, a testamentary disposition. Everything that is required of us toward God is at the same time a gift from Christ to us, for our faith and our repentance flow as fruits from His active obedience.

The conception of the covenant as testament is limited to this one place. But if one considers more than the word "testament," the concept is anything but rare. It is one of the most well-known concepts in the New Testament. And this cannot be otherwise. The sonship of believers was not unknown in Israel. But yet it first received its full revelation in the new day. Sonship, however, immediately causes us to think of inheritance. And the inheritance is nothing other than the content of the testament. Therefore, wherever there is mention of inheritance, or of adoption as children, the idea of a testament underlies it, with this distinction: For an inheritance, there is no thought of the death of the testator. For a testament, there is. So the members of the covenant are heirs of God, joint-heirs with Christ (Rom 8:17). There is an inheritance of the saints in light (Col 1:12).

This, in turn, leads to another thought. If for us the covenant of grace has a side that is testamentary and makes it appear as an inheritance, then the question arises whether it can also be called that for Christ the mediator. It is said that we are *joint*-heirs with Christ. Is He then also an heir? Scripture answers in the affirmative. Luke 22:29: "I bequeath to you (by testament or last will) the kingdom, even as my Father has bequeathed it to me." No doubt this has in view the mediatorial glory of Christ. And likewise, He now shares that glory as an inheritance with His own. Thus there is warrant for ascribing a testamentary aspect both to the counsel of peace and to the covenant of grace. But this is only one side of the matter, and this does not preclude the covenant from remaining essentially a covenant. We must take both sides together in order to grasp the whole.

Cocceius, especially, worked out this doctrine of the testaments— not in every respect with simplicity and transparency. The opponents of Cocceian theology (the so-called Voetians) were accustomed to understand under "testament" nothing other than an administration of the covenant of grace. For them, the covenant of grace was primary; testament was merely a modification of it. But according to Cocceius it was otherwise, for he accepted three testaments:

1. A general testament that applies to all ages.

2. An ancient Israelite testament that applied to the giving of earthly Canaan as an inheritance.

3. A New Testament inheritance that has in view the giving of the spiritual inheritance to the Gentiles.

Concerning this, Mastricht complains (VIII, I, 35) that Cocceius has made subordinate to this first testament: (1) the decree of foreordination; (2) the covenant of grace; (3) both Testaments, the Old and the New. Prior to Cocceius, he says, Reformed theologians began with election and made the covenant of grace subordinate to it, as a guideline for the implementation of the decree of election; the administration thereof (of the covenant) they called a testament.

On this issue we observe:

1. That Cocceius undoubtedly was wrong in making foreordination subordinate to testament. The older theology was entirely correct in its judgment that election is the source of the whole order of grace, and that nothing can be antecedent to it. The counsel of peace itself can only follow it in order and not precede it. Here Cocceius in fact departed from the Reformed conception.

2. In itself one can certainly derive from Hebrews 9 the right to apply the name "testament" to the administration of the covenant of grace, thus to something that is subordinate to the covenant of grace itself. Here in the New Testament it is spoken of as something that has been introduced through Christ's death. Therefore, it is equivalent to the New Testament administration of the covenant of grace. Also, what came before Christ is equivalent to the Old Testament administration of the covenant of grace.

3. In no way does it follow from this that one may not speak of the old and new covenant. It is true: The old theologians did not do this. In their theological vocabulary, only the term "covenant" is reserved for what old and new have in common. But the Old Testament

Scripture already speaks of a "new *covenant*" (Jer 31:31, 33). Thus one may also say: Covenant can be covenant *administration*.

4. Scripture nowhere calls the disposition of the Father concerning the Son and concerning the elect a testament. But if one wishes to call this disposition a testament in its origin (= election) or in its formal elucidation (= the counsel of peace), then we do not see what is misunderstood by doing that. A testament is equivalent to a hereditary disposition, and Scripture speaks of an inheritance, as we ourselves have seen, both in relation to believers as well as of the Mediator. Regarding the distinction made by Coccejus between Old and New Testament, see below.

34. *Is the covenant of grace unilateral or bilateral?*

By this question is meant whether there is one party or two parties in it. Properly speaking, every covenant requires two parties. A unilateral covenant is a *contradictio in adjecto* [contradiction in terms]. There was, however, an element of truth when some theologians insisted on the unilateral character of the covenant. After all, what is on man's side viewed as covenant obligation is at the same time God's covenant gift. Moreover, this covenant is entirely designed by God Himself. It is not that God and man meet each other halfway in order to approach each other. God comes to us and gives His covenant, establishes it sovereignly with us. Finally, it is only man who benefits from it, and so in that sense one could also call it unilateral. In earthly, human covenants, each of the two covenant-making parties gives and receives. Here God alone gives; man alone receives.

On the other hand, it must be maintained that in its realization the covenant is bilateral, because from his side man in fact enters this covenant by believing, repenting, fulfilling the covenant requirement. Although God works this requirement in man, through this working he is enabled to do it himself. To Abraham the requirement comes in Genesis 17:1, "Walk before My face and be upright"; and then the declaration in v. 2, "I will make My covenant between Me and you."

35. *What are the promises of the covenant of grace?*

The principal promise, which includes all the others, is, "I will be your God" (Gen 17:7–8). It reoccurs when again and again believers say, "The

Lord is my God" (Psa 33:12). Considered more closely, this one promise appears to include:

a) The promise of righteousness for acquittal and for eternal life.

b) The promise of the Spirit and of sanctification by the Holy Spirit.

c) The promise of glorification.

36. *In what form does the consent of man to the covenant of grace appear?*

This is determined by the promises of God.

a) God says, "I will be your God," so man says, "I will belong to Your people."

b) To the promise of righteousness, man responds by saving faith.

c) In general, the relationship between God as God of the covenant and the believer, whether the individual or believers together, is portrayed as a covenant between husband and wife, bridegroom and bride, father and children.

37. *In the covenant of grace, has Christ become the surety toward God for us or also the surety toward us for God?*

The Socinians argued very strongly that the latter was the case—naturally at the expense of the former. Christ's suretyship would then consist in this: He vouches for God toward us in order to assure us of God's faithfulness in fulfilling the promises of the covenant. On this question, see Owen, *Justification*, VIII. There it is rightly observed that this argument derived from the giving of Christ by God lacks all force. That a surety is given by someone by no means proves his appearance as surety for the giver. God can give Christ for the elect, and the given Christ can still be surety toward the giver for the elect.

It is a thought unworthy of God that He would need a surety, as though He were not completely trustworthy by His word alone. One could say: We need someone who assures us that something is in fact a word from God. But that is not the task of a surety. It belongs much more to the task of a witness. A surety for God would presuppose that if God does not do it, I will do it. We also find that the Son appears as a witness of the Father, but not as a surety (John 18:37; Rom 15:8). Christ cannot deserve more credence than God, as, however, would have to be the case with a surety for God.

Hebrews 7:22, where ἔγγυος occurs of Christ (the only place where it occurs in the New Testament), states how Christ has become the surety of the much better covenant by the swearing of an oath [v. 21]. That involves that He does not serve as surety in order to attest the promise of God to us, for God Himself attests His promises, and that indeed by an oath where He already gives Christ to us as surety. Again in this passage, the suretyship is mentioned in connection with the priestly office of the mediator. Now, however, the priestly office, according to Hebrews 5:1, is something performed for people toward God. But then that is also suretyship.

38. *What are the most important characteristics of the covenant of grace?*

   a) It is a *gracious* covenant. The grace consists of the following: (1) that God permits a surety; (2) that the surety is God Himself, so that God in His own person executes the ministry of the covenant; (3) that the fulfillment of the covenant obligation on the side of man comes about through grace, that is, through the Holy Spirit. Thus, here again it is God who upholds the covenant. So from beginning to end, everything is grace, a work of God par excellence.

   When we say that it is a covenant of *grace*, then we must consider specifically the relationship of guilty man before God in this covenant. When one considers the Mediator of the covenant, then naturally no grace is shown to Him. Considered in Christ, everything is a matter of carrying out the demands of the covenant of works according to God's strict justice, though in another form. Grace never consists in God abandoning anything of His justice, taken in general. But He does in that He does not assert His justice against the same person against whom He could assert it. God shows grace to us when He demands from Christ what He can demand from us. Considered in Christ, everything is strict justice; considered in us, everything is free grace.

   As a covenant of grace, this covenant also has a Trinitarian character. The entire Trinity is active in it. It flows from the election of the Father, is founded in justice by the suretyship of the

Son, and finds its complete realization through the application of the Holy Spirit (Eph 2:8; John 1:16).

b) It is an *eternal* covenant and primarily *a parte post* [with reference to the future] (cf. Gen 17:19; 2 Sam 23:5; Heb 13:20). In this eternity, permanence is also implied, because in Scripture these two concepts are interchangeable. This is one of the reasons why the designation "testament" can be applied to the covenant of grace. Taking this together with what has been said earlier, we thus obtain as grounds for usage: (1) that the benefits of the covenant are an inheritance granted from the Father to His children; (2) that these covenant benefits are accomplished through the death of Christ; (3) that the covenant, like a testament, is fixed and unmovable. Hebrews 9:17 combines the latter two of these viewpoints.

Of course, the eternity of the covenant of grace must be related to the fellowship of the covenant. The covenant bond in itself, if it does not pass over into covenant fellowship, is not eternal, but becomes broken.

c) It is a *particular* and not a *universal* covenant. This means:

1. That it is not realized in all, as universalists maintain, and also that with the will of the decree God did not will that it would be realized in all, as is held by the Pelagians, Lutherans, Remonstrants, and others.

2. That even as a covenant relationship, it does not extend to all to whom the gospel is preached, for not all accept being taken into the proffered covenant.

3. That the offer of the covenant does not come to all, because there have been and will be many peoples and individuals who will die without knowledge of the covenant of grace.

In other words, there is an election of peoples as well as individual election. In contrast, the Lutherans and some (German) Reformed maintain that the covenant of grace in this sense has a universal purport, since at various points in time it is offered to the entire human race, and it would thus have depended only on the covenant faithfulness of those persons living at that time for the covenant to be kept universally. This happened in Adam, Noah, and even later through the apostles. We say: There is no basis to make Adam and Noah representative recipients of the offer of the covenant in this manner. Neither is there proof that Adam treated Cain less faithfully than Abel, or that Noah fulfilled his covenant obligation to Ham less faithfully than to Shem. Here one must simply acknowledge God's sovereignty, which is righteous but is in no sense to be explained by the actions of man. Already in the first promise by which the covenant of grace is revealed, there is a prophecy of a separating between *the seed of the woman* and the *seed of the serpent*. In this, the particular character is implied. Finally, one gains nothing with this abstract universality. To be sure, one must acknowledge that for numerous persons and peoples to whom the covenant was offered for the first time in Adam or Noah, there was a second offer added at a later time, while for other persons and peoples this offer was lacking. So, for the one group, a universal offer plus no offer later; for the other, first a universal offer plus a repeated offer later. That is to say, regarding the second offer, it is yet again a particular offer.

We must distinguish this universality of the covenant of grace in the proper sense from another that was taught by some older Reformed theologians. Szegedin, Musculus, Polanus, Wollebius, and others make a distinction between the *foedus generale*, the general covenant, which God established with all creatures, animals as well as men, and the *foedus speciale ac sempiternum*, the special and eternally enduring covenant that is made with the elect. For the first, the covenant with all creatures, one can appeal to God's covenant-making with Noah. With that, God promised that the orderings of heaven and of earth would not again be disrupted by a flood and placed the rainbow as a sign and a seal of it.

Finally, one can also say that the new dispensation of the covenant of grace is universal in distinction from the old, which in a particularistic fashion was limited to the Jews.

d) The covenant of grace is *one* through all its dispensations, however the form in which it is administered may change. This is contested by all those who teach that the Old Testament saints were saved in a different manner than those of the new day; for example, the Pelagians, the Socinians, the later Remonstrants, the Roman Catholics, who thought the fathers to have been in limbo until the descent of Christ into hell, and in principle the Cocceians, when they have these believers existing under a *paresis*. Many modern theologians regard Christianity as something specific and new that transcends Judaism.

Recently, however, more emphasis has again been placed on their affinity, although naturally for most the tie is taken as entirely evolutionary and natural, and one grants a supernatural origin as little to the religion of Israel as to Christianity.

That the covenant of grace is one is shown by the following evidence:

1. It was demonstrated explicitly by the Apostle Paul against the Judaizers that one and the same rule held for Abraham as held for the Christians from the Jews and the Gentiles under the new day (cf. Gal 3:7–9, 17–18). Also, in other passages it is called the same covenant that was established with the fathers—for example, Luke 1:72, "[S]o that He would remember His holy covenant"; Acts 3:25, "You are children of the prophets and of the covenant that God established with our fathers."

2. As a summary of the covenant of grace in both Old and New Testaments, the expression occurs, "I am your God" (Gen 17:7–8; 2 Cor 6:16; Rev 21:3). Everything is contained in this summary. In His answer to the Sadducees, Christ proves from the expression "the God of Abraham, Isaac, and Jacob" that these patriarchs must possess eternal life since God is not a God of the dead but of the living [Matt 22:32; Mark 12:27; Luke 20:38].

3. Scripture teaches that there is but *one* gospel by which one can be saved, and inasmuch as the gospel is nothing other than the revelation of the covenant of grace, there can be only one covenant of grace. This gospel was already present in paradise. Paul says that it was proclaimed to Abraham (Gal 3:8) and curses those who, in a Judaizing manner, would wish to place another imagined Old Testament gospel in opposition to it (Gal 1:8–9). Scripture also calls it, in brief, the *eternal* gospel (Rev 14:6).

4. The Mediator of the covenant is the same yesterday and today and into all eternity [Heb 13:8]. Salvation is in no other, and there is no other name under heaven given among men through which one can be saved (Acts 4:12). He is the seed of the woman already promised in paradise; likewise, the seed promised to Abraham (Gal 3:16). All prophecies look toward Him.

5. The *way* and the *condition* of the covenant are the same, namely *faith* and *repentance* (Gen 15:6; cf. Rom 4:11; Matt 13:17). That was likewise true for the promise of the covenant (Acts 3:25–26; Gen 15:6; Psa 51:10; Ezek 36:26). Finally, the *sacraments* of the covenant are changed in form with the change in dispensation, but in essence have remained the same (Rom 4:11–12; 1 Cor 5:7).

39. *How is the covenant of grace related to election?*

As a covenant of fellowship, thus *in its essence*, it extends no further and is not wider than election. There is, however, a difference. Election starts from individual persons, A, B, and C, and then from them forms a people, so that one can say that election forms the covenant organism. Conversely, the covenant in its realization starts from this organism and then moves to the individual person.

    As a covenant relationship the covenant is wider than election, for it also lays claim to those who never attain to true covenant fellowship and a true enjoyment of the benefits of the covenant.

40. *Where is the covenant of grace first revealed?*

In the mother promise, Genesis 3:15, "I will put enmity between you and this woman, and between your seed and her seed. It will crush your head and you will crush its heel." Some have disputed that we are dealing with a covenant here. It must be conceded that the formal conclusion of a covenant is lacking, which, moreover, would have been incomprehensible to Adam and Eve. Only later, when the idea of a covenant had developed on natural terrain, God Himself used the term with Noah and Abraham, etc. But as far as the essence of the matter is concerned, the covenant was certainly with Adam since that mother promise. It was a protevangelium, a "first gospel," and the gospel is in itself a revelation of the covenant of grace. One should note the following:

a) Through a powerful word, God establishes enmity between the seed of the serpent and that of the woman, between the serpent and the woman herself. He thereby creates a relationship. This agrees completely with the manner in which He always acts in the realization of His covenant. Later, He says to Abraham, "I institute," "I establish," "I give my covenant."

b) Enmity between the woman and her seed, on the one hand, and the serpent and its seed, on the other, points to a relationship of friendship with God. After all, man had renounced friendship with God and had allied himself with Satan. Where friendship with Satan has now turned into enmity, this can mean nothing other than that friendship with God has been restored. So here the covenant relationship is clearly included.

c) It has been rightly noted that the promise of sanctifying grace was also included in this promise. How else could enmity have arisen where friendship existed? God Himself must reverse the situation through re-creating grace. He apparently worked at the same time, or already before that time, in the hearts of Adam and Eve, adding the grace of the covenant to the gospel of the covenant.

d) When God thus, through His omnipotence, brings about enmity against Satan in man, then this includes that God chooses man's side—expressed in our current language, that He becomes man's ally in the conflict against the serpent. An offensive and defensive covenant is present here in substance, although one should acknowledge that Adam could not immediately have clearly understood this relationship. In fact, this did not also need to be the case immediately. The protevangelium was not only there for the initial moment; it was there as a treasure to be preserved and pondered.

e) This relationship between God and man on one side and Satan on the other is a relationship that is not limited to individuals, but extends to the seed. And that is an essential element of the covenant concept, as we have already seen more than once.

The covenant encompasses the generations. Here, too, that is true. It does not extend only to the woman, but to the woman's seed. Adam and Eve were instructed by this how this enmity against Satan, which God graciously willed to work in them, would also continue in their posterity. There would be a never-broken line of fighters against the serpent.

f) In opposition, however, there will also be a seed of the serpent. It is not a conflict against the serpent in himself, but also against the followers whom the serpent will acquire among men. In this, one finds expressed that the covenant of grace is particular, that it draws a dividing line through humanity, and that not all are reckoned as the seed of the woman to whom the promise extends. And here, too, there is a certain bond—it is a seed of the serpent.

g) The conflict that was established by God's powerful word between the woman's seed and the serpent will not remain unresolved. Indeed, the serpent shall crush the heel of the woman's seed. And, conversely, the woman's seed shall crush the serpent's head. Therein is present, in principle, the doctrine of the atonement. The evil one and the power of evil can be overcome only if they are permitted to harm their foes. It had to be permitted that the serpent wound the woman's seed in the heel. The serpent has to bite His heel and so pour the poison of death into Him, so that He becomes the serpent lifted up (John 3:14–15). But just because the serpent strikes at His heel with its bite, He has been given the opportunity to bring down His heel on its head. It can strike Him only from below, that is, in such a position that it becomes possible for Him to kill it when it bites. This is linked to the curse pronounced on it: "On your belly you shall go, and you shall eat dust all the days of your life" [Gen 3:14]. Because sin is cursed, the serpent can kill, but because it kills from the power of a curse and not by a blind law of nature, the possibility exists that killing *by* sin becomes the killing *of* sin. Since the serpent bites in the heel from the earth, it can be pushed down into the earth by the heel of the Serpent Trampler and crushed.

h) Among the seed of the woman we understand not only, but certainly in the deepest sense, Christ. He is the seed of the woman, as He was the seed of Abraham. In Him, all who are at enmity with the serpent have their unity. In fact, it was already not the natural seed in the wider sense that was meant by the seed of the woman. It was the spiritual seed that would not be the serpent's seed. And as Paul says (in Galatians 3) that Abraham's seed consisted partly in believers and partly in Christ, without the one excluding the other, so it will also be here. In a deeper sense, only the natural descendants of the woman are the true seed of the woman, since they belong to Christ. And Christ is also in a literal sense the seed of the woman. In order to triumph in the conflict against the serpent, He had to be born from a woman, from the mother of all living, and share in our human nature, and at the same time be more than man. After all, it was a conflict not against human powers but against the serpent, thus against a higher, spiritual, demonic power that must be crushed here. Clearly the evil one is in the background.

The fact that our ancestors did not understand all this in detail is not relevant. But without doubt they would have grasped the heart of the matter. And no one with an eye for this protevangelium can deny that, in its substance, the covenant of grace was already present in paradise.

41. Where subsequently is mention made of a covenant of God with man?

In Genesis 6:13; 9:9; and the following verses, between God and Noah. Here, however, it is said repeatedly that it is a covenant between God and every living soul, not excluding the animals. Thus it is not simply the covenant of grace. It is a covenant of nature.

42. What distinguishes the relationship in which God has placed Abraham to Himself?

a) It was a formal covenant relationship. Not only were the elements of a covenant present, but it was now also openly called a covenant.

b) It was the formation of a church separated from the world. Earlier there was nothing like that. There were gatherings of believers, but there was nothing delineated and separated from the rest of the world that one could call a church. Abraham receives a sacrament, by which in itself a line is drawn.

c) It was the beginning of the particularistic administration of the covenant of the Old Testament, which later came out still more clearly. The church is limited to one race. Earlier, that was not the case.

d) It comes out clearly that man, too, must appear as a party in this covenant. Abraham believed God, and God again and again repeats His appearances and His promises, as it were, to lead Abraham to believe and to act in faith. Therefore, Isaac was also born through miraculous power.

e) It comes out more clearly than with Adam what are the spiritual benefits that God grants in His covenant. The Apostle Paul has taught us that Abraham was granted justification, adoption, conversion, etc. (Gal 3; 4:28).

f) The covenant with Abraham already had a double side, one that had in view temporal benefits—like the promise of the land of Canaan, numerous descendants, protection against earthly enemies—and one that had in view spiritual benefits. Nevertheless, this is to be so understood that the earthly and temporal were not for their own sake, but rather so that they would provide a type of the spiritual and heavenly. Thus the Apostle Paul can say that the spiritual promises did not apply to all the seed, but to the spiritual seed, to those included in Christ. By that he meant that the physical children of Abraham with their temporal blessings were an exemplar of the people of God who through faith receive the spiritual benefits.

g) One must not assume that by the establishing of the covenant with Abraham, his descendants only entered into an external covenant. They were in the full covenant of grace. But they were also in it in such a form that they entered into certain external relationships, something that became still more robust later at Sinai. The one does not exclude the other.

43. How is the covenant at Sinai to be assessed?

On this question, the most diverse opinions are prevalent. We first give the correct view. The Sinaitic covenant is not a new covenant as concerns the essence of the matter, but the old covenant of grace established with

Abraham in somewhat changed form. The thesis that it must be a new covenant is usually derived from the fact that Paul so strongly accents the law over against the promises as different from them (e.g., Gal 3:17ff.). But thereby one thing is forgotten. Paul nowhere sets the Sinaitic covenant in its entirety over against the Abrahamic covenant, but always the law insofar as it came to function in the Sinaitic covenant. There is only one place that appears to be an exception to this: Galatians 4:21ff. Here, in fact, two covenants are set over against each other. But they are not the Abrahamic and the Sinaitic covenants. Rather, they are the earthly and the heavenly covenants—the covenant that originates from Mount Sinai and has its center in the earthly Jerusalem, and the covenant that originates from heaven and is concentrated in the Jerusalem that is above. This is very significant. Paul has not said: two covenants, the one originating from Mamre and the other from Sinai. He knew well that already with Abraham something of the Sinaitic side of the covenant was also present and that, conversely, after Sinai there was a continuation of the heavenly, spiritual side of the covenant of grace with the people of God. So with this passage, one gains nothing.

The children of Israel were in the covenant when they set out from Egypt. Precisely because they were in it, they were delivered from Egypt (Gen 15:13–14). There is not one word mentioned of a new relationship. The old was altered. And at the same time, there was something new. It consisted in the following considerations:

a) Now, for the first time, the covenant with Israel rightly became a national covenant. The social life of Israel, its civil organization, its existence as a people, were brought directly into contact with the covenant of grace. These two were inextricably linked. One cannot say, "I want to leave the Jewish church but remain in the Jewish state." Whoever left the church left the state. And one could leave the state only by being exterminated from the people. Properly speaking, there is discipline through censure in a certain sense, but not, properly speaking, discipline only through excommunication or cutting off from the church. The sanction was the death penalty. All this first came about at Sinai. Earlier, God Himself had cut off Ishmael and Esau from the covenant administration. Judicially, this is later no longer permitted.

b) The covenant with Israel served in an emphatic manner to recall
the strict demands of the covenant of works. To that end, the law
of the Ten Commandments was presented so emphatically and
engraved deeply in stone. This law was not, as Cocceius meant,
simply a form for the covenant of grace. It truly contained the
content of the covenant of works. But—and one should certainly note this—it contains this content as made serviceable for a
particular period of the covenant of grace. It therefore says, for
example, "I am the Lord your God." Therefore, it also contains
expressions that had reference specifically to Israel and thus are
not totally applicable to us (e.g., "that it may be well with you
in the land that the Lord your God gives you"). But also, beyond
the Decalogue, there is reference to the law as a demand of the
covenant of works (e.g., Lev 18:5; Deut 27:26; 2 Cor 3:7, 9). It is for
this reason that in the last cited passage, Paul calls the ministry
of Moses a ministry of condemnation. This simply shows how the
demand of the law comes more to the fore in this dispensation
of the covenant of grace. This ministry of the law had a twofold
purpose: (1) It is a disciplinarian until Christ. (2) It serves to
multiply sin—that is, both to lure sin out from its hidden inner
recesses as well as to bring it to consciousness (cf. Gal 3:19; Rom
4:15; 5:13). Paul teaches expressly that the law did not appear here
as an independent covenant of works in Galatians 3:19ff. That
the law is also not a summary of the covenant of grace appears
from the absence of the demand of faith and of the doctrine of
the atonement.

c) The covenant with Israel had a ceremonial and a typical ministry,
fixed in its details. That was also already so in part for the earlier
administration of the covenant of grace. But to the degree that it
now came about, that ceremonial ministry was something new. A
formal gospel preaching was offered continually by symbols and
types. A priestly class came into existence. Earlier, every father
of a family was a priest. Now, particular persons are separated
and consecrated for this function. One must consider all these
types and symbols from two points of view: (1) as demands of
God on the people; (2) as a proclamation of God to the people.
God had appointed them to serve in both respects. But the Jews

overlooked the latter aspect more and more and made the types and symbols exclusively serve the former purpose. That is to say, they used them only as additions to a self-willed covenant of works, and misunderstood the ministering significance they had for the covenant of grace. So the opinion arose that righteousness had to be obtained by keeping that law in the broadest sense of the word, including the ceremonial law. And by this misuse, the covenant of grace of Sinai was in fact made into a Hagarite covenant, a covenant giving birth to servitude, as Paul describes it in Galatians 4:24. There he has in view not the covenant as it should be, but as it could easily become through misuse.

d) The law given by God also served as a rule of life for Israel. So, we obtain a threefold law: the moral, the ceremonial, the civil law. This civil law was a particular application of the principles of the moral law. For example, in the moral law God says in general, "You shall not steal." The civil law further elaborates what constitutes stealing, what penalties apply, etc., etc. At the same time, this law as a rule of life for civil concerns was elaborated in such a way that it provided a model for the spiritual relationship to God of the members of the covenant. Israel must bring its tithes, firstfruits, drink- and vow-offerings; and in doing that the dedication of the covenant member to God was also foreshadowed in the covenant of grace. No one from Israel may be a slave, for every Israelite is as such already totally God's possession. Even the land of the children of Israel is God's property; they are merely sojourners and aliens toward God, who live from what is His. So, too, in civil relationships in Israel, in the civil side of the covenant, the essence of the covenant of grace is mirrored.

44. *Is this covenant that God established with Israel capable of being broken or not?*

It is not only capable of being broken, but also has been broken repeatedly. Then a covenant renewal is necessary, as comes out in Exodus 34:10ff. and 2 Kings 33:3.[3] Actually, all sin is covenant-breaking, but still this covenant is such that God Himself has ordained a means to preserve the covenant in spite of those sins. This means are the sacrifices. They are

---

3 *Sic*; 2 Kings 23:3.

applicable to sins that are not committed with uplifted hands; that is, sins through error, unintentional sins. But, also, even when an intentional sin is committed, God still does not forsake His covenant. Where the appointed means of propitiation is lacking, God comes with extraordinary seeking grace, remembers His covenant, maintains it in spite of Israel's unfaithfulness (Exod 32; Psa 106:23; Num 16:45–50). Finally, it is expressed clearly that the covenant with Israel is eternal (1 Chr 16:17; Isa 54:10; Psa 89:1–5), a covenant to which God has pledged the honor of His name (Isa 48:8–11; Num 14:16). In this pledge, therefore, it is essentially settled that God guarantees the continuation of the covenant of grace, that it is eternal in a different sense than the covenant of works, that however much individuals may fall away and be lost, the core of the covenant remains and must remain—so, entirely the same thing we established earlier about the covenant of grace in general.

45. *How can it be said in Deuteronomy 5:2 and 3 that God did not make the covenant at Horeb with the fathers, if it is still one covenant?*

This must be understood not of the substance, but of the form of the covenant closure. With Abraham and the patriarchs, God had not established the covenant of grace in its Sinaitic design—that is what Moses means here. Thus by "the fathers" is meant the patriarchs, not the forefathers in Egypt (Calvin) or those who perished in the wilderness (Augustine). It is clear from subsequent places how Scripture regards the Sinaitic covenant as a continuation of the covenant with Abraham: Exodus 2:24, "And God remembered His covenant with Abraham, Isaac, and Jacob"; Leviticus 26:42, "Then I will remember my covenant with Jacob, with Isaac, with Abraham" (Deut 4:31; 2 Kgs 13:23). Again and again, there is a continual pointing back to the covenant with Abraham to show that the children of Israel were in that covenant.

46. *What are the deviating positions regarding that Sinaitic covenant of grace?*

    a) The view of Cocceius and his followers. Cocceius was a proponent of a trichotomy, that is, a three part division of administering the covenant of grace. There was:

        1. An administration from Adam to Moses.

        2. An administration from Moses to Christ.

3. An administration after Christ.

Or, expressed otherwise: *ante legem—sub lege—post legem*, that is: before the law, under the law, after the law.

The last period unfolds in seven stages that correspond to the seven letters, seven trumpets, seven seals of Revelation.

Regarding the establishing of the covenant at Sinai, Cocceius taught that the Decalogue was a summary of the covenant of grace, made especially applicable to Israel. However, after the establishment of this gracious covenant upon the 10 words, when Israel became unfaithful and fell into worship of the golden calf and broke the covenant, then as punishment the legal covenant of ceremonial institutions was established, that is, the covenant of grace as a much more rigorous and harsher administration. The servitude of the law first appears after the worship of the golden calf. And the element of servitude is found in the ceremonial law; that of grace, on the other hand, in the law of the Ten Commandments. The fathers who lived before Sinai were under freedom, under promise. According to the Cocceian understanding, the Old Testament first begins at Sinai. God did not give a law to the patriarchs. Cocceius taught of the pre-Mosaic sacrifices that they were not commanded by God but were free ceremonies that could be neglected without guilt. The Cocceian view of the Sabbath was also related to this judgment about the pre-Mosaic freedom and the Decalogue as a temporary formulation before the covenant of grace. It was thought that the Sabbath was not mandatory.

b) A second conception does better justice to the legal nature of the Ten Commandments. They are regarded as a form of a new covenant of works that God established with Israel. God did not establish it with the intent that by it Israel could earn life, for through sin that had become completely impossible. The aim was to allow them to attempt it in their own strength. In Egypt, they had lost the awareness of their impotence. This awareness had to be revived, and the new covenant of works served that end. "They were puffed up as it were with an absurd confidence in themselves and said, 'All that the Lord has said we will do.' "[4] God then gives them the law. But when they saw the terrifying display of the smoking and burning mountain, of the dark cloud and the lightning, they soon perceived that they could not live by this covenant of works and therefore asked for Moses to be their mediator. In connection with the consciousness of guilt awakened in this way, God renewed with Israel the Abrahamic covenant of grace, as recorded in Exodus 24, to which the Levitical laws also belonged. "The Book of the Covenant" was thus the summary of the covenant of grace, not the Decalogue engraved on stone tablets. In the ceremonial laws that were added later, the gospel element was resident. This is thus an opposite view from Cocceius and his school.

c) According to a third conception, at Sinai God established not *two* but even *three* covenants with Israel:

1. A national covenant.

2. A covenant of nature or of works.

3. A covenant of grace.

The first of these was made with all the Israelites, without exception, and was a continuation of the setting apart of one nation, the extension of the particular line that begins with Abraham. In this covenant, God promised Israel temporal blessings, and required in turn civic, external obedience. The prophets lament the violation of this national covenant through idolatry.

The second covenant was a repetition of the covenant of works and was established by the proclamation of the Decalogue. The promise of life and the threatening of death were solemnly uttered anew.

The third covenant was the renewing of the covenant of grace established with Abraham and was sealed through the announcement of the ceremonial law (thus Mastricht, VIII, Chapter II).

---

4 The source for this quotation is not given, but it is reminiscent of a passage in Edward Fisher, *The Marrow of Modern Divinity*, 1.2.2.3: "They swelled with mad assurance in themselves, saying, 'All that the Lord commandeth we will do.' "

47. *What objections must be made against all these proposals?*

a) That they are against the presentation of Scripture in multiplying the covenants. Never and nowhere is it presented as if more than one covenant was established at Sinai.

b) That they are in part wrong where they wish to limit the moral law or the ceremonial law entirely to one of these covenants. This cannot be achieved. We have already seen how, for example, the ceremonial law had a double aspect. These were demands that had to be fulfilled and that, through the impossibility of complete fulfillment, should drive people to Christ. At the same time, they were types and symbols that pointed to Christ and pictured Christ. Thus the ceremonial law of itself already appeared under the two covenants that one wishes to separate. It is likewise so with the moral law. In it occur features that recall the covenant of grace. It is not simply a law of the covenant of works. The promise of eternal life is not clearly expressed in it. And explanations that do present this promise occur in the midst of the ceremonial law.

48. *Does the covenant of grace continue in the days of the New Testament?*

Yes. This is already repeatedly foretold in the old day, for example, in Jeremiah 31:33. The Savior assumes this in the institution of the Lord's Supper, where He speaks of His blood of the covenant. In the Letter to the Hebrews, it is said in so many words (ch. 9). Also, the continuity of the Old Testament and the New Testament church is taught everywhere in the New Testament. The church of the New Testament has not come about as a new aggregate of individuals next to the old covenant people, but developed from it in a covenantal manner. Zacchaeus was converted because he is a son of Abraham, and with that conversion, salvation came to his house [Luke 19:9]. The Jews for the most part apostatized, but they were not all put aside so that the Gentiles simply take their place. Rather, the Gentiles were grafted as branches on the domesticated olive tree to share in the rich oil of the covenant (Rom 11). "The promise is to you and your children" (Acts 2:39; 3:25). The name "people of God" also continues in use. From all this, it is clear that the covenant continues.

49. *Is the covenant under the administration of the new day different from the earlier covenant?*

Not in essence; certainly in form. It contains greater blessings. Its essence and its benefits are more clearly revealed. It extends to all nations. It no longer has a ceremonial and typological service. The record of sin that was against us has been destroyed or nailed to the cross [Col 2:14]. There are no longer intermediaries between the believing covenant member and God, except the one Mediator, Christ. The Holy Spirit has been poured out. The glory of Christ Himself is beheld in the mirror of the gospel. There will be no more change in administration until the end of the world.

50. *Should the administration of the covenant of grace be divided into two or three parts?*

The division into two is the best and the oldest. There was an administration *before* Christ and an administration *after* Christ. It is true that there is a noteworthy difference to be observed between the administration *before* Moses and the one *after* Moses, but this was not such a difference that what these two time periods had in common, in contrast with the new dispensation, was lost. What is common to the time before Christ consists:

a) In the conception of the Mediator as a seed that was still to come, thus a pointing forward to the historical Christ. So it was with Adam as well as Abraham and throughout the whole Old Testament.

b) In the foreshadowing of the Mediator through ceremonies and types. These may have become more systematic after Sinai, but they were already there earlier.

c) In the foreshadowing of the destiny of the spiritual members of the covenant in the earthly fortunes of the covenant communities among whom God carried out His covenant. The liberation from Egypt, the occupation of Canaan, etc., all pointed forward to higher spiritual events. The points of difference between the pre-Mosaic time and the post-Mosaic time are the following:

1. In the patriarchal era, the gracious character of the covenant was more obvious (cf. Gal 3:18). Precisely because Israel was

once more deliberately reminded of the demand of the covenant of works, there existed the possibility of misunderstanding, as if this was the way to salvation. And in fact, the Israel
of a later era fell into this error.

2. The spiritual nature of the benefits of the covenant was better
understood in the patriarchal era (Heb 11:9–10). Abraham and
the patriarchs were sojourners and not owners of the land.
The temporal promise had not yet been fulfilled for them. But
just for that reason there was less danger for them that they
would look exclusively on the temporary, as the Jews did later.
They still had a clear vision of the Jerusalem that is above, the
future city (Gal 4:25–26).

3. The *world-encompassing* goal of the covenant of grace came out
more clearly. To Abraham it was said that in his seed all families of the earth would be blessed (Gal 3:8). Later, the Jews lost
sight of this, and then they thought that salvation was tied to
their nationality. Only later, during the flowering of prophecy,
the awareness was also more enlivened that God's promises
were world-encompassing.

The last two characteristics, the *spiritual* and the *catholic*,
moreover, go together. Paul is raised up by God as the great champion for both.

We therefore distinguish:

I. Before Christ

   a) From Adam to Abraham—no sacrament

   b) From Abraham to Moses—one sacrament

   c) From Moses to Christ—two sacraments

II. After Christ, until the end of the ages.

VOLUME THREE

CHRISTOLOGY

Translated and edited by

Richard B. Gaffin, Jr.

with

Jonathan Pater
Allan Janssen
Harry Boonstra
Roelof van Ijken

VOLUME THREE

CHRISTOLOGY

Contents

CONTENTS

PREFACE

My thanks to Harry Boonstra, Allan Janssen, and Jonathan Pater for their invaluable help in providing base translations for the various parts of this volume. As with the previous two volumes, I have reviewed and revised their work and given the translation its final form. The few editorial footnotes are mine. Again, thanks are due to the project manager, Justin Marr, and to the copy editors for their work.

The heart of any sound systematic theology or dogmatics is its treatment of Christology. Christ as the center of the entire saving self-revelation of the triune God finds full and rich expression in this present volume. There is much here to be read and reflected upon with great profit.

In the preface to volume one, I noted that with this translation English readers will be able to compare the early Vos of the *Reformed Dogmatics* (which was completed by the time he was 30) with his subsequent work in biblical theology. My statement then that such a comparison "will substantiate deep, pervasive and cordial continuity" is certainly proving to be true.

Still, there are some differences. One noteworthy difference is that in this volume (as he did in volume one), he cites Romans 1:4 as a proof text for the deity of Christ. This contrasts with the position—expressed in 1912 in "The Eschatological Aspect of the Pauline Conception of the Spirit"—that Romans 1:4 refers to the transformation of the incarnate Christ by the Holy Spirit in His resurrection. Also, he does not yet appear to have a clear understanding of the "already-not yet" structure of biblical eschatology, with its overlap of the two world-ages (aeons) in the interadvental period. He would later provide a now-classic articulation of this understanding in chapter one of *The Pauline Eschatology*, which informs his biblical theological work as a whole.

On the other hand, in this volume he already holds, as he argues convincingly in his later biblical-theological work, that in the description of the resurrected Christ in 1 Corinthians 15:45 as "life-giving Spirit," the reference is to the Holy Spirit.

R. Gaffin, Jr.

May 2014

CHAPTER ONE

Introduction

The Surety (Mediator) of the Covenant of Grace
The Name "Surety" or "Mediator"

1. *Of the two designations, "Surety" or "Mediator," which is most suitable to highlight the relationship of Christ to the covenant of grace?*

The name "Surety" has this advantage: that it renders more accurately what is meant by μεσίτης in most places in the New Testament—that is, one who, by assuming obligations and the guaranteeing of their fulfillment, brings about unity between separated parties. The name "Mediator" does emphasize the establishing of unity but leaves indefinite the manner in which this takes place (namely, by assuming obligations). Conversely, the meaning of the word "surety" in legal usage contains an element that suggests only the payment of an outstanding debt and loses sight of the other aspects of the work of Christ. It is therefore important with the use of both words to emphasize constantly that element that does not yet become clear in the usage of the word in itself. When one speaks of Christ as Surety, then one should remember that He does more than pay the outstanding penalty for the guilt of His people. When one speaks of Him as the Mediator, then one should accent that He is more than a means of mediation and only mediates by putting Himself in the place of the members of His body as their covenant Head. Thus both terms serve to supplement and explain each other.

2. *How can one develop the notion of Surety (Mediator) from the concept of the covenant of grace, as described above? In other words, how can you derive from the covenant of grace what Christ must be as Savior?*

   a) The covenant of grace was established with the Son, not as *Logos* apart from His incarnation, but as the Son to-become-incarnate. Thus one must deal here with the *Logos* as incarnated *Logos*. We must speak of the incarnation and the God-human existence of the person of the Son of God.

   b) As God-man, Christ is the Head of the covenant who not only effects the covenantal unity between God and man but must also possess it as a reality in Himself. There is thus a close connection between the concept of unity that must be established through the covenant of grace and the concept that one must form concerning the person of Christ in relation to His divine and human natures. On this point, too, Christology may not be detached from the doctrine of the covenant of grace but must stand in a living relationship with it.

   c) Christ is not the natural covenant Head of His people but the covenant Head in a covenant of grace. He does not begin His work as something completely new that has nothing to do with what was earlier. In back of the covenant of grace lies the covenant of works, which may not just be pushed aside but must be removed judicially—that is, the debt incurred through the breaking of the covenant of works must be discharged. At the same time, however, this covenant of works, which was violated by Adam, must be carried out. The benefits of the covenant of works must be obtained. This gives us the distinction between the passive and active obedience of Christ.

   d) Both passive and active obedience, taken together, entail a state of humiliation for Christ that He, as God-man, must enter into according to His human nature. If now Christ were only the procurer of covenant unity in a judicial sense, then one could speak only of a state of humiliation, and after having endured that, the Mediator would have to put off His humanity in order to retain only the state of divine glory belonging to Him from eternity. This, however, is by no means the case. There is more than a judicial representative unity between Christ and His people. On the basis of this, there is also a life-unity. He must not only establish covenant unity with God in a judicial sense, but also possess it in Himself and transmit it from Himself to the members of His body.

From this it follows that according to His humanity Christ must move on to a second state besides that of humiliation. All the benefits of the covenant, as they were acquired in the state of humiliation, must be exhibited in His human nature. The state in which this takes place is called the state of exaltation. According to this view, the doctrine of the states of Christ follows directly from the concept of the covenant of grace. It follows from the consideration that Christ is not the founder of the covenant but in a strict sense the Head of the covenant and thus, according to His human nature, shares in the benefits of the covenant.

Usually, the doctrine of the states of the Mediator is derived from the doctrine of redemption or salvation in general, in that one says: In the state of humiliation Christ had to earn salvation for us; in the state of exaltation He had to apply it. This explanation no doubt has great value for practical and catechetical use, and is perhaps more useful and transparent than that just given. It is, however, not completely logical. After all, it still by no means follows in itself from the fact that Christ must apply the accomplished salvation that He Himself must possess the benefits of the covenant to be applied. As far as we can judge, He could apply them without that. On the other hand, it follows from Christ's attribute as covenant Head that His human nature must be exalted. Naturally, then, this exaltation is connected with the application of salvation to the members of His body, but the application in its full extent cannot be explained from exaltation. The state of exaltation does not follow from application in general, but from the particular manner of the application of the merits of Christ (from the Head to the members). And the two states of Christ will also have to be treated in connection with the doctrine of the covenant, as a consequence of what has been said.

e) From the consideration that the Mediator must not only earn but also apply salvation, something else follows directly. If He were merely Mediator of reconciliation, debt-paying Surety, then He could appear exclusively as Priest and there would be one office. Now, however, the Mediator does much more than that. He does not stand at a distance, in between God and man, but as covenant-head of the covenant He has a personal interest in the further realization of the covenant, for which His atoning sacrifice has laid the basis. He has, in relation to the Father, taken upon Himself this further realization and, conversely, received the promise of a glorious body.

From this it immediately follows that His role as Mediator has a much wider scope than only that which flows directly from the payment of debt. In other words, there is a multiplicity of offices: Christ, besides priest, must also be prophet and king.

We find, therefore, that the doctrine of the offices of Christ, as well as that of the states, may be developed from the concept of the covenant of grace. Further support for the threefold division of the offices and the relationship of the three offices to each other can only be discussed later.

3. *Which topics must be dealt with, in succession, in this area of doctrine?*

    a) The names.

    b) The God-human existence, that is, the person and the natures.

    c) The states.

    d) The offices of the Mediator.

CHAPTER TWO

Names

1. *Why does the discussion of the names come first here?*

   a) Because in the revelation of God the name is never a meaningless sound, but expression of a reality. It is therefore a foregone conclusion that the names of the Mediator have something to tell us about His significance.

   b) Because the names do not merely serve in general to express one or other aspect of the being, but what is the core of the being. They summarize the essential characteristics of a concept. Thus when God's Word introduces the Mediator through names, then the intent—in the midst of the multiplicity of the traits with which His figure is delineated for us—is to fix our attention on what is primary, what before anything else must enter our consciousness. The richness of the Mediator is so great, and the relationships of His work are so numerous, that we have need of the help the names provide us in order to survey all of this and to place it under single, small viewpoints.

   c) Before the appearance of the Mediator in the flesh, the names were the great means of making Him into a living and personal figure. The various ways in which He was typically portrayed were summarized into a unity through the name. Thus within Israel a very specific thought was associated with what was to be understood by the name of the Messiah and of the Son of

God. When Christ actually appeared, He therefore did not begin by saying, "The Messiah, the Son of God is this or that," but by declaring, "I am the Messiah, the Son of God." He associated Himself with what the Old Testament had revealed about Him, and this association took place by means of the name.

2. *What may be observed about the meaning of the name Jesus?*

a) Matthew 1:21 and Luke 1:31 report how at God's explicit command this name was given to the Mediator. In the first mentioned verse, the explanation is also added, "for He will save His people from their sins." That care was intentionally taken, for this name-giving had a twofold purpose: (1) The name had already been borne by certain persons in the old dispensation and so already had a history in back of it as a type. (2) The derivation of the name provided an insight into the work of the Mediator.

b) The name Jesus, Ἰησοῦς, is the transcription in the Greek of the Septuagint of a later Hebrew form יֵשׁוּעַ, which occurs, for example, in Nehemiah 8:17 (of Joshua the son of Nun) and in Ezra 2:2 and 3:2 (of the high priest, son of Jozadak). The name is therefore not of Greek but of Hebrew origin, and its derivation from the verb ἰάομαι, "heal," can only be regarded as popular etymology based on its sound.

c) The older form of the Hebrew for יֵשׁוּעַ is יְהוֹשׁוּעַ, also transcribed by the Septuagint with Ἰησοῦς. The derivation of this must be יְהוֹשׁוּעַ, "Jehovah is salvation." Some have attempted to derive the name directly from יֵשׁעַ, without accepting composition with "Jehovah," but there are preponderant objections against this. For example, that such a form cannot be constructed from the root ישׁע in any of its forms, that the similarity with the name אֱלִישַׁע argues for the joining with "Jehovah," and especially that the change in name that took place in regard to Joshua ben Nun, according to Numbers 13:16, must have had significance. According to the text cited, he was previously called הוֹשֵׁעַ, "Hoshea," *hip'il* infinitive absolute of ישׁע. If the new name that he received were not composite with "Jehovah," then a meaningless change of the infinitive to the future tense would have taken place, for יְהוֹשׁוּעַ would then be understood as a *hip'il* future, "He shall deliver." This is unacceptable. The change must rather have been that through the introduction of "Jehovah," emphasis was placed on a new element in the significance as a type that Joshua the son of Nun had. In place of "salvation" in general, his name is now made very specific, "Jehovah is salvation."

d) One does not have to look far for the basis for this change. According to Hebrews 4:8 and the general representation of Scripture that the earthly Canaan is a type of the rest of heaven, the typical significance of Joshua the son of Nun lay in the fact that he brought Israel into the land of Canaan. As the Mediator delivered His people from the misery of sin, so Joshua delivered the Israelites from the misery of the wilderness. Since Joshua, however, was a mere human being and this deliverance was brought about (or might seem to be brought about) through human means, type and antitype did not agree completely. The Mediator would be more than man. He would be Jehovah, the self-existing God, and with the omnipotent strength of His deity bring His people into heaven. So that this would be seen clearly, Hoshea's name is changed and becomes Joshua so that it would be evident how also for Israel's entry into Canaan more than just human power was at work—how God through His miraculous deeds was the originator of their typical liberation and, consequently, even much more, the great and antitypical salvation pictured by that typical liberation.

Thus the meaning of the name Jesus evidently includes that a divine salvation will be wrought through Him. It is not correct to find expressed in Jesus' name exclusively the human side of the Lord's being. The name speaks to us of the divine omnipotence of salvation. The modern usage, endemic especially in the English-American world, that associates purely human predicates with the name of Jesus and puts the Mediator close to man in so familiar a fashion that all the splendor of His deity disappears, in order to make place for a sickly sentimentality, is not scriptural. One need not fall into the opposite extreme, however, and say that the name of Jesus expresses the deity of the Lord directly. One must, however, maintain that there are two elements that point to the deity of the Lord, namely:

1. The salvation to be brought about by Jesus would be a salvation planned and wrought by God. God Himself would provide the ransom. "Jehovah, salvation" is thus on a line with "Jehovah, our righteousness." And in the time of the New Testament it would be revealed more clearly that righteousness and salvation would be planned and wrought by God Himself so that the Second Person of the Triune Being would appear in the flesh as Surety. For *us*, then, there lies in such expressions nothing less in fact than the deity of the Mediator.

2. The salvation that Jesus also wrought according to and in His human nature would not take place without a communication of gifts of grace and support from the side of His deity. As Jehovah would support and protect Joshua (and therefore his name was changed), so also the deity of the Lord, His being Jehovah, would equip and powerfully support His humanity for the work of salvation.

e) The Mediator was pictured through Joshua the son of Nun, especially in his kingship. He was a type of Jesus through his conquering of enemies and a powerful communication of the external benefits of the covenant.

The salvation produced through the Mediator may also be viewed from yet another side. Sin is not only a power, and not only brings about servitude. It is also guilt and demands atonement. Besides the kingly office, the Mediator also has a priestly office. In order to show this, Joshua the son of Jozadak bore the name that the Mediator would bear. He was the high priest, and specifically the high priest who represents the sinful, polluted people: Zechariah 3:3-4, "Now Joshua was clothed with *filthy* clothes," etc.; 13:1, "a fountain against *sin* and *uncleanness*." The Mediator was pictured by this Joshua to show His work in atoning for guilt, as well as liberating and providing blessedness. That this is in fact so is stated amply in 6:13 (see above on the doctrine of the covenant). The words "and He will sit and *rule* on His throne; and He will be a priest on His throne; and the counsel of peace will be *between those two*" (that is, between kingship and priesthood) mean nothing other than that the singular calling of Joshua was to picture the unity of these two offices in Christ.

It is completely in agreement with this when the angel says to Joseph, "For He will save His people from their *sins*." Here, too, saving activity is brought directly into relationship with sin. And here, too, the modern propensity to portray Jesus as a friend of wretched people in general, as a comforter of the afflicted for whatever reason, as a compassionate martyr, must be opposed. He is, in the first place, the Surety who assumes guilt and a compassionate high priest. The point of contact must always be sought in sin. He must be commended not as a *friend* of children but as the Savior of *sinful* children. The center of gravity must always be where Scripture places it and nowhere else.

f) In our language [Dutch], Jesus is translated as *zaligmaker* ["savior"]. The question is how far that translation has maintained the force of the original. *Zalig* means "happy, blessed," which is again related to the Greek ὅλος, "whole," and Latin *solus*, "sole." So, "to save" means to "make happy," "to fill with good." This expresses only one side of the original concept, for in the Hebrew the basic concept of ישׁע, "to make room," points back to the oppression and misery that preceded the salvation. Thus, if we paraphrase, "to save" is to deliver from the greatest evil and to bring to the greatest good. Then the warrant for this paraphrase does not rest on the Germanic etymology of *zalig*, but on the Semitic meaning of ישׁע. It may also be noted that the derivation of *zalig* from words such as *gelukzalig* ["blissful"], *armzalig* ["pitiful"], etc., as if *zalig* meant "full," appears to be wrong.

If we now recapitulate, we find the following elements in the name Jesus: (1) He is deliverer from the oppression and anxiety of sin as guilt, the reconciling high priest. (2) He grants the space in which the happiness of man exists as the King conquering all enemies and saving His people. (3) He does this not as mere man but as "Jehovah of our salvation," both according to His deity and according to His humanity. The thought that He has earned salvation is not exclusively present in the name Jesus, but also certainly the thought that He applies it. That is, the name has not only a general but also a particular meaning. In the fullest sense, it can be used only by the elect: "He will save *His people* from their sins" [Matt 1:21].

3. What is the specific meaning of the name Christ?

The difference between this name and Jesus can be expressed best by saying that Christ is the designation of an office, while Jesus is derived from the *benefits* of the office acquired by Christ. From this flow different things, as we will see later.

Χριστός means "anointed" and is the verbal adjective of χρίω, "smear," "anoint." Χρίω is the Septuagint translation for the Hebrew משח, of which מָשִׁיחַ is a passive nominal form, which accordingly corresponds with χριστός. In the Old Testament, it is said of many things that they are anointed—mostly, however, of persons who are called to an office in the theocracy. The high priest is called הַכֹּהֵן הַמָּשִׁיחַ, ἀρχιερεὺς ὁ κεχρισμένος, "the anointed priest" (Lev 4:3). Most frequently the term מָשִׁיחַ occurs, in short, for kings, "the anointed" or "the anointed of Jehovah" (1 Sam 2:10, 35).

An anointing of the prophets occurs only in 1 Kings 19:16, where Elijah receives the command to anoint Elisha. The reason for this seems to be that for the priests and kings there was an ordered succession, and there were appointed persons, even office bearers, to perpetuate the office. This was not the case for the prophets. They did not form an order with succession but were called immediately by God, and where this direct call took place, there was no longer need for anointing, since the gifts of the Spirit would also have been imparted directly. That at the time of the appearing of the Messiah the Jews mainly gave the meaning of "king" to the name Christ appears from various places in the New Testament (e.g., Luke 23:2, 37, 39; "Christ, the Lord," 2:11; "the Christ, the king of Israel," Mark 15:32).

The significance of anointing is twofold:

a) It is a declarative, explanatory act that occurs both for the person himself as well as for others and is the proof that he is authorized to exercise a certain office.

b) It is at the same time an equipping act whereby the gifts of the office are granted to the anointed person. This is to be so understood that the ability necessary for the office is effected not by the external anointing but inwardly at the same time by the power of the Holy Spirit. The anointing oil that is poured on the head or put on various parts of the body portrays legitimation by the Holy

Spirit. The expression "outpouring" of the Spirit is related to this concept of anointing.

To rightly grasp the significance of Old Testament anointing, one needs to remember that it was a type that pointed forward to the anointing of the Mediator. The prophets, priests, and kings were (1) types of Christ, and (2) His organs through which He carried out His three offices. Now, we must not derive from their offices what Christ was, but must rather infer from Christ what their offices were. They were anointed because He would be anointed; He was *not* anointed because they had been. That for them an anointing was necessary, while under the new dispensation this no longer takes place, follows from the fact that the only effective anointing—that of the Mediator become man—had not yet occurred. There still was something lacking for full mediatorship. At the same time, however, the appointing of all these organs rested entirely on the official appointment of Christ Himself. Only because He Himself was clothed with the dignity of the Messiah by the Father could they be clothed with their office. Even under the old dispensation, God's church had no other prophet, priest, and king than the only Mediator. Thus, while these office-bearers point forward as types to the body that would come, at the same time they point back as organs to the eternal image of this body as it was present in God's counsel of peace. That is to say, His anointing, insofar as it was equipping, Christ received in time; His anointing, insofar as it is appointment, He did not first receive in time, but from eternity, since by the power of this anointing He already exercised His threefold office through the service of the shadows.

If we so understand anointing, it means the following, and the following elements are contained in the name Christ:

a) The Mediator is an office-bearer who has received an appointment and appears in the world on behalf of the Father. An office always presupposes someone higher who appoints and installs. It is something that requires a formal mandate. Christ has received a mission from the Father. He has not set Himself up as covenant Surety, but He has become Mediator in complete subjection to the will of the Father. His mediatorship stems from the Father, since in its entirety the covenant of grace has its origin in the inscrutable love of the Father. Every thought as if God the Father first had to be moved to pity through the work of Christ is excluded, for the Christ who satisfied God's righteousness is a Christ of *God*, that is, given to us by God for our complete salvation. This fact that He was chosen by the Father and appointed from eternity in the counsel of peace, and that consequently in all His work the good pleasure of the Father rests on Him, gives a singular coloring to the covenant of grace in its entirety (cf. 2 Cor 5:19–20).

b) Sovereignty attaches to every office. Toward the one who is superior, who confers it, it includes submission; toward the persons on whom it is conferred, it bestows official authority. Christ as anointed comes to us in each of His offices with authority, and demands submission. That is true in the first place in His kingly office, but it is also true of His priestly and prophetic activity. Everywhere Christ appears as having authority over us. In the realm of truth He is king (John 18:37). He teaches as one who has authority and not as the Pharisees and scribes. For everyone who scorns Him as high priest, no other sacrifice remains. As a consequence of His anointing, Christ cannot appear otherwise than with this sense of office, and the office bearers who speak on His behalf may not be satisfied with anything less. They must not preach a Christ who still has to obtain authority but always such a one who has been ordained by the Father and sent into the world (John 10:36; 6:27: "Work for the food ... which the Son of Man will give you, for God the Father has *sealed* Him"). Christ does not come as a philosopher who commends or presses His ideas but as the anointed of the Father. And because all preaching is an official task that is performed in His name, it may never depart from these claims. It may not at any cost deny Christ's sovereignty of office; and where it nevertheless does, it will soon become evident that it has lost its power.

c) Also belonging to the anointing is an equipping of the human nature of Christ by the Holy Spirit for the exercise of His offices as Mediator. This equipping, unlike His appointment, cannot be related to the person of the Mediator according to both His natures, but only to His human nature. As such, however, the equipping was real and not merely apparent. The human nature of the Lord was weak and frail because of our sins and accordingly was not able in itself to perform His offices. Therefore, it was endowed in an exceptional manner with gifts of the Spirit and equipped for the work of Mediator. This occurred especially on two solemn occasions: at the baptism in the Jordan and at the transfiguration on the mountain. On both occasions, the equipping was accompanied by an open declaration from God. See Matthew 3:17, "a voice from heaven saying, 'This is my beloved Son, in whom I am well pleased' "; Matthew 17:5, "Behold a voice from the clouds saying, 'This is my beloved Son in whom I am well pleased; hear Him.' " See also what is said about this anointing of the Son by the Holy Spirit in the discussion of the economic work of the Spirit.

d) As the Mediator, Christ stands in a relationship to the members of the covenant of grace in which He cannot stand to them as Jesus. Being anointed is something that He has not only for His members or for the benefit of His members but also in fellowship with His members. Saving, in contrast, belongs exclusively to Him and takes place entirely outside of them.

On the other hand, believers, like Him, are sealed and anointed by the Holy Spirit (2 Cor 1:21–22; Eph 1:13; 4:30). In particular, they are prophets, priests, and kings because something of the Holy Spirit, whose fullness dwells in Christ, has flowed down upon them, so that they, in turn, proclaim God's counsel, dedicate themselves to God as a thank offering, and reveal the power of grace in the warfare against enemies (Rev 1:6; Acts 2:17).

4. *Which name for the Mediator, besides Jesus and Christ, occurs most often in the writings of the New Testament?*

The name κύριος, "lord." Κύριος is the Septuagint translation of the Hebrew אֲדֹנִים, אֲדֹנִי, both where this is used of men as well as where it occurs in an absolute sense of God (cf. Gen 18:12, Sarah calls Abraham her lord; 18:3, Jehovah is so addressed by Abraham). In the Septuagint, κύριος also occurs where in the Old Testament יהוה is used, not to serve as its translation but simply since it had already become the custom not to speak aloud the name יהוה and to put *Adonai* in its place. In the New Testament, too, κύριος occurs of God in general or of God the Father = Jehovah; for example, ἄγγελος κυρίου, "an angel of the Lord" (Matt 1:20, 25; cf. v. 22, "what was spoken by the Lord").

When now in the New Testament the Mediator is called κύριος, "Lord," then the question arises for us whether this is to be understood in the same sense in which it refers to God, or in a changed sense. Does the relationship in which He is our Lord stem from His being one in essence with the Father, in terms of the divine nature, or from His worth as Mediator that He possesses in both natures as God-man? When the question is posed in that way, we must answer: the latter. Christ is called Lord not in the first place as the Second Person in the Divine Being, but as Mediator. This is sufficiently clear from the expression ὁ θεὸς καὶ πατὴρ τοῦ κυρίου ἡμῶν Ἰησοῦ Χριστοῦ, "the God and Father of our Lord Jesus Christ" [Rom 15:6; 2 Cor 1:3; Eph 1:3; 1 Pet 1:3], where God the Father is thus called the God of Christ as Lord, and "Lord" therefore cannot mean His deity but only His worth as Mediator. It is to be understood in the same sense when Paul says ἡμῖν εἷς θεὸς ὁ πατήρ ... καὶ εἷς κύριος Ἰησοῦς Χριστός, "We have one God, the Father ... and one Lord, Jesus Christ" (1 Cor 8:6), where existence as God and existence as Lord are clearly distinguished, without it therefore being denied that in Himself Christ is God and the Father is Lord.

Christ is therefore called our Lord as Mediator:

a) By the gift of the Father in election.

b) By His suffering and death He has obtained an exclusive right of possession to believers, before which all other rights must give way.

The name "Lord" accordingly expresses approximately the same thing as we found in the name "Christ," namely, the idea of "authority" (*potestas*, to be differentiated from *potentia*, "might"). Still, "Lord" is not completely synonymous with "Christ." The latter recalls the origin of the Mediator's capacity for power and reminds us that it is derived from the sovereignty of the Father; Christ is the anointed of God. The former, in contrast, places the emphasis on the relationship between Christ and His servants, without, in doing that, the thought being so much on the origin of that relationship. The significance of the names comes out clearly in the following texts: Luke 6:46, "Why do you call me 'Lord, Lord,' and do not what I say?" John 13:13–14, "You call me Master and Lord, and you are right, for so I am" (cf. 2 Cor 5:15; Rom 14:8).

Although the lordship of Christ over us is in the first place a mediatorial lordship and does not have in view His divine sovereignty, still, on the other hand, it must also be granted that it proves indirectly the deity of the Mediator. It would be impossible for a mere man to exercise that sovereignty and to possess that unlimited right of possession over soul and body that is attributed to Christ as our Lord. These are rights that are due God alone and that cannot be transferred to another, unless this other is Himself God. It is only the deity of Christ that enables Him in this respect to be the Mediator.

5. *Does the name "Son of God" also have reference to Christ as Mediator, and if so, what reference?*

It has been said repeatedly that the name "Son" in its deepest significance indicates an eternal-essential constitutive relationship between Father and Son—thus within the Triune Being—that exists entirely apart from the work of the Mediator and does not first flow from it. If Christ had never become Christ, He still would always have been Son, since it was not a positive, free ordaining of the Father that made Him Son, but an immutable, immanent law of the Divine Being itself that must exist in three hypostases [persons].

Still, on the other hand, it must be maintained that Christ's existence as Son has significance for His mediatorship. That He was the Son is in part the basis for His appearance as Surety and Mediator of the covenant of grace. The relationship in which this Surety and Mediator had to appear was fitting for the relationship in which the Son by nature stands to the Father. When one will be sent, anointed, made subservient, glorified, and endowed with an inheritance, then one expects that it is the Son to whom all of this happens on behalf of the Father. As eternal Son of the Father, He can accomplish and undergo these things without anything abnormal taking place.

From this it follows that in Christ's role as Mediator something of His eternal sonship shines through at the same time; and to the degree that the former appears increasingly in the full daylight of revelation, the latter will come out more clearly. In His wisdom, God has been pleased to bring the eternal relationship between Father and Son to clarity by degrees, by means of this shadowing of it in the mediatorship. Already in the days of the old covenant, God had so spoken about the relationship that He intended to establish with the Messiah that one had to sense how from such promises an eternal Fatherly love was expressed and how the person to whom they applied must be more than an ordinary man. God called the Mediator, the future theocratic king, "Son," since He would receive an inheritance (Psa 2 and 2 Sam 7:14).

Consequently, it came about that the name "Son of God" became synonymous with that of "Messiah." However, as the pious, the spiritual Israel, saw more and more the glory of the eternal sonship of the Mediator radiating through this designation, and furthermore as the revelation of the New Testament expressly pointed back to this inner-Trinitarian relationship as the basis for the economic relationship (Gospel of John, Letter to the Hebrews), Israel according to the flesh remained attached to the theocratic sense of this name and expected in the Son of God nothing more than a human king, on whom the good pleasure of Jehovah would certainly rest in an exceptional measure, but who, without preexistence, would still be born in the ordinary manner from the seed of David. The starting point for the Jewish and the biblical-Christian conception was therefore the same, but from that point on the lines ran in different directions.

In the mouth of the people, the name "Son of God" in the Evangelists usually has the meaning in which it is synonymous with "Messiah" (Mark 14:61). In the mouth of the Savior, it usually has a much deeper meaning, since He apparently connects it with His eternal sonship. This is especially the case in the Gospel of John. Occasionally, the Jews also realized that Jesus, by calling Himself "God's Son," ascribed to Himself more than human worth as Messiah. They therefore accused Him of blasphemy (John 10:36; 19:7). On the other hand, Christ Himself sometimes employed the customary usage of the word and called Himself "Son of God" in the sense in which this name was already used in the Old Testament—that is, as Mediator on whom the good pleasure of the Father rested (cf. John 10:36; Matt 26:63).

The relationship between Christ's sonship and His mediatorship is seen in what follows, which in part has already been discussed earlier:

a) The reason why Christ has become our Mediator and our covenant Head is in His eternal sonship (Gal 4:6). He is the firstborn among many brothers (Heb 2:11–12; Rom 8:29).

b) Christ has assumed human nature into the unity of His person. His human nature is therefore borne in the person of the Son of God. Through this human nature and the Holy Spirit indwelling it, He is one with all the members of His body, so that there is therefore a bond between His sonship and theirs. Still, there always remains the difference that He is Son from eternity through generation, and therefore only Son (Mediator) through foreordination and the preparation of His human nature, while they are children of God exclusively through adoption and re-creation according to the image of Christ.

Already in the Old Testament, it was clearly depicted that there existed such a connection between the eternal Son of the Father and the members of His body. For more than once, all Israel is called the Son of God (Exod 4:22; Hos 11:1; Isa 63:16; Jer 31:19–20; Mal 1:6; Deut 14:1–2). At the same time, the Messiah-king of the future was called God's Son (2 Sam 7:14). And in the New Testament, what was said of Israel as a whole is simply transferred to Christ (cf. Matt 2:15, with Hos 11:1). The explanation of this phenomenon is that Israel is a type of the spiritual covenant people and the Messiah, again, the unity and representative of the covenant people, so that as Mediator and covenant Head He is also called the Son—not, however, without the coordinate thought that it is precisely His metaphysical sonship that qualified Him to be invested with this office of Mediator.

6. *What is the significance of the name "Son of Man," with which Christ designated Himself?*

This name is also derived from the Old Testament, specifically from Daniel 7. After the description of the four world monarchies, portrayed by as many animals (a lion with eagle's wings, a bear, a panther, a beast not mentioned by name), reference is made to one "who is like a son of man" and who by the "Ancient of Days" is given "dominion and honor and a kingdom that all peoples and nations and languages should honor him; his dominion is an everlasting dominion that shall not pass away, and his kingdom shall not be destroyed" [Dan 7:13–14]. It is not subject to doubt that the Messiah is intended here, although not the Messiah by himself. Since the Son of Man comes to supersede the earlier world-kingdoms, he must be taken here, together with his kingdom and its subjects, as ruler over Israel representing his people. He is called a son of man because over against the wild and animal-like world-kingdoms he represents true humanity as it must be in God's kingdom.

Thus, in part, the question of what may have given Christ occasion to make use of this name for signifying His office is already answered.

He apparently wanted to counter the faulty conceptions that people had formed about the Messiah as an outward king. The kingdom in which He is Messiah and King is not according to the manner of the kingdoms of this world—which find their image in an animal-type, but it bears a human countenance—is like a son of man. If Christ had repeatedly called Himself Messiah, He would have given support to the fleshly expectations, with drawn bow, of his contemporaries. He therefore could use the title that let the emphasis fall on the human and less warlike nature of His kingdom, and, moreover, that was not understood by most people in its Old Testament messianic significance and gave less occasion to draw erroneous conclusions from it.

At the same time, there is in the name a not-unclear pointing to the deity of the Lord. He is *the* Son of Man, ὁ υἱὸς τοῦ ἀνθρώπου, who is thus distinguished from all other men through something special, as comes out clearly in the predicates that are ascribed to Him as such: "So that you may know that the Son of Man has power on earth to forgive sins" (Matt 9:6); "From now on, you will see the Son of Man seated at the right hand of power and coming on the clouds of heaven" (26:64); "For the Son of Man will come in the glory of His Father with His angels, and then He shall repay every man according to His works" (16:27); "For the Son of Man is Lord, even of the Sabbath" (12:8). For the mysterious nature of this title, as a consequence of which the multitude did not comprehend Him, see the question in Matthew 16:13, "Whom do men say that I, the Son of Man, am?"

7. *Is the name* παῖς, *"child," used with reference to the Messiah, and if so, what is its distinguishing significance?*

Παῖς expresses the relationship of child to parent, and also, by inference, the relationship of one who serves to the one who commands. In this derived sense, it is thus synonymous with δοῦλος, with the difference that the latter places more emphasis on constraint and servitude, while παῖς simply indicates subordination without compulsion. In the Septuagint, παῖς is the translation of the Hebrew עבד, "servant," specifically of עֶבֶד־יהוה, "servant of the Lord."

In the last-mentioned sense, it occurs repeatedly of Christ (Matt 12:18, citation from Isa 42:1); "The God of Abraham, Isaac, and Jacob has glorified His child (better, 'servant') Jesus" (Acts 3:13). In these places, one should not understand the name "child" in the sense of "Son," as if the reference were to the eternal sonship of Christ. "Child" is here exclusively a name of the Mediator, which mainly in the latter part of the prophet Isaiah is ascribed in a distinctive way to the Mediator, namely insofar as He represents the people of Israel and accomplishes that to which the nation had been called, but it had not been able to accomplish because of its sins and imperfections. In the concept of "servant of the LORD," as it is developed in this prophecy, the following elements are present: (1) The Messiah is God's possession and on the basis of confidence in Him is like a trusted servant with his lord. (2) He carries out God's work on earth, as the servant does the work of his lord. (3) He is lowly and needy in carrying out this servant work, and appears in the form of a servant. That the Messiah here appears so closely tied to spiritual Israel will have its basis in the distinctive nature of the prophecy that is intended to portray the Mediator as prophet and priest. Especially as priest, the Messiah is Head and representative of His people, so that He can easily be identified with them. This also allows explaining the error as if the term "servant of the LORD" were no more than a symbolic term for the people of Israel as a *collectivum* [collective]. This may be the case in a few places, but in most by far the reference is to one particular person, who can be none other than the Mediator.

8. *Was there another name by which Jesus was frequently called and that He acknowledged?*

The name "Son of David," by which allusion was made not only to his lineage according to the flesh from David, but above all to His royal worth as successor of this king. Among the Jews, "Son of David" had become a fixed title of the Messiah, like "Son of God" and "Anointed" (Matt 9:27; Mark 10:47). When the Lord did not protest against the use of this name, more was involved in that than an accommodation to the ideas of the people. Only when the scribes understood the term in such a limited sense that the principal aspect of His messianic glory was eliminated did Jesus see it necessary to remind them that this Son of David was at the same time also David's Lord and that His kingdom is of a higher order than that of an ordinary, earthly successor of David (Matt 12:35–37).

Chapter Three

Person and Natures

1. *As a result of the meaning of these different names, what can already be established provisionally concerning the person of the Mediator and His natures?*

   a) That He is truly God. We found that included:

      1. in His name Jesus;

      2. in the name Lord and the absolute sovereignty expressed by that;

      3. in the name "Son of God," insofar as that also has an official meaning and is synonymous with Messiah.

   b) That He is truly man. This is implied:

      1. in the official name Christ, since at least equipping for an office can only take place in His human nature;

      2. in the name "Son of Man."

   c) That in these two natures He is anointed to three offices, as is clear from the name Christ.

   d) That for exercising His work as Mediator, He had to pass through a state of humiliation as well as a state of exaltation, as is to be derived from the names "Servant of the Lord," "Son of David."

2. *How may one derive the deity of our Lord from the requirements for His work as Mediator?*

a) At every point of his existence, every man (human person) is claimed by the demands of God's law such that there remains no area where he would have no need of those demands for himself and would be able to be at the disposal of others. God claims him entirely, and if he gives himself entirely to God, then the measure of his own righteousness is only just full and so never overflows it.

Through the covenant of works, guilt was personally imputed to all human persons. Consequently, whoever is born as a merely human person has personally imputed guilt and cannot pay for the guilt of others. It was otherwise for Adam. With the establishment of the covenant of works, there was no personal guilt for those who were included in it, and God was therefore free, through a gracious determination, to let Adam's deed and situation be determinative for the status of all. This does not at all mean, however, that Adam earned more (quantitatively) than he needed for himself. The latter is the case only with Christ. This can never happen with man, and therefore Rome's doctrine of *opera supererogationis* [works of supererogation], with everything connected to it, must be rejected.

b) When we consider the same issue from a different side, we can formulate it as follows: Not only is no one in a position as mere man to act as a substitute for other men, but neither is anyone *sui juris* ("by his own right") in the sense that he can freely give himself as surety. Since, in the final analysis, every man is not his own but God's possession, he cannot give himself. But it is precisely in this free giving up of self, in this giving away of self, by one who was completely *sui juris*, and as eternal God possessed Himself perfectly—it is just in this that the value of the suretyship of the Mediator lies. Scripture teaches everywhere that the Father gave the Son, but that same Scripture also teaches that the Son gave Himself. And because this voluntary character is noteworthy throughout the work of the Mediator in its entirety, this characteristic must no less be sought and presupposed in the initial origin of that work. This may be assumed only if the Mediator Himself is the independent God, the eternal source of all right.

c) Considered apart from the natural relationship of man as man to God, a merely human person cannot be excluded from the covenant of works. This was established with all human persons. If Christ had been a human person, He would have fallen under that covenant. Now one could ask whether, by possessing a (nonpersonal) human nature, He is not already placed beyond the pale of the covenant of works, so that there would be no need of deity—in other words, whether a (nonpersonal) human nature could not in itself be our Mediator. This question must be answered in the negative. God cannot deal in justice with an abstract nature. There must always be a person underlying nature, a *suppositum* [subject] upon whom justice terminates and from whom it originates. So here, too, we reach this result: The Mediator cannot be a human person (otherwise he would fall under the covenant of works), and at the same time must be a person (otherwise he could not act for us in justice). Therefore, He must be a divine person.

d) The covenant of grace is so ordered that the Mediator who makes reconciliation is at the same time also the Mediator of the application of the accomplished salvation and that all those who share in the covenant must be placed in a direct relationship to Him. They do not draw near only to God the Father in Christ, or to the triune God in Christ the Mediator, but also to Christ Himself. Their faith, their love must embrace Him; they are subject to Him in body and soul. He is their "Lord" who has absolute sovereignty over them. In everything His word is the final decision, from which no higher appeal is possible. He must make disposition of the Spirit, who Himself is God, must send the Spirit into the hearts of His members, regenerate them with omnipotence, unite them to Himself, sanctify, and glorify them. It is completely impossible that all these predications could be attributed to one who is a mere man. No man can place himself in this way between God and the sinner and presume from the latter the service that is due only to the former. The Arian heresy, even in its most developed form (Socinianism), has therefore always seen itself compelled to have Christ elevated, after His ascension, to the status of deity. It did not wish to ascribe to Him original, preexistent deity; He had to be created or born as an ordinary man. But still it did see that His position as Mediator, in the state of exaltation, is elevated far above the limits of the purely human. Therefore, recourse was taken to an apotheosis, to a divinization of the man Christ. He was said to be clothed with divine power and majesty by the Father.

We, on the other hand, conclude from this entirely unique, more than human place that Christ occupies in His exaltation, back to His more than human origin, His eternal deity. After all, everything that exists is one or the other: God or creature. Scripture does not recognize intermediate stages. Even a creature made to be God could not be a mediator nor assume that relationship with the redeemed in which the Mediator must stand to them.

e) Likewise, the covenant of grace is so constructed and arranged that the honor for the salvation of men resides not with man but with God. The triune God—as the one who elects, as Savior, as applier of salvation—is here the one who does everything and secures the covenant in every respect. Man may not ascribe to himself anything of the glory of the covenant of grace. In it, all things must be from God, through God, to God. The entire Triune Being must be revealed in it; the Trinity must be reflected most clearly in its economy.

Now with all this it is incomprehensible that the Mediator who occupies such a prominent place in the covenant of grace would be a mere man. The beautiful order in the work of grace would then be disturbed. No longer would a triune God reveal Himself in it, but it would be a work shared between God and man. When the faith of the sinner is directed to Christ and he is justified before God through faith, the significance of that is that by faith he acknowledges and becomes conscious how all salvation is located in God. Faith is the subjective side of monergistic divine grace. Therefore, a faith that is directed to a man is a *contradictio in adjecto* [contradiction in terms]. The object of saving faith cannot be a man, but must be God.

f) Christ's work as Mediator must possess an infinite value, since that work must extend to the satisfaction of the eternal wrath of

God. A mere man can never endure this wrath, as is already apparent from the eternal punishment of those who are lost. We would have to remain under that wrath eternally simply because our human nature is not able to endure its intensity. What we thus lack for bearing this wrath in its intensiveness must (for the lost) be paid for extensively; they bear the infinite wrath of God through their endless punishment. Christ, however, did not have to be swallowed up in this death. He had to come through it victoriously; it had to become evident that death could not hold Him. For His humanity, that would have been impossible. His deity could cause the bearing of the burden of the endless wrath by His humanity without this humanity succumbing or being destroyed.

One must also note that it was the person of the Son of God who suffered in this humanity, and that thereby an infinite value was placed on His merits. Indeed, the value of the merits was determined by two things: (1) by their inherent properties; (2) by the person to whom they belonged. The humanity of the Mediator had its existence in the person of the Son of God. All the suffering and all the active obedience, although accomplished in His humanity, was nevertheless divine suffering and divine obedience—that is, of infinite value. Therefore, we find that, in agreement with the two points mentioned above, His deity was necessary for two reasons: (1) to support His humanity in bearing the infinite wrath of God; (2) to put an infinite value on the merits of the Mediator. With that said, then, yet a third reason may be appreciated: (3) only a divine person is able to bring about righteousness for *so many*.

3. *Can a similar derivation of the humanity of the Mediator be given [from the requirements for His work as Mediator; see question 2]?*

This follows directly:

a) From the necessity that a real satisfaction be made by the Mediator. This presupposes the duration of a certain phase, the transition from one state into another, the experiencing of certain transient conditions, entry into time, and participation in history. Of God Himself one cannot say that He has a history, for He is the eternal One, with whom there is no variation or shadow of turning.

Everything in Him is an unchanging presence. Salvation or satisfaction, on the other hand, is not an eternal process but something temporal, occurring in the human sphere. Even though it originates with God and has reference to God, it must still take place in what is finite and created. Every other conception rests on a pantheistic view. Because we hold satisfaction to be a single historical fact and not a transition in the eternal development process of the Absolute, for that reason we have need of the genuine humanity of the Lord—and as a basis for that, an incarnation taking place at a particular point in space and time. Not an apparent incarnation but only a genuine humanity distinguished from deity can avail here. The Mediator must be God, and still He must have a history. With these givens, the only way one can escape pantheism in Christology is by establishing that Christ, along with His true deity and unmixed with it, also possesses genuine humanity, from which all the mutability mentioned above can be predicated.

b) From the necessity that payment for guilt must also take place through the same nature in which sin against God was committed. It is true that guilt is reckoned to persons, and no legal relationships may be conceived of vis-à-vis a totally abstract nature. Thus it must be granted that it is not the human nature of Christ that makes satisfaction, but the *person* of the Son of God. But while it is the person on whom the obligation rests, He can have this obligation only to the extent that He is joined to the nature. The possession of the nature is *conditio sine qua non*, for the nature (as the inclusion of attributes common to all) first places the person in that particular relationship to others on whom these obligations are incumbent.

Our guiding principle must therefore read: The nature without the person *is* not subject to the duties, but the person without the nature *cannot* be subject to them. Adam, for example, represented the whole human race. This representation did not, in the first place, rest on the fact that he had the same nature as all other people. It rested on all human persons being personally reckoned in him through the covenant of works. That is, the nature without the person would not have been subject to the obligations.

On the other hand, it is equally certain that the personal Adam could not have represented us if he had not possessed the same human nature with us. An angel would have been a person as well as Adam, and thus, as far as being a person is concerned, would have been able to become our representative Head equally well. But that angel did not possess our human nature, and therefore could not have represented us as covenant Head. That is, the person without the nature cannot be subject to the obligations.

If we transfer this to Christ, then it follows immediately how He, although our Surety as divine person, nevertheless at the same time had to share in human nature if He was to be our Surety and Mediator. A human nature without a person was not able to save us any more than a divine person without a human nature.

c) From the necessity that the Mediator would reveal God to men in a complete, immediate manner. If He had possessed only the divine nature, He would have remained above the sphere of humanity, and a means would have been necessary to do this revealing apart from Him. He would then have had to make use continually of subordinate office bearers—who would have carried out the work of revelation for Him—or portray His priestly activity and His kingly glory, as He did before His incarnation in the days of the old covenant. Now, in contrast, through His incarnation this need has passed away. In Christ, and through His human nature, God speaks to us directly so that we can hear Him with our human ears. The person who speaks in Him is the person of the Son of God, who does not have a derived knowledge of the secrets of the divine counsel, but who is initiated into those secrets from eternity and thus speaks the things of God because He is from God, God "revealed in the flesh," "the great mystery of godliness" [1 Tim 3:16].

d) Since Christ as Head of the covenant must form one body with believers and precede them in their glorification, from this it also follows that He must possess a human nature. Joined to this human nature through the Holy Spirit, and through this human nature to the person of the Son of God, all the redeemed constitute that mysterious body that was determined in election. Christ is also allied with the angels; He would also have been in a certain relationship with humanity if it had not fallen into sin. But that bond would not have been as close as it is now, since the Son of God as Mediator has taken on human nature. It is not a divine life in the strictly metaphysical sense of the word or a divine-human substance that is to be shared with the redeemed, for that would lead to a mingling of God and man, between whom the ontological separation may never be eliminated. A pure human life—which, however much a product of God's supernatural power of grace, still remains a pure human life—had to pass from Christ to the members of His body. For this reason, too, it was therefore necessary that Christ possess this pure humanity. This demand flows no less from the significance as an exemplar that Christ's exaltation has for believers. If, after satisfying God's righteousness, He had put off His human nature, then believers would no longer be able to look to Him as the firstfruits of those who had died [1 Cor 15:20], as the supreme leader and finisher of faith, who is now seated at the right of the throne of God (Heb 12:2). Conversely, in the state of exaltation Christ is also, through the memory of the weakness and the suffering that He bore in His human life, a merciful and compassionate high priest (Heb 4:15).

4. *Can one prove from Scripture that the Mediator is truly God?*

The proof for the deity of the Son was presented in detail earlier. Since the Son is primarily revealed as Mediator, and through His role as Mediator His eternal sonship has also come to greater clarity, most of the proofs produced can also be used to prove the deity of the Son as Mediator. Virtually everywhere it is the Mediator who speaks and who ascribes to Himself (that is, His divine person) omnipotence, omnipresence, omniscience, who permits Himself to be named with divine names, to receive divine honor, and to be attributed divine works.

5. *How can one demonstrate from Scripture the true humanity of the Mediator?*

   a) By showing that Christ possessed everything that belongs to true humanity, namely:

   1. A *human body*: Hebrews 2:14, "So He likewise partook of the same" (namely, of flesh and blood); Luke 24:39, "See my hands

and my feet, for it is I myself. Touch me and see, for a spirit does not have flesh and bones, as you see that I have.'"

2. A *human soul* as the principle of willing, feeling, thinking life: Matthew 26:38, "My soul is exceedingly sorrowful, even unto death"; John 12:27, "Now is my soul troubled, and what shall I say?"

3. A *human spirit,* namely, the soul insofar as it is the principle of the enlivening force and of the animation of the body: John 19:30, "And bowing His head He gave up His spirit."

b) By showing that things are said about Christ that are completely irreconcilable with deity and consequently can have their truth only in His human nature. All affects belonging to human nature are attributed to Him, so that He was sorrowful even unto death (Matt 26:38); He was hungry (Matt 4:2) and thirsty (John 19:28); He was tired and sat down by the well (John 4:8); He fell asleep (Matt 8:24); by looking on people He was filled with love and compassion for them (Matt 9:36); He was afraid (Heb 5:7); He wept [John 11:35]; He rejoiced in spirit (Luke 10:21); He had need for prayer (Matt 14:23).

c) By demonstrating that in the Mediator, as He was revealed in the flesh, a true, human development took place. However deep the mystery of the unity of His humanity and His divine person may be, this is certain: This unity did nothing to diminish the true humanity of the Lord, and instead of impeding or disturbing human development has rather sustained and guided it. His deity did not communicate more knowledge and power to His humanity than was in accord with its age, and just by reckoning with this the Gospel narratives differ from embellished and distorted tradition. Of Jesus it is testified that He increased and grew and became strong in spirit; that He questioned others; and that He increased in wisdom, and in stature, and in favor with God and man (Luke 2:40, 46, 49, 52). It is impossible to attribute all these things to His deity, for with deity all development is excluded. One must consider, however, that this development in the human nature of the Lord did not happen in a natural manner, inasmuch as the human nature in Him was not personal but was borne through the person of the Son of God. What for others is grounded in the natural law of development that governs all that is created, and what for man is independent development of a personal life, for the Mediator was inseparably tied to the divine person, so that development cannot count as a second, independent principle in addition to that tie.

d) In Christ there was present not merely a human soul (or spirit) in general but a complete soul, insofar as it concerns the capacity that every human soul possesses. In Him there was a knowing, a willing, an emotional life. He knew, and that in a human manner—that is, according to His humanity He was not omniscient (Mark 13:32). He had a will, which He knew to distinguish from the Father's will (so also from His divine will) when He prayed, "not my will, but yours be done." (For the emotional life in the human nature of the Mediator, see above.)

e) He expressly calls Himself a man (John 8:40, "A man who has told you the truth"). It is testified about Him that He became flesh—that is, He assumed a human nature in its entirety as it is in contrast to God, that He died, that He stands as second man alongside of Adam, is of the lineage of David, etc. (cf. 1 John 4:2).

6. *What problems arise from this data of Scripture that Christ is truly God and also truly man?*

The following two:

a) How in this case the divine and the human can remain distinguished as is demanded by the difference throughout Scripture between creature and Creator.

b) How, nevertheless, their coexisting in the Mediator can be circumscribed so that there are not two persons, two mediators.

7. *How has one sought to solve that problem?*

The church has come to firm conceptions in this matter only through a continuing struggle against heretical misunderstanding and distortion of the data of Scripture. Repeatedly, where error emerged, with rejection of the error there was the incentive to establish the truth positively. It is therefore impossible to understand orthodox church doctrine on this point well if one is not knowledgeable of the various heresies that, one after the other, have beset this part of Christian truth. Church doctrine holds to the middle between extremes, because here it is also true that there is no effective heresy that does not derive its strength for exercising influence from an element of the truth, which it attempts to develop one-sidedly and elevate at the cost of all other truths. Especially in a doctrine like this, where the middle way is so narrow and one is continually in danger of slipping to the right or to the left, it is not sufficient to know the truth positively. In order to proceed safely, one must also be acquainted with error. It is therefore necessary that we here provide a brief sketch of the course of the development this dogma has passed through, in contrast with its heretical distortion.

8. *In how many ways has one fallen into error regarding the doctrine of the Mediator?*

In two ways:

    a) By trying to dismiss the problem simply by denying the data that create it. Christ is truly God and truly man. Therein lies the problem. For those who deny one of these two propositions, the problem disappears immediately—how deity and humanity are to be kept from merging and how they are to be united. Or one may not deny deity or humanity completely but deny some part of it, in order to bring deity and humanity closer together and to reach an apparent unity between both in the Mediator.

    b) By accepting the scriptural data for the dogma unconditionally but then bringing deity and humanity into relationship in such a way that either the first problem is not solved (deity and humanity do not remain at scriptural distance) or the second has no solution (no genuine unity between deity and humanity results).

9. *How, according to this scheme, can you arrange the various heretical opinions about the Mediator?*

    a) Into those that:

        1. Deny the deity of the Mediator—*Ebionitism*, in older and newer forms, the Alogi.

2. Deny the humanity of the Mediator—*Gnosticism*, particularly Docetism, Modalists (Sabellians).

3. Deny the *complete* deity of the Mediator—*Arianism*.

4. Deny the *complete* humanity of the Mediator—*Apollinarism*.

b) Into those that:

1. Keep the deity and the humanity so separated that no unity obtains—*Nestorianism*.

2. Commingle the deity and the humanity, (a) by creating a third entity from their joining—*monophysitism*; (b) by letting the one devolve into the other—the doctrine of kenosis in its modern forms.

10. *What was the conception of the Ebionites concerning the person of the Mediator?*

The Ebionites (at least the more strict line designated with this name) regarded Christ as the natural son of Joseph and Mary, as a ψιλὸς ἄνθρωπος, "a mere man," who was gifted with the Holy Spirit at His baptism and thereby became Christ (Messiah). Ebionitism expresses the one-sided-ly developed, specifically Jewish element of truth that God is one and cannot be two or three. The Old Testament also taught that, but it had also indicated that this one God is not an abstract unity and how within this divine being there is room for distinction. Ebionitism lost sight of the latter and therefore dropped the deity of the Lord. Its basic error was a deistic conception of the relationship of God to the world. And wherever in modern times Ebionitism is revived, it flows from a similar deism, as with the Socinians. The less-strict line of Ebionites (also called Nazarenes) maintained the supernatural birth of the humanity of Christ but likewise denied His deity.

11. *What particular view did the gnostics have about the Mediator?*

Gnosticism is the opposite of Ebionitism. The latter is Jewish; the former is pagan. The one holds that God and the world are sharply divided, while the other brings them together as closely as possible. The heretical in Gnosticism is evident in two points:

a) Christ was made into an aeon, an emanation of the divine, as everything in the final analysis is reduced to aeons. In other words, His deity is maintained, but it was conceived of in pantheistic terms. It was not the true, absolute deity that Scripture attributes to Christ, for according to Gnosticism, He did not remain within the essence of God, but He emanated from it in order to enter into creatureliness.

b) The humanity of Christ was made into a semblance, for according to the pantheistic scheme a distinction is not made between human spirit and deity, and since the human body as material is *per se* evil, it may not be ascribed to Christ in reality. This is gnostic Docetism (from δοκεῖν, "appear"), which can be developed in various forms. The most elaborated system is that of Valentinus, according to whom Christ did not inhabit a fleshly body (except in appearance) but only a physical body, which was not formed from Mary but only brought forth through her as through a channel. At His baptism, the higher, spiritual Christ was united with this lower Christ. Against Gnosticism, see Colossians 2:9; 1 John 4:2–3.

12. *What were the opinions of the Alogi concerning Christ?*

The doctrine of the self-contained preexistence of Christ had the beginning of its dogmatic development through Irenaeus and Tertullian. Therefore, the two heretical lines mentioned above (represented by Ebionitism and Gnosticism) necessarily came into renewed opposition to this development since they saw God's unity threatened. This opposition manifested itself in the deistic heresy of the Alogi and in the more or less pantheistically colored Modalists (Sabellians). Alogism attempted to maintain the unity by denying the deity of Christ, Sabellianism by denial of His personal existence. So here again we find orthodox doctrine moving between two extremes.

The Alogi (around 170 AD) did not deny the supernatural birth of Christ but regarded Him as a man who did not have a real existence before this birth and was distinguished from other men in that He was sinless; that a ray of the *Logos* (that is, the mind of God) dwelt in Him; or that He possessed the Holy Spirit to an extraordinary degree. They are called Alogi because they rejected the Fourth Gospel (and Revelation) as well as the *logos* concept, while in their name a wordplay is also present: *alogi*, that is, "without *logos*," "lacking reason."

13. *What was the heresy of the Modalists or Sabellians?*

They did recognize that in Christ there was something essentially divine, but they conceived of this as a manifestation mode of the absolutely one divine personality that had appeared as Father and Spirit in other modes. There was something docetic present in this conception, inasmuch as the soul of Christ was replaced by deity, and His body can only be called a temporary theophany. The Modalists are also called Monarchians, since they stood for the unity of God.

14. *What is the value of Origen with respect to the development of christological dogma?*

His construction of the doctrine of generation and his subordinationism has been discussed earlier (doctrine of the Trinity). Over against the extremes just discussed, he endeavored by the one or the other of his views to maintain both the unity of the Divine Being as well as the deity of a personally existing eternal Son. Here it should be noted how Origen was the first to accentuate with clarity how the humanity assumed by the *Logos* consisted not only of a material body, but that an *anima rationalis* (a rational soul) also belonged to it. Previously, there had been much doubt about this point. Most were constrained by the concept that Christ's deity had dwelt in the body (*sarx*) as His soul. Even in Tertullian one can find such a concept. Unhappily, this better idea of Origen was so closely related to his doctrine of preexistence that it did not spread outside the circle of his own school. According to Origen, the human soul of Christ, too, is preexistent. So it was that Origen did not advance the development of the doctrine on this point much further.

15. *What form did the dogma take in the Arian heresy?*

Earlier we discussed Arianism in detail. Since according to it the deity of Christ is only a half deity, and He belongs within the sphere of time or among beings created in time, the first of the problems mentioned above disappears. God and man were so strongly separated by Arianism that they thought Christ had to be denied deity, and through this idea the second problem also disappeared. If that of Christ which preexisted—the *Logos* created before all things—is already something creaturely, then, given that, it becomes entirely superfluous to assume a human soul. Arianism therefore says that the preexistent *Logos* only assumed a body in the incarnation and denies the existence of a human soul in the incarnated *Logos*. This denial is extremely significant since it shows how much the Arian was serious about the creatureliness of the *Logos*. Basically, Arianism was a modified Alogism. It finds its principal content in the fact that Christ is a creature, and thus adheres to the essentially Jewish concept of the abstract unity of God. It is Judaistic. And still it teaches that this creature became flesh, attained to the status of deity through moral development, and must be worshiped. That, as well as the concept that the *Logos* is the instrument of creation, since the Father could not create directly, is pagan-pantheistic. The *Logos* becomes a kind of lower God. Thus in Arianism both poles of heretical Christology, which thus far had been opposed to each other, were united.

16. *Who through his heretical opinions has helped the orthodox doctrine to develop further?*

Apollinaris of Laodicea. In the Arian controversy, the full deity of Christ was now established beyond question. Now, however, whoever despaired of the possibility of reaching a unity between full deity and full humanity obviously had to question the completeness of the human nature. Apollinaris did this, proceeding from the thesis that a complete human nature besides the divine nature results in two Sons of God— one by nature and eternal, another through incarnation and adoption. This cannot be true. Therefore, in Christ only His living flesh derives from humanity. The higher principle in man—the *nous* [mind, intellect], according to Aristotelian philosophy—was lacking, for His deity filled that place.

So, since the full humanity of Christ was attacked successively from two sides, first through Arius and now through Apollinaris, the church saw itself compelled to express its faith in this matter emphatically. If Christ only assumed a living body, then He also only redeemed our living body, and our higher spiritual capacities do not share in redemption. If Christ did not possess a human *nous* and everything that is said about Him in the Gospels must be attributed to His deity, then this did not remain the unchangeable, blessed deity but was subject to suffering. So the deity is also impaired. In addition to this, the teaching of Apollinaris cohered with the philosophical conception of the indwelling of the divine *Logos* in every human *nous*. Semipantheistically, the higher principle in man was regarded as a piece of the divine *Logos*. If now the complete divine *Logos* already lives in Christ (so Apollinaris reasoned), why would we still suppose a part of the *Logos* in Him? In this aspect, Apollinarism pointed back more to Gnostic speculations. The church rightly condemned this in 381 (Synod of Constantinople).

17. What point had the church now reached?

At the solution to the problem of how this divine nature and human nature, both complete, could exist together in the one person, Christ.

18. Is the same antithesis occurring earlier to be observed in the two heresies that sought to solve this problem in the wrong way?

Yes, the Jewish-deistic and the pagan-pantheistic error again were in opposition to each other—the first represented by Nestorianism, the latter by monophysitism.

19. Give the main elements in Nestorian Christology.

The Nestorians think of the unity of the human and divine natures of Christ according to their own interpretation of a moral unity between God and man. God lives in every saint, not essentially, but through an agreement of will and inclination. Thus there is a unity in the sense of unanimity. Now, Nestorius did acknowledge that the unity between God and man in Christ was something else than what takes place in every believer, but still there is a likeness between the two in his interpretation. Out of grace and good will (κατὰ χάριν and κατ᾽ εὐδοκίαν), God has united Himself with the man Jesus; and with Him this union was complete, while with everyone else it was incomplete. This union (συνάφεια) was not immediately complete; it kept pace with the development of the moral nature of humanity. In the end it was complete, and through the exaltation of His human nature it has now become possible to pray to Christ, who consists of two natures (persons), as to one subject, for deity and humanity are completely in harmony—what the former wills, the latter also wills. There is no other unity between the natures than those of names, honor, and worship. Closely connected with this is the conception one must form of the saving work of the Mediator. Emphasis is placed on *free will* and *moral development* in Christ. Through that, He was united with God. It took place according to His humanity. Therefore, He can accomplish salvation for us in no other way than by enabling us for a similar moral development. Therein lies the Judaistic-deistic aspect of this position.

20. What trend is the opposite of this?

Over against the Antiochian-Nestorian line, the Alexandrian school maintained that deity and humanity in Christ were *naturally* one and not just *morally*—that is, there must be a deeper unity between the two natures than a moral agreement. This deeper unity had to be natural (ἔνωσις φυσική), but not of that sort that the natures were intermingled. Up to and including Cyril, the Alexandrians remained within the bounds of orthodoxy. Cyril himself insisted on the unity, because otherwise our human nature is not redeemed and God has not suffered for us in humanity. He sought it, however, completely in agreement with what was later established as orthodox church doctrine, in the person of the Son of God. He therefore taught that in Christ there was not an individual (personal) man, but an (impersonal) human nature, although he also maintains that there was nothing lacking in Christ's human nature, since it had its existence in the person of the Son of God. With this, in fact, the correct way was found to the solution of the problem, insofar as it could be found.

One cannot accuse Cyril of monophysitism. However, Cyril had also already made the statement, "Before the incarnation two natures existed, after the incarnation only one." By this he meant that before the incarnation the human nature that Christ assumed had existed separately, while subsequently it found its existence in the person of the Son of God and thus existed individually, no longer as an abstract nature, so that one could only speak of one nature. The Alexandrians, however, were Platonic Realists who believed in the real existence of the natures. In this statement of Cyril, we now have the beginning of the monophysite heresy that was then further developed consistently in Eutyches into the assertion that there was only one nature in Christ. This meant more than it had meant for Cyril, even though it sounded similar. It included that, through its union with deity, the human nature had not only lost its abstract character (Cyril had also taught this), but that in addition it had been changed, so that now a sort of in-between entity had originated.

Under the influence of the West by the Roman bishop Leo, this Eutychianism was condemned by the Synod of Chalcedon in 451, and the famous Creed of Chalcedon was accepted. The Greek church in its entirety had in principle already fallen into monophysitism. That it did not also do so officially resulted, under God's leading, from the timely intervention of Western orthodoxy. Already for a long time salvation had been understood by the Greeks as a deification of human nature in general. Just for that reason, one could not continue to accept a unity of the natures in the person but wanted a unity in the natures themselves. It could not be a personal but had to be a metaphysical unity. The God-man was not there in order to bring God and man, initially separated judicially, together again judicially (personal unity), but in order through the incarnation of God to effect the deification of man (metaphysical unity). This pagan-pantheistic error was halted, to its credit, by the more biblical, less philosophical view of the Western church. If this had not happened, Christianity would have completely degenerated into pantheism.

21. How does the Creed of Chalcedon read?

"Following the Holy Fathers, we teach that, with one accord, all must confess the Son, our Lord Jesus Christ, as One, perfect in deity and perfect in humanity; truly God and truly man, consisting of a rational soul and a body; of one substance with the Father according to deity, of one substance with us according to humanity; like us in everything, sin excepted; begotten before time of the Father according to deity, at the end of times, for us and our salvation, born of Mary the Virgin, the Mother of God; according to humanity, one and the same Christ, Son, Lord, Firstborn, to be understood in two natures (ἐκ δύο φύσεως; another reading, ἐν δύο φύσεσιν), inconfusedly, unchangeably, indivisibly, inseparably, so that the distinction in natures is in no respect removed by the unity, but rather the property of each nature remains preserved, yet concurring in one person and *hypostasis*, not divided into two persons but one and the same Son and Firstborn, who is God the *Logos* and the Lord Jesus Christ; as from the beginning the prophets and Jesus Christ

Himself have taught us and the confession of faith of the Fathers has handed down to us."[1]

With this creed, ecclesiastical doctrinal development was closed. It is the basis on which the whole orthodox Christian church has stood since that time, no matter how otherwise divided it also is; Greek, Roman, Protestant churches agree with each other in this Christology.

Only on one point does the creed leave its meaning in the dark. It does not say explicitly that the human nature assumed by the *Logos* does not have a personal existence in itself. This remained reserved for later dogmatic development to address.

22. *On which points has John of Damascus further developed the dogma?*

He established that the human nature of Christ (a) is not the abstract nature of man in the sense of the Realists, in which all men are said to share, (b) is also not an individual humanity that in itself possesses personal existence, but (c) is an impersonal human nature, assumed by the *Logos* in the unity of the person from the first moment of its existence, so that it never has existed on its own.

At the same time, John of Damascus taught a mutual penetration of the two natures (περιχώρησις) from which followed a mutual communication of attributes (ἀντίδοσις). On this point, conflict later ignited between Lutherans and Reformed.

23. *Have all Christian churches continued to maintain this position (of Chalcedon) or has deviation also still manifested itself later?*

Deviation has also manifested itself later, with the following parties:

a) The Ebionite heresy was revived by Socinianism, which recognizes only a human nature in Christ and wishes to speak of deity only in the sense of transmitted competence for office. Socinian soteriology, as we will see, completely accords with this Socinian Christology.

b) The Lutheran Church took a step back from Chalcedon in the direction of Eutychianism, without, however, formally abandoning

---

1   This appears to be Vos's own translation of the Greek original; I have not researched whether he is quoting an existing or ecclesiastically adopted Dutch translation.

the standpoint of the Chalcedon Creed and without letting this conception work itself out consistently soteriology.

c) Modern Christology of the speculative *Vermittelungs* [mediating] theologians has in principle abandoned the standpoint of Chalcedon (deity and humanity complete and at the same time side by side) and in various forms accepted a changing of deity into humanity and a changing back of humanity into deity. This is the doctrine of kenosis.

d) While (a) errs on the Jewish-deistic side and (b) and (c) incline toward the heathen-pantheistic side, here and there has appeared sporadically as a private opinion the position that Christ's humanity did not first originate in time, but preexisted eternally in heaven—thus a renewal of Origen's Christology as far as the humanity is concerned. One finds this opinion in Swedenborg and Isaac Watts.

We turn now to a discussion of the Reformed doctrine, in order after that to come back to these errors.

24. *Give the most important positions that we must maintain concerning the Mediator after His incarnation.*[2]

a) In the Mediator there is only one person, one subject, although there are two natures. The problem that we meet here is therefore the reverse of what confronted us in the doctrine of the Trinity. There it concerned the possibility of one nature, the Divine Being consisting in three persons. Here, on the other hand, the question is how two natures can exist in one person. It may be recalled that the standard theological definition of a person reads: *substantia individua intelligens incommunicabilis non sustertata in alia natura neque paro alterius*: "an indivisible, rational, incommunicable substance, not sustained by another nature and not a part of another." This, however, is not entirely applicable to the divine persons in the Trinity, since "not sustained by another nature" is not correct here. So, for the Trinity one has to be satisfied with a simple definition: "A person is through the divine substance in

---

2   Points (b) and (c) are the answers to questions 25 and 26, respectively.

a specific *hypostasis* and through this specific mode of being distinguished from that substance and from the remaining persons." A divine person is not entirely the same as a human person.

While this is true, on the other hand it must be no less maintained that there must be similarity in a formal sense between a divine and a human person. As we shall see, this already follows from the fact that in the covenant the divine person of the Mediator represents the persons of the elect legally. This relationship of legal representation that exists between the Mediator and His members cannot exist between two entirely dissimilar entities. The similarity that exists between divine and human personality must be found in the fact that neither is upheld by another person. This is true of both. Even though the person of the Son of God is a mode of existence of the being of God and so in a certain sense is upheld through the being, through the divine nature, still this divine nature is, *qua talis* [as such], not personal but only comes to personhood in the three *hypostases*. However, there is not another person who upholds the person of the Son, in whom He subsists, in whom He exists hypostatically. It is true that from eternity the Son is generated by the Father and so has His mode of existence continually from the Father, but this still says nothing other than that as *hypostasis* He exists in the Father. For man, too, a son receives his personal existence from the father through generation, but the persons of father and son remain separate, and one cannot say that the one exists in the other. If that were the case, then the one who exists in the other, just because of that, would cease to exist as a person. We thus have these two cases: (1) In the being of God common to the three persons, the person of the Son exists eternally from the person of the Father, but not in the person of the Father; He is and remains a separate *hypostasis*. (2) In the creation of a new being by God, for man the child exists as a person through generation from the parents, but not in the parents; it is and remains a separate personality.

Divine and human personalities have *in common* that they do not exist in another person. They are *different* in the following respects: (1) A divine person can have in common with the other divine persons the same, undivided being; Father, Son, and Holy Spirit are one and the same—God triune. A human person cannot in this way have in common the same being with other human persons. With man, being comes into existence repeatedly from God's creating hand. When we say that all men have one and the same nature, this is not at all meant in the same sense as in the Trinity. For man, it means similarity; for God, identity. All men have the same nature insofar as they alike possess the sum of essential attributes. For example, all have a sinful or all have a pure nature. Among God the Father and God the Son and God the Holy Spirit, there is only one and therefore the same nature. (2) A divine person has His existence from the other person or from the other persons not only temporally, with a beginning, but also eternally, without cessation. That, therefore, with the similarity, is the difference: In the Divine Being, the bond of origination remains unceasing; for man, it does not endure.

This one person, this one subject in Christ, is vested with all the legal relationships that are due the Mediator. He, the person of the Mediator, has been established from eternity as Surety, for although having not yet assumed human nature, He—the same person who later became flesh, suffered and died—was then already present. To Him, the person, the guilt of the elect was imputed, not to the human nature that He possessed in the abstract. He, the person, who as a divine person was not subject to any law, placed Himself freely under the demand of the law and earned eternal life. He, the person, was exalted after He had fulfilled all righteousness. Everywhere a legal relationship is involved, we have to do with the person of the Mediator, the Son of God. For carrying out His functions as Mediator, both natures are certainly necessary, as has been shown abundantly above, but the legal capacity could only be provided for through the existence of these natures in the person.

25. *Is this one subject, this one person in the Mediator, a divine or a human person?*[3]

b) This person is divine, and not human or divine-human. In order to be immediately convinced of this, one may take the following into consideration. In the *Logos*, a divine person, who is immutable, is present from eternity. If now there can be but one person in the Mediator, and the divine person cannot be eradicated or changed, then it is self-evident that this one person is the divine person of the *Logos*. One can only maintain the immutability of God if one holds to the deity of the person in the Mediator. The choice lies between two persons or one divine person.

26. *What follows from this for the human nature of the Mediator?*[4]

c) That it may not at the same time be called a human person. After all, if it were a human person, then along with the divine person there would be a second person in Christ, and we would have two mediators instead of one. Nestorianism would be introduced. Between two persons no other unity is possible except a moral unity, as Nestorianism conceived of it, or a mystical unity, such as takes place between Christ and the members of His body. However, in any case, that does not produce a unity of subject. Personality is that which is deepest and most independent in man that cannot be combined with anything else. Were there now in Christ's human nature this personal feature, then it never would have been able to be joined with the deity of the Lord as one subject—such as was absolutely necessary for the execution of the work of the Mediator. This is one of the reasons why personality may not be ascribed to the human nature of the Mediator.

27. *Is it permissible, then, to say that the human nature of the Mediator was impersonal?*

No, for doing that would create the appearance that something were lacking in the human nature of the Lord, and in a questionable manner one would incline toward Docetism, as if in Christ there were only an

---

3   See the note at question 24.

4   See the note at question 24.

apparent humanity and not true humanity. Subsequently, the best teachers in the church have always avoided the expression "impersonal human nature" and rather have taught that the humanity of the Mediator has its personal existence in the person of the Son of God, whereby it is not an abstraction but is provided with personality. This is not to be so conceived of as if the person of the Son of God provides the impersonal humanity with a human person, for then that would be a lapse again into Nestorianism. It means, rather, that the person of the Son of God serves as person for the humanity as well as the deity, that He lends personality to both; or, expressed still more accurately, that as a divine person, by assuming human nature into the unity of the person, He also elevates this human nature above the terrain of impersonality. By and since the incarnation, there is in the Mediator a human nature that—not of itself personally—has its personal existence in the person of the Son of God. In a certain sense, the person of the Mediator, the *Logos*, is twofold (not a composite) since He fills two functions, namely: He serves as person both for the deity and for the humanity.

It is the merit of John of Damascus that he so clearly enunciated this "impersonation" of the human nature by the divine person, if we may so designate it. He formulated his conception as follows: The human nature of the Mediator was not properly or inherently personal (ἰδιοσύστατος), nor impersonal (ἀνυπόστατος), but rather in-personal (ἐνυπόστατος).

It must, therefore, be called inexact when Charles Hodge, in *Systematic Theology* volume 2, page 391, says, "Human nature therefore ... is in the person of Christ impersonal." This should read, "does not possess a human personality." In Junius, *Thesis* 27:16, it is formulated quite correctly. Here it is seen in which manner each of the two natures is involved in this union: The divine assumes, the human is assumed—not so that from these two a sort of third is forged together, but the human nature, at the outset ἀνυπόστατος, was assumed by the *Logos* into the unity of the person, and thus made ἐνυπόστατος.

28. *May one infer from this that the human nature of Christ is imperfect, since personality is lacking in it?*

This objection has in fact been introduced against church doctrine on this point, and even been called a refined Apollinarism. (Dorner's great work on the person of Christ is the best that has been written historically about this dogma, although the author himself believes in the error of kenosis.) The purport of this complaint is that, as Apollinaris had the divine nature take the place of the higher spiritual capacity—the *nous*—in Christ, so we let the divine person replace human personality. Against this charge, however, the following should be observed.

a) It makes a great difference whether one denies the *nous*, the higher spiritual faculty, of human nature in order to put deity in its place, or whether one replaces human personality with the *hypostasis* of the Son of God. That higher moral life—to which mind, will, and higher emotional life belong—really constitutes what is essential in man, so that whoever removes that takes away the core of the humanity—of the human nature—from Christ. The same cannot be said of the person. No matter how important it may be, it does not belong in the same sense to the essence of the nature as the higher spiritual faculty but is rather to be viewed as the individual enfolding that the nature has received in every single human being. A connection is made with modern philosophy when one places such great emphasis on the personality and then, proceeding from that, lodges the charge of Apollinarism against the church doctrine.

b) In spite of the difference that exists between divine and human personality and what is mentioned above, one cannot prove that there is such a formal difference by which the divine person is not able to elevate the human nature to a state of perfection or wholeness. The question that arises here is this: Does a *hypostasis* have qualities apart from the nature that subsists in it? That is, is a divine person, as such, distinguished essentially from a human person? Or is personality a more neutral entity, so that a human nature, even a complete human nature, is involved even if the place of the personality in it is occupied by a divine person—that is, by a person in whom deity subsists from eternity?

It will be extremely difficult to answer these questions decisively. But as long as they are not answered decisively or cannot permit a decisive answer, then neither can one assert decisively that, according to our conception, the humanity of the Mediator is incomplete in an Apollinarian fashion. There is an essential difference between divine spirit (mind–will–affections) and human spirit (mind–will–affections). In His mind, God is omniscient and all-wise; man is limited in knowledge and wisdom. In His will, God is omnipotent and absolute holiness; man is limited in power and possesses only derived holiness. In His emotion, God is eternally blissful; man enjoys only an effect of this bliss. To say that the deity in Christ takes the place of the *nous* in fact makes His humanity incomplete. But everyone sees at once that, between a divine person and a human person, such contradictions as those mentioned here cannot be determined in the same manner.

c) Many find it impossible to conceive of the human nature of the Mediator without a human personality, since they identify personality with self-consciousness and free will. It is undeniable (as the church has learned to confess in the struggle against the monothelites, and as Scripture assures us) that in Christ there is twofold consciousness, twofold will, twofold emotion—on the one hand a divine consciousness, on the other a human consciousness; a divine will and a human will; divine emotion and human emotion. Now, if for someone consciousness, or even self-consciousness, coincides with personality, then he will have to ascribe personality, along with consciousness, to human nature.

Against that we should note that it is wrong to identify these two. It is true that personality is inconceivable without self-consciousness. However, in no way does the reverse follow from that: that there cannot be self-consciousness without personality. And one is least of all entitled to the conclusion that in a certain (say, human) nature there can be no self-consciousness without personality existing in the same nature. Personality lies much deeper than self-consciousness; the latter is the mode of disclosing the former, a mode of disclosure that can be interrupted temporarily, for example, during sleep, without the personality thereby ceasing to exist. Hodge says correctly, "It follows that the human nature of Christ, separately considered, is impersonal. To this, indeed, it is objected that intelligence and will constitute personality, and as these belong to Christ's human nature personality cannot be denied to it. A person, however, is a *suppositum intelligens* [rational subject], but the human nature of Christ is not a *suppositum* or subsistence" (*Systematic Theology*, 2:391).

29. *Can one also show from Scripture that there was only one subject, one person in Christ, and that this was the divine person, the* Logos?

The proof for this from Scripture may be provided in the following way:

a) The strongest proof is found in the absence of any traces of a twofold personality in all that is communicated to us about the Mediator. Also, it is revealed to us about God that He is one God, as it is revealed to us that Christ must be called one Mediator (cf. 1 Tim 2:5). Notwithstanding the existence of this strong presumption for the oneness of God, we and the church have seen it necessary to accept a trinity of persons in this one Divine Being, since repeatedly the one person is properly distinguished from the other and introduced as speaking to the other.

Now, if two persons existed in the Mediator, we would expect something similar. There would have to be traces that the deity had spoken to the humanity, and the humanity to the deity, using "Thou" and "Thee," as occurs between Father and Son. Nothing of this nature can be found in the New Testament. This must have its reason, and the reason can be none other than that human personality is not present in the Mediator.

b) A positive proof is present in the fact that the Mediator always speaks of Himself as one and the same person, regardless of whether what is said about Him refers to His divine or to His human existence. It is the same, identical subject that speaks in both relationships, both when it is said, "My soul is exceedingly sorrowful, even unto death" [Matt 26:38], and when it is stated, "Before Abraham was, I am" [John 8:38]. Oneness of persons and duality of natures, therefore, is also the result here.

c) That the person in Christ is the divine person, the *Logos*, appears most clearly in those places in Scripture that deal expressly with the incarnation, as, for example, John 1:1-4; 1 John 1:1-3; Philippians 2:6-11; Hebrews 2:14. It is most noteworthy that in all these passages Scripture does not proceed from two natures in the Mediator—in order then, given this coordination, to obtain by their fusion a *tertium quid*—but always chooses its point of departure in eternity, in the person of the Son of God. Modern Christology takes the opposite path. In all its constructions of the

God-man it starts from the two natures as coordinated and has the two mingled or the one devolve into the other. So, John first speaks of the Word that was with God, indeed was God; Paul, of Him who was in the form of God, and who was rich, in order then to come to speak of the humanity of the Mediator. And it is no less noteworthy that Scripture, where it speaks of the union of the divine Person with the human nature, always conceives of this as an action of the former, where the *Logos* was not passive but active. He became flesh (σὰρξ ἐγένετο); He took on the seed of Abraham; He humiliated himself; He became poor, etc. Thirdly, it may not be overlooked that the humanity of the Mediator is never spoken of in personal terms but in terms of nature. It is not a man that He assumed but flesh; He was sent in the likeness of sinful flesh [Rom 8:3]. "Flesh" [here] means specifically complete human nature, including soul and body, but without personality needing to be included.

30. *Why was it necessary that the Mediator be only one person or, expressed differently, that in Him human nature (in itself) did not possess personality?*

For the following reasons:

a) Because already in the *Logos* there was a divine person who could not change, and so His humanity had to be impersonal or there would have been two subjects in existence.

b) Because all human persons are included in the covenant of works. If Christ had been a human person, then He would also have possessed original sin and could not have been our Surety. He was, however, a divine person, who as such could not be reckoned in Adam, and so also could not have been born through ordinary generation from Adam (through the will of man).

c) In Christ as Mediator, His human nature, as by a miraculous grace, must be most closely united with God. This must occur for more than one purpose—both so that in the Mediator as the Head of His body the covenant of grace is realized not only juridically but also really, and as well so that revelation through the Mediator is a direct revelation of God in the flesh. When the humanity of

Christ speaks, then in it speaks the person who is God, because the subject is one.

d) His deity must be united with His human nature such that it could add infinite value to His merits. A union other than personal union could not suffice here, since only this union is a judicial union.

e) Only because the divine person is the subject in Christ does His mediatorial work obtain the stability required by an eternal, immutable covenant of grace. Without doubt, the human nature in Christ was in itself weak and mutable. We now know, however, that this human nature in itself is an abstraction that did not exist for a moment without personal subsistence in the *Logos*. Thus the person of the *Logos* with its personality provides His human nature with the steadfastness and immutability by which the covenant of grace is distinguished from the first covenant, the covenant of works. The oneness and the deity of the person are of importance for the affirmation that Christ could not sin.

31. *What follows for the Mediator from this personal unity between human nature and the* Logos?

a) That Christ the Mediator may no longer be prayed to and worshiped exclusively as God, apart from His humanity. As the Word become flesh, He is the object of our worship. His human nature is personally united with Him; it is taken into His *hypostasis*; one may no longer separate it from His deity. Just as the Triune Being of God exists only as triune being, and we do not worship an abstract Godhead but the triune God, even so the *Logos* may not be venerated in His abstract deity but in His concrete personality, which is both God and man. Even before His incarnation, it was only possible to believe in Him as the one who would become flesh.

And still something else is related to this. For us, Christ can only be the object of worship as the God-man, as possessing human nature in the unity of the person and as He is the Mediator as the God-man. It immediately follows, then, that worship of Christ must be directed to Him as Mediator. That is, He may not become the one who is final in our worshiping, on whom it terminates and in whom, as it were, it remains at rest. Rather, one goes through Christ as Mediator to the Father. Whoever speaks to the Son speaks to Him as Mediator, and as Mediator He directs all worship over to the Father. The latter in fact represents the Trinity, so that in Him we, in turn, worship the Son. But one prays directly only to the Son as Mediator, since the humanity assumed in the unity of His person can no longer be separated from His person. It is for that reason that all revelation of the covenant of grace under the old dispensation had to point forward; that [which was] presented was not the *Logos qua talis* [as such], as Head of the covenant who had secured it from eternity, but always the *Logos* who over the course of the centuries was to come and was to become flesh.

To the question of how Christ is to be worshiped, the answer therefore must be: as Mediator who is both man and God. To the question of why or on what basis He is to be worshiped, the answer must be: on the ground that He is the person of the *Logos*, the divine person. In other words, one must distinguish between the object of worship and the ground for worship. It goes without saying that the creaturely as such, apart from personal existence in the Son of God, can never be the object or ground of worship. But a nature in the abstract cannot be worshiped. For that a person is necessary, and this person is in the Mediator a divine person.

b) That in Christ the Mediator there occurs the unique appearance of one and the same person who at the same time exists in two completely different natures. According to His deity, the person of the Mediator is omniscient, omnipotent, omnipresent; but according to His humanity the very same person of the Mediator is limited in knowledge and power and circumscribed by space. The deity has not ceased to be deity and is not in the least altered or changed by the incarnation, except insofar as it through the person has entered into a new relationship. Nor is the true humanity elevated on the supposition of the eternity of the person, except insofar as it has entered into a new and entirely unique relationship. The two spheres in which the person of the Mediator moves lie next to each other; or rather, the one lies above the other. But they do not merge together. Their unity lies solely in the person.

c) The person works through, in, and behind the fully human nature of the Mediator. The unity of the person is not merely verbal but answers to a reality. The human nature, though it has self-consciousness and will and feeling, does not operate of itself but is at every moment the instrument of the person who bears it. It does have substance but no subsistence in itself. The much-used image of the relationship between soul and body in man can serve here. Of the body, too, it must be said that it has substance but no subsistence in itself. It is not a mere accident of the soul (this would be Idealism) but is ontologically and substantially distinguished from it. At the same time, it cannot operate of itself but finds its operating principle in the spirit, which uses it as an organ.

All this may be transferred to the relationship between the divine person and the human nature in the Mediator. It is the *Logos* who makes use of the human nature existing in Him as its organ. And this is so not merely through indwelling, as, for example, the same *Logos* in the days of the old covenant made use of a creaturely form in order in it to reveal Himself at the moment. The early Fathers denied that the divine person was present in human nature like a captain in His ship. Such a local indwelling can be thought of only in material things and would therefore be applicable only to the body of the Mediator, and would lead to the Arian conception. On the other hand, it is completely impossible to think of such an indwelling for the soul, for it makes no sense to say that the divine person dwells in the human soul, if this has a different meaning than the mystical sense in which the indwelling is true of all believers. In a completely different, secret manner, the *Logos* is the person for the human nature, the starting point for all its thoughts and emotions. Here for us lies the mystery in the doctrine of the Mediator as God-man. We cannot explain how human understanding, human will, and human feeling were joined to and united with the person of the Son of God.

We can say only this: (1) The person, who was God, was conscious of the human nature belonging personally to His person, so that He appropriated it as a part of His self-existence.

The *Logos* knew every moment (if His eternity permits us to speak in such a way): It is *my* human nature that suffers and dies. (2) The consciousness of the human nature was a consciousness of not having independence (subsistence) in itself. The human nature knew that it possessed its personality in the person of the Son of God. The person of the Son of God was not positioned over against the human nature as alien any more than the human nature with its consciousness was positioned over against the divine person as alien. When the human nature spoke, it was conscious of speaking as the Son of God. "Before Abraham was, I am" [John 8:58], says the human mouth of the Lord and thinks the human soul of the Lord, which shows how a consciousness of divine "I-ness" was present in the human soul. By this is not at all asserted or meant that the entire content of Christ's divine consciousness was also present in His human consciousness, for that would obviously erase the border between the divine and human and mingle the two natures. Only at this one point must there have been commonality or, speaking more precisely, identity of consciousness, because there was identity of the person. The consciousness of personality was one and the same for Christ's divine nature and for His human nature.

This, as it occurs to us, is as far as we may and must go in the explanation of this mystery. And the final step that we take here is already a step toward that which Scripture inclines us but whereby it still does not lead us directly. All other and further explanations of this great mystery (1 Tim 3:16), however, are to be seen as inadvisable and even dangerous. Still, such explanations are not lacking. Here we mention only the Cartesian speculation, which one can find in Reformed theologians such as Wittich, Burman, and Braun, that the unity of natures was located in the mutual penetration and communication of thoughts that are possible between the two since they both (according to Cartesianism) consist essentially of thinking. Mastricht and Maresius have rightly written against such speculation. Without doubt, a communication of thoughts from the divine to the human nature takes place, but there can of course be no question of a reverse sharing by the human to the divine nature; nor does the personal unity of the natures lie in the former.

All erroneous conceptions regarding the uniqueness of this unity are carefully rejected by theologians. They are accustomed, for example, to deny that the union consists (1) in a unity of being, as is the case with the persons of the holy Trinity (συνουσιωδῶς), because in the Mediator there are two essences, two substances; (2) in a unity of essence and power, as the *Logos* with His divine nature and power is present in all things (οὐσιωδῶς καὶ δραστικῶς); (3) in a unity of support or only by the presence of grace (παραστατικῶς); (4) in a unity of nature, as form and matter are united (φυσικῶς); (5) in a unity of relationship, as a friend is to his friend (σχετικῶς); (6) in a mystical unity, as exists between Christ and believers (μυστικῶς); (7) in a sacramental unity, as is present in the Lord's Supper.

Not one of all these modes of union matches that which is within Christ, for the latter is a hypostatic union (ὑποστατικῶς), as the result of which the human nature is borne by the divine person. Here, however, it must still be carefully noted that this is not that general divine capacity with which, by *providentia generalis* [general providence], the Son sustains all things, but a special sustaining that can be compared to nothing else. In general providence the subjects remain separate, He who bears from the one who is borne; here there is properly unity of subject. Many call humanity the human organ (ἀνθρώπινον ὄργανον) of the person.

32. *What must be noted about the analogy of this personal union with the unity between soul and body in man?*

That in fact at many points it casts much light on this truth that in the abstract is so difficult for our human understanding to comprehend. Already at a very early point, this analogy was pointed to for clarification. One may compare the confession of faith of Athanasius. Calvin still found this analogy useful (*Institutes,* 2.14.1).

Later there was more objection against it, and on a basis that hardly appears satisfactory. One raised against it that human personality comes into being only through the joining of body and soul, since both body and soul are essential parts of man. One must admit, however, that the personality of man is located in the soul, as Christ's is located in His deity, and therefore that in that respect the analogy is entirely fitting.

It is true that, for man, specifically human nature (not the person) only exists through the joining of soul and body, but one can likewise say that Christ's specifically mediatorial nature (not His person) only comes into existence through the incarnation; thus there is also similarity here. Only this much remains of the objection: that the person of the Mediator existed as perfect and was unimpaired before and apart from the incarnation, thus that the latter does not belong to the idea of the *Logos*, as is taught by modern theology, and that, on the other hand, a human soul, although personal, is a fragment that does not correspond to its idea if we think of it apart from the body. The *Logos* had His perfect divine nature from eternity, in which He subsisted; the souls of those who have died have a violated, incomplete human nature as long as they are not reunited with their bodies. Therefore, one must not appeal to the analogy for help to clarify the relationship of the *Logos* ἄσαρκος to the σάρξ assumed by Him, but only to bring clarity to the *Logos* ἔνσαρκος in the σάρξ.

The points on which the analogy can shed light are the following:

a) There are two substances: matter and spirit, divine and human substance. It makes no difference that with the humanity of the Mediator the human substance consists of both matter and spirit, for here these two must combine into one unity and be placed on one line, since they, as creaturely substance, come to stand in contrast to the deity of the Mediator as uncreated substance.

b) In man there exists a union between soul and body, spirit and matter, which is very close and yet does not lead to the merging of the two. Spirit does not become matter, and matter does not become spirit; each maintains its specific qualities. This union between the two substances is not a mere indwelling, as if the soul merely resides in the body as in a tabernacle, but a personal union. All of this can be applied to the unity between the divine person and the human nature in the Mediator.

c) With man, the principle of unity, the subject, the person, does not come about by a fusion of both natures. Soul and body do not each provide a part, but that subject resides in the one substance of the soul, which has assumed the body, or at least from the first moment of life on has entered into the body as the principle of unity. In the body, there may be a kind of organic unity apart from the soul; the true unity of life, that of feeling, enters only through the soul. All of this can be transferred without difficulty. The subject, the person, is in Christ a divine person; in His human nature there is a unity similar to that in the body of man—a unity of feeling, will, and consciousness in general. But the higher unity, that of personality, is lacking in His humanity, or rather would have to be lacking if it remained by itself.

d) As it is impossible for us to explain the operation of spirit on matter and of matter on spirit, it is likewise impossible to show how in particular the organic unity of soul and body, the former in the latter, causes life and sensation. In the same way, it is not only inexplicable in general how the infinite affects the finite, how the divine affects the human. But, most specifically, the highest of all mysteries is how the person of the Son of God could so appropriate human nature that He is said in truth to exist in this humanity while conversely this humanity has its *hypostasis* in Him.

e) In man, a communication takes place of characteristics of both natures or substances to the person. Person A or B shares in all that can be said about his soul or his body. It is not his body that is sick or his soul that is depressed, but *he* is sick or dejected. The same is also true of the person of the Mediator. To His person belong all the predicates that are associated with the divine and human natures. There is, to use the terminology of the theologians, a κοινωνία ἰδιωμάτων, a communication of attributes, about which we will need to speak in more detail later.

f) From this communication of attributes, it follows that the subject can sometimes be designated according to the one nature, while, however, the predicate with which this subject is associated belongs to the subject only according to the other nature. And so arise apparently absurd and contradictory statements in which subject and predicate seem to exclude each other. When one says in English, "Everybody knows," then the person is designated according to the material nature as "body," while, however, to this person a predicate is ascribed that is incompatible with the idea of "body," namely the idea of "to know." Conversely, in the statement, "Twenty souls perished," the subject is designated according to the spiritual nature and a predicate associated with it that is only applicable to the material nature. Similar statements can be found in Scripture about Christ, as when it said that the Son of Man is in heaven and that they have crucified the Lord of glory [1 Cor 2:8], etc.

g) As the body, by its organic unity with the soul, is elevated above the sphere of the natural and material in terms of its status, even though its substance always remains that of matter, so too the humanity of the Mediator is situated in a completely unique status through union with the Son of God, even though its substance always remains creaturely, which can never transition in essence into what is uncreated. Human nature, as Christ possesses it, shares in an honor that it possesses nowhere else, just as with us the body shares in the glory of the soul and serves as the organ of its disclosure.

These are all points of striking correspondence. Still, one has always rightly felt that the analogy was a faulty one and that it does not shed light on the one mysterious point that otherwise also evades us in our study. The question of how soul and body can be one contains a problem, but the problem is different from the question of how two consciences can be one subject. The body as matter, or also as an organic aggregate, does not already have that unity in itself, which would seem to make it unsuited to be taken up as an integrated part in another unity. It leaves room for the soul as a unity-forming principle. It is otherwise with the conscious human spirit, with the consciousness of the humanity of the Lord. This appears already to possess a unity in itself, for what is consciousness other than a summing-up of many perceptions into a unity? And now it is inexplicable for us how this unity can be present where nevertheless the deeper-lying unity of the person, which exists in a different consciousness, a divine consciousness, is joined with this unity. Two consciousnesses appear to exclude one another. Here the analogy does not provide us with the least explanation, and we must, as reminded above, acquiesce in the mystery, believing that what we cannot comprehend nevertheless in reality exists.

33. *What then are the consequences for the Mediator of this personal union?*

a) A *communicatio gratianum sive charismatum in naturam*, a communication of the gifts of grace to the human nature.

b) A *communicatio proprietatum utrisque naturae cum persona*, a communication of the attributes of both natures to the person.

c) A *communicatio operationum* or *a communicatio* ἀποτελεσμάτων, a commonality of the works of redemption, according to which the actions of both natures are those of the person.

34. *How many are the gifts of grace communicated to the human nature?*

These are twofold:

a) The *gratia unionis cum persona* τοῦ λόγου, the grace of union with the person of the *Logos*, to whom the *honor adorationis*, the honor of worship, is tied. This grace has already been discussed above. It is a "grace," since human nature, even apart from all weaknesses and sin, *qua talis*, is so far below deity that it can be united with deity personally only by an extraordinary favor.

b) The *gratia habituales sive charismata* [habitual graces or gifts]. Extraordinary gifts of knowledge, will, and power were communicated to the human nature, which it did not possess in itself. In and by that human nature, too, the Mediator has to carry out His offices. At the same time, however, it is established that the very same human nature had to be beset with all natural weaknesses (except sin), in which it shares with others. The latter is inseparable from the state of humiliation in which Christ had to suffer.

The question thus arises: How can the Mediator be in this state of humiliation and at the same time possess the gifts of grace that are necessary for exercising His offices? The answer to this must be that He did not possess a human nature that included in itself these capacities as its own natural possession, but these were communicated to it as gifts of office by the Holy Spirit. Also, this communication did not occur directly from the side of the person but by mediation of the Holy Spirit. If the former had been the case, then the humiliation of human nature would have ceased, for then the gifts would have become its own personally because it has its personal existence in the person of the *Logos*. What someone has of his own person is not lent but one's own possession, and this possession cannot be viewed as a humiliation; indeed, it is incompatible with humiliation. Now, on the other hand, for fulfilling His offices, the Mediator receives these gifts from the Holy Spirit, who also was already at work in the office bearers in Israel. Although these capacities become *habitus*, "habits" of understanding and will, still they are communicated to Him from the outside (not directly from the person). They continue to possess the character of something communicated and are thereby compatible with humiliation. So, for example, the human nature of the Mediator was unable to carry out the highly weighty office of prophet. It was limited in its knowledge and its insight in its bestowed gifts, since it was our weak nature (always without sin). As in the old dispensation God endowed His weak and sinful prophets by communicating spiritual gifts for functioning in their office, so He also equipped the weak but sinless Christ by a communication of spiritual gifts for His official work, naturally with this difference: that Christ was the perfect prophet, the only one who has realized the full ideal of prophet, and that to Him therefore the Spirit was communicated without measure, that is, in an unprecedented fullness. Meanwhile, this fullness in no way eliminates:

1. that there remains a measure of gifts of grace, as that is compatible with the finiteness and true creatureliness of the human nature of the Mediator—we must not think in terms of a Lutheran communication of divine attributes;

2. that they were always granted gifts, which were not communicated directly by the person of the *Logos* but by the Holy Spirit;

3. that their communication did not occur at one time but gradually and over the course of time, all according to what was necessary for the fulfilling of the activities of the Mediator. That is why a special anointing (equipping) of the Mediator took place at His public appearance, namely, in His baptism in the Jordan.

35. *What can one add about these communicated gifts?*

Usually three kinds are mentioned: gifts of holiness, gifts of wisdom, and gifts of power.

a) Concerning the first, in the human nature of Christ, though it was pure from all indwelling sin, there was without doubt an extraordinary degree of spiritual grace. Without the influence of the Holy Spirit, there can nowhere be spiritual good, not even in the will of the human nature of the Mediator. Still, one must be on guard for two things:

1. For the view that no spiritual good was found in the human nature of Christ, since He had to assume our weak and miserable human nature. The likeness with our sinful flesh does not extend so far that this absence of spiritual good may be attributed to it. Human nature is constituted such that it cannot be neutral, and so with the absence of spiritual good must immediately turn to evil. A nature without spiritual good would be a sinful nature, which may not be attributed to Christ. On the other hand, we may assume that in the humiliation of the Lord, through an extraordinary influence, the Holy Spirit drew out and developed the habits of grace that were resident in His human nature. That is why it is reported of the Mediator that He learned obedience and through the eternal Spirit offered Himself to God (Heb 5:8; 9:14).

2. For the view that for Christ the impossibility of sinning rested on these gifts of grace of the Holy Spirit. Rather, it rested much more on the fact that in Christ's human nature there was not a mutable human person but the person of the Son of God. Will or intellect or emotion in the human nature could not have sinned unless the underlying person had fallen from a state of moral rectitude. There can naturally be no thought of the latter for the Mediator, considering the deity of His person.

b) Gifts of wisdom and knowledge are also communicated to the human nature as well, as appears from Luke 2:40, 52; 4:14, 18. In analogy with what took place with the prophets in general, the Mediator received His prophetic knowledge, as far as His human nature is concerned, from God and not from Himself.

Still, a distinction must be maintained here. With Christ there was something that, apart from Him, was not found with any prophet—namely personal unity with the *Logos*, who reveals all things. While the Holy Spirit had to make the human nature of the Mediator receptive and to enable it in all respects to receive and transmit revelation to its recipients, the real work of revelation was reserved for the person of the *Logos*; compare Matthew 11:27, where the ability of Christ to reveal the Father is derived from His entirely unique position to know stemming from the fact that He alone knows the Father, with John 3:31, 34, where both qualifications are set beside each other.

c) No less are the gifts of power bestowed on the human nature. The superhuman authority expressed from the words of Christ, the splendor of the deity, which now and then radiated through His humiliated humanity in displays of power, the authority with which He executes His offices—all this must be derived from this source.

Usually, one brings up the ability to perform miracles. With some reflection, however, it is clear that, taken strictly, this ability lies above the scope of the human nature, and that it would be the Eutychian error to consider these miracles as acts of His humanity. It was the subject of the *Logos* that performed the miracles, and it was divine power that was at work in them. To the extent, however, that the *Logos* thereby used the human nature as an organ to display these miracles, that nature was mediately active and in this respect a kind of communicate power can be ascribed to it. There naturally belonged to the human nature a sense of power to command the miracles, although it itself did not need to perform them. That the Mediator performed His miracles by the strength of His deity also appears from the fact that He never performed them in the name of God, but always in His own name. The apostles, on the other hand, in doing their miracles, speak in the name of Jesus Christ. And when, on a single occasion, the Lord prayed to the Father in performing a miraculous work and thanked Him after accomplishing it, then this must be explained by His position as Mediator. That is, He prayed to the Father, representing the Trinity, so that it would be clear to the crowd how

He, as anointed and sent from the Father, thus as Mediator, had performed this deed (John 11:41, 42).

d) In agreement with what was said above, the question may be answered whether the human nature of the Mediator exercised faith. On the basis of His full humanity, faith cannot be denied of Him insofar as it is an act of understanding, which also influences the will and the emotions insofar as it is an accepting as true upon the witness of God. To the deity of the Mediator belongs a *scientia visionis*, "a knowledge of sight," that excludes all believing. But this knowledge does not belong to the human nature. With its creaturely limitations, it cannot see immediately into the world of the eternal thoughts of God and so remains receptive, even toward the knowledge communicated to it by the *Logos*. The essence of faith lies in this receiving, in this accepting as true of something into which we ourselves have no immediate insight (cf. Acts 2:26–27; with Psa 16; Matt 27:43). On the other hand, of the specific form that faith, as saving faith, takes within the sinner, nothing can be seen in the sinless Christ. This faith, which was in the Mediator, cannot be exercised outwardly without the influences of the Holy Spirit. The same thing is to be said about hope.

36. *What should be noted about the communication of the attributes of both natures to the person?*

a) That we are dealing here with a *communicatio realis*, a real, and not a *communicatio verbalis*, a merely verbal, communication. The person really possesses both natures, and what belongs to these natures may accordingly also be attributed to the person. Were the unity between the person and the human nature a unity in appearance, then the *communicatio idiomatum* would also be an apparent communication. There is no other subject in the human nature to which its attributes can be ascribed than the subject of the Son of God. Thus, when one designates something that occurs with the human nature according its subject, one must say that it has occurred with God the *Logos*.

This explains why the Nestorians deviated from the sound position when they refused to call Mary θεότοκος. The birth certainly occurred according to the human and not according to the divine nature, but as its subject it is not permissible to indicate the latter other than by means of the *Logos*, in which it alone had its *hypostasis*. It must in fact be said: Mary gave birth to God (according to His human nature); that is to say, the subject, who is God, has undergone the process of being born by the Virgin Mary. When the Nestorians did not admit this but wished to speak of the χριστότοκος, their heresy is fully expressed in this contrast. For them, the Christ is something other than the *Logos*-God; the former is the abstraction of human and divine persons taken together. For us, the person of Christ is the same as the person of the *Logos*.

b) With this *communicatio idiomatum* a distinction must be made between the abstract and the concrete. With the abstract are meant deity and humanity; with the concrete, God and man. Now, however, the rule holds that two abstracts cannot be combined in one pronouncement. One cannot say deity is humanity or humanity is deity, for this would result in a mixing of the natures. Neither can one say that deity is man or humanity is God. That is to say, the abstract of the one nature cannot be joined together with the concrete of the other in one pronouncement. On the other hand, two concretes can be joined with each other. For example: God is man, or man is God. And likewise, the attributes of both natures may be joined with the concrete regardless of whether this concrete is derived from the divine or the human nature.

c) In this way, we obtain the following kinds of instances of this *communicatio idiomatum* [communication of attributes]:

1. The predicate in the expressed pronouncement does not belong to one of the two natures in itself but to the person by virtue of His work as Mediator. This applies to every instance where Christ is called our Savior, Lord, and King. Here the subject can be derived from the human nature: Acts 3:13, "The God of Abraham ... has glorified His child (servant) Jesus." It can also be derived from the divine nature: 1 Corinthians 15:28, "Then the Son Himself will also be subjected to the one who subjected all things to Him."

2. The predicate in the expressed pronouncement is only applicable to the divine nature but is attributed to the person, given that the person is designated according to the divine nature (Matt 11:27, "No one knows the Father except the Son"), or given that the person is designated according to the human nature (John 3:13, "The Son of Man, who is in heaven"). In the case of the latter, one can speak of a *genus majestaticum* of the *communicatio*. That is to say, something is said of the human nature that is only due it insofar as it can be used to indicate the person of the Mediator, in so doing conferring to it a great honor, for it is thereby recalled how it is personally united with the *Logos*.

3. The predicate in the expressed pronouncement is only applicable to the human nature but is ascribed to the person, given that it is designated according to the divine nature (1 Cor 2:8, "And so they would not have crucified the Lord of glory"; Acts 20:28, "To shepherd the church of God, which He has purchased with His own blood") or given that the person is designated according to the human nature (Matt 17:12, "So also the Son of Man will suffer at their hands"). In the first case, one can speak of a *genus humilitativum* of the *communicatio*. That is, something is said of the divine nature that only applies to it insofar as what is said can be used to designate the person of the Mediator who is also a man. And in doing so it is subjected to a certain humiliation, for therein is a reminder that it has been united with a weak, suffering humanity in the unity of the person.

4. The expression "communication of attributes" is not only in itself erroneous, but is also an erroneous translation of the Latin term *communicatio idiomatum*. The attributes are not communicated as if initially only the humanity possessed them by itself and then conveyed them to the person. The human nature of the Mediator did not exist for an instant apart from the person of the Son, so that from the beginning on the person also possessed the attributes. Instead of "communication," we may thus speak of "making common."

Still, by the incarnation it occurred that the person of the *Logos* took on participation in the attributes of the human nature. He has become κοινωνός [sharer] of these attributes by accepting them. As in the eternal generation, the person of the Son did not first exist without the Divine Being or outside the Divine Being in order then to receive this being through communication of being, but from eternity was generated within the being and from out of the being in order to become κοινωνός of the being. Even so, the human nature of the Mediator does not first exist outside the person of the Son in order then to be communicated with its attributes to the person, but it originates in time in the closest union with the person, who thus becomes κοινωνός with it with its attributes. *Communicare = communum facere* [to make common]. Any other view of the *communicatio* is not Reformed, but Lutheran.

37. *What is understood by the commonality of the works of redemption* (communicatio ἀποτελεσμάτων) *[communication of operations]?*

What is meant is the concurrent working of both natures in the unity of the person in all acts of the Mediator. The doctrine of this commonality of the works of redemption is, as it were, the ripe fruit of the entire development of biblical Christology. The reason why Christ had to be God and man in one person was so that a salvation could be achieved that could truly benefit us. Thus what is called for is not the metaphysical union of man with God but the judicial reconciliation of man with God. What can save is not that mankind is furnished with divine attributes or, conversely, that deity becomes humanity, but only that deity and humanity work concurrently through the unity of the person in such a fashion as is necessary to satisfy all the demands of righteousness. Thus it is that this doctrine of the *communicatio* ἀποτελεσμάτων has become a specific Reformed doctrine. It is not what Christ *is* but what He, as κοινωνός of both natures, *does* that saves us. Our salvation is a salvation by *deeds*, not by modes of existence. As we will see, in the Lutheran view the emphasis falls at a different point, and this difference in viewpoint is a distinguishing characteristic of both positions.

The following is comprised in this *communicatio* ἀποτελεσμάτων [operations]:

a) The operative cause of every work of salvation is the person of the Mediator. It is He who became Surety, became flesh, subjected Himself under the law, suffered, died, was buried, and rose. Everything originates with Him, and its merit traces back to Him. There is no particular point of departure outside of this divine person in His human nature, and nothing that occurs in it can remain at rest in it. What occurs must be reckoned to the person. The person is ὁ ἐνεργῶν, the one from whom energy originates.

b) This person works by means of the two natures, which are therefore called ἐνεργητικαί, the two organs through which action is exercised.

c) Each of the two natures only works in common with the other nature, so that, in truth, every act of salvation is an act of the whole Mediator. Nevertheless, each nature works in such a way that befits it as either divine or human nature. In the incarnation, it is the divine nature that assumes, the human nature that is assumed. In doing miracles, it is the eternal power of the *Logos* that alters the course of nature, but it is the tangible-visible and audible humanity that announces the miracle and commands the miracle. Nowhere does the one nature work without the co-working of the other. Thus, in every act of salvation there are two ἐνέργειαι or actions.

d) Nevertheless, there is only one work or ἐνεργούμενον [thing worked], ἀποτέλεσμα θεανδρικόν [theandric operation], consisting in what belongs to the person as a consequence of His working by and in both natures. If, says Mastricht, we apply this schema to our redemption, then we obtain one redeemer (λυτρώτης), who, through the coaction of both natures as redeeming (λυτρωτικά) principles, with a twofold action (λύτρωσις), brings about one ransom (λύτρον).

38. *How manifold is the union that has been assumed between the two natures in the Mediator?*

a) The *unio immediata*, the immediate union of the human nature with the *Logos*.

b) The *unio mediata,* the mediate union of the two natures, which comes about through the Holy Spirit and communicates all the gifts of grace to the human nature, discussed above.

There are, however, objections to speaking of such a mediate union of the two natures. The impression thereby arises that unity in the Mediator may come about through an intermediate factor—in other words, as if it is not a personal union but a loose placement next to each other of two disparate parts. This can lead to Nestorianism, for it was specifically the Nestorians who thought of union as moral concord. On the contrary, one must say that the communication of gifts to the human nature had an entirely different purpose than to effect unity between the two natures. It served only for equipping the human nature for its office. On this point, however, there is here and there a lack of clarity among older theologians, as also is to be concluded from the fact that they wish to derive the gifts of grace directly from the personal union of the *Logos* with the human nature.

39. *From what does the deviation of the Lutherans from this scriptural and old-orthodox [Reformed] teaching stem?*

It is not at all to be viewed as something accidental but rather as an unavoidable consequence of the distinctive way of thinking of Luther himself. Luther had at heart something mystical in his nature, which, among other ways, manifested itself in his high esteem of German mysticism. According to this German mysticism, the purpose of all religion is the union of man with God, not in an ethical or judicial sense, but substantially, so that the difference between God and man disappears. Corresponding to this is a Christology that does not have its main concern in the unity of the person but in the communication of the deity to the humanity. Accordingly, we see that Luther judges it possible for human nature to contain the divine, that he views the one as being disposed toward the other. To express this, he even makes use of philosophical propositions (for example, the Aristotelian *"materia appetit formam"* ["matter seeks form"]); and later, realizing the deficiency of this, he says, "Christ must be spoken of with new tongues and in a new language." Sometimes it even appears that Luther meant to deny the impersonality of the human nature in itself—like Calovius, for instance, who teaches the communication of personality, with that of other attributes, to the human nature.

There is no doubt that his doctrine of the Lord's Supper influenced Luther's Christology. If Christ, also according to His humanity, is present in and with bread and wine, wherever these are used, then in every instance a power must be communicated to the humanity that it ordinarily (outside of Christ) does not possess. The doctrine of the Lord's Supper thus presupposes the communication of something by the deity to the humanity, and in fact in his conflict with the Swiss over the Lord's Supper Luther made use of the doctrine of the *communicatio idiomatum*. Later he dropped this argument, not because he had a change of view, but probably because he judged the argumentation was less suited to convince. If Luther had only made his Christology clear prior to his view regarding the Lord's Supper, and if an independent principle had not been at work in the former, then he could have been satisfied with attributing divine attributes to the humanity of the Mediator after His exaltation. However, he did not leave it at that but began with the root of the matter, that is, in the incarnation. The human nature first received divine attributes not through the exaltation but through union with the deity. This is a clear indication that an independent principle is certainly at the foundation of Luther's Christology.

40. How did opinions divide after Luther's death?

In spite of the *communicatio idiomatum*, Luther had still always tried to maintain a true humanity of the Mediator in which there could be growth and development. However, he had made no attempt to show how these two were compatible. After his death, Lutheranism divided into two factions:

a) The Saxon faction, with Chemnitz as its head, adhered to Melanchthon, who never went along with the teaching of Luther on the *communicatio* and maintained that the finite was unable to contain the infinite (*finitum non capax est infiniti*).

b) The Swabian faction, led by Brenz and Andreae, were strong on the *communicatio idiomatum*. The *Logos* communicated to the human nature what one called the *majestas*, the "majesty"—which is the epitome of all divine attributes, except for *aseitas*, self-existence, for this is not communicable. Already at the moment of its origin, the humanity possessed this majesty in its entirety and this being exalted to the right hand of the Father, so that the incarnation became an ascension. Already within Mary, the body of Christ was omnipresent. If He went anywhere, according to His humanity He was already at that place in advance. When He had risen from the grave, He was still with His body in that grave. While He hung on the cross, He was present in Athens and ruled the world omnipotently.

The conflict between the two factions was eliminated temporarily in the sense that the divine attributes in the human nature of Christ during the state of His humiliation were *secret*. Difference continued to exist, however, insofar as Chemnitz wished to know only of a secret possession (κτῆσις), but the Swabians thought it necessary to assume a secret use (χρῆσις) as well.

41. *What is the Christology of the Formula of Concord?*

That is best given by the following propositions:

a) The unity in Christ is more than a *unio personalis*. There is a real unity of both natures through the communication of attributes.

b) This communication of attributes rests on the principle *humana natura capax divinae*, "human nature is capable of containing the divine."

c) The *proprietates essentiales* [essential attributes] of both natures are possessed in common with each other, with the understanding that the *substance* of the natures remains unchanged and unmixed.

d) Also, the attributes were not communicated in such a fashion as if, for example, the divine attributes could become *proprietates naturales* [natural attributes] for the human nature. As communicated, the *idiomata* [attributes] are for the other nature only *modi perpetui*, "permanent modes of existence," and not *idiomata* in the strict sense of the word. Thus omniscience does not become an *idioma* [attribute] of the human nature, as it is of the divine nature, but only a permanent mode of existence.

e) Christ did not first receive the divine majesty in His human nature in His exaltation but already by the personal union of the *Logos* with His humanity within Mary.

f) In the state of His humiliation, Christ divested this majesty so that He could truly increase in age, wisdom, and grace with God and man [Luke 2:52].

g) Nevertheless, in this state of humiliation He also made use of these communicated attributes as often as He thought it proper.

h) After His resurrection, He was confirmed in the full use and complete revelation and display of His divine majesty and thus entered into His glory.

i) Consequently, it must be said of Him that He, not only as God but also as man, knows all things, is able to do all things, and is present with every creature and exercises authority over all things.

j) This attribute of omnipresence, which is communicated to the human nature, must not be understood as if the human nature would be extended locally over heaven and earth, for something like that cannot even be maintained of His deity.

42. *What should be observed concerning these data?*

a) That, in a very circumspect manner, it is not specified what the divine attributes are that the humanity of Christ received. Four in particular are mentioned: omniscience, omnipotence, omnipresence, and all-encompassing sovereignty. About the others—for example, eternity—there is silence. Nothing need be said about why there is silence.

b) That it is not indicated exactly in what the humiliation[5] of the Mediator really consisted. He disposed of it, only used it at times; its use depended on His will. Later, He is confirmed in its full use and in its full manifestation. It appears in this that before the ascension there was only a secret possession and not a secret use, so

---

5   *Sic*; apparently "exaltation" is intended.

that Chemnitz would have been more or less in the right against the Swabians. Still, the Formula of Concord is not so conceived and also need not necessarily be so understood. The conflict between the two positions was not decided and must in time break out anew.

43. Between which parties did the conflict break out anew?

Between the theologians of Tübingen (the Swabians) and the theologians of Giessen. The former wanted to allow only for a *concealment* of the use of divine attributes (κρύψις τῆς χρήσεως), while the latter thought that Christ *disposed* of their use (κένωσις τῆς χρήσεως). The Saxon Decision of 1624 sided mainly with the Giessen theologians, so that here, too, one arrived at the standpoint of Chemnitz, according to which in the state of humiliation the human nature possessed the divine attributes in secret but did not actually use them. Thus the human nature possessed omnipresence hypothetically—that is to say, if the *Logos* so desired, it could be omnipresent. Kenoticism, as the teaching of the Giessen theologians was called, spread among Lutherans in northern Germany.

44. What has the further development of Lutheran theology in the 17th century added to the completion of this doctrine?

In the main, there was no change. Only that now in the *communicatio idiomatum* a distinction was made into three classes, namely:

a) The *genus idiomaticum*, to which belong all statements that derive from the consideration that both natures lend their predicates to the person.[6]

b) The *genus apostelesmaticum*, to which belong all statements that attribute all the works of salvation, in which both natures cooperate, to the person.

c) The *genus majestaticum*, to which all statements belong that ascribe divine attributes to the humanity.

Of course, the Reformed acknowledge only the first two classes, not the third.

---

6 This first point is missing in the transcription. I have supplied it from the handwritten edition of 1890.

Only at one point was there a further stipulation in Lutheran theology. It began to teach explicitly that the so-called dormant attributes (eternity, etc.) of God were not communicated to the human nature, but only the so-called active attributes (omniscience, omnipresence, omnipotence, etc.).

45. What is your critique of Lutheran Christology?

One can subject every doctrine to criticism in two ways. Scripture must of course be the standard for all criticism, but every doctrine admits to a twofold comparison with Scripture. First, one can inquire after the inner meaning, after the principle of the doctrine, and if this is discovered, pose the question how it accords with the basic truths that Scripture teaches throughout and makes prominent. Or, one can ask *in concreto* what Scripture teaches us in regard to the dispute in question when it expressly speaks of these things. The first approach, where it can be applied, gives us not only the *fact* of the erroneousness of the doctrine but also provides us directly with the *reason*.

a) Applied here to Christology, it teaches us that the Lutheran conception is in conflict with the pervasive demand of Scripture to keep deity and humanity strictly separated and not permit a mingling of the natures with each other. The chasm between God and man concerning what is metaphysical and substantial is an absolute chasm. That God and man can be united in a judicial or ethical sense, or even by mystical action, does not narrow this gulf. The ethical separation between both is something abnormal; the ontological separation is what is normal and can never be missing.

It has been precisely the Reformed church and Reformed theology that has maintained this principle of the absolute difference between the Creator and the creature by everywhere beginning with God and standing for His honor and infinite transcendence. On the basis of Scripture, it has not been willing to grant that the impulse of the creature for bliss can or must be satisfied insofar as the *communicatio idiomatum* presupposes that God would communicate His divine attributes to humanity. That can be demanded only by a theology that does not choose its starting point in God and the honor of God but in man and his bliss. So there are two motives that have led to the Lutheran formulation of the doctrine: (1) the pantheistically inclined mysticism of which Luther retained something; (2) the predominantly soteriological character of Lutheran theology.

b) According to Scripture, the emphasis in the first place must not be on the subjective change of human nature but on the objective justification of man before God and the satisfaction of the justice of God. Now on this point the Lutheran Reformation, insofar as it arrived at an awareness of its own character, proceeded clearly. Luther himself was the great champion raised up by God for the justice of God. If satisfaction is at the center of our doctrine of salvation, then the person of the Mediator will have to be such as is demanded by this satisfaction. Now, everyone immediately sees that for the locus on satisfaction, which belongs in the legal sphere, two natures mingled with each other are not necessary, but the unity of the person in two unmingled and intact natures. The emphasis should have fallen on the personal union and not, as now, on the *communicatio idiomatum*. In other words, Luther's Christology does not fit with the central place that he assigns to the doctrine of satisfaction and of justification through faith. It stands to reason that this can only be explained by the unconscious co-action of another principle. This, specifically, was the mystical principle that laid emphasis on the subjective transformation and deification of human nature and thus required a Mediator in whom the attributes of the natures were communicated.

c) One could ask, then, whether Lutheran theology has abandoned the *unio personalis* and replaced it with the *communicatio idiomatum*. To be fair, one must acknowledge that it did not do this. The Formula of Concord begins from the *unio personalis*. Still, the following should be kept in view:

1. That here and there in Lutheran theologians one can find the notion that the personal union was not the basis for the communication of the attributes, but its consequence.

2. That here and there the notion also surfaces that the divine nature, with its attributes, also communicated the attribute of

personality to the humanity and that the unity of the person had thus arisen from these two natures.

3. That thus the *unio personalis* has in fact moved more into the background and lost its practical value for Lutheran theology.

d) The Lutheran doctrine contains a series of contradictions and impossibilities, of which the following are the most serious:

1. On one hand, one maintains that the substances of the natures remain separate, and, on the other hand, that nonetheless the attributes of those natures are communicated. Here, then, the attributes are detached from the substances and tied to something else. It is indeed added that, for the other nature, they are not attributes but only a mode of existence. This, however, does not make the matter any more comprehensible or plausible. It is in conflict with reason that an attribute can exist other than as bonded with the substance to which it belongs.

2. If human nature is to preserve its limitedness—that is, its true humanity—it cannot share in such transcendent divine attributes. It is forever bound to time and space, regardless of whether this limitation is of the same kind as that in which it occurs for us or perhaps allows for conceiving of another relationship to space and time. In any case, there must be a relationship. The concept of being human and the concept of being elevated above time and space exclude each other. Thus it is of no help to the Formula of Concord when it rejects the view that the omnipresence of the humanity of the Mediator is local. Any form of omnipresence—whether it be local or dynamic—is for humanity, as such, impossible.

3. For the state of humiliation, Lutheran doctrine leads to more than one impossible conception. One need only reread what is said above about the opinion of the Swabians to see immediately that the state of humiliation becomes an illusion that amounts to sheer Docetism. What is one to think of a limitation that permits the thing that has to be limited to be everywhere at the same time? Further, there is the following objection: According to the Lutheran conception, humiliation is not an act of the person of the *Logos* as such but of the assumed

human nature, consisting in this nature setting aside the use of the communicated divine attributes. What constitutes the humiliation is not that the *Logos* joins Himself with the weak human nature but that the humanity lays aside its divine majesty. The question, however, arises: When has this occurred? At the incarnation, everything was already humiliation; otherwise the state of exaltation would have been earlier (albeit then for a short time) than the state of humiliation. The only escape is that one posits the preexistence of the human nature of the Mediator in an exalted state before the incarnation and so makes His humanity eternal.

4. The Lutheran viewpoint suffers from vacillation and inconsistency on the following points: To begin, it does not venture to make the *communicatio idiomatum* mutual. This, however, had been necessary according to its principles. If the Mediator could not be our Savior unless the divine nature with its attributes penetrates the human nature, one maintains with every right that the divine nature must assume the attributes of the human nature—in other words, discard its deity and enter into all human weakness and limitations. In doing that, it would have been necessary for the Lutherans to make a fourth class along with the three classes of the *communicatio idiomatum* mentioned above, namely a *genus* ταπεινοτικόν, a class of "statements of humiliation," in which human attributes are attributed to the deity. Happily, Lutheran theology shrank back from doing this, but it was a faulty inconsistency.

Next, the Lutherans do not venture to have all divine attributes communicated to the human nature, but stay with three or four. The absurdity would have been much too apparent if, for instance, one wished to maintain for the humanity of the Mediator that it was eternal and still hold that it was assumed from the flesh and blood of the Virgin Mary. So here, too, one remains vacillating.

It is no less a vacillation if one thinks a distinction can be made between the possession and use of certain attributes. It becomes impossible to ever obtain a true humiliation. For some attributes, that may be possible. For example, one could speak of a hypothetical omnipresence and by that understand the potential, the dormant capacity of making oneself omnipresent. However, with an attribute like omniscience, this does not work. Whoever is only potentially omniscient is *ipso facto* not, and no one is able to say, with its use lacking, what remains of the possession of such an attribute.

e) The Lutheran doctrine is lacking a scriptural foundation. In order to prove the doctrine, one appeals to statements in which divine predicates are attributed to the human nature (better: to the person designated according to the human nature). However, as was shown earlier, all that is to be explained from the unity of the person. And when the Lutherans do not accept this unity and think they have to insist on a literal explanation, then one may rightly ask them why they do not apply this same literal explanation when human things are predicated of the deity. This occurs just as often. The Lutheran principle is that after the incarnation, *Logos non est extra carnem, et caro non est extra Logos.* In other words, the *Logos* is not outside the flesh, and the flesh is not outside the *Logos*. Both are coextensive. If this is so, the *Logos* must be limited.

f) Lutheran Christology is Eutychian and does not do justice to the true humanity of the Mediator. If one throws a drop of water into a sea of fire, where will it be? What remains of a humanity that is swallowed up in the infinite sea of deity?

46. *What is characteristic of the Christology of the Modern (German) theologians?*

To understand this Christology well, one should start with Schleiermacher—not that it agrees with his view of Christ but because it has received its characteristic direction and shape through him. According to Schleiermacher, all religion is a life. A Christian becomes conscious of having assimilated this life within himself. At the same time, he knows that it did not have its origin in himself or in the church. There must be a beginning point for this life outside the ordinary development of humanity. Historically, this beginning point is given in the sinless, absolutely perfect man Christ, who though a creative act must have become what He is. In Christ, the idea of humanity is fully realized.

But the same ideal human Christ is as such also divine. This must be so understood that man is the *modus existendi* [mode of existing] of God on earth. God exists on earth in the form of a man. However, while with all other men this mode of existence is only deficient and a conflict takes place within them between consciousness of the world and consciousness of God, there was no such conflict within Christ. Consciousness of God completely ruled Christ's internal and external life. Since this was the case, He could not sin. In this His unique nature also now lies the possibility that He is our Savior. He works on us not so much by what He *does* as by what He *is*. He awakens in man the dormant consciousness of God and so is the source of life for others. Through Him, all believers become, to a greater or lesser degree, God revealed in the flesh. This new life of Christ is the principle that forms and enlivens the church.

47. *What should be noted in this system of Schleiermacher?*

   a) That the whole is organized along pantheistic lines. God is not a person. His attributes are forms and conditions of our consciousness.

   b) That it has no place for the Trinity. What becomes man here is not the person of the *Logos* as distinct from the Father and the Holy Spirit; rather, abstract, primal deity comes to self-consciousness in man.

   c) That it does not allow for an essential difference between Christ and believers. He is perfectly what they are in principle and in part.

   d) That as essentially pantheistic, it does not allow for any personal relationships between God and man, and so cannot find the heart of the work of the Mediator in restoring violated judicial relationships. The work of redemption becomes an ethical or religious process that takes place within man.

   e) That in order to save the supernatural and unique character of Christianity, the appearance of Christ is still explained by a creative act, although no one can explain how such a creative act originates with an impersonal God. In all these respects, the Christology of Schleiermacher has set the tone for the following development.

48. *What are the basic tenets of the more theistic Christology that has obviously developed under the influence of these principles of Schleiermacher?*

Before we address this in detail, it should be noted that for these theologians a distinction is to be made between the conscious content and the hidden impetus of their teaching. The former is theistic; the latter stems from pantheism. They are themselves theists—that is, they explain God as a personal, conscious being, and nevertheless they teach things regarding the incarnation that only fit with a consistently thought-out pantheism.

The basic tenets of this Christology are:

a) In Christ there is only one nature, whether immediately or at the end of a certain development that one attributes to Him.

b) This is possible because the divine nature and the human nature are not so sharply contrasted with each other as one in the past considered it necessary to think. Rather, they are disposed to each other such that they can devolve into each other and can combine with each other.

c) While all these theologians agree with the thesis that human nature can take the divine into itself (*humana natura capax naturae divinae*), they do not all allow that the opposite is true—namely, that the divine nature can change into the human nature. As a result, there are two lines. Those who affirm the latter stand over against those who deny it. The former are called kenoticists; their teaching is the doctrine of kenosis. The name is derived from Philippians 2:7, where Paul says of Christ, ἑαυτὸν ἐκένωσεν, "He emptied Himself." Many prominent theologians belong to these kenoticists: for example, Liebner, Hasse, Thomasius, Gess, Ebrard, Edmond de Pressensé, among others;[7] among the exegetes, Meyer (on Philippians 2). Of those who deny the view in question (namely, that the divine nature can change into human nature), Dorner is the most prominent.

---

7   The 1890 handwritten edition also lists the following (after Ebrard): Kahnis, von Hofmann, Luthhard, Delitzsch, Oehler, Godet.

49. *What distinguishes this modern kenosis-doctrine from what bore this name in the past?*

Historically, the one word "kenosis" has acquired two meanings, which one must distinguish in order not to get confused. Orthodox Lutheran theology understands by kenosis that act of the Mediator by which, according to His human nature, He has set aside the use or open use of the divine attributes communicated to this nature. Here, for the state of humiliation, the human nature empties itself of something communicated.

The modern kenosis, in contrast, is an act of the *Logos* whereby He, according to His divine nature, divests Himself of the attributes of deity, so that He no longer possesses them, not even according to His deity, which rather has ceased to exist. Of course, the old Lutheran theology did not think of something like that, that the deity could change or lay aside its attributes. Its kenosis was different *toto genere* [of an entirely different kind] than what at present bears that name.

50. *What is included in this recently fashioned kenosis doctrine?*

It displays two forms:

a) Some teach that the eternal *Logos* did not divest Himself of all, but only of the relative, divine attributes, and thereby was enabled to go through a process of divine-human development as a true man with one nature. This line has its representative in Thomasius.

b) Others go further and teach that the *Logos* not only divested Himself of His divine mode of existence but also of His full divine being and became a human soul with all its limitations in order to develop Himself from this point into perfect deity. This line is represented by Gess.

51. *Give a further description of the ideas of the first line (that of Thomasius).*

Thomasius himself provides this description in the following words:

That He, the eternal Son of God, the Second Person of the Godhead, put Himself into the form of human limitation and thereby, within the limits of space and time, subjected Himself to the conditions of human development, to the confines of a historical existence, in order, without thereby ceasing to be God, to experience with us, in the fullest sense of the word, the life of our race in our nature. Only in this way does there come about a genuine entering into humanity, a becoming truly one with it, an incarnation of God. Only in this way do we obtain as the result the historical person of the Mediator, about whom we know that He is the God-man. As is self-evident, the transition into this state is for the eternal Son of God a self-limitation, a laying aside not of what is essential for the Godhead to be God but a laying aside of the divine *modus existendi* (mode of existence) for the human, creaturely mode of existence and *eo ipso* [of itself] a distancing from the divine glory that He had had from the beginning with the Father and had exercised toward the world, by ruling and governing it.

In order to comprehend this well, one must give attention to the distinction Thomasius makes between two kinds of divine attributes: There are *immanent* and *relative* attributes in God. To the former he reckons absolute power and holiness, absolute truth and love; to the relative attributes, omnipotence, omnipresence, omniscience. God cannot abandon those attributes of the first kind because He would thereby lose His essence. He can, however, abandon the second kind because they express His relationship to the world. And these are not necessary for Him, since the world itself cannot be said to be necessary for God.

In this way, in the Mediator there is not only one subject, one person—the *Logos* who set aside His omnipotence, omnipresence, and omniscience—but also only one consciousness, one mind, one will. In this one consciousness, this one will, this one mind, are absolute power, truth, holiness, and love, as they were previously in the omnipotent, omnipresent, and omniscient *Logos*. And it is a free act of will by which the *Logos* sets aside these relative attributes. The emptying of the relative occurs by means of one of the immanent attributes, namely, by absolute power or freedom.

52. What must be noted against this kenosis as it is taught by Thomasius?

Its main error is a pantheistic distortion of the concept of God. If I attribute immanent and relative attributes to God, I thereby declare the former to be essential and the latter to be nonessential or accidental. God's essence, then, consists in this: that He has love, possesses truth, and is power. In other words: As to His essence, He is not different from man, for man can possess all these attributes. Thus one can see that here God-humanness as one nature is only attained by placing God and man on the same line and by seeking the essence of God in what is common to Him and man. This, however, is the basic error of pantheism. In opposition to that error, we must maintain that even with respect to the communicable attributes, an irremovable difference remains between God and man. God is powerful, holy, and true, but in an entirely other sense than man is all these things. He is that absolutely, and man is that in dependence on God, and between these two modes of existence there is a gulf that is just as great as that between God's eternity and the being of man in time. A God-man, as Thomasius construes Him, is only an apparent man, because He must be the one who is absolutely powerful, true, and holy—all of which are attributes that are incompatible with genuine humanity. Even in the most perfect, inalterable state, man still does not acquire this absoluteness.

Also, the basis on which Thomasius attempts to show the possibility of laying aside the relative attributes is inadequate. These attributes do not merely express a relationship to the world, so that one might infer their accidental character from the accidental existence of the world. This relationship to the world is only one side of their conception, and—insofar as the world is accidental—an accidental side. The heart of their conception lies much deeper than this relationship and exists entirely independent of it. In God's eternity, omnipresence, and omnipotence lies much more than that He is not limited by the passing of time, by the space of the universe, and by the powers in the universe. Beyond that there is a positive element, and the *Logos* can in no way discard this positive element without eradicating His essence, something that is completely excluded by the concept of the immutability of God. Besides this, as we have seen, in God the metaphysical (Thomasius: the "relative") attributes determine the so-called ethical attributes. God is eternal, infinite, true, holy, etc.—what, again, cannot be said of any creature.

On closer examination, then, it is evident how what must constitute the unity between divine and human nature in this system is different in God and man, and what would have to be put off or set aside to produce the unity demanded cannot be put off or set aside. It has been rightly noted that this kenotic Christology is gnostic and docetic; it neither retains true deity nor reaches true humanity. God in Christ is a God who has divested Himself of all His absolute divine attributes—a God rendered impotent. The man, Christ, is a man with absolute love and truth—in other words, not a man with a nature like ours.

53. *Provide a description of the other form in which the doctrine of kenosis appears—that of Gess.*

According to Gess, the person and the divine nature may be separated from each other, and the person of the *Logos* can distance Himself from the divine nature and exclude it from Himself, so that nothing remains but the formal point of personality, now in the possession of the human nature. Gess says, "The Jesus who lived on earth as a real man, who suffered and died, is the same person who, as the *Logos* of God, was with the Father from the beginning, was God, and through whom all things are created." This, however, is to be so understood that in His incarnation the Son, by an act of self-emptying, extinguished His eternal self-consciousness in order to receive it back as a human self-consciousness. He became a truly human, entirely humanly developing soul. This transition is conceived of further as follows: One may view the reception of deity by the *Logos* within the Trinity not as a constitutive, eternally necessary act but as an act of will, from which it must immediately follow that the *Logos*, if He wills it, can close off this influx of deity, and in doing so can set aside His deity. His generation by the Father will still remain an eternal, necessary act (to deny this would lead directly to Arianism), but from the side of the Son His being generated is voluntary.

54. *What is your criticism of this conception?*

In it, the pantheistic trait of the kenosis emerges in its clearest [form]. Here God, while maintaining His personality, is changed into man. He has extinguished His consciousness, as if such a thing were possible in eternal, immutable deity. A god who has it within his freedom no longer to be god due already to this will can no longer be called god.

Also taught here is a connection between person and nature, or rather a lack of connection between the two, that cannot pass the test. A person cannot exist apart from his nature. When he abandons his nature, he thereby, *ipso facto*, ceases to exist. He cannot make the transition from one nature to another without eradicating himself. Thought through consistently, the theory of Gess cuts the continuity and the identity of the subject in Christ. There is one person in the divine nature before the incarnation and one person in the human nature after the incarnation, but those two cannot be one and the same person.

The entire construction of Gess also rests on a wrong conception of the Trinity. He speaks of the inflowing of deity into the person of the *Logos*, which He Himself can cause to cease. This is conceived of as if the Son existed apart from the Father and then received the divine essence from Him. From this it naturally follows that the Son can continue to exist even if it pleases Him to shut off this inflowing of deity by an act of self-emptying. In reality, it is entirely the opposite. Within the divine essence, the person of the Father is the cause of a second person's existence, which then of Himself shares in the same indivisible divine essence. The person is generated, not the essence communicated. Thus if the *Logos* cuts off or lays aside what He has received from the Father, then the *Logos* can exist in no other way than that He casts aside His personal existence, ceases to exist as a person. So here too is the same result: The continuity is no longer the same subject as God the *Logos*.

55. How does the conception of Dorner differ from these systems properly called kenotic?

Dorner contends forcefully against kenosis and deems it impossible that God would change. Thus the *Logos* must remain absolute and unchanged. Nevertheless, Dorner, too, wishes to arrive at one nature and not to be content with two natures in one person. He also cannot agree with the impersonality of the human nature. The humanity must be complete, up to and including a human person. How then does Dorner combine these givens? By saying that in His communication of the humanity, the *Logos* limited Himself according to the measure of human nature as it developed normally, so that the complete God-man (= one nature) was not the beginning but the outcome of the Lord's earthly life.

56. What objection is there to this Christology?

That at bottom it brings together the two errors of Nestorianism and Eutychianism. Its end result is a Christ with only one nature—therefore Eutychianism! Its starting point, on the other hand, is two persons: a divine *Logos* that must remain immutable and a human subject that must grow and develop—thus Nestorianism! When Dorner speaks of a successive communicating of the divine nature to the man according to the receptivity of the latter, then one does not rightly know how that is to be understood. If something of the *Logos* is transmitted to the man, then the *Logos* must gradually be shunted into the man, so from these two becomes one. So then the change in the deity, against which Dorner contends so vigorously, would nonetheless take place. If, on the other hand, it remains at a mere inflow of power or at an ethical working on the man Jesus by the *Logos*, then the unity is lost and we cannot see how it may be attained, even if the development of the humanity were to continue forever.

57. *How does Dorner otherwise attempt to avoid this discrepancy to some degree?*

He has attempted in his A *System of Christian Doctrine* to overcome the difficulty by a transformation of the doctrine of the Trinity. If the human person of Christ has to be maintained at any cost and nevertheless no discrepancy may arise, and further, if a self-emptying of the *Logos* is impossible, then nothing remains but to deny that before the incarnation the *Logos* was personally a subject. This is why Dorner speaks of the deity as existing in only one person, and along with this one person refers to points of ego. This makes this already-dense construction even much more unnatural and unacceptable and at the same time makes the questionable pantheistic outlook of all these speculations to appear in a clearer light. God Himself is drawn along, as it were, into the process of development of the world. He does not in this way acquire His personality in an absolute sense, but acquires His absolute personality only through the incarnation—in other words, by appearing in conjunction with something created. The Trinity is changed; it becomes complete. A man is taken up into God, and by that the being of God was made even more complete than it was previously! One almost fears to utter such assertions.

Not only how much more balanced and more restrained, but also how much simpler, then, is the time-honored church dogma of the duality of natures in the unity of the person. Here, too, theology does not need to trade its old treasures for the results of modern wisdom.

58. *Finally, how can you compare Reformed, Lutheran, and modern kenosis teaching with each other?*

The problem was to so unite deity and humanity that no separation remained at any point. It is entirely understandable that we do not produce that problem. When, however, the old Lutheran Christology deifies Christ's humanity, it causes separation between Him and us to exist. When kenosis theory humanizes the deity of the *Logos*, it leaves this separation between humanity and God undiminished. We, in contrast, bring deity and humanity immediately into contact with each other through the unity of the person, and in this person we do not permit a separation but allow for an impenetrable mystery.

59. *Who in later times taught a preexistence of the humanity of the Mediator?*

Among others, Swedenborg (1688–1772) and Isaac Watts.

60. *What was the view of Swedenborg?*

He rejected the orthodox church doctrine of the Trinity. There are not three persons in the being of God; there is only a triad of principle. This uni-personal God consists of being; His form is divine and human at the same time. In other words, He has a body from eternity. According to Swedenborg, this body is not the crude material body that we men possess, but a spiritual body. However, this makes no essential difference between God and man, for, besides a material body, the latter, too, has a more refined, spiritual body. Moreover, Jehovah-God (Christ), who already possessed this spiritual body from eternity, in time also assumes from the womb of Mary a material body, with the psychical life of the same. This material body, then, is later glorified and refined, so that it becomes one with the spiritual body.

61. *What did Isaac Watts write in defense of the preexistence of Christ's humanity?*

He wrote three discourses on "The Glory of Christ as God-Man" (1746). His view was of an entirely different nature than that of Swedenborg since it did not intend to challenge the church doctrine of the Trinity. As grounds, he produced the following:

a) That Christ appeared repeatedly in a visible form before His incarnation.

b) Christ is called "the image of God."

c) Nowhere does Scripture speak of Christ having assumed a human soul in His incarnation, but always uses corporeal language.

d) The covenant between God the Father and the Son is from all eternity. This requires that both parties are present. However, in the Trinity there is only one mind and one will, which therefore cannot make a covenant. The covenant can only be made between God and the human soul of Christ. Watts also understands generation to be the creation of the human soul, and at this point at least comes into conflict with the orthodox doctrine of the Trinity.

62. How is this view to be assessed?

There is an element of truth in it. That element consists in this: that due to the eternal counsel of peace, the humanity of the Mediator was eternally and ideally present. In other words, the Son of God assumed His suretyship not as the *Logos* in the abstract, but as the *Logos* who would become flesh in time. He did this as *Logos incarnandus* [to be incarnate], and His human nature was thereby taken into account as if it were really present.

The latter, however, was not the case. It was not necessary, as Watts judged, for establishing the covenant that the actual soul of Christ existed. The establishment of the covenant was a work of the person, and this person is in the Mediator, the Son of God, as such eternally present. On the other hand, Scripture teaches us that the humiliation of the Mediator consisted in His becoming man, in His "taking on the form of a servant" (Phil 2:7). According to the view of Watts, there was first an exalted humanity, then a humiliated humanity, and later again an exalted humanity. Incarnation comes to mean "taking on a body" and no longer retains its accustomed meaning of "assuming a complete human nature." The bond between the human nature of Christ and ours is thereby severed if He in no sense assumed its primary part from us but already possessed its exalted state from all eternity. Also, such a human soul, created from eternity or at least before the incarnation, has very much of the Arian Christ, especially when one ventures with Watts to connect the idea of generation with the creation of this soul. Further, it may be observed that modern exegesis attributes this teaching of Christ as a preexistent man particularly to Paul based on 1 Corinthians 15:45 and following verses, as well as on several other places.

Chapter Four
Offices

1. *How many offices did the Mediator occupy and still occupies in His natures?*

Three: the office of prophet, of priest, of king.

2. *How do we arrive at this threefold division of offices?*

It has been shown earlier how we can derive the necessity of more than one office from the fact that Christ is head of the covenant. The question now is: How do we arrive at three offices? Is this something arbitrary, or does it have a rational ground? This question may be answered as follows:

a) This division is not arbitrary, inasmuch as it was pictured in the threefold theocratic office. Within Israel there were prophets, priests, and kings. We cannot say here that three offices were attributed to Christ in order to imitate the Old Testament institutions. But, on the contrary, we must confess [that] such offices were established within Israel because the Messiah would occupy these three offices. This division is to be explained by the preparatory and imperfect character of the Old Testament dispensation. So that it would appear that these office-bearers were not the full sun but only radiated reflected light; they did not possess the light in all its colors. Only here and there did they come nearer to the fullness, what can be considered an extraordinary grace (cf. Melchizedek in Genesis 14 and Psalm 110).

‹ 447 ›

b) There are three spheres in which human beings live and must live: the spheres of truth, of power, and of moral relationship toward God. Because of sin, abnormality has occurred in each of these spheres. Thus the Mediator must restore a state of normalcy in a threefold way. In the sphere of truth, He must be our Prophet; in the sphere of power, our King; and in the sphere of moral relationship between God and us, our Priest.

c) One can consider man in three kinds of relationships. First, one can descend from God to man; then one can ascend from man to God; and finally one can conceive of man in relation to his environment. Each of these relationships corresponds to one of the offices of the Mediator. He stands for God before us as Prophet, for us before God as Priest, and to our benefit toward our environment as King.

d) By faith there is a reflection of the Messiah for our consciousness. It is intended by God to cause us to enclose Christ in our hearts from all sides, with all His features in the fullness of His offices. Now it appears, however, that this faith has three sides—namely, knowledge, assent, and trust—of which each corresponds to one of the offices of the Mediator. Through the knowledge of faith it is Christ the Prophet who works on us by teaching and explains Himself in His mediatorial work. Through the assent of faith it is Christ as King who rules over our souls so that we give ourselves captive to His truth. Through the assurance of faith, which we call trust, it is Christ who as Priest ministers reconciliation to us and grants us peace with God or places upon us the blessing of God. Just three offices are necessary here, and there is no place for more than three.

e) Scripture itself here and there summarizes the different aspects of the mediatorial work of the Lord in this manner; for example, when it speaks of how He has become to us wisdom from God (prophetic office) and righteousness (priestly office) and sanctification and redemption (royal office) [1 Cor 1:30].

3. Is this threefold division of offices an old one in theology?

Yes, it is already found in the church father Eusebius. The Reformed theologians, Calvin foremost, were the first to give it a formal place after the treatment of the doctrine of the two natures in the one person. It was introduced among Lutherans by Johann Gerhard. Only in later times did people begin to entertain doubts about the correctness of this division. Ernesti, a Lutheran theologian, was the first, and his objections have been repeated by Schleiermacher and Schweizer.

4. Are these objections to this division well-founded?

They concern either its correctness or its completeness. It is argued that the offices do not exclude each other and also that they do not comprise in themselves all that Christ does as Mediator. We must grant the first objection, if what is meant is that in the activity of the Mediator no single moment can be pointed out where He acts entirely in the capacity of either prophet, or priest, or king, so that He only functions in one office and the other offices are excluded. It is throughout the one, indivisible Christ, in possession of the threefold office, who speaks. When as Prophet He reveals the counsel of God, He also does this with the authority of a King. And when as Priest He sacrifices Himself to God, He is, at that same moment, working prophetically by His own sacrifice. All this must be granted. The offices interpenetrate each other, and it is in a certain way similar to the unity of the natures in the person of the Mediator. These, too, can never be separated, as is shown by the *communicatio idiomatum* ["communication of attributes"].

However, if, with the objection mentioned above, one means that the offices are not logically separated and flow into each other, that one office could be removed while retaining completeness, or arbitrarily with equally good right other functions be substituted for it, then this objection is sufficiently refuted by what has been said previously concerning the derivation of the three offices. The other objection, that the classification is incomplete, is the result of ascribing unscriptural functions to the Mediator, as if the incarnation is for the perfecting of mankind and for realizing its ideal apart from sin. With the disappearance of these views, this objection also disappears. Finally, if it is asserted that we are not dealing here with something essential but merely with form, then we should answer that essence and form are closely related. And if we dare to abandon the latter unnecessarily, then we will find how the former has slipped through our fingers unnoticed. All error and heresy begins in this way: with a clamor that form is not essential. This is how the doctrine of the covenants was set aside as outdated, before long with the doctrines of substitution and satisfaction as well.

5. *From what does it appear that these offices must be thought of in the closest unity as penetrating each other?*

From the fact that the old theologians not only and not always spoke of the offices but of the Mediator's *office*, in the singular (*officium Jesu Christi Mediatorium*).

6. *Can one show from the New Testament that the Mediator holds this threefold office?*

In part, this is found already in the name Christ, "Anointed," as was demonstrated above. In part, the offices are explicitly ascribed to Him (cf. Acts 2:22; Rev 1:5; 3:14; John 18:36; Eph 1:7, 20; Col 1:12–20; Phil 2:5–11; Heb 7–9).

7. *How is the threefold office related to the reality of sin?*

Sin is a darkening of the mind; it is guilt in the conscience; it is, as inherent corruption, a power in the individual and moreover, by organizing itself, a power in the world. To this threefold action of sin corresponds the threefold office of the Mediator. It comes down to the same thing when one begins with the image of God that has to be restored in us. This consists in knowledge, righteousness, and holiness, each of which belongs to one of the offices.

8. *How can you demonstrate that one-sided or heretical views of the work of the Mediator are related to the failure to appreciate one or more of His offices?*

By pointing to:

   a) The Socinians and the Rationalists, who, concerning Christ's time on earth, only acknowledge a prophetic office. This presupposes that sin consists only in an aberration of the intellect, or at least that the will can be changed by means of the intellect. From this it follows that an incarnation is unnecessary, and that for function-ing in this exclusively prophetic office a mere man is sufficient. Compare the way in which Christ Himself corrects the Socinian-Rationalist view of Nicodemus by pointing to His priestly and kingly office (John 3:1, 2–3, 10, 14).

b) Mystics of various persuasions, who believe that a mystical transformation can be effected within man apart from a due functioning of his consciousness. Antinomians also suffer from this evil insofar as they are satisfied with an atonement for guilt without a correspondingly thoroughgoing sense of guilt in the sinner who is saved.

c) Romanism and every hierarchical system like it, besides arro-gating to itself the rights of Christ as kingly, generally places one-sided emphasis on His kingly office to the detriment of the prophetic office. The external and visible organization of the church is then pushed to the forefront, and knowledge is deemed of secondary importance.

d) Thus we see that an appreciation of the three offices is the touch-stone of the versatility and integrity of our Christianity. Only those who honor Christ as Prophet, Priest, and King have the whole Christ according to the Scriptures.

9. *How do the three offices of the Mediator stand in relation to each other?*

They have an aspect by which they are subordinate to each other and at the same time an aspect by which they are exercised more independent-ly for completion of the mediatorial work. In the first respect, the prophetic office serves the priestly office, since it lends meaning to the sacrifice of the Mediator and puts it in the proper light. Similarly, the prophetic serves the kingly office, since it proclaims Christ's kingship and brings it to the attention of men. Conversely, the priestly office, in turn, underlies both of the other offices; for the gift of enlightenment, which Christ imparts as prophet, and the other gifts of grace, which He works with kingly power in those who belong to Him, are all acquired by His priestly self-sacrifice. No less does the kingly office serve both of the other offices; for example, when Christ confirms His teaching with miraculous power or institutes the sacraments with the kingly mediatorial authority.

In the second respect, each of the offices has an independent significance and abiding worth, so that it will not do to make one of them subordinate or secondary. It is not merely to make His priestly activity possible, or to introduce saved souls into the knowledge of reconciliation, that Christ works prophetically. The knowledge of the counsel of God communicated by Him has independent significance. Also, His priesthood is not transitory in nature, for although the work of satisfaction has ended with His stay on earth, still we know that Christ remains forever in a permanent priesthood and ever lives to pray for us (Heb 7:24–25). And His kingly office, too, will never be taken from Him entirely, although He now certainly occupies it in a form that at one time will cease. Even then, when it will be found to be unnecessary for the exercise of the other offices, it will still shine on Him with its own underived splendor.

10. *How do the offices stand in relation to each other with regard to order in time and in relation to the states of the Mediator?*

   a) For God in His eternity, the completion of the mediatorial work is eternally given, and by the suretyship of the Son it is established from eternity. Every thought as if the Mediator occupied His offices only after His incarnation must therefore be rejected. Rather, we should say that He has occupied His three offices during two dispensations: during the shadowy and the embodied dispensations of the covenant of grace. Believers who were saved during the old day could not have been saved otherwise than by the official activity of the Messiah. Earlier, it was already pointed out that the prophets, priests, and kings in Israel were not only shadows or types but also messengers and representatives of the great antitype. They derived their official authority from the person Himself whom they as office bearers proclaimed in a shadowy fashion. Certainly, it is true that at that time Christ did not yet have a human nature. But His person was still the person of the one anointed from eternity. According to God's counsel of peace and His own voluntary *sponsio* (suretyship), He was the *Logos incarnandus* ("the *Logos* to become flesh").

b) Neither may a distinction be made for the state of His humiliation, as though in this state He would have occupied only a part of His offices and not yet participated in the fullness of the threefold office. Compare what has been said above concerning the Socinians. It is true that Christ in His exaltation received a kingdom that He did not possess before, but the significance of His kingdom is not exhausted in that. He was already King before in a sense in which He always was ever since His appointment as Mediator. Neither is His priestly office excluded from His state of exaltation, for He *now* appears before God for our benefit. It can be said that in the state of humiliation His kingly power and majesty receded into the background, as was to be expected. But He has always had the three offices and will possess them forever.

c) The theologians point to a certain succession in the public exercise of the offices by the Mediator (not in the *possession,* but in the *exercise* of the offices). First He appeared as Prophet, teaching and preaching, then at the end of His life He offered His sacrifice as Priest in order after the resurrection to receive His reward and to reign as King.

This order is certainly not to be considered accidental. It is the usual order that God maintained in His dealings with man, which was already prefigured in creation. First, the truth of things and their significance must be brought to light. When this has been done satisfactorily, the elaboration of the moral and legal relations must occur in this light, and only then on this foundation can an enduring fellowship be established. That is also typical for the work of God with the individual sinner, by which He brings the sinner to an awareness of the covenant of grace. Just as in the work of Christ, here prophetic enlightenment, priestly justification, and kingly sanctification and glorification follow one another.

11. *What is the prophetic office of Christ?*

His activity, which He performs as the authoritative representative of God, to reveal the counsel of God for the salvation of His people in connection with His other mediatorial work.

12. *Which biblical words are used to express the term "prophet"?*

In Hebrew נָבִיא, in Greek προφήτης. The first word seems to come from an (Arabic) root meaning "to speak." A *nabi*, therefore, is a speaker, but not in the sense of someone who speaks of or for himself. Rather, the word must have the meaning of someone who speaks as a representative of others (cf. Exod 4:16; 7:1; Jer 15:19; 2 Chr 6:4). Even clearer is the Greek word προφήτης, provided that one discards the temporal idea of the preposition πρό, which is certainly false in this connection. The prophet does not bear this name because he sometimes foretells certain things. This is only a subordinate aspect of his activity. A προφήτης is someone who passes on the words of another by repeating them in his name. Therefore, two elements belong to the concept of a prophet: (a) an infallible insight into the counsel of God; (b) an authoritative communication of that counsel of God to others.

13. *How has the Mediator exercised this prophetic office?*

a) He has done and still does that in two ways, namely by His word and His Spirit, outwardly and inwardly at the same time. Thus the office has an external and an internal exercise. Christ is not a human messenger who has to be satisfied with conveying objectively the words of his commission. He has at His disposal a means to make them powerful subjectively and to cause them to be understood in the hearts of those to whom He is sent. This should especially be noted now that Christ according to His humanity is no longer on earth. The impression could arise that, along with His personal presence, the most glorious aspect of His prophetic ministry has been taken away, as if He who formerly spoke Himself must now let other and lesser persons represent Him. This is not the case, for in reasoning in this way one does not reckon with the Holy Spirit, who is able to make the voice of the Word resound inwardly and apply it such that in His messengers one hears Christ Himself as prophet. In the ministry of His prophetic office, Christ is immanent through the Holy Spirit.

b) So far as the external ministry of the office is concerned, this, too, has occurred in more than one way. The following modes may be distinguished:

1. The ministry of the Mediator who must still become flesh. At all times it was of course Christ Himself who was the only Prophet. The difference between earlier and later, before and after the incarnation, is only a matter of clarity. Before the incarnation, this ministry occurred either *personally*, or *mediately* but *infallibly*, or *mediately* and *fallibly*. The first was the case when the Mediator appeared in a visible form as the Angel of the Lord or otherwise spoke directly; the second when He let His word be proclaimed by the inspired prophets; the third when He appointed priests and others to expound, officially though fallibly, His words already made known.

2. After the incarnation we again find this same distinction, with this difference: that now the Messiah appears personally not just now and then, but assumes flesh forever and in that flesh appears on earth to speak as prophet to the Church of all ages.

3. Both before and after the incarnation, the Mediator has also exercised His prophetic office in a particular way by causing the origination of Scripture and all that pertains to that. This Scripture has originated by His Spirit (1 Pet 1:10) and displays His image. Likewise, it is Christ who is at work in the explanation and unfolding of the content of Scripture.

4. Finally, it must be noted that there is also a prophetic ministry through deeds, as one can distinguish between word and deed revelation. Prophecy through deeds entails the following: (1) Independent deed-prophecy. When Christ arose from the dead, the fact of the resurrection by itself, even without further elucidation through words, is already a disclosure of the counsel of God and a fact with independent significance for all time. (2) Ministering deed-prophecy. When Christ Himself in person, or through His prophets and apostles, works miracles, these are also revelations—that is, they are signs of God. They have something to say to man from God. However, they are not independent but serve only to confirm the truth spoken by words. (3) Ceremonial deed-prophecy. Under the old dispensation of the covenant, Christ spoke in large part through deeds and signs, with which the word of prophetic declaration from the mouth of the priests was associated as well. Under the new

dispensation, He still speaks through the sacraments or seals of the covenant. (4) Historical deed-prophecy. Israel's history did not only have significance for the nation itself; it was also a type of the dealings of God with His covenant people through all ages. So God's counsel concerning His people was partially manifested in this history. For that reason, in the sectioning of the Old Testament the historical books are also called prophetic, namely, insofar as through history they proclaim the counsel and the plan of God.

14. *What is Christ's priestly office?*

His appointment and authorization by God to satisfy for all who are His through sacrifice and intercession before God.

15. *Where is it described for us what a priest is?*

In Hebrews 5:1: "For every high priest, taken from among men, is appointed on behalf of men in things that pertain to God, that he may offer gifts and sacrifices for sin."

16. *What is included in this description?*

    a) That the work of a high priest is not so much to represent God before men as it is to represent men before God. He is appointed for men in those matters that have to do with God.

    b) That therefore this high priest must be taken from among men— that is, must share in human nature, because otherwise he could not represent men.

    c) That his work is twofold: (1) to offer gifts for sin; (2) to bring sacrifices for sin. So what he does is closely connected to the existence of sin.

In all of these respects, the priestly office is evidently distinct from the prophetic office.

17. *Is there still another point of difference between these two offices?*

Yes, for Christ has also permitted the prophetic office to be exercised by His representatives the office-bearers in an indirect way. It remains true that the source is always in Him and that all prophecy or proclamation of the counsel of God has flowed from Him. But still a mediation for others truly takes place. The same thing cannot be said about the priesthood of the Mediator. There are no true priests besides Him. The Old Testament priests were so in a typological sense and not actually (see Heb 7:23–24). This shows how unbiblical the Romanist conception is, as if the office bearers of the New Testament were priests. This conception rests on the error of transubstantiation. Christ indeed gave some to be apostles, prophets, evangelists, pastors, and teachers (Eph 4:11–12), but He did not give anyone to be a priest, since He himself remains a priest forever.

18. *Why is it important at the outset to have this difference keenly in view?*

Because it shows the great divide that there is between the modern view of satisfaction and the biblical doctrine. That divide surely consists precisely in a totally different idea of priesthood. Scripture says a priest is appointed in those matters that have to do with God—that is, he exists for God's sake, because there are in God demands that must be fulfilled, because *He* is to be reconciled. The modern theories answer in a complicated fashion: because something must be done for mankind, because *its* well-being demands that certain conditions be satisfied, because *it* must be reconciled with God. The question, stripped of all side questions, simply reads: In the work of satisfaction, is man there for God, and consequently the sacrifice of Christ is a satisfaction *toward God* and a reconciliation *of God*? Or is God there for man, and consequently the entire priestly ministry of the Mediator is a utilitarian measure for the sake of mankind?

Hebrews 5:1 answers this question with absolute finality by teaching us two things: (a) a high priest is appointed *on behalf of* mankind; (b) in those matters that have to do *with God*.

19. *Can this be demonstrated as well from an explanation of the different terms used in Scripture in connection with the priesthood and the sacrifices?*

Yes, the most important of these terms are:

a) καταλλάσσω and καταλλαγή.

b) כָּפַר, ἱλάσκομαι, ἱλασμός.

c) ἀγοράζω, λυτρόω, λύτρον.

d) The usage of the Greek prepositions ὑπέρ and ἀντί.

20. *Demonstrate this from the meaning of the words* καταλλάσσω *and* καταλλαγή.

These words are translated with "to reconcile" and "reconciliation." This can create a misunderstanding. For us, "to reconcile" has the general sense of causing someone to move from a hostile attitude to a friendly attitude. The emphasis thus is on the subjective. This is not the primary meaning of these words as they are used in Scripture. There the verb means "to bring about a change in the legal relationship between two parties by removing legal claims." This sense can be seen most clearly in 2 Corinthians 5:19–20, "For God was in Christ reconciling the world to Himself," where it is further added how that reconciliation of the world happened: "not reckoning to them their sins." God reconciled the world, not by moving it out of a hostile attitude into a friendly attitude, but by a non-imputing of sin, by removing the legal demands that He had against the world, and doing this in Christ. This is made abundantly clear by the fact that here a settled fact is spoken of: God *was* in Christ doing this. Subjectively, the world for the most part was still living in hostility toward God when Paul wrote that. If, therefore, the καταλλαγή was a subjective change, then he would have had to write "God *willed* in Christ to reconcile the world to Himself," that is, He had Christ undergo certain things in order to make such an impression on the world that it would allow itself to be reconciled with Him. But this is not the meaning here. Similarly, what follows in verse 20, "Let yourself be reconciled with God", does not mean "abandon your subjective hostility," but "accept this legal relationship of reconciliation that God has established." Hence Romans 5:11 speaks of "having received the reconciliation." Here the *katallagē* appears as something completely objective that man can *accept* and *receive*.

However, the most conclusive evidence for this original meaning of these words is found in Romans 5:10, "For if, while being enemies, we were reconciled to God through the death of His Son, much more, being reconciled, we will be saved by His life." As enemies—thus when and while they were enemies—believers are reconciled—that is, transferred into a reconciled relationship. Our result, therefore, is:

a) *God* is the *subject* of the reconciling act.

b) *Mankind* is the *object* of the reconciling act (namely, insofar as they are those who are elect).

c) What has happened to that mankind, however, is not a subjective change of attitude but an objective exchange of the legal relationship toward God.

d) The use of this word confirms our assertion that the priestly work of Christ is performed before God, that is, in order to satisfy the demands God has against mankind.

e) The distinctiveness of the word καταλλάσσειν, by which it is distinguished from other words, is in the fact that it presents God Himself as satisfying and removing these demands. Thus it teaches us the great and important fact that God does not first need to be moved by something external to Him for the exercising of grace, but that grace comes from within Himself and functions precisely that, in order to assert His grace, He sees to a satisfaction of His righteousness and ordains that in Christ.

21. *Give an explanation of the Hebrew term* כִּפֶּר *and the Greek* ἱλάσκομαι, ἱλασμός.

The verb ἱλάσκομαι originally means "to make favorable, benevolent, well-disposed." In pagan Greek usage it occurs for all transactions, especially sacrifices through which one sought to make the deity favorably disposed. Here man is the subject of the action, the deity the object to which it is directed. The fundamental thought in the pagan notion is that the gods of themselves are not favorable toward men (even apart from guilt) and first need to be persuaded by all sorts of means to show favor. This construction of the verb with God as object also occurs occasionally in Scripture, for example in Zechariah 7:2, "to entreat the face of the Lord."

In the vast majority of cases in Scripture, the word has another construction; for example, Leviticus 5:18, "make atonement for someone on account of his ignorant mistake," whether this "for" is expressed either by *peri* or by an objective accusative (Lev 16:33). Also, iniquity is atoned for (cf. 1 Sam 3:14).

Whence this distinction? Why is it not said in Scripture, "to reconcile God" and "God is reconciled"? The answer is because ἱλάσκομαι is the Greek translation of the Hebrew כִּפֶּר, and so has also assumed the constructions of the latter. Now כִּפֶּר means "to cover" either the sinner or his sin by means of sacrificial blood. Hence Scripture says that sin must be atoned for; Hebrews 2:17, "a faithful high priest in the things that pertain to God, to make propitiation for the sins of the people."

Sin or the sinner is covered when something is interposed between God and it or him, so that only what is interposed is visible for God. Atonement, therefore, is payment by means of substitution, whereupon security and forgiveness result for the guilty one.

The subject that makes atonement is the priest. The object upon which it effects covering is the sinner and sin. The reason why this is necessary is because God's eye sees something in man on which His punitive justice must be exercised if there was no covering between them. In other words, the necessity of atonement lies in a demand of God's nature; the priestly work occurs for God's sake.

The difference between καταλλάσσειν and ἱλάσκεσθαι consists in the former being viewed as an act that originates with God, the latter as an act that a guilty man, not in his own person but through a priest, performs toward God. God was in Christ reconciling the world to Himself, but Christ as High Priest has propitiated sin. Therefore one must always carefully compare the word used in the original, since both verbs are translated the same in our language [verzoenen].

Ἱλασμός means "propitiation," "covering," and Christ is so designated since He Himself was a sacrifice, and thus a covering was effected in Him. He is at the same time the act and the means of covering; hence the abstract noun, "And He is a *propitiation* for our sins" (1 John 2:2).

22. *Explain the words* ἀγοράζω, λυτρόω, λύτρον.

Ἀγοράζειν means "to purchase something for a price." Christ is the purchaser according to Acts 20:28; 1 Corinthians 6:20; 7:23. It is God to whom the purchase price was paid. Before God, sinners are like debtors who must pay off a sum due Him—that is, they fall within the scope of His justice and in relation to it represent a certain price. They have to be removed from being under this justice by Christ. For this to happen so that God's justice suffers no impairment, Christ must pay for them the price that they owe to it. From this it follows that they become the property of Christ, who paid the price for them, and, insofar as He is God's Son, God's children are adopted in Him.

All this is more than mere metaphor. Human beings are there *for God* and must devote their entire lives to Him. If they fall short in this because of sin, their lives must still be offered to God in the sense that they must be manifested as objects of His justice. They then become slaves of God, from whom He, in severity, takes what is His. Should they now cease to be slaves and return to the status of children, then the price that these slaves represent in relation to justice must be paid. Should this be done, then the slaves are freed from all claims of punitive justice. Hence Christ's work is called not merely an ἀγοράζειν but also an ἐξαγοράζειν, namely, a "buyout," by which they escape from the curse of the law; Galatians 3:13, "Christ has redeemed us from the curse of the law, having become a curse for us." Still, on the other hand, this redeeming from God's curse can also be called a purchasing for God; for example, Revelation 5:9: "You have purchased us for God with your blood." That is, only by redemption from God's justice do believers come again into relationship with God as children; Galatians 4:5, "in order to redeem those who were under the law, so that we might receive the adoption as children."

The meaning of λυτρόω in the New Testament agrees with this. It means "redeeming by means of a sacrifice as the price" (1 Pet 1:18–19). Λύτρωσις is the act of ransoming or redeeming, but is only used passively in Scripture as "being redeemed" (Heb 9:12). Λύτρόν is the "ransom" that is paid by Christ. This is more strongly expressed by ἀντίλυτρον, "a ransom in the place of something else" (Matt 20:28; Mark 10:45; 1 Tim 2:6). The affinity between the concept of ἱλάσκεσθαι and that of λυτρόω and ἀγοράζειν can be seen most clearly in the Hebrew כֹּפֶר, for this means "ransom" specifically. It, however, derives from the same root as כִּפֶּר, "atone," and is originally nothing else than a "covering." The ransom covers a prisoner or a slave so that the demands of the conqueror or the harsh master can no longer touch him. In the same sense, "to atone" means "to cover someone in such a manner that the punishment of the righteousness of God can no longer touch him."

23. *What can be derived from the use of the prepositions ὑπέρ and ἀντί with reference to the priestly work of the Mediator?*

The usual meaning of ὑπέρ with the genitive is "for the benefit of." Now if, in the New Testament, only ὑπέρ were used to indicate the relationship of Christ's priesthood to those whose priest He is, that would indeed give the appearance that He did not pay for their guilt before God in a *substitutionary* fashion, but only did something for their benefit. But now, besides ὑπέρ, ἀντί also appears, which always means "in the place of" (Matt 20:28; Mark 10:45). Obviously, ἀντί in no way excludes ὑπέρ. That Christ gave Himself as a substitute for His own is not only well understandable along with the fact that He gave Himself for their benefit but also directly includes the latter consideration. In addition, moreover, is the fact that in more than one place ὑπέρ itself has the full force of ἀντί (cf. 2 Cor 5:20–21; Phlm 13; 2 Cor 5:14). Here, too, we again have the same result: What Christ did as priest, He did as the substitutionary Surety of believers and, precisely for that reason, did before God and not toward man.

24. *What is our first means to determine more precisely in what the official priestly work of the Mediator consisted?*

A study concerning the work of the Old Testament priests. It is true that only by a consideration of the body does one learn to distinguish what the shadow is. If, however, one thinks that we wrongly view the body itself, as the Socinians and others claim, it can be useful to go back to the shadow and show how by it the conception of these opponents is already assessed.

25. *What may be noted about the origin of the sacrifices?*

That the attitude toward them is closely related to the understanding of their significance. If they are viewed as substitutionary, then there is no escaping the conclusion that in one or another way they must have been instituted by God. The notion of substitution is not something that springs up naturally from the guilty human heart. In any case, man does not deserve to appear with it before God on his own initiative. As it is God's sovereign prerogative to exercise grace, so it is also His prerogative to announce the possibility of demonstrating grace and to have it be presented in ceremonial acts. If it is already said of the priestly ministry that no one should presume on it for himself (see Heb 5:4), then this is certainly also true of the most important part of the priestly task: the offering of sacrifices. Already the first time that we have a report of offering sacrifices, they are presented as being approved by God (Gen 4:3–4). Faith was present in Abel's sacrifice, and from that it could be inferred that there was a divine revelation on which this faith rested (Heb 11:4). Nothing can be concluded with certainty from Genesis 3:21. The earliest church fathers, Outram, the Socinians, the Rationalists, Maurice, and Bushnell deny the origin of sacrifice from divine revelation. Most orthodox theologians advocate the opposite opinion. So also the Unitarians Priestley and Young.

26. *Should the sacrifices be viewed as real expiatory sacrifices, or is their significance found in something else?*

They must be regarded as real expiatory sacrifices.

27. *What erroneous conceptions about their significance should therefore be rejected?*

   a) The view of von Hofmann and others that all sacrifices were gifts for the deity. Scripture itself objects against such an anthropomorphistic explanation (Psa 50:12–13). Of course, one need not deny that part of the sacrifices can be viewed as gifts of grateful devotion to God. The law, however, knows to distinguish very carefully between thank offerings and other sacrifices.

   This view assumes a slightly modified form with those who, like Spencer, speak of the sacrifices as a feast, which man prepares for God and in which he then deals with God. This, too, makes a single feature into the whole (Psa 50:5).

   b) The opinion of Keil that the sacrifices are symbols for restored fellowship with God. The laying on of hands is explained as a transferring onto the animal sacrifice of the feeling, the attitude, the intention that animates the sacrificer. With some limitation, this could be acknowledged, and one could say that not only the guilt but also the feeling of guilt is transferred onto a substitutionary sacrifice. Keil, however, further denies that the slaughtering of sacrificial animals has the significance of a punishment. It happens in part as a means of obtaining blood and in part to derive the transition from a life of separation to a state of fellowship with God. He weakens the significance of the sprinkling of blood by saying that in and with the blood sprinkled on the altar, the soul of the sacrificer appears in the place where God is considered to be present with His grace. In other words, the blood appears here not as the means of covering (atonement) but as the object to be covered. For Keil, the burning of the parts of the sacrifice is a symbol of the power of holiness that purifies and eliminates what is transitory. The flesh that is burned represents the body of man as the shed blood stands for the soul.

Against this conception, it must be noted that the sacrifices everywhere appear as offerings of penitence and not as symbols of restored fellowship. It is the blood of the sacrificial animals that effects atonement for the soul of the sinner. Keil's main argument is that it is not the priest, as the representative of God, who slaughters the sacrificial animal, but the sacrificer himself. We reply: It is in all respects natural that the slaughtering is done by the sacrificer. This shows that he realizes that he has forfeited his life. He can do that. However, sprinkling the blood and bringing to the altar and burning the parts of the sacrifice he cannot do, because as an impure guilty person he is unfit to do that. Thus the priest does this for him. Moreover, the entire view that the priest is in the first place a representative of God is wrong. He represents man before God.

c) The old Socinian opinion, at a later time defended by Bähr. According to it, the death of the sacrifice has no significance in itself but is merely a means to obtain the blood. The sacrifice means nothing more than thankful devotion to God of the entire life of the sacrificer. The blood thereby serves as a symbol for life. This explanation also misses the fundamental significance of the shedding of blood and the slaughtering in the sacrificial ritual.

28. *Indicate in its main features the correct view of the Old Testament sacrifices.*

a) In each sacrifice there is substitution, the exchange of what is sacrificed for the person bringing the sacrifice. Therefore, even in the thank offerings those actions from the sacrifices of atonement were repeated in order to demonstrate that there can be no peace and fellowship with God other than on the basis of satisfaction. That the actions in view here signify substitution is shown by the following.

In Leviticus 17:11, it is said in so many words, "For the life of the flesh is in the blood, and I have given it to you upon the altar to cover (atone for) your souls, for the blood covers by means of the life." The animals that were sacrificed were tame animals, those that were closest to man and so could best represent his life. The sacrificial animals had to be without defect and clean, and yet they were called "sin." This may only be explained by the idea of substitution. The laying on of hands has this significance. Compare Numbers 8:10, 16, where the Levites act as substitutes for the firstborn of the children of Israel, and the people must lay their hands on them to symbolize this. The same also appears from the fact that again and again the person to whom the guilt belonged had to lay on hands. If the individual Israelite trespassed, then he had to perform the laying on of hands; if the entire community sinned, then the elders did it (see Lev 4:15). This principle comes out even more clearly in what took place on the Day of Atonement (see Lev 16:7–22), where the one male goat appears as bearing away the iniquities, and in 16:21 it is said in so many words that the laying on of both hands by Aaron signifies the transfer of the iniquities of the children of Israel onto this animal. Also, the slaughtering of the animal can only be explained satisfactorily from this perspective. That this was truly of the greatest importance for the sacrificial act may already be inferred from the single fact that the altar derived its name from it; in Hebrew it is called מִזְבֵּחַ, "place of slaughter." Throughout the whole of Scripture, death is the punishment for sin, and therefore here too [it] may not be considered a point of transition into fellowship with God, as Keil thinks. The sprinkling with blood, which in the sin offering followed the slaughtering, had the same significance. The substituting life is thereby brought into fellowship, into contact with God, whether it be on the horns of the altar or on the mercy seat.

b) While the just-mentioned characteristics (with the exception of the sprinkling with blood) were common to all sacrifices, the burnt offering and thank offering each had their distinctive significance. The idea of total destruction (a continuation of the slaughtering, as it were) was not involved in the burning of the entire burnt offering, nor the thought of a purification associated with destruction (Keil), but rather the dedication of life to God. God must have the best, as is apparent from those portions that are due to Him from the other sacrifices. He must have the whole of life, as the burnt offering shows. The offering ascends by the fire and provides for God a pleasing aroma.

The word used for burning an offering is not שָׂרַף, which indicates a destructive burning, but הִקְטִיר, which means "to go up in fume and smoke." The fire in which the offerings ascend comes from God Himself (Lev 9:24), and the command is given that this original fire may never go out on the altar. The significance of this is that the fire must be regarded as a fire from God and the burning as a burning by God. That is, depicted in the sacrifices is not only how the entire life is brought to Him, but also how He receives it. From all this it now appears clearly how in the burning of the sacrifices there was a symbol, as a type, of the active obedience of the Mediator, who sacrificed Himself to God as a fragrant aroma.

c) The thank offerings (according to others, peace offerings) have the distinctive goal of depicting the condition or state of peace in which God and man are after the accomplished reconciliation. This is why they follow, in order, after the sin offering and burnt offering. First come passive and active obedience—the sacrificing of life in death and devotion—then as its fruit comes peace with God. Furthermore, belonging essentially with the thank or peace offering is the sacrificial meal, in which the justified person enjoys his fellowship with God. Therefore, it must be said that this class of sacrifices was typological for the Mediator, namely in the sense that He likewise, through the communication of His own flesh and blood, grants us to enjoy peace with God. After first shedding His blood and offering His life to God, He gives Himself to us, so that we, being personally united to Him, may attain to the awareness of the reconciled relationship into which He brought us as a sin offering and burnt offering.

d) These sacrifices had a twofold purpose.

1. They were types, and as such depicted the perfect sacrifice of Christ, which alone could effect true atonement. They did not atone with regard to the moral law. The blood of bulls and goats could not take away actual sin.

2. They were ceremonial, that is, they also had a significance for the church-state of Israel. In this sense, they brought about a real atonement and were the means ordained by God to maintain a state of external covenant righteousness—or where that was broken, to obtain renewal.

29. *Can it be proved from the New Testament that the work of Christ includes sacrifice in this Old Testament sense?*

a) The entire Epistle to the Hebrews is full of this sense. In it, Christ is called "priest" 6 times and "high priest" 12 times. It is said of the Old Testament priests and sacrifices that they were "a shadow of the good things to come" (10:1). The reality, the body, is in Christ. He is a priest after the order of Melchizedek, that is, "not according to physical descent, but according to the power of an indestructible life" (7:16), forever Priest, Prophet, and King together (Psa 110). The same Christ who is High Priest is also the sacrifice, for Hebrews 10:10 speaks of "the offering of the body of Christ accomplished once." Christ can be priest and sacrifice at the same time because even where His human life enters into death, His divine life still continues, for He offered Himself through the eternal Spirit (9:14). The sacrifice of Christ is a definitive act, which is not to be repeated (7:27). It is comparable to the killing of the sacrificial animal by the typological high priest on the Day of Atonement. It is brought before God because Christ Himself enters into heaven, just as the high priest entered the holy of holies. It corresponds to the covenant sacrifice of Exodus 24, wherefore Christ is called the Mediator of the new covenant (Heb 9:15). That the sprinkling with the blood of Christ was necessary before God is expressed in Hebrews 9:23, such that the heavenly things had to be purified. That is, their guilt is present in the dwelling place of God, before His face, in His tabernacle, and that guilt must be removed from heaven before the people of God can enter into heaven. The transgressions committed under the first covenant demanded atonement by death if the promise of the eternal inheritance would be obtained. That is, the guilt of the covenant of works must first be cleared away before the blessings of the covenant can be imparted. Where there is no sacrifice for sin, there is a fearful expectation of judgment and fury of fire (10:27). During His earthly life, Christ appeared *with sin*—that is, as a sacrifice upon which sin was transferred—but He will appear again without sin (9:28). The result, finally, of the priestly activity of the Mediator is the taking away of the stains on the conscience, that is, the removal of guilt objectively and of the consciousness of guilt subjectively (9:14; 10:22; 12:24).

If we briefly summarize all this, we obtain as the result that according to the Epistle to the Hebrews, Christ is: the true, only, eternal, kingly, self-sacrificing, atoning-toward-God, substituting, and actually guilt-removing High Priest.

b) In the letters of the Apostle Paul, we are taught entirely the same in principle, although in them the priesthood of the Mediator as such is not mentioned explicitly. Christ gave Himself freely out of love, and God *gave* His Son freely out of love (Rom 8:32; Gal 2:20). This was done for the benefit of man and on behalf of man (ὑπὲρ οὗ in Rom 14:15; δι' ὃν in 1 Cor 8:11); on account of their transgressions (Rom 4:25, διὰ τὰ παραπτώματα ἡμῶν); for sin (1 Cor 15:3, ὑπὲρ τῶν ἁμαρτιῶν ἡμῶν). This, however, was done no less than by means of substitution, for treating the sinless Christ as a sinner was the means by which treating sinners as sinless was made possible (2 Cor 5:21). If, then, the transmission of righteousness from Christ to us is an act of imputation (which nobody can doubt), then here the transmission of sin to the Mediator must also be an act of imputation, for both are put on par with and directly connected to each other. If one died for all, then they all have died (2 Cor 5:14–15). Concerning the ground of this substitution or of the necessity of the punishment, we are taught that it is to be found in the curse of the law (Gal 3:13). Christ had to die for there to be righteousness, for if there were another way to obtain righteousness, His death must be said to be in vain (Gal 2:21). That is, His dying as a Surety was the only means to establish sinners as righteous before God. The curse of the law, however, is simply a paraphrase for the curse pronounced by God, and God's curse implies a claim of guilty by the punitive justice of God. In view of this, Galatians 3:13 states, "Christ has redeemed us from the curse of the law, having become a curse for us." In other words, what Christ did as a Surety was to pay a ransom to God as recompense in order that we might escape the consequences of divine justice. Compare 1 Corinthians 6:20; 7:23: "For you have been bought at a high price, therefore glorify God in your body and in your spirit, which are God's." Here at the same time is confirmed what has been said above. Precisely through redemption by God, believers become the possession of God in the fullest sense of the word. By escaping His justice, they become His beloved children and their bodies and spirits can be called God's. Indeed, through their redemption (διὰ τῆς ἀπολυτρώσεως [Rom 3:24]), which is in Christ Jesus, they have moved, justified, into a state of sonship.

In all this, it is true that the idea of sacrifice is not mentioned directly. Still, it is not lacking in Paul. In Romans 3:25, it is said that redemption in Christ Jesus is effected because God has openly presented Him as a means of propitiation (ἱλαστήριον) in His blood through faith, and that (in His blood) in demonstration of God's righteousness. A propitiation in blood can be nothing other than an atoning sacrifice. Paul says that this was necessary because the sins previously committed under the old covenant had been tolerated without actual satisfaction being made and it could now seem as if God were not just. God's forbearance was the ground for this tolerance but did not in the least intend that these sins remain unpropitiated. Therefore, before God can justly acquit, there had to be an open display of Christ on the cross as a propitiation. Other places where Paul speaks of Christ as a sacrifice are 1 Corinthians 5:7—"For our Passover lamb has been sacrificed for us, namely Christ"—and 1 Corinthians 11:25, where the institution of the Lord's Supper shows how the blood of Christ is the basis of the new covenant. The thought of the sparing of the firstborn was clearly present in the Passover, for the name means "passing over," "sparing." According to Ephesians 1:7, we have redemption and forgiveness of sin through the blood of Christ. According to Ephesians 5:2, Christ gave Himself for us as an offering and sacrifice to God as "a sweet savor."

c) The same is true for the remaining books of the New Testament. In the Gospel of John, Christ appears as the Lamb who takes away the sin of the world, that is, first takes it upon Himself and then carries it away (1:29, in connection with Isa 53:11; cf. also 1 John 3:5; 2:2; 4:10). Caiaphas prophesies the suffering of the Lord as a Surety (11:50).

Particularly clear is John 3:14, where Christ is compared to the uplifted serpent and where the entire doctrine of satisfaction as Surety is summarized in only a few words. (1) The snake pictures sin as a seductive, poisoning, cursed animal. (2) As the snakebite in the desert was cured by the copper snake itself, so sin, which is a curse and an abandonment by God, is cured by the curse and abandonment by God that rested upon Christ. Guilt can only be removed by the principle resident within it being carried out to its full extent. (3) The snake in the desert had to be lifted up; likewise the Son of Man had to be lifted up. The bearing of sin is necessary. God's righteousness demands it. (4) The snake in the desert was not a snake in itself but was made to be such at God's command and by His gracious determination. To demonstrate this, Moses did not take one of the many living snakes that were biting Israel but a snake of pure metal, in which the curse of the snake as a species was indeed visible but its fiery venom was not present. Likewise, there is in Christ the likeness and curse of sinful flesh [Rom 8:3] but not the sinful flesh itself. That is, the Mediator was made to be sin, not in a real, personal sense, but in an ideal sense, in the sense of a Surety; guilt was imputed to Him. (5) After this guilt was laid upon Him, He had to bear it. He had to be lifted up on the cross and be displayed as an atoning sacrifice. (6) To be able to serve as an atoning sacrifice, He had to possess a human nature, for it is the Son of Man who had to be lifted up.

The epistles of Peter do not teach anything different. First Peter 3:18; 2:24; 1:19 are three classic texts. Christ was an unblemished and spotless Lamb, completely without sin. This lent to His blood that character by which it could count as a ransom and for which it is called precious blood. It was a sacrifice entirely unique in kind that could not be repeated. Christ has also suffered once (ἅπαξ) for sin. It was a vicarious suffering: for sin, He the righteous for the unrighteous, who *Himself* carried our sin in His body on the tree. One should take note here of the contrast between "Himself" and "our sins" (τὰς ἁμαρτίας ἡμῶν αὐτός, 2:24). Those sins have been carried *onto* the (cursed cross-) tree by Christ *in* or *with* His body. The goal of this bearing of guilt was to bring us to God, that is, as priest to open up access to God for us. Here this bringing to God should be understood objectively of the atonement, which is brought about by His suffering as Surety.

According to 1 Peter 1:2, the elect are predestined to obedience and sprinkling with blood. This refers back to the establishment of the covenant (Exod 24:7-8). Christ's suffering is a covenant-sacrifice, and those who enter into the covenant are obliged to obedience and sprinkled with the blood to atone for their guilt.

Finally, these things are taught to us—though not as explicitly and plainly, yet clearly enough—by the words of Christ Himself. A man who has incurred death cannot give anything to redeem his own soul. But the Son of Man has come to give His life as a ransom for many [Matt 20:28; Mark 10:45]. That the guilt-atoning significance of Christ's suffering is not more prominent in the Synoptic Gospels is to be attributed to the limitations of the apostles and disciples, who even later had to be called ignorant and slow of heart in this respect [Luke 24:25].

30. *How is it to be related to each other that Christ is priest (High Priest) and sacrifice at the same time?*

The distinction between priest and sacrifice is not original. What man must bring to God is his own life, and of course he can only do that in his own person, so priest and sacrifice truly coincide. In a state of rectitude, it can only be a question of a priesthood in which everyone devotes himself as a living sacrifice of gratitude to God, at best of a representative priesthood of the progenitor of a family. This is not altered by sin as far as the actual priesthood of the Mediator is concerned. The Surety, the Priest, must dedicate Himself to God as an atoning and covenantal sacrifice. It is otherwise with the priesthood that was instituted as a type to prefigure and presage the real priesthood. Here priest and sacrifice had to be separated for the following reasons:

a) A sacrifice consisting of an animal (or a lifeless object) cannot bring itself. Thus, along with what is brought there has to be someone who brings it, since otherwise the element would be lost in which the offering is a willing sacrifice of life.

b) However, one could ask, Why does the guilty Israelite himself not bring his sacrifice? In a certain sense, as we have seen, he does in fact do so when he slaughters it, and in doing so acknowledges that he has forfeited his life. He, however, is the guilty one and therefore not fit to bring his sacrifice. To begin with, he is precisely the person who has to be covered by the sacrificial blood or the life of the animal. If, then, he were to come with that sacrificial blood into the presence of God in his own person, then that would involve a contradiction. Furthermore, the sacrifice must be brought not only willingly but also in a state of purity. For these reasons, a priest is necessary. The priest is holy and set apart from out of the Levites. In his life as a whole, he had to conduct himself in such a manner that in him is seen a symbol of the purity that the sacrificer must possess. And when he appears before God with the blood, only then does he effect the covering or atonement by which it becomes possible for the guilty person to draw near as well.

c) A true sacrifice must be efficacious—that is, the ideal priest, who at the same time is a sacrifice, must also apply the effects of his service. He must do more than sacrifice—not only appear before God but also bring before God. Thus being a priest has a wider scope than being a sacrifice, although they in fact coincide in one person. Now it goes without saying that for this latter part of the priest's task—the bringing before God, the application of the priestly reconciliation—the sacrifice could not serve to symbolize. For this typological sacrifice loses its life and thereby becomes unsuitable for further representing something. It is otherwise with Christ. In Him was the eternal Spirit; His being a priest was not undone or made impossible by His being a sacrifice. In Him, therefore, what was separated in the ceremonial ministry of the Old Testament is returned to its natural unity.

From all this it appears that we should not be surprised by the union in the Mediator of being sacrifice and being priest. This only appears as strange because we have accustomed ourselves to reason from the usual Jewish or from pagan priesthood, in which priest and sacrifice are separate. This separation, however, is a defect necessitated by human weakness. The ideal union appears in Christ. Even with the separation, the ministry of shadows was not yet able to depict everything faithfully. Even a high priest, no matter how ceremonially clean, remains a morally guilty person, so that he had to make atonement for himself on the Day of Atonement. But all these defects and inner contradictions are not present in his antitype. No matter how inadequate and impossible the shadow may have been, when the body came nothing was seen but perfect harmony.

31. Were the Old Testament priests real priests?

In a ceremonial sense, yes. That is, they were really intermediaries between the people and God. The Israelite could not approach Jehovah in sacrifice or public worship other than through the mediation of a priest. It is essential to a true priest that he is an indispensable intermediary. On the other hand, however, in a moral sense, Old Testament priests were only types of the only priest, Christ. Compare what was said above concerning the double meaning of the sacrifices.

As has already been mentioned in passing, Rome sees its ministers as true priests for the following reasons:

a) They are indispensable intermediaries between God and man. Apart from the priest, Roman Catholics cannot receive the benefits of salvation over which the Church disposes. The priest has to grant them access to these benefits.

b) They bring a real sacrifice to God in the Mass. Thus here again the ideal priesthood of Christ, which had reached its unity in Him, is torn in two; priest and sacrifice are again separated from each other, and one returns to the first, weak principles of the world.

c) They provide people actual acquittal through absolution.

We assert that on all of these three points no one else stands between God and our soul than our only High Priest, Jesus Christ.

32. *What is the foundation of the priestly office of Christ?*

   a) The merciful consent of God that He take the guilt of the elect upon Himself.

   b) The willing assumption of this guilt from the side of the Mediator Himself.

33. *What, viewed from God's side, is this act called?*

The imputation of sin (Isa 53:6). Scripture speaks of an imputing of sin, a making to be sin, a laying of sin on Christ (2 Cor 5:21; Heb 9:28; 1 Pet 2:24). This is connected to the fact that the word "sin" itself has the specific meaning of "guilt," *reatus* [liability]. To make someone to be sin, then, does not mean to actually change him into a sinful being or to transmit the blemishes of sin to him but simply to make him personally responsible for the penal consequences of sin. The same thing is meant by the term "imputation." It occurs with respect to both the penal guilt that the sinner himself has accrued and the guilt transferred to him from someone else. The biblical words for this concept are in Hebrew, חָשַׁב and in Greek, λογίζομαι; Luke 22:37, "For I tell you that this, which is written, must be fulfilled in me, namely, 'and he was numbered with the transgressors.'" This is a quotation from Isaiah 53:12. In Romans 4:3 it is said of Abraham, "He believed God, and it was counted to him as righteousness." In Psalm 32:2, we have a passage where holding someone responsible for his own iniquity is called imputing: "Blessed is the man to whom the Lord does not impute iniquity."

34. *In how many senses can one speak of the imputation of guilt to Christ?*

   a) In a judicial sense, in the judgment of God. This has taken place in the counsel of peace when Christ assumed the suretyship for those belonging to Him. In the judgment of God, He then became responsible for their guilt.

   b) In an effective sense, in the suffering that the Mediator underwent during the state of humiliation and in the demands of obedience that at that time were made of Him by God.

35. *Was this imputation of sin to Christ an act of righteousness[1] or an act
of grace?*

It was both simultaneously:

a) From the side of God, granting a Surety and the taking over of
guilt by the Surety was an act of grace. God could have held every
sinner personally responsible. As will be shown in more detail,
moral guilt always adheres to the person who has committed evil,
and the giver of the moral law is not in the least obliged to remove
it from him. If we imagine the possibility that man himself would
have been able to find a mediator who can fully satisfy for him in
the same sense as Christ has now made satisfaction for him and
he were to have come before God with this mediator, it would still
remain an act of God's grace to be pleased with this substitution.
However, the act of imputation appears to us as an act of grace in
a still deeper sense when we consider that here it is not substitution in general but quite specifically self-substitution. God has
not imputed guilt to a third party but to His only begotten Son,
who is of one being with Him. Therefore, the Socinian objection
that there was no grace in the substitution of Christ lacks all
force. This objection functions entirely on the Unitarian position
in which Christ is actually a third party. On the Trinitarian position, in contrast, the Judge who transfers the guilt and the Surety
who assumes the guilt are, with regard to their being, the same
God. That God does not spare His only begotten Son and so gives
Himself up and sacrifices Himself for our sin constitutes grace.
First John 3:16: "By this we know love, that He gave His life for us."

b) Seen from man's side, it was an act of pure grace inasmuch as
by it the person who is reckoned in Christ is himself discharged
from all guilt, without he having done anything for that himself.

c) Seen from God's side, it was at the same time an act of punitive righteousness.

---

1 The Dutch *gerechtigheid* (akin to the German *Gerechtigkeit* and the Latin *iustitia*) can
mean either "righteousness" or "justice." Throughout I have rendered it in almost all
instances with the former, which Vos clearly intends.

36. *How should this divine righteousness be viewed here?*

It is described above as "the natural impulse of God's holiness to assert itself against sin." The exercise of righteousness is an essential necessity. His righteousness is an active side of His being that He cannot set aside. Above all, one must guard against identifying it with the love of God or attempting to derive it from that love. Love is certainly compatible with righteousness but yet not identical with it. God's righteousness is exercised toward the sinner for God's sake alone apart from all His concern for the well-being of the sinner. It is entirely possible that through the exercise of righteousness some sinners are also benefitted, but that is something derivative that must not be confused with the main purpose.

37. *Show that this righteousness of God is compatible with His grace and His love for sinners, from which this grace flows.*

The difficulty in grasping the compatibility of these two lies in our own psychological experience. In our limited minds, attitudes of anger and love at the same time with regard to the same subject generally exclude each other. Even in the most favorable case conceivable, that of a loving father toward his child, we do not have complete likeness to what is present in God. A father can indeed be angry and punish his child and at the same time love his child. His punishing, however, is not an exercise of justice in the same sense as the punishing of sinners is for God. It is rather a chastising that he administers to the child precisely because he loves it in his heart and seeks its well-being, although a God-given paternal authority is also expressed in this chastisement. Also, if we imagine the case of a judge passing sentence on his son, whom he loves, it is not completely the same, for the judge does not pronounce judgment of himself as if both love for his child as well as the impulse to sentence and to punish came from his own heart in the same sense. It is rather the case that his sense of justice arises from his sense of official responsibility toward God. He pronounces judgment before God; he loves of himself.

With God, on the other hand, both love and the impulse for righteousness flow directly from His own being and not from any relationship to something else. He loves, is merciful, gracious, kind—and at the same time, with equally the same spontaneity, He is angry with the sinner and in His righteousness wishes to punish him. That this is so incomprehensible for us stems not only from the fact that we cannot find a perfect parallel for it in our own experience; it stems much more from the fact that evidence against this concurrence seems to occur again and again in our sinful experience. When we feel angry toward someone, then there is not room in us for favor toward him. Self-centered, human anger cannot coexist with it. Our anger "does not work to bring about the righteousness of God" (Jas 1:20). That is precisely because it is an anger that occupies our entire spirit and with the mist of passion clouds our vision so that we can no longer see and judge impartially. The anger of man is always so little a holy anger that, once inflamed, it derives new strength from the entirety of the object against which it is directed. Every virtue that we note in our enemy can incite us to new rage. That was the case with the Jews and Christ.

For all these reasons, we have to be very careful not to think of God's righteousness in a worldly fashion. In Him, it is not something that in any respect would need to exclude love and mercy. God did not first need to be made disposed toward being merciful and loving by the Surety and satisfaction of the Mediator. He was that toward His people from the beginning. That He was appears most clearly by the fact that He Himself devised the plan of salvation. God who is angry toward sinners is also the God who Himself ordains a satisfaction for His wrath. Every thought of bloodlust in a wrong sense must be excluded here. It is quite true that God desires blood—not in the mad passion of human anger but rather with the resolute energy of His holy will. He wills to maintain both sides of His being: both His righteousness as well as His love. He had to maintain His righteousness; He could sovereignly withhold or communicate His grace toward sinners as He pleased. The wonder of grace is not that God abandoned His righteousness but that at the cost of His own Son He maintained His righteousness so that it would not strike down man. Scripture itself teaches us to emphasize this truth and consider the matter from this perspective: "God has reconciled us to Himself through Jesus Christ"; "God was reconciling the world to Himself in Christ" (2 Cor 5:18–19). It has pleased the Father to reconcile all things to Himself through the blood of the cross of Christ. In this work of reconciliation, God is therefore subject and object at the same time. And both must be maintained—the latter so that we may avoid the error of seeking the meaning of satisfaction in something subjective; the sacrifice of Christ above all affected God, not man. We must maintain the former so that grace in its costliness might be preserved for us and satisfaction might be seen to come from God.

38. *To what extent can one say that the transfer of this guilt to Christ corresponds to assigning a debt in a commercial sense, that is, of a monetary debt?*

Scripture itself leads us to make this comparison. The discussion of the term λύτρον above showed that the suffering borne by Christ is viewed as a ransom by which believers were redeemed from the servitude of punishment. Now it only comes down to finding the *tertium comparationis* [point of comparison] in this comparison, emphasize it, and guard against transferring other traits that do not possess any similarity. The essence in a pecuniary debt is the following: (a) It means the obligation of one person to pay its monetary value to another person; (b) it represents an intrinsic monetary value, that is, there exists a certain proportion. The way in which the debt was incurred determines its size and the manner of payment.

In both respects, penal guilt and pecuniary debt accord with each other: (1) Where sin has been committed, there is an obligation of the sinner toward the lawgiver to pay something. That this payment consists of monetary value here, of suffering there, is beside the point. In both cases, something has to be done or produced. (2) The penal guilt as well as the pecuniary debt is proportional. To the extent the sin is more or less severe, there exists an obligation to lighter or more severe suffering.

However, besides these points of agreement, there are also several points of difference. The most important are the following:

a) In the case of a monetary debt, what has to be paid is originally in the possession of the creditor, has been transferred by him to the debtor, and so a relationship of debt is created. If A owes 50 dollars to B, this means that B first had 50 dollars or something representing the value of 50 dollars, and that through a transaction with A this sum is subtracted from him and that the obligation now rests on A to repay this same sum to B.

    This is not the case with moral penal guilt. When the sinner transgresses God's law, God does not thereby change. He does not lose anything or become poorer in any respect. It simply means that God is deprived of the occasion, through the keeping of the law by man, to express His holiness in a positive sense, and that now, in order to compensate, an implementing and carrying out of God's holiness in a negative sense—that is, of his punitive retributive justice—will have to take place. God did not lose something, but rather an action in a certain direction originating with God is stopped and the broken balance must now be restored as the same action moves in another direction. Despite this difference, however, here, too, the point of correspondence remains that an obstacle has occurred. This, then, is common to the origination of penal guilt and pecuniary debt. The difference is that in the former instance the obstacle took place with regard to a passive, receptive activity; in the latter instance, with regard to an active, transitive activity.

b) In a monetary debt, it is completely indifferent who pays the amount due, whether it be person A who incurred the debt or someone else. All that need be done is the repayment to B of the sum that was received from him. Here the debt is related solely to what is received and not in any way to the person receiving it. If a guarantor, who offers to pay the debt, appears for the debtor, then the creditor has no right to refuse this guarantor and to insist that the debtor amass the requisite sum by his own effort. His rights extend to the repayment of the sum and not an inch further.

Again, it is entirely different with penal guilt. It cannot be separated from the person in the same manner. In moral matters, every personal being stands in a personal relation to the lawgiver and accordingly has a personal guilt. Accordingly, here it is not merely a matter of "God must receive a certain amount regardless of whether He receives it from me or from someone else," but "God must receive this amount from me, and I am personally accountable for it." It should be noted that by this it is not being maintained that God *must* punish the person himself who has transgressed. If this were true, the suffering of Christ as a Surety would be an impossibility. All that is being maintained is that God *can* punish the transgressor himself and is not *obligated* to accept a Surety. Moral guilt has a personal significance, and God has every right to keep this significance strictly in view regarding the collection of the debt. Of this personal aspect, we accordingly say that it belongs to righteousness, but we do not go so far as to maintain that it must be considered to be the immutable essence of righteousness. God can perhaps exercise His righteousness in such a manner that He foregoes this personal aspect, and we know from experience that He has actually willed to do this. He has permitted the sinner, who must pay personally, to do that through His Surety. However, it follows from what has been said that this was an act of mercy, which the debtor could not have claimed as his right. Furthermore, there are two other things that follow: (1) If God can set aside the personal character of guilt, then this cannot happen arbitrarily. If we entertain the possibility that the debtor himself was in a position morally to bear his own penal guilt and to satisfy anew the covenantal conditions imposed on Adam, then it could hardly be called just if God, overlooking this possibility, simply transferred the guilt to the Surety. One senses that as long as the possibility of a personal satisfaction exists, the guilt must also remain with the person. Only where this possibility does not exist, as in the case of sinful man who cannot at all make satisfaction for himself, can this personal imputation of guilt be removed. (2) Even when the transfer of guilt from one person to another is permitted, certain conditions must still be met. It must be ensured that the personal origin of the guilt will never entirely disappear from the awareness of the guilty person. So the guilt is never simply required of the Surety and the original guilty person left to his lot. It is brought to the awareness of the latter that he is the guilty one, that the Surety suffers on his behalf, and that the transfer from person to person is an act of grace. Likewise, this relationship is communicated to the awareness of the Surety so that he knows that he is suffering as a Surety. Christ was aware that a world of iniquity, not His own, brought the pains of suffering upon Him. The punishment did not strike Him as a blind destructive blow of fate but was borne in light of the real relationship involved. Thus, although the guilt is not borne by the person who incurred it, still it is borne with that person kept in view and mind. The personal tie between him and his guilt is never entirely lost by being forgotten.

This is what theologians have meant when they spoke of two kinds of guilt, namely, of a *reatus culpae* ["liability to guilt"] and a *reatus poenae* ["liability to punishment"]. By the latter is meant the obligation to suffer, insofar as that can be detached from the original debtor and transferred to the Surety; the former reminds us of the original personal obligation to punishment, which can never be entirely lost. Therefore they said that the *reatus culpae* could not be transferred from the sinner to the Surety, that is, that the fact cannot be undone that the sinner and not the Surety committed sin and would therefore have to repay for the guilt to God if the Lord had wished to require that. The stain of the original guilt incurred could not be transferred to the Surety. He could not be made to be sin in that sense, as if God, and He Himself, and those for whom He suffered, would forget that here is a surety-ship permitted by grace and thereby think that they no longer had anything to do with enduring this guilt. In heaven, a sinner, even after he is completely cleansed and glorified, will still re-alize that it was his personal sins for which Christ suffered as a Surety. And far from finding the remembrance of this obligation as something painful, by it he will be continually reminded of the grace of God. Likewise, it can never be erased from his conscious-ness that it was the personal merits of Christ that earned eternal life for him. There, too, the fact that the Surety, not he himself, was the original meriting person, cannot be annulled. The *reatus poenae*, on the other hand, is removed from the sinner and trans-ferred to Christ, and likewise the legal entitlement to eternal life is, in turn, transferred from Christ to the elect.

c) A third point of difference consists in the fact that whether or not the monetary debt is collected is at the pleasure of the creditor. If he demands payment of the debt, then this is his right; but if he waives repayment, he does no wrong by doing so. This follows from what is specific to the notion of monetary debt, which rep-resents something that the creditor may receive: his property. Someone can do as he pleases with what he possesses.

It is entirely different, on the other hand, with penal guilt. The judge is not free to choose whether he demands reparation for criminal guilt. It *must* be compensated. Righteousness is a transitive attribute that must work outwardly and will assert itself no matter what happens. In relation to it, guilt represents an effect and not a possession. Therefore, it is vain to ask if God could have redeemed sinners without satisfaction. The possibility for something like that presupposes that God is able to set aside or contain His righteousness. If that were so, then Christ would have died in vain and grace is no longer grace (Gal 2:21).

d) Yet another difference concerns the acquittal that must follow the payment of a pecuniary debt or recompense for penal guilt. For the former this is unconditional and immediate; for the latter it is conditional and mediate. If the satisfaction of Christ had been a commercial payment of a monetary debt, then acquittal should have immediately followed in the conscience of all sinners, as in paying a sum of money a receipt is handed over immediately. The sacrifice of the Lord would then have had to apply also to all the world, since one who pays the debt for a group of people thereby, *ipso facto*, releases the entire group from obligation for the debt. We see now, however, from God's Word and from experience that both of these things do not happen. The entire world is not relieved of guilt by Christ's sacrifice, although in a certain sense one may say that His death showed how God exercised righteousness toward the guilt of the world. Neither does this death immediately remove from the elect the accusation of conscience. Rather, they realize that, as long as they have not consciously accepted the merit of Christ by faith, God demands the satisfaction of guilt from their hands. Thus here the recompense for guilt by the Surety was of such a nature that under certain circumstances it did not exclude the demands of guilt from the initial debtor.

e) As noted above, every monetary debt is proportional, equal to the amount received when the debt was incurred, and corresponds in this respect to penal guilt. However, there is a difference in the manner in which the proportionality is measured and determined. For monetary debt, only the intrinsic value of the money comes into consideration and is not calculated by some extrinsic consideration. Monetary debt is based on *quid pro quo*, so much for so much, and although one does not repay the same coins that one received, it must still be something that represents complete-ly the same amount. Whether it be an emperor or a day laborer who pays the sum, the intrinsic value remains the same.

For penal guilt, it is different. Here intrinsic value is only one of the factors taken into account. Equally reckoned with must be the person who makes restitution for guilt and the manner in which restitution is made. If the atoning Surety is the eternal God Himself, then by that an infinite value attaches to the punitive suffering, and the guilty person cannot and need not bear the same identical suffering that all sinners together for whom He suffered would have had to endure. This suffering includes elements for which there is no room in a divine being, such as pangs of conscience, sinful despair, and so forth. Thus what Christ has paid is not the *same*, but of *equal value* for God's righteousness as what sinners themselves would have had to pay. In His grace, God not only permitted that the Surety takes the place of the first guilty person. In connection with that, He also permitted that the one manner of payment takes the place for others. Nevertheless, in this regard it should be maintained that the value has remained the same. What Christ paid was a full equivalent. Grace consists in that, not that God accepted as full what in itself was not full. In the meting out of punishment—and in determining the form that the punishment assumed for the Surety—not grace but righteousness was determinative. It is not possible for us to measure this righteousness and show in detail how Christ's suffering was a full equivalent. This was only possible for an omniscient God. But we know that no matter how much the form of suffering might have been changed, God has provided a complete equivalent.

Finally, that the satisfaction of guilt by Christ did not have a commercial character is immediately clear when one considers that in this way God would have paid Himself what was owed. In the case of a monetary debt, this would have been a meaning-less display. Thus here the distinction between pecuniary debt and penal guilt is sensed clearly. That for sinners Christ (that is, God) satisfied God's righteousness was not a mere spectacle but a necessity if they were to be saved.

39. *Is not the difference between pecuniary debt and penal guilt that for the former, but not for the latter, payment can be made by another party?*

No, properly formulated one must say: For pecuniary debt, payment by another must be accepted as legitimate; for penal guilt, that need not be but can be permitted by grace.

40. *On what basis can this be if, as we have seen, guilt has a personal significance?*

In answering this question, the criticism of those who reject atonement by the Surety should especially be kept in view. They insist that punishment, if it is necessary, is inseparable from the person of the transgressor. It is unjust and absurd that an innocent person should be punished for what someone else has committed. This conflicts with all principles of justice and morality. Conversely, the actual guilty party cannot benefit from what someone else has suffered for him. He must offer personal satisfaction to God, not that of someone else who is a stranger to him. This objection against the orthodox doctrine of satisfaction has been introduced in various forms. It is found among Unitarians and Trinitarians, in Socinus, Crellius, Bushnell, and many others. Although here we are not yet discussing deviating theories, still this objection should be addressed with an eye to them.

The following may be noted against this objection:

a) Guilt is a relationship in which a sinner stands to God, something that clings to the sinner—neither something that clings within the sinner, like a stain, nor something, as in the Manichaean conception of sin, constituting his essence. If either of these latter positions were true, then it would immediately follow that *only* the person to whom guilt clings or whose essence consists in guilt could be punished. Guilt, then, would be completely inseparable from the transgressor. However, since guilt is a relationship with respect to God, one cannot assert *a priori* that it is nontransferable, that God cannot transfer this relationship from one person to another.

b) If God's righteousness were like human, impassioned anger, if it included rancor and hate toward the sinner, then substitutionary atonement would be impossible. The element of passion is always personal and loses its significance as soon as it may move from one person to another in its operation. As we have already seen above, God's righteousness is free from all such passions and is nothing other than the calm resolute energy of His holy will to address Himself to evil and maintain Himself against evil. Who then will argue that such an expression must necessarily be directed toward the person of the transgressor himself, that it is incompatible with substitution?

c) Concerning the first part of the objection—that it is highly unjust to impute sin not one's own to the one who is punished in the place of another—it may be granted that under normal circumstances this would be so. To punish an innocent person instead of a guilty person is indeed contrary to every sense of justice. However, it should be kept in mind that it is entirely different if the substitute undergoes this suffering not unwillingly but willingly, if he takes it upon himself freely. Then there can be no question of injustice against him. Now, this was the case with Christ. He was completely willing in accepting the role of Surety, in putting Himself in the place of sinners. No injustice of any kind occurs when the righteousness of God causes Him to suffer for these sinners.

d) In the abstract, one can grant that where no unity of any kind exists between different persons, there is no place for substitution with regard to criminal law. If a citizen of Michigan, who has broken the law by committing murder and is sentenced to lifelong forced labor, has a savage brought out of the heart of Africa in order to send that person to prison as his substitute, everyone senses that this is absurd. There is not the slightest communal connection between him and the savage. One would not be able to consider this arrangement a satisfaction of the law. Any unity on which to base substitution is lacking.

If, on the other hand, such a unity exists, the matter assumes an entirely different form. This unity is not lacking between Christ and those He represents. It is grounded in the eternal agreement between the divine persons in the counsel of peace. There Christ and believers were united as one body, not only legally with regard to guilt-atoning suffering but also for their entire destiny for all eternity. In reality, ever after they form a single organism that, by a mystical union, keeps all its members joined with each other, and in which the one member cannot be treated apart from the other.

This mystical union, as it is called because of its mysterious nature that cannot be completely clarified by human analogies, comes out in everything that happens with the believer. In Scripture, it is pictured by all kinds of metaphors: as a foundation and what is built on it (1 Pet 2:4–6); as a tree and its branches (John 15:4–5); as a body and its members (Rom 12:4–5; 1 Cor 12:12, 27; Eph 5:30, 32). Its result is that what took place for them objectively in Christ repeats itself subjectively in believers in a meaningful way as a kind of symbolism. They are buried with Christ in baptism (Col 2:11–12), raised with Him through the power of the Spirit (Rom 6:4), are seated with Him in the heavenly places (Eph 2:5–6); indeed, they were chosen in Him before the foundation of the world (Eph 1:3–5). So if one objects to the satisfaction of Christ as Surety, one will have to attack the issue at its roots and reject the mystical union, which is rooted in eternity. One will have to say that the divine persons did not have the right to bind the destiny of Christ and believers together such that Christ could satisfy for them. But who will prescribe to the triune God what is right and how He should have acted in His eternal counsel?

e) From what has been said, it follows that, although satisfaction takes place in Christ, this satisfaction is nevertheless applied to the consciences of those for whom it is intended in such a manner that any appearance of injustice vanishes. Believers are not left with the illusion that personally they have always been free of guilt and that Christ is really the sinner. In the cross of the Mediator, they see the exercise of God's justice against their sins and in their minds identify with the crucified Savior. They behold in His perfect obedience the sacrifice that God could require of them. Thus by the mystical union provision is made that all false notions to which substitution could lead are avoided. That is, the order of salvation [ordo salutis] is so arranged that the believer applies to himself personally what is done for him in Christ, his Surety.

41. *If, then, substitution is permissible in the penal justice of God, how is it that it is not allowed in earthly penal justice?*

Because of the following reasons:

a) If a person would undergo the death penalty for another, he would thereby evade the performance of other duties that are incumbent upon him personally. He has his own place in society, his own duties in this life toward God. He would not be able to fulfill these if he put himself in the place of another.

b) Nobody is able to put himself in the situation of another with a complete sense of guilt. His love for his fellow man may be strong enough to sacrifice himself for him. As a sinful person, he does not possess that moral sensitivity demanded of a surety pleasing to God. Satisfaction in this way would not become a true satisfaction, but a kind of martyrdom that was accepted and endured in a heroic animation.

c) A surety under normal earthly penal justice would not be able to arouse a profound acknowledgment of this satisfaction in the person whose place he took. A hardened criminal would perhaps admit that another person suffered for him and yet not in the least be consumed by this self-sacrifice and would remain devoid of any deeper insight into the essence of righteousness. Earthly authorities may bear the sword on God's behalf, but they do not have the inward power that God has over minds. In the case of a potential substitution, they are unable to ensure that in that substitution the guilty party will acknowledge justice toward himself. It is true that they cannot ensure that with absolute certainty even when the offender is punished in his own person. Still, it is usually the case that where penal suffering and accusation of conscience coincide, the subjective sense arises that is essential to the exercise of justice. But it is not usually the case that this is brought about by the concurrence of remorse and witnessing another's suffering.

d) The earthly dispensing of justice should be distinguished from God's absolute dispensing of justice. The former is not final, not decisive. If a criminal is punished for murder here, it does not mean that justice is thereby satisfied. He still must give an account of himself to God in the judgment and will receive from God what he deserves according to his deed. He has paid for his crime only insofar as his relation to civil society is concerned. God as highest civil lawgiver has exercised His wrath against him (by the agency of the government), but He has not yet dealt with him as moral lawgiver. It is easy to see, then, how the partial and provisional administration of justice that takes place in the civil sphere has its own characteristic demands, and that in it not everything applies that applies to God's final administration of justice. In the former, substitution may be impossible or unadvisable, while in the latter it is still entirely in order.

42. Have no cases of substitution occurred in earthly penal justice?

Yes, such cases have in fact occurred. However, for the reasons mentioned above, they cannot be considered legitimate—not, however (and one should note this), because substitution in criminal cases is wrong in principle but simply because the sinful person is not a proper object for substitution as he figures in the earthly administration of justice. Jurists have never recognized such cases as valid. Grotius, world famous as a jurist, fully recognizes the principle of substitution when he says that it belongs essentially to the notion of punishment that it is imposed for a sin, but does not belong essentially that it is imposed on the same person, if, namely, such a unity exists between the Surety and those represented that the imputation of their guilt to Him can be justified by that unity.

43. Should allowing for a surety be considered a relaxation of law or of justice or, rather, as a matter of strict justice?

[It should be considered] as an act of grace and, as such, not as an act of strict justice toward the initial guilty person. Insofar as He is concerned, God has let go something of His justice—not, however, insofar as it concerns the law that was violated, for nothing of the punishment that is due is diminished. The direction in which justice is directed is changed, but its action is not reduced in strength. This is what is meant by the theologians who called permitting a surety a relaxation. Owen, for example, does this.

However, those who speak in this way mean something entirely different than what the Scotists, and later Grotius, meant by the same term *relaxation*. According to the last named, God drops something of the content of the punishment itself and, by a sovereign decree, declares something to be complete that does not possess full value. That, of course, diminishes the righteousness of God. It has rightly been observed that if God can drop a part of the punishment in this manner, He can also drop the entire punishment, and so in principle the necessity of satisfaction is abandoned.

44. *Is there a basis to deny the designation of penal suffering to the suffering of a surety?*

Some have argued this. They assume that one can only speak of punishment with respect to a personally guilty person—that is, with respect to a person in whom *reatus culpae* [liability to guilt] in the above-mentioned sense is found. The subjective element of a personal sense of guilt must thus constitute the essence of punishment. This goes directly against Scripture, which declares of Christ, "The punishment that brought us peace was upon Him" [Isa 53:5]. So we may say that the purpose of the suffering is sufficient to stamp it as punishment. All suffering that has the aim of satisfying the demands of divine righteousness we call punishment, regardless of whether it is accompanied by a subjective sense of personal guilt. That this is so also appears from the following consideration: There is no other name by which we could designate this suffering than penal suffering. It is distinguished by its aim from discipline and from a blind calamity. All suffering, however, must belong to one of these three categories. Thus, if one denies that it is penal suffering, one furthers the impression that it belongs to one of the other two categories. It is therefore dangerous to deny this name to the suffering of Christ. The addition "substitutionary" sufficiently guards against the misunderstanding that Christ's suffering is to be considered a punishment personally deserved by Him.

45. *Has the Mediator stood in the place of the elect only by discharging penal guilt or also by keeping the law for them?*

He has also kept the law for them; besides His passive obedience there is also an active obedience.

46. How in this distinction is the term "passive obedience" used?

Not in the sense that Christ in His passive obedience would have been merely receptive (passive) and did nothing Himself. His suffering included in itself an activity that was voluntary. Here "passive" should be understood as "pain-enduring." Thus by the passive obedience of Christ we designate all those experiences in which He, according to His humanity, endured pain to satisfy the punitive righteousness of God.

47. How do you define this active obedience?

As everything that Christ has done in perfectly keeping the law; as the stipulation of the covenant to which the promise of eternal life was tied.

48. What is included in this definition?

a) Active obedience consists in an actively assertive act, the object of which is the law of God. Passive obedience consists in an actively receptive act in which the law—that is, the punitive righteousness of God—is also at work. In passive obedience, the law acts on Christ with its curse; in active obedience, Christ acts on the law.

b) Here the law is not kept insofar as it is the natural demand of God's holy nature on all moral creatures. If Christ had taken away that demand by substitution, then it would follow that believers no longer stand under the requirement to keep God's law and do His will. That would be antinomianism. A rational being can never be free of this moral duty regardless of what state he is in. What Christ has kept is the law as a covenantal requirement—that is, as the means, sovereignly ordained by God, for obtaining eternal life that cannot be lost.

c) Accordingly, one must distinguish three kinds of relationships in which man stands to the law:

1. The natural relationship of a rational being. No due possession can be earned from God by this relationship. Even if a person in this relationship does all that is demanded from him, he is still an unprofitable servant [Luke 17:10].

2. The covenantal relationship. God can, out of voluntary favor, enter into a covenant with man and make the keeping of the law, under specific conditions, a means to obtain eternal life.

This second relationship does not annul the first just mentioned but gives it a specific character for a period of time. When it ceases, the first still remains, regardless of the cause of the cessation—be it the fulfillment of the covenant or its breaking. The natural demands of the law come both to believers as well as those who are lost.

3. The penal relationship. Man enters into this relationship as soon as he breaks the law. This brings to an end the covenant relationship but not the natural relationship. God still demands of a transgressor that he keep the whole law, but He is no longer obligated to tie that demand to the promise of eternal life that cannot be lost.

49. *What is the nature of the distinction between passive and active obedience?*

It must be strongly emphasized that we are dealing here with a logical distinction and with a distinction in purpose. In concept, passive and active obedience are not, and cannot be, identical in concept, but they also divide in the purpose for which they are intended. The concepts have been discussed above. The distinction in purpose has likewise been highlighted. The stability disrupted by sin is restored by passive obedience; eternal life is gained by active obedience. Neither of the two would be sufficient in itself to save the children of God.

If now, however, we wish to attempt to extend this distinction in logic and purpose into its realization, it will soon become clear that this is completely impossible. No single instance in Christ's state of humiliation can be pointed to in which He made satisfaction in a way that was either exclusively passive or exclusively active. The assumption of a weak human nature was already a suffering for His person, and this already covers the entire state of humiliation so that no place remains for a deed of purely active obedience. However, one must go even further. Not only are both coincident and accompanying each other at every point, they are also necessary for each other, and at no point can they do without each other. Without active obedience, passive obedience would not have been acceptable to God as satisfaction of His punitive righteousness. Imagine that Christ had borne His punitive suffering without for a time actively keeping the law perfectly. What would have been the consequence? Simply that penal satisfaction would have had to be obtained for His own sin that He committed by this lack in active obedience. It would then not have made satisfaction for others.

One can likewise reason in the opposite direction. If Christ had kept the law perfectly, and that had occurred without suffering, then His active obedience would *ipso facto* have lost its worth because of this deficiency—for perfect obedience in the Surety requires that He enters fully into all relationships in which the sinner stands in relation to the justice of God and that He is entirely of one will with God, even in this demand that God's punitive righteousness should have its free course. An active obedience without suffering accompanying it would betray a lack in moral rectitude in concurring with the justice of God. So from both directions we reach the same result: that passive and active obedience cannot do without each other.

50. *In what respects was active obedience necessary to make passive obedience acceptable to God?*

a) Active obedience was in itself a humiliation for the Son of God, and—to that extent—suffering. For a human person, it is not a humiliation to keep the law of God, for law-keeping befits his status as a creature. For Christ, it was different. Although He possessed a human nature, it nevertheless stands in relationship to the law through the person; and this is the person of the Son of God. God's Son, as very God, is not subject to the law but is Himself the eternal foundation of all law and justice. Thus for the lawgiver it is a humiliation to become a law-keeper. So then, one should also judge that Christ's incarnation and His submission to the law are two conceptually distinct acts. His incarnation can be logically conceived of without being tied to a submission to the law. For even in his human nature, He always remained the Son of God. We also see, then, that the Apostle Paul distinguishes between these two concepts: "God has sent forth His Son, born of a woman, born under the law, so that He might redeem those who were under the law, that we might receive the adoption as children" (Gal 4:4–5).

b) Active obedience was necessary to enable Christ to make satisfaction for others in passive obedience, as has already been shown above.

c) Active obedience also lent to passive obedience that quality by which it became a sacrifice well pleasing to God. Those who are lost are also the objects of God's punitive righteousness, but, unlike Christ, not in such a sense that God's good pleasure can rest on them. They suffer as evildoers and not in full assent to the demands of God's justice. Hence their sacrifice (if one would so designate it, for it cannot properly be called a sacrifice; Heb 10:26–27) is not accepted, and they never escape punishment. In contrast, the passive obedience of Christ is accepted in its entirety by God as a sacrifice well pleasing to him. Here is an exercise of righteousness that accordingly, despite every similarity, is nevertheless distinguished at this one point from the righteousness that will strike down the one who is himself guilty.

51. *Have all acknowledged that the satisfaction of the Mediator has these two aspects?*

Although it was already present in substance very early in the faith-consciousness of the church, the clear, theoretical distinction was first made by Thomas Aquinas. He gave the passive obedience the name *satisfactio*, "satisfaction," and the active obedience the name *meritum*, "merit." One can object to these designations because *meritum* is at the same time *satisfactio*. Nevertheless, this is exactly what was meant when later Protestant theology adopted this distinction in its confessions.

Later, however, reservations arose here and there. On the Reformed side, it was above all Johannes Piscator (professor at Herborn, 1546–1625), who opposed the active obedience of the Mediator as substitutionary. He was followed among the theologians by Paraeus, Scultetus, Alting, Cameron, Blondel, Capellus, and others. In this dispute, Piscator started from the proposition that Christ owed His active obedience for Himself and so could not accomplish it for us. He appealed to Philippians 2:9–10. From that, he further drew the conclusion that man also has no need of active obedience; or, stated differently, that God demands only one of the two, keeping the law or punishment but not both at the same time. Reformed theology, however, has not let itself be led off course by these objections but has maintained this distinction as legitimate and necessary.

52. *Show that the active obedience of the Mediator is necessary for the salvation of those He represents.*

a) Everyone will have to agree that for Adam, perfect keeping of the law for a fixed period of time was the means to acquire eternal beatitude that cannot be lost. When the covenant of works was broken, God could have rescinded this promise. He was no longer bound to honor it. Nevertheless, He allowed the promise and the condition to stand and repeatedly be published anew, especially by the proclamation of the Sinaitic law (Lev 18:5, "The one who does them will live by them"; cf. Rom 10:5, "For Moses describes the righteousness that is by the law," etc.; Gal 3:12). Fulfillment of this condition from man's side was no longer conceivable; thus the repetition must have had a different significance. This significance can only be that after the fall God gave His covenant of grace, in which the same demand and promise are fulfilled in the Mediator.

b) God's requirement cannot simply be set aside and remain unfulfilled. One should bear in mind that the requirement of the covenant contained the natural requirement of perfect keeping of the law. God's justice must be carried out in man both positively and negatively, both by righteousness of works and by penal righteousness. Thus if God were satisfied with the passive obedience of the Mediator, something would be lacking in the complete carrying out of His justice. And this would be so irrespective of all covenantal relations.

c) This stands out even more clearly when one bears in mind that those who are in Christ do not only receive acquittal from guilt and punishment but also the right to eternal life. Concerning this acquisition of eternal life, the following four possibilities may be considered:

1. God makes an essential change in the way in which He grants eternal life to His creatures. At one time, as far as we know, this always happened by a test in which obedience had to be demonstrated. Now He does this otherwise by simply clearing

away the ruins of the overturned law, without reestablishing
the law itself in all its beauty. This is what it comes down to
when we only assume a passive obedience.

2. If God does not change His conditions, then the possibility
can be considered that we are only freed from punishment
but remain forever destitute of the blessings of life, that we
are not sanctified and glorified but are brought into an in-between state—one that lies between salvation and its opposite
but is neither of the two.

3. The possibility also exists that the passive obedience of Christ
only removes legal obstacles, and it is now left to us to carry
out what is lacking, to earn eternal life by our own strength.
Then we would be accountable for achieving active obedience.

4. The fourth and final possibility is that Christ not only restores
the violated justice in its majesty by suffering but also by
obedience earns all the benefits of eternal life for those who
are His.

Now it is immediately apparent that the first two possibilities are purely abstract possibilities that cannot be taken
into consideration in reality. God cannot grant to fallen sinners, worthy of damnation, what He refused to the holy
Adam—namely entrance into eternal life without perfect
keeping of the law. This would be an unparalleled violation
of the majesty of His law, a relaxation in the bad sense of the
word. The second, that the redeemed would remain in an
in-between state, is totally unthinkable. Our choice, therefore, remains only between the third and fourth possibilities.
And then it is immediately apparent where the rejection of
the active obedience of the Mediator ends up: in nothing other
than that the covenant of grace is again made into a covenant
of works for the sinner, in which he has to earn salvation for
himself. Here Arminianism and Calvinism stand opposed to
each other. All Arminians, if they thought this through logically, have thrust aside active obedience, at least insofar as
it was an imputed obedience. The Roman Catholic theory of
joint effort in justification is based on the same idea. Those

who vacillate between a full-fledged Arminian and a more Calvinistic position also vacillate on this point (so, e.g., John Wesley). The choice here, therefore, cannot be in doubt.

d) Scripture teaches and everywhere presupposes the necessity of Christ's active obedience. It does this as often as it speaks of believers as coheirs with Christ, or gives them a share His mediatorial glory. That Christ Himself received this glory as a reward for His suffering is not subject to doubt (cf. Phil 2:8–9). Now if the glorification of believers is a direct consequence of the exaltation of their Mediator, then that also involves that this glorification was earned by Him. It is the Spirit, obtained by Christ, who effects all the workings of grace in the sinner (Acts 2:33). In Christ, they are blessed with all spiritual blessings (Eph 1:3). He has given Himself up for the church so that He might sanctify and cleanse it and present it to Himself as a church without blemish and without wrinkle (Eph 5:25–27; cf. also Titus 3:5–6, a very clear proof text). The apostle contrasts the disobedience of Adam and the obedience of Christ with each other and declares that by the latter many are made righteous (Rom 5:19). A contrast is also made between the righteousness of God and the self-righteousness of man (Rom 3:20–26). Thus there is something brought about by God Himself that corresponds to what man vainly tries to bring about. As it is witnessed of Christ that He was made sin (i.e., bearer of penal guilt) for us, so it is also said in so many words that He is given to us by God as "righteousness" (1 Cor 1:30).

e) Finally, reference should still be made to the Old Testament sacrifices. We have found earlier that they were not only types of penal suffering, but just as much of an active devotion to God. Accordingly, it is said of Christ that He gave Himself for us as an offering and sacrifice to God, a "sweet-smelling aroma" [Eph 5:2].

53. *How should the objections brought against the active obedience by Piscator and others be answered?*

That Christ had need of His active obedience for Himself is a misconception that does not take into account the deity of the person of the Mediator. It has already become clear to us why Christ did not require obedience for Himself.

As far as the other objection is concerned—that God cannot demand suffering and satisfaction at the same time, but only one of these—this rests on a confused conception of the actual state of affairs. The question here is not what God must necessarily have from man so that He Himself might not be in want of something. If that were the case, one could in fact say with Piscator: God must have either one of the two, and with either of them His justice is satisfied. From those who are lost, God does not receive anything other than satisfaction of penal guilt. The question, however, is an entirely different one—namely, what God must have from a person for that person to escape judgment and enter into a reconciled, peaceful relationship to Him. Even if after the fall a covenant of grace were not established, and Christ had borne only penal guilt and had again placed man there where Adam stood—even then, in order now to stand before God on his own account, man would have been in need of an ongoing active righteousness in order to continue sharing in the favor of God. How much more, then, now that there is a covenant!

54. What is the best designation to refer to passive and active obedience together?

The term "satisfaction" (*satisfactio*) includes both and emphasizes precisely what is common to both. However, the distinction mentioned above between "satisfaction" and "merit" is also found, following Aquinas, in some Reformed theologians. Owen, among others, has adopted it. However, it is less precise.

55. From the fact that satisfaction is a priestly work, does something also follow concerning the persons for whom satisfaction is made?

Yes. A priest does not advocate in general for everyone but sacrifices for a specific family, or tribe, or a specific people, which he represents and for which he is appointed. This causes us to expect that the satisfaction of the Mediator as a priestly act will also apply to a specific people for which God has made Him priest. In other words, we are led to the presupposition that satisfaction is not universal but particular.

56. *Is this question whether satisfaction is universal or particular*
    also connected to the conception that one forms of the nature of
    satisfaction itself?

Yes, it is closely connected. If one maintains with the Arminian that
Christ has only borne penal guilt and thereby opened up the possibility
for man to obtain the right to eternal life by the obedience of faith, then
this naturally entails that satisfaction pertains to all men. Here salvation is not tied to satisfaction, and the inference from all not being saved
to not having satisfied for all is unwarranted. If, on the other hand, one
considers faith and the subjective application of the merits of Christ
in general as a fruit of those merits, then it immediately follows that
where this fruit is lacking, the root must also be lacking. That is, Christ
cannot have made satisfaction for the person who is not saved. So it is
already apparent that particular satisfaction and active obedience in its
full meaning stand and fall together.

57. *What was the old principle concerning the extent of the satisfaction*
    of Christ?

The old theologians were accustomed to saying: Christ died *sufficienter*
pro omnibus, sed efficaciter tantum pro electis [sufficiently for all, but efficaciously only for the elect]. That is, as far as the sufficiency of Christ's
work is concerned, there was nothing lacking in its intrinsic worth in
order to save all mankind. If it had pleased God to apply this satisfaction
to the entire world, then it would have not needed to be any different
in itself than it now has been. Therefore, every thought that there is
a limitation in the worth of the obedience of the Savior—and that the
particular character of the satisfaction follows from this limitation—
must be rejected as absurd. Those who teach the universal satisfaction
of Christ cannot be more copious in praise of the all-sufficiency of the
work of the Lord than the most rigorous spokesmen of Calvinist particularism. Turretin, Witsius, Owen, and whomever one reads—they all
vie with each other in declaring that the satisfaction of the Mediator
was sufficient to save every sinner.

58. *Apart from the issue of intrinsic value, is there anything that precludes
    the satisfaction of the Mediator from being applicable to every sinner
    without distinction?*

No. Not only is the intrinsic value sufficient to save all, but also the mode
of satisfaction did not need to be another in order to make it applicable
for all. It we presuppose for a moment that God could change His purpose with respect to election, this would not involve any kind of change
in satisfaction. Apart from God's election, from God's side satisfaction
makes possible the salvation of every man. It is not possible, however,
that God would be able to change His will.

59. *Does the question at issue concern the universality or particularity of
    the offer of grace?*

No, for as proponents of particular satisfaction we acknowledge that
this offer is made to all and that it applies to all. Provided that you appropriate it by faith, all the fruits of this satisfaction are yours. Indeed,
we hold that this universal offer of grace goes forth not only with the
purpose of bringing it to the elect, who are hidden amidst the masses,
but also certainly to demonstrate to unbelievers that it is their unbelief
and not the lack of a sufficient ransom that causes them to be lost. If
the gospel were not offered, many would be able to say in their own
blindness, "We would have certainly repented and been saved if only
a message of salvation had come to us." Now a sinner cannot speak to
God in this way. If a nonelect person knew how to find a way to acquire
faith for himself, God would surely keep His word, and he would not
be lost because Christ had not died for him. But this entire supposition
naturally belongs to the realm of impossibilities.

60. *If we speak of particular satisfaction, is it then our intention to deny
    that any benefit results from this satisfaction for the nonelect?*

This, too, is not our intention. It is self-evident that the destiny of humanity, out of which God calls His elect, and the destiny of these elect
themselves cannot immediately be separated from each other. One
recalls our exposition of Romans 9:22–23 in our treatment of the doctrine of election [in volume one]. There, Paul infers the forbearance of
God toward the vessels of wrath from His merciful purpose with the
vessels of mercy. And insofar as this purpose concerning the vessels of

mercy rested on, and was related to, the satisfaction of the Mediator, who could not satisfy until the fullness of time—to that extent this satisfaction became a cause of the patience of God in putting up with those who are lost. All that results from the delay of judgment, all external blessings that mankind enjoys, all that befalls them beyond curse and death, the common grace at work throughout, with all the fruits of external righteousness that it fosters—all of this is an indirect result of the satisfaction of the Mediator.

Still, it would be more or less wrong to say that Christ earned these things for the nonelect. The correct formulation would be that these benefits for others result as side effects from His merits for the elect. Earning presupposes a direct, personal connection that obviously is not present here. It is certainly true that all these side effects are intended side effects, for everything that Christ has purposed with His work has actually resulted from it. Its direct purpose, however, did not lie in the well-being of others but in the salvation of believers. All other things are attendant on that purpose, as they are given with it.

61. *As a consequence of all these limitations, how should the question be properly formulated?*

We should ask: For which persons did God the Father and the Mediator intend His satisfaction as the certain and effecting cause of their eternal salvation? Thus the issue here is one of purpose and nothing else. When we speak of universal and particular satisfaction, the adjectives "universal" and "particular" do not express one or another property that satisfaction must have in itself but simply the relationship in which it stands to the purpose of God. It can perhaps lead to greater clarity if one explains "particular satisfaction" by "particular salvation" in the sense of "particular redemption." This last expression shows more clearly that it is a question of purpose and not of the intrinsic worth of the ransom (Owen, e.g., contended against the teaching of the Arminians of "universal redemption").

62. *On what grounds is it possible to deny that the satisfaction of Christ in the sense just described was particular?*

    a) One can deny this because one is a consistent universalist. One then assumes that all will be saved or are saved *per se* by the work of the Mediator, regardless of any further explanation one gives of this work.

b) One can deny this because one lets the application of the work of Christ depend in part on the working of the Holy Spirit, in part on the attitude of man toward it. In His election, then, God did not sovereignly limit this application, but men themselves limit it by their unbelief and by not cooperating with grace. The purpose of God when He had Christ make satisfaction, and of Christ Himself when He made satisfaction, was to save all if only they would willingly accept it. God did have foreknowledge that only a portion would accept it, but as a mere cognition this could not be of influence on His active purpose. This is the position taken by the Remonstrants.

c) One can also deny it on the basis of hypothetical universalism, which we discussed earlier. The doctrine of Saumur maintains that the objective satisfaction of Christ stems from a universal ordaining of God's grace that pertained to all mankind. This initial plan, however, was in vain, since not one person could satisfy God's command to believe. Seeing this, God then devises a second plan. Out of free grace He decrees to give faith to some. By thus postulating two plans in God, one can say simultaneously that, according to God's purpose, Christ has died for all without distinction and that it still depends on God's free decision for whom His satisfaction extends for salvation and will become effective. Objective grace is for all, not only in its offer but also in the actual purpose of God. Subjective grace is for some, not from the beginning but only in the plan devised later.

63. *What evidence can be advanced for the position that the satisfaction of Christ is in fact particular in nature?*

a) This follows directly from a proper conception of election. If everything that has been said about this doctrine earlier is correct, then all universalism in the doctrine of satisfaction is cut off at the root. We say that the election of particular persons to save them from sin and death comes first in the work of salvation as the beginning of everything, and that we cannot go back further than this; we can find nothing behind it. This, however, also determines the purpose that God had in all that follows.

Now we can also see why it is of importance to let the counsel of peace follow in order after election. The counsel of peace is at the root of satisfaction, and it cannot suffice to inquire about the purpose of God and Christ in bringing about satisfaction. Rather, one must inquire about their purpose in determining satisfaction. If satisfaction is particular, then the reason for that always lies in the particular suretyship of the Mediator. For whom did Christ become Surety in the counsel of peace? To this no other answer can be given than "for all those whom the Father has given to Him as elect." Then, however, election must also lie in back of suretyship and not follow it. If one posits the latter, then everything immediately takes on a different shape. Then the counsel of peace did not have in view particular persons; Christ assumed His work without having had particular persons in mind; and everything becomes universal. The acceptance of the suretyship is made universal, and its execution is inseparably joined to this.

It is for this reason that we make salvation and all that belongs with it subordinate to election, but then also permit ourselves to draw the conclusion that the former can no more exceed the limits prescribed for it by election concerning its establishment in eternity than it can concerning its execution in time.

b) The reverse conception is unworthy of God. If one does not start from Arminian or Amyraldian concepts, then this is truly less dangerous, but one still ascribes to God a manner of determining that is irreconcilable with His perfection. On this viewpoint, taken strictly, one cannot even really say that salvation is universal in intent. As soon as one asserts this, one has already crossed over onto the terrain of Amyraldus, for what was initially universal and has later become particular betrays a change of purpose. If one wishes to put the counsel of peace before election and wishes to do that as a Calvinist, one will have to be satisfied with saying that the former was no more intended to be universal than particular; that it was not at all concerned with either limitation or nonlimitation; that it was undetermined regarding extent; and, humanly speaking, that God had not yet put to Himself this question of extent. One, however, sees immediately that this entire train of thought is based on anthropomorphic thinking.

c) Nothing needs to be said about the Arminian conception. Amyraldianism lapses into the incongruity of making the suretyship of the Mediator end entirely in fruitlessness, so that it is to be ascribed to a timely measure of God taken subsequently (that is, particular election) that the entire plan did not collapse. Here election becomes the final effort of God to prevent the total failure of His counsel. If such things are possible, then all certainty has disappeared from heaven and earth, and we may certainly fear that even now the outcome of the work of salvation is still uncertain.

d) The giving of Christ by God and Christ's giving of Himself appear in Scripture as the acts of supreme love, by which the sinner becomes aware that all other things will certainly be granted to him. If God did not spare His own Son, then nothing can be too great or too difficult for His love. Now, however, the question arises how this surpassing love should be conceived of: as personal or as general. Must this supreme love lack a personal nature and have the nature of a general love of mankind? This is impossible. Every believer is accustomed to value the gift of the Mediator as a gift personally intended for him. He must relate to each other these two most precious of all truths, the majesty of God's love and its personal intent, and only by doing that does he receive his full salvation. Scripture also brings these two aspects together when it says "by faith in the Son of God, who loved me and gave Himself for me" (Gal 2:20).

e) If Christ's satisfaction is a general one that obtains for all in the same sense, then He is able to earn the subjective operations of grace for those who receive them. And, on the contrary, if the subjective operations of grace are personal and do not come to pass for everyone, yet have the character of merited benefits, it then follows that Christ has acquired something for some that He did not acquire for all. Now, there can be no doubt regarding the following two considerations: (1) that this subjective grace is not magnified in all but only in some; (2) that it is nevertheless an earned benefit, for it is entirely the result of the work of the Holy

Spirit, and the Holy Spirit is always presented as a gift earned by Christ. Thus the particular nature of satisfaction is inescapable other than by denying the fact that the Holy Spirit is a gift that was earned. And involved in that denial is a denial in principle of the active obedience of the Mediator, since with the elimination of the Holy Spirit and His gifts there remains nothing for the earning of which the active obedience would be necessary.

f) If all that has been said above about the nature of satisfaction and its substitutionary character may be deemed to be correct, then no doubt can be entertained about its limited scope. A surety can only make atonement for those who are in fact atoned for by His work, those on whom the wrath of God no longer falls. That Christ would substitute for those who later still themselves have to bear punishment is a *contradictio in adjecto* [contradiction in terms]. God can establish as a condition that as long as the elect do not actually believe in Christ, He may demand satisfaction from them (although in fact it has already been made), but this is not a punishment in the real sense, and it is not at all equivalent to His requiring satisfaction from the lost themselves. For the latter, a prior satisfaction is excluded. Substitution includes dealing with persons; as there is a specific person who substitutes, there must be one or more specific persons for whom he substitutes. If one denies the personal aspect, the judicial aspect is omitted and one will have to invent a theory of satisfaction other than that found in Scripture, in which it is just the judicial aspect that stands out so prominently.

g) All deviating views basically come down to this: that Christ's satisfaction is restricted to removing certain obstacles—that He does not actually save all but enables all to be saved. So He should not be called Savior, but one who makes salvation possible. This, however, goes against the explicit testimony of Holy Scripture, which says of Christ that He came to save what was lost (Luke 19:10), to deliver us from the present evil world (Gal 1:4). His purpose in placing Himself under the law was not to make us redeemable in a general sense but to cause us to obtain adoption as children (see Gal 4:5). When all these expressions are robbed of their force to such an extent that they merely express "making savable," then one can rightly say that the content of salvation is sacrificed to the extent of salvation. However, nothing of its glory remains.

h) The high priestly work of the Mediator is a whole, and its different parts may not be separated from each other, including what concerns their purpose for the persons whom they benefit. From this it follows that Christ atoned for all those for whom He intercedes and prays before the Father and for no one else, since the one is simply the completion and fulfillment of the other. Now, it is taught that the Mediator does not intercede for everyone in general but only for His sheep ("I pray for them, I do not pray for the world but for those whom you have given me"; "Neither do I pray for these only but also for those who will believe in me through their word" [John 17:9, 20]). The same consideration is included in the fact that His intercession is efficacious, never without its effect. A priest who intercedes in vain is not a real priest but a suppliant. The work of a priest is infallible, and of Christ we know that He intercedes "as a priest on His throne" [Zech 6:13], that His Father "always hears" Him [John 11:42].

That the high priestly work as a whole makes the salvation of the persons to whom it applies absolutely certain can nowhere appear more clearly than in the reasoning of the apostle in Romans 8:33–35: "Who will bring any charge against God's elect? It is God who justifies. Who is it that condemns? It is Christ who died, indeed more than that, who has also been raised (that is, justified), who is also at the right hand of God, who also intercedes for us. Who will separate us from the love of Christ?" This also agrees with the nature of His intercession, which, as Owen rightly observes, cannot mean a humiliation or abasement of the Mediator with crying, tears, and pleading—indeed, which cannot even be understood as a comprehensible or oral prayer but consists entirely in a presentation of Himself before the throne of grace for our benefit. This intercession is, as it were, only a continuation of the sacrifice. As the Lamb was slain from the foundation of the world, so by this presentation it remains slain until the end consummation of the ages, with ever-atoning sacrificial blood.

Finally, one can also reason the other way around, as follows: If the satisfaction of Christ were universal, then this would also have to result in universal intercession—for satisfaction without intercession, sacrifice without the sprinkling of blood, is an incomplete work from which no one gains anything. Although one might say that objectively Christ has died for all persons, still this can only mean that for the first half of His priestly work He included everyone in His intention in order for the second half to lose sight of them forthwith and so leave them without benefit.

i) If the satisfaction of Christ is given a general scope, then the incongruity arises of a payment of penal guilt of which the results are uncertain. This is conceivable for a monetary debt. One can pay a certain sum for someone else on the condition that certain demands will be met, while it nevertheless naturally remains uncertain whether these conditions will be satisfied. But if they are not lived up to, then there is the possibility for the moneylender to recover the amount paid. It is otherwise for penal guilt. Here, who gives back to the surety the value of his satisfaction? Who reverses all the pain endured, the groaning and tears, the indescribable suffering, the groaning of soul? All that is irrevocably buried in the past and nothing in this world can undo it. Thus for every satisfaction of penal guilt a fixed and certain determination must be made concerning its effectual and infallible working in order to avoid this incongruity. And this determination lay precisely in the fact that in the purpose of God and Christ the priesthood had reference to the elect, whom it also certainly benefits.

j) All must already admit a certain particularity in the scope of Christ's satisfaction. If we say that Christ died for the sins of the world, we do not take the word "world" in its broadest sense. Everyone (except the most insistent universalists) excludes the devil and demons. Everyone who holds to Christ's own words will likewise exclude those who have committed the sin against the Holy Spirit, for which there is no forgiveness and no sacrifice remains. Thus if one must already concede a restriction in the purpose of God on these points, then in principle one cannot entertain an objection against the restriction to the elect. The satisfaction of Christ would also have been sufficient for those who have sinned against the Holy Spirit, but in His sovereign good pleasure God has not foreordained that.

k) Finally, we can still point to those passages in Scripture in which it is explicitly said that Christ died in an entirely specific sense for particular persons and not for all; compare John 10:15; 11:51–52; 15:13; Ephesians 5:25; Matthew 1:21.

64. To what do the opponents of particular satisfaction appeal?

Mainly to three things:

a) To the universal offer of the gospel, concerning which all agree.

b) To a series of Scriptural passages that speak of bearing the sins of the entire world and of dying for all.

c) To some passages that make mention of a death of those for whom Christ has already died.

65. How should the first of these (the universal offer of the gospel) be judged?

The objection is that the presentation of the gospel becomes a meaningless form for those who do not share in the satisfaction of Christ. If we look more closely, this general objection involves three specific objections that are usually not sharply distinguished from each other, yet are essentially different.

a) It is irreconcilable with the truthfulness of God that He would offer the gospel and the merits of Christ in it to those for whom He Himself did not intend them. God would thereby give the impression that He wills to do something that in fact He does not will.

b) On our position, ministers of the gospel, one thinks, lose the right to direct a general invitation to people.

c) The hearers of the gospel could not have confidence to rely on the suretyship and the satisfaction of Christ as long as they have not received infallible assurance that they personally belong to the elect. My confidence in believing can only rest on the fact that Christ has suffered for me. If He has not suffered for all, then I will first need to know whether I belong among those for whom He has surely suffered before I can have solid ground under me.

66. *What may be said to counter the first form of this objection?*

a) That the offer of the gospel is not and does not present itself to be a revelation of God's secret will or of the will of His decree. If this were so, a contradiction would in fact exist that would detract from God's love of truth. If the following had to be concluded: God has the firm intention to bring them personally to salvation and now it depends on A or B whether you will meet God's purpose or disappoint Him—if this was the content of the gospel—then particular election and satisfaction would indeed be excluded. This, however, is not the content of our gospel or of the gospel of Scripture. This gospel does not express itself concerning the secret will of God but speaks of His revealed will. We understand this revealed will to include the command of God that comes to man and in each particular instance is determined by the specific relationship of man to God. Now, there is no doubt that it is the obligation of man to accept the possibility of redemption that is offered to him in the gospel, hopefully and gratefully. God can make that demand, and the gospel comes with that demand to all men.

b) That the content of the gospel, as it is presented to all without distinction, is a declaration of the will of God that A and B, etc., may personally be saved, but that still in this regard should always be considered a conditional will. It is not only that we are not dealing with God's secret will; we are also dealing with His revealed will under a specific condition. In God there is no unsatisfied desire that has silence imposed on it by His secret will. The desire of God can be understood as follows: If you believed, then the good pleasure of God would rest upon this act of faith. This conditional character is thus always to be kept in view and kept in the foreground.

c) It is true that in the sense just described the gospel comes to many for whom Christ has not died. But at the same time it is true that these are precisely those who willfully despise the sacrifice of Christ. It may never be portrayed as if countless sinners who, eager for salvation, are seeking a ransom [and] now have to be dismissed with the explanation, "This ransom was not meant for you." In doing that, one would be entertaining purely abstract possibilities that under the present circumstances could never become reality. The truth is that not a single instance of this kind can occur. God's ordaining is such that all those for whom Christ in His purposing has not died are precisely the same as those who reject Christ by their unbelief. Even if satisfaction were universal, this can make no difference regarding their personal attitude toward it. In reality, they would no more share in it then than now.

d) As noted above, the gospel is intended to deprive man of every excuse and to place the magnitude of his corruption in the clearest light. That is why God does not let the gospel be proclaimed only to the elect but also brings it indiscriminately to all men (as far as it in fact reaches them and, in principle, as far as we can bring it to them). Now a sifting takes place. But now, too, sin in its inner essence comes to full flowering because it becomes unbelief in the face of grace. It belongs to God's righteousness toward sin that it will also reveal its true character to sinners themselves. The preaching of the gospel contributes to this. This came out most clearly at the time of the appearance of the Mediator on earth in the flesh. Unbelief reacted against Him, the incarnation of grace, in the most decisive way. Naturally, aggravation of guilt is inseparable from this reaction of sin and its related development. However, no one can dispute God's right to bring man into contact with the gospel, even if by that his judgment becomes more severe. Whoever disputes this right takes an Arminian standpoint and tacitly assumes that God owed satisfaction to man. It is the obligation of man to accept in faith everything that God presents to him. And once this obligation is present, God cannot act unjustly when He punishes the failure to meet this obligation, regardless of whether man is able to fulfill his duty.

e) Preaching has as its goal to call everyone it reaches: "If you will, take freely from the water of life" [Rev 22:17]; and "If you come, He will by no means cast you out" [John 6:37]. But it has neither the calling nor the right to make of this "willing" something other than Scripture means by it. It is not to be presented in a

Methodistic manner as a sudden, uncaused act of will, a kind of experiment that can be independent of all antecedent conditions. The willing to which Scripture alludes is the willing of faith, of saving faith, the deepest act a person can do, in which his entire being shares and concurs—an act that becomes entirely impossible and incomprehensible without a prior attitude of repentance, to which it is linked and from which it in part results. Thus to will, along with putting aside all confidence in one's self, is to have such a delight in the work of Christ and such an inner conviction of its sufficiency that we reach out for it with all the strength that is in us.

Now, the freest preaching of the gospel must make clear that such a willing is the only means by which we can become partakers of Christ. If one will not be untruthful, then the significance of faith may never disappear. And the preventive against this difficulty is a preaching of the law accompanying the preaching of the gospel. Whoever does not first bring the sinner to an awareness of his lost condition will also not elicit true faith in his heart by preaching. It is simply not true that everyone has a right to Christ who just chooses to believe at whim. The faith to which the recent methods of evangelism incite is something irrational. The faith of Scripture is a faith supernaturally wrought by the Spirit of God but still not an unnatural faith.

67. *What should be said concerning the second objection: that with particular satisfaction ministers of the gospel could not have the confidence to bring the offer of the gospel to all?*

a) That, as ordained ministers, they do not have as their charge to carry it out according to their own reasonings and reflections. It is God's concern to reconcile their calling and His decree with each other. They have only to follow the commission given them. That alone determines the scope of their work. And that reads: "Preach the gospel to *all* creatures" [Matt 24:14].

b) The message of the gospel does not entail that one must assure everyone, head for head: God wills your personal salvation with the will of His decree. Then one would be proclaiming an untruth. Rather, it entails:

1. Setting forth the demands of God on every sinner and the work of Christ as intrinsically sufficient and suited to satisfy for every sinner.

2. Unfolding the nature of repentance and of faith as that which is necessary to obtain the personal application of the merits of Christ.

3. Giving certain assurance that everyone who comes to Christ conscious of guilt and in faith may appropriate all the benefits of the covenant of grace as his personal possession.

c) Inasmuch as God has chosen to have His gospel ministered by men and has not chosen to give them insight in advance into His secret counsel, it is entirely understandable why the gospel must be preached to everyone. The elect are hidden among all these. Universal preaching is also a means of reaching the particular objects of satisfaction.

d) Also, it may not be forgotten that the gospel does not bypass unbelievers without a trace. It becomes to them a scent of death unto death [2 Cor 2:16]. Its preaching is a crisis in which all the depravity of the heart develops to full fruition and by which the measure of wrath at the day of God's retribution is made full.

The third objection mentioned above has been sufficiently removed by what has been said.

68. *How should we assess those texts that are cited against particular satisfaction and that appear to teach that Christ died for everyone?*

a) To begin with, one should envision the historical conditions of the time when the New Testament was written. A period of particularism, willed by God, had scarcely ended. The limitation of the dispensation of grace was a principle that was resident in the Jews to the bone. Many could not conceive of any other than a particularistic religion. Now, suddenly the dispensation of the New Testament arose with its universalism—that is, with its principle that by grace all ethnic boundaries fall away, that in Christ there is neither Jew nor Greek but only a new creature. It was in all respects obvious that under these circumstances all emphasis had to be placed on how Christ has died for all. We should rather wonder that more such passages do not occur. Passages such as 1 John 2:2 (cf. John 11:51–52); Hebrews 2:9 (ὑπὲρ παντός); Titus 2:11; 2 Peter 3:9; etc., are to be considered in this light.

b) When here and there it is said that Christ has died for the world or is an atonement for the sins of the whole world, then one should be extremely careful about arbitrarily drawing the conclusion: He has made satisfaction for all men. The word "world" has a number of meanings and is certainly not plainly synonymous with "all people." It can mean the universe, or all people in the world, or all kinds of people, many or the majority of the people, or the Roman world, or humanity as alienated from God and under the curse, etc. It is unnecessary to put forward evidence for all these different meanings. Anyone can open his concordance and be convinced. Therefore, if one wishes to derive a proof for the universality of satisfaction from the expressions mentioned above, then one will only be able to do this by considering the context and carefully demonstrating that in fact a satisfaction of Christ for all, head for head, is taught. And then one will perceive that nowhere is this the case.

c) Our principle should always be that Scripture is to be explained by Scripture. Now, if we have a series of texts that teach the particular or restricted scope of satisfaction, and beside them a series of texts that seem to mention a universal intention, the one must agree with the other. Now, everyone can see that the texts of the first category lose their meaning and become totally inexplicable when one forces through the universal scope of Christ's work. But one cannot maintain the reverse. The passages of Scripture with a more universal ring still retain a clear meaning and by no means become inexplicable when they are considered from the standpoint of particular satisfaction.

d) That these universal-sounding passages may not lead us to conceive of a universal satisfaction appears from the following consideration: They speak not only of a universal satisfaction but also of a universal salvation. "As in Adam all die, so in Christ will all be made alive" [1 Cor 15:22]. Most proponents of universal satisfaction, however, do not maintain that all people are in fact saved by the sacrifice of Christ. Thus in all the expressions referred to here they must subject the general terms themselves to a certain restriction. Not all people are made alive by Christ, but all who are entitled to that life, who are born spiritually of Him, as all who are naturally born of the first Adam inherit death from him. This, however, is nothing other than the explanation that we apply to other passages as well. Compare John 12:32; 1 Corinthians 15:22; Colossians 1:20; 2 Corinthians 5:14; Ephesians 1:10; Romans 5:18. When it comes to such passages, Arminians immediately say, "All, all who believe in Christ."

69. *What passages are advanced by the opponents of particular satisfaction to prove that Christ has died for those who are nevertheless lost?*

For this they appeal to Romans 14:15; 1 Corinthians 8:11; 2 Peter 2:1; Hebrews 10:29.

70. *Do these passages in fact contain what is sought in them?*

No. As far as the first is concerned, it does not speak of the nonelect at all. The apostle rouses the stronger believers not to grieve their brothers by what they eat, if these are weaker. He then adds, "And do not destroy by what you eat the one for whom Christ has died." That is, do nothing that has a destructive tendency or can have destructive consequences for one ransomed by the Lord. Eternal destruction is not in view here but an offense that would hinder the development of spiritual life.

In 1 Corinthians 8:11, mention is made of the perishing of a brother for whom Christ died because he sees another brother with more knowledge go into a temple of idols. The context, however, shows how this perishing, literally "becoming destroyed," is to be understood. It consists in violation of conscience and moral ruination, but this is not all the same as "being lost forever." The following verse explains further what is meant by speaking of wounding the conscience of the brother.

Concerning 2 Peter 2:1, there are two explanations. First, one has pointed to the difference between κύριος and δεσπότης. The passage reads, "And there will also be false prophets among you, who will secretly introduce destructive heresies, even denying the Master who bought them and bringing upon themselves swift destruction." This first interpretation understands δεσπότης, translated here as "Master," not as Christ but as God the Father. "Bought" is understood as liberation from idolatry, false teachings, etc. Thus the sin of the false prophets becomes so great because they deny God by false teaching when it is the very same God who had delivered them from error by the light of truth. The other interpretation, however, seems more plausible to us. It has the apostle speaking here from the standpoint of the heretics themselves. They claim that Christ has died for them and has ransomed them. But they deny that same Lord about whom they profess that. Their sin is great precisely because it is committed against the light and better knowledge, in and even within the circle of the Christian church, in the bosom of the congregation. Such persons bring a swift destruction upon themselves. Accordingly, all is clear and unforced, and one does not need, with Turretin and others, to appeal to the difference between κύριος and δεσπότης.

Hebrews 10:29 reads, "How much more severe punishment do you think he will deserve who has trampled on the Son of God, and has regarded as unclean the blood of the covenant by which he was sanctified, and has insulted the Spirit of grace?" This, too, should be understood from the standpoint of those who could become apostate. Their rejection of Christ would be a rejection of a ransom that they had first openly accepted. This is worse than scorning the Savior without first confessing Him. There is a greater degree of wickedness inherent in renouncing something in which one has first lived, even if only outwardly, than in not accepting something to which one has not yet had a relationship. And as the wickedness becomes greater, so also the punishment will become more severe. In all these instances, however, it is not at all that such persons have been converted in their heart and so have actually been redeemed from sin by Christ.

71. *What aberrant theories concerning satisfaction need to be noted and discussed briefly here?*

    a) The distinctive view of some church fathers

    b) The moral or ethical theory

    c) The governmental theory

    d) The mystical theory

72. *What was distinctive about the conception that some church fathers had of satisfaction?*

The conception of many church fathers since Origen and Irenaeus had a dualistic cast. They presented it as if the ransom did not have to be paid to the righteousness of God but rather to Satan. Thereby the latter came to be a second, independent principle next to God and appeared as a person with whom God must negotiate, who has certain claims that are to be respected. He has man in his power as a prisoner and cannot be forced to let him go unless he receives compensation, a ransom. This has been called a military theory of satisfaction, not without good reason, for it is based on a kind of military law. The notion of the Christian life as military service may have contributed its share to this view.

As far as the details are concerned, a great deal of difference reigns. According to some, Christ took the place of imprisoned men and then broke the bonds of Satan. According to others, He attacked Satan directly and was victorious. According to still others, He broke the power of the evil one by letting Himself be killed by him. Satan was only allowed to kill those who were guilty. By attacking Christ, he overreached himself, exceeded his rights, and forfeited them.

73. *What is to be said with this theory in view?*

It contains an element of truth and can appeal to passages in Scripture like Hebrews 2:14 and Colossians 2:15. Guilty man has fallen prey to death. With the permission of God, demonic power under the direction of the devil can carry out part of this punishment on man. Both sin itself as well as the consequences of sin are presented in Scripture as servitude to Satan.

The Fathers, however, overlooked to too great a degree that Satan is merely an instrument of God and that we are only freed from his power by its basis in God's righteousness being removed by the satisfaction of Christ. Furthermore, it appears clear enough from this theory how far removed the Fathers were from a moral conception of satisfaction, according to which only something in man would need to be changed. They agree with the orthodox doctrine insofar as they seek the necessity of satisfaction in something outside of man.

74. *What do you understand by the ethical or moral theory concerning the satisfaction of Christ?*

That conception according to which the purpose and efficacy of Christ's priestly work are sought in causing a moral impression on man, more specifically by presenting Christ as an example worthy of imitation, or by having Him appear as an evidence of the love of God, who desires to suffer with the creature. The first view is that of the Socinians. They see the death of Christ as the death of a martyr who by dying has sealed His teaching, providing us with a powerful proof of its truth and leaving us a beautiful example of a love of truth, while at the same time they acknowledge that death for Him was the point of transition to His glorification. The second view is that of Bushnell (1876) in America; Robertson, Maurice (1872), Campbell (1872), Young in England; and Ritschl with his school in Germany. The latter all assume that Christ suffered to convince man by actions that nothing stood in the way of their reconciliation with God. When one further inquires of them how the suffering of Christ can hold good as evidence for the love of God, then the answers are different. Some say that love was manifested by Christ not allowing Himself to shy away from the misery to which He was exposed by entering into a sinful world. Others answer that God wished to impress on man that He felt sympathy for them and could enter into their suffering. By that the heart is softened and made loving. Still others let the significance of Christ's work consist of feeling remorse for the sin of man, a remorse that was fully sufficient to take away guilt.

75. *What objections are to be raised against the Socinian form of this theory?*

a) It rests on Socinian rationalism, which explains the will, sin, divine righteousness, and everything related to these in an entirely superficial way, in conflict with the thoroughgoing witness of Scripture. It is untrue that man only has need of a good example in order to become good instead of evil. He needs to be re-created and so cannot change his own will by imitation. The righteousness of God is a reality and may not be viewed, as the Socinians want, as a form of benevolence. Sin is guilt and not only moral error. On each of these points, the Socinians judge in a Pelagian fashion.

b) There are elements of the suffering of Christ that cannot be explained as imitative martyrdom. One expects from a martyr that he will bear his suffering cheerfully and heroically. The opposite is seen in Christ. Although He endured patiently and purely, there is not a trace of the martyr's enthusiasm that transcends the pains. He had to be immersed in sorrows and with cries and groans offer prayers and supplications with tears [cf. Heb 5:7]. Also, being forsaken by God cannot be explained with this theory. It has rightly been observed that whoever regards Christ as a martyr must look for a higher ideal and undoubtedly will be able to find a higher ideal in the history of science or religion.

c) If the significance of Christ's work is to be sought in providing an example, then it remains completely unexplained how the emphasis in Scripture can fall on His death instead of His life. To say that Christ's death occurs as a validation of His life does not resolve this problem, for everywhere it is the fact of the death itself that is presented to us in Scripture as most important and not this fact in relation to something that preceded it.

76. *How can you refute the other form of this moral theory?*

a) If, as this theory assumes, only a subjective change in the attitude of man is necessary, then God is powerful enough to bring that about by His Holy Spirit, without Christ having to suffer all those afflictions. Indeed, it would be cruelty in God if He let His Son suffer where this is not absolutely necessary and the goal can be reached in another way.

b) Now this consideration also removes the foundation to the moral theory. For if Christ did not have to die, and it was God's free choice to end the hostility of man precisely in this manner, then in the delivering up of Christ one can no longer see an extraordinary gift of love. It is this only if it is *necessary* for the sake of man and ceases to be that as soon as the thought of possible secondary purposes in God occur to us.

c) It is established psychologically that tragic suffering does not make an impression on human nature when it has a premeditated character—that is, if one knows that it was brought about with the goal of making an impression. In this respect, the older Socinian theory provided greater advantages than this newer form. In fact, according to Socinus, the suffering of Christ was something unintentional and accidental that befell Him since He was unwilling to vacillate or yield when it came to fulfilling His duty. Such a martyr's simplicity could make an impression. A tragedy devised in advance, on the other hand, cannot. Now Scripture tells us that Christ's suffering was in fact conceived and devised in advance, that He would come into the world to suffer. He was delivered up by the determinate counsel and foreknowledge of God [Acts 2:23]. What God's counsel and hand had determined beforehand would occur [cf. Acts 4:28] happened to Him. Given this, it is impossible to believe in earnest in the suffering of Christ as an impressive tragedy unless one also believes in a divine righteousness that made this tragedy objectively necessary.

d) Bushnell, one of the leading defenders of this form of the moral theory, had to concede that Scripture always presents the work of Christ as a sacrifice to make satisfaction. This was necessary, as he said, in order that man, for whom the fruit of this work is intended, does not become overly self-assured. That is, this theory naturally entails that the sinner purposefully comes to contemplate the suffering of Christ—adopts various attitudes toward it in order, in doing that, to induce in himself the requisite impression. Thus, not only does the work itself become an exhibition, the appropriation of it by the sinner, too, is time and again in danger of becoming an exhibition. That is why, Bushnell says, the Bible speaks of it more or less covertly, so that we can absorb its impression in a less self-aware manner. This acknowledgement exposes in a striking fashion the weaknesses of the entire theory.

e) Against the particular form of this theory that seeks the significance of Christ's work in repentance for the sins of the world, we recall that repentance is precisely what is nontransferable in sin. No one can repent for someone else; certainly one can bear penal guilt for someone else. Only, then, when the substitutionary character of Christ's satisfaction is acknowledged, could one speak, in a modified sense, of repentance in Him—that is, as of insight and whole-hearted recognition that the punishments that He suffered as Surety were deserved. This, however, is still not repentance in the proper sense of the word. The theory of Campbell is consequently untenable, despite its attempt to understand satisfaction more objectively.

77. *Give an exposition of the so-called governmental theory.*

This theory was first developed in principle by Hugo Grotius in his work *A Defense of the Catholic Faith concerning the Satisfaction of Christ*. This apology was directed against the Socinians. Grotius wished to uphold the objectivity of satisfaction—that is, it must serve in support of God's principles of moral government. Imperceptibly, however, Grotius himself lapsed into the subjectivization he contested in Socinus. Later on, this theory was further elaborated especially in New England around the end of the last century. Its major arguments are the following:

a) The core of all reasonable religion is benevolence—that is, endeavoring to promote the happiness of others. All reasonable qualities may be reduced to this. When something does not aim at the happiness of others, it is thereby condemned as unreasonable, and when something occurs in God that is seemingly in conflict with the needs of creatures, then we should form a conception of it that avoids this appearance. Punitive righteousness must be explained in such a manner that it resolves into benevolence, into a fitting provision for the well-being of the creature.

b) The entire relationship between God and the creature must be explained by this principle of benevolence. God seeks the well-being of rational beings, and for Him everything is subordinate to this. That is why He prescribes laws and requires obedience. The basis for this is not that He, as the highest good and eternal Creator, is entitled to our service, but is nothing other than the impulse of His nature to make us happy. Thus, while for us the good in God is love for justice, according to this theory justice is taken up in love and becomes a more or less arbitrarily chosen aid to cause love to prevail.

c) Certain sanctions were attached to the laws that God prescribed out of love. God deemed that He could best achieve His goal if He connected certain positive punishments to transgression of the law. Punishment is suffering that is attached by God to sin in an extrinsic way, without there being a logical or rational connection between the two. The connection consists entirely in association. Men become aware, by the revelation of God or by experience, that where there is sin, there is also suffering, and that God follows this fixed rule. By this awareness, they will gain an instinctive aversion to evil. Thus God gambles, as it were, on the self-love of men, on their aversion to suffering, and thereby seeks to deter from transgressing the law. All this He does, however, with no other purpose than to promote the well-being of His creatures.

d) God could have punished all sinners who have transgressed the law. But had this happened, the exercise of punishment would have missed its goal since evil has spread universally. Therefore, for promoting the well-being of the creature it makes no sense to punish transgression of the law, for the goal, namely deterring others, can never be attained. Still, on the other hand, punishment cannot simply be remitted. The majesty of the justice would thereby be lost, and man would lose all reverence for the lawgiver. It is therefore necessary that God at the same time spare the sinner and provide a clear example of the execution of punishment. This was done in Christ. By having Him die, God has shown that He was serious about the maintenance of the sanctions associated with the law.

e) The suffering undergone by Christ, however, should not be viewed as strictly or literally the same or of equal value as that which sinners themselves would have had to suffer had the threat of the law been carried out on them. It is not, however, a punishment by substitution but something that substitutes for punishment. God had only to see to it that the suffering of Christ would produce the same impression that the personal punishing of the guilty themselves, who now go free, would have caused. Thus a relaxation takes place.

f) The result of this suffering consists in the possibility that now God may enter anew into a moral relationship with men and can again seek, by the majesty of His justice and the threat of punishment, to move them to doing good. He does not now need to look back on His initial experiment as a failure, for He has carried out

His threats in Christ. Justice has lost nothing of its moral gravity. For all, the opportunity is now open anew to earn the eternal life that as a positive sanction was joined to keeping the law. The covenant of grace, which rests on the death of Christ, is nothing other than a new covenant of works. The suffering of Christ is not so much its foundation but is much more a preparatory means to eliminate certain obstacles. It saves no one actually, but makes all salvable.

78. What is our criticism of this theory?

a) Its foundations are totally unscriptural and, moreover, philosophically untenable. It needs no demonstration that the doctrine of benevolence as the essence of all moral good, described above, is in conflict with Scripture. It is erected on philosophical principles from entirely outside the Bible. Apart from that, however, it must lead to eudaemonism or return to our standpoint. One could pose the following question to its proponents: If the morally good is known by the fact that it wills to promote happiness, does it not then also derive its value, morally considered, from this purpose? It will be difficult to give a negative answer in response. A morally good being must seek the happiness of others. Why must he do this? Because happiness is the highest good in the world; it must be sought for its own sake. That is clearly eudaemonism, the apotheosis of happiness, the reduction of the good to the pleasurable. If, on the other hand, one says that in the first place benevolence should not strive for the happiness of others but for their moral improvement, then one has thereby acknowledged that moral rectitude carries its value in itself and is neither dependent on happiness nor to be identified with benevolence. Then, however, it will also follow that sin carries within itself its own condemnation, which must be carried out not for the sake of happiness but apart from all consequences. That is exactly what we maintain when we say that God must punish sin.

b) The theory is modeled on a certain conception of the goal of the earthly administration of justice. Since it is within the purpose of punishment administered by earthly civil government to promote the well-being of society and elevate the happiness of its citizens, one thinks that therefore: (1) Punishment must be considered entirely from this point of view; (2) God's punishing can also have no other significance.

This reasoning, however, is false, both in its premises and in its conclusions. It is false in its premises, for it is not at all the case that government punishes exclusively in order to protect society. The state is more than a utilitarian institution. It has value and significance in itself, and accordingly its administration of justice is also of independent significance. This reasoning is false in its conclusions, for what is true for this earthly and temporal dispensation may not therefore be transferred to what is eternal and final: the administration of justice by God.

c) The theory rests on an unworthy conception of God and of the manner in which He deals with His creatures. He first tries, by sanctions that threaten personal punishment, to maintain the majesty of justice and to induce fulfilling the law. This experiment, however, is a total failure. If God now willed to carry out His threats, He would achieve precisely the opposite of His intention: the misery instead of the happiness of His creatures. He is therefore compelled to withdraw His threats, insofar as they were personal, to grant a compromise between full enforcement and total violation of the law, and to set an example in Christ. By doing this, reverence for the law among His creatures is salvaged and God can begin with a new experiment. However, what if this also should fail? Is it not natural for transgressors to hope anew for a relaxation in the future? After God did not strictly carry out the threat in the past, who will provide a guarantee that He will do so in the future? The possibility exists that He will no more be deterred by the action of Christ from a third experiment than He was held back by the transgression of the law from showing grace in Christ. All moral seriousness in His tendencies disappears, and the satisfaction of the Mediator leads exactly to the opposite of what it was supposed to effect according to this theory. Additionally, because of this God repeatedly assumes a false attitude toward His creatures. He says, "If you transgress, then you will be punished," but His deepest thought and intention in this is, "By saying this man will be deterred from transgressing, and if that does not avail, the law can always be relaxed."

d) According to this theory, God counts on the self-interest of man. The sanctions attached to the law are effective only insofar as they cause man to fear punishment. Now, it is true that earthly governments can and must also make use of this motive on their sinful subjects to maintain social order and keep sinful tendencies in check. But it is entirely incredible that God, who is not only concerned with outward decorum but with truth inwardly, would settle for observance of the law effected in this way and would make it the foundation for the eternal well-being of creatures.

e) The defender of the governmental theory, however, could say, "Punishment for sin and the satisfaction of Christ should not be viewed exclusively as a deterrent." It is not our meaning that God only intends to work on man by fear. We maintain that in the suffering of Christ God has left an impressive statement concerning the abhorrent character of sin. By this execution of punishment, He has not so much said—or at least not only said—what the consequence of sin is but rather what sin is. And by awakening insight into the abhorrent character of sin, satisfaction does its work and God reaches His goal.

Our answer to this should be that if God can show how abhorrent sin is by bringing suffering upon the sinner or upon Christ, then this can only find explanation in a punitive righteousness that *must* be carried out. In itself, suffering in no way has as its purpose to highlight the abhorrence of sin. If we presuppose that God does not necessarily possess righteousness that works retribution, then there is nothing in the least in the character of physical suffering that proclaims: sin is such a great evil. There are only two ways in which punishment can be related to sin: (1) as a deterrent, and (2) as just punishment. So when the advocates of the theory discussed here speak again and again of the suffering of the Lord as a proclamation of how abhorrent sin is, then they unwittingly take our position and use terms that only have meaning within our system.

The same thing can also be made clear along the following lines. Regarding its relation to sin, suffering can be considered in three ways:

1. By virtue of God's unimpeachable righteousness, it is connected to sin by God positively. One then adopts our position.

2. It is arbitrarily connected to sin by God as a deterrent, so that man, by the force of the principle of association, would be restrained from sinning. God then counts on the fear of man.

3. It results from sin itself as its natural outworking. Sin yields its own punishment. In Christ, God willed to demonstrate what sin by its nature leads to if it continues. In this case, however, God again counts on the self-centered fear of man. He wishes to move him to cease from sin, not because of its own heinousness but because of the heinousness of its consequences. The lesson of the cross of Christ may then be expressed in the following words: By doing good one gets ahead the furthest, and evil is a disastrous and dangerous principle!

f) Finally, this theory makes the suffering of our Lord more a display than a reality. It was designed to create an effect, not to satisfy righteousness. In no way is this in accord with what is reported to us concerning the suffering of Christ. With that, the emphasis is always on the sorrow and anguish that Christ lived through in His own consciousness, not on what He appeared to others to be. Think of the struggle in Gethsemane, of the refusal of the Lord to take the wine mingled with myrrh [Mark 15:23].

79. *What conception does the mystical theory have of the work of satisfaction of the Lord?*

It agrees in one respect with the moral theory already discussed, namely, insofar as it seeks the purpose of satisfaction in a change that must take place in the creature, not in the fulfillment of a requirement of God. However, while the moral theory limits this change to the consciousness of the creature and finds its essence in a change of the subjective state of man, the mystical theory conceives of the situation more deeply and allows for a reversal to take place in an unconscious change. Christ intervenes in life in the organic existence of man, and what occurred through and after the incarnation in Himself, in His human nature, was the beginning of a conversion of human nature. Only as such does His suffering have significance. Sin is to be viewed not as guilt but as power, as indwelling corruption that must be countered and purged. While this grounding is common to all forms of the mystical theory, they differ from each other in their further elaboration.

a) The Platonizing Greek church fathers spoke of a deification of human nature through the incarnation of the *Logos*. We have seen how the orthodox doctrine of the two natures in one person can be misused in this way. Deification means, in the first place, removal of perishability, to make immortal. In this view, the element of guilt naturally recedes into the background.

b) Others, especially in more recent times, put more emphasis on sin itself than on the consequences of sin. Sin is a power resident in the flesh of man, that is, in his corrupt nature. Christ with His human nature, with His flesh, had to take this power into Himself, let it have its effect on Him, and thus abolish it. One can see how this makes it necessary to think of Christ as sinful, for only by having sin within Himself could He expel sin. Instead of being a barrier that would preclude Him from being our Redeemer, for this viewpoint sin becomes an indispensable requirement for Christ to be able to become that Redeemer. This also entails, however, that only overcoming and expelling sin as a stain is at issue, and sin as guilt does not need to be reckoned with. One cannot have both in view at the same time, for precisely by assuming a sinful nature, the possibility ceases for Christ to pay for the guilt of the sins of others. Hence guilt is simply pushed aside. Sin is a poison that has entered man apart from his guilt. All that is required is an antidote that consists in the poison losing its power in someone who lets it subside within himself and at the same time does not succumb to it. This is the theory of Irving in England; of Menken, Stier, and Strok in Germany. According to Irving, Christ possessed original sin but no actual sin. By the power of the Holy Spirit, he suppressed the flesh and gradually purged it so that finally only spirit remained.

c) The conception of Schleiermacher. According to Schleiermacher, the work of Christ consists in His taking believers up into the communion of His life—that is, in part into communion with His powerful God-consciousness, in part into the enjoyment of His perfect salvation. The former is called redemption, the latter reconciliation. The suffering of Christ consisted in nothing other than sympathy with human guilt and in patiently bearing the evil that the sinful world inflicted on Him. While He thus suffered with sinners, at the same time He was completely at peace with God.

Those who become members of the church of Christ receive some of this same life, which knows itself to be at peace with God; they are redeemed and reconciled. Guilt as an objective relationship toward God is not at all taken into account. For Schleiermacher, sin is merely the ascendancy of world-consciousness, or the flesh, over God-consciousness, caused by the fact that the former develops earlier, and if the God-consciousness is awakened, has already gained an influence that prevents the latter from coming to its fullness. The punishment that is linked with sin is not recognized as such by Schleiermacher. Punishment is only the natural consequence of sin. In the exercise of His work as Mediator, Christ has become a partaker in the consequences of sin that was not His own sin. Thus He has become acquainted with suffering as separable from personal sin. Those who are brought into the fellowship of His life also become acquainted with it as such, with the result that they no longer feel it to be a disturbance of their salvation. Their reconciliation consists in this. It is not reconciliation with God but a reconciliation with the suffering of this life.

80. *What objections are to be brought against these mystical theories?*

a) That they reverse the scriptural order. This order is that man cannot be delivered from sin as a power if he is not first freed from guilt as a burden outside himself. These theories maintain that guilt cannot be removed other than by the power of sin being broken within man himself.

b) Everything that belongs to the sinful past of the man delivered in this way is simply consigned to oblivion, as if a just demand of God did not attach to that past. However, if guilt can only be removed by taking away sin, and the sins of the past can no longer be taken away, then the guilt of the past must forever continue to testify against us. One can only get past this consideration by pushing aside the entire scriptural notion of guilt.

c) All these theories limit the efficacy of the satisfaction of Christ (if His work may still be called that) to the period after His incarnation and suffering. Salvation becomes a mystical process tied to the humanity of the Savior as actually existing. The human life of Christ cannot be effective before it actually existed. Given that, it follows that all generations living before the incarnation of Christ, both in Israel and among the pagans, have died off unredeemed and unreconciled—contrary to the express testimony of Scripture, which assigns a true salvation to God's covenant people already under the old dispensation based on the suretyship of Christ.

d) The attribution of an actual sinful nature to Christ makes Him utterly unfit to be able to be our Savior. This is not only the case when one adopts our legal standpoint, but would still have to be the case even on the standpoint of Irving, Menken, et al. By the power of sin in His nature, the person of Christ, too, must become unavoidably sinful. A sinful person, however, cannot save himself. To claim this is equivalent to Pelagianism. To claim the opposite, that the human nature of Christ can be sinful without His person sharing in that sin, amounts to Nestorianism.

e) This entire conception of the work of the Mediator fits within pantheism, as appears most clearly in the beliefs of Schleiermacher. Here sin, punishment, guilt all become unavoidable conditions. Instead of being an expression of the righteousness of a personal, transcendent God, the suffering in the world becomes a necessary state of affairs in nature. When man is reconciled, this does not consist in a legal acquittal by which he is relieved of suffering for his sins, but in stimulating a fresh consideration of this suffering so that man learns to recognize that suffering is not punishment. This terminology of Schleiermacher, then, is completely misleading. What he calls reconciliation would have much more properly been called redemption.

81. On what important issue do many who otherwise share our view of satisfaction depart from the time-honored doctrine?

On the point of the basis of the imputation of our sin to Christ. We have seen earlier how realism and traducianism, when they are used to explain the transmission of hereditary guilt and hereditary corruption, lead to insurmountable problems in Christology. It is surely well established that Christ assumed our nature from the flesh and blood of the Virgin Mary. If original sin is automatically transmitted with this nature, then it was also transmitted to Christ. As for corruption, one may avoid that by referring to the purification of this nature by the Holy Spirit before it was assumed. For guilt, however, the situation is completely different. That cannot be waived by some act of power, and if it continues to exist, it also makes the purification of the nature impossible. If Christ has sinned in Adam, then God cannot justly purify human nature on His behalf. For if He can do this with Christ, He would also be able do this with every sinner, and then salvation through payment for guilt would be unnecessary.

Despite these substantial objections with which realism and traducianism are burdened, many not only retain these positions, but in more recent times it is claimed from more than one side that they provide the key for understanding the solidarity of the Savior with us. To be able to bear our sins, it is argued, He not only has to possess our human nature but, moreover, has to share in the first act of original sin, so that it can be rightly affirmed that He does not assume sin alien to Him but that of a race in which He shares personally. One sees that this view is considerably different from that of Irving and his followers. According to Irving, habitual sin was inherent in Christ; according to the advocates of this view, there was only adhering guilt. The Holy Spirit purified His human nature such that this hereditary guilt did not result in hereditary corruption. So Christ could suffer for us as sinless, and it could nevertheless be affirmed that it was not an absolutely alien guilt that was imputed to Him—for at one point, the point of His own hereditary guilt, He shared in that guilt personally.

82. Why is this conception utterly untenable?

     a) It rests on a weakened conception of hereditary guilt as the source and root of all evil. One thinks that hereditary guilt can be attributed to Christ and that everything else can be denied to Him. That is to nullify the organic bond there is between hereditary guilt and inherent corruption, not only in a real but also in a legal sense. Whoever keeps this close bond in view, and is deeply imbued with the conviction that no sin of any kind may be attributed to Christ, will instinctively recoil from making the origin of all sin, the guilt of Adam, to adhere to Christ. By this, a dangerous line is crossed. Scripture speaks of that guilt as fully sin, as disobedience, and contrasts it with the obedience of Christ as the second Adam.

b) Those who champion this opinion think that the close bond between hereditary guilt and inherent corruption can be abolished by an act of God's power, by the purification of His human nature by the Holy Spirit. This, however, is a fallacy. If the guilt of sin in its consequences can be stopped by such acts of power, the entire work of the Mediator is superfluous. God can then do the same for every sinner and thus render harmless the consequences of guilt. However, He deals with the Surety not according to power but according to justice. Thus a justification must lie in back of the sanctification of human nature. If one goes on to accept that, then it becomes immediately clear to what disastrous consequences this false idea leads. We then have a Surety who must first be justified and sanctified—and that on the basis of his own merits, as it were by their imputation in advance, before He could intervene for us.

c) The great error of this conception is that one does not take with sufficient seriousness the notion of covenant attribution. This free attribution that unites Christ and us, initially separated, into one body, not only for suffering but for the entire future, must remain the point of departure. The apostle does not teach us that Christ could be made to be sin for us because He was already guilty, but that He who knew no sin was made to be sin for us so that we might become the righteousness of God in Him [2 Cor 5:21]. Because, however, this mystery, which came to pass in the counsel of God, has been lost sight of, all sorts of other means are seized on to fill its vacant place. Then realism and traducianism must serve to eliminate the problems that arise.

And if one looks more closely, one will note that in the end nothing is gained by this. Surely, one will not be able or want to deny that Christ has been a divine person from eternity. If now He is not capable of suffering for our sins by sharing in our nature without partaking in our personal guilt, then we may rightly ask whether in fact He is capable—as purely God, without sharing in our nature—of assuming that nature by a legal act and identifying with us in such a manner that now guilt for Adam's sin also becomes His own. In other words, there is not only an attribution of Christ to us but also an attribution of us to Christ, and that took place in principle when Christ entered into our nature. Now, if the latter can be free without having to be based on unity in nature, then why not the former as well?

83. *Does the priestly work of the Mediator consist exclusively in His satisfaction, or does something else belong to it?*

Belonging to it as well is intercession, mediating activity, or being an advocate.

84. *Which words in Scripture indicate this intercession to us?*

a) He is said to appear now in the presence of God for us, ἐμφανισθῆναι (Heb 9:24).

b) It is said that He intercedes for us with God, ἐντυγχάνειν (Heb 7:25).

c) He is called our Substitute or Advocate. He is α παράκλητος, Paraclete (1 John 2:1). One should note that the word *paraclete* is used in a double sense in the New Testament. It is originally a passive form and means "someone who is called to help"—that is, an advocate. Since, however, an advocate can also take the place of someone whom he helps, the word at the same time also takes on the meaning of "substitute." It is so used of Christ in the passage just cited (1 John 2:1): "And if anyone sins, we have an advocate (a substituting intercessor) with the Father." This is the first meaning.

At the same time, the word is taken in a somewhat different sense when Christ calls Himself "Paraclete" for believers and promises them the Spirit as another Paraclete (John 14:16): "And

I will pray to the Father, and He will give you another Paraclete, that He may be with you forever." Here the Paraclete is "counsel-giving advocate." The Holy Spirit, too, is now called a paraclete in this sense, especially because He fills the place of Christ with believers now that Christ has departed. Of course, the principal work of the Holy Spirit as Paraclete is to bring comfort, but the translation of the word itself as "Comforter," however common, appears to be incorrect and cannot be justified. Παρακαλεῖν does mean "encourage," "comfort," but παράκλητος is a passive, not an active, form. The explanation that most presently give it and that is supported by this active form, namely, "counselor," is also that of Augustine, Calvin, Beza, Lampe, and many others. The concept "comforter" is too narrow.

85. What is the significance of this intercession of the Mediator?

Already in the Old Testament, the high priest had not finished his work when he had performed the sacrifices. The blood, as the principal part of the sacrifice, had to be presented before Jehovah in the holy place or the holy of holies, and only by doing that was full atonement accomplished so that he could return to bless the people. The sacrifice, once brought, must be kept in remembrance constantly by the sprinkling of blood, and by being kept in remembrance must effect the continuance of the favor of God for the sinful people.

This is also the essence of the significance of the intercession of the Mediator. It is not the case that His sacrifice, once brought, was a forgotten or lost fact by which God in the past removed some obstacles but whose power no longer continues. Such a view would fit the governmental theory of satisfaction but not a system based on Scripture, in which satisfaction retains its full validity. God's righteousness, which is an always-active impulse in His being, rests now and rests forever in Christ as the meritorious sacrifice. For the divine consciousness, the memory of satisfaction is continually present, and the demands of righteousness and the sacrifice of obedience continually come together in the person of the Mediator. That Christ ascended into heaven and appeared in the place where God's glory dwells means that He presented His sacrifice to the Father, and on the part of the Father that He received it, accepted it as well pleasing. Christ did not come there as an isolated person who had left behind Him what had taken place on earth. The entire priestly activity that He had performed here below clung to His person. He came in a strictly official capacity. And as the Father's consciousness of justice now rests on Him in this official capacity with satisfaction, so Christ in His priestly consciousness comprises all the past experiences, all the struggle endured, all the accomplished merits of the priestly ministry in order to place them before God. This is in Him an act that continues permanently, is not interrupted for an instant, and His divine omniscience enables Him to perform it. All of the gifts that come to believers from God result from the harmony of this twofold consciousness. They are claimed by Christ on the basis of His merits and granted by the Father on the basis of those merits.

But there is more than this. Christ not only presents His own work in the abstract, but the specific needs and prayers of believers are also included in His consciousness, so that all that is impure and imperfect in them is removed and they appear as sanctified before God. That is why they pray only in the name of their Lord Jesus Christ, which means more than that they appeal to His past. They also rely on His living activity for the present. Therefore, they expect every blessing and every gift through their Lord Jesus Christ, which again means more than that they find the basis and effective cause for this in His historical work of satisfaction. They also believe in a presently existing causality for it, joined with the former. One is dealing here with realities, and should avoid every appearance that these are merely abstractions or ideal relationships. Scripture takes these matters with full seriousness and derives from them a compelling reason to approach the throne of grace with complete confidence. We can do that, not only because Christ's work once completed is behind Him and its fruits now follow of themselves, but much more because He now still lives and works to produce its fruits. That our weaknesses will find pardon and strengthening is likewise derived from this. Christ is a compassionate High Priest, who still carries the memory of weakness and suffering in His human consciousness, who can therefore put Himself in our circumstances and can have the merciful compassion for us that is entirely unique in its kind (Heb 4:15–16).

86. How then can you paraphrase this intercession of Christ?

It is the steadfast will of the Mediator by which He presents His satisfaction to the Father and keeps it in His remembrance, and by which He claims its particular application for all the members of His body.

87. Do we know much about the specific manner in which this intercession is made?

As good as nothing of this has been revealed to us, and we can also say very little about it because of our faulty conception of heavenly things in general. In this regard, one must again be on guard against two extremes. On the one hand, there have been those who, from the impossibility of giving concrete content to the idea of intercession, have drawn the conclusion that they were dealing here only with an abstraction. Accordingly, it is said that "Christ intercedes for us" is the expression in Jewish ceremonial form of the idea that the fruits of His merits benefit us. This, however, is an undue nominalism, for in the things of God it is the case that realities correspond to such ideas. God does not comfort us with abstractions; and when we pray on the basis of the intercession of our Mediator, that is not self-deception. And God does not accommodate Himself to our limited comprehension, but reality corresponds to our conception. If one will not acknowledge a real intercession, then everything that we are taught about the high priestly sympathy of the Mediator becomes meaningless. And once it has become permissible to let this matter evaporate into an idea, then one will also be able to presume this same right with regard to many other things of which we also cannot form a concrete conception. One can certainly ask why it is still necessary for Christ to present His merits and recall them to the Father, since the Father surely knows from eternity what these merits are and from eternity is disposed to grant their validity. With equal right, however, one could ask why it is necessary for the Father and the Son to negotiate formally with each other in the counsel of peace, since for them each other's thoughts are clear and open from eternity. Whoever indulges in such questions and considerations will quickly see his concept of God harden into the rigidity of pantheism. He is left with a God through and in whom nothing more occurs. Our first thought, therefore, should not be, "What is necessary for God?" Reasoning in such a way, we could set aside intercession along with many other things. Rather, we should ask,

"What is becoming and appropriate for God?" Then Scripture teaches us that there is a heavenly existence of forms, in which the thoughts of God are majestically embodied. Heaven is the place where all that is humanly faulty and untrue remains banned but from which, nonetheless, in no way does what is true and purely sensory about those forms—which are also prevalent among us men—need to be excluded. Thus we must not form an all-too-spiritual and meaningless conception of the things of God.

All this, however, is not said to cause one to lapse into the other extreme, where the Lutherans have ended. They think they have to insist that this intercession is *vocalis, verbalis, et oralis*—that is, with voice, words, and mouth, concerning which many other things are assumed. We have no right to go so far—not because such things are impossible in themselves, or unworthy of God, but simply because Scripture makes no mention of them. In what has been said above, we think we have given the sense of the biblical data correctly. We do not know how exactly these things occur, and it is of relatively little importance as long as our conception of the heavenly things must also remain vague and nebulous in other respects.

88. *Can you show from some Scripture passages that something like what is described above in fact takes place?*

Romans 8:33–34, "Who shall bring any charge against the elect of God? God is the one who justifies. Who is He that condemns? It is Christ who died ... indeed, who also intercedes for us" (ὃς καὶ ἐντυγχάνει ὑπὲρ ἡμῶν).

Acts 2:33, "Being therefore exalted to the right hand of God, and having received from the Father the promise of the Holy Spirit, He has poured out this, which you now see and hear." Here the outpouring of the Holy Spirit is linked with the fact that Christ appeared before the Father in heaven. Only when He entered the holy of holies through the torn veil could the great gift, acquired by His sacrifice, be distributed.

Luke 22:31–32, "Simon, Simon, behold, Satan greatly desired to have you that he might sift you like wheat, but I have prayed for you that your faith may not fail." This is an instance of particular intercession.

Isaiah 53:12, "Because He poured out His soul to death and was numbered with the transgressors, and He bore the sins of many, and interceded for the transgressors."

89. *In how many ways has Christ exercised this work of intercession?*

Two different ways are usually distinguished, corresponding to the two states of the Mediator.

a) Intercession made here on earth, which through the nature of His entire work in His state of humiliation was itself also given the form of a humiliation. Christ prayed then on the basis of His merits, made eternally certain by His suretyship, but at the same as a supplicant who humbles Himself, both in His inner mood and in His outward gestures.

b) The intercession made in heaven since the ascension of the Lord, which is no longer accompanied by humiliation but by majesty and regal glory.

90. *Who are the persons whom this intercession benefits?*

Lutherans are accustomed to make a distinction between the universal intercession of the Mediator, which applies to all people, even those who are lost, and His particular intercession, in which only believers share. They mainly appeal for this to the prayer of Jesus on the cross for His enemies (Luke 23:34). Of course, this view is closely connected with the entire Lutheran system. In the specific sense, Christ can only make intercession for the elect, for His intercession is not a mere beseeching where it remains uncertain if it will be heard, but it is an ever-active steadfast will, which the Father is always ready to oblige. Therefore, intercession extends as far as the saving fruits of satisfaction reach. This, of course, does not exclude that Christ otherwise has also prayed for those who are excluded from this specific intercession. Compare with the text mentioned above, John 17:9–20, where the scope of intercession is indicated for us both positively and negatively: "not for the world ... for those who are sanctified by Him, and for all who will believe in me through their word."

91. *Can anyone other than Christ make intercession for us?*

No. If His intercession is nothing other than the continuation of His priesthood and its ideal conception, then it will immediately follow that one who is not a priest also cannot make efficacious intercession before God. Only the one who has sacrificed may appear in the sanctuary. Since

now, however, the Roman Catholic church has repristinated the priesthood and has the sacrifice of Christ repeated, it has by analogy with that
also invented a multitude of intercessors. It canonizes certain so-called
saints, to whom it attributes a degree of excess in merits and refers to
them as intermediaries able to influence God. With the basis on which
this doctrine rests, the dogma of the *opera supererogationis* [works of
supererogation], the doctrine of the intercession of the saints itself also
falls. It is true that Scripture stirs believers to pray for each other and
to intercede before God—and the Hebrew word for "pray," הִתְפַּלֵּל, even
means "intercede"—but by this is not meant an official act of an office,
only an intercession by brothers, who are equal, for each other. One can
request the intercession of a brother but may never interpose him as a
mediator between God and one's own soul. This would be deification of
man. There is but one Mediator, who can bring our prayers before God,
and every notion as if there were others who could do something like
this unavoidably leads to clothing these persons with divine attributes.
The Roman Catholic public actually conceives of its saints as omniscient,
omnipresent, etc.

92. *By what is the priestly office of the Mediator in intercession
    distinguished from the work of the Holy Spirit as Paraclete, as that is
    described especially in the Gospel of John?*

Both activities, that of Christ and that of the Holy Spirit, are designated
with the same words (e.g., Rom 8:26–27, "The Spirit Himself makes intercession for us with inexpressible groanings [ὑπερεντυγχάνει στεναγμοῖς
ἀλαλήτοις]; "because the Spirit intercedes for the saints with God [ὅτι
κατὰ θεὸν ἐντυγχάνει ὑπὲρ ἁγίων])." Still, there is a great difference between the two. The intercession of the Holy Spirit is not an intercession
that takes place outside of believers, but one that is made by them in
themselves. They themselves pray by the Holy Spirit, or the Holy Spirit
prays from within them. The work of the Holy Spirit in the economy
of salvation is precisely to identify with believers and to dwell within
them. It is otherwise with the intercession of Christ, which takes place
outside the believers and remains sharply separated from their own
prayers. Therefore, we do not pray to the Holy Spirit but to Christ, and
not by Christ but by the Holy Spirit.

King[2]

93. What is the kingly office of the Mediator?

His official appointment and activity on behalf of God to rule and protect His church.

94. Is Christ already king apart from His mediatorship?

Yes. As sharing in the Divine Being, He also possesses from eternity the royal power over all creation that belongs to God. This continues with His true deity through all that befalls Him. In a strict sense, however, one cannot speak of this as a *munus regium*, a "kingly office." After all, an office always presupposes delegated authority exercised in the name of another. Divine kingly power is absolute. Hence one was accustomed to speak of a *regnum essentiale*, an "essential rule," and place next to it the *regnum personale*, the "personal rule." The latter, then, means the official kingship of the Mediator.

95. Can one delineate further within the mediatorial kingship itself?

Yes; it includes more than one aspect.

Dominion over the church that the Mediator exercises by His word and Spirit. He prescribes laws by virtue of His office. He sees to it that these laws are lived up to by the working of His Spirit. All office-bearers in the church derive their authority from Him and receive their appointment from Him. Nothing can be done with authority without this authority being granted by Him. Christ received this kingship when He was appointed as Mediator in the counsel of peace. As far as its essence is concerned, it was not tied to the actual performance of His suretyship, for this essence has existed from the first beginnings of the church on up to the incarnation as well as afterward. It is called the *regnum spirituale*, the "spiritual kingdom," because it is established by spiritual means and is governed by spiritual power alone. "Spiritual" here, however, is to be understood in a deeper sense. The act of regeneration is also a spiritual act and one of the spiritual means by which Christ rules as King. Nowadays, people have become too much accustomed to an excessively

---

2   There is a "King" heading here in Vos' manuscript, but earlier "Prophet" and "Priest" headings were not present.

ethical conception. Concerning this *regnum spirituale,* the following can be distinguished:

1. Its *basis.* This consists in the salvation or redemption of believers by Christ. He has paid the ransom for them, and through this they enter into a wholly unique relationship with Him. They are no longer their own possession but with body and soul the possession of Jesus Christ.[3] Faced with His will, they have none but only unqualified submission. Whether they live or die, they are the Lord's. In this way, the believer stands in a totally unique relationship to Christ, unlike the relationship in which He stands to the Father and the Holy Spirit, and which ultimately can only be explained by the deity of the Mediator.

2. Its *nature.* It is a spiritual kingdom, but that notwithstanding, a real kingdom. That is, no external physical force is used, as is the case with the kingdoms of this earth. But neither does everything in it happen according to the dictates of a permissive love. There is authority, power, and sovereignty—in the first instance in Christ and then entrusted by Him to His servants.

   It is most necessary to keep this in view in order to avoid wrong conceptions concerning the essence of the visible Church. It does not originate from a voluntarily arrived-at contract that its members enter into mutually until its termination at a later point, so that in time one can withdraw from it. That theory is not applicable to the state, much less to the Church. One does not join the Church from desire or inclination but as a subject of the kingdom of the Lord, conscious of one's obligation to have fellowship with other subjects and to acknowledge the servants of the Lord. This position, if it is well thought out and consistently applied, is naturally rich in its implications. Among other things, it includes that the Church does not lose its power over a person if this person deliberately leaves its bounds. In an earthly kingdom, nobody would think a subject is free to terminate its dominion. The state does this, not the individual. Neither is one free to withdraw from the Church arbitrarily. The Church retains its power (within the limits prescribed to it by God) as long as it

---

3   See the Heidelberg Catechism, question and answer 1.

has not loosed the subject of the Lord, and it cannot relinquish the exercise of its discipline. Whether the secular government is willing to acknowledge this right is irrelevant. Christ has granted to His Church an independent right that does not first need to be enacted by secular law. It is better for the Church to violate the command of secular government than to leave unfulfilled the commandments of its own King.

3. Its *scope*. To the spiritual kingdom of the Lord belong all those whom He has redeemed or if according to the rule of the word of God we have to assume that to be the case; therefore, all believers. Still, not all of them stand in the same relation to Christ the King. All of them are subjects and, to that extent, equal. But some of them are more than subjects; they are also servants with official authority. However, this authority of the servants in the kingdom of God is not a magisterial but a ministerial power. That is, it is not absolute but bound to certain regulations that God has revealed in His word and illuminates by His Spirit. Only Christ Himself has absolute power—that is, the right to act as He sees fit—for He is the only King. But within these limits, the servants of the kingdom still have real authority with all its aspects. They have not received this authority from the people, although the people choose them. This power descends from above and does not arise from below. One must guard against being led astray by the prevailing ultrademocratic ideas concerning the source of civil authority into making the Church into an absolute democracy. That the Church is not. Its servants are accountable not to the Church as such but to Christ. The Church is a kingdom.

4. Its *significance*. The kingdom of the Savior may never be viewed as a utilitarian institution that exists entirely for the individual. This conception of the state is also widespread and sometimes transferred to the kingdom of Christ. The state, however, is much more than that sort of institution. It is one of the independent organisms that God has created, a body that, like all bodies, has meaning in itself. The state exists to realize certain things that cannot be achieved by the individual: to administer justice, to represent visibly God's virtues as ruler. The same may be said about the kingdom of the Mediator. It may not be viewed solely

as a well-organized association set up entirely for the expansion of power but apart from that is lacking any positive value in itself. The Church exists to embody and represent in visible form the dominion of King Christ. On the basis of God's Word, it must organize itself and prescribe certain laws. It does not have the freedom to live without restraints, without there being something of the resemblance of a kingdom in its visible form. It is not permitted to organize its laws according to the changeable conditions of the world. The principal features of its government are given in Scripture and outlined in the organization of the apostolic church, and that pattern has binding authority. Within those principal features there may be a certain latitude, but they themselves may not be eliminated.

5. Its *duration*. Christ did not first acquire His rights as King over all believers by the actual act of redemption but already by assuming His work as Mediator. Hence this spiritual kingdom also reaches back to the first days of creation. As soon as there were believers, the exercise of dominion by the Mediator began. Although the form of that dominion may have changed according to the different dispensations of the covenant of grace, its essence was the same. Also, for the future, this kingdom will remain the same for all eternity as to its essence. It cannot cease to exist any more than believers can cease to be the property of their Savior. As Christ is Priest and Prophet forever, so also will He be King eternally (Psa 89:4, 36–37; Luke 1:33; Dan 2:44–45).

6. Its *instruments*. Ultimately, its instruments are the Word and the Spirit. Through both, Christ is present in His church. Here attention should be paid to the fact that the Spirit works along with the Word. When the dominion of Christ is exercised by His servants, that does not mean that the Mediator Himself is at a distance in a deistic manner and absent from His place of jurisdiction, for it is He who engenders both authority and respect, both in ministers and in subjects of the kingdom.

7. Its *epochs*. A distinction is made between the *regnum gratiae* and the *regnum gloriae*, the "kingdom of grace" and the "kingdom of glory." The latter begins on the day of judgment. It will be distinguished by the fact that it includes all believers in the same state

of glory and none but believers, since the separation between wheat from chaff will have taken place. Christ will no longer rule by providing Himself with servants but will exercise His kingly power in His own person. His power will be perfected in His subjects, and nothing more will be lacking in the full unfolding of the kingdom of heaven.

96. *What is the connection between the two concepts of Christ's headship and kingship over the church?*

a) *Headship* is the term for the mystical union that exists between Christ and believers. It expresses an *inward* relationship between Christ and those who belong to Him. *Kingship* is the term for the legal unity present between Christ and believers by authority and obedience. It thus expresses an *outward* relationship.

b) Headship also concerns the church as a whole, but is nevertheless established in such a manner that each of the members is connected to Christ with a separate bond and only through Christ joined to the brothers. The peculiarity of kingship, on the other hand, lies in the fact that one stands before Christ the King only as a fellow-subject in connection with the brothers. A multitude of subjects is essential to the idea of a kingdom.

c) Headship is not an official but an organic concept. Christ is King on behalf of the Father, so that the outlook of His kingship is upward as well as downward. On the other hand, He is the Head not so much in relation to the Father but in relation to the members of His body.

d) Nevertheless, both things are not to be separated from each other. Headship serves kingship, for precisely because Christ is organically one with His people He can govern and rule them outwardly. Conversely, this outward dominion also serves to implement His headship until finally it will become fully realized, and all those who were reckoned in Christ will be brought in as members of the body. Also, in the Old Testament the word "head" occurs with both meanings: (1) organic head; (2) royal ruler.

97. *In how many senses does Scripture use the expression "kingdom of heaven" or "kingdom of God"?*

It is well known that the designation βασιλεία τῶν οὐρανῶν, "kingdom of heaven," usually occurs in Matthew's Gospel. In Mark and Luke, one only finds βασιλεία τοῦ θεοῦ, "kingdom of God." The latter designation is also found in John and Paul. The addition "of heaven" serves to indicate the heavenly origin and the heavenly character of this dominion. The Mediator, who was anointed as King, was in heaven from eternity and has returned to heaven, and heaven is the center of all His activities. This corresponds to the fact that the coming of the kingdom is equated to the coming of Christ. He also possessed this dominion earlier, but in secret, and only let it be represented by kings—David's descendants—as types. He was only known as the future King. As the covenant of grace had indeed already long existed and yet can be said to have been instituted by the coming and sacrifice of Christ, so too for the kingdom of heaven these things do not exclude each other. From out of heaven, as it were, the king has brought His royal worth with Him in order to reveal it (cf. Gal 4:26, "But the Jerusalem that is above is free, which is the mother of us all").

Furthermore, the word βασιλεία can have three meanings:

a) Kingly worth or kingship. Compare 1 Corinthians 15:24, "when He will have delivered over the kingdom to God and the Father," and Matthew 16:28, "until they will have seen the Son of Man coming in His kingdom" (i.e., "with His kingship"). "Your kingdom (= kingship) come!" [Matt 6:10; Luke 11:2].

b) The kingly realm extensively, thus kingdom in the proper sense. This is meant when speaking about entering into the kingdom of heaven or being cast out of it.

c) The sum of the obligations and privileges that come with being a subject in this kingdom. So it is said that we must seek the kingdom of God, that it can be possessed by us, that it is a treasure, a pearl of great value, etc.

98. *What kingdom has Christ received besides this* regnum spirituale
[spiritual kingdom]?

The *regnum potentiae*, the kingdom of power. This extends over the entire universe. According to Matthew 28:18, to Him has been given all authority in heaven and on earth. The apostle says that God has seated Christ at His right hand in heaven, far above all rule and authority and power and dominion and every name that is named, not only in this but also in the coming world (Eph 1:20; cf. further Phil 2:9–10; and Psa 8, with Heb 2:6–9). Concerning this kingdom of power, we should note:

a) That Christ has not always possessed it but first received it after His ascension, when He went to sit at the right hand of God. The spiritual kingdom has always existed from the first beginning of the church; this kingdom of power began with the third stage of Christ's exaltation. From this it follows, in the second place:

b) That it will cease when its goal is reached. This is taught by the apostle in 1 Corinthians 15:24, 28. In the end, the Son will hand over the kingdom to the Father when He will have destroyed all dominion and authority and power, in order then also to be subjected Himself to the One who has subjected all things to Him, so that God may be all in all.

c) The specific purpose of this all-encompassing kingship is found in the spiritual kingship that Christ has over His Church; Ephesians 1:22, "and gave Him as Head over all things to the church." This entails: (1) Christ is the Head of the Church; (2) as such He is above all things, exercises unlimited dominion.

d) More specifically, this unlimited dominion is necessary to protect the Church from its enemies. The Church is in the midst of the world and still has the evil of the world in its own bosom. So, if it is to be secure, then its Head must have dominion over the world. Its history is intertwined with the history of the world. Consequently, only who governs the latter will be able fully to lead the former. Christ has therefore assumed dominion over the world for the benefit of His Church. He exercises it on behalf of God, for this kingdom of power, too, is and remains an official kingdom.

e) That Christ received this kingdom of power at the same time had consequences for His spiritual kingdom, since, as the exalted God-man, He can now by His Spirit also work everywhere in order to assert even the power of His exalted humanity.

f) Also, for Christ Himself this royal power has the significance of a reward, which He received for His redemptive work. Scripture calls it an inheritance, which the good pleasure of the Father assigned to Him as Son (Heb 1:2). It was the person of the Mediator who, according to both His natures, received this kingly majesty: according to His human nature, because it was perfectly glorified; according to His divine nature, because it can now radiate all its splendor unhindered by His humanity, which previously had been the cause of its concealment.

CHAPTER FIVE

States

1. *What is a state and what must be understood specifically by the states of the Mediator?*

A state is the relationship to the judicial power within which one stands. One needs to grasp this concept precisely and to distinguish it clearly from every other concept. Without a relationship to a judge that determines a state, one could not speak of a state. A sinful condition can always be conceived of as an inherent quality, even if there were no God in the world—although, of course, sin as a condition would then assume a different character. But guilt is completely inconceivable without a God before whom one stands guilty. Guilt, then, is a state. In its original meaning, then, a state is nothing other than an imputed condition. The condition effects the state as it reflects back upon us in the judgment of God. When God takes note of our condition and accordingly determines our relationship to His justice, He assigns a state to us. So, when God created Adam pure, he was in a state of rectitude, and when he had sinned, he was moved by God's judgment into a state of guilt. In both cases, the state was nothing other than the objectification of his condition.

Now, however, since guilt is a state—that is, an objective relationship—God, by grace, has been able to permit the transfer of the state of one person to another who becomes a Surety for him. Where this transfer takes place, then the situation occurs that the state is not only distinguished from the condition but also that they are not in accord.

This was the case with Christ the Surety. His state—at least the state of humiliation, the state of being guilty by the effective imputation of God—was transferred to Him from those whose Surety He became. With regard to His condition, He was completely perfect and without sin; with regard to His state, He was completely guilty and cursed. And conversely, the state of righteousness into which He entered by the satisfaction He made is transferred from Him to believers, so that they, although being in a sinful condition, still, with regard to their state, stand before God as those who are fully justified.

However, we must go one step further. As state originates from condition, it also produces a condition. Whoever is in a state of guilt before God must, unless that state is removed from him, enter into a condition of misery. And whoever is in a state of justification before God must enter into a condition of salvation and glorification. Thus it is the case that state, although it is to be sharply distinguished from condition, is still sometimes used of a condition, but then only insofar as it is a direct consequence of the state that is reflected in it. Christ was not limited to the state of obligation for guilt or the state of righteousness. A corresponding condition was joined to both.

2. *How then can we further describe "state" as specifically applied to the Mediator?*

A state of the Mediator is the status in which He stands as Surety before the justice of God, along with its corresponding condition.

3. *How do you define the state of humiliation?*

The state of humiliation is the status of guilt of the Surety before the justice of God as that is manifest in the corresponding condition of misery.

4. *How do you define the state of exaltation?*

The state of exaltation is the status of righteousness of the Surety before the justice of God as that is manifested in the corresponding condition of glory.

5. *Who is the subject of the state of humiliation?*

This is none other than the person of the Mediator, the Son of God. His humiliation does not refer to a nature in the abstract but is something that applies to the person. Here, too, Scripture begins with the divine person (Phil 2:7–8).

6. *By what is the state of humiliation brought about?*

By the act of humiliation. Christ humbled Himself and freely entered into the state that He had taken upon Himself through His suretyship.

7. *Which two parts are further distinguished in this act?*

It is customary, on the basis of Philippians 2:7–8, to make a distinction between:

    a) Κένωσις, "emptying."

    b) Ταπείνωσις, "humiliation."

By *emptying* we understand the act of the person of the Mediator by which He submitted to the assumption of the human nature in the form of a servant, without this human nature being equipped with the glory befitting His divine Person.

By *humiliation* is understood the subjection of the so-assumed submissive human nature under the curse and the demand of the law.

8. *What judgment is to be made about the question whether the incarnation of the Mediator in itself belongs to His humiliation?*

Opinions diverge considerably on this point. Authorities may be produced for two views. On the one hand, one points to the language of Scripture. The apostle says Christ has emptied Himself (ἑαυτὸν ἐκένωσεν) by assuming the form of a servant (μορφὴν δούλου λαβών). How this is to be understood is then further explained by the words, "being made in the likeness of men" (ἐν ὁμοιώματι ἀνθρώπων γενόμενος). So it seems to be established without question that the μορφὴ δούλου is nothing other than the human nature as such, and to assume it was, according to the apostle, an emptying of Him who was in the form of God. Accordingly, the incarnation is thus the first step in humiliation.

On the other hand, one has rightly pointed out that the Mediator never again puts off His human nature and now also possesses it in His exalted state. Now, if the possession of the human nature as such were a humiliation, then Christ would remain eternally humiliated. So it appears that the express witness of Scripture conflicts with its no-less-clear pronouncement of the exalted state of the Mediator.

9. *In what way may these two truths be reconciled with each other?*

First, we must distinguish properly between human nature in the abstract and human nature in a specific form. Although human nature, as Christ possesses it following His exaltation, is suffused fully by the radiance of His deity and is transformed into a suitable organ of revelation, still it was not in fact the human nature that He assumed in the incarnation. Now, from this one can certainly draw the conclusion that the assumption of human nature in itself or in the abstract need not include humiliation. But then one may never forget that abstract nature without specificity never exists. What Christ assumed was our nature in a specific form, the form of servanthood, yet not one as it has become weakened by sin. The act of assumption itself occurred with the purpose of making that nature an instrument of servanthood and was already a humiliation. Conversely, in His exalted state, the human nature of the Mediator is raised to a degree of glory that goes far beyond the glory of the first Adam and far exceeds that to be received by the redeemed.

10. *To what extent did the divine nature share in this act of self-humiliation?*

The deity assumed human nature in the unity of the person, so the latter is something that belongs to the divine person. Now, however, humiliation is included for a person who is God if He has something in Himself that is imperfect and subservient and in which His glory cannot shine through fully. Hence it appears further that humiliation is certainly possible without a change of condition, for in the blessed condition of deity no change can take place. It was a humiliation of relationship, originating through relationship to humble humanity.

11. *Was not the Mediator's appearance as Surety, prior to His incarnation, already a part of the state of His humiliation?*

No, for the μορφὴ δούλου, "the form of a servant," of which Philippians 2:7 speaks, was not associated with that appearance. Christ did not put Himself in the position of one guilty but only promised that He would be willing to assume this position. The effective imputation of guilt had not yet begun. And the activities that the Mediator carried out prior to

His incarnation did not bear the character of humiliation; they were all anticipations of His prerogatives as Mediator to be obtained through His humiliation.

12. *What is intended by* μορφὴ δούλου *in Philippians 2:7?*

As demonstrated earlier, it means: (1) neither the essence of God nor (2) the state, the position, of God in Himself, but (3) certainly the form or mode of revelation for others—thus that in which the essence unfolds itself outwardly. Now, this text teaches that prior to His incarnation Christ possessed the form of God—that is, His likeness as a whole revealed His deity; essence and form agreed with each other fully. By the incarnation, however, He assumed the form of a servant, the μορφὴ δούλου. Δούλος here means nothing other than man as servant and forms a contrast to θεός, "God." By also assuming human nature—as all men possess that as a subservient form—with His deity, the *Logos* acted such that one could no longer designate His form as entirely corresponding with the essence. There was now something in Him that was no longer in conformity with His divine essence, and that was His humiliation. Thus the expressions used by the apostle agree completely with the description above that we have given of the concept *state*.

13. *What are the stages of the state of humiliation of the Mediator?*

These are summed up differently by different persons, without there being an essential difference. It is otherwise with the difference that exists between Reformed and Lutherans on this point and to which we return below. We can sum up the stages of the state of humiliation in order as follows:

   a) Incarnation, including birth

   b) Subjection to the law

   c) Suffering of death

   d) Burial

   e) Descent into hell

14. *What may be noted concerning the incarnation in particular?*

   a) That it relates to the *Logos* and not to the triune God as such. Thus to express ourselves properly we must not say, "God has become human," but, "the *Logos* has become flesh." It is not the being of God as existing in the Father and the Holy Spirit that has assumed human nature but the being of God in the existence mode of the Son.

b) Nonetheless, the entire Trinity had something to do with this incarnation because it was an "external work." The Father, the Son, and the Holy Spirit worked together here, and each of these three worked in His particular way, carrying out the task that was appropriate to His place in the Trinity.

c) The incarnation was not so much something to which the *Logos* was subjected and that was done to Him by another as it was something to which He subjected Himself and He did Himself. Thereby it received its value before God and made up a part of His passive as well as active obedience.

d) The incarnation takes place from the Virgin Mary. In ancient times, that had to be maintained against Docetism. In later times, it has become necessary to emphasize that in opposition to the Mennonites, who only grant that the *Logos* assumed flesh in Mary without there having been a real connection between His human nature and ours except for their similarity. We believe that the Mediator not only has a nature like ours (sin excepted) but also has taken a nature, derived from ours, *from* that nature.

e) It was an incarnation. As was touched on earlier, that includes two things:

1. Not only a body, but a reasonable soul, was assumed from Mary. The term *flesh* in Scripture, when it appears in a connection like this, never means the body in itself but body and soul in their organic union. This does not mean, however, that the human soul of the Mediator separated itself in a realistic mode from the soul of the Virgin Mother or in a traducianist mode was transplanted through an action of her soul. Rather, as in other cases the soul is organically united to the body, which develops from the body of the mother, so too that occurred with the incarnation of the Mediator. His human soul was created by God, not apart from the body in order to be united with it but rather in the closest union with the body.

2. From Mary the Mediator assumed a human nature, not a human person.

f) The incarnation occurred from the *Virgin* Mary—that is, without the participation of a male—through an immediate, immanent action of the Holy Spirit. And that is so for the following reasons: (1) Because all sin must be excluded down to the root in the origin of His human nature. Sexual intercourse between a man and a woman is tainted with sin. (2) Because what is personal in human nature, it would seem, is linked with the act of generation by the father, wherefore this act, where a human person did not need to originate, must be omitted. Whether Mary knew a man after the birth of the Savior from her and whether the brothers of the Lord, who appear in the Gospels, were really His brothers in the ordinary sense of the word, is a question about which there is a great deal of dispute and which, dogmatically as well as exegetically, does not appear to be susceptible to a solution and moreover is of secondary importance.

g) The incarnation is accompanied by a sanctification of the human nature received from Mary. Luke 1:35 teaches us this: "Therefore (that is, in accordance with the fact that the Holy Spirit will come upon you, inferring back from the result to the ground), that holy one who will be born to you will be called God's Son." That the Son of God must be born of Mary as a *holy something* (neuter: τὸ γεννώμενον ἅγιος) makes necessary a special action of the Spirit. If we now knew precisely how the stain of sin transfers to human souls at their origin, then we would also know how to identify precisely in what the specific work of the Holy Spirit consisted when He purified the human nature of the Mediator. Now, however, we know little concerning that and must limit ourselves to conjectures, and the present point remains in the dark. That the body must be kept pure from certain affects speaks for itself; for although no sin lurks in what is bodily considered apart from its enlivening, it nowhere exists outside of union with the soul, and something that is of physical or physiological origin can become sin for the soul. Consequently, there is a connection between soul and body by which the latter pollutes the former—not only by having something in itself for which the soul, as the seat of personhood, becomes responsible, but also by making the soul sinful in itself. Finally, the most generally accepted opinion is that the sinful condition of human souls, which already dates from conception and birth, takes its origin in the withholding of the Holy Spirit on account of original sin. In all three of these respects one may speak of a purifying activity of the Holy Spirit.

15. *Where do Roman Catholics seek the basis for the sinlessness of the human nature of the Mediator?*

In the "immaculate conception of the Virgin Mary." The decree of Pope Pius IX (promulgated in 1854) says "that the doctrine that states that the Blessed Virgin Mary, from the first moment of her conception on, by a singular grace and privilege from Almighty God, in view of the merits of Christ Jesus … has been kept from every stain of original sin, is a doctrine revealed by God, and therefore must be certainly and continuingly accepted by all believers." One may note that here the stain of original sin is spoken of, but of course the absence of actual sin is also intended. The latter was in fact already taught by Augustine, although he had posited original sin in Mary.

Against this view are the following preponderant objections:

a) It contains a contradiction. Mary is freed from the stain of original sin because of the merits of Christ. The merits of Christ, however, are only for the guilty. So, then, Mary was guilty.

b) If it was necessary for the immaculate conception of Christ to assume an immaculate conception of Mary, then one can with equal right require an immaculate conception of Mary's mother in order to maintain hers. And so one would regress infinitely. Conversely, if it is sufficient to curb the stain of sin in the conception of Mary, then it is equally sufficient to curb it in the conception of Christ, and one need not go back further.

c) In order to be thought through consistently, the immaculate conception of Mary would have to be an entirely miraculous conception as with Christ Himself—that is, without the participation of a male. The Roman Catholic church itself, however, does not yet teach this.

d) The roots of this doctrine do not lie where they lie according to Rome's pretensions. It does not in the first place have to do with protecting the sinlessness of Christ. The interest that one has in this doctrine is concentrated in Mary herself. The place that she has come to occupy in the idolatrous veneration of the Church makes her sinlessness imperatively necessary. To posit her as sinful and still to venerate her *as such* would be an anomaly. In practice she stands above Christ and in theory is beneath Christ—what the Holy Spirit is, in fact, according the Scripture. The dogma elevates Mary above the natural connections of humanity, but it does so because she no longer occupies her place within humanity. She was taken up into the heavenly divine economy, deified.

16. With what is the assertion that the incarnation was not a humiliation for the Mediator usually connected?

With the pantheistic idea that God and man are not essentially different from each other but have an affinity for each other.

On the contrary, however, modern kenosis doctrine, itself pantheistic in origin, has explained the incarnation itself as a extinction or emptying of deity.

17. Do the poverty and the outwardly insignificant setting in which Christ was born also belong to His humiliation?

Certainly. One has wanted to deny this on the superficial ground that poverty is no shame. This, however, is a misunderstanding. For a person who only lives in this sinful and cursed world, it may not involve a particular reproach to be poor; in itself, poverty is a consequence of sin. Man is not disposed to suffer want and to make do with little. He has been created to rule and to possess. Especially for the king of the universe, it was a humiliation to be poor.

18. What does the subjection of Christ to the law mean?

That He, from the beginning of His incarnation on, has freely surrendered Himself to the curse as well as to the requirement of the law of God in order to fulfill all passive and active obedience. Subjection to the law does not begin later than the incarnation but coincides with it in the same point of time. What, however, is simultaneous in time is separated logically.

19. What follows from the fact that this subjection to the law already began with the incarnation?

That the suffering of the Mediator does not date from the end of His stay on earth. In fact, subjection to the law includes suffering, since its subjection is to the curse as well as the requirement of the law, and the two may not be separated. It appears from His circumcision that Christ, as concerns the requirement of the law, subjected Himself not only subsequently but from the beginning. And it is rightly observed that the blood of the Savior's circumcision is as much atoning blood for us as is the blood shed on Golgotha. His entire life was a continual suffering. Accordingly, in enumerating stages we have made a distinction between subjection to the law and the suffering of death.

20. How, further, must the suffering of the Savior be distinguished?

a) The first distinction is that between the suffering that He bore His entire life and the suffering of death at the end of His life. This is a distinction in gravity. It was the purpose of Christ to bear fully the wrath of God against sin, to undergo both temporal and eternal death. But just as with man and in humanity the process of death takes a slow course, likewise the burden of the wrath that death brought upon Christ intensified by degrees. There was an increase of the power and the force of death upon Him, an increase that accelerated as He came closer to the end of His earthly life. Thus, shortly before His transfiguration on the mountain, He could say to His disciples, "I must depart in order to suffer," as if only now was the suffering to begin. This, however, was not so. He suffered before that time as well.

b) One may distinguish between suffering of body and of soul. Here one must take care not to stress either one of the two one-sidedly but to retain them both in their indissoluble connection. Earlier, one has sometimes looked too much at the bodily suffering, while it is well established that not blind pain as experience but precisely pain accompanied by distress of spirit and consciousness of guilt as Surety that constitutes the essence of suffering.

At present, many incline in the opposite direction and maintain the hyperethical demand that a spiritual thing, as sin is, must also be atoned for by exclusively spiritual suffering, that what is physical is by its nature not adequate to counter the ethical. This, too, is a half-truth that becomes an untruth. Our body is not merely an appendage but belongs to our being. So if there is to be punishment for sin, this organic connection of our being requires that it also affect the body. And this is all the more the case since it is always the soul that suffers in the body, since the body as bare matter, considered naturally, can feel no pain. It is thus necessary to hold to both—to the suffering of the body and to that of the soul.

c) One can distinguish according to the causes of suffering:

1. The suffering that flows from His servitude to the law. The contrast between the deity of His person and the servant-form of His human nature must be one of the causes of suffering.

2. The suffering that arose from the contact He had with the sinful, corrupt environment of mankind. For a holy soul, every expression of sin that it observes must be painful. For a soul that was conscious, as Surety, of bearing the guilt of men, every memory of the magnitude of their guilt must cause pain.

3. The suffering connected with the prospect of the bitterness of His final days for the Savior. He not only had a clear grasp of the immense extent of the guilt but also of the intensity of the punishment consequent on that guilt. In every sacrifice brought under Israel's ceremonial worship, He could contemplate an image of that guilt and a prophecy of His own pains. Already from of old He saw Himself pictured with the most vivid characteristics as a man of sorrows, visited with illnesses, from whom everyone hid their faces, who must endure in anguish and judgment [Isa 53:3]. Accordingly, He spoke of a baptism with which He must be baptized and of a pressuring with which He must be pressured until it would be completed [Luke 11:50]. This suffering of death lay in the background of His consciousness throughout the entire time of His stay on earth.

d) One can make a distinction concerning the *kind* of suffering and then speak of an ordinary and an extraordinary suffering. Under the former, then, is understood the pain that came upon Christ mediately through the different causes of misery there are in the world. All that was just detailed under 3 can be called suffering in this ordinary sense—not as if it would not have to be distinguished in gravity from the suffering of others, for in this respect the suffering of the Mediator was always extraordinary, completely unique in kind, but insofar as it was brought about through ordinary causes.

Scripture teaches, however, that besides this ordinary suffering, there was an extraordinary suffering that assailed Him through the direct and immediate action of God. God specifically permitted our unrighteousnesses to be laid on Him with great violence. What took place in Christ was not at all a natural process of misery; it was not the unavoidable consequence of His participation in our nature. There was a positive element in it that may only be explained by a positive action of God. To this belongs, for example, the temptation by Satan in the wilderness, to which the Lord was led by the Spirit "to be tempted" [Matt 4:1]. As was the case for His suffering in Gethsemane, it is written that the angels came and ministered to Him. Later, too, the evil one appears to have been at work on Him, for we read that he left Him for a time (Luke 4:13).

Above all, however, the suffering in Gethsemane and on the cross belongs here. No natural causes are sufficient to explain the degree of suffering that was wrestled with by the Mediator in these two places. This is spoken of in the strongest expressions. He sweated drops of blood, felt Himself abandoned by God, was astonished and deeply alarmed. In Greek, the words used here are ἐκθαμβεῖσθαι and ἀδημονεῖν [Mark 14:33], which originally mean "terrified," "driven wild." It was for these reasons that we spoke earlier of an efficacious imputation of guilt to the Mediator. This latter suffering is completely incomprehensible to us because nothing like it falls within our consciousness. Parallels may be produced for ordinary suffering; any resemblance for this suffering is lacking (cf. Zech 13:7; Isa 53:5, 6, 10).

21. *When we speak of the suffering of death, does that only mean the separation of the soul and body for the Mediator?*

No. This expression must be understood to be not only about that temporal death but also eternal death. Christ must bear death fully insofar as it was threatened as punishment for sin and insofar as His sinlessness makes that possible. Now, as was noted earlier, the concept of death includes three things:

a) Separation of the source of life for the soul so that it becomes a spiritual death. There can be no thought of that with Christ, for the condition of spiritual death is a sinful condition.

b) Separation of the source of life for the body, because the soul can no longer retain it in its organic connection. This was also the case with Christ.

c) Separation for the consciousness from any favor and a full awareness of the infinitely severe wrath of God. This is eternal death, and we believe that this too befell Christ.

22. *Can we state precisely in what this eternal death consisted for the Mediator and in what sensations it manifested itself?*

This eternal death belongs to the extraordinary suffering that befell Christ and so is of course inexplicable. As human nature existed in Him in a completely singular manner, so this suffering must have also assumed a completely unique form that we cannot imagine for ourselves. We may only make the following observations:

a) This eternal death was certainly an exact equivalent of what the sinner himself will have to pay to God if he is personally punished, but in its nature it is not the same. If with Witsius we assume that there are four elements in the eternal punishment of the lost— (1) privation of divine love, (2) sense of the divine wrath, (3) the worm of conscience, and (4) despair—then it appears that at least the latter two cannot be attributed to Christ.

b) Eternal death also does not consist in the personal union between the *Logos* and His human nature being terminated. This union cannot be broken, and would, were it broken, have caused the entire work of redemption to fall to pieces.

c) Nor can eternal death consist in the deity of the Lord being abandoned by the Father. The bond among the three persons of the Divine Being is not susceptible to being broken or disrupted.

d) That also means that eternal death cannot lie in the love of the Father and His divine good pleasure being withdrawn from the person of the Mediator. Just when He drank in the bitterest aspect of this death in obedience and suffering, He was for that reason an object of greatest good pleasure to God, a sacrifice of sweet-smelling aroma to the Lord. Witsius says of this, "To be the beloved Son of God and at the same time to bear the wrath of God are not such contradictory things that they could not coincide. For as Son, as the Holy One, who obeyed the Father in all things, He was always the beloved—yes, more than ever when He was obedient unto the death of the cross, for this was so pleasing to the Father that He has therefore raised Him to the highest degree of honor (Phil 2:9). Although laden with our sins, He felt the wrath of God burn, not against Himself but against our sin, which He had taken upon Himself." Expressed otherwise, even in the moment that He died an eternal death, His active obedience was not permitted to be separated from His passive obedience, and by the former He was still the object of the good favor of God.

e) Positively, it can be said that eternal death manifested itself for the human consciousness of Christ in the feeling of being forsaken by God. Since now, however, the person for the human nature was the Son of God, this consciousness could have no reality to it if the humanity had not momentarily lacked the conscious comfort that there was for it in this personal unity with God. Thus it momentarily missed an awareness of divine love, felt the full divine wrath, and cried out, "My God, my God, why have you forsaken me?" [Matt 27:46]. Still there was not an element of despair in this, for were that so, we could no longer explain the "my God." One who is lost would call, "O God!" Also, the "why" may not be taken as indicating ignorance, for the worth of the suffering lay just in the fact that Christ knew why He was thus abandoned. Owen says: "These words express wonderment, not ignorance or unbelief or complaint. Christ knew very well why He was abandoned in this hour and had perfect faith and confidence in His

Father. ... But He was astonished and silenced in the experience of His unspeakable anguish."

23. Was it necessary that the Mediator died a temporal death?

Yes, for this constitutes an essential part of the process of death, by which God's righteousness is avenged on sin. If the concept of death is separation, dissolution, then this characteristic must come to light in the strongest possible way. Hence soul and body must be torn apart. Still, one may not view this temporal death as the end of the process, for in those lost a union will follow separation. Soul and body will be reunited, and only then will they experience in themselves the full working of eternal death. With Christ, too, eternal death acted on soul and body while these were not yet separated from each other. But the sequence with Him was different; first came eternal death, then temporal death.

24. Was the form in which this temporal death came upon the Mediator immaterial?

No, it must strike Him in such a form that the meaning of death would thereby come to light. If it had been a death by blindly operating secondary causes, one could have taken it for a calamity. Or if in the zeal for God that consumed Him, Christ had caused His own suffering and death, one could then have seen in that the ideal of a martyr's glory. Both these ideas, however, are excluded, for:

a) He did not die by accident but was formally condemned and executed by both clerical and secular power. Whether or not this was a just action makes no difference here, for legitimate government speaks with God's authority even when it passes sentence unjustly. Thus by its verdict the death of Christ was a legal death. It thereby came about that the sentence was pronounced by the highest power in the world of the day, by the Roman government. If now, finally, one bears in mind that the Romans were the people of law and justice par excellence, then one will understand that in no other way could the significance of the death of the Lord been shown so clearly than in the manner in which it happened.

b) He was not executed in a relatively reputable way by beheading or a similar execution, which would express a certain sparing of the condemned. Were this the case, then one could think that the punishment applied not so much to Himself as to the onlookers; it was then more a display than an execution that bears its meaning in itself. But He was crucified—that is, the curse and the God-forsakenness of His death have found expression in the mode of His death. For the Romans, crucifixion was the most despicable form of punishment, by which only slaves and the most heinous criminals were punished. A crucified person was an infamous person. Although punishment by crucifixion was not Jewish, the Jews still had something that corresponded with it in principle— namely, the hanging on a tree of one already condemned to death and executed. Regarding this, Deuteronomy 21:22–23 states, "And if someone has committed a sin worthy of death and is put to death and you hang him on a tree, then his body shall not remain on the tree overnight, but you shall by all means bury Him on the same day, for the one hung is cursed by God (כִּי־קִלְלַת אֱלֹהִים תָּלוּי), so that you do not defile your land which the LORD your God gives you as an inheritance." The thought contained here appears to us to be twofold:

1. By elevating and publicly displaying the body on a tree, most of the time in a naked condition and in the most shameful way, the criminality and heinousness of the transgression are displayed. Here the punishment is also in conformity with the essence of sin. As inwardly shameful as the latter is, the former is outwardly notorious.

2. The one hanged was, as it were, expelled from the earth and hung in the air as one cursed and disposed of from before the face of God. From ancient times, the land was holy to Jehovah. As a result, whoever highly offends Jehovah must not only be killed but also distanced from the holiness of the Lord. He was a personified curse, and even after he was elevated above the earth, such an odor of curse emanated from him that before the evening arrived he must be taken away in order that the land not be defiled.

We find both these strands in Christ. He suffered as one marked by infamy and as one forsaken by God, as one cast off. And it is on that ground that Paul says in Galatians 3:13: "Christ has redeemed us from the curse of the law, having become a curse for us, for it is written, 'Cursed is anyone who hangs on a tree.' " The law expresses a curse on all transgressors. The law depicts the essence of this curse by the shame it assigns to the greatest criminals. This arrangement was a type and looked forward to the Mediator, who as Surety would suffer as one who is most guilty. This type has found its antitype in the cross of Christ. And inasmuch as in that cross, as in a single point, it is displayed the clearest, the cross of our Savior has become the meaning-laden symbol of His mediatorship and of all of Christianity.

Judaism has grasped that significance instinctively. The two principles—salvation through curse and suffering and salvation through the fulfillment of the law—are irreconcilable. The cross is the death of the law as a means of justification, the abrogation of the legalistic dispensation, the dissolution of the salvation-by-works [werkheilig] covenant between the sinner and the law. The crucifixion of the Mediator is therefore an offense to the Jews, and from this fact is already to be explained that the Apostle Paul gives the cross such a central place. He is brought to that by his polemic against salvation-by-works Judaism. This was not a conflict about a minor point but a conflict about the essence, the heart of religion, about the point of justification. Here, too, God has consequently used historical conditions in order, by way of antithesis, to place this central truth in the immediate foreground. In Jewish legalism, the sin of unbelief is brought to its deepest expression. In contrast, Paul must inevitably reach for the most pointed manifestation of the other principle, the utter helplessness of and curse upon man. And by doing that, he reached for what is true not just for that time but what is true for all times, the heart of the matter as long as there are sinners to be justified. And led by the Holy Spirit, he became the eloquent apostle of the cross.

One cannot better sense the antithesis between Judaism and the cross than when one recalls the Jewish exegesis of Deuteronomy 21:22-23. Their explanation is that the one hung is a curse before God—that is, a shame and one marked by infamy before God, something by which He is dishonored and blasphemed. The genitive אלהים is thus taken as an objective genitive. And by that they think to have passed judgment on the cross of the Mediator. That is the typical expression for the offense of the cross (for what is developed here, cf. Gal 6:14; 5:11; 2:20-21; 1 Cor 1:23).

25. *Does Scripture also present the cross of the Mediator to us under still other viewpoints?*

Yes. Although what has been said is the main point, the cross appears here and there under one or another aspect.

a) The elevation on the cross was the symbol of elevation above the narrow limits of Jewish particularism. By the cross, an end is made to the dispensation of the ceremonial law. From now on, salvation comes to Jews and Gentiles alike. The ascension of the Lord had the same meaning, for, exalted above all, He is the savior of all believers. So in a most meaningful way, Holy Scripture links to each other the two—the crucifixion and the ascension—in order under this viewpoint to posit them as in principle the same exaltation; John 12:32–33, "And I, when I will be lifted up from the earth (on the cross and by the ascension), will draw all men to myself (that is, all sorts of men)." One should bear in mind that this statement was spoken on the occasion when certain Greeks wished to see the Lord (vv. 20–21). "He said this signifying the manner of death He would die" [v. 33]. A similar thought is present in Hebrews 13:12–13, "Wherefore Jesus too … has suffered outside the gate. Let us then go out to Him outside the camp, bearing His abuse."

b) The elevation on the cross was also a public display, not only as a divine punishment (already pointed out above) but at the same time as a liberating act. Sin masks its true character. God displays it in all its terrible consequences. It begins its dominion with a lie. God begins His triumph over it by maintaining the truth. For this view of the cross, compare John 3:14–15; Romans 3:25 ("Whom God has displayed"); Colossians 2:15 ("Having disarmed the authorities and powers, He has openly put them on display and in doing that, triumphed over them").

26. *Did it emerge from the conduct of Christ Himself that His death must take place in such a way?*

Yes, for He expressly explained that as long as all these circumstances were not yet a fact and suitable for sacraments, His hour had not yet come. Consequently, it was not irrelevant how and when He died. He had a time, a particular hour. The crucifixion was predicted along with what preceded and belonged with it. So the scourging (Isa 50:6; 53:5); the disrobing (Psa 22:18); the crucifixion with the piercing of hands and feet (cf. vv. 16–17).

27. *Does the burial of Christ belong to the state of His humiliation?*

Yes. This is shown from the following considerations:

a) Being laid in the ground as a return to dust is a punishment threatened for sin. On account of the unity of the person, everything that happens to the body must be seen as a humiliation of the soul. Soul and body are really separated by death and rent asunder, but nonetheless continue to belong to each other. The bond is not broken for eternity. It is the same body that will be raised that was first buried, however much flesh and blood may be changed. Now, if this humiliation of the body is a punishment for sin, then it also could not have been otherwise for Christ. One need only keep in mind what was said above concerning the concept of a state in order to see immediately that the burial belongs to the state of humiliation.

b) The state of exaltation begins with the resurrection, for according to the representation of Scripture it is the public justification of the Mediator by which He obtained acquittal from punishment and the right to eternal life. Now, however, acquittal and the awarding of rights as judgment necessarily precede actual release and the real communication of privileges. If we must now assume that the burial did not belong to the humiliation, then we would have to assume that it was either an intermediate state— neither humiliation nor exaltation—or that it belonged to His exaltation. The first view, however, is as little possible as the second, for if the work of the Mediator was in fact completed, then it was inappropriate that He must wait for exaltation. The justifying pronouncement must immediately follow satisfaction, for the righteousness of God does not tarry.

c) We have already come to recognize earlier, as a fixed general rule, that the facts of salvation as they follow each other in the Mediator find a sort of shadow and repetition in the order of salvation [*ordo salutis*], by which His benefits are appropriated by believers. If Christ is crucified for sins, the sinner is crucified to sin and the world; if Christ has risen for the justification for all His own, the sinner, too, rises out of his spiritual death in sin to walk in newness of life with Christ. There is a dying off of the old and an enlivening of the new man.

We have now only to ask whether the burial of the Mediator also has a similar shadowing and, if so, to which of the two series it belongs: to the doing away of the old or to the origin and development of the new. If it falls within the first series, it will then also have to be reckoned in Christ to the state of His humiliation, for the state of humiliation had just this purpose: to do away with the old, the guilt and the power of sin. The apostle teaches us in Romans 6:4 that we are buried with Christ through baptism, in death, so that as He is raised from death by the glory of the Father, so we too should walk in newness of life. That is to say, our old man is put to death and perishes completely in that death, and that is reflected in the symbolism of baptism. This, however, is in connection with the death and burial of Christ. This connection can lie in the fact that in the death and the burial of Christ the old man of the sinner is done away with *legally*. In this regard, the burial appears as the extreme realization of death. Accordingly, "Christ was buried" says: He has died completely, through and through, been taken away from among the living, removed from their midst. Only through the burial of a dead person does it become obvious that he is gone, that he is no longer numbered among the living. Christ, as the Surety taking on guilt, must be buried in order that the curse of God would come upon those who are guilty fully, and it, in their Surety, would be completely done away with from before the face of God. That this was less a suffering than a symbolic declaration is beside the point. What we maintain in the first place is not that the burial of the Savior belongs to His suffering as that it must certainly be reckoned to the state of His humiliation.

d) The separation of soul and body in the Mediator, and its continuing separation, was certainly something abnormal, an imperfection, and every imperfection had for Him the character of humiliation and so also belongs to the state of humiliation. From this viewpoint, one can even maintain that staying in the grave included a certain measure of suffering for the Savior. The soul was conscious that its body, which had to be viewed as belonging with it, was humiliated and certainly felt the dishonor of this humiliation. Although a state of dishonor is not in itself suffering, still the sensing of that state becomes a matter of suffering.

e) In prophecy, Christ is strikingly introduced as one who confidently expects His deliverance from the power of the state of death but nonetheless also perceives that He has come under the power of that state. Peter in Acts 2:25-31 and Paul in Acts 13:34-35 apply the passage in Psalm 16:10 to the Mediator. Both teach that the prophecy came true when Christ rose from the dead. Therefore, what constituted His deliverance and the object of His confidence was not that He would not die but that He could not be held by death. He was certainly given over to death but not abandoned or left in death. From this it also follows that being given over in death was the ultimate limit of humiliation—that is, that burial, descent into the grave, brought His humiliation as far as it could go. That Christ rose, not that He sank into the grave, was the beginning of His deliverance.

f) The word "humiliation" in itself already contains a powerful argument for the Reformed view. In its original sense, it means *localiter* [locally], "to go below." Movement downward in Scripture, however, is always a symbol of dishonoring, as movement upward expresses being honored. This metaphor is hardly accidental. It rests on the order of creation that goes from above to below. God is said to dwell above us; the cursed spirits dwell in the depths. Man is drawn up out of the dust of the earth, and that is his honor. When the curse of sin smites him, he must go back below again into the dust. This order would have to be completely reversed if the burial may no longer be validly considered as humiliation.

28. *How does this view comport with the Savior's crying out from the cross,* τετέλεσται, *"It is finished"?*

a) One has rightly noted that this cry may not be understood as if it strictly excluded all further suffering and all further humiliation. If this were so, one would arrive at the absurd position that giving up the spirit, actually dying, did not constitute part of His suffering. When the Savior cried out as He did, He had not yet died, for shortly before His death He still cried out with a loud voice. The cry is thus a cry of expectation. After He had given up His spirit and closed His mouth, He could no longer speak, and so He spoke beforehand, without desiring to exclude the suffering of temporal death and the dishonor of burial.

b) What was finished was not the full suffering of humiliation but the active bearing of pain. The word "finish" already includes that in itself. What occurred after this finishing was more something that happened to the Mediator than something that He did Himself. He gave His spirit over into the hands of the Father— that is, relinquished control of His body. Whatever happened now with the lifeless corpse, the soul no longer senses in and through the body.

29. *By the death of the Savior, was a separation made between His divine person and His body?*

No; His deity remains united both with the separated soul and the buried body. So, too, what occurred with His body in humiliation is attributed to the person of the Mediator.

30. *Does Scripture itself also present to us the burial of the Savior in this light (as a humiliation)?*

Yes. The Savior Himself has presented His resurrection after a stay of three days and three nights in the heart of the earth as a sign like to that of Jonah the prophet. Now, with Jonah there are two considerations:

a) A living sojourn in the fish. Although he was swallowed up, he did not thereby perish. Likewise, the Lord was surely swallowed up by death; He still did not perish from that. He saw no corruption in the grave [Acts 2:27].

b) At the same time, it was a deliverance for Jonah and for the Mediator when they were freed from their dungeon. If there were no deliverance here, there would be no sign.

It is true that as in many other cases, here, too, the type falls short of the antitype; for Jonah was not really dead but only as good as dead and buried, while for the Savior burial was in fact the seal on His death and its realization.

31. *Is there unanimity concerning the last stage of the humiliation, "the descent into hell"?*

No; opinions on this diverge greatly. The difference concerns the following two points:

a) Whether the descent into hell, of which the Apostles' Creed speaks, is to be regarded as a real descent to the place of demons and the lost or to a similar place, or should be understood less realistically.

b) In connection with this, whether the descent into hell is to be reckoned to the state of humiliation, to that of exaltation, or to an intermediate state that follows the humiliation and precedes the exaltation.

32. *How does the expression at issue here read in the creed?*

In the received form, it reads in Latin, *descendit ad inferna*; in Greek, κατελθόντα εἰς τὰ κατώτατα. Some manuscripts have *ad inferos* (masculine plural). The Greek form sometimes has εἰς ᾅδου or εἰς τὸν ᾅδην.

33. *What can be established concerning the antiquity of these words in the Creed?*

They appear for the first time in the text of the creed given us by Rufinus (390) and in the text of the church of Aquileia, not in the old Roman form. Likewise communicated to us by Rufinus and dating from before the year 341, the old Roman form read, "was crucified under Pontius Pilate and buried; the third day He rose from the dead." The form of the creed that we find in Marcellus of Ancyra, which is likewise earlier than the year 341, reads similarly. The Church of Hippo Regius in Africa, where Augustine was bishop, possessed the Apostles' Creed without this article around the year 400. In addition to this, even in the churches of the province of Aquileia two other forms were used, perhaps of an older date than the form given by Rufinus, in which the article on the descent into hell is lacking. Rufinus himself says, "One should know that in the Creed of the Church of Rome, this addition, '*decendit ad inferna*,' is not found." Also, the churches of the East do not have these words. The force of the expression, however, appears to be the same as what is contained in the statement that He was buried.

34. *What is apparent from this historical overview?*

a) That the article "descended to the lowest places" is of relatively late origin. It is not found in the oldest forms of the creed accessible to us.

b) That also the explanation of the words was at the same time uncertain. Rufinus speaks of it with an "appears," as if to him the sense was not entirely clear and indubitable.

c) That we can dismiss for ourselves the complicated historical question what the words originally meant in the Apostles' Creed for the person who first inserted them. It is not even certain whether the one who did this attached a particular thought to the expression. In any case, this is not the place to speak of what is historically correct. When we acknowledge the Apostles' Creed as a part of our confession, we do so with the understanding that it may have the sense that our other creeds give to it. Only what official view the Reformed Church has formed of the words needs to be considered here.

35. *How many views are there concerning the meaning of this article of faith?*

Five and still some:

a) The *Roman Catholic* view. When His soul was separated from the body, in this soul Christ went to the *limbus patrum*—that is, the border region of the Fathers, the place where souls who had died previously find themselves. The purpose of His appearance in this place was to bring these souls into heaven. The place of glory could not be open for them previously because the true Christian sacraments, which actually communicate grace, were lacking under the old order. There was at that time no genuine and perfect salvation, and that lack was supplied through the saving act of Christ.

b) The *Lutheran* view. In the Formula of Concord, this is described as follows (article IX):

"A dispute has arisen among those who have subscribed to the Augsburg Confession concerning this article: When and how did our Lord Jesus Christ, as our catholic faith teaches, descend to hell? Did this occur before or after His death? Further, one has asked whether He descended only according to His soul, or only according to His deity, or actually in body and soul, and whether this occurred spiritually or bodily. Also, it has been disputed whether this article should be reckoned to the suffering or to the glorious triumph of Christ. Now since this article, as also the preceding, can be comprehended neither by our senses nor by our reason, but must be accepted by faith alone, we have unanimously approved that there shall be no dispute concerning this point, but that one shall believe and teach it in all possible simplicity. Let us in this respect follow the godly teaching of Dr. Luther, who in his sermon at Torgau in 1533 has unfolded this article in a most godly manner, cutting off all curious questions and awakening all Christians to the godly simplicity of faith. For it should be enough for us to know that Christ descended into hell, destroyed hell for all believers, and that by Him we are snatched from the power of death and of the devil, from eternal condemnation and even from the jaws of hell. But in what way these things have come to pass, let us not ask about that curiously but rather await the knowledge of these things in another world, where not only that mystery but also many other things will be made clear— things that we must simply believe here, things that go beyond the reach of our blind reason."

This still sounds very modest. In reality, however, what is intended is an "actual, real and supernatural movement" of Christ, "by which having wrestled Himself free from the shackles of death and having again become alive, He went with His entire person to the underworld in order that He might show Himself to the evil spirits and damned men as victor over death" (Hollaz). Christ also preached in hell, but it was not the preaching of the gospel of salvation but rather a legalistic preaching of damnation.

c) The view of Aepinus (1499–1553) and others. According to Aepinus, Christ had traveled to hell really and locally to endure hellish punishments there in our place. This descent had reference only to His soul, as also, for that matter then, the orthodox Lutherans do not appear to want to deny that Christ's body remained in the grave. With Aepinus, the descent into hell in the strictest sense falls under the humiliation.

d) The view of Ebrard, Schenkel, and many recent theologians. They maintain that Christ went to Sheol to preach the gospel there, not in the Lutheran sense of a preaching of curse, but with the goal of converting the inhabitants of Sheol. Sheol (שְׁאוֹל; Greek ᾅδης) is not hell as the place of final damnation but the realm of the dead in which Old Testament believers at one time were gathered with pagans and unbelievers from Israel after their death and in which dead pagans are now located with unbelievers who die among Christians. At present, the doctrine of the so-called probation after death is voiced in this explanation of the *descensus*.

e) The view among the Reformed that explains the *descensus* as the hellish anguish that Christ has suffered in His soul, especially in Gethsemane and on the cross, when He felt Himself forsaken by the Father. Thus our [Heidelberg] Catechism, question 44; Calvin, *Institutes*, 2:16, 8–12; Wollebius, Bucanus, Wendelin, Burman, Voetius, Pictet, Polanus; more recently Dr. Kuyper, who also gives his own explanation of the order of the articles in the creed. That the descent into hell comes after the death and burial has its basis, according to Dr. Kuyper, in that eternal death follows temporal death and burial for the lost. What Christ has done for us is summed up here in the same sequence as would have taken place if we had had to bear it personally.

f) The view among the Reformed that explains the descent into hell as a forceful expression of the fact that both in body and soul Christ found Himself in the state of death. That He descended into hell simply means to say He entered fully into the state of death. The Westminster Larger Catechism, 50, asks, "Wherein consisted Christ's humiliation after His death?," and answers, "Christ's humiliation after His death consisted in His being buried, and continuing in the state of the dead, and under the power of death till the third day; which hath been otherwise expressed in these words, He descended into hell." Charles Hodge (*Systematic*

Theology, 2:616–17) defends this view with an appeal to the derivation of the English word "hell" from the Greek ᾅδης, which means
"what is invisible," "what is covered," as well as by explaining the
insertion of this article in the creed from an attempt to illumine
further the article on the burial. According to A. A. Hodge, the
article intends to say nothing other than that Christ has really
died: "Crucified, died, buried, dead-dead!"

g) With many Reformed theologians, one finds the fifth and sixth
opinions combined. They allow for the descent into hell, which
concerns the person of the Mediator, to apply partly to the body
and partly to the soul. It means that in His body the Mediator remained in the Sheol of the earth and in His soul suffered hellish
pains. So Olevianus, Witsius, Mastricht, and many others.

36. Does Scripture itself speak of a descent into hell?

No. The expression in Latin and Greek that is translated by these words
reads, as we said above, "*descendit ad inferna*, κατελθόντα εἰς τὰ κατώτατα,
descended to the lowest parts." This expression appears to be derived
from Ephesians 4:9, "This 'He ascended,' what is it other than that He
had also descended to the lower parts of the earth (εἰς τὰ κατώτερα μέρη
τῆς γῆς)?"

To understand what the apostle intends with these words in
Ephesians 4, one must compare the immediately preceding citation
from Psalm 68:18. This psalm pictures how Jehovah, after having under-
taken a victorious expedition against His enemies, returns in triumph
to His dwelling on the top of Zion. He has brought with Him booty from
the war, which He, as kings are accustomed to do, distributes among
His servants. This all has significance as a type, the apostle assures
us. Jehovah's going up to Zion was a type of the ascension of the Lord.
His expedition coming down from Zion and His struggle with enemies
found their antitype in the gigantic struggle of the Mediator with the
power of sin death and darkness. The distribution of the spoils of war
represented the giving of the gifts of the Spirit, from which everyone
receives from the measure of the gift of Christ, by which some are
equipped to be apostles, others prophets, etc.

From this, it is now apparent what the apostle will have understood by the words "descend to the lower parts of the earth." It simply

serves to show that Christ has not gone to heaven without the fruits of His glorious victory. He ascended, but not without something having preceded. He first went down for battle. The ἀνέβη may not be viewed as a stand-alone act but must be viewed in the light of the preceding κατέβη. This ἀνέβη, "what is it other than that He had first descended to the lower parts of the earth?" The one who descended is Himself also He "who ascended above all heavens so that He might fill all things." The fullness of the gifts, then, which the Mediator has at His disposal following His ascension, is measured by the apostle according to the depth of His humiliation. Because He came down to the lower parts of the earth, therefore, having ascended above all heavens, He could fill all things, and as the identical person who had lived through all these things (καὶ αὐτὸς, v. 11) give apostles, prophets, etc.

One sees that for the apostle the expression εἰς τὰ κατώτερα μέρη τῆς γῆς is the measure of the humiliation of Christ. Given that, however, it becomes wholly unusable for Roman Catholic and Lutheran dogmatics. For in both, one is accustomed to view the descent into hell as a triumph belonging to His exaltation and not as a humiliation into the depths of the world of the spirits for a personal struggle with Satan within his very own domain. The triumphal exaltation *here* is the ascension—and not the ascension of Christ's separated soul from hades to paradise, which one has imagined, but just *that* ascension on which the outpouring of the gifts of the Spirit followed, the ascension from the earth on the 40th day after the resurrection. This already provides us with the occasion to make the point from which the ascension begins as the endpoint of the descent, for both are commensurate in depth and height for the apostle. As deep as He has descended, so high has He ascended. The expression itself leads us to the same thought. It means "the lower part of the earth." The earth has two halves: a visible side, on which the living walk, and an invisible side, in which the dead lie, namely, the grave. Christ has descended even to the invisible lower part of the earth. He was laid in the dust of death, not in parts under the earth, the underworld, but in the lower part of the earth itself.

That we are correct to understand the words in this way may be proven, finally, from their origin. They are derived from Psalm 139:15, where the poet says that he is wondrously wrought "in the lowest part of the earth" (בְּתַחְתִּיּוֹת אָרֶץ), that is, in his mother's womb. This is designated as a hidden, invisible place. Therefore, one need not assume that here Paul, too, means a mother's womb by the lower parts of the earth and so would have thought of the incarnation from Mary as the deepest humiliation. Psalm 139 is poetic, and the mother's womb appears there not as something *low* but as something *hidden*. Here, on the other hand, where the comparison is between ascending and descending, a spatial image must be assumed. Thus Paul very appropriately chooses the burial of the Savior as the image of His deepest humiliation in order to place it over against the ascension as His greatest exaltation. Nothing is said of an actual descent to the place of the lost or the demons.

37. *Is not a local descent into hell taught in 1 Peter 3:18-19?*

In the Greek this passage reads: θανατωθεὶς μὲν σαρκὶ ζωοποιηθεὶς δὲ πνεύματι, ἐν ᾧ καὶ τοῖς ἐν φυλακῇ πνεύμασιν πορευθεὶς ἐκήρυξεν ... [translated as Vos understands it: "being put to death in the flesh but made alive in the spirit, in which also He went and preached to the spirits in prison..."].

It is explained very differently, and without going into all the questions that can present themselves, we limit ourselves to two areas:

a) The conditions under which a local *descensus* would in fact be taught here would be:

1. That σάρξ here means "body," and πνεῦμα, "soul." Then the explanation would be: In His body Christ is dead, but in His soul is made alive, and He has preached to the spirits in Sheol.

2. That the datives in both parts of the sentence must have the same sense and each must be translated by "in which": "in His body dead," "in His spirit made alive."

3. That the word ζωοποιηθεὶς does not mean "made alive" but "kept alive," for the proponents of the local descent must understand it this way. They cannot and will not assume that the soul of Christ also died and then was brought back to life again.

   Now, it appears that none of these conditions are supported by the text. To begin with the last, ζωοποιεῖν does not mean "to keep alive," but always "to bring back to life." So Christ is brought back to life. With that, the translation of πνεύματι by "in the spirit" falls, for Christ did not die according to the spirit in contrast to His body. We are compelled to translate, "*by* the spirit." And this changed translation now necessitates that another sense than "body and soul" be given to the contrast "flesh and spirit." It is a contrast between divine and human nature, as it appears in Romans 1:3-4, "who is born from the seed of David according to the flesh, but declared to be the Son of God with power according to the Spirit of sanctification"; Romans 9:5, "From which is Christ, as far as the flesh is concerned, who is God over all to be praised forever"; John 1:14, "The Word became flesh." Here "flesh" always means the whole of human nature, inclusive of soul and body.

b) The explanation of the passage required by the context.

1. The point of departure is the admonition of the apostle that Christians must suffer patiently, witnessing by their proclamation of the faith, witnessing by their behavior, to those who oppress them. This is urged by the example of Christ. In Him it was apparent how much better it was to suffer than to oppress in an unrighteous way. His enemies could kill Him in His human nature; by the Spirit, by His divine nature, He was raised again to immortality. So it will also be with believers who suffer oppression for the sake of their faith.

2. This will happen among believers not only in following Christ but as a working out of Christ's life in them. The deep thought that the likeness of the lot of believers to that of Christ rests on a fellowship in lot—that in Christ is not only the example but also the causation of what takes place with His members. This deep thought also appears here. Christ therefore goes with His members through oppression to the life of glory.

3. That this in fact is so the apostle proves in a most meaningful way, as follows: The flood was a symbol and type of baptism, and baptism signifies and seals the salvation of Christians through oppression of them leading to life. What took place at the flood? The Spirit, the deity of Christ, worked in Noah, "the preacher of righteousness," and testified through him against the unbelieving world. The same water of the flood, through which Noah with his eight was saved, became destruction for unbelievers. This can be seen from the fact that those to whom the gospel was preached then are now spirits in prison. They

were disobedient at that time, however long the patience of God waited, and have received the payment of their hardening.

Noah himself was saved by Christ, for the water of the flood from which he was saved pictured the death of Christ from which He arose. Taken all together, then, the same history that is already observed in the flood is now seen when Christians suffer oppression:

a) The suffering of Noah was an aftereffect of the oppression of Christ, or if one wishes, a prelude to it. Since Christ testified in him, he was ridiculed and reviled.

b) The suffering of Noah was, as such, the cause of the destruction of the world. Since Christ testified in him and was rejected in him, the unbelieving spirits were imprisoned.

c) The salvation of Noah was a result of the resurrection and glorification of Christ. Therefore he was saved through water (v. 21). God could have saved him in a different way, but it must be made known, as a type, that his deliverance resulted from the great deliverance of the Mediator from suffering and death, to which the water of baptism points.

All this is repeated in the same order in the present time:

a) The suffering of believers is an aftereffect of the suffering of Christ, since they witness for their Savior, sanctify Him in their hearts, always give account for the hope that is in them (v. 15), and are therefore ridiculed and reviled. So it transpired with the Savior Himself: Since He bore witness against the world, it nailed Him to the cross and killed Him.

b) The suffering of believers is, as such, the cause of the destruction of the world. Since the world fights against Christ and rejects Him in believers, it will imprison itself. The same end that struck the world in Noah's days is to be expected for it. Nothing different already transpired with the Lord Jesus. When the world caused Him suffering, it sinned against Him most grievously and sealed its own doom.

c) The salvation of believers is a result of the resurrection of the Lord. For Him, the same death that brought judgment to the world was at the same time the passage to eternal life. It is the same with Christians. The oppression of the present produces an entirely surpassing gain of future glory, and that this is directly an effect of the glorification of the Mediator appears from their baptism. This baptism is, according to v. 21, "the appeal of a good conscience toward God, through the resurrection of Jesus Christ."

38. What explanation is required by the context of 1 Peter 4:6?

This passage reads: "For this reason the gospel was preached to the dead, in order that they would be judged according to man in the flesh but would live according to God in the spirit." The apostle admonishes his readers to forgo all pagan wantonness, in which they had walked long enough previously. They may also not thereby allow themselves to be misled because the world speaks evil of them when they do not share in the same riotousness, for the world will one day have to give account for that before the Judge of the living and the dead. It will be punished for that as certainly as Noah's contemporaries were punished for that. They also ate and drank and made merry and ridiculed the godly patriarch, whose modest life testified to the seriousness of judgment. God's admonition came to them too. The gospel was preached to them, and its content was, "Be judged by men according to the flesh, accept the slander of the world, choose the reproach of the people of God (v. 6), in order that you might live according to God in the spirit." They did not listen, and the result has been that they are now dead. Thus it will be with everyone who places the approval of the world above being scorned with God's children.

39. If, then, there are no grounds for belief in a local descent, are there also weighty objections to it?

Yes.

    a) All mediatorial acts are executed by Christ as God-man so that both natures work together, each in its own way, and then not a half nature, but the human nature according to body and soul. If we say that the burial of the Savior was an essential part of His humiliation, then we include both soul and body in the humiliation. They were separated from each other, and the dishonor and the abnormality of that condition clung to both. If we would maintain the contrary—that Christ went with His soul to hades while His body remained resting in the grave—then this would be a mediatorial act in which only half the human nature participates, something that would thus stand completely on its own without analogy. We need not go so far as to say with some Reformed theologians that in such a state of being separated, Christ was not man (Burman, Wendelin, et al.). We can certainly say, however, that in this state of being separate, the soul was not qualified to carry out the sort of mediatorial act that this *descensus* must be.

b) One has rightly noted that the time when Christ was still held by the bonds of death was not the appropriate time to celebrate a triumph over hell and the devil. The sting of death and the victory of hell were removed by the resurrection of the Mediator, and only someone who has completely triumphed holds His victory march. Scripture, then, also so presents it that the resurrection of the Lord was His victory over the powers of destruction. As long as He lay in the grave, it still appeared as if the evil one had really taken Him off to his dark place of residence. With the resurrection, the glory of God descended with the angels into the grave. Christ has led away captivity captive when He went up into the heights. When He arose from the dead, it was apparent that He could not be held by the grave.

c) Before His death, Christ commended His spirit into the hands of the Father. That is more than a way of saying that He died. It meant the condition of His [body and soul] being separated as a condition of relative passivity. Where previously there had been active suffering, now came more of a resting and resignation, in the hands of the Father, in what of the humiliation must still follow. The descent into hell does not accord with this passive character. The former presents us with the Mediator as active and working, triumphing over the depths of the universe and bringing His power to bear in the farthest abysses of the world. Christ promised the murderer that he would be with Him in paradise, and that indeed "today." If the soul of Christ thus ...[1]

---

[1] The section ends with this sentence fragment in the handwritten original as well as the transcription. It seems plausible to surmise that the missing thought intended is that if the soul of Christ descended into hell, then Christ could not have made the promise to the murderer in the terms He did ("today") because the promise would not be true.

40. *Is there sufficient ground to label the severest suffering endured by Christ with this designation, "descent into hell"?*

Yes, the Scripture sometimes speaks of an extremely severe suffering as a suffering unto Sheol, to the state of the dead: Psalm 18:5, "The bands of hell were around me, the snares of death came over me"; Psalm 116:3, "The bands of death surrounded me and the pains of hell laid hold of me"; Psalm 88:6, "You have put me in the lowest pit, in the dark places, in the depths"; Psalm 30:3, "LORD, you have brought up my soul out of hell." The word שְׁאוֹל, here translated "hell," can have two meanings in Hebrew: (1) The state of death in general with what belongs to it; (2) the place of torment. Now one could say that in the passages cited here, the word has the first sense, that thus there is no mention of "hell" in the usual meaning, and that from it we can only infer the right to speak of severe pains as a descent into death. However, one would then overlook that Scripture, by choosing one and the same word for these two concepts, has wrongly intended to teach that the grave for the sinner is a gate of hell. The state of death and that of torment stand in the closest connection with each other. Now since it is in fact said of Christ there that He was grieved *unto death*, we remain entirely within the limits of biblical usage if we describe the pains of eternal death as a descent into hell. And that, finally, is also what the apostle means when he speaks of the "lowest parts of the earth" (Eph 4:9). The "grave" is taken there as an image of the deepest humiliation. We concur with the opinion of the Reformed who understand the descent into hell as the anguish of eternal death. Still, we do not wish to maintain that the expression is originally so intended in the creed, for this cannot be proven.

41. *Have all theologians among the Reformed reckoned the burial and being buried to the state of humiliation?*

No, some have wavered on this point. Bucanus, for example, says that one can attribute being buried both to the exaltation and to the humiliation. The ground for this vacillation lies in an unclear conception of what the exaltation of the Mediator was. If one conceives of this entirely negatively as a removal of the misery that accompanied His humiliation, then there is in fact reason for saying that the grave was the entrance to His exaltation. As for believers, the state of separateness is a putting-off of the state of corruption that clings to them here, so for the Savior the burial of His body was a putting-off of the defective tabernacle in which He had dwelt here. We do not know whether the re-creation of the corruptible body into an incorruptible one first came into existence at the moment of the resurrection or already beforehand.

The analogy makes us expect the former. Still, on the basis of Psalm 16:10, one usually assumes that the body of Christ saw no corruption and was not given over to decomposition. Thus there must have been a miraculous power that preserved it from decomposition and thereby also prepared it for the glorification of the hour of resurrection. By this preparation it was in a certain sense freed from its natural inclination to decompose, and it is that thought that has compelled some to include the grave with the exaltation, or at least to place it between the two states. But removal of what is corruptible is not yet exaltation; liberation from weakness is not yet endowment with glory. Therefore, we draw the line between humiliation and exaltation with the resurrection of the Lord.

42. *What distinguishes the Lutheran conception of the state of humiliation from that of the Reformed?*

a) Concerning the subject, the Lutherans maintain that this is to be sought in the human nature. The divine attributes were communicated to it by the incarnation, and by the act of self-humiliation it has divested itself of their use (Chemnitz) or of their open use (the Zwabians).

The Reformed maintain that the subject of the act of humiliation is the divine person as the person of the Mediator, although humanity naturally was the means for that, the nature in which the humiliation took place. One must keep this clearly in view, for the Reformed also did not deny that the condition of misery connected with the state of humiliation could only occur in the human nature, because the divine nature is immutable. What the Reformed, on the contrary, do deny is (1) that humanity can divest itself of something that belongs to it as a communicated divine attribute; (2) that the incarnation in itself, because it would have been accompanied by the communication of the divine attributes to the human nature, would not have been a humiliation but an exaltation for the Mediator.

According to the Lutherans, there are two distinct acts, not only logically but also actually: the assumption of human nature, of which the subject is the Son of God and which does not include humiliation, and the divesting of the use or open use of the divine attributes, of which the human nature is the subject and in which the humiliation consists.

According to the Reformed, these are only two sides of one and the same act, although it is the case that one can logically distinguish them. For the Lutherans, the humiliation begins with the conception. Thus they distinguish further between assuming human nature and conception and come very close to teaching a preexistence of the human nature. The already incarnate *Logos* subjected Himself to conception in the womb of Mary. It goes without saying that "the conception of an already incarnate person" is a *contradictio in adjecto* [a contradiction in terms].

b) Lutherans also differ on the concept of humiliation itself. At least some Lutheran theologians teach that the humiliation was a concealment of use and not an abolition of use. Here the humiliation vanishes in a concealment. It consists of an appearance that does not agree with the reality.

c) The third point of difference concerns the duration of the humiliation. As already seen, for the Lutherans this extends only to the burial, since this in itself and the descent into hell, which occurred at the time of being buried, are included in the exaltation.

Many Lutheran theologians have affirmed the descent into hell in a figurative as well as the local sense.

43. *What is the connection of the exaltation of the Mediator to His humiliation?*

The connection of legal consequence. Christ is Mediator not as a private person but as an official person, as Head of His members. Hence He must receive the fruits of His merits in Himself. And as He did not suffer for Himself, so too He was not glorified for Himself.

44. What is the subject of the exaltation of the Mediator?

His person as Mediator, and that, again, according to both natures. As it was a state of humiliation for the deity to have something joined with it in which it could not reveal its full glory—namely, humble humanity—so it was a restoration in honor when this humanity was made a suitable instrument for the revelation of its glory.

45. In what does exaltation consist?

According to the definition of the concept "state" given above, in two things:

a) In coming out from under the curse and wrath of God, under which the Mediator had been in the state of His humiliation. This was followed by an entrance into the favor and full good pleasure of God that rested on Him as Mediator. The opposite of curse is blessing, and He is the Blessed of the Father.

b) In a change of condition coinciding with this exchange of legal position. Both in body and in soul it must be made clear that the curse had ceased and that the Mediator found Himself basking in the good pleasure of the Father. His exaltation is therefore at the same time glorification, just as the humiliation was also at the same time a shattering for Him.

46. Do these two elements accompany each other in all stages of the state of exaltation?

Yes; every stage has a significance that applies to the one element as well as the other. When Christ rose from the dead, this was both a fact that had judicial significance and an act of God that brought about a powerful reversal in His human nature. When He went to heaven, a declaration of God in the judicial sphere was also involved, and at the same time we must assume that the ascension of the Lord had a continuing change for His humanity as a consequence. Besides His judicial exaltation, a real glorification for the Mediator may not be assumed—only for His return for judgment and for taking His place at the right hand of God.

47. *How manifold is the significance of the exaltation of Christ?*

Threefold:

a) *Declarative*. This is true of all stages, as was just indicated.

b) *Exemplary*. This is true of the two first stages, the resurrection and the ascension. In both there is for the members of the body of the Lord an example of what will happen with them.

c) *Instrumental*. This is again true of all stages insofar as they are used as means for the complete glorification of the body of Christ.

48. *What in particular is the significance of the resurrection of Christ?*

a) *Declarative*. The death of the Mediator had been the open manifestation of the curse that He bore as Surety. From the inmost part of His being, the dissolution process of death had surged outward and had separated soul and body from each other. Now, if that death had thoroughly done its work throughout, then the visible restoration of that outward unity of soul and body will also have to be the initial proof. As long as the rupture continued, the power of death continued to be at work and ever further ruptured and dissolved. It is not by the initial tear but by the lengthening the tear once made that death manifests its power. If, therefore, a restoration of what death has ravaged also takes place at but one point, then this is sufficient proof of the undoing of death. The resurrection is the death of death. By letting it be exhausted in Himself, Christ destroyed the power of death. The Father, when He brought Christ again from the dead, derived the declaration that there was nothing more to bear and to die, that the passive obedience in all its parts had been perfectly provided.

However, this was still only one side of the matter. The resurrection also relates to the active obedience of the Mediator. It is a positive act. The power of death was contained so that it not only could not continue working further, but soul and body are brought together and reunited through a new outflow of life. There was a communication of life, and indeed a communication of eternal life—of that life that was promised upon the perfect keeping of the law. In the Surety, passive and active obedience had accompanied each other at every point, and so it was required that they both also be declared sufficient at one and the same point. This happened in the resurrection of the Lord. Had something been lacking in the suffering of Christ, then it would have been impossible that the violence of death had ceased even for a moment. Had there been something imperfect in the active obedience of the Mediator, then in no way could an enlivening have taken place in His soul and body. The resurrection must be viewed as God's *de facto* declaration of the perfection of Christ's work in both respects.

b) *Exemplary*. The resurrection of the Mediator shows by way of example what will occur with all the members of His body.

1. In their justification. As Christ is acquitted of guilt and has received the right to eternal life, so too those who are Christ's, each in his order [1 Cor 15:23], will share in these same privileges.

2. In their spiritual resurrection or regeneration. Just as in Christ the old sinless nature, nevertheless ravaged by the consequences of sin in which death had hitherto reigned, is replaced by a nature in which immortal life reigns, so too for believers the law of sinful flesh will give way to a law of the life of the Spirit.

3. In their bodily resurrection. With the Mediator, the life that He received in His soul was at work organically; it received power to act upon the body and to enliven it anew. Likewise, too, the re-creation that first begins in the soul of believers will then reach its end when the corruption of the body will have put on incorruption.

c) In all these points, the resurrection of Christ at the same time works *instrumentally*. There is a causal connection between the justification of Christ and that of those who belong to Him, between the making alive of His soul and the regeneration of the children of God, between His resurrection and their resurrection.

1. The justification of Christ is a justification of the Head, and to that extent of all the members who are in this Head. By

the resurrection, the judgment is pronounced that the body made up of the elect is righteous before God. Therefore it is said that Christ was given up for our sins and raised for our justification [Rom 4:25], and that were Christ not raised, we would still be in our sins [1 Cor 15:17]. What comes to pass with the individual believer in his justification is nothing other than the personal realization of this justification of the Surety. We hope to come back to this point in connection with the doctrine of justification.

2. The enlivening of Christ is an enlivening of the Head, and to that extent of all the members who are in the Head. In it resides not only the legal ground for the regeneration of the elect, but in a certain sense its active cause as well. It is not as if there had been no regeneration before the Mediator rose from the dead, for the saints of old also received the grace of regeneration on the basis of the merits of Christ. But since the exaltation of Christ has taken place and the outpouring of the Spirit has followed it, this regeneration must be seen as an implanting into the body of Christ. Earlier, the Spirit operated in a more separate manner in each individual and not directly from Christ as glorified Mediator. Now it is the Spirit of the one body who from the Head acts upon the members. Scripture in fact views the regeneration of believers as a consequence of the resurrection of Christ; Ephesians 2:4–5, "But God who is rich in mercy, through His great love with which He has loved us, even when we were dead through trespasses, has made us alive with Christ"; Romans 6:5, "For if we have become one plant with Him, planted in the likeness of His death, so will we also be in the likeness of His resurrection." Baptism as the bath of regeneration points to the resurrection of Christ from the dead (Rom 6:4; 1 Pet 3:21).

3. In a similar way, the resurrection of Christ functions instrumentally for the resurrection of the body of believers. He has become the firstfruits of those who are asleep [1 Cor 15:20]. As death is through one man—namely, has been brought about for us causally by Adam—so the resurrection of the dead through one man [1 Cor 15:21]. The first man, Adam,

has become a living soul, the last Adam a life-giving spirit.[2] All these statements appear in 1 Corinthians 15 [vv. 20–21, 45], where the apostle speaks specifically of the resurrection of the flesh. And in Romans 8:10-11, he says, "If the Spirit of the one who raised Jesus from the dead dwells in you, so will He who has raised Christ from the dead also make alive your mortal bodies through His Spirit who dwells in you." Finally, in John 5:25-26, the Savior Himself says, "Truly, truly I say to you, the hour comes and now is when the dead will hear the voice of the Son of God, and they who have heard it will live; for as the Father has life in Himself, so He has also given to the Son to have life in Himself" (cf. vv. 28–29). The raising of the body of believers, therefore, stands in connection with the resurrection of the body of the Mediator, and it is the Spirit of Christ who effects this connection. One must, however, note that it is not the resurrection as a bare fact that is referred to here, for that occurs as well for those who have died outside Christ. They, too, will leave the grave at His voice. It is rather the resurrection as re-creation of the psychical [cf. 1 Cor 15:44] body of believers into a pneumatic body—the change from the corruptible into the incorruptible, from dishonor into glory, from weakness into power—that is to be viewed as a fruit and consequence of the resurrection of Christ.

49. *Does the resurrection of the Mediator consist solely in the reunion of His soul and body?*

No; that such is not the case may be shown from the following considerations:

The resurrection was the beginning of the exaltation. Now, the humiliation of the Mediator consisted not only in the fact that His soul and body were slowly torn apart, but at the same time dissolution manifested itself within the orbit of the life of soul and body itself. Whoever is of the opinion that the essence of death lies in the separation of soul and body makes an extremely superficial judgment. Death also works within

---

2   Here "spirit," lowercase; below in the answer to question 50 [original question 221], again quoting 1 Corinthians 15:45, "Spirit," is capitalized, referring to the Holy Spirit.

the soul, and all the suffering and the weakness that were encountered in the life of Christ's soul were phenomena of death. The same death was at work in His body long before it was separated from the soul, and all the imperfections of the body were the effects of death in Christ. Consequently, the abolition of death will have to consist of three things:

a) The restoration of the perfection of the human soul of the Savior. This nature had never possessed sinful weakness, and in this respect no change was required. Considered apart from sin, on the other hand, inherent in it were all natural, though no personal, weaknesses. It had to be made suitable by special official grace from the Holy Spirit for its work. In a certain sense, one can even say that in it there had been a split and dissonance of life as long as Christ bore the sin of the elect: He was at the same time the object of the wrath of God and the object of the good pleasure of the Father. His personal relationship to God as Son and that as Mediator did not coincide.

Now with the resurrection, all this was otherwise. First, all sinless weaknesses were removed from the soul of the Lord. Further, the split in life, which was inseparable from the work of satisfaction, gave way for undivided reception and drinking in of the love of God, which a feeling of wrath could no longer disrupt. What the apostle says in Romans 6:9–10 has this in view: "Knowing that Christ being raised from the dead no longer dies; death no longer rules over Him. For the death He died, He died to sin once for all, and the life He lives, He lives to God." Only after the completed task of salvation can the soul of the Savior live to God in this fullest sense of the word. Prior to that, besides the attracting action of the love of God, proceeding from the righteousness of God there was also an unsettling action upon it, and that for it was death.

b) The restoration of the perfection of the human body of the Mediator. In bodily life as well as in the soul, the true unity of life was lacking; it existed during the state of humiliation in a continual disintegration, and above all during the anguish of eternal death was subject to violent shocks that must have disoriented and shattered Him physically. And apart from that, it was from the outset a body of death, just because it was our dying and corrupted flesh and blood that the Mediator assumed. With the resurrection there came, in principle, a perfect body in which everything worked harmoniously, in which nothing discordant or disturbing was left. The resurrection is more than a return to life of the one buried; it is simultaneously the re-creation and the transformation of that person. Christ, according to His human nature, came out of the grave as a new creature, for whom everything old is past and a new law of life has begun. It cannot be decided with complete certainty how much of this re-creation of both soul and body coincided with the resurrection and how much remained delayed for the ascension. In any case, what was imperfect was removed at the resurrection, even though the glory that had to replace it followed in stages.

c) The restoration of the organic bond between body and soul. The re-creation of the body must be taken in the closest connection with that bond. As spiritual death in general draws the body after itself, so too the spiritual resurrection will exerts its influence in the sphere of the bodily. The soul will draw the body to itself again and make it a living unity.

50. *Are we taught further about the nature of the resurrection body of the Lord?*

Yes. In general we can say that it has the nature of all resurrection bodies, which the apostle describes in 1 Corinthians 15:42–49. There it is taught of the resurrection body, in sequence, that it is incorruptible (ἐν ἀφθαρσίᾳ), glorious (ἐν δόξῃ), powerful (ἐν δυνάμει), spiritual (πνευματικόν). Here, in the first place, the resurrection body of believers is spoken of, but this will be like the glorified body of Christ (cf. Phil 3:21). The first three predicates refer to the antithesis to the body at burial. At that time, it is abandoned to dissolution (ἐν φθορᾷ); as a corpse it is unsightly (ἐν ἀτιμίᾳ); in being dead it is weak (ἐν ἀσθενείᾳ).

The fourth antithesis reaches back further into life prior to burial. In contrast to the σῶμα πνευματικόν stands the σῶμα ψυχικόν: "There is a natural body and there is a spiritual body." To understand this antithesis correctly, we will have to take into consideration that here in opposition to "spiritual" Paul does not set "fleshly" but "natural." A fleshly body is a body that becomes sin for its possessor; a natural body, then, is not a body of sin. A fleshly body bears the seed of death within itself; a natural body is in itself not yet mortal, so that it must die. In agreement with this is the fact that the natural body does not originate with the entrance of sin but has its origin in creation, "The first man Adam has become a living soul (εἰς ψυχὴν ζῶσαν), the last Adam a life-giving Spirit." With that, reference is made to the creation account, Genesis 2:7, "and blew into His nostrils the breath of life, so the man became a living soul." Apparently, then, three bodies are possible: a natural, a fleshly, and a spiritual body. The natural, psychical [*psuchikov*] body becomes a fleshly body as soon as man sins. The fleshly body becomes a spiritual body in the resurrection of the dead.

The question still remains to be answered why the apostle distinguished the body as Adam possessed it and the resurrection body of Christ specifically with the terms "natural" and "spiritual." The psychical, natural body is such as it derives its organic life from the *psuchē*, from the soul of man, thus certainly possesses life, but still not immutable and irrevocable life, which ultimately always rests on the indwelling of the Spirit of God as the principle of eternal life. Now in the state of rectitude Adam possessed irrevocable, eternal life as little in his soul as in his body. In that consisted the psychical nature of his body. Prior to His resurrection, Christ possessed that same psychical body and in it, moreover, carried around the seed of death, by which it thus received a certain likeness with the fleshly body. In contrast, after His resurrection His human nature shared in the full enlivening of the Spirit, and that not as a bestowed benefit but as its own possession; the Spirit was given to Him fully and dwelt in Him. Related to that, His body too received an imperturbable, incorruptible life. It was suffused with the power of the Spirit, and thereby the material from which it consisted received a higher quality, so that it can not longer be called flesh and blood, while not ceasing to be material. An immaterial body is a *contradictio in adjecto*; a spiritual body is a possible concept. That the spiritual body is no longer flesh and blood follows in [1 Cor 15] verse 50: "But I say this, brothers, that flesh and blood cannot inherit the kingdom of God, and the corruptible cannot inherit the incorruptible." The flesh and blood of which Adam's body consisted was vulnerable to corruption and dissolution, which is still something entirely different than saying it must undergo corruption. Corruptible here is a contradictory contrast to no-longer-corruptible, completely incorruptible. Further, it is a consequence of this spiritual existence of the body of Christ that He is "life-giving Spirit" (v. 45). Through the possession of the power of eternal life, Christ could also give life to others and guarantee the resurrection of the bodies of believers. Adam could only be called a living soul, but he could not communicate life to others; Christ does the latter and therefore He is life-giving Spirit.

That the explanation given here is correct appears from what the apostle adds as further explanation: "The spiritual is not first, but the natural, then the spiritual" (v. 46). In the order of God, the body that could still be corrupted comes first and then only secondly follows the body that is no longer vulnerable to corruption. Adam must not from the outset be placed in the state of immutability and of eternal life. Although created completely right, without there being anything wrong or any principle of death in him, he still awaited the confirmation and completion of His beatitude, which was attached to keeping the covenant of works as a condition. Had he sustained the test, he would have become the first and second Adam in one person. But the principle would still have been valid: "The natural first, then the spiritual." Now that he falls, Christ enters as the second Adam—and besides restoring what Adam had ruined, He also carries out gloriously where Adam has failed. He became the progenitor, the covenant Head of the spiritual and highest order of things that must arise on the basis of the natural order. Christians bear His image in their re-creation as they bear the image of the first Adam in their creation. "The first man is from the earth, earthly (ἐκ γῆς χοϊκός); the second man is from heaven" [v. 47]. Inasmuch as Adam's body was taken from the earth and had not yet been made into a spiritual body by the Holy Spirit, it also shared in the attributes of earthly materials. These would naturally be susceptible to change. Adam's body was not such that external disturbing influences, if they were present, would have had no effect. It is otherwise with the body of the resurrected Savior, at least in His consummate glorification. It is incorruptible, and that certainly because a heavenly power, the power of the Spirit, has affected it. Therefore, the second man is ἐκ οὐρανοῦ, for heaven is the realm of immutable, immovable things, while here on earth everything moves and is mobile.

One must not interchange what is said here concerning the contrast between ψυχικός and πνευματικός with the ethical meaning that the word ψυχικός has in 1 Corinthians 2:14, "The natural man does not understand the things that are of the Spirit of God, for they are foolishness to Him." There the concept of what is natural includes in itself the characteristic of sinfulness, something that did not appear to be the case in the pericope just explained.

51. *Do the facts related to us in the Gospels agree with this?*

They show in part that a total change had really taken place in the body of the Lord.

   a) He was not immediately recognized by those with whom He had been intimately associated earlier (John 20:15; Luke 24:31; John 21:7).

   b) In an inexplicable way He appeared and disappeared, covered distances, went through closed doors (John 20:19; Luke 24:36).

   c) He did not resume an intimate association with His disciples again, but kept them at a reverential distance. A higher majesty lay over all His action, as if He lived in a higher sphere and was no longer suited for a stay within the common sensory perception of this world. This comes out so strongly in the Gospels that it has led some to the strange surmise that immediately after the resurrection of the Lord He dwelt in heaven and that each appearance must be held to be a descent, immediately followed by a new ascension.

     On the other hand, the body that the Lord possessed did not completely coincide with the resurrection body as that is delineated for us by Paul in 1 Corinthians 15. Jesus declared it to be flesh and bone (Luke 24:39), while Paul expressly asserts that flesh and blood will not inherit the kingdom of God [1 Cor 15:50]. Consequently, we appear here to have to think of a middle state that formed the transition to His fully glorified humanity as He possesses it in heaven. During these 40 days He could eat, although it is not to be assumed that He had need of food. Augustine has said of this, "It is in one way that the thirsty earth absorbs water, in another way that the rays of the sun burn; the first through deficiency, the other through power."

52. *Is the body of Christ a material body that as such is bound to space?*

Yes; it must be material if it will truly remain a body. And as material it must also be subject to the limitations of matter, circumscribed in space. The conditions for its movement through space will differ considerably from those that apply to us, but in principle the relationship is the same. We do not believe with Lutherans in a ubiquity of the human nature, neither of the soul nor of the body. Nor are we despisers of matter, as if in this in itself lurks a profane principle that must be eliminated and purged. Matter can be glorified so that divine glory permeates it at every point and the Spirit of God governs it completely. That is realized in the resurrection of Christ. That His body is truly matter appears from:

a) The analogy of sowing and harvesting elaborated by the apostle in 1 Corinthians 15. One does not sow the body that will become, but there is still an organic connection between what is sown and what is harvested. The new is present in principle in the old; there is a thread of identity that runs through the harvest. So, too, in the resurrection of the dead. It is a re-creation of the old, not a destruction of it. There would not be an organic connection between the buried body and the resurrected body if they were detached from each other as material and nonmaterial.

b) All the appearances of Christ were in the mode of space, however extraordinary they otherwise were. What is visible in the mode of space is material. And this applies not only to the time before His ascension; it also applies to the time afterward. He appeared to Stephen, Paul, and John as visible in space.

c) If one appeals to Matthew 22:30 to prove the immateriality of the body of the resurrection, one seeks the point of comparison where it does not lie. Those raised are compared with the angels because they will no longer marry and procreate and because they are immutably confirmed in their state forever.

53. *Who was the acting cause in the resurrection of the Mediator?*

Generally and preferably it is attributed to God as the one who fashions it: Romans 6:4, "Christ has been raised from the dead through the glory of the Father"; Acts 13:30, "God has raised Him from the dead." According to Ephesians 1:19–20, sinners must be born again by the same strength of divine power that He wrought in Christ when He raised Him from the dead. This agrees fully with the meaning of the concept. As a declarative justifying act, it must be an act of God the Father, who maintains the violated law and proclaims the restored law. Since, however, the human spirit of Christ, filled with new power of life, acted on His body to reassume it as His instrument, and since it was the power of His own life as Mediator that set the body in motion and caused it to rise, so the resurrection can just as well be viewed as a work of Christ. He said, "Tear this temple down and in three days I will build it up again" (John 2:19); "I have power to lay it down (namely, life) and to take it up again" (John 10:10).

Finally, if the Holy Spirit works life everywhere and calls it out, both in the sphere of creation as well as in that of re-creation, and insofar as He has poured out the fullness of eternal life into the human nature, the Third Person of the divine Trinity can also appear as the cause of the resurrection. Romans 8:11 includes, at least by implication, that the Father has brought about the resurrection of the Mediator through the Spirit.

In all their external works, the three persons act together. And the work of the resurrection finds a parallel in the act of the incarnation, in which the same conjoint working of the divine persons manifests itself.

54. Does the resurrection of the Mediator include a proof of His deity?

Yes. By raising Him from the dead the Father sets the seal on His mediatorship—and since this includes His deity, His seal on the latter itself. In this, He is powerfully shown to be the Son of God according to the Spirit of sanctification by the resurrection of the dead (Rom 1:4). Moreover, the fact that He could bear eternal death, without succumbing in that struggle, is in itself irrefutable proof of His divine nature. A mere creature would be swallowed up by that death and would never again be able to hold his head high. He, in contrast, could not be held by that death.

55. What is the second stage in the state of exaltation?

The ascension of the Mediator. It is to be defined as the local passage of the person of the Mediator, according to His human nature, from earth to heaven.

56. *Our conviction that heaven is a place is supported on what grounds?*

a) First, it follows from the fact that heaven is the dwelling place of created beings. The angels reside there. The human nature of the Mediator also resides there. All these are created natures. Again, all that is created stands in a certain relationship to space and time. Only God is elevated beyond these two modes of being. The residence of such beings that exist in relationship to space must bear a local character. It is quite possible that the laws that govern in heavenly space are not entirely the same as those that apply in our earthly space. But there must be similarity, just as surely as similarity existed between the body before and after the resurrection of the Lord. His body is marked by extension. Though we did not at all know an answer to give to the question where heaven is, still the knowledge that the Mediator has brought His exalted humanity into heaven would provide us a fixed point for the determination of heaven, and we could answer, "Heaven is the place where the humanity of the Lord dwells."

b) The contrast, "heaven and earth," which we already meet in the creation account, continues through the entire Scripture. In this contrast, the one member determines the meaning of the other. It is absurd to make mention of earth and heaven as the juxtaposition of a place and a condition.

c) Scripture teaches us to depict heaven in a local manner when it turns our gaze *upward*, as it suggests for us to think of hell as a place below. This would make no sense if something local did not cling to the conception of both heaven and hell.

d) Entrance into heaven is described as an ascending, thus again in local terms. For the ascension of the Lord, that comes out very clearly. He rises in the air, is intercepted by clouds, and vanishes from sight.

e) A distinction is made by the apostle between the third heaven and what lies beneath it [2 Cor 12:2]. This presupposes the application of the category of number in the sphere of heaven, and the means by which this application happens can only be distance.

f) All that is reported to us of heaven—may the description of it also be ever so figurative—still demands the presupposition that there are local relationships. The tabernacle was made after the pattern of heavenly things, a shadowing of the higher reality. What is said of heaven is not an image derived from the arrangement of the Jewish sanctuary. The reverse is the case: The Jewish sanctuary in its arrangement has been determined by holy things that are above.

57. What is the significance of this ascension of the Lord?

Again, like the resurrection, it has a threefold significance:

a) *Declarative.* Heaven is the place of God's holy dwelling, where He reveals His glory more than elsewhere, while the earth is only a footstool for His feet. That Christ, after having completed His work as Mediator, went to heaven showed first of all that His work as Mediator concerned God, was a sacrifice brought to Him, which must be presented to Him.

Further, if entrance into heaven was granted to Christ, then this was all the more a declaration of God that His work was complete and acceptable. Man is driven from the blessedness of God by sin, which was symbolized by his expulsion from the earthly paradise. Had he retained the favor of God, he would have been transferred into heavenly regions. Now that he has lost the right to appear there and hell draws him below with the bonds of darkness, the thought of a future salvation involuntarily takes this form: "When will I, a sinful creature, again appear before God in Zion?" So it was necessary that the great High Priest, who alone can appear before God, also actually enter heaven and so as the Head of the redeemed come before God as righteous.

Finally, the ascension of the Mediator was the strongest possible expression of the depiction that His work is not limited to Israel but has a wider scope and significance. By not establishing His royal throne in the earthly Jerusalem but exalting that throne far above it to a height for which earthly boundaries are no longer visible, Christ showed that He was anointed over a spiritual Israel. His royal city is the Jerusalem that is above, the free, the mother of us all [Gal 4:26], in which Philistine, Tyrian, Moor are born.

Had the Mediator remained on earth, Jewish messianic expectations would have come true. But now His Kingdom is not of this
world (Eph 4:9–10).

b) *Exemplary.* The ascension of Christ is prophetic for the ascension of all the redeemed. They are seated with Christ in heaven
(Eph 2:6). He prays and petitions that where He Himself is, they
who are given to Him by the Father may also be. According to
Hebrews 2:6–9, in Christ is fulfilled the prophecy that the psalmist had expressed concerning man.

c) *Instrumental.* He has entered heaven to prepare a place there for
the members of His body. They all will come there not only *as* He
is there, but also *because* He is there. The Head draws the members after Himself, for the body is the fullness of Him who fills all
in all [Eph 1:23]. And because the Head is there, both in body and
soul, the members have the assurance that their flesh too, which
they must put off here, is not lost and will not become identified
with the earth, but that it again will sprout and, like the plant that
grows upward, will seek heaven.

58. Was there also associated with the ascension of Christ a further glorification that concerns His condition?

Yes; His human nature was now made fully suited for the heavenly environment in which He would live from now on. Here on earth it had
already been exalted above the power of earthly elements but had still
not yet received its heavenly glory. The apostles to whom He appeared
did not see Him as, later, Stephen, Paul, and John saw Him in His glory.
In what further this change consisted is not revealed to us.

59. What do the Lutherans teach in distinction from the Reformed concerning the ascension of the Mediator?

For them the ascension is the point at which the communicated divine
attributes, which the human nature possesses, break through into full
revelation. Christ is ubiquitous, not by a pulling apart or diffusion of
the material particles of His human body but in an entirely unique way.
The *Logos* is not outside the flesh, and the flesh is not outside the *Logos*.
The realistic impulse to have the humanity of Christ present of itself is
also at work here in the Lutheran system.

Apart from this change in condition, Lutherans clearly cannot grant a local ascension. The human nature was in heaven since the incarnation by virtue of the *communicatio idiomatum* [communication of attributes]. Nevertheless, local movement from earth to heaven is taught. The contradiction at this point is no greater than with respect to every local movement that Christ made during His stay on earth. There are also Lutherans, however, who are consistent in teaching that Christ has brought about the end to His visible presence here on earth and that His ascension consists in that.

60. Is Christ still on earth with His human nature after His ascension?

No, we reject, in sequence: (a) the just-outlined opinion of the Lutherans, who make both body and soul ubiquitous; (b) the opinion of some who make at least the soul ubiquitous.

The Mediator's person is certainly on earth according to His divine nature. This divine person also possesses human nature. A person is therefore with us who at the same time is human, but He is not with us according to His humanity. Another question is whether there cannot be a powerful action of the humanity of the Mediator, even where that human nature itself is not present. As one knows, Calvin assumed something like that for the Lord's Supper. Polanus, a Reformed theologian of good name, says, "Christ is present with His church not only according to His divine but also according to His human nature, but then in a spiritual manner, as a head is with the members, with which it is united, and who makes them alive." And the form for our Lord's Supper says, "[I]n order that we through the same Spirit, who dwells in Christ as the Head and in us as His members, would have true communion with Him and partake of all His benefits, of eternal life, of righteousness and glory." Such a dynamic action of the humanity of the Lord, however, is not intended as immediate but is expressly ascribed to the mediation of the ubiquitous Spirit.

61. What is the third stage in Christ's exaltation?

His being seated at the right hand of God—or, expressed actively, taking His place at the right hand.

62. *Is the human nature alone the subject of this exaltation?*

No, the person of the Mediator, and that surely: (a) according to His deity, insofar as in the new dominion that Christ receives, it can assert its omnipotence and can reveal all its glory; (b) according to His humanity, insofar as it received power and glory that it had not previously possessed.

63. *Is this exaltation a work that God executes, or does the Mediator exalt Himself?*

One can properly say both. It was naturally of the Father that He occupied this place. The fullness of power that devolved to Him was official (cf. Acts 5:31, "God has exalted Him to His right hand as Prince"; Heb 2:7). The Mediator also actively assumed that power and honor, sat, has taken a seat at the right hand of God. Christ could *ex pacto*, by virtue of the covenant, also claim this exaltation: Psalm 2:8, "Ask of me, and I will give you the nations as your heritage, the ends of the earth your possession"; Isaiah 53:12, "Therefore I will give Him share among the many because He has poured out His soul in death."

64. *What distinguishes sitting at the right hand of God as a stage of the exaltation from the ascension?*

The ascension had a twofold significance. In part, it had an independent significance as the transition of the Mediator from the sphere of the earth into the sphere of heaven according to His human nature, and concurrent with that, the change of this nature. In part, it was preparatory for sitting at God's right hand. The lordship and majesty associated with the latter could only be exercised in heaven. For these reasons, it is impossible to speak of the ascension and to highlight its significance without bringing in the kingdom of power with it. Nonetheless, as a distinct stage of exaltation the ascension must be sharply separated from the reception of kingdom power, and the latter reserved for sitting at the right hand.

65. *How is the expression "sitting at the right hand of God" intended?*

   a) First, we must note that it is to be taken figuratively and not literally. It is a total misconception when Lutherans, under the appearance of excluding a local "there," nevertheless drag it in again by saying "*Dextra Dei ubique est*," "The right hand of God is everywhere." The expression has nothing to do with what is local. Nor does it teach that Christ is ubiquitous as He is that in one particular place. One can derive the former only by deduction, and then only with regard to the deity.

b) The metaphorical speech of God, however, also has a deeper sense here than one usually thinks. It is here as little as elsewhere derived only afterward from the relationships of creaturely things but rests on an eternal reality of which created things, in their turn, are the image. There is something in God, insofar as man is the image of God; in Him is the same as ectype, and of this likeness with God there is an imprint in His material nature.

c) The right hand is the seat of power. God has willed that for man it would be the instrument of the most natural and noble exercise of power. It is extended to command, holds the scepter for rulers, is a direct reflection in man of both the might and power that God possesses.

Thus to sit at God's right hand is for all things to be in the closest communion with His divine power and might. Whoever sits at someone's right hand is connected with that of which the right hand is the symbol. Thus divine authority and divine power flow over, as it were, into Christ. For this significance of the right hand, one may compare passages like Isaiah 41:10, "I also support you with the right hand of my righteousness," and 45:1, "Cyrus, whose right hand I hold."

d) Inasmuch as the preeminence of a king lies in his power, or in general power is something excellent, so the right hand is a symbol of honor, of virtue as well, and connection with the right hand, the sign of glory and high esteem (cf. Psa 80:17, "Your hand be upon the man of your right hand"—that is, upon Him who is in great honor with you—Eccl 10:2, "The heart of the wise is toward his right hand, but the heart of a fool is toward His left hand"). The blessing communicated by the right hand is viewed as the most excellent, for which reason Joseph placed his son Manasseh at the right hand of Jacob [Gen 48:13]. The elect will be placed at the right hand of the Mediator in the day of judgment [Matt 25:34]. This is the sense to be understood when Bathsheba is set at the right hand of Solomon (1 Kgs 2:19), when the mother of the sons of Zebedee requested that her two sons might sit, the one at His right hand and the other at His left hand, in the kingdom of the Lord [Matt 20:20-21]. For Christ, there is not only authority and power but also honor. The apostle includes both when he says, "has set Him at His right hand in heaven ... above every name that is named ... and has subjected all things under His feet" [Eph 1:20-22]. Honor is referred to separately in Hebrews 1:3-4, "at the right hand of majesty in the highest heaven, having become so much more superior than the angels as He has inherited a more excellent name above theirs."

e) The *sitting* at the right hand of God has distinctive significance. Sitting is something other than standing. Someone who serves stands in the presence of the one he serves (1 Kgs 10:8, "Blessed are these your servants who continually stand in your presence"). The angels are always presented as standing (Isa 6:2; 1 Kgs 22:19). In Hebrews 1:3, it is apparently in contrast to the standing posture of the angels that it is said of Christ, "He has sat down." The Hebrew word for priest, כֹּהֵן, is derived from standing before God to serve (Heb 10:11, "And every priest stood daily serving"). So Christ, too, stood during the bringing of His satisfaction. Now, however, He has *sat*, as the sign of His efficacious exercise of the priestly office and kingly rule (Zech 6:13, "And He will sit and rule on His throne"). Of the man of sin, who arrogates to himself the rights and honor of God, it is prophesied that "he will *sit* in the temple of God as a God, displaying himself that he is God" (2 Thess 2:4).

f) From what has just been noted, it appears that sitting at the right hand of God is not exclusively related to the kingdom of power but also indicates the point at which His glorious intercession begins. Or, expressed more accurately, it indicates that stage of exaltation in which the kingdom of power and the priestly intercession begin to interpenetrate one another. It is described prophetically from this point of view in Psalm 110. The emphasis there falls on the fact that Melchizedek was king and priest at the same time. In Israel, the two positions of dignity were separated. David, the head of his people, could not provide the gift of atonement for his people. The priest, the one atoning for the people, could not rescue Israel with kingly power. In the awareness of this imperfection, David rises prophetically to the ideal mediatorial office of his Lord, who will unite priesthood and kingship in Himself, and to whom the Lord says, "Sit at my right hand until I will have put your enemies as a footstool for your feet" [v. 1], whose scepter of strength will be sent from Zion (v. 2), at whose right hand is the Lord Himself (v. 5), who does justice among the nations [v. 6], who is priest forever according to the order of Melchizedek [v. 4].

g) The sitting, finally, also has judicial significance: Psalm 9:4, "You have sat on the throne, O Judge of righteousness"; Joel 3:12, "But there I will sit to judge all the surrounding nations" (cf. Matt 19:28).

66. *What does it mean that Stephen saw Christ standing at the right hand of God [Acts 7:55-56]?*

This in no way conflicts with sitting at the right hand, since this is only a figurative expression for what has just been described. We can on no account imagine the humanity of the Lord as immovable and unchangeable in one place. Standing expresses readiness to help and to protect and to receive into the eternal dwelling places: Micah 5:3, "And He will stand and shepherd the flock in the power of the Lord"; Psalm 94:16, "Who will stand for me against the evildoers?"; Genesis 19:1, "And when Lot saw them, he stood up to meet them and bowed down with his face to the ground."

67. *Is there an essential glorification of the human nature that also accompanies taking His place at the right hand of God?*

Insofar as this coincides with the entrance into heaven, yes. Or one could even divide the question and say that the comprehensive transformation of the humanity of the Lord from an earthly to a heavenly accompanied the ascension, and that now this heavenly humanity received a special investiture with glory by which it was raised to the zenith of honor. If we take into consideration that Paul and John on Patmos received an overwhelming impression of the glory in which Christ appeared, so that repeatedly they were trembling, astounded, and left as dead, then we are certainly forced to consider something that far surpasses all our imaginings and exceeds the glory that believers as members of the body of the glorified Christ will themselves one day receive. They will, it is certainly true, become conformed to the image of the Son as His first-born brothers (Rom 8:29), but there is, nonetheless, a glory of the sun and of the moon and of the stars, and the mediatorial glory of Christ must be as much greater than that of His own, as the head is greater than the members.

68. *Has the exaltation of the Mediator ended with His session at the right hand of God?*

No. Its highest stage is not reached during this dispensation, but only at the end of the ages. So Paul says that Christ is seated far above every name that is named, not only in this but also in the coming world—that is, at the end of this dispensation [Eph 1:20–21]. Still to follow session at the right hand and is return for judgment.

69. *Does Scripture reckon this return for judgment as a great turning point along with the remaining steps of exaltation?*

Yes; Hebrews 6:1-2 reads, "[N]ot laying again the foundation of repentance from dead works ... of the resurrection of the dead and eternal judgment (κρίματος αἰωνίου)." Here the doctrine of the final judgment is reckoned among the fundamental articles of faith.

70. *With what words does Scripture indicate this final exaltation of Christ?*

a) It calls it a παρουσία, from παρεῖναι, "to be present." *Parousia*, however, means not only "presence," but "appearance to remain present from now on." An absence and distancing that now still exists will then cease. Now, according to His divine nature Christ has never been absent from His church but is with her to the end of the world. In contrast, according to His humanity, He has indeed departed. As long as this dispensation lasts, there is a split between the militant and triumphant church, and only of the latter can it be said that they have Christ present with them in the full sense. Believers on earth dwell apart from the Lord and long to dwell with Him. Christ is in them and yet they still look for His coming. The work of their salvation awaits its completion. They have the firstfruits of the Spirit and still sigh in themselves, looking for the adoption as children, the redemption of their bodies (Rom 8:23). This suffusion of their bodies now with the Spirit of Christ so that they will be with the Lord according to their material nature coincides with the bodily appearance of Christ Himself. Therefore, Paul says quite strikingly (Phil 3:20–21), "But our conduct is in heaven from which we also await the Savior, namely, the Lord Jesus Christ, who will change our humble body in order that it will be conformed to His glorious body, according to the working by which He can subject all things to Himself." The body that rests in the earth is an essential part of the believer, and yet it is always separated from the Lord as long as He has not come. Having returned to dust, it lies on the periphery, on the outermost circumference of the circle of re-creating action that proceeds from the Mediator. It is the last in its turn to be renewed. But the power of Christ reaches out into ever wider circles, and when finally all believers are gathered, the working by which Christ can subject all things to Himself is complete. This final act, however, must be viewed here not in its significance for believers but in its significance for the Mediator Himself. It makes His body complete, sets the crown on His saving work, positions Him as victor over the last bulwark of sin, brings death under His feet. Paul says very clearly, "The last enemy that is destroyed is death" [1 Cor 15:24].

So it is certainly wrong to limit the significance of this last stage of exaltation to the judgment. It is equally wrong to eliminate the local and the bodily from this conception of the return of the Lord. The most important part of its significance lies precisely in glorifying the material nature by eliminating local separation.

b) Another term for this stage of the exaltation is φανερωσθεῖναι, "to appear, be manifested"; ἀποκαλυπτέσθαι, "to be disclosed, revealed": 1 John 2:28, "so that when He appears, we will have confidence and not be made ashamed of Him at His future coming." Here "being revealed" and "the future coming" of the Lord stand as parallel concepts beside each other: 2 Thessalonians 1:6–7, "Therefore, it is just for God to repay oppression to those who oppress you, relief with us at the *revelation* of the Lord Jesus from heaven with the angels of His power," and verse 10, "when He will have come to be glorified in His saints and to be marveled at in all who believe" (cf. 1 Pet 1:7). Finally, the term ἡμέρα τοῦ κυρίου, "day of the Lord," has the same significance. This is a day, then, that will be completely given over to the Lord, whose significance will be concentrated entirely in Him, the day in which His justice will appear and His glory will break through as never before (2 Thess 2:1–2).

With these three terms, the return for judgment is indicated as a glorious vindication of Christ and His own in the sight of their enemies. Despite His unlimited kingly power, until that day a segment of creatures will be permitted to oppose Him and fail to appreciate Him. Many will deny that He is glorified and exalted as the militant church believes Him to be glorified and exalted. But in the end, His glory will be revealed in a visible form on earth, in the same sphere in which He endured His humiliation and shame. At His name will bow every knee of those who are in heaven and on the earth and under the earth, to the glory of God the Father (Phil 2:10–11). He, at one time condemned by the world, will in His turn judge the world—and, as is evident from 2 Thessalonians 1:6–7, this appearance will comprise in itself, both for Himself and believers, a satisfying of their deepest sense of justice.

71. *Does this final exaltation of the Mediator apply to both His natures?*

Here, too, both natures work together. According to the human nature, He appears openly and makes that appearance perceptible to creatures. According to His divine nature, He pronounces sentence with omniscience and omnipotence. Only a Mediator who is Himself truly God can execute such a judgment. Still, this highest and most glorious act also remains an official mediatorial act executed on behalf of the Father: John 5:27, "And He has given Him power also to execute judgment, because He is the Son of Man"; Acts 17:31, "Because He has appointed a day on which He will judge the earth righteously by a man whom He has ordained to that end."

VOLUME FOUR

SOTERIOLOGY

Translated and edited by

Richard B. Gaffin, Jr.

with

Kim Batteau
Harry Boonstra
Annemie Godbehere
Allan Janssen

VOLUME FOUR

SOTERIOLOGY

Contents

CONTENTS

PREFACE

Thanks are due for the indispensable help of those who provided base translations for the various parts of this volume: Kim Batteau, Harry Boonstra, Annemie Godbehere, and Allan Janssen. I take special note of Ms. Godbehere, who also worked on volume one and has now passed away. Let this volume be in memory of her and of her contributions to this project, as considerable as they were conscientious. As with the previous volumes, I have reviewed and revised their work and given the translation its final form along with a few editorial footnotes. Again, my thanks also go to Justin Marr, the project manager at Lexham Press, and to the copy editors.

In the preface to volume one I asked, concerning the identity of theologians contemporary to Vos or recently past, who may have had a direct influence on his thinking or perhaps shaped his presentation of material.[1] Volume four continues to leave this question unanswered. Regardless, readers of this volume who have also read the previous three will hardly miss the impressive coherence of its treatment of the application of salvation with the treatments of Christology in volume three and the covenant of grace in the latter part of volume two.

R. Gaffin, Jr.
September 2015

---

1   *Reformed Dogmatics*, vol. 1, *Theology Proper* (Bellingham, WA: Lexham Press, 2012), ix.

CHAPTER ONE
The Ordo Salutis

1. What is understood under the ordo salutis, the "order of salvation"?

The series of acts and steps in which the salvation obtained by Christ is subjectively appropriated by the elect. In Scripture σωτηρία, *salus*, has a double meaning, one more subjective and one more objective, according to whether it includes the act of saving or of being saved. In the first sense it naturally extends much farther than in the subjective appropriation of salvation. Christ is called σωτηρία not merely because He applies His merits but because He has likewise obtained them. His satisfaction was the principal act of salvation. In the second sense it is narrower in scope and in fact covers what one understands under the designation "soteriology."

2. What is further contained in the term ordo salutis, "order of salvation"?

That the subjective application of the salvation obtained by Christ does not occur at once or arbitrarily. In the abstract, it would be possible for God to take hold of and relocate each one of the elect into the heaven of glory at a single point in time. He has His good reasons that He did not do this. There are a multiplicity of relationships and conditions to which all the operations of grace have a certain connection. If the change came about all at once, then not a single one of these would enter into the consciousness of the believer, but everything would be thrown together in a chaotic revolution. None of the acts or steps would throw light on the others; the base could not be distinguished from the top or the top from the base. The fullness of God's works of grace and the rich variety of His acts of salvation would not be prized and appreciated.

The opposite of all this is true. There is order and regularity in the application of salvation as well as in every other area of creation. The acts and operations each have their own fixed place, from which they cannot be uprooted. They are connected to each other from what follows and from what precedes; they have their basis and their result. Consequently, the Scripture gives us an ordered sequence (e.g., Rom 8:28–30). At the same time, this order shows us that even in what is most subjective the purpose of God may not be limited to the satisfaction of the creature's longing for blessedness. If this were so, then the order that is slow and in many respects tests the patience of the children of God would be lost. But here, too, God works first of all to glorify Himself according to the principles of an eternal order and an immanent propriety.

3. *Does unanimity rule among the theologians in the identification of the different steps that belong to the order of salvation?*

No, a great variety rules in sequence as well as in completeness. All do not enumerate the same steps. When they all have the same things, they are given in a different sequence. Different terms are used for one and the same thing.

4. *Enumerate some points of difference that are important for proper differentiation.*

    a) An important point is the varying and unclear definition of the concept of regeneration. For many theologians the locus on regeneration is completely lacking, although many federalists are an exception here. At the same time these theologians do of course know of regeneration, and its specific character has not escaped them entirely.

        1. Some identify "regeneration" (*regeneratio*) with "conversion" (*conversio*). This is quite customary with the dogmaticians of the 17th century. The Canons of Dort teach in chapters 3 and 4, article 11: "Furthermore, when God accomplishes His good pleasure in the elect or works true conversion in them ... He not only powerfully illumines their mind by the Holy Spirit ... but by the effective power of the same regenerating Spirit, He

penetrates to the inmost parts of the man, opens the closed heart ... infuses new qualities into the will, and makes the dead living ... (article 12) and this is that—so often proclaimed in the Holy Scriptures—regeneration, new creation, resurrection from the dead and making alive, *which God, without us, works in us*."[1] Owen also expresses himself in a similar way.

Some, however, sought to avoid the lack of clarity that may originate from this usage by a more precise distinction between two kinds of conversion. So Turretin makes mention of a double *conversio*. The first is habitual and passive. It consists in producing a habit or disposition of the soul: "Habitual or passive conversion occurs through the infusion of supernatural habits by the Holy Spirit." The second conversion is called active and effective conversion. It is the exercising in faith and repentance of the already implanted *habitus*: "Active or effective conversion occurs through the exercise of those good habits by which the acts of faith and of repentance are both given by God and elicited in man." He then adds, however, that it is better to call the first kind of conversion "regeneration," because it refers to the new birth by which man is renewed according to the image of his Maker, and to limit the term "conversion" to the second kind, since in it the activity of man is not excluded.

2. The majority by far summarize regeneration and conversion under the concept of internal calling. Wollebius says, "Particular calling is termed: (a) new creation, (b) regeneration, etc." In the schools it is called (a) effectual election, (b) effectual calling, (c) internal calling. Accordingly, some speak first about calling, then about faith, then about conversion, so that calling apparently takes the place of regeneration (e.g., the Leiden *Synopsis*). Calling is often enough described as an implanting into Christ, a union with Christ, an indissoluble joining of the person of the elect with the person of the Mediator, all of them concepts that bring regeneration to mind clearly enough.

---

1 Emphasis added by Vos.

3. Others take the concept of regeneration in a very wide sense, as almost completely synonymous with *sanctificatio*, "sanctification," and under that notion understand the entire process by which the old nature of man is transformed into a new nature resembling the image of God. Calvin says (*Institutes*, 3.3.9), "Therefore, in a word, I describe *poenitentia* [repentance] as regeneration, of which the goal is none other than that the image of God, defiled and nearly wiped out in us by the transgression of Adam, is restored in us. ... And this restoration is not completed in one moment or in one day or one year; but with continual, yes, even slow steps God removes corruption from his elect." Later we will see why this wider use of the term has a certain right.

b) Another important point that lacks clarity lies in the concept of calling. While for this concept some still have all the emphasis fall on the immediacy of the action and thus identify internal calling with regeneration, others hold to the obvious thought that calling already presupposes a life and the capacity to hear, and so must be distinguished from the initial begetting of life.

c) Also, the concept of *poenitentia*, "repentance," is not always clearly distinguished. Sometimes this word is taken to mean long processes that accompany the whole of life here on earth, sometimes for instantaneous actions at a critical moment.

As seen above, Calvin identifies *poenitentia, regeneratio, sanctificatio*.

5. *Does one also find here and there an attempt to divide the different stages of the way of salvation in an orderly manner?*

Yes, we can find an example of that in the classification of Voetius. He distinguishes three kinds of acts of God as belonging to the application of salvation:

a) Acts that only effect a change in our state in relation to God. To these belong *reconciliatio*, "reconciliation"; *justificatio*, "justification"; *adoptio*, "adoption as children."

b) Acts that are directed to the will of man with moral suasion but do not take hold or transform inwardly and omnipotently, such as external calling and what belongs to it. Voetius calls these "moral acts."

c) Acts that bring about a real and inherent change in the subject. Regeneration, glorification, etc., are counted among them.

As we will see, the main features are drawn quite correctly here.

6. *What distinctions must we make with a view to arriving at a clear overview of these different acts in their mutual connection?*

a) The first great distinction that needs to be kept in view is the one between *judicial* acts, which change a judicial relationship of man, and *re-creating* acts (in the widest sense of the word), which bring about a change in the actual condition of man. An act of the first kind, for example, is justification; one of the second kind is sanctification. The first kind changes the status; the second changes the condition of the one regarding whom or in whom it takes place.

b) Another distinction of equally great importance teaches us to divide between what occurs *under*, and *in*, or *for* the consciousness of the sinner. Some acts in the application of salvation derive their meaning completely from the fact that they are executed in the light of the consciousness, be it by God or by the man in whom God works. Others, by their nature, can only affect the deeper essence of man that does not appear in the light of the consciousness. Accordingly, they occur without man himself being able to understand and observe them. An example of this latter kind is regeneration. A sinner is as little conscious of his rebirth as a child is conscious of its birth, apart from the consequences by which it makes itself known. An example of the other kind is justification, consisting in a communication to the sinner's consciousness of acquittal and the merits of Christ.

c) Next, one can distinguish between the removal of the old and the establishment of the new in man. Sin is not a mere lack. If it were this, it could suffice for the Holy Spirit to make up what is lacking, and the distinction in view here would make no sense. Sin, however, is more—a positive power that must be removed and destroyed—and in its place must be introduced a positively operating principle of good. Regeneration, preferably, is an act that belongs to the establishment of the new. Repentance, by contrast, we can better reckon to the removal of the old, although here, as in the two earlier cases, we cannot sharply separate the two. Rather, these two—removing the old and establishing the new— accompany each other at every point of their way.

d) Finally, one must carefully distinguish between the beginning, the sudden breakthrough, of an act of grace and its further impact and development. The beginning of God's work of grace always has something distinctive by which it is sharply delineated from the development that follows. Now, in a certain sense one can maintain that regeneration and sanctification are parts of a great process of renewal that begins where the Holy Spirit first lays a hand on someone and ends where the heaven of glory is reached. Still, regeneration and sanctification are essentially distinguished. No less different from each other are the initial crisis in the conscious life of man that one is accustomed to call conversion and the further killing of the old man that continues throughout the whole of life.

7. *What may be established further concerning the relationship between these different groups?*

a) Our first principle is that the judicial relationships are the basis on which the moral acts of re-creation rest in their entirety. However, one should be completely clear what is intended here: it is not that justification as it takes place in the consciousness of the sinner must precede his regeneration in time. This would presuppose an impossibility. Justification surely occurs by faith, and faith as an expression of life in no way tolerates separation from the principle of life that is imparted in the essence of man. Believing without regeneration is no more conceivable than consciousness in a child without natural birth. So, in relation to time, the change of the unconscious condition certainly precedes the change in the conscious state. In contrast, it is completely otherwise if we ask about the logical relationship and put the question as follows: Is someone justified because he is regenerated, or is he regenerated because he will be justified? The answer here according to all of Scripture and according to the Protestant principle can only be the latter. For God, justification in His view is the basis, regeneration the consequence. If wrath and a relationship of punishment continued to exist, no new life would be able to germinate. God cannot communicate subjective habitual grace unless objective satisfaction of His justice is offered with specific application to the individual person. And not only does God, in infusing habitual grace, have in view the judicial relationship, restored or to be restored, but also in his conscious justification the sinner receives the insight that all that is habitual, which is already or will be worked in him, has its basis and origin in acquittal for the sake of Christ. And, accordingly, in the consciousness of God and in the consciousness of the sinner what occurs outwardly in the sphere of justice precedes what occurs inwardly in his moral condition.

b) It is equally necessary to hold firmly that for habitual grace, action on the unconscious essence precedes action on the conscious life. This is but an application of the general rule that what lies on the surface of life stems from the hidden impetus of the depth of life. From the root comes the mysterious life that is at work in the stem and the branches and causes fruit to ripen. So, if we place regeneration and conversion, or regeneration and faith, next to each other, conversion and faith cannot be first in time; on the contrary, regeneration precedes. If one sometimes hears the opposite sequence defended, this rests on a misconception to which we will have to return later.

c) One certainly needs to pay attention to the fact that the two distinctions, of acts that fall within the sphere of justice and acts that fall within the sphere of habitual grace, on the one hand, and of acts of grace that affect the root and acts of grace that affect the branches, on the other, do not run in parallel. Certainly, a saving act that falls in the judicial sphere is always a conscious act, in the original sense for the consciousness of God, in a derivative sense for the consciousness of the sinner. An act that produces habitual grace, however, is not always an act that works in the unconscious life. It can do so, and does, for example, in regeneration, but it need not do that and does not in sanctification and glorification. These two distinctions intersect each other.

8. *What questions need to be addressed regarding each step of the order of salvation?*

   a) Is this particular act of God a judicial act or an act that effects subjective grace?

   b) If the latter, is it an act that works beneath or in the consciousness?

   c) Is its purpose the removing of the old man or the bringing to life of the new man?

   d) Is it an act that stands at the beginning of a long development and produces a crisis, or does it include a long series of similar acts?

   e) Is it an act that is executed by God immediately or an act in which He works mediately?

9. *Are the distinctions made here based on Scripture or are they merely human attempts to bring about an order in the multiplicity of phenomena of the work of grace?*

They are based on Scripture and not only have practical significance but also reflect real relationships that exist between the different virtues of God. Therefore, one cannot change them without the greatest danger, for what one changes is not a subsidiary viewpoint, a perspective, but the fundamental conception of religion. That can be shown in particular on each of the points advanced above.

Concerning the first, the distinction between judicial actions and re-creating acts of grace, on this point the Roman Catholic and the Protestant churches diverge. The former thinks that the changed judicial relationship must have for its basis a change in the moral condition of the sinner, and so with that reintroduces the principle of justification by works that the Apostle Paul so powerfully combated. The latter maintains that all improvement and conversion must have acquittal in God's tribunal as its starting point, and so, on the contrary, makes works a consequence of justification. In the first case, man gets part of the honor for himself; in the second, God gets all the glory. But danger threatens here not only from the side of historic Roman Catholicism.

There is a neo-Romanism that unconsciously honors the same principle. The endeavor is fairly common at present to deny the necessity of change in the judicial sphere as a condition for moral improvement. Almost all the emphasis falls on the ethical, on the reformation of man, as if there is no need to take account of God's justice. This is the opposite of antinomianism; it is a denial rather than a misuse of free grace. The character and capacities of man are elevated as a measure of the favor of God, and moral perfection is insisted on with full force. One would characterize this direction as moral legalism and distinguish it, as such, from the ceremonial legalism of the Jews and the Roman Catholic legalism that coincides with it. Under the appearance of holding high the moral ideal, it is in fact active in attacking this ideal at its heart, for only one who has a thorough sense of the guilt and inner accursedness of evil can possess an unadulterated appreciation and admiration of the good, which is a normal consequence of the former. Whoever preaches transformation without justification does not have the right conception of sin and improvement. He reckons only with the external side of sin under a utilitarian aspect; its deeper spiritual significance totally escapes him. By far the greatest part of the ethics presently preached from pulpits is of this kind. It demands a sanctification under which the indispensable foundation of justification is utterly lacking. From this, in part, is to be explained the ease with which some, despite the clear witness of Scripture, eliminate the doctrine of eternal punishment. The foundation of this doctrine is lacking in the conscience—namely, a deep sense of the necessity that God's justice be maintained. And the end of all this will be the weakening and falsifying of all moral distinctions.

It is almost superfluous to show that Scripture never loses sight of the order indicated above against Roman Catholicism and neo-Romanism. Paul's entire teaching rests on this distinction between sanctification and justification. A Christian loves much after much has been forgiven him, not the reverse: that much has been forgiven him because he loves much. The lost son received forgiveness before anything else. And the same thought recurs everywhere, so strongly in Paul that his opponents could take the occasion to hurl at him the recrimination of antinomianism (cf. Rom 6:1ff.), and he was forced to show expressly how moral transformation infallibly followed imputation—indeed, how in one and the same baptism both were pictured and the images of both fused together.

Also on the second point, Scripture does not leave us in the dark. It always distinguishes between what occurs *beneath* and *in* the consciousness. Romans 8:28–30 presents the chain of salvation with its different links. The practical purpose that the apostle has with this is to strengthen the believer in the consciousness that future glory cannot elude him. In line with that, he now enumerates precisely the acts of salvation that fall within the light of the consciousness, which enable looking forward and backward—namely, calling and justification as lying between election and glorification. This is a proof, therefore, of the genuinely biblical character of the distinction made, for what moves Paul here to limit himself to calling and justification is nothing other than the principle of that distinction that while some operations of grace are recognizable by the consciousness, others are not.

This principle, too, is of utmost weight. Whoever doubts that, along with the influence of grace in the conscious life, God's acts of grace intervene much more deeply and affect the inner essence of man, can do so only on the basis of a superficial view of sin. To allow everything to terminate in conscious life presupposes a Pelagian view of sin and all that is connected with it. What occurs in the consciousness naturally works mediately, persuasively, countering resistance. Only insofar as it surges from the inside out is grace entirely grace, a supernatural operation of power, an exclusive work of God.

The distinction between foundational acts of grace at the outset, which intervene in a creative manner at critical moments, and the further ongoing uniform activity of grace is in no need of demonstration as scriptural. It is necessary, however, to emphasize that distinction because here, too, some seek to substitute slow development from natural causes for a sudden change worked by God.

10. *What points must be examined in general before we proceed to discussing the particular acts of grace?*

a) The relationship between these operations of grace and the work of the Holy Spirit in the sphere of nature.

b) The relationship between the operations of special grace and common grace, *gratia communis*.

c) The relationship between special grace and Holy Scripture.

d) The relationship between special grace and the person of the Mediator and the person of the Holy Spirit.

11. *What is the nature of the relationship between the work of the Holy Spirit in the sphere of nature and that of grace?*

a) A relationship of *analogy* or *correspondence*. In the kingdom of nature the Holy Spirit has His specific task, as well as the Father and the Son. He is the person who by His working leads things to their destined goal and development—who creates and maintains life in the realm of the organic, the rational, the reasonable. Likewise, in the kingdom of grace the Holy Spirit is the one who leads the elect sinner to his destined goal and development by creating and maintaining new life in him.

b) A relationship of *subordination*. What God does for someone through the Holy Spirit in the sphere of nature is not unconnected with what He intends for him in the kingdom of grace. The entire life of the elect, including that part that precedes their implanting into Christ, is ordered by God with a view to its final destined end. It is not immaterial how and where someone is born, which influences work on him, how he is raised, which direction the development of his life takes. Since the place to be occupied by someone in the kingdom of grace is determined by God and coheres closely with all of his earlier development, the latter cannot be left out of consideration in determining the former.

c) Notwithstanding this analogy and this subordination, there exists an essential difference between the working of the Holy Spirit in the sphere of nature and in the kingdom of grace. The latter is a new order of things that cannot be explained by the former, but rests on an immediate intervention of God's Spirit. Grace is not nature. It is certainly true that one also calls grace the natural guiding actions of God, with which He deals with the elect before their regeneration (*gratia praeparans*). But taking the word in this broad sense is not meant to deny the specific difference between the operations of the Spirit in nature and in grace. The word "grace" still has a twofold sense: (1) An attribute in God is called grace; (2) an influence on man that transcends natural influence bears that name. If now something that falls within the sphere of nature is called grace, then it is because the gracious purpose of God adheres to it. One and the same act can occur with respect to two persons and be grace in this sense for the one but not for the other. Still, the act remains specifically the same, and by this purpose is not set outside the sphere of nature. It is absolutely necessary to maintain the sharpest contrast between nature and grace.

12. *What is the relationship between the operations of common grace and the special grace of the Holy Spirit?*

To understand correctly the difference between these two in connection with the preceding distinction, we must move out of the sphere of nature into the sphere of revelation. This revelation is itself the product of a wholly supernatural act of grace. The announcement of the truth of God and the inspiration of the Holy Spirit lie both beyond and above nature. At the same time, however, that truth is given in natural forms. It is expressed in words written with letters, words that can be heard by the natural ear and read by the natural eye. As we hope to see, it is not the most proper and highest end of the truth to accomplish its work outwardly in this way; rather, it reaches its proper goal only when an entirely supernatural work of the Holy Spirit accompanies it. That it works *in this way as well*, however, no one can doubt. The only question, though, is how? If it were simply directed to man and nothing more, this encounter would only result in opposition and reaction from a soul that is sinful and hostile to God. That this nevertheless does not occur, but that even in those who are not regenerate the moral power of the truth is manifested, shows that there is an accompanying working of God's Spirit. That working of the Spirit is given to all in greater or lesser degree. It comes down, then, to separating it sharply from special grace, in which only the elect share. So that the distinction would already appear in the term, it has been called *common* grace, and what contrasts with it, *special* or *particular* grace. One further needs to give attention to making distinctions on the following points:

a) Common grace brings about no change in the nature of man as special grace does. Whatever may also be its external manifestations, it does not regenerate man.

b) A second distinction is connected with this. Common grace is also limited to making man receptive to the influence of the truth that works on him from his consciousness. It works persuasively, by offering motives to the will and by making use of inclinations that are already present, not by creating new habits in man. It can certainly bring the external good still present in man to development, but it cannot produce what is spiritually good from that. It can cause a seed of external righteousness to germinate, but it is not capable of implanting the seed of regeneration.

c) All that works in this manner can also be resisted. Since it is directed toward individual motives from outside, the possibility always exists that the unrenewed nature will overrule all these motives and render common grace powerless. It is otherwise with efficacious grace. It does not offer motives for doing good to a will that in its nature is evil, but transforms the will itself from the innermost recesses of its nature, not by countering it but by re-creating it. Hence, common grace is termed resistible; efficacious grace, with a somewhat oblique label, irresistible.

13. *Does one sometimes also speak of "common grace" in a still broader sense?*

Yes, one sometimes also applies the word to the restraining action of the Holy Spirit that, where revelation is not known, is joined with the natural knowledge of God and hinders the breaking out of sin in its most dreadful extremes.

14. *From what may we discern in some measure what should be ascribed to the operation of this common grace?*

We have seen in the doctrine of election that God's Word rightly ascribes the hardening of sinners to the withdrawal of common grace. It calls this being given over to a perverse mind and shows from experience what dreadful dimensions sin assumes where this hardening sets in. On the other hand, it also describes for us the fate of the lost who are devoid of common grace. Consequently, everything that hinders the process of death that sin brings in producing the complete dissolution of moral and social life for the individual and for society is to be ascribed to *gratia communis* in the broadest sense of the word.

15. *Can you show that Scripture teaches such an operation of the Holy Spirit?*

Yes, it is said of the generation that lived before the flood that God's Spirit contended with them and contended in vain, that the patience of God at the time of this contending held back His punishment, but that finally this operation of grace ceased since it was resisted and scorned (Gen 6:3; cf. 1 Pet 3:19–20; 4:6). Stephen cried out to the Jews, "You always resist the Holy Spirit; as your fathers did, so do you" (Acts 7:51). Also, Isaiah 63:10 mentions a grieving of the Holy Spirit.

16. *How far can this common operation of the Holy Spirit go?*

We must assume that it always remains distinguished specifically from regenerating grace. So, concerning the operation itself, one really cannot speak of it approaching the grace of regeneration. What lies between these two is not a gradual but a principial difference. Whatever else one may do to a dead person, one cannot say that actions are performed on him that *bring him close to life*. Since, however, the infusion of life eludes our sight and we can judge it only by its outward manifestation, so the possibility always continues to exist that common grace reveals itself in forms that are hardly to be distinguished from the actions of the regenerate. Temporary faith, of which Scripture speaks in very strong terms, must be counted among these cases. And often the sole criterion for recognition lies in the passing of time itself.

17. *Are the effects of common grace divorced from any connection with regenerating grace, which works only in the elect?*

No; if by common grace someone has received a certain measure of insight into the truth prior to his regeneration, be it then also in a non-saving way, its fruits are not lost. When saving grace comes upon us, it imparts new worth to all the old that was already present with us earlier. It only must be maintained that it never is the old as such that continues to work after regeneration, but the old is placed in a new light and with completely new qualities. The knowledge of saving faith is very much connected with historical knowledge that someone gained prior to his regeneration, but it would still certainly be wrong to maintain that a regenerate person does not know, in his faith, in an essentially different way than the unregenerate person.

18. *Has the doctrine of common grace also been misused?*

Yes, some have wished to find in it a solution to the question why saving grace befalls only some and not all—in other words, an explanation of God's sovereign election. Shedd says the following: "The nonelect receives common grace, and common grace would incline human will if it were not defeated by the human will. If the sinner should make no hostile opposition, common grace would be equivalent to saving grace. To say that common grace if not resisted by the sinner would be equivalent to regenerating grace is not the same as to say that common grace if assisted by the sinner would be equivalent to regenerating grace. In the first instance, God would be the sole author of regeneration; in the second He would not be." Yet in another place he maintains, "Regeneration rests upon God's election ... upon special grace and not upon common grace." Thus it is not very clear what he intends. If, of themselves, all sinners already resist common grace, then it makes no sense to say that it would regenerate them if they did not resist it, for nonresisting means the same as being no longer sinful. If, on the other hand, a sinner is able to resist and not resist common grace, and some are really in the latter category, then for them, according to this conception, regenerating grace becomes completely superfluous. Common grace should work on them and regenerate them. This idea is completely false. God's election lies above every consideration of the use of common grace. One can only go this far: Those who resist common grace such that God withdraws it do not belong to the elect. They are then abandoned to the hardening from which salvation is no longer possible. On the other hand, it cannot be maintained that a good use of common grace always leads to receiving saving grace or is even a characteristic of election. Certainly in a negative sense, if someone resists common grace, then this is a bad sign. But we may not go further.

19. *What is the connection of special grace to Holy Scripture?*

A very close connection. It is not the destiny of man to be re-created in his nature without there being knowledge of God and his relationship to God in his consciousness. Man is a rational being, and there must be for him an objective knowledge of the truth, besides the operation of grace that affects him below his consciousness. The rule, then, is that the saving grace of God works only where Holy Scripture, the Word of

God, is present. Here it is like natural birth. God does not allow children to be conceived and born into a world without light, air, or food. Neither does He regenerate His children without a divine Word that can supply them with the content requisite for consciousness.

This, however, does not imply at all that regenerating grace only occurs mediately through the Word. To maintain this would evidently lead again to confusing saving with common grace. Regeneration does not occur without the Word—that is, where the Word is not present—but just as little by the Word as a *causa efficiens* [efficient cause]. Air, light, and food are necessary conditions for the birth of a child, but no one will maintain that they are sufficient active causes for birth. Again, a child is not born without the involvement of father and mother, but a creationist does not therefore believe that father and mother as secondary causes can give rise to the soul of the child. Creating the soul is the prerogative of God's omnipotence in the kingdom of nature; re-creating the soul is the exclusive work of His sovereign omnipotence in the kingdom of grace. And that He is independent of the Word can best be seen when one considers the regeneration of children. Those who die at a young age and enter heaven have most certainly experienced the saving grace of God, and for them there surely cannot be talk of a mediate working by God's Word. Since their consciousness is still dormant for the most part, regeneration need not be preceded and accompanied by the preaching of the Word.

20. *Does the rule strictly apply for adults that there is only regeneration where the external Word of God is preached?*

We do not have the slightest reason to depart from this rule. It conflicts with every analogy that God would engender life where all further conditions for the feeding and development of life are entirely lacking. One could only ask: Is it absolutely necessary for God to fulfill those conditions by means of Holy Scripture? Can He not set the necessary truth directly before the consciousness outside the sphere of the dissemination of Scripture and outside the bounds of the church or of its influence, and then bring about regeneration in connection with that? There have been some Reformed theologians, specifically Zwingli, who have been willing to leave open the possibility of something like that in order not to judge the pagan world too harshly.

If, however, we read Scripture in an unprejudiced way, then we will have to agree that the basis for such a view is lacking. Paganism is always presented as a state of absolute darkness, into which no ray of light penetrates. Those who do not have the gospel are without hope and without God in the world, without a share in the citizenship of Israel and strangers from the covenant of promise [cf. Eph 2:12]. Naturally, we must let God be free and can arrogate for ourselves no judgment on what He *could* do. At issue here is only the question what He, as far as we know, actually does. Also, all Christian zeal for missions presupposes that grace closely follows God's Word and cannot be detached from the ministry of the Word. With election itself God has established the means of election, and even what happens with someone in the kingdom of nature is regulated with that in view. So, if He had willed to elect pagans, He certainly could have had them born under the light of the gospel.

Some have pointed to the conversion of Paul and to similar facts. Paul, too, was not acquainted with the gospel through the ministry of the Word that already existed in the church but received an immediate revelation accompanied with internal renewal (Gal 1:12). So, it is thought, God can also do that with a Socrates, a Plato, or with other pagans, and we are advised not to be too narrow in our thinking about them. Especially the broad outlook of our century, which spans worlds, can no longer be satisfied with the old, narrow particularism of national election.

There is only one answer to all that: God's Word does not teach us otherwise. The case of Paul is not at all suited to derive something from it. That he received an immediate revelation was not, in the first place, necessary for his personal renewal but primarily for his official calling as apostle, and only in connection with that for the work of grace. At that time, too, Paul was in no way outside the sphere of revelation but was a Jew of the Jews [cf. Phil 3:5], a member of the covenant nation, one of the great branches from the stem of Israel that was not cut off when the rest fell and into which the pagans were grafted.

21. *Between what extremes does this legitimate Reformed conception of the connection between Scripture and the operation of grace lie?*

Between, on the one hand, the mystical conception that, without prior contact with objective truth, has manifestations of grace emerging everywhere—manifestations that themselves create conscious content in a capricious way. The truth, then, emerges from the subjective working of grace, and no means remain to test the latter. We, on the contrary, hold that Scripture is not only a necessary condition for the growth of spiritual life, and to that extent also for its creation, but moreover that the experiences of this life can be gauged as legitimate only by Scripture. What does not accord with the objective Word and in its general features is not approved by it and is false experience.

The opposite extreme is that of rationalism, which ascribes everything to the common operation of the Word. This is deism applied to the personal relationship between God and man. As God works in nature from without through second causes and not immanently, so too He works in man through moral and religious truths and not from within, in the heart. In this deistic standpoint one cannot even grant the operation of common grace, for this already lies on the line of immanence; much less, then, regenerating grace.

We say: not without the Word, but also not exclusively through the Word.

22. *How do Lutherans think about the connection between the Word and saving grace?*

They, too, reject all mysticism that detaches grace from the ordained means of grace. At the same time, however, they fall into the error that God works instrumentally through the Word at every point, both in regeneration and otherwise. Now, to avoid all misconception in a rationalistic sense, they teach that there is latent in God's Word a power higher than moral power—a supernatural power. A human word works by generating certain thoughts and setting in motion a certain series of ideas, but it is not therefore able to create something new in the soul. With God's Word it is otherwise, according to the Lutherans. It works through a *vis inhaerens*, "an inherent power," operative on all who come in contact with it. Lutherans certainly do not maintain that this supernatural power of grace is resident in the written letters or the audible sounds of the Word, but in the ideas that are expressed and represented thereby. Between the latter and grace there exists a *unio mystica*. This, then, is also transmitted from the Word, and by means of the Word to the sacraments.

23. *How do the Roman Catholics think of the connection between the external means of grace and the internal operation of grace?*

They, too, accept an instrumental and not only an accompanying connection. Power is latent in the sacraments as such and is not to be obtained apart from them—and then in the sacraments as *res*, "things," not in the Word that accompanies them, as the Lutherans intend. The *gratia praeveniens*, "antecedent grace," in which adults share without any merits, works persuasively. It teaches an adult to know his sinful condition and the righteousness of God, consider the mercy of God, and be confident that God will be gracious to him for Christ's sake. Accordingly, he is enabled to cooperate with this grace, which disposes him to love God and brings him to the hatred of sin and the contrition that must precede baptism. Finally, this antecedent grace also moves him to desire baptism and to receive it for himself, and in baptism the actual re-creating power of grace appears.

One sees from this that Rome rejects semi-Pelagianism, at least in theory. Antecedent grace is necessary. Man cannot begin by himself. But this antecedent grace is still not re-creating in nature but is more of a persuasive kind. From that it is sufficiently clear that no account is taken of the impotence of man. Man cannot learn to abhor sin, practice true repentance, etc., by persuasive grace. These are always acts that cannot arise from the dead and unregenerate heart.

For children, there is naturally no need for these prior actions. They receive baptism without preparation.

24. *Do all God's operations of grace have the same relationship to the Word of Scripture?*

No, there is a difference here between one operation of grace and another. Concerning the begetting of life in the soul, regeneration, the external Word has only an accompanying connection with internal grace. It is impossible that the light and the things that appear in it would beget the capacity for sight or would be useful as means to that end.

It is otherwise once the principle of life is infused and manifests itself in the consciousness. Then it immediately comes into contact with the Word of God. Just as with a child the capacity for sight is developed and reaches its completion only by repeated seeing, so too the spiritual sight of the regenerate is sharpened by this contact with the truth.

In fact, the latter here works instrumentally. God makes use of it to nurture life. And for all acts of grace that occur in the consciousness, it is the case that they are connected with Scripture. Justification and calling, for instance, occur in the consciousness. In both, God comes and speaks to man. In both, the content of the truth is introduced into his consciousness. The correct conception is that this truth is not the product of a new, completely self-standing revelation. God does not call with an audible voice and does not express His judicial sentence through a special revelation, but in both cases He makes use of the once-for-all revealed Word of Holy Scripture, and surely He does this by a particular application of it to the consciousness, effected by the Holy Spirit.

Here, too, we must sail between the reefs of deism and mysticism. Calling and justification are more than the deducing of a consequence from a few general lines of Scripture. For God's work of grace, reasoning and reckoning in this way do not suffice. Neither, however, is it a mystical inspiration flowing from feeling or the will, detached from the objective truth of Scripture. They both rest on the truth of Scripture, made personal by the Holy Spirit. Grace in the consciousness is not independent of the Word. But the Word, in turn, is not detached from the Holy Spirit.

25. *What kind of connection is there between the operation of God's grace in the special sense and the Mediator?*

In this connection lies the most characteristic distinction between the operations of particular, saving grace and all that lies outside. Regarding God's purpose, saving operations and other operations of grace can sometimes coincide. Also, there can sometimes be agreement concerning their miraculous and immediate character. One thinks, for example, of the miracles, all of which occur immediately, of supernatural revelation, of the inspiration of Scripture.

But all this is different from saving grace at one point: Saving grace effects at its onset a personal bond with the Mediator, Christ, and in its further realization rests on the continuation of that bond. The one in whom no saving grace has worked is apart from Christ; the one in whom this grace has in fact worked, or even begins to work, is joined to Christ. The bond with Christ brings saving grace with it, and where the latter is found the first must also be found. Consequently, we have here something objective by which particular grace can be delimited from all the rest. It is grace from Christ and to Christ.

26. *What is the name that is given to this bond between persons in whom special grace works and Christ?*

This bond is called the mystical union, *unio mystica*. It bears this name because it lies beneath the consciousness. It does not consist in a fellowship or exchange of thoughts, but in a real though incomprehensible fellowship of life. *Mystical* stands here in contradistinction to the rationally transparent. In a certain sense, all the deeper actions of life are mystical, mysterious, but this union is so in double measure.

27. *What in general is the significance of this union with Christ?*

It serves to form a glorious body for the Mediator, of which He Himself is the head. For the Savior it is an honor as mediator to be so joined personally with those for whom He has become their surety and to live with them in a fellowship of destiny never to be dissolved. Coming into consideration here, however, is not so much the significance that this *unio* has for Christ as its meaning for the work of grace that takes place in the believer. Put more precisely, the question is this: Why does grace work from now on in the sinner from Christ and only in union with Christ?

In answering this question, one will need to guard against a great misconception. Many continue to propose that the bond with the Mediator is the legal basis on which God permits His merits to benefit the individual sinner. The reasoning goes as follows: Christ has certainly satisfied for sin and earned eternal life, but all this does not help me and is not valid for me as long as Christ is a stranger who is outside me. God cannot declare me just on the basis of what the Mediator did as long as the Mediator remains a stranger to me. Such a declaration of justice would be unjust. Thus God ensures that a real fellowship between Christ and my soul is brought about. He implants Christ in me, and now declares in agreement with my actual condition that I am just. Indeed, by this implanting I have truly become a member of Christ's body, so that it is now the righteousness of the body, whose organic member I am, that is imputed to me. Union with Christ is, so it is thought, therefore the indispensable juridical basis for the justification of sinners.

This reasoning sounds fine, and has misled many by its attractiveness. Despite its fine appearance, it falsifies the fundamental element of the Christian doctrine of salvation: the element of justification by free imputation. Justification is always and everywhere in Scripture a declaration of God, not on the basis of an actually existing condition of our being righteous, but on the basis of a gracious imputation of God that is contradicted by our condition. While we in ourselves are unrighteous, God's judgment acquits us. Justification is a paradox. The old theologians, therefore, always rightly stood for the proposition that the sinner is justified *qua talis*—that is, *qua impius*, as sinner, as godless. His justification is an act of grace insofar as it concerns himself, not an act of justice. If, then, we must assume that it occurs on the basis of his actual being in Christ through mystical union, then it could only be a declaration of what really is, a taking note of the actual condition, and the element of grace would be lost.

The intended proposal must accordingly be rejected, and one must endeavor to be completely clear where the error in it is. It reverses the relationship between grace in the justice of God and grace in the life of the sinner; it makes the former rest on the latter. This cannot be. Concerning the legal relationship, being reckoned in Christ precedes, and only from that does being in the Mediator follow. The mystical union is not the basis on which I appear just before God but a gift that is extended to me from God's justification. When one reasons otherwise, one constantly reasons secretly in a circle. If all the actions of grace following upon the mystical union become mine on the basis of this union, the question must still always be asked: On what basis do I share in the *unio mystica* with Christ Himself? If it is true that no grace can come to me on the basis of Christ's merits as long as I am not in Christ, how is it ever possible that I would be implanted in Him? This implanting cannot occur on the basis of being in Christ, for it is precisely the implanting that effects being in Christ. One will thus be compelled to say that implanting occurs by way of anticipation in view of impending justification. A clear circle, for now we have justification on the basis of being in Christ and being in Christ on the basis of justification.

It rests on this misconception when some maintain that regeneration can only follow faith, for first faith unites to Christ and the gifts of grace only come from Christ, regeneration not excluded. One need only ask where faith comes from. If from Christ, then one has in principle abandoned the thesis that all subjective grace rests on being in Him.

The correct conception of matters is as follows: The legal basis for all grace lies in being reckoned in Christ by the judgment of God. This actual relationship in the justice of God is reflected in the consciousness of the sinner when he believes, for by faith he acknowledges that there is no righteousness in himself, and that the righteousness by which he stands righteous before God is transmitted to him by imputation. Now as far as what is judicial is concerned, it could have remained at this. Without effecting a life-union between Christ and believers, God still could have transmitted His righteousness to them. Then, however, imputation would only appear in the consciousness. Grace would have only been revealed as grace to the consciousness, without its imprint having been stamped deeper into the life of the believer. Now, however, God acts otherwise. He does not stop with this acknowledgment in the consciousness that righteousness is transmitted and that, consequently, each gift of grace is given for Christ's sake. To strengthen this impression, He also has all grace actually come from Christ and establishes a life-bond between the Mediator and believers. The legal fellowship reflects itself in a fellowship of destiny. All that the sinner receives flows from the living Christ. The result is that the sinner not only knows as an idea that he will receive everything for Christ's sake but also *experiences in life* how everything comes from Christ. He is regenerated, justified, sanctified, glorified, but all this is in the closest bond with the Mediator.

However, far from leaving him with the illusion that as a member of a great body he has a right to these things, this arrangement of God serves as a constant reminder of the fact that he personally had no right to them, that this right is earned by Christ, and that the right has been passed on to him in the judgment of God, just as the gifts have been passed on to him, both from Christ. We therefore reach exactly the opposite result. The mystical union is not ordained in order to eliminate the idea of free imputation but to keep the memory of this idea rightly alive. If the gifts of grace were distributed directly, the consciousness of their real origin would all too easily be lost. Now that possibility is cut off. The receiving of life from Christ reminds at every moment that that life is earned by Christ.

For Christians the doctrine of the *unio mystica*, correctly understood, is the best means of protection against salvation by works. It shows how foolish and unnecessary it is to bring the covenant of works back into the covenant of grace and to again allow the sinner to merit something for himself. All self-meriting assumes the idea that a separate fountain of life exists in the meriting self. If Adam had merited eternal life, he would have had the fountain of life in himself. Now that, on the contrary, the fountain is in Christ, no one can doubt that the merits reside in Him as well. The Roman Catholics with their system of salvation by works have no place for the *unio mystica*.

28. *What can we establish further concerning this union with Christ?*

a) It is not a unity that resides in the ordinary concursus of God. God is present in every creature by His co-action. And insofar as Christ as Logos sustains all things, He also has a certain immanent association with all created spirits. This, however, is a union of the Logos-God with the creature as creature. The mystical union is a union of the person of the Mediator with the regenerate person as such.

b) Neither is it a unity that rests on an agreement of consciousness by which the doctrine of Christ is accepted in faith. Faith as an act of consciousness is only the surface manifestation of the unity of life that lies much deeper. Socinians and Arminians have such a concept of the union with Christ as is rejected here. The former think of a unity of doctrine, the latter of a unity in love.

c) It is also not a merging of being such that the separate existence of either Christ or the believer would come to an end. This was the error of the mystics. Some of them went so far as to teach the identification of Christ and the believer, and led the latter to say the words, "I am Christ Jesus the living Word of God; I have saved you through sinless suffering." On the contrary, we believe that personal identity is not in the least impaired by mystical union, but first comes to its full right. Every believer is joined by a particular and distinctive bond to Christ, and only by that bond becomes what he should be and what God has destined him for. So little does the fellowship of life with the Mediator negate this distinctiveness that the apostle can say instead, "To a perfect man, to the measure of the stature of the fullness of Christ" (Eph 4:13). "But to each of us is given grace according to the measure of the gift of Christ" (Eph 4:7).

d) It is not a union that can be wrought or brought about by any external means. Sacramentarians—that is, those who tie the essence of Christianity to the use of external, physical means—maintain such a view. This is the grossest misconception of all. The *unio mystica* lies far beyond the scope of any material substance.

e) Concerning the essence of this union in a positive sense, we can say that it is:

1. An *organic* unity. Accordingly, Scripture compares it with the connection there is between the vine and the branches, the head and the body (John 15:1-6; 1 Cor 6:15, 19; 12:12; Eph 1:22-23; 4:15-16; 5:29-30). The essence of the organic consists in the fact that there is a reciprocal connection of goal and means between the differing parts of a thing that nonetheless has an abiding significance in itself. So it is with Christ and believers. He is there for them, yet they also are given to Him as instruments for His honor. And the body that they form with Him is not a creation of temporary duration by which a passing goal is to be reached; it will remain eternally in its organic connection. Also, it cannot be dissolved; no member having once been engrafted can fall from it (Rom 8:35, 39). Even those who die still die in Christ, and even their bodies that are entrusted to the earth are not torn away from the organic connection with the *unio mystica* of the Lord, for they are sown (cf. 1 Thess 4:14, 17; with Rom 8:11; 1 Cor 15).

2. A unity of *life*. The power of the new life that is in believers comes from Christ. Christ lives in them. Someone must show that he is a Christian by whether Christ is in him (Gal 2:20; 2 Cor 13:5). When the life of the Christian develops fully, then Christ is formed in him [Gal 4:19]. And it is said directly that Christ is *in* the believer (Rom 8:10). All these expressions can only have a single significance: The life of Christ exercises a secret action on the life of the regenerate sinner, in

consequence of which the latter receives its direction toward God—that is, becomes spiritual life.

3. A *spiritual* unity. The *unio mystica* is wrought by the Holy Spirit: "For we are all baptized with one Spirit into one body" (1 Cor 12:13). The Spirit is called "the Spirit of the Lord" in 2 Corinthians 3:18. Indeed, verse 17 says directly, "Now the Lord is the Spirit." In Romans 8:9–10, "to have the Spirit of Christ," "to be in the Spirit," and "Christ is in you" are parallel. Therefore Christ is in someone by the Spirit: "The one who is joined to the Lord is one Spirit with Him" (1 Cor 6:17). Consequently, it is not subject to any doubt that the bond between Christ and the members of His body is the Holy Spirit. Still, it must surely be observed that the Holy Spirit is present here, strictly speaking, as He is given to Christ at His exaltation and after that is poured out on the Church. It is the Holy Spirit as *gift* that we are to think of here. Before the Holy Spirit was poured out, He had already worked subjective grace in believers throughout the entire old dispensation. But still, the result of that work was not what could properly be called a mystical union. When Christ became the glorified Head, He took this gift and imparted it to all who are members of His body. Just because the indwelling of the Spirit is in Christ— what is referred to here—this mediate unity must at the same time hold true for the closest bond. The Holy Spirit is in the human nature of Christ and works from there out on believers to dwell in them. By placing the emphasis on this, we also avoid imagining that there is an identification of being between Christ and believers. The unity between the divine person and human nature in the Mediator is a personal unity and therefore also immediate, not first wrought by the Holy Spirit. It is otherwise with the unity established between Christ and believers. This is not a personal unity in the sense that a unity of person would flow from it. Christ and those who are of Christ remain different persons, so that for that reason, too, the mystical union can never be the legal basis of their justification before God. Rather, it is a unity of life that neither removes nor makes impossible the distinction of

persons. And therefore it is wrought and maintained by the source of all spiritual and eternal life by God the Holy Spirit.

4. A *reciprocal* unity. Establishing this unity is of course a work of Christ. Man does not take the initiative here by taking hold of Christ and drawing Him to himself or bringing himself to Him. The impossibility and inconceivability of that follows from what has already been said. How by any act from his side would man ever be able to make himself master of the Holy Spirit? It is entirely the reverse: Christ sends His Spirit, who, in the first grace that befalls man in the grace of regeneration, establishes the mystical bond. After this has happened and has also penetrated into the consciousness, one can certainly say that faith reaches out reciprocally to Christ, and the activity of faith and the nurturing of the spiritual life resident in union with Christ keep pace. But faith in itself, as subjective habit or subjective act, is not able to effect unity with Christ. It is one of the manifestations of the life of the Savior in us rather than the source of this life itself. When Scripture speaks of a union with Christ by faith, then this always applies to unity in the consciousness or the consciousness of unity: "so that Christ may dwell in your hearts by faith" (Eph 3:17), where, however, precedes, "so that He might grant you though the riches of His glory to be strengthened with power *by His Spirit* in the inner man." The Spirit's activity, therefore, is antecedent, and only as a result of it does Christ dwell in the heart by faith. It is the drawing power of Christ Himself that in our faith draws us to His life. In this sense, then, Scripture clearly teaches that a reception of life from Christ by faith is possible for us— indeed, is necessary (John 6:47, 51). There is not merely a life of Christ in us but also a life of ours for God in union with Christ. According to Romans 7:4, the believer knows himself to be as closely united to the Mediator as husband to wife, and according to 2 Corinthians 11:2, the church is viewed as a bride presenting herself to her bridegroom, Christ. "The Spirit and the bride say, 'Come!'" (Rev 22:17).

5. A *personal* and thereby *corporate* union with Christ, the Head for all believers. Because they all are united with the exalted

Mediator and engrafted into the same branch, in Him they also have a bond with each other. Still, this may not be understood in the modern pantheistic sense, as if life resides in the church and is transmitted from the church to the individual. Everyone who is regenerated receives his life directly from Christ. A communication of life from one man to another is unthinkable. It is only the second Adam who has become a life-giving Spirit [1 Cor 15:45], so that He can cause power to issue from Himself in order to beget life in others. The communion of the saints is a fruit of grace, not a means of grace.

6. Union with Christ is a *transforming* and *conforming* union. Here, too, it appears how close the connection is with the person of the Mediator according to His humanity, for there can be no thought of conformity to the divine nature of Christ. What Christ effects in the members of His body is a likeness of what has taken place in Himself. They are buried with Him, rise with Him [Rom 6:5], are oppressed with Him and glorified with Him [Rom 8:17], are ordained to be conformed to His image and, as subsequently born brothers, to follow Him, the firstborn [Rom 8:29]. But all this is not a mere similarity, for the apostle teaches in Romans 6:5 that one becomes one plant with Christ in the likeness of His death and in the likeness of His resurrection. That is, because it is one Spirit of life who works in Christ and us, so the likeness of His resurrection must also follow the likeness of His death: "That I know Him and the power of His resurrection and the fellowship of His suffering, being conformed to His death" (Phil 3:10); "And in my flesh I fill up the remnants of the afflictions of Christ for His body, which is the church" (Col 1:24); "But as you have fellowship in the sufferings of Christ, rejoice" (1 Pet 4:13).

CHAPTER TWO

Regeneration and Calling

1. *What is regeneration?*

Regeneration is an immediate re-creation of the sinful nature by God the Holy Spirit and an implanting into the body of Christ.

2. *Is it a judicial or a re-creating act?*

The latter. In regeneration the condition and not the state of man is changed.

3. *Does regeneration occur in the consciousness or below the consciousness?*

Below the consciousness. It is totally independent from what occurs in the consciousness. It can therefore be effected where the consciousness slumbers.

4. *Is regeneration a slow process or an instantaneous action?*

It is an instantaneous action that is the basis for a long development in grace.

5. *Is regeneration concerned with the removal of the old or the enlivening of the new?*

Regeneration includes both. However, one can rightly maintain that the latter has prominence.

6. *Is regeneration a mediate or an immediate act of God?*

It is immediate in the strict sense. No instrument is employed for it.

7. *Which words in Scripture designate regeneration?*

    a) The first term is γεννηθῆναι ἄνωθεν, which appears in John 3:3, 7; γεννηθῆναι ἐξ ὕδατος καὶ πνεύματος (John 3:5); παλινγγενεσία (Titus 3:5); ἀναγεννηθῆναι (1 Pet 1:3, 23); ἐκ θεοῦ γεννηθῆναι (1 John 2:29; 3:9; 4:7; 5:1, 4, 18).

       1. Concerning the places where *gennēthēnai* appears, the passive meaning of this term must be noted first. It literally means "to be generated." By this is expressed as strongly as possible that regeneration is an act of God, in which man remains passive. When one considers the birth of a child it could perhaps still be maintained that it is accompanied by some movement of the child itself. But "to be regenerated" excludes any such movement in principle and fixes us on the activity of the one who regenerates.

       2. Ἄνωθεν γεννηθῆναι does not mean, as Meyer and others assert, "being born from above." It is certainly true that ἄνωθεν can have this local meaning, but the context shows that this is not the case here. After all, in John 3:4 ἄνωθεν is replaced by δεύτερον, "for the second time." And Nicodemus is not surprised by the fact that this birth must come from above, but by the fact that it must take place a second time. If he had thought "from above," he could not have posed the question, "Can someone enter a second time into his mother's womb and be born?" "Again," however, has the deeper meaning "anew" here, so what is required is an absolute beginning. Not that half of what is connected with generation or birth must be repeated, but man must again undergo being born anew. Compare Galatians 4:9: "which you want to serve again [πάλιν] anew [ἄνωθεν]."

       3. Thus, something occurs that is a repetition of the first birth. The point of similarity is this: In natural birth man has received from his father and mother a carnal, corrupt nature: "What is born of the flesh is flesh" (John 3:6); "... are born not

of blood, nor of the will of the flesh, nor of the will of man" (John 1:13). In regeneration he receives a spiritual nature. The similarity does not go further. It is by no means being denied that the first birth is connected with the *genesis of the substance of the soul* and the *formation of the person*, while by regeneration the substance is not removed and replaced by another, but, like the person, it remains the same as it was before.

4. It is a birth ἐξ ὕδατος καὶ πνεύματος, "of water and Spirit." This refers to baptism, and, according to a sacramental manner of speaking, what is attributed to the sign belongs to the thing signified. Baptism portrays two things: the washing away and cleansing of what is sinful, and the imparting of what is pure and new. "Water" and "Spirit" thus stand for the two sides of God's re-creative work: "the removal of the old" and "the imparting of the new." Compare Ezekiel 36:25–27, where they are likewise placed side by side: "I will sprinkle clean water on you, and you shall be clean. ... And I will give you a new heart, and a new spirit I will put within you. ... And I will give you my Spirit." One should note that "water" and "Spirit" occur here without an article, because baptism does not so much have in view a specific application of water and a specific activity of the Spirit as the character of water and Spirit in general. The water is the cleansing element; the Spirit is the generator of life. Thus, all told: "For someone a renewal of nature must take place, in which he is cleansed of sin and receives new life within himself."[1]

5. The same sense is present in Titus 3:5. Baptism is a bath from which one emerges washed and renewed. Thus, the work of regeneration has two sides: cleansing and renewal. The Holy Spirit is the one who effects this, and He is richly poured out by Jesus Christ the Savior (Titus 3:6). The *palingenesia* spoken of here puts the emphasis more on what occurs in man; it is literally "regeneration."

We believe, accordingly, that by regeneration is to be understood: (1) an act done exclusively by God; (2) a renewal of nature;

---

1 No source is given for this quote.

(3) an act that has two sides—the removal of the old life and an imparting of a new life; (4) an act in which the Holy Spirit appears as the one who produces this new life; (5) an act in which the Holy Spirit works out of Christ and jointly with Christ.

b) In Paul we have a series of terms that clearly express the same matter: "For neither is circumcision anything, nor uncircumcision, but *a new creation* [καινὴ κτίσις]" (Gal 6:15). "Therefore, if anyone is in Christ, he is *a new creation*" (2 Cor 5:17). "For we are *His* workmanship, *created in Christ Jesus* for good works" (Eph 2:10). "Even when we were *dead* in trespasses, He made us *alive* with *Christ*" (Eph 2:5). "*From Him* you are *in Christ Jesus*, who has become to us wisdom from God and righteousness and sanctification and redemption" (1 Cor 1:30). "For the law of *the Spirit of life in Christ Jesus* has set me free from the law of sin and death" (Rom 8:2). "We then were *buried with Him* by baptism into death, so that as Christ was raised from the dead by the glory of the Father, we too should walk in *newness of life*" (Rom 6:4).

Here, too, we reach the same result: (1) Regeneration is an immediate work of God by which man is totally passive, a new creation; (2) it effects a renewal of nature; (3) it has two sides, a burial of the old man and an enlivening of the new; (4) the Holy Spirit is the one who produces this new life; (5) the Holy Spirit does this jointly with Christ; it is the law of the Spirit of the life in Christ that frees from the law of sin and of death.

c) Particular mention is due those scriptural passages that speak of regeneration as a renewal of the *heart*. "Create in me a clean heart, O God, and renew a steadfast spirit deep within me" (Psa 51:10). "I will remove the heart of stone from their flesh and give them a heart of flesh" (Ezek 11:19). It is necessary at this point to keep in view accurately the biblical concept of "heart," לֵב, לֵבָב, καρδία, in contrast to ψυχή and πνεῦμα, נֶפֶשׁ, and רוּחַ, which were already discussed earlier.[2] The heart is the seat of the potency that determines our nature, the center of our being that indicates the direction and predisposition of all that occurs in our spiritual life. It is therefore something that lies still more deeply than

---

2   Vol. 2, ch. 1, q. 5.

personal self-consciousness, for the latter is merely the reflection in the conscious life of the unity and uniformity of the soul, as we saw earlier in the scriptural terms ψυχή, נֶפֶשׁ. What is meant by "heart" can become clear from Proverbs 4:23, "Keep your heart with all vigilance, for out of it flow the issues of life." The heart is therefore also the place where the Holy Spirit, who renews the nature and governs the new life, makes His abode. "The love of God has been poured into our hearts through the Holy Spirit who has been given to us" (Rom 5:5). "God has sent the Spirit of His Son into your hearts" (Gal 4:6). To the heart is ascribed the predisposition and basic inclinations in which the personality and nature manifest themselves: "according to your hardness and your impenitent heart" (Rom 2:5); "an honest and good heart" (Luke 8:15); "love from a pure heart" (1 Tim 1:5); "an evil, unbelieving heart" (Heb 3:12); "a true heart" (Heb 10:22); "the pure in heart" (Matt 5:8). In all these cases, ψυχή could not be used. The "heart," therefore, is something that man cannot judge, that evades our observation, and that only God in His omniscience knows and searches (Matt 15:8; Luke 16:15). All that is good wells up from the heart, and all that is evil arises from the heart. "The good man brings forth good out of the good treasure of his heart" (Luke 6:45). "For from within, out of the heart of man, arise evil thoughts, sexual immorality, etc." (Mark 7:21).

It is now of the greatest importance for the doctrine of regeneration that it is presented as a renewal of the *heart*. Over the heart lies the veil, and in the heart shines the light (2 Cor 3:15; 4:6; 2 Pet 1:19); with the heart one believes (Rom 10:10); the heart is directed to the love of God (2 Thess 3:5). Therefore, by this, every conception that in the renewal of man God works from the circumference to the center is excluded. On the contrary, He works from the center to the periphery, regenerates the heart, and by this in principle the nature is reversed in all its expressions, or at least given a formative capacity that works against the old nature.

8. *How is the usage of scriptural language regarding "calling" connected with the doctrine of regeneration?*

As we know, many older theologians treat regeneration under "calling." They speak of a twofold calling: an *external* calling (*vocatio externa*) that occurs through the preaching of the Word, and an *internal* or *effectual* calling (*vocatio interna, vocatio efficax*) that occurs through the operation of the Holy Spirit in the heart. These terms are not chosen arbitrarily. They occupy a rather large place in scriptural usage, and since theological terminology ought to keep as closely as possible to God's Word, we may not push them aside. However, the question arises whether in Scripture "calling" is in fact understood as the same thing that we have come to know as "regeneration." The answer to this must be twofold: *yes*, concerning the essence of the thing; *no*, concerning the viewpoint from which the same thing is considered. The difference is in the following two points:

a) Regeneration occurs *below the consciousness*; it cannot be observed by man himself and is altogether independent of every relationship that he could adopt toward it. To speak with complete precision, one cannot assume a stance toward his regeneration, since it is not placed objectively before his consciousness. It is otherwise with calling. This occurs *in the consciousness*, is directed to the consciousness, and demands a certain relationship to the consciousness. This is already contained in the term "*calling*." A calling comes from outside; a rebirth works from the inside out.

b) Connected with this, regeneration is a *physical* act. Calling is a *teleological* act, directed to a certain end. One is regenerated *from* one condition into another; one is called *to* something. With calling a certain endpoint is brought into view, with the prospect that one would reach this endpoint, or also a certain rule prescribed that one should follow. One would now be able to say that if this representation is correct (as will presently be shown in detail), then it is a contradiction *in adjecto* [in terms] to speak of an "internal calling." If "calling" is always something that comes from outside and presupposes a hearing, then calling cannot be internal, and it is a misuse of the word to indicate regeneration by it.

It cannot be doubted that by the use of "calling" in the sense described above, the older theology has obscured the two points of difference mentioned. Still, in this use it was led by a correct consideration. What drove it was the conviction that the working of God's grace may not be detached from the Word of God. If one speaks solely of regeneration, that still does not include anything that recalls that the Word is a necessary concomitant element of re-creating grace. If, on the other hand, one speaks of calling, everyone immediately senses that saving grace closely follows the proclamation of objective truth and does not go beyond the limits drawn by this proclamation, even though it is not coextensive with the external hearing of the gospel. Hence some have spoken of an "external calling." To that is then tied the internal calling, in order by the similarity of the name to be reminded anew what connection God had laid between His Word and grace.

With that, however, the use of the term "internal calling" for "regeneration" is not yet fully justified. While a thing may be always accompanied by another thing, I still have no right to designate it by the name of the other, especially if the specific essence of the thing is thereby overlooked. Thus, there must be another ground for the designation "internal calling." That ground is as follows: One can present God's work of grace under two viewpoints—as it occurs below the consciousness, and as it is reflected in the consciousness. The former is a more complete and theological view, the latter a more partial and practical view.

Now, the fact that the first Christian congregations were mostly gathered by the sudden conscious addition of believers led inadvertently to the last, more practical view. The implanting of life in the heart and the hearing of that newly awakened life at the calling of the gospel occurred practically in the same moment. There were no reasons to presuppose a passing of time between the two. Because it coincided in this way with calling, regeneration could appropriately be termed "calling." Or, expressed more precisely, regeneration, as the invisible background, could for the moment be left out of consideration. The first thing one noted about it was calling. And now it needs to be granted that calling did not enter the consciousness as an external, general conception and offer of the gospel. It entered the consciousness of those who were being added as it was applied (made personal and compelling by the Holy Spirit), so that they immediately realized that an internal change had taken place that had been accomplished by an act of God's power. When a sinner hears this calling of God, he does not deliberate or reason, but is drawn and irresistibly compelled to follow. Thus a certain reflex of the nature of regeneration appears in his consciousness, and that is calling. One will therefore easily perceive what ground there is for continuing to speak of an internal calling and to place it next to external calling as distinguished from it and yet closely connected with it by name. When regeneration has worked on the consciousness, it immediately manifests itself as a totally new perception of the omnipotent might of the Word of God, to which one must submit, a Word that speaks as a word of power and, as it were, creates the obedience of faith. Thus, as one is *called* with power in his conscious life and comes, so at the center of his being one is called out with creating omnipotence from death and brought over into life as by a powerful creating word of God. And both lie so closely to one another that one may designate them with one name.

By this, however, is indicated the particular limitation of the concept of "calling." It cannot be applied everywhere. Only in a place where, without remaining hidden for a long time, internal re-creation immediately manifests itself in the consciousness can one rightly speak of regeneration as "internal calling." [It is] not with the same right, on the other hand, when one has to do with children. For them, regeneration does not as yet take the form of a calling—that is, it does not manifest itself in their consciousness as an act of God by which, also for their own awareness, they are called out from the one condition into the other. Of a child one says that it is regenerated and not that it is called.

The question now is only whether one has grounds to assume for adults that regeneration and calling are separated by a considerable period of time. A further distinction must be made here. For those who do not yet live under the administration of the covenant of grace, there is no ground to suppose such an interval. There the seed of regeneration is implanted and usually sprouts immediately. With the children of the covenant, the possibility always exists that they were born again long before their consciousness is awakened. If such is the case with those who die before they are able to comprehend, it is difficult to see why this could not also be the case with many who later give evidence of true godliness and yet who are unable to point to a specific time in their conscious life at which they were effectually called. Conversely, however, there is no evidence that such early regeneration is the rule for children of the covenant. We cannot bind God here. In particular, the idea that someone would be regenerated, and yet in his own consciousness would remain uncalled for years on end, seems unacceptable, for it presupposes an illusory connection between what is internal and what is external.

9. *Show from Scripture that calling is viewed in this way.*

a) First, concerning the use of the term for external calling, that is, the proclamation of the gospel, we have the use of the word as of an *invitation* to a wedding (Matt 22:3, 9; Luke 14:8; cf. John 2:2, "and Jesus was also called," that is, invited; 1 Cor 10:27). In Matthew 20:16 [Textus Receptus] we have a contrast between the many "called," κλητοί, and the few "chosen," ἐκλεκτοί. Here, external calling is not only distinguished from internal calling but even separated from it. What is spoken of is a calling of sinners to conversion (Luke 5:32).

b) That calling is a work of grace taking place in the consciousness is established from Romans 8:30, as developed above. Besides, it follows from the imagery of 1 Peter 2:9: "So that you may proclaim the excellencies of the one who called you out of darkness into His marvelous light." Clearly, light nowhere stands for life as something unconscious, but always for life as it manifests itself in the consciousness. To be brought out of darkness into the light thus means to be brought from the alienation of the consciousness from God into clarity in the awareness of being allied with God, and to a clear knowledge of the truth.

c) Next, as we have said, calling is an act directed to a certain goal and revealing that goal to the consciousness of the one called. Also, where the word of internal efficacious calling is present, it clearly never loses this character of a concept of purpose, as already appears from the fact that it can be connected with the preposition "to," εἰς, or "in," ἐν. God calls believers "to" eternal life (1 Tim 6:12); "into the fellowship of His Son Jesus Christ our Lord" (1 Cor 1:9); "to freedom" (Gal 5:13); "not to impurity but to sanctification" (1 Thess 4:7); "to peace" (1 Cor 7:15); "to one hope of calling" (Eph 4:4); "in one body" (Col 3:15); "so that you may inherit blessing" (1 Pet 3:9).

Calling, then, is also always presented by Paul as a ground of comfort for the believer that enables him to look beyond his own shortcomings and instances of unfaithfulness and to the unfaltering faithfulness of the God who calls. In calling, God, as it were, has bound Himself to the believer and established the covenant bond, so that from now on there is no longer any doubt whether he will reach the goal. "The gifts and calling of God are irrevocable" (Rom 11:29). "He who calls you is faithful, who will also do it" (1 Thess 5:24). The idea of calling deserves more attention than it has so far had. The fact that it has become the general name for regeneration has caused its specific meaning to be lost from sight. And yet in its distinctiveness it is a rich concept that in the letters of Paul, for example, occupies a prominent place.

d) Naturally, all this does not detract from calling as an act of power. This is already included in the word. "Calling" is not persuading or discussing, but bringing about an instantaneous effect by a word or the naming of a name, so that the one who is called comes. In this sense calling—as internal, efficacious calling—extends just as far as election. "Those He foreordained, these He also called, and those He called, these He also justified" [Rom 8:30]. The called are the same as the elect. They are "called according to His purpose" (Rom 8:28); named "called saints" (1 Cor 1:2; Rom 1:7; 1 Thess 2:12; 4:7). It is expressly said, then, that calling is an act of omnipotence: "God calls the things that are not as though they were" (Rom 4:17, where the reference is to the extraordinary birth of Isaac). And in Romans 9:11, it is said "that the purpose of God according to election might stand, not of works *but of Him who calls*." Here calling stands as God's work *par excellence* over against man's work, and it is testified of God's election that it is intended to reveal how salvation is entirely of the God who calls.

10. *How then can you define external calling?*

As the presentation of the gospel to sinners in general by the preaching of the Word.

11. *How, on the other hand, can internal or effectual calling be defined?*

As the transferring of the elect sinner in his own consciousness from the state of alienation from God into the state of fellowship with God (the covenant of grace), and that certainly by means of the external word, applied internally by the Holy Spirit.

12. *How can one relate internal calling and regeneration to each other?*

By saying that:

a) If we consider the *one who calls*, God, regeneration is an effect of calling. "Calling" then means the act of *calling*, as it is in God and as it embraces the sinner.

b) If we consider being called as what occurs in the one who is called, then calling is the effect of regeneration, for the ear is first opened by the latter so that it can recognize the voice of the God who calls. "Calling" then means being called and knowing oneself to be called.

c) If we take the matter in its full scope, we must say that calling, as it were, encompasses regeneration from beginning to end. It precedes and follows it, according to whether one draws attention to the consciousness of God or to the consciousness of the sinner who is called. It hardly needs to be mentioned that this preceding and following is not to be taken in a strictly temporal sense.

13. *Is it necessary to say that the sequence of the acts of grace is: (1) calling, (2) regeneration?*

Some have proposed that in order to, in this way, arrive at a clear distinction. Although one can now readily say, in the sense just described, that regeneration follows calling, there are still objections to this manner of representation.

a) In doing this one runs the danger of losing sight of the fact that calling has an essential significance for the consciousness of the sinner. In fact, one then restricts the name to the action of God in order to call the other, the effect of the action as that which causes change, regeneration.

b) On the other hand, it is wrong to so restrict regeneration that
it becomes only the product, the outcome, the transition, while
the activity of God is omitted. Scripture emphasizes that we *are*
regenerated, that *God* regenerates us according to His will, etc.
(Jas 1:18).

14. *What ground does one have to understand the concept of regeneration in*
the wider sense, which, for example, Calvin ascribes to it?

This is based on some scriptural passages that do not speak directly
of regeneration but of "a putting off of the old man" and "a putting on
of the new man" and "a being renewed in the spirit of the mind" (Eph
4:22–24). Romans 12:2 speaks of the same thing. Second Corinthians 4:16
speaks of a renewal in the inner man that takes place day by day.

All these expressions, however, have in view more the transformation of something old than the creation of something new. And it is just
the new principle of life poured into the sinner that in its outworking
brings about this transformation of the old. Renewal is not regeneration,
but presupposes regeneration. Thus the command can come to man that
he must make for himself "a new heart and a new spirit." However, nowhere in Scripture is the command directed to someone that he must
regenerate himself. That command always comes in the form of "arise
from the dead."

15. *Who is the author of regeneration?*

a) It is God the Father by way of eminence. Since regeneration appears as something completely new, it fits with the economy of
the Father that regeneration is ascribed to Him. "According to his
great mercy, the God and Father of our Lord Jesus Christ has begotten us again to a living hope through the resurrection of Jesus
Christ from the dead" (1 Pet 1:3; cf. also Jas 1:18; Eph 2:5; and the
expression "born of God," 1 John 5:1, 4, 18).

b) The Son is related to regeneration in more than one way.

1. He is the meriting cause. He has obtained the Holy Spirit, who
works all subjective grace, and so has also obtained regeneration (Rom 5:18).

2. He is the head to whom believers are joined as members by regeneration, and who thus lives in them and expresses His life in them (Gal 2:20).

3. He is the image into which the believers are transformed in regeneration and to which continually they are also being increasingly conformed (1 Cor 15:49; Gal 4:19).

c) The Holy Spirit is the one who effects regeneration for the sake of the Father and the Son in the heart of the sinner, as He in general organizes the mystical body of Christ.

16. *Is regeneration a mediate or immediate act of God? Is it or is it not brought about by any instrument?*

God does not use any kind of instrument in regenerating a sinner. An instrument is never used to create something new, but always only to effect a change in what already exists. With a surgical instrument some part of a living body can be treated, a diseased part removed, but the most advanced instrument cannot possibly produce life in a dead body.

17. *Is not the Word of God an instrument by which regeneration is achieved?*

No. On the one hand, this would lead us to the Pelagian or semi-Pelagian view, or, on the other hand, cause us to revert to the Lutheran idea of an inherent magical capacity for the Word of God. In order to reach clarity on this point, one must make plain how truth works on man. It in fact works in a spiritual sense, as every physical instrument does in a physical sense, but then not in such a way that the act would lie entirely in the cause. It is always the case that the cause acts, and that to which it is directed then reacts, and so the effect occurs. The result, therefore, depends as much on the object that undergoes the action as on the acting cause.

Now, if the truth is the cause, then it will only produce effects in us because our soul responds, reacts to it. If the truth is to have an effect in which there is life, then this can only be as it brings about an expression of life in my soul as the response. So, in order for the truth to become effective instrumentally for life, I already need to have life in me. Therefore, anyone who has the truth accomplishing regeneration through motivations teaches that man *is not entirely dead*. That is, he teaches in a Pelagian or semi-Pelagian fashion. A motivation works on me only through what I am. A motivation that awakens a reaction in me will leave my neighbor unmoved, not because the motivation is different, but simply because the person with whom it is brought in contact differs from me. If we want to escape this Pelagianism, then nothing remains except, with the Lutherans, to locate life in the Word.

However, one may then perceive clearly that every analogy between the Word as *causa efficiens* [efficient cause] and every ordinary *causa instrumentalis* [instrumental cause] collapses. Not one instrument works in this way, by causing an overflowing of an inherent power. On close inspection, then, for Lutherans, too, the Word is no longer a means of grace or an instrument of grace; it has become a source of grace. It takes the place of God, for it belongs only to God to act so immediately on things that His effective power does not engage their reaction. Rather, as He works entirely alone, He imparts qualities to them or changes their habits. Basically, therefore, the Lutherans gain nothing when they suppose they are maintaining the instrumentality of the Word. The Word slips out of their hands and becomes a magic wand.

18. What by nature is the disposition of man toward the truth?

Scripture declares that by virtue of his natural birth, man is flesh, and the mind of the flesh is enmity against God [Rom 8:7]. Now, it is in the truth that God Himself is brought into contact with this sinful flesh. For this reason already, the result of this contact cannot be the beginning of spiritual life. Indeed, it cannot change hate when the hated object is brought nearer. That would rather incite hate. Yet, according to this instrumental understanding of regeneration, it would be sufficient to place the object of enmity before the inimical consciousness in order immediately to change enmity into love.

19. Does the concept of truth allow that one may consider the Holy Spirit as a higher power bound to it at certain times?

No, the concept of truth includes in itself the elements of immutability and universality. Truth remains fixed and is objectively the same for all. Thus it will not do to confine the efficacious action of the Holy Spirit within the truth and yet still want to maintain that the Holy Spirit does not work everywhere in the truth or by the truth. Once accepting this concept, one must be consistent and say, "Everywhere this supernaturally equipped Word is and works, there the Holy Spirit also is and works." The Spirit, then, comes and goes with the Word and is in the wake of the Word. And then from that it follows further that, again, the reason why the one and not the other is regenerated must be sought in man. After all, the same power of the Spirit comes to all, and nothing comes other than it. Yet it is not effective in all. Thus, the one must act differently toward it than the other.

20. *Does Scripture teach that there is a working of God in the heart of man that is not instrumentally connected with the working of the truth?*

Yes. Of Lydia it is said, for example, that the Lord opened her heart to pay attention to what was said by Paul (Acts 16:14). The psalmist prayed, "Incline my heart to your testimonies" (Psa 119:36).

21. *Does not James 1:18 teach that the word is God's instrument in regeneration?*

At a first glance this passage indeed appears to teach that. It reads, "According to His will He gave birth to us by the word of truth, so that we should be as the firstfruits of his creatures." However, we observe:

a) That in the context itself the word for "give birth" occurs in a broader sense. In verse 15 we read, "Desire, having conceived, gives birth to sin, and sin being complete, gives birth to death." Here there is naturally no mention of the absolute beginning of sin, for desire is already sin, and death, too, is already resident in sin. To "give birth," then, means to "bring into the world," and is in fact something already present in principle and with which one is pregnant.

b) In the Greek here, in both verses 15 and 18, a word is used that expresses the feminine act of "give birth to," and not so much the masculine act of "generation" or "begetting of life." In verse 18 the wording is βουληθεὶς ἀπεκύησεν ἡμᾶς λόγῳ ἀληθείας. Now κύω or κυέω means "to be pregnant," and ἀποκυέω means "to bring out of the darkness of the womb into the light of the day."

With these two observations, the argument that some intend to derive from this text fails. The words simply mean that the life generated within believers is drawn outwardly and brought to light by the word of truth. Everyone will agree that Scripture is instrumental for this, and that God does this through the Word. But "giving birth" is something entirely different from "generating life" or "regenerating." It is somewhat regrettable that our [Dutch] word *wederbaren* does not do justice to this distinction as well as, for example, the English "regeneration." In 1 Corinthians 4:15, Paul even says that *he* had "fathered" the Corinthians in Christ through the gospel (γεννάω is used here). This, too, is of course only to be understood of drawing life outward by the preaching of the Word, as he speaks in Galatians 4:19 of "being in travail" (ὠδίνω), because through his work with them Christ ought to be formed in them.

22. *Does not 1 Peter 1:23 teach that the Word is instrumental in regeneration?*

Here, too, this interpretation has no more than the appearance of truth. The text reads, ἀναγεγεννημένοι οὐκ ἐκ σπορᾶς φθαρτῆς ἀλλὰ ἀφθάρτου διὰ λόγου ζῶντος θεοῦ καὶ μένοντος: "Being born again not of perishable but of imperishable seed, through the Word of the living and (eternally) abiding God." One should note that two things are distinguished here: (1) a "from which," "out of" imperishable seed; (2) a "whereby," "through" the Word of God. But the "from which" is not the "whereby." The light that shines on the field and the sunshine that warms it are not the seed that is buried within it and germinates and sprouts under their influence. That Peter does not equate the two can already be inferred with certainty from the fact that, according to 1 Peter 1:3, he sees in the resurrection of Christ from the dead the instrumental cause of regeneration. The "seed" must therefore be the seed of life from Christ, planted in us by the Holy Spirit. This seed is incorruptible because it communicates the eternally abiding life of Christ. Viewed in this way, this much-misused verse from Peter also does not teach regeneration through the Word of Scripture.

23. *Is there perhaps another instrument than the Word used in regeneration?*

The Roman Catholic, Episcopal, and Lutheran churches teach that baptism is the means ordained by God to effect regeneration.

   a) According to Rome, regeneration, which is given in baptism, includes: (1) removal of the guilt and pollution of sin—so, justification as well as the source of sanctification in a negative sense; (2) the infusion of new qualities of grace—that is, sanctification in a positive sense, at least in principle; (3) adoption as children—that is, the positive side of justification as we understand this word.

b) According to many in the Episcopal church, regeneration, in distinction from conversion, is accomplished by baptism. It also makes conversion superfluous, except for those who after baptism again fall into great sin. All this, however, is not the official confession of the Episcopal church.

c) The Lutheran opinion has been discussed above.

24. *Why is this conception, that baptism achieves regeneration, unacceptable?*

a) Scripture nowhere teaches that baptism brings regeneration, but only that the church presupposes internal calling and regeneration for adults to whom it administers baptism. For baptism it still demands faith, and true faith is only possible where God has worked a new source of life in the heart. "If you believe with all your heart, then it is permissible" (Acts 8:12, 37).

b) There is absolutely no concurrence between the means and the effect. This already applies to the Lutheran view, but still more to the Roman Catholic view. Water is physical in nature and, unless its nature changes, cannot possibly cause other than a physical activity. It can cleanse the body but cannot touch the soul.

c) When Scripture sometimes speaks as if baptism stands in the closest connection to the grace of regeneration, then this can be satisfactorily explained from a sacramental way of speaking. This sacramental way of speaking reflects that sometimes what is only present in the thing signified is ascribed to the sign and seal itself. Baptism is the bath of regeneration; one is regenerated out of water and Spirit because the symbolism of baptism in fact points to regeneration. Inasmuch as the water of baptism and washing with the same have in view both inner cleansing by the Holy Spirit as well as the cleansing of guilt by justification, it is in all respects fitting when Scripture mentions baptism and regeneration together. That, however, does not at all mean that baptism effects regeneration.

25. Is regeneration a renewing of the substance of the human soul?

No, this view has its home in the system of the Manichaeans. It demands as its opposite that sin is something substantial. If regeneration produces a change of substance in the soul and at the same time is a renewing of its nature, a removing of the old nature, then this old nature, which is replaced by the new substance, must have also been something substantial. At a later time it was Flacius Illyricus (1520–1575) who advocated this view. He arrived at it as a reaction against the weakness of the synergistic conception of many in his time. It has already been shown above[3] how in his battle against the Manichaeans Augustine went somewhat too far when he taught that sin is a mere privation. It is not substance; in that, Augustine was no doubt right. But it is also not a mere privation. Between the two views, sin is a positive moral quality or disposition that inheres in the substance of the soul. From that it directly follows: Regeneration is not the renewing (more precisely, the changing) of the substance of the human soul, but the renewing of the inherent nature or moral disposition of the soul.

One can still ask: How is the renewing of the nature or the disposition possible without the renewing of the substance? The answer to this must be: Man is not simple in the sense that the disposition of his soul could only be changed by a change of his substance; he is not absolutely simple. Absolute simplicity is only an attribute of God. With God, being and attributes coincide such that we cannot conceive of a separation between them. Therefore, if a change were possible in God's nature, this would at the same time be a change in His being. He is the absolute good by virtue of His being. And if He could cease to be good, He would also change in being. With man, it is entirely different. He is composite. His attributes cohere with his being, but not as that is so with God. The omnipotence of God can change them without therefore needing to create a new being, a new substance. It really lies already in the concept of substance that it can be detached from attributes that form antitheses, like good and evil. But precisely for this reason we do not ascribe a substance to God, but rather speak of essence, "being."

---

3   Vol. 2, ch. 2, q. 35.

26. *Does regeneration consist in a change of the soul's capacities, of either one or more of these capacities?*

This, too, cannot be said. Such a change does indeed flow from regeneration. When God re-creates man, there is in fact an enlightening of his mind, a reversing of his will, and a purifying of his affections. But these three sides of the spiritual life of man are most closely tied to each other; in its root, they are one. That unity may be incomprehensible and inconceivable for us, since it never comes into the light of our consciousness. And all of which we ourselves are aware is always thinking, willing, and feeling. But still, that unity exists as surely as the unity of our soul exists. There is a hidden source from which our life springs where these three streams are one, a stem from which these three branches sprout. At this source, God performs His miracle of regeneration. There He infuses the new principle of life. And since it is the source that pollutes the water, the stem that sends up the sap of life into the branches, so from this implanting of life a new disposition and efficacy flows for our understanding, our will, and our affections (Matt 12:33, 35; 15:19).

27. *Can you show that the re-creation of a single capacity is not sufficient to regenerate the sinner if God does not renew the root of his life and thereby also regenerate the other capacities?*

This can easily be shown. If we assume, as some have done, that God produces only an enlightening in the intellect of the sinner and leaves the person's will unchanged, what will be the consequence of this? Man, with his enlightened intellect, will then see for himself the things of God, all the truths of salvation in their proper objective relations, and be able to explain the ins and outs of everything in the minutest detail, as a mechanic takes apart a machine and puts it together. His will, however, will directly oppose the truth, even though he grasps with his intellect the obligation to submit himself to it. The intellect alone cannot overturn the will or incline it. One is indeed accustomed to saying [that] the intellect pronounces its judgment, and then the will follows the final judgment of the intellect. This, however, is very misleading without further explanation. Clearly, the will follows the judgment of the intellect in a moral being, but what this final judgment of the intellect will be depends again, in turn, on the will. In expressing its judgment, the intellect is subservient to the will. Our will has a certain tendency: good or evil, holy or unholy, acting with God's will or against it. Our intellect judges what decision of our will squares with it, and on that basis the will follows this judgment of the intellect. The opposite view is purely rationalistic. Our will does not simply let itself be commanded by the intellect. The known truth always works through the reaction of the inclinations of our will. If, now, every good tendency is lacking in the will, then there is nothing on which the truth can act and to which it can react, and all the knowledge of angels will not produce a better disposition of the will. A sinner whose intellect was enlightened and who kept his old, completely sinful will would be the most miserable and terrifying creature in the world—the victim of the most dreadful disharmony—for his sinful will and his sinful pure knowledge would constantly work against each other. But such cases do not occur. God gives no one a saving enlightening of the intellect without at the same time renewing the will.

The situation is no different with the relationship between the will and the affections, or the capacity for emotion. Our will does not work apart from our emotional life any more than the intellect works apart from the will. In all the operations of the will, the impulse of the emotions plays a part that accompanies every spiritual function to a greater or lesser degree. He whose will is united with God's will engenders a delight in the law of God according to the inner man [Rom 7:22]. On the other hand, he whose will works against God's will finds enjoyment in sin.

If we now were to assume that God has re-created the will but left the capacity for emotion unchanged, the result would again be an untenable situation. Man would will what God wills, but it would leave him entirely unmoved and unfeeling, without any involvement of the heart. He would fulfill the commandments of the Lord with his will like a machine. Every warmth and ardor would be absent. Indeed, worse than this, if his uncleansed affections were still in him, at the same time he fulfilled the Lord's will he would detest it, so that his condition would be called most lamentable.

Finally, without an enlightened intellect neither a sanctified will nor a cleansed emotional life would avail. It is true: Someone who has a good will and pure emotions knows more and better than someone whose will is hardened and whose emotions are depraved. But that is only true where the condition of the intellect is the same for both. The best will and purest emotions cannot enlighten a darkened intellect. The light must come, not from within the will, but from outside it. And as long as that is lacking, the will and the emotions cannot work rightly.

28. *To what extent can one say that the enlightenment of the intellect precedes the operation of the will and emotions?*

It does not precede so far as proper, immediate regeneration is concerned. In regeneration, the re-creation of intellect, will, and emotion occurs simultaneously in a single moment, without one of these three preceding the others. On the other hand, certainly one can speak of a precedence concerning the manifestation of regeneration in the consciousness. The will and the affections cannot operate unless they have content, an object with which they are occupied. This object, this content, must have been given to them by the capacity to know, and certainly been given in the right form—that is, by an enlightened intellect. For this reason, the enlightened intellect is first in order of the three capacities in which regeneration manifests itself. And so it can appear that the will only need be suffused with the light of the intellect in order to reach out immediately toward what is known. However, this is no more than appearance. Basically, the will was already changed, for that will, too, was embedded in the root of life, in which the miraculous change was wrought by God's Spirit.

29. *Show that regeneration produces an enlightening of the intellect.*

This is presupposed everywhere, even to the extent that the images in which regeneration is pictured to us are often derived from the noetic life. "For God, who said that light should shine out of darkness, has shone in our hearts, to give the light of the knowledge of the glory of God in the face of Jesus Christ" (2 Cor 4:6). "The natural man does not understand the things that are of the Spirit of God ... and he cannot understand them because they are spiritually discerned. But the spiritual man judges all things, but he himself is judged by no one" (1 Cor 2:14–15). In this last passage it is even said of believers that they have the mind, the gift of spiritual discernment, of Christ (1 Cor 2:16; cf. further Eph 1:18; Phil 1:9; Col 3:10; 1 John 4:7; 5:20).

The difference between this knowledge of one who is regenerated and that of a natural man may only be experienced and can never be sufficiently described. It does not exclusively consist in the degree of more or less clarity, but it is a difference in quality. It rests on the entire change of being. Before regeneration, one can certainly have in himself and reproduce logical concepts and the connection of these concepts—indeed, make himself thoroughly familiar with them—but the right consciousness of the reality to which they correspond is lacking. One cannot empathize with them and penetrate them. It is, in a word, an external and not an experiential knowledge that one has of the truth. This analogy cannot be maintained in all respects, but still it has been said: As someone blind from birth cannot form a conception of colors, so someone who is unregenerate has no comprehension of the spiritual sense of God's truth.

30. *Show that regeneration produces a renewing of the will.*

This is taught, among other places, in Philippians 2:13: "It is God who works in you, both to will and to work for His good pleasure." If this applies to the continuation of spiritual life, so will it apply all the more to its beginning (cf. Heb 13:21; Psa 110:3; 2 Thess 3:6).

31. *How does God move the will of man?*

In a manner that accords with the freedom and the spontaneous character of the will—not, therefore, by placing Himself against the will and bending it with force; also not by a physical or unspiritual power that occurs in baptism, as the Roman Catholics contend; but by bringing about a reversal in the root of life, out of which the will itself arises. The result of this, then, is that the will of itself works in the opposite direction than was previously the case, and that no longer unwillingly but spontaneously, willingly.

32. *Do we mean that the Holy Spirit only changes the expressions of the will—"willing"—or that He also renews the more deeply lying will, the direction of the will, the tendency of the soul?*

The latter is meant. What takes place is not merely a change in actions but a change in the permanent disposition of the will. Even if for an instant there is no expression of the will—if, for example, a regenerate person is in an unconscious condition—even then there is a great difference between him and an unregenerate person in an unconscious condition. The will of the former is directed toward God; the will of the latter away from God. Single actions of the will are only manifestations of this difference in disposition. The so-called "exercise scheme" of Emmons teaches that there is nothing in the soul but a succession of expressions of the will, "exercises," and that to initiate such a succession is the work of regeneration. This is both theologically and psychologically wrong. There is much more in the soul than its substance and expressions of conscious life. The substance has its capacities, and these have their dispositions that must first be reversed before a good action can begin.

33. *Show that regeneration also produces a re-creation of the emotional life of man.*

Scripture speaks of believers having a joy in Christ Jesus that is inexpressible and glorious (1 Pet 1:8). Through regeneration, a life comes into existence that can hunger and thirst after God and His righteousness. Hunger and thirst presuppose not merely a tendency of the will toward God but also that emotion accompanies it. Natural hunger and thirst create a physical feeling; spiritual hunger and thirst a spiritual feeling (Psa 42:1-2; 63:1-2). No less is spiritual sorrow mentioned as the characteristic of a regenerated person (Matt 5:4; Psa 34:18; Isa 66:2).

34. *Is the entire nature of man renewed by regeneration, so that nothing remains to be renewed?*

No, for everything would then be included in regeneration, and sanctification would become superfluous. The conception of Scripture is much more that the renewing activity of the Holy Spirit does not immediately remove all evil from us and replace it with a completely holy and good person, but that He effects renewal at one point in order from there to cause His renewing and sanctifying work to take hold in increasingly wider circles. Thus, there is sin within the regenerate as well as within the unregenerate. Also, as long as the former is here on earth, he cannot perform anything into which sin does not flow. His best works are still tainted with evil. But while in the sinner before his regeneration there cannot be a single thought or motion of the will or expression of emotion that arises from a good foundation, since evil always lurks in the deepest foundation of life, in the regenerate person another foundation has now been laid, a new principle created; spiritual life is present. Now, it does remain true that all the actions of this spiritual life, as soon as they press toward the circumference of life, inevitably become tarnished by the sinful remnants of his nature. But in their origin they are still something entirely different than the most pleasing deeds of the sinner dead in sin. It is also true that this new principle of life, worked by the Holy Spirit, does not have the power in itself to be able to survive. If it were left to itself, it would soon be overgrown and smothered by the weeds. But it does not exist on its own. The eternal power of life of the Holy Spirit is behind it and works in it. Therefore, not only can it not die, but it must also prove to be more powerful than the sin that has remained in its nature.

Every attempt, however, to try explaining psychologically how this new principle of life relates to sin committed after regeneration will certainly have to fail. We only know from Scripture and experience that in the regenerate a noticeable conflict exists, so that occasionally some have spoken of two persons, which of course can only apply in a very figurative sense. Still, to make the matter clear, one perhaps gets the farthest with images. We are reminded of the grafting-in of a cultivated sprig on a wild stem, by which the latter, although not immediately becoming completely cultivated, still so functions that it produces cultivated fruit. Some have used the image of a body maimed, damaged, and already in the process of disintegration, in which by a miracle the principle of life has been restored. The body will start to move and raise itself up; a dead body cannot do that. In no way, however, will the mutilation and the traces of disintegration therefore disappear. More likely, for a long time these will still recall death and will hinder the body in its expressions of life. Although such images remain deficient, they still provide a general idea of the characteristic situation in which the regenerate is placed by his re-creation.

The apostle has depicted the discord meant here in Romans 7:14–25. The facts established by him here are the following:

a) In the regenerate there is sin not only existing in single actions but a deeply rooted evil: "I know that no good dwells in me, that is, in my flesh" [Rom 7:18]. The apostle has called this sin "indwelling sin" (Rom 7:17, 20), which proves sufficiently that it is continually present; it is a sinful disposition, inherited pollution. It is a *law* in the members, thus *something permanent*.

b) Yet in the regenerate there is also something good. That already appears from the specific form in which the previous statement was expressed—"in me, that is, in my flesh" dwells no good (Rom 7:18). Thus, the apostle can speak of himself from two angles. If he spoke of himself as he was in himself, apart from the activity of the Holy Spirit, thus as flesh, then no good dwells in him. If, on the other hand, he spoke of himself insofar as the Holy Spirit maintained a new life in him, then there was something good in him.

c) This new principle, worked by the Holy Spirit and based on the indwelling of the Holy Spirit and only maintained by that indwelling, touches the deepest ground of his life. It was deeper than indwelling sin. That appears from the words with which the apostle sets these two against each other. *He* no longer does it (namely, the evil), but the sin *that dwells in him*. Thus: *he* over against the sin *that dwells in him*. This is not said to excuse the evil, but only to show that the power of sin was still so great and even at work against the new life. So, in verses 22 and 23, the "inner man" and "the mind" are against "the members." The "inner" here is what is regenerated and new in man (cf. 2 Cor 4:16; Eph 3:16; 1 Pet 3:4). The "members" are the same again as "flesh"— that is, the depraved nature as it is apart from the new implanted principle of life. The "mind" is the same again as the "inner man." All this shows that the new principle of life in the regenerate Christian confronts his still-sinful nature (both soul and body) as a living soul confronts a dead, decomposing body. This, then, is also the image the apostle uses in verse 24. Indwelling sin is like a body of death. It is as if a hideous corpse embraces and captures him. He cannot save himself from that embrace.

d) Nevertheless, the new life within him also pervades his conscious thinking, willing, and feeling. After all, in him there is a willing of the good (Rom 7:19) and a not willing of the evil, a taking delight in the law of God after the inner man, a disapproval of what he himself does, a consenting that the law is good. These are all expressions of the new life, however much the apostle also had to add that it was not granted to him to fulfill this good to which his new man testified.

e) The conclusion that the apostle finally draws from this state of affairs is that only the grace of God can deliver him from this indwelling corruption. It is not by the native activity of the new life in obedience to the law that the corruption is purged, but by the continuing grace of God. The law *alone* does not bring about sanctification. As the Holy Spirit has created the new life, He must also continue working it out and mortifying the flesh (cf. Gal 2:20; 5:17).

35. *Is regeneration to be viewed such that in it this new principle of life is infused into man and what is contained in that principle now comes to expression of itself?*

No. Also, this coming-to-expression of the life once given—its impact on the intellect, will, and emotional life—cannot occur independent of the ongoing grace of God. But the difference lies in this: that in regeneration proper, the soul is wholly passive. It does not work, but is worked on, undergoes change, while in further stages this soul, made alive by God, becomes itself the subject of its expression of life. Nevertheless, it is also the case that it must be continuously enabled for these expressions by the grace of the Holy Spirit.

36. *In what relation does regeneration stand to the subsequent saving actions of God?*

It has already been noted that in these subsequent actions man himself is made the thinking, willing, and feeling subject of what takes place in him. Conversion and faith, worked by God, do not merely pass from God onto the root of his life (like regeneration), but through the root of his life outwardly. It is man himself who repents of his sins, who exercises faith, is with Christ, etc., while it is not man himself who regenerates himself or lets himself be regenerated. Clearly, these spiritual activities of repenting, believing, etc., presuppose a principle of spiritual life that in fact has become man's own. The renewed life must be his life if he is to be able to manifest repentance and exercise faith. However, to possess life in general is not sufficient. Or, expressed more precisely, life in general and in the abstract without some determination of powers and capacities does not exist. It belongs to the nature of life that it comprises a multiplicity in unity. In every seed the functions of life are present, and therefore we must assume that in the regenerate and in the life of the regenerate God also gives the capacity in principle to be able to perform the different activities of life. Thus, regeneration first makes possible all that subsequently takes place in a sinner. It not only precedes but is in a living connection with all that takes place subsequently. However, one may not think of the capacities of this spiritual life as developed dispositions. They are only present as a predisposition, as potentiality in seed form. Indeed, the seed of what a child learns to do later is given at its birth. But that does not mean that the *habitus* to perform certain activities is the same with a child as with an adult. This is the same in regeneration. With and in the spiritual life infused, a regenerated child certainly receives the disposition to believe. But that disposition develops. A regenerate adult, who has exercised faith for years on end, possesses that disposition in a much different condition. And yet in principle, the *habitus* in both is one.

37. What distinguishes more recent views concerning regeneration?

a) First, we have here the theory of trichotomy, which develops a distinctive doctrine of regeneration from its basic tenets. There are three parts in man: "body," "soul," and "spirit." In general, sin has its seat only in the life of the soul, not in the *pneuma*, or "spirit." As soon as it penetrates to the spirit, man becomes incapable of being saved, for that is to commit the sin against the Holy Spirit. The angels are incapable of being saved, since being only spirit, they are completely imprisoned in sin. In regeneration the Spirit of God produces a strengthening of the *pneuma* in man. This is no longer sinful, but still weakened. All that is necessary exists in this strengthening. When the spirit, thus strengthened, begins to govern the lower passions again, man has become "spiritual."

One sees immediately that this is merely a "refined rationalism." Sin in man, the depravity of his nature, is sought in a discrepancy between the lower and higher capacities. He is saved as the higher capacities of his reason (for this concept of "spirit" finally amounts to that) suppress the lower. He is called "spiritual," not because the Holy Spirit has made His abode in him, but because he again is led by his own "spirit" or "reason."

b) Then we have the decidedly pantheistic or pantheistically tinted soteriology of the "mediating theologians." Their Christology is false and, like it, their soteriology also proceeds from the idea of the unity between God and man. In the Mediator there are not two unmixed natures, but one mingled divine-human nature. God and man are melded together into a third entity: a divine-human life. This is the same life, then, that is communicated to man in regeneration. He partakes of the life that is in Christ. Not in *our* sense—as he is united to Christ the Head by the Spirit and as the Spirit, who is at work from Christ, works and maintains a personal life in him—but literally, as a part of the life of Christ passes over into him. Here, therefore, the mystical union is misused in a pantheistic sense.

It is accompanied, further, by another misconception: that this life, since it is the same in substance in each regenerated person as in Christ, need not be generated anew each time by the Holy Spirit, but that it is resident in the Church and passes from the Church to the individual. Communion with the Church brings the higher life. This is a return to Romanism. The entire judicial work of the Mediator is pushed to the background.

Finally, on this view, one cannot speak of regeneration so long as the divine-human life of Christ did not yet exist. During the Old Testament dispensation, no one was regenerated. All this is sufficient to make us see that here we no longer have to do with a Christian but with a philosophical system that, as much as it still can, uses Christian terms in order to be accredited within Christian circles and to preserve for itself the name of Christian.

38. *What name do the theologians use to express the uniqueness of regenerating grace?*

They use the word "physical." Regeneration consists of a physical action wrought by God. "Physical" here contrasts with "moral." They intend with that to emphasize that God's work is not morally persuasive. Currently, however, the word "physical" is currently used in a sense that can lead to misunderstanding. Physics is a natural science, and it is usually knowledge of material nature. Physical is what works in a natural or material way. In that sense, regeneration is the opposite of physical. It is therefore better to say that it is supernatural, hyperphysical. Also, God's omnipotent activity is not the same everywhere as to its manner of working. It works differently on matter than on spirit. But on the spirit it can work in a twofold fashion: by means of the consciousness, and below the consciousness. The latter occurs in regeneration.

39. Is regeneration resistible—that is, can a person resist it and undo it?

It is irresistible. And not in the sense that regeneration is merely more powerful than all resistance, but that even the thought of resistance is out of the question. Regeneration lays hold of the subject that would wish or be able to offer resistance, even in its deepest depth, and changes it. Saying that it can be resisted would always be based on the conception that it confronts its object. It does not do this, but works immanently within the heart of man.

Chapter Three

Conversion

1. *What words in Scripture are used for the concept of conversion?*

The first and most important word is μετάνοια. The verb that belongs with it is μετανοεῖν. Both words are composed of the preposition μετά and the noun νοῦς. *Metanoia*, therefore, is a change, an alteration of *nous* [mind]. Now we need only to specify what is meant by *nous*. *Nous* is related to γιγνώσκειν, Latin *noscere*, English "to know." This already points us to conscious life. Conversion is a change of what occurs in our consciousness. However, one would take the concept of *nous* far too narrowly if one were to limit it to intellectual, theoretical consciousness. It is much wider. *Nous* is synonymous with συνείδησις, "conscience," moral consciousness: "both their mind and their conscience are defiled" (Titus 1:15); "one person regards one day above the others, but another regards all days alike. Let each one be fully convinced in his own mind [νοῦς]" (Rom 14:5). When one changes his *nous*, this means more than receiving new knowledge, new concepts, and a new conscious content. The direction, the quality of his conscious life is changed. While previously all his thinking and endeavoring moved apart from God and something else stood in the center, now it is so reversed that it moves around God and for God, and He comes to stand in the center. The word *metanoia*, however, does not put the emphasis so much on the point of departure and the point of arrival as on the change and reversal.

The change expressed by this word has reference further:

a) To intellectual life, thus theoretical consciousness: "with meekness instructing those that oppose, if God may someday grant them repentance leading to a *knowledge of the truth*" (2 Tim 2:25). The unconverted consciousness finds itself entangled in a world of erroneous concepts. For that person, God's truth is not the highest reality. His train of thought does not revolve around God. Through conversion, that becomes different. The consciousness, insofar as it involves thinking, loses its worldly sinful independence and submits to the wisdom of God. In this respect, conversion thus coincides with the faith of the regenerate. Above it has already been pointed out that what the regenerate knew and believed previously in a solely historical way he now also knows and believes in an essentially different way.[1] His faith, which has now become spiritual, is directed entirely to the testimony of God. Thereafter, the knowledge of saving faith and all that accompanies it must also be brought to bear. The doctrine of sin and grace in the consciousness of the converted sinner receives the weight due it. The knowledge of spiritual faith in the wider sense belongs essentially to the manifestation of conversion. Faith is a part of conversion.

b) By no means, however, does *metanoia* remain limited to the consciousness of the intellect. The consciousness of the life of the will likewise shares in it. In the conscious willing of the unconverted there is an impulse that is active against God and self-seeking. In the conscious volition of the converted there is an impulse that is active toward God and away from himself. The will was first turned away from God and is now *converted* to God. On this point, too, faith coheres most closely with conversion. In all believing, there is a letting go of ourselves and a resting in another. In conversion, faith—of which the seed was given in regeneration—turns to God to rest in His testimony. The will, insofar as it is involved in believing, now turns to God (Acts 8:22, "Therefore repent of this your wickedness; Heb 6:1, "Not laying again a foundation of repentance from dead works").

---

[1]   Ch. 2, q. 29.

c) Conversion also extends to the life of the emotions. While for the unconverted the spiritual things of God are an arid desert, for the converted they become a source of lively delight. While formerly the reality of the relationship to which he stood toward God left him cold and indifferent, his heart now reacts immediately to it.

d) In all three respects, however, *metanoia* includes a conscious opposition to the former condition. This is an essential element in the concept, and one should therefore attend to it very carefully. Being converted does not mean simply going from one direction of consciousness to another so far as the intellect, will, and emotions are concerned. It means, in doing this, that at the same time there is present in the new direction of intellect, will, and emotions a conscious aversion to the former direction. In other words, *metanoia* has a positive side, but it also has a negative side. A new knowledge arises in the one converted, but at the same time he is conscious that his old knowledge was foolishness and ignorance. A new volition impels the one converted, but at the same time he becomes conscious of a deep aversion toward his old volition that worked against God. A new emotion controls the one converted, but in it he similarly has a consciousness of a deep sorrow over his former condition.

Conversion, therefore, looks back as well as forward. In their functioning, the new capacities that are now turned toward God look back in a conscious fashion on their former activity that was turned away from God. This is the *element of repentance* in conversion along with the element of *faith*. All the activities mentioned under (a), (b), and (c) go back to faith, insofar as it has its seat in the intellect and will, and at the same time is accompanied by the emotions. What is meant here is repentance—that is, a true, deep-seated knowledge of and a strong aversion, an active abhorrence, toward the earlier relationship toward God. "Now I rejoice, not because you were grieved but because you were grieved leading to repentance [εἰς μετάνοιαν]. For godly sorrow produces repentance without regret that leads to salvation, but the sorrow of the world produces death" (2 Cor 7:9–10). "And if he sins against you seven times in a day, and returns to you seven times in a day saying, 'I repent' [μετανοέω], you must forgive him" (Luke 17:4).

2. *What is another word used in Scripture for "conversion"?*

The word ἐπιστροφή, which occurs only once in the New Testament, in Acts 15:3. On the other hand, the verb ἐπιστρέφειν is used much more. It has a somewhat wider scope than μετανοεῖν. It not only puts the emphasis on the change of direction in the conscious life, but it also expresses that a new relationship comes about by this change. Hence it can be used with μετανοεῖν; for example, "Repent [μετανοεῖν], therefore, and turn back [ἐπιστρέφειν]" (Acts 3:19). While μετανοεῖν is sometimes used exclusively for repentance, in ἐπιστρέφειν faith is necessarily included. Repentance (μετάνοια) and faith can be mentioned together, but not conversion (ἐπιστροφή) and faith: "repentance toward God and faith in our Lord Jesus Christ" (Acts 20:21)—here one finds μετάνοια. Where these two words [ἐπιστροφή and μετάνοια] are distinguished, the former lets the focus fall more on the positive direction of faith, the latter more on the retrospective attitude of repentance.

3. *What word does the Hebrew use for conversion?*

The noun שׁוּבָה and the verb שׁוּב. In the Septuagint this is nearly always translated by ἐπιστρέφειν (1 Sam 7:3; 1 Kgs 8:33).

4. *Is there still another word that is used by the New Testament?*

The word μεταμέλεσθαι. This literally means "to be concerned about something afterwards": "and afterward he repented and went"; "and even when you saw it, afterward you did not repent in order to believe" (Matt 21:29, 32). Thus the emphasis here is on the element of repentance. However, from the texts just cited above, it appears that it is incorrect to understand the difference between this word and μετανοεῖν as if the former merely indicates a sensation of emotion by which the will is not yet changed—thus superficial sorrow, worldly sadness, that is a result of the common grace of the Holy Spirit but that faith need not follow— while the latter always indicates heartfelt conversion that presupposes regeneration. *Metanoia* can occur a few times for regret. For example, "And if he is sorrowful, forgive him" (Luke 17:3). The difference lies only in this: that μεταμέλεσθαι points exclusively to the negative, retrospective side of repentance. *Metanoia* is richer in content. Included in it is the element of will; it consists of a firm intention, of an active change of the will; there is action. Hence, μετανοεῖν appears in the imperative mood: "be converted." But, in contrast, μεταμέλεσθαι, "be sorrowful," never does, for emotion as such cannot be commanded.

5. *What is distinctive of most of these words?*

They are almost always active terms, something by which they are distinguished in use from the words for regeneration. There it was "to be regenerated" (ἀναγεννᾶσθαι). Here it is "to convert *oneself*"—a proof that after regeneration, as soon as it penetrates into the conscious life, the gracious activity of God makes the subject itself active. Here, man is no longer purely passive; he is not only acted on but impelled to action.

6. *What is conversion called in Latin?*

In Latin three words are used:

a) *Poenitentia*, "having remorse," connected with *poena*, "punishment." In it the element of "penitence," "contrition," comes to the fore. One may compare this with the English word "repentance" (from *repoenitere*). In the Roman Catholic church, however, *poenitentia* more and more received an external sense. "Penance" was placed as an independent sacrament alongside the others. It has reference to a Christian who has fallen into mortal sin, and so does not have initial conversion in view. It consists of three parts:

1. *Contritio*, sincere remorse, to be distinguished from *attritio*. The latter abhors and hates sin because of its terrible consequences; *contritio*, on the other hand, for its own sake. If, however, *attritio* is concerned with the eternal consequences of sin and not merely its temporal consequences, it is also sufficient.

2. *Confessio*, or "confession," acknowledgement of sin before an ecclesiastical judge.

3. *Satisfactio*, "satisfaction" of temporal punishment, likewise prescribed by an ecclesiastical judge. Through this wholly external understanding, the word *poenitentia* acquired a bad sound, so that some preferred not to use it any longer.

b) Another Latin word is *conversio*. This is essentially the same in meaning as *epistrophē*. It comes from *convertere*, "to turn around," and therefore points to the about-face and the changed direction that comes into the life of the sinner at conversion.

c) A third term is the much-used *resipiscentia*, literally, "becoming wise again," from *resipiscere*, "to return to one's senses." It agrees to a great extent with *metanoia*. The difference is only that the prefix "re-" calls to mind the abnormality of the former state of the consciousness. What supervenes in becoming wise again is not something new but just what should have been present originally—what is normal.

7. *How do you best describe conversion according to what we have found?*

It is active: that act of God by which He turns the regenerate man in his consciousness to Himself by faith and repentance.

It is passive: that conscious act of the regenerate man in which by God's grace he turns to God in repentance and faith.

8. *Does conversion take place in the judicial sphere, or in the sphere of dispositional re-creating grace?*

Properly speaking, conversion lies in the sphere of re-creating grace. It does not change the state but the condition of man. However, in conversion, an awareness that the sinner is worthy of damnation is awakened in him, and in connection with that, faith is given, which in its turn leads to justification. Conversion, therefore, is also connected with what occurs in the judicial sphere.

9. *Is conversion an act of grace that takes place below the consciousness or in the consciousness?*

As we saw from the name *metanoia*, conversion does not take place below the consciousness but in the consciousness. There is, of course, a transition of the activity of life from the new principle of life into the consciousness. The first dawning of conversion must thus start from below the consciousness. But, as the whole work of God, it is itself reflected in the light of man's consciousness.

10. *Does conversion have in view the removal of the old man or the enlivening of the new man?*

Actually, already in regeneration the old is replaced at the core of our being by a new principle of life. And, conversely, conversion flows from the outworking and penetration of this new life into the consciousness.

Thus, to this extent one cannot say that conversion removes the old; rather, it is a continuation and extension of the activity of the new.

Still, with that, not everything is said. When a new principle of life has been introduced at the core of a man's being, then his entire existence is still not yet reversed by it. In his consciousness, particularly, he still holds on to the old, lives in the old, and turns away from God. The center of the circle of his life may lie in God, while he does not see or seek that center in God but elsewhere. This, then, is what is changed in conversion. In his consciousness, in his own awareness, the sinner learns to see the lostness and untenability of his former position and his former condition, and the result of this is that he is also loosed from the old in his conscious life. And conversely, he learns to understand and appropriate with a clear consciousness the permanency and safety of his new position and his new condition. He adopts the standpoint of someone who lives for God. Thus we find that, for the consciousness, conversion in fact has the same two sides that we encounter in regeneration, but nevertheless for both the second, positive side of regeneration is the basis.

11. *Is conversion something that occurs at once in a crisis or does it consist of a slowly continuing process?*

Different answers must be given to this question. For regeneration, it was impossible to speak of a continuation or repetition. By the nature of the case, someone can only be born once. On the other hand, the consciousness of man goes up and down—is now darker, then clearer, subject to fluctuations and changes. It lies on the surface, on the outside of life, and consequently can be seized by the still-continually-impure nature, so that in a certain sense it again turns away from God. Thus, the possibility exists for a continuing and repeated conversion. The Christian needs to die daily in repentance and made alive in faith. The old man must be crucified anew again and again so that the new man can arise with all the more power.

Still, it remains true that in its specific sense, conversion is something that occurs once and can only occur once, and that consequently it stands out as a crisis in the life of sinners. Thus, the old theologians had every right to bring conversion into the closest connection with regeneration and to regard conversion as the reverse side of the latter.

Only where the consciousness is wholly fallen and turned away from God can it experience this great reversal, to which some give the designation of "first conversion." Afterward, the contrast between the old and the new can no longer appear with the sharpness that it has in the first days of the activity of the new life. And at a later point it is tempered by the consciousness of justification that can never be entirely lost where it has once occurred. Although one must thus agree that the distance between first conversion and continuing conversion is not the same as the absolute difference between regeneration and the development of life, there still remains sufficient place for a distinction.

12. *Is conversion exclusively a work of God, or is man also active in it?*

In it, man is worked on by God's grace such that he *converts himself*—that is, consciously turns from sin and turns to God. The subject that is active here is, however, the regenerated man, not the old, natural man.

13. *What is the connection of conversion to effectual calling?*

The closest connection. Conversion is the direct consequence of this calling. It is not as if the sinner converted himself to God by his own hand. Rather, conversion is always accompanied by a lively awareness that it is God who calls us to Himself. In the concept of calling, precisely that is expressed as clearly as possible. The difference between true conversion and a superficial moral improvement lies precisely in this point. The moral reformation of which the unregenerate speaks is a work that he himself performs and by which he places himself against the Lord. It is something, moreover, by which he continually relies on himself and exclusively considers himself and his own interests. It is a sorrow of a sinner according to himself.

In genuine conversion, man feels that he is under the working God. It may be that under the crushing and the death of repentance, he does not draw from conversion the comfort that he should be able to draw from it. But with that, he already senses that he is still placed in a direct relationship with God, *to be approved by Him*. And no less does the converted person reckon with and think of God, and is primarily concerned for His holy rights. In discussing calling above, it was pointed out how the man in whom the consciousness of the new life awakens for the first time is under the impression that God effectually draws him to Himself and omnipotently calls forth life from him. He says, "Convert me, so I shall be converted!" Precisely by that it comes about that, for his consciousness, regeneration and calling nearly fuse.

14. What is the connection of conversion to faith?

Conversion consists of repentance and faith. So faith is a part of conversion. Still, to arrive at clarity one needs to make a twofold distinction: There is a faith in the wider and in the narrower sense.

In the wider sense, we understand faith to be an acceptance as true of all that God declares; in the narrower sense, it is an acceptance as true of the declaration of God that in Christ He will forgive sin. By the former is not meant ordinary historical faith that can also be present in a sinner apart from regeneration and conversion. With conversion, a new faith awakens in the sinner with respect also to what he formerly believed in a merely historical fashion. An unconverted and unregenerate sinner can know that he is a sinner and deserving of condemnation in Adam. He knows this by historical faith. When conversion comes, however, he now begins to believe this in a much deeper sense, so that it becomes a reality for him with which he reckons and that is effective in his life. This is not saving faith in the narrower sense of the word, but it is still something entirely different than historical faith. Here, for the consciousness of the sinner by the action of the Holy Spirit, the content of historical faith is made into living, active truth, to which he must react. He knows it differently and agrees to it differently than was the case previously. Now, that truth is directly addressed by God to his consciousness and the power of the presence of God speaks from it. Also, it is now regarded as a truth that has a special, personal application to the sinner himself, while previously it was regarded as a general, collectively applicable truth. It is indifferent what name one gives to all this, whether one calls it conviction, repentance, or awareness of sin, provided one only recognizes that it falls under the general concept of the illuminating and enlightened knowledge that is only encountered in the regenerate in conversion and by which they learn to take into account the relationship in which they stand to God.

In this wider sense, one will have to say that faith accompanies conversion from its inception. Conversion is never a blind impulse by which man, without knowing why, would be driven to God. Knowledge is an essential element that never can be completely missing. It is a *calling* that draws and impels man, not a mystical something that has nothing to do with the truth.

It is another question how far saving faith in the narrower sense belongs to conversion. If someone is under conviction of sin and the reality of his situation is placed before his eyes by the faith just described, that does not yet actually include that he also exercises a faith that surrenders. Awareness of sin and of deserving damnation is logically a different concept than trusting in the Mediator. It is not only a different concept, but also a concept that must precede the latter. Without the conviction of sin, the act—the exercise—of faith is unthinkable. Also, believing in Christ is something reasonable that occurs in the light of truth, not a blind, mystical urge. Thus it is not subject to any doubt that, in order, repentance and the knowledge of sin precede surrendering faith. However, one should keep the following in view:

a) That this can only apply to the act of faith and not to its disposition. The latter is given in regeneration and so, in order, also precedes repentance. It underlies faith in the wider sense as well as in the narrower sense. Only by this disposition does it become possible for the sinner to see the reality of his relationship with God. It is the basis of both the activity of the intellect of the converted person, by which he sees the things of God correctly, and the inclination of his will, by which he agrees with God's declaration. Indeed, when God declares that the sinner is lost and deserving damnation, then there belongs to believing this witness not only an enlightened intellect but also a will bent to His. And the disposition that is the root of both of these can only precede repentance if it is to be the true repentance of conversion.

b) The distinction made here is a logical one and not a chronological one or a distinction in time. It is not as if the sinner is first brought to the knowledge of himself, of his lost condition and of his relationship as a sinner toward God, and then, after having spent considerable time in this situation, suddenly comes to the knowledge of Christ and His righteousness. Without doubt such cases do occur. There have been those converted who have wrestled before God for days and weeks almost without hope as lost, without the glimmer of faith occurring in their consciousness. But we may not make the presence or absence of such a condition a distinguishing mark of true conversion. One can even assume that this experience does not occur in the majority of those converted. Still, it is so that a historical knowledge of Christ is present from the outset in all those converted who come to repentance. God's way of proceeding is such that He only works conversion where one lives under the ministry of the Word, and so where a certain degree of knowledge of the truths of salvation is found. Where the notion of the Mediator is already in the consciousness, then from the first moment of conversion on it will generate a lesser or greater activity of the faith that accompanies repentance. In this way the activity of repentance and faith can coincide chronologically, and the one can affect the other. The knowledge of Christ and His righteousness do not remain without influence on the sinner's consciousness of guilt, but shape it. And in many cases it will be impossible to indicate precisely what first entered the consciousness clearly: repentance, or faith.

c) Conversion also includes the source of sanctification. Now, the rule is firm that there cannot be genuine Christian sanctification that does not grow on the root of justification. And justification, in turn, is only given to saving faith. At the same time, this includes that conversion as a source of sanctification presupposes the activity of faith. It is also entirely impossible that the sinner would try to do something good for God and devote himself to God as a pleasing sacrifice as long as he feels that he lies under the curse and does not have the consciousness, at least in principle, to be cleansed by the merits of Christ and to be accepted by God. The entire positive side of conversion—actively turning toward God—is inseparable from justifying faith. We see here again how the various saving acts of God, however much they can and must be distinguished logically, nevertheless may not be separated from one another as if they did not affect each other. Rather, they involve each other at every point and are interwoven with each other. We found that regeneration is included in effectual calling. We now find, in approximately the same sense, that justification is surrounded by the various activities of conversion.

15. *Who is the author of conversion?*

God, as we are taught in Acts 11:18: "So then to the Gentiles also God has granted repentance unto life." Here, it is called a gift of God. "Whether God may at some time grant them repentance leading to a knowledge of the truth" (2 Tim 2:25).

16. *In conversion, does God work solely through means, or is there in addition also an immediate working?*

In conversion there is a twofold working of God:

a) Mediate working through the Word of God. Both through the law as well as through the gospel, God affects the consciousness of sinners in order to bring about conversion in them. Through the law, repentance is generated, for by the law is the knowledge of sin [Rom 3:20]. Through the gospel, faith is generated, for faith is by hearing [Rom 10:17]. Still, one must not separate these two too sharply. In the law there is already an adumbration of the gospel, and in the gospel there is an eloquent testimony to, a crushing proclamation of, the law. The cross of the Mediator not only proclaims that satisfaction is accomplished and pardon may be obtained, but at the same time points to what the sinner had deserved for himself and what would happen with him if God were to deal with him in justice. Hence, Scripture describes the crisis of repentance, in which man abandons himself and learns to distance himself from all self-righteousness, as a "being crucified with Christ," a "mortifying of the old man." "For through the law I died to the law"—something that is further clarified by the words, "I have been crucified with Christ" (Gal 2:19–20). "Knowing this, that our old man was crucified with Him, so that the body of sin might be abolished, so that we no longer serve sin" (Rom 6:6). In baptism there is a picturing of this repentance as death: "Therefore we were buried with him by baptism into death" (Rom 6:4).

b) Besides this mediate working of God, in conversion there is also a direct, immediate working—a working linked with the new principle of life already infused into the soul but that then directly, without the intervention of any means, implements this principle. Also, this new principle does not possess in itself the capacity to flow outwardly and lay hold of the consciousness of the sinner. It is Lutheran and Remonstrant to think that God gives powers in the regenerate man over which he can now dispose freely, which he can use or can leave unused or, if need be, can discard and lose. Conversion is as little an uncertain work as regeneration. God works in His children to will and to work for His good pleasure. Even the best seed does not germinate and grow without the fructifying and nourishing working of the Spirit. In this working of the Spirit, there is an immediate working (Phil 2:13). Not only the disposition of faith but also the act of believing is sustained by the working of God's grace. The old theologians distinguish these two acts of conversion, or of the converting God, as moral and physical, ethical and material action. The word "physical" is used here in the same sense as in regeneration.

17. Is the word "conversion" always used in the same sense in Scripture?

No, it occurs with more than one meaning, and one must take the greatest care not to confuse these with each other or to apply to the one what is meant by another.

a) Conversion is used for a change in the outlook of a nation—thus, in an external religious sense. So, for example, it occurs of the Ninevites, who were converted by Jonah's preaching (Jonah 3:10; Matt 12:41; cf. Isa 19:22).

b) A godless person can convert in his outward life to a virtuous one without being regenerated (Psa 7:12; Jer 18:11).

c) After being caught in a condition of lifelessness and barrenness, a believer can convert from it to a new faith (Rev 2:5; Jas 5:19–20).

d) A regenerate person can come for the first time to exercise repentance and faith. This is conversion as discussed here.

18. Is conversion absolutely necessary?

Everyone who is saved must come to a true knowledge of his sins and to a believing appreciation of the merits of the Mediator. If he is regenerated in adult life, he has lived in a conscious estrangement from God. It can therefore not be otherwise than that the about-face of this consciousness must be registered very sharply in his life, and in such a case, one beholds the crisis that is called conversion.

The possibility exists, however, that children are regenerated before they come to exercise discernment. To what extent that takes place cannot be decided. The Bible provides us with only two instances: namely, those of the Prophet Jeremiah and John the Baptist. However, where such a case occurs, the possibility also exists that the child does not first need to be brought over from a conscious condition of estrangement from God into that of conversion to God, but that of its own accord, in growing up, it already lives in the latter condition. There are young people who cannot point to a particular time for their conversion, and who can recall that, as far back as their consciousness reaches, they have always been active for God with a repentant and believing heart. There, the course is not marked by crisis, but is more protracted. Still, there too the essential elements of conversion are present. But they are more diffused.

✧

CHAPTER FOUR

Faith

1. *What order should be followed in discussing faith?*

   a) Its scriptural names in both the Old and the New Testament.

   b) Its psychological nature. The following question should be discussed: What is faith as an activity of the soul? This is one of the most difficult psychological questions, which becomes even more complicated by its theological ramifications.

   c) Its soteriological meaning as a link in the order of salvation. Scripture does not speak solely of faith in general but it occupies a very special place as saving faith.

2. *What word is used most in the Old Testament to express the concept of believing?*

The verb הֶאֱמִין, *hip'il* from אמן. The *qal* means "to strengthen," "to support," "to uphold," but does not appear other than in the participle. The active participle אֹמֵן means someone who cares for and raises a child, a pedagogue. The passive participle has the sense of the *nip'al* and means "strong," "lasting," "to be permanently trustworthy," thus approximately the same as the *qal* passive participle. The specific sense of the *hip'il* is rendered best by "demonstrating faithfulness" or "generating faithfulness," "establishing oneself." Without doubt, we are shown by this an active disposition of the soul, an action that produces change.

הֶאֱמִין is connected with the preposition בְּ and the preposition לְ. The difference between the two constructions appears to lie in this: that the latter is used preferably for holding something to be true, the former for a trustful resting in a person or in a truth. Both appear for believing God or in God. "So you rebelled against the mouth of the LORD your God and did not believe him" (Deut 9:23; לְ is used here). "Then Moses answered and said, 'But behold, they will not believe me nor listen to my voice, for they will say, "The LORD did not appear to you" ' " (Exod 4:1). Genesis 15:6, the verse repeatedly cited by Paul, which speaks of the justifying faith of Abraham, has בְּ: "And he believed the LORD, and He reckoned it to him for righteousness." Of course, in the case of Abraham, something different and something more is meant than that he held the promise of God to be true. As this promise was a matter of life for Abraham, so this promise was also a living testimony for him, and his faith was not merely concerned with the truth in the abstract but with the God of the truth. A personal relationship came about between the consciousness of Abraham and God. Thus we may already say in general that הֶאֱמִין בְּ is the trustful acceptance of the testimony of a person that becomes a basis of certainty for us through the conscious conception of that person.

The independent substantive that would mean "faith" does not occur with הֶאֱמִין. It is true that אֱמוּנָה appears, but this word does not belong in the *hip'il*. It belongs in the *nip'al* and the *qal* passive participle; hence it is rendered as "steadfastness," "permanency," "trustworthiness." This can already be seen from the fact that in most cases the Septuagint translates it with ἀλήθεια, "truth." It is also applied to God Himself, "For the word of the LORD is right, and all His work is faithful ['emunah]" (Psa 33:4); of men, "O LORD, do not your eyes look for faithfulness ['emunah]?" (Jer 5:3). In Habakkuk 2:4, the verse in which 'emunah certainly comes the closest to the New Testament concept of "faith," the latter is surely not meant simply in general but specifically as steadfast in unwavering faith. Talmudic Hebrew is the first to adopt a separate word for the concept of believing as a noun—namely, הֵימָנוּתָא.

3. Does the Old Testament use still other words for the same concept?

Yes it has:

   a) בָּטַח, "to be sure," in construct with בְּ, thus to trust in someone. "But I have trusted in your lovingkindness" (Psa 13:5); that is, "I consider myself safe and reassure myself in the consciousness of your lovingkindness." "In him my heart trusts" (Psa 28:7). Here, too, the personal relationship comes out. Depending on the testimony is accompanied by and derives its strength from this personal relationship.

b) חָסָה, "to hide," "to take refuge in," likewise in construct with בְּ. Here again the emphasis is on the trusting side of faith and not on the purely intellectual "accepting as true." "Be merciful to me, O God, be merciful to me, for my soul trusts [חָסָיָה] in you and in the shadows of your wings I take refuge [אֶחְסֶה]" (Psa 57:1).

c) קָוָה (from the *qal*, only the participle קֹוִי), properly, is to be "intense," "strong," "taut." In the *pi'el* קִוָּה is intensive, "focusing the mind on something." This can be taken more in the sense of "hoping." However, it can also be taken as an intensive focusing of the intellect that definitely expects the realization of what is desired. Faith is thus again indicated from its active side. קִוָּה is in construct with the accusative or with אֶל. "But they who wait on the LORD will renew their strength" (Isa 40:31). "Wait on the LORD; be strong, and He will strengthen your heart; yes, wait on the LORD" (Psa 27:14). This waiting, therefore, is not a passive state, depleted of all expressions of life. Rather, it is an extending and securing of the heart, a reckoning on Jehovah connected with the inner strength of the soul.

4. *What are the various elements belonging to the concept of believing that we can gather from these various designations?*

   a) Faith is an activity of the intellect as it accepts the testimony of another (הֶאֱמִין לְ).

   b) Faith can be much more than an activity of the intellect. As trust it is that deeply moral action by which, in order to have stability, man, as it were, puts himself into another (הֶאֱמִין בְּ).

   c) As such, faith does not have a passive but an active, dynamic form (חָסָה בְּ).

   d) As trust, faith is accompanied to a greater or lesser degree by a sense of security. Faith not only seeks certainly but finds it and also produces certainty. It knows itself to be certain and safe (בָּטַח בְּ) and lives in a reality with its conceptions that is not yet present (קָוָה).

5. *Which are the words for "faith" and "believing" in the New Testament?*

Πίστις and πιστεύειν, which are related to πείθειν, "to persuade"; πείθεσθαι, "to be persuaded"; πεποιθέναι, "to trust."

6. *What two meanings does πίστις have in Classical Greek?*

a) It means "a conviction," based on the trust of a person that as such differs from knowledge resting on one's own research. By Plato, "faith" is set against "knowledge," πίστις against ἐπιστήμη. A conviction concerning the existence of the gods is called *pistis*, faith.

b) It means such *trust itself*, as that on which the above-mentioned conviction is based. Such trust is more than an intellectual conviction that someone is trustworthy. It presupposes a personal relationship with him whom one trusts, a sharing of life, a forsaking of oneself and resting in another.

7. *Is the word in this latter sense also used with reference to the gods by the Greeks?*

No; according to the Greek understanding, the relationship between the gods and men is not of such a nature that one can speak of an intimate contact, of a resting of man in the gods. "Belief in the gods" (πίστις θεῶν), therefore, nearly always means theoretically holding to be true what is asserted regarding the gods or by the gods. The gods are not favorable or inclined toward men. They must be moved to friendship by sacrifices and gifts, and never condescend to the degree that man can conceive of truly trusting them. Compare this with what was noted about ἱλάσκεσθαι in connection with the doctrine of satisfaction.[1] This notion of having confidence in the gods is so far removed from the Greek spirit that even in the first of the meanings mentioned above, in the sense of "believing in the gods," the verb πιστεύειν τοὺς θεούς is not yet used. This would have in itself too much of the sound of trust. Thus, the Greeks chose a purely

---

[1] Vol. 3, ch. 4, q. 21.

intellectual word, in which every personal element is lacking, and called it νομίζειν θεούς, "believing in gods."

8. *From where, then, did the New Testament derive its usage of the words* πίστις *and* πιστεύειν?

For the translation of the Old Testament concept of הֶאֱמִין it chose a word that was used by the Greeks chiefly of the mutual relationship between human beings and only partially of the relationship between divine and human beings. Thus the sense of the word is determined not by the pagan Greek but by the Old Testament meaning. The concept of faith toward God comes from the thought world of revelation and not from Hellenic life. But the word that, as a substantive, expresses this act of faith comes from Greek vocabulary. As we saw, the Old Testament lacks a separate noun that means "faith."

9. *With how many meanings do* πίστις *and* πιστεύω *occur in the New Testament?*

a) Here, too, they not uncommonly have the meaning of testimony that is brought to us by another person for acceptance as true. This is a cognitive conviction regarding the reality and trust-worthiness of what someone says and that cannot be verified by us, for which we must therefore rest in a personal trust that we place in that person. "I told you, and you do not believe it [namely, that I am the Christ]. The works that I do in the name of my Father, those bear witness to me" (John 10:25). "Look, you scoffers, marvel and perish; for I work a work in your days, a work that you will not believe even if someone tells it to you" (Acts 13:41). "You believe that there is one God; you do well; the demons also believe and tremble" (Jas 2:19). "Now if we have died with Christ, then we believe that we will also live with Him" (Rom 6:8). "For if we believe that Jesus died and rose, even so God will bring with Him those who sleep" (1 Thess 4:14; cf. John 3:12; 6:36; 10:37–38). The usual construction with this meaning is with the accusative of what is accepted as true and the dative of the person on whose testimony one relies. Naturally, a clause with ὅτι can replace the accusative: "For I believe God that it will be so, even as it was told me" (Acts 27:25); "Woman, believe me, the hour is coming" (John 4:21). Here we clearly have both elements: the personal and the natural, and the first as the basis on which the second rests. Also, where faith is used in a cognitive sense, trust is included. Faith can never be a purely cognitive act. It is always only a question of which of the two elements comes most to the fore.

This meaning applies to all those who speak of faith in contrast to seeing and perceiving: "Unless you see signs and wonders, you will not believe" (John 4:48); "For we walk by faith, not by sight" (2 Cor 5:7). In other places, however, it seems again that faith and sight do not exclude each another but go together: "And he saw and believed ... and Jesus said to Thomas, 'Because you have seen me, you have believed'" (John 20:8, 29). In such cases, *pisteuein* is apparently either synonymous with being convinced—knowing—entirely apart from the ground on which the conviction rests, or it refers to believing in something invisible on the basis of seeing something else; for example, "We no longer believe because of what you said, for we ourselves have heard Him and know that this is truly the Savior of the world" (John 4:42). Here, then, believing the testimony of the woman ceased and was replaced by hearing, where believing the witness heard from Christ continued.

Hebrews 11:1, which provides a definition of faith, deserves special discussion. However, it is not a definition of faith in its specific form in which it appears as saving faith, but in its most general sense. This appears already from the fact that it is not "faith" with the definite article (namely, specific, justifying faith) but without an article—"*faith* is." Of this faith it is now said that it is a ἐλπιζομένων πραγμάτων, "a substance of things hoped for." The substance of a thing is what manifests the stability and durability of its existence, what makes it real. The characteristics of a thing may change; the substance lasts. When there are things hoped for—that is, things that one does not yet possess but of which one still has knowledge through the testimony of another—then faith is what imparts to us proof and reality. When we believe something, then by that faith we have a distinctive reality before us. It has an effect on us that in a certain sense corresponds to the reality. In this, then, lies in part the certainty and in part the activity of the conviction of faith. By faith we learn to reckon on the things we hope for as if they are really seen by us.

Further, faith is an ἔλεγχος "of the things one does not see." An ἔλεγχος is "a proof," a thing from which the reality of something else is proven. If I believe something that is not seen, then my faith fills the place of proof, evidence. By my faith I am assured of an invisible entity, as I am assured of something by a proof.

What then is the distinction between "things hoped for" and "things that are not seen"? It appears to be the following. Things hoped for can become visible sometimes; they are not so only for the moment. On the other hand, things that cannot be seen can already be present at this moment, but by their nature they are unsuited to become objects for observation—thus spiritual, imperceptible things. For the former, which have the goal of being seen and observed, a substance is necessary by which they receive a certain reality for us until such a time as the full reality dawns. When that substance itself comes, then the faith-substance that temporarily replaced it ceases; faith is exchanged for sight. For this contrast, compare Romans 8:24-25: "Now hope that is seen is not hope. Why will someone also hope for what he sees? But if we hope for what we do not see, we wait for it with patience." It is otherwise with invisible spiritual things. These cannot and may not have a substance for us but a proof or evidence—that is, we must be fully convinced of their reality but not feel the unspiritual urge to want to touch and see them. With respect to them, faith can never cease to be faith. Thus, while on the one hand faith is one of the things that pass away, on the other hand it is also something permanent. For example, that the world was made by the word of God nobody other than God Himself beheld, and also its beholding cannot be reproduced for anybody but for all eternity must remain a matter of faith. Hebrews 11:7 speaks of "things that are not yet seen," which roughly corresponds with "things that are expected."

b) At the same time, the concept of "faith" does not lie entirely within the cognitive sphere. Even when one admits that faith is a conviction in understanding that rests on a personal relationship of trust, one has not yet expressed everything that the New

Testament means by faith. There is an *antecedent trust* and *consequent trust*. If I trust a person completely, then in a given case I will be prepared to accept the testimony he gives as true. Here, trusting is first and believing second. If now, however, he has provided testimony that affects my life interests, then I am presented with a unique situation by which I am engaged with him under this particular aspect, reach out to him, abandon myself to him. This, then, is no longer the general trust that I place in him but something new and special. This is consequent trust.

Now, when in an array of places Scripture speaks of believing as such a trust, then the two other elements are evidently presupposed by that. I cannot rely on someone and put my trust in him if I do not (a) possess a trust in general in the trustworthiness of his person, and (b) maintain a conviction concerning the truth of the particular testimony that constitutes the object of my consequent trust. In all trusting faith, these three elements are present and connected. If a doctor assures me that I will be regaining my health, and if this assurance is to put me at ease, I must first have a reasonable trust that he means it and does not have an untrustworthy character; further, the conviction that his statement contains the truth; and finally, the complete peace of mind that results. However difficult it may be to analyze this last element precisely, it is in any case something special.

The Apostle Paul in particular elaborated this side of the concept of faith. In John, the emphasis is more on attaching faith to the testimony that Christ gives of the Father, thus on the confidence that Christ is the true Messiah and holding His message to be true. In Paul, all the emphasis is on the trust that His merits are a sufficient ground of righteousness, a trust that releases us from all further striving after a righteousness of our own. For Paul, believing is opposed to doing, and everything associated with this opposition belongs to the essence of faith. From this it already follows that believing must be something other and more than accepting a testimony to be true, for in the latter in itself there is not an opposition to doing. Neither could Paul have regarded faith as a moral work that had become a replacement for the works of the law. Finally, his meaning also cannot be that believing is internal obedience to the law of love, while the law itself would merely demand a legalistic external obedience. The latter is precisely not the case. The law demands inner form. The man who is mindful of his justification before God wishes to give it to God. The man who believes learns, in the wrestling of his soul to offer God righteousness, to look away from himself and to rest in the Mediator for his standing before God, on which his entire destiny hangs.

Thus we see that for saving faith the will in any case has an important part, and at the same time we can already say in advance that the whole man with all his capacities will be involved, for believing is a life issue in which it is a matter of death or life for the awakened sinner. For the opposition between faith and works, compare Romans 10:5–6; Galatians 3:23–25; Romans 4:13–14; 3:28. This faith that trusts in another can now be directed to God insofar as He declared the merits of Christ to be sufficient when He raised Him from the dead. When we rely on that declaration of God—not merely acknowledging God in general as true or believing this declaration theoretically but making it the ground of our trust in the face of the just demands of God—then we exercise saving faith. So God appears as the object of faith in Romans 4:24, "But also for our sakes, to whom it will be imputed, namely to those who believe in Him who raised Jesus our Lord from the dead" (cf. Col 2:12).

Usually, however, faith is presented as something that is directed to the Mediator, Christ. It is called "believing *in* Christ" (πιστεύειν εἰς Χριστόν)—actually, "into Christ" (cf. Rom 10:14). That is, the action of the soul by which it abandons its own doing and relies on the doing of Christ is presented as a local movement of the will into Christ. There is a relocation of the resting point of life. Where it formerly lay in the self-righteous sinner himself, it now comes to lie in Christ. It is also called "believing *in* Christ" (πιστεύειν ἐν Χριστῷ). The thought here is not so much of a movement into Christ as of its result, "resting in Christ" (Gal 3:26). Also occurring is πιστεύειν ἐπ᾽ αὐτῷ, "believing in Him" (Rom 9:33; 10:11, in a citation from the Septuagint of Isa 28:16), which has approximately the same meaning as εἰς Χριστόν. Finally, the apostle also speaks of a "faith of Jesus Christ" (πίστις Ἰησοῦ Χριστοῦ) with the objective genitive—thus a faith of which Christ as mediator is the object, a trust by which one depends on Him (Rom 3:22, 26; Gal 2:16; 3:22).

Above, we have already seen that in the letters of Paul, too, the wider meaning of faith—that of holding to be true on the basis of antecedent trust—is not absent. However, in every place where the reference is to justification by faith, faith has the sense described above of consequent trust. Where that is not the case, it can very well be trust in the veracity of the person and the faith that results from His words. In 1 Corinthians 2:8 it occurs in this wider sense, and so in many other places. Now, it is natural that in practice both meanings, although logically distinct, flow imperceptibly into each other at the same time. Whoever trusts Jesus Christ as mediator and believes from the heart that He speaks the words of God, that person will also accept the main part of His message: that one must abandon self and be justified by believing. And, conversely, whoever does the latter cannot do that without at the same time unconditionally submitting to all the truth that Christ proclaims. "No one can say 'Jesus is Lord' except by the Holy Spirit" (1 Cor 12:3). In Romans 1:17, therefore, it is said of the gospel that in it "the righteousness of God is revealed from faith to faith." That is, from the faith that Christ is the Mediator ordained by God—if this is at least more than bare historical faith and worked in the heart by God the Holy Spirit—flows of itself trusting, justifying faith. It goes from faith (antecedent trust, plus holding to be true) to faith (consequent trust).

10. *Is faith also described sometimes in other terms in Scripture?*

Yes, Scripture uses a number of images in order to make the act of faith clear.

a) One of these is the image of seeing that occurs in John 3:14–15, compared with the account of the lifted-up serpent that the bitten Israelites must see. In this example, faith was represented by seeing. In fact, all the elements of faith are resident in seeing. First, it includes a rational element, for all seeing is a cognitive act. Seeing includes separating, distinguishing. Further, it includes an element of the will, for to pay attention to something, to feast one's eyes on something, observing it, is a sign of delight in what one observes. Finally, there is an element of satisfaction, of trust, for continually paying attention to something includes letting one's gaze come to rest, withdrawing it from all else and concentrating on one point.

b) Another image is that of eating and drinking, of hungering and thirsting (cf. Matt 5:6; John 6:48, 50, 53–58). This image is most suited to illustrate for us the essence of faith, and includes the following:

1. Hungering and thirsting, eating and drinking are expressions of life. Likewise, faith is the expression of the regenerate life.

2. Eating and drinking are actions by which one takes to himself nourishment from the outside and identifies with it. Likewise, faith draws the Mediator to one's self.

3. Eating and drinking occur not only with the conviction that the food or the drink is available but also with a more or less strong conviction that it will satisfy our hunger and our thirst. Similarly, appropriating the Mediator is always accompanied by a certain degree of trust that He saves us.

c) A similar image is that of "accepting," in which a movement of the hand is in view. In John 1:12, this accepting of Christ is put on the same line with believing in His name.

11. *What, therefore, is our result concerning this New Testament linguistic usage?*

According to the New Testament, "believing" includes:

a) Antecedent trust in a person with whom one comes into contact (πιστεύειν τινί).

b) Holding as true a testimony that is brought to us by such a person (πιστεύειν τι).

c) Consequent trust in that person in connection with a testimony that affects our life interests (πιστεύειν εἴς τινα, ἔν τινι, ἐπί τινα).

12. *Is the word* pistis *also found in the New Testament with another meaning than that of "faith"?*

Yes, it also has the meaning of "faithfulness," "steadfastness," "trustworthiness"; thus when the apostle asks, "For what if some were unfaithful? Does their faithlessness nullify the faithfulness of God?" (Rom 3:3); likewise *pistis* for "faithful" (e.g., Rev 2:10).

13. *What word did Latin use for the concept of "believing"?*

The verb that seemed most suited to translate *pistis* was *credere*. But it lacked a related noun and adjective for "faith" and "faithful." Therefore *fides* and *fidelis* were taken over to fill this gap. Originally, the meaning of both is more like "trustworthiness" and "trustworthy" than "trust" and "trusting." Nevertheless, already before the rise of Christianity their meaning bordered on that of πιστεύειν. According to Cicero, *fides* is *firma opinio* [a firm belief]. Another Latin word is *fiducia*, which has more the active meaning of "trusting" but is only used to any extent by later writers.

14. *What is the derivation of the Dutch word* gelooven?

Gelooven comes from a word that appears in Gothic as *galaubjan*, as its adjective *galaubs*, connected with *liubs*, "dear," "precious." Therefore, *galaubjan* originally meant "regard as precious." One may compare "to you who believe He is precious" [1 Pet 2:7]. Our *gelooven* is related to "to betroth," "to promise," "to permit." The English "belief" is the same word. The English "faith," on the other hand, comes from the Latin *fides*, and therefore also has a double meaning: "trust" as well as "trustworthiness."

15. *What needs to be discussed in treating the psychological aspect of faith?*

We have to deal here primarily with two questions, namely:

a) What is the ground of certainty on which one in faith accepts certain things as true, and what is the nature of the certainty that is thus obtained?

b) What capacities of the soul are involved in the act of faith, or what is the proper center of the act of faith?

16. What different answers have been given to the first question?

Some have answered that faith is being subjectively assured, and then in distinction from being objectively assured, for which there are other terms. This distinction is connected with a popular usage known to us all. It is said, "I only believe that but don't know it for sure." So according to this view, believing lies between decisive certainty—resting on reliable, objective grounds—and a loose, superficial opinion on which one hardly relies. Locke described faith in this way. In the same sense, the skeptic Hume replaced knowing, which he regarded as impossible, with believing. Still later, Kant followed the same path in his famous distinction between "believing" and "knowing," although he did not so much seek the difference in the differing degrees of certainty. According to Kant, my faith in God, freedom, and immortality have rational certainty but are not objective knowledge. I can certainly say, "*I am* rationally certain that these three exist," but not, "*It is* rationally sure that they exist." Certainty always remains within myself and can never be transferred to another. We can constrain anyone of a sound mind to accept a judgment that rests on objective grounds but cannot force anyone to believe. To believe must be given to him as it is given to us. In the Netherlands this view is defended by Doedes, among others.

17. What should be noted against this conception?

a) That it limits the significance of faith entirely to the terrain of the intellect. It is then only a subjective weighing of grounds and the question of how much worth I wish to ascribe to one or other ground. Faith becomes the result of adding or subtracting evidence. However, this is a very unspiritual and unworthy view of faith. Scripture and experience both teach us that faith is a deeply moral act and not a detached conviction that we have formed on grounds satisfactory to us.

b) In this view, faith becomes something that has less certainty than knowledge. The grounds are not strong enough, one thinks, to justify an assertion of knowledge, and therefore we say that we merely believe something. But according to Scripture, a characteristic of faith is precisely firmness of conviction. One may read Hebrews 11 and ask whether the men of God whose faith is described there acted as they did on the basis of something that they did not regard as certain enough to know it (cf. also 2 Tim 1:12).

c) If we consider the matter in this way, then the essence, the distinctiveness of faith lies in something entirely negative—namely, in the absence of sufficient objective grounds. In this view, accepting something as true where there are not sufficient grounds that would be valid for everyone is faith. This of itself cannot be. If this definition is to have even a semblance of being correct, one must bring to light the character of those subjective grounds that compensate for the absence of objective grounds. And then it will be evident that faith certainly bears a positive character that is derived precisely from this character of its grounds.

d) That the popular use of "believe" in this sense is warranted must be granted. Whatever may be the basis for this usage, in no case may it be made the basis for our determining the concept of faith.

18. Is there still another way one can seek the distinguishing characteristic of faith in something subjective?

Yes, some wish to bring faith into a close connection with the will. Kant, for example, already did this, as do presently, following him, the neo-Kantian theologians in Germany. Our sense of our own worth, our moral significance, demands the truth of certain things that we do not know objectively and cannot prove. I consider the connection of virtue and happiness as the highest good; therefore, I must also believe in a God who causes this connection, in a future life in which it will be able to be realized. One speaks therefore of "value judgments" that need to be distinguished from "purely intellectual judgments." A value judgment is a judgment concerning a thing that rests on my assessment of the value of that thing. Thus, here the will becomes the mother of the judgment; I believe in something because I am pleased to do so.

19. What is your objection to this explanation of faith?

a) That it ascribes something to the will that cannot rightly be its due and that a person who loves the truth will never grant to his will—namely, to pronounce a judgment on what is true and what is not true. That task falls to the intellect. It is certainly true that the desire for something all too often becomes the mother of belief in it. But that is a defect in us, and when there are matters of great importance at stake we are not at all blind to the groundlessness of such a mistake. The most fervent desire for something has brought no one to a firm, unshakable faith.

b) The accord of our will with a person belongs in fact to the trust in general that we put in him. If our will directly opposes his, our trust will never reach that degree of believing him at his word. At the same time, it should be noted that in many a case this general prior trust can amount to a minimum. If a criminal acknowledges his crime, which up to that moment he had stubbornly denied, shortly before his execution, I will very probably believe his confession. Yet one could hardly say that this belief is based on a great deal of trust in his love of the truth, or on the assent of my will to any extent.

c) In a great many cases, people are compelled to believe what they are extremely grudging to believe. According to the view being discussed here, one would just about have to be able to believe whatever one wanted. This is not so. In certain circumstances, the objects of belief present themselves with equally compelling force to our consciousness as do what one likes to call the things of science. Many who lack the gift of faith and wander about in the wilderness of skepticism have voiced the wish, "O that I may believe more, but I cannot!"—clear evidence that it does not depend on the will.

20. *Has it also been attempted to seek what is characteristic of faith in the uniqueness of its object?*

Yes. In connection with Hebrews 11:1 and some other passages mentioned above, it has been maintained that believing is accepting as true something that is invisible. However, the word invisible can be taken in more than one sense. In the first place, it can mean something that by its nature cannot be seen—that is, cannot be observed—whose reality cannot come directly into contact with my cognitive capacity. Further, it can mean something that by its nature is not unsuited to become an object of observation for me but in fact has never been subject to my observation. Thirdly, it can also mean something that previously, perhaps even countless times, has been observed by me, but now at this moment, while I assent in faith to its reality, is outside the scope of my observation.

Concerning the first meaning of invisible, this must always remain an object of faith for me. For example, the fact that in my own soul there are depths of life that I can never observe is established for me by faith—that is, on the basis of the testimony of the Word of God. Here, what is invisible and what I believe coincide. This can also be granted for instances of the second meaning. I am convinced of the existence of many visible, observable things that I have so far never observed myself or never will observe. None of us have ever seen Peking [Beijing]. Yet we all accept that a town of that name exists. We are assured of the truth of something invisible to us, and can call that faith. For the third meaning, however, it is clearly different. That a great lake is located on the west side of the state of Michigan is an established fact for us all. However, we are not inclined to call this faith, although we are only relatively seldom in a position to convince ourselves of its reality by personal observation. And so there are many invisible things that we nonetheless know. Every perception of our senses in the next moment, as soon as it has passed, will have become an object of believing.

Only in the case of the first two meanings, therefore, is what is invisible an object of faith. But solely because it is invisible, or for another reason? Apparently the latter. We speak of faith with respect to things that are completely invisible or never seen by us, since their existence can become known to us only by the testimony of another. The entire invisible world that comprises the object of our faith, which becomes a reality for us by faith and in which we live by faith, can only be placed before our spiritual gaze by the declaration of God's Word. It not only lies behind the world of phenomena, but above it is a higher world than that in which we go about observing. But from this it is evident how it is not so much what is invisible that we call the object of faith, but in a broader sense what is *inaccessible*, what for us is *personally inaccessible*, with which we can have contact only by the intervening testimony of another person. If one wishes to stay with what is invisible, many things may be enumerated that cannot be seen and yet are not really objects of faith. General propositions that are derived with deductions from other propositions and into whose truth we thus have an immediate logical insight represent a reality that can never be observed by us as such. That the three angles of a triangle equal two right angles is a proposition that is only thought of in its universality but can never be seen in its all-inclusive reality. Yet no one says that he believes this, and everyone asserts that he knows it. The reason is that here we do not rely on the testimony of another but independently have a logical insight into the truth of this proposition. Therefore, here is something invisible that is not an object of believing but of knowing. It is, however, not something that is unattainable in the sense described above, for we can reach this proposition with our capacity for logical reasoning; we can arrive at it directly.

With the objects of faith that is not so. They lie outside and above us, and no reasoning in the world brings us in proximity to them. Therefore, criticism of this definition—that believing is conviction about what is invisible—has at the same time shown us in which direction we will have to seek the right definition.

21. *Must what distinguishes faith be sought in the object that is believed or in the particular way in which one holds to be true what is believed?*

Both views are, as has now been amply shown, untenable and one-sided. We will therefore have to say that what distinguishes faith is to be sought:

a) Not in the nature of its object. One and the same thing, without changing, can be an object of faith now and an object of knowledge tomorrow. If a good friend tells me about San Francisco, I believe that those things are true; if I visit the city tomorrow, my believing changes into knowing.

b) Not in the nature of the subject alone. It is not possible for me to pass randomly from a state of knowing into that of believing by an arbitrary change. It is not up to me whether I will to know or believe something. In the one as well as in the other case, there is something objective outside of me that compels me either to know or to believe.

c) Certainly in the nature of that by which my knowledge of something is mediated. If this knowledge is realized by immediate contact with the object in my experience or by logical reasoning, then I speak of knowing. If this is not the case, but the personal testimony of another intervenes between me and what in itself is inaccessible for me, then I speak of believing.

d) Certainly in the subjective activity that results from this personal mediation. It is wrong to say that believing is a subjective holding to be true that lacks the certainty of objective knowing. But it would be no less wrong if one wished to deny that faith has its distinctiveness as a subjective disposition and act in man. The difference does not lie in the greater or lesser degree of firmness or certainty. But still there is a subjective difference between the way in which in my knowing I accept something to be true and the way I assent to it in believing. In the latter the activity of my soul is different than in the former. The result may be the same in both cases, but the path along which it was reached was not the same, and the subjective experiences also differed. That we are no longer able to see this difference clearly is to be ascribed to the fact that in our daily living the experiences of believing and knowing are mingled at every point. Anyone, however, if he makes some effort, can reflect on the difference.

This subjective difference of which we have spoken follows directly from what is objective. The mediation between the truth and me by another person is the reason that I am brought into a distinctive disposition toward this truth. By this the one-sidedness, which we need to reject in the opinions discussed above, has disappeared.

22. *On the basis of what has been said, how could we define "faith" in general?*

Faith is an acceptance as true by which we do not rest in ourselves but in the testimony of another.

23. *According to this definition, what must already be reckoned as objects of faith?*

With some reflection it will be apparent that our entire human society, all spiritual communion with others, and by far the greater part of our thinking and acting rests on faith. Faith is the warp and woof in the fabric of human life. Without faith no one could exist in society. Life is a large ocean of which only a small segment falls within our horizon, and this small segment is nearly endlessly suffused with what we can know only by faith.

a) The highest truths, the roots of all our knowledge, the propositions that are not subject to further argumentation are objects of faith for us. It is not true, as the Rationalists maintain, that for this knowledge our reason rests self-sufficiently in itself. It rests in God. He is the ground of our knowing, and His veracity is for us the guarantee for the trustworthiness of this foundation of all knowledge. If one considers how these highest truths are interwoven through all our thinking and knowing, how nearly all things at every point are dependent on it, then from that alone is already to be derived how much in our consciousness rests on faith. At the same time, it is evident from this how absurd it is to elevate knowledge at the expense of faith or to despise the latter for the sake of knowledge. There is no knowledge that in its deepest ground would not rest on faith. As creatures, believing is a law of life for us. We stand on the terrain of a world for which in its necessity we can only demonstrate by far only the smallest part. The greater part we accept on the basis of testimony. We are not constituted to rest in ourselves but to rest, with our convictions as well as in all other respects, in God.

In these matters, faith will never cease or be eradicated. Viewed in this way, it is a characteristic of being a creature that never can be lost. The angels have such faith. Man had it before his fall, and has to exercise it after his fall. Only God does not believe, since He has no one greater than Himself in whom He can believe and rest. He is immediately in contact with things by His omniscience, and all truth has its ground in His being. He does not rest in the truth, but the truth rests in Him. He knows and understands everything in His own being.

b) In our sense experience, too, there is an element of faith. With some reflection one will recognize that even our knowledge that seems to be the most immediate is nevertheless mediate. How do we know that our senses are not deceiving us? That they are fitted to reflect the world in our consciousness as it really is? How do we know that no idealistic appearance deceives us? Only by faith in God our Creator, who has given us this nature and this capacity to know, can man be kept from skepticism in the face of all these questions. Therefore, present in all skepticism is defection from God, a falling away from Him, that has moral significance.

c) All spiritual communion with our fellow creatures rests on faith. Cooperation with others would be completely impossible if God had not given us the capacity to accept as true the testimony of others and rely on it, if He had not so curbed the deceitfulness inherent in all men by nature, at least on its external side, that a reality corresponds to this faith. However often our trust may be disappointed, without faith we cannot live at all, and every day we trust, more or less, most people with whom we come into contact.

d) Our knowledge of the past, no longer present, rests on the testimony of previous generations. All our historical knowledge rests on faith. None of those historical facts allows for direct investigation, for time has borne them away. Yet among them are facts that are perhaps more certain for us than many a thing that we observe with our eyes.

e) For what is meant under (a) and (b) above, we depend on the veracity of God, and so our faith is a *fides divina* [divine faith]. For what is meant under (c) and (d) above, we rely on the fidelity of men, and our faith is a *fides humana* [human faith]. In a certain sense, both faiths go together and follow each other so far as divine revelation is concerned.

Historical faith in revelation, as long as the testimony of the Holy Spirit in the heart is lacking, is in large part a faith that also arises within us by the mediation of men. In the first instance, a child believes Scripture because it has been taught that by its parents and teachers. Some who lack a deeper faith have spoken of believing the content of Holy Scripture on historical grounds that support the fact that here one has a divine revelation. This historical faith is not to be despised, and once one has recognized what an important role authority plays in our human life, then one will not find it at all strange that an element of historical authority is mixed with our conviction concerning the truth of Scripture. This, however, is a provisional position and not the foundation on which a Christian must rest in life and in death.

This can only be by a direct faith in God, resting on the testimony of the Holy Spirit. It is good to believe historically in revelation because miracles accompany it and guarantee it as divine. But it is better to believe directly because of the testimony the Spirit gives through the Word. Still, in the first case, too, there is really a testimony of God, at least if one sees the miracle itself. But however one may come to the conviction that Scripture is the revelation of God, in any case its content as a whole can only be an object of faith. The state of affairs is as follows: Some accept the divine origin of Scripture on historical grounds; others accept it on the basis of the testimony of the Holy Spirit. In both cases one believes the *contents* of Scripture as God's testimony since God addresses us through it.

24. After deducing all this, does much still remain for knowing?

What has been said has shown that a conviction in which we would have to rest entirely in ourselves really does not exist for us human beings. With the deepest roots of our knowledge we are anchored in the truthfulness of God. And inasmuch as not one conviction is entirely detached from those roots, it too rests on the same basis. Now, however, one can in his reasoning momentarily abandon this foundation of faith. One can presuppose as true the general grounds on which everything depends without bearing in mind their distinctive character as truths of faith. And then, taking those grounds as a point of departure, one can assume other derived truths on account of their connection with those grounds. One has a logical insight into these derived truths and is convinced of them, not on the basis of a testimony but on the basis of his own reasoning. Here, then, one has to do with knowledge, but it can only appear to be true knowledge since one has lost sight of and not taken into account the basis of faith on which these derived truths, too, ultimately rest. One sees now how very limited the area of knowledge is, and that in real life believing and knowing are blended.

25. What is the second question regarding the psychology of faith that needs to be considered?

The question of what capacities of the soul are involved in the act of faith. This question, of course, stands in the closest relationship to the other: Of how many parts does faith consist? It is really another formulation of the latter question. Believing is an expression of the human spirit, and so includes as many parts and acts as there are capacities of this spirit in operation.

26. Is the question posed here easy to answer?

No; down through history, it has been answered in various ways and currently still divides theologians. This does not surprise us. Faith is an expression of life, and everything that relates to life has this character-istic: that to our consciousness in experience it is simple and uncom-plicated; for our intellect, in contrast, [it is] complex and complicated. Thus it does not involve a contradiction if we maintain that faith is at the same time extremely simple and extremely complex. The same may be said of a number of other activities of the intellect or the soul. In order to bring about a simple—an apparently entirely natural—ac-tivity, many factors have often been involved that we usually do not observe. How wonderful is the composition of our eye; how natural is the act of our seeing for our own perception! This is so, too, with faith. The simplest Christian can exercise it without taking into account what he thereby does. But all this does not relieve us from the obligation also to consider faith more closely and analyze it, and, insofar as it is given to us, to understand it. For regeneration there can be no thought of doing that, but certainly for faith, an act that falls within conscious life.

27. Is faith something that presupposes a new capacity of the soul? That is, is it not the case that one does not believe with the capacities with which one performs all other spiritual acts?

Some have assumed that, but entirely wrongly. It is certainly true that our capacities must be worked on by the Holy Spirit in a supernatural manner before we can exercise saving faith. But this does not prove that the Holy Spirit implants a new capacity within us besides the others that we already possess. The Holy Spirit regenerates the heart; and as the intellect, will, and emotion flow from the heart, this root of life, so they have in principle received at regeneration the capacity to be active believingly, each in its own way. Neither in the natural man is there a separate organ for faith. By giving us a threefold capacity of the soul, God has so equipped us that we can do all the actions that belong to our spiritual life without having the need for a new organ. And if one were to once begin to assume a separate capacity for faith, one could do that with the same right for other expressions of life: for love, hope, etc.

28. *If we ask about the capacities operative in faith or about the parts in which faith consists, do we then have in view faith in general or saving faith in particular?*

Both. We cannot assume that the word "faith," when it is used for various things, would have nothing in common in each of those senses. However much historical faith and saving faith in the narrower sense also differ from each other, they must still have the general form of faith in common with each other, or they could not be designated by the same name. So, if one says that saving faith has these or those parts, that these or those capacities are active in it, then this could apply in the main to everything that is called faith. The difference derives from the content of what is believed and the relationship it has to our living. In saving faith, both are such that it is completely impossible for an unregenerate person, with his capacities, to act on them in faith. If we say that faith consists of knowledge, assent, and trust, we usually mean saving faith. However, this also applies to faith in the widest sense. By no means, then, do we maintain that the unregenerate person cannot exercise knowledge, assent, and trust in earthly matters or toward God historically. As often as he exercises faith in any connection, this general form of faith is present. On the other hand, we maintain that he cannot be active with knowledge, assent, and trust toward the objects of saving grace, toward the Mediator, applied to his own soul. In this specific connection he does not have saving knowledge, or assent, or trust.

29. *Do all agree in enumerating the actions that belong to faith?*

No, although most speak of three actions or aspects of faith: (1) knowledge (*notitia*); (2) assent (*assensus*); (3) trust (*fiducia*).

Some wished to reduce these three to two, either by removing knowledge as first or trust as last. They maintained, namely, that knowledge was certainly the necessary prerequisite for faith, but therefore was still not yet identical with faith—not a piece or part of it. Others said that trust (*fiducia*) certainly flowed from faith as its necessary consequence, but that this did not give the right to confuse it with the core, the essence of faith, or to include it within faith. All this is still apart from the unscriptural view of the Roman Catholics, who not only wish to exclude knowledge from faith itself but also even deny that it is the necessary prerequisite of faith.

Others again did not limit to these three aspects but extended them. Witsius, among others, considers faith to include seven actions, after he first has recalled in a rather nominalistic fashion how there are not really separate capacities in the soul but ultimately they are all one. He enumerates in succession: (1) knowledge, (2) assent, (3) love, (4) hunger and thirst for Christ, (5) accepting the Lord Christ, (6) leaning on Christ, (7) surrendering ourselves to Christ; to which then the conclusion is added, as the closing act of faith accompanied by a blessed peace of the soul: (8) Christ is mine!

One sees immediately that here is a very penetrating and complete enumeration of the differing aspects of faith, but not an exact psychological classification.

30. Does knowledge belong to the essence of faith?

Yes; and to understand this well, the sentiments of the Roman Catholics, which in more than one respect deviate from Scripture, must first be rejected. Rome eliminates the great difference there is between historical and saving faith. It demands nothing more than a historical assent to the truth, without a heartfelt trust having to be included. This means that it has also applied its principle of externalization to faith and thereby adapted it to the masses.

The second peculiarity in Rome's view of faith is that the element of knowledge is eliminated and everything included in assent. If only assent is present, knowledge may be lacking, and there will still be faith. In order to accentuate this, Rome makes a distinction between *fides implicita*, "undeveloped faith," and *fides explicita*, "developed faith." The first works without knowledge of the truth, the second with knowledge of the truth. If only one is ready to believe what the church believes, this counts as faith for him. That is the principle of clericalism applied to the concept of faith. As the clergy performs many other things for the laity, so they can also believe for them, and a blind assent is all that is demanded of the laity itself. The result is that an independent quest of the divine testimonies is unnecessary for the common people and is opposed rather than promoted by the church. The language of the church is an alien language that the people do not understand. The preaching of the Word moves into the background, the rite into the foreground, and the latter works on the emotions more than on faith.

The third point, finally, that characterizes Rome's doctrine of faith is the distinction between *fides informis*, "unformed faith," and *fides formata*, "formed faith." The former is the bare assent to historical faith described above. Formed faith is faith formed and perfected by love so that it becomes justifying faith. This is connected with the error of the Roman church in the article of justification. Because they do not view this as a judicial act of God that imputes to us the merits of Christ but as an infusion of subjective righteousness, as a *making* righteous, so too a character must be ascribed to faith that accords with that doctrine. Now, love is the root of all Christian virtues. Faith that makes righteous (holy) subjectively will therefore be able to consist in nothing other than love. This distinction between formed and unformed faith is therefore nothing other than the principle of works-holiness applied to the concept of faith. And we see that by its three fundamental errors of externalization, clericalism, and works-holiness, Rome has transformed faith into its own caricature.

Concerning the second point of difference, which is only at issue here, we hold that the act of faith is completely impossible without knowledge. The disposition to believe something can be present without knowledge, but not the act. Thus it is not at all apparent what would remain of the act of faith if one removed knowledge. If one says that a conscious intention remains to accept as true all that someone says, then we answer that this can only be called trust in a person in the most general sense, but it cannot bear the name of faith. And furthermore, even this, too, will still include a certain measure of knowledge, for this general trust in the person also undoubtedly stems from knowledge of the person and of certain statements that he has made. However great or little the knowledge may be, there is always knowledge where there is faith. The danger resident in Rome's conception is just this: It makes this knowledge of faith, which it cannot do without, into knowledge of the authority and trustworthiness of the church instead of knowledge of the authority and trustworthiness of God. So, as the object of faith, the church comes to stand in the place of God. Man is not made aware of God and the Savior so that trust might develop from this knowledge. He is simply placed before the church and the clergy, and from what is proclaimed to him about their authority, a blind submission must develop in him that is called "faith."

The scriptural view of faith is a completely different one. It includes that a thing, in order to be believed, must be known. This is sufficiently evident from the manner in which, for example, in the Gospel of John, knowledge of God is interchanged with faith in God, knowledge with faith in the Savior. In this way, to know God and Christ is eternal life. Faith comes by hearing, and hearing by the Word of God (Rom 10:14, 17; John 6:69). Believing is accompanied with confession, but then there must be something to confess and something made known. One is warned in Scripture that by lack of knowledge one can be destroyed (Hos 4:6). That God accompanies the operations of His grace with external calling presupposes the same principle. And that believing is characterized by the image of seeing also allows no other view. In Isaiah 53:11, it is said that by His knowledge the Servant of the Lord will justify many, a proof that saving faith includes a certain degree of knowledge.

31. *Can we establish in advance how great must be this knowledge required for faith?*

No, we can only say in general that the knowledge must be sufficient to produce a conception of what one believes. For every exercise of faith, only knowledge of the particular object to which faith is directed and with which it is inseparably connected is necessary. To the degree that someone has a clear historical understanding of the content of Scripture, to that degree will he also be able to exercise faith in a historical sense with respect to Scripture. To the degree that someone has a clear and distinct knowledge of the person of the Mediator, of His offices and states, to that degree his exercise of faith will also be richer and more comprehensive. Therefore, knowledge is not only essential for faith, but also the criterion for the extent of faith and for its inward riches. Still, it is true that saving faith can be accompanied by a minimum of knowledge. In any case, we must hold that its object is not the truth of God in general but specifically the Mediator of the covenant of grace. Of course, everyone who believes savingly in the Mediator will also be prepared to believe all of the testimonies of God. Still, in the first place, his faith is not directed to them in general, and a great ignorance of the truth in detail is in itself not a proof of the absence of saving faith.

32. *With what things must this knowledge of faith not be confused?*

a) In the first place, it must not be confused with comprehending the things that one believes. Comprehending means having a clear discernment of a thing, of the basis from which it exists, and of the necessity with which it derives from that basis. At the same time, however, it is evident from this that comprehending and believing are not the same. What we believe is something positive; what we comprehend is a natural-logical conclusion.

b) Neither must the knowledge of faith be confused with a bare portrayal of things. To portray is not to know. And were the knowledge of faith a bare portrayal, then it would not belong to the essence of faith. This may already be ascertained from the fact that someone can have a picture of certain things without having faith in these things. If this portrayal was knowledge, and knowledge an essential part of faith, then unbelievers would have an essential part of faith. And the above-mentioned reasoning of those who would exclude knowledge from faith would then in fact be conclusive. They do say that knowledge is required for faith and necessarily precedes it, but it is therefore not a part of faith. But that is not what is meant. Our knowledge that we intend to have viewed as an essential part of faith is more than a bare portrayal, in which case it would still be completely in doubt whether or not a reality corresponded to it. The knowledge of faith is of that sort that it immediately places things as real to our view. Any divide between the portrayal of the thing and the reality of the thing is alien to it. That is exactly the deep sense of the statement in Hebrews 11:1: "Faith is the substance of things that one hopes for, and an evidence of things that one does not see." From the outset, the representation of the knowledge that we carry in our consciousness of the objects of faith is colored by this distinctive reality. The knowledge of faith is a cognizance of truths inseparably connected with the thought that those truths express realities. It is not as if, like a judge, we first hear the testimony of God and, in the meantime, maintain our intellect in a neutral attitude in order only later to decide calmly how great the evidence is and what may or may not be true of what is testified. If it really happened in this manner, knowledge would have to go its way alone for a time, without being accompanied by that consciousness of reality. In other words, it would not be knowledge, but only cognition. Believing presupposes antecedent trust, by which all questions are cut off regarding whether or not the testimony is to reality. As soon as God opens His Word in order to address us, the knowledge of faith begins to work and immediately therefore also appears as faith-knowledge, bears in itself the character of faith, and has a distinctive coloration. It is extremely difficult to analyze this uniqueness psychologically, but one can appeal to each experience. We hold, therefore, that knowledge is an *essential part of faith*, is resident in faith, even at the risk that it will be difficult for us to differentiate knowledge and trust.

33. *Does what is said here also apply to saving faith—namely, that knowledge is an essential part of faith and not merely its prerequisite?*

Yes, this applies both to saving faith as well as to faith in the wider sense. This saving faith also begins with a knowledge that presents the truth to our view as real. By this knowledge it brings us, as it were, into contact with the living Christ. The picture of the Mediator that we receive in our consciousness is a picture based on knowledge and not a portrayal of fantasy. We do not regard it as a portrait of a stranger, who as far as we are concerned can be the creation of the fantasy of the painter, but with the active interest of seeking sinners, we drink in His features; we become cognizant of the truth as the only means that can bring us into a relationship with Christ. Hence this knowledge is an essential part of saving faith. It is the first act of receiving the Savior into our soul. He enters within through the gate of our thought-life in order also to be appropriated immediately by our will and to rule over our affections.

And knowledge, as belonging essentially to faith, also becomes here the criterion for the extent of faith, if not the plumb line of its depth. Since faith begins with receiving the figure of the Savior, so believing fully would have to begin with taking in that figure in all its fullness, from all sides and with all its features. To admit Him as prophet, priest, and king, as our rich, full messiah through the windows of the intellect into the heart, would be the first act of an ideal and perfect faith.

From this it at the same time follows that in saving faith there is something different and more than the old knowledge of historical faith. Many imagine it as if assent and trust came with that old historical faith, in order then with these three to form saving faith. This is not the case. On the basis of that earlier knowledge a new knowledge arises—completely different and to be compared with nothing else— with which only a true believer, regenerated by God's Spirit, knows. In this is also a new proof how, for those who have saving faith, knowledge is not merely a *conditio sine qua non* of faith but also a part of the act of faith itself. If it were merely the old historical knowledge augmented with assent and trust, then there would be no difference, as far as that knowledge is concerned, between those who have saving faith and those who do not have it. And from this it would again follow that knowledge was not included in faith but preceded it. Clearly, it is the reverse. For the regenerate, faith is irradiated and permeated with knowledge; it radiates knowledge; it is a seeing and knowing faith.

34. *To what extent can one still say that the knowledge of faith precedes saving faith?*

The distinction has already been made above between faith in a wider and in a narrower sense. All agree that the object of saving faith in the narrower sense is the Lord Christ, the Mediator. To believe in Him is what justifies us before God. On the other hand, having knowledge of our sins and that before God we are worthy of eternal damnation— namely, a spiritual knowledge—belongs to faith in the wider sense. Someone who is convicted of his guilt and his depravity has that conviction, since he believes God's declaration concerning it. Now, it is obvious that the knowledge present in the latter is necessary for the knowledge of saving faith. A certain degree of consciousness of sin is necessary for the exercise of justifying faith. But it would clearly be wrong to say that justifying faith includes this knowledge as a part of its essence. The knowledge that is a part of justifying faith focuses, as does that faith as a whole, on Christ, the Mediator. It does this under the impression of the knowledge of sin. But still, if we wish to speak accurately, this knowledge of sin does not belong with it as a part. The faith that justifies and saves looks on the Savior, not on the danger. Surely, when one desires to look with interest on the Savior, a view of the danger precedes. And surely, looking to the Savior may be continuously interchanged with looking to the danger. Yes, even more: Since the Savior in His quality as savior is completely the opposite of the danger, looking on Him naturally includes the idea of the danger. His suffering and death can only be viewed in direct connection with sin. We may therefore say that in practice this more nuanced distinction between faith in the wider sense and faith in the narrower, saving sense very rarely becomes conscious. But that is ultimately so with all the elements of the act of faith, and therefore this experience can never hinder us from distinguishing as accurately as possible. We say, therefore, that consciousness of sin precedes saving faith as an indispensable requirement but does not belong to the knowledge of faith itself.

35. *How is the definition of saving faith that our Catechism gives to be understood?*

The [Heidelberg] Catechism [21] says: "A true faith is not only a certain knowledge, whereby I hold as true all that God has revealed to us in His Word, but also an assured trust," etc.[2] However, by this is not meant that all the truths revealed in God's Word are directly the object of saving faith, and that even where knowledge of them is lacking one would still need to speak of believing them. Only opposition to Rome is expressed in the definition. Rome said: "Believing is only a certain knowledge, whereby I hold as true all that God has revealed." Protestants: "Not *only* a certain knowledge, but also," etc.

36. *Can one also put too much emphasis on knowledge as part of faith?*

Yes, the Rationalists do that. They have the whole of religion occupied with rational conviction. There is also a dead and deadening orthodoxy that has this feature in common with Rationalism. No one side of faith may be elevated at the expense of the others. Such one-sidedness always calls forth a reaction that degenerates into the opposite extreme, and so balance is never reached. Schleiermacher's doctrine of feeling followed the rationalistic religion of reason.

---

2   Apparently Vos' own slightly loose rendering.

37. Is it easy to distinguish the assent of faith from knowledge as described above?

No. As we have seen from the start, knowledge is present from the outset with the awareness that it takes note of truth and that it has to do with realities. That is already an implicit assent. It is precisely assent that makes this knowledge such a unique act. In order to distinguish both clearly, we could limit knowledge to becoming cognizant of the truth. Against that, however, are two objections:

a) In distinguishing in this way, one obtains a conception of the knowledge of faith that is falsified by reality. Nowhere is there such knowledge of faith that it would not be under the formative influence of assent. One can compare our sense perception with the knowledge of faith. In the former, two elements are also present: the reception of sense impressions and the assent that a reality outside us corresponds to them. Now, however, the knowledge that we have by our sense perception nowhere appears detached from the assent that what is perceived is real. With that knowledge, assent is given automatically. It seems absurd to us to think that we would know and not agree. Likewise with faith. When we have someone whom we trust completely, then it does not occur to us first to consider his words in the abstract. We know already assenting and assent already knowing; the one permeates the other. Someone who with us heard the same thing but did not assent would also know it in a different way. Knowing in the way we do is equivalent to assenting.

b) In distinguishing in this way, one could also lose sight of the distinction between historical and saving faith. The knowledge of these two differs precisely in this: that the latter is a knowledge that is accompanied by the warmth and glow of conviction. And precisely by that, it becomes a wholly new knowledge that is permeated by this saving assent that casts a new light on everything. When by His illumination the Holy Spirit makes the truth clear to the eye of our soul, it can no longer be denied. Receiving its impression in the consciousness coincides with assenting to it.

For this reason, it is better to say that knowledge and assent are not two different acts, but two sides of one and the same act. They work reciprocally on each other and are simultaneous, and we cannot say that the one is independent of the other. In the same moment that the one begins to be active, the activity of the other begins. Furthermore, knowledge is the receptive and more passive, assent the expressive and more active side of the act of faith. And for the consciousness, both are fused together as an indissoluble unity.

38. *Show that according to Scripture assent belongs to faith as an essential part.*

John 3:33 reads, "The one who receives his testimony has sealed that God is true." Here the verb λαμβάνειν is used—literally, "to long for something in order to take it." This expresses very precisely the more active side of assent. It is still more than a receiving; it is an accepting and assimilating (cf. also Col 2:5-6).

39. *Is this assent an act of the intellect or an act of the will?*

This is very difficult to decide. One could say in general that the decision on the truth or the reality of a thing is due to the intellect. Everything about whether it is true or untrue belongs to the sphere of the intellect and not under the jurisdiction of the will. This is why many discuss the assent of faith as a purely intellectual act, certainly an act of the enlightened intellect effected by God's Spirit, but with that still an act performed by the capacity of the intellect. In fact, some go even further and draw not only assent in its entirety but also trust within the intellect, so that they insist on viewing the whole of faith not as an act of the will but as an act of the intellect. Now, it is certainly clear that knowing as such, when faith is excluded, is a purely intellectual act. The conviction that this or that conclusion follows from premises does not include an act of the will. It is otherwise when the testimony of another is the ground on which I assent to the truth. A moral element is present in that assent. This appears, above all, in such cases where my assent to testimony that someone gives stems from an antecedent trust in general that I place in his person. Man in his sinful condition has an inclination to withdraw into himself, and this sinful, selfish directing of his will also reveals itself in his intellectual life. If now he does not seek the basis for a judgment of the intellect within himself but in another, then that is a turning from himself and a resting in another. We believe that this does not occur without the will. The assent of faith is an act by which man submits to the authority of another. That demands an act of the will. Of course, the expression of the verdict itself—"this or that is true"—is reserved for the intellect. To say that the will does this would be a confusion of concept and would make faith an arbitrary act. But no one will be able to deny that in any case this act of the intellect is preceded and accompanied by a movement of the will. Also, in the assent of faith the capacities of the soul concur and penetrate each other in their activity.

40. What question is connected with what has just been posited?

The question regarding the actual formal act of faith. While some placed it in the assent of the judging intellect, others thought that it was to be sought in consequent trust. The objection that Brakel and others had against the first view resided mainly in the fact that faith was thus made a matter of the intellect. It is already evident from what was just said above, however, that in every act of faith something more than the intellect is at work: the capacity of judgment that decides what is true and not true. And, conversely, as will be still further evident below, a true trusting of faith is unthinkable apart from intellectual assent. Thus we can already note provisionally that the pending dispute appears to rest again and again on a one-sided emphasis on one act of faith.

41. Which is the third act or side of faith?

Trust, which we can describe as resting in the testimony of another for anything significant that affects our lives.

42. Describe in more detail in what this trust consists.

a) It is not an exclusively intellectual act. If I believe the statement of the doctor that I will be healthy again, and this intellectual act now becomes the starting point of a trusting disposition, then in the latter there is already more than an intellectual judgment. Without the judgment, "that is the truth," the disposition of trust cannot be present. Also, the former could not be present where the latter is lacking. They are inseparably connected with each other, but still not the same.

b) It is also not an act of the feeling. Of course, the doctor's statement above, for someone who hovered between life and death, exercises a great influence on his emotional life. The emotions of fear and anxiety, agitation, etc., will disappear to make room for the opposite emotions. There is thus most decidedly an effect of faith on feeling, or rather a retroactive effect of feeling on the consciousness of faith that will nowhere and never be entirely absent. Nevertheless, feeling is not trusting. Two people can be endowed with faith in different degrees. Faith in A can be stronger than in B. But B is an impassioned person in whom emotional life has developed much more strongly than intellectual life and the life of the will. The result will be that B, with his lesser degree of faith, at the same time has more emotional activity in connection with this faith than A. His joy, his delight, his praise will be much stronger. But no one would gather from this that more inward power of faith is at work in him than in his more calm and sedate brother. A strongly trusting faith is certainly compatible with certain natures where strong emotional activity is absent. Trust is not resident in feeling.

c) So then, nothing else is left but to locate trust in the *will*. Not, however, in the will as the capacity for particular expressions of the will, but understood more deeply as the direction and disposition of the soul. There is in man an impulse by which he moves out toward certain things. There must be a certain object for this impulse in which he comes to rest. In a sick person there is an irresistible yearning, a tendency in which his entire life participates. If the doctor declares that the sick person will get better, this yearning lays hold of that declaration, rests in it, and finds its end for which it reached out. Trust exists in this. This may also be applied to saving faith. In the awakened sinner is an impulse, a desire, a striving, a hungering and thirsting after God's righteousness. The soul extends itself toward this, moves itself in this direction, so that the whole life is drawn thither. Now when God, as the physician of the soul, testifies that in Christ satisfaction of His righteousness is obtained, then this urge for righteousness that God approves finds its rest in this testimony and settles itself in it as its end point. And that is the trust of saving faith.

d) One now sees clearly in what the uniqueness of this trust is to be sought as distinct from a bare act of the intellect and a mere movement of emotion. An intellectual judgment of the truth or untruth of something—also of the testimony of another—can occur for me without my having a direct interest in it. The fact remains outside me. Antecedent, personal trust certainly does not occur without an act of the will, but it is an inclination of the will of a different sort than that meant here. The trust spoken of here always presupposes an interest, a being involved with the truth communicated by the testimony. This interest can be greater or smaller, depending on whether it affects a less significant part of my life or my life at its core. For saving faith, at issue is a question of life and death for the sinner: How can I, a sinner, live before God? Hence, trust is a trust for life that affects the soul at its core. Emotion, on the other hand, does share this distinctiveness with the trust of faith in that it interests me personally and is not outside me, but it is purely subjective; emotion causes me to rest in myself. The trust of faith, in contrast, is the resting of the impulse of my life in something that lies outside me, is distinguished from me, something objective.

43. *Is it correct to say that the intellect is active in the knowledge of faith, the will in the assent of faith, and emotion in the trust of faith?*

No, this idea must be rejected. Emotion can on no account be taken as the seat of faith. Moreover, the activities of the intellect and trust and those of the will and trust may not be so separated. On the whole, it is true that, in the knowledge of faith, the intellect comes to the fore; in assent and trust, the will; but also, a complete separation may not be maintained here. Our result, in general, is this: The seat of faith, as far as its activity is concerned, is in the intellect and in the will, while these expressions are always accompanied more or less by emotion. On the other hand, the seat of faith, as disposition, is in the heart as the common root of intellect and will.

44. *How many types of faith are distinguished?*

One is accustomed to distinguish (a) faith that is believed (*quae creditur*); (b) faith with which one believes. The first, then, stands for the content of faith, as we speak, for example, of "the Protestant faith." The question, however, is whether Scripture uses the word "faith" in this sense. It appears at least to come close to it a few times (cf. Jude 3, 20; both explanations are possible in 1 Tim 1:4, 19; 2:7; 3:9; 4:1, 6; 5:8; 6:10,

21). Faith with which one believes (*qua creditur*) is faith as disposition and act of man. It is further distinguished into: (1) historical faith; (2) temporary faith; (3) faith in miracles; (4) saving faith.

45. *What is historical faith?*

A mere assent to revealed and known truth. The designation "historical faith" does not mean that the object of this faith is only history—that is, a description of bygone things and past events—for to it also belong truths that are still valid at this moment. Neither is the meaning that one accepts certain things as true *on the testimony of history*, for one can have the living witness before him. In a certain sense, Nicodemus exercised historical faith when he said, "Rabbi, we know that you are a teacher come from God" [John 3:2]. The designation means, rather, that one accepts divine truths as one accepts history for which one does not have a personal interest, and one nonetheless gives credence. History is taken here in the sense of something that we stand apart from and only instills in us theoretical interest. Other designations that have been proposed are: "*contemplating* faith" or "faith of bare assent" (Witsius); "speculative faith" (Hodge).

46. *On what grounds may this historical faith rest?*

On more than one. It can be a merely authoritative faith—that is, holding something to be true based on the testimony of parents or a teacher or public opinion in general. It can also rest on historical research into the hallmarks of divine revelation. Finally, it can also have its basis in inner evidence that the truth possesses as coming from God and, for which, by common grace, the eye of man is more or less opened.

47. *Where does Scripture speak of this faith?*

Among other places, in James 2:19, some have "a faith of the devils"; Matthew 7:26, "hearing and not doing"; John 11:42, "that they may believe that you sent me"; Acts 26:26, "I know that you believe them [the prophets]."

48. *What is "temporary faith"?*

It is assent to the truth for a time with an application to oneself, not without some emotion and fruit, but out of an unregenerate heart.

49. *From where is the designation derived?*

From Matthew 13:20–21, "But as to what was sown in rocky places, this is the one who hears the word and who immediately receives it with joy, yet he has no root in himself but *endures for a time* [πρόσκαιρός ἐστιν]," etc. What is said there of seed sown among thorns (Matt 13:22) also must be understood of temporary faith.

50. *To what extent is this designation "temporary faith" applicable?*

Insofar as temporary faith is not finally lasting in duration. In death, it is surely taken from a person, and he learns to know himself as an unbeliever. However, it can also continue until death if there are no particular circumstances that intervene in order to bring his unrighteousness to light. In oppression and persecution, it is immediately revealed in its true character. Conversely, it can also arise in extraordinary circumstances—for example, in times of great distress, of war and contagious diseases—and then, as soon as these dangers have blown over, it disappears again. Some have wanted to call it a hypocritical faith, but incorrectly, for conscious hypocrisy is not at issue here. Those with temporary faith in fact think that they have true faith. The designation "presumed faith" would then be better, but not, as Witsius wants to call it, "an arrogant or conceited faith."

51. *By what is temporary faith distinguished from historical faith?*

By the personal interest it shows in the truth and by the retroactive effect of feeling on the truth. The word is *received*, that is, personally appropriated, and received *with joy*, that is, appropriated with emotion.

52. *By what is temporary faith distinguished from saving faith?*

It is very difficult to specify or ascertain this difference for a third party, although there is a profound difference. Christ says, "It has *no root* in itself." Thus, saving faith is embedded in the regenerated root of the soul and is an expression of spiritual life that originates from this depth. Temporary faith is an action of the soul that has been brought about externally at the periphery, on the exterior of the consciousness. It is precisely for this reason that it vanishes as soon as this activity from the outside ceases, and the unregenerate ground of life can reveal itself as it is in reality.

Now, however, since no one can scrutinize the root of his own life, the question then arises how he can be assured that the faith he exercises is not temporary but saving faith. Many characteristics are enumerated by theologians, and since the assurance of faith is possible through self-examination, and Scripture stirs us up to examine whether we are in the faith [2 Cor 13:5], there must be signs. The main issue will reside in this: Temporary faith runs on feeling and has a subjective basis. It rests on the enjoyment that the activities of faith bring along with the truth and, to this extent, is selfish in nature. Where it is no longer sustained by this pleasurable caress of feeling, it becomes vexed and ceases. Thus, there do not always need to be external advantages by which it is driven, and the allure of a more inward caress of soul can be the cause in back of it. A believer has therefore to ask himself whether he is being led and driven in his activities of faith by this subjective urge for enjoyment, this craving for false assurance, by antinomian, transitory sympathies, or by a passion for the honor of God by hungering and thirsting after His righteousness. The latter is always something that can only be worked by the regenerating operation of the Holy Spirit in the heart.

53. Is there more in this temporary faith than ordinary historical knowledge?

There can be knowledge in it that is different not in principle but still in degree than ordinary historical knowledge. Scripture speaks of "having once been enlightened" (Heb 6:4). This certainly falls under the rubric of temporary faith, although this is not to say, conversely, that all temporary faith falls under the rubric of Hebrews 6:4–8. If the latter were so, the exercising of temporary faith would exclude obtaining saving faith. Thus, a special, enlightening work by the Holy Spirit is possible by which the truth makes a deep impression on man, and one or other aspect of the truth begins to work on his will so that delight in the truth results. Normally, then, this temporary faith will not be directed to the truth in general but very specifically to the heart of the truth, to the gospel of redemption. In this, too, it is different than historical faith, for the latter makes no distinctions and treats all truth with the same indifference.

54. *Who have eliminated the distinction between this temporary faith and saving faith?*

All who teach an apostasy of the saints and thus suppose that the difference lies only in time. If someone's faith continues until death, then it is saving faith, for then the possibility of apostasy ceases. Conversely, if it vanishes earlier, then it is not saving faith. So, in particular, the Remonstrants, who lack the deeper concept of faith and whose saving faith is basically nothing more than an extended and enduring temporary faith. According to us, the two are specifically different.

55. *What is miracle faith?*

The assurance on the testimony of another that a miracle will certainly occur by me or to me (Matt 17:20; 1 Cor 13:2; Acts 14:9–10). It appears from some of these passages that this faith was in relation not only to miracles, in the narrower sense, but is associated with the extraordinary gifts of grace in general. Man has a natural confidence that he can perform this or that activity. God, however, can grant to him to perform activities that as such lie beyond the reach of human nature and for which he feels himself unable. Every attempt to do them must happen in faith. This is even clearer when man is merely the instrument or proclaimer of a miraculous work performed directly by God Himself. Then he must trust absolutely the miracle proclaimed, that God will not put him to shame.

56. *Is this miracle faith in an active sense always accompanied by saving faith?*

No, for it only includes trust in God in the physical realm, while saving faith is a trust in God and Christ in a spiritual respect. This miracle faith is certainly a glorious gift, but does not so affect the root of human life so that it could only be given to someone who is regenerate. To be elevated above the limitation of our material nature by trusting in God's miraculous power can be accompanied by unbelief in the deeper sense (Matt 7:22–23, 27; cf. Matt 10:1, 4).

57. *Is miracle faith also spoken of in a passive sense?*

Yes; then it is the certainty that a miraculous work will be done to me (John 11:40; Acts 14:9). Since the miracles of the Lord undoubtedly have a symbolic significance and picture His work of spiritual deliverance, it was in all respects fitting that faith was required in the recipients. Thus this passive miracle faith appears as a direct reflection of saving faith. In some instances, it merges with the latter, so that implications are drawn from it that are connected with saving faith (cf. Matt 8:10–13). Still, in no way is it to be identified with saving faith, and it can be present without it. The multitude that followed Jesus because of bread certainly possessed miracle faith but otherwise was unbelieving; compare John 11:22 with 25–27, where both kinds of faith are clearly distinguished.

58. Is there still a place for such miracle faith at the present time?

Roman Catholics affirm this and substantiate this affirmation with stories of miracles that serve for defending their church. Protestants would rather answer negatively. If miracle faith will be real faith, then there must be a specific promise of God to which it can point. The Roman Catholic church believes that such a promise has been given once for all to the church in general—that is, to the clergy. It is entirely fitting that in a church that extends the line of revelation and lays claim to infallibility for itself, miracles occur as accompanying signs of revelation. For us, this is *a priori* improbable. We lack the promise of God that in one or other particular case He will do miracles. Otherwise, it is not entirely right to say, "Miracle faith no longer exists," and to claim, "Miracles no longer occur."

59. From what standpoint must saving faith be discussed?

From a soteriological standpoint. With that in view, we have thus come to the third part of our treatment. In order to understand well what this saving faith is, one must relate it to the rest of the steps of the order of salvation. Light can only be shed on its mysterious nature if one poses the question: What is the reason why this faith occupies such a prominent place in the order of salvation that it overshadows all the other aspects? What is there in faith by which it is suited to be the great condition of salvation? Why are we saved by faith and not in any other way? That is, we cannot arrive at clarity here by a penetrating psychological analysis or by examining the activity of faith within ourselves, but only by considering faith objectively on the basis of God's Word as an appropriate phenomenon whose uniqueness corresponds to the uniqueness of the way of salvation along which God saves sinners. However much that is mysterious faith may otherwise possess, on this point it must be clear and comprehensible.

60. How can this saving faith be defined?

The best definition is that of the [Heidelberg] Catechism [21]: "A true faith is not only a certain knowledge, whereby I hold to be true what God has revealed to us in His Word, but also a sure confidence, which the Holy Spirit works by the gospel in my heart, that not only to others, but to me also, remission of sin, everlasting righteousness and salvation, are given by God, out of pure grace, only for the sake of the merits of Christ."

61. In what does the significance, the form, and the essence of faith lie?

Not in a single one of the three aspects that it possesses—not in knowledge, assent, or trust in itself—but in the unique relationship to God in which these three—knowledge, assent, and trust—place us.

62. In what, then, does this unique relationship consist?

In this: that our consciousness, worked upon by the Holy Spirit, turns away entirely from our own doing as the ground of our righteousness before God, and to the triune God, and specifically to the Mediator, as they appear in the covenant of grace, in order to rest in that.

63. What is the result of this?

That precisely by this consciousness of faith within us God receives the honor that is due to Him by virtue of His plan of grace, and that we appear to ourselves stripped of all honor and merits.

64. Is it therefore incidental that salvation is tied to true faith?

No, this is far from incidental and, if one looks at it from this standpoint, in all respects natural. God saves sinners without their contributing anything. His plan of salvation is a plan of grace, His way of salvation a covenant of grace through and through, by which He alone can lay claim to honor. True, God also treats men as rational beings in this way of salvation—that is, the manner in which He saves and blesses them must be reflected and recognized in their consciousness. The sinner must know how he is saved, what his righteousness before God is, that nothing is to be ascribed to his own merits, that all his salvation lies in Christ. If this did not happen—if God transferred the sinner at once out of his state of misery into the state of blessedness—then man would surely be saved but God would not be glorified in His work of grace. Man must recognize that it is God who as the triune God of the covenant accomplishes his salvation. Faith is that gift of God's grace by which this recognition is brought about in man, in a manner to be described presently in more detail.

The absence of faith in a person who is being saved would be equivalent to the absence of any recognition of God's grace. The covenant of grace and faith presuppose and demand each other as the objective and the subjective. *For man*, there is no covenant of grace if there is no faith. And as he lives out of and in faith, to that extent he lives out of and in the covenant of grace. Now, however—since on this point man may not be considered completely neutral—we must go a step still further and say: The absence of faith in a sinner is equivalent to the presence of a being-holy-by-works, self-righteous condition of the soul. The supposition entertained above that someone could simply be transferred from the state of misery into the state of beatitude is fundamentally an unthinkable, an impossible supposition. Man is so created by God that he cannot simply have salvation; he must furthermore have a basis for salvation on which it rests. Now if faith in the Mediator is not this basis, then there is another basis, namely, faith in one's own merits, faith in oneself, the caricature of faith, self-righteousness. Therefore, the only choice here is between a consciousness of holiness by works and a consciousness of faith. One will see that this is said with a view to fallen man, man as a sinner, and not with a view to man in the state of rectitude. It was otherwise for Adam before the fall. This dilemma was not applicable to him. He could be right before God without saving faith. But a sinner cannot. He must be one or the other, *either* ascribing to himself the honor of his righteousness and salvation (and then he does not believe), *or* giving the honor to God (and then he exercises saving faith).

65. *Must it be inferred from this conception that believing is nothing other than an insight into, a conception, a correct idea of the relationships of the covenant of grace?*

By no means. Faith is not something that plays out in the intellect and bypasses the life of man. As saving faith, its uniqueness is just that it is a consciousness in which the deepest longing of the soul reaches closure and in which, therefore, the whole man is involved. To exercise saving faith means to have a conviction of the gracious action of God in Christ, but then with a living, personal application to myself. That is, saving faith may only be conceived of from the standpoint of an awakened sinner who has become sensitive to the justice of God. Where this sensitivity to God's justice is lacking, the yearning in one's life to stand as just before God and to be saved in His judgment is also inconceivable. Where, on the other hand, this sensitivity is restored, then too that yearning will immediately begin to be active and become for the sinner the greatest—as it were, the only—concern, in which his whole life concentrates and focuses itself in his consciousness. Thus, providing that one starts here and does not for one moment lose sight of this, one may certainly say that for the awakened sinner faith is the conviction that *his* salvation lies in Christ as a free gift of God's grace.

66. Does one then have the right to say that faith is an act of the intellect?

This question must be answered in different ways. If one means that saving faith remains enclosed entirely within the sphere of the intellect and contains nothing other than intellectual activities, then this is certainly incorrect. If one means that a firm conviction of the intellect is the terminus of the activity of faith, where, as it were, it ends up, then that can be granted. There has been considerable dispute about this question, and even Reformed theologians diverge here. Some insisted that saving faith was to be understood essentially as a cognitive, intellectual act. Others—in fact the majority—sought the essence of the activity of faith in an act of the will. The former make up the line that, as Kuyper says, runs from Calvin through Voetius to Comrie and, in Kuyper's judgment, is the purest. The second conception is found in the definition of our Catechism given above, and furthermore in the majority of Reformed theologians. In *de Heraut* [*The Herald*] of May 31, 1885 (no. 388), one can find quoted the grounds presented by Brakel for the second view and by Comrie for the first.

Concerning the question itself, it seems to us impossible to accept either one of these two conceptions to the exclusion of the other. Saving faith is neither a bare intellectual nor a bare volitional act. If I were to say the former, then I would sever the root of life in which the conviction of faith grows. If I were to say the latter, then the danger threatens that faith again appears as a work, as a deed, and not as a recognition of God's doing for me.

If, on the other hand, I accept both conceptions and keep them in the closest connection, then they correct each other's one-sidedness. One realizes then that believing is more than the conviction that something is true. It is a resting of the deepest longing of spiritual life in such a conviction, and in that the will is certainly involved. However, one also realizes that believing is not a new work that has replaced the works of the law and by which I now should be justified before God. By believing, my will must not be put into motion to accomplish something before God, but at issue is that the movement of my will should coincide with the judgment of my intellect, in which I am convinced of the gracious imputation of God. So, although faith in its final ramification is a conviction of the intellect, yet it would not have any significance if the direction of my entire life were not expressed in that conviction. My heart must concur that God declares me to be righteous in Christ, and in the conviction that God does that every longing of my heart must participate. Only so does it become a whole-hearted conviction by which the imprint of the honor of God is not only impressed into my intellect but into the whole of my consciousness.

It is evident already in the manner in which the defenders of the first opinion express themselves that they really do not exclude the will. They say, for example, that believing is being persuaded, and that this being persuaded is the essence of faith that the various forms of faith have in common. But however much being persuaded occurs in the intellect, everyone still understands that this does not happen without the will. That is expressed [in Dutch] in the preposition over- [in overreding, "persuade"]. There are no logical grounds that God advances to persuade me. Rather, He places His testimony before me and by the Holy Spirit inclines my consciousness to hold that testimony to be true in a whole-hearted manner.

67. *Of how many parts does saving faith consist?*

Of three parts: knowledge, assent, and trust.

68. *How is this knowledge of faith to be viewed?*

a) As far as its *nature* is concerned, it is a spiritual knowledge that must be distinguished as such from the knowledge of historical faith. The believer possesses a different knowledge of truths than someone who accepts them as true merely historically. This has already been discussed sufficiently above.

b) As far as its *object* is concerned it focuses on the Mediator of the covenant of grace. One could perhaps think that the object should be taken more broadly. For one thing, saving faith surely accepts the testimonies of God concerning the satisfaction obtained by the Mediator, as Paul expresses it [cf., e.g., Rom 10:9], to believe in God who has raised Christ from the dead. But everyone recognizes that this amounts to the same thing. This testimony of God is a testimony concerning the Mediator, so that ultimately our faith still focuses on Him as its object. On the other hand, one could say that the sinner must surely believe much more than what is connected with the Mediator. He will have to express sincere faith and be wholeheartedly convinced of the truth of the declaration of God concerning his own lost condition. So here is an object for his faith that is not the Mediator.

We answer here as follows: Such faith is indeed prerequisite to saving faith, and without accepting the testimony of God concerning his lost condition, no one can exercise true faith. Still, it is less correct to reckon all this to the essence of saving faith itself. It precedes and accompanies it, but does not in the strict sense belong to it. It is necessary to hold to this, since otherwise one would have the sinner look too much within and at himself just when he needs to look away from himself and to Christ. We say, therefore, that saving faith has the Mediator as object, and its knowledge consists in knowing the Mediator in the broadest sense of the word.

Here there must now be noted the connection that exists between faith as accepting as true the testimony of God in a broader sense, and faith as accepting as true the testimony of God regarding Christ, thus in a narrower sense. This connection is very close. If we say that Scripture is the object of faith in the first sense and Christ, as mediator, in the second sense, then we can express the connection in this way: The Mediator is the principal content of Scripture; the entire Scripture is so arranged as to bring the image of the Mediator before our eyes. Someone who believes savingly therefore no longer regards Scripture as a loose amalgamation of parts that he should accept piecemeal without an inner connection. This is the Roman Catholic mechanistic understanding of faith. A Roman Catholic believes in bits and pieces, time and again, as much as the church dispenses to him and approves as advisable for him. The genuine believer takes the whole of Scripture as a living organism produced by the Holy Spirit to present Christ to him. On every page of Scripture, he finds traits and traces of the Mediator. He regards each declaration of God in this light. One should purpose to grasp this close connection vividly—that we recognize and know nothing of Christ other than through and from Scripture. Thus, there are not two objects of our faith standing independently next to each other. It is not Scripture plus Christ, but Christ in Scripture, and Scripture in its center, Christ. While on the one hand, for the eye of faith, the word of Scripture changes imperceptibly into the image of a person, on the other hand that person bears completely the traits of a word, for we do not yet behold Him in concrete form but know Him only from the Word. Once we see Him Scripture will thereby become superfluous, and He Himself in His visible appearance will be the object of our beholding. But for the present we still have the Scriptures concerning Him and Him in the Scriptures. That is already expressed by the designation "Word of God." The Mediator is the eternal and eternally abiding Word. Scripture is also Word of God, but then a Word appearing in time and passing away again with time. For us, both are inseparably connected.

c) The *extent* of this knowledge of saving faith can differ considerably. For one it can be very great, very slight for another. All considerations being equal, however, one can say that a richer degree of knowledge will lead to a richer development in the life of faith, while limited knowledge will always have to hinder the development of that life.

d) The knowledge of saving faith is not a bare cognition of things that are its object. If we were to posit this, we would also have to say that knowledge is prerequisite for and not part of faith. But we do not say this. According to our view, in knowledge the essence, the uniqueness, of faith already emerges. We have seen above that knowledge of a thing always includes awareness of its reality. By knowing something we come into contact with it as with a reality. When now in this way one comes into contact with the gospel concerning the Mediator as with a reality, then the activity of the principle of faith already lurks there—still imperfectly, but at the same time unmistakably. Our self-righteous heart does not want it to be that salvation will be obtained in this way. It still has in itself by nature, its sinfulness notwithstanding, an impulse to be something before God. It will not allow itself to be persuaded of the reality of the free imputation of the merits of the Mediator. That God would declare the sinner righteous without his own help seems foolishness to the natural man. Even where the Holy Spirit has initially enlightened the eye of the soul, and thus deep knowledge of sin is present, there still can be a struggle because of the natural aversion that asserts itself against such a procedure of God. Thus, *before there is present in the sinner such knowledge of faith that makes the grace of God in Christ appear to him as an absolute reality, he must be dissuaded of his own righteousness.* Thus, one sees how already in the knowledge or in the assent of faith—for these may not be separated here—there is an element of the true essence of faith. This knowledge is being persuaded of something against which the natural mind testifies with all the force of its works-holiness. In historical faith, knowledge and assent naturally do not have this significance, for they are thoroughly superficial and reside merely in the intellect, without a personal, living interest being involved. Because it occurs apart from this interest and the ignorant sinner does not concern himself with his right standing before God, it is relatively easy for him to agree that God in Christ forgives the sinner and deals with him according to grace. But as soon as his right standing before God becomes a personal question, he will also be much more involved to know this action of grace as a reality. And only by the grace of the Holy Spirit will he be able to possess this knowledge of saving faith.

e) Furthermore, as far as the uniqueness of the object known is concerned, saving faith is something invisible in the absolute sense, *something that cannot be seen.* That God for Christ's sake manifests grace, that He transferred our sins to Christ and transferred the righteousness of Christ to us, are invisible things that we can believe only because of God's testimony. Thus it is not only the case that in the covenant of grace God takes away the meriting of salvation and obliges man to look away from himself and to rest entirely in the work of God, but the sinner must also accept God's Word that He in fact maintains this way of salvation with him. He cannot observe God and look into the depth of His divine consciousness. Even if he had been able to see Christ suffering on the cross with his own eyes, apart from faith he would still not be able to see that this suffering was a suffering that He bore as mediator for the sins of His people, a suffering as surety. Even then, everything would ultimately still come down to the testimony of God concerning the meaning of those sorrows. Therefore, for this faith man from the outset must bring his consciousness captive under the authority of God. Already in the initial stage, he must entrust himself unconditionally to God with no other certainty than that God cannot lie. The one who receives the Mediator by faith has sealed that God is truthful. This aspect of faith, too, is in all respects normal. The principle of the first sinful act was unbelief and made God a liar. In the same way, the principle of the act of faith that saves and justifies is a principle of faith by which, without reservation, we acknowledge the truthfulness of God in a matter that concerns us personally and in which our highest interests are at stake.

f) Regarding the activity of this knowledge of faith, it is twofold: one more *active*, and one more *passive* or *receptive*. The following is meant by this distinction. The genuine believer not only approves of the truth of God when, without his action, it is placed before his consciousness, but he is also actively engaged with that truth, to probe it, to be acquainted with it, to draw it into his consciousness. The knowledge of faith is effective knowledge. Although it is true that with every new acquaintance with the content of truth the believer must once again bow before the convincing power of that kingly word of his God and thus once again maintain the receptive character of faith, this still does not in any respect hinder the other side from constantly revealing itself. Faith seeks out the truth to which it wills to submit.

It is not something that sits silently, not something passive, not a lifeless mirror that catches what is placed before it, but a stream of living water, an active consciousness incessantly in motion to embrace the truth. It is completely impossible to understand the nature of saving faith correctly if we do not keep this difference in mind. By faith a union of the soul with the Mediator arises in the consciousness. To believe, then, is not to have a conviction concerning the Mediator as a third party based on the testimony of God, but to be engaged with the Mediator Himself as a living person, to go to Him, to take in His image as it is delineated by Scripture, and to feast on beholding Him—acts that are all of an active nature. By these two poles we can recognize faith, and for each healthy, well-developed faith, they both must be present. If someone says that he submits believingly to the testimony concerning the Mediator and yet is not actively engaged with the Mediator, his faith cannot be genuine. We will not merely have read to us a document that acquits us of terrible punishments and gives us the right to great possessions, but we will want to have it in our hands—to touch it and reread it. Likewise, someone who believes in the Mediator will not be satisfied with having that Mediator depicted by someone else. He will, as it were, have Him in his hands, inspect and examine Him, actively embrace Him, familiarize himself with Him in all respects.

Therefore, one can best distinguish bare historical faith from saving faith by keeping in mind this twofold character of faith. Idle assent, too indifferent to offer resistance, can be found sufficiently with the ignorant. Also, with such people it is not uncommon to encounter a theoretical interest in and search for the truth. But the unity of these two characteristics—active search for the truth and passive submission at every point to the overpowering impact of the truth—is a mark of true, saving faith. This two-sided character, moreover, is not limited to the knowledge of faith but pervades all the activities of faith. We will meet this again in *trust*. It also comes out in the images Scripture uses to depict faith. "Accepting" is more an expression for faith as receptive; "hungering and thirsting" are images referring more to the outgoing activity of faith.

69. *Does trust also belong to the essence of saving faith?*

Yes, as the definition in our [Heidelberg] Catechism 21 says, it is an *assured* confidence (*certa fiducia*) that not only to others, but to me also, remission of sin, everlasting righteousness, and salvation are given by God.

70. *Show from Scripture that this is so.*

In Ephesians 3:12 the apostle says, "In whom [that is, in Christ Jesus] we have boldness and access with confidence through faith in him." Hebrews also speaks of the "boldness" of faith (Heb 4:12), of a *plērophoria* of hope in connection with faith (Heb 6:11–12); "Let us draw near with a true heart in full assurance of faith" (ἐν πληροφορίᾳ πίστεως; Heb 10:22). *Plērophoria* really means "full-spiritedness." Further, there is a boast of faith (Rom 5:11; cf. also Matt 14:31–32, where Peter's lack of confidence is called "little faith" by the Lord; Luke 8:25; Jas 1:3). In Galatians 2:20 the apostle describes the object of his faith as "the Son of God, who loved me and gave himself for me."

71. *Should we understand this trust of faith as an intellectual conviction that may be summarized in the sentence: "I am justified before God?"*

No; although this could seem so according to our Catechism, it is nonetheless not so. It cannot be, for the reason that one then comes into conflict with the teaching of Scripture that says that justification is by faith. According to this conception, justification would precede faith. Faith would be nothing other than the conviction by which we become informed subjectively of objective justification. Further, it would follow from this that someone lacking this firm conviction cannot possess the trust of faith. How few are there who perceive such conviction in themselves and still exhibit all the marks of possessing and exercising the genuine trust of faith?

72. *What has occasioned conceiving of the trust of faith in this sense?*

a) All those who teach a doctrine of eternal justification must certainly end up forming this conception of the nature of faith. Justification is then complete from eternity, and nothing remains for faith other than accepting it. Faith is then understood as the firm assurance that one is justified in Christ from eternity.

Connected with this is when theologians such as Comrie and Holtzius, who taught an eternal justification, also put greater emphasis on the intellectual character of faith and thought that every activity of the will should be excluded. This was demanded by their entire system. However, in treating the doctrine of justification we will see how speaking of an eternal justification completely conflicts with the conception of Scripture. Consequently, the correlate of this misconception, this peculiar one-sided view of faith as trust, must be abandoned.

b) The Reformers also put great emphasis on faith as consciousness of assurance. Most of them maintained that *fiducia* was the essence, the heart of the act of faith, that this firm assurance, "I am justified," was in fact what God demanded of the sinner. On this point their statements are very strong. For example, Calvin says, "We will obtain the right definition of faith if we say that it is a firm and certain knowledge of God's good pleasure toward us"; "that we not only judge that the promises of mercy that God offers are true apart from us but not with regard to us, but rather that we make them ours by embracing them inwardly"; "in a word, only he is a true believer who, being fully convinced that God is a gracious and kind Father to him, hopes all things from His kindness; only he who affirms the promises of divine favor toward himself has an undoubted expectation of salvation" [*Institutes*, 3.2.7, 16]. Compare also the definition of our [Heidelberg] Catechism.

How did the Reformers arrive at this conception? In order to understand this we need to realize what Rome had taught the people. With all the aids at its disposal it had kept the conscience in fear and a state of tension and denied in principle the possibility of absolute assurance concerning one's state of justification. The standing of sinners before God goes up and down with their works. The normal, desired situation is that one lives in constant anxiety, in continual fear for his salvation. However, this anxiety and fear have essentially a character of salvation by works. They accompany the consciousness that one must earn salvation and that it will never be complete. The Reformers protested against that unrest of salvation by works. They could not do this better than by putting the emphasis on calm, unshakable trust as the foremost part of faith. Whoever exercises this trust stands at the furthest possible distance from Rome's error. This is why they brought rest to the consciences of people and insisted that one must hold firmly to the conviction of forgiveness in Christ. Thus, the truth is that the Reformers placed in the foreground that aspect of faith that was useful to them for their polemic against Rome. In doing that, however, they did not want to deny in the least that faith as trust also had other sides. And one may never understand their description of faith other than as a *protest against the uncertainty resulting from salvation by works.* There is an uncertainty, a lack in faith as trust that rests directly on principles of self-righteousness. There is also a lack of assurance that can have other causes. Only the former is a criterion for the weakness of faith. The latter, on the other hand, is a product of misunderstanding and ignorance.

One now sees that the motive by which the Reformers were led when they sought the essence of faith in *fiducia* was entirely different than that by which Comrie, et al., were led. The line Calvin-Voetius-Comrie can certainly be drawn formally, but on their differing points differing principles were also at work.

73. To what extent can we say that trust belongs to the essence of faith?

Faith must show in all its parts and aspects that distinctive quality that causes us to renounce ourselves and to rely on the work of the Mediator. Now, it is easy to see that many doubts are possible concerning the application of the work of the Mediator to myself that flow directly from a salvation-by-works tendency of the soul. If someone says, "Christ certainly died for sinners but not for such a great sinner as I am; my unrighteousness is too great; I may not apply His merits to me," then one senses that here a lack of trust comes to light—in other words, that someone who speaks like this still has to learn to abandon himself completely and has to learn to surrender himself to Christ. On the contrary, if someone can silence all such whisperings and has a firm trust that his sins do not have to stand in the way—if he may also triumph over this last vestige of self-trust and, freed from his own fears and cares, may lay down to rest in Christ—then no one will be able to deny that here the power of faith is manifested. Thus, there is a point where trust and faith merge, where distrust, unbelief, and lack of assurance is lack of faith. And one may safely determine that there is no saving faith where this assured trust is totally lacking.

Usually, a twofold distinction is made between (1) trust that takes refuge, and (2) assured trust. What is meant with the first is turning to and being occupied with the Mediator as meeting one's needs; with the second, the posture of the soul that finds stability and certainty in (1). We need, however, to say that there is no saving faith without a certain measure of trust in both senses. The believer who is occupied with Christ and pleads His merits for himself cannot do this without more or less relying on them and drawing security from them. It does not matter whether he brings that to his consciousness; it is still present. And one will be able to convince a person of this presence if one poses the question to him: "If at this moment Christ as mediator vanishes, would your anxiety and lack of certainty then become greater or not?" To that even the least trusting person will have to answer, "Much greater." But with that answer is also granted that a certain measure of assured trust was present that had not entered the consciousness. If it were possible for someone to be occupied with the Mediator and behold His image without that being accompanied by minimal assurance and confirmation, then we would have to say that person does not have saving faith. But such a case cannot occur. The awakened sinner lays hold of the Mediator and is occupied with Him because he is constrained to do that by the longing of his soul for certainty. He needs to find security somewhere, for man cannot exist without certainty or he will fall into despair. Therefore, where utter despair is not present and at the same time man no longer trusts in himself, trust in the Mediator must be in him.

74. *Can one also misuse the proposition that in all saving faith there is a certain degree of assured trust?*

Yes, this proposition has sometimes been misused in an antinomian sense. If someone is settled in the certainty of "I am saved" and, at the same time, lives in indifference about all other things, then this would be sheer antinomianism. Therefore, two things must be pointed out, both of which are of the greatest importance:

   a) That also in the trust of faith the honor of God must impel us. For the sincere believer it is never only a matter of the salvation of his soul in a hedonistic sense. If that were the case, a sense of assurance must lead to passivity. But this should not be. The believer is under the impact of having violated God's law, of missing the mark concerning this law, of everything coming down to fulfilling the law. If now he arrives at the assured trust that the merits of Christ will be applied to him, too, then it is an assurance that not only includes "I am safe" but that simultaneously includes "I stand righteous before God." Thereby the root of all antinomianism is cut off. The confident trust that leads to antinomianism is self-deception, *not the trust* of saving faith.

b) The trust of faith has two sides: a more active and outgoing and a more receptive side. Faith is not only insistent on the assurance that it has security in Christ, but it also seeks that security, relies on it, and rests in it. By this, too, that genuine faith that would lead to false passivity is excluded.

75. *What is the object of this trust of faith?*

Again, the Mediator, in the most extensive sense of the word, or "the Mediator as ordained by God in His mediatorial work for the salvation of lost sinners and as presented for that end in the promise of the gospel" (Owen [in *The Doctrine of Justification by Faith*, chapter 1]).

76. *Demonstrate that in this is encompassed everything that one is otherwise accustomed to propose as the object of this trust.*

a) Many say that the object of this trust is the grace, love, and mercy of God. So, as seen above, Calvin and the Reformers in general. This was also connected with their reaction against the error of Rome. The mercy of God had almost completely disappeared from Rome's horizon. It was only about works and merits. Therefore, it was necessary to stress that the sinner needs to believe that there is grace and forgiveness with God. On the other hand, however, one may never forget that this grace is possible only in Christ. Faith, therefore, does not trust in God's mercy in general, as a mercy that as such can simply overlook sins, but on God's mercy as a mercy such that it arranges for a ransom—thus on the mercy that is made possible by Christ's merits.

b) Others say that the righteousness of the Mediator is the object of our trust. This, too, is somewhat one-sided. For, (1) the righteousness of the Mediator must be imputed and granted to us by an act of God's grace. Thus, if our trust of faith did not include the grace of God, it would be an unfounded or premature trust. (2) The righteousness of the Mediator is not all there is to the Mediator. The believer abandons himself to the Mediator totally and under every aspect, since He has been given to us by the Father for wisdom, righteousness, sanctification, and complete redemption [cf. 1 Cor 1:30].

c) Still others say that the promises are the object of faith. In a certain sense, that is true. One should note, however, that according to the ordering of God, faith is not directed to ideas but to a living person, in whom those promises are "yes" and "amen" [2 Cor 1:20]. The promises only have the purpose of presenting the living Mediator before us in His true stature. Compare what is said above concerning the connection between Scripture and Christ.

77. How is this trust of faith worked in the sinner?

Our [Heidelberg] Catechism [21] says, "Which the Holy Spirit works in my heart by the preaching of the gospel." Two things are present here:

a) Faith, the principle of which is given in regeneration, does not come to outward expression other than by contact with the preached gospel. The gospel is not only the object on which it focuses, but also the instrument by which it is put into operation.

b) Beside this mediate operation of the gospel, however, there is also an immediate working of the Holy Spirit in the heart, by which the sinner is moved to put his trust in the gospel. This trust of faith always has the character more or less of something simple, unreasoned. One will not be brought to it by a syllogism, but the Holy Spirit works in us such that we cannot do otherwise than trust the Mediator. There will always remain an element here that cannot be made entirely clear by reasoning.

One can, however, indicate somewhat further the different steps along which the believer comes to this trust. It will appear that the trust of faith is not only the last and most complete expression of faith, but also that it accompanies the activity of faith from the beginning—in other words, that it is not trusting "I am justified," for the latter can only be construed as the ripest fruit of faith.

a) Before anything else one must see the sinner as convinced of being worthy of condemnation and of being lost.

b) The sinner convinced of this receives spiritual insight into the fitness of the Mediator to meet his needs.

c) In connection with this, the initial trust of faith develops, for the thought, "There is a mediator," cannot but produce a certain degree of trust and keep from utter despair.

d) In being engaged further with that mediator, the sinner is placed increasingly in the situation of those to whom He is commended by the promises of the gospel. The promises of God are that for such who are so disposed, Christ is intended. The sinner recognizes his own image in the sinner so portrayed; in the Mediator, he recognizes the counterpart of his needs. All this does not so much occur by logical reasoning as by an immediate empathy with the truth of Scripture.

e) In this way, the general promises of God contained in Scripture are in a certain sense made personal for the believer, so that for him it is as if God came to him personally with the Mediator. A personal relationship develops between him and the Mediator. It is no longer a matter of truths about God and concerning the Mediator with which he engages speculatively, but it is the living God and the living Mediator Himself before whom he is placed.

f) Placed in this personal relationship, the sinner cannot neglect to make firm his trust on what is thus addressed to him by God in Christ. Lack of all assurance would be distrust. The way of salvation in which the glorification of God shines has his approval so fully that he accepts it completely and in trust assents to the promises, saying, "Lord, it is so, just as you say."

From all this it is evident that there are various things with which the trust of faith is linked: the urgent need of the sinner, the fitness of the Mediator, a personal relationship with God. But behind and above all these things is the Holy Spirit, who produces the trust of faith in a way that can never be entirely explained.

78. Does the trust of faith focus on the promise, "God has loved you personally"?

This is certainly involved in the trusting activity of faith. That is, if a believer undertakes to reason about his trust, he will have to come to the conclusion that by trusting he is also bound to accept such a promise. But one cannot claim that this belongs to the essence of faith itself. The conclusion follows not so much from an analysis of the object of faith itself as from a comparison of it with other known truths. *Election is not the object of saving faith.* If there were no election and God would save all sinners, then the character of saving faith could nonetheless be the same. All that the sinner must have as the ground of his trust is that there is a special mercy in God, a love of good pleasure distinguished from His love of benevolence. That certainly belongs to the object of the trust of faith. The believer does not trust in God's benevolence in general, for he perceives that despite this he could perish but that a wonderful, wholly unique love for sinners was necessary to ordain the Mediator. However, whether this love is extended to many, to few, or to all is a consideration with which the believer is not concerned in the first place.

This is not to deny that there is also an activity of faith with regard to election. In this, too, the believer learns to glorify God's free grace that he is saved and not others. This, too, is an acknowledgment of faith, inasmuch as it compels him to deny every ground of salvation in himself. But it is not the heart of justifying faith.

Similarly, a judgment needs to be made about the other question much discussed by theologians: whether it belongs to the essence of faith that Christ died for me personally, or if this is to be considered as a consequence of faith. The answer given was that it does not belong to what faith consciously conceives that Christ died for me personally in distinction from dying for A or B; certainly, on the other hand, it was answered, there was a personal reckoning in the death of Christ that was not a matter of course but flowed from the free love of God. And, finally, also involved in the trust of faith is that this particular reckoning also applied to me.

79. *What is understood by the "syllogism of faith"?*

The syllogism of faith, also called the *actus reflexus* [reflexive act], consists in this reasoning:

a) Major premise—God has promised salvation to all believers.

b) Minor premise—I am a genuine believer.

c) Conclusion—Therefore, I can count on my salvation, certainly and firmly.

Scripture mentions this *actus reflexus* frequently. For example, "Examine yourselves, whether you are in the faith; test yourselves. Or do you not know yourselves that Jesus Christ is in you? Unless somehow you are rejected" (2 Cor 13:5).

Now, many thought that the trust of faith was only obtained by this syllogism and that what our [Heidelberg] Catechism [21] means by its "assured trust," and what the Reformers mean by trust, is nothing other than the conclusion of this reasoning. However, one senses why this cannot be and also cannot be meant by the Reformers or our Catechism. The object of faith cannot be some mode or the condition of our soul, but only the testimony of God. So, if I base my trust on the presence of faith within my own soul, then this would involve trust itself falling outside faith. There is then: (a) faith, and (b) trust, resting in the fact that I have faith. My trust, therefore, is not the trust of faith (trust exercised by faith), but trust in the presence of faith. We therefore say:

a) This *actus reflexus* is not something that is joined with faith and follows on faith but does not belong to faith itself.

b) On the basis of Scripture, our Catechism and the Reformers have taught that there is an assurance that does not rest on reasoning about faith but flows directly from faith, an *actus directus* [direct act] of faith.

c) This direct assurance is involved in the essence of faith, not merely in its well-being. That is, there is no saving faith in which it could be entirely lacking. In a great many instances, the believer himself would recoil from forthrightly professing what is already involved in his trust. Therefore, one may not make the confidence of faith, in order to confirm it as certain, the distinguishing mark of faith. The negative criterion is better.

80. Is this trust of faith the bare recognition that there is no salvation other than in Christ the Mediator?

No, this was the contention of the Remonstrants, who yet again made faith so defined into a work that man must perform. The recognition that salvation lies in Christ alone is indeed included in faith, but is only a part of it. Rather, the trust of faith consists in this: that I become personally engaged with this conviction. If it remained with that conviction, saving faith would not be present.

81. Is the trust of faith directed to testimony about the Mediator, or to the living Mediator Himself?

The latter, although that does not exclude the former. We ought to consider the matter as follows: The entire mediatorial work of Christ is the object of faith. Although a part of this work as mediator is now already in the past and can never be repeated, from that it may nonetheless not be inferred that we put our trust in an abstract fact. The same Mediator, who fulfilled this work in the past, also lives now to keep it in lasting memory and to make it effective by His intercession. Christ as the heavenly high priest embodies at the same time the suffering Christ—that is, all the fruits of His sufferings are at His disposal. And saving faith is focused on this Christ. God's ordaining is such that trusting in the work of the Mediator and trusting in the person of the Mediator may not be separated. The former without the latter is of no value at all. And they are therefore so closely connected that, through this personal relationship to the Mediator in which the believer is placed, his awareness would be strengthened that he has everything from the Mediator. The unity in life of mystical union and the consciousness of that unity in the personal trust of faith thus both serve the same end, namely, to give us a deeper impression of imputation by free grace.

82. Does the essence of faith then consist in love for the Mediator?

To maintain this would bring us onto Roman Catholic terrain, because, as has already been noted, for Rome love is seen as the "form" of faith—that is, love is what gives faith its distinguishing character. Still, there are some who have called faith an unfailing form of love (cf. the enumeration above of the acts of faith in Witsius). There is evidently a difference in principle between believing and loving. It is true that saving trust in the Mediator may not be conceived of without it being accompanied by love for Him. But this does not at all prove that faith and love must be regarded as identical. The difference is this: that love is an act by which I devote myself to the beloved object, while faith, conversely, resides in an appropriation of the object of my faith for myself. In faith I seek for *myself* a certainty on which *I* can live before God, and so in faith there is always an element of personal interest. In love, on the other hand, I am not inquiring after such a personal interest. This does not mean that, in a selfish manner, saving faith is only concerned with its own salvation. Rather, it has this distinctive quality: that in the work of salvation, too, its concern before everything else is the glory of God, so that the faith of Abraham can be portrayed as giving glory to God (Rom 4:20). But this seeking the glory of God *for my person and by my person* is precisely the reason why I exercise faith in the Mediator. In order that the glory of God may shine in my personal relationship to God, I take hold of the Mediator as the means established by God to that end and put my trust in Him. Out of the personal relationship of faith in which I have hereby been placed to Him, love naturally develops as a fruit of faith. In the same way, all the other Christian virtues are resident in faith as in a root. But they do not contribute to the formal perfecting of faith, although in retrospect they can serve as grounds for recognizing the genuineness of faith.

83. Is faith a deed, a work?

Yes. Although one can speak of faith as a disposition or as a principle that has not yet developed, faith is usually presented as an activity of the soul. But in the justification of a sinner, faith, although an act, does not occur in the quality of a deed or work. The Remonstrants maintained the latter. The Reformed say: In no respect does faith as a deed have the power to justify us, for like all the deeds of the human soul before death, it is defiled by sin and itself has need of the righteousness of the Mediator. The connection in which it stands to justification can only be indicated further in discussing the latter.

84. Who is the author of faith?

Mentioned as such is:

    a) *God.* It is the Father who draws the sinner to Christ (John 6:44). For the sake of Christ it is given by grace not only to believe in

Him but also to suffer for Him (Phil 1:29). Ephesians 2:8 says expressly, "By grace you have been saved through faith; and that not of yourself; it is God's gift." Although one may think that "this" (τοῦτο) does not refer to "faith," which is certainly possible, in any case it must have reference to *all that precedes*—namely, to *"by grace you have been saved through faith,"* whereby faith is obviously included. In Colossians 2:12 mention is made of "the faith of the *working of God.*"

b) Further, *God the Holy Spirit*. According to 1 Corinthians 12:3, no one can say that Jesus is Lord except by the Holy Spirit. The Spirit, therefore, is called, "the Spirit of faith" (2 Cor 4:13).

85. *How is this faith effected—mediately or immediately?*

As to its principle, immediately in regeneration; as to its outward expression, in part immediately in the direct act of conversion, in part also mediately through the preaching of the gospel. Our [Heidelberg] Catechism [21] alludes to the latter when it says that faith is worked in the heart by the preaching of the gospel.

86. *Will it not do to have faith originate with the sinner in a completely mediate manner?*

No, this is Pelagian or semi-Pelagian. One must then grant to the natural or at least unregenerate man the capacities for an expression of life such as believing is.

87. *What is the difference between a "seed of faith" and a "disposition of faith"?*

The former is given in regeneration, and thus is faith as an undeveloped potentiality. A disposition, on the other hand, is the inclination developed by the activity of faith that furthermore now underlies this activity. From this it follows that for adults, when they are regenerated, the principle or the seed of faith also immediately becomes a disposition of faith. For children it is otherwise. Children who die before years of discretion and are children of the covenant are regarded as having also received the seed of faith with regeneration. For them, however, one can hardly speak of a disposition (*habitus*), although some theologians do use this terminology. Those who express themselves more accurately speak of a *seed* of faith (*semen fidei*).

CHAPTER FIVE

Justification

1. *What words are used in Scripture for the concept of "justification," and what can be derived from this usage for the doctrine to be treated now?*

a) The Hebrew term is הִצְדִּיק, *hitsdiq*, which in by far the most cases means "to declare judicially that someone's status is in agreement with the demands of justice." "For I will not justify the godless" (Exod 23:7). "If there is a dispute between men and they come for judgment that the judges decide between them, they shall declare righteous the one who is righteous and condemn the one who is unrighteous" (Deut 25:1). "Those who justify the godless for a gift and deprive the righteous of their righteousness" (Isa 5:23). "He who justifies me is near" (Isa 50:8). The *pi'el* forms of the verb can have the same meaning, צִדֵּק, *tseddeq* (cf. Jer 3:11; Ezek 16:50–51). That the meaning of the word is strictly judicial and nothing else appears most clearly from Proverbs 17:15: "The one who justifies the godless and the one who condemns the righteous are both indeed an abomination to the LORD." Were one now to maintain that here "justify" means "to change someone into an upright person by infusing good qualities," one would then get the result that to make an evil person into a good one is an abomination to God.

When, in a few places, the concept includes more than "to declare just," these are exceptions to the rule. And even then, the meaning is not simply synonymous with "to make good, holy" but means, rather, "to place in such a condition that a judgment of justification can be pronounced." That is, it is not the changing of disposition *in itself* that is designated "to justify," but rather the changing of disposition *with an eye to a judicial pronouncement*, whereby that change is taken into consideration and credited. This is the case in Daniel 12:3: "Those who are wise shall shine like the brightness of the sky above, and those who justify many like the stars forever and ever." Here the term is used of the instrumentality of the ministers of the gospel by which those who hear them come to be in a state of justification, that is, believing, whereupon God can pronounce on them His verdict of justification. Similarly, Isaiah 53:11: "By his knowledge shall my servant, the righteous one, make many righteous, for he shall bear their iniquities." Here "justify" is certainly more than "declare just." It means to bring about everything that is necessary to make possible such a declaration of righteousness. The Servant of the Lord does this by His suretyship, and in doing that, He justifies. Usually, however, it is God the Father as judge, who, pronouncing the verdict, justifies; who, taking note of a status of righteousness—whether as one's own or by imputation—announces the corresponding status.

b) The New Testament word is δικαιοῦν. This also means "to let justice take place by a formal declaration," "to declare just or righteous." For example, "the tax collectors justified God" (Luke 7:29)—that is, they acknowledged God to be righteous, as having the right that was due Him. "But he, desiring to justify himself, said to Jesus, 'Who is my neighbor?'" (Luke 10:29). The meaning here is, "to present someone as δίκαιος [righteous, just]." The passive has the meaning of "to be presented or known as δίκαιος." "For by your words you will be justified and by your words you will be condemned" (Matt 12:37). In extrabiblical Greek δικαιοῦν can mean "to pronounce a just verdict on someone," both in a good as well as a bad sense: (1) for the evildoer, punishment; (2) for the one who does good, reward. In the New Testament, however, the word is used exclusively for acquittal—thus, in a good sense, never in a bad sense for condemnation to punishment. This is also already the case in the Septuagint.

Δικαιοῦν is a term whose soteriological meaning comes to its full rights in Paul. From Romans 4:5, it is evident that we have to do here with a judicial pronouncement and not with a transforming act. "But to him who does not work but believes in Him who justifies the ungodly, his faith is counted as righteousness." This is no less evident from the terms that are the antithesis of "justify." For example, Romans 8:33-34: "It is God who justifies. Who is the one who condemns?" From Romans 4:5, it is also evident that justification does not depend on the condition of the person himself, but on what is imputed to him by grace.

Here, too, a few texts are produced that appear to deviate from this normal usage. These are principally Revelation 22:11, "The one who does wrong, let him still do wrong; and the one who is filthy, let him still be filthy; and the one who is righteous, let him still be justified; and the one who is holy, let him still be sanctified."[1] For "let him still be justified," the Textus Receptus has δικαιωθήτω. Since Bengel it is fairly common to read δικαιοσύνην ποιησάτω ἔτι, "let him do more righteousness" (so, too, Wescott and Hort). Here, then, justification is not spoken of as a transforming action by which a person gradually makes himself more and more righteous, but of the exercise of righteousness in life.

First Corinthians 6:11 is also a passage to which appeal is made to prove the ethical meaning of δικαιοῦν. There we read, "Such were some of you; but you are washed, you are sanctified, you are justified in the name of the Lord Jesus Christ and by the Spirit of our God." It is said that here justification is presented as occurring through the Spirit of God, and from this it should then be evident how "justify" is synonymous with "sanctify." But that here, too, that justification cannot simply be equivalent to "sanctify" is apparent from the fact that this concept immediately precedes, and the apostle cannot have wanted to say the same thing twice. Nor does the fact that the Spirit justifies prove anything, for besides the fact that He is certainly the creator of justifying faith and the one who applies justification to the conscience, one need not have "by the Spirit of our God" refer to justification.

1 The quotation is from Statenvertaling, which Vos proceeds to correct.

It can refer exclusively to "you are washed, you are sanctified." The apostle apparently alludes in this text to baptism, in which justification is signified and sealed "in the name of Christ."

A third passage appealed to is Titus 3:5–7: "He has saved us, not because of works of righteousness that we had done but according to His mercy, by the washing of regeneration and renewal of the Holy Spirit, whom he has poured out on us richly through Jesus Christ our Savior, so that we, being justified by his grace, might become heirs according to the hope of eternal life." It is said that here the rich outpouring of the Holy Spirit, which effects regeneration and renewal, is presented as the cause of justification because "so that" is in the text. We respond: Here, "so that" ought not to be connected with "poured out," but with the preceding, "he has saved us." And furthermore, the clause does not have in view "being justified," but reads, "so that after having been justified [that is, after having received the right of inheritance], we [actually] would become heirs according to the hope of eternal life."

2. *What is the specific meaning of the adjective δίκαιος contained in the verb δικαιοῦν?*

Δίκαιος never expresses what a thing is in itself but what it is in relation to something else, a norm that is outside it and to which it ought to correspond. It is thereby distinguished from αγαθός, "good." It can, for example, be connected with concepts like "wagon, horse, ox," etc., and means then that these things correspond to the demands that one has for their usage, while to say that they are "good" is something completely different—namely, that they correspond to their ideal. Man, then, is "righteous" if in his entire life he is as his judicial relationship to God requires of him, and *consequently is pronounced righteous by the judgment of God.* That someone acts righteously or is righteous can include the concept of being good or doing good, but that is always included in terms of a certain aspect—namely, that of a judicial relationship to God.

3. *Does the word "justification" itself also occur in Scripture?*

Yes, δικαίωσις occurs with this meaning in Romans 4:25, "who was delivered up for our trespasses and raised for our justification." Likewise,

Romans 5:18: "So also through one act of righteousness grace comes upon all men for justification of life."

4. *What is the meaning of the Latin word* justificare?

As its derivation already shows, this word means *justum facere*, "to make someone a righteous person." Now, one could say that this always entails a change in the person, because a "making" is spoken of. For this reason, some have objected to the translation "to *make* righteous" and wished for it to be avoided, and that instead "justification" and "justify" be used. This, however, is without grounds. The meaning of the word *facere* is just as general as "make" [in Dutch and English]. We speak of "making someone a king," "making money," making mention," etc. In each particular case, "to make" has a meaning that corresponds to that particular case. Where one has to do with a relationship, "make" does not mean to change the thing itself inwardly, but to create this relationship by a declaration. To make someone king does not at all mean to furnish him with the particular qualities that a king should have, but simply to declare him to be king, to create between him and his subjects a relationship that is called kingly rule. To make righteous is to be understood similarly, and in terms of this point of view may be defended fully. It is to effect, to create, to make the relationship of righteousness. This can occur (1) by taking the subjective condition of someone into consideration and making it the basis of a justifying judgment; or (2) by transferring to him the objective relationship of righteousness from someone else.

Previously it has been demonstrated how it is precisely in this objective character of righteousness or justness that the possibility of imputation has its basis. One can "sanctify" someone, at least in an ethical sense, only by changing him subjectively. Holiness cannot be transferred because it is something resident in a person. Righteousness, in contrast, may indeed be transferred, because it is something that exists between that person and another, something *in which he stands*.

5. *To what does justification have reference: to the judicial state or to the condition of man?*

To the former. When someone is justified, his condition is not thereby changed. A change may precede or follow, because God has set it in an inseparable relationship with justification. But justification itself never consists in that change. Thus, on this point, justification is utterly distinct from regeneration and sanctification. In order to grasp this difference well, it is necessary that one clearly present the two relationships to God in which man stands.

First, there is a relationship of *similarity* to God, consisting in this: Man is God's image-bearer; more specifically, he possesses the image of God in the narrower sense, is holy, completely good. Second, there is a relationship of *subordination* to God, consisting in this: Man has obligations toward God, owes Him something; his entire moral condition is seen as being subject to the claim of God. Regeneration and sanctification belong to the first sphere, and justification to the second.

Now, it is true that our moral goodness and our righteousness can be in the closest relationship, that someone good and holy is righteous *per se*. But still one must be careful to note that righteousness only stems from moral goodness by means of a judgment of God. *One's condition taken into account by the judge yields that person's judicial state.* Pollution becomes guilt because it passes through the judgment of God. If Adam had remained unfallen and kept the probation command, then God would have justified him—that is, God would have taken into account Adam's holy and steadfast condition and would have had a state of immutable righteousness follow. Conversely, when Adam sinned, it was the condemnation of God that followed on the heels of this sin that transferred him from a state of rectitude into a state of damnation.

6. *How, consequently, can you describe justification?*

It is a judicial assigning to the sinner of the status of righteousness on the basis of the merits of Christ, imputed to him by God, and in which, in faith, he places his trust.

7. *Indicate the points by which this justification is distinguished from sanctification.*

   a) Sanctification serves to take away the pollution of sin and to replace it with what is good as an inherent disposition; it restores in us conformity to the image of God. Justification serves to take away the guilt of sin and to replace it with the right to eternal life in relationship with God.

The usual description—sanctification takes away the pollution of sin, justification the guilt of sin—is not incorrect but still incomplete, because only half of the matter is taken into consideration. In both, in sanctification and justification, there is a second half—namely, what is positive. To take away evil does not yet say what good is given in its place. Likewise, to abolish guilt does not yet mean to grant full rights.

b) Sanctification takes place *within us*, justification *outside relative to us*. The former is an action that changes one's being; it must therefore intervene within our being and bring about a subjective change. The latter is a declaration that changes one's status, a judicial word, and therefore does not affect our being but our standing; it does not take place within us but before God *in His tribunal*.

c) Sanctification, which begins with regeneration, has to do in the first place with the unconscious part of man. It changes, though not only but still first of all, his heart, his disposition, and from there moves to his thoughts, words, and work. Justification, which takes place in the tribunal of God, is intended to address the consciousness of man. Take note! We are not saying that justification takes place in our consciousness, although that may be said of justification in the widest sense. We are only saying that justification in the tribunal of God is intended to be perceived by the consciousness of man. That already follows from its character as a *declaration*. An act without a word can be applicable to unconscious life, but an act in a word, an existing verdict, must find its significance in the consciousness. Justification is thus intended to be introduced into the consciousness of man, to be brought to understanding in him.

d) Sanctification is a slow process that is never entirely completed in this life; justification, in contrast, occurs once and is complete. The former can regress; the latter cannot. Once declared, justification remains secure forever.

e) Sanctification and justification differ in their cause. The meriting cause is the same for both, namely, the merits of Christ. But the difference is to be found in the effecting cause. While *God the*

Father as judge declares the verdict of justification in the divine tribunal, it is *God the Holy Spirit*, as our sanctifier, who works subjective holiness in us.

8. *Who loses sight of the difference between regeneration-sanctification on the one hand and justification on the other?*

Roman Catholics. Under justification they do not understand an *actus forensis*, a judicial act, but an *actus physicus*, a physical act, better still an *actus hyperphysicus*, a supernatural act. Now, one could think that this is merely a verbal difference and that it does not matter whether the one word or the other is used, if one simply means the same thing, and that Rome does not need to be in error materially when it designates sanctification with the term justification. When we look closer, however, it is soon clear that this formal difference is caused by a deeper material difference. One should note the following points:

a) Although the Roman Catholic church does not deny that there is an imputation of the merits of the Mediator, it nonetheless makes this imputation something subordinate, pushes it completely into the background, and makes the subjective change of man the be-all and end-all. Rome does not deny that all grace comes to us on the basis of the merits of Christ. The Council of Trent teaches: "Although no one can be righteous unless the merits of the suffering of Christ are communicated to him, still this takes place in this justification of the ungodly so that by the merits of the most holy suffering of the same, the love of God is poured out by the Holy Spirit in the hearts of those who are justified, so that it inheres there," etc. And again: "The meritorious cause [of justification] is His dearly beloved Only Begotten, our Lord Jesus Christ, who, when we were enemies ... earned justification for us by His most holy suffering on the wood of the cross," etc.[2] But all that is merely preparatory. It is the basis and the starting point, according to Rome, not the substance of the matter. It takes place outside of individuals and is really vested in the church. What happens to the individual himself is that he is made subjectively righteous and holy by the sacrament. If one now takes into consideration

---

2   These and the quotations below are from the Council of Trent, session 6, *Decree concerning Justification*.

that, according to Scripture, the justification of man before God is the principal part of the order of salvation, really the cardinal point about which everything turns and on which everything is focused, then the use of this term for something else acquires an extremely dangerous meaning. Indeed, the importance and the weight of the matter, which adhere to this term, are transferred with the term to this totally different meaning. Thus, what, superficially considered, could appear to be a mere change of name is in fact a shift in principle of the center of gravity of religion, a total falsification of the relationship between God and man. For Rome assigns all the weight that Scripture attributes to forensic justification to physical justification. If in the former it is the grace of God—the free imputation of the merits of the Mediator—that shines, for Rome, man—the inner condition of man, what he is and does—comes to the fore.

It is not otherwise with the concept of faith. This, too, as we saw, has a central significance in Scripture. Faith is precisely what it is so that God's glory in the sinner might come into its own. Therefore, faith precedes justification logically; we are justified in and by faith. But Rome splits faith in two, speaks of a *fides informis* and of a *fides formata*, an unformed and a formed faith. The former, consisting of bare historical assent, precedes justification; the latter, as far as its seed is concerned, consisting in love as the root of all virtues, is given in justification itself. "In the justification mentioned, man receives through Jesus Christ, in whom he is engrafted ... faith, hope, and love." And, "we are therefore said to be justified by faith, because faith is the beginning of human salvation, the foundation and the root of all justification." Thus, there is transferred to faith as a good, ethical property of man what Scripture says of faith as a trusting acknowledgment of the soul that salvation is wholly in Christ.

b) Catholics deny in principle the imputation of the active obedience of the Mediator in justification. It is on the basis of the suffering of the Savior that new qualities are infused into us, and by exercising these new qualities and putting them into operation we must merit eternal life for ourselves. Thus only in a very indirect sense can one say on the basis of the Roman Catholic standpoint that the merits of Christ are the foundation for obtaining eternal life. They are that foundation insofar as they have made it possible for the sinner himself to receive the necessary means to merit eternal life himself. Here, too, Christ is therefore more a means and a preparation for our justification than its foundation, its real meritorious cause. The work is divided between God and man. The former does the negative, the latter the positive half. The covenant of grace serves merely to restore the covenant of works.

c) In connection with this, the Roman church teaches that there is a decrease and increase of justification, that one must progress from virtue to virtue, that only the works that one does bring justification to perfection. As faith, love, and hope multiply, so justification also increases. One can fall from justification and then must receive it again by the sacrament of penance. It is lost not only when faith ceases but also by each mortal sin that is committed. From that, then, it follows further that there is no absolute assurance of justification and that in the Roman Church one always continues to be in an uncertain, wavering condition.

9. *What propositions must be set in opposition to this Roman Catholic teaching?*

a) In what Scripture calls "justification" nothing is changed with respect to our subjective condition. In justification we appear as *sinners*. It is a *justificatio status externus*; only our external status is exchanged; our *status internus*, our internal state, is not changed. The Apostle Paul teaches this expressly when he says (Rom 4:5), "But to the one who does not work but believes in *him who justifies the ungodly*, his faith is counted as righteousness." This follows as well from the objection that Paul's Jewish opponents again and again raised against Paul's teaching on justification. They said, "According to your scheme, justification is something that takes place entirely outside a person; subjectively, someone can be the greatest sinner and still be completely righteous before God." To that objection Paul never answered, "My righteousness is *at the same time* a subjective change and a re-creation of man." But he always answered, "Regeneration and sanctification are always joined with my justification as something distinct from it and as a fruit of it." That is the reasoning that is used by the apostle in Romans 6. According to Rome, he should have reasoned in a completely different manner.

b) Not only the works that we do in our own strength, or that we do before regeneration, or that we do without the merits of Christ, but *all works, of whatever sort, are excluded from justification*. This is so repetitively certain in Scripture that proof is almost superfluous. Galatians 2:16 reads, "... nevertheless, knowing that a man is not justified by *law*-works [ἐξ ἔργων νόμου]." In no way is the reference here to works prescribed by one or another specific law, because the article is missing. All law-work as such is excluded from justification. According to Paul, faith and works form an absolute contrast in the matter of justification (Rom 11:6). This must be maintained against the Roman Catholic teaching about the instrumentality of works in justification, as well as against Pelagians, Rationalists, and Remonstrants. The first two mentioned, the Pelagians and Rationalists, maintain that Scripture excludes only the works of the Jewish law, that is, the ceremonial law, but that the moral law certainly has to be observed by us for justification. The last, the Remonstrants, go one step further, and in place of the moral law in all its severity put a lighter form, the law of the obedience of faith. They speak of a *fides obsequiosa* [submissive faith] and of an *obedientia evangelica* [evangelical obedience], which, while in itself not perfect, is accepted by God as perfect.

c) Justification is not in the first place designed to save man and make him better, but to reveal the free grace of God in which His glory is displayed. According to us, justification is also meant to exalt God's honor. And since in the covenant of grace the honor of God consists in the fact that He Himself alone is at work, this must also emerge in the case of justification. Hence Paul teaches how, in justification, all boasting on man's side is excluded (Rom 3:27). But with Rome that does not come out in an absolute way. Man himself is a coworker; the work of God remains limited to eliminating obstacles and to providing means for man's working. That reverses the right relationship. We say: The judicial aspect, in which the honor of God as the sole source of salvation shines so powerfully, precedes. Rome says: The ethical aspect, which is directed to man and achieves something in man, precedes, and then from man, thus restored, the judicial aspect proceeds.

10. *Show that justification takes place in the tribunal of God* (in foro divino).

This is apparent from the expressions used by Scripture—for example, "before God [παρὰ τῷ θεῷ]" (Gal 3:11), "in his sight [ἐνώπιον αὐτοῦ]" (Rom 3:20). Both of these expressions include a standing before God as before the judge who sits on His throne, a standing before His face.

11. *What takes place in this divine tribunal when a man is justified?*

In order to understand this well, the less-accurate answers must first be rejected.

a) Some say: In His eternal decree or in the eternal counsel of peace, God determines that the sinner who is elect will be regarded and dealt with in the Surety. This is eternal justification, taught by many theologians, such as Voetius, Comrie, Holtzius, and, presently, Dr. Abraham Kuyper. Justification is thus the determination of God that the judicial status of the sinner will be separate from his own personal condition, and will be determined by the merits of the Mediator. One usually reasons for this on two grounds:

1. Everything that occurs in man subjectively must have its objective basis antecedently in the merits of Christ, imputed to him personally. Now, it is undeniable that when a person is regenerated, he already received this gift of God as the fruit of the imputed merits of Christ—indeed, going back still further, that the workings of preparatory grace have also been given to him, because the merits of Christ have been imputed to him personally. In fact, God's dealings with him from the beginning of his life on and even in his ancestors have been determined by divine deliberation. He has been included in the Surety from eternity. Thus one cannot say anything other than that the justification of the sinner has its origin in eternity.

2. The second ground on which one reasons is that justification is not an inward act in man—that is, not an act that occurs within man and hence transpires in time. It takes place in the divine tribunal, within the being of God, and does not take place outside of His being. Therefore, it is of itself eternal, for everything that occurs within God's being is elevated above time.

It may not be denied that Reformed doctrine, by seeking to find the certainty of all things in God and requiring a foundation for all that is temporal in eternity, teaches such a view of justification much more easily than other systems. The Lutherans have always reproached the Reformed that their doctrine of election must lead to this conclusion. If it is determined from eternity and absolutely for whom the merits of the Mediator are reckoned and to whom they will be applied in time, then the actual imputation, the establishing of a bond between the believer and Christ, has already been realized in eternity and there is no longer a need to establish this bond in time. Conversely, one might say that only the doctrine of universal satisfaction escapes this conclusion. Then Christ has died in general for all sinners, and now it must be determined in time, by faith, which specific persons His merits will benefit. Thus we see the need for a temporal justification.

There are preponderant objections against the doctrine that justification is from eternity:

1. Everywhere in Scripture it is taught that justification is through and by faith. It cannot, therefore, precede faith. Although faith is not the meriting or the effecting cause of justification, these two surely stand in a certain inseparable connection. As certainly as faith is something that originates in time, so certainly does the justification of the sinner before God, which is tied to faith, occur in time.

2. In Romans 8:30, where the steps in the order of salvation are enumerated, justification comes between two temporal acts of God, namely, between calling and glorification. And these three things stand together as consequences of a pair of other acts, which are distinguished as eternal from what is temporal. At the same time, in verse 29, the specification is expressly

added for the foreknowledge and predestination of God that they took place *beforehand*, that is, before time. That is not the case with justification.

3. To affirm justification from eternity can lead to approximately the same results as the Roman Catholic error in this area of Christian doctrine. What does Rome do? As has been seen, they take the term "justification" and apply it to something entirely different, something that is true in part but still is never called justification by Scripture. However, with the name they also transfer many characteristics of justification to this other entity. As a result, what remains for them of true justification is without sharp and vital features. The imputation of the merits of Christ remains in the dark for them. The same thing can happen with us if we teach eternal justification. No one will deny that in fact there is something like Comrie and others speak of when they speak of an eternal imputation of the merits of Christ. But Scripture does not call this justification. Now, one could think, as with Rome, that we have to do here merely with a faulty designation that amounts to a verbal difference. But that is not the case. Temporal justification, as Scripture teaches it, has certain traits and particularities that are inseparable from its temporal nature. Thus, whoever applies the word "justification" to an eternal act of God will not be able to do it justice. And at the same time, what he would then still believe about the temporal justification of the sinner would be much less clear and defined in his view than it should be according to Scripture. The teaching of eternal justification, therefore, even has serious objections practically. It will lead people to transpose their life of faith back into eternity and to turn away from the display of God's favor at this present time. It will remove justification from being in opposition to the consciousness of sin, for if in this manner the sinner viewed himself as justified from eternity, then it is not possible that he view his ideal personality in God's counsel with the same conviction of sin and lostness as his real personality in time.

4. As far as the second of the grounds, on which the defenders of eternal justification reason, is concerned—namely, that all acts of God, which are in God, must be eternal—this ground is thoroughly deficient. If in this way one infers the eternity of justification, then one must also infer the eternity of condemnation, for this too is a judgment of God about man, not an act that occurs in man. In the same way, creation as an act in God is eternal. But all these acts, although not transpiring for God in the form of time, are nonetheless eternal in a somewhat different sense than God's decree is eternal. They terminate in time. God's eternal act of creation does not give us an eternal creation as its product. Neither does eternal justification, if by that one only means that the judgment of God does not transpire in the form of time. By paying close attention to this distinction, all the conclusions fall away that the defenders of eternal justification wish to derive from this eternity of God's acts. So some say, for example, even when a sinner does not yet believe and still lives in the world alienated, he is already the object of God's good pleasure, for he is justified from eternity. We answer: In this sense, he is just as well condemned from eternity. But in both cases the use of the word "eternity" is misleading. That God's acts lie above the form of time does not eliminate the fact that in their relationship to us they appear in temporal sequence and are to be viewed as such by us. That is why Scripture teaches that both condemnation and justification are temporal acts for us, and that the former always precedes the latter. Paul declares to the Ephesians not that before their calling they were already the objects of God's good pleasure, but that they *were children of wrath* like the others (Eph 2:3). If someone believes in the Son, wrath is removed from him, but if he disobeys the Son, the wrath of God *remains* on him [cf. John 3:36].

5. Finally, concerning the first ground—namely, that the merits of Christ have already been imputed to the sinner before he believes, since on that basis, workings of grace take place within him—this too is deficient. The concept of imputation does not always have the same meaning. (a) In election,

imputation was the determination that Christ would be the surety for believers. (b) In the counsel of peace, imputation was the agreement that the Mediator would pay for all the guilt of the elect. By this imputation, their salvation was made firm and certain. It was not a conditional suretyship but an absolute one. And on the basis of this absolute suretyship, the elect can receive regeneration, conversion, and faith. All this, however, was determined with the provision that the judicial relationship of God to them would not be changed personally until they believed. In a gracious arrangement, as the establishing of the Mediator as surety was, the creditor has every right himself to determine when the consequences of the agreement will become effective. (c) In time there is the personal, judicial imputation for believers that is only called justification in Scripture.

b) There are others who do not place justification in eternity, but find it in the satisfaction of Christ. Thereby the just demands of God were satisfied, and where there is satisfaction of demands, the claim *eo ipso* [of itself] disappears. Some say that this then is conclusive, since in God's plan Christ suffered for the elect, and thus—in the suffering that struck Him and in the obedience that He supplied—God with full consciousness received and obtained the justice due Him from the elect, and thereby at the same time declared that they were just before Him.

This view, too, must be rejected for the following reasons:

1. Earlier we have seen that a pecuniary debt and a punitive debt are to be distinguished precisely by the fact that payment of the former by a surety *ipso facto* [in itself] releases the original debtor, while for the latter such is not the case.

2. If justification has taken place in the satisfaction, or more precisely, in the resurrection of Christ, then it was incomplete for Old Testament believers. They were not really justified then. This cannot be. There is, therefore, a complete justification that is not present in the resurrection.

3. It is certainly true that the resurrection of the Mediator is a factual declaration of God that He had fulfilled all righteousness,

and there is no objection to calling this the collective justification of the body of Christ. But it was not personal justification. Romans 4:25, "who was delivered up for our trespasses and raised for our justification," is to be understood as follows: Christ was raised so that later, when we are justified, it would be even more certain for us that a complete satisfaction had been accomplished.

c) A third view is that justification takes place when God begins to treat the sinner with effectual grace. It would then be not so much a verbal declaration as a change in procedure that is expressed through actions. Formerly, God treated a sinner without workings of grace; then there comes a point where He works in him regeneration, repentance, and faith. This transition is justification.

Against this view must be noted:

1. Scripture always seeks justification in a judicial pronouncement and not in a change of treatment.

2. The change of treatment begins beneath the consciousness, while justification is an act intended for the consciousness of the sinner.

3. Justification follows faith logically and so cannot precede faith.

4. A ground adduced for this view is that justification always has one who is *ungodly* as its object. Now, if a person is not justified before he exercises faith and is regenerate, then he is no longer a suitable object for this justification of the ungodly. That is why some will have Scripture teach "justified *to* faith" instead of *by* and *through* faith. But, to begin with, Scripture never says "*to* faith." Further, the objection just mentioned also disappears if one only takes into consideration that faith within man is not the basis of merit on which man is declared just. In justification, God declares to the believing sinner that he in his capacity as entirely without rights is nevertheless endowed with all rights. Faith and regenerate life are thus certainly present but are not taken into consideration in the judgment—for which, moreover, they, imperfect and stained by sin, would also in no way be adequate.

d) The correct conception is this: As soon as the sinner exercises saving faith, God absolves him personally in the heavenly
tribunal, and He declares that now He will no longer be seen
by anyone in the world, *not even by the sinner himself*, as being
wrathful against him, or as expecting from him the fulfilling of
any demand for obtaining eternal life, but rather as gracious and
as giving him assurance of eternal life, and all this on the basis of
the merits of Christ as the only meriting cause. This declaration
of God in His tribunal, intended for the believer personally, is
justification proper, and it is evidently distinguished specifically
from everything that has preceded. It can occur only now, since
only by faith is the possibility of an antinomian misuse of grace
cut off. God can indeed deal with the sinner in his unconscious
life favorably—for example, grant him regeneration before he
exercises faith—but His intention is not to say to the sinner in
His tribunal, "You are righteous in Christ and I no longer consider you as a sinner," before faith began to function in him.
Before that time, God addresses the sinner as an angry judge.
Thus, one must sharply distinguish these two: (a) the treatment
of the sinner from the side of God by actions; (b) the treatment
of the sinner from the side of God by a judicial declaration that
is intended to be announced to the consciousness of the sinner.
The former begins much earlier than when faith is present.
The latter does not begin before faith is present, and in it we have
to seek justification proper.

12. *In what, explained in more detail, does this justification consist?*

To begin with, it is to be distinguished into (1) active justification (*justificatio activa*) and (2) passive justification (*justificatio passiva*).

Active justification occurs in the divine tribunal. It is the declaration
as God makes it. Passive justification, in contrast, is the application
and announcement, or rather the carrying through, of this verdict in
the conscience of the believer, in the tribunal of the conscience (*in foro
conscientiae*). Further, as far as active justification is concerned, the following should be noted:

a) The declaration of God that we are righteous does not consist
merely in the *forgiveness of sins*. The expression "forgiveness of

sins" can even be used in a way that excludes it entirely from justification. Sometimes it is understood as overlooking sin, simply not taking account of it. God, however, cannot exercise such forgiveness because of His righteousness. There must be a ground on which acquittal from guilt—forgiveness—rests. That ground is to be found in the merits of Christ, and more specifically in His passive obedience. Therefore, when God justifies the sinner, He declares that, viewed on the basis of those merits, He will no longer be reckoning his sins to him. In other words, God makes an open declaration that the merits of the Mediator are imputed to the believer personally. There is thus a transfer of merits. Just as in the suretyship of the Mediator there was a transfer of obligations from the elect to the Surety, just as in the satisfaction of Christ there is a transfer of the punishments and demands in the same direction, so, now, in justification there is a transfer of merits in the other direction.

b) In justification, God appears in a twofold respect: first, as a righteous judge, who takes account of guilt and must take account of it; then, as a gracious God, who does not insist that guilt be charged personally to that person who contracted it. Insofar as the first is the case, justification that takes place under the covenant of grace is no different than justification under the covenant of works. The old theologians expressed this by saying that gospel justification did not differ from legal justification *quoad essentiam*, "as to essence," but *quoad circumstantias*, "as to circumstances." If one considers the activity of God insofar as it takes place with a view to Christ and takes into account His merits, then we have justification in the strict sense of the word. That God justifies the sinner freely never means that God permits the violation of justice. No sinner who has arrived at a proper insight into God's justice would have anything to do with such a justification. If, on the other hand, one considers the action of God with a view to the sinner himself, then it is pure grace. One who is ungodly is declared righteous. Thus, what on the one hand is the fullest justice appears on the other hand almost as a paradox. But both are true.

c) The *effective* cause (*causa efficiens*) of justification is God, more accurately God the Father, and still more accurately His grace and righteousness. The *meritorious* cause is the obedience of Christ the Mediator (*causa meritoria*). The *instrumental* cause (*causa instrumentalis*) is faith worked in the heart through the Holy Spirit and then put into action. The *final* cause (*causa finalis*) is the glorification of God regarding all His virtues related to justification.

d) Justification, both as active and as passive, has two parts that correspond to the two aspects of the satisfaction of Christ. Passive obedience is the basis for remission from punishment due to guilt; active obedience is the basis for attributing the right to eternal life.

There is some difficulty in finding suitable terms for these two aspects of justification. The first aspect is generally called *forgiveness of sins*, the second *adoption as children*. This is possible only as one keeps in view that both rest on one act of imputation that also belongs to justification. Not simply forgiveness, but forgiveness on the basis of imputation. So, too, for adoption.

When Calvin and others among the old theologians sometimes have justification amount to the forgiveness of sins (*remissio peccatorum*), then one must keep the following in view as the explanation of this phenomenon. First of all, in their opposition to Rome, that aspect of the doctrine that the Catholic church misunderstood had to be given prominence. That was not the aspect of justification in the strict sense, but, quite to the contrary, the aspect of grace and forgiveness. Furthermore, this description agreed with the Old Testament phraseology, which very often speaks of justification as a blotting out of sins, a forgiving of sins, a no longer remembering of sins, a carrying away of sins, etc.—all of these expressions in which the second aspect is not mentioned. In general, in the Old Testament the second aspect of justification remained more obscure. There was, certainly, an assurance of eternal life, but this occurred through the typical promise of a blessed temporal life, and only by degrees came to greater clarity (cf. Psa 51:4; Jer 31:34; Psa 32:1; Isa 43:25; 44:22; Zech 13:1). This does not mean that the believers in the Old Testament did not have a complete justification, as the followers of Cocceius maintain, who on the grounds of Romans 3:25 ascribe to them only a *paresis* [passing over] and not an *aphesis* [remission of sin]. This certainty of satisfaction was completely guaranteed by the immutability of the divine Surety, and so in no way did justification need to wait for the accomplishment of the work of redemption. The difference was gradual—a difference in clarity, not a difference in principle, as the distinction just mentioned between "passing over" and "forgiving" would have it.

Neither is it entirely right when our [Belgic] Confession of Faith, in the heading to Article 23, seeks justification in the forgiveness of sins plus the imputation of the merits of Christ. These two cannot be coordinated in this way. Rather, the merits of the Mediator are the basis of forgiveness plus adoption as children. In this article, however, no mention is made of the latter.

13. *Do all agree that justification rests not only on the passive but also on the active obedience of the Mediator?*

No. Besides the view just mentioned, which places less emphasis on this aspect, there is also a systematic denial of this element. Naturally, all those who deny active obedience as a part of Christ's satisfaction must also deny its application to the sinner, and so develop a one-sided, incomplete doctrine of justification. This happens in Piscator and in all theologians who have followed him. It is not necessary here to repeat the arguments that have been raised against this misconception in discussing the doctrine of Christ's satisfaction. With necessary changes made, they can all be used here. The principal issue comes down to this: that one does not distinguish properly between negative not-being-unrighteous and positive being-righteous in the sense of having the right to eternal life. If God forgives someone his sins, he is not yet thereby automatically placed in the position of someone entitled to eternal life. Between the two extremes of someone guilty and condemned and someone fully justified, a third state can very well be imagined. God could have forgiven people, namely their guilt, because of the merits of Christ, and then further could have entered into a new covenant relationship with them in order to let them earn eternal life for themselves. But then they would not have been justified as believers are now justified. Justification is not merely the act of God whereby He puts the sinner in a position to open a new page in his life's book, which for the time being would still be blank, and on which he himself would still have to inscribe new merits. All the pages are opened by God at one time; on all pages, the handwriting of sin against him is wiped out [cf. Col 2:14], and in its place the promise of eternal life is written.

14. *Can you show that in justification a granting of the right to eternal life*
    in fact takes place?

Yes. In Galatians 3:13–14, these two things are clearly placed next to each
other: (a) being redeemed from the curse of the law that has occurred
because Christ became a curse for us; (b) the coming-upon us of the
blessing of Abraham. That the latter cannot be located merely negatively in the redemption from the curse is clear from Galatians 3:11–12,
where it is described as a fruit of justifying faith that the person lives by
it, and this life of faith is set in opposition to living by the works of the
law. See also Galatians 3:5, where "the Spirit" as the principle of eternal
life is presented as the gift of righteousness that follows faith. Again,
in Galatians 3:21, that the law would make alive and that righteousness
would be by the law are juxtaposed as synonymous.

In Acts 26:18, both aspects of justification are placed next to each
other in just so many words: "in order that they may receive forgiveness
of sins *and an inheritance among those who are sanctified by faith in me*
[Christ]" (cf. also Zech 3:4–5; Isa 61:10). No less weighty is the declaration of the apostle in Romans 5:18–19, where of justification it is said: "by
one act of righteousness grace comes on all men for justification of life,"
and "by the obedience of one many will be made righteous."

15. *Do those who think like Piscator deny this and other truths of Scripture?*

No. They maintain only that all this is to be seen as a fruit not of the
active obedience of the Mediator but exclusively of His passive obedience. By covering sin, Christ has obtained life. One simply does not
intend to think of a middle state. From this, it is clear that one must
make a distinction between the worse thinking of the Roman Catholics,
the Remonstrants, et al., on the one hand, and this one-sided thinking of
Piscator on the other. The latter was in principle more a misconception
than a heresy. For the others, the error derives from a deeper, heretical
principle.

16. *How should we explain it when now and then Scripture also presents the*
    positive blessing of justification and the gift of eternal life as a fruit of
    the death or the blood of Christ?

This should be taken synecdochically—that is, so that the one part is
included in the other. We have noted earlier that the two aspects of the

obedience of the Mediator may be distinguished but not separated from each other. The one is repeatedly contained in the other. His obedience is precisely that obedience by which He gave Himself over to death (Phil 2:8). And since the passive obedience was the indispensable condition for the validity of the active obedience, as a part it can designate the whole. This occurs, for example, in Romans 5:9, "being justified by His blood," and in Romans 3:25, "as a propitiation by faith in His blood, for a demonstration of His righteousness."

17. *What should be noted concerning the second part of justification, "adoption as children"?*

a) That it occurs in a forensic, judicial sense, as is required by the nature of justification. One should above all distinguish this adoption as a judicial act from the ethical act of God by which He restores to sinners, who were His enemies and fought against Him, the attitude of a child and the likeness of a child to its father. Of course, in this ethical significance the doctrine of adoption does not belong to justification but to regeneration, conversion, and sanctification. It stands to reason that this judicial adoption and ethical adoption cannot exist totally separated from each other. In Galatians 3:26-27, both meanings occur in the immediate context next to each other. First, children by faith in Christ Jesus (= forensic sense), then actually having put on Christ, thus having become one body with Him and possessing the Spirit of the Son who cries, "Abba, Father" (cf. also Gal 4:6). But the distinctive factor is that in Paul, *adoption as children* always appears as a legal concept and, as such, is continually the basis of the subjective ethical sense of adoption. Paul calls it υἱοθεσία, literally "a placing as children," from υἱός and τιθέναι. In classical legal language, this was a sharply delineated concept, and never meant to bestow on someone the characteristics of a child subjectively but always to place someone objectively in the status of a child, just as one still today adopts a child as his own. The concept occurs with the same legal meaning in John 1:12: "To as many as have received Him, He has *given the right* to become children of God, namely, those who believe in His name." Here it reads ἐξουσίαν ἔδωκεν, "He gave legal authority," although directly following that, allusion is made to regeneration again as the second cause of adoption.

Otherwise, adoption is generally considered ethically in John. For this reason also the word used is not υἱός but τέκνον, which points more to origin (τίκτειν, "to beget, to give birth") than to a legal relationship (cf. 1 John 3:9–10). This adoption, as is evident from this passage, is related more to sanctification than to justification.

b) If we now ask further what this judicial adoption includes, then the following should be noted:

1. It implies that, on account of the suretyship provided by the Mediator, believers are discharged from all obligations to satisfy God's justice. The son must still serve the Father and obey His laws, but he does it out of love and no longer has need to do that in order to earn something. Believers are thus under the law as a rule of life, but no longer under the law as a means of justification. As far as their persons are concerned, they receive all the riches of the Father without having to do something for them. It is a free gift. Under the curse of the law they were slaves; now they are sons (Gal 4:7).

2. The son nevertheless has rights—namely, the right to inherit the treasures of the Father. This right of inheritance is conveyed in justification. Believers are coheirs with Christ and heirs of God (Rom 8:17). This inheritance includes all the subjective benefits of salvation. Reckoned to them in Galatians 3:14 is "the promise of the Spirit"; in 4:6, "the Spirit of the Son, who cries, 'Abba, Father!'" But not only present but also future gifts belong to these subjective benefits. In Romans 8:17–18, the glory that the coheirs with Christ receive comes only after the oppression of the present time. In Romans 8:23, the redemption of the body, directly called the "adoption as children," belongs to that future glorification. According to Romans 8:30, glorification is connected directly to justification as a link in the chain of salvation; it is the consequent fruit of justification. From all this, it is clear that in his justification a person receives a legal entitlement from God to all the benefits of the covenant of grace, temporal and eternal, bodily and spiritual. Justification is not the imparting of those benefits, but the granting of the right to them.

18. *Is justification an act that takes place once and for all, or an act that can be repeated?*

a) The Roman Catholic church makes a distinction between a *first* and a *second* justification. The first consists in the infusion of habitual grace, by which original sin is suppressed and expelled (see above). The formal cause of the second justification is to be sought in good works that man himself performs. This is a confusion of sanctification and justification, and makes the fruits of the former meritorious. As justification becomes sanctification, so sanctification again becomes justification in the hands of Rome—naturally, a legalistic justification.

b) Also among those who hold to a sound doctrine of justification, a difference of opinion is prevalent concerning the question whether justification can be repeated. Some think that justification repeatedly follows each confession of sin, and so explain this repeated justification with respect to what is said about the forgiveness of the sins of believers. Others—and they are the majority of the Reformed theologians—hold that justification is an *actus individuus et simul totus*, that is, an indivisible act that occurs only once. This latter view is certainly the only tenable one, and for the following reasons:

1. Scripture itself nowhere says that the judicial act of God, which it calls justification, would be capable of repetition. Rather, it always presents justification as occurring at one point in time. As there is one predestination, one calling, one glorification, so there is also only one justification, and this stands between the other acts of the order of salvation (Rom 8:30), of which it is certain and generally agreed that they occur but once.

2. The idea of sonship implies that we cannot lose the state of justification once we have obtained it. A son can certainly sin and transgress against his father, but he does not therefore cease to be a son. By adoption as children, the legal position of believers in relation to God is loosed once for all from their own doing and working. Note: not their moral position but their legal position. A believer remains under the moral law, and for him every transgression of it is sin, which must be

confessed. But his status before God is no longer determined by those things.

3. If justification must be constantly repeated, then it is not clear how a sinner could ever come to be in a state of being justified. In each fraction of a second a new sin is committed; there is never a sinless moment in the life of believers. They are therefore, according to this view, repeatedly outside of justification and never within it. Their life is a matter of constantly becoming justified and never being justified. This differs considerably from the situation of one justified as that is portrayed for us by Scripture in Romans 5:1 and 8:33–34.

4. It will naturally not do to say that one does not need a new justification for all sins committed after the first justification, but only for those that occur in the consciousness and so are confessed. The consciousness of sin can never be made such a basis for distinguishing. One could with as much right maintain that in the so-called first justification all those sins were forgiven that appear in the consciousness.

5. One might say that it is an absurd idea that future sins, which are not yet committed, would be forgiven. But this idea contains nothing absurd if one only considers that for the Judge who pronounces forgiveness, the record of sins, their guilt, does not lie hidden in the darkness of the future but in the full light of His divine omniscience. Furthermore, it cannot be more absurd to forgive sins in advance than to atone for sins in advance. The latter has taken place in Christ. He bore millions of sins that were not yet perpetrated and for which the perpetrators were not yet in existence. This is possible because for God's eternal view all that, too, was present.

6. The testimony of Scripture is that *all* our sins are forgiven by the imputation of the merits of Christ (Col 2:13), that nothing more can be charged against the elect of God (John 5:24; Rom 8:33–34; cf. also v. 1, according to which there is no longer any condemnation for those who are in Christ Jesus). The same thing holds for the second aspect of justification. Not a part of the rights is granted to us, but at once in their

entirety. In Ephesians 1:3, it is said that we are blessed with *all* spiritual blessings in Christ. Also, it is completely unthinkable that the one Christ, who surely becomes ours in justification, would only be imparted to us by degrees and in parts. We receive Him completely, and therefore our justification must be complete from the outset.

19. *What, then, is the correct view regarding the state of the believer after he is once justified?*

In justification, all sins—past, present, and future—are forgiven at once with regard to the liability to punishment or the curse of the law, under which those sins stand. In this sense, the forgiveness of sins precedes the committing of sins (Psa 103:3–4). Still, sin as it actually exists certainly retains its character as sin as far as its inherent character is concerned. If this were to be removed, then the law of God would have to be abrogated and sinners would be *ex legis* (outside the law)—something that would be antinomianism and is contradicted by Scripture and experience alike. Moreover, when the consciousness of sin awakens in the believer, again and again there must be a renewed application of justification to the conscience. To that extent, one can say that justification is repeated. In the forum of heaven or before God it occurs only once, but the application of this single pronouncement to the conscience occurs again and again in renewal. Scripture calls that the forgiveness of sins (1 John 1:9; Matt 6:12; 1 John 2:1). At the same time, however, resident in this forgiveness is the consciousness that it is an application of the absolute justification that is granted with the first exercise of faith. The believer does not regard himself as fallen away from Christ, but makes use of the Mediator, who all along has been his possession. "We *have* an advocate," John says [1 John 2:1]—not, "We *obtain* Him." Hence some say: In justification future sins are not forgiven *explicite* [explicitly] and *formaliter* [formally], but *vertualiter*, that is, in principle and potentially. In initial justification resides the root of all subsequent forgiveness of guilt, so that in any case it is wrong to make a coordinated series of justifications. One cannot say that the initial forgiveness of sins that occurs in justification proper is as dependent on later forgiveness as vice versa.

20. *Does the second aspect of justification also have a retroactive purpose?*

In general, one can say that this aspect looks forward to the future insofar as it grants the right to the inheritance. However, insofar as the principles of that inheritance are already given prior to justification, it also reaches backward. The believer is already regenerate and converted. In his justification he learns to see and to confess that this, too, has been given him on the basis of the merits of Christ imputed to him in justification.

21. *What is the relationship between faith and justification?*

Opinions diverge considerably on this question. Naturally, those opinions must be set aside that rest on an erroneous conception of justification itself:

a) The Roman Catholic view that faith formed by love, being infused into us in first justification, enables us to merit eternal life by doing good works.

b) The Socinian view that faith includes obedience to the commandments of Christ.

c) The Remonstrant view that here faith counts insofar as it produces good works and is their root.

d) The view of the Rationalists of varying shades that in justification faith functions as the inward attitude demanded by God in antithesis to outward acts.

e) The view of many recent theologians that in a mystical manner faith is the principle of the life of Christ in us. This life of Christ, then, is the ground of our justification, not as imputed to us but rather as transplanted in us. This transplantation or overflow is certainly not yet complete, but still it is potentially present by faith. From this conception, then, naturally flows a falsification of the concept of faith as well as a falsification of the concept of justification. The former is divested of its conscious character and ethicized, mysticized, and made into a life within man. All who make the imputation of the merits of the Mediator dependent on mystical union, as discussed above, move in this direction; so, for example, Ebrard.

All these views mentioned so far agree in denying the imputation of the merits of Christ as the sole basis of justification. But even after eliminating these errors, a difference of opinion still remains among adherents of the orthodox doctrine regarding the role of faith in justification. Various terms have been proposed and used; for example: instrument, condition, *conditio sine qua non*, preparation in the subject, etc.

The term *causa instrumentalis* [instrumental cause] was at first generally in use freely. Later, that was otherwise. It was said that the expression "instrument of justification" was not found in Scripture. This in itself is not sufficient for rejecting the term, for there are more theological terms that are not used in Scripture and that we would be loath to do without. Further, it was said that if faith is the instrument of justification, then the question arises, "Whose instrument?" Naturally, either God's or ours. It cannot be the former, for faith is not an activity of God but an activity of man. Neither can it be the latter, for what is in us can never be an instrument of an act of God. To say that by our believing we cooperate instrumentally with God in bringing about justification appears to denigrate the honor of God.

Against these objections it must be observed:

a) That Scripture in fact says that we are justified πίστει (Rom 3:28); we are justified διὰ πίστεως (Rom 3:22, 30; Eph 2:8). These expressions cannot be understood other than in an instrumental sense. Here the dative case is evidently *casus instrumentalis* [an instrumental dative]. According to Greek usage it cannot have another meaning. And that this is not accidental is clear from the further description διὰ τῆς πίστεως [e.g., Rom 3:30]. *Never* is it said, on the other hand, that we are justified διὰ τὴν πίστιν, "on account of our faith."

b) From this it is sufficiently clear that faith has a certain instrumentality in justification. But one may go still further and must even say: Faith appears as an instrument of God in justification. Scripture also states that explicitly: "inasmuch as God is one, who will justify the circumcised by faith and the uncircumcised through faith" (Rom 8:30). Thus there is a sense in which one may say that God justifies us by the instrumentality of faith.

c) No less can it be said that faith appears here as instrument on our side, used by a person who undergoes justification. Of course, this does not mean that by faith we become the cause of God pronouncing the verdict of justification in a physical sense, but certainly that insofar as God, when He declares us just, takes faith into account. If there were no faith, there would be no verdict of justification. There is a bond between the two according to the ordaining of God.

The question now arises, "To what extent can faith be *God's* instrument in our justification?" This can be so in more than one respect. In the first place, faith is the *indispensable prerequisite for justification*. In His sovereignty, God has simply established this rule: that He will justify no one on the basis of the merits of the Mediator other than the one who believes. Now, if we posit that there simply is this rule and also that God Himself acts in accordance with it—that, further, man cannot exercise this faith of himself but only if God works it in him—then it is immediately obvious that by giving man faith, God Himself calls into existence the indispensable prerequisite of justification, and to this degree He thus uses faith as a means to bring about justification. Faith is His means, since it is His gift. At the same time it is *our* means, since by grace He has granted it to *us* to exercise this faith. Both go together very well.

Further, it should be kept in view that, as an act of God, justification has two aspects—namely, the pronouncement in the forum of heaven and the application of this pronouncement in the forum of conscience. The latter occurs mediately by faith that focuses on the declaration of God made in His Word. In order for justification to reach its endpoint and also be proclaimed in the consciousness of man, there must be an activity of faith. Now, this is not the proclamation itself, but it belongs so inseparably to the proclamation that one may safely say that God justifies us in the forum of conscience by faith.

22. *In how many respects, then, does faith occur in relationship to justification?*

In two respects. As was described above in detail, it is—as knowledge, assent, and trust—the indispensable prerequisite of justification. Scripture appears to indicate that by the expression ἐκ πίστεως that occurs along with διὰ πίστεως. So viewed, faith precedes justification logically (not chronologically). But in the second place, there is also a point where assured trust becomes the means of our passive justification itself—or, expressed more properly, of the consciousness of this passive justification, its acceptance by us. That is what the older theologians meant when they said that believing itself is man's being justified. That is why they also distinguished carefully between different acts in justifying faith:

a) The *actus dispositivus or praeparationius*, "the dispositive or preparatory act." Meant by that is faith, insofar as it logically precedes justification.

b) The *actus justificationis formaliter*—that is, that exercise of faith itself by which my assured trust becomes an understanding of the proclaimed justification. This is "the formal justifying act" of faith.

c) The *actus consolatorius*, "the trusting or consolation-bringing act"—that is, the exercise of faith by which I accept that in the past all my sins have been forgiven and that I have been transferred to a state of being just before God, a doctrinal assertion as Paul states in Romans 5:1, "Being justified by faith, we have peace with God." That, too, is the language of faith.

Maresius, who makes this distinction, says further that in the first aspect faith *precedes* justification, in the second aspect it is *simultaneous* with justification, and in the third aspect it *follows* justification. Burman expresses himself similarly.

Both aspects must be maintained. There is an exercise of faith that assures me, "You are justified," and there is an exercise of faith that must precede justification. The danger simply lurks in this: that in describing faith one begins with the first aspect and leaves no room for the second. It is necessary, therefore, to emphasize the sequence in which the steps of faith occur: (1) faith with a measure of trust that takes refuge and is assured; (2) active justification in the tribunal of God; (3) passive justification, the announcement of God's verdict in the tribunal of conscience; (4) coinciding and merging with this, the most mature assurance of faith, the most assured trust. Naturally, by this it is not at all maintained that these four stages can be distinguished in the consciousness of the believer himself. It may very well be that he passes imperceptibly from the one stage to the other. But the logical order is such, and if one foregoes seeking the exact point of transition, one will be able to discern the distinctions involved.

23. How can one further designate faith in relation to justification?

As the organ that possesses, the *organon lēptikon* (ὄργανον ληπτικόν). This is meant as follows. By faith the sinner appropriates the merits of Christ to himself, and there thus arises in his consciousness a unity between Christ and himself. These merits are the δικαίωμα, the "legal ground," upon which God's pronouncement is based. It follows, then, that the sinner by faith makes his own a righteousness on the basis of which he can be justified before God. Faith justifies insofar as it possesses Christ.

This description has good sense and can even serve to eliminate dangerous errors. So, to say in general that faith is an instrument in justification always evokes the idea that different things collaborate in justification, of which our faith is one. An "instrument" usually contributes something from its own capacity by the fact that it produces a certain change in the material on which it works. That, of course, cannot be said of faith. The merits of Christ, the only ground of our justification before God, do not first have to undergo processing before they can serve as our righteousness. They are not changed by our faith. It is not these merits as material plus the form given to them by faith that justify. With this in view, one certainly cannot be surprised that objection began to be raised against the use of the term "instrument." That objection falls away as soon as we use the expression "possessing organ." This does full justice to the scriptural expressions discussed above, and to those texts that speak of believing as a λαμβάνειν (ληπτικόν derives from λαμβάνειν).

Still, there is another side to this matter. It is certain that God's ordaining is such that no one is declared righteous except the person who by believing accepts the merits of the Mediator. The question, however, is whether this subjective, accepting act is the real ground of the unity between Christ and us in the tribunal of God. One senses that this, strictly speaking, cannot be. That in justification God imputes to us the merits of Christ does not occur apart from considering faith, but still not on the basis of faith as a *per se* and unavoidable functioning legal basis. That we believe in Christ, viewed in the abstract, is not a sufficient basis to identify ourselves with Him in terms of rights. The basis for that is not in us or in any act of ours, but exclusively in an act of God. This act of God is the judicial act of imputation (חשב, λογίζομαι, *imputare*), by which the merits of the Mediator are reckoned to us for our benefit, credited to our account, and their fruits allocated to us as if these merits were personally our own. The certainty of this resides in God's act, not in ours. This is all the more striking when one considers that these merits are intended for us personally already before justification, namely, in the counsel of peace and in the satisfaction of Christ. There, of course, the basis of justification cannot be faith, but on the contrary, faith is the future gift of this intention. One must thus avoid viewing the situation as follows: Prior to faith, the Mediator and the sinner are detached from each other without any legal bond; by faith, a legal unity arises; on the basis of this legal unity, God pronounces the verdict of justification. Rather, the correct conception is this: Already prior to faith the merits of the Mediator were intended for the elect sinner; at the same time, however, there was a determination of God that the formal act of imputation would not be carried out before the sinner by faith came subjectively to the consciousness of this free, sovereign imputation. When this takes place, then, *on the basis of His free, sovereign intention* (which naturally is completely in accord with His justice), God pronounces His formal verdict that the sinner is justified *in consideration of his faith*.

It occurs to us that, for these reasons, a not-entirely-incorrect consideration underlay the proposal to call faith a *conditia* [condition] or *causa* [cause] *sine qua non* of justification. These expressions certainly exclude every possibility that one would come to view faith as the judicial origin of imputation. Still, it is not advisable to adopt and substitute them for the terms "instrument" and "possessing organ." They can lead to misconception on the other side, since they sound much too vague. To say "condition," moreover, can lead to thinking of a meritorious condition. "*Causa sine qua non*" leaves the issue of the relation between faith and justification completely undefined. It evokes the thought that occurrence is mechanical in this matter, as if we merely have to do with a blind sequence: first faith, then justification, about which nothing more is to be said. That is not at all the case. There is resident in the nature of faith something by which it can be this *causa sine qua non*. Where there is a *causa* at work that is indeed *sine qua non*, there must also be a genuine relationship. That two things constantly accompany each other must have its meaning. Such a *causa sine qua non* must be either a meriting cause or something like that. So that is also true of faith. Faith is the subjective side of the objective imputation of the merits of Christ, which is the sole judicial basis of our justification. By our believing we identify ourselves with this imputation or transfer; we approve it, accept it. By our believing activity with respect to the Mediator we appropriate to ourselves personally what God objectively imputes to us. Faith as a whole is thus a faithful image in us of the gracious activity of God outside us. And it is on the basis of this that Scripture conjoins these two so closely and even speaks of faith as being reckoned as righteousness (λογίζεται ἡ πίστις αὐτοῦ εἰς δικαιοσύνην, Rom 4:5; cf. Gal 3:6). It was a complete misconception and misunderstanding of the nature of faith when the Remonstrants deduced from this that faith, now replacing works as in fact the judicial basis, is reckoned to us as righteousness. Faith here stands for the object of faith. This can be because faith receives and accepts Christ, mirrors Christ, and places itself in Christ, so that it itself, as it were, retreats from view and only presents its object to us. Since all true faith flows out like a stream into Christ and loses itself in Christ, Scripture can say without danger of misunderstanding, "Faith is reckoned as righteousness."

24. What has been treated so far?

The judicial relationship *of the sinner* (*justificatio peccatoris*).

25. Do the theologians speak of still another justification?

Yes, they also speak of the *justificatio justi*, the justification of the just, and describe it as the declaration by which the person who has been justified by faith, revealing his status of righteousness and the genuineness of his faith in good works, is declared to be one who lives uprightly.

26. What should be noted concerning this?

    a) That without doubt there is a testimony of good works and conduct from which believers themselves and others can draw strengthened assurance that they truly are children of God, that Christ's power is working in them, and that they are increasing in living righteously.

b) That without doubt that testimony drawn from the life of a Christian can be joined with the *justificatio passiva* [passive justification], the pronouncement in the forum of conscience that we stand righteous before God.

c) That nevertheless, the word "justification" used in this sense takes on another meaning than that previously used. It now means to manifest as righteous; passively, to be manifested as righteous to oneself and to others. This belongs more to the application and the results of justification proper than to justification itself.

d) Some attach a somewhat different meaning to the term "justification" in this connection. Where there is justification, there must naturally also be an accusation, a charge. Now it is the devil who constantly disturbs believers and brings accusations against them that their faith is feigned, "as if it were but an artificial and white-faced mask." To this, God now declares, by the testimony of His Holy Spirit, that this accusation is false and in doing so absolves them from this fear of insincerity. This is the way Witsius, for example, sees it. Justification is thus simply the declaration of God to reassure our conscience that this particular sin is not present in us and in no way to base further judicial consequences on it. While for the previous view the *justificatio justi* [justification of the just] is seen as a manifestation of the *justificatio peccatoris* [justification of the sinner], here it appears more as an exoneration from the sin of hypocrisy. Moreover, this and the previous view do not exclude each other. It is only a question of the basis on which, in this connection, we use the word "justification."

e) This distinction between the justification of a sinner and the justification of a just person has also been applied to the Letter of James and used as a means to reconcile its statements with the declarations of the Apostle Paul. When James says that someone is not only justified by faith but also by works (Jas 2:24), he means, according to this view, that the works of this person have been for himself and for others a demonstration in God's name that he is in the state of justification by *faith alone*. Justification proper, then, is *sola fide*; its manifestation (which here is also called justification) is *fide et operibus* [by faith and works]. In support of this view it is argued that James cannot have in view initial and proper justification, since he cites an incident from Abraham's life—namely, the offering up of Isaac—that took place long after his initial justification; so, too, with Rahab the prostitute.

Others say no, James is speaking of initial justification, the *justificatio peccatoris* [justification of the sinner]. He means to say that this justification is not wrought by a dead faith. If someone has such a dead faith, in which works are not virtually present, then he does not obtain justification. That is expressed as follows: A person is justified by works, not only by faith. Abraham's faith was such a living faith, for *as was clear later*, the seed of works was in it. "*The Scripture was thus fulfilled*, 'Abraham believed God and it was reckoned to him as righteousness'" (Jas 2:23). That is, it turned out that the declaration regarding Abraham, "He believed God," was true, that this faith could indeed be called genuine, living faith, in distinction from dead faith, demon-faith, the antinomian faith spoken of in the previous verses.

Both explanations of this pericope from James provide a satisfactory sense and remove the basic contradiction between him and Paul. It is difficult to choose between the two. Both can be reconciled with the aim that James clearly had in view when he wrote in this way. His argument is aimed against libertines who used the teaching of grace of the gospel as a cloak for their licentiousness. They reasoned, as all antinomians do, in this fashion: Good works are not regarded as the basis of our righteousness before God; therefore they are (in every respect) superfluous—yes, even dangerous—and also cannot be ordained by God as marks of the genuineness of faith. According to the first explanation of James above, this apostle is zealous against the position just mentioned—namely, that good works cannot be the criterion for the sincerity of faith. According to the other explanation above, James is zealous against the basic error that lurked in the view of faith itself, not that of a faith that denies itself but that of a passive, dead faith, and in its passivity, self-centered faith.

In his Letters to the Romans and to the Galatians, Paul naturally had to do with entirely different opponents—namely, with Pharisaic proponents of salvation by works, who replaced faith with works. That is why his polemic turned out differently.

His watchword, though not expressed with the same words, is still in its intention *sola fide*, "by faith *only*." The watchword of James is *sed non fide solitaria*, "but not by a faith that is solitary, standing alone." The one watchword does not exclude the other.

27. *Is this* justificatio justi *[justification of the just] discussed here synonymous with the so-called "second justification" of Roman Catholics?*

No, it is altogether different. The Catholics naturally use the Letter of James to maintain this distinction. What the Reformed understand as the justification of the just is not an act of God by which He allots some reward to the sinner. According to the Catholics, that surely happens, and then on the basis of the good works of man. This Catholic second justification thus looks ahead; our *justificatio justi* points back. Theirs is according to merit; ours is by grace.

28. *Is the word* righteousness *and its corresponding adjective,* righteous, *used in Scripture of inherent righteousness in already-justified sinners?*

Yes. First John 3:7 reads: "Little children, let no one deceive you. Whoever does righteousness is righteous, as he is righteous" (cf. 3:8–10, where committing sin is the opposite of doing righteousness). Of the parents of John the Baptist it is said, "And they were both righteous before God, walking in all the commandments and statues of the Lord, blameless" (Luke 1:6). In some places it is difficult to decide what is meant: "standing as righteous before God" or "being righteous by inherent righteousness."

29. *Can this inherent righteousness ever be or become the ground upon which one is acquitted in the judgment of God?*

No, the covenant of grace excludes that. That this is still called righteousness follows from the fact that it is required of us. It is in that sense an obligation that we have toward God, only not an obligation that is considered in justification. A believer is obligated to fulfill the entire law, and he is not exempt from a single commandment. But he has come out from being under the law as a means of justification.

30. *Can you show that the inherent righteousness of the regenerate*
does not come into consideration with God as the judicial basis for
their justification?

a) This follows first of all from the fact that the active obedience
of Christ is imputed to us and the benefits of righteousness are
granted on the basis of it. If now our own inherent righteousness
were to also come into consideration, then there would be a re-
dundancy of judicial grounds—two where only one is necessary.

b) Inherent righteousness is imperfect in every respect and therefore totally inadequate to be the basis of our justification before
God. Inherent righteousness that is valid in legalistic justification
must be completely perfect and must be equal to the law in all its
parts (Heidelberg Catechism 62 ["… the righteousness which can
stand before God's judgment must be absolutely perfect and in
complete agreement with the law of God"]; Gal 3:10–11). No one
approaches that in this life.

c) This inherent righteousness itself is not a product of our own
works but is a gift of God's grace—a fruit, in turn, of the imputed
obedience of Christ. Otherwise, one would have to assume that
God flattered the pride of man by imparting an apparent righteousness and granting life on that basis, while in reality his righteousness comes from Christ—similar to the way one pretends
to a child that it has done and accomplished something when in
reality it has not done anything. God does not mislead believers
in this way. They know full well, as far as their persons are concerned, that they are justified *freely* (δωρεάν, Rom 3:24).

d) The polemic of the Apostle Paul is not directed in the first place or
exclusively against those who asserted that the works of the unregenerate person are his righteousness before God. In particular,
the Judaizers, whom he opposes in the Letter to the Galatians, certainly agreed that faith was necessary. But, they said, faith plus
the works of the believer are necessary. By contending against
this view, the apostle clearly expressed that he also intended to
exclude works done after regeneration. His antithesis between
faith and works is absolute.

e) The justification of a sinner before God takes place entirely by grace: "and are justified freely by his grace, through the redemption that is in Christ Jesus" (Rom 3:24). If a part of our justification waits on our works, then just to that extent grace decreases. No boasting remains for us (Rom 11:6; 3:27, Eph 2:8–9).

f) The opposite view confuses the two covenants: the covenant of works and the covenant of grace, legalistic and evangelical justification.

31. *Is it not true that on the day of judgment believers will be justified as possessing an inherent righteousness?*

a) The final judgment will indeed be pronounced on persons who possess an inherent righteousness. But this in no way means that this judgment will grant them eternal life on the basis of this inherent righteousness. Rather, Scripture teaches that then they will be addressed as blessed of the Father and as heirs of the kingdom prepared for them from the foundation of the world [Matt 25:34]—in other words, as objects of God's free love that is granted to them in Christ Jesus and with regard to His merits.

b) On the day of judgment the good works of the righteous will certainly enter into the judgment of God, as well as their inherent righteousness that has been given to them at their death—not, however, as the basis of their righteousness before God but as the marks of the genuineness of their faith. And that not so much for themselves, for besides the fact that they have already been completely justified in this life, they, for the greater part, will also have already tasted for a considerable time the blessedness of heaven. This justification on the day of judgment will thus be an open justification, a *justificatio publica* [public justification], before the eyes of the world. God will declare that these, His elect, first consumed by unrighteousness so that Satan could accuse them of everything, are now completely rescued from that plight and are freed from all the consequences of unrighteousness. Naturally, this will also include the declaration that sin has been completely removed from them, that they possess a perfect inherent righteousness and thus *can* enter heaven, but not that they therefore *may* or are *entitled* to enter. In eternity, too, the child of God will have no other right of inheritance to the benefits of the kingdom than what has been obtained by Christ. Perfect holiness in the glorified state always remains a fruit of the merits of the Mediator.

c) On that judgment day, believers will be granted a reward of grace on the basis of, or rather in proportion to, their good works. After God has once given this promise to those who are His, it will naturally be a matter of His justness to fulfill it. But this reward does not take place according to merit; it takes place by grace (Heidelberg Catechism 63; cf. also Heb 6:10, "For God is not unjust that He would forget your work").

32. *Is it true that this doctrine of imputed righteousness opens the door to antinomianism?*

a) No, for the imputation of the merits of the Mediator is not something that remains outside of us but has as a consequence our subjective re-creation. Justification is thus in a judicial sense the root of our sanctification. Where the former is present, the latter cannot remain in abeyance.

b) As far as the temporal order is concerned, regeneration even appears, along with conversion, before justification. No one says that he is aware of standing righteous before God who is not regenerate and has not received a new principle of life. From this it follows that his conviction regarding justification will also be governed by this new principle that seeks God's glory in all things (cf. Gal 2:19, "... so that I might live to God").

33. *What should we answer when someone says that in justification, declaring us to be righteous, God does not act according to truth, since in ourselves we are still full of sin and unrighteousness?*

a) God's judgment pronounced in justification does not mean that we possess a perfect inherent righteousness. If God said that, He would be making an untrue declaration. But He does not do that.

b) God's judgment would likewise be untrue if He imputed to us an imperfect righteousness of the Mediator as if it were perfect.

This would be *ex injuria* [by injustice]. But this, too, is not the case. Nothing at all is lacking from the righteousness of Christ.

c) God's judgment would be precisely untrue if He declared us righteous on the basis of our persistently imperfect subjective righteousness. On Rome's position, a justification according to truth during this life is impossible.

d) The truthfulness of God's judgment rests on the truthfulness of imputation. This is no fiction. In reality, God ascribes the merits of Christ to our account. To deny that this is a reality is also to deny the reality of the atonement, in which, conversely, our sins are imputed to Christ. If the Mediator can occupy our legal position without that detracting from the truthfulness of God, so also we can occupy the legal position of the Mediator, and God's judgment concerning that can be fully according to truth.

e) Scripture declares with emphasis that in this action, its paradoxical character notwithstanding, God is fully righteous: "so that He might be just and the justifier of the one who has faith in Jesus" (Rom 3:26).

34. *What is to be said to the objection that the Mediator as man needed his righteousness for himself?*

It is said that Christ, by becoming man, placed Himself *eo ipso* [in itself] in all the relationships in which a man is related to the law. Therefore, His active obedience was His obligation for Himself. It should be noted, however, that:

a) The righteousness of Christ imputed to us in justification is that of His person. This person is clearly a divine person (Acts 20:28). This divine person was not under the law, ὑπὸ νόμον, but was the law in His own person, the law itself. When, in freely humiliating Himself by means of His assumed human nature, He places Himself under the law, in this way He obtains a righteousness that is not for Himself but can be imputed to others. Galatians 4:4, therefore, says that Christ has been "born under the law" (γενόμενον ὑπὸ νόμον), in distinction from being "born of a woman."

b) In His work as mediator, Christ was entirely a *persona publica* [public person] and not a *persona privata* [private person]. That is, we may not regard Him as a man alongside of other men, but His significance was taken up entirely in His official calling. Nothing of what He was or did, He was or did for Himself. From the beginning on, His official significance rested on everything. From this it follows that there can be no thought that His righteousness was necessary for Himself.

c) The best answer to this objection will remain the observation that now Christ is certainly not under the law as He was during the days of His servitude here on earth. From this it is abundantly clear how "being under the law" was not something inseparable that derived of itself from His human nature but something that He voluntarily accepted, and therefore also lasted but for a time and ceased of itself as soon as the particular relationship ceased by which it was caused—namely, the state of His humiliation.

35. *In what did the error of Osiander consist in the matter of justification?*

Andreas Osiander (1498–1552) made a sharp distinction between our redemption through Christ and our justification. Of the former, he acknowledged that it occurs by the merits of Christ, but he denied that this belongs to justification properly called. The latter was understood by him subjectively in the sense of "making inherently righteousness." To this extent, then, Osiander went along with Rome. "To free a thief from the gallows does not mean to make a thief good and righteous" was his watchword. His divergence from Rome (and of course from the Reformation) comes when the question is posed how man obtains this inherent righteousness. Rome said: by the working of the Holy Spirit, who gives us *fides formata* [formed faith]. Osiander said: by the communication of the essential righteousness of God, from the divine being, from God Himself. In this lurked a pantheistic principle, and the rest of the Reformers were on guard not to develop their doctrine of mystical union in this direction. According to them, to belong to the body of Christ meant something entirely different, and to take into oneself the essential righteousness of God meant to participate in a mingling of being with God. The pantheistic origin of this speculation of Osiander also came out in that he made Christ, the God-man, even apart from sin to be the ideal, the perfect realization of God. God is disposed to become man. By the entrance of sin the course of the process is changed, but the terminus is not essentially altered. Adam was already created, not as the image of God, but as the image of Christ, the ideal God-man.

36. *Is it not true that in Scripture our righteousness by which we are justified is called "the righteousness of God"?*

Yes, this expression occurs several times: "For the righteousness of God is revealed in it [the gospel] from faith to faith"(Rom 1:17); "for a demonstration of His righteousness"(Rom 3:26); "namely the righteousness of God" (Rom 3:22). This δικαιοσύνη θεοῦ [righteousness of God] is either righteousness as an inherent attribute in God (Rom 3:26), so that it can be said to be revealed in the gospel or in the atonement of Christ, or by it is meant the righteousness of a sinner that obtains before God (= *genitivus objectivus* [objective genitive]), or, finally, the righteousness that is provided, effected, produced, applied by God (= *genitivus subjectivus* [subjective genitive]. The latter is the most probable. In any case, by it cannot be meant an essential righteousness of God, poured out or communicated. See Philippians 3:9, "And be found in Him, not having my righteousness that is by the law, but that which comes through faith in Christ, *namely, the righteousness that is from God through faith.*"

37. *Are there still other grounds to which appeal is made in defense of this false view?*

Yes, use is made of everything that Scripture teaches regarding the mystical union between Christ and believers. Above all, statements in the Gospel of John are forced to do duty for this pantheistic mysticism. Even the figurative language of the Savior, when He says, "I am the way, the truth, and the life, the light," etc. [John 14:6], is misused for this purpose.

38. *What consequences did the error of Osiander have?*

Some went to the opposite extreme. They began to be afraid of the assertion that it is the righteousness of Christ as God that is imputed to us and tried to limit the righteousness that becomes ours by imputation to His human nature. However, that likewise cannot be. If the divine person had nothing to do with it, then it would not be the righteousness of the Mediator, and it also did not possess that worth that it had to possess for the justification of sinners. The line between error and truth is not the line between the divine and the human nature. It is rather the line that runs between inherent essential righteousness and the adherent righteousness of merits. What is imputed to us is not a part of the being of the Mediator but an objective possession of the Mediator, the treasure of His merits. These merits were once in the Mediator—or, to speak with complete accuracy, what they flowed from was in the Mediator, namely, His passive and active obedience. Still, of themselves the merits cannot be something inherent, but always signify an objective relationship, a judicial pronouncement. That was also the case with Christ. He did not *have* His merits. He *was* His merits. Still, it remains true that the only way for us to have these merits imputed to us resides in what the Mediator Himself has obtained. But that, too, only means that those merits follow the Mediator to whom they adhere, and in no way means that the merits are the being of the Mediator himself. It is necessary to make these distinctions, which for many will perhaps appear subtle, since at present the danger of a confusion of essential righteousness and the righteousness of merits is especially great.

39. *What view do the Socinians have of justification?*

According to them, it consists in the forgiveness of sins and endowing with eternal life. Since, however, they do not teach a satisfaction of Christ to the demands of God's righteousness—indeed, even eliminate this attribute—this description must have a totally different meaning for them than it does for us. By justification, they understand that God, out of pure mercy and benevolence, gives us these two things. Further, they maintain that faith (understood as obedience to Christ) is the indispensable condition for justification. This, however, is not so meant as if God declares us righteous on the basis of this faith-obedience as its meriting cause. Faith is a *conditio sine qua non* [indispensable condition], nothing more. Socinus says, "So that we must be on guard not to hold the holiness and innocence of life as the effect of our justification before God, and also not to affirm that faith is the effecting or moving cause of our justification before God, but only the cause without which God has determined that that justification will not become ours." One sees here how justification is a sovereign, rather arbitrary act that has no further judicial basis than God's free will.

40. *What do the Arminians teach regarding justification?*

According to them, justification is only a *forgiving* of sins. This forgiveness of sins they see as identical to the imputation of righteousness. The basis of this forgiveness does not reside in the imputation of the merits of Christ, since they deny that Christ has brought about a genuine satisfaction for sin. What is imputed to us is not the righteousness of Christ, for Scripture nowhere teaches "that the righteousness of Christ is imputed to us, *but only that faith is reckoned to us for righteousness,* and that for the sake of Christ [*propter Christum*]" (so Limborch). And Curcellaeus says, "Nowhere does Scripture teach that the righteousness of Christ is imputed to us. Also, that is absurd. Surely no person unrighteous in himself can be formally righteous with the righteousness of another any more than a Moor can be white with the whiteness of another." The difference between the Socinians and the Arminians appears at two points:

a) The latter understand the meaning of the death of Christ somewhat differently than the former. Although not a complete satisfaction, it was still accepted by God as a revelation of his governmental righteousness. It removed obstacles that otherwise would have made justification impossible.

b) They substitute something else for the imputed righteousness of the Mediator, which the Socinians do not do. As we saw, Socinus protested against regarding our obedience of faith as the effecting, meriting cause of justification. The Remonstrants are not so reticent. They assert their *fides obsequiosa or evangelica* [obedient or evangelical faith] as the grounds of justification. A new covenant of works is thus established on the ruins of the old, by means of the work of Christ. Thus, while the Socinians no longer have what may properly be called justification, the Arminian justification is a legalistic justification.

The image used by Curcellaeus is, of course, completely irrelevant. Whiteness for the Moor is not a relationship but would necessarily be an inherent characteristic. No one can be declared white. For righteousness it is otherwise. That is a relationship. In the same sentence Scripture calls Christ sin, as we are called the righteousness of God in Him. This, of course, does not mean that He is made sin subjectively in the sense of a quality. But it does mean that He is in the legal position, the legal relationship of a sinner. *Sin*, therefore, has two meanings: (a) an inherent quality; (b) an adherent relationship. In the latter sense, Christ was a sinner for our sake, although to prevent misunderstanding it is always advisable not to make use of this way of speaking. But that does not mean that someone white was declared to be black, that a black robe was put on him and the pronouncement made, "He is black." The entire image of skin color and a robe is mistaken (cf. 2 Cor 5:21; Gal 3:13).

41. *Is it true that Scripture nowhere teaches the imputation of Christ's righteousness, as the Remonstrants claim?*

No, in Philippians 3:9 it is taught in nearly so many words that it is not his own righteousness that the sinner possesses, but the righteousness of Christ. Romans 3:25–26 teaches the same thing. The expression "faith is counted as righteousness" [Rom 4:5] was explained above by the nature of faith itself.

42. *What distinguishes the justification concept of the more recent speculative theologians?*

a) A disdain for the concept of "imputation" and of the "transfer of merits." This old conception is called mechanical, external, magic, unreal, and unsatisfactory. It is maintained that it leads to a fiction, as if the mind and verdict of God were not the highest reality.

b) For this old, despised principle of forensic reckoning, this view substitutes the ethical principle of the infusion of righteousness. It seeks to secure for faith its old place by saying that it is that attitude that makes the sinner receptive for the righteousness to be infused.

c) Not all have the same conception regarding the nature of what is infused into the believer and taken into him by faith. Some offer a completely pantheistic explanation for that. Others keep more within theistic limits. The former provide a repristination of Osiander's heresy, against which the Reformers expressed themselves so decisively. In any case, everything transpires entirely within the sphere of being and not within the legal sphere.

No place remains for the Mediator as surety. The Mediator as a philosophical intermediate being, to unite God and man, becomes everything.

d) Some recent theologians identify regeneration with justification. This is related to the fact that they, carried along in part by the pantheistic direction described above, make the mystical union (transformed into a unity of being) the judicial ground for our justification. Since, according to them, this unity in being originates in regeneration, justification proper must also take place there. This is Ebrard's opinion, who therefore also declares both propositions to be the same in meaning: Christ justifies us; faith justifies us. He denies that Scripture speaks of an imputation of the righteousness of Christ (just as the Remonstrants deny that) and wants to replace that with the scriptural expression: "By justification grace *comes over* us." And that will then be taken in the most real sense. We become united to the person of Christ through a substantial unity of life.

43. *What should be said to refute this most recent form of the doctrine of justification?*

a) This conception is more dangerous than the other mentioned earlier, since it presents itself as more attractive and apparently leaves untouched the background of the atonement of Christ. The pantheistic principle is at work in it in a more hidden manner.

b) Scripture opposes this entire conception as forcefully as possible. Faith is not the kind of mystical receptivity that is taught here. Believing is a conscious act, an appropriating of the merits of the Mediator with one's consciousness, not a mysterious imbibing of the being of Christ. The most unclear and nebulous conception that one forms of faith arises precisely from the fact that this idea of a mystical union with Christ hovers in the background. It is therefore most necessary to describe faith precisely and to analyze it as closely as possible, lest in place of the scriptural idea of faith another that differs from it totally be imposed on us. Here too, as always, vagueness and generality expose us to error.

c) In this viewpoint, it is true only in a figurative sense that faith justifies us. The receptivity to take in food does not feed us and does not provide for our growth. However, those who hold this view will have faith understood in this way. Faith, which is a subjective deed, is supposed to have this wonderful capacity to draw to itself the objective Christ with all His treasures and gifts of grace. Note carefully: Faith draws out of heaven and takes into itself not the merits of Christ but the living Christ Himself. This is a mystical and completely impossible concept.

d) The motive that prompts the formation of this theory, even apart from its pantheistic origin, is not an innocent motive. The imputation of Christ's righteousness solely in the judgment of God, it is thought, is too mechanical, too little real. But why? Apparently because in it man is not judged according to what he himself is, but according to what Christ has done for him. The mechanical here thus lies in the transfer involved. In other words, man can only take satisfaction in a justification before God that he himself has earned. That, however, is a holiness-by-works principle. Moreover, it cannot be sustained, for in any case the payment of prior guilt must be provided for by means of imputed merits. Thus it is either one or the other: One must either deny that atonement for sins is necessary, or here one must admit the so-called mechanical. Even through mystical union with Christ, the payment for prior guilt can never become our own in this completely real sense. Those sins are in the past and the merits of Christ are in the past; and so it is impossible to see how a connection between the two could be established other than by the act of God's imputation. Thus one sees that this protest against the external and mechanical results in a protest against the heart of the doctrine of the atonement.

e) The result of this modern view must be that man is dissuaded from trust in Christ and led to trust in himself. If in a real sense righteousness becomes his own, then he also no longer needs to go outside himself; faith and the trust of faith in the scriptural sense have become superfluous.

44. *How are they justified who do not arrive at a conscious activity of faith;
for example, the children of believing parents who die in infancy?*

For them one must assume that God's justifying act follows immediately
upon the implanting of the seed of faith, and thus upon regeneration.
Scripture, however, does not speak expressly about such a justification,
because justification belongs to the conscious side of the *ordo salutis*.
There can be no thought of consciousness in this life for children dying
in infancy.

Chapter Six

Sanctification

1. What words are used in Greek for the concept "sanctification"?

There are mainly five words, more or less synonymous with each other, even though, as we will see, there are certainly differences along with the similarity. These are: ἱερός, ὅσιος, σεμνός, ἅγιος, ἁγνός.

2. Which of these five is used most frequently in the New Testament?

The word ἅγιος. And it is just this word that is used the least of all these in secular Greek. There must be a special reason that this relatively unfamiliar word became the most familiar.

3. What, in the first place, is evident from this phenomenon?

That the concepts that the Greeks (and pagans in general) formed of the holiness of the gods differed greatly from the biblical concept. This concept must have even been so great that the most commonly used words to express this pagan concept were, by this frequent use, considered unsuitable to serve as the vehicle for the divine idea. Also, our [Dutch] word *heilig* ["holy"], one surmises, was first formed under the influence of divine truth, that is, after the Teutons had come into contact with Christianity. Thus, in its origin it is a concept of revelation, a Christian term.

4. *What was the main element in the meaning of the Greek words mentioned above?*

That of sublimity, sacredness, venerability. They completely lack, on the other hand, the moral element that, just in contrast, comes to the fore in Scripture.

5. *Indicate in general the meaning of the terms mentioned.*

a) Ὅσιος is used for everything that by divine or human right has acquired a kind of devotion. It is not used exclusively for religious things. It never serves to translate the Hebrew קָדוֹשׁ in the Old Testament. In the New Testament it occurs in 1 Timothy 2:8, "lifting up *holy* hands"; Titus 1:8, "temperate, just, *holy*, chaste"; Acts 2:27, "not to hand over your *Holy One* to see corruption." Ὁσιότης means faithful in carrying out the duties of piety (Luke 1:75); ὅσιος of God (Rev 15:4; 16:5).

b) Σεμνός (from the stem σεβ in σέβομαι) means what instills reverence and awe. It is also used of human things worthy of honor; for example, clothing. It does not occur in the Septuagint. In the New Testament it occurs in only four places: "all that is true, all that is *honest*," that is, all that is honorable (Phil 4:8; cf. 1 Tim 3:11; Titus 2:2). It is not used of God in Scripture.

c) Ἱερός is all that is divinely exalted, since it belongs to the gods. It is never used of the gods themselves. The word seldom occurs in biblical Greek: of trumpets (Josh 6:8); of the temple [Ezek 27:6; 28:18]. In the New Testament τὸ ἵερον is the temple—that is, the whole temple (not only "the holy place"), with everything that belongs to it, including the forecourts (1 Cor 9:13); "the Holy Scriptures" (2 Tim 3:15). The meaning is thus entirely external, apart from any moral quality.

d) Ἅγιος is not used by the Greeks for *either* gods or men. It means that which is an object of religious veneration (from ἅζομαι). The Septuagint chose it for translating the Old Testament קָדוֹשׁ. In Scripture it then became the basis for a series of new words formed from it, such as ἁγιότης, ἁγιωσύνη, ἁγιάζειν, ἁγιασμός, ἁγιαστήριον, καταγιάζειν.

e) Ἁγνός is used by the Greeks for both gods and things. In the former instance the meaning is "what must be venerated with sacrifices"; for the latter, "consecrated." In the New Testament, however, it has obtained the particular meaning of "chaste" or "pure" (e.g., 2 Cor 11:2; Titus 2:5; 1 Pet 3:2; also in a metaphorical sense).

6. *What is the derivation of the Hebrew word* קָדוֹשׁ, *"holy"?*

It comes from a root that means "cut," "separate," and thus originally expresses being "set apart," "separated."

7. *What is the opposite of this concept?*

In contrast to קָדוֹשׁ, "holy," is חֹל, which means "loose," "common."

8. *Is this contrast completely synonymous with that between "clean" and "unclean"?*

No. That this is not the case can already be seen from the fact that for the latter contrast the Hebrew uses a different pair of words—namely, טָהֹר for "clean" and טָמֵא for "unclean." Now the connection between these is such that all that is "holy" must at the same time also be clean, and all that is unholy is also unclean, but the opposite is not true. "Holy" means more than "clean."

9. *Is the concept of "holiness" merely that of "separation," completely undetermined, or is there an additional determination?*

There is a further determination. That something is set apart does not yet make it something holy. It becomes holy because it is set apart for God and His use.

10. *Is the concept first applied to created things or to God Himself?*

The former has been maintained and the matter presented such that certain things "dedicated to God" were called holy. But then it becomes completely impossible to explain how one arrived at conceiving of holiness also as an attribute of God. "Being-dedicated-to-God," applied to God Himself, no longer makes any sense, at least not if one has to think of its origin in this way. It is also completely wrong with such a significant concept applied to God so frequently to choose its starting point in what is creaturely. We, on the contrary, therefore say: God in the first place is called the "Holy One," and only from that does it follow that holiness can also be ascribed to other things apart from Him. Thus we say that the concept of holiness came from above to below, not the opposite.

11. *How then is it possible to speak of God as "set apart"?*

We must think of this as follows. With created things there are two moments present in the concept of being set apart, namely, a point of origin and an end point, a *terminus a quo* and a *terminus ad quem*. Whatever is holy is *set apart from the unholy world* and dedicated to God. Now it becomes self-evident how it can also be said of God Himself that He is set apart from the profane, the unholy, and determined for Himself. In this way, holiness can be ascribed both to God and to creatures without the word having to be changed in meaning.

12. *Is holiness a purely formal concept? That is, is there nothing in it other than the thought of setting apart without there also being the thought in what respect that setting apart occurs?*

This formal concept has a positive content also when it is being used of God Himself. Holiness is not merely "God's sublimity above the world," nor merely "God's power," nor "the consuming majesty of His being." In all these ideas, the moral element is lacking. It has been rightly noted that where the insignificance of the creature over against God is portrayed in the strongest terms, this is never taken back to holiness as a cause (cf., e.g., Isa 40:12–17; 45:9; 64:8). Conversely, when God appears in His holiness as it is described in Isaiah 6, then the thought that overcomes the creature is not, in the first place, "how weak and of little meaning am I." Rather, the creature feels seized by the awareness of his uncleanness and exclaims, "Woe is me, because I am defiled." For this reason, the angel takes the coal from the altar and touches such a person on the lips, an act that naturally must have ethical significance.

On the other hand, it is a kind of exaggeration of the moral element that is present in the concept of holiness when one has identified holiness and grace, condescending kindness. This conflicts entirely with the derivation of the word that indicates being set apart. One must therefore be on guard against both extremes.

13. *What then is contained in this holiness of God?*

   a) That God loves Himself as the highest moral good.

   b) That God as such turns away from all evil.

In fact, in God, too, holiness is therefore a being separated—a being separated from the world, but not the world in the abstract. It is a separation from the unclean, sinful world. And thereby it must be kept in view that this separation derives from a positive principle, since God seeks and loves Himself as the highest good.

14. *Is this holiness of God always manifested in the same manner?*

No; as it comes into contact with different objects, its manifestations are also different. This explains why such unsatisfactory concepts concerning God's holiness have been formed. This arose from the fact that people proceeded from a single manifestation of the holiness of God and wanted to derive everything from that. In this way not only one-sided but also false conclusions arose.

   a) Sometimes God's holiness is manifest in the judgments He exercises over the nations: "Who is like you—glorious in holiness, fearful in praises, doing wonders?" (Exod 15:11).

   b) Sometimes His holiness becomes manifest in the special adopting of His covenant people. By redeeming them and making them His special possession, and setting them apart from the unclean world, God has, as it were, registered His protest against the latter and created the core of a new world. God's redeeming activity is thus a consequence of His holiness. From this it results that one can think that holiness equals grace. This, however, is only apparently so. Holiness is at work in redemption, not insofar as it forgives sin but insofar as it removes from the sinful world and redeems from sin (cf. Ezek 20:39–44; 38:16).

   c) Since in this way God has especially united Israel to Himself and has proposed a holy purpose for His people, it thus also becomes a matter of His holiness to reach this goal, even through the failure and unfaithfulness of His hallowed people (cf. Isa 49:7 and all the places in Isaiah where, very significantly, "Redeemer" and "Holy One of Israel" are next to each other). God redeems His people *for*

His own sake, to display His own virtues. It can therefore hold as a consequence of His holiness that He seeks out and forgives and accepts them again (cf. Hos 11:9, "I will not execute the fierceness of my anger; I will not return to destroy Ephraim, for I am God and not a man, the Holy One in your midst"). In a momentary fit of anger a man would allow it to destroy his work, but God keeps His holy purpose in view (Psa 33:21; Ezek 20:9, "But I did it for my name's sake, so that it would not be defiled in the eyes of the heathen").

d) Thus, although righteousness can and must be seen as a direct result of His holiness, there are still manifestations of holiness that appear to stand over against righteousness, as when it is ascribed to God's holiness that He does not destroy His people because of their sins. After all that has been said, the reason will be clear. However, the holiness of God does not work redemption without righteousness being put into operation. For the close tie between these two, see Isaiah 10:17: "The light of Israel becomes a fire, and his Holy One a flame, which will set on fire and consume its thorns and thistles in one day" (cf. also Isa 5:16).

15. *With what meanings does the word* ἅγιος *appear in the New Testament?*

a) Except for a few citations from the Old Testament, one finds it used of God in general only in the Apostle John (John 17:11; Rev 6:10; 1 John 2:20).

b) The reason for this is not far to seek. It is the Spirit of God who is given the name "holy" in the New Testament, something that happens in the Scriptures of the old covenant only a few times (cf. Psa 51:11; Isa 63:10–11). Through the Spirit, God sanctifies His people, for the Spirit is that person in the Holy Trinity through whose work it can be said that all things are *unto* God, for which reason He is also called *Holy* Spirit (cf. Titus 3:5: "the renewing of the Holy Spirit"; 2 Thess 2:13: "sanctification of the Spirit").

c) Holiness occurs in an official sense for those who have been set apart for a special service: "holy prophets" (Luke 1:70); "holy apostles" (Eph 3:5); "holy men of God" (2 Pet 1:21); "holy covenant"

(Luke 1:72); "holy Scriptures" (Rom 1:2); "commandment" and "law" as "holy" (Rom 7:12).

d) Holiness is used in an ethical sense, for example, when it is said in 1 Peter 1:15–16: "But as He who has called you is holy, so also you be holy in all your walk. Therefore it is written, 'Be holy for I am holy'" (Eph 1:4; 5:27; Col 1:22).

It is this last-mentioned meaning that has its place in the doctrine of sanctification.

16. *From what two concepts, therefore, must the concept "holy," as Scripture uses it, be sharply distinguished?*

a) From the concept of *purity* taken in itself. Someone is called good and pure if, considered in himself, he has no pollution.

b) From the concept of *righteousness*. Someone is called righteous if either his own merits or the imputed merits of another cause him to be in a state of acquittal before God. Thus, righteousness not only means that there is a relationship of his moral condition to God but also that that relationship has worked retroactively upon him.

Holiness is to be distinguished from both of these concepts. From purity in the abstract, first of all, for holiness means a relationship with God, a dedication to God. To be holy never means something that one is in himself, apart from God. But holiness is likewise distinguished from righteousness, for it is an inherent attribute and not a status granted to us again by God. It is something that we have *in ourselves* and not something *in which we stand*.

17. *Is this delineation of great importance for establishing the concept of sanctification?*

Yes, since at present one is accustomed to completely losing sight of this element of consecration to God and to regarding holiness anthropocentrically. One thereby starts with man and assumes that to sanctify is to make someone better or much better. This idea is already excluded by the term. Once someone has gained a correct insight into the biblical concept of "holiness" in its original meaning, as an attribute of God, in its theocentric character, that person will find it impossible to proceed in such a humanly oriented fashion. The moral transformation of man, too, his subjective change, must from the outset be regarded from this point of view: It is for God and not for ourselves. It serves for God's glorification and to carry out His holiness, not to remake us for an ideal that would have independent significance and would bear in itself its own standard.

Thus, on this point, despite every difference between them, sanctification and justification agree in that both happen to us for God's glorification. It is not wrong to stress sanctification along with justification, for on that Scripture itself leads the way for us most emphatically. But it is certainly wrong to stress sanctification that is cut off from the root of God's holiness, that is not for God, so is unscriptural. That is what must be repudiated in the ethical preaching of our day. However, by no means is the corrective against such preaching a one-sided emphasis on objective justification and a neglect of subjective sanctification. True sanctification must again replace false sanctification. Once this happens, dead and deadening ethicism will be replaced by a moral earnestness that will express the warmth and ardor of true religion. "Be holy, *for* I the Lord your God am holy"; not only, "*as* I am holy" [Lev 11:44–45; 19:2; 1 Pet 1:16]!

18. *What is the meaning of the word ἁγιότης?*

It means holiness as an inherent attribute. It appears only in Hebrews 12:10, "He chastises us for our benefit, so that we might share in His *holiness.*" Thus it is used as an attribute of man as well as God.

19. *What does ἁγιωσύνη mean?*

This is also derived directly from ἁγνός and accordingly means "holiness." Some have wanted to derive it from ἁγιόω = ἁγιάζω and then also wanted to give it the active meaning of "sanctification" (as deed), but this cannot be proven. In 1 Thessalonians 3:13 it is applied to people. Rather difficult is the explanation that the word must have in Romans 1:3, "who is powerfully shown to be the Son of God, according to the Spirit of sanctification, from the resurrection of the dead (κατὰ πνεῦμα ἁγιωσύνης). Here it appears to mean the deity of the Lord as *Spiritus summe venerandus,* "Spirit to be worshiped."

20. *What does the verb ἁγιάζω mean?*

In general, this word means "dedicate to God," "take up into the fellow-ship of God" (said of God Himself). This, however, can occur in more than one way:

   a) By investing with an office, to entrust with a mission: "Do you say to me whom the Father has *sanctified* and sent into the world?" (John 10:36). Christ is therefore called "the Holy One of God" in several places (Mark 1:24; Luke 4:34).

   b) By producing the inherent attribute of consecration to God in someone. For example, "Sanctify them through your truth; your word is truth" (John 17:17; cf. 1 Cor 6:11); "And may the God of peace Himself sanctify you completely, and may your whole spirit and soul and body be preserved blameless in the coming of our Lord Jesus Christ" (1 Thess 5:23).

   c) The sanctifying of people, that is, performed by people, occurs partly with respect to something that is already *holy* (e.g., in the Lord's Prayer, "Hallowed be your name"), partly with respect to something that must still be devoted to God (e.g., 1 Tim 4:5). In the first instance, it means that the holiness of something must come to expression in word and deed and in all of life.

   d) Sanctification also occurs in a special sense, namely, of the Mediator of the covenant of grace. "Because both He who sancti-fies and those who are sanctified are all from one" (Heb 2:11); "So that He might sanctify her, having cleansed her with the washing of the waters by the word" (Eph 5:26); "In whose will we are sanc-tified through the offering of the body of Christ, taken place once for all" (Heb 10:10).

      One could gather from these passages that sanctifying is equivalent to atoning or making satisfaction, since sanctifying is brought into connection with sacrifice and blood. This, however, is not so. Sanctifying here amounts to obtaining an objective state through sacrifice. Believers are therefore sanctified in principle by the satisfaction of Christ; their sanctification is firm in Him, as will be argued later. From Hebrews 9:14 it appears that a sub-jective cleansing belongs with this sanctification, that therefore it cannot be identified with justification.

e) Finally, it is also said of the Mediator that He sanctifies Himself for His own (John 17:19). This, of course, is not to be understood as a change in the Savior, as if this sanctification presupposes a previous lack of holiness, but as the consecration of His life in mediatorial obedience (passive and active) to God. This was an official holiness that is the basis of the sanctification of believers but must not be confused with it.

21. *What is the meaning of the word* ἁγιασμός?

It means "sanctification" and is the proper Greek word for what we call sanctification. But now the question arises whether the word is to be taken actively or passively—that is, whether it means the act of sanctifying or undergoing this act, being made holy. Both senses appear to be the case: active in 1 Thessalonians 4:3, "For this is the will of God, your sanctification, that you abstain from fornication"; also, "in the sanctification of the Spirit" (2 Thess 2:13; 1 Pet 1:2); on the other hand, certainly passive in Romans 6:19, "in order to be of service ... for sanctification," and so in other passages.

22. *How do you define sanctification?*

The gracious work of God whereby, under the immediate operation of the Holy Spirit, the justified believer is renewed by degrees in his whole nature, so that Christ is formed in him and he lives for God in good works.

23. *Is it correct to say that the righteousness of the Mediator is imputed to us in justification and infused in sanctification?*

Although there is certainly a working of Christ in us through the Holy Spirit in sanctification, this formula could give rise to misunderstanding. In any case, it is not the same righteousness of Christ that occurs in its two parts. When I speak of an imputed righteousness of the Mediator, then I mean that righteousness that He obtained by means of His suffering and dying and obedience *in the state of humiliation*—not, however, the righteousness of life of the human nature of Christ, that is, that Christ in His human nature now possesses. The latter is not imputed to me. And, conversely, the former cannot be infused into me; it can only be reckoned to me. Really, one cannot even say that the righteousness in which Christ now lives is infused into me. This always rests on a more-or-less unclear mystical conception. It is not the personal righteousness of Christ that is infused into the believer, for, as an inherent quality, righteousness cannot be detached from the person.

In 1 Corinthians 1:30, where the apostle enumerates what we have in Christ, there is no mention that Christ would be our holiness (ἁγιωσύνη or ἁγιότης), but it is simply said that He is our *sanctification* (ἁγιασμός).

24. Is then no "holiness" of Christ imputed to us?

Yes; by that term, if one wishes, one can designate His active obedience, imputed to us in justification. As our [Heidelberg] Catechism states in the answer to question 60, "How are you righteous before God? ... God grants and imputes to me the perfect satisfaction, righteousness, and holiness of Christ," etc. In this sense, one may thus then say that Christ is not only our sanctification but also our *holiness* before God.

25. Is sanctification something that occurs in the judicial sphere or does it have reference to a subjective change in the disposition of man?

The latter is the case, as was explained in detail above in the distinction between it and justification.

26. Does sanctification occur in the conscious level of the life of believers or below that level in depth?

It occurs below the level of conscious life and works out of the regenerate root of the soul on its dispositions and inclinations to sanctify them.

27. Is sanctification a mediate or immediate work?

As it takes place below the consciousness, it is primarily an immediate work. That, however, does not take away from the fact that in its manifestation it is tied by God to the use of certain means.

28. Does God Himself work in sanctification or is it man who does the work?

God is the author of sanctification and not man. The latter can only be maintained by proponents of so-called free will. Here again, however, it must be noted that the outward manifestation of this sanctification is not apart from means that the believer has at his disposal.

29. *Is sanctification a work that occurs all at once or is it subject to a long passage of time?*

In the normal course of things, sanctification covers a long period of time. It can happen, however, that it is completed in a single moment, namely where regeneration-conversion and temporal death coincide, or at least where the latter quickly follows the former. Because it is certain that with the death of believers, or rather immediately after their death, their sanctification is complete, then it must follow that in such cases it is immediately perfect in its full extent. It then takes on the nature of a critical transformation in place of a gradual process. And even where gradual sanctification has preceded, temporal death still always retains the character of a crisis.

30. *What is the relationship between justification and sanctification?*

a) Justification precedes. That is the sequence in the covenant of grace, by which it is distinguished from the covenant of works. Adam, as he was in the covenant of works, was perfectly holy; in all his characteristics and inclinations there was perfect devotion to God. Still, on the basis of this perfect holiness, righteousness had first to be acquired by Adam; his condition expressing itself in works would be indicative of his state, of his righteousness. In the covenant of grace, this is reversed. Here, by faith, the sinner is first transferred into the state of righteousness, so that he is much further than Adam before the fall; inasmuch as Adam's state was not secure, the sinner's is. And now, following on this righteousness, the state of holiness appears, produced through the work of sanctification. In this respect, the justified believer is not above but below Adam, for in him is unholiness, as sanctification continually presupposes.

In the Letter to the Romans there is this sequence: first justification, then sanctification, indicated by the successive treatment of both parts—chapters 1 and 2, sin; chapters 3-5, justification; chapters 6-7, sanctification.

b) The legal ground for sanctification lies in justification. Sanctification must be viewed as a gift. It belongs to those things that God can require of us, which, however, we are still not able to produce, and which are now, through the merits of Christ, produced in us through the grace of God. For this reason, as indicated above, sanctification is more than once connected with the suffering of Christ, His blood.

c) Justification excludes that in our sanctification there could ever be any mention of obtaining rights to eternal life. Sanctification remains completely outside the legal sphere. Justification has completely taken over this sphere for itself, so that nothing remains for sanctification.

d) Conversely, justification remains completely outside of our being, and therefore may never contest the distinctive task of sanctification. To stand righteous before God is not enough; the believer must and also will be holy before God. All traces and remnants of sin must be removed from him, the pollution completely purged, as well as the guilt entirely wiped out.

31. *What connection and what difference is there between regeneration and sanctification?*

a) Regeneration happens all at once. A person cannot be more or less regenerated. He is, or he is not. Sanctification happens gradually, and there are degrees.

b) Nevertheless, regeneration is the beginning of sanctification; Philippians 1:6, "Being confident of this, that He who has begun in you a good work shall *complete* it at the day of Jesus Christ." All the sanctifying of our nature takes place in connection with the new principle of life that God has produced in regeneration.

32. *What relationship is there between initial conversion and sanctification?*

Conversion is the first outward manifestation of sanctification, just as continuing conversion may be called its renewed manifestation.

33. *What is the nature of sanctification?*

Sanctification has a *supernatural character*. Many think of sanctification as if it is taken up with awakening, activating, drawing out and exercising the principles of grace present in the heart as that happens in an external, persuasive manner by presenting motives. Sanctification would then be a kind of spiritual pedagogy, and God would then deal with believers as a schoolmaster treats his pupils when he seeks to develop their intellectual and moral life. Now, the great difference lies in the fact that the schoolmaster cannot inwardly touch the child's soul and expressions of life. He must confine himself to gaining access to the child's life along conscious routes. As a result, he can introduce nothing specifically new into the child, but only develop what is already present in principle. At the most, by the exercise of the better qualities of the child he can suppress evil and silence it temporarily; he cannot eradicate it at its root. But God's relationship to the soul of the believer is totally different. He works from within and from the outside at the same time. Direct supernatural working and indirect working accompany each other. Therefore:

a) The principle of life, bestowed in regeneration by a special supernatural work of grace, is, with all the dispositions contained in it, strengthened and increased. It does not receive that strengthening and increase from itself. Already in nature, creation of life and causing the growth of life are two different actions of God, to which two different immediate activities correspond. God's providence in the world of living beings works directly. But it is likewise the case in relation to spiritual life. Growth is brought about by God immediately.

b) In connection with this, it is also the case that the remnants of sin in the nature of man are not just suppressed or silenced but are also eliminated, removed. The root from which they thrive is cut off. It is obvious that this also must be attributed to a supernatural work of God. The one thing has in itself no power over the other to banish it. That is above all true of sin. Its power is so great that it cannot be killed by mediate means alone. Only because God banishes and kills sin does the new life receive the power to replace it.

c) Thus, while the actual killing of sin and the growth of the new life remain the immediate work of God, there is also another side in sanctification. First, a difference is to be made between a disposition, even the most developed disposition, and its activity. Someone who has not spoken a certain language for many years need not for that reason have lost the habitual capacity to speak that language. But he is out of practice. And when he speaks, all kinds of defects will mar his speech. Similarly, if the believer does not exercise the dispositions of grace present in him in a conscious manner and constantly, they will not be able to be manifested in his life but will continually be overcome by evil dispositions. Thus, sanctification is furthered by good works, and has its impact in all branches of life.

d) As the believer can never recognize his regeneration other than as it is worked out in repentance and faith, so too progress in the knowledge of sanctification is tied to the exercise of sanctification. Only *then*, and *insofar* as he makes progress toward honoring God in his works, can a child of God have the assurance that he is sanctified and becomes sanctified.

e) This activity coming from the outside, too, may not be viewed as detached from the grace of God. It is God who works in us both the willing *and* the working according to His good pleasure [Phil 2:13]. The result is therefore that in sanctification God not only works in certain respects, but the believer nowhere works alone in any respect.

34. *Show from Scripture that there is a supernatural activity in sanctification, and that not everything happens through moral exercise.*

a) This is taught explicitly in passages that have sanctification taking place in the inner man, thus, from within: "that He would grant you, according to the riches of His glory, to be strengthened with power through His Spirit in the inner man, so that Christ may dwell in your hearts through faith and that you be rooted and grounded in love" (Eph 3:16); "to be strengthened with all power" (Col 1:11).

b) This is taught no less in those passages that view sanctification as preeminently a divine work. For example, "and may the God of peace sanctify you completely" (1 Thess 5:23); "now may the God of peace ... make you perfect in every good work ... working in you what is pleasing to Him, through Jesus Christ" (Heb 13:20-21).

c) It is also shown from the fact that the sanctification of the believer is viewed as a fruit of life-union with Christ. Because of that, sanctification immediately receives a deeper sense than one can connect with an external exercise. The Savior says that without Him we can do nothing, that He is the vine and we are the branches [John 15:5]. That relationship is, in the first place, organic, not moral. And there are a number of texts that derive sanctification directly from that relationship (Eph 2:20–22; Gal 2:20; Eph 5:28–32).

d) It is confirmed by the fact that in the first place sanctification is not attributed to the external means of grace but to the Holy Spirit, who works within the heart. The Spirit is therefore called the Spirit of grace, of joy, of love, of faith, etc., and in general the Christian virtues are called the fruits of the Spirit (cf. Gal 5:22–23).

35. *Who deny that sanctification is a supernatural work of God in the sense described?*

First of all, Roman Catholics, because they hold that through regeneration all sin, properly speaking, is eradicated from a person, and that there is thus no further need for a supernatural action for removing sin. They therefore must have sanctification turned into a purely human work, the performing of good works. And insofar as these good works flow from a purified nature, a meritorious character can more easily be ascribed to them.

At an even further distance from Scripture are the views of Pelagians and Rationalists, who deny the inner corruption of sin and so, moreover, have no need for sanctification. The good slumbering by nature in every man needs only to be awakened and brought to development.

36. *To what parts of man does sanctification extend?*

To the whole man as he exists organically. To soul and body, to all the capacities of both. First Thessalonians 5:23 sums up all the parts of man in the terminology of that time: "your whole spirit and soul and body." Second Corinthians 5:17 emphasizes that to be in Christ Jesus means to be a new creature in every respect, so that all the old has passed away (cf. also Eph 4:24). Further, one can say that sanctification extends:

a) To the *mind*. There is in the natural man, also in his thought-life, an inclination to evil, a congeniality with sin and an aversion to the good. Through sanctification this disposition and inclination is removed and the opposite put in its place (John 6:45).

b) To the *will*. In the unbeliever the will, too, is opposed to the holiness of God. But it is reversed, so that he now reaches out for that holiness with inward pleasure (Phil 2:13; Ezek 36:25–27).

c) To the *passions*, from which all selfish desire is removed and which are relocated in God as the source of all true enjoyment: "But those who are of Christ have crucified the flesh with its passions and desires" (Gal 5:24).

d) To the *conscience*. Through the working of sin in the soul, the conscience is defiled. If the soul is sanctified and cleansed, it involves a cleansing of the conscience (Heb 9:14). But the conscience is sanctified in still another sense—namely, because it is made sensitive and tender and judges us more dependably according to God's holy righteousness. A defiled conscience is in this sense a conscience that is so stained by sin that it has become impervious to sin, just as one can no longer see new stains on a stained garment: "But both their mind and conscience are stained" (Titus 1:15).

e) To the *body*, in which—insofar as it is the organ of the sinful soul—sinful inclinations have created a fixed form. This, too, is removed by sanctifying grace. This working, however, is largely limited to the crisis that for the body coincides with temporal death and the resurrection of the dead. This is also the only point at which one may say that sanctification is not limited to this life. However, life is, as it were, something that at death remains in this life and remains behind on earth in order to become completely sanctified at the last day (1 Cor 6:15, 20; Rom 6:12).

37. Of how many parts does sanctification consist?

Two; the same two that we find in principle in regeneration. As there was in regeneration a mortifying of the flesh at its root and an implanting of a new principle of life, so too in sanctification there is a continuation of this double work.

a) *The putting to death of the old man*, that action of God whereby the pollution and corruption of nature, flowing from sin, are gradually diminished and removed in believers.

b) *The enlivening of the new man,* whereby the same corrupt nature is more and more renewed according to the image of God in Christ.

38. Are these terms scriptural?

Yes, they are used repeatedly in Scripture to portray the sanctification of man. "Knowing this, that our old man is crucified with Him, so that the body of sin might be destroyed, so that we no longer serve sin" (Rom 6:6). "But those who are of Christ have crucified the flesh with its passions and desires" (Gal 5:25). Thus one sees that not only the death in general but most specifically the *crucifixion* of the old man is presented in Scripture as the one side of sanctification. Therein lies the double notion of (a) misery and (b) shame. In continuing penitence and sorrow before God, the dying of the old man enters into the consciousness of the believers. But from the other side, the struggle with the death of the old man is nothing other than the birth pangs of the new man. And coupled with the dying of the old is an inner aversion to the old. This is a proof that the holiness of God makes its impression in the soul of man. In it something occurs that, at a great distance, resembles the divine repugnance that is awakened by all uncleanness. In the eye of believers sin becomes shameful, so that they abhor it not only because of guilt and punishment but because of the pollution itself. This is one of the characteristics by which true sanctification is distinguished from moral reformation.

That the old man must be slain and crucified also expresses in a striking manner how at issue is not a partial renewal but a total, organic re-creation. It is man in his entirety. Thus this expression must never be taken in a personal sense, as if in the believer two "I's" are opposed to each other, but more extensively: The man in view is human nature, being human in its entirety. And the same thought is present in reverse: namely, that it is a new man who must be made alive. Here, too, it is not a matter of single expressions of life but of obtaining a complete formation, an image in all its dimensions. In the beginning, over against the strong, mature old man, the new man is like a weak, newly born infant. This relationship must be reversed.

39. *Can this putting to death of the old man also be described in another way?*

Yes. One can describe it as the removal of the pollution of sin. The distinction involved is that the putting to death of the old man has in view more the conscious side of sanctification, while the removal of the pollution also includes the subconscious. The pollution of sin is what stands precisely over against the holiness of God, what in the spiritual world answers to physical contamination. Pollution and guilt correspond respectively to God's holiness and to His righteousness. And in man, conscious shame answers to pollution, conscious fear to guilt. We thus see this double set:

Righteousness	Holiness
Guilt	Corruption
Fear	Shame

Even feelings of physical shame serve to portray this moral fact of pollution. As soon as Adam sins, he is ashamed and acknowledges his nakedness. And in the same way, the ceremonial laws of clean and unclean serve in order to impress this consciousness of pollution deeply in the soul of the Israelite sinner. All these things could only cleanse the flesh, but they pointed to a higher cleansing, that of the soul through the blood and the Spirit of Christ (Heb 9:13–14). Thus, there is something in sin that casts a spiritual stain on the soul, and it belongs to true repentance to feel this pollution as something detestable, unbearable. Whoever is used to bodily cleanliness and is aware that some uncleanness sticks to him has an aversion to his situation. This feeling accompanies the consciousness of sin to an even much greater degree when it is awakened in the sinner by God's Spirit. And being freed from this feeling already belongs to the cleansing of conscience, of which Scripture speaks.

The opposite of this pollution is a spiritual beauty and splendor of the soul. Not only cleanliness in a negative sense, equivalent to the absence of pollution, but holiness in a positive sense, as holy adornment, replaces the pollution. The Church that is sanctified is presented to her Savior without spot or wrinkle [Eph 5:27] (cf., for the portrayal of the pollution of sin and of sanctification in this sense, Hab 1:13; Psa 5:4–6; Jer 44:4; Ezek 36:25; Isa 4:4; Mal 3:2–3; Psa 51:7).

40. *How is the disposition designated that originates through the second work of sanctification?*

Scripture calls it "a living for God" (Gal 2:19; Rom 6:11). It is expressed very strikingly in this how true holiness is completely different from self-interested reformation, insofar as the goal of its striving is not in man but in God.

41. *Is there also a link between faith and sanctification?*

Yes, and it is a tie that is closely connected to what has just been said. Sanctification is one of the benefits of the covenant of grace, and so will also bear the features of the covenant of grace. It is true that holiness cannot be anything other than conformity to God's law, since this is the complete expression of God's nature, and that, in turn, is the norm of all genuine holiness. This, however, does not diminish that restored obedience to that law, according to the varied circumstances under which it appears, also assumes a particular coloration. Adam also, when he was in the covenant of works, possessed holiness. In a certain sense, one can even say [it was] a holiness in which faith in a broader sense was not entirely lacking. But this was a legal holiness, as that was resident in the covenant of works. It was accompanied by the awareness that this inherent disposition, this personal condition, was the basis for obtaining eternal life. For Adam, there was no thought of saving faith as the elect sinner learns to exercise it. After all, this faith, as we have found, is nothing other than that activity of the soul by which it separates its legal standing from all of its own doing and works and makes it to rest in the merits of Christ. Now, however, it cannot be other than that this form of faith must be at work in sanctification. Faith becomes the root of all Christian holiness, since at every point of our striving for improvement and conformity to God it fills our hearts with the thought that all this cannot ever be the ground on which we could stand in God's judgment. It teaches us true humility, which in the covenant of grace is inseparable from true holiness. Thus, faith is not solely something that accompanies sanctification, but something that permeates it; and that, properly seen, is the heart of everything in our holiness that is pleasing to God. Without faith it is impossible to please God (Heb 11:6). One is sanctified by faith in Christ (Acts 26:18). Our hearts are cleansed by faith (Acts 15:9; cf. also 1 Pet 1:21–22; Col 2:12–14; 3:7–11).

Thus, the question sometimes discussed—whether faith is necessary for our sanctification—must be answered according to what has been said. The answer must be decidedly affirmative. That there could have been disputes about this stems from a misunderstanding. It is feared that from this conception confusion between justification and sanctification can arise. This cannot be, if one only keeps in mind that in sanctification faith functions in a different manner than it does in justification. In justification it is the instrumental cause or the possessing organ through which we appropriate the merits of Christ. In sanctification, on the other hand, faith is the humble form of the soul by which all self-righteousness is banished from our inward holiness and from our good works. Furthermore, it is one of the characteristics of good works that they occur *by faith*. The relationship of the sinner to God brought about by the covenant of grace is such that the absence of faith stamps everything as sin. Whoever performs any good work without the conviction that all merit is excluded, by that already becomes the object of God's displeasure. We may and must therefore say: Faith is not only necessary for the sanctification of a believer, but the form faith assumes constitutes an essential part of his sanctification itself.

42. *Is this true only for the conscious exercise of faith, or does it also count for the disposition of faith that is produced and maintained in the soul through God's Spirit?*

It is true for both. As there is unconscious holiness, so there must also be unconscious faith that makes it pleasing to God. What does not enter into the consciousness is therefore surely present. A believer does not cease being sanctified if he loses consciousness. Between a sleeping worldling and a sleeping child of God is just as great a difference as between a David who sings psalms and a blasphemer who curses his Creator. Holiness and sanctification are not matters that can be repeatedly interrupted; they remain constantly present. And thereby is also shown the necessity of the dispositional aspect of faith for sanctification. The entire life of the soul, down into its unconscious depths, is for the regenerate person a life of faith. Faith penetrates and sanctifies everything.

43. Is faith present in sanctification in yet another connection?

Yes, insofar as it unites us in our consciousness with Christ and keeps us in union, which is our sanctification. Thus, in his faith the believer recognizes:

a) That sanctification, received by him as a gift of God's grace, rests on and flows from the merits of Christ. Faith not only works negatively by keeping us mindful of the unmerited nature of our holiness and our good works, but also by reminding us of the origin of both in Christ.

b) That sanctification not only flows from the merits of Christ as its *judicial* wellspring, but also from the living Christ as its fountain. According to the Apostle Paul, it is the life of Christ in him on which his life rests before God (Gal 2:19-20). After their regeneration, believers do not serve God in their own strength. They know that for every good work they perform, the strength of Christ flows into them and is at their disposal. Through His intercession, Christ is continually active for their holiness (John 17:17). He prays for Peter that his faith will not fail [Luke 22:32]. All this can only be appropriated from our side by faith. So, an activity of faith with respect to sanctification is indispensable.

c) The Mediator is even more than the meritorious and effecting cause of sanctification. In the third place, He is also the guarantee of its permanency. In the holiness in itself that the believer possesses, there is no basis for saying that it can never be lost or die off. Neither is there a guarantee that it will ever reach its perfection. Christ is the guarantee for both: for not becoming lost, and for becoming perfect. Thus by faith the initially sanctified one contemplates his holiness as it will be perfect in the future (Gal 2:20).

d) At the same time, Christ is also the *model* of our sanctification, the image in which we are formed (Rom 8:29), the form that must be born in us [Gal 4:19]. In Christ all the virtues and all the gifts of holiness are perfectly present. He is the living law, according to which our living must be directed. We must not form ourselves according to a self-formed ideal, but the Holy Spirit forms us according to the image of Christ as Scripture portrays it, so that we can also recognize the likeness and find the traits of the Savior in ourselves. From Christ one must learn how to be (Eph 4:20). Beholding the Savior is what is necessary for realizing this conformity in us, a beholding of faith, so that here too faith appears as instrumental for sanctification: "And we all with unveiled face, *beholding* the glory of the Lord as in a mirror, are being changed in form according to the same image from glory to glory, as from the Spirit of the Lord" (2 Cor 3:18); see also "the light of the knowledge of the glory of God in the face of Jesus Christ" (4:6); "everyone who has this hope in Him purifies himself as He is pure (1 John 3:3; cf. also Phil 3:21; Heb 2:14–15; Phil 2:5–7).

Although many now wrongly find in this transformation according to the image of Christ the only use that we could make of Him as mediator, this should not cause us to fall into the opposite extreme, as if we had nothing to do with Him as an example. Scripture explicitly portrays Him as such. Only He is not an example in that superficial sense in which older and newer Pelagians take it. He is an example who possesses the power of the Spirit in order to affect and impress Himself into our life, in order to reproduce His form in us, in order as the Head to have issuing from Him formative power that determines our image: "In every way to grow up in Him, who is the Head, namely Christ, from whom the whole body, being fitly joined and held together, through the supply of joints and marrow, according to the working of each part in its measure, maintains the growth of the body for building itself up in love" (Eph 4:15–16). This being given the imprint of Christ in us also has, since it coheres with mystical union, the secret nature of the latter, so that it cannot be fully conceptualized. But it is a reality.

To this conformity to Christ also belongs a part of the Christian life on which older theologians rightly placed great emphasis— that is, self-denial and cross-bearing (cf. Calvin, *Institutes* 3.8, "Of the Bearing of the Cross"). Scripture provides the occasion for this (Isa 31:9; 48:10, where it speaks of a fire of purification and a "crucible of affliction"; 1 Cor 3:13; "He chastises us for our benefit, so that we may become partakers of His holiness" [Heb 12:10]). The cross sanctifies:

1. Because it becomes the reminder and measure of our remaining sin. While not a punishment for sin, it is still in many respects proportional to sin. That, of course, is not to be understood as if the full punishability of sin would be depicted.

2. The cross, insofar as it is a deprivation of earthly pleasure, leads the believer to seek his only enjoyment in God. It removes from us whatever besides God occupies a place in our hearts; "I am crucified to the world and the world to me" (Gal 6:14).

3. Through the cross, faith, hope and all gifts of grace are brought to more than usual expression, so that they are strengthened and through exercise, developed.

44. *Is sanctification in this life complete, so that all the pollution of sin is removed from the believer?*

No; that is an error of Pelagius, some Roman Catholics (Trent), Socinians, Arminians, many mystics of all sorts (Pietists, Labadists, Quakers, Herrnhutters) and a number of sects at present.

45. *What does the Reformed theologian mean when he teaches the incompleteness of sanctification in this life?*

a) He does not mean it is incomplete in its *parts* (*qua ad partes*), as if only a portion of a holy person was created in regeneration. It is an entirely new man—but then an undeveloped new man—who is placed within the old, in order further to reach growth and maturity. A newly born child is a complete child, if it is properly formed; it lacks nothing in that regard. Similarly, at the beginning of his sanctification, the believer receives every capacity for holiness: a mind enlightened in principle, a will inclined to God in principle, and, in principle, a pure emotional life.

b) He does mean that it is incomplete in its *stages*. A "stage" here refers to the degree of development that the new man has reached. This degree can be more or less. It is determined in part by the influence of the remnants of the old nature that hamper growth. And, in particular, the new man, even with the most powerful development, cannot manifest outwardly whether in his expressions of life all sorts of sin overflow from his evil nature. Thus, the question is only whether already during this life the latter, the evil nature, is removed completely by sanctification. Here in the first place the negative side of sanctification comes into consideration. The positive side is perfect in principle and imperfect according to stages. The negative side is also given in principle, for at regeneration, and consciously in conversion, the old man has received its deathblow. But the question is simple: Does its dying cease during this life so that it can be called completely dead? To that opponents answer, "Yes," and we, "No."

The perfectionist no longer reckons with the dying of the old man, thinking that he has gotten beyond that and that it lies behind him as an overcome position. Of the two parts of sanctification that should always accompany each other, he lets one fall away. He thinks that since the old man has in principle suffered a mortal wound, and since it appears to have lost the power to assert itself strongly, that therefore it now no longer lives and draws breath.

A second error of the perfectionist is that he has formed a lowered concept of the demand of the law of God, as if it does not press for holiness in the depths of our living, in our heart, in our entire inner outlook, but requires only external purity of conduct. Many perfectionists do not call sin what, according to our view, is intrinsically sin. They will acknowledge that they frequently perceive the same thing in themselves—things about ourselves with which we are displeased and are humbled before God—but for them that cannot become a source for self-accusation, since their conscience does not cause them to recognize it as sin. From this it is clear, then, how it is not a matter of perfectionism but of a great imperfection in tenderness of conscience. Such people can call themselves perfect while in reality they are still so imperfect. Precisely this belongs to ongoing sanctification as a prominent part—namely, that our conscience becomes more and more sensitive about the least lack of conformity to the law of God, thus that the object of our self-criticism gradually shifts from the outside to the inside.

Roman Catholics give us a clear example of a perfectionism that first pulls the demands of the moral law downward in order then the more easily to attain to its full height—indeed, even go beyond it. Through regeneration, everything that is considered intrinsically sin in man is eradicated. But Rome acknowledges that concupiscence (*concupiscentia*), evil lust, also remains in the person baptized, only not as sin. Neither do forgivable sins strictly count as sins. The Christian is thus clearly subject to a law that is not the same as the pure expression of God's holy nature, but a law that will be satisfied with less.

The Arminian judges similarly. It is not the law of Adam under which Christians live, but the law of Christ, the law of the obedience of faith. Sin is not every departure in state, inclination, or act from that original law of God, but as Wesley says, conscious and willful violation of a known commandment. Faults, mistakes, and weaknesses are not sins.

46. *To what do perfectionists appeal to substantiate their doctrine of perfection in this life?*

   a) To the repeated commands of Scripture that make our striving for holiness a duty. If complete holiness were an unattainable goal, these commands, it is thought, would lose their meaning.

   b) To passages in Scripture where, without further stipulation, sanctification is simply attributed to the people of God: "and you are perfected in Him" (Col 2:10); "so that you may be blameless and upright, children of God" (Phil 2:15); "as many of us as are perfect, let us have this mind" (Phil 3:15).

   c) To examples of children of God who according to Scripture have attained this perfection, such as Noah, Job, Psalm 119:10; 139: 23–24.

   d) To the express declaration of the Apostle John that those who are born of God no longer commit sin (1 John 3:6–7, 9; 5:2–3, 18).

47. *What must be observed against these assertions?*

   a) That the command to be holy cannot prove anything since it is a command that comes to every person, to the unregenerate sinner as well as to the believer. The law of God must demand holiness of us. If, then, one wishes to infer from the command the possibility to obey it, one must do so for every person. That, however, can only be done if one teaches perfectionism in a Pelagian sense. On the other hand, as soon as one acknowledges that only believers can attain to this perfection, this argument also becomes useless.

b) When the congregation is addressed as holy or sanctified, this need not at all include that it may be called perfect in a perfectionist sense. It can be called holy because in Christ (1) it possesses the holiness of His active merits as imputed; (2) it has at its disposal the power of sanctification, and so is sanctified in principle.

c) Likewise, it proves nothing in favor of perfectionism when Scripture sometimes speaks of those who are "perfect." The contrast to "perfect" here is not "impure" or "unholy," but rather "immature" or "childish." For this, Scripture uses the words τέλειος, "perfect," and τελειοῦν, "to make perfect." These mean "to bring something to its full size or ripeness." It is applied, for example, to the Mediator Himself; He has been made perfect (Heb 2:10; 5:9). From this it is immediately apparent how "to make perfect" cannot simply be a synonym of "to sanctify." In James 2:22 it is said that by works the faith of Abraham was "made perfect," that is, became a mature faith. Thus, one must distinguish between "perfection" in this scriptural sense and complete sanctification. In the life of the believer there no doubt comes a period in which he ceases to be a child and becomes an adult. Then he must be treated as an adult, no longer fed with milk but with solid foods [cf. Heb 5:13–14]. The error of the perfectionist consists in this: that he confuses maturity with perfect holiness. By properly distinguishing these two concepts, many passages adduced in support of the theory vanish (Phil 3:12, 15; 1 Cor 2:6).

d) The Scripture passages that attribute perfection to the believer in the sense of no longer sinning have in view the new principle in the believer. One can in fact say that the new man in them does not commit sin. The Apostle Paul says, "So then now I no longer do it, but the sin that dwells in me" [Rom 7:17]. This is not said as an excuse, but, on the contrary, to show that the new life can even be said no longer to sin, while in the same breath can be added, "the sin that dwells in me." If one only had the first half of this statement, then one could also maintain that Paul was a perfectionist. Now we know better.

Now, however, while Paul gives prominence to the coexistence in the believer of these two principles, flesh and Spirit, in John, on the other hand, the believer is regarded as in the deepest ground of his life to be alienated from and crucified to sin. According to him there are only two kinds of persons: those who have the new life and those who have the old life. For the sake of that great antithesis, the phenomenon that the old man is not completely dead but still constantly dying moves to the background; his death sentence has been signed. Besides this, the same Apostle John, whom some have teaching perfectionism in 1 John 3:6, 9, speaks entirely differently in other places, where he no longer has this great antithesis in view: "And if anyone has sinned, we have an advocate with the Father, Jesus Christ, the righteous" (1 John 2:1). "If we say that we have no sin, we deceive ourselves, and the truth is not in us. If we confess our sins, He is faithful and just to forgive our sins and to cleanse us from all unrighteousness. If we say that we have not sinned, we make Him a liar, and His word is not in us" (1 John 1:8–10).

It has also frequently been overlooked that a literal view of the texts adduced from John by the perfectionists are not even applicable to themselves. What does the apostle say? "Whoever is born of God does not sin, because His seed remains in him, and he cannot sin, because he is born of God" [1 John 3:9]. It does not say, "The believer *can* be without sin" (what perfectionists maintain), but the believer is always without sin. If one now applies that to the believer's actual condition, then that would include that not a single regenerated person commits a single sin. After all, the apostle ties not-sinning to being born of God and having the seed of God. From this it would then follow further that for the regenerated, no apostasy of the saints were possible. Apostasy in itself, and that by which it would be brought about, can be nothing other than sin. Now it is the case that by far the most perfectionists are at the same time proponents of the doctrine of the apostasy of the saints. Thus, it appears to us that the literal explanation of the texts from John is impossible for perfectionism itself, and that perfectionists must also concede that these texts are intended relatively. And if that is once conceded, then everything supports the interpretation that we have given above and is against the perfectionists. To be born of God, having the seed of God within, not being able to die, are expressions that show clearly what the apostle was thinking.

e) Of none of the persons who are commended to us as examples of perfection does Scripture say that any one was or could be entirely without sin. We are told of the most prominent saints that they fell into sin. Noah, Abraham, Job, David, Peter, Paul, John—there is not one among them for whom blemishes cannot be pointed out. Of course, this does not yet prove that they were *always* blemished, but it is certainly noteworthy that, when it is reported of all these men how they have committed sin, not once are we presented with how they were completely holy.

f) There is, however, more than this. Scripture declares expressly that there is no one on earth who does not sin (1 Kgs 8:46; Eccl 7:20; Jas 3:2, "For we all stumble in many ways [things]"). Believers must pray daily, "Forgive us our debts" [Matt 6:12], must confess their sins to each other, again and again make renewed use of the intercession of Christ. All of this is inconsistent with the view that now they are already in a state of perfect holiness.

48. *Is sanctification something indispensable, like justification, or can it be dispensed with?*

It is absolutely indispensable. To deny this is libertinism and antinomianism. Still, sanctification is indispensable in a different sense than justification. The latter stands in a judicial relationship with salvation, so that salvation is grounded in it. Sanctification, on the other hand, is a portion of the bestowed salvation itself, a part of the way along which one comes to salvation. As is known, in the Lutheran church a conflict was carried on about the necessity of good works. Agricola taught that good works were not necessary for salvation and that the law should not be preached in ministering the gospel. According to him, true repentance did not flow from preaching the law but from presenting the gospel. The believer has nothing more to do with the law. Sometime later, Major lapsed into the opposite extreme by maintaining that no one could be saved without the performance of good works. Against these extremes we must note:

a) That good works cannot be said to be necessary as conditions for obtaining salvation.

b) That neither can they be considered to be means for retaining salvation. Our salvation and the perseverance of the saints are secure in an act of God and not in any act of man.

c) That, strictly speaking, it cannot be asserted that *good works* are the only way to salvation. After all, children and those who die immediately after their conversion are not able to do any good works. Thus the assertion in view would shut them out of heaven.

d) Scripture nowhere teaches that no one can be saved without good works. Certainly, on the other hand, without sanctification no one shall see the Lord [Heb 12:14]. There is a difference between sanctification and good works. The former can occur at once without any passage of time, as in a crisis moment; for doing the latter, time is necessary.

e) If someone does not do good works and allows the flesh that is in him to fester unhindered, then he does not have any reason to remain assured of his salvation. Scripture addresses such people as being in danger of becoming lost (Rom 8:12-13). Thus we see here the conclusion drawn from the lack of good works—that a true regenerate life cannot be present (Eph 2:10; Heb 12:14, "Pursue peace with all, and sanctification, without which no one will see the Lord").

f) The proposition that good works can be *harmful* to salvation (Agricola) is a dangerous error. It rests on a view of good works [that is] wrong at its root, and on their severing from faith and from Christ. To the same degree that someone exercises faith, he will be safe from the danger that by doing good works his salvation will be damaged. If one looks carefully, the proposition under discussion here rests on a principial denial of sanctification itself. If the selfish and self-righteous dispositions in man are not changed, then it would indeed be impossible to bring him to the performing of good works that could not harm him. Outward holiness, then, could not reveal itself without being polluted by inward unholiness. But Scripture does not teach such external holiness. It presents God's work of grace as moving from within outwardly. The best works are the most humble works, where the most faith is and is expressed.

49. *Where does the difference between sanctification and good works lie?*

 a) Sanctification is a work of God in us; good works are acts of ourselves for God.

 b) Sanctification is the source out of which good works come; good works are the waters that flow from this source.

 c) Through sanctification something is brought into us that was not there previously; through good works something is expressed outwardly that was already present in secret.

 d) By confusing these two, one makes sanctification into something pietistic, that man must now perform by himself, while God is said to be at work in justification. If this were obviously right, then of course sanctification would have to be removed from theology in order to find its place in ethics, for theology has to do with the acts of God. But it is not right. In their variety, good works belong within ethics and only come into consideration here insofar as they are in an organic relationship with the sanctifying work of God in us. But sanctification has always been viewed as an essential part of the saving activity of God.

 e) Good works are also in response to the holy disposition that is implanted in man by God. By being expressed and activated, this disposition is developed and strengthened inwardly. It is to be understood in this way when believers are urged to cooperate in their sanctification (2 Cor 7:1; Rom 6:19, 22; 1 Thess 3:13). However, a distinction has to be made here. In the natural order, where man has powers at his disposal, a disposition can originate through repeated activity and exercise. Something like that cannot happen in sanctification. Good works do not create holiness originally, although they promote its further development. The opposite is the Pelagian error. In this respect, holiness is distinguished from what is its opposite—sin. Through his first fall man can cause the sinful disposition, but he is not able by a leap in the opposite direction to restore the sanctified disposition. Desecration is his work; sanctification, in the final analysis, is the work of God. However, as actual sinning makes inherited pollution greater and increases inner corruption, so too the contrary is the case with good works and sanctification.

50. *What are the characteristics of good works, and how is this designation meant?*

a) The first characteristic of a good work is conformity to the law of God. As we define sin according to its departure from the law of God, so here, what is the opposite of sin. It is not possible for us to determine materially what sin is, nor to determine materially what good is. Something becomes good by its agreement with the law. Through sanctification, the regenerate person acquires a delight in the law of God according to the inner man [Rom 7:22]. The law is written on the tablets of his heart. And because it flows from this inward conformity to the law of God, it can be called a good work. On this basis, the Savior speaks of a good tree that brings forth good fruit (Luke 6:43-44). Thus, these works are not called "good" because they conform to the law externally. With "work" here is not meant the product of material lying outside of man, but the action itself as it stems from his consciousness, "working." Neither are they called "good" because in all aspects they were free from sin, and within them nothing wrong lurked. There is not one believer who can do such a good work. But certain works are called good insofar as they arise from the new man, and so in their point of departure they agree with the law. Scripture itself speaks of good works in this way (Acts 9:36; Eph 2:10; 2 Tim 3:17; Titus 2:14).

Expressed negatively, this proposition says that nothing can be a good work that does not conform to God's law and is not commanded by it. This holds true against Rome when it teaches that believers can do more than keep the law perfectly. By complying with the *concilia evangelica*, "gospel counsels" (in distinction from the *praecepta*, "the commandments"), the believer can gain extra merits. To this belong celibacy, monastic obedience, and voluntary poverty. In opposition to this view we observe:

1. That the law of God requires complete obedience and lays claim to all of human life. Thus all that is in fact well pleasing to God falls under the law. By this we are not saying that every good work must be prescribed in so many words in the law, but the principles and rules from which it flows are resident in the law.

2. That, conversely, when it cannot be derived from the law and thus falls outside the law, it also cannot be well pleasing to God and is not to be regarded as a good work.

b) The second characteristic of a good work is that it is done by *faith*. This was discussed above.

c) The third characteristic relates to the *goal*, which is the honor of God. In good works, too, the true character of holiness and sanctification must come out, that is, that the center of regenerate living is in God.

51. *Can these good works be considered meritorious?*

No, and the reason why not has already been demonstrated in general above. Concerning the meritorious character of good works in the strict sense, theologians teach that what would be needed for that is:

a) That we are not required to do them. This cannot be said of the good works that a believer does because they are not only an aspect of the gratitude that he owes to God, but they are also required by the natural relationship in which he, as a moral creature, stands toward God's law.

b) That they are entirely our own. Now, it is the grace of God, who puts what is good in us and draws it out from us. God has prepared our good works beforehand, so that we would walk in them (Eph 2:10).

c) That they are completely perfect, what again does not hold true for a single good work in this life.

d) That they are proportional to the reward—that is, inherently proportional. We know that God has instituted a certain proportion between the reward of grace and the good works done by believers. But this proportion is again by grace. The good even for

Adam in the covenant of works, the great gift of grace of eternal life promised him by God for his obedience, far surpassed his obedience in value. This is much truer of the good works of believers. If God granted believers eternal life for them (something that He does not do), as Rome maintains, with Rome it could still not yet be held to be *meritum ex condigno,* "by worthiness," or inherent merit.

e) That they are worthy of reward not *ex pacto* but *ex natura.* This is also not true of any work. All payment or reward takes place by covenant and not according to natural necessity.

[Perseverance][1]

52. *Can sanctification, once caused by God, still be completely lost?*

This is the same question as to whether there is an apostasy of the saints. To answer "no" here is unique to the Reformed church, since not only non-Protestant Christianity but also the Lutherans give an affirmative answer to this question. One may even say that through Reformed doctrinal development, starting with Calvin, justice was first done to the perseverance of the saints as a scriptural doctrine. Augustine, who otherwise was in many respects the precursor of Reformed theologians, could not accept this doctrine but, strangely enough, stood with Pelagius on this point. But still there was a difference. According to Pelagius, there is no difference in principle between the believer and the unbeliever. The former does not have a higher life that is lacking in the latter. There is only a different use of the powers that every natural man possesses. Augustine, on the other hand, certainly taught that a believer and a nonbeliever differ in principle: In the one, there is a new life that is lacking in the other. But even according to Augustine, that life can be lost. To be regenerated does not necessarily include remaining regenerated. One can be regenerated initially and then can return again to the position of the unregenerate. Yes, one can even be *elect* and still fall from grace—of course, not finally, for all time, but in order later to be taken into that number again. So, a result of this view is that also

---

1   Vos does not have a separate chapter heading on perseverance, but he treats it beginning with chapter 6, question 52.

for Augustine the believer cannot use his election as the basis of his certainty, simply because there are no evidences of election in this life other than being actually saved at the end. That one is regenerated no longer provides any guarantee for election. Thus one sees what a great difference there was between Calvin and Augustine, notwithstanding all the agreement there was. With the former, election has become the firm ground for the assurance of the individual believer.

The Roman Catholic church also teaches an apostasy of the saints. This already follows from the human character that it ascribes to the work of justification (for Rome, equal to sanctification). Whatever is in human hands naturally cannot be absolute and incapable of being lost. Next, for Rome, this view follows unavoidably from its conception of the Church and the means of grace. Since salvation rests with the Church and is distributed through the means *ex opera operato*, "by the worked work," in certain cases scorning or not using the means must naturally lead to being lost. By a mortal sin justification is lost; by the sacrament of penance it is restored. Whoever makes no use of this sacrament dies unjustified and is lost.

That the Socinians and Remonstrants teach an apostasy of the saints is well known.

However, on this point the Lutheran church, too, is against us. Faith is not compatible with a mortal sin. With Augustine, it teaches that there is an apostasy from faith, but not a final apostasy of the elect. However, the faith that the elect possess is not specifically different from the faith in many who are finally lost. For the Lutherans, this error is connected to their overall conception of the resistibility of grace. Man can resist or not resist when, through the mystical power of the Word of God, the action of grace impinges on him. Man himself settles the matter, makes the decision, notwithstanding his complete inability for any good. It would be nonsensical, then, to place the man who made the decision at the outset in a position subsequently where nothing more remains to be decided. For the sequel, too, it depends on him whether or not he will persevere. In their last period the Lutherans, as we have seen earlier, have gone over completely to the Remonstrant point of view and so no longer hold to absolute election.

Modern theologians for the most part also teach an apostasy of the saints; for example, Ebrard.

Over against these parties the Reformed church now stands virtually alone. Only Luther in his early period, when he opposed the free will of Erasmus, was untainted. True, there are also among most recent theologians those who deny an apostasy of the saints, but they do this on a pantheistic basis. It goes without saying that on such premises as this theology proceeds, there can be no thought of change. If the life of the Christian is the life of God in him, in a real substantial sense, infused into him by a mystical process, then it can no longer be expelled or suppressed; God does not let Himself be driven out by man. But thereby the doctrine becomes completely changed and assumes a totally other character.

If someone Reformed is asked on what his perseverance in the state of grace rests, then he will not answer, "On something in me, on the power and the capacity for withstanding of the new life that I possess," but, "Solely on the preserving faithfulness of God." Thus he reasons theologically, from God and His free election, on the basis of Scripture; not psychologically, from himself, on the basis of spiritual experience that he has gained for himself. Hence he knows very well how to explain when God's Word frequently speaks with warnings as if an apostasy of the saints were possible. Where this occurs, the matter is simply being looked at psychologically, from the side of man, and accordingly man is roused to be on guard against this psychologically possible apostasy. This is not thereby denying that from the side of God apostasy is inconceivable and never occurs. With modern theologians, these two sides now become one. God does not act as a free and self-conscious being on man's soul, but passes over with His life into man. The distinction between a theological and psychological viewpoint has then lost its meaning.

53. *What is meant when we say that there is no apostasy of the saints?*

That the regenerate life with the dispositions flowing from it and at work in sanctification cannot be driven out of the believer. Even if all the activities of faith would cease, even if someone would be robbed by insanity of the ability to exercise faith, the new life would still endure and his dispositions would continue to exist.

54. *What is the principal error of those who teach an apostasy of the saints?*

They confuse the state of believers in the covenant of grace with the state of Adam before the fall, as if these two were completely the same.

The difference lies precisely in this: Adam possessed a perfect but mutable holiness, since he was in a covenant of works in which the decision is suspended from the will of man; the believer is in a covenant of grace, in which God has made all things secure so that there is no longer any thought of vicissitude. For this reason, believers have a holiness that is imperfect but is still incapable of being lost.

55. *Is then perseverance something that adheres in man as a moral disposition?*

No, it is a gift of God's grace. As long as we look at man and limit ourselves to man, there is nothing that would make us suppose that he would remain constant. Life is certainly present, but it has no inherent attribute of constancy. It remains because God constantly keeps it present: "whom God will also sustain to the end, to be without blame in the day of the Lord Jesus Christ" (1 Cor 1:8). Hence perseverance is not something that originates by degrees and is acquired slowly. There are those who think that the believer on the lowest level of his sanctification is still exposed to apostasy, but that having progressed further, he has escaped this danger. In doing so, however, they suppose that perseverance is a disposition in man. Scripture always attributes it to God as an act of grace (Phil 1:6; 1 Thess 5:23).

56. *What are the evidences for the doctrine of the perseverance of the saints?*

a) The principal ground is the doctrine of election. If this is (1) an election to eternal salvation and (2) the sole source of faith and regeneration, it must follow that, therefore, where sanctification has once begun, it must certainly reach its completion. One could now still ask with Augustine if it is not possible to posit an interruption in the life of grace in the elect, or if it is necessary to teach its uninterrupted continuation. Our answer to this is that in Scripture the doctrine of election is not at all related only to final salvation but also certainly with the impossibility of a temporary apostasy. Scripture does not comfort us by saying: "Come what will, and although your regeneration is lost multiple times, in the end you will still enter heaven." On the contrary, it says: "God is faithful, and He will never allow you to be tempted beyond your ability" [1 Cor 10:13]. Be assured that no one can snatch us from the hand of the Father. Not, "Finally we will still return again into the Father's hand," but, "We remain there all the time" (John 10:28–29; Rom 11:29; 2 Thess 3:3; 2 Tim 1:12). It is not only that salvation is kept in readiness for the believer, but also, conversely, that the believer is kept in readiness for salvation (1 Pet 1:5; Rev 3:10).

One must also pay attention to the fact that Scripture everywhere presents the doctrine of election as a ground of confidence and trust for the believer. If this is so, then the possibility must exist to be assured of his election. But the only possibility lies in this: that faith and election presuppose each other, that the one points no further than the other. As soon as one says to the believer that there are nonelect believers, for him comfort is gone from election. Therefore, each use that Scripture makes of the doctrine of election as a basis of comfort for believers is a proof of the perseverance of the saints.

b) A second argument for perseverance is found in the immutability of the covenant of grace. As noted above, in the covenant of grace God also guarantees for man himself that everything is accomplished that must happen. Therefore, this is called an eternal covenant (Jer 32:38–40; cf. Jer 31:32–33; Gen 17:7). This is true for all who share in the essence of the covenant, though not for all who are reckoned objectively under the covenant. But this latter consideration does not matter here, for the question is about the apostasy of those truly *sanctified* (Heb 8:9–12).

c) The work of Christ as mediator, His eternal suretyship, is also a ground that confirms the perseverance of the saints—and that in more than one way. First of all, His suretyship is not provisional but absolute. He pays for the debt of His own. Now, if there is an apostasy of these believers, if they are finally lost, then either the payment of Christ counts for nothing or the one debt is paid twice. Next, at regeneration a life-union comes about between Christ and believers, as a result of which they form one body. To assume that a believer, one initially sanctified, can fall away, even if it were only temporarily, involves the unbecoming notion that members can fall out of the mystical body of the Lord, so that it is disfigured and desecrated. Insofar as the members themselves are concerned, nothing is impossible, but certainly not insofar as the body is concerned. Its beauty, its proper proportions, must thereby be lost. From all this it appears that in our union with Christ, He—not we—is the governing factor. It is He who lives in us. Turning off that inflow of life that comes from Him, as the head to the members, would have to happen from His side, which again cannot be, since He is faithful.

Further, Christ through His merit has also acquired sanctification for us. If now this can still be lost, then His acquisition would have been conditional or powerless. The sin of apostasy would then be a sin for which He would not have gained our holiness. There would remain in us a series of deeds that are not covered by the merit of the Mediator. But Scripture teaches that in all His work He includes us completely in every aspect of our lives. After our justification, there is nothing in which we stand on our own account. Even our unfaithfulness and our deviation with respect to Him are forgiven on His account, and by His power we are redeemed from that and sanctified (2 Cor 1:20–21; John 6:37; Gal 2:20).

d) There is a no-less-firm basis in the work of the Holy Spirit, who makes His dwelling with believers. Through His presence, there is in them a higher and divine principle that does not permit being supplanted by the stirrings of the old nature. In back of grace, as it has become their subjective possession and has become intermingled with their lives, stands the personal Holy Spirit, who cannot be harmed through their subjective ups and downs but continues His work with eternal power. The Spirit as comforter abides with believers *forever* (John 14:16; Eph 1:13). He is at the same time a seal and a pledge of the future benefits of salvation, and an earnest, the firstfruits to which the full harvest will follow [2 Cor 1:22; 5:5; Eph 1:14; Rom 8:23]. It would therefore involve a dishonor for the Holy Spirit, as well as for Christ, if He had to withdraw from His temple and to abandon what He had once taken possession of to a renewed pollution of sin. Therefore, not only final but also temporary-total apostasy is impossible (Eph 4:30).

e) The doctrine of justification automatically brings with it the doctrine of the perseverance of the saints. The justification of a sinner is absolute. It places him forever in the status of a child, covers both his future life in its entirety as well as all of the past. Now, if we must assume that there is a temporary apostasy of the saints, then from that it will follow that there can be justified children of God without any grace in their hearts, without any faith, without any union with Christ, without being subjectively distinguished in any respect from the unjustified sinner. This of course cannot be. The apostle teaches us that there is no justification without sanctification. We say: no continuation of the one, then, without continuation of the other. See Romans 8:33–39, where the conclusion drawn from complete justification is that nothing will be able to separate the Christian from the love of Christ, and from the love of God in Christ.

f) At his regeneration the believer receives a life that is, in principle, *eternal* life. Eternal life means not only what is communicated in eternity but also what extends from now on into eternity (John 3:16; 5:24; 6:40; Rom 5:4–5, 10).

57. *What objections are brought against this doctrine of the perseverance of the saints?*

a) First, it is said that the repeated warnings against apostasy presuppose the possibility of such an apostasy. To this we answer:

1. That such warnings, as they are directed to man, are meant psychologically and consider the matter from the side of man. From that, one may not conclude that apostasy really occurs with those who possess true faith. One could just as well conclude from the demand for faith that comes to people that it is within their own power to give themselves faith. Believers can no more give themselves supernatural grace than they can deprive themselves of it.

2. Scripture clearly indicates that if there are those who appear to apostatize, this is only *a posteriori* evidence that their faith was not genuine—that is, that it was no more than an apparent apostasy preceded by an apparent faith (1 Cor 11:19; 1 John 2:19).

3. At the same time, such warnings also serve to awaken believers to self-examination whether their faith is true faith, or

whether they are perhaps deceiving themselves with a temporary faith. They must examine themselves whether Christ Jesus is in them [2 Cor 13:5]. But to be assured of that also gives them a firm basis of certainty for the future.

4. If one remains aware that perseverance is not an inherent state but a constant act of grace, then it is immediately apparent to what end those warnings serve. They are intended and formulated precisely to cause believers to persevere. In this, too, God makes use of means by which He awakens us and causes us to persevere. Quite rightly some have pointed to the case of the shipwreck of Paul as a picture to illustrate this issue (Acts 27:21-31). The apostle first declares emphatically, "There shall be no loss among you of anyone's life." However, later he says to the officer, "If these men do not remain in the ship, you cannot be saved." But he uses just this statement as a means for the soldiers to keep the sailors from fleeing and to prevent a total shipwreck. In the same manner, God declares categorically already in advance that none of His children will be lost, but this does not prevent Him from directing extremely serious warnings to them as if it could in fact happen.

b) It is said that there are statements in Scripture that directly teach an apostasy of saints—instances of persons who in fact suffered shipwreck from the faith. Here one points especially to Hebrews 6:4-8 and to the case of Judas, Ananias, David, and others. Against this view, we say:

1. That the persons of whom such an apostasy is recorded either were not regenerated and did not possess true faith but only an apparent faith, or they did not completely lose their faith but only fell into sin temporarily, whereby gloom descended over their conscious state. The former was the case with Judas, who is called a "son of destruction" [John 17:12], whom the Savior knew from the beginning, of whom not once was it said that he truly believed. The latter was the case with David, whose repentant and believing attitude appears to be sufficiently present, even after committing his sin.

2. Hebrews 6 has already been discussed more than once. We recall only in general: (a) that in this passage none of the terms used necessarily cause us to think of saving faith; (b) that on the contrary, temporary faith is spoken of; (c) of temporary faith, however, not in the general sense but in a entirely specific form as was perhaps possible only during the apostolic age, accompanied by extraordinary gifts and powers and under the ordinance of God that their loss made further conversion impossible.

The context of the words is as follows: At the close of Hebrews 5 a complaint is made about dullness in knowledge. The Hebrews, who ought to be teachers, were again in need of teachers and needed milk instead of solid food. They were children where they could have been mature (= perfect). This, however, is not a reason to despair. If they would only leave behind the elementary teaching of Christ and continue on to perfection, then the future can bring them to the required perfection. The apostle himself progresses in this (Heb 6:3). And then follows (Heb 6:4) the basis for this progress. "*For it is impossible for those who were once enlightened, and who have tasted the heavenly gifts, and have become partakers of the Holy Spirit, and have tasted the good word of God, and the powers of the coming age, and fall away—those, I say, it is impossible to renew again to repentance, as those who crucify again to themselves the Son of God and openly put Him to shame.*" To repeat the elementary principles and to lay again the very first foundation is, in the given circumstances, useless work, for those who have sunk to that are not renewed again to repentance.

Now, one should note that it is not said of the Hebrews here that they were in this situation. They were certainly dull, but not apostate; the foundation had remained. Hebrews 6:10 says, "God is not unjust, that He would forget your work and the labor of love that you have shown in His name, as those who have served the saints and still serve." In Hebrews 6:4–8, on the contrary, no mention is made of the gift of grace that regeneration of the heart would presuppose. There is no mention of faith, of justification, of sanctification. This is most remarkable, for if an apostasy of the saints were taught, one would certainly expect such. Over against this is the fact that in Hebrews 6:12 and following, which speak of the promise of the covenant of grace, completely the opposite of apostasy is taught—namely, the unchangeable faithfulness of God through which believers can have a strong consolation [Heb 6:18]. God wished to demonstrate to the heirs of the promise more abundantly the immutability of His counsel, and therefore He interposed with an oath [Heb 6:17]. This is not *apostasy* but perseverance of the saints in the strongest terms.

As to the nature of the gifts ascribed here to those who can fall away, these gifts are spoken of as:

a) "Enlightenment." By this is meant an extraordinary and supernatural degree of knowledge of the truth. This enlightenment is between historical knowledge and the knowledge of saving faith. It is distinguished from the former by deeper insight, from the latter by the absence of the experiential element (cf. 2 Cor 3:18).

b) "Having tasted the heavenly gift." The heavenly gift is the gift of the Holy Spirit, also so named elsewhere in Acts 2:38; 8:20. Especially the latter text sheds light. Simon thought that the gift of the Holy Spirit was obtained for money. That was the gift to do extraordinary things, which the possession of the Holy Spirit enabled. This gift is called heavenly because it is sent from heaven by Christ.

c) "Having become partakers of the Holy Spirit." This expresses the same thought in other words for further clarification.

d) "Tasting of the good word of God." This of itself reminds us of the description of the temporary faith given by the Lord in the parable of the sower: "the one who hears the word and immediately receives it with joy." With that, however, it is expressly said that such people have no roots in themselves. Thus one can taste the good word of God without being regenerated at the root (Matt 13:20–21).

e) "Tasting of the powers of the coming age." By this is meant the exercise of the power of the Spirit mentioned under (b) and (c).

Thus one sees that (d) corresponds to (a), and (e) with (b) and (c). The subjective effects of the enlightenment consist in tasting the good word of God. Those effects of becoming partakers of the Holy Spirit consist in tasting the powers of the coming age. The coming age is the dispensation of the New Testament, the age of the Messiah in distinction from the Old Testament dispensation, in which those powers were not seen but presented as something future (Joel 2).

The question is raised whether the words, "These, I say, to renew again to repentance," do not imply that initially genuine repentance was present. "Again" and "re-" in "renew" look back on an initial repentance of which this would have to be the repetition. However, this objection immediately fails as soon as one poses the question of who is in view here as the subject of the renewing. If it is God, the meaning would be: It is impossible that God would again renew such persons to repentance, that He would repeat the act of renewal that He had once done in them. Then it would be difficult to avoid the conclusion that the reference here is to an apostasy of those who have truly repented, for, without further stipulation, the repentance that God produces in a sinner is true repentance. But the question takes on an entirely other complexion if men, ministers of the Word, teachers, of whom the writer himself is one, are seen as the subject of the renewing. Then the meaning becomes: It is impossible, after they have fallen away, that we would renew again to repentance such persons whom we at one time have brought to an outward repentance and moved to a confession of Christianity. Without doubt this latter understanding is the correct one. Were the other correct, then it would have to include *that God* would renew such people again. The context does not speak of the work of God but of the work of men, of a progressing to perfection, of not re-laying the foundation, etc. Thus, all that can be rightly derived from this expression comes down to this: If there are such apostate persons, then with this their apostasy our calling toward them ceases; God has not directed us to continue working on such people. By that, strictly speaking, it is not yet said that God, too, could not bring back such people, but that He generally does not do so and therefore also does not will to have the instrumentality of the ministry of the Word used for that. It is similar to what the Apostle

John says about the sin unto death—namely, that one shall no longer pray for it [1 John 5:16].

That this is the correct conception appears, finally, from the image used in Hebrews 6:7-8, used to clarify what has been said. The soil that drinks the rain receives God's blessing, but that which produces thorns and thistles is rejected and thereby shows that it is not good soil for growing. The former is therefore also continually cultivated; the latter is considered rejected and one no longer bothers about it.

58. Is there sanctification after this life?

No. This opinion must be rejected just as much as its opposite, perfectionism. The grounds are these:

a) Scripture says that the spirits of the blessed in heaven are completely perfect (Heb 12:23); that to see the Lord as He is involves being like Him (1 John 3:2); that those who die in the Lord are blessed in the full sense of the word (Rev 14:13).

b) Sin does not let itself be separated from misery. Therefore, to bring sin into heaven means to bring misery into heaven, which is nothing other than abolishing the concept of heaven.

c) The contrary opinion rests on the idea that change can still come about in the condition of the sinner after this life. If such is possible with holiness, then it is not to be rejected for regeneration and repentance. The doctrine of a "second probation" will then be the result.

d) Thus we posit that at death a crisis takes place in sanctification, in which every blemish of sin is at once completely taken away from the believer. This, of course, does not mean that a child who dies immediately receives the fully developed holiness of one who is mature (an adult). But all sin will be removed from the soul. This last point, however, belongs to eschatology.

VOLUME FIVE

ECCLESIOLOGY
THE MEANS OF GRACE
ESCHATOLOGY

Translated and edited by

Richard B. Gaffin, Jr.

with

Kim Batteau
Allan Janssen

CONTENTS

Contents

PREFACE

The appearance of this volume has been facilitated by initial translations of its different parts by Kim Batteau and Allan Janssen. As with the previous volumes, I have reviewed and revised their work and given the translation its final form. The editorial footnotes are mine.

The relative distribution of attention to the topics treated in this volume is striking and will likely be surprising to many familiar with Vos' interest in eschatology prominent in his later work in biblical theology. Here less than one-fifth of the whole is devoted to eschatology, the rest to the church and the means of grace. Approximately 60 percent more attention is given to baptism alone than to eschatology, and only slightly less attention given to the Lord's Supper than to eschatology. Still, in this treatment of eschatology we find a clear recognition of the two-age construct, including the present interadvental overlapping of this age and the age to come, and the structural importance of this construct for biblical eschatology as a whole—an insight that he subsequently develops so magisterially in works like *The Pauline Eschatology*. The in-depth discussion of the church and of the sacraments will repay careful reading in any number of places. Even those who disagree at points—say, in the case made for infant baptism—will be stimulated by the challenge to their own thinking.

As noted in the preface to Volume One,[1] the *Reformed Dogmatics* does not include a section on introduction (prolegomena) to systematic theology. In that regard, the answer to question 11 in part two, chapter

---

1 Page x, note 9.

three in this volume, "In how many senses can the expression 'the word of God' be understood?," warrants careful consideration not only in its own right but also because it provides an indication of key elements that surely would have marked Vos' formal treatment of the doctrines of special revelation and Scripture.

This is the final volume of the *Reformed Dogmatics*. With the completion of the translation as a whole, several points made in the preface to Volume One bear repeating. The goal throughout has been to provide a careful translation, aiming as much as possible for formal rather than dynamic equivalence. Nothing has been deleted, no sections elided or their content summarized in a reduced form. Vos' occasionally elliptical style in presenting material, meant primarily for the classroom rather than for published circulation to a wider audience, has been maintained. The relatively few instances of grammatical ellipsis unclear in English have been expanded, either without notation or placed within brackets.

At the same time, it should be kept in mind that this is not a critical translation. Only in a very few instances has an effort been made to verify the accuracy of the secondary sources Vos cites or quotes, usually by his referring to no more than the author and title and sometimes only to the author. Also, no exact bibliographic details have been provided, and explanatory footnotes have been kept to a minimum.

The *Reformed Dogmatics* makes a welcome addition for anyone wishing to benefit from a uniformly sound and often penetrating presentation of biblical doctrine. Also, English readers will now be able to explore the relationship between the early Vos of the *Reformed Dogmatics* and his subsequent work in biblical theology. With this translation now completed, I am confident in saying that whatever differences such comparisons may bring to light, the end result will confirm a deep, pervasive and cordial continuity between his work in systematic theology and in biblical theology.

Who were teachers or other theologians, contemporary to Vos or recently past, who may have directly influenced his views and his presentation of material in the *Dogmatics*? That question, raised in the prefaces to several of the preceding volumes, so far remains unanswered, for others perhaps to examine.

From its beginning in 2012, this translation project has been a collaborative undertaking that would not have been possible without the substantial help of others. Those mentioned above and in previous volumes have provided initial translations of its various parts and, in some instances, reviewed them. Thanks are also due those who have been involved with the copy editing, Elliot Ritzema and Abigail Stocker—their careful work has also added a measure of smoothness to the translation at a number of points—as well as those who prepared the extensive and useful indices, Dustyn Eudaly and Spencer Jones. Finally, my heartfelt thanks go to Justin Marr, the project manager at Lexham Press, for all his help and for serving as a continuing source of patient encouragement throughout this project.

May God be pleased to grant that the value of the *Reformed Dogmatics* be duly appreciated. May it be used for the well-being of His church and its mission in and to the world in our day and beyond.

R. Gaffin, Jr.
May 2016

PART ONE

Ecclesiology: The Doctrine of the Church

Chapter One

Essence

1. *What is the nature of the transition from soteriology, handled previously, to the doctrine of the Church?*

Everything discussed so far has had reference to the individual believer and to what the Spirit of God brings about in him as an individual. As such he was called; as such he was regenerated; as such he believed and was justified; as such he is an object of sanctification. But the individual believer cannot remain by himself. The work of the application of the merits of the Mediator also has a communal side. A root of unity is latent among those individuals. This unity originates not only in retrospect but existed beforehand. Believers were all reckoned in Christ, regenerated by the Spirit of Christ; they were all implanted into Christ in order to form one body. Therefore, now that what concerns the individual has been handled, what is communal ought to be discussed. This takes place in the doctrine of the Church.

Evidently connected with this doctrine is that of the sacraments, for they, too, do not have an individual character. They are inseparable from the Church, proceed from it, and point to it. By baptism a relationship to the Church is represented and established. One is not baptized as a solitary individual but in connection with the Church of Christ. Likewise, no one can hold the Lord's Supper by himself and for himself; the Supper refers to the communion of the saints.

Now, one could still ask whether it is not necessary to deal with the doctrine of the Church before individual soteriology. Does not the individual Christian exist from the outset if he is born into the covenant of God, according to and under what is communal? This would, in fact, be the case if we taught, with modern theology, that the life of the children of God resides in the church and is passed on from the church to those who join it. With Rome, too, that must be the sequence. Here it is not believers who form the church, but the church forms believers, and that not only in an external sense through the ministry of the Word and sacraments in the covenant of God, but in the most real sense, to the extent that all grace must come through the material substance of the sacraments, which the church has at its disposal. Someone is regenerated through his baptism, and in the array of sacraments he receives in succession from the treasury of the church all the grace necessary for his salvation.

This is not the case according to the Reformed conception. Although we believe in the ministry of the covenant of grace and attach great value to that ministry, it is still firmly established that real re-creating grace passes not from one believer to another, not from the church to the individual, but from Christ directly to the one called. Through this unity with Christ, believers also become one with each other. In this way, too, the ministry of the covenant of grace originates. God calls efficaciously, and then establishes His covenant with them and with their seed. He has done so with Abraham. This is why we have the doctrine of the Church following soteriology.

2. *Which words in Scripture are used for the concept "church"?*

The proper word for "church" is *ekklēsia* (ἐκκλησία), from *ekkalein* (ἐκκαλεῖν), "called out." For the Greeks this *ekklēsia* is the gathering of free citizens who make decisions about matters of the state and who are called together by a herald.

In the Old Testament, this word is now used by the Septuagint for the translation of the Hebrew *qahal* (קָהָל), which has the similar derivation: "gather, call together." It means, then: (1) the Israelite nation in its entirety as a church-state, even when it was not called together (e.g., Lev 4:13, "If now the entire *congregation* of Israel will have gone astray"); (2) an assembled gathering of this Israelite nation (e.g., 1 Kgs 8:65, "At the same time Solomon also held the feast and all of Israel with him, a great *congregation*").

In the books of Moses, *qahal* is rendered, where it appears, as *synagōgē* (συναγωγή). However, in these books it is mostly replaced by another Hebrew word, namely, *'edah* (עֵדָה), which likewise means "assembly."

For the New Testament use of the word *ekklēsia*, attention must now be paid to different things, namely:

a) The use of the word in antithesis to the name that the Jews used for their assembly.

b) The use of the word in the mouth of the Savior in the Gospels.

c) The connection between the concepts "church" and "kingdom of heaven."

d) The differing meanings in which the word itself appears in the New Testament.

3. Is there a contrast with the assembly of the Jews in the word ekklēsia?

Yes, a few times in the New Testament the term *ekklēsia* also appears for the Jewish church; for example, "This is he [Moses] who was in the *congregation* of the people in the wilderness" (Acts 7:38). But here it looks back to the old Israelite church. On the other hand, for the present Jewish assembly, *synagōgē* is generally used: "And when the *synagōgē* was dismissed" (Acts 13:43). In antithesis, on a single occasion the gathering of believing Christians is called a *synagōgē*: "If a man with a golden ring on his finger comes into your gathering" (Jas 2:2). But those are exceptions. As a rule, it is the case that the assembling of Jews and of Christians are contrasted with each other as "synagogue" and "church."

Thus it must be of significance when the Lord and His apostles refrained from the use of the word *synagōgē* and reverted to a word that, although entirely scriptural, had nonetheless fallen more and more into disuse by the Jews. That the Jews made use of *synagōgē* had various reasons. For them the word *ekklēsia* had a pagan flavor. Moreover, the word *synagōgē* was the usual word in the law of Moses. Since Judaism after the exile now thought it had to focus on keeping the law with the exertion of all its powers and so had degenerated into a legalistic Judaism of holiness by works, it surely had to give preference to this term from the law. When we take this into consideration, then the choice of *ekklēsia* by the Lord acquires a deeper sense. He chose a word that transcends the legalistic meaning of Israel, that points to *the call of God*, that causes one to think back to the call of Israel, that thus from the outset places the New Testament dispensation of the covenant of grace on a basis that is no longer limited to a single nation; see Acts 2:39: (a) for the promise comes to you and to your children, and (b) to all who are far off, as many of you as the Lord our God will call.

With this it is not maintained that the synagogues of the Jews fell outside the circle of the Old Testament dispensation of the covenant. This was clearly not the case. Christ himself went into synagogues; later the apostles found a point of contact for their missionary work in the synagogues. They did not break off the line of the ministry of the covenant, even after the resurrection of the Lord and the outpouring of the Holy Spirit.

One thing must not be lost from view here. The synagogue of the Jews was not a solely religious gathering *everywhere*. The Jews in the Diaspora naturally had no civil power, and when they gathered it was as a religious community. This was the case even in Palestine, everywhere where a mixed population was found. There were, however, many places where the civil government of the elders and the administration of the synagogue coincided. Thus, in such cases, notwithstanding the abolition of the Jewish state, the Old Testament identification of state and church continued. In this respect as well, the concept of the church will have formed a antithesis to that of the synagogue.

4. *What is the distinctive meaning of the word "church" in the mouth of the Savior?*

In the Gospels, *ekklēsia* is used by the Lord only twice:

a) Matthew 16:18: "And I also say to you, that you are Peter and on this rock I will build my *church*, and the gates of hell will not overcome it" (ἐπὶ ταῦτα τῇ πέτρᾳ οἰκοδομήσω μου τὴν ἐκκλησίαν).

b) Matthew 18:17: "And if he does not listen to them, then tell it to the church (εἰπὲ τῇ ἐκκλησίᾳ), and if he also does not listen to the church, then let him be to you as a pagan and tax collector."

Here, both times, the congregation in view—that is, "the *church*"—is spoken of as something future: "I will build my church." In Matthew

16, almost immediately following the Word of the Lord cited, is the prediction of His suffering, His death, His resurrection. The building of the church is thus indisputably related to that. Earlier, it was always "kingdom of heaven"; now, where the prophecy of the suffering and the resurrection occurs, it suddenly becomes "church." It is likewise so in Matthew 18:20—"For where two or three are gathered in my name, there I am in the midst of them"—something that evidently refers to the absence of the exalted Mediator in His human nature. Thus, on the one hand, the church is something future. On the other hand, there is present in the word itself, pointing back clearly enough to the church of Israel, that it is not something absolutely new. It has existed earlier but will now come in a new form; it will now be *His* church par excellence—that is, the church in the form that He Himself, having appeared in the flesh and as duly authorized by the Father, has given it. In essence, the church under the old and new covenant is the same; in form and manifestation there is a difference. And this difference resides in more than one thing.

a) The church under the old dispensation was more than church; it was equally state. The Old Testament covenantal dispensation had two faces, something that at the same time had the dependence of the church as a consequence. Just because the church was more than church, it could not be completely church. The church did not receive its own form, was not something separate and distinguished from all other things.

b) The church of the old covenant was not only a state church; it was also essentially a national church—that is, limited to one nation. A pagan who wanted to belong to it could only join by becoming a Jew. It is certainly true that this particularism is used in the design of God for a purpose encompassing the entire world, but in itself, it was still a limitation.

c) The outpouring of the Holy Spirit, as it is specific to Pentecost and could only follow the accomplished work of the Mediator, likewise distinguishes the Old and New Testament church. It is not as if earlier there had been no activity of the Spirit. Prior to that outpouring, the Spirit also regenerated and led to the Mediator and effected being united to Him by faith. But in the particular form in which this now happens, it forms a distinction between the Old and the New.

5. What does it mean when the Savior says, "I will build my church"?

In the first place, this image is without doubt suggested by that of the rock, which is applied to Peter's confession. At the same time, there appears to be yet another thought present, namely that of the house-family connection. For the person in the Middle East, house means his family as well as his dwelling. That the church is a house connects it with the administration of the covenant. It is continued by God in the line of families. In Scripture, then, the church appears in this sense as the "house of God" (cf. 1 Tim 3:15; Heb 3:6, 10:21); the members of the church are "family" (Gal 6:10; Eph 2:19; Matt 10:25).

6. What is the connection between the two concepts "kingdom of heaven" and "church"?

This connection is twofold:

a) On the one hand, "kingdom of God" is the narrower, and "church" the wider concept. While the Church has both a visible and invisible side, and so can often be perceived of an entire nation, the kingdom of God in its various meanings is the invisible spiritual principle. It is the lordship Christ exercises over our souls if we truly belong to Him, our submission to his sovereign authority, our being conformed and joined by living faith to His body with its many members. It is the gathering of these true members and subjects of Christ. It is called the "kingdom of heaven" because it has its center and its future in heaven. All the spiritual benefits of the covenant are linked to it: righteousness, freedom, peace, and joy in the Holy Spirit [cf. Rom 14:17]. As such a spiritual entity, it is within man and does not appear with an outward face. Understood in this sense, the kingdom of heaven equals the invisible church, but then in its New Testament particularity, for Christ preached that the kingdom of heaven had come near, namely, through His coming. He is the king, and through His clear self-revelation and through His completed work, the invisible church also receives a new glory that it did not have previously, so that even the least in this kingdom is still greater than John the Baptist [Matt 11:11].

b) On the other hand, the "kingdom of God" or "of heaven" is a broader concept than that of the church. In fact, it is presented to us as leaven that must permeate everything, as a mustard seed that must grow into a tree that with its branches covers all of life. Plainly, such a thing may not be said of the concept "church." There are other spheres of life beside that of the church, but from none of those may the kingdom of God be excluded. It has its claim in science, in art, on every terrain. But the church may not lay claim to all that. The external side of the kingdom (the visible church) must not undertake these things; the internal essence of the kingdom, the new existence, must of itself permeate and purify. It is precisely the Roman Catholic error that the church takes everything into itself and must govern everything. Then there appears an ecclesiastical science, an ecclesiastical art, an ecclesiastical politics. There the kingdom of God is identical with the church and has been established on earth in an absolute form.

According to us, it is otherwise. The true Christian belongs in the first place to the church, and in it acknowledges Christ as king. But besides that he also acknowledges the lordship of Christ in every other area of life, without thereby committing the error of mixing these things with each other. The Old Testament church-state, which comprehended the entire life of the nation, was a type of this all-encompassing kingdom of God.

If now one compares the visible church and the kingdom of God viewed from the first side, then one can say that the former is a manifestation and embodiment of the latter.

If one compares the visible church and the kingdom of God viewed from the second side, then one can say that the former is an instrument of the latter.

If one looks to the final outcome, then one must say that the church and kingdom of God will coincide. In heaven there will no longer be a division of life. There the visible and the invisible will coincide perfectly. Meanwhile, for now the kingdom of God must advance through the particular form of the church.

7. *With what meanings does the word "church" occur in the New Testament?*

a) In the sense of the totality of those internally, effectually called, thus all who by faith are united to Christ the Head—the sum of true believers. The New Testament concept of the Church emerges from that. What is internal and invisible is what is first, and then not as it is limited to one place but as it extends to all places where the body of Christ has its members. In the first place, it is those called by Christ and to Christ, not those called together to a particular assembly. That already follows from the fact that, in the mouth of the Savior, "church" was also connected with the Old Testament *qahal*. And this *qahal* always comprised the entire nation. Thus, "Church" comprises all the people of God, where they are in heaven and on earth; for this meaning see Acts 2:47, "And the Lord added to the *church* daily those being saved." "And God has placed in the church first apostles," etc. (1 Cor 12:28); "because I persecuted the church of God" (1 Cor 15:9; cf. Gal 1:13); "to shepherd the church of God which He has obtained through His own blood" (Acts 20:28). In all these passages, the reference is to the church of the elect called on earth. In Hebrews 12:23, it also refers to those who have already entered heaven, "to the general assembly and the church of the firstborn who are enrolled in heaven."

b) The second meaning of the word "church" is that of the local, visible church—thus, the gathering of believers who meet in a particular place or city. In this sense it occurs numerous times: for example, the church in the house of someone, "Greet also the church (congregation) in their house" (Rom 16:5; cf. 1 Cor 16:19; Col 4:15; Phlm 2); the church of Antioch (Acts 13:1), of Jerusalem, (Acts 8:1), of Thessalonica (1 Thess 1:1); "*no* church" (Phil 4:15); "everywhere in all the churches" (1 Cor 4:17); "the churches of the Gentiles" (Rom 16:4). So throughout, the local church.

c) The question arises whether besides these two meanings the word *ekklēsia* has yet a third, namely a collective, meaning, so that it would stand for the union of a number of local churches in a certain region or country. The resolution of this question depends on a single text—namely, Acts 9:31, where one reads, "Then the churches throughout all Judea and Galilee and Samaria had peace," etc. Here the *Statenvertaling*[1] follows the reading αἱ ἐκκλησίαι, plural. If this is correct, then it must be said that there is no text in the New Testament where "church" appears for a number of churches taken together. There are, however, manuscripts that have the singular, and these, it would seem, are the oldest and best. Westcott and Hort also read ἡ ἐκκλεσία, "the church." But that reading is not entirely certain. For this generally current use, one could appeal to the Old Testament, where the visible gathering of all Israel in its unity is called a *qahal, ekklēsia*. Still, this appeal is not sufficient to legitimize the more recent use. Indeed, the Jewish church was in fact centralized in a sense in which the Christian church under the new covenant is not and may never be. Thus it will not do to draw a conclusion from that. And the usage of our fathers, who preferred to speak of "churches," has in fact a scriptural foundation. On the other hand, however, one must also not forget that the churches as they appear in the New Testament history had their unity in the apostolate. To begin with, they did not yet need to form a unity of themselves and among each other through representation. Thus there existed no occasion to speak of "church" in the singular. Later, it was otherwise.

It seems to us that for these reasons no well-founded objection can be offered against the application of the term "church" to the totality of local churches. To say something does not appear in the New Testament is not equivalent to saying it is in conflict with the principles of church government laid down in the New Testament.

One will have noted that in the two places where the term "church" is used by the Savior, both meanings are found. In Matthew 16:18, it is the universal church of those called of which the Lord speaks, the church that He will build everywhere. In Matthew 18:17, on the other hand, it is the local church to which the brother to be censured and his accuser belong. This is seen in "tell it to the church," something that can only refer to the local church.

---

1   The "States-translation" of the Bible authorized by the Dutch government, first published in 1637.

Finally, there is still the question whether in the New Testament "church" is used of the place, the building where the church gathers. "Synagogue," as is well known, is used in this way. In our usage, "church" in this sense has almost completely superseded the use of the term for the local church. Roman Catholics maintain that there are examples of this in the New Testament—wrongly. The first Christians had no church buildings but gathered in houses or where they were best able to. Appeal is made to 1 Corinthians 11:18 and 22, but here "when you come together in the church" is equivalent to "when you come together as the gathering of believers."

d) To the three meanings discussed, one could still add that of Matthew 18:17, since "say it to the church," according to many, will have to refer the representatives and rulers of the church, thus the so-called *ecclesia representativa*. Roman Catholics even derive from this passage that "church" can be equivalent to the Pope. If, then, the Pope would obey what is said here to Peter, he would have to understand "say it to the church" in the sense of "say it to yourself." Bellarmine too, then, does not hesitate to explain the matter in this way.

Presently we are accustomed to making a distinction between "congregation" and "church"—and then, in this sense, that the former is local and the latter general, inclusive of a number of "congregations." The old usage of our language was the reverse. Preference was given to calling the local gathering of believers "church" [*kerk*] and to calling the universal gathering of believers in all places "congregation" [*gemeente*]. Still, this too was not followed strictly. When one consults the *Statenvertaling*, one will see that it uses both *gemeente* and *kerk* of the one as well as the other, apparently without a fixed rule. Only for this usage, one should take note that throughout, the Greek word is the same [ἐκκλεσία] and that there are not two Greek words that correspond to these two Dutch words. Naturally, one need not therefore reject the distinction.

8. *What is the derivation of our word "church" [kerk]?*

This comes from the Greek κυριακόν, the neuter of κυριακός, "what is of the Lord," "what belongs to the Lord." Some have doubted this derivation, but it still appears to be correct.

9. *Is it easy to give a definition of "the church"?*

No, for as the matter is considered from differing viewpoints, the definition will also come out differently. The concept of the church is many-sided, and what matters is that one does justice as much as possible to all sides and aspects.

10. *From what three viewpoints has one attempted to define "the church"?*

For this some have begun from election for one viewpoint; from baptism for another; then again, from confession.

a) From *election*. Some say that the essence of the Church is not latent in any external institution but in internal unity with Christ. As has already been observed repeatedly, Rome works from the outside to the inside. For it, what is outward imparts a share in what is inward. We cannot reason this way. And so to show that the true essence of the Church lies in what is inward, one would have it delimited through election. The elect, be they already in heaven or still on earth or yet unborn, would then as such fall within the Church. One easily sees that the concept can be exchanged with that of the invisible church. At the same time, it already has within itself as a subdivision the distinction between the church militant and triumphant. Many of the theologians also begin with election in defining the church.

Against that, however, is one objection: election comprises all who belong to the body of Christ, regardless of whether they are already engrafted into the body of the Lord or are still completely estranged from Him. Now, one can scarcely say of the latter that they belong to the Church. The concept of Church does not refer to being destined for the body of Christ but actually being in this body. Election as delimiting the Church must thus be replaced by effectual calling. When we substitute the latter, there is no longer anything against saying that the invisible church is the gathering of those effectually called by God's Word and Spirit, who are bound by true faith and by mystical union with Christ and in Him with one another. This concurs completely with the term Church itself. The *ekklēsia* still is the gathering of those called (from ἐκκαλεῖν, called out).

b) From *baptism*. Engrafting into the body of Christ and belonging to it are outwardly signified and sealed in baptism. Thus here we no longer have to do with the invisible church, but with a visible form that it assumes. Naturally, in consideration here must be a Christian baptism that can be recognized by us as legitimate. However, one of the most difficult questions is where the line must be drawn here. Roman Catholic baptism is recognized by us as baptism, and yet it would be difficult to call members of the Roman Catholic church believing brothers and to have Christian communion with them as such. In any case, there is a visible church where faith manifests itself, the genuineness of which we have no ground for doubting. God has put at our disposal certain external signs that we have to evaluate and to treat someone as Christian without legitimating further expression of judgment over his condition. Wherever, then, the obligation is incumbent upon us to presuppose the presence of faith by these external signs, we also have to recognize the existence of the visible church.

c) Finally, some have begun from *confession*. Insofar as confession is the principal external means to manifest the invisible essence of the church and to cause it to materialize outwardly, it already belongs under the preceding approach. Confession, however, is also a bond that binds the members of the church together in the external form of the church. To this extent, it is what is characteristic for the visible church in its institutional form. One can define the visible church as "the gathering of those who, through the external Word, the use of the sacraments, and ecclesiastical discipline, unite into an external body and association." To such a visible church belong the ministry of the Word, the administration of the sacraments, the office of rule, and discipline. Only through this union in a fixed form does the visible church actually appear. What is discussed above under (b) can certainly be called a sporadic manifesting of the one invisible church. The visible church as such, it is not. To be able to retain the designation "visible" over the long run, the church must be organized, assume a fixed form; it may not exist in a completely disjointed manner. That is the duty incumbent on it for this earthly dispensation, and where that duty is continually omitted and willfully neglected, one has well-founded reasons to doubt the presence of the invisible church as well. Thus the major distinction that remains for us is that between the visible and the invisible church.

11. *What then is the connection between these two?*

As is well known, Rome starts from the absolute identification of these two. Through the visible church—that is, through the Roman Catholic church as institution—one also gains access to all the invisible benefits of salvation. Everything is tied to the church. Only joining the external institution makes someone a full member of the Church. For consistent Roman Catholics, catechumens who are not yet baptized, excommunicated persons, and schismatics do not belong to the Church, although some, like Bellarmine, would consider them as potential members, like a child who is conceived but not yet formed and born. Rome will not acknowledge an invisible church, and its spokesmen constantly charge Protestants with deliberately fashioning this concept to evade the difficult question of where their church was prior to the Reformation. Naturally, that is not so. That Protestants start from the concept of the invisible church has a much deeper basis—namely, that they desire to have no mediator between God and the believer. For the deepest thought of Rome comes down to that: that the church places itself between us and Christ, as Christ stands between the Church and God. Since now Christ, although visible in His humanity, is still absent from us according to the flesh and is only to be seen by faith, since also union with Him is something spiritual, not in the sphere of the sensible-visible, so this standpoint, once taken, directly includes that the Church is invisible. Therefore, this doctrine of the invisibility of the Church is not an aid in the polemic against Rome, but the deepest expression of the antithesis to Rome. The invisibility of the Church must be further defined:

a) It is not ascribed to the Church in an absolute sense, as if the Church raised to its perfection and having reached its goal would still be an invisible entity—that is, something that by its nature cannot be seen. Such a dualism would be completely intolerable.

The invisible is oriented toward the visible and vice versa, as the soul to the body and the body to the soul. When the Church is perfect, it will also be entirely visible as well as invisible, and the former will be an adequate manifestation of the latter. The Church does not consist of angels but of men, and men are visible beings. But the re-creation, which is invisible, is during the present dispensation still resident within the visible creation, which is unrenewed. Believers do not have a different body than unbelievers. If they did, we could easily distinguish between the two, and the invisible church would coincide with the visible. In this respect, Rome, accordingly, anticipates the heavenly and the perfect as it in other respects repristinates—that is, draws out the old again from the days of the old covenant.

b) To begin with, there is invisibility in the *form* of the Church (*invisibilitas formae seu essentiae*). By that is meant that the essence of the Church, faith, does not come within the scope of the senses, that therefore we can never specify determinatively and infallibly this or that person belongs to the Church in the deepest sense of this judgment. Only for God, who sees and knows all things, is the Church manifest according to this form, according to this its essence. He sees and searches out the entire organism of the body of Christ in all its parts. We see only here and there a trace of a few points on the surface from which we can form an idea of its shape in general, but we do not see the body as such.

c) Next there is an invisibility of *parts* (*invisibilitas partium*). By that is really meant "the incalculability" of the Church. The church is spread over the entire earth. Apart from the fact that its inner essence is invisible, if we keep ourselves to what is external it also remains the case that the greatest part of the catholic (universal) church falls outside our purview; we cannot survey it all. In this sense, even Rome would have to grant that the Church is invisible, if, in the Pope and the clergy with an ascending order of ranks, it had not fashioned a means to concentrate the entirety of the body of the Church within a small compass. In the Pope, the entirety of the Roman Catholic church is visible to itself. But we do not believe in such invisibility. Perhaps it will be possible in heaven. For the present, it is excluded.

d) The Church is also invisible, or can be invisible, when error or persecution hinders its outward manifestation. One calls this the invisibility of marks (*invisibilitas characterum*). It has its basis in accidental and temporal conditions. With the previously mentioned meanings of the word "invisible," the basis in part of invisibility lay in something else. That the Church therefore does not adequately possess its outward-sensible form of manifestation lies in the development of the plan for the world. That it cannot be seen by us in all its inward ramifications, in its deepest essence, lies in the limitation of our knowledge. That it cannot be surveyed in its entirety is bound up with our finitude.

It is the invisibility intended under (b), that of the form or the essence, that is at issue between Rome and us. And here, too, one must take note that it has not become a question of terms. It finally comes down to the following issue: Scripture speaks of a Church. Certain goods are granted to this Church. Now the question is, to what are these properties and goods given? Rome says, to the visible church. Thus it follows that salvation and all that belongs to it attaches to external things. We say, to the invisible church; thus, the opposite follows. The entire way of salvation belongs to it. That the Church viewed in its essence or its form is invisible appears from the following:

a) The terms by which the Church is designated in Scripture are such that they do not coincide with outward, visible things. It is called the body of Christ. But this is a body that is formed through mystical union. The question is not whether in the organized, visible church there are members who do not belong to the body of Christ, but the question is only whether it can be said of the mystical body of Christ that there are dead members in it. Further, the Church is called the bride of Christ, to whom He is betrothed in righteousness, in truth, forever, whom He cares for and loves as His own flesh, with whom He will one day celebrate the eternal wedding (Eph 5:23; Hos 2:19; 2 Cor 11:2; Rev 19:9). That too may not be said of the external, visible hope, but only of the invisible, spiritual Church hidden within it. The Church is a spiritual temple built from spiritual stones, from *living* stones, which are not visible in their quality as living stones [1 Pet 2:4-5]. The Church is called *holy,* and we therefore describe it in the

Apostles' Creed as "the communion of saints." It can now only be holy through the possession of the Spirit and through its union with Christ—again, both invisible things.

b) That the Church is invisible in its essence the Apostle Paul has clearly taught in his dispute with Roman Catholics before Rome, with the Judaizers. They also taught that the essence lay in external things, in circumcision, etc. In opposition, Paul says in Romans 2:28, "For one is not a Jew who is that openly, nor is circumcision that which is open, in the flesh; but one is a Jew who is that in secret and the circumcision of the heart, in the Spirit, not in the letter, whose praise is not from men but from God" (cf. Rom 9:6; Gal 6:15; Phil 3:3; 1 Pet 3:4; Rev 2:17; 2 Tim 2:19).

c) All that constitutes the essence of the Church belongs to the realm of invisible things: regeneration, righteousness, union with Christ.

d) What is said in the Apostles' Creed accords with this: I *believe* a holy, universal Christian Church. Faith has as its object something invisible, not something visible. The Roman Catholic church must therefore say, if it will be consistent: I *see* a holy, universal Church.

If then it is established that one may not identify the invisible church with the visible, the question still remains unanswered: What is the connection between the two? One may not place them beside each other dualistically as if there were two churches. The Reformed have always taught that the distinction between the visible and invisible church is not a bifurcation of a generic concept into two species, but simply the description of one and the same subject from two different sides. On this point one must be careful, because here many are caught in a great misconception. There are not two churches, (a) an invisible and (b) a visible, but there is one Church that must be defined from the one side as invisible and from the other as visible. If one grants the dualism just noted, then one would have to allow that a visible church of Christ is also there where no believers are present. God has not placed on earth alongside His invisible church a salvation association, an external institution, so that it would be permissible for us to establish a visible church everywhere men are inclined to unite with a part of such an institution.

It is completely the other way around: God, through His Word and Spirit, begets believers in a place, or sends them there from elsewhere, and on the basis of the confession of these believers that they desire to belong to Christ they can now form a visible church. The visible thus everywhere presupposes the invisible, rests on it, derives from it its right of existence. It is called "church" because it is thought to stand in connection with what the essence of the Church is, to be a manifestation of the body of Christ. By that it is not at all denied that in such a visible church members can appear who do not belong to the invisible church. But this coheres inseparably, as we will see, with the unique calling and goal that the visible church has on earth. Someone has quite rightly observed that although sand is mixed with gold, still the gold is not therefore called gold because of the sand mixed in it but because of its own quality.

This, however, is not the only relationship in which the invisible and the visible church stand to each other. If the former is what is primary, the antecedent of the latter, there is also a reverse relationship. In a certain sense, one can say that again and again the visible church is used by God to form and continue the invisible church, insofar as the former precedes the latter. Theologians express this by saying that the visible church is twofold: (1) the company of believers (*coetus fidelium*) — that is, the manifestation of the body of Christ in visible form through the assembling of the individual members; (2) the mother of believers (*mater fidelium*) — that is, the matrix of the seed from which the church of the future grows.

Now, both of these characteristics of the visible church must be retained and are in need of each other to present the concept of the visible church fully. Rome separates them by ascribing one to the clergy and the other to the laity; they both belong to the church as a whole. Neither of these two can be overlooked where a true, pure church is. Where God's Word is purely proclaimed by a true church, this church is also propagated.

From what is said it now follows that the visible and the invisible church do not perfectly coincide. For (a) the triumphant Church as a whole belongs to what we call invisible and not to what we call visible; (b) it always remains possible that someone here on earth is regenerated and united with Christ who has not had the occasion to join with a visible church; (c) a true believer can fall into sin and be excluded from the visible church through discipline; (d) there will always be hypocrites in the church, false members, who as members are not right before God but who nonetheless cannot be excluded by the church. So, in each of these four respects the visible and invisible church diverge.

12. *Is the visible church in its essence a visible entity, or is its form of organization something accidental that may also be set aside?*

There are many at present who view the organization of the church with its offices and its ministry, etc., as accidental, as a purely human creation, as a form that the Church gives to itself to reach its goals. Of course, some then grant that in the life of believers the impulse to unite must necessarily be at work, and that in the long run union without organization is impossible, but still will acknowledge no higher authority for the institutional character of the Church than this necessity. The refutation of this notion of the Church is really already given in what is said above. Precisely because the church must be both the gathering of believers and the mother of believers, it must appear from the outset not only as a visible body but also as an organization. Its continuation is guaranteed by the fixed form it receives. Thus we also see already at the beginning of the founding of the church that the Lord instituted the office of the apostolate. That was an extraordinary office. But it comprised in itself everything that was later distributed among the other ordinary offices. Other office-bearers were appointed by the apostles, or they allowed their election by believers, and so new offices originated. This clearly shows that the church was intended to be an institution, and that a loose gathering of believers without a tighter connection has no right to arrogate to itself the name of church. Certainly, the government of the church is not prescribed in all its details in the New Testament, but that there must be a government is established, and its outlines also drawn clearly enough.

13. *What is meant by the attributes of the Church?*

The features that are peculiar to the invisible church. To that end, one usually recognizes the following:

a) *Unity.* The Apostles' Creed already speaks of *one* church. By that Rome naturally means unity of organization, subjection to one external authority, presently to the Pope. According to Protestants, it is a spiritual unity, not one of place or time or ritual,

3. One can also take the catholicity of the Church intensively; that is to say, from the religious life of a Christian, insofar as it is manifested in the church, an influence must proceed in every area of life, so that everything is Christianized in the noblest sense of the word. Where religion is reduced to a matter of secondary importance, as something for Sunday, then that is the opposite of catholicity. We have already seen above that Scripture designates this side of Christianity with a particular name—namely, with that of the kingdom of God. For Rome, catholic = Roman Catholic.

d) The Church is imperishable (*perennis*). It can never completely disappear from the earth. The number of members of the true Church who fall within the church militant may continually change—are now more, then less; it is always there. The Socinians deny the imperishability of the church militant. This is related to their denial of the perseverance of the saints (Matt 16:18; 28:20).

14. *What are meant by the marks of the Church?*

The marks (*notae*, γνωρίσματα) refer to the visible church and not, like the attributes, the invisible church. A mark by its nature is something that must fall within the sphere of what is visible. Although the Church, viewed in its entirety, can never disappear from the earth, there is still no guarantee that its individual parts will continue to exist. They can completely degenerate and deteriorate; believers who are still therein can die off so that only apparent members remain. But the presence of true members does not let itself be recognized. We cannot see into the heart of men. There is accordingly a need for external visible data, from which we can make out that we indeed have to do with a manifestation of the body of Christ in which for us there will be a communion of saints, in which office is ministered in the name of Christ, and in which we can discharge our Christian calling. If the Church on earth were also one externally, then marks would naturally be superfluous. However, it is divided. This results from different causes:

a) Division of insight into what is recognized as divine truth. The one has this view of truth, the other yet another view, and there is no one who entirely avoids being one-sided. That is the case for both churches and individual persons. One could now say that such difference of insight may not lead to division in individual churches, since the one side needs to be completed by the other, and so they should continue to exist alongside each other. But in fact that is not so, and it would appear to be completely impossible to have paedobaptists and Baptists live together ecclesiastically.

b) The difference in language and nationality makes ecclesiastical coexistence impossible in many cases.

When now for these reasons the church appears split and broken apart into a number of churches, then it is self-evident that there will be differing degrees of purity. A more accurate knowledge of the truth is granted to the one part of the body of Christ than to the other. Again, the practice of piety will shine in another church more than in this one. Consequently, the question arises here not only whether in the particular situation in which I am, I have to do with a true church, but also which church is the purest, so that the calling is incumbent on me to unite with it. The marks are thus in part about whether or not a true church is present, in part about the greater or lesser purity of a church.

What, then, are these marks? Usually three are given:

a) the pure proclamation of God's Word;
b) the orderly administration of the sacraments;
c) the faithful exercise of ecclesiastical discipline.

Not everyone, however, accepts just these three marks. Some are content with two—namely, Word and sacrament. So, for example, Calvin. Still others, like Turretin, limit themselves to the Word alone. It must be admitted that these three marks are not neatly coordinated. If the pure proclamation of God's Word is more than a semblance and sham, one will inevitably also be serious about the administration of the sacraments formulated according to the institution of that Word. And so with discipline. Submission to the Word is thus in the deepest sense the sole mark. But, of itself, this one mark divides into three when one recalls that each visible church must be the gathering and the mother of believers at the same time. That they have the pure proclamation of the Word must now serve as a mark for the one as well as for the other. Thereby the church still declares that it obtains its salvation on no other foundation than that given in the Word. The pure proclamation is at the same time a pure confession. At the same time, however, the church shows through this proclamation that it understands and exercises its calling as the mother of believers. The ministry of the Word is the means ordained by God to maintain the church and continue it. A church that would abandon this ministry, at least in its fundamental elements, would cease to be mother of believers. It strikes at the sign and seal for the continuation of God's covenant. To abandon this ministry is equivalent to endangering the continuity of the church. Baptists allow for a congregation to originate through the ministry of the Word but reject infant baptism. One may now imagine the situation where all confessing members of the church die out. According to the Baptists, there is then no longer a church. The administration of the second seal of the covenant is also a mark. When, likewise, in the Lord's Supper—the communion of the saints with the head—Christ is confessed and exercised, then here the inward essence of the church emerges directly in a visible phenomenon. When the celebration of the Lord's Supper with preparation is neglected, the church denies its essence and lacks an essential mark. Finally, the exercise of discipline also belongs to the marks. It is the calling of the church to manifest itself as true Church both in walk and confession. Now the walk always remains imperfect on account of the piece of the world that is still present in believers. But there must be a limit. To leave all sins unpunished and unjudged in its midst would involve, for the church, a failure of a principal part of its calling. Consequently, through discipline it is determined to what extent holiness of the life is demanded of the church.

15. *Can one show from Scripture that the pure proclamation of the Word is a mark of the true Church?*

Yes, the Lord says that His sheep and His disciples can be known by the fact that they hear His voice and abide in His Word (John 10:27; 8:31-32, 47; 14:23). "The disciples persevered in the teaching of the apostles, in fellowship, in the breaking of the bread and in prayer" (Acts 2:42). Here Word and sacrament are joined. On the contrary, the false, feigned church is known by the falsehood of teaching from the fact that it does not subject itself to God's Word. "To the law and to the testimony; if they do not speak according to this word, it will be that they will have no dawn" (Isa 8:20; cf. Deut 13:1-2; 1 John 4:1; 2 John 9). In Galatians 1:8, a curse is pronounced upon those who proclaim a different gospel.

The words of God are entrusted to the Church, both in antiquity to the Jews and now to the Church of the new covenant (Rom 3:2). Where now the words of God are to be found, the Church, too, will have to be sought. If the candlestick is removed from its place, the Church ceases to exist (Rev 2:5), and although the believers who are in it are saved as by fire, one will still have to fear that God will not carry out His covenant but cause the church to perish.

16. How far must this mark of the pure ministry of the Word be carried out?

A church does not immediately cease to be a true church with every deviation on a subordinate point of doctrine. The possibility even exists that, in a church with impure doctrine, more true believers are present than in a church that remains closer to Scripture. Purity of doctrine is not always a measure of the number of believers. But it is a mark for us to which we need to hold ourselves objectively. Where the pure proclamation of the Word exists, there the church is revealed. There is gold among the sand. Whether there is more or less sand does not matter for us. We do not have the freedom to make the all-or-nothing presence of spiritual life a mark of the church. There can be a dead orthodoxy where all true communion of saints appears to be lacking. And on the contrary, there can be a church that in spite of all sorts of errors and false notions in the area of doctrine, displays spiritual power. But the church that is pure in doctrine is the church that, all things considered, can satisfy the existence of its calling; that has a guarantee for the future; that in the long run must engender the greatest number of believers, will be the most fruitful mother of children. It is in no case permissible to make what is doctrinal a subsidiary or incidental point, as many in our days wish to do. The true Church is a teaching church, a confessing church. Whoever comes in contact with its word also comes in contact with the Root of its life, its holy walk. It is completely impossible to give the church an objective content without the Word and apart from the Word, by which it is clearly distinguished from the world and heretics. Churches that abandon or dispense with their confession are in a process of dissolution. There are differing degrees in purity of doctrine. But there is a null point where its Christian character ceases. Paul himself indicated that where he speaks of another gospel (Gal 1:8-9). If the Word of God is completely absent—as, for example, in a Socinian congregation—there the Church is also missing, and one does not have the freedom under any circumstance to engage in fellowship with such a church. Such a church, which abandons the fundamental truth and no longer rests on the catholic ground of Christendom, is called a heretical church. Socinians are heretics. On the other hand, one could not rightly call the historic Lutheran church a heretical church. However, one cannot draw a sharp line, and it is difficult to say where precisely impurity ceases and heresy begins. In any case, it remains the calling of every Christian to join with the church about which he is convinced, according to God's Word, that it has and maintains the purest doctrine.

17. *What are the marks of the true church according to the Roman Catholics?*

They are presented by them in different ways. The Catechism of Trent speaks of only two. Others, however, make mention of many more than these two (catholicity and apostolicity). One finds a full statement in Bellarmine:

a) Catholicity and the name Christian Church. This is meant in an external sense. That is, the church that calls itself catholic and excludes others from catholicity is the true Church.

We answer: Exclusivism and arrogating to oneself an external name is not true catholicity. This must be viewed as we have described it above. That church is catholic that recognizes all as Christians who submit to the Word of God and confess Christ as the only savior. Rightly grasped, this mark consequently falls under the first.

Roman Catholics say: The church as an external visible body is a better-known entity than doctrine, than the Word of God; thus you maintain that the better-known must be distinguished from the lesser-known. The church must lead us to doctrine and not, on the contrary, doctrine to the church. In this, as to the actual state of things, there is an element of truth. That the church is the mother of believers already involves that each individual does not find the truth on his own through independent inquiry, and then through individual judgment finds the true Church. But the question at issue here is not at all about how one comes to the truth or to the church historically, but simply how logically and rightfully these two stand in relation to each other.

And then we say: for us the power and the authority of the church are based on God's Word. Rome says: The power and authority of the church is the foundation of my faith in God's Word. That is ecclesiolatry, "church-idolatry." This error, however, goes back very far, as far as Augustine and even farther. In its protest against heresy and schism the ancient church allowed itself to be driven so far that it maintained (also in the mouth of Augustine), *Extra ecclesiam nulla salus*, "Outside the (visible) church there is no salvation."

b) Antiquity (*antiquitas*) is not a good mark, for the kingdom of Satan is also old. Freemasonry also calls itself old. Thus antiquity cannot be a mark, since it is established only by a wide-ranging historical inquiry, an inquiry that lies beyond the reach of most. The antiquity of doctrine can only be proven from Scripture, so that here too the Word appears to be the only true mark. Measured by that, the entire Roman Catholic system of doctrine has been built up from innovations.

c) Permanent duration, again naturally of the visible institution of the church. This is antiquity that also extends forward. That in this way the visible church cannot be broken off is true only in a relative sense, and does not apply to an institution. Heresy, too, is sometimes persistent and spreads ineradicably like cancer.

d) The great number of believers. This is an accidental mark. When the church began its course, it was a small flock, and it was still the true Church. There have been times in which the great majority deviated and became heretical (Luke 12:32; Matt 7:14; Rev 13:3, 16). Arianism appeared for a long time to occupy the entire church.

e) The unbroken succession of bishops. This is not a mark. Annas and Caiaphas were the followers of Aaron. Arian bishops were the followers of orthodox fathers. The entire Greek [Orthodox] Church, which the Roman Church declared to be schismatic or even heretical, maintains succession on equally good grounds as Rome. Thus the church is not necessarily where succession is. The church can exist without succession. If all the presbyters in a church were to die at once, it would not thereby cease to be a church. Succession in its entirety cannot be demonstrated, not even by the most exacting historical inquiry. One should be clear that one single gap in the succession makes the entire following series of bishops illegitimate. Whoever attaches the authenticity of the church to the unbroken line of bishops hangs by a hair. It is apparent that by such reckoning not a single authentic church exists.

One speaks of succession in another sense—namely, *successio doctrinae*, "the continuity of doctrine." So understood, this mark naturally comes down to our first [the pure proclamation of God's Word], and it is a good mark. Only, one must take care that it is not understood all too formally and externally. True doctrine has always been implicitly present and has always lain in Scripture. But the church has not always had it in conscious dogmatic formulation. It is a futile undertaking to seek our formulas for the doctrine of the Trinity and Christology in the patristic writers of the second century. Nonetheless, at work in the faith of the church were all the factors from which these dogmas are composed, and only one heretic needed to arise who attacked one or other element, or the church reflected directly on the content of its faith, and it began to formulate that content.

f) Agreement with the ancient church and the postapostolic fathers in doctrine. Not only does Rome make much of that, but the Anglican church also places weight on it. One must consider, however, that a distinction is to be made between the individual opinions of many fathers and the consensus of all. The fathers often groped in darkness; they wrestled for light. In them it is not the truth but the process of finding the truth that is to be noted. Someone has said it well: "They were not church fathers but church infants." On the other hand, when one sees that the fathers were as good as in agreement on a point, this had much weight, for in this way the church arrived at the formulation of its dogma and is still continually at work for greater clarity. In this sense, our confession also connects with Nicaea and the church councils that followed. Still, this authority of the ancient church may not be separated from God's Word. We do not have to do here with an independent mark. The consensus of the fathers is based on Scripture. It is the outline of Scripture itself that they have traced. For this reason, and this reason alone, someone is excluded from Christianity who, for example, will not stand on the ground of Nicaea. So the Socinians.

g) The connection of the members mutually and with the head. Applied to Christ, this is a mark of the invisible church; applied to the Pope it is not a good mark. Mutual unity among believers can be disturbed by many things without the essence of the Church thereby disappearing.

h) Holiness of true doctrine.   Both these ultimately coincide with
i) Efficacy of doctrine.   our mark, the pure proclamation of the Word. Every word of God is holy and powerful (Psa 19:7; Heb 4:12; John 17:17).

j) Holiness of life. True holiness effected by God is invisible; external holiness is not always to be trusted. Gross unholiness is naturally negative, since manifested unhindered it is an evidence that the church is not present. But for that reason, we also speak of discipline as a mark.

k) The glory of miracles. This only comes into consideration insofar as it accompanied the Word in the beginning and so is subservient to the Word. Therefore, from the Word, too, an answer must be found to the question whether continuing revelation is still to be expected and whether this will be accompanied by miracles. Scripture does not know of miracles without revelation, simply as a mark of the church in history. In order to extend miracles, one must make the church into a church of revelation. This cannot now be done. God has spoken in the last days through His Son, and the Son has given the apostles authority to speak in His name, and with that, revelation is finished. Moreover, Scripture itself says that false doctrine—that is, feigned revelation that is in conflict with earlier revelation—cannot be accredited, not even by a miracle. The Word stands above the thing (cf. Deut 13:1–5).

l) The light of prophecy. This, understood as a real prophecy, is not a characteristic of the church. Only the Old Testament had prophets, and not always. Prophecy, in the broader sense of the interpretation of Scripture, falls under the proclamation of the Word.

m) The significance of opponents. The impossibility of letting this be valid as a mark is obvious.

n) The woeful end of enemies and persecutors. As to that end, no judgment is to be made. True believers, too, sometimes die in doleful ways.

o) Temporal success. The opposite is true, for "in the world you will have oppression" [John 16:33].

CHAPTER TWO

Organization, Discipline, Offices

1. *How many views are there concerning the organization and government of the visible church?*

   a) The view of those who declare every external form as unnecessary or even illegitimate. So judge the "Plymouth Brethren," or Darbyists, who have separated themselves from all organized churches. They think that every church formation necessarily corrupts and leads to results that are irreconcilable with the spirit of Christianity, and that therefore it is not only unnecessary to form a visible church, but positively sinful. Of itself, then, office also falls with external formation. All believers are priests, and the Holy Spirit is the only bond that may bind them as one (Darby 1800-1882). The Quakers have a similar view. They too reject office.

   b) The Erastian system. This teaches that the church as such is entirely spiritual, and that it belongs to the state to provide it with an external organization, to exercise the power that there must be in it. Erastus (1524-1583) had taken over his ideas from Zwingli. The sin of confessing Christians may not be punished by ecclesiastical office-bearers by denying them the use of the seals of the covenant. Only the civil government may concern itself with sin. The church cannot make laws or decrees. It can only instruct, admonish, convince. This Erastian system can be applied in different ways.

1. The application found in England, where it is connected with Episcopalianism. At the time of the Reformation, the English king had assumed for himself the power of the Pope as head of the church. All the bishops had to swear allegiance to him and to receive their office from his hands. Some said that by virtue of his office the king had also received the mandate from God to care for the spiritual concerns of his subjects. Others said that Scripture does not provide a form of church government, and so the church is completely free if it wishes to permit itself to be governed by the state. They are not strictly Episcopalian. The "high churchmen" tried in one way or another to diminish the authority of the crown.

2. The application of the Remonstrants. They too were zealous proponents of the authority of the state in ecclesiastical matters. This was connected with the political conditions of those days in Holland, but, moreover, also had a still deeper basis— namely, a weakening of the concept of the church and, in connection with that, of the kingship of Christ.

3. The application of the Lutheran church. In Germany, the Reformation certainly did not originate with civil power but still was taken up and advanced by it. The Reformers allowed consistories, which were charged with ecclesiastical discipline, to be appointed by the electors. The ruler of the land consequently received the power to appoint instruments for the government of the church and in fact became *Summus Episcopus*, "Highest Bishop." Some have the following theory for the explanation of this actual situation: the ruler is not the highest governor of the church on the basis of his civil position but only as its most eminent member. In the execution of his power, however, he is bound by the judgment of the clergy and the people. Others, however, are consistently Erastian and ascribe ecclesiastical authority to the ruler as such.

c) The episcopal system. This teaches that the unity and authority of the church resides with the bishops in their totality. It views the bishops as the successors of the apostles and thinks that authority has come by transmission from the latter to the former. Thereby an ordering naturally appears among the clergy, for the apostles certainly had a wholly unique position. Whoever thinks that the apostolate has been perpetuated in the episcopate must thus place the bishops higher than others who work in the church under their control. From this, it further follows that all the clergy must be ordained by the bishops if they are to be recognized as legitimate ministers of the church. The episcopal system is thus insupportable to other churches that reject its basic conception. That is, the episcopal system is schismatic in nature; it hinders practicing communion with other manifestations of the body of Christ on earth. It is said that the Episcopal Church of England rebaptizes children who were baptized in Presbyterian churches, and reordains ordained ministers from such churches. For a long time the episcopal system was the system of the Roman Catholic Church, first generally and later in opposition to the ultramontane theory. The French church appeals to bishops over against the Pope.

d) The system of the present-day Roman Catholic Church. This has already been discussed in part above. Since the Vatican Council,[1] it is a complete system. The Roman Catholic Church is an absolute monarchy. The Pope is accountable to no one; he stands above the church; indeed, the church is dependent on him. In a certain sense, he *is* the church. This system involves a great transformation, since it imports something absolute and tangible into our world of relativities and abstractions. If the church must surely be an institution, many say, then preferably it should be a perfect institution that acts with authority and finality. But this is an utterly unscriptural system, as is shown in detail in the introduction to dogmatics. It may be maintained neither exegetically nor historically nor dogmatically.

e) The system of the Independents. To begin with, this system agrees with the Puritan principle. One conceives of the church too much as a spiritual body of believers only, without reckoning

---

1   The First Vatican Council, 1869–1870.

with the calling that the church has to fulfill as an organized institution. Owen was an Independent or a Congregationalist. According to him, then, the individual visible church consists of those regenerate who are united by a specific relationship for the service of God and to exercise mutual oversight of one another. Believers are the material of the church, and this relationship is the form of the church.

Now it is self-evident that when in this way one limits the significance of the visible formation of the church, unity among the local churches is out of the question. Each church stands by itself. When a kind of union between different churches comes about, then this is completely accidental and not *jure divino*, "by divine right."

At the same time, internally Independentism also has its own distinctive mark by which it is distinguished from other systems. It has office ministry permanently bound to the choice of all believers; that is, it is absolutely democratic in its government of the church. There are no office-bearers in the Presbyterian sense of the word. The people, the sum of believers, invest with office and therefore can also, when they desire, withdraw it. Further: only confessing believers are subject to ecclesiastical discipline, for only they make up the church, properly speaking. On this point one can perhaps best see the difference between the Independent and the Presbyterian-Reformed concept of the church. Finally, many Independents also allow ordination to the ministry of the Word only in relation to the local church in which it took place. According to this understanding, when a teacher has left his church in which he was ordained, he becomes an ordinary member and must be ordained anew to be able to minister in a new local church. It is said that such ordinations regularly occurred among the Puritans in New England. According to the Presbyterian concept, ordination does not only apply to a local church. An elder is only an elder in the one congregation that chose him, but a minister of the Word is minister of the Word wherever he proclaims the Word in the church of God. The system of the Independents must in fact exclude missions to pagans.

f) The collegial system. This is the system developed by Samuel Pufendorf (1687), by Christoph Mattäus Pfaff (1719), and J. H. Böhmer (1744) in Germany. The old Roman guilds were called *collegia*—free associations that originated out of a particular interest but that were recognized by the state as such. So Christian churches, which in the beginning had been *collegia illicita* [unlawful associations] for the Romans, later became *collegia licita* [permitted associations]. The collegial system will have churches viewed as such free societies. They originated by a contract.

However, this is a more or less rationalistic conception of the matter. It is certainly true that one obtains his full rights in the visible church only by confession, but still one is already associated with the church earlier, apart from his own doing. That the church has originated through a contract is equally quite as mistaken as the theory that the state had come into existence in that way. As the state rests on the basis of the family and the clan in the sphere of natural law, so also in the spiritual sphere the church rests on the ministry of God's covenant. To wish to derive its right from a free act of man is completely Pelagian. The collegial system is usually connected with the idea that the local churches are parts of the visible association as a whole and not, in antithesis, to be viewed as a product of the gathering of local churches through their representatives in larger assemblies.

One can compare the collegial system with the partitioning of France. France is a republic, and the separate provinces are determined from Paris. The whole is greater than the parts, and all power and jurisdiction comes from above. One can compare the Reformed-Presbyterial system, on the other hand, with the union of the states of North America. Here the parts precede the whole and authority rises from below, from which then it further follows that the state has rights that it has not ceded to Washington, and, conversely, those rights that the individual states can no longer exercise.

g) The Reformed system of church government. This is based on the following fundamental theses:
   1. The church, in its deepest essence, is a *kingdom*, for Christ is anointed king over it. Accordingly, no authority may be

exercised in the church unless it is derived from the kingship of Christ and remain bound to it. To want to make the
church entirely into a free association shortchanges this kingship. Believers are not free to unite or not to unite, but from
the outset stand under the command of Christ, their king.

2. This kingly authority of Christ over the church is connected
to the kingly word of Christ. Christ is in the church, and He
rules over the church through His word. Therefore, no one
can do anything in the church that would be right and conflict
with that word. All believers owe unconditional obedience to
the word of their King, and that obligation takes precedence
before all other things. In this way, all despotic authority is
excluded. There are no truly sovereign rulers in the Christian
church. Christ is the only sovereign. In the Roman Catholic
Church, the Pope claims that he is such a sovereign and then is
also called the representative of Christ on earth. He is bound
by nothing, does not live according to the law of Christ, but
produces the law of Christ in a sovereign manner. In the Reformed church, something like that is completely inconceivable. In God's Word we have the commands of Christ once for
all. In it, also, the outlines of government are drawn, while
what is subordinate is left to Christian wisdom according to
time and circumstances. But the main thing is to carry out and
to apply the word of Christ. Thus, insofar as the church itself
is concerned, it is entirely a ministerial and not a ruling power.

3. Christ as King has invested the church with power (*potestas*).
However, this *potestas* does not reside, as the Roman Catholic and the Episcopal system would have it, with a separate
class that would possess it without the church and beyond
the church. It resides with the church as a whole. The whole
church has received this power from its King. The power of
the keys resides with the church. Everywhere the church is,
there is the power of the keys. Everywhere the church originates or manifests itself, there the power of the keys appears.
In Matthew 18:18 it is said to the congregation, "All that you
will bind on earth shall be bound in heaven," etc. The church
can exercise this power through the ministry of overseers as

it generally does, and it is even its calling to choose such over-seers and to subject themselves to their direction, to maintain a special ministry of the Word, but all this does not negate the fact that the church as a whole is the seat of power that is exercised in it on behalf of Christ. Voetius expresses it like this: "that the ministering key of authority and government is in the whole body of the church as such *virtualiter* [virtually], but only in the ministers *formaliter* [formally]."

Viewed from this angle, Reformed church government is a democracy in antithesis to the oligarchic and despotic charac-ter of the Roman Catholic and Anglican system. Voetius asks "whether the *potestas* [power] resides in the church council [consistory] or with the ministers of any particular church, or with the people in distinction from the church council, or in the entire church body consisting of people and church coun-cil?" His answer is, "We deny that all the power resides either with the church council alone or with the ministers alone. This would still be oligarchic and papist, so that the people as laity would be excluded from all power and everything would be guaranteed to the clergy and that certainly a hierarchical clergy." Subsequently, "We deny that all the power resides with the people as distinct from the church council, with them as first and sufficient subject, so that it would devolve from there to the ministers and the church council with regard to its possession or at least with regard to its use, namely, be-cause the people choose and appoint ministers and elders, and transmit to them power, or rather, the exercise of power; just as if they possess no proper power in themselves or through themselves by virtue of their ministry or work by divine right." (This is the Independentist theory, indicated then in the con-text as the teaching of the Brownists.) Consequently, "We deny that all power in the same sense belongs to the church council and its members and to the people head for head or taken col-lectively." Finally, "We affirm that ecclesiastical power taken universally and collectively resides with the whole body of the church, as that consists of church council and people as its proper and sufficient subject; that it is not passed from the body of the people to the church council and also not the reverse—no more than my right eye is the real, first, immediate and nearest subject of my sight and this sight passes over to my left eye, nor the reverse."

Therefore, the conception is this:

a) Power resides with the church as a whole.

b) The exercise of this power cannot occur other than by the office-bearers in the church connected with the congregation. It is not legitimate for a congregation to act without government in the manner of Independents

c) Neither can a government act apart from the congregation.

d) Church as institute and government originate with each other, for the individual church is organized as a separate body by the election of overseers—that is, church and church council originate with each other.

e) The power that the church council has is not transmitted from the individual members of the church by election and installation. Calling or election is nothing other than the concrete application of office to this or that person, and only to this degree is it a *causa sine qua non*, "condition without which not."

f) Conversely, the power that resides with the members of the church does not first descend from above and derive from the church council. When the office-bearers admit someone to the visibly Reformed church, this act of reception is naturally indispensable, but it is not the source of ecclesiastical power.

This conception is in fact supported by Scripture. At its beginning, the church existed with the apostolate. The apostles were of course much more than ordinary ministers of the church, but still their office also included ordinary authority.

These apostles were not chosen by the church but by Christ, who gave power both to them and the church. The eleven apostles did not choose a new apostle as though they had formed a college that could refill itself. They had two chosen by the congregation, while the final choice

remained to the one who knows the heart. Later, too, it was
Christ Himself who called the apostle Paul. Thus, if one
were to drop the apostles, one could say that the church
was there before its office-bearers. But that one cannot exclude the apostles and view them merely as missionaries
appears certain from Matthew 16:19, where the keys of the
kingdom of heaven were given to them.

4. This *potestas ecclesiastica* [ecclesiastical power] is distributed
in different ways. Some speak of (1) a dogmatic power, and
(2) a juridical power. To the first, then, belong the preaching
of the Word, the administration of the sacraments, and all
that serves these as means: the gathering and organization
of churches, the choosing of ministers, the calling together
of assemblies, etc. To the second belong ecclesiastical discipline and all that pertains to it. Hence one speaks of two keys:
a key of knowledge and a key of government (*clavis scientiae et
regiminis*). Others make a threefold distinction: (1) a dogmatic,
(2) an ordering, and (3) a judicial power.

5. Dogmatic power, like all ecclesiastical power, is naturally a
ministerial power and bound to the Word of God. It includes:

a) The preservation of Holy Scripture. The words of God are
entrusted to the church. It preserves the Scripture not only
as a Bible society does, but it is its official calling (Rom 3:2).

b) The ministry of Holy Scripture. This happens through the
ministers of the Word. They speak on the basis of the Word
and from the Word, and so open or shut the kingdom of
heaven. This is a declarative power that then is only valid
before God when it agrees with Scripture and when the situation to which it is applied is in fact as one assumes it to be.
Consequently, there is a distinction in this power between
mere scriptural interpretation by a private member and
the official ministry of the Word. God or Christ speaks to
the congregation through the latter, through such who are
called by Him to that end. Christ has given them the ministry of reconciliation, and they are ambassadors on behalf
of Christ, who implore: Be reconciled with God (2 Cor 5:20;
cf. 1 Tim 4:13; 2 Tim 2:15; cf. [Heidelberg] Catechism, 84).

c) The explanation and determination of the meaning of
   Holy Scripture by means of creeds and confessions, especially against erroneous opinions. Accordingly, the
   church is called a pillar and ground of the truth (1 Tim 3:15).
   Of course, the Word of God has its ground in itself, and this
   Word is not unlocked, as Rome would have it, only by the
   church. But through the ministry of the church the truth
   is expounded and upheld; its certainty is made manifest.

   There are many who deny to the church the power and
   right of making creeds, and think that to do so is in conflict
   with the sufficiency of Holy Scripture. Hence, too, there
   are many communions that hold to no confession, such as
   the Quakers, Darbyists, etc. One should grant that creeds
   are not absolutely necessary. A church, if one wishes to
   reason in the abstract, can exist without confessional
   documents, and has existed without such. These, however, were exceptional situations. It is impossible to guide
   someone through Scripture in its entirety or to ask him his
   opinions concerning the whole of Scripture. The essential
   things must be gathered together in order that the church
   may show how it understands Scripture in the light of the
   Spirit. The authority of these creeds is always bound to
   Scripture; they are susceptible to improvement, but may
   not be lightly revised, inasmuch as they are not a compen-
   dium of theology but the ripe fruits of the spiritual development of the church, sometimes obtained through a long
   struggle. A true revision does not tear down the old but
   explains and confirms it and further illumines it in connection with new times and circumstances. But it remains
   true that the Scripture is the *norma normans* [norming
   norm], the confession the *norma normata* [normed norm].

6. According to some, what we have already enumerated above
   as parts of the dogmatic power of the church belongs to the
   potestas ordinis [power of order], since one limits this power
   to the official ministry of the Word. If one takes the first part
   more broadly, as we have done, falling under the *potestas ordinis* is the making of laws and rules, thus of a *church order*

and the implementation thereof; in short, all that occurs in the church apart from the power that is related to the Word and that belongs to discipline. The ordinances that the church makes are distinguished from the ordinances that God Himself has prescribed in His Word. The latter bind the conscience, something that cannot be said of an ecclesiastical ordinance. That there must be gatherings in which God's Word is proclaimed and the sacraments are administered is a "law" that obligates the conscience; how those gatherings will be further organized in detail is an ordinance of the church, a *canon* or *constitution*. If the latter are transgressed, then it is not sin because they are binding in themselves, but only because by transgressing them one devalues the ecclesiastical power by which they are established. The laws are only *declared* by the church; the ordinances are *made* by it. Laws are spoken of in Matthew 28:20, "teaching them to keep all that I have commanded you." Of the ordinances (at least in part), there is an example in Acts 15 (cf. with 1 Cor 8:9, 13 and 10:23, 25, 27; cf. also 1 Cor 14:40; 11:34; 16:1).

Now, every church order consists of two different parts. In it are elements that belong to the most fundamental parts of scriptural government; thus church laws. In it are also elements that are freely made and about which Scripture is not decisive, at least gives no direct command. A good church order must include both, since free stipulations can only be made on the basis of the foundations of scriptural church government and so be suitable. Thus there is also an unalterable element in the church order, derived from God's Word, to which the human element is added. The latter too, however, must be followed, although on a different basis than the former, namely, since the church has also bound itself to that element by its own rulers. Whoever acknowledges ecclesiastical power to make ordinances must also keep those ordinances, even when he may consider them less useful or serviceable. A canon that need not be followed *eo ipso* [thereby] ceases to be a canon.

Discipline[2]

7. The third part of ecclesiastical power is the *potestas judicialis* or *disciplinaris*, "ecclesiastical discipline." Not everyone acknowledges that the church has this power to maintain oversight of its members through discipline or to exclude from its fellowship by excommunication. Erastians deny every such action, maintaining that such discipline belongs to the sphere of the state and that therefore the church must keep itself out of it entirely. Only if the state does not fulfill its duty, or cannot since it is unbelieving, may the church, according to some, take discipline into its own hands.

It was Calvin who brought to the fore specifically ecclesiastical discipline, as something distinguished from civil discipline, in connection with the presbyterial office. And for these two things—discipline and the office of elder—the Reformed church is indebted, under God, to him. However, in Geneva, according to the church order introduced in 1541, on more than one point ecclesiastical discipline was still dependent on the power of civil punishment. Elders were chosen from and by the government. Only in lands where the government stood over against the church was this good principle developed with complete purity.

The question is where and to what extent Scripture teaches discipline in the narrower sense—that is, the sort of handling of the members that ends up in public and official excommunication. It is not sufficient to appeal to the character of an association, for the church is more than an association. It acts not by its own hand but in the name of its King. May it in His name proceed to banish? Theologians (such as Turretin) appeal to the Old Testament. Fallen man is thrown out of paradise and eating from the tree of life is denied him. Paradise was a type of the congregation, the tree of life a sacrament, as was what happened with Cain (Gen 4:14). The uncircumcised, lepers,

---

2   Still addressing the question of the organization and government of the church, this subpoint (7) provides a lengthy treatment of discipline, and the following subpoint (8) a similarly lengthy treatment of offices.

the impure were excluded from holy places within Israel (Lev 5, 6, 7, 10); also from the use of holy things. Priests and Levites had to separate the pure and the impure (Ezek 44:28; cf. also 44:9). One may understand all this as a type, but the question is whether it is a type for the visible church or for the invisible, the kingdom of God. At that time there could not be a real excommunication as it exists under the New Testament. Church and state were one. Therefore, someone could not be put out of the church or he must also be eliminated from the state, that is, be eradicated from his people and punished with death. Only later, when the Jews lost their independence and this law could no longer be exercised, did actual excommunication, the termination of religious communion, originate. "And he himself would be separated from the congregation of the exiles" (Ezra 10:8). After the exile, the maintenance of this excommunication was an issue of its existence for Judaism. Surrounded on all sides by the pagan world, they had to rigorously exclude all pagan elements so that they were not gradually absorbed completely into paganism. The Jews made a distinction between נִידוּי and חֵרֶם, "temporary" and "final" excommunication. In the New Testament, this Jewish excommunication is spoken of in Luke 6:22; John 9:22; 12:42; and 16:2. The right to excommunicate resided with the elders of the synagogue ("the Jews had already made a decision together"; John 9:22).

This excommunication was the application in new situations of the principles prescribed in the Old Testament. Through Ezra it had received divine sanction, which Christ connected with the power of the keys that He gave to His church. Matthew 16:19 and 18:17 is the communication of this power. Its application is found in 1 Corinthians 5; 2 Thessalonians 3:14–15; Titus 3:10–11 ("Reject a heretical person after the first and second admonition, knowing that such a person is perverse and sins, having condemned himself"); 2 John 10; 1 Timothy 1:20 ("Among whom are Hymenaeus and Alexander, whom I have handed over to Satan in order that they would learn to no longer blaspheme"); and Romans 16:17.

Does all this have to do with the ordinary exercise of terminal discipline as this is understood to take place even now, or is this something that was only legitimate for the apostles? In 1 Corinthians 5, Paul says that the church should remove the incestuous person from its midst and that only if they did not do so, he himself intends to intervene with his apostolic authority (1 Cor 5:2–7). But even then it is not a solely apostolic excommunication that will be pronounced on such a person, for the apostle intends that his spirit will be present when the church is assembled, with the power of the Lord Jesus Christ. Accordingly, there are two elements here: (a) excommunication by the congregation, which the apostle urged and in which he participated through his spirit; (b) handing over to Satan for the destruction of the flesh (5:5). By that it is evident that something quite extraordinary is meant. We may not say that the church that applies discipline to someone and cuts him off hands over such a person to Satan. Our formula for removal does not use such expressions. Likely the apostle refers to bodily suffering, to which he had then gives over the one guilty (cf. the case of Elymas, Acts 13:9–11). First Timothy 1:20 is to be judged similarly. At the same time, we see from this case that the terminal exercise of discipline still has a remedial significance. Handing over to Satan also happened in order that the spirit may be saved in the day of the Lord Jesus Christ. The other texts mentioned above also place that in the foreground.

But this is not the sole purpose. If discipline has reference to the individual member, no less does it have reference to the body of the church. It serves to remove such members who, by remaining in the church, would infect others, would completely pollute the body, and would defile the table of the Lord. About that 1 Corinthians 5:6–7 says, "Do you not know that a little yeast leavens all the dough? Then clean out the old yeast that you may be new dough." But these two things do not necessarily exclude each other. As long as someone lives in sin and does not repent, he can be a dangerously sick member of the congregation and it can be necessary to cut him off while he still is and remains truly a child of God. Then he will return with confession, and discipline will have accomplished its double purpose. Of course, it may also be that he belonged among the hypocrites, who ought not to be in the congregation.

But the church cannot say that decisively when it pronounces excommunication; it must leave to God the judgment on what is inward. Its excommunication is always on the basis of God's Word and declarative—that is, if the person does not repent and his inward state corresponds to his outward conduct, then he will be excluded from the kingdom of God, as he is now excluded from the fellowship of the visible church. Thus, while those in the church are judged objectively according to their confession and are to be dealt with as Christians, the church has no further judgment to pronounce over someone who is excommunicated, for those who are outside God judges. Also, in subsequent dealings with such a person the church must reckon with both possibilities: that he can be a true member of the body of Christ who has taken a wrong path, and also that he can have been an apparent member. If he returns with repentance and confession, then the church deals with him (again objectively) in the first sense.

Connected with this is the question whether one can apply discipline to someone who puts himself outside the church. This question is difficult to answer. On the one hand, one can say that the individual has not become a member by a free act of the will, that by virtue of God's covenant he belongs to the church by his baptism and is under the oversight of the church, that he therefore cannot withdraw by a free act of the will. Consequently, if a freely self-willed separation from the church eliminates the further exercise of discipline, nearly nothing of discipline remains. If someone silently permits his being cut off to happen, then in most cases he will also not hesitate to sever the bond beforehand. In the worst illness, the radical cure has to remain unused.

However, there is also much to be said on the other side of this question. If one would carry out the execution of discipline strictly, then one must not only proceed if a member under censure separates himself, but also once a member free from censure takes this step. Indeed, even members by baptism must then come under censure if they withdraw, and the entire process of discipline must be carried out with all its steps from beginning to end. That smacks more or less of Rome. One can also say that by the self-willed withdrawal of a person the goal of discipline is in part reached, in part made unreachable. As far as the *surgical* aspect of discipline is concerned, this has become superfluous; the offender has freed the congregation from himself. As to the *healing* aspect, there is little chance that someone who of himself evades exclusion from the seals of covenant and from the termination of ecclesiastical fellowship will cause much disturbance. It seems to us that discipline must be exercised in ordinary circumstances. Many who have the sad intention to separate arbitrarily can perhaps be affected by official admonition or even by formal removal. Such cases have taken place. However, it is not advisable here to lay down a rule that must be valid for all instances. In any case, to say that one *may not* deal with someone who has separated goes too far.

Does this discipline also extend to those baptized who are not members by confession? That question is judged differently. The examples of discipline described for us in the New Testament concern those who were baptized as adults. This question is connected with another: whether the children of the covenant, the children of the confessing members of the church, belong to the institutional church. Voetius poses this question, "Whether the children of covenantal members are of the visible church and help to constitute it? Answer: They are called members of the church by the Netherlands Liturgy in the formula for the administration of baptism, in the first question put to the parents ("as members of His church ought to be baptized"). And that is shown from 1 Corinthians 7:14 and Acts 2:39. But this must be understood with a qualification, as Ames expresses it very well: The children are not in this sense mature members of the church that they ... are able to share in all privileges." This, however, may not be understood as though the church had no calling and no right to deal with the children and to admonish them. There is, therefore, a kind of discipline. But when someone becomes a confessing member, he promises that he will subject himself to ecclesiastical discipline. Formal, proper discipline, then, is designed for mature persons who have reached years of discretion, and not for children. The latter are members of the visible church, fully members and not half-members, but immature members who do not have the full right of members. But this in no way proves that the church does not possess its full rights with respect to them.

Discipline does not concern all sins, but so-called public sins—that is, those that openly give offense. Thus, by public sin is not meant a sin that is committed in the clear light of day, for there are many unrighteous acts that by their nature seek darkness and ecclesiastical discipline would thus become completely useless with such a limitation. Something becomes a public sin *ipso facto* [in itself] as soon as it openly produces offence in the congregation, even if it would also be committed behind closed doors. One may imagine what an untenable position the church would occupy against all the secret societies of our time if it would take "secret sin" in the strictest sense of the word. A sin can be secret and public at the same time, according to how it is understood. The demand that for a censurable sin one must be able to specify the day and the hour is completely untenable.

How the process of discipline should proceed is prescribed in Matthew 18:

a) Brotherly admonition between the one who has become aware of the sin and the sinner alone.

b) If this does not avail, admonition in the presence of one or two witnesses in order that it is clear later how the personal handling of the affair has taken place.

c) If this too does not help, the sin is presented to the congregation. The question here is whether by "the congregation" the church council is to be understood. Beza and our formula for the induction of elders understand it that way ("which by no means can be understood of each and every member of the congregation"). The truth appears to be that here it is not the particular form of government of the congregation that is in view, since that still lay in the future. By saying the church council, one says the congregation. In Corinth too, moreover, the entire church appears to have taken part in the exercise of discipline (cf. Heidelberg Catechism, question 85).

d) As soon as a sin is brought before the church council, it becomes public if the admonition does not avail. If the admonition does avail, the sin need not be made public further. If, on the other hand, it has been public from the outset, the church council naturally need not wait for someone to be concerned with it in private but must press for public confession. Public sins must be confessed publicly, whether they were originally public or become so by scorning ecclesiastical admonition.

The first step following fruitless admonition by the church council is the minor excommunication (*excommunicatio minor*), denial of the use of the Lord's Supper. Between this minor excommunication and the final removal fall three admonitions, according to article 77 of the Church Order of Dort. In the first, the name of the sinner is not mentioned; in the second, his name is mentioned with the recommendation of the classis. In the third, his removal is finally declared, in order that it can take place with the silent agreement of the church. This removal is called "major excommunication" (*excommunicatio major*). Reinstatement must also take place with the prior knowledge of the congregation.

Only individual persons are objects of discipline, not collective bodies, as Rome would have it when it excommunicates entire lands and nations. The consequences of discipline are not civil, as if one may not have any sort of contact in civil life with a censured or excommunicated person. Paul has expressly warned against this excess in 1 Corinthians 5:9-12. One must have no religious fellowship with such person. In a religious respect, he must be as a pagan or publican. But one may certainly work with a pagan and a publican. The church is also obligated to that after the exercise of discipline (2 Thess 3:15).

One sees that in general, with respect to its foundational principles, discipline rests on God's Word. Individual steps, on the other hand, possess no biblical authority and so do not belong to laws but to ecclesiastical regulations. Matthew 18 says nothing more than that those who do not listen to the church must be kept from all fellowship. However, discipline in stages is already very old in the church. A first and second admonition is already spoken of in Titus 3:10, after which a heretic must be expelled. The ancient church was rigorous not only in exclusion but also in readmission, which occurred in four steps (πρόκλαυσις, ἀκρόασις, ὑπόπτωσις, σύστασις). There were even parties that would not readmit the fallen. One who was placed under church discipline was excluded from office. In later times discipline fell into disuse, especially in the Roman Catholic Church through trafficking in indulgences.

It is almost superfluous to observe that excommunication does not exclude from the scope of the ministry of the Word but only from the ministry of the sacraments. Someone who is excommunicated has accountability toward the Word as much as do pagans and publicans when it is brought to him.

Ecclesiastical and civil dealing with sins do not exclude each other but run parallel. That someone has borne his civil punishment and so is once again right with the civil authority does not vindicate him before the church. It can also occur that in one way or another civil law does not condemn him while there are still reasons to deal with him ecclesiastically. The church need not conform to the opinions of worldly justice. It has its own administration of justice, and is itself responsible to God.

Offices[3]

8. To exercise the government of the church Christ has instituted offices. "He has given some to be apostles and some to be

---

3   See the preceding footnote.

prophets and some to be evangelists and some to be pastors and teachers" (Eph 4:11). "And God has placed some in the church: first apostles, second prophets, third teachers, after that miracles, after that gifts of healings, helps, governments, various kinds of tongues" (1 Cor 12:28). "Whether prophecy, according to the measure of faith, whether service, in serving, whether the one who teaches, in teaching, whether the one who admonishes, in admonishing, whether the one who distributes, in simplicity, the one who is an advocate, with diligence, the one who shows mercy, with cheerfulness" (Rom 12:6–8). From these passages one should start with the distinction of offices in the New Testament church. They are in part ordinary and in part extraordinary—Calvin (*Institutes*, 4.1.1 and following) divides them as follows: apostles, prophets, and evangelists are of an extraordinary and temporary kind; pastors and teachers have an ordinary office that is permanent. Teachers have to do with the interpretation of Scripture, pastors with the preaching of the gospel and the administration of the sacraments. Further permanent offices (derived from Rom 12:7 and 1 Cor 12:28) are government (κυβέρνησις) and care for the poor (ἀντίλημψις). Government resides with the elders, and care for the poor with the deacons. There are two sorts of deacons, those having to do with good for the poor and those having to do with the persons of the poor.

Apostle (ἀπόστολος), from ἀποστόλλειν, properly means "envoy," "one sent." It can be used in a general sense (cf. 2 Cor 8:23). Usually, however, it has a quite specific meaning. Jesus designated the twelve whom He chose with this specific name (Luke 6:13), which thus implies the particularity of their office. They were not called apostles as ordinary missionaries (cf. Acts 1:2, 8). Paul certainly did not merely claim the position of an ordinary preacher when he defended and established his apostleship with such emphasis and so frequently.

The apostles are chosen, twelve in number, as representatives of spiritual Israel. Thereby it was meaningfully indicated that the New Testament church rested on the ground of the

Old and that it was built upon that ground. They are at the same time stones that, with the prophets, form the foundation (Matt 19:28; Luke 22:30). When one considers the matter from this viewpoint, the election of Matthias (Acts 1:26) cannot be called a mistake or hasty action. Paul did not appear in the place of Judas, but stands outside the circle of the twelve (cf. Rev 21:14). He was the Gentile-apostle, ἀπόστολος ἔθνων (Rom 11:13), ἀποστολὴν ... εἰς τὰ ἔθνη (Gal 2:8).

An apostle has an office that not only extends over his lifetime but is valid for the entire earthly dispensation of God's covenant. Presbyters and deacons in the New Testament are no longer our deacons and presbyters. For us, they are past historical persons. It is otherwise with the apostles; they are our apostles as well as the apostles of the first Christians, sent to us, authoritative for us. There is no knowledge of Christ other than through the word of the apostles. Christ prays for those who will believe in Him through their word. Whoever withdraws himself from the authority of the apostles places himself outside the pale of Christianity. Paul says: my gospel is the only, genuine gospel, and if an angel or whoever else proclaims another gospel to you, let him be cursed.

The marks of an apostle are:

a) That he must have a mission directly from Christ. That is implied in the name. He is not an "envoy" in a general but a specific sense, an envoy directly from Christ. The Gospels say, "Jesus sent out these twelve" (Matt 10:8; 11:1; Mark 6:7; Luke 9:2). One could say then that Matthias could not be an apostle since he was chosen by the church. But the church chose two then, and left the decisive choice to Christ. Paul, too, was directly called by Christ (Gal. 1:1).

b) The apostles had to be witnesses of the life of Christ during His state of humiliation, of His mediatorial work in that state, of His suffering, and above all of His resurrection (John 15:27). "It is necessary then that of the men who accompanied us during all the time in which the Lord Jesus went in and out among us, beginning with the baptism of John to the day in which He was taken up from us, that one of these become with us a witness of his resurrection" (Acts 1:21–22). Hence Paul asks, "Am I not an apostle? Am I not free? Have I not seen Jesus Christ our Lord?" (1 Cor 9:1). And accordingly, his seeing of the Lord on the way to Damascus must have been a real seeing and not merely a leaving of his senses. Elsewhere, then, the apostle also puts it on the same line with a series of other bodily appearances of the Lord (1 Cor 15:8).

c) An apostle spoke and wrote by inspiration. The Lord promised that to His apostles (Matt 10:19; Luke 12:12). The Holy Spirit, whom the Father would send in His name, would teach them all things (John 14:26), lead them into all truth (John 16:13). This promise is fulfilled in Peter (Acts 4:8). Later they could say, "It seemed good to the Holy Spirit and to us" (Acts 15:28). "So then whoever rejects this, does not reject man but God, who has given us His Holy Spirit," Paul says in 1 Thessalonians 4:8. An apostle can certainly sin and make mistakes, but he cannot proclaim false teaching. When by his conduct Peter appeared to teach the obligation of the Gentiles to keep the Jewish law, he acted hypocritically but did not err (Gal 2:13).

d) An apostle possesses the power to work miracles. That too was promised them in their sending, and they made use of it (Acts 3:15–16; Heb 2:3–4).

e) An apostle receives validation from God by the success of his work. Paul, at least, has repeatedly appealed to that for his apostleship, and others have acknowledged it as a verdict of God (Gal 2:8; 1 Cor 9:1–2).

These facts are sufficient to settle the question whether there are still apostles or can be. Episcopalians make the apostolate something transmissible and think they may view their bishops as apostles. But they cannot say that they have seen the Lord, are not inspired, work no miracles, and are not chosen by Christ Himself. Hence they maintain that besides the qualities mentioned above, the apostles had this as well: that they could ordain and govern, and that is passed down to the bishops. Now it is certainly true that the apostles possessed this power. They rule with absolute authority over the churches, appoint elders, deacons, etc. But only they? This is evidently not the case. By virtue of its entirely unique character, their office included all these other things (cf. 1 Tim 4:14 with 2 Tim 1:6).

In recent times, the Irvingites have sought to revive the apostolate. According to them, the gift of tongues has also returned. The return of Christ is about to take place. Hence the name: "Catholic Apostolic Church." There are prophets, apostles, evangelists, and pastors.

A second office reckoned as extraordinary is that of *prophet*. Under the Old Testament there were two sorts of prophets: those who stood on the same line with the New Testament apostles, that is, who were infallible proclaimers of the counsel of God, and those who applied and further disseminated the truth proclaimed by the former. In the New Testament, prophets appear along with the apostles (Eph 3:5; 2:20; 4:11; 1 Tim 1:18; 4:14; 1 Cor 14:3; 13:8; Rev 11:6). From these passages, it appears that in the apostolic era the gift to speak for the edification of the congregation was developed in an extraordinary way, that through the Spirit mysteries were revealed, future things sometimes foretold (Acts 13:1–2; 11:28). To that extent, this prophetic office was temporary and extraordinary. In the broader sense of "speaking for edification," it is permanent and was also in use in old Reformed churches.

A third office is that of *evangelists*. This designation is easily misunderstood. Biblical evangelists were essentially distinguished from ours. They are connected with the apostles. They were their associates, traveling companions, fellow workers. Philip, Timothy, Titus, Mark, Silas belonged to this group. The seventy disciples whom the Lord sent out are also to be noted here. Their work consisted in preaching and baptizing. To that extent they corresponded to ordinary pastors, except that these served in a set place. But at the same time, they appear to have had special power. Titus appointed elders (Titus 1:5) and exercised discipline (3:10). Timothy laid on hands (1 Tim 5:22). From all this it appears that there was something extraordinary in the office of evangelist. Jerome already said, "Every apostle was an evangelist, not every evangelist an apostle." The popular notion that an evangelist stands a little lower than a pastor is, in any case, unbiblical. If this office of evangelist can still exist, there is much more reason to place them higher (cf. also "helps," 1 Cor 12:28).

We come now to the ordinary offices. Here different questions must be discussed: (a) The relationship in which the offices of elder (presbyter) and bishop or overseer (*episkopos*) stand to each other, and whether this is one and the same office. (b) The relationship in which the office of pastor (*poimēn*) stands to the two mentioned in (a); that is, whether within the eldership there is a distinction between those who are pastors and those who are not pastors. (c) The question concerning the office of teacher and whether this was a particular office, distinct from the office of pastor. (d) The question concerning the office of deacons and deaconesses. (e) The question concerning calling to the offices and the way in which one is invested with office.

a) The relationship between the episcopate and the presbyterate. Advocates of the episcopal system say that the two offices of bishop and presbyter are different. Bishops are higher than presbyters. They have the power to ordain and to govern the presbyters. The latter cannot ordain each other. Some go much further, as we saw, and make bishops successors of the apostles.

In antithesis, we posit the thesis: bishop and presbyter, overseer and elder wholly indicate the same office. An overseer is an elder and an elder is an overseer. If there was a distinction in the eldership and in the overseership, this had nothing to do with the double name. One called the two kinds of elders that there were both overseers and presbyters. It is reported of Paul (Acts 20:17) that he summoned the elders of the church of Ephesus and then addressed them as overseers (20:28). In Philippians 1:1 overseers appear next to deacons, as in other places elders are next to deacons (cf. also 1 Tim 3:2 with 3:8); "that you should appoint elders from city to city" (Titus 1:5) and "for an overseer must be above reproach" (1:7). Consequently, nothing is clearer than the identity of these two offices. The only difference lies in these two points: elder (presbyter) is a Jewish term derived from the synagogue, which was also administered by the eldest men; overseer (*episkopos*) is a Greek term. Elder refers to the *dignity* of the office, overseer its *work*.

b) The second of the questions above concerns the distinction within the eldership itself. Were there two kinds of elders? It appears from 1 Timothy 4:14 that in one and the same church there was a plurality of elders, and that they formed a closed whole, a college, "presbytery," "eldership." From 1 Timothy 5:17 it appears further that there were elders who worked in the Word and teaching, and so also elders who were not occupied with such work. The distinction between teaching elders and ruling elders rests on that.

We will now have to think about the matter as follows. Originally all the emphasis with the eldership fell on ruling, maintaining oversight. The reason for that was that the extraordinary office of prophecy and the extraordinary χαρίσματα (*charismata*), in general, as well as the continuing presence of the apostles and evangelists made the need for an ordained office of teacher less visible. Elders could all teach and speak the Word, but there were many besides them who also taught and prophesied in the congregation. Later, when extraordinary gifts had already waned, there arose of itself the need for a regulated office of teacher. In the Pastoral Epistles of Paul this already appears as an established structure. Still, it seems to us that one derives too much from the data if one argues that all the elders were not free to be active in teaching in the congregation. Only this follows with certainty: there were a number of elders who had the specific duty to teach. The others may have had the freedom; they did not have the duty. Hereby, in fact, the Reformed distinction between two kinds of elders is legitimized in principle.

Some difference prevails concerning the office of ruling elders. According to one theory, they must be viewed as representatives of the people. The church is then governed by two sorts of office-bearers: (a) ministers of the Word, who are clergy; (b) ruling elders, who are laity. Both have identical rights in all ecclesiastical bodies to which they are delegated. But the elders who only rule bring along these rights from the people whom they represent; teaching elders have those rights, as it were, in themselves. From that it follows that the latter also continue to possess them in ecclesiastical assemblies when they do not represent a church council or congregation. A teaching elder without ministry nonetheless has a vote in assemblies. The Presbyterian Church of the United States says in its "Form of Government": "The ordinary and permanent office-bearers in the church are overseers or pastors; the representatives of the people are commonly called ruling elders and deacons." And again: "Ruling elders are properly the representatives of the people and are chosen by the people to exercise government and discipline in connection with the pastors and ministers of the Word" (ch. III, 2, and ch. V).[4]

There are substantial objections to this view:

1. It could be inferred from it that the congregation that chooses these representatives can give them a specific mandate—now broader, then less broad—all according as it chooses. Strictly speaking, one can give instruction to a representative and say: you must act *so*. Now, it is clear that in this sense ruling elders are not representatives of the people. They have received an office from Christ; the Holy Spirit has appointed them as overseers of the flock; they are not accountable to their constituents but to God and His Word.

---

4 Translation of Vos' Dutch translation. I have not verified either the edition of the Form of Government cited or the accuracy of the reference. It is not clear which Presbyterian denomination Vos has in view; most likely the Church in the North.

2. It cannot be proven that the New Testament makes such a distinction with respect to the power of the teaching and ruling elders. They apparently form one institution, bear the same names (bishop, elder), and it is completely impossible to explain this if there is such a profound difference as this theory presupposes. Some of its advocates (Charles Hodge, among others) would then retain the term *presbyter* in a specific sense for ruling elders—completely without support, in our thinking. If anything is clear, then it is this: that in 1 Timothy 5:17 both kinds of elders are specifically called presbyter.

3. It is certainly true that power is given by Christ to the church as a whole, but this must be understood in the sense described above and not as if it is transferred democratically from the congregation to the elders, who govern. Elders have their power to rule from Christ as they belong to the organism of the congregation.

4. That elders are chosen by the congregation does not mean that they are representatives of the congregation. It is well established that even in electing an apostle the congregation is consulted for its choice. No one would infer from this that an apostle represents the congregation. And the congregation likewise takes part in the election of a teaching elder. Conversely, it would seem, sometimes the apostles also appointed both ruling and teaching elders directly or had them appointed by their evangelists. If the office of ruling elder were in its essence an office of representation of the congregation, then one must say: a ruling elder chosen by an apostle is a contradictory notion. But the matter becomes completely otherwise if one abandons this idea of representation. Then it becomes clear how there are two ways along which Christ chooses office-bearers, both to rule and to teach—namely, sometimes

directly by His apostles, sometimes by the choice of the congregation.

Nevertheless, there is some truth in this theory. It has already been noted above that a ruling elder can only serve in the particular congregation that chose him. He cannot function in another congregation. But a minister of the Word can certainly do that. This, however, does not prove that ruling elders get their authority from the congregation. That simply follows from the limitation on their work. Ministers of the Word have a general or a limited mission. But they too, for example, can be delegated by a classis to a broader assembly.

While a ruling elder does not have the rights and duties of a teaching elder, in antithesis a teaching elder certainly has the rights and duties of a ruling elder. Those who teach likewise govern, but not the reverse. The installation formula for ruling elders specifies their activities as follows: (1) having oversight of the congregation; (2) to be helpful to the ministers of the Word in exercising the governing power of the church (see above); (3) having oversight of the doctrine and conduct of the ministers of the Word.

On the other hand, teaching elders have: (1) the ministry of the Word; (2) the accompanying administration of the sacraments; (3) the public invocation of the name of God on behalf of the entire congregation; (4) the exercise of governing power; (5) oversight and discipline of the congregation.

Is there a particular term that is standard for teaching elders in Scripture? For that some have wanted to take the term "shepherds" (ποιμένες). From that come our "pastors," which is no longer applied to ruling elders. But Scripture does not make this distinction. In Ephesians 4:11, the "pastors" are put next to the "teachers," and by the former are apparently to be understood "elders," "overseers," without further specification or division. In Acts 20:28, again, it is said of all the presbyters that they are appointed as overseers to shepherd (ποιμαίνειν) the congregation of God. Also, that concept includes a twofold shepherding: (a) feeding; (b) leading or ruling. In all its dimensions, it is therefore only applicable to teaching elders, and to that extent one has a certain right to call them "pastors" preeminently, as those alone in whom the concept of "pastor" is realized in full. On the other hand, there is another term for overseers and elders that then lets more emphasis fall on the ruling element alone, namely, "upholder" (προιστάμενος, προεστώς, from προιστάναι, Rom 12:8; 1 Tim 5:17); see also "administrations" (κυβερνήσεις, 1 Cor 12:28).

c) The third question concerns the office of teacher. "Teachers" are spoken of in more than one place in the New Testament. Ephesians 4:11 has ποιμένας καὶ διδασκάλους, ["pastors and teachers"]. Is that one concept, one office, characterized from two sides? Calvin (*Institutes*, 4.1.5; 4.3.4) separates the two. "Teachers" (*doctores*) have only to do with the interpretation of Scripture, in order that the pure, biblical truth endures; "pastors" have to do with the preaching of the gospel and the administration of the sacraments and discipline. In a similarly but less decisive vein is his *Commentary on Ephesians*, on 4:11. It is best explained (according to Calvin): pastors are at the same time teachers, but, conversely, to be a teacher one need not at the same time be a pastor. Most Reformed theologians follow Calvin and speak of a specific doctorate (cf., e.g., Maastricht, [*Theoretico-practica theologia*] 2.7.20). But there is no proof that something like that existed in the New Testament as a regular office. One could rather identify the teachers who appear there with catechetical instructors. If one would view professorship as a separate ecclesiastical office, one can infer that from the general concept of a teaching office. The Church Order of Dort also speaks of doctors or professors in theology (article 18). They, however, are not appointed by the church. In any case, the scientific degrees granted by the universities may not be confused with ecclesiastical offices. An ecclesiastical office must be granted by the church. The question here simply comes down to this: Is this teaching office that the church confers on some a particular alteration of that of the minister of the Word, or is it a new office that someone can occupy without being a minister of the Word? So far the church has not given a clear answer.

d) In the fourth place, deacons and deaconesses should be spoken of. Διάκονες (from διακονεῖν) is in general a "servant." It can be said of all office-bearers in the church that they are servants. Paul calls himself a "deacon" [διάκονος] (Col 1:25). The government is God's minister (Rom 13:4; cf. 2 Cor 3:6). But "deacon" also appears in a narrower sense along with the office of "elder," "with the overseers and deacons" (Phil 1:1; cf. 1Tim 3:8, 12). Mention is made of a woman as a deaconess, "Phoebe, a deaconess of the church at Cenchreae" (Rom 16:1; according to some, 1 Tim 3:11 as well).

In Acts 6, one finds the establishment of the office of deacons. There are, however, not a few who dispute that.

1. According to some, in Acts 6 we do not have the origin of the diaconate but of the presbytery [body of elders]. One gathers that from the fact that according to Acts 11:30 the congregation in Antioch sent aid to Jerusalem, which was handed over not to deacons but to elders. If there had been deacons, it is said, these must have received it. So judge Lange, Lechler, and others. But this conclusion is hasty. It was no more than natural that representatives from a different congregation approached the elders as the leaders of the congregation, not the deacons. It is also said that if this is not the institution of the office of presbyter, where then is this to be found? But we can just as well ask, vice versa: if the diaconate is not instituted here, then where?

2. Others say that what is first instituted in Jerusalem according to Acts 6 was a mixed entity that united in itself the functions of both eldership and deaconate. This too is not plausible. It is not said there that the

men who were chosen must do the work of a presbyter. They must serve tables.

3. According a few (Vitringa), we have to do here with an extraordinary, temporary office that may not be confused with our diaconate. But there is also no proof for this. It is difficult to see where that great difference would have consisted between these and later deacons.

We have Acts 6 for the institution of the ordinary diaconate throughout history. It arose through the pressure of circumstances. The apostles could not "serve tables," that is, not busy themselves with the distribution of foodstuffs, when their principal work of the ministry of the Word of God and prayer had to suffer by doing that. Hence the designation "deacon, "serving," had the specific meaning of "serving table" (John 2:5, 9). The office is designated according to what had first been given it, the ministry of tables. From Romans 12:8 and 1 Corinthians 12:28, Calvin inferred that there were two kinds of deacons.

e) Finally, the question must be discussed how these offices were continued in the church after they had once been instituted. Accordingly, this is an inquiry concerning the calling of office-bearers in the church. All authority of office comes from Christ. But Christ does not speak from heaven and does not appoint directly the persons by whom He would be served in His church. Provision, therefore, must be made by external means to make this appointment in a fair and orderly manner. The church must have grounds for believing of its servants that God calls them. Calling is to be viewed not as an absolute transfer of power but as an appointment of those who will exercise power. They are distinguished in differing ways:

1. Into an *external* and an *internal* call. In the latter, God works through His word and through His Spirit directly on the heart of the individual person to give

rise in him, more or less strongly, the conviction that he is intended for official service in the church. Paul speaks of that in 1 Timothy 3:1: "If someone *aspires* to the office of overseer, he *desires* an excellent work." To that desire belongs a consciousness that one is impelled to the office not by fleshly ambition or greed but by love for God and zeal to build the church; further, with the conviction that the gifts necessary for occupying the office and the exercise of its ministry are not completely lacking; finally, that by providence the paths are also opened and paved for us to reach our goal by external calling. Where these things are present, one ought not to expect something additional and extraordinary.

Christ has made external calling to reside with the congregation. Here, too, we come into conflict with Rome. According to Rome, it resides with the bishops as far as the lower clergy is concerned, with the Pope for the bishops. We say that the church normally has the power of calling exercised by its already-installed ministers, by presbyters, both teaching and ruling, but that this is not at all absolutely necessary, so that if the circumstances demand, a church should not call a teaching elder directly as it normally calls ruling elders. One may imagine that a number of believers suffer shipwreck during a storm and land on an isolated island in the midst of barbarians, and that they have to remain there without communication with Christian churches in Christian lands. Have those Christians the right to call from among themselves a teacher to administer the Word and sacraments? To that all Reformed theologians answer affirmatively. We surely say that no one may arrogate an office to himself without a call. Still, the calling of the church is sufficient, and that of the ministers of the church is not absolutely necessary. That Rome answers differently is connected with the distinctive understanding it ascribes to calling and ordination.

For Rome, this is a sacrament (*sacramentum ordinis*).
The common folk of the laity cannot administer the
sacrament. Further, a sacrament impresses with
a *character indelebilis*, "an imperishable character."
Something granted in this way can only be ascribed
to the bishops.

Our arguments are: the power of the keys is
given by Christ to His entire church (Matt 18:17).
The church is also sent by Christ into the world in
such a way that it bears in itself the fullness of power
necessary to discharge its calling. It must be able,
if necessary, to call its ministers if it would be and
remain a true church. The ministry of office-bearers
may not be a stumbling block that drags the church
down on its way and that impedes it in its movement,
but must be an instrument and means through
which it reaches its goals—naturally not a purely
human means but one commanded and approved by
God. It is not a legitimate or illegitimate office that
makes a true church, but the reverse. Paul appeals to
the congregation, "Whether Paul, whether Apollos,
whether Cephas ...; all are yours" (1 Cor 3:22). Thus,
there is order in the congregation prior to office,
even though temporally they both have existed side
by side. The church abides eternally; office ceases
when the militant church ceases to exist (1 Cor 4:5).
The congregation must expect false teachers and distinguish between false and true teachers (Matt 7:15;
John 10:14, 27; 1 John 4:1; Gal 1:8).

The practice of the apostles also teaches us this.
If with anyone, then with them the right resided
to appoint office-bearers directly in the congregation. They have apparently also made use of that
right. But still by no means always, as one would
have to expect according to the Roman Catholic view.
It has already been noted that the congregation at
Jerusalem was consulted even for the choice of an

apostle (Acts 1:23). In Acts 6, the entire assembly of believers again chooses the seven men who were intended by God for the diaconate. How the presbyters in the Jerusalem congregation were appointed is not mentioned. They appear for the first time as something known (Acts 11:30). In Acts 14:23 we read, "And when they had chosen elders for them in each congregation, with the raising of hands, having prayed and with fasting," etc. (χειροτονήσαντες δὲ αὐτοῖς κατ᾽ ἐκκλησίαν πρεσβυτέρους). Two things are apparent from this: on the one hand that the congregations had existed for a time without having chosen presbyters. It was only on their return trip that Paul and Barnabas did what is recorded here. We will therefore have to assume that with their initial visit, on their outward-bound journey, they will have entrusted leadership of the nascent congregations to a few persons. But now with their return, where the congregations were sufficiently mature for such a choice, they must themselves designate their presbyters. For the power of choosing with "the raising of hands," one may compare 2 Corinthians 8:19. It indicates a choice that took place freely, by which each of those choosing raised his hands. Raising hands does not intend to say laying on of hands, as the Roman Catholics hold—namely, for ordination. Another word is used for that, on which below (cf. Acts 15:22, 25). Even of Timothy it is said that a gift has come to him through the laying on of hands of the eldership. It is possible that Titus 1:5 may speak of the placing of elders by Titus as an evangelist, but it may also be that we must explain this as analogous with Acts 14:23.

All this is very clear for ruling elders. There the individual congregation calls externally, but for teaching elders or ministers of the Word one must differentiate somewhat further. A teaching elder must satisfy certain requirements. An examination must take place whether he possesses those requirements. By the nature of the case, that is difficult for the presbyters of a single congregation. That was different in the apostolic era. Then there were extraordinary *charismata* and the weight of office rested less on individual persons. There was also a gift of the distinguishing of spirits. Now that conditions have become ordinary, recourse must also be taken to ordinary expedients.

With that there is still another consideration. A minister of the Word is minister not only for a single church, but can be called by all churches, can speak with authority and administer the sacraments anywhere. Thus where his office is more general, the nature of the case also demands that examination by the aggregate of churches will initiate his calling, or at least a part thereof. Thus it occurs that not a single presbytery but an assemblage of them (classes or presbyteries) institutes an examination, grants freedom to the examinee to preach in public, proposes him as eligible for a call. In the distant past it was the custom first to institute an examination after the candidate was called in the congregation, thus immediately prior to his ordination. The classis did this. Later, this inquiry was divided in two. First came the examination after someone had left school, by which he received the right to preach in the congregations. Then, after a call was extended by the congregation, came a final examination, upon which ordination followed. The examination that granted someone access to the ministry of the Word resided in any case with the classis and not with the school where he was educated. Conditions are now markedly changed. Earlier the schools did not stand in that direct connection with the church in which the theological schools of the free church stand toward it. Accordingly, the church is represented in the school. The church looks into the examinations at the school. Still, along with that the peremptory examination remains, so that we now have twice what naturally should only be once. If the church believes that it may not take the examination out of the hands of its ordinary assemblies, then these assemblies must properly examine in everything. The right admitting to preaching in the congregation must reside with them. In any case, there is much to be said that the latter should not depend on the faculty of the school but on the classes or the curators. That is good old-Reformed practice.

The proper call is the call of a congregation, that is, of a local church. Prior or subsequent examination also belongs there, but the crux of the matter is still the choice of the congregation, by which it desires someone as its minister. See the Church Order of Dort, article 4 and article 7, in which the latter article says: "No one shall be called to the ministry of the Word without placing him in a specific location, unless he is sent to preach here and there within the Church under the Cross or otherwise to gather churches." In ordinary circumstances, where one does not have to do with mission work, the work of the local church in the external calling of ministers is therefore essential. It does that with the prior knowledge of the classis, but still does it itself. It can do it through its governance (church council and deacons) when that appears advisable to it, without the whole congregation itself voting. But even then the congregation has a silent voice in the matter, for the final confirmation may not take place unless the name of the minister is first announced in the church for fourteen days (cf. Church Order of Dort, article 4). Ordinarily, however, already at the outset the entire church is also consulted in the choice and the call.

Most old theologians also ascribe to the civil government a right to involve itself in the call. Voetius disputes this as a principial right. For most, however, such a notion of the connection between church and state reigns that they acknowledge the right of the government without scruple (cf. the Church Order of Dort).

2. Calling is also distinguished as *ordinary* and *extraordinary*. Ordinary is the calling of priests under the old covenant, that of pastors under the new. Extraordinary was the calling of prophets under the old dispensation, that of apostles under the new.

3. External calling may be distinguished as *immediate* and a *mediate*. Prophets and apostles were called immediately (Gal 1:12–22). God calls ordinary ministers of the church mediately. Immediately calling can be absolutely immediate (e.g., for Moses and John the Baptist) or relatively immediate (e.g., for Elisha, who was called by Elijah at the command of God).

A heated polemic was conducted by the Roman Catholics against the validity of the call of Protestants. Rome says: In part, the first pastors at the time of the Reformation never had a legitimate call; in part, they lost it when they exited from the Catholic Church and became apostate. The answer to that is that by their struggle against Rome and by leaving the Church, the Reformers who had been office-bearers in the Catholic Church—for example, bishops—have only done what accompanies their office according to God's Word; that they, however, by faithful fulfillment of the obligations of their office could not lose their office but remained legitimate ministers of the church. It is noteworthy that they did not maintain that Rome's call was no longer a legitimate call. Apparently, they deemed the continuation of the obligations of office to be compatible with the deeply debased condition of the Church and its hierarchy. Turretin, for example, writes: "Here again two kinds of call must be distinguished. First, one that on account of its particular institution is false, in every way illegitimate insofar as it serves entirely the propagation of godlessness and idolatry. Then, a call that in its institution is holy and right, but is corrupted and perverted by the abuse of men and is directed by them to the propagation of error. The first must be absolutely rejected because there is nothing good in it. But the second is to be improved and purified so that after the removal of error and corruption introduced by men, only the institution and use of Christ remain, according to the intention of God. Such (namely, like the second), now, is the call of presbyters and bishops in the Roman church" (*Institutes*, XVIII, 25, 8). When Roman Catholics say: but that was dishonest, for you were certainly not ordained and have not let yourself be ordained with the intention that you would oppose the church that ordained you and do injury to it, then one responds: one must first heed the command of Christ, for He is the one who calls and ordains in His church. The *finis primarius* ("the supreme purpose") in every calling is the purpose of God. Only in the second place does the intention of the calling instruments come into consideration.

From this reasoning, however, the old theologians did not intend to infer that Rome was a true church. Certainly, where the true church is, there is legitimate calling; but not the reverse: where legitimate calling is, there is the true church. With this matter, one says, it is like baptism, which can also be legitimate in a heretical church. Augustine: "It matters little whether the water is conducted through a stone channel or a silver pipe."

For other cases, namely, where ministers of the Word did not bring their call with the from Rome but set to work themselves, one appealed to the office of believers in connection with the fact that a reformation of any kind could not be expected from the rulers of the church. As long as the ministry of the Word in a church is pure or gives hope for reformation, it must be purified in order to call and ordain new ministers, and in ordinary conditions it is not permissible to make ministers of the Word outside the body of teaching elders. But in extraordinary circumstances it is different. There must be a ministry of the Word; that is a *necessitas salutis*, "something that is necessary for salvation." But that already serving presbyters shall participate in calling is a *necessitatis ordinis*, "a necessity of order." The former takes priority over the latter.

Ordination, of course, must be distinguished from calling. When a minister of the Word is ordained, he must be called beforehand and the question proposed to him whether he believes himself to be called by God's congregation and therefore by God Himself. Thus ordination appears as the validation and public declaration of the call. For ordination in the apostolic church the laying on of hands was practiced (ἐπιθέσεως τῶν χειρῶν, 1 Tim 4:14). Laying on of hands was an ancient ceremony. The Lord Himself sometimes laid on hands to heal and to bless. The apostles also did so to devote to a certain task in the service of the church. After the congregation had chosen deacons, they were placed before the apostles and they laid hands on them (Acts 6:6). Ananias laid hands on Paul (Acts 9:17). In Antioch, where Paul and Silas were sent on their first missionary journey, the prophets and teachers laid hands on them (Acts 13:3). In this case, as with the ordination of deacons, prayer or fasting and prayer preceded. Laying on of hands was also used to communicate the Holy Spirit (Acts 8:17; 19:6). The body of elders laid hands on Timothy (1 Tim 4:14). Thus New Testament laying on of hands was evidently of two kinds—namely, extraordinary and an ordinary. By the former something special is communicated; the latter was a solemn and public setting apart for an ecclesiastical office. Rome lost sight of this distinction and invested the laying on of hands with a sacramental character. With us, too, the laying on of hands is used in the ordination of pastors and missionary-teachers. A more than symbolic significance cannot be attributed to this. It belongs to the non-essential parts of introduction into office. Accordingly, the question of who is permitted to take part in this laying on of hands is also of secondary importance. In the New Testament, the whole body of elders took part. But, as we have seen, in this first period the offices of ruling and teaching elders were not sharply separated. Thus one can not necessarily conclude: according to Scripture all elders can participate in the laying on of hands.

Once the presbyters divided in two, it appears in every way proper that the laying on of hands took place by those who serve in the same work as the minister to be ordained will be occupied. Accordingly, ministers of the Word lay on hands at the ordination of a minister of the Word. Hands are not laid on elders, although according to Acts 6 it even occurred with deacons, namely, by the apostles.

According to Hodge, in the Presbyterian Church it is not permissible for ruling elders to take part in the laying on of hands at the ordination of a teacher (*Church Polity*, pp. 288ff.).

Up to this point, only the government and the offices of the individual church established in a particular place have been discussed. The Bible does not contain a worked-out church order concerning the mutual relationship of local congregations. It was said above that the unity of the visible church was embodied in the apostolate. But this is not to be understood as if the apostles had formed a college that could rule over the churches either by its full number or by majority. Every apostle had apostolic power personally, even apart from the others. Paul, chosen as an apostle, did not consult with flesh and blood, that is, with the other apostles, but felt himself called independently by God. But at the same time it remains true that whoever resists the apostles or an apostle excludes himself from the church.

But even apart from that fact, there is sufficient evidence that the New Testament does not portray for us independent churches. There was a lively interaction among the differing congregations. There was a certain unity that was felt as binding, even in external things. The Christians at Jerusalem felt in solidarity with those at Antioch, and vice versa. In particular, that bond had to be felt between the Jewish-Christian congregations. They all looked to Jerusalem in Palestine. Paul knew a still-higher Jerusalem, the Jerusalem that is above, mother of us all (Gal 4:26). Also between congregations from the Gentiles and those from the Jews real fellowship was maintained through collections and in other respects. In his congregations, Paul continually emphasized that they may not stand alone and may not act arbitrarily. "But if someone appears to be contentious, we do not have such a custom, nor does the congregation of God" (1 Cor 11:16). And in 1 Corinthians 14:36 he asks very sharply, "Has the word of God come from you? Or has it come to you alone?" That is, you must hold to the things that are generally in use with all Christians. From Acts 15 it appears that matters of common concern may and must be deliberated on communally. Present were the apostles, elders, and the congregation at Jerusalem; Paul, Barnabas, and a few others from Antioch. It may not be concluded from verse 6 that it was a separate gathering of apostles and elders; the church was present, as is sufficiently clear from verses 12, 22 and 25. Together they chose the representatives who would deliver the decrees. In Acts 15 we have in principle the example of a classical or synodical meeting, but in a special form. The participation of the congregation in the voting may not be transferred to the present. Also present there were infallible apostles, who now are no longer. One may note, however, that the decision is not merely a matter of giving advice but has binding validity. Gentile Christians must conform to it. This is contrary the system of Independents (cf. vv. 28-29).

The mutual government of the churches rests on the autonomy of the congregation. That is, each individual church is a complete church that, if the need demands it, can do everything that belongs to the essence of the church. And when the churches gather, such gatherings are not *higher* but *larger* assemblies. The churches gather as equally entitled. This principle also carries with it that the rights and power of the larger assemblies are not unlimited. They cannot proceed to rule over individual congregations or members by setting aside church councils. If the classis and synod would wish to proceed without more ado to order things that belong to the internal governance of each congregation, the church council should not put up with that. When the individual churches take up correspondence with each other and enter into connection, mutual rights are defined. The church order serves that end. This order at the same time says not only what the churches have to hold themselves to mutually by virtue of their alliance but also guarantees the rights of the congregation that may not be infringed by the churches jointly. The idea that a classis or synod could impose anything on a congregation is completely un-Reformed and of Roman Catholic origin.

But the matter also has a reverse side. If the church order is a kind of constitution that guarantees the freedoms and privileges of the congregation, then, on the other hand, it is no less a valid norm to whose maintenance one has solemnly bound oneself. Things that appear in it and that are not left to the consent of individuals are things in which all have interest. The organism of the church is so interrelated that the one member shares the fate of the other. The States of the Union have their freedoms and rights as states, but from this autonomy of the state it may never be concluded that the Constitution of the United States does not need to be obeyed. There is autonomy in principle, but not autonomy that in its scope extends to every point. If by its own hand the State of New York proceeded to create money and to maintain its own rate of currency, it would soon turn out that the central power would have to intervene; otherwise the financial system of the other states would be jeopardized. It is so, too, *mutatis mutandis*, in the churches of God. Autonomy and strict compliance with mutual alliances do not exclude each other, but go together.

The object of the deliberations of the larger assemblies (classis, synod) is:

a) What all churches have in common. This is absolutely left to the larger assemblies, since the smaller ones naturally cannot undertake it.

b) What belongs specifically to individual churches. Naturally, this can only be taken up by the churches jointly in *particular* instances, namely: (a) in case of inadequacy, when the local church is unable to discharge its own affairs; (b) in case of irregular or illegitimate conduct, as when a disease that is spreading must be counteracted by all in contact with it; (c) in case of appeal, when one or another party believes itself to be wronged by the smaller assembly (So Voetius, III. I. 4).

PART TWO

The Means of Grace

CHAPTER THREE
Word and Sacraments

1. *In how many senses can one speak of grace?*

In three senses:

a) As an *attribute* of God. Then in a broader sense grace is unmerited favor and in a more specific sense, that favor toward sinners. This grace has no means by which it is induced or brought about. It chooses and creates its own means. The entire plan of salvation, not excluding the Mediator, is a fruit of this grace.

b) As an *objective gift in Christ*. In Him as the exalted Mediator is found the basis of all manifestations of favor granted to the sinner. From His fullness we have all received grace for grace [John 1:16]. The means by which this grace was obtained and brought about are found in the satisfaction of the Savior.

c) As a *subjective action in us*. Everything that happens in us or to us as the outworking of the attribute of God and the gift of grace in Christ is called grace in the specific sense of the word. And this third grace is in view when we speak of the *means of grace*. There are certain instruments by which God wills for us to come to know and to apply His favor residing in Christ. These are means connected with the communication of grace. Grace is hereby taken in its widest sense, so that it is not limited to effectual, seeking, or regenerating grace, but includes everything that happens subjectively in or below our consciousness.

2. *What follows when we understand the word "grace" in the expression "means of grace" in this way?*

A certain indefiniteness that makes it difficult for us at a first glance to delineate sharply the concept of the means of grace. Everything that God uses as a means in order to show me any unmerited favor and by which He acts for my good then becomes a means of grace. There is common grace and special grace. But what serves for receiving and granting the former must also count as a means of grace. What occurs in the sphere of God's providence cannot be excluded. Through the particular circumstances of life, God can act on me, and it is grace from Him when He does this. However, one senses that we cannot let the expression depend on this indefinite sense. The concept, taken so generally, would lose its theological significance for us.

3. *In what way can one place some limits on this generalization?*

a) By showing that many of these things that one would like to call means of grace, in the widest sense, are not such in an independent way and by virtue of their own content, but only through the connection into which they are brought with instrumentalities that are the proper means of grace. One or another experience that I have in my life can certainly be used by God to strengthen the life of grace in me, but it could not do this by itself. It does this only because it brings me anew into contact with the Word of God and has as its consequence a new application of that Word to my life. It is therefore not a means of grace in the proper sense.

b) By saying that not every connection with preparatory grace or with common grace makes something a means of grace, but only the specific connection with the regenerating, effectual, converting, justifying, sanctifying grace of God. Said more succinctly: its connection with the beginning and the continuation of special grace. If something is not connected with that in one way or another, it may not be called a means of grace.

c) By saying that something must be linked with the gracious working of God not just incidentally on a single occasion but that it must be the regular, ordained means that accompanies that working. The means of grace are *constant*, not exceptional.

If we accept these three conditions, then it appears that they only apply to the Word of God and the sacraments. These two are the only means of grace in the narrower sense.

4. *Is the concept "means of grace" (media gratiae), so understood, valued equally by all?*

No, varying value is attributed to it. There are those who deny all ordered working of grace, who compare it to the blowing of the wind, in which man can discover neither a law nor a norm. Grace is then tied to nothing—neither to the church nor to office, neither to Word nor to sacrament. It comes and it goes, just as God wills it (mystics).

Others go less far but will not acknowledge an organic connection between inward grace and outward means. The former works, according to them, not unrestrained and arbitrarily but nonetheless completely controlled by its own secret law, as life that spreads and proliferates in a certain sphere (the Ethical theologians).

Still others will have grace bound completely to the means, and then in different ways. In the first place, one can identify it with the natural significance of the means. The Word of God then works, for example, through its reasonable, moral content, convincing and admonishing (Rationalists). One can also let it flow into the outward means in a supernatural way, so that they actually cease being natural means but change into something higher, so that, for example, in the sacrament of the Lord's Supper bread and wine become flesh and blood, or the water of baptism washes away sin *ex opere operato*, "through the worked work" (Roman Catholics). Finally, one can bind grace completely to its means in a secret manner, so that it does remain distinguished from these means but still occurs nowhere separated from them (Lutherans).

The Reformed doctrine of the means of grace may never be confused with any of these views.

5. *Where does the difference between us and the Ethical theologians lie?*

In this: that the order and regularity that God follows in the working of grace is not a mystical inward one, set for it by a life process, but an objective, outward one, determined by the ministry of God's covenant according to Scripture.

6. Where does the difference between us and the mystics lie?

In this: that we do not acknowledge any working of God's grace other than in the orbit where the Word of God from Scripture is present. God works sovereignly, but not in a disorderly or arbitrary manner. In general, He has circumscribed the working of grace by the means of grace.

7. Where does the difference between us and the Rationalists lie?

In this: that according to us grace makes use of the means, and is served by them, but is not identical with the means. When under the preaching of God's Word sinners are regenerated, then it is still something other than the convicting moral power of the Word that causes the change in them from death to life. The working of grace as the action of God and the means of grace are things that accompany each other organically, but nevertheless in no sense coincide.

8. What is the difference between Rome and us on this point?

a) When we say that the means of grace are ordained by God in order to keep us in union with Christ in an objective way, and so to cause grace to flow to us from Him objectively, then it is immediately apparent of how great importance it is not to place something else in back of the means of grace that intervenes between them and Christ. Rome does exactly that. Behind the means of grace, between these and Christ, stands the Catholic Church. That is why it always speaks of "the means of grace of the Holy Church." Grace is deposited in it; therefore it has the means of grace at its disposal.

b) From this first difference flows a second. One can easily see that the Word of God does not lend itself easily to the Roman Catholic concept of a means of grace. A means of grace, as Rome conceives it, must be, strictly speaking, a thing, a work, an action, not a thought, a word that brings God's thoughts to our souls. Only the sacraments really fit in this system. They are means of grace as Rome requires them to be. The Word has something general, something unofficial, something extra-ecclesiastical about it that Rome does not know what to do with. The result of this is that for Rome it must recede into the background. For Rome the Word is not honored half as much as it is for the church of the

Reformation. If the latter is the church of the Word, Rome is the church of the sacrament. Not as if Rome in theory would deny the value and the significance of the Word, but in practice it comes down to that denial. The worship of a Roman Catholic constantly gravitates to the sacrament.

c) This is not all. The Word thus forced into the background cannot remain what it is and ought to be for Rome. It is externalized. The gospel is changed into a law. Faith, as was seen earlier, becomes historical faith instead of saving faith. And Word and faith, both, no longer bring real grace; they belong to the preparatory stage. Grace in the specific sense first begins where a person receives his first sacrament from the hands of the Church. However much happened to him previously, he cannot have received grace before or apart from the sacrament; he has remained without grace. With us, precisely the reverse occurs. The Word is the beginning, middle, and end. If necessary, we can think of Word as a means of grace without sacrament, but it is impossible to think of sacrament as a means of grace without Word. The sacraments depend on Scripture, and the truth of Scripture speaks in and through them.

9. What is the difference between the Lutherans and us?

Initially, Luther stood where Calvin stood. Later, in reaction to a fanatical trend, he took a step back toward Rome and taught something about the Word similar to what Rome taught about the sacraments. The Holy Spirit has become incarnate—flesh, as it were—in Scripture. Since Scripture has come into existence, the power of the Holy Spirit resides only in Scripture. Even when that Word of Scripture is not spoken, not preached, not read, it still has the power of the Spirit in it. As the power of procreation is in a seed, the power of sight in the eye, so the power of conversion is in the Word. In the controversy with Rathmann (1612–1628), who challenged these conceptions, the Lutheran view was developed in all pointedness. Rathmann said that it meant dishonor for Christ and the Holy Spirit to so interpose something between Him and man. It may not be denied that in this he was right. The theologians on the other side went so far as to maintain that the Word is God, a "piece of God" (*verbum Dei esse aliquid Dei*), "an outflow of God." We have to do here with a divinization of Scripture, a communication of divine attributes to Scripture, as it were. It began to be asked whether Scripture could still be called a *creature*.

Connected with this great significance ascribed by the Lutherans to the Word as Word is the fact that they had a separate locus in their dogmatics for "the Word of God," that is, not only at the beginning, where the Word of God must be discussed as the source of knowledge of theology, but immediately before the doctrine of the sacraments. The Reformed, of course, also discussed the Word of God at the beginning, but generally did not have a separate treatment of the Word insofar as it is a means of grace. From the doctrine of the church they generally went on to the doctrine of the sacraments. This was something of a lacuna. One may not overlook, however, that the two parts of which God's Word consists, law and gospel, also had to be discussed elsewhere. The law, then, is the requirement within the covenant of works, and the gospel has its place within the covenant of grace. It appeared therefore less necessary to dedicate a special discussion to the unity of these two as the Word of God. Lutheran dogmatics was not covenant theology, as was Reformed dogmatics. Hence the difference.

See the Heidelberg Catechism, answer 65: "From the Holy Spirit, who works faith in our hearts by the preaching of the gospel, and strengthens it by the use of the sacraments" (cf. also the Belgic Confession, article 33).

10. *What is distinctive about the Reformed doctrine of the means of grace?*

     a) That effectual grace only works where the means of grace are present.

     b) At least at one point it works directly, without any means being used—namely, in regeneration.

     c) Even when it works mediately, it is not bound up entirely with the means but accompanies them and causes the soul to be receptive to them, so that there is a concurrence of two factors, each of which does its particular work; and they belong with each other.

     d) The Word of God is never separated from the sacrament—not only because the sacrament is a word, conveyed in an image and intended for the eye, but also because a spoken word always accompanies the sacrament.

e) All knowledge given to the person granted grace is taken from the Word of God. There is certainly an immediate working of grace, but not an immediate communication of knowledge.

11. *In how many senses can the expression "the word of God" be understood?*

a) The Word of God can mean the Logos, the personal Word (John 1:1).

b) The word of God can be every word of power spoken by God. At the creation God spoke such a word, and subsequently He has so spoken repeatedly. This word of God is thus something other than Scripture. Mention is made of such words of power in Scripture, but not all of them are recorded for us. Some wish to see that the word of God is spoken of in this sense when regeneration is attributed to it (e.g., Jas 1:18). With this, they say, the Word of Scripture is not meant but the word of God's power that proceeds out of His mouth and effects re-creation. See, however, what was noted regarding these texts in treating the doctrine of regeneration.

c) All revelations that God has given to man and in which He communicates His counsel can be called the word of God. Those revelations are contained in Scripture, and to the extent this is the case one can say: God's word is in Scripture. But this may never lead to a denial of the other affirmation, that:

d) Scripture as a whole is the Word of God. In a plain and clear manner one must give an account of the basis on which Scripture is called this. It is called this in its entirety for two reasons:

1. Because it is inspired by God. It makes no difference what is communicated in it, whether the words of men, of angels, of Satan, or of God Himself. God Himself vouches for each of those words as if it were His own account to us. If the Evil One is presented as speaking, then it is certainly his words that form the content of the discourse, but it is God who recounts these words to us as spoken by Satan. The account is God's word to us.

2. Because the various parts of this inspired Scripture have been so ordered and arranged that the whole, however manifold and diverse it may be, forms one discourse of God to us. The one part functions with the others such that it becomes the whole: all that God wishes to convey to our minds in order to bring us to understand His entire counsel for salvation. The account of the fall thus forms an integral part of the Word of God, not only because it is an inspired account, for the truth of which God vouches word for word, but also because it makes up a part of what God wills to bring to our understanding in connection with law and gospel.

12. *In what sense is God's Word a means of grace?*

In the sense in which we use it of the whole of Scripture. It is then usually differentiated into two parts, namely, law and gospel.

13. *In how many ways is the law contained in the Word of God used as a means of grace?*

One usually speaks of a threefold use of the law:

a) A *usus politicus* and *civilis*: a *civil* use. The law serves to prevent a profuse outbreak of sin. It is a restraint on sin, an aid to promote civil righteousness.

b) A *usus elenchticus sive paedagogicus*: a *convicting* use, by which it serves as a disciplinarian, convicts man of his sin and inability so that he might go to Christ, who has fulfilled the law.

c) A *usus didacticus, normativus*: a *didactic, normative* use for the believer. For him the law becomes a rule of life, according to which he orders his life out of true thankfulness. This is the so-called *tertius usus legis*, "the third use of the law," about which conflict arose in the Lutheran church between Agricola and his opponents.

Reformed dogmatics laid the emphasis, above all, on this third use of the law. The law is not treated so intentionally as promoting repentance, as happens with the Lutherans. Our [Heidelberg] Catechism treats the law in its teaching on gratitude, and so do many dogmaticians who treat the Decalogue under sanctification. Only in the second and the third use can the law be seen as a means of grace. In the first use it only accompanies common grace, not special grace.

14. What is nature of the relationship between law and gospel?

We saw earlier that there is a sharp division, indeed an antithesis made in Scripture, especially by Paul, between the law and the promise. Proceeding from this, many theologians say that everything in Scripture that relates to demands and commandments belongs to the law; everything that relates to unconditional promises belongs to the gospel. So, if "believe," "repent," etc. is spoken of, then because it is in the form of a demand, it must be reckoned as belonging to the law. The result of this would be that much that we usually reckon as belonging to the gospel must be removed from it.

This issue is connected with another, namely, the question whether the covenant of grace is conditional or unconditional. Due to the error of the Remonstrants, who had made a second law of the gospel, and faith a second keeping of the law ("evangelical obedience"), many of the older theologians were extremely averse to the term "conditional covenant." Witsius says: "When God presents the formulation of the covenant of grace, then the words that belong to its substance are solely promises ... (Jer 31 and 32). For this reason our teachers, who after the clever contrivances of the Socinians and Remonstrants learned to speak very carefully, indeed rightly stressed that the gospel, strictly speaking, consists of pure promises of grace and glory." And in another place, "The covenant of grace or the gospel, strictly so termed, ... really prescribes nothing as an obligation, demands nothing, commands nothing, not even 'believe, trust, hope in the Lord,' nor any more such obligations. Rather, it tells, proclaims, and signifies to us what God promises in Christ, what He wills to do and will do. All prescriptions of obligation belong to the law—as in a similar manner, after others, the esteemed Voetius most certainly inculcated. And that is to be maintained in all respects, if we, with all the Reformed, wish steadfastly to defend the perfection of the law, comprehending within its scope all the virtues, all the obligations of holiness."

Thus, the view of the one party. In opposition were those who pointed out, for one thing, that the law had its promises, that the gospel presents its demands, and that it was completely impossible to realize such a sharp division.

Practically, it seems to us, the question comes down to this: When someone is brought into the covenant of grace by personal assent to the covenant relationship that exists between God and the believer, is he then completely passive or does he in fact recognize as well that accepting this covenant is an obligation that rests on him, a requirement that can be rightly put to him? If the former must be maintained, then the separation will be made, then nothing of the law enters into the gospel; it is accompanied solely by promises and not by requirements. If, on the other hand, the latter is true, then it will not be possible to make the separation, since a promise comes to us that at the same time lays hold of us as an obligation and immediately assumes the form of a command.

The answer will have to be as follows:

a) Law can be taken in more than one sense. It can indicate a natural obligation toward God that is incumbent on us and must always be incumbent on us. It can also indicate a specific obligation, determined by a pact, to which certain consequences are linked if it is kept or transgressed. The latter, for example, was the case with the law in the covenant of works. In Scripture, then, the antithesis between law and gospel is meant such that the law as the condition of the covenant of works and the gospel exclude each other. Thus, if in Scripture the law as such occurs, then that is not gospel. When Christ said, "You know the laws," etc. [Mark 10:19], He did not speak as preacher of the gospel but as exponent of the law; likewise Moses when he said, "The one who does them shall live by them" [Lev 18:5].

b) The matter is different if we understand the law as the natural obligation that man as creature has toward God. It is completely impossible to think of man being in a state in which he would be *ex lex*, "outside the law." That would be antinomianism. That is not the case after his conversion and in his sanctification. It is also not the case in his accepting the covenant of grace. The law of God lays claim to the entire life of man and to every act in it. It also lays claim to the relationship in which man is faced with the gospel. The natural relationship of man to God entails that when the Lord comes to him with a covenant of grace, he is obligated to accept it. Now if one wishes to label that law and maintain that there is law in the gospel, then that should be allowed—only if it is clearly understood how here there is no thought of the law as an instrument of the covenant of works. Of itself the law cannot yield the covenant of grace, for it knows of no grace. As to its content, the covenant of grace is not in the law. But formally the law lays claim to the covenant of grace; that is, after the covenant of grace has come to us from God's free determination, it falls under the general terms by which the law establishes norms for our life. Theologians call this the serving of the law within the covenant of grace, a term that should not be confused with the service that the same law has with respect to the covenant of grace insofar as it is a disciplinarian to Christ. For this entire question, see Witsius, *The Economy of the Covenants* 3.1.8 and following.

When someone meets the demand of God to believe, to be converted, etc., then that is not a fulfilling of a condition upon which he can demand the benefits of the covenant; rather, the path is simply followed along which access to the benefits of the covenant is opened.

15. *May the difference between law and gospel be interchanged with that between the Old and the New Testament?*

No, for the gospel is just as properly in the Old Testament as in the New Testament, the law just as properly in the New Testament as the Old. One need only think of the Sermon on the Mount, where the demands of the law are held high and the comfort of the gospel nevertheless follows closely upon them. And the gospel runs like a stream through the entire Old Testament.

16. *What is there along with the Word as a means of grace?*

The sacraments. Here we are faced with this question: *why* the sacraments along with the Word? This cannot be by accident. But while all agree with this and seek a rationale, the explanations of the fact turn out to vary greatly:

a) The Roman Catholics, of course, say that the sacrament is the beginning and end, and needs no explanation. It is the normal, indispensable instrument of a church that is the mediatrix of grace and has in its possession the treasures of salvation. Here it is much more necessary to ask why a Word along with the sacrament than the reverse.

b) There are those who say: because in the sacrament a special, specific grace is dispensed to us distinct from the grace effected by means of the Word. For two kinds of grace there are also, accordingly, two means of grace. Since Gerhard, the Lutherans have spoken of the *materia coelestis*, the "heavenly matter" in the Lord's Supper.

c) Amounting to approximately the same thing is a distinction made by recent Lutherans. In the sacraments, they say, God works directly by physical means on the nature of man, on his so-called psycho-physical essence (whatever that may be), without the agency of his intellect and will. In this way the sacraments transplant us into Christ. They are church-forming instruments. The Word, on the other hand, works upon the self-conscious personality, upon the intellect, thus gradually. One easily sees that this is a pantheistic idea that at the same time goes back to the Roman Catholic conception. It is completely untrue that Word and sacrament are distinguished in this way, as if the latter addresses itself only to the unconscious and the former only to the consciousness. The sacrament has meaning for conscious life because it is always a sign and seal, the meaning of which God wants us to understand. And, conversely, the invisible grace of the Holy Spirit, who changes and renews our nature, also works with and through the Word. But that nature is not a psycho-physical nature, not a third entity elevated above matter and spirit. Word and sacrament are both intended for our spiritual nature. They are spiritual things, and as such they pertain not only to the grace of renewal (regeneration, etc.), but also to the grace of forgiveness (justification, etc.).

d) Still others say: The Word apportions grace in a multiplicity of thoughts and passages, and how richly and fully they will come to us in the ministry of the Word so much depends on the capability of the minister. Further, the Word goes out to all the hearers of the Word without distinction. In that, it is lacking in personal application or there is a personal application that is not suited for everyone.

On the other hand, there is the sacrament, which (1) concentrates grace; and (2) applies it specifically. In the sacraments, the heart of the gospel is summarized in a single sign, or in a pair of signs, and in a simple action. Here we have the whole Christ. And flowing from this of itself is the second result: now that the believer is thus brought into union with the whole, personal Christ, he can take from His fullness what, according to time and circumstances, meets his needs.

This conception, too, is mistaken, although it may not be denied that there is some truth to it. As far as the first point above is concerned, in preaching the *whole* counsel of God must be proclaimed and also be focused in such a way that what is essential is distinguished from what is secondary, what is absolutely indispensable from what belongs to well-being. It is true, however, that this happens in the sacraments in a particularly striking way. Only, one thing must not be forgotten: it is only through the Word that the sacrament has this focusing power. As far as the second point is concerned, it is not clear why the sacrament would work in a more specialized way than the Word. It is true that the sacraments are administered to us personally, while the Word does not speak directly to us as individuals. But by the Holy Spirit we can be brought to the point where we apply the proclaimed Word personally. And in the same way the Holy Spirit must move us to the believing use of the seals of the covenant. The one is not more personal than the other.

The true view is this: God has so created man that he obtains the knowledge of things in a higher sense by two of his senses. These two are sight and hearing. Through these two capacities, the higher attributes and ideas resident in things come to our knowledge. Speech, word answer to faith; form, image, to sight. This distinction is already felt very early. Augustine already said that the sacrament is a visible Word, a picture as it were of the Word (*pictura verbi*), having the same meaning as the Word. See also the Belgic Confession, article 33: "visible signs and seals"; "better to present to our external senses."

While now, on the one hand, the normal state of man brings with it this dual nature of his capacity of perception, there is also, on the other hand, something involved that is connected with the sinful state of man. Some say: the Word is spiritual, the sacraments involve the senses, hence the distinction. But the Word, too, involves the senses, for it must come to us through sound; there is no direct speech to our soul. It is true, however, that the Word is closer to the realm of spiritual things than the image. It is less tangible and involving the senses than the latter. Mysticism, for example, virtually drifts between sound and thought. Man feels that difference especially in his sinful state. His weakness makes him long for something more tangible than the fleeting sound of words. And it is to be so understood when "our ignorance and weakness" [Belgic Confession, article 33] are named as the motivation for God to ordain the sacraments.

17. *Will it do to associate Word and sacraments coordinately, or is there certain subordination between them?*

Strictly speaking, there is not coordination. The Word is resident in the sacrament. The Word is accompanied with the sacrament. If one takes away the Word, there is nothing left of the sacrament. If one takes away the sacrament, because of that the Word is still not lost. If we do not take children into consideration, there is no salvation without the Word of God. But we cannot assert the same thing of the sacraments. All this shows how there is some difference between them.

18. *Show in what respects Word and sacraments agree and in what respects they differ from each other.*

They agree:

   a) In the *author*, God, who is the one who institutes both.

   b) In the *content*, Christ, who is brought to us in both Word and sacrament. This is a point to which attention must be given. In the Word Christ is wholly present, and in the sacrament Christ is wholly present—as in 1 Corinthians 1:30 He is called our wisdom, righteousness, sanctification, and complete redemption; the Christ, who is the same yesterday, and today, and forever [Heb 13:8].

c) In the *manner* in which the content or the object is received. For both Word and sacrament this is faith. Without faith we cannot share in the thing signified by the sacraments. But also without faith we have no enjoyment of Christ, who is presented in the Word.

They differ:

a) In their *necessity*. The Word is absolutely necessary; the sacraments are not absolutely necessary. Expressed otherwise: the necessity of the latter does not lie on the side of God but on the side of man.

b) In their *purpose*. The Word serves to produce faith; the sacraments serve to strengthen faith.

c) In their *extent*. The Word of God is brought and comes to everyone we are able to reach with it. The sacrament is a seal of the covenant and comes only to those who belong to the covenant.

19. *In how many ways can we proceed in treating the doctrine of the sacraments?*

One can begin with the general concept of a sacrament, that is, apart from the bifurcation into baptism and the Lord's Supper, and seek on the basis of Scripture to establish what a sacrament is and what belongs to a sacrament.

Conversely, one can treat baptism and the Lord's Supper separately and then see what is common to both, in order to bring this to a focus in the concept of a sacrament.

The first method of treatment is somewhat problematic. First, Scripture never speaks expressly about the concept of a sacrament in general. So one must deduce from some general data what a sacrament in a scriptural sense is. By doing that, one can easily err. This historically is the error of the Roman Catholic Church. Starting from a general concept of sacrament, established *a priori*, it has proceeded to falsify the individual sacraments. For us, too, a danger exists in this approach. Whatever is said here should accordingly be seen as something tentative; it is factually derived from teaching regarding baptism and the Lord's Supper, and so must be tested by this teaching in order to see whether it is in fact appropriate in every respect.

20. Does the word "sacrament" occur in Scripture?

No, it is from a Latin word, *sacramentum*. Originally it meant an amount of money that people deposited with each other in a civil lawsuit. When two people, for example, had a dispute about a piece of land, one might say to the other, "Since you wrongly lay claim to this property, I challenge you with a sacrament of 500 *asses* [copper coins]." This money would then be paid to the priest by both parties. The winner received his money back, the convicted person had to give up his amount, and it was then used for a religious purpose. At a later time, one did not ask for money but only for a guarantee that it would be paid. Opinions diverge about the purpose that one had with this demand for a monetary deposit. Most judge that it was to prevent rashly initiating a lawsuit. Others say that the matter had a religious origin. Both persons had to swear an oath (*sacramentum*) that their statements corresponded to the truth. If the oath of the loser proved to be false, an appeasement for the gods was necessary. And the deposit would then originally have served for that.

Whatever the case may be, the thing in question could only be called a *sacramentum* because it was related in one way or another to the gods. The lawsuit itself was also called a *sacramentum* because it had a religious meaning. The transition from the pagan to the Christian use appears to have been located in two things in particular:

a) In its military meaning. A *sacramentum* is the military oath by which the soldier solemnly binds himself to obedience to his commanders. Tertullian alludes to this military oath when he writes, "We are called to military service of the living God in our answer to the words of the sacrament (at baptism)."

b) In its more specifically religious meaning. *Sacramentum* was the Latin translation of the Greek word *mustērion* (μυστήριον), "mystery." Thus the Vulgate speaks of the "sacrament of godliness" (1 Tim 3:16); "the sacrament of the seven stars" (Rev 1:20); "the sacrament of the woman and the beast" (17:7). In Latin translations older than the Vulgate, it occurred in many other places where *mysterium* is found in the Vulgate (Rom 16:25; 1 Cor 13:2). Now under "sacrament" it was indeed possible to understand every mystery, but it was also quite obvious to see the term referring to certain kinds of mysteries that had a certain resemblance to Christian signs and actions. First, there was a similarity in form between the pagan mysteries (washings, etc.). Further, there was a kind of secret character in both. This led to a slowly more limited use of the term. Tertullian speaks of the sacraments of baptism and the Lord's Supper, Cyprian of "each of both sacraments," referring to baptism and confirmation; again, others speak of the sacrament of marriage (Eph 5:32). One sees how this loose use of language can contribute to leading Rome down a false dogmatic path. When baptism and confirmation and marriage are all called sacraments, then it was no longer easy to keep the difference clear and alive in the consciousness of the people.

21. *Is the word to be rejected because it is not scriptural?*

No, for it shares this character with many other terms that we nevertheless cannot do without. Time and time again there have been those who have expressed objection to its use, but in spite of all criticism the word has remained.

22. *Who is the first to have begun giving a definition of the concept of sacrament?*

Augustine. He said, "A sacrament is the visible form of an invisible grace"; sometimes as well, "A sacrament is a sign of a holy thing." Both of these definitions sound too indefinite. Although by them Augustine is thinking mostly of baptism and the Lord's Supper, he nevertheless still uses the word with other meanings. (Some say that the first definition first occurs with the Scholastics.) For present-day Roman Catholic theology, these definitions no longer apply. In the sacraments of penance and of marriage, for example, the *visible* thing is lacking. Moreover, it is not said that the sacraments *communicate* grace. The Catechism of Trent meets both objections by saying: "A sacrament is a thing that is perceived by the senses and has the capacity not only to portray grace but also to effect it."

23. *How do Reformed theologians define the concept of sacrament in general?*

From Calvin come two definitions (*Institutes* 4.14.1): "An outward sign by which the Lord seals to our consciences the promises of His goodwill toward us in order to sustain the weakness of our faith, and by which we in turn attest our commitment to Him, both in the presence of Himself and His angels and before men." The other: "A testimony of divine grace toward us confirmed by an outward sign and sealed from our side with a reciprocal attestation of our commitment toward Him."

We may say: "Holy, visible signs and seals instituted by God, by which the grace of God in Christ is signified and sealed to the participants in the covenant of grace, and they, in turn, attest their faith and obedience toward God."

24. *With reference to this latter definition, what should be noted further?*

a) The outward material of the sacrament, the visible sign and seal—for example, water in baptism and bread and wine in the Lord's Supper—and what is done with them.

b) The inward, invisible material of the sacrament, the spiritual benefit that is signified and sealed by the outward material.

c) The connection or relationship between these two, how that is conceived of by others and how it is to be conceived of by us.

d) The characteristic modes of speech that flow from this definition.

e) What belongs to the essence of a sacrament, and in connection with that, the question concerning the number of sacraments.

25. *What is understood by the outward material of the sacrament?*

The external material (*materia externa et sensibilis*) is that side of the sacrament that is perceived by the senses, specifically what reaches our sight and our hearing. Now it all depends how one defines a sacrament, whether or not one will be able to speak of outward along with inward material, visible along with invisible material. If one describes a sacrament as is done in the two definitions above of Calvin and in the other added to them, then a sacrament is the outward material plus an action. It then makes no sense to speak of an inward material of the sacraments. There are, however, many among the theologians who take a sacrament in a broader sense. It is then the thing that signifies plus the thing signified. So, for example, Turretin. And then one can appropriately distinguish between the twofold materials of the sacrament.

The difference ultimately comes down to a difference in words. If one but knows what one means by a sacrament and always remembers that, there is no objection to either view. But if one forgets this, misunderstanding can easily arise. If one proceeds from the broader concept and poses the question whether the unbelieving partaker receives the sacrament, then he will naturally have to answer *no*. He has already said himself: a sacrament is the thing that signifies plus the thing signified. The unbeliever does not receive the latter. But one would be equally mistaken if from this one wanted to draw the conclusion that no objective signs and seals of God's covenant of grace remain when subjective faith is absent. He intends only to say that it is not a sacrament in the full sense of the word.

26. *Do only the inert elements belong to this outward material, or does still more belong to it?*

More belongs to it. The outward material is twofold:

a) The elements themselves: water, bread, and wine. These have not been chosen at random, but by their particular nature are suited to serve as elements. In general one can say that they have a certain relationship of resemblance to Christ, who is the invisible matter of the sacrament. Their natural use corresponds to the use that is made of Christ spiritually. As we will see, their being a sign is based on this natural resemblance. That they are seals, on the other hand, is based on the institution of God. For the sealing, God could just as well have chosen other elements, but not for their significance, simply because other elements did not possess the suitability to depict.

b) The action done with these elements. This action is essential to the material. Water as such is not a sacrament. It must be water that is sprinkled. Bread and wine as such are not sacraments. The bread must be broken, the wine poured out, and both must be used by those who sit at the table. That is the reason that even the definition of the sacrament speaks about an "action" instead of a sign. But the word "sign" is broad enough to also include the action. The sign is not only what one sees; it is also what one sees happen.

27. *Does Scripture itself take the lead in calling the sacraments signs?*

Yes, it speaks of them as "signs of the covenant" (Gen 9:12–13; 17:11; Exod 12:13; אוֹת הַבְּרִית).

28. *How is a sacrament further designated?*

It is not only called a sign but also a "seal." This, too, is scriptural. In Romans 4:11 the apostle says of Abraham that he received the sign of circumcision as a "seal" of the righteousness of faith (καὶ σημεῖον ἔλαβεν περιτομῆς σφραγῖδα τῆς δικαιοσύνης τῆς πίστεως). A seal is thereby distinguished from a sign in that it confirms and not only portrays something (for this usage of the seal, cf. texts such as Rev 7:2; John 6:27; 2 Tim 2:19; 1 Cor 9:2; Rev 5:1, 9:4; 2 Cor 1:22; Eph 1:13; 4:30).

29. *Does this sealing character of the sacraments mean only that they apply a promise of God to our consciousness theoretically and also confirm it for our consciousness?*

That too belongs to it, but not only that. The sacraments are no *nuda signa*, "bare signs," no *signa theoretica*, "theoretical signs." They are also *signa practica*, "practical signs." When they are used in faith, the user actually receives, by the working of the Holy Spirit, the grace that they portray and seal. The sacraments are means of grace. The Zwinglians and Remonstrants deny that, making them into bare symbols, whether of the grace of God or the confession of man. As other symbols work by the association of ideas and by means of imagery, so too do these symbols. That is not the biblical and Reformed teaching, as will appear in treating baptism and the Lord's Supper.

See the declaration of our [Belgic] Confession (article 33): "For they are visible signs and seals of an inward and invisible thing, by means of which God works in us by the power of the Holy Spirit." There is a *materia interna*, an internal material of the sacrament. But it has already been pointed out above that this is not otherwise with the Word. On the other hand, however, this does not do away with the fact that it is essential and must be distinguished from the moral influence that the truth has on every receptive person. With the Word, too, the latter is only incidental. God has associated the working of His Spirit with the Word so that something much higher comes about. It is the same with the sacraments.

30. In what does the form of the sacrament (forma sacramenti) *consist?*

This lies in the relationship of the outward material to the inward, of the thing that signifies to the thing signified. In this relationship or connection, surely, lies the essence of the sacrament, what makes it a sacrament, for the expression *forma* is meant in this sense. And then the answer to the question about this form is that it is not *physical* or *natural*, through bodily contact, as if grace flowed into us by contact with the outward sign. Also it is not *local*, as if grace accompanied the sign, bound to it within the same space, as if it were. But it resides *relatively* and *sacramentally* in three things, namely, in signifying, in sealing, and dispensing (*exhibitio*).

The first negation is directed against Rome, the second against the Lutheran confession. One can express the difference between these two no better than by saying: Rome materializes grace, Luther localizes it. That is, the Roman Catholics maintain: this bread and this wine *are* the body and blood of Christ, the entire Christ. Luther says: within the same space is the entire Christ—in, with, and under the bread and wine. In both the Reformed find an unscriptural and unspiritual outlook. Grace does not allow itself be changed into matter, but neither does it allow itself be drawn within the confines of space.

We say, therefore: *where* the sacrament is used in faith (this applies at least for adults), there at the same time the grace is sealed. But *where* is not taken in a localized sense. Luther spoke in a localizing way: *where*, etc. Rome says even more than that. And while we make faith a condition for the presence of the working of grace, the Lutherans make it only the prerequisite in relation to the recipient for the working of grace that blesses. If there is no faith, grace works therefore in a localized connection with the sacrament as well. It is in fact so, too, with the Word. Preached or not preached, believed or not believed, the Word has supernatural, mystical power as something that is inherent. Rome, finally, even makes the working of grace that blesses independent of faith, and must certainly do this since it has identified grace and sacrament.

According to the Lutherans, there is a *vis inhaerens* ["inherent power"] of the Holy Spirit. The Holy Spirit works "in the sacrament." According to the Reformed, there is a *virtus Spiritus Sancti extrinsecus accedens*, a "power of the Holy Spirit added from outside."

It has already been said above that on this point a difference prevails among the Lutherans before and after Gerhard (1582–1637). Before Gerhard grace was in the sacrament through the Word; after him one spoke of a heavenly matter that was distinguished from the Word. One then attributed power to the Word in order to unite the earthly matter with the heavenly matter. It was an acting cause for joining these two into one sacrament.

31. *What results from this union or relationship between the sign and the thing signified?*

The so-called sacramental phraseology, or "way of speaking," which one can compare to some degree with expressions resulting from the personal union of the two natures in the Mediator. Because by the institution of Christ the sign and the thing signified have come into a certain relationship to each other, what belongs to one can be attributed to the other.

a) The thing signified is designated by the name of the sign. So Christ is called our Passover (1 Cor 5:7); true faith, circumcision of the heart (Rom 2:29; cf. 1 Cor 11:24).

b) The sign is designated by the name of the thing signified. So circumcision is called "the covenant" (Gen 17:10), and as a result things are attributed to the sign that belong to the thing signified (Acts 22:16: "Let yourself be baptized and wash away your sins"), as if outward washing in water can wash away sins, while surely only inward grace, which is thereby signified and sealed, is able to do this.

32. *What is the nature of the relationship between the word spoken with the sacraments and the sacraments themselves?*

a) The word that accompanies the sacraments belongs essentially to them and is a part of the sacramental action; it may not be omitted. Sprinkling at baptism, without the baptismal formula, is not permissible. And the same is true at the Lord's Supper. This applies at least for the sacraments that have been ordained for us by the institution of Christ, although it cannot be proven for those in the Old Testament, something that is perhaps bound up with the overall character of the Old Testament dispensation of the covenant of grace. This was surely not a speaking but an acting and symbolizing dispensation (cf., however, Exod 12:27).

b) The word of institution as it was originally spoken by Christ is the basis of the sacrament as sacrament. This is the sole guarantee by which we are assured that God wills to have His grace joined with these means. For the sealing part, this link, as we have seen, is undoubtedly a positive link. Naturally there is nothing in the sacrament that can cause us to rely on the thing signified when we see or use the sign. But because Christ has so instituted it and so willed it, it is so. Augustine already said: *Accedit verbum ad elementum et fit Sacramentum.* "The word is added to the element, and thereby it becomes a sacrament."

c) This institution of Christ has two parts:

1. A word of command. By that the sacrament becomes necessary for believers, with a necessity of command. Christ says, "Go therefore and baptize," and, "Do this in remembrance of me." And this command has been transmitted to us by the agency of the apostles. "For I received from the Lord what I also delivered to you" (1 Cor 11:23). And the apostles had to teach all whom they would make disciples to observe all that Christ had commanded them.

2. A word of promise. Christ says: If you do according to this my institution and obey my command in faith, then the grace signified and sealed in the sacrament will surely be given. "Whoever believes and is baptized will be saved" [Mark 16:16]. "This cup is the new covenant in my blood, which is poured out for you" [Luke 22:20].

d) Both of these words of institution—the command and the promise—are repeated in carrying out the sacrament. Thus it is Christ who makes use of His servants in order to continually speak the same words that He once spoke at the time of institution.

But while all agree so far, here at once the difference begins. The Roman Catholics clearly maintain that this sacramental word is a consecrating and effective word that, spoken by the priest, really changes the elements. It infuses grace into them. That is why that word does not need to be spoken loudly; the priest can

whisper them to himself, and the mystical working of transubstantiation, etc., will still follow. The Reformed, on the contrary,
maintain that it is a *verbum praedicatum*, a "preached word," that
as such must be spoken out loud so that the gathered congregation may hear it. The purpose of the preached word is not to
change the elements substantially but to set them apart for a holy
use. Before the pronouncement of the words, it is nothing but
ordinary bread; afterward it is still ordinary bread, but ordinary
bread that became a sacramental sign and seal. The sacramental word is a part of the sacramental sign. The sacramental sign
serves to depict the invisible thing. An image must be seen, a
sign must be observed. Therefore the words, too, insofar as they
are part of the sacrament, must be perceptible, spoken with an
audible voice. Christ himself, at the institution of the sacraments,
spoke to His disciples so that they could understand it (1 Cor 11:28).
Even, for example, at infant baptism where the recipient of the
sacrament cannot understand the spoken words, they may nevertheless not be omitted.

33. *How far does the import of the word extend with the sacrament?*

It can only hold for the use of the sacraments. As soon as this use is over,
the signs, too, have lost their sacramental design and are no longer distinguished from ordinary elements. After the celebration of the Lord's
Supper, someone who uses the elements that are left over does not
receive the sacrament in them. For Rome this, too, is otherwise. Grace
remains materialized in the elements, and therefore they are carefully
stored so that they may be kept from being profaned. The Lutherans,
reasoning consistently, would have to arrive at such a conclusion.

34. *According to Rome, is more needed than the word spoken according to
the institution of Christ?*

Yes, the intention, the aim of the ministrant to do what the church intends with the sacrament, must also be present. If this is lacking, then a
real sacrament does not occur. Accordingly, here the sacrament is bound
to a person, and then to something in the person over which he alone has
control and that no mortal in the world can verify other than himself.
Not all Roman Catholics agree regarding the character or the degree of
this intention. Some speak of a *habitual* intention, others of an *actual*

intention, and still others of a *virtual* intention (see Hodge, *Systematic Theology*, 3:515). Now a great difficulty arises here for Roman Catholics themselves. They are accustomed not even to rebaptize children who, for example, have been baptized in Calvinistic churches. But when this baptism in a Reformed church was administered, the minister certainly did not have the intention to do what the (Catholic) Church intended to have done by baptism. Thus it turns out that Rome, contrary to its own teaching, must acknowledge a sacrament in which the intention was lacking.

We teach, on the contrary, that the validity of a sacrament is not to be judged subjectively but objectively, and that if it is administered in a congregation of God, and the proper intention is missing, it nevertheless retains its validity by virtue of the institution of Christ. It is no different with the Word. In Philippians 1:16–18, Paul says that Christ can be preached in all kinds of ways—in pretense, with evil intentions, out of envy and rivalry—but that still a preaching of Christ remains in which he rejoices. It is no different with the sacrament. This, too, is not tied to the sin of man but depends entirely on the faithfulness and the powerful working of God.

Naturally, in saying this it is not being denied that the absence of the proper intention is sinful for the ministrant himself, but that this does not impair the sacrament. And conversely, the objective requirements for the validity of the sacrament must always be kept in view. The administration of the sacraments belongs to the ministry of the Word, and the ministry of the Word belongs to the gathering of believers in an organized church.

According to Rome, in the sacrament of ordination the priest receives a *character indelibile*, "an indelible stamp," as a result of which he always retains the capacity to impart sacramental grace and to let it flow through him. Having once become a priest, for his entire life thereafter he can physically distribute grace where and when he wills. This position, together with the preceding one that everything depends on his intention, shows to what absurd consequences the Roman Catholic system leads.

35. *What must be taught regarding the necessity of the sacraments?*

According to Rome, with the sacraments there is a *necessity of means* (*necessitas medii*). They are the only means that God intends to use in order to communicate His grace. Excluding the sacraments excludes grace. The unbaptized children of believing parents do not go to heaven but to the *limbus infantium*, where they do not endure positive punishments but still lack salvation. Lutheran dogma, too, makes the sacrament of baptism necessary, at least for children, with a necessity of *means* (not for adults, for their regeneration precedes baptism, which seals it). Still, Lutherans do make a distinction and say that only "contempt" for baptism (not the deprivation of baptism in itself) is already the cause of being lost.

For Rome, not all sacraments are absolutely necessary for salvation. But they are the only means to receive that specific grace that is connected to them by the Church. If someone wishes to be a priest, then this is only possible through the sacrament of ordination. Baptism is absolutely indispensable.

According to the Reformed, the sacraments are necessary with a necessity of *command*. Contempt for them and neglect of their use is a sin, for they are not human ordinances but institutions of Christ. But they are not absolutely necessary for salvation. Not the outward sign but the inward grace that is signified is indispensable. "The one who believes and is baptized will be saved, but the one who does not believe will be condemned" (Mark 16:16). "Unless one is born of water and the Spirit, he cannot enter the kingdom of God" (John 3:5). Only the Word is absolutely necessary for salvation—that is, for adults, hearing the Word, and for children, being born under the ministry of the covenant by the Word.

36. *Is there a difference between the sacraments of the old and the new covenants?*

Rome maintains that there is. As the Old Testament priests were not priests in a proper sense but only priests as types, so also the sacraments of the old era were only typical sacraments. The full reality of the sacraments depended on the sacrifice of Christ, so for this reason believers who died before that sacrifice remained in the abode of the fathers [*limbus partum*] until Christ freed them from it and brought them into full glory.

We say from our side that there is a sameness of substance between the sacraments of the old era and those of the new, with differences in circumstances. The author is the same, the thing signified is the same, the organ of application is the same, the sacramental word has the same double content, although the wording differs, and the purpose is the same.

The difference lies:

a) In the fact that in Israel the sacraments, besides their significance for the covenant of grace, also had a national aspect, from which a difference in practice arose between them and the New Testament sacraments on a few points. For us, one comes to the table of the Lord only after one has learned to discern the body of Christ. In Israel the children also ate the Passover. This was because the Passover together with its covenantal significance had national significance. The same is true for circumcision. Baptism in the New Testament is administered to both sexes of the children of believers. In the Old Testament, circumcision was only for infant boys. Indeed, in the national life of Israel only the men counted and represented the women, and this also had to come to light outwardly.

b) In the Old Testament there were different symbolic representations of the truth, which, even if they could not be called full sacraments, still came close, more or less, to being sacraments. To these belonged the sacrifices, the purifications, etc. In the New Testament there are just two sacraments, and one may not add any others to them, not even in a secondary sense.

c) The Old Testament sacraments portray a Christ who was to come and they sealed benefits of salvation that still had to be obtained, although certainly those benefits were already granted to believers at that time by virtue of the suretyship of Christ, which is eternally valid. The New Testament sacraments signify and seal the benefits of salvation that have already been obtained.

d) At the same time, resulting from this there is a greater degree of grace attached to the sacraments of the new covenant than to those of the old era. Sealing can now come with greater power where the fullness of the Spirit has been obtained, for the Spirit Himself is the seal.

37. *Show that there is no difference, as Roman Catholics think that there is, between the sacraments of the old and the new covenants.*

a) In 1 Corinthians 10:1–4, Paul ascribes to the Old Testament church our baptism and our Lord's Supper, so far as the thing signified is concerned. The fathers were all under the cloud and all passed through the sea, were baptized into Moses in the cloud and in the sea, ate the same spiritual food, drank the same spiritual drink, etc. Now if these spiritual benefits of salvation were present, then they certainly must have been signified and sealed by the usual sacraments. The purpose of the apostle is to warn the Corinthians that they must not allow themselves to be misled by the possession of their great privileges to think that God cannot reject them. The Israelites in the wilderness also possessed those privileges, and yet God was not pleased with most of them.

b) Concerning circumcision, Paul showed intentionally how for Abraham it was a sign and a seal of the righteousness of faith (Gen 17:7; Rom 4:11; cf. also Heb 11:16).

c) The names of the sacraments of both dispensations are interchanged with each other. Circumcision and the Passover are ascribed to us (1 Cor 5:7; Col 2:11), and, conversely, as seen above, baptism and the Lord's Supper to Old Testament believers.

All this does not detract from the fact that the sacraments of the old covenant had their typological side. In the old covenant, everything had two aspects (Heb 10:1; Col 2:17). But they were types of Christ, and not of our sacraments. The shadow is a type of the body, not of the sign of the body. The latter are called antitypes by Peter (1 Pet 3:21, ἀντίτυπα). But this intends only to say that they are counterparts of the Old Testament sacraments insofar as they, in a sacramental manner of speaking, represent the thing signified. Not baptism itself but what is signified and sealed by baptism is really the antitype, and then insofar as baptism portrays this, baptism itself.

38. Do all recognize the same number of sacraments?

No, Scripture knows only two in the new era. The Roman Catholic Church, in part under the influence of a vague definition of terms, began quite early to multiply the number. After much wavering, bishop Otto of Bamberg (1124) fixed the number at seven, and the Council of Florence sanctioned this in 1439. The Greek [Orthodox] Church, as well, has its seven mysteries. There was a time when the Lutherans, too, displayed a tendency to admit a third sacrament along with baptism and the Lord's Supper, namely, *poenitentia*, "penance." However, it has never gone that far. The Protestant churches all accept that there are only two sacraments, and reject the other five that Rome wishes to place beside these two.

The five sacraments that Rome adds to ours are (1) confirmation, (2) penance, (3) ordination or consecration of priests (*ordo*), (4) marriage (*matrimonium*), (5) the last rites, anointing with oil (*extrema unctio*).

39. In what does the sacrament of confirmation consist for Rome?

It is an anointing or spreading of the anointing oil on the forehead of a baptized person in the form of a cross, done by the bishop with the words: "I mark you with the sign of the cross and confirm you with the anointing oil of salvation in the name of the Father, of the Son, and of the Holy Spirit." The result of this anointing is the increasing of sanctifying grace and the impressing of an indelible stamp.

40. What must be observed against this?

That the essential requirements of a sacrament are lacking here: institution by Christ, the element, the rite, the word of promise—everything is unscriptural. Confirmation has to be elevated at the expense of baptism, as if it were not sufficient to seal to us the grace of the Holy Spirit.

Appeal is made to the laying on of hands that followed upon baptism in the apostolic age (Acts 8:16–17; 19:6). In the first instance, baptism and the laying on of hands do not even coincide in time. This is generally seen as something extraordinary that only took place in the apostolic church. The Holy Spirit stands for "extraordinary gifts of the Holy Spirit." It does not mean the Holy Spirit as indwelling in believers, thus in a personal sense. In order to receive the Spirit as indwelling Spirit, no laying on of hands was necessary. Hence, too, the expression: the Spirit *falls* on them (ἐπιπίπτειν), something that completely befits this extraordinary situation, but not what is ordinary (Acts 8:9–19; 10:41, 46). In Acts 19:1–2 it is also meant in this sense. That is why Simon Magus desired the laying on of hands of the apostles (Acts 8:19).

Protestants have replaced the Roman Catholic confirmation with a confirmation of their own. However, they make no claim that it is a divine institution; it is something purely human that may not be elevated at the expense of baptism. Baptism and the Lord's Supper belong to each other as sacraments; the so-called profession [of faith] or confirmation indicates only the time when the right to the Lord's Supper, constantly held forth, becomes actual, is in force. It may not be denied that, by a more-or-less watered down conception of baptism, profession has so risen in value for many that the heart of the matter is now sought entirely in it. One senses that faith belongs at the Lord's Supper and, since faith does not come into consideration in infant baptism, profession compensates for this lack.

By noting this, it is not being claimed that profession need merely be a profession of the mouth. In it the heart must certainly be speaking too. But one may not proceed from the presupposition that only now is it to be ascertained who are truly members of the church—as if one had been dealing with unbaptized persons who came out of paganism.

41. *What is the sacrament of penance, and what end does it serve?*

Penance serves to obtain forgiveness for those sins committed after baptism. The *material* of the sacrament of penance consists of three parts: abasement of the heart, confession of the mouth, and satisfaction of works. The *form* is absolution granted by the priest, which should be seen as a judicial act.

Against this: In penance the sacramental sign is completely lacking. Only in an extremely forced manner can one claim that the three parts constitute a sign. They are not visible, only in part audible. Abasement of the heart is something within the sinner himself, and cannot help form a sacrament. The same can be said of the satisfaction of works. Absolution is not a judicial act, for God has reserved to Himself to forgive sins judicially. In this the church has only a ministering role.

There is and may be a confession of sins by believers to each other (cf. Jas 5:16). When someone feels burdened by the consciousness of trespasses not known to anyone else, then it can be a relief to share them with a brother. A deep sense of sin always awakens a longing for truth, and to be known to be as bad as one really is can be more satisfying than to have an undeserved good name. But such a confession of private sin must always remain something voluntary, whether expressed before an ordinary brother or before a minister. The person himself must judge if he needs to do this. There even exists the danger that the comfort and the exoneration of men may replace the absolution that only God can give (cf. Calvin, *Institutes* 3.4.12).

Rome binds the forgiveness of sins to the confessional, the confession with the mouth. This is one of the many means by which it unsettles the conscience. Instead of holding forth the omniscience of God as a basis of comfort, forgiveness is made dependent on the limitedness and fallibility of human consciousness. The distinction between mortal sins and venial sins is not always easy. No one can be completely sure that he has completely searched out his sinful heart and that nothing has evaded his notice (Psa 19:12).

42. What is the sacrament of extreme unction?

This is anointing a dying person with oil by Rome with the aim of removing the remnants of sin that baptism and penance have left in the believer, and with the subsidiary aim of sometimes restoring the sick person to health. The material is oil. The form is the formula: "Through this holy anointing and His most holy mercy, may God forgive you whatever sins you have committed by sight, hearing," etc. The oil, consecrated by the bishop, is spread on different parts of the body. This sacrament can be repeated.

In fact, in two passages in the New Testament something is found that resembles such a sacrament. The first is Mark 6:13: "And they cast out many demons and anointed many who were sick with oil and healed them." This is said of the Twelve, who were sent out two by two with a special authority to perform miracles (v. 7). The second is James 5:14-15: "If anyone among you is sick, let him call for the elders of the church, and let them pray over him, anointing him with oil in the name of the Lord. And the prayer of faith will save the one who is sick, and the Lord will raise him up. And if he has committed sins, he will be forgiven." As far as the first passage is concerned, this was a gift of healing; that is:

a) an extraordinary, miraculous gift only given to the apostles;

b) a gift that they exercised on all kinds of sick people, and not, like a sacrament, only on certain people;

c) exercised not only on those whose lives were in danger;

d) not exercised with the intention of taking away sins.

As far as the second passage is concerned, here too something is described that differs considerably from the Roman Catholic ceremony. The apostle does not make a distinction between fatal diseases and other diseases, and directs the anointing to apply exclusively to the healing of the body. The forgiveness of sins is connected to the prayer of faith, which has great power. Perhaps there is also an allusion to particular sins, for which sickness was a special chastisement, so that the healing in fact would be linked with restoration to God's favor (1 Cor 11:30).

43. What is the sacrament of ordination?

This consists in the rites customary at the ordination of Roman Catholic office-bearers. Rome has three *ordines majores*, "higher orders," four *ordines minores*, "lower orders." To the first group belong: sub-deacons, deacons, and presbyters; to the second: *ostiarii*, *sectores*, exorcists, and acolytes. Only the bishop can consecrate for the *ordines majores*. This consecration of priests is one of the three sacraments that leave an indelible stamp. The other two are baptism and confirmation.

With this sacrament there is no outward, visible sign, unless one sees it in the laying on of hands. This, however, is no more than a symbolic practice. It is not an element but an action, and in a true sacrament both—element and action—are always united. There is no institution by Christ. What an odd sacrament that must be, moreover, in which material and form differ according to the seven different ranks of clergy for which it opens access.

44. Can one call marriage a sacrament?

Rome can do this on the basis of a dualistic view of human life. What is natural is as such unholy, unconsecrated, but the Church can take it and consecrate it so that it becomes holy. The Church also does this with marriage. It views marriage as a means for propagation of the Church and has a special grace accompany it, insofar as it is concluded ecclesiastically. The marriage of Roman Catholics is thus something other in the eyes of the Church than the marriage of people who are outside the saving activity of the Church. Otherwise one would say that marriage common to all is not in the least suited to serve as a sacrament. According to Rome, marriage is indissoluble without a dispensation from the Pope.

For this sacrament, the outward sign is again completely lacking. Some say that this is found in the words of assent of both contracting parties. Others say that the persons themselves form the sign. Both views are absurd. The material of the sacrament and the persons who receive it cannot be the same.

The most noteworthy thing is that Rome denies this sacrament to priests. The two sacraments of ordination and marriage thus exclude each other. One would expect that marriage, thus sanctified and elevated above the natural sphere, would be holy enough to be used by priests. But Rome does not deem it so.

We do not view marriage in the first place as something ecclesiastical. It rests on the basis of creation (Gen 1 and 2). But from that it does not follow that marriage is unholy. There is no specific grace needed to consecrate it. Of itself the kingdom of God also permeates marriage, so that it again answers to its natural ideal. Besides that, it also has an ecclesiastical side because it is connected with God's covenant.

CHAPTER FOUR
Baptism

1. *What were the two ordinary sacraments for the Old Testament dispensation of the covenant of grace?*

Circumcision and *Passover*. These were ordinary sacraments. Certainly some are accustomed to speaking of more sacraments and add, for example, the rainbow, the flood, the exodus through the Red Sea. But the covenant established with Noah was not a covenant of grace, although it was related to the covenant of grace. The flood and the exodus were facts that only occurred once, and thus could be types of later salvation facts, thereby acquiring a certain sacramental significance, but they were not ordinary sacraments that were repeated and used at set times (cf. Calvin, *Institutes* 4.15.18; our Form for Baptism).

Others go back still further and even speak of the "casting out of paradise" and "denying access to the tree of life" as a sacrament (cf. Witsius, *Economy of the Covenants* 4.7.3). But a sacrament is always a means of grace and not of punishment or of threatening. That man was driven from paradise, and the covenant of works was thus closed for him, was in itself no assurance that a covenant of grace was opened, and could not confirm Adam's faith in it.

2. *What is the term for circumcision in Hebrew and Greek?*

Hebrew = מוּלָה, *mulah*, Exodus 4:26, from the verb מוּל; Greek = περιτομή, from περιτέμνω, "cut around." In Hebrew the foreskin, which was cut off, is called עָרְלָה, *arlah*; in Greek, ἀκροβυστία, "the tip of the male member," or according to others, "stopped up from the front" (from βύειν); as some think intentionally formed to remind by the sound the Hebrew, בֹּשֶׁת, *bosheth*, "shame" (cf. Cremer on this word).

3. Is this circumcision something original with the Jews?

We read of its institution in Genesis 17:11 (cf. vv. 25–27). It appears here for Abraham and his family as something new that was not in use previously. From this many Reformed have immediately drawn the conclusion that there was no circumcision in the world previously, even in the outward sense, and that everything of this sort found in other peoples in earlier and later times was a corruption of the sacrament that Jehovah gave to Abraham and his seed as a sign and a seal of the covenant of grace (Witsius, *Economy of the Covenants* 4.8.11: "But in all peoples who have been estranged from the true service of God, circumcision was nothing other than pure superstition and evil imitation of the sacrament that God had given to those in His covenant"). The facts, however, show that in this they judged incorrectly. The Egyptians were circumcised, the Arabs (boys between their tenth and fourteenth year), the Phoenicians and other Canaanites, for in the Old Testament the term "uncircumcised" refers specifically to the Philistines. For the Egyptians, circumcision existed before the Jews came into Egypt. Origen says that only the priests in Egypt were circumcised, but although in his day that might have been so, initially that was not so, and nowadays too it is still otherwise. But there is more. Circumcision is found in Central America, among a few races in the Pacific Ocean, in many tribes in Australia, in Africa among the blacks.

In all of this there is nothing extraordinary. When it is also established of baptism that it has different analogies among pagan peoples and that these were partly in use before Christian baptism itself, then it is not apparent why it has to be otherwise for circumcision. One should not therefore say that God took over a pagan practice. But like causes have like results. That is, there is something in the sign of circumcision, as there is something in the water of baptism, that possesses a natural appropriateness to portray a religious truth. That natural appropriateness has at all times struck the most diverse peoples in all parts of the world, and so circumcision arose, probably in different places in an independent manner. But that circumcision was not a sacrament. It could become a sacrament only because God attached the seal of His approval to that natural idea and made circumcision a divine institution for His covenant people.

It is not impossible that many of the tribes surrounding Israel took over circumcision from Israel, such as the Arabians and the Midianites. But it seems to us hazardous to link to this the further thesis that the descendants of Israel and Esau were within the pale of the church until the making of the covenant at Sinai and even still later. Even Witsius does this: "And it is not to be doubted that He had his elect among the other children and descendants of Abraham. And there is nothing more certain than that within the four centuries, circumcision, and with circumcision, the visible church or congregation was propagated within all those eastern peoples who could have had their origin from Israel and from the sons of Keturah and from Esau," etc. (*Economy of the Covenants*, 4.8.5).

4. *What was signified and sealed by circumcision?*

   a) Some associate circumcision with the motif of purification. Herodotus speaks in that vein about Egyptian circumcision. Philo the Jew speaks about four reasons given by tradition, among which purity occurs. This may have been a secondary motif, but circumcision is not explained satisfactorily as a purity and health measure.

   b) Others have regarded circumcision as a bloody sacrifice, or as a remnant of earlier human sacrifices, or as a symbol that God has a claim on human life. Here too there is an element of truth. Circumcision is distinguished from baptism precisely by this— that it is accompanied by the shedding of blood—and this is a feature that coheres most closely with the character of the Old Testament dispensation as a whole.

   c) We will have to hold ourselves to what Scripture teaches on this point. And this comes down to the following:

     1. Circumcision is a sign of the covenant of grace (Gen 17:11) and is called "the covenant in your flesh" (v. 13).

     2. It points to the impurity of man in his natural state. That natural state must be changed before man can be received into the covenant of God. That is why circumcision is instituted before

the birth of Isaac, the seed of the promise. One could ask why the impurity of the natural state of man is signified specifically by this shameful member. There appear to be three reasons. First, the genitals in themselves are already connected to the pollution of sin. The feeling of shame, including physical shame, points back directly to sin (Gen 3:7). Second, original sin is connected with the propagation of the human race. It is the nature that is corrupt, and nature comes from *nasci*, "to be born." Third, God has connected the administration of the covenant of grace with the sexual relationship. The promise is for Abraham, and always "to you and your seed."

3. It signifies and seals the removal of this natural impurity, is a symbol and seal of the renewal and cleansing of the heart as well as the removal of guilt: "Circumcise, then, the foreskin of your heart, and no longer be stiff-necked" (Deut 10:16). "And the LORD your God will circumcise your heart and the heart of your offspring, so that you will love the LORD your God" (Deut 30:6). "Circumcise yourselves to the LORD; remove the foreskin of your hearts" (Jer 4:4). Compare also Leviticus 19:23, were mention is made of a circumcision of trees. "Circumcision of the heart, by the Spirit, not by the letter" (Rom 2:29). "For we are the circumcision, who worship in the Spirit" (Phil 3:3). "In whom also you were circumcised with a circumcision made without hands, in putting off the body of the sins of the flesh, by the circumcision of Christ" (Col 2:11). "And you, when you were dead in your transgressions and in the uncircumcision of your flesh, He made alive together with Him, having forgiven you all your trespasses" (v. 13). Some think that in this last text the death of the Savior is spoken of as a "circumcision of Christ." This could be, for in the death of Christ was the true and actual cutting away and rooting out by which guilt is wiped away and the handwriting of sins is taken away out of the midst [Col 2:14]. But this interpretation is still doubtful. The "circumcision of Christ" will surely have to have in view the origin of spiritual circumcision. It is Christ who works this by His Spirit, and therefore it is called the "circumcision of Christ."

Finally, Paul tells us expressly that circumcision was "a sign and a seal of the righteousness of faith" (Rom 4:11).

5. When did circumcision take place and how?

It took place on the eighth day, with sharp stones or with a knife (Exod 4:25; Josh 5:2). The person who performed it at first was the father of the household (Gen 17:23-24). Later, other persons appear to be appointed specifically for that. There are those who believe that the priests ordinarily performed the procedure. But John the Baptist was not circumcised by his father, who was a priest (Luke 1:59, 62). The giving of a name usually occurred on the very same day with circumcision.

6. Was circumcision a temporary thing or a sacrament that would not be eventually abolished?

It was intended to remain valid during the entire old dispensation of the covenant of grace. Against this it has been objected that God says to Abraham: "And my covenant shall be in your flesh an everlasting covenant" [Gen 17:13]. To this the answer has been that the word translated "everlasting" refers to "this age," that is, the time before the coming of the Messiah. But it is better to say: the covenant sealed by circumcision was an eternal covenant, not the sign. In the same sense it is said that the Lord gave the land of Canaan as an eternal possession. That, too, is meant as a type. The spiritual benefits that are depicted by the land would be an eternal possession of God's covenant children. The same is true of circumcision. It is abolished in the New Testament dispensation, and baptism has come in its place (Col 2:17; Gal 5:6; vv. 2-4: circumcision regarded as a means of justification cuts off from Christ). However, circumcision still lived on in practice for a time among Jewish Christians.

7. Where should the origin of Christian baptism be sought?

In answering this question, three points should receive attention:

  a) The pagan practices that display similarity, more or less, with baptism.

  b) Proselyte baptism, and whether historically it has any connection with the Old Testament washings and with the baptism of John.

c) The baptism of John and the connection between it and Christian baptism.

8. Were there practices among pagans that had some similarity with baptism?

Yes, we find religious washings among the Egyptians, the Persians, the Hindus, and others. They were customary especially in the mystery religions. However, finding a general analogy is something completely different than intending to establish a historical connection. Whatever of this sort is encountered with pagans will have to owe its origin to the dictates of conscience that there is guilt and uncleanness that must be taken away before one can have communion with the gods. It is said that in Norway and Iceland such a pagan baptism existed for a long time alongside Christian baptism. In any case, the baptism of the Bible originated entirely independent of such pagan practices.

9. What was proselyte baptism, and what was its connection with the baptism of Scripture?

Gerim (גֵּרִים) or proselytes (προσήλυτος) are those pagans who by circumcision and keeping the law were received completely into the community of the Jews. In the Old Testament, the gerim are none other than "strangers," "sojourners"—that is, those pagans who, without becoming Jews, still lived continually in the land of Israel. And the Septuagint, therefore, uses the word "proselyte." Consequently, later both words changed in their meaning. In the Talmud a distinction is made between two sorts of proselytes, between a "righteous stranger," who keeps the entire law, and a "stranger who is a sojourner." Still later, the latter were called "proselytes of the gate." When a proselyte of righteousness was received into the Jewish congregation, three things had to take place: (1) circumcision; (2) baptism; (3) a sacrifice. Baptism was called טְבִילָה, tebilah.

The question now is how old this use of proselyte baptism is. Since the beginning of the eighteenth century the opinion has arisen among scholars that it has a much more recent origin than Christian baptism, and is probably only an imitation of it. At present, opinion is divided. Lightfoot, Danz, Bengel, Delitzsch, Edersheim, Schürer maintain that this baptism is very old and existed already at the time of Christ.

According to Meyer and others, the usage only arose later, in any case after the destruction of the temple in Jerusalem by the Romans (commentary on Matt 3:6).

The truth seems to be as follows. A pagan who lived as a pagan is impure in numerous ways. Thus, when he is received by circumcision into the Jewish community, this is not sufficient to cause him to participate fully in the community of the pure Jews. To that end, he must undergo a washing, bathe himself, as it is demanded of Jews themselves in the law when they have made themselves impure in one way or another (Lev 11–15; Num 19). Now, it may well be that later various usages were attached to this water bath that were not yet connected to it at the time of Christ. But there is no doubt that the essence of this proselyte baptism is nothing other than the usual Levitical cleansing demanded in this particular case. And as such, baptism will have existed at the time of John, indeed even before that time.

But from that, then, it also follows that it is incorrect to want to explain the baptism of John historically from this practice. John appeared with his demand of baptism in order to indicate that Judaism as a whole was apostate and not any better than paganism; that, consequently, they all had to undergo what the pagans underwent when they became Jews, namely, proselyte baptism. It cannot be proven that at that time the baptism of a proselyte took on such an important place in the initiation ritual that this view could be called correct. It must have still been something more or less subordinate then, to which one could not simply connect the idea of becoming a Jew. Jewish baptism will have only gained this importance as an initiation ceremony at a later time, perhaps under the influence of Christian practice. John himself did not present his baptism from this point of view. Rather, he associated himself with the same Levitical purifications of which the proselyte baptism was a particular application.

10. How should the significance of the baptism of John be assessed?

The Council of Trent has said: "If anyone says that the baptism of John possessed the same power as the baptism of Christ, let him be anathema" (session 7, canon 1). The Reformed maintained the opposite. While Rome thus said that those baptized by John had not received the dispensation of grace of proper baptism and later were baptized again or baptized as

Christians for the first time, the Reformed insisted that such a rebaptism did not take place.

It can hardly be denied that there was some difference between the baptism of John and baptism in the New Testament dispensation of the covenant of grace. But the question is whether it was an essential difference, so great that the new baptism was necessary. There was difference:

a) In the way in which baptism pointed to Christ. John was not yet in the kingdom of heaven. He stood at the dividing line. The Law and the Prophets were until him [Luke 16:16]. He was the forerunner who announced that the kingdom of heaven was nigh. His baptism, therefore, had to look forward to Christ. Christian baptism points back to the same Christ.

b) A second point of difference is connected with this. Although forming the transition, the baptism of John still belongs to the Old Testament dispensation and derives its features from the latter. The entire Old Testament dispensation places the law in the foreground as a disciplinarian until Christ. It was a dispensation to awaken repentance, consciousness of sin. Accordingly, we also find then that the baptism of John was a baptism for repentance. But this may not be understood as if it had only had a negative meaning, and as if the positive side had been totally lacking. True repentance is not possible without faith.

c) The baptism of John was still national and not catholic. It was a baptism for the Jews, while Christian baptism is a baptism whereby every distinction between Jew and Gentile, barbarian and Scythian, disappears.

d) In the degree of gifts that baptism sealed, the baptism of John naturally ranks below the later baptism of Christians. The Spirit having not yet come, all the special gifts that depended on the Spirit's outpouring had to be missing at that baptism. But this does not justify saying that in the baptism of John no special gift was sealed that was already available and obtainable at that time.

Alongside of the difference, however, there was essential agreement. The one who instituted the baptism of John was God Himself (John 1:33; Luke 3:3–4; Matt 21:25). Similarly, Christ, out of the fullness of His power as Mediator—by which He, Himself God, represented God—instituted

Christian baptism. The thing signified and sealed was the same, namely, forgiveness of sins and regeneration (Matt 3:7–8; Luke 3:3; Mark 1:4; cf. with Acts 2:38). The conversion that John, already preaching, would effect was conversion to faith, for of him it was said that he would convert many of the children of Israel to the Lord, their God (Luke 1:16), that it took place in order to make ready for the Lord a people prepared (v. 17). That thereby John pointed to Christ is apparent from everything (John 1:20, 23, 26–27, 30). The same thing is evident from the fact that Jesus Himself was baptized with this baptism of John, as well as His apostles, and that nowhere are we informed of a rebaptism.

It is asked, however: If this is so, how then can John himself make the sharp distinction he does in Matthew 3:11? He distinguishes there between his baptism, which is a baptism with water, and the baptism of Christ, which is a baptism with the Holy Spirit and with fire. How is that to be understood? Obviously, two outward baptisms are not set over against each other here, for just as John's baptism was a baptism with water, so the baptism of Christ would be a baptism without water. But contrasted with each other are the outward baptism of John and the special gifts of the Spirit that were signified and sealed by that baptism, and that could only follow later when Christ would have sent the Spirit from the Father. Thus the fire would also have to refer to the dispensation of the Spirit, and it is perhaps added to accentuate the distinction between this extraordinary and ordinary communication of the Spirit. Certainly, the regular activity of the Spirit is described in John 3:5 as *"water and Spirit."* Others see this fire as referring to the fiery tongues on the day of Pentecost; sill others to the fire of Gehenna, so that curse and blessing would be set over against each other. Both these interpretations are less satisfactory. Thus we see that nothing can be derived from this saying of John to establish a difference between his baptism and that of Christ. The same thing can also be said of the baptism that Christ had His disciples administer before His suffering (John 4:2; 3:22), namely, that it was not a baptism with the Holy Spirit and with fire. But it was still Christian baptism.

Another objection that is made is that later there were so many who were baptized on Pentecost that there surely must have been those present who had also been baptized by John: thus, rebaptism. So even Charles Hodge, who on this basis in particular expresses himself in favor of a difference between the two baptisms (*Systematic Theology*, 3:594). But it is not susceptible to proof that all present there had already been baptized by John, and that those who were already baptized by him were baptized again.

The principal objection, however, lies in Acts 19:1-7. There it is reported how in Ephesus Paul found some disciples who had not received the Holy Spirit—indeed, had not even heard if there were a Holy Spirit—who had only been baptized into the baptism of John. Then Paul says: "John baptized with the baptism of repentance," etc. Then there follows in verse 5: ἀκούσαντες δὲ ἐβαπτίσθησαν εἰς τὸ ὄνομα τοῦ κυρίου Ἰησοῦ, ["and when they heard this, they were baptized in the name of the Lord Jesus"]. "And when Paul laid hands on them, the Spirit came on them, and they spoke in strange languages and prophesied."

The understanding of this difficult passage depends entirely on the meaning of the words just cited in Greek.

a) The old and most accepted explanation is that these words (v. 5) are not the words of Luke the writer, but the words of Paul the speaker addressed to the disciples. So he intends to say: It is certainly true that John's baptism was chiefly a baptism of repentance, and that thereby repentance came to the fore, but still those who heard John were also baptized in the name of the Lord Jesus, and therefore it is not necessary that they be baptized again; it is sufficient for you that we lay hands on you and you will receive the gift of the Spirit. So, then, these disciples were not rebaptized. This is the explanation that our *Statenvertaling* [Dutch State Translation] favors by the added "him," which refers to John. This is the explanation of Beza, Calixtus, Calov, and many others, including the majority of the dogmaticians.

b) Another explanation is that verse 5 does in fact give the words of Luke, and not of Paul. But, it is said, according to Luke the baptism that the disciples received here in addition to their baptism by John was not a repeated water baptism; it was the baptism of the Holy Spirit, thus baptism in a spiritual sense. This is said to be explained further in in verse 6 by the laying on of hands and what followed, speaking in tongues and prophesying. This is the explanation of Calvin.

c) A third explanation is that of Zwingli, also followed by Dr. [Abraham] Kuyper (*De Heraut,* no. 643). Zwingli says: These twelve were rebaptized, not because they had received the authentic baptism of John and this was not sufficient for a Christian, but because one or another disciple of John had misled them by baptizing them in the name of John himself and not in the name of Jesus. The meaning of verse 4 then becomes as follows: John certainly baptized unto repentance but also in the name of Jesus, that is to say, "that they should believe in the one who came after him, that is, in Christ Jesus." You have not received the true baptism of John, but a counterfeit baptism. Verse 5 then becomes the account of Luke. The disciples were baptized by Paul, not rebaptized.

For this latter explanation, an appeal is made especially to verse 3. "And he said to them, 'Into what then were you baptized?' And they said, 'Into John's baptism (ε baptism (aid, β baptis).'" That will then have to mean: "baptized in the name of John." But it is totally uncertain that the words can mean that. Baptism in someone or into someone is never called the baptism *of* someone. For this explanation we would simply expect "*into* John."

d) Others say that the baptism of John was certainly authentic, but that these disciples were not sufficiently instructed regarding the future gifts of the Holy Spirit, the extraordinary charisma, and that this is meant by their saying: "We have not even heard that there is a Holy Spirit." That this certainly cannot mean "We have never heard of the existence of the Holy Spirit" is self-evident (cf. John 7:39). And now, supposedly, Paul, taking their weakness into consideration, rebaptized them at their request, which did not happen in normal circumstances. That they desired this is supposedly indicated by the words, "on hearing this" (v. 5).

One must grant that this, in light of the context, is the most natural explanation of all. The rebaptism will then be based on the dual character that Christian baptism initially had, on the charismatic aspect. If one accepts this explanation, then it in no way follows that therefore rebaptism is permissible, as Anabaptists propose, who have always attempted to make capital of this text. That Apollos was baptized by Aquila cannot be positively proven (Acts 18:26).

However, the objection remains to this view, too, that the laying on of hands followed baptism. Usually one assumes that this laying on of hands had specifically as its aim to communicate the charisma of the Holy Spirit. And here too that is the case, for they immediately begin to speak in tongues and to prophesy. One could still say: baptism and the laying on of hands belong with each other.

The first explanation would be the most preferable if we could translate the Greek of verse 5 as "those who heard him." But one would expect that then the text read: οἱ δὲ ἀκούσαντες αὐτόν. This text is and remains a *crux interpretum* ["crossroads for interpreters," a passage difficult to interpret]. Turretin acknowledges that rebaptism is possibly spoken of here, but that nevertheless an essential difference need not exist between the baptism of John and Christian baptism. He says that John perhaps did not use a formula such as was used later, and that thereby the repetition was warranted. One can hardly prove that John used a set formula, but with no less difficulty that this in itself gave rise to repetition.

11. *What word in the New Testament is used for baptizing, and what is the force of that word?*

Βάπτω (*baptō*) means "to dip," "immerse," for to baptize and to immerse are related to each other (cf. the English "to dive," "to dip"). In John 13:26 it is used for the dipping of the morsel by Jesus that he gave to Judas. See also Ruth 2:14 [Septuagint] for dipping the morsel in vinegar by Ruth; Luke 16:24 for dipping Lazarus' finger in water. In all these passages, the word used is βάπτω, so that positively no doubt need exist about the original meaning. When a Baptist says that *baptō* means "immerse," then one should grant him that without reservation.

A strengthened form of *baptō* is *baptizō* (βαπτίζω), and this is the usual word in use for "baptize." This, too, is originally "immerse." Actually, *baptizein* means "immerse repeatedly"; it is an iterative form. Hence it is used instead of *baptō* in 2 Kings 5:14 [Septuagint], which recounts how Naaman dipped himself seven times in the Jordan. But this iterative meaning is not always maintained, so that often enough *baptizein* is equal in meaning to *baptein*. Now, however, this *baptizein* appears at the same time to have been the usual Greek translation for the Levitical washings and purifications, which again may be connected with the fact that this took place generally by bathing—that is, by immersing the body in water. One may compare, for example, Matthew 15:2, "For they do not wash their hands when they eat" (οὐ γὰρ νίπτονται τὰς χεῖρας), with Mark 7:4, "unless they first wash" (ἐὰν μὴ βαπτίσωνται).

With this, the concept of *baptizō* is placed directly under the viewpoint of "washing," a fact of the highest importance. That this "washing" was in most instances a washing by immersion appears as something accidental that could also be something else, and that, if it had been something else, nothing of substance would have changed. The Levitical purifications were washings of the whole body, also where a sprinkling accompanied them (Num 19:19; see also v. 18; Lev 11:24–28 and following; 17:15; 14:2–8; 15:16–18, 19–24, 25–29, 2–15). That in all these purifications the whole body had to be washed and not just a part had to do with the ceremonial and burdensome character of the Old Testament dispensation. If an easy sprinkling had been sufficient, then perhaps it would have quickly become an outward form. The bathing of the whole body did not easily become a meaningless custom. Then one should also not forget that for the Levitical purification its symbolic character came to the fore. It was therefore in all respects fitting that in the case of uncleanness the whole body was subject to a washing. By that was certainly pictured how the entire person is polluted by sin and how complete renewal is necessary. However, from that it may not be inferred that at baptism as a sacrament, too, complete immersion of the body is necessary. With baptism, not the sign but the seal is surely in the foreground. The New Testament sacraments are not in the first place symbols; they are above all seals of the covenant. Thus it is in no way necessary that the entire symbolism of the purifications of the Old Testament be transferred to the baptism of the New Testament.

The error the Baptists make when they insist that *baptizein* is immersion and nothing else lies in overlooking the fact just mentioned. Words have their meaning by their use, not by their etymology. One can safely grant not only that originally *baptizō* means to immerse; indeed, one can even go so far as to say that initially immersion was the customary mode of baptism, without playing into the hands of the Baptists. The point at issue between them and us surely lies in this: whether immersion constitutes the heart and essence of the symbolism of baptism, so that abandoning it would be the same as abandoning baptism itself. When one asks a Baptist, "Why did Christ institute the sacrament of incorporation into the Christian church in *this* way?" then his answer is: "Because it had to be portrayed by descending into and emerging from the water." That thereby washing takes place at the same time, since one cannot immerse someone without the water at the same time washing his body is, according to him, something incidental. Baptism would be baptism, and its essence preserved, if one could immerse someone in something else that does not have a cleansing quality. If one poses the same question to us, then we answer: The sacrament was instituted by Christ in this way because He intended to have washing and purification portrayed. The fact that this ordinarily took place in a land like Palestine and according to the Jewish law by immersion or bathing was something incidental and subordinate. If a washing takes place without immersion, then baptism retains its essence.

Thus the issue between us and Baptists is not at all whether *baptizein* means to immerse or to sprinkle. One can grant, and probably will have to grant, that nowhere in the New Testament has it completely lost its original meaning of "immersing" or "dipping." The issue is simply whether immersion was the main point or something incidental. And then we say the latter. It was immersion with the purpose of washing, and in order to portray purification. We rely on this when we claim that baptism by sprinkling is just as much the ordinance of Christ as baptism by immersion. From their side, Baptists believe that the Reformation has taken half measures, that Luther and Calvin did not fully clean out the Roman Catholic leaven, and that on them the duty rests to restore original Christianity in its purity.

One should preferably not combat Baptists with weak historical arguments from the New Testament. One can appeal to Mark 7:4: βαπτισμοὺς ποτηρίων καὶ ξεστῶν καὶ χαλκίων καὶ κλινῶν, "washing of cups and pots and copper vessels *and couches*." It is said that cups and pots and copper vessels could be immersed, but not couches. It is a question, however, whether these words (*kai klinōn*) belong in the text. Westcott and Hort omit them. The Revised Version does also. One can also point to Acts 2:41–42. There were 3,000 people added to the church, who for the most part were also certainly baptized. Was that possible in so short a time if baptism took place by immersion? It is not impossible. An equally large number of converts have been baptized in a relatively short period of time by immersion. The appeal to Acts 10:47 is also not strong, since we evidently have to do there with a figurative expression. Peter intends to say: the Holy Spirit has already come upon them; can anyone still forbid water, by which they are signified and sealed? From Acts 16:33 it has generally been inferred that the jailer and his family were not baptized by immersion but simply by sprinkling. But Baptists say that the jail, like most of the large buildings in the Middle East, had a fountain and a cistern. First Corinthians 10:1–2 states that all the fathers were under the cloud and passed through the sea and were baptized into Moses in the cloud and in the sea. The fact that they went through the water, and that certainly with dry feet, can, it is said, be called already being baptized. They were simply sprinkled with the spattering drops. But there is no mention of sprinkling in the account of these events. The apostle apparently conceived of them such that the sea and the cloud surrounded the people, and so became an element in which they were located. The sea was on both sides, the cloud was over the Israelites; that was their baptism.

Appeal is also made to passages that speak of a baptizing with the Holy Spirit: Matthew 3:1 (ἐν πνεύματι ἁγίῳ καὶ πυρί); Mark 1:8 (ἐγὼ ἐβάπτισα ὑμᾶς ὕδατι, αὐτὸς δὲ βαπτίσει ὑμᾶς ἐν πνεύματι ἁγίῳ); John 1:33 (οὗτός ἐστιν ὁ βαπτίζων ἐν πνεύματι ἁγίῳ); Acts 1:5; 11:16 (ὑμεῖς δὲ βαπτισθήσεσθε ἐν πνεύματι ἁγίῳ); 1 Cor 12:13 (καὶ γὰρ ἐν ἑνὶ πνεύματι ἡμεῖς πάντες εἰς ἓν σῶμα ἐβαπτίσθημεν). The question is how this "in the Holy Spirit," as it literally stands in all these passages, is meant. Is the Holy Spirit the element in which one is baptized, in which God, as it were, immerses, or is it to be understood as a being baptized with the Holy Spirit? In the latter case, ἐν, equivalent to בְּ in Hebrew, would be an instrumental preposition. In Mark 1:8 it is without doubt "by means of water ... by means of the Holy Spirit." But from this it does not yet follow that sprinkling is thought of, for one can also call baptism through immersion a baptism by means of water. In 1 Corinthians 12:13, the translation "by means of one Spirit" appears to us the most natural, but sprinkling is not proven by it. By all of these things one can only deprive Baptists of proofs, not obtain proofs for his own views. See the commentaries on these passages.

12. *What is the testimony of the history of the postbiblical period regarding the question of immersion or sprinkling?*

It appears that sprinkling was already in use early, especially in so-called "clinical baptism," namely, for sick persons who had to receive the sacrament. For them immersion was excluded. It appears, however, that in the earliest times many superstitious persons did not regard such a baptism as being complete. Those who were baptized by sprinkling were called "clinici." At first it was thought that there was no proof from the second century for baptism by sprinkling, because a few texts in Tertullian are regarded as uncertain, and also the age of certain pictures in which sprinkling occurs cannot be determined precisely enough. But change has come through the discovery of the Didache of the Twelve Apostles. From it, it is certainly evident that even in the very earliest times no offense was registered if sprinkling replaced immersion. Still, here it is also added that there had to be an objective grounds that made immersion impossible or inadvisable; for example, if there was no running water in the vicinity. Along this path, too, one cannot prove the apostolic origin of sprinkling.

13. *To what, finally, can one still appeal against the Baptists?*

To the universal character of Christianity. Christianity is catholic, that is, intended for all times and places. That must come out in its sacraments too. Hence, the signs in these sacraments are such as are to be found everywhere: water, bread, wine— the most common products of nature that can be kept everywhere. But the same thing will also have to apply to their manner of use. Immersion is something that is sometimes feasible in Middle Eastern lands, but then again in many regions, not. If Christianity is thus bound to something like this, then in this respect it is the same as Islam, which obligates all its adherents to a pilgrimage to Mecca. But Islam is then also particularistic; Christianity is universal, catholic, intended for all times, countries, circumstances, and conditions.

14. *Is it only Baptists who have immersion?*

No, the entire Greek Church also maintains baptism by immersion. It took a long time in the Roman Catholic Church before immersion and sprinkling were recognized as equally legitimate (the end of the thirteenth century). The English Church appears to have practiced immersion for a time. The Westminster Assembly said, "sprinkle or pour" [Westminster Confession of Faith 28.3]. Earlier, when immersion came into use by the Baptists, it was seen as a novelty.

15. *In what does the outward matter, the outward sign consist for baptism?*

In washing with water. Pure water must be used, and not, as Roman Catholics propose, oil, salt, saliva, honey, or what have you. The water must be used in such a way that an image of washing away emerges. It must be brought into contact with the body of the person to be baptized. There are those who insist that this contact of the body with water must be a threefold action, in order to accord with the Trinitarian baptismal formula. Tertullian, Cyril, Basil, Ambrose speak of a threefold sprinkling. Turretin says: "We hold presently to a single sprinkling, and believe that we need not dispute with anyone in the world about this matter, since there is no express command for the number one or three" (*Institutes*, 19.11.12). Exorcism, consecration of the water, making the sign of the cross on the forehead and chest of the person baptized, hanging a lit wax candle over him—all of them Roman Catholic practices—are rejected.

16. *Indicate further how this water and the action performed with it in baptism becomes a sign.*

a) The water is that element in nature that has been created by God for the purpose of physical cleansing. The idea of cleansing has been placed by God in water. This choice of water was not made in retrospect, but water was created for that beforehand. The cleansing in a spiritual sense refers to two things: first, the removal of guilt; further, the removal of pollution. There is a washing of justification; there is also a washing of sanctification. The contact of the water refers to both. One, however, can ask further: What is it, then, that produces this twofold cleansing in a spiritual sense? The answer is: the blood and the Spirit of Christ. These two must therefore also be portrayed by the water of baptism. This is so obvious for the blood that it scarcely needs demonstration. But 1 Corinthians 6:11 also has the Spirit in view: "And this were some of you. But you are washed, you are sanctified, you are justified, in the name of our Lord Jesus Christ and by the Spirit of our God"; Hebrews 10:22: "our bodies being washed with pure water"; Revelation 1:5: "and has washed us by his blood"; 1 Peter 3:21: "of which the antitype, baptism, now also saves you, which is not a putting away of filth from the body but an appeal of a good conscience to God, through the resurrection of Jesus Christ." That the Holy Spirit is also signified in baptism comes out, among other places, in Titus 3:5: "by the washing of regeneration and renewal of the Holy Spirit"; John 3:5: "unless one is born of water and the Spirit." See also Matthew 3:11 as this text has been interpreted above. Here John contrasts the sign and the thing signified with each other and says that he can only give the former, that Christ must and will give the latter.

Scripture does not indicate further how the Spirit is portrayed in the sign of the water. There is no need to be reminded that the outpouring of the Holy Spirit is a common image in Scripture. But outpouring is something that makes us think of water. So, there is nothing in itself incongruous that the Spirit is portrayed by water and His action signified by sprinkling with water. Some have pointed to the life-giving power of water, but this surmise appears to lack scriptural grounding.

The blood of Christ applied to the soul justifies. In the shedding of that blood is both the passive as well as the active obedience of the Mediator. That is why the sign of baptism is also a sign, not of a half, but of a complete, perfect justification. Baptism, says Peter, is the appeal of a good conscience to God through the resurrection of Jesus Christ. In baptism there is the appeal, but also the response to it from the side of God.

b) The Baptists and all who insist on the necessity of immersion proceed in a completely different way in their explanation of the symbolism of baptism. They say that baptizō is "dipping." "Dipping" is putting something in water so that it first goes under water and then comes out of it again. The movement down and up, then, is what is essential. The movement signifies entering into death and emerging from death. The death into which one enters and from which one emerges is in the first place the atoning death of Christ. The believer must enter into it in order to share in it; that is, he must have fellowship with it—the death must be imputed to him. Christ therefore called His death a baptism: "Are you able to drink the cup that I drink, or to be baptized with the baptism with which I am baptized?" (Mark 10:38); "But I have to be baptized with this baptism, and how distressed I am until it is accomplished" (Luke 12:50). That is why Paul speaks of baptism as follows: "Or do you not know that as many of us as were baptized into Christ Jesus were baptized into his death?" (Rom 6:3).

But that is not the only thing about the symbolism of baptism that we, in the estimation of the Baptists, fail to appreciate and omit. There is more. When the baptized person descends into the water and is baptized downward, that symbolizes the destruction of his own old man. When he makes the movement upward and rises, it signifies the resurrection of his new man. Further, between both of these symbols of death there is now a connection. Baptism signifies that only through fellowship in the death on the cross and the resurrection of Christ (in a juridical fashion) can the killing of the old and the resurrection of the new man take place in us. Our burial and our resurrection are only possible because we enter into the death and the resurrection of Christ, thus into the water of baptism.

And the conclusion is that only immersionists possess the unimpaired sacrament, that, on the other hand, aspersionists [those who sprinkle] have a corrupted sign and are disobedient to the ordinance of Christ. A Baptist writes: "It is a sad thing that those who follow the practice of sprinkling in place of immersion say by that symbol that a man can regenerate himself, or at least that his regeneration can take place without being connected with Christ's death. ... Purification is made to be the essence of baptism, and one concludes that any form of purification corresponds to the purpose of the ordinance. But if Christ's death is the meriting cause of our purification, we may expect it will be pictured in the ordinance that attests that purification; if the death of Christ is the central fact of Christianity, we may expect

it will also be symbolized in the initiating rite of Christianity"
(Strong, *Systematic Theology*, 529)[1]

Our answer to this view is as follows:

1. That abundance of water and entering into it is a special
    image of the death of Christ cannot be proven from any place
    in Scripture. What Christ says in Mark 10:38 and Luke 12:50,
    cited above, certainly does not look ahead to Christian bap-
    tism but is a figurative expression. The thought is probably
    connected to Old Testament expressions, such as Psalm 69:1–2,
    14–15; Psalm 42:7; 124:4–5; 144:7; Isaiah 43:2; Revelation 12:15.

2. When the water of baptism is brought into contact with the
    person being baptized, then a connection between him and
    the death of Christ comes about just as well as it does by im-
    mersion. This baptismal water surely signifies, as we have
    seen, the blood of the Savior. Blood causes one to think im-
    mediately of death. And sprinkling with blood shows clear-
    ly enough that the death of Christ has something to do with
    our washing and purification. It is therefore a completely un-
    justified accusation against the aspersionists when it is said
    that they detach subjective grace from its origin in the death
    of Christ. As long as there is an application of water in bap-
    tism, in whatever particular way that may be, something like
    that detachment is naturally impossible. The death of Christ
    is symbolically there in the water.

3. The Baptistic symbolism is not simple and clear enough to be
    able do service for the kind of rite that must be generally un-
    derstandable. The submerging of the person baptized must

---

1   Translation of Vos' translation of Strong. The earliest publication of Strong that I
    was able to access postdates Vos. It reads: "It is a grievous thing to say by symbol, as
    those do say who practice sprinkling in place of immersion, that a man may regen-
    erate himself, or, if not this, yet that his regeneration may take place without any
    connection with Christ's death. ... Purification is made to be the essential meaning of
    baptism, and the conclusion is drawn that any form expressive of purification will
    answer the design of the ordinance. But if Christ's death is the procuring cause of our
    purification, we may expect it to be symbolized in the ordinance which declares that
    purification; if Christ's death is the central fact of Christianity, we may expect it to be
    symbolized in the initiatory rite of Christianity" (Strong, *Systematic Theology: Three
    Volumes in One* [Revell, 1907], 944).

signify two things at the same time: namely, the death of Christ and the death of the sinner that flows from it. Cause and result merge here. The water in itself, the quantity of water, cannot represent the death of Christ, for, if one admits that, it becomes a purely quantitative question and there are no longer any grounds for saying that the small amount of water that we use does not depict the death. But neither does submerging, for it is the submersion not of the Savior but of the sinner. But few people can understand such a complex symbolism.

4. The passage primarily appealed to from the Baptist side is Romans 6:1–10. One must agree that here Paul here links his argumentation to the symbolism of immersion. He aims to show that justification by faith does not lead to licentiousness, that thereby one does not learn to say, "Let us continue in sin that grace may increase." The proof lies in the fact that a subjective reversal in the consciousness of man accompanies entrance into the state of objective justification. And for this the apostle finds proof in the ceremony of baptism—that baptism was a baptism into the death of Christ because it was a baptism into Christ. As many of us as were baptized in (into) Christ were baptized into his death. Because by his baptism the Christian has been brought into union with Christ, that union must continue in all its aspects and parts. It must be a union in death. Now it is self-evident that this cannot be understood in an entirely literal way. Our death is not totally the same as Christ's death. There is only a kind of likeness. The dying of Christ was the dying of sin; our death is a dying to sin. The comparison between these two is thus not so much a comparison between two similar facts as a meaningful allusion. Baptism reminds us that the death of Christ must be at work in us, that the sin that was judged on the cross must now further also be pursued and driven out until its last traces have disappeared. The center of gravity of the discourse, therefore, lies in union with Christ.

Now, however, no one will maintain that baptism loses this element as soon as it ceases to be an immersion. After all, sprinkling, too, *takes place into* Christ. When the blood of

Christ is applied to us in baptism, that signifies not only that guilt but also pollution must be cleansed. The *shedding of blood* becomes a *washing with blood* in a double sense, namely, for justification and sanctification. If now in Paul's day baptism by sprinkling was usual, he could just as well have reasoned from this practice as from baptism by immersion. He could have spoken as follows:

a) In baptism as the sacrament of incorporation into the Christian church, what it means to become a Christian comes out.

b) In baptism the blood of Christ is not only shed *outside* of us as a sacrifice that is effective for us; it is also sprinkled *upon* us as blood that cleanses.

c) Baptism signifies and seals, therefore, that the blood of Christ, as the sign of His death, also works *in* us, that it sanctifies and regenerates us.

d) It is therefore slander if one disseminates that a Christian could say: Let us commit sin, so that grace may increase!

There is, however, more that stands in the way of Baptistic reasoning. One is accustomed to represent this descending into and arising out of the water of baptism as a symbol of regeneration. But Paul is not speaking about regeneration here. It is without doubt that he has conversion in view. Repentance and faith as the source of good works correspond to this descending and arising. It is something that occurs in the consciousness, a breaking with and a crucifying of sin that has the character of something shameful, something painful. Because the Christian, before he came to the peace of justification, had to wrestle through this process of dying, because sin was revealed in him in all its hideousness and is always a disgrace for him, it is therefore impossible that he would ever fall into the frightful error of wanting to commit sin so that grace would increase. Not regeneration, but conversion is thus portrayed here by descending and arising. And now we must agree that for this symbolism immersion alone is fitting. Only submersion with water, plunging into it, produces the thought of something painful and grievous. Paul then also speaks of being buried with Christ, a being crucified of the old man with him, but he never says that the essence of baptism is to be found in that. In Titus 3:5, where he mentions regeneration, he finds the symbolic element in the bath, thus in washing, not in something painful but in something refreshing and enlivening.

The result for us, therefore, is that baptism by immersion can be used with a richer symbolic significance than by sprinkling, but that the latter also is a complete baptism; and that in the institution and origin of baptism, not burial and resurrection but cleansing and washing were in the foreground. Paul used immersion in a meaning-filled way to express a profound thought, but nowhere did he say that he thereby indicated or explained the mode of baptism.

17. Where does one find the institution of Christian baptism?

In principle it already received its divine institution with John the Baptist. But this institution is ratified anew by the Mediator before His ascension (Matt 28:19).

18. What is the meaning of these words of institution?

a) They must be related to verse 18: "And coming to them Jesus spoke, saying, 'To me is given all authority in heaven and on earth.'" As the powerful one, that is, as the one who is fully authorized, who possesses mediatorial power, Christ instituted the sacrament of baptism. It is authority granted, thus the authority of the Mediator.

b) "Having gone out, make disciples of all nations." This is the literal translation of the word that our translations have rendered with "teach" (μαθητεύσατε). In "all nations" lies the catholicity of Christianity, which with the exaltation of the Lord would receive its full rights. But the Jews are not excluded from this "all the nations." From now on, Israel is an ordinary nation alongside the other nations. One great Christian people takes the place of the people of fleshly Israel. The Vulgate already translated with docete, "teach," and thereby this incorrect translation has come into and remained in use.

c) The question further is: What is the connection between the three things: "make disciples," "baptize," and "teach"? Evidently, the connection is this: that making disciples takes place by baptizing and by teaching. Accordingly, it has two parts. First, by baptism someone is placed in the relationship of a disciple of Jesus, and then he is taught accurately concerning everything that the Lord has commanded so that he may keep it. By this it is not said, but neither is it excluded, that the persons to be baptized must first receive some instruction. If their baptism is their becoming a disciple, then they must know what that means. For adults that is the case, but if, as for children, instruction is not possible immediately, baptism can precede and the instruction in its entirety allowed to follow. This is important for infant baptism.

d) "Baptizing them in the name of the Father and of the Son and of the Holy Spirit." By this baptism, water baptism is to be understood, not, as the Quakers hold, Spirit-baptism by Christ. Father, Son, and Holy Spirit are here mentioned next to each other, and the one word "name" applies to these three together. If the text had read "in the names," then that could give rise to the impression that each of the three divine persons bore more than one name. The question, however, is: What is meant by this "into the name" (εἰς τὸ ὄνομα)?

1. The Vulgate has translated it *in nomine*, "in the name." Luther has followed this translation, "in Namen." That would mean: "by order of, by the authority of Father, Son, and Spirit." But this cannot be so for various reasons. Then nothing would be said about the purpose of baptism, about its signifying and sealing power, and only the person who administers it and his mandate would be mentioned. Further, neither can εἰς τὸ ὄνομα mean "*in* the name" (בְּשֵׁם), but will have to be understood otherwise, equivalent to לְשֵׁם, "*into* the name." And this "into the name" does not mean "unto the honor of the name," neither simply "for the confession of the name," nor "so that the person baptized may be called by another name." Rather, the meaning is that by baptism one comes to stand in a personal relationship with the triune God, who is called by the name Father, Son, and Holy Spirit. The name is the revelation of the

being; the being of God is in His name. Thus, to be baptized into the name indicates entering into that relationship with God whereby His being becomes the full truth for us. By baptism the first person of the Trinity becomes for us (always sacramentally) a Father who "adopts us for His children and heirs, and promises to provide us with all good and avert all evil or turn it to our benefit" (Form for Baptism). Likewise with the Son and the Holy Spirit. These three names occur here economically in their meaning that they have for the covenant of grace. Of course, at the same time a Trinitarian confession is included, but that is still not all. To be baptized into the name of the triune One speaks of much more than being bound by baptism to believe in the Trinity. It speaks of coming into a practical personal relationship with the Trinity. Baptism is not just a general symbol of Christianity; it is a seal of the covenant of grace. And the covenant of grace is in essence a Trinitarian covenant.

2. We thus avoid two extremes in the explanation of these words. The first extreme is that of the explanations mentioned above; the other is that one understands "into the name" as the sphere into which the baptized person enters. Here it is not in the first place a sphere with which we have to do, but a relationship. Of course, that relationship brings consequences with it. But that stems from the fact that it is not we ourselves who place ourselves in this relationship; it is the Triune God who does this. That is the starting point of our Form for Baptism. The Father declares, the Son declares, the Holy Spirit declares, and that is the meaning of our being baptized *into* their name.

3. In many respects, one has wished to translate: "immersing them in the name of the Father," etc., as if here the name occurs as the element in which one is immersed. But then the water must picture the name of the Father, of the Son, and of the Holy Spirit. But for that any further basis is lacking in Scripture. The water in which one is immersed is never anything other than the blood and the Spirit of Christ. Thus the entire expression will have to be understood as follows: "Baptize (in water) into the fellowship of the covenant of grace

with Father, Son, and Spirit." And in this is contained the thought that what is signified and sealed by water is the sole means for gaining access into fellowship with Father, Son, and Holy Spirit. One must be brought into contact with the water, into the water, and only in this way is it possible to come to the triune God. In baptism we have to see in the sign not so much the goal as the means to that goal. The blood, as blood of the covenant, as the blood of the Mediator, opens to us the entrance to the covenant relationship with God.

e) Are these words, "into the name of the Father, of the Son, and of the Holy Spirit" to be regarded as a formula that must be pronounced at baptism and that may never be changed? Tertullian maintained that the form was prescribed; Origen declared that no baptism was legitimate other than that in the name of the Trinity, as did Athanasius. The latter two, however, appear not to have insisted on the precise form. But Augustine, going along with Tertullian, did. Thomas Aquinas also agreed with them, and required the use of the words as a formula. He says that when the apostles sometimes used other words, they had special permission for that from Christ that we do not have. The Roman Catholic Catechism doubts that the apostles ever baptized with any other formula than the full formula. Bellarmine does not appeal to Matthew 28:19 but to tradition and the church to prove the necessary use of the formula.

On the other hand, there are not a few others who declare a baptism in the name of Christ as legitimate, since in the name of Christ that of the Father and of the Son is already implied. We mention only Ambrose, Bernard of Clairvaux, and Peter Lombard.

Luther denied that the strict formula is demanded and that baptism in the name of Jesus Christ would not be valid. Zwingli denied that Matthew 28:19 is intended for use as a formula. Calvin judges otherwise (*Commentary* on Acts 2:38 and 1 Cor 1:13). He reasons from the thought that Christ certainly intended to prescribe a formula. Voetius said that at baptism there must be an audible word including the command and the promise of God, and for that one does best to keep to Matthew 18:19, but that one may not seek the form and the essence of baptism in the use of those words and in their sequence. Cloppenburg calls it an error to think that Christ gave a command to use precisely these words. Beza, Gomarus, Maresius, Heidegger, and Turretin, in contrast, are in agreement with Calvin. Cocceius said that no formula was prescribed, as do most Cocceians. À Brakel, too, does not hold the formula to be necessary.

One sees that the theologians, in the Reformed church too, answered the question differently. Can it be shown that the apostles used another formula? In Acts 2:38, Peter does call his hearers to let themselves be baptized in the name of Jesus Christ, but it cannot be demonstrated that by that he intended to indicate the formula that was to be pronounced at baptism. Bengel thought that the Jews only needed to be baptized in the name of Jesus, while for the Gentiles, who were completely alienated from the true God, the full formula would have been used by the apostles. In Mathew 28:19, then, "all the nations" would have that in view. But, as already has been said, this expression does not at all exclude the Jews. We believe that nothing can be proven from Acts 2:38, nor from Acts 8:16. Acts 10:48 has "in the name of the Lord"; in 19:5, "in the name of the Lord Jesus." Apparently here throughout the purpose of baptism is described, with the baptism formula cited, and in order to describe the purpose nothing was more suitable than to say, "into the Mediator," "into the name of Jesus Christ."

It is otherwise in Matthew 28:19. Certainly here, too, emphasis is placed on the purpose of baptism, but this time intentionally, in instituting baptism. Thus we may assume that the words found here are the formulation of our Savior regarding the purport of baptism. And if it is now established that at baptism something must be pronounced, and that this pronouncement must express in a few words the purport of the sacrament, then we rightly ask, Where could one better find the words required than in this commission of the Savior? Although it is true that there is no command here to use that specific form of words, still it borders on audacity even to desire to give a better formulation for the meaning of the sacrament than that Christ has given us here. There is not even the slightest reason conceivable why one would deviate from it.

May one say, however, that baptism not administered with that formula is illegitimate? Here one should make a distinction. If omitting the formula takes place out of a deliberate denial of the Trinity in the church that administers baptism, then that baptism is certainly illegitimate. If, on the other hand, the intention was none other than to baptize into the fellowship of the Father, of the Son, and of the Holy Spirit, then one may not attach such significance to the words in themselves that by their omission the baptism could be altered.

At the same time, it follows from this that in our day the use of the formula is of more weight than in earlier times. If there were no Unitarians in the world, then the omission of the formula would not provide an occasion to regard anyone with suspicion. But now that the Trinitarian confession is being denied most strongly from many sides, there is a great probability that something more is lurking behind the falling of the formula into disuse. That is why it is not permissible for anyone to change the words or omit any of them lightly.

19. *What question is related to what is being discussed here?*

That concerning the one who legitimately administers baptism. Roman Catholics, following in the footsteps of Augustine, posit an absolute necessity of baptism for salvation. Since it appears cruel to tie the salvation of a person on occasion to the accidental presence or absence of a priest, Rome has seen itself compelled to allow for baptism by laypeople, even by women in cases of emergency. That is called emergency baptism. Even a nonbaptized layman can baptize others in case of an emergency. Rome will even recognize the baptism of heretics, although in the ancient church there was an intense conflict about that. Cyprian and the African bishops rejected the baptism administered by heretical and schismatic churches, and rebaptized. The Donatists insisted on this even much more strongly and developed this divergent belief into heresy. The Church of Rome, in contrast, did not rebaptize those who had received a heretical baptism. At the Nicene Council this latter standpoint was adopted, but an exception was made for heretics who denied the Trinity.

Regarding the one administering baptism, the Reformed have always held to the rule that the ministry of the Word and the administration of the sacraments belong together. In the institution of baptism is a command to the apostles to make disciples. Baptism belongs to this making of disciples. It is a part of making disciples. Teaching precedes and follows it. This teaching is official teaching, teaching first entrusted to the apostles, but in them entrusted to the whole church, its dogmatic power. It is natural, then, that those who occupy this teaching office also perform baptism. It goes without saying that it was not entrusted only to the apostles to baptize. The command in its generality, "make disciples of all nations," could only be carried out by the church of all ages. The sacraments are seals of the King of the church, but it is inherent in the nature of a seal that it cannot be used by just anyone. The king appoints his lawful servants to affix it for him to those items to which he wishes to have it affixed. Roman Catholics appeal to Zipporah (Exod 4:25). But the cases are not the same. At that time, there was no regular ministry of the Word, and circumcision was ordinarily done by the father of the household. Finally, since we do not teach the necessity of baptism in order to be saved, we also cannot concede that in any instance it would be necessary to depart from the rule that baptism must be administered by ministers of the Word.

Baptism is not a private matter. As a sacrament, it belongs to the church. Therefore it should be administered in a public meeting of the congregation, when believers are gathered for the ministry of the Word.

Of course, it cannot strictly be proven from the New Testament that only ministers of the teaching office administered baptism in the first Christian churches. At Pentecost, some of the disciples could have assisted the apostles in administering baptism. Philip (deacon and evangelist) baptized. Ananias baptized Paul in Damascus, and we know nothing more about him than that he was a disciple (Acts 9:10, 18). In 1 Corinthians 1:7, Paul says that Christ did not send him to baptize but to preach the gospel. That is, what was specific, what distinguished the apostles from others, what others could not do just as well, was not found in baptizing but in the apostolic proclamation of the word of God—proof that Matthew 28:19 was directed to the church as represented by the apostles, and not to the apostles as such. In Acts 10:48 Peter, too, appears to have left the baptizing to others.

Regarding heretical baptism, the Reformed church also takes the standpoint mentioned above by distinguishing between fundamental heresy and non-fundamental deviation in doctrine. We do not recognize a baptism by Arians and Socinians. We do recognize baptism by Roman Catholics and Remonstrants. When someone comes over to us from the first two groups, we do not rebaptize. We baptize for the first time, for he has not been truly baptized. The point is not whether or not the person who administers baptism has been corrupted by fundamental heresy; at issue is only the standpoint of the church in which and for which he has administered baptism. But it is obvious that this is an area where one could raise many hard questions. When the church tolerates a heretical teacher, is it not then itself partly accountable and accessory to so-called heretical doctrine? Can one acknowledge the baptism of a so-called Reformed church that permits someone who denies the deity of Christ to continue to minister the Word and the sacraments? If the heresy of the minister has remained hidden heresy, then that of course is not an issue for the validity or non-validity of the baptism.

20. To whom should baptism be administered?

Its institution makes clear that those should be baptized who are able to be disciples (Matt 28:19). Thus men, not clocks or buildings or the like, as Roman Catholics maintain. Linked permanently to 1 Corinthians 15:29 is the difficult question whether dead persons may also be baptized, at least representatively—that is, whether someone can be baptized on behalf of the dead. There the apostle says, "Otherwise, what will those do who are baptized for the dead (Ἐπεὶ τί ποιήσουσιν οἱ βαπτιζόμενοι ὑπὲρ τῶν νεκρῶν), if the dead are not raised at all? Why then are they baptized for the dead?" Already long past there have been no less than 23 explanations of these words.

a) Calvin and others take this "letting oneself be baptized for the dead" as meaning "letting oneself be baptized in the state of dying, as such who certainly will die, who are as good as dead." In view then must be sick Christians who had not yet received baptism but still wished to die as baptized persons. It is apparent, however, that the words cannot possibly mean this.

b) Luther and others take ὑπέρ in a local sense: "above the graves." He says that Christians in Corinth carried out the ceremony of baptism above the graves of those who had died. But ὑπέρ in such a sense does not occur in the New Testament, and that baptism was administered above the graves cannot provide proof for the resurrection of the dead, for which the words of the apostle must surely contain a proof.

c) Chrysostom: "be baptized for the resurrection of the body," that is, under the circumstance of confessing the article of Christian faith that speaks of the resurrection of the dead; so the view of many others. But neither can the words mean this.

d) The most natural and, as it appears to us, only tenable explanation seems to be as follows: In the Corinthian congregation a misuse must have existed whereby Christians let themselves be baptized vicariously for unbaptized deceased persons, probably in the superstitious belief that from this baptism the latter would gain an advantage on the day of the resurrection. Thus this misuse included belief in the resurrection of the dead. And to the extent that the practice included this faith, Paul could make use of it as an ad hominem argument. By this, however, it is not being maintained that Paul approved of this superstitious use. Under other circumstances Paul could have remonstrated with the Corinthians about this practice and taught them better. In any case the apostles opposed it, for it did not continue in the church. It is found later only in heretical sects such as, for example, the Marcionites.

One should grant that only this last mentioned explanation does justice to the natural sense of the words. No one will be able to claim, however, that it removes all difficulties. It remains abidingly strange that Paul could make such a dreadful misuse of baptism the basis for his argument without a single word of disapproval.

21. *How can one further categorize the recipients of baptism?*

Into two groups:

a) Adults who were not baptized in their infancy.

b) Children of the covenant who were baptized as such.

It is necessary to treat the meaning of baptism for these two classes separately. The question of infant baptism is a question of such great importance that it should be discussed independently. It is granted by all that where the New Testament deals with baptism *ex professo* [by profession], the baptism of adults is meant. In a time of missions, as the New Testament was, that should naturally come to the fore. We first seek, therefore, to establish what meaning the New Testament attributes to baptism as administered to an adult.

22. *To what adults was baptism administered according to the ordinance of Christ?*

To those who were in truth His disciples. Through baptism one became a disciple of Jesus. One was baptized into Him in order to enter into the fellowship of the covenant of grace with Father, Son, and Holy Spirit. Nowhere is there a hint to be found that by this only an outward relationship is meant, an obligation to be present for or to do this or that. To the words of the Ethiopian eunuch, Philip says: "If you believe with all your heart, it is permitted" (Acts 8:37). Here it is implied that baptism would not be permitted if this heartfelt faith were lacking. Now, Philip is not setting himself up as the judge of the inward condition of the eunuch. Rather, he puts the responsibility completely on the eunuch himself. "If you believe, it is permitted." The eunuch, knowing that he did not believe, would have had no right to receive baptism. Whoever believes and is baptized will be saved. Thus, saving faith must precede the baptism of an adult. The church may give the sacraments, the seals of God's covenant, to no one other than believers. There must first be a credible profession of faith.

Whether the profession accords with reality, the church need not investigate further. It is not only possible but also likely in advance that in many cases the reality will not accord with the profession. But even in those cases, the church proceeds freely when it administers the seal of the covenant on the basis of profession, for Christ has not commissioned it to investigate the genuineness of a profession. It only has the commission to take note of a profession and to act on it. And its judgment about that profession itself is purely negative. That is, it may and must put to itself the question: Is there anything that absolutely compels us to doubt the sincerity of that profession? It is self-evident that this question must be posed. It is impossible and would amount to self-mystification, if, for example, one would want to regard as sincere a profession that is openly contradicted by the person's conduct. Besides that, however, such an investigation is negative—that is, it proceeds from the position that sincerity must be accepted wherever its opposite cannot be shown. It is not the calling of an office-bearer to set himself the task of proving the genuineness of someone's faith. That is precisely the Labadistic method that demands that, with the help of all possible means, one should obtain moral certainty regarding the inward state of someone who presents himself for the reception of the sacraments. But the Reformed position is to distance oneself completely from doing that after the candidate is satisfactorily instructed regarding the import of the step he is to take. In this entire matter the church does not act in a discretionary manner; it acts by mandate. Fixed rules have been prescribed to it, to which it is to adhere strictly. It is a judge in this sense: it may not rely on subjective impressions or moral convictions that it has formed by itself but must submit to the divine right of its King. And as a judge does not ask himself: Can I regard that man as innocent or trust him? But rather: Is or is not what that man has done within the terms of the condemnation of the law? So, too, does the church. A judge can see himself forced to acquit someone of whose guilt he is morally convinced. The church can see itself forced to permit someone to be baptized about whose sincerity it entertains reasonable doubt. In both cases, any lack of absolute proof benefits the person who is under suspicion.

One can also express all this as follows: the church has no right to withhold the sacrament of baptism from someone if for the same reason it would not be entitled, if the person were already baptized, to excommunicate him. And since now someone is not excommunicated on moral suspicions or subjective convictions but only on objective grounds, so also only the latter are sufficient to warrant withholding the sacrament. The profession that should precede baptism is a profession that *can* be believed, not one that *compels* us to believe it.

Our Form for Baptism, in that section that is to be used for adults, understands the matter in this way. It begins with the words: "And although the children of Christians (apart from the fact that they do not understand this) should be baptized by virtue of the covenant, nevertheless it is not permissible to baptize adults, unless they, with a prior sense of their sins, make a profession of their repentance and faith in

Christ." This is then proven by an appeal to the baptism of John, to the institution of baptism, and from the practice of the New Testament. With the questions that the adult to be baptized is asked also belongs this one: whether he believes that by the power of the Holy Spirit he has become a member of Christ and His church. Thus this profession certainly implies a subjective change in the one who makes it. That is no Labadism, but biblical prescription, and common Reformed practice.

On this point one can best distinguish the significance of the sacrament. For the baptism of young children, it is naturally much more difficult. But for adults, no Protestant church has ever doubted that only true, saving faith can entitle to baptism. Here all Protestant churches stand together against Rome. Rome administers baptism to the masses as soon as they are but inclined to receive it, baptizes on the basis of historical faith only, and then also on the basis of a *fides implicita* [implicit faith]. The Brownists (Puritans in the narrower sense) instituted a Labadistic investigation of the inward state of the person to be baptized. The Reformed church stands midway between these two extremes. It always insists earnestly on truth in one's relationship toward God and in receiving His covenant seals, and never by word nor action gives the impression that baptism is merely an outward ceremony or that mere historical faith is sufficient. Baptism on the basis of historical faith alone is not permitted. But the church does not permit itself to be used as a discerner of hearts that must distinguish historical faith from saving faith.

What further is contained in such a credible profession cannot be specified so easily. Knowledge of the fundamental truths of Christianity is required. The baptism of an adult takes place on the supposition that there is grace present in the heart. But the presence of that grace can only be revealed by words. Where every expression of knowledge is lacking, the basis for the supposition just mentioned would be lacking. God has so ordained that the inward life of a Christian can only emerge by a conscious profession. But a difference of opinion can exist regarding the extent of the knowledge required. That extent can vary according to the person. In the Formula, the following doctrines are enumerated in sequence as those in which faith is required: the Trinity–creation–providence–sin–redemption. But before that a private profession has already preceded, and also at the conclusion assent is asked to all the articles of the Christian religion.

23. *What is the efficacy of this is baptism for adults?*

This question is identical to the other: is baptism a bare sign and seal, or is it also a means of grace by which Christ, along with the Word, ordained to really convey grace to us?

From this then of itself another question develops: What grace may be communicated by baptism?

Regarding the first question, we have already seen how the Reformed conception makes the sacraments to be real means of grace. The Zwinglian doctrine, according to which they are bare symbols of God's grace and signs of our commitment to God, is rejected decisively. But one need not appeal to exclusively confessional grounds in order to reject this view. Scripture, too, rejects it. It is not probable that Christ would have carried out the institution of a mere symbol in such a serious and solemn way in His last commission to His disciples, more specifically to His apostles. At such a moment we expect more from someone who speaks in this way. Also, in the New Testament dispensation there is really no place for symbols that are not means of grace, since the shadows have passed away and the body has come. The sacramental expressions of Scripture, which present the thing signified and the sign in such close conjunction, become completely inexplicable if one continues to adhere to the concept of symbol.

So, if baptism is a means of grace, then the question arises: What grace is imparted by it? Once again, it should be recalled that here we are only speaking of the baptism of adults. Infant baptism is discussed later. We can establish the following:

a) According to the teaching of Scripture throughout, for adults, receiving baptism presupposes the presence of saving faith, and, consequently, the presence also of everything that saving faith brings with it or presupposes. So, regeneration, conversion, justification. And it is therefore an unbiblical doctrine that in an adult baptism works regeneration, conversion, justification. Even the Lutheran church, which places such a great emphasis on the sacrament as an effective means of grace, has not let itself be misled to depart from this scriptural basis. Although seemingly attributing all these things to infant baptism, the Lutherans teach nevertheless in their Large Catechism: "Only faith makes the person worthy to receive the salvific and divine water with profit. ... If faith is absent, baptism remains merely a naked and ineffective sign."

b) Consequently, one must understand in another way the passages in Scripture that appear to present regeneration as achieved in adults by baptism. Scripture cannot be in conflict with itself. It cannot say in one place, "In order to be baptized, someone must first believe!" and in another place, "Baptism effects regeneration and faith." The passages that could be considered here are primarily John 3:5 and Titus 3:5.

The first passage has already been discussed earlier. There are various explanations of it. Calvin says, "He applies 'Spirit' and 'water' to the same thing. ... It is a common and everyday mode of expression in Scripture when reference is made to the Spirit, in order to express His power. ... The water, therefore, is nothing other than the inward cleansing and enlivening of the Holy Spirit." Others (for example, Meyer) believe that here Christian baptism is spoken of directly and is made a condition for entering the kingdom of heaven. Still others think of the baptism of John. The correct explanation will be as follows:

Regeneration is delineated here according to its two aspects: the doing away of the old man and the raising up of the new man. These two aspects are described in terms of the most prominent part specific to each. By the doing away of the old man, washing, in particular, is meant—namely, washing that does away with (guilt and) pollution. By the raising up of the new man an implanting of a new life principle, in particular, is meant. The first aspect precedes the second in order. Now to express the first aspect, Jesus uses the image of water that cannot have been strange to Nicodemus. He was well-acquainted with the Levitical washings and, moreover, with the baptism of John. The latter all the more, since with the baptism of John it was just the negative aspect of regeneration, the doing away of the old, that was prominent. Nicodemus would thus have immediately understood what was meant by a regeneration by water.

To express the second aspect, the Lord speaks of a regeneration by Spirit. Spirit occurs here without the article because it is very closely connected to water, "water and Spirit." It must thus be taken as that which, like water, has a specific function. Water purifies, Spirit makes alive. Water plus Spirit makes pure plus alive. Nicodemus could know that, too, as a teacher in Israel. The Spirit as life-giving was not an unknown concept in the Old Testament.

Thus, our result is that in view here is regeneration with its two aspects, but not baptism. But one can certainly say that the images used here by the Savior are likewise made the foundation for the signifying and sealing of Holy Baptism. Nevertheless, with this distinction: that *there* [in baptism] water portrays not just the blood but also the Spirit of Christ, while *here* [in John 3] water and Spirit are differentiated.

In Titus 3:5, there appears to be much more of a basis for the idea that baptism is a means of grace for regeneration. Many think that the washing spoken of here must be baptism. And now there is said to be a washing of regeneration and a renewal of the Holy Spirit. But we observe:

1. It is entirely uncertain that here the apostle is speaking of baptism. "The washing" can be a figurative expression for regeneration. The two genitives that follow serve then as a further clarification of what washing is meant, namely, the washing that consists of regeneration and renewal. The genitive "of the Holy Spirit" says who the author of this washing is, or we could take Him as the instrument of the washing. God is the author who saves us. He does this through a washing, a bathing, and He does this as He richly pours the Holy Spirit over us through Jesus Christ, our Savior. These last words cause us to think even involuntarily that here a washing of the Holy Spirit is in view.

2. However, if by "washing" one wishes to think of "baptism," it still in nowise follows that regeneration by or in baptism is taught here. The genitive could express multiple relations. It could be: the baptism with which the regeneration and renewal of the Holy Spirit are accompanied. But it could also be:

the baptism, in which regeneration and renewal of the Holy Spirit are signified and sealed.

Calvin understands it in the latter sense: "Baptism seals to us the salvation obtained by Christ." The apostle says that God has saved us through baptism, since in sacramental phraseology the thing signified can be expressed by the sign. Our [Heidelberg] Catechism understands it in this last sense (question 71). The two concepts, "regeneration" and "renewal," are not to be sharply divorced. They serve to complement each other. It is a regeneration that at the same time is a renewal.

3. Thus if faith (regeneration, conversion, etc.) must precede the baptism of adults, is there perhaps another special grace that has been linked to baptism by God and is granted in baptism? This has been maintained by not a few. There are those who acknowledge that baptism must follow faith, but that nevertheless at baptism something happens to the believer by which he is essentially changed. He receives the Holy Spirit, is brought into fellowship with Christ by the Holy Spirit, and thereby undergoes a work of Christ that causes him to die according to his old man and to rise according to his new man. It is obvious that on this viewpoint one must assume a twofold possession of the Holy Spirit. *In the first place*: a being wrought by the Holy Spirit by which faith is produced, a new life principle is infused, and testimony to justification is given. To divorce all these things from the work of the Holy Spirit runs entirely counter to the rule of Scripture. A person must be regenerated by water and Spirit. "And to another, faith by the same Spirit" (1 Cor 12:9); "Since we have the same Spirit of faith" (2 Cor 4:13). *Further*: a possession of the Spirit as an indwelling person who makes us to be temples of God, unites us to Christ the head, establishes the communion of saints, and forms the mystical body. Now it is supposed that the latter possession of the Holy Spirit is given in baptism, not the former. Appeal is made to texts like the following: "For as many of you as have been baptized into Christ have put on Christ ... for you are all one in Christ Jesus" (Gal 3:27–28); "For by one Spirit we

all have been baptized into one body ... and all were made to drink of one Spirit" (1 Cor 12:13).

This would therefore be a special baptismal grace, which nevertheless leaves the principle of faith as a prerequisite for receiving the sacrament completely intact. However, the difficulty of giving the sacrament a specific content of grace lies just in this: by doing that, one is so easily in danger of slipping away from the Reformed basis and making baptism an instrument of generating faith instead of viewing it as a means of strengthening faith. And conversely, one so easily reasons: If faith is already present before the use of the sacrament, what then still remains for the sacrament itself? This theory attempts to navigate between these two difficulties by making the distinction noted above.

This theory has been worked out by Dr. [Abraham] Kuyper in a particular form. He says (*De Heraut*, no. 638): "If now one asks wherein the special, singular, distinctive and distinguishing characteristic of the strengthening of faith by sacrament lies, then this must undoubtedly be sought in the fellowship of the body of Christ. Holy Baptism ushers our faith into this fellowship and the Holy Lord's Supper nourishes and maintains this fellowship." However, this is not meant as if the Holy Spirit is first imparted by the sacrament. "This cannot be, for whoever does not already partake of the Holy Spirit ... cannot receive the sacrament. ... The Holy Spirit now exercises this singular and special activity in the sacrament, so that he frees our faith-consciousness from its sinful self-containedness and enriches and strengthens it through the faith-communion of the saints." In number 647, a distinction is made between grace in the root (regeneration), grace in the branches (further development of this life in its diversity), and grace in the fruits (good works). But the grace of baptism is not found in any of these three; it bears a character entirely its own. "If it is already so that Holy Baptism causes reception of the Holy Spirit, this must be so understood that the Holy Spirit appears here in a special sacramental action that as such must be distinguished from all other actions of the Holy

Spirit." And again: "That by your regeneration you are indeed organically joined with the body of Christ through a mystical bond of life is not enough; that bond of life must also become a bond of faith. ... By it you first come to know that you ... are a member of a body."

No one who has attentively read the texts in which the New Testament (in particular, Paul) speaks about baptism will be able to deny that there is truth in this view. But still we believe that it cannot be shown that this grace is exclusively the property of baptism or the Lord's Supper and that it can be called a specifically sacramental grace. On the one hand, it is established that faith, apart from every sacrament, already unites to Christ and, in Christ, with the saints. When Christ dwells in hearts through faith, one learns to fully comprehend with all the saints what is the breadth and length and height and depth (Eph 3:17-18). In the Word is the whole Christ, and where the whole Christ is, there, too, is the fellowship with the body of which He is the Head; there, too, is the consciousness that faith has of this fellowship. Thus, to say that the grace of the sacrament is a special grace always amounts to saying that in the sacrament Christ offers us another side of Himself than in the Word. And if Christ offers us another side of Himself in the sacrament than in the Word, and vice versa, then He does not offer Himself completely in each of these. It occurs to us that this is a great objection to this conception. It does not have the sacraments solely strengthen faith, but at the same time—and that is the primary part—it has the sacraments give to faith a new aspect and direction that it cannot get from the Word. And on the other hand, everywhere baptism is discussed, the emphasis is never put on the communion of the saints. Now it is the grace of justification, then the grace of regeneration as inward renewal, then again the grace of regeneration as joining to the mystical body of Christ that is indicated. In still other cases, the bond of the mystical union, the possession of the Holy Spirit, is made prominent. Sometimes conversion, as well, is at the center.

From all of this, it is clear that the grace of baptism cannot be limited to a single specific point. In our Form of Baptism it is understood in this way, and in connection with the Trinitarian formula the entire content of the covenant of grace is developed sequentially. And this is likewise the case in the Form for the Lord's Supper. Although it is undeniable that the sacraments may only be administered in the gathering of believers, still this in itself does not give us the right to concentrate their function as means of grace on the strengthening of faith's consciousness of the communion of saints. After all, it is true of the Word, too, that its official ministry belongs there in the gathering of believers.

We may not speak of a twofold possession of the Holy Spirit. If there are passages that appear to teach that, then they must be explained as referring to the Spirit as the author of extraordinary gifts. That the reception of these gifts could accompany baptism in the apostolic church appears from Acts 2:38 and other passages. But more than once baptism appears as full baptism where, nevertheless, the gifts were absent and were only added later by the laying on of hands (e.g., Acts 8:16–18).

4. If we nonetheless speak of a grace that is given by God by means of baptism, then this occurs in the following sense:

a) It is not a grace that could not also be received through the Word. Sacramental grace is the regular grace of the means of grace. Baptismal grace is the same grace as grace apart from baptism. The whole Christ is present in both Word and sacrament.

b) It is specifically a grace of faith that is given in the sacrament. All else is joined to it and flows from it. If the use of the sacraments also has significance for the other steps of the *ordo salutis*, this may be explained from the many-sided significance that faith itself has. Faith does not allow itself to be excluded from anything. It is joined with sanctification as well as with justification, and every strengthening of faith must finally benefit the entire development of the Christian life.

c) It is a grace that is not worked by the outward sign itself. It proceeds directly from Christ. For an adult, too, baptism does not work *ex opere operato*, as Roman Catholics maintain. Here, again, Word and sacraments stand on the same line. As the Word in itself is not able to produce faith in principle, so baptism in itself is not able to strengthen that faith. In both cases there must be the accompanying action of Christ by the Holy Spirit.

It is also not an action that results in a natural manner from the idea that is symbolized in the sign. The Lutherans teach that the grace in baptism is worked by the power of the Holy Spirit residing in the Word. Luther says in his Small Catechism: "Indeed it is not the water that brings about such great things, but the word of God that is in and with the water, and faith that trusts the word accompanying the water. ... When the word of God accompanies it, it is a baptism, that is, salvific water of grace and of life, and a washing of regeneration in the Holy Spirit, as Paul says (Titus 3:5)." To say that the image of water does not work grace is ultimately the same as saying that the spoken Word of itself does not work grace. The Word heard or the image seen differ then only in form, and apart from the Spirit of God the one can do no more than the other. But the Lutherans believe that just in the idea expressed by the Word a supernatural power works in a magical way. This power works, according to the Lutheran conception, *per se*, when there is no resistance. Hence, too, it is that in children who cannot offer resistance, baptism works regeneration.

d) It is a grace that for adults can only work through a conscious exercise of faith. It is settled for all that faith is necessary for the use of the sacraments by adults. But this is not meant in the sense that the capacity for faith or the disposition of faith must be present; it refers to the activity of faith. This activity is the *conditio sine qua non* for the recipient in order to receive the blessing of the sacrament. Calvin says: "They [the sacraments], however, impart nothing unless they are received by faith." He compares faith in this working of the sacraments to the mouth of a vessel in which wine or oil is poured. If the mouth is closed, even though the pouring be ever so copious, the vessel remains empty (*Institutes*, 4.14.17). "Faith is the only mouth." In this respect, too, the sacraments must be kept on the same line as the Word. According to the Reformed view, the Word does not work other than with active exercise of faith.

e) Nevertheless, it is a grace that not only or in the first place benefits the conscious side of faith. It is often thought that with a sacrament it has to do with a momentary conscious strengthening of faith. Someone sits at the table of the Lord who thinks that he has already often received all the rich blessing of the sacrament, when for a few minutes he has an exceptional enjoyment in his consciousness of the benefits of the covenant, which, by recalling it, perhaps lingers on in his spiritual life for two or three days, only then to disappear as an impulse that has faded away.

Now for the sacrament of the Lord's Supper something may be said for this view. This sacrament indeed is continually repeated so that the need for an inward strengthening produced in the disposition of faith is less noticeable. But an adult receives baptism only once, not to mention infant baptism. Thus, if in fact baptism has to do with a working of grace, then that should certainly occur in the disposition of faith. And, conversely, if it does not occur in the disposition of faith, then it must follow that the working of grace at baptism is of secondary importance. What is essential must lie in the symbolic significance of baptism. From this alone it can be explained that baptism is administered only once. But baptism certainly has more than symbolic significance; it is a sacrament and therefore a means of grace.

So we assume that an adult, making use of baptism in faith, is also strengthened inwardly in his faith. But it must be carefully noted that it is a strengthening of faith. It is not a matter of being joined to the mystical body of Christ or of being gifted with the Holy Spirit. Those are things that underlie faith and precede faith. When we deny that in baptism grace has as its purpose the conscious exercise of faith at the time of baptism, at least only has that as its purpose, then by that we are in no sense denying that it is intended for enriching and deepening the *ongoing* conscious exercise of faith. The point at issue here is not *purpose* but *means*. By saying that the sacraments serve to strengthen faith, it is already granted in principle that their ultimate goal lies in their acting upon conscious faith. Faith, as to its nature, belongs to the conscious life of a Christian. It must turn its unconscious power outward, appear in the light of consciousness, and its worth lies in that. The disposition of faith that does not become activity is dead capital. So, when in the use of the sacraments someone desires a strengthening of the activity of faith, then this is completely proper. The sacrament is disposed to do that. But many are caught up in the misunderstanding that this strengthening of the activity of faith by the idea of the sign must work on that activity in a completely conscious way, and that by this conscious activity the *habitus* [disposition] must be strengthened. To us, the correct view appears to be this: By the use of the sacraments in faith, strengthening is imparted to the disposition of faith, and from there reacts on its active exercise. From there, as well, this strengthening is not merely a momentary one, acting as a passing impulse; but faith, strengthened inwardly in its depth, is now able, again and again, to supply new strength to the conscious exercise of faith.

f) Thus, by the right use of the sacraments, by the right use of baptism, one receives an inward strengthening of faith. This strengthening is connected, in advance and in retrospect, with the conscious exercise of faith. In advance, for this exercise, as *conditio sine qua non*, must precede. In retrospect, for all strengthening of faith must result in this exercise. Now, saving faith directs itself to Christ the Mediator. Therefore, the strengthening of faith must also consist in a close tie of the life of faith to the Mediator.

We have already found that this is the significance of being baptized into Christ. Although baptism as a seal of the covenant of grace joins us with the triune God, still entrance into and strengthening of this bond is always through the Mediator. Christ must dwell in our hearts by faith [Eph 3:17]; we must be one plant with Him [Rom 6:5 KJV], baptized with Him into one body [cf. 1 Cor 12:13]. All of this refers to the bond of faith.

Now, although the activities of faith, which are strengthened with the proper use of the sacraments, are many and various, still in this root they are all one; they rest on a closer tightening the bond of faith that binds to Christ. A sacrament does not bless; nor does baptism bless if it does not enhance the blessing of the bond with Christ. And from this enhancement and strengthening in the root flows of itself the enlivening of the individual acts of faith that are related to particular aspects of grace. So, an enhancement of justifying grace can result from baptism, used in faith. Only by faith does the Christian have access to the grace in which he stands [Rom 5:2], to the consciousness of justification that in God's tribunal has been pronounced once for all as soon as faith has been quickened in his soul. Faith is before all things justifying faith, and it is that in the same degree as it may be closely bound to Christ. The strengthening of faith and of the bond of faith to Christ is thus the only means that can put us more firmly in the consciousness of justification. It is not even excluded that in many cases the strengthening of faith by baptism has been so great that it coincided with the transition from taking refuge to assured trusting. The *justificatio passiva* [passive justification] was in that case connected temporally to baptism. Thus it could be said to those just converted, in whom the exercise of faith had just begun and was not yet very developed: "... be baptized and wash away your sins" (Acts 22:16). And the apostle can address the Corinthians: "And such were some of you. But you were washed, you were sanctified, you were justified in the name of the Lord Jesus Christ and by the Spirit of our God"

[1 Cor 6:11]. That the subjective appropriation of the grace of justification can coincide with receiving baptism does not remotely prove, however, that baptism is the sacrament of justification and that, like faith, so too justification does not usually precede.

It is the same for conversion. Conversion has two parts: repentance and faith, the dying of the old man, the enlivening of the new. But faith is already resident and at work in repentance. The strengthening of faith must always work fresh conversion. Therefore in Romans 6 the apostle Paul connects the crucifying of the old man and the raising up of the new with baptism. He does this, however, again in a specific way, namely, by viewing it as a result of the bond with the Mediator Christ. We have been baptized into Christ, baptized into His death, "... buried therefore with Him by baptism into death ...," etc. That is, by the right use of the sacrament of baptism we are so closely bound to Christ in our faith that we feel the obligation concerning the sin, which has been judged in His death on the cross, also to crucify and oppose it in ourselves. And no less: so closely bound to Christ that the impulse works in us, concerning the new life that He leads since His resurrection, to live together with Him for God, to walk and to work in it. Even the dying of the old man and the enlivening of the new is thus seen here as a fruit of the bond of faith with the Mediator. And now, again, it is not excluded that for those first called in times of missions, this consciousness of conversion coincides with the reception of baptism. It is possible that for them it is as if at the time of receiving the seal of baptism, precisely then their old man was truly buried and their new man raised. Thus, in retrospect, for them it will be as if they were converted at their baptism. But again, that in no sense means that baptism is the sacrament of conversion in the specific sense, or, even less, the sacrament of regeneration, as Baptists claim. Romans 6 does not teach that the crucifixion of the old man and the resurrection of the new man is achieved by baptism as a special grace, but only that the strengthening of faith is also significant for this part of grace. And since, for those suddenly converted, that significance had come to light very clearly, the apostle could appeal to baptism to refute the claim that on Paul's standpoint someone could commit sin so that grace might increase.

It is no different, finally, with the communion of the saints. Faith is a faith that all Christians have in common with each other and that also binds them together in their consciousness. Strengthening faith must result in strengthening the communion of the saints. But in this aspect, too, faith is directed in the first place to Christ. A closer bond with the saints can only be obtained by a closer bond with Christ. He is the Head, and through their fellowship with the Head the members are in an organic connection. And since the connection with Christ by faith becomes closer in baptism, so the awareness of the communion of saints will naturally be strengthened. Scripture, then, also lays emphasis on this point in passages like Galatians 3:27–28 and 1 Corinthians 12:13. In both the Forms for Baptism and the Lord's Supper this is pointed to as part of the grace of the sacrament. But only as a *part*, not as the main thing. Finally, here too it could appear to those just converted as if it were through baptism that this communion of saints and this connection with the body of Christ had first begun for them. But we have no right to derive from that the proposition: as a specific grace baptism produces the connection of faith to the faith of all.

g) Finally, it should be noted that the conscious exercise of faith is strengthened not only at the moment of receiving baptism but also later. God has not bound the blessing, which He intends to impart by baptism, to one moment; it can come much later. Our [Belgic] Confession says: "Neither does this baptism avail us only at the time when the water is poured upon us and received by us, but also through the whole course of our life" (article 34).

24. *Does baptism or receiving it also have significance as an act of man toward God?*

Yes, for all covenants contain two parts. By his baptism the candidate for baptism commits himself, solemnly and publicly, to all that the status of a member of the covenant brings with it in the covenant of grace. He does this not in his own strength but on the basis of the promises of God made to him in baptism, which he accepts in faith. In all his covenant activities, God is the First, who promises grace, including the grace that ought to enable us to keep His covenant. But it is presupposed of man that he accepts this in faith. So, baptism is not only a seal of the free promises of God, but the administration of baptism with its reception is also a seal of the established covenant. Someone who is baptized as an adult may not judge that he carries about in his person an offer of the covenant that he has not yet taken up and at an opportune time can still accept. He is in the covenant, has from his side submitted himself to it, and is regarded and treated as a member of the covenant. Baptism for adults is not a means of regeneration or conversion. He who receives baptism declares publicly that he will "cleave to this one God, Father, Son, and Holy Spirit, trust Him, and love Him with his whole heart, soul and mind, and with all his strength, forsake the world, put to death his old nature, and walk in a new godly life." Baptism is for him a and undoubted testimony that he has an eternal covenant of grace with God. It was so under the Old Testament when someone was incorporated into Israel; it is so under the New Testament when an adult receives Christian baptism.

At the same time, for the adult who receives it, baptism is incorporation into the organized church, by which he receives the rights of a full member and sees access to the table of the Lord opened to him. There are those who on the basis of a peculiar view of the covenant deny this, but according to the correct scriptural view, these two sacraments belong together. The baptized person, then, places himself under church admonition and church discipline in entirely the same sense as someone who makes profession of faith. In the Form he is asked expressly whether he has resolved from the heart to subject himself to that admonition and discipline, and he answers that by assenting.

25. *To what question have we now come?*

To that of infant baptism.

26. *What is the historical witness of the New Testament in the matter of infant baptism?*

By historical witness we mean what the New Testament teaches regarding the baptism of young children presented as fact—not what the New Testament otherwise teaches dogmatically, or what data it offers us for deriving from them something for infant baptism.

Regarding this historical witness, we will have to acknowledge that a positive, incontestable proof for infant baptism as fact is not to be supplied from the New Testament. Many exegetes then also assume that infant baptism was not an apostolic practice, and that at first only adults were baptized. This has led even Reformed theologians to view infant baptism as something *permissible*, the strict necessity of which cannot be proven from divine command and apostolic exercise. To that others have rightly answered that the import of this matter is too profound for it to be regarded as a matter of indifference. An adiaphoron like baptism would truly be extremely dubious, since it throws open the door for all kinds of superstition. It is therefore necessary that here one does not take the position of being content with probabilities.

The conflict about infant baptism is carried on between almost the entire catholic Christian church on the one side (Roman Catholic Church, Greek Church, the historic Protestant churches), and on the other side, the Baptists, the Socinians, and the Quakers, with this distinction that the last mentioned (the Quakers) reject all sacraments, even for adults, while the Socinians wish to retain baptism as something allowed for those who become Christians in their adult years. The Arminians stand between the two parties, in that they teach the permissibility (not the necessity) of infant baptism.

The Anabaptists make much use of the silence of the New Testament as a historical witness for the existence of infant baptism. One need consider this fact only somewhat attentively in order to be convinced immediately that it is completely useless for a Baptistic argument. The position of the Baptists is that children born of believing parents may not be baptized as long as they are children, but only such who, having become converted in their adult years, thereby give evidences of being regenerate. Now one would expect, were this the apostolic view, that there would be traces of the Baptistic practice in the New Testament. Not only would one have to show negatively that no children were baptized, but one would have to show positively that adults were baptized who with their parents had previously entered into the circle of the church and for a considerable time had lived in the church. The origin of the New Testament covers enough time to make such positive demonstrations possible. But they are entirely lacking. Certainly baptism is mentioned frequently, but either baptism administered to new converts from Judaism or paganism, or in an undefined manner. Baptists are completely silent about this in their argumentation. They assume that it appears that the New Testament speaks against our practice and for theirs. The truth is that as a historical witness, the New Testament does neither of these two things. It focuses its attention exclusively on those who come over from Judaism and paganism to Christianity. Thus, the dispute between Baptists and paedobaptists cannot at all be decided on this basis.

This remark was necessary beforehand in order to remove the unfavorable impression that all too easily arises when one must make the concession to the Baptists that the New Testament does not positively teach infant baptism as fact. We answer, first of all, that the New Testament does not teach the Baptist practice either. Further, nowhere does the New Testament teach that children were excluded from baptism. Repeatedly, mention is made of households that were baptized: Lydia and her household (Acts 16:15); the household of Stephanas in Corinth (1 Cor 1:16); of the jailer: "and he was baptized, he and all his family immediately" (Acts 16:33). And in these passages it does not say that the entire house believed, or had to believe in order to be able to be baptized, as we would expect if the entire household consisted of adults. But it is simply said: "Believe in the Lord Jesus, and you will be saved, you and your household." Lydia paid attention and she was baptized, she and her household.

27. *What is the witness of the postapostolic church regarding infant baptism?*

Here too one cannot produce any strict proofs from the first period. Irenaeus speaks somewhere of a sanctifying of children by the Redeemer, but does not explicitly mention the baptism of these children.

The Teaching of the Twelve Apostles [the Didache], discovered a few years ago, and which some even locate in the first century, does not appear to mention infant baptism. Tertullian, as is well known, was a vehement opponent of infant baptism, but one should take into consideration that he never says that it is a novelty. In his day, infant baptism apparently existed as a fairly common followed practice. Origen says plainly that the church had received infant baptism from the apostles. Augustine says that the custom of infant baptism is an apostolic tradition. In his conflict with the Pelagians he appeals to infant baptism as a proof for original sin. Now Pelagius would certainly have responded that infant baptism was an unapostolic innovation if he had been able, with even an appearance of legitimacy, to do so in the light of history. But it does not appear that he gave this answer.

The silence in the time that immediately followed the apostles is certainly somewhat strange. That much must be granted. There will probably be a historical basis for that, although that is not easy to specify. Infant baptism appears to have fallen into disuse early on. This fact could be related to the common tendency to postpone baptism, but we do not know if there are evidences that that tendency existed so early. Later when the practice once again became more common, there were not always clear Scriptural grounds from which one operated. In this Augustine has led the church in a wrong direction by teaching the necessity of baptism for salvation.

According to some, the existence of infant baptism can be demonstrated in the time of Justin Martyr (about AD 139). He says: "By means of baptism we, since we have been sinners, have received spiritual circumcision by the grace of God ... and it is commanded to all to receive it in the same way." The latter words will mean that, differently than circumcision, baptism relates to both genders. One should grant that these words appear to assume infant baptism.

Tertullian opposed infant baptism not with historical grounds but from a principle of usefulness. It is dangerous to baptize the young and unmarried, for temptation is so great. "If one knew of what great weight baptism is, one would be more afraid to receive it than to postpone it." His argument is not only applicable to the baptism of infants but applies to the baptism of young people in general. This moves within the well-known stream of sacramentalism that attributed a completely unique value to baptism. It was thought that sins committed after baptism could no longer be forgiven.

Here, too, weight must be given to the fact that the church fathers tell us nothing about the time when young people in the church should be baptized. That would have been necessary if infant baptism had been totally absent. It is explainable when one assumes that the time of baptism varied, that some had their children baptized earlier, others later. That a great deal of arbitrariness prevailed is certain.

28. *What two matters are there to consider in the further discussion of infant baptism?*

    a) The foundations on which it rests for us.

    b) The significance that is to be attributed to it.

It is certainly not possible at every point to keep these two matters separate from each other. Still, for the sake of clarity, we will endeavor to do this as much as possible. There are grounds for infant baptism that everyone will have to grant regardless of what significance he wishes to give to infant baptism.

29. *What is the first ground for baptizing infants?*

The fact that under the Old Testament dispensation of the covenant of grace, young children of the covenant people were circumcised. If it can be shown that circumcision was a sign and seal of the covenant of grace in entirely the same sense as baptism is that now, then infant baptism follows from circumcision.

One easily sees that this argument can only be advanced by maintaining the spiritual character of the Old Testament dispensation. Baptists are intent on making this dispensation terminate in what is external. What God established with Israel was a national covenant, nothing more. This national covenant had national covenantal seals, a national continuation in the line of natural propagation. It was a covenant that everyone could keep with his natural capacities, so that without his knowledge, by virtue of his birth he could be obligated to it and taken up into it. The significance of circumcision accords with all that. But in the New Testament, it has become completely different. Now, what is external and national has ceased to be valid. Something spiritual and universal has come in its place. Birth from certain kinds of parents no longer settles status in the kingdom of God. One is what one is by personal choice, whether of God or the person himself. To say that a child of Christian parents as such must or may be baptized means bringing back Old Testament distinctions that are completely terminated.

This is the Baptist position. We deal with it here only to the extent that it is based on a faulty view of the Old Testament. That the Old Testament had a national aspect is certain. For Israel, church and state were merged. The one aspect was embodied in the other. There was thus an external entity that there now no longer is in the new dispensation of the covenant of grace. One can certainly make that external again by establishing a state church, but then one does that contrary to the spirit of Christianity. Neither is it to be questioned that there is also a national aspect to the Old Testament sacraments. By circumcision a Jew was not only a member of the covenant of grace; by circumcision he was also a citizen of the Jewish state. And that, too, is gone from the New Testament sacraments. Baptism no longer has a political significance. Certainly that tie sometimes exists, when, for example, an Englishman baptized in the Anglican Church has access to certain offices in the state. But that is contrary to the character of baptism.

Now the Baptist would naturally have to show that the sacrament of circumcision had an exclusively national significance, or at least that the circumcision of children derived from the national significance of the sacrament. Actually, both assertions amount to the same thing. Circumcision was a complete circumcision of the children (apart from proselytes). The path is cut off to saying that for adults circumcision was a sign and seal of the covenant of grace; for children it was solely a sign and seal of the national covenant. Adults, however, were not circumcised in Israel. The Baptist must then also maintain that circumcision did not possess any signifying and sealing power for the covenant of grace. But if not circumcision, then what? Passover, perhaps? Its administration was just as general as that of circumcision. So we see how the Baptist must come to completely despiritualize the Old Testament dispensation of the covenant of grace. Nothing of it remains other than the form of a national covenant.

According to Scripture, circumcision (= circumcision of children) was more:

a) According to Romans 4:11, it was given to Abraham as a seal of the righteousness of faith. Now, someone could say: that was circumcision for an adult. But it is surely the same circumcision of which God commands that it must be administered to all baby boys eight days old. For them, it cannot have been something different than it was for Abraham. Thus, it was a sign and seal of the covenant of grace.

b) It was instituted when God formally founded His covenant of grace with Abraham. That was a long time before the covenant people were organized as a theocratic state at Sinai. According to the Baptist view being contested here, circumcision should have come at Sinai, and not already with Abraham. But now, it does not come from Moses but from the patriarchs, as the Lord says [John 7:22]. There is no basis, then, for making its national significance—which the sign received later—its only significance. The promises of the covenant in Genesis 17 were spiritual: "I will be God to you and to your offspring after you" [v. 7]. It is not therefore that some external privileges were sealed to them by circumcision, but that God willed to be their God, and would be, and would be that for the children as well as for the adults.

c) The spiritual significance of circumcision is asserted with emphasis again and again in the Old Testament (Deut 10:16; Jer 4:4; Ezek 44:7). Being uncircumcised is used as an image of a spiritual state deserving condemnation (Exod 6:12; Lev 26:41; Acts 7:51). In the New Testament, too, the thing signified by circumcision is spoken of (Rom 2:28–29; Phil 3:3).

d) Even the national bond of the Jew to Jehovah his God may not be so sharply distinguished from his spiritual responsibilities, as the Baptists wish to do. One may really not say that the spiritual relationship of the covenant of grace and the national relationship of the national covenant were side by side but detached from each other, so that the one was independent of the other. God did not say to the Israelite: I require of you that you (1) fulfill your civic duties, and (2) if you can still do something additional, your duties relative to the covenant of grace as well. Rather, again and again it was given to the Israelites to understand that even in their national position they were not right before God if the spiritual truth of that position was lacking. To the Jews in the exile the reproach is added that they are called by the name Israel, have come from the waters of Judah, swear by the name of the Lord, and make mention of the God of Israel, but not in truth nor in righteousness (Isa 48:1). And there are many such texts.

e) Baptism has come in the place of circumcision: "a circumcision made without hands, by putting off the body of the sins of the flesh, by the circumcision of Christ, being buried with Him in baptism," etc. (Col 2:11–12). Therefore, those who received circumcision must also receive baptism, and the young children may not be excluded.

30. Where is a second proof for infant baptism found?

In the fact that God's Word everywhere recognizes children as being fully human, notwithstanding their situation of being underage and their use of reason not yet developed. If one is a Pelagian and makes everything dependent on the conscious choice of the will, then a child will have to be regarded more or less as something neutral that does not count in the kingdom of heaven, that has no status in the church, about which there is nothing to say. If, on the other hand, one recognizes that conscious life as it emerges on the surface has a deeper invisible background, that there is more to a person than he can say and reveal, then we must also take account of children. When now it is said that the kingdom of heaven belongs to children, then this shows clearly enough what the answer of Scripture is, and on which side it is positioned. The question here is not whether the kingdom of heaven belongs to every child that is baptized, but simply whether children fall under the terms of this kingdom of heaven.

The Baptist admits that they can. A child can be regenerated—but, he says, we have no basis for assuming that this is the case. In other words, he maintains that children constitute an area that does not count for the visible church. Nothing may be said about them. They are neutral territory. They cannot be received into the organism of the congregation.

But we say: if it is once established that children can be regenerated and partake of the kingdom of heaven, then there must be one way or other by which the status of these children can be objectively settled and they are placed in a definite relationship to the visible church. We do not have to do here with a small minority but with a large majority. And it is impossible to assume that they must grow up entirely without an objective relationship to the visible church.

31. *Where is a third proof found?*

In the character of the covenant of grace as it continues in history. God maintains His covenant of grace with the believer. But when He gives the promises of the covenant to that believer who is brought into the covenant as an adult, these promises are not only "for you!" but they are also "for your seed after you." Involved here is a link between the natural relationship between parents and children, on the one hand, and the benefits of the covenant of grace, on the other. This link is not such that it works as a natural law. Grace is not an inheritance that one receives without exception because one has been born of parents who are members of the covenant. In His election God always remains free. But nevertheless the rule remains that He has His covenant continue in history, builds the church from the seed of the church. Thus there is not a founding of a new covenant again and again, but the one covenant is administered throughout the ages and generations.

The opponent of infant baptism has no eye for that. He thinks that nature and grace have not been brought together in an organic connection. According to him, grace comes again and again in each particular instance as something supernatural from above, without it being connected historically with what preceded. It is, moreover, something wholly individual that is not concerned with the connection between generations.

This view is totally wrong. Against it we assert that natural life with its natural context is taken up into the context of grace and receives a corresponding significance. God does not reckon solely with individual persons in an atomistic manner. His covenant is established with the children and their children into distant generations. This is already taken into account at the institution of baptism. It does not read "Baptize people from all nations," but "Make disciples of *all nations*, baptizing them," etc. When Zacchaeus is called, then the Savior says: "Today salvation has come to this *house*, since he too is *a son of Abraham*" [Luke 19:9]. This call is based on the promise given for Abraham's seed, and from it flow further blessings for Zacchaeus' seed too. Cornelius was a devout man "with all his household"(Acts 10:2); "by which you will be saved, and all your house" (Acts 11:14); see also Paul's answer to the jailer (Acts 16:31, 34). These households turn to Christianity as entire households (1 Cor 1:16; "in the Lord," Eph 6:1; 1 John 2:13–14).

32. *Where is further proof for infant baptism found?*

In the characteristic use that is made by the New Testament of the term "people of God." Jesus will save His *people* from their sins (Matt 1:21). John's work serves to prepare for the Lord an equipped people (Luke 1:17); "That which was not my people I will call my people, and that which was not beloved, my beloved" (Rom 9:25; cf. v. 26); "and I will be their God, and they will be my people" (2 Cor 6:16); "to purify for Himself a people for His own, zealous for good works" (Titus 2:14); Hebrews 8:8–10, citing Jeremiah 31:33, where specifically the new dispensation of the covenant of grace is spoken of; "a holy nation, a peculiar people" (1 Pet 2:9); "and they will be His people, and God Himself will be with them and be their God" (Rev 21:3).

From all these examples it is sufficiently clear that the New Testament covenant community is not an aggregate of individuals but an organism of a people that continues. A people is a nation, and a nation ([Dutch *natie*] from [Latin] *nascor* [to be born]) is a connection perpetuated by birth. God has not chosen an association of individuals, but a people, chosen under the old era in order to entrust His words to them and to establish His covenant with them. And Paul teaches us that the root of this old people has continued to exist, although the majority of the branches are cut off. Converts from paganism are grafted into the good olive tree. They are grafted in as branches from which new branches ought to grow [Rom 11:17–24].

This entire view is based on the participation of children in the covenant. The Baptist must exclude children from the covenant. He will certainly say that the church must care for its children, work with them, teach them, urge them to conversion, and then, in general, the church will be replenished from them. But the fact remains that these children, during all the time of their being underage, are regarded as being outside the church. If they enter later, this happens apart from any connection with their parents as a *churchly* connection; they come from outside the sphere of Christianity, from out of a kind of paganism.

The Baptist church in its entirety is a missionary church. It must therefore also direct its preaching to its own children as it would direct that preaching to pagans.

Peter says in Acts 2:39: "For the promise is for you and for your children and for all who are far off, as many as the Lord our God will call." Here a distinction is made between: (1) adult Jews who are in the covenant; (2) their children to whom, with them, the promise came; (3) those from among the Gentiles, as many as God in His omnipotence calls. In other words, the Baptist principle is only valid with regard to Gentiles who are worked with in missions, not with regard to those who are already in the covenant. It does not say: "As many of your children as God will call" (the Baptist says that with respect to his own children). But it says: "You and your children."

33. Is there still another proof for infant baptism?

Yes, in the New Testament little children are regarded as members of the church of Christ. Baptism belongs with the membership of the congregation. Those who are members of the church have a right to baptism. Christ permitted little children come to Him; He has taken them in His arms and blessed them. Paul says of the children of believing parents that they are holy, even when only one of the parents is a believer (1 Cor 7:14).

Much has been written and disputed concerning the meaning of the "holiness" of which the apostle here speaks. Opponents of infant baptism say that it is a holiness that even an unbeliever can possess, for in what immediately precedes it is said that the unbelieving husband is sanctified by the wife, and the unbelieving wife is sanctified by the husband. Now, it would surely not have entered Paul's mind to grant that such an unbelieving husband can be baptized on the basis of this holiness. But the two cases are not the same. The unbelieving husband is holy enough to remain the husband of a believing wife. He is holy in his capacity as husband, and everything that is connected to this capacity shares in this holiness. So, if a child is born to him and his believing wife, then for this birth he does not count as someone unholy, and one cannot say of the child: it has been born of someone holy plus someone unholy. Then, too, the child has been born to holy parents. Thus one sees that the holiness of the husband is relative in a certain respect. But that

of the children, to which Paul points, is absolute. They are holy with
the kind of holiness that is in their entire status, and not only from a
certain vantage point. Their holiness is then, for Paul, the established
fact on the basis of which he argues against the Corinthians. One should
pay attention to the fact that in his argument he does not derive the
holiness of the children from that of the parents, but, on the contrary,
from the generally recognized truth that the children are holy, he determines the holiness of the marriage relationship between a believer
and an unbeliever. So, at that time the children were regarded as holy.
And "holy," when so used without further definition, was synonymous
with "member of the church." It is the members of the church that are
addressed by Paul in his letters as elect saints [holy ones]. He has therefore undoubtedly regarded the children as members of the congregation.

34. On what does the meaning one attributes to infant baptism depend?

This depends entirely on the conception one has concerning the covenant of grace. Baptism is a sign and seal of the covenant of grace. Infants
who are baptized are members of the covenant. The meaning that one
associates with the baptism of infants will vary according to what one
thinks of the covenant. Here we will only discuss the various views that
have been defended in the Reformed church, and to that end begin with
the least tenable.

35. What is the first view that can be discussed here?

That of a twofold covenant, corresponding to the visible and invisible church. In the defense of this theory one usually links to the Old
Testament. However, instead of giving the one covenant in the Old
Testament two aspects, one ascertains two covenants there. The one was
completely external. The sacraments belong to the external covenant.
The obligations of the external covenant are also external obligations.
God can also make this subservient to bring someone over into the internal covenant. But formally and officially the covenant member has
bound himself to the external covenant. By his entrance he professes
only that he possesses historical faith, will be subject to the ordinances
and regulations of the church, and make use of the sacraments. He can
make use of both baptism and the Lord's Supper, and in both cases on
entirely the same grounds. What gives a right to the one sacrament also
gives a right to the other. Christ uses this institution of the external

covenant in order to form the internal covenant of His mystical body. For more on this theory one may compare Hodge, *Systematic Theology,* 3:562–63.

The objections to the view are as follows:

a) It is true that the Old Testament dispensation had such an external side. But that was a political side, and with the new age the covenant of grace has lost all of its political character. There is not a trace of evidence that Christ has established an external institution, has founded a double church.

b) The theory is in conflict with the clear requirement of the New Testament that for adults baptism presupposes sincere saving faith. On this point of view, adults ought also to be taken into the church upon a profession of historical faith. But Scripture teaches that for adults the faith upon which baptism follows is a faith that saves (Mark 16:16).

c) In this conception, the unique character of the sacraments is completely misunderstood. They are made means of conversion. The scriptural and Reformed view is that they serve to strengthen faith. Here baptism, as well as the Lord's Supper, serves to bring someone into an external sphere and to keep him there, where he is under favorable influences and perhaps will be able to attain to regeneration and faith.

d) The question is not whether the external administration of the covenant of grace and its internal essence coincide, but only whether one has the right to separate them in this dualistic way and to make two covenants of them. This must necessarily lead to a falsification of the concept of the church. And the invisible church then lacks its outward manifestation; the visible church is something different, something independent.

36. *What is the second view that is associated with the one just mentioned?*

This is the so-called Half-Way Covenant. Here a distinction is made between the two sacraments, baptism and the Lord's Supper. The former becomes the sign and seal of the external covenant, the latter the sacrament of the internal covenant. When someone receives baptism, he does not make a profession of his faith. When he comes to the Lord's

Supper, he does. The result is that someone can also be entitled to request baptism for his children and nevertheless not have access to the Lord's Supper. In this way, it is believed, a great difficulty is removed. A great number of parents do not dare to come the Lord's table and still desire to have their children baptized. Now if baptism and the Lord's Supper are on par as sacraments, then it immediately follows that he who is not entitled to the one for himself is not entitled to the other for his children. Conversely, if baptism and the Lord's Supper are completely different, then one can partake of the one and be denied the other.

This view, too, is untenable. It separates what God has joined. Scripture nowhere gives us occasion to think that baptism and the Lord's Supper can be torn apart in this way, to be signs and seals each of a covenant of its own. The designation Half-Way Covenant is also less precise for expressing what is meant. The external covenant is not half of the internal one. It is something next to the internal covenant. All the objections that are valid against the previous view must then also be brought against this view. Here, too, the external institution is something independent. Someone can be born in the church, live in the church, and die in the church as a good, honored member, without having proclaimed the death of the Lord one single time. No one can maintain that this agrees with the teaching of Scripture.

This view was officially accepted by the Congregational churches of New England about the middle of the seventeenth century. However, it also found many opponents there (cf. Hodge, *Systematic Theology*, 3:567).

37. *Can this last view of a Half-Way Covenant still be presented in a modified form?*

Yes, one can also apply the distinction between an external and an internal covenant exclusively to infant baptism. This goes one step less far than the two preceding theories. The first view makes the external covenant applicable to all and involves both sacraments. The second also makes it applicable to all but only involves baptism. This theory again makes it applicable to all, but only involves infant baptism. The reasoning is as follows: All who enter the church as adults do this upon profession of a sincere faith of the heart. In consideration of such a profession, they are baptized. This baptism is twofold: (1) a sign and seal of the internal covenant of grace; (2) a sign and seal of the external church covenant. The former they can naturally enter only for themselves, for saving faith is something entirely personal, in which the father or mother cannot act vicariously for their child. The latter, however, the external covenant, they can also enter at the same time for their children. And on the basis of that established external covenant, the young children receive baptism as sign and seal. If in growing up they come to personal faith, then for them, too, baptism will gain the double significance that it has for the parents. They are then in both the external and the internal covenant.

One sees that this does not differ essentially from the preceding view. The dualism of external and internal covenant remains, without true unity between these two being established. And if baptism for children can be a sign and seal of something completely external, then it is not to be seen why it could not also be that for adults. Or if it is halfway for adults, then why not also, if necessary, for adults only? Expressed here too, in the requirement that, at least for adults, baptism must presuppose the possession of true faith, is the awareness how sacraments are more than seals of a national or external contract.

38. Which views are at the extreme opposite of those just mentioned?

Here and there in some Reformed theologians a conception intrudes that appears to function at the boundary of the orthodox system, so that one may doubt that it may still be called Reformed. There have been those who posit a kind of justification and regeneration at baptism, signified and conveyed to all the children of covenant members, without exception, but then not necessarily connected to salvation, since it can be lost through the fault of the children in growing up. Pareus taught that all children of the congregation are justified and regenerated by the Holy Spirit, to the extent that befits their age, without that, however, infringing upon God's counsel, which customarily is first disclosed during adult years. Baron and Forbes, English theologians, had a similar view. The latter appealed to Augustine and Prosper. These, too, maintain that all baptized children are justified, and that thus original sin is forgiven them in baptism; nevertheless, with the difference that Augustine assumed a forgiveness that could be withdrawn and for reprobate children is withdrawn infallibly, while Prosper held this grace to be irrevocable. According to the last mentioned, a person who after his baptism apostatizes from Christ and ends his life alienated from grace certainly comes into damnation. He is not damned, however, because of his original sin. Rather, on account of his later sins he is punished with that death to which he was also subjected on account of the sins that are forgiven him.

Davenant, delegate of the English church at the Synod of Dort, taught something similar. According to him, all children baptized into the covenant are not only adopted and justified but also regenerated and sanctified. But he distinguishes this justification, adoption, and regeneration from the benefits of salvation, incapable of being lost, that adults share in at their regeneration. For the children, he says, those gifts are sufficient to place them in a state of salvation. If they die in childhood, then on that basis they go to heaven. But for adults it is not sufficient. When a baptized child grows up, it may not be regarded as a living member of the church on the basis of the grace of baptism alone. Not that it has lost its initial grace, but it has lost its status as a child, and thereby its condition is changed. If no true conversion follows, then a baptized person who dies as an adult is lost.

We can clearly discover in this outlook the endeavor to give a real, tangible content to baptism. But it is, as Witsius observes, a failed endeavor. In undertaking it one envelops himself in greater problems than one is attempting to evade. First of all, in undertaking it one teaches a grace of baptism that does not really comport with the Reformed doctrine of the sacraments. Baptism does not exist to effect regeneration, justification, and sanctification. Here it becomes, in a Lutheran sense, the means ordained by God for begetting new life. Further, that there would be a partial forgiveness of sins and a partial justification is irreconcilable with Reformed principles. It will not do to say that original sin is taken away but the guilt of actual sin remains. Also, it cannot be that the merits of Christ would be applied to someone for regeneration, justification, and sanctification without the one to whom they are applied being included in election. There is no application (though certainly an offer) of the merits of the Mediator except for those who have been given to Him by the Father. Finally, with the subsequent loss of these gifts of grace one comes into the greatest difficulties. Christ has suffered for that forgiven guilt, for on that basis it is forgiven. But now that forgiveness is lost again, and the person in view is punished for it personally. There is then a double retribution, first borne by Christ and then by the person himself.

In conclusion, grace does not permit itself to be meted out quantitatively, as Davenant intends. As far as regeneration, justification, and sanctification are concerned, a child can do with nothing less than an adult. The true spiritual life that is given in regeneration is sufficient for an adult to live for God. It cannot be made insufficient by the development of natural life. One would then have to assume that it was really lost again, and that would be equivalent to teaching an apostasy of the saints. For all these reasons, the view mentioned is not tenable for one who is Reformed.

39. *What, in general, is the view of the Reformed concerning the meaning of infant baptism?*

On this there are two views that have both had defenders, though not both equally. We first give, in some propositions, the most common view that on good grounds can be called the historic-Calvinistic view.

a) By the fall of our first parents the entire human race has fallen into sin and damnation. Consequently, all men are conceived and born in sin and are by nature children of wrath.

b) Out of this corrupt human race, God wills to redeem certain persons known to Him, accept them in grace, justify them through Christ, sanctify them by His Spirit, and bring them to salvation.

c) In the dispensing or withholding of this grace God is not obligated to a person, but, since grace is free grace, demonstrates this grace to whom He chooses.

d) God therefore would do no one, old or young, an injustice if He would cause them all together, without distinction, to be lost.

e) Communion in this grace can only be made known to us from certain fruits and marks.

f) No one, and so also the church, can judge with certainty who those are who share in this grace and the essence of the covenant of grace. Only believers themselves by the witness of the Holy Spirit have a direct assurance of that.

g) The church, as ministers of God's covenant, has to observe certain external marks of the grace of God and to act thereon according to the judgment of charity, without concerning itself further with the question, never to be settled, whether the inward state corresponds to that grace.

h) This judgment of charity concerns all the members of the visible church, and only them. To these members belong not only the adults who profess Christ, and do not contradict this profession by their conduct, but also young children born of believing parents belong by virtue of the promise made to Abraham and his descendants and by which they, like their parents, are included in the covenant of God.

i) Consequently, with regard to the judgment of the church, birth from believing parents (at least one) is the equivalent of what for the parents their profession of faith is.

j) Therefore, according to the judgment of charity, salvation is ascribed to these children and they are regarded as elect, as their parents are regarded when they make profession of faith, and continue to be as long as they in fact do not give evidence to the contrary.

k) Believing parents must raise their children as members of God's covenant in the fear and knowledge of the Lord, just as adult believers are admonished to increase in faith and to advance in godliness.

l) On this basis the children, as members of God's covenant, are entitled to the sign and seal of the covenant and ought to be baptized, as born into the covenant and, by virtue of the promise of the covenant, members of the congregation.

m) As adult believers who die professing faith and calling on the name of God are held to be saved, so too the same should be judged of the children of believers who die in their infancy.

n) This judgment of charity could nevertheless be mistaken according to the Word. They are not all Abraham's children because they are Abraham's seed, nor are they all Israel who are of the father of Israel [cf. Rom 9:6–7], just as in growing up, it is often apparent that the most reprobate children are born from the most pious parents, and the most pious children from the most ungodly parents. But with that we do not concern ourselves further. That is God's concern, who has commanded us to administer His sacrament in this way, and according to whose command exclusively we are to conform. With adults, too, the same thing appears repeatedly. There are those who upon profession of faith are received into the congregation, whom one thus has to regard as fellow citizens of the saints and of the household of God, who upon the profession of their faith are admitted to the sacrament of baptism and the sacrament of the Lord's Supper, and who nevertheless later fall away, so that we can no longer, even according to the judgment of charity, regard them as brothers. But the Word of God has not failed because of that. It has only become evident that, in the faithful administration of the ordinance of God, the church can make a judgment that does not always correspond with someone's inward state. The church never has certainty, no more for adults than for young children. The difficulty here is thus the same in both cases; and if we can accept it in the one case, we can also do so in the other.

40. *Can you provide some citations that show that this conception of matters is what is generally found in Reformed theologians?*

Yes. First of all Calvin, *Institutes*, 4.16.17–18, where he argues extensively that the children of believers *can* receive regeneration and the Holy Spirit. One should pay attention to the fact that he bases baptism on this *can* in connection with the promise of God: "to you and to your seed." He points to the example of John the Baptist and how he was sanctified from his mother's womb. Then he takes note of the objection of opponents to infant baptism that this only happened once. "But we are not arguing in this way either (that is, as if the Lord is generally accustomed to deal with infants in this fashion). Our purpose is solely to show that they unjustly and wickedly shut God's power within these narrow limits to which it does not permit itself to be confined." And in section 20: "This objection can be refuted briefly, namely, that infants are baptized unto the repentance and faith that they will have hereafter, the seed of which two gifts are already in them by the secret working of the Spirit, even though those gifts themselves have not yet taken shape and been formed in them."

Further, Ursinus (*Commentary on the Heidelberg Catechism*, question 74). He answers the objection of the Anabaptist (those who do not believe ought not to be baptized) as follows: "This is only true of adults..., for in them faith is demanded before baptism..., but for young children, for baptism it is enough that they are sanctified and regenerate, and their faith and profession is that they are born to believing parents.... Further, it is so that a right decision cannot be made from this that such ought not to be baptized, for here only those are spoken of who do not believe at all, neither in fact nor by profession nor by disposition. But of young children, although they in fact do not believe, one can nevertheless not say that the children are entirely unbelieving. And they have this disposition not from the flesh or from nature, but from the Holy Spirit and from the grace that is promised to them."

Beza: "There is a special situation with children who are born to believing parents. For although they do not have in themselves that quality of faith that is in adult believers, nevertheless it cannot be otherwise than that those whom God has sanctified from their mother's body and marked off from the children of unbelievers have the seed and the bud of faith.... With what right, then, would someone deny them the sealing of the thing that the Lord has already imparted to them? If someone objects that those who are born of believing parents are not all elect and consequently not all are sanctified, ... we do not lack an answer: for although we do not deny that it is so, nevertheless we say that one must let this hidden judgment remain with God, and, in general, by virtue of the formula of the promise, we hold them all to be sanctified who have been born of believing parents, or of which one of the two is a believer, unless there is something in the way from which one could decide to the contrary."

Peter Martyr Vermigli: "Because we may not out of curiosity investigate God's hidden providence and election, we hold the children of the saints to be holy as long as, in growing up, they do not show that they are alienated from Christ. We do not exclude them from the congregation but accept them as parts of the same, hoping that, as they are the seed of the saints, they also share in divine election and have the grace and the Spirit of Christ. And we baptize them on that basis. One should not listen to those who make difficulties of this and say: 'Is the minister deceived?' or, 'Could it be that in truth the child is not a child of the promise of divine election and mercy?' For one can also bring up such derision about adults. Of them, too, we do not know whether or not they come deceptively, whether they truly believe, whether they are children of election or destruction.... Why do you baptize them? You will say: 'I do it because I follow their outward profession'; so we also say that the church therefore receives and baptizes our children because they belong to us. And so that is for them a sign of God's will, as the outward profession is for adults."

Franciscus Junius answers the objection of the Anabaptists that children are not capable of regeneration: "Regeneration is viewed in two senses—namely, as according to its foundation, it exists as a disposition in Christ, and as it is in fact present in us the former regeneration, which can be called the transplanting of the old Adam into the new, is the cause of the latter, which follows as the fruit. Elect children are regenerated in the first-mentioned sense when they are implanted into Christ and the sealing of this becomes theirs in baptism."

The Leiden Synopsis: "We do not tie the efficacy of baptism to the moment in which the body is sprinkled with external water, but, with Scripture, require faith and conversion beforehand of all those baptized, at least according to the judgment of charity, and that both in the children of the covenant, regarding whom we maintain that in them the seed and the Spirit of faith and conversion must be assumed, by virtue of the divine blessing and the evangelical covenant, as well as for adults in whom an active profession of faith and conversion is necessary."

Witsius: "Further, we also say that the young children of believers have received the Spirit. Otherwise they could not also be holy, which Paul nevertheless attests to (1 Cor 7:14); nor could they be Christ's, to whom no one belongs who does not have His Spirit (Rom 8:9).... From this it follows that the water cannot be refused them by injecting that young children should not be baptized.... I go further. God is not only free to impart the grace of regeneration to elect children before baptism, but it is also likely that He generally does so."

Burman: "Regarding the faith of children, investigation is very obscure, since there is no memory of that age, and the working of the Spirit takes place in secret so that we cannot determine its mode. The elements of regeneration and the seeds of new life do not occur in children any less than the pollution and the evil of the corrupt nature that they have received from the forefather of the human race. It is sufficient that the thing signified in baptism is due them, which can be sealed to them so that no one may think that a blank piece of paper, on which nothing is written, is sealed in that baptism."

Braun: "To the one who shares in the thing signified, the sign is also due; but children partake of the thing signified—namely, the forgiveness of sins, regeneration, and eternal life—since they belong to the covenant and have the promises, and the kingdom of heaven is given to them."

Heidegger: "As far as adults are concerned, outward baptism does not seal inward grace to all, but only to those who have in their heart and profess with their words a sincere faith. Also, baptism does not seal regeneration and spiritual grace in its all-inclusive scope to all children and to every child of believing parents, but only to the elect. Although it is right and good concerning each one of these children in particular to hope for the good according to the judgment of charity, still we are not free to do this with an eye to all children taken together."

A distinction is then made between those children who die before the age of discernment and the rest. Regarding the former, Heidegger maintains that they are already sanctified in the womb and that baptism seals to them this grace already present. Those who grow up are generally endowed with faith in the usual way, that is, by hearing the Word, and so for them baptism was not a seal of present grace.

Marckius: "From the absence of faith (the opponents of infant baptism reason), as well as from the absence of a confession of faith and sins. We require both of these prior to the baptism of adults, but judge that it is sufficient if, with the judgment of charity, they are expected to follow in children. They also reason from the absence of sealed benefits, such as sanctification. These, however, are in fact present according to their measure, such as sanctification, which can just as little be denied as the corruption of nature antecedent to it."

Turretin: "The same judgment must be made about the faith of the children of the covenant as their reason. They possess both in the first act, not in the second ... in the root, not in the fruit."

41. *What is the second view that has existed along with the other in the Reformed church?*

The following: In the Word of God, there is an offer of the benefits of the covenant on the condition of faith and repentance. By external calling, the Word says: all these benefits are for you, presupposing that you believe. That is the universal offer of the gospel. But now the sacraments are added. They seal this offer of the gospel—however, not to everyone to whom it comes without distinction, but only to those of whom it is apparent by their profession and conduct that they do not reject and despise it. *Olevianus* says: "In order that out of this whole multitude would emerge a church, which God unites to Himself in Christ, God thus begins in that solemn transaction, as in a marriage contract, not with the sealing of grace offered in general (for many reject that grace openly and therefore it cannot be sealed to them; on the other hand, the Lord also does not will to bind Himself to hypocrites, who secretly harden themselves, which would happen if He first gave His seal); but with what in the manner of the offer of grace was the last, He makes in its establishment a beginning by visible signs, etc.... Then there follows the sealing of the first in the grace offered in the gospel and the special bond of God" (p. 502).[2]

Now one must pay close attention to what is implied in this conception. Here in the sacrament there is an offer of the benefits of the covenant, but in what sense?

a) Not as an offer that can still be rejected or accepted, and whereby man is free or remains free. When the sealing takes place, man is bound. The sacrament seals the established covenant.

b) Also, not merely as an offer that *must* be accepted by virtue of the law and its demand applied to the promises. Every man who hears the gospel is under this obligation. The covenant of grace is not only offered to him, but he is also obliged to accept it and to live according to it. Still, the sacrament cannot yet be administered to him on this basis. The natural obligation to enter into God's covenant provides no basis for the administration of the seals of the covenant.

2 Only the page number is given. Presumably the quotation is from *De substantia foederis gratiuti* ..., either the Latin original (Geneva, 1585) or possibly a Dutch translation.

c) There must thus be something else, and evidently this other thing is located in the fact that the recipient of the sacrament has solemnly bound himself to live in the covenant and to fulfill the covenant. He has concerned himself with the covenant and has entered into the covenant. It is an established covenant. If he does not walk the path of faith and of repentance, he therefore becomes a covenant-breaker and will be treated as such by God. And he has a weightier responsibility than do those to whom the word of the gospel has merely come, and have never been in relationship with God.

d) This view is thus distinguished from that of an external covenant. In the latter, merely the general offer of the gospel is sealed. Here there is a seal on the promises, whereby it is presupposed that one accepts them in faith. And the basis of that presupposition is the profession of the recipient of the seals that he desires to live in the covenant and from the covenant. Therefore, not merely: if you believe, the benefit of the covenant is for you. But: since you, according to your own declaration, acquiesce in God's covenant, there is sealed to you here the right to all the benefits of the covenant in the way of ongoing faith and continual repentance. The difference between the doctrine of an external covenant and this view can best be seen in the baptism of adults. And only this view is in agreement with our Form for the baptism of adults.

That principle is now extended to the baptism of the children of believers. By virtue of their birth from believing parents, they are also included in the covenant; one can even say, on the basis of Scripture, born into the covenant. Thus by this relationship the obligation is incumbent on them to live in the covenant and to live out of it. Again, not in the perfunctory sense in which the obligation to believe is incumbent on everyone to whom the gospel comes, but in the very specific sense that the children are no longer free, are members of the covenant, must keep the covenant, and, should they not do so, become covenant-breakers. Incumbent on them is a wholly unique and particular responsibility. On this basis, that is, on the presupposition and with the expectation that they accept and keep the covenant, the seal of the covenant is administered to them. If, in growing up, they show that they do not fulfill it, then they take a step backwards; they are idle and neglectful in keeping the covenant, or they in fact show that they are not willing to keep the covenant and break it.

One will notice that this conception also avoids the danger present in the doctrine of an external covenant. Here the demand of spiritual truth is held high. The internal is kept in contact with the external. The dualism, however much it may remain in practice, is in theory not legitimized and taught systematically. The ideal character of the covenant, its essence, is kept constantly in view.

42. *Are both views, as now described, found beside each other in Reformed theologians?*

Yes, in many of those mentioned above one at one time finds expressions that recall the first view, and then again expressions that recall the other. Anyone can be convinced of that by reading attentively. And the more one reads, the more one comes to the conviction that proponents of neither view have the right to commend theirs as the only historical Reformed view. Witnesses for both views can be produced in abundance.

43. *How then should we judge concerning the meaning of infant baptism?*

a) We observe, first of all, that there is a large objection to the first view if it teaches that all children are to be held to be regenerated and to possess the principle of faith until the opposite is apparent. If one assumes that, then one must also carry it through in his dealings with children and work only on the development of their new life. Also, one then cannot, with reason, pray for their regeneration as a thing that they must still receive or still need. The children themselves, in growing up, will be under the illusion that they possess regeneration, and the truth that without regeneration no one can see the kingdom of God will lose its force. It will gradually be seen in the congregation as something self-evident that whoever lives and dies within its circle is saved, since he has come into the world virtually as a regenerate person, is renewed and sanctified from his mother's womb. This is extremely dangerous. One is also tempted to think that the resoluteness with which this view was expressed by some old

Reformed theologians is connected with the pure church-state of their day, or also is to be explained in part by Roman Catholic reminiscences.

b) Further, this view also brings one more or less into conflict with reality. It is ever apparent, as they grow up, how many of those children possess an unregenerate or at least unconverted heart. What then must one think of this supposition of baptism? One answers: that can also happen later with adults who are baptized. Although this is true, there is still a difference. With adults we have a personal profession, and God seals His covenant to those who mean this in truth, who believe. With young children we do not have such a personal testimony. Here it is God who commands us to baptize them. If now He had added, "on the basis and with the presupposition that they are regenerate before their baptism," then we would have to acquiesce in that. But He does not say that. He has nowhere bound Himself to do that in general, although no one, of course, has the right to assure us that He never or seldom does that. It is a matter that simply cannot be verified by us. Only a positive promise would give the right to assure ourselves of something as certain. Naturally, if it *could* not happen, then infant baptism would be condemned. For thereby the lifetime of a child in its entirely would be placed outside the circle of God's supernatural working of grace. Hence the argument of the old theologians repeated again and again: the children partake of the thing signified, therefore also of the sign and the seal. One may not infer from this that they always only meant that all children of the covenant are regenerated by baptism. They only intend to say that children *can* be regenerated. Compare what we have cited above from Calvin.

c) The seals of the covenant are not foreordained to seal the possession of grace subjectively, but to seal the promise of grace in the broadest sense—to seal to the believer both justifying and sanctifying grace. By saying that children must be regenerated beforehand, one shifts this viewpoint. One wishes to maintain: if they have a right to the sacraments, they must be believers, and they cannot be believers without regeneration. But this applies, however, only *as long as* and *as soon as* there is an activity of faith that can be directed to the seal. An adult, therefore, may not properly receive the seal without a profession of faith. For the children, in contrast, it is different. For them it is sufficient that: a) The promises of God are sealed as promises in the widest sense, entirely apart from the question whether or not a subjective appropriation of the promises has already begun. God says to the children who are baptized: "I, God, will be your God; yes, I *am* your God." b) The well-founded expectation can be entertained that the children will appropriate the promises for themselves with the use of their understanding, and therefore the demand of the covenant to do that can also be addressed to them.

d) Thus we do not maintain that the children of believers are already regenerated at an early age, but leave that completely undecided. And nevertheless, we assume on the basis of the promise of God that the young children of the covenant who die before the use of their understanding, receive eternal salvation. On what basis do we make this assumption?

1. We should note that Scripture does not offer us any grounds to entertain this expectation for *all* children wherever they are born among pagans, Mohammedans [Muslims], or Christians. It is clear that one can only reason here from the covenant. Where no covenant relationship exists, every basis for such a verdict is lacking. One need not for that reason preach with emphasis that all such children are lost. But there is no basis for their salvation. All the reasons that are produced for their salvation proceed from a weakening of the concept of original sin. It is believed that original sin (inherent pollution) in itself is not sufficient to consign a child as damnable before God, or at least to cause it to be lost. If the child dies before it commits actual sin, then it is saved. Our answer to this is that original sin is certainly sufficient for damnation, and one may not make this difference in degree between it and actual sin. Further, too much is deduced from the premises. One might only conclude that the children are not lost. To say that they are saved can only happen on the grounds that the merits of Christ are imputed to them. And for that there must be solid grounds. Where those are lacking, then logically one

could only draw the conclusion that the children are in a middle state that is neither heaven nor hell. And that would be Roman Catholic.

2. All salvation of young children, therefore, is based on the gracious imputation of the merits of Christ. How can we now hope that the children of the covenant who die before the use of their understanding have received this imputation? This is inferred from their being in the covenant. Now, if this were nothing other than a formula for the fact that they live under the offer of the gospel, then it would not be possible to see how one could draw that conclusion. Every possibility to decide whether they acquiesce in that offer would then be lacking. And we would have to end with saying that we know nothing about that. The comfort of the covenant promise would then be gone. But now that is not how things stand. The covenant is an established covenant. God wills that for adults we regard it as accepted, and as it will and must be accepted by the young children of the covenant. This is now—and we should certainly pay attention to this—not only a bond of obligation by which He has a certain claim to the children; it is also a divine promise. It includes that where believers raise their seed for the Lord, He will continue His covenant from that seed, will build His church. Thus, not only "It is expected of those children and required of those children that will live in my covenant," but also: "I, God, will to give it to them, and make true my promises to the parents." Here, therefore, is a firm divine foundation.

God's covenant is a giving covenant. It also includes, along with other promises, the promise of regeneration. Suppose, now, that this promise is not fulfilled in young children who die before the use of their understanding. The result would then be that God has given us a promise and prescribed a seal of the covenant, but He does not allow us to cling to it and to draw comfort from it, even where every ground for removing it is lacking. He has caused the sacrament of baptism to be administered to young children. That sacrament sealed the established covenant, and so it was given to the child in the expectation, based on God's promise, that the child would truly live in the covenant. If the child dies, then we have to cling to that expectation, and from it may assume for our solace the child's salvation.

3. With that said, it is of course also assumed that the child is regenerated before it gains salvation. Without regeneration, no one will see the kingdom of God, and that applies to young children as well as adults. But *when* the child is regenerated, no one can determine. Whether before baptism, or at baptism, or after baptism—who will say? It can be regenerated at its entrance into heaven, as subsequently the adult believer is completely sanctified as in a crisis. As far as we know, positive data are entirely lacking here.

e) We think, therefore, that one cannot go further than to say that on the basis of the promise it is expected and required of all the children of the covenant that they will fulfill the covenant. That expectation includes that, if the parents honor their promise, God, in His own time, wills to work in their children through His Spirit, and from those who grow up will build the church and further His covenant. And at the same time, that expectation includes that those children who die before the use of their understanding are saved. Both expectations are sealed in baptism. And so there is more in that sealing of baptism than a conditional offer of the covenant; there are positive promises of God. These are the two highly comforting facts. And with an eye to this, no one will be able to say that infant baptism is meaningless.

But we may not individualize. If we knew now which of the children of the covenant would die before the use of their understanding, then from the outset we could say: "This child and that child have the essence of the covenant." But we do not know that. And even if we did, we could still not say: "They have the essence of the covenant in subjective possession." In no way, however, do we know who these children are. Only their death gives us a definite answer in this regard, and thus becomes a fact that turns our general expectation into an individual confidence. As far as the other children are concerned, namely those who grow up, these must be prayed for, that in them God may make the promises of the covenant a matter of the truth, may bring those promises to fulfillment where that has not yet occurred. As long as they have not come to an age of discernment, we do not make an individual judgment about them. This, precisely, is the difference. In its official dealings with adults, the church can do nothing else than deal with them as believers. On that basis, it must not only admit them to the Lord's Supper, but must encourage them and require them to participate. The congregation is officially a believing congregation—something that in the meantime does not take away the fact that, again and again, there must be an insistence on self-examination, to the end of everyone deciding between God and his conscience whether his official status corresponds with his actual relation to God. Through these two means—formally dealing with the members of the visible church as believers and insisting on truth in the believer's relationship to God—church life must be kept pure, and protected from its two extremes.

f) The children of the congregation belong to the congregation; children of the covenant to the covenant. They are a part of the visible church. And the visible church must be operative as the manifestation of the invisible church. We say, then, that the invisible church is manifested in the children as well as in the adults; it is what is there behind and in the visible church. It is not limited to adulthood but has its ramifications in every age, in that of children too. In the matter of the covenant, there is always a seed for the Lord. But the children are taken as a group, as it were, and we do not speak of them in an individualizing way as we do of the adults.

g) The question now is how the children of the covenant are to be regarded when they come to years of discernment. This question is extremely difficult to answer, especially with respect to practice. The covenant has been sealed to them in the expectation and with the requirement that it be followed; that is, that as soon as the years of discernment would come, faith and repentance would be manifested. The first requirement is that one point to the distinctive obligation that a baptized person has toward the covenant. He may not be brought to the illusion or left in the delusion that in what is external he has enough to be right before God. The error is that one insists entirely too exclusively on making profession, as if it were a requirement that only now is in effect and did not apply previously. That conception is completely wrong. Before making profession, too, there was a *covenantal call* to show faith and repentance. Making profession is, as has already been remarked earlier, something negative; it is no longer being kept from the Lord's Supper. If one deals with young members before their profession as if they were unconverted, though living in good standing in the church as loyal covenant members, then the result will be that, being pointed especially forcefully to the spiritual requirements of the covenant in making profession, they draw back. And then the baptized members come. In their profession, then, is compressed, as it were, what should have been spread over the years past. It takes on the character of a crisis. The idea of gradually identifying consciously with the covenant and gradually living in the covenant with one's consciousness is lost. What is needed is more urging of the truth day by day, in the official cultivation of the children of the covenant as they grow up, and less pressing for a profession at a particular moment.

But not only the requirement; the promise of God must also be pointed to. The positive promise of God certainly remains in effect for the children too as they grow up, that God will further the covenant from the seed of His covenant members. Thus they, too, have a direct relationship to the invisible church. They know that they find themselves in the workplace of re-creating grace, that God's gifts of grace lie within the sphere in which they were born. They come into contact with the essence of the covenant, its invisible benefits. The kingdom of God is, as it were, among them and in their midst.

The impulse of exhortation and the power of consolation that are present in it are not always noted sufficiently and summoned for help. One can stress the obligations toward the covenant too much and overlook the giving side of the covenant too much. The one needs the other. Only presenting the obligations is deadening; only pointing to the promises causes indifference.

How to proceed if all this does not produce fruits, and after persistent faithful dealings, all spiritual response to the promises

of the covenant must be found to be lacking? In such cases, discipline should be applied properly; for that a baptized person lives
on year in year out without coming to the Lord's Supper, or that
he desires baptism for his children and does not desire the Lord's
Supper for himself, is a completely false situation that cannot be
excused, although in practice one may attempt to make an excuse
for it. But we believe, first of all, that with faithful dealings that
do not occur spasmodically and expect everything in the making
of a profession, such cases will be extremely rare. If that were not
the case, then God would have given us a rule that in practice is
unusable or must lead to the extinction of the congregation and
to the removal of the covenant. For in all such cases, many or few,
one would have to come to the conclusion that the covenant had
failed, while God promises specifically that His covenant will not
fail where it is faithfully administered. If, however, such a case
does occur, then one should not act precipitately. Slow, persistent,
careful dealing, coupled with earnestness, may be just the means
to bring such a person to repentance. For we do not know when
the patience of God ceases to surround someone like this with
the promises of the covenant. If he in his dying hours comes to
repentance, we would still have to view it as a fruit, a subsequent
effect of the covenant. Even where a generation has passed away
that was apostate, God can still remember His covenant in children's children. And we may not be less patient than God.

44. *In what sense, then, is baptism a means of grace for young children?*

Judgments on this question are quite diverse. If one is committed to the
view that as a means of grace baptism works specifically at the moment
of its administration and thereby keeps focused on the requirement
that the sacraments serve to strengthen faith, then one will necessarily
have to come to the conclusion that young children are generally regenerated before baptism. This, then, appears to be the principle from
which Dr. [Abraham] Kuyper reasons in his view. He also applies to
infant baptism the affirmation that there is a special internal grace associated with the external sacrament that differs specifically from grace
in root, branches, and fruits: the grace of the forming of faith for the
communion of saints. Where that happens, the children must naturally
be regenerated, for otherwise they could not possess the seed of faith. It

is true that Dr. Kuyper is not alone in affirming the presence of regeneration before the baptism of children. That is sufficiently clear from the citations given above. But as far as we are aware, no one among the Reformed theologians has taught this specific baptismal grace, either for the baptism of adults or for the baptism of young children.

One may observe the following:

a) Those among the Reformed theologians who ordinarily put regeneration before baptism divide into two groups:

1. Those who suppose this only for children who die before their use of understanding. So, for example, Witsius. After first having argued that the grace of regeneration is not tied to baptism, he says: "I go further: not only is God free to grant the grace of regeneration to elect children before baptism is administered, but it is also likely that He ordinarily does this. This is deduced in this way from what has been said. Since already beginning at birth God has received elect children into the fellowship of His covenant, has united them with Christ, has reconciled them with Himself, has forgiven them the guilt of original sin, no reason can be produced why at the same time He would not regenerate them, unless they are not to be regarded as suitable objects for regeneration.... Further, I believe that no single example or witness can be produced of the removal of the guilt of sin by forgiveness, without at the same time the dominion of the same sin being crippled, so that where it loses the power to condemn, it also loses the power to rule. Now where the dominion of sin is diminished, sin is slain. Where sin is slain, the soul is made alive. The enlivening of the soul is nothing other than regeneration."

But it is otherwise with the children who come to the use of their understanding. For this, Witsius cites the following statement of Beza with approval: "Concerning children who are born in church and in God's name are elect (and after careful deliberation I have said that all must be held to be such) and die before the use of their understanding, I could easily assume, on the basis of the promise of God, that they are incorporated into Christ at birth. However, what we can establish about the others, without being rash, is that they are first regenerated when by hearing, they are endowed with true faith" (Witsius, *Miscellaneorum sacrorum libri II*, 633).

One sees that there is no mention here of baptismal grace. Witsius and Beza reason from the seal. They conceive of this (always presumptively) as a positive sealing of God that the children are elect. Thereupon they then draw the conclusion that those dying before they understand are already regenerated before baptism. But how they come to that conclusion is not clear. It cannot be logically deduced from the premises. They surely regard all baptized children as the same, as elect. Perhaps their reasoning is as follows: God wills in general to work regeneration under the hearing of the Word. There is therefore no basis for God to deviate from His rule, and certainly a basis to suppose that He holds to it. But there is no basis at all to say that He would will to regenerate a child who will not come to a conscious use of the means of grace at the age of three rather than immediately. Ergo: it is most probable that He does this forthwith, already at birth. It seems to us that this is the thought process by which one unconsciously lets himself be led. But it does not come out clearly in the words used.

2. Those who suppose the priority of regeneration to baptism for all elect children. This is the view of Voetius. He says: "The teaching of Reformed theologians regarding the function of baptism is well-known, namely, that it does not consist in causing regeneration, but in the sealing of regeneration that has already been caused." But, as one sees, Voetius, too, does not connect a special grace to baptism. Baptism seals the regeneration that is already present. The power resides, according to him, in the *seal*.

b) Of course, those who have connected regeneration to the moment of baptism have not been lacking. This view, however, is too strongly Roman Catholic and Lutheran for it to gain many supporters. It found approval in the Anglican Church and with some among the French theologians. Here there is in fact a baptismal grace, but it is not a specific grace following regeneration.

c) It has been said that on this point Dr. Kuyper is Lutheranizing. This is true insofar as he teaches a specific baptismal grace through which baptism is the normal, ordained means. This is what is new in his conception, not known until now among the Reformed. The rest, then, is not *the* Reformed but still *a* Reformed view, and represents a line that is not at all new but may be traced back to the first development of Reformed theology. Only it seems to us to be less accurate to present it as *the doctrine* of the fathers. For the rest, we should pay attention to the fact that there are three great points of difference between Dr. Kuyper's theory and Lutheran doctrine. The Lutherans say: baptismal grace is granted by baptism to every child; Dr. Kuyper says: only to elect children. The Lutherans say: it is the grace of regeneration; Dr. Kuyper says: a specific grace through which faith already present is formed for the communion of the saints. The Lutherans say: grace is worked by the water in the word [spoken]; Dr. Kuyper says: grace is worked by Christ and the Holy Spirit, not by means of but along with the sign.

d) Here too it appears to us that a Scriptural basis is lacking for the doctrine of a specific baptismal grace. We will have to maintain that baptism is a means of grace, but that its being a means of grace is linked to its being a seal. That is what it was in the baptism of adults. Now, however, the question arises: If this is so, can infant baptism then remain a real means of grace? A seal only has meaning and significance for its conscious use. It is intended to be seen, touched, read. Sealing must pass through the consciousness. And if grace is tied to conscious sealing, how then can baptism be a means of grace for young children?

Our answer is twofold:

1. Because this objection was felt and nevertheless it was desired to maintain baptism as a means of grace, from the Reformed side it has been repeated time and again that the efficacy of baptism is not tied to the moment in which it is administered externally. As far as we know, baptism as a means of grace can only begin to work directly for the child itself, when the child begins to understand something about it. And then it must be assumed that it works in entirely the same way as baptism

for adults. That working starts with the conscious exercise of faith and leads back to the conscious exercise of faith. But to that end, it is necessary that the child learn to understand the meaning of his baptism. Here two factors are always working together: sealing coming from God, and faith worked by God, which makes the sealing personal for us. Baptism is a seal of God apart from faith, but it only gains sealing power for our own consciousness as our faith is occupied with it.

2. Baptism as a means of grace has significance not only for the baptized child. The church, too, in whose midst baptism is administered, is concerned with it. Therefore baptism is administered in the gathering of believers. Therefore it is said in the Form that baptism is an ordinance of God to seal His covenant to *us* and our seed. Prayer is offered beforehand that the holy ordinance may be done for our comfort and for the edification of the congregation. Therefore the parents are asked if they believe what is proposed to them in the questions.

From all of this, it is sufficiently evident that baptism has sealing power for the parents as much as for the baptized children. There is then also a covenant requirement for the parents as there is a covenant promise for them. They must have faith with respect to God's covenant if before God they will rightly ask for and receive baptism for their children. Also, if there is no faith with respect to the covenant, there can be no prayer with respect to it. That the parents have faith, then, is certainly required. That does not mean, as it has sometimes been propounded, that the faith of the parents is in the place of the children who are not yet able to believe. That cannot be, because faith is something personal, for which no substitution is possible. The faith of the parents is necessary for themselves, in part so that they may make use of the sealing in baptism for the strengthening of their faith, in part that they may fulfill the promises that are asked of them. Again and again when an administering of baptism takes place, it is sealed anew to the congregation that God's covenant is present in its midst, that with that dispensing, God also wills to maintain and continue the covenant in its midst, that He wills to make its seed to be a holy seed. And when this sealing is appropriated in faith, God thereby wills to increase His grace in the sense described earlier.

45. Which children may or should be baptized?

The children of believers—that is, those who are in the fellowship of the visible church and so are presumed to be believers. At least one of the two parents must be a believer in this sense. And it can be expected of a believer that he or she fulfills the obligations of a believer and values his or her privileges as a believer. Thus, someone who is a member only by baptism and does not make use of the other sacrament is, strictly speaking, not a believer in good standing. But in practice it is very difficult to deal with such persons.

Also, the question whether, in certain circumstances, other children may not also be baptized has already been much debated. On various grounds, the right to the sacrament has been extended more widely.

a) One ground is in the declaration of God, as it is thought, that He makes His promises to children and children's children until the thousandth generation (Hodge, *Systematic Theology*, 3:561). An appeal is also made to Isaiah 59:21: "My Spirit who is upon you and my words that I have put in your mouth, shall not depart out of your mouth, or out of the mouth of your offspring, or out of the mouth of your offspring's offspring" (*De Heraut*, no. 664).

b) Another ground is naturally the teaching that the sacrament is necessary for salvation and imparts grace that cannot otherwise be obtained. Roman Catholics and ritualists must inevitably come to baptizing, without discrimination, all children who are brought within their reach and not asking about the state of the parents.

c) Externalizing the covenant by causing it to coincide with the state, in a state church, leads to entirely the same result. An Englishman, then, has a right to baptism in the Anglican Church just as he has a right to citizenship, regardless of whom he was born. Discipline can naturally not be exercised in such a church, which is wed in this way to the state and must conform to the state.

d) Still another view holds the baptism of the parents who come with their child as merely necessary, without asking about their relationship toward the covenant. Carried out consistently, this naturally leads to two kinds of members in the church. If it is possible in the first generation, then it is also in the second, and third, and so on. It is then possible to have a series of a hundred or more generations who were in the church as those who were baptized but who still have not valued God's covenant—indeed, have scandalously profaned it. The latter will naturally occur less often, for whoever lives in gross sins will probably no longer desire baptism for his child. But the first case occurs frequently, namely, that parents bring their children for baptism who are in the church by baptism but do not come to the Lord's Supper. It is said that the Presbyterian Church in Ireland and Scotland follow this practice. The Presbyterian Church in the United States, on the other hand, appears to hold to the practice that only parents who come to the Lord's Supper can receive baptism for their children.

e) The principle of adoption has been applied to obtain baptism for children who otherwise would have no right to it. Orphans or children of parents who are unfit or unwilling to be parents, to bring them up in the Christian religion and to lead them into a consciousness of the covenant, can, it is said, be accepted on their behalf by others who then vouch for a Christian upbringing. Thus, Abraham had also to circumcise his slaves who were born in his household, including even the slaves who were bought with money (Gen 17:12–13). The Presbyterian Church decided in 1843 that children from paganism can be baptized if they are connected with one missionary or another, such that they are guaranteed a Christian upbringing. The Synod of Dort also debated this point. Some were for it, but the majority decided against—in our opinion, correctly. That believers intend baptism for their children is based on something other than their being willing to raise them in a Christian manner. It is based on the command and the promise of God. And that reads, "to *you and to your seed!*" not "to all to whom you can give a Christian upbringing." With Abraham and those born into or bought to be part of his household, it was somewhat different. Although it was in fact the same covenant of grace administered there that we still have, at the same time we must not forget that the basis was laid there for the national existence of Israel. And this was a direct divine command to receive all the servants into the covenant. With that it was not intended that Abraham could bring an indefinite number of pagan children under his oversight and circumcise them. That was decidedly excluded by the Old Testament particularism. Only the Jews shall have the covenant. The Old Testament church was not a missionary church as we are.

f) So we can only hold to this rule: the children of believing parents have the right to baptism. It is very difficult to make a further determination and establish how many generations may be skipped. The church has not always remained the same on this matter. It wishes to baptize even the children of those who are excommunicated (See the Synod of Dort, 1574, question 9). À Brakel ([*The Christian's Reasonable Service*], 39.23) says: the children of covenant members born of harlotry too, the children of members under censure too, for the son will not bear the guilt of the father. Reasoning from this, it is fair to ask: Is there anything to be said, then, against baptizing the children of members by baptism only? Generally the reasoning is that members by baptism only are certainly covenant members, but members who do not honor their covenant obligations. And those who are excommunicated and censured for other sins do that much less. This, too, is a consideration: suppose that one admits such baptized members to the sacrament of baptism for their children, what means are there left to exercise discipline over them? Keeping them from the Lord's Supper is of no avail, since they do not desire the Lord's Supper for themselves. Denying them baptism for their children appears to be the only means. But that is a means that at the same time affects the children along with the parents, and over against this one must acknowledge that à Brakel is in the right when he says: "The son shall not bear the guilt of the father."

46. What is understood by baptismal witnesses?

Baptismal witnesses are those who are present at baptism, either to provide testimony regarding the persons who desire baptism for themselves or their children, or to bear witness to certain obligations that they take upon themselves with respect to the one to be baptized. Tertullian makes the first mention of this under the term *sponsores* [sponsors, sureties] in connection with infant baptism. Later the Roman Catholic Church legalized this use of having *sponsores* and specified that the parents may not serve as such at the same time. The *sponsores* were gradually transformed as spiritual guides into *paters* [fathers] and *maters* [mothers], and the idea arose of a spiritual kinship between them and those to be baptized that then had as a result a covenant of union between these two parties.

There were also witnesses for adults who came for baptism, at least already in the fourth century. The practice was taken over by the Protestant churches, as well as by the Reformed Synod of Dort, 1574, articles 61 and 62: "Because we have no command of the Lord to receive patrons or witnesses in order to present children for baptism, one may not impose this on anyone as a specific necessity." The purpose of being a witness is specified: to bear witness to the faith of the parents and the baptism of the child, to take upon oneself the task of instructing the child in case his father or mother has died. Also, in order to maintain mutual fellowship and the bond of friendship among the believers, one may not make this a matter of dispute but should abide by the old practice.

47. How many views are there regarding the baptismal Form?

As many as there are views of baptism:

a) Some say the Form takes the standpoint of those who assume regeneration as having preceded baptism. Witsius: "It can scarcely be doubted that the affirmation of the regeneration of young children, at least according to the judgment of charity, is the accepted view of the Dutch [Reformed] Church. Certainly in its baptismal Form this question is addressed to the parents who offer their child for baptism: whether they do not confess that they [the children] are sanctified in Christ," etc. Then everything naturally acquires an absolute sense. Being sanctified is understood as initial regeneration; new obedience is such that only those are able to manifest it who are regenerated and in whom grace is already at work. The child is without its knowledge adopted into grace, just as without its knowledge it participates in damnation in Adam. All of this is very strongly expressed, as everyone will have to acknowledge.

Only, one comes into difficulty with the prayer: "That you would graciously look upon these children and by your Holy Spirit incorporate them into your Son, Jesus Christ." How is that to be explained when the children are already regenerated? Various explanations have been given. Dr. Kuyper: It refers to the specific baptismal grace whereby faith obtains that union with the body of Christ that later will enable the child to live in the communion of saints. But it seems to us that it cannot be shown that this view of baptismal grace existed when the Form was composed. Witsius: This must only be understood of sacramental incorporation and of the confirmation of real incorporation, of its increase and fruits. Otherwise the baptismal Form would be contradictory with itself, and that may not be assumed of a Form so closely examined, so generally accepted, so many years in use. The same Form does say that they are sanctified in Christ.

Another solution: The Form speaks in general of *us* and *our* children. It does not individualize. But the prayer now applies personally to these children, asks thus that God would make them to be the seed of the congregation to which the promises aim. But the distinction between *our* children and *these* children does not hold in the face of the Prayer of Thanksgiving, for there it is said first "that you have forgiven us and our children all our sins through the blood of your beloved Son Jesus Christ and by your Holy Spirit have received us as members of your only be-gotten Son, and so adopted us to be your children." And then the same Prayer of Thanksgiving continues: "We also pray that you will always govern *these* baptized children by Your Holy Spirit." That is again personal, and so also for this explanation the Form would not remain the same.

b) Others say that the Form presupposes not that the children are already regenerated but that they are elect, and that baptism is a seal only for the elect. "Sanctified in Christ" then intends to say: "That by virtue of that covenant, the children of covenant members ... have a right to its benefits and will participate in possessing it." So à Brakel, with which one may compare his affirmation: "Baptism seals only the elect."

c) Still others understand being sanctified not only in an objective sense, but also in a lesser sense as meaning "dedicated to God." If this should mean that the parents intend before the Lord that the children are not Turks or pagans but grow up in the Christian congregation, then this certainly does not do justice to the other expressions of our Baptismal Form.

d) One can also take it in the sense of "sanctified by God for His service and taken into a covenant relationship with Him." Sanctification stems from God. It is a characteristic of the entire church, the visible church, and to that extent, of all who belong to it and who are born in its fold. The children are holy then, since it is expected and required of them that they live in God's covenant. But this explanation, too, is not entirely satisfactory, since it does not accord with other expressions of the Form, especially in the Prayer of Thanksgiving.

e) The only thing that we are able to say about this issue is:

   1. The Form speaks of *us* and *our* children where it says, among other things, that we have been made members of Christ by the Holy Spirit. This appears to have the congregation in view to the extent that God realizes the covenant in it and from it— that is, effects the fellowship of the covenant. Here it is expressed in the past tense, not as if it had already occurred for all children before their baptism or even will surely occur, but because throughout all ages God has been true to His promise to the congregation.

   2. The prayer "that God look graciously upon *these children*" applies this general promise to them personally and assumes at least the possibility that they are not yet regenerated; "incorporate into Jesus Christ" can refer to nothing else than regeneration.

3. The prayer "that God always govern these baptized children by His Holy Spirit" also applies the promise to the children personally—without, however, definitely presupposing that the Holy Spirit has already been given to them.

4. The expressions in the Form itself—that God the Father establishes an eternal covenant of grace, that God the Son washes us in His blood, incorporates us into the fellowship of His death and resurrection, that the Holy Spirit wills to dwell in us, appropriating to us what we have in Christ—all these do not mean that the benefits promised here have their beginning just now or that they will first begin in the future. That cannot be, because the first part of the Form for Baptism is also used for adults; and for them, as appears from the questions, the beginning of subjective grace is assumed. Thus it can only mean that the triune God promises all these benefits to His congregation in general; and this is done without specifying a time when they will begin to be bestowed, also without specifying persons, other than according to a judgment of charity and according to the expectation that is based on the promise. For the individual, there is no other way to have the promise applied to oneself than the way of faith. If A has been baptized as a child and the Holy Spirit has sealed to him that He wills to sanctify him as a member of Christ and to apply to him what he has in Christ, then, as he grows up, he can have a well-founded assurance that that promise also concerns him only to the extent that he believes it.

48. *How do we explain the statement in our [Belgic] Confession that by baptism original sin is not entirely abolished or completely eradicated?*

a) It was thought that this is an incorrect translation of a statement present in the French copy of the Confession. "Not entirely" should say "not at all." And that would then refer to Roman Catholic teaching. This teaching includes that by baptism original sin is abolished, and also that remaining *concupiscentia* [concupiscence] does not have the character of genuine sin. In the English translation of the Confession (adopted by the Reformed Church [in America]) we read: "Nor is it by any means abolished or done away by baptism" (article 15). But when the statement was also modified to have this sense in the Dutch printings, our fathers, in revising the Confession, expressly restored it again to the original. Thus there is more to this statement than a protest against Rome.

b) Dr. Kuyper connects this expression to baptismal grace. By that grace, original sin is broken in the child since it comes into fellowship with the body of Christ. Fellowship with the old Adam is consequently cut off and fellowship with the new Adam, with Christ, entered into. But the words do not cause us to think of such an explanation.

c) The article explains itself further. (a) The root of original sin, as inherent corruption, remains, for new sin always wells up from it as from an unholy fountain. This is against Rome. (b) This original sin is no longer imputed to the children of God as placing them under damnation (although they in themselves naturally remain guilty and worthy of punishment). Take note: the children of God. If someone is a child of God, he accepts in faith the attestation of God directed to him in baptism. He thereby receives the strengthening of grace as well as of justifying faith—a new and solemn assurance that, for the sake of the blood of Christ, all his sins have been forgiven him. This refers not only to past and present sins but also to those that are future. It covers his entire life, just as justification covers his entire life. And original sin, no less than actual sin, is subsumed here. So it can be said that for him baptism is a removal of original sin, namely, from the aspect of hereditary guilt. Now, everything said subsequently in the article fits with this explanation. Indeed, one could think that when a Christian receives such an exemption for the guilt of all his sins, then that would lead him to live a dissolute and careless life, and he would not concern himself very much about remaining corruption. But that by no means follows, the article says: "not in order to sleep easily in sin, but that the sensing of this corruption would often make them groan, longing to be delivered from this body of death."

49. *Give a definition of baptism.*

Baptism is a sign and seal of the covenant of grace in which, by the washing with water in the name of the triune God, to believers and in the way of faith their participation in the benefits of the covenant is signified and sealed, and they in turn commit themselves to a life in obedience of faith to God.

40. Give a definition of baptism.

Baptism is a sign and seal of the covenant of grace in which, by the
washing with water in the name of the triune God, to believers and in
the way of faith their participation in the benefits of the covenant is
signified and sealed, and they in turn commit themselves to a life in
obedience of faith to God.

CHAPTER FIVE

The Lord's Supper

1. *Under the old dispensation, what corresponded to the sacrament of the Lord's Supper?*

The Passover. For its archeological particulars, one may consult biblical archeology. Here we only have to do with its dogmatic meaning as a sacrament.

2. *From how many points of view can the Passover be considered?*

Primarily from four:

   a) As a sacramental meal of remembrance.

   b) As a sacrifice with a sacramental character.

   c) As a sacramental meal.

   d) As a harvest feast.

3. *To what extent was the Passover a sacramental meal of remembrance?*

As we can see from Exodus 12:1–13, 21–23, 28, 43–51, the Passover was instituted at the liberation of the people out of Egypt. Thus it is a meal of remembrance of that, and when the children ask, "What do you mean by this service?" then the answer must be: "This is a Passover sacrifice to the Lord, who passed over the houses of the children of Israel in Egypt," etc. (Exod 12:26–27). But we may not conclude from this that it was solely a memorial meal, tied to that fact as a historical fact. Rather, that fact itself had significance as a type. The liberation out of Egypt was a picture of liberation out of the slavery house of sin. In this way the memorial meal at the same becomes time a sacrament, for in the historical liberation out of Egypt Israel could not see anything else portrayed than the spiritual liberation that would be achieved by the Messiah. The name Pascha, then, refers to this, an Aramaic form of the Hebrew פֶּסַח, "overlooking" or "rescuing." God says (Exod 12:13): "When I see the blood I will pass over you." There was therefore in the Passover a sign and seal of God's pardoning mercy. The firstborn of the Egyptians were struck down, but Israel was delivered from this and other punitive judgments, although Israel also certainly had deserved death.

4. In what respect was the Passover a sacrifice?

Although against the Roman Catholics the Reformed have sometimes disputed that the Passover was a sacrifice, one can nevertheless not deny that they were mistaken in this. They feared putting a weapon in the hands of Roman Catholics for defending their mass, which is a sacrifice. But wrongly. That the sacrament under the old dispensation was a sacrifice does not entitle one to the conclusion that it is so now. Christ is the only true sacrifice. The sacrifices of the Jews were only shadowy sacrifices. When the body came, the shadow ceased [cf. Col 2:17]. Therefore we now no longer have sacrifices. But the Passover lamb is certainly a sacrificial lamb in completely the same sense in which all the Old Testament sacrifices were sacrifices. As a sacrifice, it is a type. And since the sacrifices reminded that the true sacrifice was still to come and still had to be brought, so too did the Passover lamb. It portrayed the only sacrifice of the covenant Surety, but then as one that was still to come; hence also the bloody character of this sacrifice. With circumcision there also blood. But with baptism and the Lord's Supper, now that the true blood has flowed, there is no longer shedding of blood.

That the Passover was a sacrifice appears clear. In fact, it is called a Passover sacrifice (Exod 12:27). It is not so easy to decide what kind of a sacrifice it was. Some say a thank offering, others a sin offering, and still others a peace offering. Keil says it unites the meaning of the later sin and thank offerings; this appears to be correct. The meal reminds of the thank offering, of the sin offering, though not the offerer. But what was otherwise unconnected was here kept separate. The sacrifice upon which sin was put could still be eaten; it was still declared by God to be clean and holy. It is so with Christ too. As a surety He was fully a sinner, and yet He emerged from that sin-bearing completely clean, without sin, so that He could be true food for the soul. In the Passover, the sacrifice precedes the meal and leads to the meal. The suffering and the self-sacrifice of Christ form the basis on which fellowship with Him by faith is based.

The Passover lamb had a definite relationship to the household. The father of the house had to obtain it for his family. In Egypt (after that no longer) the blood had to be spread on the posts and the lintel of the door. And the father of the house himself had to do that. So in a certain sense, he was a priest. Later in Palestine, however, the blood was sprinkled on the altar by the priests.

5. *What was the meaning of the Passover as a sacrificial meal?*

The Passover lamb had to be eaten. It came to the table in its entirety. No bone in it could be broken. Also it was not boiled in water, but roasted or grilled. It is not possible to state with certainty the meaning of all these things, but without doubt all these features point to the unity of the church, which is grounded in the unity of Christ. That is why, as well, the Passover lamb may not be divided.

If it was not possible for one household to eat it all, more households could join together. Nothing of the meat could be taken outside the house. What was left had to be destroyed. Always eating the same meal already indicated a certain fellowship, but this comes out here very strongly in the eating of the one unbroken lamb. Further, the eating of the lamb had to take place with bitter herbs. On this point, the commemoration recalling Egypt and the general sacramental meaning coalesce. Without doubt the bitter herbs referred to the bitter Egyptian slavery (Exod 1:14). But that was not all. The bitterness of sin in the sinful life was thereby portrayed, and the thought that therefore resides in this is that eating of the meal of God's grace is associated with eating of the bitterness of sin, that repentance accompanies faith.

For the Passover meal one must distinguish between what is based on a direct divine command and what on human authority was added to it later. According to divine command, the food consists of meat and bread. These are, at least for sinful man, ordinary foodstuffs. The bread had to be unleavened bread. This referred, for one thing, to the hasty exodus out of Egypt (Deut 16:3: "For you came out of the land of Egypt in haste"); for another, it also had a deeper symbolic meaning. The yeast (although also occurring with the opposite significance) is still in general a symbol of corruption. It is what is old, what must be purged from man (1 Cor 5:8; Matt 16:6, 12). That the Israelites were fed here with unleavened bread indicated as well how the new life, which was nourished sacramentally by God, was no longer a life of sin and corruption but a holy life in which sin could no longer have dominion.

Later, other features were added to these. These added features are therefore of importance, since they are connected with the institution of the Lord's Supper, and so after the fact received a certain sanction from Christ. A cup of wine was poured at the beginning of the Passover and blessed with a prayer of thanksgiving by the father of the home. Then they drank from it one by one. After this, hands were washed and they ate some of the bitter herbs, while a passage was read out loud. Then a second cup of wine was poured. The son asked about the purpose of the meal; the father explained it to him (Exod 12:26-27). The Hallel was sung, as well as Psalms 113 and 114, after which the second cup was drunk. Only then came the actual meal. At its conclusion the father of the house washed his hands, thanked God, and took a third cup. This was also blessed and was called "the cup of blessing" *par excellence* (1 Cor 10:16). Finally, after this third cup was emptied by the guests, a fourth cup was poured. Again, the Hallel and Psalms 115-118 were sung. The father blessed this fourth cup with the words of Psalm 118:26, and one drank from it. Altogether, then, there were four cups.

It was not necessary that wine appear as a sign and seal in the Passover, for the Passover lamb called to mind directly the shed, the sprinkled blood. When, with the dispensation of the shadows, the Passover lamb as well fell away and only the thing signified, "*our* Passover lamb," Christ, remained, it became necessary that there also be a visible sign for this aspect. Christ then linked Himself with the use of the cup just described. He took that cup from the Passover meal and made it to be the cup of the Lord's Supper.

In the meal, Jehovah is the host. The father of the house, who leads, does priestly work, appears on behalf of Jehovah. Those sitting at the table are Jehovah's guests. This appears most clearly from the fact that later the Passover is not killed and eaten in everyone's house but in the sanctuary, thus in the place where Jehovah dwelt and to which He called and invited the people to Himself. Only those who were Levitically clean could sit at His table; the uncircumcised, who did not belong to God's covenant people, were excluded. For the concept of the table, compare what the apostle says in 1 Corinthians 10:14–21.

6. Was the Passover also a harvest feast?

Yes, already before the institution of the actual Passover Israel celebrated a spring feast that was related to the natural benefits of God. This was the Feast of Unleavened Bread, to be celebrated from the 15th to the 21st of Abib or Nisan. On the second feast day, the 16th, the sheaf of the first-fruits of the new harvest was offered. On the first and the seventh feast days there were solemn gatherings of the congregation. All yeast had to be removed from houses and from within its borders. The name *Passover* was also given to this feast, as well as to the sacrifices that were offered at the feast (cf. Deut 16:2; Luke 22:1). This Feast of Unleavened Bread, in the meantime, also had a national-historical significance. It pointed back to the liberation out of Egypt and, to that extent, forward to the liberation that would be accomplished by Christ. In Egypt, Israel had begun its new existence. That was a type of the spiritual and holy existence of the people of God. And the fact that the feast commemorating that liberation was associated with the harvest by which the natural life of Israel was nourished, indicated in a tangible manner how the natural and the spiritual must permeate each other, how the former must also be sanctified by the latter. The creation and the re-creation are joined with each other here in the most intimate connection.

7. Does the second sacrament of the new dispensation have a specific fixed name like the first?

No, the name "baptism" is fixed and is also retained by everyone. With the Lord's Supper it is otherwise. There are various names in use for it, by which sometimes the theoretical view one has of this sacrament is clearly reveals itself. The most common are:

a) "The Lord's Supper" (Δεῖπνον Κυριακόν). It is called a "supper" because it was instituted and celebrated for the first time in the evening. This of course is connected with the institution of the Passover as a sacramental meal, which had to be partaken of in the evening (Exod 12:8). Also, meals in the temples of idols were generally called "evening meals" by pagans since they were generally eaten in the evening. And in Middle Eastern lands the evening meal was the principal meal, otherwise than with us. That it was eaten in the evening is therefore not essential for the Lord's Supper. It is called *the Lord's* Supper because the Lord Christ, the institutor, is the thing signified, the object of this sacrament.

b) "The table of the Lord" (τράπεζα κυρίου, 1 Cor 10:21). This is to be understood as a metonym. The table stands for everything that belongs to it and is used from it. The table of the Lord stands in opposition to the table of idols. Evidently, then, it is the table at which people have fellowship with the Lord and realize a close unity of life with Him and witness to that realization (cf. v. 20). By eating in the temple of idols, the Corinthians would have witnessed to desiring to have fellowship with idols.

c) "The breaking of bread" (κλάσις τοῦ ἄρτου). Some wish to have this refer exclusively to the Lord's Supper. It is, however, likely that wherever it occurs in the New Testament what is meant is the communal love feast plus the Lord's Supper that followed it. In the apostolic church, then, these two meals were regularly celebrated together, so that the one inevitably turned into the other (Acts 2:42; 20:7, 11; 27:36).

d) "Thanksgiving," "Blessing" (*Eucharist, Eulogia*). The apostle says, "The cup of thanksgiving that we bless with thanksgiving" (1 Cor 10:16). Here the apostle alludes to the blessing that is pronounced over the cup and by which it is set apart for sacramental use. "To bless" means "to devote," for by the blessing that comes upon something, it is intended for something. *Eucharistein* is something else again. It is said of Christ that, both before distributing the cup and before dispensing the bread, He "gave thanks" (Luke 22:17, 19; Mark 1:23; Matt 23:27; 1 Cor 11:24). This was a thanksgiving that to a certain extent recalled the thanksgiving or the prayer of thanks in the Passover meal. Over the third cup was indeed said: "Blessed are you, O God, our eternal King, who has caused its fruit to come forth from the earth, who has made the fruit of the vine." There is thus a double blessing, a blessing of God and a blessing of the sign.

e) The terms mentioned thus far have a scriptural origin. But there are also others: for example, *synaxis*, "bringing together," because the sacrament is administered in the public gathering of the church; *leitourgia*, "ministry," because it constitutes a part of the ministry of what is holy; *thusia*, "offering," in the first period of the church, not because the Lord's Supper was considered to be a repetition of the sacrifice of Christ, but because at the occasion of the celebration one brought an offering of charity through his alms or also gave bread and wine.

The word *mysterium* ["mystery"], which stood for secret, religious ceremonies and for the sacraments in general, was also applied to the Lord's Supper in particular.

Finally, the word "mass" (*missa*), used by the Latins. *Missa* is originally nothing other than the word that was spoken to dismiss the gathering. "After the sermon," Augustine says, "let the catechumens be dismissed; the believers shall remain." These catechumens should not be present for the sacrament and the sacrifice connected to it. After the celebration of the sacrament, the believers were also dismissed, and the minister said: "*Ite, missa est*" ["Go, dismissal is made"]. It is not difficult to see how the word "mass" naturally had to transfer onto the ceremony that was closed by two such "masses" ["sendings"].

We note that the word "communion" is taken from 1 Corinthians 10:16: "The cup of thanksgiving that in giving thanks we bless, is it not fellowship (communion) in the blood of Christ?"

8. *In the first period in the Christian church, what was associated with the Lord's Supper?*

The love feast, the so-called *agape*. This was an ordinary meal at which food was eaten and at the same time witness given to the unity of all believers in the Lord. The Passover meal, the pagan sacrificial meals, had their influence here; also the custom of gathering together in a house of one of the brothers supported this practice. Paul speaks explicitly about these love feasts in 1 Corinthians. Initially they preceded the celebration of the Lord's Supper itself. Later, it appears, it was determined, in order to prevent abuse, that the Lord's Supper must come first and only then the love feast. Indeed, already in Corinth the situation had occurred that people, hungry or drunken from eating the *agape*, proceeded to the celebration of the holy sacrament of the Lord. Paul alludes to this when he says that a man must examine himself before he eats of the bread and drinks of the cup.

9. Where is the institution of the Lord's Supper described for us?

We find it described in the first three Evangelists, Matthew 26, Mark 14, Luke 22, and again separately in the apostle Paul, in 1 Corinthians 11. John speaks of eating the Lord's Supper before the Passover (13:1–2 and following), but not of the institution of the sacrament.

First of all, we observe that the cup of Luke 22:17 is not yet the cup of the Lord's Supper but the cup of the Passover meal, probably the first of the four. Jesus says: "Take this, and distribute it among yourselves. For I tell you that from now on I will not drink of the fruit of the vine until the kingdom of God comes." It has been asked whether the Lord first let the entire Passover meal run its course in order then to replace it with the new institution, or whether He has let the one flow into the other. The latter is certainly the most probable. The Passover meal will have transitioned imperceptibly into the sacrament. In the hands of the Lord, the sacrament of the old dispensation changed, as it were, into the sacrament of the new dispensation. According to Luke (22:20) and Paul (1 Cor 11:25), Jesus took the cup of the Lord's Supper after eating, that is, after eating the Passover meal (μετὰ τὸ δειπνῆσαι). This also involves then that the taking, the breaking, the distributing of the bread, took place during the Passover meal. Now we have seen above how the eating of the Passover meal took place between the second and the third cup. So it will have been the third cup that was taken by Christ and made into the cup of the New Testament; compare also verse 26 in Matthew: "Now as they were eating, Jesus took bread." Thus, that part of the Passover meal that followed the third cup was of itself omitted here.

In the words of institution, as they are given by the three evangelists, agreement in substance prevails, with some differences in form. As to their completeness, more or less, we can maintain that the four complement each other. Concerning the small difference in form, one must bear in mind that in inspiring Scripture, the Spirit of God could render the words of the Lord in various ways, according to what appeared useful to Him, without the meaning really having been changed. When we take everything together, we get: "Take, eat; this is my body, which is given/broken for you. Do this in remembrance of me."

And with the cup: "Drink of it, all of you. For this is my blood, the blood of the new covenant (or This cup is the new covenant in my blood), which is poured out for many/you for the forgiveness of sins. Do this as often as you drink it, in remembrance of me."

It is certain that Paul, too, received the words of the institution of the Lord's Supper, not by tradition but directly by revelation from the Lord, as that was the case with his gospel in general (cf. 1 Cor 11:23; Gal 1:13).

Before the Lord said these things with respect to the bread, He "took," He "thanked," He "broke," He "gave." Matthew says that He took "the bread," the others that He took "bread." The former indicates the unleavened bread that was used in the Passover meal. From the latter, however, we see that this bread was not considered unleavened but ordinary bread. Later the Roman Catholic Church returned to unleavened bread (that is, to the Old Testament).

That Jesus "took" bread means that He set it apart for sacramental use, and indeed for this new sacramental use. The same thing took place by the act of "blessing" (εὐλογήσας, Matthew and Mark), "giving thanks" (εὐχαριστήσας, Luke and Paul). It has already been noted above that giving thanks and blessing are two aspects of the same thing. The prayer of thanks is offered to God, the blessing is meant for the element. In the Passover meal, too, God was thanked and the bread, which He had caused to come from the earth, blessed. Here God is thanked, and the sign and seal of that spiritual bread that derives not from nature but from his dispensation of grace for us, blessed. It is of course not possible to determine what words the Lord spoke in this giving of thanks. That 1 Corinthians 10:16 is used is not to be disparaged, but there Paul does not say to us that the Lord spoke these words with the cup or that He said such words with the bread. The bread thus replaces the Passover lamb as sign and seal. Now that the true lamb was about to be slain, the lamb as a type had to cease. The Passover lamb also had a national significance that recalled the liberation of Israel out of Egypt, but from now on the national aspect in the administration of the covenant of grace disappeared. Bread is ordinary and universal foodstuff found everywhere. One may also note how the Roman Catholic doctrine of transubstantiation and also, in part, the Lutheran doctrine makes this replacement of the lamb by bread inexplicable. If it had had to do with an eating of the Lord's flesh and the blood with the mouth, then the animal flesh of the lamb would have been a much more fitting element than the plant-based food of bread. But in the fact that bread was chosen there is then also, on the contrary, an intimation of how here we have to do with a sign and seal of a higher spiritual eating of faith with the mouth. He "broke" it (cf. Acts 2:42; 1 Cor 10:16). The Jewish father of the household also broke the bread in order to be able to distribute it. But here this breaking has a deeper significance. This is evident: (1) from the fact that all three Evangelists and Paul have: He "broke" it. (2) That Paul says, "The bread that we *break*, is that not the fellowship of the body of Christ?" that is, the breaking of the *one* loaf of bread refers to the fellowship of the saints in the *one* body of Christ. (3) Because it reads: "which *is broken* for you," with respect to the body. The breaking of the bread is thus an essential element of the sacramental act that may not be omitted. It refers to the breaking of the body of Christ in His suffering for our good. And therefore it is to be condemned when the Roman Catholic Church distributes the unbroken wafer. Luther initially held to the necessity of breaking the bread, but subsequently ceased doing that. The Socinians also insist on the breaking of the bread.

He "gave": that, too, belongs to the action. Christ takes the lead with us. First He gives and then we receive. The one who administers the Lord's Supper gives it in Christ's name, to himself too.

Following these four actions, or rather the first three, follow the last accompanying words: "Take, eat." The bread is thus already consecrated bread. It does not first become that by the following words: "This is my body." The Roman Catholics generally maintain that the consecration takes place by the latter words, which then the priest need only murmur to himself softly. The Reformed say that the consecration is not located in these specific words but in the preceding activity as a whole—more specifically, in the giving of thanks or blessing.

Taking is an act that has significance, as does eating. Both are conscious acts, and they picture the conscious exercise of faith. Here we have the imperative mood: "Take, eat." Thus the word of command in the institution of the Lord's Supper. First addressed to the apostles, this word of command comes through them to all the disciples of the Lord as well. But this word of command does not merely have an external sense. That the communicant must take the bread into his hand and into his mouth is something so self-evident that there is no need of a separate command. Rather, implicit in this command is its symbolic sense as well: take with the hand, eat with the mouth of faith. The faith that is required here is a willing faith. One *comes* to the Lord's Supper, certainly in obedience to the command of the Lord, but surely in willing obedience. Actually, at this point the views regarding the Lord's Supper already begin to diverge. The Roman Catholics and the Lutherans act as if it did not say "take, eat," as if faith had nothing to do with the receiving of the spiritual benefits.

The word of command is followed by the word of promise, for here, too, in the sacrament these two must be next to each other: "This is my body." These words have led to conflict among the churches:

a) The view of Carlstadt that by τοῦτο, "this," Jesus would have indicated His body, must naturally be rejected. With τοῦτο nothing else can be meant than the bread, which was spoken about directly before this. Carlstadt appealed to τοῦτο as neuter, which otherwise should have been οὗτος, since ἄρτος is of course masculine. But that was entirely unnecessary. Something like bread can be regarded by us as a thing, neuter. The Lord therefore means: "This thing, this bread, which I have here in my hands, is my body."

b) The Roman Catholic view: "This thing, which possesses the accidents and the outward characteristics of bread, is my body," that is, by transubstantiation it has become my body in its substance. This view is based on or at least is defended by the literal interpretation of the word "is." But if the Lord spoke Aramaic, as then is to be assumed, the copula was completely lacking. The Roman Catholics then also come into difficulty because they cause transubstantiation to take place by these words themselves. But how can that be? In the words by which something should take place, it would at the same time be presupposed that it has already taken place.

c) The Lutheran view: This is less literal than the Roman Catholic view. It acknowledges that it is a figure of speech and not literal language. But when one asks, "What figure of speech?" the answer is given: not a metaphor at any price, so that the words would come to mean "this thing signifies, symbolizes, and seals my body." It must be understood differently, namely, synecdochically. This is my body therefore means: "Where you have this, you have my body. My body is in it, with it, under it." The two are linked in such that the one can stand for the other, synecdochically. Therefore the τοῦτο is also already understood as referring to the real presence of the body of the Lord. The synecdoche exists both in the "this" as well as in the "is," or really even more in the former than in the latter. "What I give you here (with, in, under the bread) is my body." The "is" is taken as just as real as it is by the Roman Catholics; the "this" is understood differently than the Roman Catholics. For the latter, it is only apparently bread. For the Lutherans it is a composite entity, in which bread and Christ's body are present together in a way that is conjoined locally.

The great objection to this is that the apostles would certainly not have grasped such a meaning. Such a synecdoche is not self-evident. When two things belong together naturally and always go together, then a synecdoche is easy to understand and no elucidation is necessary. But that was not the case here. Thus there ought to have been added a specific and extensive explanation if the Lord had wanted to be understood in this way by the apostles. Some then say that a miraculous enlightenment of their understanding by the Holy Spirit also accompanied these words of the Savior. This Lutheran view must also be rejected in its entirety because it is based on the untenable Lutheran Christology and leads to the banal teaching of a *manducatio oralis* ("eating with the mouth"). That teaching is banal; the idea that the body of another would be eaten by our physical mouth is abhorrent. Why would it not be? Must then food for our spiritual life be fed to us by our bodily organs? Such a conception is at home in materialism but not in teaching that clearly distinguishes between soul and body, as Scripture does everywhere.

d) The Reformed view is exegetically the only tenable one: "This thing (the bread) *signifies* my body." That the apostles could understand. By that understanding one is not in the least forced into the Zwinglian view. Nowhere is it determined that we must derive everything that we know regarding the sacrament of the Lord's Supper from that "is." If that were so, then the explanation "signifies" would in fact carry us into the arms of Zwinglianism. But there are other data that teach us that more is connected with this "signifies," about which further presently.

"This is my *body*," says the Lord. *Soma*, "body," is the organic whole, and to that extent the blood is already included. And yet the blood comes separately later under the sign and seal of the wine in the cup. Why does the Lord not say "flesh" (*sarx*)? Apparently because here the emphasis must fall on "broken," "given." Now if "flesh" were said, then we would have before us flesh torn out of its organic context. "Body" causes us to think immediately of the yet-unbroken corpse that is then broken violently. The breaking must be specifically the breaking of something *whole*, not merely a distribution.

In a very striking way the words "broken for you"/ "given for you" in Luke and Paul complement each other. In the one ("broken") is the *manner*, in the other ("given") the *origin* of what is about to happen with the Lord's body. With "broken," one thinks instinctively of Isaiah 53:5, 10. With "given," we think of John 6:51. Neither of these aspects should be lost sight of. First of all, it is a broken body that is signified and sealed. That is, fellowship, by imputation, in the suffering and the suffering merits of Christ occupy first place here. The judicial precedes. To eat and drink Christ means, in the first place, to receive His merits by faith. But that broken body is also "given" to us. He gives it away, gives it away to us, in order that soon we would also truly have fellowship with Him by faith—not just with His merits but also with His person as Mediator, as Mediator become flesh.

In Luke and Paul still follows finally: "Do this in remembrance of me." With "this" is meant this eating (and drinking) of the bread as sign of my body (cf. 1 Cor 11:26–29). The Roman Catholics understand "do this" as spoken to the priests, so that in the institution of the mass the institution of the sacrament of priestly ordination is included, as if it had meant: "As I now bring and effect and hand the sacrifice to you, do likewise, and as priests perform this sacrificial ritual authorized by me for that purpose." The passage does not at all suggest something like this.

The bread must be eaten "in remembrance of me." Thus: in order to remember Him and keep His memory alive. This, however, is not to be understood in the personal sense—that one ought to think about Him as one thinks of a distant friend—for the Lord had already given the promise that He would be where two or three were gathered in His name. It is a meal of remembrance, but a meal of remembrance as the Passover was. There, too, the Israelites were to think back on the liberation out of the house of slavery in order, then, at the same time to enjoy the blessing and nurturing that was opened for them by this liberation. It is like that here. It is obvious that the disciples will have the Lord present with them. But they had to focus their remembrance specifically on the cause of this gracious presence, on the source from which all these spiritual blessings flowed, on the suffering of the Lord. As Christ is present in heaven as glorified Mediator but still His sacrifice brought in humiliation is constantly held in memory through His intercession, so in the faith-consciousness of those who are His this sacrifice must always be the starting point from which their fellowship with Him begins. His glory grew out of His suffering; enjoying the former can only grow out of remembering the latter. Paul therefore also calls this eating and drinking in remembrance of the Lord "a proclaiming of the death of the Lord until he comes." From remembrance flows proclamation. So the Lord wills in fact to have the sacrament viewed as a public, external confession. Still, this comes afterward. It is not the first and only purpose, but only one purpose.

We come now to the *cup*. "Likewise, the cup," both Luke and Paul say. This is a strong reason over against all wishes to have the Lord's Supper celebrated *sub una specie* [under one kind], as Rome does. Implicit here is that the same thing was done by Jesus with the cup that occurred first with the bread: "take," "give thanks," "bless," "give." In Matthew and Mark the giving of thanks is also stated. However, it is not also said explicitly that Jesus poured out or poured the wine into the cup. And yet the analogy with the broken bread, upon which so much emphasis was put, causes us to expect that. One should be careful to note, however, that subsequently it is said not of the wine (the sign) but of the blood (the thing signified) that it is poured-out blood. Luke even says with a distinctive construction: "This cup ... that is shed for you." Although one cannot now say that as the bread ought to be broken, so also the wine ought to be poured out before the eyes of all, still as much should be retained such that the flowing of the wine, in drinking, is a sign and a seal of the bloodshed of our Lord. The distinction here is in the fact that the bread in itself does not yet recall the breaking of the body, and therefore must still be broken deliberately; the wine, in contrast, already by its particular appearance recalls the breaking, so that being poured out visibly is no longer necessary.

Why the double sign of bread and cup next to each other? Various answers have been given: to supplement the idea of sustenance with that of refreshment; to show, along with sustenance, the enhancement of life. As bread sustains life, so wine elevates life since it makes the heart of man glad [Psa 104:15]. The principal reason, however, resides in this: The separating of flesh and blood, of bread and wine, places before our eyes, in the most vivid way, how we have to do here with a suffering, crucified Savior. It has been noted that in the Old Testament the drinking of wine was missing, not only at the Passover meal but at all sacrificial meals. In contrast, pagans drank wine at such occasions.

Which wine is meant? Red or white? Mixed or unmixed? In Palestine wine is usually red, and it would have been red wine that Jesus took from the Passover table. But this is not essential, and nowhere are we told with even one word that it must be red wine. The latter surely portrays the blood better than white wine. According to later sources, mixing of water with the wine was prescribed for Passover, and soon a symbolic meaning was sought in this. It referred, it was said, to the union between Christ and His own. They were the water, and He was the wine, and the two were mixed together as one (Cyprian). Others find here a symbol of the union between the divine and the human natures of the Mediator. Both the Roman Catholic Church and the Greek [Orthodox] Church mix wine with water. Against this practice: (a) It is very uncertain that at that time the wine of the Passover meal was mixed with water. (b) If it did happen and were of significance, it would have been explicitly mentioned, as with the breaking of the bread.

"Drink of it, all of you" (Matt). "And they all drank of it" (Mark). Calvin rightly observed that these words seem to condemn in advance the error of the Roman Catholics. They all must drink of the cup. With the command to take bread and eat it, this "all of you" is lacking. This omission here must have its special significance. Some say: Jesus did not say "all of you" with the bread because He wanted to give Judas a cue to refrain from eating or to withdraw, and now that he had nonetheless taken the bread, he also had to take the wine, to his judgment. It is not impossible that there is this consideration for Judas. From John's Gospel one could draw the conclusion that Judas left before the celebration of the Lord's Supper. But the words of Luke (22:21) are decisive in this regard. Judas did partake of the Lord's Supper (so also Calvin and many Reformed interpreters). It is natural to find in this a proof that, in admitting or refusing to admit to the Supper, those who administer the Lord's Supper in Christ's name must not act according to a subjective criterion but according to an objective criterion. The subjective criterion that Jesus had was infallible, for His divine omniscience showed Him clearly who Judas was. Still, He did not unmask Judas before but after the Lord's Supper, and in a completely objective manner treated him as an apostle among the apostles. This is something, however, from which in no sense does it follow that someone should gain confidence from Judas's behavior to go and sit at the table of the Lord with unconfessed and unforgiven sins in his heart.

For Roman Catholics, the *communio sub una specie* (withholding the chalice from the laity) is consistent with the doctrine of transubstantiation. The Council of Constance issued this highly remarkable declaration: "Although Christ instituted it after the meal and administered this venerable sacrament to His disciples under the double signs of bread and wine, nonetheless the authority of the holy Canons ... has established that such a sacrament ought not to be celebrated after the meal, and ought not to be received by believers who have previously eaten." Only the celebrant priest takes the chalice; the rest of the priests and the laity receive the wafer. In a few cases the Church makes exceptions to its rule, such as for civil rulers, cardinals, etc.

Exegetically, Rome appeals to 1 Corinthians 11:27, "So, then, whoever eats this bread *or* drinks the cup of the Lord in an unworthy manner will be guilty concerning the body and blood of the Lord." Here, then, "or" is understood disjunctively and viewed as proof that in the apostolic church communion under one sign occurred—wrongly. What is spoken of here is not the use of one element but an unworthy manner of use that need happen even for only one element to make someone guilty. By the Roman Catholic separation the meaning of the sacrament is lost. If drinking is not added to eating, the breaking of the body of the Lord does not come to light; our nourishment is not complete.

The words of the promise with respect to the cup are: "This is my blood, that of the new covenant, which is shed for many for the forgiveness of sins" (Matthew, Mark). "This cup is the new covenant in my blood, which is shed for you" (Luke and Paul). In treating the doctrine of the covenant it has already been pointed out what these expressions recall. The blood of the new covenant points back to the blood of the old covenant (Exod 29). The latter was covenant blood as a type; the former is the real covenant blood. The making of the covenant with Israel was, as it were, by these two facts: the slaughtering of the Passover lamb and the formal, solemn confirmation of the covenant with accompanying sacrifices. The wine in the cup *is* this blood of the new covenant. The "this" can again not refer to anything else but the *wine*. When Luke and Paul say "this cup," the content of the cup is meant, that which is to be drunk, as Scripture speaks elsewhere of the drinking of a cup. Here "is" also means "signifies." But at the same time implied here is that the wine, as sign and seal of the covenant blood, from now on takes the place of all the typical sacrifices that followed one after the other under the old dispensation. Here is the end of ceremonial service. The covenant will not be made again with sacrifices but with bread and wine.

Had not this blood that was portrayed by the wine also been the blood of the old covenant? Had it not taken away sin throughout all the centuries, even before it was shed? Without doubt. And still here the Lord calls it the "blood of the new covenant." Thus it occurs here in the specific sense as it only occurs in the new and not in the old dispensation, namely, as actually shed, with all then that is further connected with it. The wine did not portray blood that still had to be shed but blood that was already shed. Indeed, the institution of the sacrament here was anticipatory, pointed ahead, looked to the time when Christ would have suffered. While the blood of Christ had exercised its retrospective power from the beginning of time and had brought about the redemption and the justification of the pious, it began now to work in a more glorious and powerful way now that it was actually shed. Now came the removal of the dividing wall between Israel and the Gentiles; now came the outpouring of the Spirit. The bloodshed of the Mediator marked the dividing line between old and new covenants. As shed blood, His blood could thus be called preeminently the blood of the new covenant. The Form for the Lord's Supper: "Finally, by His death and the shedding of His blood, the new and eternal testament, the covenant of grace and reconciliation was settled, when He said, 'It is finished.'"

Luke and Paul have: the cup is the new covenant by means of his blood. The blood is, in general, as blood of the Mediator, the essence of the covenant of grace. In that the covenant of grace has its validation, its stability. Only in this blood can God and man come together and live together. The blood is, in particular, as shed blood, the essence and the validation of the New Testament dispensation of the covenant of grace. All that is specific to the New Testament dispensation derives from this blood. Thus both things can be said: the cup was the covenant of grace through the means of the blood, and the cup was the new covenant (= the New Testament dispensation of the covenant of grace) by means of the blood. Here the emphasis is on the latter, but at the same time the former is included in it.

This blood was "shed for many/for you for the forgiveness of sins." As with the bread, this also points ahead. There it was: "my body that is given/broken." It is no longer blood that is about to be shed, but the shedding is now present. "For you" means "on your behalf," "for your benefit" (ὑπέρ, Luke; περί, Matt and Mark). One should pay attention to "for many," "for you." Not, then, for *all*. There is evidently a restriction. But for all who appear at the table, the Lord here says, "for you." For they come there as those who seek their salvation in Christ as His disciples. And for all of these He has shed His blood. Even with Judas there is no intention here to exclude him from it. The Lord says in general: for you. In "for many" there is without doubt a reminder of the wide scope that the administering of God's covenant of grace would take in the new age in contrast to the national particularism of the old dispensation.

"For the forgiveness of sins" (Matt). This is not to be understood as if there were no forgiveness in the old dispensation. Here the primary benefit of the covenant of grace is placed in the foreground, as that belongs to the essence of the covenant of grace (cf. Jer 31:33-34: "But this is the covenant. ... For I will forgive their iniquity, and I will remember their sin no more"). One can ascertain a difference here between the old and the new dispensation only to the extent that in the former a reminder of sin takes place again and again (Heb 10:3), and now God makes the promise that He will no longer remember sins at all, will also no longer remember them through sacrifices (cf. Heb 8:12-13).

Finally, in Paul we still have: "Do this as often as you drink it, in remembrance of me." By this the institution of the Lord's Supper is shown to be an institution that is for all times—not for that one meal, but for the future as a whole, "until He comes" (1 Cor 11:26). "As often as" clearly presupposes that it will not occur infrequently, although there is no express stipulation how often it should take place. In this there is latitude.

10. *How can you briefly show what is included in these words of institution?*

a) In the Lord's Supper there is a signifying of the suffering and death of the Lord (the "broken body" and "shed blood").

b) This suffering and death appears here as the foundation of the covenant of grace ("the new covenant in my blood").

c) At the same time, however, this signifying is also a sealing of the covenant of grace on the side of God ("for you").

d) At the same time there is consent here on the side of the believer, by which he again and again enters into the renewal of the covenant ("take," "eat," "do that," "drink of it all of you").

e) At the same time this covenantal fellowship is also a public profession of the Lord, a proclamation of His death, a remembrance of what He has done for His own ("do this in remembrance of me"; "proclaim the death of the Lord until He comes").

f) At the same time the exercise of this covenantal fellowship has as its purpose the nourishing of the spiritual life of believers. The sacramental covenantal action is also a meal. This resides in the fact that the Lord has given the bread and the cup. As one prays for the blessing of God on earthly food before eating it in order that it may serve the purpose for which He has ordained it, so, too, in connection with this sacramental food it is blessed and blessing prayed for.

11. *What questions should be discussed further in relation to the Lord's Supper?*

a) In what sense are the body and blood of Christ received in the Lord's Supper?

b) What are the major departures from scriptural teaching on this point?

c) Who ought to come to the Supper of the Lord?

d) How is the Roman Catholic mass to be adjudged?

12. *Give an elucidation of the first question.*

We have already seen how the signs of bread and wine in the Lord's Supper set before our eyes the Mediator as suffering and dead. We have also seen that taking and eating are simply scriptural expressions for believing. Thus in the Lord's Supper our faith is directed to the suffering and dead Mediator. And to eat His body and to drink His blood would be nothing else than to appropriate in faith the merits of His suffering and His dying. That, then, has in view fellowship in being right with God. It is to the grace of justification that the Lord's Supper points as a means of grace. This grace is sealed to us, and our faith, which takes possession of this, should be strengthened.

Without doubt, this is the purpose of the Lord's Supper. The fact that here Christ appears before our eyes under the signs of broken bread and poured wine is already sufficient to show that. The question is only whether one can stop with this consideration. Or is there more that takes place in this sacrament than such an application of the merits of Christ by faith? If now, for the time being, we leave aside Roman Catholic and Lutheran teaching, then it appears to us that in the Reformed church itself there has been an effort to give a still deeper sense to the sacrament of the Lord's Supper. We will (a) highlight historically which views have been formed in this regard; and (b) inquire after the scriptural grounds on which this view is based.

13. *Who among the Reformed took the least mystical viewpoint with respect to the Lord's Supper?*

The Reformer Zwingli. He said: "To eat the body of Christ spiritually is nothing other than with our spirit and our understanding to trust in the goodness and the grace of God through Christ." What distinguishes this view consists of two things: (a) The eating is solely an eating of faith; that is, it is done by an exercise of conscious faith. (b) It is an eating, not so much in an exercise of mystical fellowship with the living Christ, as an eating that consists in looking to the saving events of the suffering and the death of the Lord.

14. *Did Calvin also remain committed to this point of view?*

No, he went further than Zwingli. Our fellowship with Christ is not only a fellowship with His merits by imputation; it is a fellowship of life through the action of the Spirit of Christ. Where this is once established, it must necessarily follow that bread and wine are not simply signs of what Christ has done in His person, but at the same time are signs of what Christ is for us now as the living Mediator who still possesses our nature. Our eating and drinking, then, is also more than an exercise of justifying faith; it is a sign of the mystical fellowship of life that we as members of His body have with Christ, the Head. Calvin says [*Institutes*, 4.17.10]: "We conclude that our souls are fed by Christ's flesh and blood, just as bread and wine feed and sustain physical life. For the sign would not correspond with the thing signified if souls did not find their nourishment in Christ. ... And although it seems unbelievable that the flesh of Christ should penetrate to us through such a great distance to become food for us, let us bear in mind how far the secret power of the Holy Spirit extends beyond all our awareness ... since He (Christ) pours his life into us, just as if it penetrated into our bones and marrow. ... The thing signified is offered and presented there by Him to all who ... sit ..., although it is received with benefit only by believers." This is substantiated with an appeal to 1 Corinthians 10:16.

Further, Calvin distinguishes between: (1) the physical signs; (2) the spiritual truth. To explain what the spiritual truth is, he says, attention must be given: (a) to the meaning; (b) to the substance or matter; (c) to the power or fruit that follows from both.

The meaning resides in the promises, which are entwined to some degree in the sign. The substance is Christ, with His death and resurrection. The fruit consists of redemption, justification, sanctification and eternal life—in brief, all the benefits. Further, it is expressly said that to receive Christ by faith is not solely to receive Him by the intellect and the imagination. For, says Calvin, redemption and justification are only to be obtained by true fellowship with Christ.

The starting point for Calvin is no different than for Zwingli. We only eat Christ properly, then, when we eat Him as crucified and lay hold of the power of His death by an animated sense. It must begin with a conscious exercise of faith. But it does not remain there. Both from the side of Christ and from our side in appropriation, there is something more. *From the side of Christ*: Christ, as a living Mediator, has in Himself the power of His death and the resurrection as something eternal and immortal. He is not a dead Christ, but a living Christ who was dead. As exalted Mediator, He has at His disposal the fruits that have grown from His suffering. *From our side*: We not only have fellowship with Christ through the conscious life of faith but also in a mystical way. The others (Zwinglians) say: the eating amounts to believing. Calvin says: one eats Christ's flesh by believing, and such eating is a fruit and effect of faith; it is a result of faith, not faith itself. Thus it is not an eating with the mouth but in fact an eating of faith—an eating, however, such that it is not only a judicial application of conscious appropriation, but also effects a mystical bond with Christ.

The question now arises: How did Calvin think of this real communion with the flesh and blood of Christ? He says [*Institutes*, 4.17.9]: it is more than sharing in His Spirit. As the Logos, Christ is already the fountain and origin of life. Additionally, by His incarnation He has become the fountain of life in a new sense. After His resurrection, the flesh, the human nature of Christ, is saturated with the fullness of life. That means, John 5:26, "He has given to the Son also to have life in Himself." Ephesians 1:23; 4:15; and 1 Corinthians 6:15 are also cited.

Still, the Spirit has a work to do here. It is not necessary that the flesh of Christ descend from heaven to us. The power of the Spirit overcomes all barriers. This is a mystery. How can flesh become life to our spirit? The power of the flesh and blood of Christ is applied to us by the Holy Spirit. In a certain sense it is a miracle.

This conception of Calvin is found most clearly in the French Confession, the Belgic Confession, and the Scotch Confession. Our [Belgic] Confession says (article 35): "In order to assure us that, as certainly as we receive and hold this sacrament in our hands and eat and drink the same with our mouths, by which our life is afterwards nourished, we also do as certainly receive by faith (which is the hand and mouth of our soul) the true body and blood of Christ our only Savior in our souls, for our spiritual life. ... In the meantime we do not err when we say that what is eaten and drunk by us is the proper and natural body and proper blood of Christ. But the manner in which we partake of the same is not by the mouth but the spirit through faith."

Our [Heidelberg] Catechism speaks less forcefully, but maintains the same principle. See questions 75 and 76. In both, two things are clearly distinguished and placed side by side: (a) the appropriation of the merits of Christ by faith; (b) the imparting of the fellowship of life and union with Christ through the Holy Spirit.

15. *What were the scriptural grounds upon which this teaching was built?*

The principal ground was found in what the Lord says in John 6:53–58: "Unless you eat the flesh of the Son of Man and drink His blood, you have no life in you" [v. 53]. "For my flesh is true food, and my blood is true drink" [v. 55]. And verse 51, "And the bread that I will give is my flesh, which I will give for the life of the world." It may be asked, What is meant by all these expressions? When Jesus spoke in this way, was He thinking specifically of the mystery of the Lord's Supper, or did He speak in a entirely general way?

Over time this question has been given very different answers, and there are almost as many views of these words as there are explanations of the words of institution of the Lord's Supper. The majority has answered: Christ is not speaking here of the Lord's Supper (so many church fathers, Luther, Calvin, and the Formula of Concord). The latter says that only a *spiritualis manducatio*, a spiritual eating, is spoken of here; and the Lutherans maintained, as is known, that in the Lord's Supper there is more, a *oralis manducatio*, an eating with the mouth, with the physical mouth. "There is, therefore, a twofold eating of Christ. The one is spiritual, of which Christ treats primarily in the Gospel of John, chapter 6, which does not otherwise occur than in the Spirit and through the gospel" [Formula of Concord, Solid Declaration 7, paragraph 61]. It is not difficult to point out what underlies this Lutheran polemic against the exegesis that understands John 6 of the Lord's Supper. It then emerges too clearly here that it could not be denied how eating Jesus's flesh and blood takes place only by faith. And the Lutherans do not want that; Luther did not want that. Unbelievers also eat Christ's flesh and blood with the physical mouth. Therefore here in John 6 something else must be meant, namely, spiritual eating, which is only attributed to believers. This is certainly a remarkable phenomenon; realistic robustness that on the one hand thinks that on the issue of the Lord's Supper it must insist on the most literal sense of every syllable and that here, on the other hand, explains the much stronger expressions—eating of flesh and drinking of blood—in a completely spiritual way of appropriation by faith.

Along with those who will not think of the Lord's Supper in any respect here are also those who understand the words exclusively of the Lord's Supper. That is another extreme that Calvin already contested—against, it seems, some Lutherans of his time (*Institutes*, 4.17.7). The words sound completely general, and nothing necessitates us to think specifically of the sacrament. Calvin says correctly [*Commentary on John 6:54*]: Christ speaks of the perpetual eating of faith. But he adds: "At the same time, however, I agree that nothing is said here that is not signified in the Lord's Supper and truly imparted to believers. Therefore Christ has willed that the holy Supper be a seal, as it were, on this preaching. And this is the reason why in John there is no mention of the Lord's Supper. And therefore Augustine follows the right order, when, in explaining this chapter, he does not mention the Lord's Supper until he comes to the conclusion. For there he teaches that this mystery is represented in a symbol as often as the churches celebrate the holy Supper."

Now one could ask whether Calvin has sought in the Lord's Supper something else than is in John 6. Is there an eating in the Supper that is essentially different from this continual eating of faith? The answer must be in the negative. In John 6, too, Calvin already sees more than the conscious appropriation of the benefits of Christ by faith. He distinguishes eating and believing. While he emphasizes that eating is impossible without faith (against the Lutherans), on the other hand he does not wish to identify the two. He says, "What some deduce from this passage, namely, that believing in Christ is the same as the eating of Christ or of His flesh, does not have a sufficiently firm basis. For these two things differ from each other as what precedes and what follows, as coming to Christ and drinking of Him differ, for coming to Him is prior. I acknowledge that Christ cannot be eaten other than by faith; but the reason is because we receive Him by faith that He may dwell in us, and that we may be partakers of Him, and so may be one with Him. The eating, therefore, is a fruit or work of faith" (*Commentary* on John 6:47).

Still, Calvin does not think that the Lord's Supper is in view here. The matter is the same, but the meaning was not directed to it.

The reason he gives is that the Lord's Supper was not yet instituted, and that it would have been uncalled for to speak of something that did not yet exist. But, in our view, this does not show that our Savior Himself was not thinking of the Lord's Supper. More can be resident in His words than His listeners understood of them. But also, apart from that, one should ask whether the thought of partaking of flesh and blood really lay so far outside their comprehension that every allusion to it had to be unintelligible to them. Some have rightly made reference to the sacrificial meals. At them there was at least an eating of flesh, and in this eating of flesh there was religious fellowship. The Jews could have thought of that. That they did not think of it lay in their blindness to the deeper meaning of the Old Testament sacrament and the Old Testament sacrifices in general, and in their blindness to the significance of the Messiah as sacrificial lamb and food for the soul. It is true, "the drinking of the blood" must have sounded strange in their ears. That was something unheard of in the Jewish sacrifices.

When now we look further at the words closely, then it is apparent that there is more than one point of similarity. Christ is speaking specifically of a bread that He *will* give, and that is His flesh. That refers to something in the future, and causes us to think of the words of the institution of the Lord's Supper, "which is given for you," which has already been discussed in brief above. For that one can think of more than one "giving": (1) A giving of sacrifices to God. The sacrifice was a giving, an offering up of self that happened willingly and derived its value from that willingness. (2) A giving of the presentation and offering in the word of the gospel, to which conscious faith responds. In this sense Christ gives Himself and imparts Himself to His disciples, as He also said at the institution of the Lord's Supper: "Take, eat, drink, this is my body, my blood." (3) A giving of impartation when He by His Holy Spirit actually becomes the spiritual life of believers. Here we are to think especially of the first giving, nevertheless such that the other two are connected as following directly from it. Although Christ had said "I *am* the bread of life" and speaks throughout this entire pericope in the present tense (cf. vv. 47–48, 50–51), still in this "*will give*" there is also a reference to the future. Although being the bread of life already, He would become that in a still deeper and special sense by giving Himself as living bread. That referred to His suffering, His death, and His glorification. And with that the institution of the Lord's Supper was also connected, as we have already seen. Therefore we may say: The Lord speaks here in John 6 not *only* of a general sense in which He, as Mediator, is the source of life for believers, but He also speaks specifically of the sense in which He, as glorified Mediator, whose sacrifice *has been* brought, becomes a source of life for believers who are members of His mystical body. And because that was about to happen shortly and was at hand, He also instituted the Lord's Supper on the night before His suffering. Both John 6 and the institution of the Lord's Supper point to this one truth.

With this is also given the viewpoint from which the rest of the passage should be explained. One may focus one's attention on the following points:

a) That the Savior can be our food and drink in a spiritual sense is connected with His incarnation. Hence the repeated speaking of "coming from heaven," "eating of flesh and drinking of blood."

b) This, however, is not to be understood as if, with the incarnation as such, our salvation was achieved in principle and eternal life guaranteed to us. The incarnation is necessary, but more is necessary. Here, as well as in the institution of the Lord's Supper, it is a matter of what is given, the broken flesh. This also comes out clearly here in that the Savior speaks separately of flesh and blood. He speaks not only of His body but of His mangled body. The question why the Savior speaks in the Lord's Supper of the "body," here of the "flesh," does not have to be discussed and decided here.

c) Christ as incarnate and as sacrificed Mediator is thus the spiritual food of believers. And the eating of Him as such must always proceed from faith. That is clear in verse 47: "Truly, truly, I say to you, whoever believes in me has eternal life." The point of contact in us thus always resides in faith. And that faith must begin where the giving of Christ begins—that is, with His suffering and death. That is what comes first in our eating and drinking of Christ, that in faith we appropriate His merits to ourselves.

d) We believe with Calvin, however, that more is meant here than a conscious exercise of faith. There are three points on which one must fix one's attention in order to see this: (1) Christ says not only that He is the bread of life but also that He is the living Bread

(vv. 48, 51). (2) He speaks of a mystical fellowship of life resulting from this eating and drinking. "The one who eats my flesh
and drinks my blood abides in me, and I in him" (v. 56). (3) That
the Lord speaks of something very real is apparent from verse
57: "As the Father has sent me, and I live because of the Father,
likewise the one who feeds on me will also live because of me."
And verse 54, "The one who eats my flesh and drinks my blood has
eternal life, and I will raise him up on the last day."

From this it is apparent, it seems to us, how the Lord refers to a mysterious fellowship of life that, viewed from our side, proceeds from faith
and cannot exist apart from faith, but that viewed from the Lord's side
must certainly have a still-deeper origin. Christ is the living bread that
works upon us in an enlivening fashion, and in and with our believing
gives itself to us so that nourishing power flows into the depths of our
spiritual life. While we are in Him through our faith, He is in us and
works in us through His Holy Spirit. As the Father had given it to Him
to have life in Himself, so He wills to grant us life. And what He gives is
eternal life, which no longer can die and must so completely transform
and permeate our entire dead and corrupt nature that on the last day
even the resurrection of the dead must follow as a consequent fruit.

One sees that these expressions are too strong to find a place in the
Zwinglian conception. And without doubt we will thus have to acknowledge that there is something mysterious here, that mystical union with
Christ is spoken of, and also that the Lord's Supper is associated with it.
But how is that mysterious nature to be formulated? We cannot do that;
for if we could, it would have ceased to be a mystery. Read what Calvin
says in this regard (*Institutes*, 4.17.7)—golden words in which emphasis
is put on both the reality of the mystery and its incomprehensibility.
One can say one thing or another about it only negatively.

We observe:

a) That faith does not focus on the Mediator as a historical person
   out of the past who suffered and died more than 19 centuries
   ago now, but on the living Christ as He still exists in our human
   nature. That has been already set forth in the discussion about
   faith. Thus, when our faith is focused on the flesh and blood
   given, then it certainly sees them in Christ as He now possesses the merits of His obedience. Our faith has to do with a living

person in whom the powers and the fruits of historical facts are present, not with a historical fact in itself. That is too much lost sight of; and when losing sight of that, one presents the eating and the drinking only as living back into that historical fact, then one ends up inevitably in the Zwinglian view. Conversely, when it comes out clearly that there cannot and may not be any fellowship of faith in the suffering and death of Christ other than that focused on Him as a now-present and now-living Mediator, then one will see immediately that it cannot remain a spiritual fellowship in thought—that it must be a genuine fellowship of life.

b) That nevertheless faith in itself does not possess the power to grant us this real fellowship with Christ. That, too, has already been pointed out. The action here must come not from us but from Christ. The only thing that matters is that one distinguishes carefully and clearly. The Lord has bound our fellowship with Him to the exercise of faith. For us there is no other means to enter this fellowship or to be led deeper into it for our conscious life than the exercise of faith. Every other means is for us useless and illegitimate. And that applies both for the Word and for the sacrament. Viewed from our side, then, faith is in fact the access to eating, in principle the eating itself. Whoever does not have faith cannot eat; and to the same degree that someone has faith, he eats and drinks. But there is another aspect to the matter. We can no more bring about the life of Christ in us by our progress in believing than we can draw Christ to ourselves by faith at the beginning of our believing. In both cases it is Christ Himself who first binds Himself to us by His Holy Spirit, and only then from our side the bond of faith with Christ follows. In regeneration Christ bestows faith and, thus wrought, we believe. Similarly in the ongoing life of faith: by His Holy Spirit Christ maintains the fellowship of life between Himself and all His members, and because He does that, we exercise faith. So, our faith is both the means by which we appropriate that life for ourselves as well as the fruit of the bestowal of that life by Christ.

c) Therefore, the eating and the drinking of Christ in fact has a twofold sense: (1) It is partaking in and obtaining His merits by faith.

(2) It is having fellowship with Him and obtaining more and more the life that is in Him.

However, one may not place these two next to each other loosely. The beautiful thing is just that in the institution of the Lord's Supper and in John 6, they are connected so intimately. Both proceed from the breaking of the bread, the separation of flesh and blood, the giving of life. And both lead on from there to fellowship with the living Christ. From our side, then, there is first an activity with the living Mediator under the aspect of a high priest who has made sacrifice. By this activity of faith a bond with Christ originates, and from this bond with Christ there flows a more assured appropriation of the merits of the Mediator. The one leads of itself to the other. One can distinguish here, but one may not separate. The believer knows that he is in a bond of life with Christ, and by the awareness of this he is strengthened in the conviction that he partakes in all the benefits that are found in Christ. Mystical union is not the judicial ground, but is certainly the means of impressing deeply within the soul the thought that the only judicial ground for our life and our salvation resides in Christ (Calvin, *Institutes*, 4.17.2).

d) One should not think that this fellowship with Christ is only granted in the Lord's Supper. It is a constant for believers that can never cease. The Holy Spirit does not withdraw entirely. Where He has once taken up His abode, He always keeps those who believe in Christ united with Him. Nor may one think that fellowship with Christ is tied to the sacrament in distinction from the Word. However the gospel of Christ comes to us, whether in Word or sacrament, it always still remains the means ordained by God for fellowship with the living Christ. Here too emphasis must be placed on the fact that the sacrament does not give any more than the Word, and the Word does not give more than the sacrament. They both give the full, whole Christ. The eating and the drinking can thus take place both apart from and in the Lord's Supper. But this does not give us any right to spurn the institution of Christ. He has clearly willed that along these two paths fellowship with Him would be established and maintained.

Not making use of the sacrament must impoverish spiritual life and cause it to deteriorate.

e) Eating and drinking are not constant activities, but take place only now and then. As it is in our natural life, so it is in our spiritual life. The fellowship of life with Christ is certainly never broken off completely, but there are still times in which it is especially strengthened. This happens through the means of grace. With the faithful use of them Christ wills to do for our spiritual life what happens for our natural life by eating and drinking. Something certainly occurs with the faithful use of the means of grace that continues to be at work in the future. It is not only that for a moment our conscious faith is strengthened and we feel that the quality of our life is elevated, but it is also the case that the wellspring of life is provided with new water by which the stream of faith can subsequently continue flowing. As one does not eat and drink for the sake of a momentary enjoyment of food and drink, so we do not go to the Lord's Supper to be refreshed and comforted for a single moment but in order to obtain something on which one can feed and from which we can continuously draw strength. And as God has established a certain order and regularity in our natural life, so too in the sound spiritual life there will have to be a regular and ordered use of the means of grace that have been given us by God.

f) Thus far everything is clear and all Reformed theologians essentially agree. But now there comes a point about which complete unanimity does not prevail, and regarding which Calvin has gone further than anyone else. Calvin, then, teaches that there is not only a mystical union and that in the Lord's Supper that union is maintained, strengthened, and nurtured by the Holy Spirit, but he has also endeavored to state more precisely how that is effected. He has presented this from two angles: Sometimes he speaks of an *emanation* of the power that is in the body of Christ on believers observing the Lord's Supper; sometimes he speaks of an *elevation* of believers to Christ in heaven, where the glorified body of Christ is, by faith. Genevan Catechism, 166[1]: "I do

---

1   Quoted from questions and answers 353–355.

not doubt that Christ makes us partakers of His substance, as is attested in the words and signs. ... Since the body of Christ is in heaven, ... He accomplishes this by the marvelous power of His Spirit. ... We must raise our minds to heaven, where Christ is, ... in these earthly elements He is sought in vain." Here the second and the first conceptions are joined.

The first conception is found in *Institutes*, 4.17.18, "as if He were present with them with His body ... so that He clearly feeds them with His own body, the fellowship of which He pours into them by the power of His Spirit. In this manner, the body and blood of Christ are given and imparted to us in the sacrament." In the Confessions, too, this conception has not remained entirely without resonance. Belgic Confession, article 35: "On the other hand, we do not err when we say that what is eaten and drunk by us is the proper and natural body and the proper blood of Christ. But the manner in which we partake of the same is not by mouth but by spirit through faith" (cf. French Confession, article 36).

Above all, one should make clear what is contained in this conception. According to it, there is a real communion with the flesh and blood of Christ. The spatial distance that there is between us and that body of Christ is filled in by the ubiquitous Holy Spirit. Not just Christ the God-man, the Mediator, but specifically the human nature of Christ exercises a mysterious activity upon us. There is a receiving, certainly not of the substance in a material sense, but nonetheless of the power of the substance of the body of Christ.

All Reformed theologians agree that in the expressions "This *is* my body"; "This *is* my blood," there is a trope in the copula. "Is" equals "means and seals." But some of them think that there is still another trope in the predicate, that "my body" and "my blood" intend to say as much as: communion with me, the sacrificed Savior. But Calvin chose to understand these words literally and not to discover a trope in the predicate. He insists on body and blood, and on true communion with them. Without doubt, on this point he stood closer to Luther than the other Reformed theologians. He held to a spiritual eating of a material thing.

The question now is, How is this distinctive view of Calvin to be judged? Does Scripture lead us to follow him as far as he has gone? To begin, we observe that of the two conceptions just mentioned, apparently only the one can be taken literally. When it is said that by faith we are elevated to heaven, where the body of Christ is, then this can only be a figurative use of language. Faith is something spiritual, and as such cannot effect a spatial movement. It cannot bring us near to the glorified Christ in a spatial sense as far as His body is concerned. It is otherwise with the other conception. No one who is appropriately humble and has a sense of mystery will presume to claim that by His omnipotent activity the Holy Spirit is unable to bring to us the power that radiates from Christ's glorified body. That this is incomprehensible is beside the point here. Calvin observes correctly against this objection that we may not choose to measure the immeasurable greatness of the power of the Holy Spirit according to the measure of our understanding.

But there is another objection against the view of Calvin. If it is based on anything, then it must be on the literal explanation of the expressions "eating flesh," "drinking blood." Now, it is more than likely that in both the institution and John 6, these expressions refer to a real communion with the human nature of the Mediator, but nonetheless are to be understood symbolically to the extent they represent this human nature as flesh and blood, as corporeality. Surely, if the broken body and the shed blood stand for the suffering of the Mediator, then in that there is already a synecdoche. This suffering had a broader scope than the breaking of the Lord's body and the shedding of His blood. Suffering in His soul was a primary part of it. The entire human nature of the Lord suffered, according to His soul as well as according to His body. And still that is represented by the sign and seal that points directly only to the bodily suffering. It is broken body and shed blood. But without doubt the reason for this inadequate representation is the following: Only the body can be shown under a sacramental action with a sensory image. When one speaks of a break-up of the soul or of a melting of the soul, then surely it is still always in bodily images. And where one must speak of something that occurred with HIs humanity as a whole, must speak using visible symbols, there that symbolic language is naturally connected with the visible, sensory side of human nature: flesh and blood. There not the suffering of the soul, but the suffering of the body is chosen as the starting point. Expressed still more generally: Since the sacraments are intended for our sense of sight, they are tied to that part of the thing signified that falls within our sense of sight—thus here on what has happened with flesh and blood. What distinguishes the appropriation of the sacrament also leads to the same thing. This happens in the Lord's Supper by eating and drinking. But one can in fact only eat and drink something material. Hence the sign in the Lord's Supper, in order to be of one part, must represent the body and the blood and not the soul.

Thus by a careful consideration we see how a figurative element is latent in this "my body" and "my blood." Flesh and blood signifies not only what has occurred in that flesh and blood but also all that that has occurred in the human nature of which flesh and blood form the outward, visible side. If we confine ourselves first to judicial fellowship with the merits of Christ by faith, then we obtain: "This is" means "this signifies" (first trope: metaphor). "My body," "my blood" means what has occurred in my body and blood (second trope: metonymy). "My body, which is broken for you," "my blood, which is shed for you" means all my suffering that I have endured in my human nature and of which the breaking of my body and the shedding of my blood is the visible indication (third trope: synecdoche). "Eat," "drink," means "appropriate for yourselves the merits of this suffering in faith" (fourth trope: metaphor).

If we now give attention to the fellowship of life with the glorified Christ, about which we established that it takes place in the Lord's Supper: here, too, "this is" means "this signifies." Here, according to Calvin, "my body" and "my blood," "which is given for you" mean, without any figurative meaning, "my glorified corporeality." "Eat" and "drink" mean "appropriate for yourselves the power of this glorified corporeality by faith."

One sees where the weak point is here. Flesh and blood are taken too literally, as if they must signify the flesh-matter and blood-matter substantially, materially, and did not stand for human nature in general. This cannot be. To have fellowship with the glorified human nature can be represented sacramentally by eating something that signifies a body and drinking something that signifies blood. But no one may conclude from this that this fellowship with the glorified Mediator was in the first place a fellowship with His body and blood. No more would one be able to maintain that fellowship by imputation with His suffering was in the first place fellowship only with His bodily suffering. But in His suffering we include the soul as well. So here, too. Eating the body and drinking the blood of the Lord are expressions that one should not force. Without doubt they have a reality as their basis, but that reality can be none other than the mystical fellowship of life, which believers also enjoy in the Lord's Supper, based on the full human nature of the Lord. There is a fellowship with the Lord as possessing human nature, a fellowship of mystical life through the Holy Spirit, and not solely a fellowship of conscious faith. It is a fellowship that must be of such a nature that it would not be possible without the incarnation (becoming man) of the Mediator, and that to that extent also is certainly bound up with and based on the bodily, material part of the human nature of the Lord. But still, as well, it in no way terminates in the latter. Flesh and blood are not everything; they are merely one aspect. The soul is the other, and that is more than the flesh.

Further than this, it seems to us, we cannot go. We acknowledge that in the Lord's Supper there is for the believing participant a true fellowship through the Holy Spirit with the Mediator become flesh and now existing in flesh. We acknowledge that this fellowship can take place in its full power only since the glorification of the flesh assumed, although previously there was certainly fellowship with the Mediator, who had not yet become flesh, through the Holy Spirit. We acknowledge that this fellowship does not proceed from us but in the first place from Christ, and that the Holy Spirit, as the entire Scripture teaches us, establishes and maintains the bond here between Christ and us.

But we do not know how this occurs further in detail, in what mysterious way the powers of life and of faith are conveyed and poured into us through the Spirit of Christ from Him, the Head. Is it substantially the same power of life that is at work in His glorified humanity or not? Does that power proceed from His soul or from His body, or from both? These, it seem to us, are all questions that are not capable of being answered. And when, nonetheless, one presses for answers, then the danger is very great that formulations will be devised that are exposed to all kinds of misunderstanding.

As is well known, a difference of opinion prevails regarding the real intention of Calvin. If he did not intend to take body and blood in a one-sided manner for the bodily elements of Christ's human nature, but, by synecdoche, to include the soul, then the biggest objection is removed. But even then, it seems to us, this objection remains: How power radiates from the humanity of Christ and is brought to us by the agency of the Holy Spirit is described all too precisely here.

If, on the other hand, what is at issue is meant corporeally, then there are two big objections against it. First of all, the literal meaning of the words *flesh* and *blood* cannot be applied to the glorified humanity of the Lord. Paul tells us that flesh and blood cannot inherit the kingdom of God [1 Cor 15:50]. It remains a body forever, but not a body of flesh and blood. The eating of flesh and blood must thus to that extent always be understood figuratively. And in the second place, one could expect from an action of His body only an effect upon our bodies. And that would be contrary to the tenor of Scripture. Throughout we are taught that the re-creation of our bodies does not begin here, that no seed of higher spiritual life has been put into our bodies, but that only after death and resting in the grave will the body be re-created at the resurrection. There can be no question of an action of the body of Christ in heaven on our bodies, nor of an action of His body on our souls either.

If it therefore appears that Calvin has gone quite far, on the other hand it cannot be pointed out enough how he has rightly rejected the Zwinglian view. We must hold fast to real fellowship with Christ in the Lord's Supper. And that real fellowship may never be sublimated into a thinking about Christ or into a conscious activity of faith with Christ. Calvin saw that, and by his view he has protected the Reformed confession from falling into that error.

One point should be addressed still further. As a sacrament, the Lord's Supper is directed to the life of faith. It serves to strengthen the life of faith. Now one could ask: What is the connection between it and the fellowship of life with the glorified Savior? In order to understand this properly, one must bear in mind that our faith does not exist in itself and is not detached from the spiritual life that is bestowed in regeneration. Rather, faith must be seen as the conscious aspect of this spiritual life. Therefore, everything that serves to strengthen this new life will also have a strengthening effect on faith. When Christ feeds us with His flesh and gives us His blood to drink, then in that feeding and the drinking, our faith, by which we appropriate Him and all His benefits, must inevitably develop. Approximately as in the natural increase of the power of life, a greater degree of hunger and thirst is produced. Not only faith in its activity but faith in its root is strengthened. And by that faith, the Christian lives consciously out of all the benefits of the covenant of grace. As little as in baptism is there reason here to limit the scope of this activity of faith. It is, in the first place, certainly focused on justification, the remission of sin, as our Form for the Lord's Supper rightly begins with that. Anyone who would benefit from Christ in the Lord's Supper without in first place and primarily availing himself of Him as High Priest, as Surety, as sacrificial lamb, would certainly miss its purpose. One must go back again and again to the broken body and the shed blood. But one need not remain there. We "share in all His blessings of life eternal, of righteousness and glory." Thus the Lord's Supper summarizes, as it were in one volume, the entire work of redemption. Here the source from which all blessings flow and the sum of all blessings themselves are compressed. It is the Lord who died and nevertheless lives into all eternity.

The Lord's Supper also points to the communion of saints. Our Form has that in view in the third place, with an appeal to the word of the apostle (1 Cor 10:17): "There is one bread, so we who are many are one body, because we all partake of the one bread." The communion of saints experienced in the Lord's Supper is based on communion with the Lord. Because everyone is joined to Christ, he is joined to believers. It is broken and nonetheless united bread, just because it represents the Mediator according to two aspects, according to two states.

16. *In what sense can one now say that Christ's body and blood are present in the Lord's Supper?*

This then concerns the question of sacramental union (*unio sacramentalis*). We have now seen what the sign is; we have also seen what the thing signified is. The sign is bread and wine; the thing signified is Christ the Mediator in the unity of His death and His life. But what is the relationship between these two, sign and thing signified?

a) It is not a material union, or, expressed more precisely, a change, as if the bread and wine ceased being bread and wine and flesh and blood replaced them (against Rome).

b) It is not a local union, as if the body and blood of Christ were joined in space through local proximity or contact with the signs.

We may not say: In this location where you see the signs, you must also consider the substance of flesh and blood present (against the Lutherans).

c) It is not a notional union that only exists in the minds of believers. With a symbol I always associate the thing signified with my conception; I represent it to myself. But that is a thing thought, something figurative. In the Lord's Supper that is the starting point in our conscious faith, but sacramental union does not terminate in that (against Zwingli).

d) It is a union by relationship (σχετικῶς). The thing signified is associated with the sign for the believing participant. It does not come through the sign itself. The sign serves only to bring its meaning and certainty to our consciousness. Only at this point, and only to that extent, is the sign an instrument for the thing signified, expressed more precisely, for an awareness of the thing signified.

e) Not the *existence* of the thing signified, but certainly its *spiritual efficacy* on the soul of the communicant is tied to faith. One must pay attention to this point, and in this regard make a precise distinction. There is a fellowship with the living Mediator as He exists in a glorious human nature for the believing participant. But what if the participant does not believe? The thing signified does not thereby cease to exist. Christ remains the same Christ. However, He is only active by His Spirit in the heart of the believer to bestow fellowship with Himself. Now everything depends on what one understands by the presence of Christ. If this means that the signs, as commissioned by Christ, are offered by Christ, and that the Holy Spirit, as God omnipresent, is present, ready to apply the thing signified, then Christ is also present in the Lord's Supper for the unbelieving participant. If, on the other hand, it means that by the Holy Spirit fellowship with the living Savior is established, then Christ is not present for the unbelieving participant. The word "presence" has more than one meaning. It can mean that something makes itself felt and causes its action to be experienced. It can also mean that something is present.

Faith is required in order to enjoy the blessing of the Lord's Supper, in order, in the sense just described, to receive the body and blood of Christ present (as active power). Still, one may not say that faith makes Christ present. Faith is the *conditio sine qua non* [necessary condition], but it does not perform a miracle; it does not draw the human nature of Christ down from heaven.

17. *In what sense can one say that Christ is eaten in the Lord's Supper?*

From the connection in which sign and thing are related, it is apparent that it is not a question of eating with the bodily mouth. The eating occurs with the mouth of faith. But as such, nevertheless, it is real. It is a receiving of Christ into ourselves by the Holy Spirit. And to this eating of Christ there follows a being fed with Christ. To that extent Calvin is entirely right when he insists that believing and eating are not completely the same. We could say: Believing is the same as eating, but both are still followed by something else. If someone eats food, by that in itself he is not yet effectively fed. The energy resident in the food must pass into his blood and his body, and this one could call a second eating, an eating in a deeper sense, since not only the mouth but the bodily system as a whole appropriates the nutritional elements, and that in such a manner that they go into the flesh and blood. It is the same with the Lord's Supper. We first eat with the mouth of faith. But following that eating of faith, an eating occurs in a deeper sense by our spiritual man as a whole when the life-giving power of the Lord, the nourishment that there is in Him, enters us, into the flesh and blood of the spiritual man—is identified with us. That eating is the fruit and result of faith, but, viewed in this way, still also more than faith.

18. *Give a description of the Lutheran doctrine of the Lord's Supper.*

One should be aware that Luther did not always take the same position. At first, he acknowledged that the signs are mere signs and that faith, as a kind of miracle-working faith, thereby creates the reality of the thing signified. Later, he adhered to the word that comes in and with the signs, and had the sacrament be a seal of this word. But soon, in reaction to Carlstadt and others, he began to take the characteristically Lutheran standpoint. Now he insisted on the literal interpretation of the "is" in the words of institution, taught a local presence, and connected this teaching on the Lord's Supper with his Christology. The Augsburg Confession expresses itself very modestly, so that the Reformed (e.g., Zanchi) did not hesitate to subscribe to its teaching on the Lord's Supper as a whole. The body and blood of Christ, it reads there, are truly present in the Lord's Supper and are distributed to the participants. The Apology of the Augsburg Confession (1531) already speaks more explicitly: the body and blood are truly and substantially present. The Smalcald Articles go a step further: the ungodly, too, receive and take this body and blood. The Formula of Concord teaches that the words of institution must be understood literally. Not the consecration of men but the omnipotence of Christ makes the local presence to exist. The humanity of Christ is at the right hand of God, and the right hand of God is everywhere. The body and blood of Christ are not only received and eaten by the mouth of faith but with the bodily mouth, yet not in a Capernaitic sense. The points already mentioned above by other confessions are also confirmed. One knows that the Lutheran formula is: "in, with, under" the bread and the wine. To describe this doctrine non-Lutherans used the term *consubstantiation*, which, however, has not been approved by the Lutherans themselves. The term can be misunderstood, since it makes one to think of a fusion or coalescence of two substances. Only an accompanying is meant, and Lutherans protest against the term when one ascribes to them that they mean to confine the essence of Christ's body and blood within the elements.

Regarding the efficacy of the *manducatio oralis* [oral eating], the views of the Lutherans also varied. Initially for Luther almost everything was focused on justification by faith, and he therefore also made this eating of the body and blood subordinate to that; thus in his Small Catechism. In the Large Catechism, he already went further. And in his private writings Luther even taught that from this body and blood a mysterious efficacy emanates upon our bodies, by which we become certain of their immortality. The flesh of Christ, being assimilated by us, re-creates our flesh (cf. Calvin, *Institutes*, 4.17.32 for something similar). But the Lutheran Church has not given confessional authority to this particular opinion, nor has the opinion of Calvin on this particular point entered into the Reformed confessions. The Formula of Concord places in the foreground as a fruit of the Lord's Supper the "true comfort and the strengthening of weak faith."

Lutherans have not made clear what they see as the difference between Capernaitic eating and the *manducatio oralis*. Luther had expressed himself rather crassly and spoken of a "biting with one's teeth."

The Formula of Concord, on the other hand, says the Sacramentarians (i.e., Zwinglians and Calvinists) wrongly and against their better knowledge accuse the Lutherans of teaching a tearing of the body with the teeth and a consuming of the same like other food. It is unnecessary to subject the Lutheran doctrine to express criticism here. The foundation upon which it is based has been treated earlier, and with that treatment the doctrine itself falls. One must not think that the exegesis of the words of institution give rise to this doctrine of the Lord's Supper. On the contrary, it was the view of the Lord's Supper that led to the well-known exegesis of the words of institution. Both in Christology and in the doctrine of the Lord's Supper the same principle was at work in Luther—a principle that did not keep God and man separated sharply enough, and in the impulse for intimate union with God obliterated the boundaries of the two natures. Using Lutheran Christology, many Lutherans, or at least those who call themselves Lutherans, have also changed the old doctrine of the Lord's Supper.

19. *What is the Roman Catholic view of the Lord's Supper?*

First of all, one must observe that according to Rome, what we call the Lord's Supper includes two distinct things: (1) a sacrament; (2) a sacrifice.

These two are certainly connected to each other but still are not the same. They are two distinct actions. In the sacrament, something is given *to us from God*. In the sacrifice, *we* give something *to God*, through the hand of the priest. Since the Roman Catholic Church arrogates to itself the role of a mediatrix between God and man, it is in its nature to put much more emphasis on the sacrifice than on the sacrament. To give something from God to man is already a great deal, but for man to bring something to God is the proper work of the priest. The mass has thus become the most important part of the Roman Catholic worship service, around which everything is concentrated.

We speak here only about the Lord's Supper as sacrament.

a) Its *basis* for Roman Catholics is the doctrine of transubstantiation. Through the words of consecration that the priest speaks, the entire substance of the signs is changed. The sensory "accidents," such as color, smell, taste, etc., remain, but the substance is miraculously changed. These accidents thus exist entirely in themselves and have nothing to which they adhere, for as substance only the body and blood of Christ is present, along with everything that is inseparable from them. Indeed, where the body is the soul must also be, and where the soul is, the Godhead must also be. That is why the Church teaches that the whole Christ is present locally where the signs of bread and wine have been changed into the substance of the body and the blood. The result of this transubstantiation, further, is that now the whole Christ is present in each ostensible sign in itself. He is in the ostensible bread; He is in the ostensible wine. And so one only needs to receive one sign in order to receive the full Christ. Christ is the bread and the wine, or the wine and the bread are Christ, not only during their use, but that also remains so after the celebration of the Lord's Supper (or the mass). This is one of the points where Lutherans also diverge from Rome. For Lutherans the local union is in effect only for the time of the administration of the sacrament. The Roman Catholics preserve the consecrated wafer, bring it to the sick, carry it around in processions, render to it religious veneration of the highest kind (*latreia*).

b) The *practice* of the Lord's Supper. The celebrating priest drinks the chalice; the others receive and eat the wafer. Unleavened bread and mixed wine are used.

c) The *purpose* of the Eucharist is not to grant forgiveness of sins. The Canons of Trent oppose the view that sees the forgiveness of sins as the principal fruit of communion. In this, then, Rome again differs from both Lutherans and Reformed. The sacrament of penance is intended to first take away mortal sin, and that sin must first be taken away before one can attend the Eucharist. Only venial sins can be forgiven by the Lord's Supper. The primary purpose lies in the mystical exchange of substances, by which it is not so much that Christ's body and blood pass into us as that these rather re-create and change us, so that we become like Christ. The Catechism of Rome appeals to the words of Augustine: "And you shall not change me into you, as the food of your body, but you will be changed into me!"

d) The *proof* for this doctrine resides primarily, it is thought, in John 6:48-65. But, as Roman Catholics themselves acknowledge, here tradition is a more firm basis than Scripture, so that the

Scriptural proof can be called almost superfluous. With John 6 Rome gains nothing. It is clearly taught there that this eating and drinking of the Lord is necessary to have life in one's self, thus for salvation (v. 53). If then the reference here is *exclusively* to the Lord's Supper (and it must be so, for, according to Rome, the eating in the Lord's Supper is a completely unique eating), then that will imply that communing is necessary to have life. But Rome itself does not teach this. Life is given in baptism; in the Lord's Supper it is assumed to be present; someone can be saved without this eating of the Lord's Supper. In John 6, therefore, it cannot be exclusively a question of the Lord's Supper.

Nor is tradition a firm basis here. The rule "*quod semper, quod ubique, quod ab omnibus*" ["what is believed always, everywhere, by all"] may not be applied here. One need only open a history of dogma to see the gradual development of the Roman Catholic doctrine disclosed.

The doctrine of transubstantiation includes a physical impossibility. Accidents cannot exist without and apart from a substance. And here they are left entirely in the air. And that the same Christ—not, we say, according to His deity but according to His delimited human nature— would at the same time be in as many places everywhere where but one priest, by the act of consecration, calls Him to appear or to be present, is nothing less than absurd.

20. *What views have been developed by modern theology regarding the Lord's Supper?*

Modern theology has the two natures in Christ fused into one divine-human nature. This divine-human nature, although individualized in Christ, is at the same time also a generic entity that can impart itself and propagate itself. It is not confined within Christ but flows over into the church and into all believers. There is no essential difference between the deity and humanity, the body and the soul of Christ. He must thus be imparted to us in His entirety if we are to receive His life. This does not flow into us in a material, sensory way, but in a spiritual way, since the bond with Christ is fixed at the center of our personality, which in itself is neither matter nor spirit, but a higher entity. The imparting of this substance of Christ takes place in the Lord's Supper. It takes place not by the Holy Spirit but by Christ Himself. According to the Reformed view, mystical union is effected by the Holy Spirit, who dwells in Christ, the Head, and in us, His members. According to this modern view, it is effected and continually maintained by the inpouring and infusion of this divine-human essence.

One can find this theory in most modern theologians. Ebrard has worked it out in detail. It does not have a scriptural foundation. It is based on philosophical-pantheistic premises, and tries to maintain itself exegetically with what Scripture teaches in an entirely different sense regarding the mystical union between Christ and believers. This, as we saw earlier, is not a union of essence but a unity of life through the Holy Spirit.

21. Who should come to the Lord's Supper?

Those who are members of Christ's congregation and examine themselves, who can discern the body and blood of Christ. Thus:

a) Not the children before they have come to years of discernment. The Greek [Orthodox] Church has child communion, which for a long time has also been in use in the Roman Catholic Church. Appeal for that can be made to John 6:53, if one maintains that this eating and drinking of Christ is only to be received in the Lord's Supper. But Rome does not maintain that the Lord's Supper is necessary for salvation. Among the Reformed, there is almost no one who has spoken with uncertainty on this point. Musculus argued from baptism, but that argumentation does not hold. In baptism, the person appears in a completely passive way; he receives something. In the Lord's Supper, in contrast, he comes actively, acting; he does something—takes, eats, drinks, does it in remembrance of Christ. It is required of those who come to the Lord's Supper that they discern the body of the Lord and examine themselves. Children cannot do that. Children did join in eating the Passover at a very early age. But it cannot be proven that later very young children had to join in traveling to Jerusalem or to the place where the tabernacle stood to eat the Passover. In any case, the Passover and the Lord's Supper are not on the same line such that what applies to the one also undoubtedly applies to the other.

It is reported of Jesus that He went along to Jerusalem at the age of 12 (Luke 2:42).

It may be noted, however, that it is not the (old) Reformed practice and also not warranted by Scripture, when making profession of faith and participating in the Lord's Supper is postponed to the age of 20. Years of discernment come earlier. In civil life one acts with discretion much earlier; why then in church life should one come to the Lord's Supper so much later? Postponing participation for a long time has not benefited Lord's Supper observance, since it has led to the illusion that life in the congregation according to God's requirement is also possible for those who are completely grown up even when they do not go to the Lord's Supper. Since profession of faith does not come at the beginning of independent living but in a certain sense in its midst, one begins to regard it as something unusual, as a crisis, as something for which something new must become apparent.

b) Not *unbelievers*, that is, those who by doctrine and life give offense in the church and who consequently by discipline must be kept from the table of the Lord. The church must exclude such people, for it is entrusted to it to be vigilant for the holiness of God's covenant according to an objective standard. Hence the listing in our Form of the Lord's Supper of gross and public sins, and the pronouncement that those who know themselves to be polluted with these sacrileges should absent themselves. Even if the church has not officially taken note of such sins, the person who knows himself polluted with them may not participate if he does not feel heartfelt sorrow for his sins and it is not his intention to improve his life.

c) Not *unbelievers* who lack saving faith entirely. But here one must distinguish:

1. Between the question of who the church should and may admit and the entirely different question of who possesses for himself subjectively the right go and to sit at the table, to eat and to drink. Regarding the first question, the church, also in the matter of the Lord's Supper, does not have to make a subjective judgment about someone's state but only to deal with members of the visible church who are improper in doctrine

or life. The church should invite all such people to the Lord's Supper and even insist that they shall come. It may never say: if you are unconverted and without faith, then you must stay away. Rather, it must enforce two things: the obligation of every member to come and the obligation of every member to come as a believer.

2. Between faith and faith. The faith that someone must possess in order to be able to come to the Lord's Supper with a quiet conscience is not the assured trust of faith. Were that so, then only very few would be able to make use of this sacrament. Surely it has been instituted by Christ for all, even for the weakest believer among His believers. No one should ask himself: "Am I assured of my justification? Can I count on it that I am regenerated?" But surely: "Is there in me sorrow over my sin and a trust that takes refuge in my Savior, even if it is so little?" Whoever has, to him can be given. The smallest faith can be fed and increased at the Lord's Supper.

d) *Not true believers in every state.* There is an unworthy eating and drinking that can take place, even for a true believer. That occurred in Corinth. In hunger and drunkenness one reached for the bread and for the cup. Thus, if a Christian is in a mood by which it is certain beforehand that he will not be able to hallow the institution of the Lord but will dishonor and profane it, then he may not attend. If such cases occur, everyone must decide for himself. According to 1 Corinthians 11, the believer, too, can eat and drink judgment upon himself. From this it is evident that the popular exegesis of this chapter is untenable. "Judgment" here does not mean "punishment," much less "eternal punishment," but "chastisement" sent by God upon His own so that they will not be condemned with the world (v. 32). Accordingly, the self-examination, which is required here, is also not so much an examination of oneself with an eye to the question whether one is regenerated or not, but rather an examination of the attitude that one takes towards God and His institution, so that one may move from a wrong attitude into a worthy one, and so eat and drink. The most painstaking self-examination must also end in this, according to Paul: in eating and drinking in the right state, in a humble attitude desirous of salvation.

22. What is one to understand about the Roman Catholic mass?

The sacrifice brought to God by the hand of the priest, after transubstantiation, consisting in the body, the soul, the deity of Christ, in the ostensible form of bread and wine.

On this point the Greek [Orthodox] Church has essentially the same view as the Roman Catholic Church. It too regards the sacrament as a sacrifice. The Roman Catholic Catechism says that the sacrifice takes place by consecration. If then the consecrated signs are preserved or brought to a sick person, then that is not a sacrifice but merely the Lord's Supper. That the two ought to be separated, at least logically, also appears from the fact that the Canons of Trent deal with the Lord's Supper in session 13, with the mass in session 22, thus with each in a separate place. There can be communion without the mass, at least in the same moment, although it appears that the mass with consecration must have always preceded. There can also be a mass without communion; for example, so-called private masses at which no participants are present.

The mass is an actual sacrifice. It does not differ in its essence from the sacrifice brought by Christ on the cross. That was a bloody; this is a bloodless sacrifice. But in both Christ is sacrificed.

Also, in both cases the priest is the same. Sometimes it is presented as if the officiating ministrant is the priest. However, it is emphasized by the Roman Catholic Catechism, among others, that it is the sacrificed Christ Himself who at the same time also does the work of a priest. This is to be so understood that Christ offers Himself through the ministry of the priest. They act for Christ in Christ's name.

The mass, as repetition of the sacrifice of Christ, works in an essentially different way than a sacrament. Roman Catholics teach concerning a sacrament that it works *ex opere operato* [worked by the work]. Baptism and the Lord's Supper of themselves do what they are said to do. The cross of Christ does not justify but merely opens justification, makes it possible, and hence the mass. It makes certain merits available that then, however, require a special application to become effective. Bellarmine makes a distinction between the sacrifice on the cross and the sacrifice of the mass. The former was meriting (*meritorium*), bringing about satisfaction (*satisfactorium*) and meriting salvation (*impetratorium*). The sacrifice of the mass is only the latter. It depends for its power on the sacrifice of Christ on the cross, so that it is not entirely correct when Roman Catholics are accused of making the sacrifice on the cross insufficient. The sacrifice on the cross has, in the sense just described, infinite power, since it lends value to everything that happens in the name of the Church over the centuries. The power of the mass is limited, for otherwise there would be no need for many masses. The purpose of the mass is to obtain the remission of sins for the living and the dead, for individual persons and for believers in general, and to make it possible to store up merits for eternal life. For those who are in purgatory, masses can be celebrated by the Church if they themselves or their relatives have made money available for that purpose. Through these masses their stay in purgatory is shortened. This is an ever-flowing source of income for the Church.

23. *What is the scriptural basis on which Rome thinks it possible to construct this doctrine?*

As seen above, appeal is made to the words from the institution of the Lord's Supper: "Do this," etc. Thereby Jesus supposedly will have motivated His apostles and given them power to do what He Himself had just done, that is, to learn to effect transubstantiation. But, first of all, the entire view is based on the impossible explanation of the words, "This is my body," as if that were a transubstantiating formula. If that is not the case, and every unprejudiced exegesis must acknowledge this, then what has been built on it also collapses—this strange institution of the sacrament of priestly consecration.

Furthermore, Roman Catholics say that Christ is priest according to the order of Melchizedek and therefore must continually repeat the sacrifice once brought by Him on the cross. But: (a) The point of comparison is not that Christ and Melchizedek sacrifice continually but rather that they do not have any successors in sacrificing, as the letter to the Hebrews says that with one sacrifice He has perfected forever all those who are sanctified [Heb 10:14]. Thus, just the opposite of what Rome maintains. (b) The comparison with Melchizedek carried through on this point must exclude specifically the priesthood of the ministers of the Roman Catholic Church.

An appeal is also made to Malachi 1:11: "'But from the rising of the sun to its setting my name will be great among the nations, and in every place incense will be offered to my name, and a pure offering, for my name will be great among the nations,' says the LORD of hosts." The Vulgate has "*sacrificatur*" here. Even if this is correct, one may not take it literally. When Isaiah 19:21 says that in the future the Egyptians will serve the Lord with sacrifice and offering, in verse 19 that in that day the Lord will have an altar in the midst of the land of Egypt and a monument established at its border, then it occurs to no one to expect a literal fulfillment of these words. It is simply the Old Testament expression for the thought that Egypt will know and serve the true God. It is the same for Malachi 1:11.

Our [Heidelberg] Catechism calls the papal mass "an accursed idolatry." This is accurate. If here what is not a sacrifice is offered to God as a sacrifice, and this thing sacrificed is venerated as God when it is not God, then one can find no other term for this than "accursed idolatry." It has been said that Roman Catholics surely do not worship the wafer other than on the supposition that it really *is* their God. But every idolater does that more or less. No one worships a stone or a piece of wood with the thought that it is nothing more than wood or stone. Thus, if this excuse were valid, then one could no longer speak of idolatry anywhere.

The Roman Catholic doctrine of the mass is the consistent expression of the idea that the church must supply the things of salvation from its treasury to believers *ex opere operato*. If the one sacrifice of Christ was there as sufficient, then it would also follow that it would be accessible outside the church. But now it is not sufficient. The church must give it its efficacy. And thereby it becomes fully true, also even for the accomplishment of salvation: *extra ecclesiam nulla salus* [outside the Church there is no salvation].

PART THREE

Eschatology: The Doctrine of Last Things

1. What is contained in the term "eschatology"?

That history, in the course of which we are situated, will have a conclusion. It is not an endless process but a genuine history that ends in a definite goal and so has a boundary and limits. As it had a beginning, it will have an ending. That ending will come as a crisis, and everything that has to do with this crisis belongs to the "doctrine of the last things."

2. Is the term "eschatology" a Scriptural term?

Yes, for Scripture makes mention of "the last days" (cf., e.g., Isa 2:2, LXX: ἔσχαται ἡμέραι; Mic 4:1; Acts 2:17), of "last times" (1 Pet 1:20, ἔσχατοι χρόνοι), of "the last hour" (1 John 2:18, ἐσχάτη ὥρα).

3. In many of these passages, is not something entirely different spoken of than what we understand by "the last days," namely, the New Testament dispensation of the covenant of grace?

Considered superficially, this is indeed the case. See, for example, Acts 2:17, where the outpouring of the Holy Spirit is spoken of as taking place "in the last days." Nevertheless one ought to maintain that here, too, the eschatological meaning is present. The explanation is as follows: From the perspective of the older prophets, the coming of the Messiah coincides with the culmination of the kingdom, the end of all things. Isaiah, for example, speaks in one breath of the return from exile, of the coming of the Messiah, of the end of the world, and unrolls all these events before our eyes as in one great scene. He sees only the peaks towering above everything. Accordingly, the older prophets reckon on only two time periods: *this* age (οὗτος ὁ αἰών) and "the *coming* age" (ὁ μέλλων αἰών). So, for Isaiah and for Micah the "last days" are the days that precede the end and at the same time precede the coming of the Messiah. The later prophets were granted in the Spirit to see more clearly how there would be a *double coming* of the Messiah, one for suffering and scorn and one in glory (Dan 7; 9; 12). Thus what in the older prophets was still combined or condensed into one coming was in the later prophets divided into two. But now from this it follows as well that the time that elapses between the first and the second coming of the Lord can be viewed from a twofold perspective. If we fix our attention on the coming that is still expected and we include everything before that in "this age," then we and all the New Testament saints live in the last days, that is, in the period that forms the eve of the second coming of our Lord in glory. If, on the other hand, we focus attention on the coming that is already past, and we draw the dividing line between the two ages at the first coming, then we in fact already live in the "age to come." Consequently, since the time between the first and the second coming of the Lord is governed completely by the thought of His coming either as already having occurred or as still having to occur, one can call it "the last days."

The first of the conceptions just mentioned is found, for example, in Luke 20:34, Ephesians 1:21, and Galatians 1:4. The other conception is found, for example, in Hebrews 2:5. The one is not in conflict with the other. Our time, the time of the new covenant, in fact bears a dual character. The old age is in us and at work in us, but also the new age and what is coming already exists in what for now is its prophecy.

4. *How is eschatology to be divided?*

a) Individual eschatology.

b) General eschatology.

The end comes at the close of world history for everything at the same time. What belongs to that end and is connected with it we call general eschatology. But for the individual the end also comes with his departure from this life, from this age. By his death he is lifted above this age in its earthly development, and in a certain sense brought closer to the age to come. Indeed, in Scripture the antithesis between the two world-*times* intersects with the antithesis between two world-*places*. The new Jerusalem, the future city, the heavenly kingdom will be revealed when this age empties into the future age. Therefore, relocation of dwelling place is always an exchange of age. On this is based the right of the above-mentioned division of eschatology, which otherwise could appear arbitrary.

CHAPTER SIX

Individual Eschatology

1. *What further brings you to this individual eschatology?*

   a) The scriptural doctrine of the intermediate state of the soul before the resurrection.

   b) The Roman Catholic doctrine of purgatory, the *limbus patrum* and the *limbus infantum*.

   c) The modern doctrine of the distinction between Sheol-Hades as a general dwelling place of all souls, on the one hand, and, on the other, heaven-hell as dwelling places at the end for those good and those evil, now separated.

   d) The doctrine of soul sleep. "Second probation." Annihilation. Conditional immortality.

2. *What does Scripture teach concerning the intermediate state of souls before the resurrection?*

   a) That after death the soul continues to exist in self-conscious immortality, that it is not annihilated, and does not lose its consciousness. This doctrine is revealed clearly in both the Old and the New Testament, although, as with other doctrines, so too with it, more light is shed by the full revelation of Christ. *Proof from the Old Testament*: the answer of our Lord to the Sadducees that God is called the God of Abraham, Isaac, and Jacob as the

God of the living and not of the dead; Psalm 73:23–24; 1 Samuel 28 (the coming up of Samuel); Isaiah 14 (the descent of the king of Babylon, where all the dead meet him); Psalm 16 (of the resurrection of Christ); Psalm 17:15; the two clearest passages: Isaiah 26:19 and Daniel 12:2 (cf. Heb 11:13–16). Proofs from of the New Testament are unnecessary.

b) That this state between death and resurrection is a state outside the body. That, nevertheless, outside the body, too, the soul retains its capacities of observing and acting, something that shows convincingly that seeing, hearing, etc., are possible outside the body, and what the prophetic ecstasy in which this occurs accordingly confirms (proof: Phil 1:23; 2 Cor 5:6, 8). After death, in a way that is incomprehensible for us, the soul is in communication with what is outside it. It does not have a spiritual body until the day of resurrection.

c) Although this intermediate state is distinguished in certain ways from the final state that will only come after the resurrection of the dead, Scripture still always presents it as a definitive state in which a change or reversal is no longer possible. As the tree falls, so it lies. If the parable of the rich man and Lazarus teaches anything, then it is that after death no change of destiny, for good or for evil, is possible. Judgment before the judgment seat of Christ has to do with what is done in the body [2 Cor 5:10], and in this there is more of the same.

d) This intermediate state is passed by believers in heaven, by the lost in hell. Thus it is not a state without locality, as some maintain, thinking that the soul separated from the body can no longer exist in relation to space. But the soul is not elevated above space, although it is not extended in space like the body. It must be somewhere; it must have an *ubi* [where]. It does not exist in space circumscriptively (in a descriptive way), but definitively (in a determinative way). That believers at their death enter heaven follows from the fact that that they go to be with the Lord. We may not be able to say where heaven is, and yet that heaven is where Christ is, namely, according to His human nature (2 Cor 5:8; Phil 1:23; Luke 23:43; Eph 2:6). That the lost are in hell follows from Luke 16:23, "being in torment"; 1 Peter 3:19, "in prison"; 2 Peter 2:9, "under punishment" (κολαζομένους), not as the *Statenvertaling* [cf. the κjv]: "to be punished"; correctly, the English Revised Version: "to keep the unrighteous under punishment until the day of judgment." Nor are the souls of those who have died elevated above time; they are and remain in time (Rev 6:11); they serve God "day and night" [Rev 7:15].

e) For believers, death is a crisis event in which they obtain perfect holiness. That was shown earlier in treating sanctification. They come into a place and into a state of blessing and rest (Rev 6:9–11; 14:13), a condition that is to be preferred far above what they share in now. It is a removal of the activity of death from the soul of the believers, an expelling of spiritual death completely and of all that takes place in temporal death. At regeneration that spiritual death is broken in principle, in sanctification the struggle is continued, in temporal death the soul is withdrawn from the terrain of the struggle and placed beyond every influence of death. In the resurrection death will also finally lose its power over the body.

What happens with unbelievers must be located within the same viewpoint. It is a further outworking of the spiritual death that comes upon them at temporal death. They are further separated from God.

Death as temporal death is for God's children something other than it is for the unbelievers. The matter of death may be the same; the form, the scope is changed. One can debate why God's children still have to die. Would it not have been more consistent if the re-creation of their bodies would have come at the same time as the re-creation of their souls, gradually, although were that then also in a crisis? One can give a twofold answer: (a) Believers must die in order by the consciousness of death to be loosed from the earth and what is temporal. Temporal death is a part of *their cross*, and the cross has this scope (Matt 16:24–25). (b) God's providential ordering unfolds such that He has willed to reserve the material re-creation for the end of the ages; and the perfecting of the bodies of believers belongs to the re-creation of material things. Their bodies are part of matter and must therefore wait for the liberation of the entire groaning creation (Rom 8:20–22).

Since now, however, believers must enter heaven, nothing else is left than that their bodies and their souls be separated.

f) Concerning the particulars of this state before the resurrection, both in heaven and in hell, for believers and unbelievers, we can say almost nothing. Only general features are described for us. The parable of the rich man and Lazarus is a parable from which one cannot or may not carry over all the features. One should keep to the point of the comparison; all the rest is setting. All kinds of questions present themselves: Can the spirits of the dead return to earth? Can they establish a relationship there in one way or another with those in the body? Do the spirits in heaven or hell know what is happening on earth? Scripture does not answer these questions. It says only as a matter of practice that we may not seek to have such fellowship with the dead in any way whatsoever, with or without magical means. Incantation of the dead is sin (Deut 18). Spiritism has something attractive to many because in the wilderness of unbelief and of materialism it promises a kind of compensation. But anything more than deception that lurks within it is not from God. It may not be used as a means of grace (Luke 16:30–31).

3. What do the Roman Catholics teach concerning purgatory?

Purgatory (*purgatorium*) is a place of suffering in which the souls of believers are purified after death, in order by this suffering to make satisfaction to God for their sins and in order to be prepared for heavenly glory. Someone can remain in purgatory till the day of judgment. Then it ceases. The Church has this purgatory among the power of the keys and can by its service shorten the time that the souls of the dead spend there. Usually purgatory is seen to be a place of physical fire, but this has not been given creedal status by the Church.

In purgatory one makes satisfaction for the sin committed after baptism, for Christ has only delivered us from eternal death. The mass can serve to decrease this satisfaction required of us. That is why the Church holds masses for the dead who are in purgatory.

4. Where is the alleged proof for this doctrine?

Primarily in tradition. The doctrine has its roots in paganism, in Parsiism and Manichaeism. The doctrine has been especially developed in the Western Church. Augustine first gave it a specific form. Gregory the Great developed it later.

Only in an extremely forced way can Scripture be cited for this dogma. Appeal is made to Jesus' words that the sin against the Holy Spirit will not be forgiven, either in this or in the world to come; hence the inference that there is forgiveness in the world to come. But this is merely a manner of speaking: "never," "not in eternity," as we say "neither in heaven nor on earth" for "nowhere." Further, Revelation 21:7–8, which needs no refutation; Isaiah 4:4; Micah 7:8; Zechariah 9:11; Malachi 3:2; 1 Corinthians 3:13–15; 15:29. All these passages speak of something totally different.

The Roman Catholic doctrine is to be judged by the false premises upon which it rests: (a) the partitioning of the work of Christ, as if we must still add something to it; (b) the meritorious character of our good works, which does not exist; (c) the doctrine of the merit in good works, so that the church disposes over a treasury of merits; (d) the absolute power of the keys of the Church in a *judicial* sense.

5. What is the limbus patrum of Roman Catholics?

The *limbus patrum* (limbo of the fathers) is the place where the believing fathers of the Old Testament had to stay in a state of expectation before the coming of the Messiah. After His death on the cross, Christ descended into Hades and freed the fathers. This goes with the Roman Catholic doctrine of the sacraments of the Old Testament, to which they do not attribute power to save, as they do to the sacraments that the Church now administers. The *limbus patrum* is a part of Hades, of Sheol, about which more will be said below.

6. What is the limbus infantum of Roman Catholics?

A place where the souls of unbaptized children dwell. These souls may not enter heaven, for this is only possible for those baptized. It is not specified precisely in the creeds how one should think further of the state of the children in this place. The *limbus infantium* is a place in Hades or Sheol. But the punishment of children differs from the punishment of adults. Whether it is *poena sensus*, "punishment of feeling," or only *poena damni*, "punishment of loss" or "privation," the Church has not decided. The Latin fathers appear to have taught mostly the former, the Greek fathers mostly the latter. The *poena damni* is a deprivation of the beatitude of heaven, of the beatific vision of God. Thomas said that these children do not feel pain or sorrow as result of this deprivation. Others said they do.

7. *What should be observed regarding these two dogmas?*

The doctrine of the *limbus patrum* collapses together with the proposition that the Old Testament saints did not partake of complete salvation. If they had justification, regeneration, the full sacraments, then there is no reason at all for denying them salvation at their death. A local *descensus ad inferos* [descent into hell] has been refuted earlier.

The *limbus infantium* rests on the Catholic concept of the sacraments. If baptism is not the means, the sole means of regeneration, then unbaptized children can go to heaven. And if they do not go to heaven, they must be sent to hell. There is no place or state in between. Children are not too innocent to be lost. The entire conception results from a weakening of the understanding of original sin.

8. *What distinction is made presently between Sheol-Hades, on the one hand, and hell-heaven, on the other?*

Many maintain that in Scripture the Hebrew word שְׁאוֹל (Sheol) and the Greek word ᾅδης (Hades) do not mean the place of suffering but a general dwelling place of the dead, in which there are different sections for the different kinds of people who are gathered there after their death. In this way, corresponding to each of the different places, a different state is also assumed, which is carefully distinguished from the state of eternal destruction or eternal blessing. Sheol-Hades is an intermediate place; they who find themselves there live in an intermediate state. The English Revised Version has adopted this view by rendering Hades not with "hell," as the King James Version does, but with "Hades." In the historical books they render Sheol mostly with "the grave" or "the pit" and in a marginal note add "Sheol," so that the reader does not think of "the grave." In the poetic books they use "Sheol" in the text and "the grave" in the margin. Only in Isaiah 14 has "hell" remained in the text.

It is not feasible here to enumerate all the conceptions that have been formed regarding the relationship of Sheol-Hades, hell, and heaven to each other. As an example, we give the view of Kliefoth, a modern German theologian, who has written a work on eschatology. He says: At the time of the Old Testament there was only one abode for all the dead. Both pious and ungodly went to it. At the descent of Christ into hell, this Sheol was emptied of all its inhabitants, that is, both of those called of the Old Testament, who had lived under the dispensation of the covenant of grace (believers and unbelievers), and of those not called under the Old Testament, who went down into Sheol from the pagan world. But Sheol does not disappear with the descent into hell. Indeed, Revelation 6:8 and 20:13-14 speak of it (under the name "Hades") as of something that will continue to exist until the final judgment (Phil 2:10; Rev 5:3 also teach that). Therefore those not called—pagans, Mohammedans [Muslims], Jews, etc.—now go into Sheol-Hades at their death. Those who are called, that is, who live under the gospel, on the other hand, now go immediately at their death to Gehenna (= hell) if they have remained unbelieving; to paradise (= heaven) if they believed. According to Kliefoth, children who die unbaptized also go into Sheol-Hades.

Against this conception we observe:

a) That with the words *Sheol* and *Hades* one cannot always think of a locality. Without doubt both occur as abstract concepts by which nothing else is meant than being dead, soul and body being separated. This takes place for believers and unbelievers under the old and new covenants, and so in a figurative sense it can be said that they all, without distinction, are in Sheol or Hades. It is meant in this way in the Old Testament; for example, 1 Samuel 2:6: "The LORD kills and makes alive; He brings down to Sheol and brings up." Here the parallelism shows what is meant (Gen 44:31; Job 14:13; 17:13-14; Hos 13:14; Psa 89:48). And many more places of that sort can be found in the Old Testament.

But Hades occurs in this sense in the New Testament too. Acts 2:27: "You will not leave my soul in Hades (= in the state of the separation of death), nor will you give over your Holy One to see corruption" (cf. v. 31). First Corinthians 15:55: "Death, where is your sting? Hades, where is your victory?" Here again the parallelism shows what is meant with Hades. And the number of such citations can also be increased.

b) Thus we do not need to show that Hades or Sheol never mean something that applies to both believers and the ungodly, but only that they do not mean a place where the souls of believers and the ungodly dwell or exist together. Every place where Sheol-Hades is meant locally, it indicates nothing other than the place of destruction, what we usually call "hell." Only the latter need be demonstrated. It is based on the following grounds:

1. Descending into Sheol is threatened as a danger and a punishment of the ungodly (Deut 32:22; Job 21:13; Psa 9:17; Prov 5:5; 15:24). The threatening sense disappears from these passages if Sheol is a place neutral in character, more negative than positive, where good and evil are found together. *As a place*, then, Sheol cannot contain two sections, Gehenna and Paradise, for here Sheol *as such* is identical with the place of destruction. The idea of a division within Sheol itself is a pagan one that first intruded into the Christian world of thought from paganism, and perhaps had already possessed the Jews during the sojourn of our Lord on earth, but is not supported by Scripture itself. Only of Sheol *as a state* can it be said that in it there are two divisions, but then one is speaking figuratively.

2. If Sheol does not mean the place of destruction, then the Old Testament has no word to designate this place, and we would have to reach the conclusion that during the time of the Old Testament there was no "hell." This conclusion, however, completely contradicts every analogy, is in conflict with the retributive righteousness of God, and so must be rejected along with its source.

3. The Old Testament, on the contrary, speaks of a place where believers who died in their Lord enjoy a state of blessing. Hence they cannot have gone to Sheol (Num 23:5, 10; Psa 16:11; 17:15; 49:15; Prov 14:32). Enoch and Elijah certainly did not go to Sheol, the land of darkness and shadows, as the pagans imagine it, and about which they declared that it must be located far below the earth (cf. Heb 11:16, 35).

4. Sheol as a place and not only as a state occurs in the closest connection with the concept "death." Thus one only need grasp this biblical concept of "death" in its depth to see immediately that Sheol cannot have been the dwelling place for those who died in the Lord. Death is not solely physical. It is also spiritual death. One may compare Proverbs 15:11; 27:20; 5:5 with Revelation 20:14 to see that in the former series of texts Sheol and death are linked, as are Hades and death in the latter passage.

c) Both meanings of the *state of death* and the *state of destruction* (= *the place of destruction*) are therefore designated in Scripture by the same word. That is not accidental. It is based on the fact that death is a punishment for sin and that in the returning of the body to dust, in the body being covered by soil, the Lord has provided an image of the *destruction of death in the broadest sense* that includes the damnation of hell. It is not to be thought that the designation Sheol for "hell" is a metaphor derived from the designation Sheol for "grave." On the contrary, since for sinners God has ordained Sheol as "hell" and consistent with the spatial order determined by God this "hell" is associated with what is *below*, He has therefore willed that something would happen with our dead bodies that called to mind symbolically eternal destruction. Hence in Scriptural symbolism the grave is the gateway to hell. Accordingly, Sheol in the one sense is the anteroom of Sheol in the other sense. But because this was so, and this plainly cannot be applied to those who die in the Lord, therefore, by the mouth of the apostle Paul, Scripture has given another sense to this "going down" for believers, connected to another symbolism. For believers, descending into hell is being sown in a furrow. Seed, too, goes down, apparently to rot, but in reality in order to come up in the glory of stem, leaf, and blossom.

In the Old Testament, Sheol more often means "grave" and less frequently "hell." In the New Testament the relationship is reversed. This is connected with the fact that in the New Testament more light is shed on the doctrine of future things.

One can conclude from what has been said how little justification there is for always translating Sheol or Hades in the same way and to decide that *a priori*. In each instance the translation should depend on the context. The English Revised Version has done something risky by taking sides here, and ultimately can itself not remain consistent (Isa 14). One should either leave Sheol and Hades untranslated everywhere or assess and decide each concrete case individually.

9. What is to be understood by the doctrine of soul sleep?

This is the doctrine that after death the soul continues to survive as a separate and indivisible spiritual being not in a clearly conscious state with continuity of consciousness but rather in a sleeping state. At the time of Eusebius there were those who advocated this doctrine. He speaks of a small Christian sect in Arabia. Such conceptions also emerge at the time of the Reformation. Calvin wrote against them; Socinus taught that after death the soul cannot have fellowship with anything outside it, although he judged that in itself it is active consciously.

Appeal is made in particular to the fact that in Scripture death is so often called a sleep (e.g., 1 Thess 4:14–15; 5:10). It is also said that the conception of a day of judgment only at the end includes that the time period between death and this judgment does not count for the soul and its conscious state. Neither of these two grounds has sufficient force to convince in the face of the express assertions of the Bible. That death is called a sleep means to say nothing else than that the connection between soul and body—and with it the connection as well between the soul and this earthly, visible world—is cut off. Suppose that someone in a rapture of the senses (ecstasy) receives a vision. He will then have the appearance of being completely asleep, and perhaps there will not be any trace of the life of his soul remaining in his body. And still at the same time, clearly his soul will be consciously active, see, hear, etc. Similarly, it can be said of the dead that they sleep. The judgment of the last day is not so much necessary for deciding as for a public proclamation of the verdict given by God.

10. What is meant by the doctrine of a so-called "second probation"?

"Second probation" is a second testing or trial. The "first probation" takes place in this life. This doctrine posits a second after this life. Usually the doctrine, described above, of Sheol-Hades as an in-between place is connected with this doctrine. In it, the dividing line for the individual between this age and the age to come is drawn not at his death but at the day of judgment. Until then nothing is decided; only then does the irrevocable decision result. The application of Christ's work reaches beyond death; the today of grace extends to the day of judgment. It is obvious that this general principle can have multiple specific applications. One can have the time of grace continue for all without distinction. One can also make an exception for those who in this life have not yet been under the administration of the means of grace, namely pagans and children. And this restriction of a second opportunity to pagans and children, then, rests again on the fact that one will know of only one sin that is worthy of damnation, namely, the sin of rejecting Christ. Original sin and actual sin, as long as they are not related to Christ and develop into the sin of unbelief, do not doom anyone (so Dorner IV, 167).[1] The sin against the gospel is *the* sin, the greatest sin.

Against this doctrine in general we observe:

a) That Scripture clearly teaches how everything is decided at death: "to die once, after this the judgment" (Heb 9:27); "you will die in your sin" (John 8:21); "night is coming, in which no one can work" (John 9:4; cf. Luke 21:34–35; 13:24–25; 2 Cor 6:2; Heb 3:7; 4:7).

b) The same conclusion follows from the fact that at death believers are completely sanctified and removed from all variation and change. For now life goes up and down, but this ceases at death. "But the one who endures *to the end* will be saved" (Matt 10:22); "Jesus Christ will sustain you *to the end*" (1 Cor 1:8; cf. Heb 3:6, 14; 6:11; Rev 2:26).

Against the particular form that applies this doctrine to pagans and children:

a) The basis is unscriptural through and through. For the slightest sin man is worthy of damnation before God. He does not become so only by rejecting Christ. The conception being objected to comes down ultimately to the view that God frees all people from damnation because of Christ's merits, and then provides them anew with the opportunity to decide for themselves. It is glossed-over Arminianism.

---

1   The reference is likely to an edition of the German original of *History of Protestant Theology*.

b) The rejection of Christ is a great and severe sin, but it is nowhere presented as the only sin that condemns.

c) This doctrine would quench all missionary spirit. If pagans have the same chances in the future world as here, then to bring the gospel to them does nothing other than to hasten the crisis. That could cause their judgment to come more quickly and make them more anxious. Why not let them rather live in ignorance then? Speaking reverently, let us leave all missionary activity to God Himself?

d) Scripture is so emphatic in teaching the decisiveness of this present life for eternity that many who assume a preaching of the gospel in the hereafter still acknowledge that the outcome of this preaching is always determined by the state of the hearer already in this life. So, for example, Kliefoth: If someone from among the pagans has acted here according to the light that he had, then he will also be converted by the preaching in Sheol; otherwise not. But why then, we ask, is preaching still necessary?

e) Scripture teaches that pagans are lost (Rom 1:32; 2:11, 14–15; Rev 21:8). As little for adult pagans as the children of pagans who die before their exercise of understanding does Scripture provide us with any data on the basis of which one could hope for their salvation. Naturally one cannot say *a priori* that is impossible. Some of the older Calvinists explicitly left this possibility open. Dr. Kuyper, too, leaves it open, although not as doctrine but only as sheer possibility. Among others, Zanchi and Bucanus may be named here. Suppose that with these theologians one would want to leave open the possibility, then there would still have to be protest made most earnestly against the superficial view that it is just Seneca, Cicero, and the like who are chosen as typical examples. Virtue is made the basis for knowing who is elect. If pagans are saved, they could just as well be found among the base as among the noble, the virtuous, and the learned. Here one measures with an unequal standard. Appeal is made to Acts 10:35, but there the terms "fearing Him (God)" and "working righteousness" are technical terms for proselytism (Acts 13:26; 17:4, 17; 16:14). First Peter 3:19–20; 4:6 have been discussed in detail earlier.

11. *What is meant by the doctrine of annihilation or of conditional immortality?*

The doctrine that at their death the souls of unbelievers are either completely annihilated or lose consciousness forever. Note "forever," for by that specifically this doctrine differs from that of soul-sleep. Usually it is said that by its nature the soul of man does not possess immortality but depends upon the body as an organism for its continuity of consciousness. In man as he is by nature (not as he has become through sin), the soul loses its consciousness as soon as the body dies. Out of grace, however, God has made His children immortal, that is, granted them a continuation of their consciousness after bodily death; hence conditional immortality. This theory accordingly denies the eternal punishment of the ungodly or says that their punishment consists in annihilation, at least of consciousness.

Objections to this doctrine are:

a) That death, in the proper sense of the word, would cause annihilation is in conflict with every analogy. God does not annihilate things but causes them to assume other forms. It is so with the body. Will it then be different with the soul? The biblical concept of death has nothing in common with annihilation. A man is spiritually dead before he dies bodily, but is his soul therefore annihilated or its consciousness diminished (Eph 2:1–2; 1 Tim 5:6; Col 2:13; Rev 3:1)?

b) Annihilation cannot be called punishment. Punishment demands consciousness of pain. And where existence ceases, consciousness obviously also ceases. At the most one could say that fear of annihilation is a punishment, but then naturally a temporary punishment and a very mild punishment. God can cause rational beings to return to nothing or cause them to lose consciousness. Would that be a punishment?

c) If the punishment of unbelievers consists in annihilation or elimination of consciousness, then no degrees of punishment are possible. All must then be punished in the same way and to the same degree. But Scripture appears to teach otherwise (Luke 12:47–48; Rom 2:12).

d) Many people see the extinguishing of consciousness as something desirable because they are tired of existing. So for them the punishment would be changed into a blessing. And if their consciousness ceased, they could not be convinced that they had erred.

Chapter Seven

General Eschatology

1. *What should be discussed under general eschatology?*

   a) The resurrection of the flesh.

   b) The return of the Lord for judgment and what is connected with that.

   c) The doctrine of the thousand-year kingdom; the millennium.

   d) The eternal punishment of hell.

   e) The eternal beatitude of heaven.

2. *Has the resurrection of the flesh also been denied?*

Yes, the Sadducees denied it. The Athenians could only scoff at it (Acts 17:18, 32). Hymenaeus and Philetus said that it had already taken place, that is, that it was a purely *spiritual* resurrection (2 Tim 2:17–18). In Corinth, too, there was a faction that doubted the resurrection (1 Cor 15:12). The Gnostics denied the resurrection of the flesh on the basis of a Platonic disdain of matter. In the face of all this, the ancient church said in its oldest [Apostles'] creed: "I believe the resurrection of the flesh."

3. *Is the resurrection of the flesh taught in the Old Testament?*

Yes, in Isaiah 26:19–20; Daniel 12:2–3. Consequently, at that time in which the Scriptures of the new covenant place us, the Jews generally believed in the resurrection—Martha, for example (John 11:24; cf. also Matt 16:14; Mark 6:15; 9:10; Luke 9:8, 19; Matt 14:2; Mark 6:14, 16; Luke 9:7). Especially what the Lord says against Sadducean skepticism (Matt 22:23-32; John 5:26, 28) may be compared for the New Testament. The *locus classicus* is 1 Corinthians 15.

4. How is Christ designated?

The firstfruits of those who have fallen asleep, the first from the resurrection of the dead, the firstborn from the dead (1 Cor 15:20, 23; Acts 26:23; Col 1:18; Rev 1:5). This is certainly meant in the first place of the order, but one can also grant it of the time. In the fullest sense no one rose from the dead before Him. Certainly there were resurrections from the dead in the Old Testament, but returning to this ordinary earthly life with a body as one had before is not yet being raised in the eschatological sense. Probably these people who were raised died again. The eschatological resurrection gives a new body that will not again decompose.

5. When will the resurrection take place?

Before the last judgment, at the return of Christ for judgment (1 Thess 4:16; 1 Cor 15:23-25; concerning Rev 20:5, see below in connection with the millennium). Most who teach a millennium divide the resurrection into two. Tertullian supposed that it was a gradual process, that during the 1,000 years one person would be raised earlier, another later, according to the person's worthiness, but that only at the end of the 1,000 years would they all receive a finer body. The later chiliasts, however, divided according to classes of men and not according to the parts of the resurrection itself. Some said: at the first resurrection, only believers; others, only believers from Israel.

Here we observe that Scripture knows of only one time of resurrection. This is clear in John 5:27-29, where *in the same hour*, at the voice of the Son of Man, those who have done good and those who have done evil come out of their graves. Matthew 25:31 requires the same thing, and no less 2 Corinthians 5:10. A double resurrection would require a double Parousia, for, as has been shown previously, the resurrection as a fact in the *visible* world is linked with the *visible* return of the Lord, with His appearance in a locality on earth.

For a successive resurrection, as Tertullian thought, every ground is lacking. The resurrection is not a process; it is a crisis and at the same time, as such, *a being assembled for the final judgment*. It cannot have this meaning as a process.

6. *Who will accomplish the resurrection?*

    a) Sometimes it is God in general who by His power makes the dead alive (Matt 22:29; 2 Cor 1:9), who gives us the resurrection body (1 Cor 15:38).

    b) As the Father makes the dead alive, so also does the Son (John 5:21). It is the will of the Father that the Son will raise the dead on the last day (John 6:38–40, 44). The dead will hear the voice of the Son of God (John 5:25; 1 Thess 4:16).

    c) God will make our mortal bodies alive by His Spirit (Rom 8:11).

The triune God, therefore, will accomplish the resurrection as a consequence of and out of the power of the resurrection of the Mediator. In Romans 4:17 the resurrection stands in parallel with the creation.

7. *Is the resurrection something already prepared for here or something absolutely new?*

Especially in recent times it has been proposed that the seed of the resurrection body is already present here in our mortal bodies. As seen earlier, this view is often connected with the doctrine of the sacraments. It will be a fruit of the Lord's Supper when this higher body originates and develops in us; so already Irenaeus, also Tertullian; in recent times, Delitzsch among others.

The consequence of all these conceptions is that the resurrection appears more and more as a natural outcome of sanctification and to that extent less the occurrence of an absolute miracle. It may not be worked from the outside; it must be worked from within. But that is confusing and mixing matter and spirit. The spirit cannot itself re-create matter, as is claimed here. We believe that the re-creation of matter is reserved for the end and will take place by a miracle. Finally, on this viewpoint the resurrection of unbelievers remains totally inexplicable. For them one will still have to think of a miracle.

8. Who will be resurrected?

According to Scripture, all men who have died before the hour of the resurrection (John 5:25, 28–29; "All who are in the graves," v. 28). Those who have not died a bodily death will also naturally not be resurrected, for example, Enoch, Elijah, and those who are living at the time of the Parousia (1 Thess 4:17; 1 Cor 15:51). For those who are still living a change will take the place of the resurrection.

The resurrection of the ungodly has been denied in earlier and later times. Some suppose that only believers will be raised, since they teach a conditional immortality; others connect the resurrection with the means of grace.

9. What will be resurrected?

In general we can answer: the *same* body that is laid in the grave. Thus there is identity. Scripture always speaks in such a way that this is presupposed. *This* corruptible must put on incorruption [1 Cor 15:53]. The resurrection of Christ is an example of the resurrection of believers. Now there can be no doubt whether the body of the Lord that rose was identical with that which was laid in the grave. It still even bore the signs of His suffering, the spear wound and the marks left by the hammered nails. The same thing is also implied in the image of sowing used by the apostle (1 Cor 15). What grows in the field is certainly not substantially the same as is placed in the furrow, but still it is also not something entirely new that is not connected with it.

The subject of the resurrection is *the body,* and that already entails that identity and continuity exist. Imagine that the soul received a new body. Could one then still say that *the body rose?* The soul would then be the subject of a transformation, not the body the subject of the resurrection. But Scripture speaks clearly of ἀνάστασις, ἐγείρεσθαι.

Those who reduce resurrection more to a gradual process that already begins in this life must also deny the identity of the resurrection body. Help is sought approximately in the following way: This spiritual body already being formed here gradually is like the kernel in the germinating part of a seed of grain. The whole seed does not change into the plant; a large part is lost, namely, the husk. Only the germinating part, the kernel, sprouts. Similarly, the higher body, like a bud, is in the earthly body, and while the husk perishes, the bud sprouts in the day of the resurrection.

But against this view it must be noted that Paul has taught us how *the material body as a whole* and not a part of it is the seed. Also, Paul has not given the image intended in order to *explain* the mystery, but only to show us by an analogy what is intended and how this is not impossible. One may not transfer all the features of the image, for from one seed of grain that is sown come many, while from each buried body only one body of the resurrection results.

However, one may also not fall into the other extreme, as if the resurrection body were completely the same as the buried body. Against this view there are preponderant objections:

a) Already in ordinary language usage all identity is not as such a material identity in every respect. We are aware of having the same body that we had 10 years ago, and yet this body is not comprised of the same matter that it had then. There is a steady process of metabolism; new matter is introduced, old matter is eliminated; the body is never stable. Why then would it be necessary that entirely the same particles of matter that are laid in the earth would be reconstituted into a body?

b) It has undoubtedly happened repeatedly that the same particles of matter that are located in the body of one man pass over after his death into the body of another man. One could ask (in a Sadducean fashion): whose will they be in the resurrection of the dead? But without doubt here, too, the Savior would have answered that it is not so in the resurrection of the dead.

c) Scripture teaches explicitly that, despite identity, there will be a difference between the body now and the body of the future. It is said in 1 Corinthians 15:50 that flesh and blood do not inherit the kingdom of heaven. By that the apostle does not mean to teach that the body of the resurrection is immaterial, but only that it is not flesh and blood in the earthly sense of these words. The apostle also says: "And what you sow is not the body that will be but a bare seed, perhaps of wheat or of some other grain. But God gives it a body *as He wills*, and to each seed *its own body*" (vv. 37–38).

d) Great and radical changes occur with the body in the hour of the resurrection. The mortal puts on immortality, the corruptible incorruption, what was weak becomes strong, what was in dishonor comes again in glory. Concerning two organs, at least, we are taught that they no longer will serve for their present use; namely, the sexual organs (Matt 22:30) and the digestive organs (1 Cor 6:13). In the latter passage it even says that God will destroy both the stomach and food. Both these organs are connected with this earthly dispensation and the work to be done by man in it, and if they are preserved will be intended for a higher use. Finally, we also have the explicit explanation that the resurrection body (at least for believers) is a pneumatic, a spiritual body, and no longer a psychical [ψυχικόν, 1 Cor 15:44], a natural body.

e) So we say: There is *identity* and there is *difference* together. The difficulty is only in determining in what that identity consists. To be noted is the following:

1. There will be an identity of *form* and *shape*. Each body has something personal and characteristic, but additionally each kind of body also has something typical. How far one can go regarding the former aspect is difficult to determine, but with regard to the latter one can say with certainty that the *typus* [type] of the human body will be preserved. The conception of Origen, who attributed a spherical shape to the resurrected person because the sphere is the perfect mathematical figure, should be called banal. That after His resurrection Christ had a human form settles everything here.

2. In the case of the believers, all defects and imperfections will be removed from the body. Some have thought that a cripple must first rise as a cripple and then be transformed. But Scripture presents the situation differently. It does not speak of resurrection plus glorification as two divergent things, but says: it is raised "in glory" (1 Cor 15:43).

3. We must be modest here and not wise beyond what is taught in Scripture. Augustine and others supposed that *all* matter that had ever been present in the body, all nails and all hair that had ever been cut off, would help to form the resurrection

body, not in the same form but nonetheless in their substance. Others were more moderate and said only the particles of matter that were in the body at death (so Thomas Aquinas). However, there are objections against this view too. For defective growths, malformations, disproportion, one should surely assume a loss of matter. Therefore it is better to maintain silence here about the precise manner *how*. One can only say this: In the resurrection body there will also be an identity of matter with the present body. In modern times this is often presented in such a manner as if only the same kinds of matter—for example, hydrogen, oxygen, etc.—enter into the body, but perhaps nothing of the same particles of these kinds. In our opinion that nullifies the identity and replaces it by a similarity of kind. Two statues made of the same kind of marble are not identical. We believe that matter transfers, but we do not know what matter or how it transfers. Scripture does not give us a sure explanation, and despite all scientific research matter itself is still a mystery. How the one mysterious thing that we try to fathom futilely will continue in the other mysterious thing—who will explain it? With God all things are possible.

4. With the Corinthians one can pose the question: "With what kind of body do they come?" (1 Cor 15:35). Does a person who died as a child expect to have a child's body at the resurrection? Or will all bodies be raised in adult form? Will the differences between the sexes remain discernible? Does the explanation of the Savior that they will be "like angels in heaven" [Matt 22:30] imply that not just the function of the sexual organs will cease but these organs themselves will disappear? Will stomach and food themselves or just their earthly use be done away with? These are extremely difficult questions, perhaps not to be settled entirely.

In a certain sense the resurrection is general and the same for all, for not only believers rise but also unbelievers rise. Still, again, this general resurrection is not the same for all, for the Lord Himself makes a distinction between "the resurrection of life" and "the resurrection of damnation" (John 5:29 [KJV]).

Resurrection "in glory" cannot be attributed to unbelievers, since it is a resurrection of a body that from then on is bound inseparably with the soul and cannot be detached from it. Spiritual death enters into our natural state and in this earthly dispensation always ends with temporal death; in the long run a sinful soul cannot remain joined with the body. Since now, however, according to God's ordinance, just this bond must exist for the lost, the body needs to be made in such a way that, as the organ and seat of punishment, it remains permanently joined with the soul. Thus, something in fact also happens to the resurrection body of unbelievers; it becomes something other than it first was. Still, one should take note that what Paul says in 1 Corinthians 15 is not applicable to unbelievers, since it is seen as a fruit of the resurrection of Christ. Our [Heidelberg] Catechism [answer 45] also says that the resurrection of Christ is a sure pledge of our resurrection as *saving* (vv. 20, 23, 45, 49). For the rest, Scripture says but little about the body of the ungodly as it will be after the resurrection. Some believe that they are able to tell us with complete accuracy what those bodies will look like. They will, we are told, bear the image of Satan, be completely repulsive and malformed; all the marks of sin will be etched in them. For one thing there is no proof for all of this; for another one will always have to distinguish between the body that unbelievers *receive* and the further deformation and malformation that body will undergo by the effect on it of their sinful, lost souls. Negatively, we can say that the bodies of the lost will not be spiritual, glorious, powerful (cf. 1 Cor 15:43–44).

For the body of believers one must distinguish two elements: (a) that by which it is distinguished from the body of sin; (b) that by which it is distinguished from the body that Adam had before the fall. Paul teaches clearly that the image according to which the resurrection body is formed is not the image of the first but that of the second Adam (1 Cor 15:49; Rom 8:29). Believers receive a body that is not designed for the earth but for heaven, at least for the new earth in which righteousness dwells. Their bodies are not only free from all corruption and from any seed of death, but also they can no longer die (Luke 20:36; John 11:26). The second death has no power over them (Rev 20:14; 21:4). The bodies of believers will be spiritual, glorious, powerful—heavenly bodies (σώματα ἐπουράνια, 1 Cor 15:40, 43-44); they will soar into the clouds and penetrate distances (1 Thess 4:17).

From Revelation 20:12 some have wanted to conclude that in the resurrection those who will have died as small children will also receive the bodies of small children. This is clearly deriving too much from a single phrase. In response to such an exegesis one may rightly ask: How can *all* small children *stand*? The passage says clearly: "And I saw the dead, small and great, *standing* before God." What is meant is plain: all the dead, without distinction of age, class, sex, etc.

Those who will be living at the return of the Lord will not die but will be changed at once (1 Cor 15:51-53; 1 Thess 4:13-18; to these passages some add 2 Cor 5:1-10, since, it is thought, the apostle supposed the Parousia to be very near). Scripture does not speak of a change of unbelievers without dying. Still, as far as we know, there are also no texts that definitely exclude this. The time of the transformation of the living coincides fully with the time of the resurrection of the dead; the one will not precede the other. Still in the same context (1 Thess 4:16-17) Paul says that, in order, the dead will rise first and then the living will be changed. In any case, this is merely a difference of a short time and neither of the two, the transformation as little as the resurrection, can be depicted as a process. It, the transformation, will occur *at one point in time, in an instant*. They who rise and they who are transformed will then be taken up together in the clouds to meet the Lord. If 2 Corinthians 5:1-10 also speaks of this change, then it is distinguished here from the "being clothed" (ἐνδύσασθαι) of the resurrection, as a "being clothed upon" (ἐπενδύσασθαι) and described further as a "being swallowed up" of what is mortal by life [vv. 2-4]. And, finally, it is added that this change is preferable to the resurrection, undoubtedly because the Christian who shares in it does not have to go through death (v. 4).

10. *What should be discussed in connection with the return of the Lord to judge?*

    a) The events that precede it.

    b) The return itself.

    c) The final judgment that follows it.

11. *What comes up for discussion concerning the events that precede the Lord's return?*

    a) The calling of the Gentiles.

    b) The conversion of the Jews.

    c) The antichrist.

    d) Signs and wonders.

12. *Where does the difficulty lie in saying something about these things?*

    a) In the need before speaking about them to make a thorough and comprehensive study of all the prophecies of both the Old and New Testaments.

    b) In the distinctive character of prophecy itself. It frequently speaks in such terms that it is only understood in its proper meaning subsequently, after its fulfillment.

13. *From what do you establish that the general calling of the Gentiles must precede the return of the Lord?*

From Matthew 24:14; Mark 13:10; Romans 11:25. These and like passages together include that the spread of the gospel to all is the goal to which history is moving and that therefore, with the reaching of this goal, history has fulfilled its task and passes over into the end of all things. The prophecies mentioned here do not necessarily mean that all nations will accept the gospel *en masse*, but only that it will come to all nations and among all of them will find its followers. It seems only that is meant even in Romans 11:25.

14. *Where is the conversion of the Jews spoken of as a sign of the end?*

In general, in all the prophecies of the Old Testament that speak of the apostasy and the return of the Jews; more specifically, in Zechariah 12 and Romans 11. Romans 11 speaks of a national conversion, that is, a conversion of the majority, by which naturally it is not also said that then all individuals of that majority will be saved. But what is meant is something as a whole, something national, for Paul clearly distinguishes the conversion of the "remnant according to election" [Rom 11:5] from the salvation of "all Israel" [v. 26].

15. *What makes the treatment of the further details of this conversion*
so difficult?

Because for one thing it has been associated with the anticipated return of the Jews to the Holy Land, for another with the millennial kingdom. This already happened quite early (Justin, Irenaeus). In reaction, the opponents of chiliasm have not infrequently denied the general conversion of the Jews (e.g., Augustine). Later, too, doubt about this conversion kept pace with the aversion to chiliasm. One was afraid of furthering chiliasm.

It seems to us that the conversion of Israel is clearly predicted. But that will not occur in order to make Israel a special nation and give it back its old, separate position; that would be an anachronism in the days of the New Testament. Nor will it be in order to return the Jews to the Holy Land.

Appeal for this view is made:

a) To the explicit statements of Old Testament prophecy. But it should be noted that Old Testament prophecy speaks in Old Testament terms, which we may not interpret literally. The Israel spoken of repeatedly is spiritual Israel. And when it is said that it shall return to its land, that the temple will be rebuilt, the office of priest restored, the sacrifices reintroduced, the entire Mosaic ritual renewed in detail, then one should either take *all of this* literally or, if one cannot or dare not do that, should also understand the return to the Holy Land less literally and more spiritually. All too literal interpretation here would undermine the perfect and final character of the work of the Mediator.

b) To the special lot of the Jews, who, despite their being scattered, have continued to exist as a separate race and do not mix with others. From this, however, it appears only that God wills to deal with the Jews at a particular time and that they must remain separate until that time. In no sense do they still have a national calling. They will become ordinary Christians, not a kind of Christian nobility.

c) To the fact that the Holy Land is empty and, as it were, seems to be waiting for the Jews. But the desolation that has come upon Palestine this land shares with other Near Eastern lands, so that from that circumstance nothing can be concluded.

16. *What does one understand by the antichrist?*

An appearance that must precede the return of Christ (2 Thess 2:1–3). This passage does not have the term *antichrist*. Daniel 7 speaks of the little horn that came up among the ten horns of the wild beast, had eyes like human eyes and a mouth speaking great things. Then thrones are set up and the Ancient of Days is seated, the judgment comes, the books are opened [vv. 7–10]. This is then explained further (from v. 24 on). The small horn is another king who will arise after the ten kings, who humbles three of them, speaks words against the Most High, harasses the saints of the Most High, and into whose hand they shall be given over for "a time, times and half a time," after which comes the judgment that takes away his dominion, and consumes and destroys him. See also chapter 11 from verse 36 on, and chapter 12. From Revelation, chapters 17 and 18 come into consideration here. Spoken of here is a woman sitting on a scarlet beast. The term *antichrist* is not mentioned. If occurs only in John, who uses it five times (1 John 2:18, twice; 2:22; 4:3; 2 John 7).

The question now is, What is meant by the phenomena delineated here? Is the antichrist a single, particular person? Or is it a power presented here personified? Does he come only at the end of time? Or is it a frequently repeating phenomenon that in its first appearance is a prophecy of its later form? Is it a worldly power or an ecclesiastical power? All these questions are so interwoven with each other that it is impossible to answer them separately.

a) In the ancient church, which bitterly oppressed and persecuted the Jews in particular, it was thought that the antichrist had to be a

Jew, and then from the tribe of Dan, because it was omitted in the list of the tribes in Revelation 7:5–8. This Jew will present himself as the Messiah. He will rule in Jerusalem and in the temple proclaim himself to be God. From there he will extend his dominion (cf. also Gen 49:17; Rev. 11:7–8). This is also the view of Bellarmine among Roman Catholics, who go to a great deal of trouble against the Protestants to exonerate the pope or the papacy from blame as the antichrist.

b) Many unbelieving modern exegetes declare the antichrist to be a Roman emperor—Nero or another ruler—from the time when the letter to the Thessalonians was written. This view rests on a denial of the infallibility of Scripture. Supposedly predictions like those in Daniel, in Paul, and in Revelation only have in view contemporary or at least not far-distant events of that time, and that all of these imaginings have now served their purpose. Paul believed, it is said, that the Roman world power, personified in one Caesar or another, was the antichrist. This theory is also applied to Revelation and so understands the antichrist to be Nero. The number of Nero is 666 (קסר נרון = 100 + 60 + 200 + 50 + 200 + 6 + 50 [Rev 13:18]).

c) The Waldensians, Wycliffe, Hus, most of the Reformers, and the Protestant theologians see the antichrist in the papacy. Here and there this view is affirmed in a confession, for example in the Smalcald Articles. The Lutherans especially take a strong stand here, so that anyone who did not accept this view was held to be heterodox. But most of the Reformed also shared this opinion (cf. Calvin, *Institutes*, 4.2.12; 4.7.20 and following).

There is much to be said for this view:

1. According to Paul in 2 Thessalonians 2:3 and following, the antichrist is an *apostate*, thus in one sense or another an ecclesiastical power, or an ecclesiastical person and not purely worldly in nature.

2. This apostate will sit in "the temple of God," thus as it were, in the church.

3. He will sit there "as God," thus arrogating to himself things that only belong to God.

4. He will come with "'signs and wonders of the lie," with the power to delude, in order to cause the lie to be believed.

5. He will be a persecuting power.

6. Although at the time of the New Testament he was still to come in the future, still the mystery of iniquity was already being wrought silently, the rudiments of his power were present and developing.

7. Verse 6–7 can be readily understood as speaking of the power of the Roman state. As long as it existed, the power of the papacy could not arise. The former was the "the restrainer" (ὁ κατέχων and τὸ κατέχον). It needs no detailed argument to show how all these characteristics are again found in the papacy.

But there are also objections to this view:

1. According to Daniel the little horn is not an ecclesiastical but a worldly power, like the empires that preceded it; someone, according to chapter 8, who finds his exemplification in Antiochus Epiphanes.

2. Revelation also generally presents the power of the antichrist as a worldly power (9:15 and following; 11:7; 13:1 and following; 17:18, cf. vv. 13–14).

3. It seems that Revelation makes a distinction between Babel and the antichrist. In chapter 17 John is shown the great prostitute who sits on the many waters [v. 1], who is called Babylon [v. 5], who is drunk with the blood of the saints and of the witnesses of Jesus [v. 6], who sits on the seven mountains [v. 9], who is hated by the ten horns, made desolate by them, and burned up with fire [v. 16]. In chapter 18 it is then said that she is fallen [v. 2]. Then chapter 19 again mentions the beast, who is captured with the false prophet, and they are thrown into the lake of fire that burns with sulfur [v. 20].

We do not believe that these objections are insurmountable and note the following:

a) That according to the explicit explanation of John, the antichrist is every place where a hostile spirit arises against Christianity.

In agreement with this, the basic principle of the power of the antichrist already began to be at work in Paul's day.

b) That the antichrist will indeed attain to its/his maximum power at the end of time, and this final appearance of it/him will be a sign of the end, but that nevertheless all kinds of phenomena during the entire time of the New Testament must be seen as antichristian in character.

c) That Daniel delineates the antichrist more according to its/his worldly side, Paul more according to its/his ecclesiastical side, but that the book of Revelation combines these two sides when it shows us a *woman* on a *beast* with heads and horns. It is most plausible to think of the ecclesiastical side for the term "woman," the worldly side for the term "beast." Consistent with this, the church is repeatedly called a woman or virgin and the apostate church an adulteress or prostitute, as the woman on the beast is called here. Finally, we must take note that in Revelation the beast first appears *alone* (chapter 3), then the beast and the woman *together,* grown into one as it were (chapter 17), and finally, after the woman is fallen and consumed, the beast *alone* again (chapter 19).

d) It appears to be implied in this that the antichrist first appears as a worldly power, then is married with the apostasy of the church, in order with or after this to perish. This undoubtedly makes us think of Rome. Rome is apostasy plus secularized church power. It has married itself to the state and by means of the power of this world has oppressed and persecuted God's children. To that extent it can very well appear as the woman on the beast, as church and world together.

e) It is not to be denied that the Old and New Testament prophecies give rise to thinking of a specific revelation of this antichristian power toward the end of the ages. We can therefore surmise that in Rome—better, in the papacy as it now is—we do not yet have the full revelation of the antichrist. Perhaps the papacy will once more ally itself with the hostile power of the world, to then be itself rejected by the latter. We do not know whether that will happen, but if it did happen, we would certainly have to acknowledge in retrospect that prophecy has alluded to it.

f) One must make a distinction between antichrist and *the* antichrist. To say that the papacy is antichrist is not the same as saying that it is *the* antichrist. And one must likewise make a distinction between the papacy and the Roman Catholic Church. The antichrist as such directly opposes Christ and is estranged from all truth; in the Roman Catholic Church elements of truth still remain.

g) One should associate the last appearance of the antichrist, as its/his appearance in general, with *apostasy*. That is clear on the basis of the predictions of the Savior Himself (cf. Matt 24–25; Mark 13; Luke 21). Unrighteousness will increase steadily; the love of many will become cold; people will betray each other; brother will hand over brother, parents their children, children their parents; false prophets and Christs will arise, etc. With this 1 Thessalonians 5:3 agrees that they will say: There is peace without danger!

One could now ask: How are the various signs of the end to be reconciled with each other? On the one hand, the fullness of the Gentiles must enter and all Israel must be saved! On the other hand, a great apostasy will occur in which antitheses come to be sharply opposed to each other and the church comes to be almost completely isolated, oppressed by all its persecutors. One should bear in mind, however, that the outward expansion of the church, which proceeds slowly, is quite compatible with internal apostasy, while also, surely, the gates from which apostasy and mission emerge ought not to be the same. One could even maintain that there is more than a temporary link between expansion and apostasy, that the former, by the externalization to which it gives rise, carries within itself the seeds of the latter. But this and more such particulars we wish to leave to its place.

17. Must signs and wonders precede the end?

Yes, for signs and wonders belong to every supernatural crisis in the history of revelation. They have accompanied the exodus from Egypt, the giving of the law at Sinai, the incarnation of the Word, and they will also precede and accompany the fulfillment of all things. Scripture presents this in such a way that in the last days there will signs and wonders (Joel 2:30–31; 3:15–16; Isa 13:6–13; 24:18 and following; Hag 2:7).

For the New Testament compare the eschatological discourses of the Lord (Matt 24; Mark 13; Luke 21). Here the apostles present two questions to the Lord, namely, (a) when the destruction of Jerusalem predicted by Him will occur; (b) what the signs of His coming are when the end will be. Apparently these questions were asked with the presupposition that the destruction of Jerusalem would coincide with the end. Hence, too, in the answer of the Savior a sharp division is not made between what belongs to the one and what belongs to the other, and it is very difficult for us to make the division. In any case it is clear that the Lord Himself did not identify the time point for these two events. Further, it appears from the presentation as a whole that the signs and wonders will certainly be grouped together toward the end, but that they will not all come at the same time; there is a certain passing of time; they will follow each other and so by their sequence show that the end is approaching more and more.

The Lord speaks of a few of these signs as ἀρχὴ ὠδίνων, "source of the sorrows" or "beginning of the birth pains" [Matt 24:8; Mark 13:8]. By that all these events are put under the viewpoint of catastrophes that accompany the birth of something new. As an infant cannot be born without pains, so too the rebirth of the entire earthly creation, which coincides with the end, will occur under terrible labor pains. The beginning of those pains consists of wars, sicknesses, famines, and earthquakes. In itself all of this would not yet be something special, but Luke 21:11 tells us that this will be accompanied by "terrible things and great signs from heaven," thus by something absolutely extraordinary, so that it will be easy to distinguish them from ordinary disasters and distresses.

Mentioned as later signs, which appear to immediately precede the Parousia, are: the darkening of the sun, the ceasing the light of the moon, the moving of the stars out of their paths and their falling from heaven, the powers of heaven being shaken, that is, the loss of balance of the powers that maintain the order of heaven. It will be as if the universe was unhinged. The result of these signs will be anxiety of the nations, great perplexity, and the failure of hearts through fear and the expectation of things that will come.

Between these two groups of signs falls the appearance of the false prophets and of false Christs, who will perform similar signs and wonders. This agrees with what we have seen above regarding the apostasy of those times.

In Revelation, too, such signs and miracles are spoken of. First come war, famine, and plague that kill a fourth of the inhabitants of the earth. Other phenomena of a celestial kind follow: the sun becomes black as sackcloth, the moon like blood, the stars fall to earth as a fig tree throws off its unripe figs, heaven disappears like a scroll that is rolled up, mountains and islands are moved from their places. Men hide themselves in the caves and among the rocks of the mountains (Rev 6:12–17). In chapter 8:7–12 still more is added to this: hail and fire mixed with blood, a third of the trees and all the grass is burned up, a third of the sea becomes blood, the a third of the water of the rivers becomes wormwood by a star that falls from heaven, those who drink of the waters die. See further the whole of the ninth chapter for the further trumpets, as well as chapter 16 for the bowls.

Many suppose that also in the last days signs and wonders will be renewed among the children of God, as Joel 2:28–29 speak of that. A great prophet, it is thought, will come before the Lord, now too as at His first coming (Mal 3:2–3). The two witnesses of Revelation 11:3–12 are associated with this. By these two witnesses Luthardt, among others, understands Moses and Elijah in connection with Matthew 17:11. But all this is very precarious.

All these signs and wonders are distinguished noticeably from earlier signs and miracles. All the miracles of the Savior were curative in nature (with the sole exception of cursing the unfruitful fig tree). The signs of the end are in order to harm and to corrupt, to terrify and to oppress. They are punitive wonders, God's judgments, plagues.

18. What does Scripture teach about the return of the Lord Himself?

Earlier [in volume three] we pointed out the significance it has as a step in the exaltation of the Mediator. Here it comes into consideration as an eschatological fact. Already in Daniel the two comings of the Lord are separated; likewise in Zechariah 13:7 and following. In the New Testament it becomes completely clear that a second coming will follow the first. The following points deserve consideration:

a) Did the apostles expect the return of the Lord soon? On the one hand, it has been maintained unequivocally that this is the case, and that in this they were mistaken and so erred in what they taught. On the other hand, it has been argued as certain that not for a moment can they have thought that. Both ideas, it seems to us, are incorrect. The apostles were at first, especially before the suffering of the Lord and even still later (Acts 1:6–8), very ignorant about these things. Also, the Savior did not deem it necessary to inform them in detail about times and season (Acts 1:7; Matt 24:36, 42, 44, 50). We have no basis for assuming that later the apostles had revelations about the exact passage of time between the ascension and the Parousia. They always speak indefinitely, although Paul certainly says negatively that the day is not yet immediately at hand (cf. 2 Pet 3:8–10). Paul knows that first the fullness of the Gentiles must come in and all Israel be saved. So it cannot be conceded that the apostles would have definitely misled their converts or entangled them in the error that the day of the Lord was immediately at hand.

Against that conclusion, appeal is made to passages like Matthew 10:23. Taught here is only the unresponsiveness of the cities of Israel. Matthew 16:28 speaks of the initial glorification of the Lord. Matthew 24:34 and parallel passages either have in view the fall of Jerusalem or with "this generation" the nation of the Jews is to be understood. Matthew 26:63 also says only that His judging and ruling, of which the last judgment is the culmination, already begins after His suffering. Philippians 3:20, 1 Corinthians 15:51, and 1 Thessalonians 4:15 are cited from Paul's letters. But it cannot be proven that the "we" in these passages is more than the general Christian "we" that includes everyone, including Christians of the future. When the reader is reminded again and again that the Lord is near, etc. (Phil 4:5; Heb 10:25, 37; Jas 5:7–9; 1 Pet 4:7), then by that it should be kept in view that for the Christian death is equivalent to the coming of the Lord.

b) The return of the Lord is meant literally, bodily, and not figuratively as the Rationalists and also Schleiermacher propose. Sufficient here, for example, is a passage like Acts 1:11. He will return "in the same way" as He departed.

c) The Lord will return only once, and not as chiliasts must teach, twice—first to establish the millennium, then to begin the eternal kingdom. Scripture knows only *one* return. Chiliasts are not agreed on the question whether after His first Parousia the Lord returns to heaven. If so, what becomes of His 1,000-year reign on earth? If not, how then can one speak of a new return? That He will come in order to judge cannot be denied.

d) Regarding the *manner* of His return, Scripture teaches that He will come:

1. from heaven

2. on the clouds of heaven

3. in the form of His human nature

4. as a man

5. not in humility but in glory

6. without sin, that is, no longer as the Surety bearing guilt

7. with His angels, the heavenly host who will serve Him in everything that is associated with His return

8. according to some, accompanied by the spirits of believers who have already gone to heaven, which, it is thought, is to be found in 1 Thessalonians 3:13 ("with all His *saints*"), 2 Thessalonians 1:10, Jude 14

9. as a thief in the night, not only for unbelievers but also in a certain sense even for believers since they never know the hour exactly

10. for all together as in the same moment, as a lightning bolt that shines from east to west

11. not only visibly but also audibly, with a shout and the voice of the archangel and with the trumpet of God

12. with His manifestation and cry, causing the resurrection of the dead and gathering them for judgment, so that at His coming believers lift up their heads with joy, meanwhile unbelievers weep.

The place of the return is not mentioned. Some expect that it will occur in the valley of Jehoshaphat on the basis of Joel 3:2, thus near the place where He arose. But that is merely a hypothesis.

e) We note further that the antichrist will be destroyed by the Spirit of the Lord's mouth and by the manifestation of His coming [2 Thess 2:8]. The hostile power that has arrayed itself against His church will collapse as soon as the Lord shows Himself. From Revelation 19:20 the conclusion has been drawn that the antichrist and the false prophet, who has served him, will, without dying first, descend living into hell (as it were in contrast with Enoch and Elijah), while the others are killed in order then again to be resurrected.

19. *What views regarding the last judgment must be rejected?*

a) That it is not a single event at the end of the ages but a slow process realized in history, *"Die Weltgeschichte is das Weltgericht"* ["The history of the world is the judgment of the world"—Hegel].

b) That what Scripture pronounces concerning it is merely Jewish, sensory dressing for the idea that one day there will be a separation between the world and the church—Schleiermacher.

c) That the determination of everyone's destiny already at temporal death, when the soul already enters then into beatitude or perdition, makes a last judgment superfluous. (One also reasons conversely: if the definitive judgment first comes at the consummation of all things, death cannot be decisive; ergo: conversion is possible after death.) But the last judgment is distinguished from that at death: (a) by its public character; (b) by its pertaining to both body and soul; (c) by its universal character.

d) That judgment at death and the last judgment must coincide for the individual in his consciousness, because after death until the resurrection there is no passing of time for departed souls. It is not true that in this sense departed souls are outside of time. We are outside of the time of this earth, not outside time in general.

20. Will the last judgment take place in one day or last longer?

One could conclude the former from what Scripture continually mentions of "the day" of judgment (Matt 10:15); "the day" of Jesus Christ (1 Cor 1:8); "the great day" (Rev 6:17); "the day" (1 Cor 3:13); "that day" (2 Tim 4:8). But, on the other hand, there is also mention of "the hour of judgment" (Rev 14:7). Thus one can only say this: (a) resurrection and judgment will be linked directly; (b) the judgment will not be a slow process but *one* act, clearly separated from the other.

21. Where will the judge and the persons to be judged be located?

It is difficult to conclude anything in this regard. The judge will certainly be visible to all. On the basis of 1 Thessalonians 4:17, the Lutherans thought that the judgment would take place in the air. The Reformed sometimes concluded from this text that believers would receive their judgment in the air, unbelievers below, on earth. But 1 Thessalonians 4 is not related specifically to the last judgment but only to the glorification of believers, which in part precedes the judgment, in part follows it, for which reason also nothing is said about unbelievers.

22. Who will the judge be at the last judgment?

Christ in His official capacity, nevertheless enabled for this by His divine perfections. His judging is a part of His work as Mediator. In that it can also be said that God is the judge of all (Heb 12:23), for what the Mediator does He does on behalf of God. John 3:17 and 12:47 of course do not exclude His judgeship but rather require it (cf. 9:39). Because Christ is the Son of Man (= the Mediator), He has received power to execute judgment over all (John 5:27). The Father judges no one but has given all judgment to the Son (v. 22; cf. also Acts 17:31; Rom 14:9–12; 1 Pet 4:5; Rev 6:16, "the *wrath* of the Lamb").

There is a series of texts in which a joint judgeship of the angels and the apostles or even believers in general, seems to be taught. To that series belongs Matthew 19:28; 20:23; Luke 22:30; Matthew 25:31; 16:27; 2 Thessalonians 1:7; Revelation 14:10; Jude 14; 1 Thessalonians 3:13; Matthew 13:39, 41, 49; 24:31; 1 Thessalonians 4:16; 2 Thessalonians 1:10; Revelation 3:21; 1 Corinthians 6:1–3. For these texts a threefold observation may be made:

a) What is said about the apostles judging the twelve tribes of Israel does not so much have in view judgment but rather the glorification that follows.

b) What is said about the angels only concerns their ministering work at the judgment: proclaiming that the Lord is there, gathering for judgment, separating good from bad, but still not the actual judgment itself.

c) Concerning believers, 1 Corinthians 6:1–3 undoubtedly teaches that they will be involved in judging at the judgment exercised by Christ. Scripture does not say further how we are to think about that. How can they judge and be judged at the same time? Perhaps the one follows the other. By "angels" [v. 3] we have to understand the *fallen* angels.

23. *Who will appear at the last judgment?*

All men and at least the fallen angels. The former is denied by consistent chiliasts, for those who have already ruled for 1,000 years with the Lord in glory can certainly not come into judgment again. There are those who only have the inhabitants of Sheol summoned at the judgment, namely, those whose destiny is first decided in Sheol, while they also have believers and unbelievers, who have heard the gospel here, judged already at death. Appeal for this view is made to John 3:18; 5:24; 12:47. But in these passages we find nothing more than that the relationship one has to the Savior already virtually decides his destiny. Their unbelief already establishes that perdition awaits them. But this in no way excludes the judgment itself, which takes note of these things and renders their judicial consequence.

Scripture teaches very emphatically that the judgment will be general (e.g., Matt 25:32; Acts 17:30–31; Rom. 2:6–16; 2 Cor 5:10).

That the evil angels will be judged is apparent from 1 Corinthians 6:3, from 2 Peter 2:4, "submitted them to chains of darkness to be kept for the judgment"; Jude 6, "kept in eternal chains under darkness for the judgment of the great day." It has been said that the devil does not belong at the judgment along with men, since grace has not been offered to him and the demons. But neither does that apply to pagans, and the devil with his demons most certainly has a relationship to the work of redemption as its great adversary, whose works Christ destroys.

24. Can we specify further how the judgment will take place?

No, we cannot envision the visible particulars in detail. Scripture says, for example, that seats are placed, etc. It may be, however, that this is merely earthly imagery. But, conversely, this does not grant the right to vaporize the whole into a metaphor. It will not be, as Origen thought, a solely inward trial in the conscience of men, but something external and objective. Everyone will see the Lord, and He, the judge, will look everyone in the eye. To its implementation, furthermore, belong three parts: (a) the *cognitio causae*, the announcement of the state of things with respect to each person in particular; (b) *sententiae promulgatio*, the declaration of the verdict; (c) *sententiae executio*, the execution of the verdict.

a) The *cognitio causae* has been portrayed symbolically as an opening of the books or as questions and answers (Dan 7:10; Rev 20:12; Matt 25:34–46). By books nothing other is to be understood than the infallible omniscience of God, who knows everything as precisely as a man knows what he has written down in his books. One speaks of the book of providence, the book of conscience, the book of predestination or of life, the book of Scripture. Similarly, one need not understand the questions and answers as necessarily literal. But in each case, at the same time everything that is the object of judgment will pass through the consciousness of the person who is judged. He will have to represent himself. How that is effected is irrelevant. In an earthly trial it happens through the examination of witnesses, audible giving of evidence. God can cause all that, as it is present in His divine omniscience, to occur immediately for the consciousness of those who are judged. This *cognitio causae* will be all-inclusive; it will concern words, thoughts, actions, habits, the deepest predisposition and orientation of the soul—faith or unbelief for those who have lived under the gospel, living according to the law or transgressing the law for those who have sinned under the law—the works both of believers and unbelievers (1 Pet 1:17; Rev 20:12–15; Eph 6:8; 1 Tim 6:18–19; 2 Cor 11:15).

That this being judged "according to works" also applies to believers is apparent from Matthew 25:34-40; 1 Corinthians 4:5; 2 Corinthians 5:10; Revelation 22:12. However, this is not to be understood in the sense that works provide the basis for the decision whether one has earned or not earned salvation. Works will come into consideration as a manifestation of genuine saving faith. Work in the scriptural sense also means not just an external display but the expression of one's life that flows out of the depth of the heart. So understood, works are in fact evidences for the presence of faith. But works occur in yet another sense than as evidences of faith. Scripture also speaks of reward for believers ("their works follow them," Rev 14:13; Matt 5:12, 16; 6:1; Luke 6:23; Heb 10:34-38). This reward comes as compensation for the cross, as restitution for what was robbed, as recompense for love shown to the servants of the Lord, etc. There will be proportion in this reward (Matt 25:21, 23; Luke 6:38; 19:17, 19; 1 Cor 3:8). It is present- ed as a reaping that corresponds to what is sown (Gal 6:7-10). Salvation will be perfect for all, but nonetheless not entirely the same for all. This is certain: the difference will not possibly provide any occasion for unhappiness. Accordingly, for believers works are a *criterion* for the glory to be received. But this is *a reward out of grace* (Rom 11:35; 1 Cor 4:7; John 3:27). And the be- stowing of salvation, as such, will take place solely on the basis of the imputed righteousness of Christ received by faith.

It is asked whether the sins of believers will also be judged. Without doubt, these too, but then immediately compensated by the righteousness of Christ. Even in what appears to be their good works a sifting will take place. It will be become manifest what is gold, silver, precious stones, and what is wood, straw, or stubble must be nullified in the fire of the judgment. If anyone's work is burned up, then he will suffer loss but nonetheless will himself be saved as through fire (1 Cor 3:11-15).

Those who have lived under the gospel will be judged not only for their faith but for all their sins, including unbelief. One's entire life will be summed up, the final outcome settled, and the result of that life registered.

Pagans who have only had the law of nature will also only be judged according to that law—not as if God would also require less than complete conformity with His strict justice but in such a way that their responsibility will not be as weighty as it will be for others judged by the knowledge that they possessed of the supernaturally revealed will of God (Rom 2:14).

The representation of Scripture throughout is that what has happened in the body falls under the judgment. This means that the existence of departed souls in heaven and hell will not be judged. Hence the existence of those in hell is to be seen as anticipated punishment—preceding the judgment in time, following the judgment in order.

b) The *sententiae promulgatio* [declaration of the verdict] follows the *cognitio causae* [announcement of the case]. What has been established for everyone must become open, public. The day of wrath is at the same time a day of the revelation of the righteous judgment of God (Rom 2:5). And of all men it is said that it must be public. A sense of justice requires this. Usually it is imagined that the Judge will at least announce the final verdict over everyone with a loud voice. This is certain: it will be made known not only to the person whom it concerns but also to all who are connected with him.

At the last judgment humanity divides into two classes, which Scripture places on the right hand and on the left hand of the Lord. Still, there are those who here too wish to introduce a threefold division. It is said, namely, that those who have not lived under the gospel here have gone to Sheol. In Sheol no preaching of the gospel was possible because there is no time for the souls of the departed. Therefore the preaching must follow on the day of judgment itself. It consists in the appearance of the glory of Christ. As soon as this glory is revealed, the souls that have come out of Hades and are now again united with their bodies are enabled to accept Christ or reject Him. And then their judgment follows. That this conception is completely unscriptural needs no argument.

c) Concerning the execution of the previous verdict, see below.

25. What is understood by the thousand-year kingdom or millennium?

The name is derived from Revelation 20:1–6. Satan is bound for 1,000 years and shut up in the abyss. The souls of those who were beheaded for the testimony of Jesus and for the word of God and who have not worshiped the beast or its image, live and reign as kings with Christ for a thousand years. The name *chiliasm* means the same thing ($\chi\text{i}\lambda\text{io}\iota$ = 1,000).

It is not easy to state what chiliasm intends. The chiliasts differ greatly among each other. Kliefoth gives the following as its main features: When the preaching of the gospel has come to all the Gentiles, Israel will be converted to Christ—and that as a people, in its entirety—the Lord will then appear and will return Israel to the land of Canaan and unite it with the believers of all ages resurrected by Him. In a glorified Jerusalem and Canaan, Israel, under the idealized and spiritualized ordinances of the Old Testament, will realize the ideal of a Christian state and will become a spiritual metropolis for all countries, from which a work of missions on a great scale will go forth. At the end of the 1,000 years the unbelieving elements of the countries surrounding it will be united, rise up against the Holy Land and besiege the glorified Jerusalem. In doing that, however, they will be crushed by the Lord, after which the general resurrection, the last judgment, and the end of this world will follow.

Besides this there is a less crass view that has a spiritual return of the Lord following the appearance of the antichrist and then a period—not exactly 1,000 years but still many years—of unheard-of prosperity and blessing for the church and of restraint of evil and Satan. Christianity will occupy a position of world dominance. In this period, then, also falls for the greatest part the universal preaching of the gospel.

Finally, there is still a third view that takes up many elements of chiliasm regarding the future of the Jews and their national preeminence, but places all this in eternity, therefore after the general resurrection and the last judgment.

Within these limits, as has been said, great differences prevail among chiliasts. Some say that the Jews will first be converted and then brought to their land. Others say that the Jews will first be brought to their land and there be converted. Some say that the resurrected saints will live in heaven, others put them on earth; still others say that sometimes they will be in heaven and sometimes on earth. Some say that they will appear visibly to those over whom they will rule, others that they will not be seen. Some see believers or saints as being angels; others hold that from them there will be reproduction and multiplication of the human race during the thousand years. And regarding the manner of contact between this glorified part of humanity and the remaining, still earthly humanity, great differences of opinion prevail.

26. What are the objections to these chiliastic theories?

a) The first objection is that the chiliasts have a wrong understanding of the concept "Israel." In itself it is not necessary that chiliasm and the expectation of an external, national restoration of Israel coincide, but in fact they do mostly coincide. And this is not accidental. If one does not hold to this national, earthly future for Israel, then one cannot imagine anything in the world that the millennium should serve to fulfill. It then becomes merely a shadow of the future glory, a thing composed of heterogeneous elements of diverse origin. If, on the other hand, it is true that Israel must be restored as a unified people with political, theocratic institutions and external national forms, then a period will have to be set apart for that before the consummation of all things, for in eternal glory there is no place for something like that. In that point lies the *nexus causalis* [causal connection] between Jewish-fleshly expectations and chiliasm.

This entire conception is in conflict with Scripture. With the incarnation and Christ's finished work of satisfaction, Israel's national calling has been terminated. That would even have been the case if Israel in its majority had not rejected the Savior. Even then it would not have been more than the first in the line of Christian peoples, a part of spiritual Israel. For according to the repeated witness of the New Testament, "Israelite" is synonymous with "Christian." The circumcision of the heart makes one a true Jew [Rom 2:29].

The chiliasts repeatedly represent the situation such that the apostasy of Israel (said with respect) was a disappointment for God and the calling of the Gentiles a surprise. Scripture speaks repeatedly such that from the very beginning it is in God's purpose to confer the covenant service of the Jews on the Gentiles.

It is one church that is built on the foundation of the prophets and the apostles; as a matter of course the spiritual Israel, the true Israel, grows out of Israel according to the flesh. One may compare how the New Testament writers assess the fulfillment of Old Testament prophecies that the chiliasts would wish to refer to the restoration of Israel. Peter [sic] says in Acts 15:16 that the reception of the Gentiles into the church of the Lord is a fulfillment of what Old Testament prophecy knows to relate to rebuilding the fallen tent of David (Amos 9:11). The letter to the Hebrews says that already at that time was fulfilled what the Old Testament says concerning the pilgrimages to Jerusalem of all peoples (Heb 12:22). All the Old Testament concepts of "temple," "Jerusalem," "Zion," are conceived of as spiritual and international in the New Testament.

b) Chiliasm robs the Christian church of its missionary privilege. It is almost as if God is bound to Israel in order to complete the work of missions and so must wait for the conversion of the Jews. Scripture speaks entirely the other way around. The fullness of the Gentiles will enter first and then all Israel will be saved.

c) In the eschatological discourses of the Lord and in the letters of the apostles not a word occurs about a thousand-year kingdom, not even where there was an occasion to speak about it. An appeal is made to various passages, for example, to Acts 3:19–20, but only by contrived exegesis can anything about a millennium be found in them.

One circumstance in particular gives an appearance of warrant for the chiliastic conception. The apostles frequently speak soteriologically about eschatology; that is, they often deal with the doctrine of the last things from the viewpoint of the significance it has for believers (so, e.g., 1 Thess 4 and 1 Cor 15). Hence they are silent about the significance these last things have for unbelievers. Consequently, it would unavoidably have to appear as though they only knew of a resurrection and glorification of believers, and there are those who are immediately ready to identify this with the so-called "first resurrection" of chiliasm. However, on closer examination it is soon apparent that also in those texts where the dark side of eschatology remains outside of consideration, the data still occur altogether irreconcilable with chiliasm. One may take 1 Corinthians 15, for example. In verse 23 the resurrection of believers with Christ is spoken of. Now in verse 24 the millennium should be spoken of. But what is there? "Then shall be the end, when He shall have delivered over the kingdom to God the Father, when He shall have destroyed all rule and all authority and power." So, here the resurrection of believers and delivering over the kingdom are directly connected.

d) There are a great number of texts that do not leave room for a millennium between the first resurrection and the consummation of all things.

1. The destruction of the antichrist and the Parousia coincide, according to 1 Corinthians 15:24 and 2 Thessalonians 2:8.

2. The resurrection and the last judgment likewise coincide, according to Luke 14:14; John 5:25–29; Heb 6:2.

3. Again, the destruction of the antichrist and the general resurrection coincide since, according to 1 Corinthians 15:24, all powers hostile to God, even death, will be destroyed together with the antichrist. So it follows then that Philippians 3:20–21, 1 Thessalonians 4:15, and other passages connect the Parousia directly with the last judgment.

e) The Lord taught explicitly that the separation of the good from the wicked will only take place at the consummation of the ages (Matt 13:37–43, 47–50); according to the chiliasts a separation already takes place 1,000 years before the end. As a disciple "in this age" one receives a hundredfold in houses, brothers, sisters, mothers, children, fields, with persecutions, but eternal life only "in the age to come" (Mark 10:30). But "this age" and "the coming age"—which Christ so sharply keeps separate here—chiliasm merges.

f) Chiliasm entangles itself in insoluble difficulties. How is it possible that a piece of glorified earth—one may well say, a piece of heaven—can exist in the midst of an unglorified earth? How can death and life coexist on the same planet in this fantastic manner? How can there be contact between these two different kinds of people? How can the Lord rule on earth without believers from all lands streaming to Him? Who would want to remain in America if he knows that his Savior is to be seen in Palestine? How at the end of the millennium will Gog and Magog dare to be so bold as to rise up against the Lord Himself and fight Him? No chiliast has ever made a successful attempt to remove all these difficulties.

g) One must acknowledge that Revelation 20:1–6 seems to speak of a millennium. We are not able here to provide an explanation of this passage. It would first be necessary to decide which interpretation of the book of Revelation must be employed, the so-called church-historical theory or the so-called groupings-theory. In any case, it is certain that the numbers in Revelation do not have a literal but a symbolic meaning. The number of the beast is 666. Even the chiliast cannot take that number literally. Why then does he insist on the literal interpretation of these 1,000 years? Also, Revelation 20 does not say anything about the Jews. Only the martyrs and the faithful are mentioned. Additionally, one ought to proceed from the principle that in more obscure prophetic passages one may not find what is in conflict with the clear meaning of other passages.

However, we would not want to go as far as some who say that if it is proven that Revelation 20:1–6 in fact teaches a millennium, then that for me is a reason to declare Revelation to be spurious. We do not have the right to reject prophecy because it appears to us to be in conflict with other portions of Scripture. For that we would have to have the supernatural gift of the testing of spirits.

27. *What names does Scripture give to the abode of the lost to which they will go following the last judgment?*

a) The names Sheol and Hades, which were discussed above.

b) The name *gehenna*, Greek γέεννα, from the Hebrew גֵּי־הִנֹּם or also גֵּיא בֶן־הִנֹּם or גֵּיא בְנֵי־הִנֹּם, "valley of hinnom," "valley of the son of hinnom," "valley of the sons of hinnom." According to some, *hinnom* is a common noun meaning "cry"; thus: "valley of crying" or "valley of the children of crying." Others, in contrast, say that Hinnom is a *nomen proprium* [proper noun], and that the valley is so named after a historical person. The issue is not important.

The Hinnom Valley lies southeast [*sic*] of Jerusalem. Under the kings Ahaz and Manasseh (2 Chr 28:3; 33:6) it was made into the place for the worship of Moloch. The place of sacrifice was called Topheth, תֹּפֶת, "place of spitting out." In Moloch worship, children were slaughtered and burnt. Later the cultic place in the valley was destroyed (namely, under Josiah, 2 Kgs 23:10) and declared unclean by the priests (cf. Jer 7:31 and following; 32:35; 19:1–6). The rabbis say that this unclean Topheth in the Hinnom Valley was used as a place to incinerate the carcasses of animals, so that there was a continual fire (cf. Jer 31:40). The Old Testament does not yet make the comparison between the place of the damned and the Hinnom Valley. The Apocrypha also uses still other names. The Talmud already speaks of גֵּהִנָּם [in Hinnom]. Hence the occurrence of the name in the New Testament. It must have been fairly common at that time.

In the name itself two elements can be distinguished:

1. It portrays the place of the damned as an unclean, cursed location, over which the fire of the divine wrath burns. Indeed, the fire that glowed in the Moloch-furnace was already a lingering trace in paganism of the unadulterated concept of divine righteousness that exercises punishment. And the fire that later consumed carrion and other impure things was even more an image of the burning that causes God's holiness to break out against all sin.

2. It portrays the place of the damned as a location where the fire of hostile hate against God in the heart of the lost is never extinguished. As in Topheth the Moloch-oven burned, so in Gehenna does the furnace of sin.

   It is, it would seem, particularly for the first reason that the name Gehenna occurs so often connected with the concept of "fire." "The Gehenna [hell] of fire" and with it, "the eternal fire" (Matt 18:8–9; cf. also Mark 9:43–48). By this, however, we do not mean that the fire in Gehenna is only meant symbolically. That God can render the concept "hell" by "fire" and "Gehenna" in our language and for our perception must have its basis rather in the fact that He originally placed in fire the image of "hell."

c) For "fire" one could think of a condition, since the local element appears to be more or less lacking. But this is amplified in other passages: "the furnace of fire" (Matt 13:42; Psa 21:9), "the lake of fire" (ἡ λίμνη τοῦ πυρός, Rev 20:14–15), "the lake of fire that burns with sulfur" (καιομένη ἐν θείῳ, Rev 19:20), and many other passages in Revelation; for that sulfur one may compare Isaiah 30:33 with 66:15. Still, it appears that something else is being thought of primarily. The lake is a pool of death; enclosed water. That makes one think immediately of the Dead Sea, which originated by the fire and brimstone rain of God's judgment. Jude 7 also makes the connection with Sodom and Gomorrah. And then again one can point out that, at least in the Apocalypse, the nations are seen as a "sea" (13:1), the nation of those saved as a "sea of crystal" [15:2]; so the lake of fire and of sulfur in antithesis to the sea of crystal. Compare, finally, also Ezekiel 47:1–12, "water that flowed from under the threshold of the house," and in verse 11, "the muddy places and marshes that will not become fresh." There, too, the wellsprings of life in Revelation are already present.

d) Another name is φυλακή (1 Pet 3:19; Matt 5:25; Luke 12:58), "prison," "repository." It contains in part the idea that the lost do not enter willingly but, as is said elsewhere, are pushed or thrown into it, in part the thought that they must remain inside it and are no longer able to go out into the rest of God's creation in order to bring in corruption and disruption. Sometimes mention is even made of jailers or tormenters, but that can belong to the elaboration of the image. Or it could refer to the devil and his demons (Matt 18:34).

e) Also spoken of is the ἄβυσσος (Luke 8:31). The "abyss" is the abode of the devil and the demons. But from Matthew 25:41 and Revelation 20:10 it is evident how these and the lost are consigned to one and the same place. According to Luke 8:13, the demons apparently abhor departing to this deep place; they would rather remain on earth, even though in the bodies of the pigs. The devil is also thrown into the abyss, which is shut and sealed over him (Rev 20:3). Conversely, it is said of the tongue that it is set on fire by Gehenna, "hell" (Jas 3:6), by which surely the abode of the demonic powers is meant.

f) Finally, the pagan term τάρταρος occurs, namely in 2 Peter 2:4 (cf. Jude 6), namely in a verbal form, ταρταρώσας, "having cast into Tartarus."

28. What is evident from all these names?

That we have to do here with a real place. We cannot, however, specify further where this place is, except that in antithesis to the height of the heavens it is called the depth of the abyss. Here too fantasy has imagined all kinds of things. From Jude 13 it has been thought possible to deduce that hell is located on the comets. The place of hell is "outside" (Matt 8:12; Rev 22:15), naturally not outside the extent of the created universe or the inhabitable world, certainly; on the other hand, outside the sphere of recreated and glorified things in which the love and the grace of God will reign. All dualistic conceptions, as if Gehenna was a creation of the devil, must be rejected. God has created the darkness, even the outermost darkness, as well as the light (Isa 45:7). In "outside" is contained the antithesis to the salvation of the "inside." "Blessed are those who may enter into the city through the gates. ... But outside are the dogs and sorcerers and the whoremongers," etc. [Rev 22:14–15].

29. In what will the punishment of hell consist?

a) In *absolute separation* from the gracious presence of God. Therefore it is spoken of as "death," "the second death"; therefore, too, as "outermost darkness," for in the salvation of God is light, as in fellowship with Him is life. However, this is not to be understood as if for the lost there would no longer be knowledge of God. They will know Him in His wrath.

b) In *endless destruction*, an endless disruption of existence, ἀπώλεια. It is impossible for us to fully delineate this concept. Destruction and endlessness seem to exclude each other. Nevertheless, the punishment of hell is often presented to us just from this viewpoint of ἀπώλεια. Another designation is φθορά [corruption] or ὄλεθρος αἰώνιος [eternal destruction] (Gal 6:8 and 2 Thess 1:9).

c) In *actual pains of the soul and of the body* (Rev 14:20; 20:10; Matt 10:28: "both body and soul" are destroyed in hell). It is a "fire," "a worm," what in any case points to actual punishment, though it is otherwise thought to be understood metaphorically.

There has also been a desire to portray it as a punishment of the lost that they will behold the glory of the saved from a distance. This would have to be based on Luke 16:23. But in this respect, too, it is forgotten that here we are dealing with a parable. It can certainly be assumed that the thought of the salvation against which they have sinned will be agonizing to the lost.

d) Along with these objective punishments, there will also be subjective ones—pangs of conscience, anguish, despair—as Scripture portrays all this for us so appallingly in the expression "weeping and gnashing of teeth" [e.g., Matt 13:42, 50; Luke 13:28]. By no means, however, may one reason from this subjective punishment as if the real Gehenna consisted in it. Some are accustomed to saying that an evil conscience will be hell, or that the lost will not so much be in hell as they will have hell in themselves. Scripture does not speak in this way.

e) The question arises how the "fire of hell" is to be understood. About this there has been a great deal of dispute. Roman Catholics say: actual fire, at least those who already maintain that of purgatory. Others, including Lutherans and the Reformed said: material fire, but not earthly fire. Still others said: certainly real, but not a fire of elements, material fire. Against material fire it was objected: (1) It is said of the fire that it is prepared for the devil and his angels; material fire cannot affect pure spirits, like demons. It seems to us this metaphysical reason is insufficient. If the body acts on the soul in man, why then would material fire not be able to act on demons? (2) Other expressions that occur along with fire must apparently be understood metaphysically, for example, the worm that does not die, the chains of darkness, the lake of sulfur, etc. It must be acknowledged that there is weight to this argument. Indeed, some of these expressions are difficult to reconcile with each other if one takes them literally. (3) Also, where the blessings of heaven are spoken of, we are not accustomed to taking the expressions of Scripture literally. Scripture must use such images in order to give us a grasp of the future things that are above or below earthly things. For heaven it speaks of "Abraham's side," "recline at table with Abraham," etc., "crowns," and many other things. There is weight to this too.

It seems to us that this question is not capable of being re-solved. One thing should be kept in view. Even if material fire is not meant, then the repeated mention of fire still cannot be a mere metaphor in the superficial sense in which it is usually taken. On the contrary, here too one will have to say: earthly fire is an image of the hellish reality that we call fire and about which further we cannot form a conception.

f) In the punishments of hell there will be a *difference of degree*. That is clearly taught in Matthew 11:22; Luke 12:47–48; "his portion," Matt 24:51 (Luke 12:46). That does not allow for determining in detail. In Matthew 23:14 [cf. KJV] it is said of the scribes and Pharisees that they will receive more severe judgment.

30. *How long will these punishments of hell last?*

Forever. Those who deny that can be reduced to the following groups:

a) Those who teach an ἀποκατάστασις πάντων, "a restoration of all things." Very early on Origen already held this view, since he viewed the punishments of hell as curative. Actually, all must teach that who, deducing the righteousness of God from His love, make punishment a benefit. An eternal punishment then becomes a *contradictio in adjecto* [contradiction in terms]. This view is also connected with the Pelagian doctrine of free will. It is thought that even the damned must retain their measure of freedom of the will, which always leaves open the possibility of restoration. In this case, however, the possibility must also be acknowledged that those who are saved can fall from heaven. Among modern theologians, Nitzsch, among others, teaches the restoration of all things.

b) Those who teach an *annihilation* of the ungodly. This view has been discussed earlier and there it was shown why it cannot be a substitute for the old view.

c) Those who in a universalistic fashion teach the salvation of all—either during this life or during a stay in Sheol-Hades—do not so much deny the eternity of the punishments of hell as rather hell itself. For someone who believes Scripture, this is scarcely worth refuting.

31. *To what grounds is appeal made to deny the eternity of the punishment of hell?*

Schleiermacher, for example, presents the following:

a) The words of Christ are figurative.

b) 1 Corinthians 15:25–26 teach that all evil will be overcome. (Response: the passage says rather, "be put under His feet.")

c) If the punishment consisted in bodily pains, the lost would get used to it; if it was pain of soul, it could not increase, for that would presuppose that the lost become ever more sensitive to it, and that would also imply that they continually become better instead of more evil. (As if there were no other pain of soul conceivable than specifically pangs of conscience, and as if all pangs of conscience presuppose *per se* a measure of moral uprightness. Scripture knows very well to distinguish between sorrow toward God and sorrow that works death [2 Cor 7:10].)

d) The ruin of the lost would intrude in a disturbing manner on the blessed state of those glorified. (But Scripture teaches us that in the last judgment a separation, a split, will be made between evil and good. This certainly implies not only that two classes of persons will emerge but also that the ties and relationships between these two will be cut off altogether.)

The scriptural grounds that are supposed to dispute the doctrine of eternal punishment are extremely weak. A few texts are wrenched from their contexts, such as Romans 5:18 and 1 Corinthians 15:22, and everything that Christ and the apostles say about eternal fire and eternal ruin is left unexplained.

32. *Can you show from Scripture that the punishments of hell are of eternal duration?*

Yes.

a) This doctrine is found most clearly in the words of Christ, the Savior and Redeemer Himself. Whoever rejects it presumes to be more merciful than the Son of Man. He warns against the one who can destroy both soul and body in hell, speaks of the worm that does not die and the fire that is not quenched, says that He will assign those condemned their place in the *eternal* fire that is prepared for the devil and his angels [Matt 10:28; Mark 9:48; Matt 25:41]. The words of Christ could have no other meaning than they must have had in the understanding of His hearers according to the common parlance of that time. And with such expressions as Christ used, the Jews certainly understood nothing other than eternal punishment. One may compare still further Luke 12:9–10, where it is said explicitly that the sin against the Holy Spirit will never be forgiven; also, what is said about Judas, namely, that it would have been better if he had never been born [Matt 26:24]. The ungodly are represented as the weeds to be separated from the wheat on the day of judgment and to be burned with unquenchable fire [Matt 3:12; 13:40]. Weeds do not become wheat in eternity. The bad fish are thrown away [Matt 13:48]. All of this is irreconcilable with the doctrine of a merely temporary punishment of hell.

b) It is said in so many words that the punishment is "eternal," αἰώνιος, ἀΐδιος (Matt 25:46; 18:8; Jude 6–7; Rev 14:11; 19:3). When the word αἰώνιος is used here, this can have no other meaning than that which belongs to the coming age, thus lying on the other side of the boundary that divides the two ages in Scripture. And what is on the other side of the boundary is *per se* endless, for Scripture knows of no other borderline that would yet again make a division within that age. Naturally, it must thereby be taken into account that the punishment of the ungodly falls in the coming age. On the other hand, it can be said of something belonging to "this age" that it is αἰώνιος without eternity as endlessness being meant. So it is said of Onesimus that he would be an eternal servant of Philemon [Phlm 15]. The mountains are "eternal" mountains because they last as long as this aeon lasts. But the punishments of the wicked are "eternal" because they extend over the entirety of the coming age. And in Scripture the αἰὼν μέλλων has no end, limit; nor is there a dividing line within it.

c) The eternity of the punishment is in antithesis with the eternity of the salvation of the blessed. And it is described as eternal with the same words. If, then, someone wishes to attribute a weaker sense to the concept "eternal" (αἰώνιος, ἀΐδιος) with respect to the punishment, then he must also concede that thereby all proofs for the *eternal* beatitude of the children of God fall away. According to Shedd, *Dogmatic Theology*, 2:688, "Αἰώνιος is employed 66 times in the New Testament. Of these, 51 relate to the future happiness of the righteous; 7 relate to future punishment (Matt 18:8; 25:41, 46; Mark 3:29; 1 Thess 1:9; Heb 6:2; Jude 6); 2 relate to God; 6 are of a miscellaneous nature."[1] It may also be observed that Scripture speaks in the same terms of the punishment of the ungodly as of the devil and his demons. Therefore, a conversion that does not also extend to the latter is no help. And the idea of a redemption of the powers of hell is thoroughly unscriptural.

33. Do the rational grounds that have been brought against the eternity of the punishments of hell have convincing force?

No, they all start either from a wrong concept of the righteousness of God or from a weakened concept of sin. Sin is committed against an infinite God, and what punishment it deserves can only be measured accordingly. Furthermore, salvation from sin is something positive that God owes no one, and where such salvation does not occur, sin continues of itself. From the flesh corruption must be reaped (Gal 6:8). If one makes the punishment of the ungodly finite in duration, then that implies that in principle it was not necessary. In fact, then it is defined not with reference to God but to man. And if punishment was not necessary with respect to God but only has its basis in man as he determines it, then it appears doubly difficult in God if He, who can surely save man without punishment, has chosen just this method. Universalism is then the only consistent view.

34. Is the punishment of the lost absolutely eternal?

Naturally *a parte post* [as to the future], not *a parte ante* [as to the past]. It has a beginning, but it will have no end.

---

1   Quotation is from Shedd, *Dogmatic Theology*, 3rd ed. (Phillipsburg, NJ: P&R, 2003), 897. The words are a loose quotation of Moses Stuart, *Exegetical Essays on Several Words Relating to Future Punishment* (Andover, MA: Codman Press, 1830), 46.

35. What will precede the consummate salvation of the children of God?

The appearance of a new world. Scripture speaks of that very clearly. In Acts 3:21 Peter speaks of an ἀποκατάστασις, a "restoration of all things." And in Revelation 21:5 He who sits on the throne says: "Behold, I make all things new." As a matter of fact, all this is inherent in the relationship to the rest of creation in which man stands. It is given to him so that he would rule over it. It has been carried along with him in his fall. It has been subjected to the groaning of futility. It is in travail, since with the dawning of the glory of the children of God it also awaits its liberation [Rom 8:19–22]. It is not solely about atonement for sin but about the removal of the results of sin. And when the devil, the demons, the lost, will be thrown "outside," then the last vestige of sin, to the extent it is "inside," will also need to disappear from the creation of God. The Old Testament in fact already speaks of this (Psa 102:26–28; Isa 34:4; 65:17; 66:22; 51:6, 16; 11:6–9). In the New Testament, one may also compare 2 Peter 3:7–13; Revelation 20:11; 21:1.

Scripture teaches further that this new world will follow the glorification of the children of God, that is, the glorious resurrection and the last judgment.

36. How are we to think of this bringing into being of the new world?

Thinking on this question differs greatly. Some propose an absolutely new world, so that in substance the old does not recur in the new and a new world comes in its place. The Lutheran dogmaticians until Gerhard were devoted to this view. But in general whenever they mention the new earth *pro forma*, they do not say much about it. The Reformed, for the most part, expressed support for the opposite view, namely that the substance of the presently existing world will be preserved but will be restored, purified in glory. Also, a host of recent theologians align themselves with the Reformed here. The grounds are:

a) Even the passages that seem to speak emphatically for the destruction of the old world are nevertheless not decisive. They are 2 Peter 3:7–13 and Revelation 20:11 and 21:1. The first passage speaks only of "passing away," "being melted," without it exactly becoming extinct; indeed, in our experience burning is never total annihilation. Revelation speaks of a "fleeing away," a "passing away," a "being no more."

b) The Old Testament passages all speak clearly of "change," not of "annihilation," for example, Psalm 102:26–27. This passage is taken up again in Hebrew 1:10–12. And accordingly, Hebrew 12:26–28 should also be so interpreted that at the shaking of the cosmos something remains that is immovable. This immovable something could be found in the heaven of God's glory, but still probably also meant is that something of what is changeable will remain in order to be made unchangeable.

c) If annihilation is assumed, then texts that speak of change are absolutely impossible to explain. If change is assumed, the texts that seem to speak of annihilation can still be explained in a very sound sense.

d) Analogy speaks for change. The body of man, too, is not annihilated and a new body created in its place. The old is changed or glorified. One should assume then that this will also take place in the wider sphere with the entire groaning creation.

37. How will that change occur? ·

Second Peter 3:7–12 says that it will occur "by fire." This cannot be meant figuratively. It is contrasted with the destruction that once came upon the earth by water, the water of the flood. So it must be just as real.

Hebrews 12:26–28 speaks, as we saw, of a "shaking" and "moving." But this and what Peter says do not exclude each other. A conflagration of the world with tremors and earthquakes would fulfill both prophecies.

The renewal of the earth does not affect heaven as God's dwelling place but heaven in the celestial sense.

38. Can we say very much about heaven and the blessings of heaven?

No, for this far surpasses our understanding. We know only:

a) That heaven is a place. Like hell, it is to be thought of as having a locality. It may be true that someone can have heaven in his heart, but his heart must also be in heaven with his body.

b) The enjoyment of heaven is in the first place the enjoyment of God, the *visio Dei*, a "beholding of God." This is not to be understood one-sidedly in an intellectualistic manner but in all its magnitude. The nearness of God will affect every capacity of man, and every capacity will react to it. Theologians usually speak of *visio* [seeing], *amor* [love], *gaudium* [joy], *gloria* [glory]; others of knowing, serving, enjoying, and glorifying God (cf. 1 Cor 13:9–13).

It has been asked whether this will be a seeing with physical eyes. This is not to be assumed. God is not visible to the senses. The Mediator certainly is. No one has ever seen God. This seeing follows on faith. It is thus something that is comparable with faith but that still does not necessarily need to be a perceiving with the senses. There will thus be a perception of God, yet such that it is not a material entity that appears to us.

c) The enjoyment of heaven in fellowship with God is eternal life in all its fullness.

d) Along with these enjoyments, perhaps other blessings will be bestowed on the children of God. But Scripture describes all that in images about which we cannot say to what extent they are purely metaphysical, to what extent they are metaphorical in the deeper sense of the word. Naturally, all defects and all misery will be banished from heaven.

e) Heaven will not be a world of uniformity; diversity will rule there. One is the glory of the sun, another that of the moon, another of the stars [cf. 1 Cor 15:41]. Not all receive the same portion. The one who has sowed much receives a rich harvest. But as already said above, diversity will not possibly function as a cause for distress.

One can think of the blessed state of heaven too much as an individual. There will be an ordering of things there. Glorified humanity will have its head in Christ and form a body under Him. In a body there are always different parts.

One can also think of the blessings of salvation too spiritualistically. Many do not reckon with the fact that the body of the believer, too, is resurrected and that the earth, too, will be re-created. In their conception there is really no place for a new earth. Still, on the other hand it should be acknowledged that we do not know what the enjoyment of God's world will be like for His children. We do not, if for no other reason because we lack any adequate comprehension of that new world itself.

INDICES

INDICES

Volume One Question Index

VOLUME TWO QUESTION INDEX

VOLUME THREE QUESTION INDEX

Volume Four Question Index

Volume Five Question Index

Subject and Author Index

atonement (*continued*)

governmental theory 514, 519–24, 531

military theory 515

moral theory 514, 516–19, 524

mystical theory 514, 524–27

particular (not universal) 497–514

purchase, ransom, redeem, redemption 460–61, 471, 515, 527, 538

and universal offer of grace 499

attributes of God 14–18, 921

classification of 16–18

communicable 17–18, 24

distinction from God's being 15

incommunicable 17–18

inherent 16–17

moral 17, 30

natural 17

negation of 16

relationship between 15–16

transitive 16–17

unity of 15–16

Augsburg Apology 1084

Augsburg Confession (1530) 1083

Augustine 49, 146, 224, 247, 249, 531, 552, 567, 590

on baptism 979–81

on the church 872, 913

on creation 176, 177, 189

on divine knowledge 27

and eschatology 1103, 1118, 1123

on the image of God 229

on infant baptism 246, 1004, 1015

on the Last Supper 1052, 1069, 1086

on perseverance 825–26, 828

and predestination 129, 153, 160–61

and the sacraments 933, 937, 943

on sin 274, 284, 290, 656

on the Trinity 54, 59, 63, 71

authority

of the apostles 896

of Christ 852–53, 880–84

of God 135

See also power

autonomy, of the local church 917–18

B

Babylon, and the antichrist 1126

Bähr 464

baptism 309, 318, 574–76, 629, 660, 746, 945–48, 954–1045

of adults 984–1001, 1014–15, 1027

and the church 858, 865, 869

and confirmation 949–50

infant 246, 282, 977, 984–85, 988–89, 1002–44

of Jesus 304, 308–9

as means of regeneration 654–55

postponement of 1004–5

rebaptism 962–65, 981–83

as a sacrament 935–37

as sign of regeneration 641, 655

See also under Lord's Supper; sacraments

Baptists

and the church 868–67

and circumcision 1005–7

and immersion 966–75

and infant baptism 1002–3, 1010–11

baptizō 965–68, 971

baptō 965–68

Baron, Robert 1015

Basil of Caesarea 970

beast, and the antichrist 1127

begetting of the Son. *See under* Christ: the Son of God

being of God 13, 16, 47, 148, 199

distinction(s) in 19

homooousios 53, 54

ousia 55

relationship to decrees of God 103

relationship to power of God 46, 58

relationship to space 22

self-existence 14, 18, 23, 36

as spirit 12, 18

unity of 15, 51, 56–57, 59, 65, 68–69, 70, 71, 78, 80

Belgic Confession (1561) 52, 103, 763, 926, 933–34, 940, 1000, 1043–44, 1067, 1076

Scripture Index

Old Testament

New Testament

Apocrypha

2 Maccabees

Wisdom of Solomon